THE COLLECTED PAPERS OF
DAVID RAPAPORT

DAVID RAPAPORT

The Collected Papers of
DAVID RAPAPORT

---

edited by

Merton M. Gill

Basic Books, Inc., Publishers

New York   London

EDITOR'S NOTE

This volume includes almost all of Rapaport's published papers, as well as some hitherto unpublished ones. Works not included are listed in the bibliography at the end of the volume. None of the omitted papers includes any important ideas not covered elsewhere in his work.

ACKNOWLEDGMENTS

I wish to express my appreciation to the people who helped in bringing out this volume. I received general guidance and advice from Drs. George S. Klein, Robert R. Holt, Sibylle Escalona, Roy Schafer, and Paul Bergman. Others who advised on specific papers are Drs. Fred Schwartz, Abraham Edel, Stuart Miller, David Shakow, Elvira Rapaport, and Mr. Erik H. Erikson.

Sue Annin performed not only the usual chores of an editorial assistant, but in addition her very careful study of the papers led to questions and suggestions which played a major rôle in the annotations I have made.

Drs. Ernst Lewy, Milton Lozoff, Karl Menninger, and Roy Schafer and Mr. Alden Weber gave permission to reprint papers on which they had collaborated with Rapaport, and Dr. Gardner Murphy made available a letter which Rapaport had written to him about the lectures on methodology (Chapter 14).

Sally Brandwein and Dorothy Bianco very efficiently carried out secretarial tasks.

Mrs. Maria Antalfy translated Chapter 1 from the Hungarian.

My work was supported by Public Health Service Grants M–5413, MH–07,424, and Research Career Award K6–MH–19,436 from the National Institute of Mental Health.

The following journals and publishers kindly granted permission for us to reprint papers: *The American Journal of Orthopsychiatry, The American Journal of Psychiatry, The Bulletin of the Menninger Clinic, The Bulletin of the Philadelphia Association for Psychoanalysis, The International Journal of Psycho-Analysis, The Journal of the American Psychoanalytic Association, The Journal of Personality, The Journal of Projective Techniques, Psychiatry, The Psychoanalytic Quarterly, Science,* The American Psychological Association, Duke University Press, Harvard University Press, Hashomer Hatzair, the Indian Psychoanalytical Society, International Universities Press, The Josiah Macy, Jr. Foundation, The Journal Press, The New York Academy of Sciences, The Philosophy of Science Association, The University of Nebraska Press, and The Wenner-Gren Foundation for Anthropological Research.

Merton M. Gill

September 1966

Contents

THE COLLECTED PAPERS OF
DAVID RAPAPORT

IN MEMORIAM

David Rapaport, 1911–1960

MERTON M. GILL

I

Though he had suffered from chronic rheumatic heart disease since child-hood and had for years been plagued by major and minor illnesses, David Rapaport's sudden death on December 14, 1960, came as a shock to his family, his friends, the psychoanalytic community, and psychologists the world over. The scope of his work was such that it cannot be assessed quickly, nor in the brief compass of an obituary.

He was born in Hungary in 1911 to a middle-class urban Jewish family. Intellectually and socially precocious, by his early teens he was already an accomplished political orator and leader in a leftist Zionist youth organization. The organization was not entirely legal, and more than once the youth-ful, fiery spellbinder was in serious danger. After four years at the University in Budapest, spent in the study of mathematics and physics, he joined his group's kibbutz in Palestine, where he lived for two years. He was sent back to run the youth group in Hungary, where from 1935 to 1938 he was psychoanalyzed and obtained his Ph.D. in psychology from the Royal Hungarian University.

First published in Journal of the American Psychoanalytic Association, *9:755–759, 1961.*

It is characteristic of his industry, rapid grasp of a field, and tendency to hide his achievements under a superior's cloak that during this period he "ghosted" two books on psychoanalysis for an analyst who was his "fatherly friend." This venture was an early clue to his lifelong interest in hoaxes, which unfortunately never issued in a publication. He was convinced that in the hoax lies an important avenue to the understanding of certain facets of creative thinking.

In 1938, in a crucial and painful decision, he decided not to rejoin his kibbutz but, instead, to emigrate to the United States. He worked briefly at Mount Sinai Hospital in New York, Osawatomie State Hospital in Kansas, and finally, in 1940, settled at the Menninger Clinic.

Incongruous as this prickly, stiff immigrant Jew from Budapest was in Topeka, Kansas, it was a tribute to his talent and to the perspicacity of the leaders of the Menninger Clinic that he rose rapidly in the organization, first becoming chief psychologist and then head of the Research Department.

In 1948, actuated by a number of reasons, not least of which was his desire to curb his propensity to develop an organization under himself so large as to hold him captive, he moved to the Austen Riggs Center in Stockbridge, Massachusetts, where he worked until his death. He leaves his wife, Dr. Elvira Strasser Rapaport, a mathematician, and two daughters, Hanna and Juliet.

Though he never practiced psychoanalysis, in 1949 he began therapeutic work with a few schizophrenics and borderline patients, primarily to study their thought organization. But beyond this he was continually steeped in clinical material. His entire professional life was spent in clinical settings, and from his early work in psychological testing to his participation in studying the therapeutic community he remained in touch with clinical data. At both Menninger's and Riggs he created for himself that unusual combination in which he could best thrive—an academic post in a clinical setting.

II

Rapaport had a brilliant mind and an astonishing memory. With remarkable speed he not only assimilated ideas in themselves but fitted them into their correct place in his whole body of knowledge. His capacity for work, the economy with which he did things, and his ability to keep many different projects going at once were remarkable.

In one of several accountings of his work, he wrote that the "red thread" of his intellectual life was his interest in thought processes, and particularly the central issue of epistemology, i.e., how thinking progresses from the drive-determined autism of the infant to the socially adaptive and veridical thinking of the adult. His doctor's thesis was on the history of the association concept from Bacon to Kant. He soon moved into psychological testing and worked out a battery of tests which he learned to interpret in the light of psychoanalytic insight and theory.

Very early he became convinced that, potentially, psychoanalytic theory offered the most illumination of thought processes but that the theory sorely needed critical systematization. A large part of his professional life was devoted to the latter task, beginning with a study of the literature entitled *Emotions and Memory,* published in 1942. He subsequently said that the major failing of that study was that it did not take ego psychology adequately into account. In 1945–1946 he summarized his testing studies in *Diagnostic Psychological Testing,* a work which, in addition to its utility for the clinical psychologist, is noteworthy for the light it sheds on the thinking process. By this time he was playing a central rôle as critic and adviser in four major research projects at the Menninger Clinic—on perception, hypnosis, infant study, and the selection of psychiatric residents. After his move to Riggs came the prodigious annotated source book, *Organization and Pathology of Thought,* and a series of studies in psychoanalytic theory —on the basic model, on thought, on affect, on ego psychology, on ego autonomy, on development, on motivation, and the comprehensive statement, *The Structure of Psychoanalytic Theory: A Systematizing Attempt.* Not generally known is the experimental work in memory and learning which he began in 1952. By 1957 he had begun a series of experiments designed to test his theory of attention cathexes as a basis for a psychoanalytic theory of learning, and at the time of his death he had planned a large-scale, ten-year program of such research which had been approved by the Board of Trustees of the Riggs Center.

While no effort is being made here to catalogue his publications, mention must be made of his important labors in translating Fenichel, Schilder, and Hartmann.

III

Rapaport exerted a powerful influence on his contemporaries. He was instrumental in the shift of psychologists in the '40s from technicians giving I.Q. tests to clinicians employing batteries of both structured and projective tests of thinking and of personality. His *Diagnostic Psychological Testing* has been and remains widely used by psychologists. He was a founder and first secretary (1946–1949) of the newly formed Division of Clinical and Abnormal Psychology of the American Psychological Association. He lectured widely in the psychoanalytic institutes of the United States, bringing about an appreciation of psychoanalytic theory in general and ego psychology in particular. His lecturing style was extraordinary and to some intimidating, especially to those accustomed to gentility in scientific discourse. He discussed abstract metapsychology with the fervor of a political orator and the thunder of a Hebrew prophet. Much of his lecture material has yet to become available in published form. He conducted a voluminous and detailed correspondence with an astounding number of people, including the leading psychoanalytic thinkers of our time, and raised around himself a group of students with whom he generously shared his insights no less than he relentlessly taught the meaning of discipline, hard work, and precision of thought. Rapaport's central goal was to make of psychoanalysis a general psychology, a psychology which could integrate ego psychology and social psychology while preserving Freud's first and revolutionary insights into id psychology. He was undoubtedly the major interpreter of the general (as against the clinical) theory of psychoanalysis to psychologists. He suffered the fate of many who bridge two disciplines: he was not completely accepted by either of them. Nevertheless, in September, 1960, he did receive from the American Psychological Association's Division of Clinical Psychology an award in recognition of his distinguished contribution to the science and profession of clinical psychology. He was a special member of the Western New England Psychoanalytic Society and a mainstay of its teaching faculty. He was a member at large of the International Psychoanalytical Association, and at the time of his death an effort was under way to make him an honorary member of the American Psychoanalytic Association. In fairness, it must also be said that Rapaport, on his part, did not "accept" the organized disciplines of either psychoanalysis or psychology. He did not have much forbearance for the degree to which all organizations are inevitably infected by the less noble human motivations.

IV

Rapaport was a complex and vivid person. His interests were many and varied, though the world of knowledge was his consuming passion.

His personality was noteworthy for striking contrasts, which, to a considerable degree, he was able to integrate. He was at once fiercely proud and genuinely humble, a firm upholder of the dignity of tradition and a fearless iconoclast, generous without stint and capable of relentless feuds, a direct and tireless fighter for his views and an adroit maneuverer backstage. It was greatly rewarding but sometimes not easy to be his friend. His intellectual life, invested though it was with the most intense passions, was superbly disciplined. He had deep roots in Rabbinical bibliophilia and casuistry, but was nevertheless capable of broad perspective and grasp of the essential core of an issue. He took life very seriously, but could relax and regale others with his endless supply of stories. He also had a remarkable ability quickly to summon up an apt story, usually a joke, to illustrate a point. He was so quick to understand and carry further another's ideas that some felt devoured by him; yet he was extraordinarily careful to respect the independence and individuality of others. His careful documentation of the forerunners of his own ideas has led many mistakenly to regard him as a scholastic systematizer rather than as a creative thinker. With none was he more critical than with himself, both in his work and in his personal life. He was highly introspective and self-aware. He laid plans with the same astonishing care and detail with which he reworked draft after draft of his writings. Despite their clarity, his writings must be studied rather than read because every ounce of excess fat has been trimmed away. He was able to be explicit about the light he hoped would be thrown on the theory of thinking by every one of his astonishingly many and actively pursued interests, however remote they might seem from the main goal—so much so that some of us suspected him of retrospective rationalization to maintain a sense of order and mastery. The fact was, however, that he wasted nothing and had an exceptional capacity for deriving something useful from the most unlikely sources. His benefactions were many and often not known. The mantle of benefactor, teacher, counselor, and sage so well suited him that most people, even his elders, found themselves tailoring their relationship to him on these terms. In fact, it was not often that he accepted an intimacy on any other terms. Yet it was also true that he constantly sought criticism and could accept correction even from a beginning student. One of his favorite images was that one had to expose one's ideas to their reflections in the variously shaped mirrors of others. He especially delighted in helping those who were breaking the yoke of the old and painfully building the new, whether they were those who dared to have a new idea, or young and struggling artists who had given up the usual societal supports, or those who were restive under a tyranny—whether political or personal—or the builders of the new society in Israel. He was uncompromisingly devoted to the truth, but he knew that there are many truths. His capacity for empathizing with differing views gave him an unusual breadth of perspective and an uncommon compassion. Despite a propensity for indirection and complication in personal relationships which made him sometimes seem crafty and suspicious, he in fact assumed the essential goodness of human beings and bowed to evidence to the contrary only reluctantly. Undiluted scorn was reserved only for intellectual dishonesty and emotional callousness. It was not possible to know him well without being profoundly influenced.

David Rapaport felt an enormous debt to the past and an enormous responsibility to the future. He labored mightily to pay the debt and to fulfill the responsibility by performing his task in the chain of generations. Though not a religious man, he was deeply attached to Jewish culture. *Zichrono l'vrocho:* His memory will be blessed.

THE STRUCTURING OF
DRIVE AND REALITY

David Rapaport's Contributions to
Psychoanalysis and Psychology

MERTON M. GILL AND GEORGE S. KLEIN

We cannot hope to do justice to David Rapaport's work in a single paper. The intricate skein of his contributions would have to be followed into the work of those who are exploring areas that he boldly, sometimes daringly, charted and with whom he was in many instances an unseen collaborator. This hints at the luxuriant variety of his thought and of his contributions. It hints also at the complexity of the man. He was so many-faceted, so made up of paradoxes, that almost any generalization about him personally is bound to be false in some critical respect. It will require a gifted biographer to do full justice to Rapaport the man.

Earlier versions of this paper were read at the David Rapaport Memorial Meeting of the Convention of the American Psychological Association in New York City, August 31, 1961; at the Helen D. Sargent Memorial Award Meeting in Topeka, Kansas, September 11, 1961, on the occasion of a posthumous award to David Rapaport for his monograph, The Structure of Psychoanalytic Theory: Systematizing Attempt; *at the New York Psychoanalytic Society, December 19, 1961; and at the Austen Riggs Center, January 1962. First published in* The International Journal of Psycho-Analysis, *45:483–498, 1964.*

Our task is more limited. We will sketch the main themes of his formal presentations. The range and complexity of these—the more remarkable for being compressed within a short twenty or twenty-five years—make the task a difficult one. We are aided, however, by the fact that an unusual unity of theme and purpose is perceptible in all that he did. In whatever directions Rapaport carried his efforts—and they are amazingly diverse, extending to many sectors of psychological theory and over a wide variety of psychological phenomena and behavior—recurrent emphases and themes can be found. Approaching concepts principally by way of their history, he was able to accomplish unique integrative feats within psycho-analytic theory and between it and general psychological theory. In the dis-cussion to follow we shall not restrict ourselves to Rapaport's contributions to theory but rather, as we believe to be appropriate on this occasion, to the science of psychology in general.

MAJOR MOTIFS OF HIS WORK

Every man's life, wrote William James to his father, can be summarized in a single cry. If one searches for the central preoccupation in all of Rapa-port's theoretical and empirical efforts, one could say it was to unravel a paradox: ". . . how man can know of, and act in accordance with, his environment when his thoughts and actions are determined by the laws of his own nature" (Rapaport, 1959a, p. 57). How does thought—this need-fulfilling, wish-fulfilling human product—become socialized, logical, and goal directed?

Around this question and this theme crystallized the central objective of Rapaport's lifework—the effort to contribute to a psychological theory that would confront both drive and reality in human functioning. In this effort the main substance was to be the phenomena of cognition and thought. "The core of my professional work has been my interest in the nature of thinking," he wrote (1960a), and the data and observational methods of the psychology of thought processes remained pre-eminent in his strategy for implementing his vision of psychoanalysis as a general theory of behav-ior.

While Rapaport attempted to keep a private *Weltanschauung* out of his psychological work, there is no doubt that the tragic view of man was con-genial to him. It was a view obviously in harmony with a conception of the innateness of both drive and drive restraint, a conception in which intra-psychic conflict is inevitable. There is also no doubt that he was profoundly concerned with the question of how to reconcile strict determinism, the coercive claims of man's inescapable drives, and immutable reality on the one hand, with, on the other, his personal belief that man does play a rôle in shaping his own destiny. He found the solution of the paradox in a principle that wise men have always known: freedom lies in control and in the awareness of necessity. "The old adage, that freedom is the acceptance of the restraints of the law, returns to us here with renewed significance" (1957c, p. 741). Hartmann had similarly said: ". . . the normal ego must be *able* to control, but it must also be *able to must*" (1939, p. 94). In the ego's relative autonomy lies a measure of freedom and a base from which to enlarge the scope of freedom. Reconciliation and modulation must always be represented by the formation or the delineation of a psychical structure. Once formed, a psychical structure brings the organism to a new level of adequacy beyond the encounter that produced it, and a certain measure of autonomy has thereby been won. Such tangible residues of encounters between motive forces and reality are not easily fixed, and the freedom won thereby is only relative, for the guarantees of autonomy are capable of subversion.

Hence the deep and abiding interest in the structuring of drive and reality which was Rapaport's guiding central theme in the later years of his life.

DRIVE AND REALITY

Observation, argued Rapaport (1947, 1957c) does not confirm the Berkeleian view of man as totally dependent on images residing within him, so that he cannot come to know an external world independent of these inner formative agents. Neither does it confirm the Cartesian conception of man as born a clean slate upon which experience writes, a conception in which man is totally dependent upon and in harmony with the outside world. The latter view, Rapaport wrote, is "emphatically contradicted by psychoanalytic observations, which amply demonstrate the survival of pathological behavior forms in defiance of environmental conditions and requirements" (1957c, p. 726). But, his argument continues, because Freud's most original and revolutionary discovery was that of the drives, the danger of underemphasizing the rôle of the environment is always present in psychoanalytic formulations. Mindful of this possibility, Rapaport traced with great care the shifting accents upon external reality that characterized the several phases of Freud's thinking (1958, 1959a); in the first phase reality occupied a central position, the theory emphasizing the memory of an actual traumatic event which was defended against; in the second phase, reality receded into the background with Freud's realization that his patients' tales of seduction were largely fantasies, to explain which he postulated innate drives; in the third phase, in the theory advanced in *Inhibitions, Symptoms and Anxiety* (1926), reality again came to occupy a place of prominence: one of the major reasons an instinctual danger is defended against is that gratification would bring danger from another quarter—reality.

Rapaport recognized and valued the contributions made by the neo-Freudians in their attempts to emphasize and specify the rôle of the environment, but he was convinced that the next major advances in the development of psychoanalysis as a comprehensive psychology were foreshadowed in the theories of Heinz Hartmann (e.g., 1939, 1950a, 1950b, 1952) and Erik H. Erikson (e.g., 1937, 1940, 1950, 1946–59). He believed not only that Hartmann and Erikson were building a theory which took account of reality without losing sight of the impetus of the drives, but also that their conceptions of reality provided flesh and blood for the skeletal formulation of the reality principle that existed in Freud's theory.

This insistence upon codetermination by both drive and environment was at the heart of Rapaport's theoretical work. The merit of this emphasis was not that it was original with him, which, of course, it was not, but in the steadfastness with which he kept both determinants in view and in his unrelenting efforts to keep them in proper balance in every theoretical formulation. He vigorously opposed those who emphasize one at the expense of the other—those for whom the psychology of the id is all-important and who conceive of the individual's world as shaped by his drives alone, and those at the other extreme who attempt to account for development solely in terms of the shaping effects of environmental encounters.

STRUCTURE

Before Hartmann (1939), interest in the ego centered mainly upon the workings of defenses, culminating in Anna Freud's (1936) classic study. The characteristics of the ego as a synthesizing and adaptive organization superordinate to the defense function received only desultory attention. Rapaport accepted the broadened concept of the scope of regulation by the ego, especially as laid down by Hartmann's formulations, and contributed to the increasing recognition in psychoanalytic theory that the issue of structure development in psychical organization extends beyond the defensive function. He accepted Hartmann's principles of primary and secondary autonomy. Ego development is not contingent on conflict alone: ego functions also have an independent origin and development; furthermore, the ego structures that evolve from conflict or from the interplay of forces pressing for and against drive-discharge themselves acquire a measure of independence from both drive and reality and from conflict between them.

In emphasizing the stable, the permanent, the delaying and inhibiting characteristics of the psychic apparatus, Rapaport laid particular emphasis upon the pervasiveness of structure in psychical functioning, a theme that became dominant in his theorizing. In this he placed himself squarely in the camp of Hartmann, Kris, and Loewenstein (1946), who concluded that Freud's gradually increasing emphasis upon structured systems of regulation (1900, 1923) marked a major advance in psychoanalytic theory. Together with these workers (Hartmann, 1939, 1950a; Kris, 1932–52; Loewenstein, 1950), Rapaport played a central rôle in placing the structural point of view in its true perspective in psychoanalytic metapsychology.

Doubtless in part as a result of his years of concentration on diagnostic testing, he gave the concept real generality as well as concreteness and usefulness, as witnessed by the various paths of experimental work that sprang directly from this emphasis in his formulations (e.g., Paul, 1959; Gardner et al., 1959; Schwartz and Rouse, 1961).

From whatever direction Rapaport's theorizing proceeded, it converged in every instance on the nodal problem of *structure*—its formation, its stability, the conditions of its weakening, of its maintenance, of its disintegration, and of its reconstitution. He was concerned not only with the major structures, or what we may call macrostructures—id, ego, superego—the usual foci of structural discussions in psychoanalysis, but with the various levels and forms of structures including those of ideas, percepts, and memories (1957a), and more complex structural arrangements like discharge thresholds, defenses, controls, and identifications (1951d). It was a crucial assumption for him that not all functions are created, as he used to say, *de novo*, on each occasion where they are needed; the structural bases of functions eventually become stabilized and the functions thereafter are reactivated automatically—a process Hartmann had formulated as the "automatization" of apparatuses of secondary autonomy (1939, see pp. 87 ff.). Such stabilized structures become the basis of new structures (and functions), in an ever more differentiated hierarchical development. The analysis of structure epitomized Rapaport's approach to issues of drives, affects, defenses, controls, channels of communication, states of consciousness, and of ego organization in general.

In Rapaport's view, a comprehensive theory of human behavior would have to stress both drive forces and structures. In a statement (1953a) to a conference on "mass communications" he said:

> Yet in the course of the development of psychological and psychoanalytical knowledge, this discovery [that basic drives are at the heart of all human psychological processes] proved to be only a partial explanation of human behavior. We have learned that no dynamics of forces alone can explain what a human being does. We know from biology, and from social studies also, that functions, once established, structuralize, i.e., they form steady states which are resistive to change. In psychological life too we find such automatized functions, which do not have to be created anew, which behave as structures [p. 518].

His basic premises about structures were straightforward. In contrast to drive processes whose rate of change is fast and whose course is paroxysmal, structures, which hold a rein upon such peremptory forces and codetermine behavior, are relatively invariant and function at a slower rate of change. Structural determinants presumably account for the observation that motivations do not determine behavior in one-to-one fashion.

The issue of a *general theory* of structure formation came to dominate

Rapaport's interest in recent years as no other issue did, and he was preparing himself to confront it directly in a long-range program that was to combine experimental and theoretical work. He viewed the solution of the problem of structure as the single most critical condition for the acceleration of psychoanalytic theory in the next decade.

> In psychoanalytic theory, structures play such a crucial rôle that as long as the propensities and changes of psychological structure cannot be expressed in the same dimensions as psychological processes, dimensional quantification is but a pious hope. In other words, the study of the process of psychological structure formation seems to be the prime requisite for progress toward dimensional quantification. We must establish how processes turn into structures, how a structure, once formed, changes, and how it gives rise to and influences processes [1959a, pp. 98–99].

RAPAPORT'S WAYS OF WORKING

Rapaport considered psychoanalytic theory to be the only theoretical guide that was comprehensive enough for an eventual illumination of thought phenomena. But, as he wrote, ". . . it was both in a chaotic state lacking systematization and in flux due to its rapidly developing concern with ego psychology" (1960a).

Rapaport firmly believed in and practiced the principle of arriving at theoretical order through exploring the historical development of a concept. Hartmann (1948, 1956) and others had likewise emphasized that some parts of psychoanalytic theory cannot be understood without a knowledge of their history. Rapaport's historical approach had no mechanical respect for chronology. Not only was the contemporary scene to be surveyed against the background of history, but history was to be surveyed against the background of contemporary development. For him the historical approach was not only a means of arriving at the most advanced understanding of a concept; it also made it possible to revive the usefulness of previously discarded concepts, which for one reason or another had not been digestible within the theory, by bringing them into relationship with later developments in the theory. Good examples are his resuscitation of Freud's earlier conception of consciousness as a substructure ("sense organ") responsible for the directing of attention cathexis, and of Breuer's "hypnoid state" (Breuer and Freud, 1893–95) as a precursor of the concept of states of consciousness (1951e, 1956, 1957a, 1959b, 1960a).

Though for Rapaport the historical approach was the guarantee *par excellence* against superficial theorizing, it also reflected his conviction about the tentative character of psychoanalytic theory. To him, psychoanalysis was anything but a final statement that simply called for appropriate deduction and application. It was an evolving system of thought, incoordinate in its parts, and so intricately webbed that adequate conceptualizing was a matter of *discovery,* not simply of a chronological arrangement of sources. The historical approach was for him a teaching device as well as an instrument of discovery. There are, he wrote, no easy introductions to a systematic statement of the theory:

> In the lack of such, the investigator has to master the primary sources and do the systematization for himself. . . . It is often said that psychoanalytic theory is a rigid and unchangeable doctrine. Although there is such dogmatism and orthodoxy in the Societies and Institutes (whether they are Freudian or Neo-Freudian or in between) in regard to the clinical theory, I have rarely found dogmatism in regard to the general theory. The attitudes range from enthusiasm, through lack of interest, to total lack of information. The general theory, far from being well-ingrained dogma, is a waif unknown to many, noticed by some, and closely familiar to few. Not the alleged rigidity of the theory, but rather unfamiliarity with it is the obstacle to theoretical progress [1959a, p. 140].

To bring the development of a concept in line with other segments of theory—this was the crux of his historical approach. His interest in history and his sense of responsibility to the psychoanalytic community for developing and preserving its archives of theory took diverse forms, such as the sponsoring of the work of a professional historian, his translations of Fenichel (1922–46), Schilder (1924), and Hartmann (1939), his active behind-the-scenes encouragement and help for a new monograph series, *Psychological Issues.*

The places where Rapaport's formulations were not only creative syntheses but also extensions and innovations are not always easily visible, for he went to extreme lengths to keep his rôle anonymous and to justify his formulations through the work of others.[1] We say "extreme lengths" because it was not uncommon for someone to find himself extensively quoted by Rapaport and to come away from the context in which his work was referred to with the feeling of Molière's hero: "I did not know it was prose I was speaking all the time." So motivated was he to avoid the appearance of innovation in the ideas he put forward, and so much did he value finding one's roots in the past, that he often engaged in a relentless search of the work of others to forge links between his ideas and another's work. Such hints even seemed to be a necessary condition for him to explore freely the possibilities of an idea. Perhaps something of the same unease with taking full responsibility for a novel idea or interpretation contributed to his pref-

[1] We have not attempted in this paper to do more than indicate some of the major sources and influences to which he was indebted. His own writings make detailed and explicit acknowledgment.

erence for commentary by footnote, a sometimes exasperating even though usually rewarding experience for his readers.

Rapaport felt acutely the need to bring together contributions which their own creators did not see as related but which in his view nevertheless included important parallels or were necessary complements for an integrated view of personality development and functioning. His remarkable capacity for such tasks is most clearly seen in his integration (1958) of the work of Hartmann and Erikson, which we will discuss below. He characteristically immersed himself in the writings of these two men, and strove to make clear their relationship to each other and their place in the total perspective, thus revealing his self-adopted rôle of interpreter, but, more important, his devotion to the advancement of science rather than his own aggrandizement. How he was led to feel this need for integration may in part be seen in the closing two paragraphs of his review of the work of Schilder (Rapaport, 1951c).

> So it is in the development of science. For every achievement we pay dearly by turning away and indeed cutting ourselves away from other possibilities and facts. No individual and no school can encompass the riches of phenomena in any science, and even less so in the science of man, with which we are concerned. . . . none of us can behold all aspects of man at once, and the one who attempts to do that will give a rich and intuitive but scattered picture He [Schilder] makes it easier for us to understand why, in exploring cultural influence in personality development, one is prone to forget basic motivation by showing us that a high price has to be paid, by every one of us, for what we would discover.
>
> This price is determined by what our interest centers on, and our interest in turn flows from our character and personal proclivities. It is a different person with partly different values who is possessed with the discovery of basic motivation, from the one who finds defensive and socializing motives to be the ultimate ones. So with Schilder too: personal proclivities, values, and urges, determined ultimately the choice of the price he paid. Let us, however, not ask what the personal proclivities of Schilder were that shaped the character of his scientific creativity; let us rather honor the man, so rare in our time, who sowed seeds richly and was little concerned with the harvest [pp. 381–382].

Rapaport, too, sowed seeds richly but he was intensely concerned with the harvest. His students well know the unrelenting demands he made on them for scholarliness and clarity of communication. But these were more than matched by the lengths to which he drove himself to reach, through draft upon draft, the maximum lucidity in his own writing, and by the painstaking preparations that preceded his every lecture and seminar.

Rapaport was not interested merely in the intellectual exercise of theory-building. He always sought the empirical datum that was responsible for a new turn in theory. And in his own theoretical work he attempted to take account of data derived not only from psychoanalysis but also from past and present academic psychology and from the other behavioral sciences. He explicitly acknowledged the responsibility of theory to be receptive to all data and observation, whatever their source.

Still, it may come as a surprise to many to learn that Rapaport was not only an empiricist but came to lean heavily, even predominantly, on experimentation. He was responsible for bringing to light and to the attention of academic psychology pioneering experiments on dreams and pathological thought processes in his *Organization and Pathology of Thought* (1951d). He carefully followed the experimental literature and had a virtually unexcelled mastery of the literature of academic psychology. Eight years before his death he had also embarked on a broad program of experimental research. It is true that he felt it necessary to devote his professional efforts mainly to theorizing and to count on his students to carry out the experimental work he considered vital. However, his over-the-shoulder participation in experimental work was close and constant. It is true also that Rapaport did not consider himself a "natural" experimenter, which perhaps further inclined him to lean upon others in fulfilling this part of his personal program—with no transfer of credit to himself.

But he saw no value in experimenting merely for the sake of experimenting. He believed that experimental work should issue from a clearly formulated theory. "However," he wrote, "our experiments so far have been designed that regardless of whether they confirm and elaborate the theory I am trying to develop they will bring new factual knowledge. I will persist in building such safeguards into every experiment" (1960a).

Experimentation was not, to Rapaport's mind, the only goal of theory. In common with Hartmann (1939), he was single-mindedly devoted to one vision, which was crucial to his work: to develop the resources of psychoanalytic concepts in such a way that from them would evolve a comprehensive general theory of behavior, one not simply founded on clinically useful concepts, but one whose formal character would provide a mooring for clinical *and* experimental observations. It is in the light of this vision that we can appreciate his efforts to use the findings of the ethologists e.g., Lorenz and Tinbergen) and Hebb's structural conceptions, and his probing and sensitive attempts to integrate Piaget's work into psychoanalytic theory (1959a, 1960b), and how he felt it to be his responsibility to bring psychoanalytic theory in a more rigorously stated form to the attention of experimental psychology, as well as to show the potentialities of the theory for illuminating neglected phenomena of thought, e.g., altered states of consciousness (1951d, 1951e, 1957a). He hoped too that psychoanalytic theory would provide an integrating focus for the training of clinical psychologists. He considered clinical psychology to have been prematurely professionalized under social influences emanating from World War II, with a resulting dearth of theory and disciplined scholarliness.

We should like now to review briefly the main phases of Rapaport's psychological contributions.

DIAGNOSTIC PSYCHOLOGICAL TESTING

Rapaport's first period of professional work was in diagnostic psychological testing. That he chose at first to work with tests rather than to experiment illustrated his gift for making one activity serve several goals at once, and to return full measure for what he was given. Testing provided him with an avenue to the study of the thought process, but in return, as he put it, "I earned my bread." That is, he fulfilled an immediately practical function in the clinical setting that was supporting him.

Rapaport regarded his work on diagnostic testing as carrying forward the efforts of Kraepelin and Bleuler to find in the *forms* of thinking the criteria for distinguishing various pathological entities. He felt that this program had been in abeyance during the rise to prominence of id dynamics which had focused interest on thought *content,* but that with the development of ego psychology a way had again been opened to a systematic approach to the structure of thinking. His first stress was on issues of drive break-throughs in thought, and the relationship of defense—again manifested in thought—to such pressures. Only later did he give equal emphasis to the relatively autonomous and adaptive aspects of cognitive functions.

Rapaport regarded thought organization as the key to the specifications of personality dynamics. He wrote:

> In the past few decades, *psychology* has become much concerned with motivation and personality. Nevertheless, it has paid little attention to the mediation-processes through which "personality structure" and "motivation" translate themselves into action or, more broadly, behavior. Thought-processes, in the wider sense, have been little studied [1951d, p. 4].

Rapaport proposed three assumptions on which to base diagnostic psychological testing, assumptions that have by now become axiomatic:

> (1) every behavior segment bears the imprint of the organization of the behaving personality, and permits—if felicitously chosen—of reconstruction of the specific organizing principles of that personality; (2) pathology is always an exacerbation, that is, decompensation, of trends existing in the adjusted personality, hence fundamentally diagnosis is always personality diagnosis; (3) the theory of diagnostic personality tests deals with the rationale of how, by which processes, the organizing principles of the personality and their pathological alterations are carried over into test performance [1950b, pp. 339–340].

These principles are not limited to the arena of "projective" testing, for Rapaport found that so-called intelligence tests are also sensitive to many of the nuances of personality functioning. For the first time, responses to the subtests of the Wechsler-Bellevue acquired meaning within conceptions of the dynamics of specific defenses, modes of adaptive control, and the workings of different forms of pathology. By his application of psychoanalytic conceptions of drive and ego structure to the phenomenology of specific thought functions, Rapaport opened the way to the study of consistency in all aspects of a person's thinking—"cognitive style"—as well as of the significance of such consistency in individual development, epitomized by research in recent years on the personality correlates of cognitive controls.

Rapaport's conceptions provide a general scheme for the analysis of how cognitive functions contribute to a behavior product. About any thought product, he laid out these main lines of analysis: What *functions* are exhibited through it? In what *form-varieties* are these functions manifesting themselves in behavior? What *conflicting forces* and *defensive constellations* are represented in them? What *reality-adaptive controls* and what *states of consciousness?* And over and above these considerations are questions of what *motivational forces*—on what level of the motivational hierarchy—are being served by them, and to what *environmental reality* is the thought product responsive? An adequate, complete accounting would refer to the *epigenetic* level of the behavior as well. Thus Rapaport established the standard of a complete functional approach to behavior in which form and content are joined by an integrated analysis. Such a program of behavioral analysis is, of course, an exacting challenge, but one that provides built-in guarantees against superficiality.

One of the consequences of Rapaport's contributions was the rescue of the psychometrist from the status of a technician and his elevation to the rôle of a truly clinically oriented psychologist, whose objective was not so much diagnosis, in the sense of classification, as an understanding of the distinctive patterning of thought functions in personality and in its pathological forms. Administering a test simply to obtain an I.Q. became a sterile occupation. Rapaport bridged the traditional gulf between psychometrics and academic psychology's search for laws of thought organization. Personality study through tests and the experimental study of thought functions shared a single objective—that of explicating the principles of personality in thought organization.

Rapaport's approach to psychological tests revolutionized clinical psychology and influenced clinical psychologists the world over. It was partly through his work that the Menninger Foundation became a symbol of pioneering advances in clinical psychology. His approach to diagnostic testing first appeared in manuals (1944–46) distributed by the Macy Foundation and widely used by psychologists during World War II, and in its final form in the two-volume *Diagnostic Psychological Testing* (Rapaport, Gill, and Schafer, 1945–46). A well-trained clinical psychologist can no longer be content with knowing how to administer tests well; he must steep himself in the phenomenology of thought functions within a rationale of personality economy—and David Rapaport's test rationales are indispensable.

STUDIES IN PSYCHOANALYTIC THEORY

The second major period of Rapaport's work was devoted to the integration of psychoanalytic theory. We have already quoted his view of the importance of systematizing it, and we have described his use of the historical approach in accomplishing this task.

It is possible to give only a brief and general review of his work in theory. While systematization may seem less creative than innovation, we believe not only that Rapaport's systematizations included innovations but that the systematizations themselves are creative achievements, as anyone who has struggled through Freud's metapsychology and then turned to Rapaport's work can attest!

Rapaport began his work in psychoanalytic theory shortly after the publication of Hartmann's *Ego Psychology and the Problem of Adaptation* (1939). Rapaport regarded this monograph as so fundamental that he devoted much labor to producing an authoritative translation (in 1951d; and Hartmann, 1939). It was also at about this time that Erikson's theories were beginning to appear.

Any effort to place Rapaport's work in perspective requires a statement of what he considered to be the contributions of both these men. We are fortunate that he himself provided it succinctly in a condensed yet comprehensive history of the psychoanalytic theory of the ego (1958). He accepted Hartmann's views on the undifferentiated phase of postnatal development, the independent roots of ego development in "primary autonomous" structures (to which he added threshold structures), the adaptedness and potentials for adaptation of the human infant to an "average expectable environment," the development of "secondary autonomous" structures by way of a "change of function" of structures (e.g., from defense to nondefensive modes of adaptation), saying that "Hartmann's theory links the concepts *change of function* and *apparatuses of secondary autonomy* (by way of the concepts *automatization* and *neutralization*) to Freud's theories of the secondary process and of (defensive) structure formation by binding of countercathexes" (1958, p. 751). He believed that Hartmann had formulated a clear-cut theory of the ego's relative autonomy from the id but had left only programmatic the ego's relative autonomy from the environment.

Hartmann's views are now generally accepted in the main stream of psychoanalytic theory. Erikson's views do not have nearly the currency or acceptance of Hartmann's in psychoanalytic circles, but Rapaport was not only convinced of their importance but believed that the theories of the two men converge and provide necessary supplements to each other, even though neither one of them had himself attempted an integration. He saw Erikson's "mutuality" as parallel to Hartmann's "adaptedness to an average expectable environment," and Erikson's "estrangement of organ modes" as an example of "change of function." He believed that Erikson's concept of ego epigenesis particularizes Hartmann's concept of autonomous ego development, as well as Hartmann's theory of reality relations, by specifying *phase-specific developmental tasks* (spanning the *whole life cycle*) which are solved through the ego and the social aspects of the ego's object relations. He believed that "The crucial characteristic of this [Erikson's] psychosocial theory of ego development, and of Hartmann's adaptation theory (in contrast to the 'culturalist' theories) is that they offer a conceptual explanation of the individual's social development by tracing the unfolding *of the genetically social character of the human individual*" (1958, p. 753).

Rapaport's first theoretical study was *Emotions and Memory* (1942), which he later (1950c; 1951d, p. 9) criticized as one-sided in its omission of ego-psychological considerations. With the studies in diagnostic testing, Rapaport's attention turned to the psychoanalytic theory of thinking. But characteristically, he could not make a systematic study of some portion of the theory without an over-all perspective. And so he worked out his view of the root models of psychoanalytic theory (1951a, 1959a). He outlined a unified scheme embracing conative, cognitive, and affective functions and under each formulated both a primary and a secondary model, thus placing in the foreground one of Freud's central hypotheses—the distinction between primary and secondary processes. The models served him in all his subsequent work. In explicating the psychoanalytic models, his main emphasis is upon development of a hierarchical sequence of structures through which the external world progressively comes to be represented. Through structural differentiation, drives themselves are transformed into more "neutralized" derivatives.[2] Finally, the stabilized structures and the motivations characterizing them become relatively autonomous determiners of thought and behavior.

Through the years Rapaport continued to be occupied with the over-all framework of psychoanalytic theory. He published (with Merton Gill) a paper (1959) on the metapsychological points of view, which proposed adding the adaptive and genetic points of view to the classic triad of dynamic, economic, and structural, suggested four assumptions on the most general level of abstraction under each point of view, exemplified these as-

[2] In the work of both Hartmann and Rapaport the concept of hierarchies in the psychic apparatus plays a central rôle, as indeed it did in Freud's earliest writings (e.g., 1895 and 1900).

sumptions in terms of the psychoanalytic theory of affects, and proposed a hierarchy for the classification of psychoanalytic propositions.

Rapaport's specialized concern with the psychoanalytic theory of thinking (1950a) resulted in 1951 in the monumental source book, *Organization and Pathology of Thought* (1951d). The form of publication expressed a good deal about the man. His ideas provided the footnotes to the papers of others. The bulk of the footnotes often far outruns the text, in a manner not unlike a page of the Talmud with its commentaries, attesting to one of the cultural roots of Rapaport's style. The book closes with a masterly integration ranging from the primary models through creative thinking to the socialization of thought. He characteristically described this final chapter as merely his "pulling together" of the scattered pieces of the theory. It includes important sections on states of consciousness, and on concepts, memory, and anticipation as cognitive structures.

Nineteen fifty-one was also the date of his first paper on the autonomy of the ego (1951b), a paper which was essentially restricted to a discussion of the autonomy of the ego from the id.

In 1953 appeared his conception of the psychoanalytic theory of affects (1953c), showing how far his grasp of the theory had advanced beyond the discussion of affects eleven years before in *Emotions and Memory*. Rapaport divided the development of the psychoanalytic theory of affects into three phases: the first in which affect was equated with psychic energy; the second in which affect was viewed as a drive representation; and the third in which affects were explored in relation to the ego, and the rôle of the ego in turn explored in the "taming" of affects. Rapaport's summary illustrates again his capacity to cut to the core of an issue and present it succinctly:

> The theory of affects, the bare outlines of which seem to emerge, integrates three components: *inborn affect-discharge channels* and discharge thresholds of drive cathexes; the use of these inborn channels as safety valves and indicators of drive tension, the modification of their thresholds by drives and derivative motivations prevented from drive action, and the formation thereby of *the drive representation termed affect charge;* and the progressive "taming" and advancing ego control, in the course of psychic structure formation, of the affects which are thereby turned into *affect signals* released by the ego [1953c, p. 508].

In 1957 Rapaport presented a full-scale study of psychoanalysis as a theory of development (1960b) at the commemoration at Clark University of the fiftieth anniversary of Freud's visit. His view was that only a psychology that postulates intrinsic maturational factors can properly be called a developmental psychology and that the central intrinsic, maturational factors of psychoanalytic theory are instinctual drives, the structures restraining them, and synthetic functions.

To the emphasis in psychoanalytic theory on the innate character of the drive forces, Rapaport was thus integrating Hartmann's and Erikson's propositions that the drive-*restraining* and drive-*adaptive* forces, themselves interrelated, likewise have an innate base. Freud had hinted at such a view as early as 1905 in *Three Essays on the Theory of Sexuality,* describing the forces that inhibit instinct as "organically determined and fixed by heredity" (1905, p. 177). It is also implicit in his ego-psychological works (esp. 1923, 1926, 1930, 1939) and is given brief mention again in one of his last writings, "Analysis Terminable and Interminable" (1937, pp. 343–344). In consistently adhering to this point of view, Rapaport (1960b) pointed out the inconsistency in Freud's reply, in *Totem and Taboo* (1913), to the question whether the original development of morality was the outcome of a deed or an impulse. Freud's reply was "deed," and in Rapaport's view Freud was thereby repeating in another form the early error of taking as deeds his patients' tales of seduction in childhood. He likewise emphasized that a consistent application of the view that the *synthetic function* (including the secondary process) has innate roots leads inescapably to the conclusion that the thinking of primitive man, animistic though it be, does not consist only of primary processes, as is sometimes assumed, but includes secondary processes as well.

In 1958 appeared Rapaport's second paper on the autonomy of the ego (1957c). Proceeding from his earlier presentation of Hartmann's theory of the ego's autonomy in relation to the id, he outlined a complementary theory of its autonomy from the environment as well, which Hartmann had implied in his concept of "internalization" (1939, p. 40). Rapaport wrote:

> . . . while man's behavior *is* determined by drive forces which originate in him, it is not totally at their mercy since it has a certain independence from them. We refer to this independence as *the autonomy of the ego from the id.* The most common observation which necessitated this conception was the responsiveness and relevance of behavior to external reality. But this dependence of behavior on the external world and on experience is not complete either. Man can interpose delay and thought not only between instinctual promptings and action, modifying and even indefinitely postponing drive discharge, he can likewise modify and postpone his reaction to external stimulation. This independence of behavior from external stimulation we will refer to as *the autonomy of the ego from external reality.* Since the ego is never completely independent from the id nor from external reality, we always speak about *relative* autonomy [1957c, p. 723].

And he concluded:

> . . . while the *ultimate guarantees of the ego's autonomy from the id* are man's constitutionally given apparatuses of reality relatedness, the

ultimate guarantees of the ego's autonomy from the environment are man's constitutionally given drives [1957c, p. 727].

The *proximal* guarantees of both autonomies are the same, and they are the apparatuses of *secondary* autonomy.

Rapaport followed Hartmann in insisting that the autonomy of the ego is only relative. In this relativity lies one of the conditions of health. For while the relativity of autonomy opens the way to reversal of this autonomy in regressions, it is only through such relativity that drive and the apparatuses of reality relatedness can serve as each other's guarantees. The issue of regression was thereby linked to "loss of autonomy," [3] and Rapaport described the conditions under which the relative autonomy of the ego may be undone. A rich lode of empirical and experimental possibility is contained in his analysis.

He dealt not only with the more usually discussed issues of how autonomy may be lost to the drives, but also with how it may be lost to the environment. Impressed with Piaget's (1936, 1937) concept of stimulus "aliment" in the formation of structures, he asserted that, once formed, structures require an optimal degree of appropriate external stimulation if they are to remain intact. Rapaport's dialectical turn of mind saved him from giving to anything the character of an absolute. In recognizing that structures require stimulation, he made clear that structure was no more absolute than anything else. He further proposed that internal as well as external sources can provide the required nutriment. On this basis he explained the capacity of some human beings to resist powerful environmental pressures, as, for example, in "brainwashing" (1957c). He suggested a hierarchy of intrasystemic (Hartmann, 1950a) ego structures which can cooperate as well as conflict with each other, as Hartmann had also proposed in his concept of the rank-order of ego functions (1939, p. 55).

The same paper outlines in schematic form Rapaport's model of activity and passivity. He considered activity and passivity not in the usual psychoanalytic sense of specific aims of drives, but as referring to "the degree of control of structure over drive" (1953b). He believed that the roots of such a conception of activity and passivity were already present in Freud's theory of the ego, that Kris had extended this conception with his concept of regression in the service of the ego, and that Hartmann had "made an important step toward generalizing this conception by demonstrating that the ego makes use not only of the highest-order secondary processes and rational regulations, but integrates and makes use both of its own archaic regulations and mechanisms and of the id's regulations and mechanisms" (1958, p. 752). Rapaport attempted a full-scale exposition of his models of activity and passivity, drawing upon clinical and other evidence to empha-

---

[3] Hartmann had similarly written, "The degree of secondary autonomy, as I . . . have called this resistivity of ego functions against regression . . ." (1952, p. 25).

size their complex layering in behavior and thought (1953b). However, he never published it, although on occasion he spoke of this work as his most original.

Only a few months before his death, Rapaport contributed a paper on the psychoanalytic theory of motivation to the 1960 *Nebraska Symposium on Motivation* (1960c). The paper is his most ambitious effort to state the psychoanalytic concept of drive and drive derivatives, and to confront the challenge to the theory of R. W. White's position (in the same symposium, 1960) that not all motives are to be referred to drives. Rapaport's solution was to distinguish between motivational instigators of behavior—those arising from drive and drive derivatives—and those of nonmotivational origin, which he termed "causes." While all motives are causes, not all causes are motives. The most critical energic source of the development of the nonmotivational "causes" of behavior was, in his opinion, attention cathexis. He believed that Freud's theory of consciousness as a sense organ functioning with attention cathexis could be molded into a theory of structure formation, and hence of the organism's relationship to the environment, and of learning. This truly bold suggestion, based on this little-known and little-developed conception of Freud's, received its only systematic exposition in this paper.[4] The hypotheses he evolved from this viewpoint underlay the little-known program of experimental work which he began about eight years before his death and about which we shall have more to say. The energic requirement of structures for nutriment he also viewed in terms of a claim for attention cathexes; the search for such nutriment he regarded as a cause rather than a motive of behavior, though he conceded that further work might show that the function of attention cathexes too has motivational characteristics (1960c, p. 902).

The list of his achievements in theory is capped by his study, *The Structure of Psychoanalytic Theory: A Systematizing Attempt* (1959a), which he undertook for the comprehensive review of theories sponsored by the American Psychological Association (Koch, 1959). Obviously, it is not possible to capture the detail and comprehensiveness of this work. Clear and balanced, it is written with an objectivity extraordinary for one presenting an area of work to which he had devoted the major part of his professional energy. Rapaport showed clearly here his talent for laying bare essentials, for seeing concepts in perspective, his ability to discern both strengths and weaknesses without unduly emphasizing either. This monograph, in the form of its systematization, reveals one of Rapaport's major contributions—that he brought psychoanalysis closer to the more general language of science. Following Koch's outline for the reviews of psychological theories, he attempted to view psychoanalytic data and hypotheses in terms of "independent," "dependent," and "intervening" variables and discussed the problem of quantification in psychoanalysis, including suggestions of how it can be pursued experimentally. But he made it plain that the

---

[4] Except for "The Theory of Attention Cathexis" (1959b).

methods of any science must be creatively tailored to its subject matter, and he decried a slavish adherence to some ideal of "the scientific method" as well as the "measuring rage."

There are two remaining important studies which will be posthumously published. The first, on the superego (1957b), includes valuable material on structure formation and a differentiation of the mechanisms of introjection, incorporation, identification, and internalization. The second (1959c), written as a memorial to Edward Bibring and based on Bibring's theory of depression (1953), tries to generalize psychoanalytic formulations of the affect of anxiety to the affect of depression.

CONSCIOUSNESS AND STATES OF CONSCIOUSNESS

A distinctly creative addition to psychoanalytic theory was made by Rapaport in his preoccupation with issues of consciousness and states of consciousness. Rapaport believed that psychoanalysis is the only theory that provides a useful conception of the nature and function of consciousness. He wrote:

> The question arises whether the narrowing of consciousness is but an epiphenomenon accompanying the narrowing range of cognitions, or whether consciousness has a function of its own in normal as well as narrowed ranges of cognition. In either case it deserves to be taken out of limbo and to be restudied: in the first case as an index of the cognitive range, in the second as an organization subserving cognition. Indeed, clinical theory has been treating consciousness as an organization through all the years in which most of experimental psychology used it as the generic term for deceptive and useless introspections. I hope that the observations I shall next present will lend support to the following theses: (1) consciousness can be usefully treated as an organization subserving cognition; (2) consciousness is not a unitary phenomenon but one that has a whole range of varieties, each corresponding to a different cognitive organization [1957a, p. 640].

Rapaport carried out important theoretical and empirical work around these two theses. He traced the vicissitudes of the concept of consciousness in psychoanalytic theory. He observed that with the replacement of Freud's topographic systems by the tripartite model of ego, id, and superego, consciousness was reduced in importance and the earlier conception of it as a structure for dispensing hypercathexis receded into the background:

> The next logical step would have been to state the obvious—that all that which had so far comprised the system consciousness would become the function of the structure termed ego—and then to explore the substructure consciousness within the structure of the ego [1956].

It was from this point that Rapaport carried forward the psychoanalytic theory of consciousness. His approach was a comparative one—to bring the function and structure of consciousness into relief by studying different states of consciousness. He undertook to observe himself in other than the alert waking state of consciousness—recording by a kind of automatic writing his own daydreams, hypnagogic reveries, dreams, and other products obtained during sleep. Through these protocols he demonstrated that there is a continuum of states of consciousness between waking and dreaming and that they differ from each other in the kind and extent of reflective awareness, voluntary effort, and forms of thought organization prevailing in them. Thus, the closer to the dream state, the more will thought be pictorial and implicative, reveal more primitive levels of the motivational hierarchy, and become, as he put it, "connotatively enriched" by the mechanisms of condensation and displacement; and the less likely will it be verbal, differentiated, and capable of "turning round" on the content of the state of consciousness (1951e, 1956, 1957a).

Rapaport reported on these studies in the context of his discussion of cognitive structures as part of a symposium on cognition held at the University of Colorado in 1955 (1957a). He argued that there are varieties of states of consciousness. Like other structures of control, they are "organized means or tools of cognition." He showed how in different states the same motif or theme can be traced in the particular cognitive garb characteristic of the state of consciousness in which it is developed.

Of the array of cognitive structures—in which he included, for example, memory organization, cognitive style, grammar and syntax—Rapaport singled out for special discussion two kinds of structures: first, those structures having to do with preserving distinctions in *modes of experience*—for example, the capacity to distinguish fact and assumption, memory and percept, hope and actuality, certainty and doubt, etc., all of these being varieties of experience that had not been brought within the scope of psychoanalytic theory, yet are basic to an understanding of reality testing; second, those structures that are formed by the organization of such varieties of experience into higher-order structures or states of consciousness.

In a paper on attention cathexis (1959b), he wrote that the workings of the synthetic function observable in dreams, reveries, and hallucinations necessitate the assumption that attention cathexes must play a rôle in these differing states of consciousness as well as in the "normal waking state." He suggested that either the attention cathexes are the same as in the normal waking state but their effects differ because of the prevailing structural conditions of different states of consciousness, or else that there are attention cathexes of differing degrees of neutralization, that is, that there are different hypercathectic "pools" for the various hierarchic levels of psychical structure.

The potentialities of Rapaport's conception of states of consciousness are still untapped. Its empirical value is shown in the recent resurgence of interest in daydreams and reverie states and the structural characteristics distinguishing these states from dreams—a view that owes much to Rapaport. His concepts of awareness and states of consciousness are being applied to the understanding of the effects of incidental and subliminal stimulation on thinking. He wrote, for example, in the paper on attention cathexes just mentioned:

> . . . The complex conditions of incidental perception . . . combine low levels of cathecting and structuralization with the consequent ready decomposition, recomposition, displacement, fragmentation, distortion, and indirect representation of percepts with motivational and structural conditions which by themselves are likely to bring about or permit (respectively) such vicissitudes of percepts [1959b, p. 791].

The concepts are proving their usefulness, too, in studies of sensory isolation, helping to bring about an understanding of the disturbances of thinking and of reality testing that occur in this and in other stressful conditions.

STRUCTURE FORMATION AND LEARNING

We come now to what was for Rapaport the most insistent and deeply preoccupying theoretical interest of the last few years of his life.

He was convinced that the most basic gap in psychoanalytic theory was the absence of a theory of learning, and he was further convinced that this gap could not be filled by any of the contemporary learning theories, which on several occasions he trenchantly criticized (1952, 1953d).

Since he defined learning as abiding change wrought by experience, learning was, for him, the theory of the organism's relation to the environment in so far as it was not determined by the innate coordination between drive and object. Only in Hebb's contributions and even more in those of Piaget did he see elements of an adequate learning theory which in his view would be, in effect, a theory of structure formation. He believed that a theory of structure formation had to account for the phenomena which R. W. White (1959, 1960) explains by postulating an "effectance" motivation. Rapaport wrote thus of his own conception of learning:

> Whether or not all structure formation (in that broad sense which takes account of the epigenetic-maturational matrix) should be considered learning (i.e., abiding change wrought by experience) is both an empirical and a conceptual problem. But it seems that all learning may be looked upon as a process of structure formation. The processes of verbal learning and habit formation may well be considered subordinate to this broader category, though their study may or may not be revealing of the relationship between process and structure [1959a, p. 99].

Rapaport believed he had found the basis for a theory of structure formation in Freud's concept of attention cathexis. He proceeded to elaborate the properties of attention cathexes, the conditions of their attraction and disposition in different structures, and the behavioral consequences of this distribution. Attention cathexis, he assumed, is critical to the raising of any idea to awareness; in order to rise to consciousness, excitations of both internal and external origin must attract a threshold quantity of attention cathexis. He further assumed that attention cathexes are available in only a *limited* amount and that, therefore, there is competition among excitations for that limited quantity. This much Rapaport found in psychoanalytic theory. He then proceeded to incorporate these fragments into a tightly reasoned conception of learning, extending the conception of attention cathexis in what he called a "reconstruction" of the theory, but which was, however, a truly innovative addition. The key proposition was:

> . . . if an excitation (internal or external) attracts cathexis in a sufficient amount, for a sufficient length of time or with sufficient frequency, a structure is formed which may be either what is called a memory trace of an idea, or a relationship between ideas, or a structure of a threshold character (for instance, a defensive structure) [1960d].

He reasoned, too, that considerable quantities of attention cathexis go into the building of a structure. Once built, however, the structure releases these cathexes, retaining in the structure itself only a small part of the amount used in its building; the rest becomes available again for attention and for further structure formation.

In placing his bets on attention cathexis as the basis of structure formation, Rapaport was taking a calculated risk. He was assuming that a quantity and the parameters of its distribution could yield propositions that would make it possible to define the *qualitative* aspect of structures. Through the rules that determine the disposition of this quantity he thought he would solve the enigma of structure—its qualitative character—the "glue" that defines its distinctiveness. It may be noted that in taking this stand he was reversing a position of Freud's. Hartmann (personal communication) has said that Freud's inability to solve the problem of quality, that is, the nonquantitative aspects of a structure, was his greatest disappointment, one that made him feel that his theories of consciousness, in their various phases, remained incomplete. We do not know whether Rapaport would have had more success with a purely quantitative notion of structure than Freud did. This much can be said, however: Its formulation in propositional and experimentally testable terms makes it a unique instance of psychoanalytic theory formulated in rigorous enough fashion to serve the needs of experimenters.

To test his propositions concerning attention cathexis, Rapaport began an experimental program in 1952. As he put it, "The question raised is not how much and how rapidly something is learned but rather how does something perceived turn into something retained."

In the first series of experiments that developed from this point of view (Paul, 1959), stress was placed on the structural style of response and upon the informational factors in stimulation rather than upon motivational, affective, and value considerations. The experimental program of his last years, carried on in collaboration with a group he had gathered together at the Austen Riggs Center, led him into issues of short-term and long-term memory, proactive and retroactive "inhibition," conditions of attraction and repulsion of attention cathexis, and, not least, a reinterpretation of experiments carried out in conventional theoretical frameworks (Rouse, 1959; Rouse and Schwartz, 1960; Schwartz and Rouse, 1961). He chose to work with relatively autonomous functioning largely divorced from motivation because he felt it was a good tactical choice. He wrote in his paper on attention cathexis (1959b):

> . . . The postulates and the observations in regard to autonomy permit us to hope that in some learning processes attention cathexes and structures may be studied in isolation from motivations. Naturally the ultimate goal, once the "independent" rules of functioning of attention cathexes are established, is that the rules of their actual functioning in relation to motivation will be investigated. Thus it is a tactical and not a strategic theoretical consideration which leads us to studies under the postulate of independence [p. 789].

Rapaport saw ahead a hoped-for decade of rigorous experimental work linked intimately to psychoanalytic theory. Just before his death, the trustees of the Austen Riggs Center had approved a ten-year plan for the expansion of the program. But like Moses approaching the Promised Land, access was closed to him by death.

These were the main and best known of Rapaport's programs of theoretical and empirical work. He had also projected for the future a number of others not well known which we can here only mention. They had already crystallized somewhat in the form of accumulations of literature, notes, excerpts from his reading, and fragmentarily expressed ideas. They especially concerned thought and communication in art, literature, and sciences, the nature of the artistic impulse, and the function of artistic form. The psychical structures involved in human communication, expressed in his concept of "channels of communication" (1951d, pp. 726 ff.; 1951f), he thought would be the basis for an eventual theory of social intercourse. Among his historical projects was "The Influence of Freud on American Psychology" (Shakow and Rapaport, 1964), a study in which he was actively engaged with David Shakow for several years. He had also recently taken on the task of organizing the files of the late Edward Bibring and preparing his unpublished material for publication.

THE PUBLIC IMAGE OF DAVID RAPAPORT

Reputation is crucial, for it conditions the approach one takes to a man's work, inclining us to take it seriously or not, poisoning or sweetening it, disposing us to read between the lines or only scan it or not to read it at all. We rely on shorthands in this busy world, and reputation is one. The hazard of being so guided is that reputation is often compounded of elements distant from or irrelevant to the work itself. The danger is great where Rapaport is concerned. The public face he presented attracted passionate pros and cons; he did not hesitate to shoot from the hip where he felt shooting was indicated; he antagonized many and aroused mixed feelings in even more. While the American scientific tradition is to keep such personal reactions out of print, this is not to say they do not exist; and they perhaps have to do with certain of the misconceptions that often appear in informal expressions and evaluations of Rapaport's work in the cocktail bars and committee rooms of conventions, where reputations are made and destroyed. There is too much value in David Rapaport's work for psychologists and psychiatrists to allow themselves the luxury of superficial appraisal. We do not feel it appropriate to do more here than to list some of these sometimes heard misconceptions. He has been called *merely* an encyclopedist, an *apologist* for psychoanalytic theory, *only* an ego psychologist, a *clinical* and not an experimental psychologist, and an abstract theoretician whose work lacked clinical specificity. As is perhaps inevitable, these public stereotypes trade upon one or another facet of Rapaport's personality. In isolation they create misleading perspectives on his work. Perhaps the best safeguard against them, and the best perspective to hold in reviewing his work, is the vision he shared with Heinz Hartmann, which we have repeatedly stressed, of psychoanalysis as a general theory of behavior that would draw freely upon and be rigorously applicable to phenomena both of the clinic and of the laboratory. In fact, it is precisely because of this catholicity—put to the service of bringing psychoanalytic theory into intimate contact with the major empirical issues and theories of the contemporary psychological scene—that Rapaport became *the* acknowledged authority—and this also is part of his public image—on psychoanalysis in the eyes of professional psychologists. It was largely by way of Rapaport that the theoretical contributions of Hartmann, Kris, Erikson, and others have come into academic psychology.

Contemporary developments in psychology were for Rapaport a matter of continuing concern because of the value they might have in deepening and extending psychoanalytic theory. Even when he rejected theories, as he did in the main contemporary theories of learning, he gave a respectful ear to the experiments and data that they generated. To only a few developments was he especially cool. He was distrustful of factor analysis because it seemed to him so easily perverted into an attempt to generate concepts by computer. He was wary of physiologizing in psychology, believing that the time had not yet come when such relations could be fruitfully studied and, further, that psychological theory could and should be developed as a self-contained realm. He privately expressed distrust and hostility toward religio-mystical influences in psychological theory, which he detected in certain contemporary extensions of existentialism, viewing these as crude misreadings of the great philosophical phenomenologists.

In general, not only did he seek to enrich psychoanalytic theory with the yield, historical and current, of academic psychology; he also influenced psychology by his effort to forge links, through theory and experiment, between the laboratory, clinic, and psychoanalytic theory.

Having arrived at the end of an altogether too cursory review of a remarkable man's work career, we are acutely aware of the inadequacy of our inventory, not simply because many subtleties of Rapaport's thinking are lost in our account but because so much has been left out of consideration entirely. We have taken no note of his discussions of purely professional problems, nor to the thought he gave to problems of therapy and pathology and their clarification in theory. Worst of all, we have given little notice to his tremendous vitality and impact as a teacher, as a man who launched many useful careers and provided a continuous source of nourishment to great numbers of younger and older psychologists who owe their intellectual momentum to his ideas. Here was a truly Faustian man, extraordinarily diverse and intense in the range of his scholarship, in his empirical and theoretical efforts, and in his unstinting personal devotion to the lives of his students and friends. "What dwelleth in men, what is desired by men; what men live by"—this was the grandeur of his quest, and we cannot conceal our bitterness at the fate which cut short his journey.

REFERENCES

Bibring, E. (1953). The Mechanism of Depression. In *Affective Disorders,* ed. P. Greenacre. New York: International Universities Press, pp. 13–48.

Breuer, J., & Freud, S. (†1893–95). Studies on Hysteria. *Standard Edition,* 2. London: Hogarth Press, 1955.

Erikson, E. H. (1937). Configurations in Play—Clinical Notes. *Psychoanal. Quart.,* 6:139–214.

——— (1940). Problems of Infancy and Early Childhood. In *Cyclopedia of Medicine.* Philadelphia: Davis, pp. 714–730. Also in *Outline of Abnormal Psychology,* ed. G. Murphy & A. Bachrach. New York: Modern Library, 1954, pp. 3–36.

——— (1946–59). Identity and the Life Cycle: Selected Papers. *Psychol. Issues,* No. 1, 1959.

——— (1950). *Childhood and Society.* New York: Norton.

Fenichel, O. (1922–46). *Collected Papers,* 2 vols., tr. D. Rapaport & A. Strachey. New York: Norton, 1953, 1954.

Freud, A. (1936). *The Ego and the Mechanisms of Defence.* New York: International Universities Press, 1946.

Freud, S. (1895). Project for a Scientific Psychology. *The Origins of Psychoanalysis: Letters to Wilhelm Fliess, Drafts and Notes, 1887–1902.* New York: Basic Books, 1954, pp. 347–445.

———— (1900). The Interpretation of Dreams. *Standard Edition,* 4 & 5. London: Hogarth Press, 1953.

————(1905). Three Essays on the Theory of Sexuality. *Standard Edition,* 7:123–245. London: Hogarth Press, 1953.

———— (1913 [1912–13]). Totem and Taboo. *Standard Edition,* 13:1–161. London: Hogarth Press, 1955.

———— (1923). The Ego and the Id. *Standard Edition,* 19:12–59. London: Hogarth Press, 1961.

———— (1926). Inhibitions, Symptoms and Anxiety. *Standard Edition,* 20:87–172. London: Hogarth Press, 1959.

———— (1930 [1929]). Civilization and Its Discontents. *Standard Edition,* 21:64–145. London: Hogarth Press, 1961.

————(1937). Analysis Terminable and Interminable. *Collected Papers,* 5:316–357. New York: Basic Books, 1959.

————(1939 [1934–38]). *Moses and Monotheism,* tr. K. Jones. London: Hogarth Press.

Gardner, R. W., et al. (1959). Cognitive Control. *Psychol. Issues,* No. 4.

Hartmann, H. (1939). *Ego Psychology and the Problem of Adaptation,* tr. D. Rapaport. New York: International Universities Press, 1958.

————(1948). Comments on the Psychoanalytic Theory of Instinctual Drives. *Psychoanal. Quart.,* 17:368–388.

————(1950a). Psychoanalysis and Developmental Psychology. *Psychoanal. Study Child,* 5:7–17. New York: International Universities Press.

————(1950b). Comments on the Psychoanalytic Theory of the Ego. *Psychoanal. Study Child,* 5:74–96. New York: International Universities Press.

————(1952). The Mutual Influences in the Development of the Ego and Id. *Psychoanal. Study Child,* 7:9–30. New York: International Universities Press.

————(1956). The Development of the Ego Concept in Freud's Work. *Int. J. Psycho-Anal.,* 37:425–438.

————, Kris, E., & Loewenstein, R. M. (1946). Comments on the Formation of Psychic Structure. *Psychoanal. Study Child,* 2:11–38. New York: International Universities Press.

Koch, S., ed. (1959). *Psychology: A Study of a Science,* 3 vols. New York: McGraw-Hill.

Kris, E. (1932–52). *Psychoanalytic Explorations in Art.* New York: International Universities Press, 1952.

Loewenstein, R. M. (1950). Conflict and Autonomous Ego Development during the Phallic Phase. *Psychoanal. Study Child,* 5:47–52. New York: International Universities Press.

Paul, I. H. (1959). Studies in Remembering: The Reproduction of Connected and Extended Verbal Material. *Psychol. Issues,* No. 2.

Piaget, J. (1936). *The Origins of Intelligence in Children,* 2nd ed. New York: International Universities Press, 1952.

————(1937). *The Construction of Reality in the Child.* New York: Basic Books, 1954.

Rapaport, D. (1942). *Emotions and Memory.* Baltimore: Williams & Wilkins.

————(1944–46). *Manual of Diagnostic Psychological Testing,* 2 vols. New York: Josiah Macy, Jr. Foundation.

————(1947). Dynamic Psychology and Kantian Epistemology. *This volume,* Chapter 23.

————(1950a). On the Psychoanalytic Theory of Thinking. *This volume,* Chapter 28.

————(1950b). The Theoretical Implications of Diagnostic Testing Procedures. *This volume,* Chapter 30.

————(1950c). Preface to Rapaport (1942), 2nd unaltered ed. New York: International Universities Press.

————(1951a). The Conceptual Model of Psychoanalysis. *This volume,* Chapter 34.

————(1951b). The Autonomy of the Ego. *This volume,* Chapter 31.

————(1951c). Paul Schilder's Contribution to the Theory of Thought Processes. *This volume,* Chapter 32.

————, ed. & tr. (1951d). *Organization and Pathology of Thought.* New York: Columbia University Press.

————(1951e). States of Consciousness: A Psychopathological and Psychodynamic View. *This volume,* Chapter 33.

————(1951f). Interpersonal Relationships, Communication, and Psychodynamics. *This volume,* Chapter 36.

————(1952). Review of O. H. Mowrer, *Learning Theory and Personality Dynamics. This volume,* Chapter 37.

————(1953a). Discussion at "Mass Communications Seminar." *This volume,* Chapter 42.

————(1953b). Some Metapsychological Considerations Concerning Activity and Passivity. *This volume,* Chapter 44.

————(1953c). On the Psychoanalytic Theory of Affects. *This volume,* Chapter 41.

————(1953d). Review of J. Dollard & N. E. Miller, *Personality and Psychotherapy: An Analysis in Terms of Learning, Thinking, and Culture. This volume,* Chapter 43.

————(1956). The Psychoanalytic Theory of Consciousness and a Study of Dreams. Lecture to the Detroit Psychoanalytic Society, January 14.

————(1957a). Cognitive Structures. *This volume,* Chapter 50.

————(1957b). A Theoretical Analysis of the Superego Concept. *This volume,* Chapter 55.

————(1957c). The Theory of Ego Autonomy: A Generalization. *This volume,* Chapter 57.

————(1958). A Historical Survey of Psychoanalytic Ego Psychology. *This volume,* Chapter 58.

————(1959a). The Structure of Psychoanalytic Theory: A Systematizing Attempt. *Psychol. Issues,* No. 6, 1960.

————(1959b). The Theory of Attention Cathexis. *This volume,* Chapter 61.

———(1959c). Edward Bibring's Theory of Depression. *This volume,* Chapter 59.

———(1960a). Research Plans: April 1960. Submitted to Medical Director, Austen Riggs Center. Unpublished.

———(1960b). Psychoanalysis as a Developmental Psychology. *This volume,* Chapter 64.

———(1960c). On the Psychoanalytic Theory of Motivation. *This volume,* Chapter 65.

———(1960d). Statement of the Research Plan: November 28, 1960. Unpublished.

———, & Gill, M. M. (1959). The Points of View and Assumptions of Metapsychology. *This volume,* Chapter 62.

———, & Gill, M. M. (1959). The Points of View and Assumptions of Meta- *ing,* 2 vols. Chicago: Year Book Publishers.

Rouse, R. O. (1959). Proactive Inhibition as a Function of Degree of Practice of the Two Tasks. *Amer. Psychol.,* 14:385.

———, & Schwartz, F. (1960). Word-Association Intrusions in Recognition Memory. *Amer. Psychol.,* 15:450.

Schilder, P. (1924). *Medical Psychology,* ed. & tr. D. Rapaport. New York: International Universities Press, 1953.

Schwartz, F., & Rouse, R. O. (1961). The Activation and Recovery of Associations. *Psychol. Issues,* No. 9.

Shakow, D., & Rapaport, D. (1964). The Influence of Freud on American Psychology. *Psychol. Issues,* No. 13.

White, R. W. (1959). Motivation Reconsidered: The Concept of Competence. *Psychol. Rev.,* 66: 297–333.

———(1960). Competence and the Psychosexual Stages of Development. In *Nebraska Symposium on Motivation, 1960,* ed. M. Jones. Lincoln: University of Nebraska Press, pp. 97–141.

THE PAPERS OF DAVID RAPAPORT

I

THE RECENT HISTORY OF THE
ASSOCIATION CONCEPT

Though this paper is of great historical interest for
Rapaport's development, that is not the only reason
for its inclusion here. It is a valuable survey in its own
right and deals with an issue still being fought on the
contemporary scene. The essential point—one to
which one might regard Rapaport's professional life
as having been devoted to demonstrating—is stated
in the final sentence: "Thus, the basic law of psychic
function is need dynamics and not the mechanics of
association."

The paper was originally published in Hungarian,
and its part II is a précis of Rapaport's doctoral thesis
on the history of the association concept from Bacon
to Kant. I have had the thesis translated, but decided
against its inclusion in these collected papers. It is a
sprawling document and, though it here and there
reveals flashes of Rapaport's insight and incisiveness,
I believe it would be of interest largely to students of

First published in Hungarian in Psychological Studies, *edited by the Psychological
Laboratory of the Royal Hungarian Peter Pazmany University, 2:159–180, 1938.*

37

the history of philosophy. Even more in this précis
than in the thesis itself does it become clear how great
a rôle was assigned to "affective-emotional-instinctual
motives behind associations" in the writings of the
philosophers through Kant.

The rest of the article is noteworthy for the breadth
of scholarship, conversance with empirical research,
and grasp of essential issues which Rapaport already
revealed in this early writing. The fruit of this detailed
knowledge of the development of psychology—including in his range philosophers and Wundt, Ziehen,
Brentano, Meinong, G. E. Müller, Ebbinghaus, Selz,
Freud, Pavlov, Thorndike, Katz, Piaget, Hull, Tolman, Uexküll, Lorenz, Köhler, Ach, and Lewin—is
to be seen in the scope of his later *Organization and
Pathology of Thought*. Perhaps especially interesting
is the attention he devotes to learning theory, a subject on which he unfortunately did not leave a systematic study and evaluation, though there are scattered trenchant comments on the subject throughout
his writings (see index). His discussion of Hull and
Tolman is a sophisticated one, even in contemporary
terms, and especially noteworthy in two respects.
First is his description of the Hullian system as following a model akin to the psychoanalytic: "As in
depth psychology, external contiguity and similarity,
as well as interoceptive stimuli or internal states, may
act as intermediary links in the sequence which starts
with the eliciting symbol and ends with the response." Second, as is also demonstrated in the quotation just given, is his recognition of the influence on
the one hand of frequency and contiguity, and on the
other hand of wish and affect as determinants of the
course of associations. That psychology must include
both ego and id is already foreshadowed—M.M.G.

I. DEVELOPMENT OF THE ASSOCIATION CONCEPT

Like most conceptual histories, the history of the association concept may
be divided into two phases. In the first phase, the facts underlying concept
formation are not yet fully recognized; during the second phase there is a
gradual recognition and more or less systematic organization of these facts,
which lead to the development of the definitive, explicit concept.

The problem of a historical accounting arises when both phases are in essence completed. This need may arise from two causes: (1) When a concept, in the course of its history, becomes public property, its popular connotations will endanger its scientific usefulness by playing the rôle of definitions and by subsuming a wide variety of concepts under one common term. (2) Another moment for historical survey arrives when new knowledge makes the presumably final formulation of the concept obsolete, requiring either that the concept embrace the new knowledge, or yield place to new concepts and definitions that explain the new facts more adequately.

Today we have reached a juncture in the history of the association concept when the need for such reformulation is imperative. The concept of association has become vulgarized and its popular usage meaningless. New facts have come to light which can no longer be explained by the classic association concept. This state of affairs has given the impetus and the background for the present paper (see Rapaport, 1938).

II. OUTLINE OF THE MODERN HISTORY OF THE ASSOCIATION CONCEPT

Although the association concept is derived from many diverse sources, the trends in its modern history show a remarkable homogeneity.

Bacon's "idols" are associations which underlie the errors of human thought. Authority, words, popular beliefs, subjective connections in thinking believed to be objective: these are the associations described as "idols" by Bacon. This, obstructing rational behavior, makes up almost exclusively the contents of his psyche ("human nature"). He introduces the inductive method for the purpose of eliminating this disturbing factor; however, the method itself rests on association by similarity. Describing learning, Bacon outlines the mechanism of association and states that *facts connected with strong feelings* (shame, fear, admiration, etc.) are more readily retained in the memory than indifferent ones. Thus he points to the relationship of association and emotional-affective factors.

Descartes attributes even greater importance to associations. Associations are the result of the activity of the vital spirits; their flow in the brain from one concept to another is facilitated by previously experienced contiguity of those concepts. Thought connections thus created are fortuitous. This is why Descartes found it necessary to conceive of the human being as divided into extended and unextended substance (*res extensa, res cogitans*). This is also the source of his skepticism, his systematic avoidance of these thought connections, and his assumption that the valid, rational truth resides in the innate ideas. *Ideae innatae* are precursors of the Kantian categories. For Descartes, the motion of vital spirits is the essence of the passions as well. *Associations and passions emerge from the same source. Several times Descartes refers to memory reproductions brought about by passion.*

Hobbes further elaborates the association mechanism introduced by Descartes as the motion of vital spirits. Perception, thinking, judgment all become mere associative mechanisms. Those aspects which do not readily allow themselves to be subsumed under this schema are excluded from the realm of psychology by Hobbes as "unorganized phenomena." He views the mind as two systems: the theoretical and the practical. The former is the system of association mechanisms; the latter that of willed actions, which take place between the two poles of attraction and avoidance; the latter system, however, is also subject to the former. *Thus, wish or instinct dynamisms are closely related to the mechanisms of association, the latter as subordinated factors.*

For Spinoza, associations express the laws of both the extended and the thinking realms. Thus for the first time a unitary law for all psychological phenomena is proposed: yet it appears to transcend the scope of the psychological law. *Spinoza is aware of the link between passions and association (memory) postulated by Descartes. His mystical goal is to avoid hatred, which hinders objective observation and understanding by determining the course of associative connections.*

Guided by the Bacon-Descartes conception of association as an error-producing agent, Locke arrives at the concept of association of ideas, for him a psychological disturbance bordering on madness. The Descartes-Hobbes mechanism dissolves; association emerges as the essence of reflection and intuition, hence, conceptualization. Association divides into two phases: sensation and reflection. This introduces the problem of the genetic method: what is the sensation that corresponds to reflection? *Pain and pleasure, the forces of the passions, are the basis of associations. They are also the foundation of habit, the association of ideas, and the flight of ideas.*

Leibnitz considered association as the primary undeveloped form of thinking and logic, in line with his general monads theory. Thus he continues Locke's genetic method, creates a uniform psychological law, imposing philogenetic unity on reason, cause, and association; furthermore, in his *petites perceptiones* he links association with the unconscious. *The already discovered relationship between emotional and instinctual life is carried even further: Leibnitz declares that "appetition" is the force leading us from one perception to another. Thus, according to him the motivating force of association is clearly the pleasure principle.*

Berkeley returns to the thinking of Hobbes, proposing a single law of perception and thinking. But, since neither man nor the world exists for Berkeley, for all is dissolved in solipsism, the law of association is a universal rather than a psychological law.

In Hume's system Locke's two phases of association—impression and idea, cause and effect—reappear. As a logical consequence, the genetic method makes its appearance, used to show that space, objects, personal identity are illusions created by associative connections. He attributes psychological experience to frequency of association and formulates an all-embracing mechanistic law of association. *There are indications that Hume considered the passions to be the driving force governing associations, will, and even rational thinking.*

Kant touches on associations in two connections. First, he attributes the activity of the imagination to empirical associations. Second, he answers the question of the validity of associations by postulating that they are valid on the level of pure intellectual concepts and pure intuitive forms by which man arrives at the laws of the universe. Transcendental deduction, by which Kant proved the possibility of synthetic a priori judgments, reveals the secondary laws of association. *Pleasure and pain are the determiners of the power of judgment; appetition is the determiner of reason, and the ability of knowing the basis of cognition, as proposed in the critique of the power of judgment; thus, appetitive strivings are the roots of associative and judgmental activities.*

It is seen, then, that every one of the above-mentioned students of the human mind, with the exception of Berkeley, *had some insight into the affective-emotional-instinctual motives behind associations. This thought then may justifiably be considered the main thread running through the history of the association concept.* Modern empirical studies of psychology have been forced back to this thread. Finding and following this line of inquiry represents the historical continuity between philosophical psychology and psychology as a specialized science in its own right.

The results summarized above are supported by quotations and interpretations of source material throughout this paper (Rapaport, 1938). The development of the problem is so manifold that my immediate goal is limited to mapping out that part of it which is related to empirical research.

III. PHYSIOLOGICAL PSYCHOLOGY AND ITS OFFSHOOTS

Physiological psychology did not advance beyond the association concept of the previous period; it merely worked on its systematization.

The school best represented by the names of Wundt and Ziehen set out to refashion Hume's concept formation and the physiological ideas of Hartley and Priestley on the pattern of modern physiology. It sided with the mechanistic finalistic philosophy of Hume's *Enquiry* rather than with the speculative approach of his *Treatise.* Consistent application of these tenets reduced the causes of all psychic events to sensory elements; the events, broken down into their elements, were then reconstructed with the help of the concept of association. According to this school, psychic events are made up of sensory elements which once had associative connections so that the occurrence of one causes the emergence of the others. Every single experience was held to be due to an associative connection (Wundt, 1874; Ziehen, 1900). Thus, this school outdid even Hume.

This line of investigation did not produce significant results, except perhaps the work to discover the common basis for associations arising from similarity and contiguity. However, the simplified approach allowed the broadening of the scope of psychology—even if it failed to answer the questions it posed. Among the investigators Ebbinghaus emerges as the most important; his extensive investigations of the statistical laws of association served as an impetus for further empirical study (Ebbinghaus, 1905).

Brentano's contributions mark the beginning of the reaction to the mechanistic conceptions. His work stimulated theories within the school which were to modify radically the concept of association. Brentano revives the medieval idea of intentionalism, causing the introduction into associative theory of two new concepts hitherto classified as associative mechanisms: *intention* and *attention* (Brentano, 1874). Brentano's immediate followers, Meinong and Benussi, took associations to be fundamental (*fundierend*) and the elicited psychological phenomena derivative (*fundiert*). The difference was held to be qualitative and of extrasensory origin (*aussersinnlicher Provenienz*) (Meinong, 1904; Benussi, 1904).

Ach tied this doctrine to Wundtian psychology and most of the later investigations follow his footsteps. *Before him, the study of intention resulted in no deeper insights than that psychological experience consists of a variety of qualities not mutually deducible from one another.* In Ziehen's system, all psychological phenomena are reduced to associations, while here just the opposite happens. More and more phenomena are declared to correspond to a unique experience, an elemental phenomenon, amenable to no further analysis. G. E. Müller (1911) speaks of judgment-experience, Meinong (1904) of attention-experience. Slowly a welter of others, such as specific-intention-experience, causality-, relatedness-, sudden change-experience, crop up. Both extremes made a contribution: one emphasized the common elements in psychological phenomena, though at the price of certain distortions; while the subtle analysis of the other brought out their differences.

Ach's psychology shows the reaction in its experimental criticism of the concepts of association and intention and not by adopting experience as the universal panacea. He does not conceive of psychology as mere description, as do the experience psychologists of his era. He attacks the theory of association within the framework of Ebbinghaus' studies (Ach, 1905). He argues that similarity and contiguity alone cannot explain the emergence of association, since every sensation and perception is multiply associated. He shows that a "determining tendency" must operate to select the elements to be associated from among the many that could be evoked; this tendency is the organizing principle of events. This is the path of Brentano, but the means are the experimental methodology of science. "Determining tendency" is a return of the selective principle whose existence I demonstrated in the association concept of the Age of Enlightenment. There it was seen to be a wish-dynamic factor, while here it is a hypothesis auxiliary to observation—Brentano's intentionalism in disguise. Its principal merit is to refute the hypothesis that the connection with the highest frequency of repetition prevails.

The era of reaction to the associationist school made its greatest contribution in showing the untenability of the explanation of thinking and experience by associative mechanisms and by associatively compiled elements. Under its influence even Wundt revised his theory, arriving at the conclusion that psychological processes are "creative syntheses" in which the end product is qualitatively different from its components (1914). Of course, this does not shed light on anything, but it does indicate the closeness of his atomistic approach to the quality-of-experience theory of Meinong and Benussi—however much the two seem poles apart.

The next stage in the development of the association concept is G. E. Müller's (1911) complex-theory. It assumes that elements evoking one another are in associative connection not only with each other but also with the starting point of the entire train of thought within which they occur. This reasoning postulates as a priori the very phenomenon it set out to prove and to explain.

Selz, who attacked this theory, does not succeed in resolving the problem, but is able to discredit the theory of complexes (1913). His investigations on thinking show that constellation as an explanatory concept makes the theory of association unnecessary. He works out a "constellation theory" showing that in thinking we anticipate results with the help of schemata and without any associative activity whatever. This is essentially the Kantian schema. The concept thus introduced is in need of an explication, such as association or an equivalent. But this is only natural. It is impossible to base a theory of sensation and perception on a psychology of thinking.

Here we arrive at a turning point in the history of the association concept. New schools begin to experiment with approaches seemingly unrelated to all that went before. Though it is always possible to trace their roots to past theories, their work leads to new, comprehensive ones. To wit: depth psychology, the biological schools, and gestalt psychology.

IV. THE ASSOCIATION CONCEPT IN DEPTH PSYCHOLOGY

The unconscious nature of the connecting and motivating force of associations, already encountered in Leibnitz's thinking, comes once again to the fore in Freudian theory, with the connection of symbolism and association becoming even more important. Mechanics are replaced by wish dynamics as the sole cause of associations.

THE UNCONSCIOUS AND ASSOCIATIONS

Psychoanalysis did not take its point of departure from previous associational studies. Freud studied psychic disturbances using at first the tool of Bernheim's Nancy school, hypnosis. He tried to elicit from the patient in the hypnotic state the cause of his illness. By this means, forgotten (traumatic) events were uncovered; he found that when he told these to the patient in the waking state, he brought about catharsis and cure. However, the effect proved temporary, the cure only symptomatic. Freud reasoned as follows: what is known to the patient in hypnosis must be present, somehow hidden, in his memory; since he is unaware of it in the waking state, the existence of the unconscious must be assumed. Freud assumed that if the patient remembered the traumatic event in the waking state the cure would be radical. He began to seek ways to make the patient's latent memories conscious (1916–17). He based his deductions on oneness of the psyche and assumed that if the patient communicated the flow of his thoughts (free associations—flight of ideas), their interconnection, their network would somehow allow insight into the patient's psychic life and furnish clues to the traumatic event. In other words, he considered free associations as the road to the unconscious. Thus he postulated the unconscious nature of associative connections and motivation. Two more of his tools, parapraxes and dreams, proved to be of decisive importance in the development of the association concept.

PARAPRAXES AND ASSOCIATIONS

Freud discovered that parapraxes are consequences of associations (1901). In the course of thinking, element a is erroneously associated with element c instead of element $b,$ but not because c is more strongly associated with a. According to Freud, b is not necessarily tied to a by associative connection. Rather, a can be followed by any element according to the instinctual, goal-, and wish-dynamic context from which it emerges. Parapraxes occur when two such strivings—wish dynamisms, as I have called them—are present, one encroaches on the associative chain of the other and disrupts the logical sequence. *Thus, associations are the products of wish-dynamic or instinctual strivings, rather than of mechanical contiguities.*

DREAMS AND ASSOCIATIONS

Locke, and even Aristotle, considered dreams to be products of flights of ideas, of associations. Freud had his patients free associate to parapraxes and dreams. With the parapraxes this gave him insight into the workings of the unconscious, the hidden causative wish dynamics. With the dreams, he arrived at the discovery that they have a language all their own (1900). He found that the smallest fragment of a dream is fraught with meaning, for it represents another, latent, associate meaning. That is, he distinguished manifest and latent dream content. One is all symbols, created by associative connections, a coded message. The other expresses a repressed striving, shunning the light of consciousness, expressed only in the symbolic language of dreams. As with the parapraxes, the associative train of thought brought about by one striving is encroached upon by another, a repressed striving; the latter is admissible to consciousness only in this way. The incoherent dream material is the manifest content; underneath is the core of latent striving creating the symbolism. Thus the dream language sheds light on the associative meaning of adequate and symbolic ideas. Here again associative connections are due to relevant wish dynamisms, not mere frequency.

ASSOCIATIVE MECHANISMS

Freud does not reject contiguity and similarity as association-producing entities. They provide the opportunity for associations connected by wish dynamisms. They furnish the possibility, the strivings, the sufficient cause for associations. Things, actions, concepts can fully substitute for one another by force of their associative connection. Such substitutions are widely observable, but the symbolism is usually highly personal; the hermeneutics peculiar to a given person can be deciphered only through an intensive study of his free associations. Common features of symbolism were found by Freud in the meaning of space, time, and causality. Some of these closely resemble those outlined by Hume (Spielrein, 1923).

V. ASSOCIATION THEORIES OF THE BIOLOGICAL SCHOOLS

Pavlov undertook to provide a firm foundation for the tottering edifice of physiological psychology by means of biological experiments. The reflexes were to provide the physiological equivalent of associations. For example, he studied the secretion of saliva on seeing food (1933). The sight of food was the "unconditioned stimulus"; the reaction the "unconditioned reflex." He succeeded in eliciting saliva secretion to unrelated stimuli repeatedly presented with the food stimulus. The new stimulus was called the "conditioned stimulus" and the attendant salivation the "conditioned reflex." Acoustical, visual, tactile, gustatory, and electrical stimuli presented simultaneously with food would after some repetition elicit salivation in animals. It appears, then, that the physiological reaction produced by Pavlov is analogous to associations. Since the conditioned reflex depends on the existence of the biological unconditioned reflex, associations must be biologically based. The phenomenon of extinction, which is analogous to forgetting, underlines the decisive importance of this relationship: a conditioned stimulus presented alone for a number of times will be less and less effective in eliciting the reflex, but if again presented with the unconditioned, it regains its force. It is also significant that only those stimuli presented before the unconditioned stimulus will become conditioned: once the animal has reacted to the unconditioned stimulus, no carryover reaction will take place.

This is a phenomenon of entirely mechanistic sequences. But it proved too narrow; if there were significant changes in the animal's environment, not even the strongest stimuli would elicit the conditioned reflex. This shows that Pavlov's experiments were conducted under highly artificial conditions and so—despite intensive theorizing efforts—they are unsuited to the interpretation of animal behavior in general.

The first theories of behaviorism adopted Pavlov's findings as "learned responses" and tried to see in them the laws of human behavior (Koffka, 1921). Watson, for example, attributed three emotions to the infant: fear, rage, and attraction, each of which may be elicited by specific stimuli (Watson, 1930). He held that all other affective responses can be elicited only by stimuli associated to these three and so are "learned" responses. His views were further developed by Thorndike (1898), who explained learning with a "trial-and-error" formula hinging solely on the frequency of experienced connections. Later, he calls the drive to learn the paramount factor in learning; thus, while using the mechanistic model, he realizes that if learning is to be analogous to the conditioned reflex, the latter must be a given, something that is prior to any trial and error. This leads to the question of the biological basis for the original tendencies (Thorndike knows many such).

The biological bases of the original tendencies of behavior were explored by the conative psychologies. To go deeply into the unsettled issues of primary and derived needs and their significance for the concept of association would take us beyond the scope of the present paper; I shall therefore limit myself to tracing the work of Katz (hunger and appetite), L. R. Müller (genesis of instincts), and Piaget (origins of intelligence), to the effect that it is the organism's objective biological needs which turn the psychological processes toward the external world (intentionalism). A two-component theory of the functions emerges: according to Katz (1932), the animal's well-differentiated biochemical needs, its general condition, and the prevailing external conditions (quantity, quality, composition of food, etc.) direct the animal without previous experience to its food. According to L. R. Müller (1926), instincts are functionally derived needs, based on biological function, hormonal and external stimuli. According to Piaget (1936), adaptation and assimilation, the subject's way to re-create the world in his own image and to adjust to it, develop habit and intellect. Bühler (1936) proposed the meeting of need and opportunity as the model of psychological experience.

Hull worked on the conditioned-reflex theory, Tolman furthered behaviorism by postulating the instinctual nature of behavior and by taking into account the animal's total situation, internal and external. The first step in

the adaptation of the conditioned-reflex approach to a theory of behavior
was substitution of "conditioned reaction" for the purely physiological "reflex." Hull (1937) introduced radical changes. The old concept of conditioned reflex was based on three factors: the unconditioned stimulus, the
conditioned stimulus, and the response. Now two new elements were
added: the interoceptive stimulus and the tracelike conditioned response.
The kinesthetic concomitants of behavior provide new stimuli for the animal and may become conditioned stimuli eliciting anticipatory conditioned
reflexes. Thus the three-factor schema becomes a chainlike sequence. With
the help of these factors, Hull and his students explained animal behavior
otherwise incomprehensible without the assumption of insight (Miller,
1935). The concept of the chainlike conditioning of all stimuli preceding
the selection (learning) "associated" with the reward-goal factor of learning or of punishment served as a solid explanatory base. If the interoceptive
stimuli which change the tripolar connection to a chainlike one are strong
enough, the animal is capable of adequate behavior almost from the start.
While the conditioned-reflex theory corresponds to the classical association
schema, the chainlike-reaction concept is formally akin to the association
concept of depth psychology. Thus, any element *c* may follow element *a* if
the process on hand links *these two*. As in depth psychology, external contiguity and similarity, as well as interoceptive stimuli or internal states, may
act as intermediary links in the sequence which starts with the eliciting symbol and ends with the response.

*Tolman, studying goal-directed behavior, clashed with the original stand-
point of behaviorism in that he set himself the goal of investigating the
animal's total situation: besides the manifest behavior, its internal state and
the external factors impinging* (1932) *on it. He came to the conclusion that*
organismic state and the individual's past are the crucial variables which
determine how the external situation will influence behavior. This is conative behavior theory, based on Tolman's experiments. Tolman showed that,
other things being equal, learning depends largely on organismic need. This
refuted the mechanistic conceptions and opened up for scientific scrutiny
what we have called "instinctual drive" or "wish dynamism" (Tolman,
1938). Thus Tolman sharpened the two-component theory of the conative
psychologies. In his detailed study of learning, he found the interoceptive
stimulus to be an abstraction accounting for only a fraction of all external
and internal factors at work.

The schools of Uexküll and Buytendijk were purely biologically oriented.
The latter was mainly preoccupied with the criticism of Pavlov's studies and
with phenomenological analyses irrelevant for our present purpose (Straus,
1935). The orientation of Uexküll's school, however, is pertinent to our
topic. Uexküll's (1931) point of departure was J. Müller's doctrine of specific energies, according to which the animal perceives the effect of the stimulus on its organism, rather than the stimulus itself. It perceives not the wave

length of the light but the specific changes occurring in its eyes. Uexküll says that this change is taken by the animal as a "signal" from the environment; it then uses it to orient itself in the external world. Thus the animal creates its own environment. Thereby Uexküll combines Kant's transcendental subjectivism and Leibnitz's monadology. He held that there is a rigid a priori relationship between perceptual signals (*Merkmale*) and reaction signals (*Wirkmale*). Experiments conducted by him and Buytendijk showed that on the basis of primary signals the animal can develop secondary ones. These differ from primary signals in that they are at once extinguished by failure. Thus Uexküll recognizes original connections inherent in the biological equipment of the animal, which are clearly identical with what we call instinctual; further, he recognizes secondary connections, those based on the instinctual.

Lorenz, his student, found nearly reflexlike mechanistic associative connections in the instinctual behavior of birds (1935). For example, in observations of the feeding of baby storks, he noted that the parent would circle above the nest before alighting to feed the young. If the parent is forced to alight directly, the young will not feed no matter how hungry, and will treat the parent as an enemy. Thus instinctual behavior functions like behavior acquired by rote. For this reason some students of animal psychology hold instincts to be learned behavior inherited over generations. Whether this unprovable assumption is correct or not, it is clear from the studies of the Uexküll school that actual learning is based on instinct. Thus their contribution to the new association concept is a biological foundation of the "wish-dynamic" factors.

VI. GESTALT THEORY AND ASSOCIATION

The final result of the reaction to the atomistic approach to physiological psychology was gestalt psychology. We discuss it last not only because it is the newest development, but also because it was meant to refute the basic principles and results of classic association theory.

KÖHLER'S THEORY OF ASSOCIATION

While classic association theory builds on sensations and perceptions, gestalt psychology accords primacy to the whole and not its parts: the whole is not the arithmetic sum (*Und-Summe*) of its components, it is qualitatively different from that sum. Instead of viewing psychological phenomena as pieced together from elements mechanically associated, gestalt psychology views them as dynamic entities within which the parts depend on self-distributive processes; therefore it is senseless to seek independent laws of the parts. Furthermore, if there are no independent parts, their associative relationship must be fictitious and merely the product of the dynamic self-distribution. Gestalt psychology does not doubt the existence of the phenomenon that the emergence of one idea may elicit that of another. But it shows that it can occur only if the associative elements belong to the same gestalt (Köhler, 1933). Consequently for Köhler, as for Locke and Hume before him, "association" designates only the connection of the elements; their recall is "reproduction." The strength of association grows with the *Prägnanz* of the gestalt containing the elements, but is not sufficient to elicit it. For if one of the elements loses its *Prägnanz* on a subgestalt it will not reproduce the other element. Thus, association is a function not only of the original connection but also of the gestalt in which it is reproduced. Köhler shows that the effect of associations is limited; while the gestalt creating the associative connection must be strong, it must not blot out the independence of the elements. The latter condition must also be met by the gestalt triggering the reproduction; elements in question must maintain relative autonomy as subgestalten.

LEWIN'S ASSOCIATION EXPERIMENTS AND NEED THEORY

Lewin varied his experiments according to the principles of gestalt psychology and redefined the association concept (1922). He looked for clues in the experimental material to refute the theory of association. His investigations were closely connected with those of Ach and Poppelreuter. A subject would learn some syllables and a prescribed way to react to them. To one list he was to react with rhyming syllables; to another with reversing its letters; to a third, he was to alternate these two reactions. Then the lists were mixed and presented to him. According to the classic theory of association experiments, the reaction to a syllable from one list, when appearing in another, would be appropriate to that syllable and not the containing list, or at least there would be a lengthening of reaction time, indicating a struggle.

This is what happened: when a syllable learned to be reversed was presented in a list of syllables learned to be rhymed to (or vice versa), the syllable was reversed (or, respectively, rhymed). But when it was presented in an alternate-reaction list (rhyme one, reverse one), the new instruction was followed without hesitation. In the second instance the law of association was not effective; in the first, it was. This proved that Ach and his school made unwarranted generalizations based on incomplete evidence. After a great deal of testing and retesting, Lewin came to the conclusion that learning and frequency of contiguity in time and space do not, in themselves, determine associations. Without a readiness to act (*Tätigkeitsbereitschaft*) there is no associating and also no errors. Supported by introspective reports, he concluded that subjects followed directions in the second experiment because variation of task precluded reproduction of learned associations, while in the first experiment, the historical homogeneity of the list promoted reproduction of the learned reaction. The essential difference between "determining tendencies" and "readiness to act" is that the former is abstract and general, the latter denotes a propellant of behavior, directly determined by the actual structure and temporal sequence of the situation, i.e., which of the possible response modalities will come to the fore and what elements will be reproduced.

This novel association concept becomes quite clear only in the light of Lewin's general theory of psychological forces (1926). According to this theory, intention (*Vorsatz, Vornahme*) creates quasi needs which imbue objects or events capable of satisfying the quasi need with positive valence (*Aufforderungscharakter*). Along with original needs, man has quasi needs. Intentions are the product of wish dynamics, necessary intermediates to attaining instinctual satisfaction (culture and civilization are just these intermediate activities); they create quasi needs which, in turn, seek satisfaction. Thus, the basic law of psychic function is need dynamics and not the mechanics of association.

REFERENCES

Ach, N. (1905). *Über die Willenstätigkeit und das Denken.* Göttingen: Vandenhoeck & Ruprecht. [In part translated as "Determining Tendencies; Awareness." In *Organization and Pathology of Thought,* ed. & tr. D. Rapaport. New York: Columbia University Press, 1951, pp. 15–38.]

Benussi, V. (1904). Zur Psychologie des Gestalterfassens.

Brentano, F. (1874). *Psychologie vom Empirischen Standpunkte.* Leipzig: Dunker & Humbolt.

Bühler, K. (1936). Die Zukunft der Psychologie und die Schule. *Schr. Pädag. Inst. Stadt Wien,* 11.

Ebbinghaus, H. (1905). *Grundzüge der Psychologie.* Leipzig: Veit.

Freud, S. (1900). The Interpretation of Dreams. *Standard Edition,* 4 & 5. London: Hogarth Press, 1953.

——— (1901). The Psychopathology of Everyday Life. *Standard Edition,* 6. London: Hogarth Press, 1960.

——— (1916–17 [1915–17]). Introductory Lectures on Psycho-Analysis. *Standard Edition,* 15 & 16. London: Hogarth Press, 1963.

Hull, C. L. (1937). Mind, Mechanism, and Adaptive Behavior. *Psychol. Rev.,* 44:1–32.

Katz, D. (1932). *Hunger und Appetit.* Leipzig: Barth.

Koffka, K. (1921). *The Growth of the Mind: An Introduction to Child Psychology.* New York: Harcourt, Brace, 1924.

Köhler, W. (1933). *Psychologische Probleme.* Berlin: Springer.

Lewin, K. (1922). Das Problem der Willensmessung und der Assoziation. *Psychol. Forsch.,* 1:191–302; 2:65–140.

——— (1926). Intention, Will and Need. In *Organization and Pathology of Thought,* ed. & tr. D. Rapaport. New York: Columbia University Press, 1951, pp. 95–153.

Lorenz, K. (1935). Companionship in Bird Life. In *Instinctive Behavior,* ed. & tr. C. Schiller. New York: International Universities Press, 1957, pp. 83–128.

Meinong, A. (1904). *Untersuchungen zur Gegenstandstheorie und Psychologie.* Leipzig: Barth.

Miller, N. E. (1935). A Reply to "Sign-Gestalt or Conditioned Reflex?" *Psychol. Rev.,* 42:280–292.

Müller, G. E. (1911). Zur Analyse der Gedächtnistätigkeit und des Vorstellungsverlaufes. *Z. Psychol.,* 5 (Suppl.).

Müller, L. R. (1926). *Über den Instinkt.* München: Lehmans.

Pavlov, I. P. (1933). *Vorlesungen über die Arbeit der Grosshirnhemisphären.* London: Bush House.

Piaget, J. (1936). *The Origins of Intelligence in Children,* 2nd ed. New York: International Universities Press, 1952.

Rapaport, D. (1938). *Az Asszocizcio Fogalomtortenete.* Budapest: Royal Hungarian Peter Pazmany University. [The History of the Concept of "Association of Ideas." Doctoral dissertation.]

Selz, O. (1913). *Über die Gesetze des geordneten Denkverlaufs.* Bonn: Cohen.

Spielrein, S. (1923). Die Zeit im unterschwelligen Seelenleben. *Imago,* 9:300–317.

Straus, E. (1935). *Vom Sinn der Sinne.* Berlin: Springer.

Thorndike, E. L. (1898). Animal Intelligence. *Psychol. Rev.,* Monogr. Suppl. No. 8. New York: Macmillan.

Tolman, E. C. (1932). *Purposive Behavior in Animals and Men.* New York: Century.

——— (1938). The Determiners of Behavior at a Choice Point. *Psychol. Rev.,* 45:1–41.

Uexküll, J. von (1931). *Die Lebenslehre.*

Watson, J. B. (1930). *Behaviorism,* rev. ed. New York: Norton.

Wundt, W. (1874). *Principles of Physiological Psychology.* New York: Macmillan, 1904.

——— (1914). *Sinnliche und Übersinnliche Welt.* Leipzig: Kröner .

Ziehen, T. (1900). *Leitfaden der physiologischen Psychologie, in 15 Vorlesungen,* 5th ed. Jena: Fischer.

2

SHOULD THE RORSCHACH METHOD
BE STANDARDIZED?

I should like to limit myself to two points: (1) I think that our question should rather be put this way: What standardization tasks have we in the Rorschach method? This is the first point I shall consider. (2) The expression "standardization" is often used instead of the expression "objectification." The second point I shall discuss is: What possibilities of objectification of the Rorschach procedure have we?

(1) The reason I feel that the question should be put the way mentioned will be clarified if we compare the Rorschach procedure with that of other psychometric tests. A good psychometric procedure uses several tests and tries to compound a picture of the personality by means of the records of these tests, comparing them and trying to find a unified representation of the abilities of the person. Each of these tests is standardized, but the conclusions drawn by psychologists are based on their experience as to the relationships of these tests and are not standardized in the common sense of the word. The Rorschach procedure contains a great many determinants, the relationships of which indicate the personality structure to the skilled psychologist experienced in using the method. It seems to me that the difference between the psychometrist composing the results of several tests to a unified picture and the psychologist working with the Rorschach procedure is not an essential one. The only difference is that the Rorschach proce-

First published in Rorschach Research Exchange, *3:107–110, 1939.*

dure cannot be handled like one of the other tests which can be standardized, because one of these tests indicates only one determinant, one ability of the person, whereas in the Rorschach procedure we deal with several determinants. We have standardization tasks here too, *but only the single scoring determinants have to be standardized and the correlation of them is to be handled and considered as we consider the procedure of the psychometrists* comparing the records of the single tests and compounding a picture of the person by means of them.

The three standardization tasks are known and recognized by most of the Rorschach workers. They are: (a) the question of F + and F − ; (b) the question of D and Dd; (c) the question of popular form. There is, however, no agreement as to the method of the standardization and its limits. On the one hand qualitative assumptions are being made, on the other the simple statistical frequency of the answers is taken as decisive. The results of both procedures are as different in the F + and F − as in the D and Dd question. My opinion is that the qualitative assumptions made up to now still lack the basis demanded by Rorschach, who stated that for the purpose of final differentiation between D and Dd, space-rhythmical experimental researches should be made. It seems to me that in the question of the forms we have the same problem. To be able to decide whether or not a rare form has achieved the form level of the statistically proved positive forms, we have to define *what form level means*. This can be done only by means of investigations of the procedure of form genesis.

On the other hand, the statistical method seems to neglect the fact that findings in 300 adolescents or in superior adults are not likely to furnish the basis for a general decision. It seems that some of the normal details determined in a statistical way are due to the age and lack of selection of the subjects and could never be normal details for normal adults.

In conclusion I want to emphasize the need for statistical research on these three determinants. But this statistical research must be refined by eliminating every record containing specific material likely to distort the results. Not *random* but *selected* material has to furnish us with statistical norms. The results of such statistical research can furnish the basis of our scoring. But only space-rhythmical and form-genetical experiments can complete these results so that we may achieve a scoring system likely to give personality pictures in accordance with clinical findings.

On the question of the popular form we are close to agreement, that it should be determined in the statistical way.

Until we have the results, showing exact determination of F + and F −, D and Dd, accumulated personal experience of investigators has to be the basis of the determination; and *it can be the basis, because statistical research together with space-rhythmical and form-genetical research will only systematize this experience. This is because this experience grows out of the comparison of the single answer with the whole record.*

(2) However, with the exception of this standardization problem, our

most important problem is the general objectification of the Rorschach interpretation. Here I see two main tasks:

(a) We must build up standards for age levels. This, however, cannot be a standardization in the common sense of the word. We must observe the changes of the Rorschach records of the same group over a long period, to be able to determine trends of evolution of the type of approach and experience balance, etc. We have to investigate average material in the several age levels, to have comparative material as a basis for our judgment. It is possible that we will be able to use more exact mathematical, statistical correlation methods, as has been done, for instance, by Ben Eschenburg or Nadine Suares. At least we must make efforts to use such methods. *But the main thing that remains is that we must deal with the relationships of the determinants and not with their simple statistical frequency.*

(b) Up to now clinical control, repetition of the Rorschach experiment, statistical standardization, were used as verification of the method. But the objectification of the procedure can be developed in an entirely different way as well. In my first point I referred to general psychological investigations on space rhythm and form genesis. Both of these problems can be investigated, for instance, under the aspect of the term *Prägnanz* of gestalt psychology. With the exception of the earliest attempts of Rorschach, Frankhauser, Furrer, etc., no efforts have been made to show the general psychological procedures underlying the Rorschach replies. We have to investigate these procedures and show how a reply is born and *why* it has the significance which it has according to the experience of all Rorschach workers.

The new instinct psychology, gestalt psychology, genetic psychology, psychoanalysis, the new psychiatric findings, the new concept of association in contemporary psychology can furnish a basis for explaining and objectifying the Rorschach experiment.

The experimental-psychological investigation—although a difficult and far-reaching task—can at least attain the same significance for the objectification of the Rorschach method as the statistical standardization. Its advantage is that it can give the basis for the parts of the interpretation of the Rorschach records which seem—unjustifiedly—to be subjective and arbitrary to many psychologists and psychiatrists.

3

NOTE ON METRAZOL

IN GENERAL PARESIS

A Psychosomatic Study[1]

WITH VIVIAN BISHOP KENYON
AND MILTON LOZOFF

Our purpose in this paper is to sum up the problems which emerged in the course of our investigations in general paresis. Despite the indubitable results of modern methods of treatment by hyperpyrexia and tryparsamide, in many cases, often even in serologically significantly improved ones, no remission of the psychosis follows. One of us[2] suggested the application of metrazol in a case of this type (see Kenyon and Rapaport, 1941). The psychosis responded to the metrazol treatment, and the patient was returned home shortly afterwards, well improved. Subsequently a group experiment was undertaken, and the results suggest that the psychosis of

---

[1] We are greatly indebted to Dr. Ralph M. Fellows, whose interest in the psychological aspects of paresis and the social problem of the "defect-cured" paretic has instigated and aided us in our study of these problems.
[2] Vivian Bishop Kenyon.

First published in Psychiatry, *4:165–176, 1941.*

general paresis can be influenced, and even greatly improved, by metrazol [3] in some cases. We propose to survey the theoretical situation in regard to the psychosis of general paresis in order that light may be shed on the theoretical significance of this result, and its implications for further research. The purpose of this paper is to seek orientation in the problem by a synopsis of theories and facts which have been thus far presented.

General paresis was for a long time removed from psychological understanding and investigation for rather obvious reasons. The organic damage was so impressive and the dementia was so outstanding that the possibilities for psychological studies seemed too discouraging. The introduction of malarial treatment centered the interest on arresting the specific disease process, rather than upon understanding its psychological aspects. As a result of early treatment the classical picture of general paresis became increasingly rare, and thus an understanding of its genesis became a more difficult problem.

General paresis still deserves special interest. The gross organic damage and the spectacular psychotic manifestations make it outstanding in the group of organic psychoses to which it belongs. It presents a basic problem from the point of view of psychosomatic research. What relation exists between the gross organic damage and the various psychological manifestations of the psychosis? Perhaps only the toxic group possesses a similar significance for psychosomatic research in the field of the psychoses. The biological background of the functional psychoses is still beyond our knowledge, and opportunities for a direct approach to the understanding of psychosomatic interrelations in functional psychoses are but slight at present. Thus general paresis, in which there are gross pathophysiological changes coincident with prominent psychic manifestations, offers an excellent opportunity to unearth at least some aspects of the psychosomatic character of the psychoses. Investigations on organ neuroses—asthma (F. Deutsch, 1939), for example—and studies on gastrointestinal disturbances (Alexander et al., 1934), have yielded similar information in the field of neuroses.

SURVEY OF THEORETICAL CONSIDERATIONS

We are not primarily concerned with the original theories of the etiology of general paresis, nor with the various speculations attempting to correlate the psychotic symptoms with pathophysiological changes. The theory that paresis is caused by a specific neurotropic strain of spirochete, Nonne's (1916) theory of individual variances as to the vulnerability of nerve tissue

---

[3] To our knowledge no other shock treatment of organic psychosis has been reported in the literature. A personal communication from Dr. D. V. Conwell of Halstead, Kansas, reveals that he has successfully treated two cases of paretic psychosis with insulin shock.

to syphilitic invasion, Bayle's (Kornfeld and Bickeles, 1893, esp. p. 337) explanation of the ideas of grandeur as due to overnutrition of the cortex, Baillarger's, Gubler's, and Meynert's theories attributing the euphoria and delusions of grandeur to central hyperemia (Hollós and Ferenczi, 1922, esp. p. 2), and Weichbrodt's (1911) formulation that a toxin of the treponema pallidum causes ideas of grandeur are a few examples.

Various remarks on the rôle of the previous personality pattern of patients developing paretic psychoses deserve to be mentioned. Näcke (1906) maintained that most paretics had previously been sanguine or choleric persons, having often been abnormal from early years. Similar ideas were expressed by Hoppe, Fauser, Schüle and Cullers, and Raecke (Hollós and Ferenczi, 1922, p. 4). Osnato (1918) found that in twenty of thirty-seven cases of general paresis, it was possible to demonstrate that the paretic psychosis occurred as a general rule in those who possessed "neurotic, seclusive, or emotionally unstable personalities," whereas in the remaining seventeen cases in which such previous personality abnormalities could not be demonstrated the physical signs of the disease were predominant.

There has been much speculation concerning the possibility that syphilitic brain damage may prematurely precipitate a latent functional psychosis. Schube (1934) maintains that the type of psychosis or psychoneurosis exhibited in general paresis is "that which the individual would have developed at that time provided syphilis was absent and any other precipitating factor (endogenous or exogenous) was present." It would be extremely difficult to advance scientifically controlled evidence to support such a theory. Although Kraepelin (1913, p. 92) considered the occurrence of other mental disease with paresis to be so rare as to be regarded as purely incidental, it is of interest that there are more recent reports of functional psychoses occurring coincident with neurosyphilis of a paretic type. Barrett (1916), House (1924), and Postle (1939) describe cases with episodic functional psychoses which later developed clinical and serologic findings of general paresis, with, as Postle stresses, psychotic manifestations identical with the previous episodes. Postle concludes that in the organic psychoses the brain disease serves to exaggerate the pattern of the individual personality features, or to release it from previous controls; that the particular type of mental symptoms in organic brain disease is determined by the individual personality organization and previous experience.

Not before Hollós and Ferenczi (1922) undertook their analysis of general paresis from the psychoanalytic point of view was there a real psychological investigation of the subject. Their main conclusions were:

> General paresis is a pathopsychosis. The general impairment of mental functions is responded to by withdrawal of libido from the functions concerned. Thus regression to earlier stages of psychic de-

velopment, in which the damaged functions were not yet existent, occurs, permitting maintenance of self-esteem, since the damaged functions do not have any significance in those stages of development to
which the patients regressed. No specific differentiation of this regression from others is given.

The organic damage only initiates the psychosis. It has a limited
rôle in the make-up of the psychosis which follows the psychological
laws of regression. The dementia as a special problem is not discussed
by the authors.

The psychosis commences with a neurasthenic and depressive
phase. While, according to Freud, the loss of love object is the cause
of melancholia, it is maintained that in paresis the losses of the ego
inflicted by the organic damage (narcissistic loss) are equated with the
loss of object and effect the depression and its compensation, the
mania.

The significance of earlier personality development for the make-up
of the psychosis is mentioned. Castration complex and incestuous
wishes are noted.

Subsequently Schilder (1930) made an extensive theoretical, experimental, and clinical study to establish the psychology of the paretic psychosis.
His main conclusions were:

Dementia is the core of the psychosis of general paresis. The damage of that *brain system* which accounts for thought production, anticipations, censure, and reality testing allows for ready penetration of
preconscious wishes. The delusional and thought material of the paretic is a banal one, as opposed to the material of the schizophrenic
which is archaic. Regression is rare and unimportant, and follows usually only the malarial treatment.

The organic damage and the concomitant dementia constitute the
essence of the psychosis. The case histories presented show that the
dementia often improves—thus it is conceived to be reversible. Regressive phenomena are admitted and explained by the dementia or by
an unknown factor introduced by malarial treatment. It is maintained
that: "If only the ego periphery is damaged, then the dementia appears and the ego ideal, when undamaged, reacts to this. If, however,
the latter is involved also, then a simple dementia results."

The assumption that initial depression generally occurs is denied; a
concession to early theories maintaining dependence of the type of
psychotic manifestations on localization of the brain damage is made,
inasmuch as a damage of the "manic-depressive brain system" is hypothesized.

The case histories show the importance of the previous personality
development for the make-up of the psychosis. The luetic damage and

psychic dissolution are equated with punishment for masturbation and incestuous wishes. It is pointed out that the psychological state of the luetic in general, which should serve as a basis of comparison, is not yet investigated.

A third contribution to the problem was that of Katan which, however, is not available to us in the original, at present. Van Ophuijsen (1933; Katan, 1931) summed up all three contributions; his viewpoint might be stated as follows:

> "Our problem may be stated as one of determining to what extent the symptoms of the organic psychoses, especially dementia, can, or must, be considered to be pathopsychotic." He adopts Hollós' and Ferenczi's regression theory. He quotes with approval Katan's opinion that "an important quantity of energy is absorbed by the fight against the paralytic virus or lost by the destruction of the brain tissue. As long as no malarial treatment comes to the rescue by a direct attack on the said virus, thus liberating again the absorbed energy, the necessity of keeping the level of psychic expenditure as low as possible continues to dominate." With the malarial treatment these energies are freed and "expansive adaptation mechanisms"—Schilder's schizophrenic features—appear.
>
> Van Ophuijsen adopts Roche's concept of axial and marginal (irreversible and reversible) dementia and appears to be of the opinion that malarial treatment has shown that "even dementia of a type which formerly would have been considered axial can be cured, or at least improved to a considerable extent."
>
> In paretic melancholia Katan found traces of the Freudian mechanism of melancholia; this melancholia, however, usually lacked self-reproach and revealed hypochondriacal ideas, often of a sexual nature and of oedipal etiology.
>
> Van Ophuijsen accepts Ferenczi's concept of pathopsychosis (1916), by inference, the determination of the psychosis by previous personality development (Ferenczi et al., 1919); he adopts further the oedipal-castration-incestuous character of the psychosis suggested by Schilder and elaborated by Katan.

A careful scrutiny of these theories shows that the one feature common to them can be summed up as follows: the psychic manifestations of general paresis might be understood in terms of Freudian psychodynamics, no matter whether the psychotic material is considered in terms of regression, as Hollós and Ferenczi, or Katan, considered it, or it is considered, as by Schilder, to be a product of preconscious wishes which easily penetrate because of the damage inflicted on the system of reality testing. There is, however, a great difference between the former and the latter approaches. If the regression is the basic phenomenon of the paretic psychosis, then its reversibility can be readily understood, since the regression of functional psychoses has been considered reversible—at least theoretically—because of spontaneous remissions, and psychotherapeutic, as well as pharmaco-therapeutic, improvements. If, however, the dementia, developing on the basis of the brain damage, is the basis of the paretic psychosis, then it is far from obvious how it can be reversible.

It seems to us that there are at least three possibilities which might explain the reversibility of the paretic psychosis.

One possibility is that brain damage is *the* cause of the dementia and this in turn is the cause for the ready penetration of preconscious wishes, constituting the delusional content of the paretic psychosis—Schilder's theory. In this case the reversibility might be explained by the regeneration of the destroyed brain tissue, subsidence of inflammatory processes, or a vicarious function of other parts of the brain, taking over the reality-testing function of the damaged parts.

Another possibility is that the brain damage is the pathological basis. The psychic apparatus reacts to this in a fashion which is clinically described as dementia, and only secondarily on the basis of this dementia does the regression with nonarchaic and archaic features of the paretic psychosis develop—Hollós and Ferenczi. This hypothesis would permit of reversibility, as the dementia itself would thus be only a part of the psychotic development. This would be consistent with Roche's concepts of "axial and marginal dementia," discussed by van Ophuijsen.

A third possibility is that the dementia is of a twofold origin, being caused, in part, by the organic damage, and, in part, occurring as a concomitant of the psychotic process. Thus, reversible and irreversible, psychogenic and organic, marginal and axial deterioration—dementia—would shade imperceptibly into each other.

It is obvious that this theoretical situation is not especially clear. The sole point of clear-cut agreement in all these theories would grant no more than an understanding of the fantasies—of the unconscious individual content—of the paretic patient; and further, a general inference that the previous personality development plays a determining rôle in the make-up of this psychosis; the concrete significance of this rôle is not clarified by any of these theories. However, the points where agreement is not present are of broader scope.

On the one hand they raise the question: what is the mechanism by which the psyche relates to the body, to its own states and efficiency, in the same manner as it does to environmental objects—reacting to damage, sometimes with castration complex and melancholia by regression to early stages of development, and at other times with simple deterioration? [4] This

---

[4] It appears that all of these changes can be brought about by changes in object cathexes also.

variety of responses to organic damage might yield information about psychosomatic interrelations in further investigations.

On the other hand, the problem is implied whether or not the dementia itself is reversible and whether and how far the dementia depends on the actual organic damage. The reversibility of functional psychoses and their dementia should be the basis for comparison. We shall see that a complete reversibility might be questioned there too.

THE FACTUAL MATERIAL

The factual material, which appears to have a bearing on the theoretical problems just described, will be surveyed.

In this section we shall advance the evidence derived from the reaction of the paretic psychosis to malaria, sodium amytal, and metrazol. In the next section the evidence obtained from investigations with psychological testing methods will be discussed.

THE EFFECT OF MALARIA

The two main problems arising for us in connection with malarial treatment are: how does it occur that some of the malaria-treated patients, although improved serologically, remain psychotic, while some others, although showing no change in serology, have a good remission of the psychosis; and, how does it occur that some of the paretic patients develop marked schizophrenic features in their psychosis, in the course of or after the malarial treatment (Dattner, 1933; Gerstmann, 1924; Krayenbühl, 1929; Kihn, 1928; Rothschild, 1940; Schilder, 1930)?

These two problems have a positive bearing on the psychogenic origin of the paretic psychosis, because they are hardly explainable on the basis of purely organic hypotheses. It might be advanced that the organic damage— parenchymatous damage and inflammatory processes—itself is responsible for the psychosis and that the remissions are explained by subsidence of the inflammatory processes, and that the lack of remissions in turn is due to the great extent of irreversible organic damage. Against this, arguments might be offered to the effect that this hypothesis would not explain the change of the psychotic picture, described under our second main problem. In addition, although we cannot exclude, on the basis of the experiences with malaria, the possibility that the remission is due to the subsidence of inflammatory processes, we have clinical and testing evidence that the quantity of the damage—if this can be measured by clinical deterioration and deterioration tests—does not account for the persistence of the psychosis; for we had cases of good remissions in which the deterioration was much greater—relatively and absolutely[5]—than in other cases showing no remission. Thus

[5] By "relative" is meant the comparison of the difference between the vocabulary and performance scores of the same person; by "absolute" is meant the comparison between the performance scores of different persons.

far, the deterioration appears to be correlated to a certain degree with the organic damage, while the persistence or nonpersistence of the psychosis seems to depend rather on a more general factor, probably on the previous personality structure.

Some light might be shed on our second problem by the reports of cases in which febrile states elicit psychoses in nonparetic cases (Menninger, 1919a, 1919b; Henderson and Gillespie, 1927, pp. 286–289). It has also been observed that occasionally there is a spontaneous remission of a functional psychosis in accidentally contracted febrile illnesses (Courbon, 1923; Jones, 1927; Munn, 1934). The beneficial effects of malaria on certain cases of schizophrenia have also been observed.[6] While there is no doubt that hyperpyrexia has a spirocheticidal effect and resolves inflammatory processes, it is conceivable that malaria has some additional action comparable with the above-mentioned effects of other febrile states reaching beyond the specific effect. The nature of this further effect is unknown, except that it would seem safe to call it a nonspecific effect.

How this nonspecific effect relates to the theory of Katan, that malaria liberates energies absorbed in the fight against the toxic virus and thus makes the psychotic display apparent, is not clear.[7] Neither is the relation to Grotjahn's (1938, pp. 156–157) findings and theory on juvenile paresis clear. He says that,

> The high and repeated fever, chills and weakness of the body fulfill the need for punishment and eliminate the feeling of guilt. . . .
>
> Also, it is now evident why a second fever cure is so seldom followed by a psychological success even if the second treatment succeeds in serological sanitation of the blood and spinal fluid. In consequence of the repetition the fever can never impress or activate the patient as greatly as the psychological experience of the *first* treatment.

To call this unknown effect a "psychological effect" or attribute it to a change in the "homeostatic equilibrium" would merely be giving it another label, unless by the term we mean something which has concrete corollaries. We suggest the consideration of some purely theoretical aspects which might be useful for all of our discussion. The psychosomatic unity of the organism becomes, from day to day, more evident. In view of this fact, is it permissible to speak about such phenomena in terms of "This is organic," and "This is psychological"? It seems to us that we deal here with a twofold phenomenology and, accordingly, with two empirical ways of approach. It is necessary to use both approaches, especially since we are far

---

[6] In the State Hospital, Osawatomie, Kansas, we have seen some striking examples of this type.

[7] See Rothschild's (1940) similar theoretical attempt.

from knowing the interrelations of both phenomenologies. However, we must not forget that when dealing with "psychological facts" we deal only with one aspect of this unity and vice versa. By "psychological effect" we certainly do not mean something which does not have physiological correlates. We should use this term only when the psychological aspect of the integrated psychosomatic process is more readily available for a demonstrable hypothesis than the physiological.

Thus, if we are inclined to call the effect of malaria therapy a psychological effect we must indicate concretely what we mean by this. It is well known that fever has the psychic effect of weakening the reality-testing mechanisms, permitting entrance of unconscious tendencies into consciousness. If both effects of malaria, remission and further regression, be considered changes in reality testing similar to those probably present in febrile psychoses and postfebrile remissions, this would constitute a concrete psychological hypothesis which awaits demonstrable confirmation. It is conceivable that such a loosening or weakening of the boundaries in the psychic make-up is of varying degrees in different patients depending on the previous personality structure (Menninger, 1919a, 1919b). This might explain the varying effects of malarial therapy on the paretic psychosis. Some paretics with a certain type of personality structure would show less weakening of the reality-testing mechanisms so that no further regression occurs, and with cessation of the febrile state[8] they tend to reverse toward normality, while those with less favorable previous personality structure, namely those with previous strong schizoid trends, regress further as a result of the weakening of the reality-testing functions, thus permitting the appearance of archaic material.

In summary, it might be said that Katan's energy liberation and Grotjahn's punishment are but other expressions of what was suggested as occurring, in general, psychologically in febrile states. It might be that all these three are but different aspects of the same process; on the other hand it may be that they mutually exclude each other. No feature of the material known to us at present seems to give decisive evidence concerning these alternatives.

THE EFFECT OF SODIUM AMYTAL

The only report on the effect of sodium amytal on paresis, to our knowledge, was published by Fellows (1932). A hopelessly deteriorated paretic patient, who did not improve with all the usual specific treatments and who refused to eat or speak, was given sodium amytal. After the first sodium-amytal administration he behaved normally, ate, spoke, was rational, tidy, and able to dress himself. After a few hours he relapsed into his earlier

[8] The beneficial effect of malaria on the paretic psychosis often does not become apparent for several weeks, indicating—if our hypothesis is applied to this fact—that the re-establishment of reality testing can occur as a slow, gradual process.

state. After a series of sodium-amytal administrations he remained improved and was paroled. Here the report ends. Available personal communication indicates that shortly after his parole the patient again relapsed and was admitted to another hospital where he died.

What is the theoretical significance of the effects summarized above? Reversibility of the psychosis of general paresis is apparent here, although the agent producing the remission probably had no effect on spirochetes or on the cerebral inflammation. The fact that the psychosis and probably the deterioration of general paresis yielded to sodium amytal in the same temporary way as the functional psychoses do, appears to indicate that the make-up of the paretic and functional psychoses may be similar. This would support the basic assumption of Hollós and Ferenczi, namely, that the psychosis of general paresis is precipitated in a response to the impairment of the ego inflicted by the organic damage, and characterized by regressive mechanisms.

It would be of great interest to have detailed data on the psychic contents of sodium-amytal twilight states of paretics and on the psychic contents and deterioration measures of such a remission period as described in the case history presented above. The clarification of the effect of sodium amytal on the psychic content of the paretic during the active defense against the disease, as well as the alterations of the psychotic content in the course of the malarial treatment, as shown by sodium-amytal interviews, might indicate whether there is an absorption of psychic energies present, bound unalterably with the somatic defense to the disease process, as advanced by Katan. Such results might give a clue concerning the nature of regression after malaria and of deterioration in general, as well as the nature of the psychic changes in other febrile states.

THE EFFECT OF METRAZOL

We described in the introduction how we came to use metrazol in the treatment of the psychosis of general paresis. We conducted this experiment on a group of sixteen patients. Four of these had received no previous specific type of treatment. The remaining twelve in the group had received specific therapy, including malaria or artificial hyperpyrexia and chemotherapy without appreciable improvement in the psychosis.

The period of time elapsing between the specific fever and initial metrazol treatment varied from one month to two years and two months. In the untreated group, two patients improved both clinically and in their objective psychological testing results; one showed a slight improvement, and one no change.

In the specifically treated group of twelve patients, three showed a good clinical improvement [9] with metrazol therapy, two of these were subse-

[9] Clinical improvement means here a favorable change in the psychotic features in the direction of remission, not implying any improvement in the organic syphilitic process.

quently paroled; four showed some clinical improvement, while five remained unimproved. The three well-improved cases had intervals of five weeks, three months, and two years and two months, respectively, between the specific fever treatment and metrazol treatment.

There can be many objections and doubts as to the significance of these results, for example:

General paresis has already been described by Kraepelin (1913, pp. 83, 92) to be of a fluctuating nature. The objection can be made that our results, as well as the above-quoted result with sodium amytal, are simply a product of such fluctuations. We have to admit this possibility. The fact, however, that there were several significant improvements and that nearly all of the patients showed some improvement in the treatment period, makes it probable that more than fluctuation is involved. It is true that we did not have a control group with neutral injections and with the same psychiatric care as that which was granted to the metrazol patients. We do not think, however, that the nature of general paresis would permit such control experiments. In our opinion no paretic patient can be deprived of the benefit of continuous treatment while in an acute stage; and to take a control group of unsuccessfully treated patients would not be of much value.[10]

Thus, the decision concerning the reliability of the results has to be sought in other ways. In accordance with modern experimental psychopathology it will be necessary, in general, to look for means of decision other than statistically reliable differences between treated and untreated groups.[11] The decision lies in the theoretical systemic consistency of the findings of clinical and psychological testing studies in systematically varied types of treatment. In our problem, malaria, sodium amytal, and metrazol treatments constitute the experimental variations; the systemic consistency of the patients' reactions to these is the topic of our discussion.

Another objection might be that the group was too small and the results too recent to permit conclusions. It must be stated, however, that the nature of the conclusions sought here is not dependent upon the size of the group and the recency of the results. The problem is not primarily the therapeutic problem, but that of the make-up of the psy-

---

The detailed psychiatric and laboratory data, as well as the data on treatments, will be published in the near future. [Kenyon, Lozoff, and Rapaport, 1941.]

[10] Even in our metrazol series, we did not feel justified in depriving the patients of the benefit of specific treatment; in order to keep the experiment as reliable as possible, bismuth sodium tartrate—an agent which we felt to be least likely to interfere with the results of the experiment—was administered biweekly during the course of the metrazol treatment.

[11] Compare this with a similar development in experimental psychology as reflected by Lewin (1927).

chosis of general paresis. In this respect our results show that the psychosis of general paresis *might* yield to the same agents as do the functional psychoses.

A third objection can be raised that in the cases which improved during the metrazol treatment, the improvement was a delayed effect of the previous hyperpyrexia treatment, rather than a result of the metrazol shock itself. This objection may have some validity, but against it the following two considerations can be raised: the improvement occurred only during the metrazol treatment, whereas it had not occurred previously despite the varying intervals between the conclusion of the hyperpyrexia and the institution of the metrazol treatment; and, the group contained, as has been described above, several untreated cases which showed especially good improvement during the metrazol treatment.

These considerations seem to indicate that the improvements were more than purely coincidental. What does this fact imply theoretically? To answer this is difficult, because the actual mechanism of the effect of metrazol shock on functional psychosis is not yet established. Is it anoxemia, anoxia? Is it destruction of the most minute nerve fibers? Is it disequilibration of the rigid homeostasis of the psychotic? Or is it punishment? Is it rebirth? Is it a deep orgastic satisfaction? It appears that the present state of knowledge does not permit any answer to these questions. If this be so, then the question must be raised whether or not it is warranted to draw any conclusion from the similarity of reaction of functional and paretic psychoses to metrazol. One positive conclusion appears to be warranted: in both there is some type of psychosomatic disturbance of reversible nature present. What the specific psychic and somatic representations of this disturbance are, is not exactly known. A negative conclusion also seems warranted, namely that it is improbable that the effect of the metrazol convulsion on the paretic psychosis was due to a specific action of metrazol either on the spirochetes or on the actual brain pathology. It seems much more probable that such a very general factor as the homeostatic equilibrium of the organism is changed by the metrazol shock. What we learned thus from these results is that many features of the paretic psychosis might be reversible and the metrazol affects not the specific paretic process, but instead appears to act in the same manner as in the functional psychoses, supporting the psychogenic theory of the psychosis of general paresis.[12]

12 Two of the previously untreated patients who made striking clinical improvements as a result of the metrazol treatment showed some degree of further improvement with subsequent hyperpyrexia therapy, while the third, who had made but little clinical improvement with metrazol, showed marked improvement following malaria. These findings might have some bearing on the twofold origin—somatic and psychic—of the paretic psychosis.

THE PSYCHOLOGICAL TEST FINDINGS

We administered three different tests before and after metrazol treatments and before and after malaria or artificial hyperpyrexia to paretics in order to check upon the changes elicited by these treatments.[13]

The tests used were the Rorschach Inkblot Test, the Babcock Mental Deterioration Test, and the Szondi Test.[14] The implications of the results of the three tests will be discussed individually.[15]

THE RORSCHACH TEST

The Rorschach Test (Rickers-Ovsiankina, 1938) of the paretic, except in cases with full-fledged ideas of grandeur, is dominated by anatomical answers, impulsive color answers, few movement answers, by failures, and by depressive characteristics. The majority of our group in which we had good results appeared to show the coarctative improvement manics usually show after metrazol treatment (Orbison, Eisner, and Rapaport, 1940). We had only a few patients who, like catatonics, increased their color scores, with more affective responsivity and release of blocking. In general, the paretics showing schizophrenic characteristics showed less tendency toward improvement.

Significant is the fact that the patients, after improvement, still manifest a bodily preoccupation—indicated by anatomical answers—depressive features, strong coarctation, and a repression of affects. This indicates that the path toward regression through bodily preoccupation and depression[16] is still present. Psychiatric investigation of these patients reveals the actual presence of these characteristics, even in those who have had practically optimal remissions. This indicates that not all of the psychosis, namely, its precipitants and sequelae, is reversible. The discussion of the Babcock results appears to shed further light on this point. What seems to be changed is the discharge of impulses which appears to be checked, as indicated by the diminished number of the color answers after improvement. The range of the affective and intellectual interest appears to be extremely narrowed after treatment, as if to avoid the reoccurrence of the regressive process.

The problem suggested by these test results is whether in spontaneous remissions we have the same coarctative process and whether the indicators of the regressive tendencies are present in them. This problem should be

[13] The whole group included a total of forty-three patients, sixteen of whom were given metrazol, and all of whom received hyperpyrexia.

[14] The description of these tests is beyond the scope of this paper. Adequate descriptions can be found in the articles to which reference will be made hereinafter.

[15] The nature of this article does not permit a presentation of the statistical data on the test results. These data will be published in the near future. [See Kenyon, Lozoff, and Rapaport, 1941.]

[16] See Hollós and Ferenczi (1922, p. 35) for the manner of onset of the paretic psychosis.

investigated before further conclusions are drawn from these findings. In
the meantime, however, the fact that a great many of our paretics reacted to
metrazol and hyperpyrexia in the same way as manics react to metrazol
might have the implication that the paretic psychosis has some relation to
the manic-depressive psychosis, and that Schilder's theory—that in consequence of the dementia, preconscious wishes penetrate and judgment is impaired in the paretic psychosis—is supported by the test findings which indicate that after improvement repression of affects results.

BABCOCK DETERIORATION TEST

The Babcock Deterioration Test (Babcock, 1930)—administered in its
shortened form—showed that the test scores of the patients who improved
by treatment, metrazol or hyperpyrexia, were also improved. Their score
averages after the treatment came nearer to their vocabulary scores than
prior to the treatment. It remained, however, true for all cases that a certain, quite significant, deterioration persisted even in the cases of best improvement. According to Babcock's classification, the measure of this persisting deterioration would fall between "poor" and "pathologically poor"
mental efficiency. These results seem to indicate that the dementia, presumably due to organic damage, although diminished, is significant and general
even after the treatment regardless of the kind of treatment used.

Does this constitute objective proof of the concepts of axial and marginal
dementia? The fact that a certain degree of deterioration persists in spite of
improvement seems to justify the concept of axial dementia. It is probable,
furthermore, that this axial dementia should be linked up with the indubita-
bly existent organic damage. In other words, it appears that in the dementia
of general paresis there is an irreversible element implied. This finding supports to a certain degree Schilder's theory. The results of the Rorschach
Test, however, shed more light on the problem. It is indicated there that
repression and depression are present even in the best-improved cases after
all types of treatment. It is known that such psychic factors diminish efficiency and give marked deterioration scores. Thus, it appears probable that
these factors play a rôle in the irreversible axial dementia—in other words,
in the persistent deterioration of the paretic. If we consider further, however, that according to Hollós and Ferenczi this psychogenic factor is a
response to an organic damage, a new question arises. Is it the persistently
present organic damage, or is it the experience-trace of the damage previously experienced, to which the person reacts by depression?

Here again we arrive at a point where psychic and somatic etiology shade
imperceptibly into each other. Investigations comparing the deterioration of
cured or spontaneously remitted functional psychoses with the deterioration of paretics might shed some light on this problem. It has already been
shown by Rorschach studies before and after metrazol treatment in the
functional psychoses that even the best-improved cases reveal latent psy-

chotic trends which might be considered irreversible elements in the psychoses (Eisner and Orbison, 1939).

THE SZONDI TEST

The Szondi Test (Rapaport, 1941) indicates basic personality trends.[17] We found that in this test our group of paretics showed characteristic features in common. These features might be described as follows: latent homosexuality or similar infantile psychosexual development, very strong latent aggressions available for manifestation, underdevelopment of the ego, primitive and blocked thinking, as well as a tendency to depression. If one compares this with the description given by Ferenczi (Ferenczi et al., 1919, esp. pp. 18–19, 23–27) on the personality of the soldier who is apt to develop a war neurosis,[18] the similarity becomes obvious.

We have no sufficient proof as yet that these are the sole personality characteristics precipitating a paretic psychosis or that there is no other personality structure which predisposes to the psychosis. The findings of this test, however, suggest investigations on the problem whether or not a specific or some specific personality structures are the ones which develop the psychosis of general paresis when afflicted with neurosyphilis; furthermore, whether these findings indicate previous personality structure predisposing toward paresis, or simply reflect features of the psychosis itself. The solution of these problems would require rather extended comparative research on the psychology of the luetic. Schilder has already pointed out the lack and need of such a research. The final word on the relation of the previous personality development and brain pathology in paresis[19] will not be said before a comparative investigation on the psychology of syphilitic and paretic patients is conducted.

SUMMARY

The survey of the literature of the psychosis of general paresis showed that already early observers felt the previous personality development played an important rôle in the make-up of this organic psychosis; that psychoanalytic literature found the content of delusions can be understood by means of psychoanalytic knowledge; that there is difference of opinion on the question whether the dementia or the regression is the essence of this psychosis; that it was rather generally agreed upon that luetic damage equals castra-

[17] [Rapaport's final estimate of the Szondi Test was not so favorable, as he briefly indicated in Rapaport (1950)—Ed.]

[18] Ferenczi described as characteristic of those persons who developed traumatic neuroses such symptoms as hypochondriacal depression, terror, anxiety, and a high degree of irritability with a tendency to outbursts of anger. He concluded that in all these persons was a partial fixation of the libido in the developmental stage of narcissism with indications of sublimated predominant homosexual tendencies.

[19] Osnato (1918). Osnato's conclusions have been previously described in this article.

tion; that the conditions of reversibility of the psychosis are unclarified, and so is the extent to which the dementia is psychogenic (marginal) or organic (axial).

The discussion of malarial treatment indicated that beyond the specific effect of this treatment there probably is another effect present comparable with that of febrile states, precipitating onset or remission of psychoses. If this be so, it would indicate that the psychosis, since yielding to nonspecific treatment, follows the laws of psychodynamics. It was also concluded that while the deterioration might be correlated, to a certain degree, with the organic damage, the persistence or nonpersistence of the psychosis seems to depend on a more general factor, probably on the previous personality development.

The discussion of the effect of sodium amytal indicated that a paretic psychotic reacted to this drug in similar fashion as functional psychotics do. In particular, the transitory lucid periods suggested the reversibility of this psychosis, appearing to support the Hollós-Ferenczi theory of regression. The sodium-amytal effect does not seem to support Schilder's theory in which the presence of organic damage plays a more basic rôle. It was pointed out that further sodium-amytal experimentation combined with deterioration-test measurements appears to be necessary in order to clarify further the rôle of dementia stressed by Schilder.

The experimental use of metrazol in a group of sixteen paretics is reported with favorable results appearing in three of twelve patients who had previously not responded to specific therapy, and in two of four patients who had received no specific treatment prior to the metrazol; some degree of improvement was noted in five others of the group. These results appear to confirm the inference from the effect of sodium amytal that in at least some cases of paresis the psychosis can be reversed to varying degrees, by the same measures used in the treatment of the functional psychoses, thus indicating the importance of psychogenic factors in the production of the paretic psychosis.

The Rorschach Test results on hyperpyrexia and in metrazol-treated paretics are discussed. It seems that the paretic patient retains after improvement the bodily preoccupation and inclination to depression, which have been described as initial phenomena of the onset of this psychosis. Thus, the way to regression seems to remain open after improvement. The tests indicate in the majority of our cases an intimate relation of paretic psychoses to the circular psychoses.

The Babcock Deterioration Test results seem to indicate that great deterioration persists even in the best-improved cases. A discussion of these results and a comparison with the Rorschach results appear to indicate that axial and marginal dementia shade imperceptibly into each other and raise the question whether the deterioration in functional psychoses does not show similar irreversible features.

The results of the Szondi Test—although tentative—appear to indicate that there might be some predisposing personality pattern in the person developing paretic psychosis.

CONCLUSIONS

The theoretical situation concerning the psychology of general paresis is described; the few convergent and numerous divergent points are discussed. It is pointed out that while the points of agreement show the possibility of psychological understanding, the points of disagreement, especially concerning the rôle of the dementia, might yield valuable information on psychosomatic interrelations in general paresis.

An experiment using metrazol in general paresis is reported. Some specifically treated—three out of twelve—and untreated—two out of four—patients responded with good improvement to this drug hitherto used only in the functional psychoses.

The similarity in the reactions of paretics to very different therapeutic agents, such as hyperpyrexia, sodium amytal, and metrazol is considered as indicative of the important rôle which psychogenic factors play in the paretic psychosis.

The results of the psychological tests—Rorschach, Babcock, and Szondi —administered to forty-three paretics are discussed. The test results appear to contribute to the affirmation of the psychogenic theory and to give preference, in general, to the Hollós-Ferenczi theory, and partially to the Schilder theory on the psychology of general paresis.

Further investigations by the use of drugs, psychological tests, and comparative researches on the psychology of the luetic are suggested for the further clarification of the large number of problems involved.

The method of using drugs and psychological tests as variations of the experimental situation is suggested as a method for psychosomatic research.

REFERENCES

Alexander, F., Bacon, C., Wilson, G. W., Levey, H. B., & Levine, M. (1934). The Influence of Psychologic Factors upon Gastro-Intestinal Disturbances: A Symposium. *Psychoanal. Quart.,* 3:501–588.

Babcock, H. (1930). An Experiment in the Measurement of Mental Deterioration. *Arch. Psychol.,* No. 117.

Barrett, A. M. (1916). Syphilitic Psychoses Associated with Manic Depressive Symptoms and Course. *J. Amer. Med. Assn.,* 67:1639–1643.

Courbon, P. (1923). The Remission of Mental Affections Just before Intercurrent Somatic Diseases. *Rev. Neurol.,* 30:237–241.

Dattner, B. (1933). *Moderne Therapie der Neurosyphilis mit Einschluss der*

Punktionstechnick und Liquor-Untersuchung. Vienna: Wilhelm Maudrich.
Deutsch, F. (1939). The Production of Somatic Disease by Emotional Disturbance. *Res. Publ. Assn. Nerv. Ment. Dis.,* 19:271–292.
Eisner, E., & Orbison, W. D. (1939). An Objective Evaluation of Metrazol Therapy: A Rorschach Study. Address to The American Psychiatric Association, Chicago, May.
Fellows, R. M. (1932). Sodium Amytal in the Treatment of Paresis. *J. Missouri State Med. Assn.,* 29:194–196.
Ferenczi, S. (1916). Disease- or Patho-Neuroses. *Further Contributions to the Theory and Technique of Psycho-Analysis.* London: Hogarth Press, 1926, pp. 78–94.
———, Abraham, K., Simmel, E., & Jones, E. (1919). *Psycho-Analysis and the War Neuroses.* London: International Psycho-Analytical Press, 1921.
Gerstmann, W. (1924). Zur Frage der Umwandlung des klin. Bildes der Paralyse in halluz paranoische Erscheinungsformen in Gefolge der Malarianimpfbehandlung. *Z. Neurol. Psychiat.,* 93:342–358.
Grotjahn, M. (1938). Psychoanalysis and Brain Disease. *Psychoanal. Rev.,* 25:149–163.
Henderson, D. K., & Gillespie, R. D. (1927). *A Textbook of Psychiatry.* Oxford: Oxford University Press.
Hollós, S., & Ferenczi, S. (1922). *Psychoanalysis and the Psychic Disorder of General Paresis.* New York: Nerv. Ment. Dis. Publ. Co., 1925.
House, W. (1924). Nonsyphilitic Psychoses in Syphilitic Patients. *J. Amer. Med. Assn.,* 83:239–242.
Jones, — (1927), Review of Courbon, P., "The Remission of Mental Disorders Just before Intercurrent Somatic Diseases." *Arch. Neurol. Psychiat.,* 12: 715–716.
Katan, M. (1931). Abstract from Dutch Psycho-Analytical Society. *Int. Z. Psychoanal.,* 17:301.
Kenyon, V. B., Lozoff, M., & Rapaport, D. (1941). Metrazol Convulsions in the Treatment of the Psychosis of Dementia Paralytica. *Arch. Neurol. Psychiat.,* 46:884–896.
———, & Rapaport, D. (1941). The Etiology of the Psychosis of Dementia Paralytica with a Preliminary Report of the Treatment of a Case of This Psychosis with Metrazol. *J. Nerv. Ment. Dis.,* 94:147–159.
Kihn, B. (1928). Über chronische paranoid-halluzinatorische Bilder nach Infektionsbehandlung der Paralyse. *Psychiat. Neurol. Wochenschr.,* 30:285–288.
Kornfeld, A., & Bickeles, S. (1893). Über die Genese und die pathologish-anatomische Grundlage des Grössenwahns bei der progressiven Paralyse. *Allg. Z. Psychiat.,* 49:332–340.
Kraepelin, E. (1913). *General Paresis.* New York: Nerv. Ment. Dis. Publ. Co.
Krayenbühl, P. (1929). Zur Halluzinose nach Maleriabehandlung der Paralyse. *Z. Neurol. Psychiat.,* 120:664–699.
Lewin, K. (1927). Gesetz und Experiment in der Psychologie. *Symposion,* 1:375–421.
Menninger, K. A. (1919a). Psychoses Associated with Influenza. I. General Data: Statistical Analysis. *J. Amer. Med. Assn.,* 72:235–241.

——— (1919b). Psychoses Associated with Influenza. II. Specific Data. *Arch. Neurol. Psychiat.*, 2:291–337.

Munn, C. (1934). Historical Survey of the Literature of Stupor with the Report of a Case of Twelve Years' Duration with Complete Amnesia for Ten Years. *Amer. J. Psychiat.*, 90:1271–1283.

Näcke, P. (1906). Erblichkeit und Praedisposition, respektive Degeneration bei der progressiven Paralyse der Irren. *Arch. Psychiat.*, 41:278–299.

Nonne, M. (1916). *Syphilis and the Nervous System*, tr. C. R. Ball. Philadelphia: Lippincott.

Orbison, W. D., Eisner, E., & Rapaport, D. (1940). Psychiatric Implications of Rorschach Studies with Metrazol and Sodium Amytal. Address to The American Psychiatric Association in Cincinnati, Ohio, May 23.

Osnato, M. (1918). Personality in Paresis. *J. Amer. Med. Assn.*, 70:434–439.

Postle, B. (1939). Pattern Features and Constitutional Susceptibility as Related to Organic Brain Disease, with Special Reference to General Paralysis. *J. Nerv. Ment. Dis.*, 89:26–36.

Rapaport, D. (1941). The Szondi Test. *Bull. Menninger Clin.*, 5:33–39.

——— (1950). The Theoretical Implications of Diagnostic Testing Procedures. *This volume*, Chapter 30.

Rickers-Ovsiankina, M. (1938). The Rorschach Test as Applied to Normal and Schizophrenic Subjects. *Brit. J. Med. Psychol.*, 17:227–257.

Rothschild, D. (1940). Dementia Paralytica Accompanied by Manic-Depressive and Schizophrenic Psychoses. The Significance of Their Co-Existence. *Amer. J. Psychiat.*, 96:1043–1061.

Schilder, P. (1930). Studies Concerning the Psychology and Symptomatology of General Paresis. In *Organization and Pathology of Thought*, ed. & tr. D. Rapaport. New York: Columbia University Press, 1951, pp. 519–580.

Schube, P. G. (1934). Emotional States of General Paresis. *Amer. J. Psychiat.*, 91:625–638.

van Ophuijsen, J. H. W. (1933). Psychoanalysis of Organic Psychoses. In *Psychoanalysis Today*, ed. S. Lorand. New York: Covici-Friede, pp. 270–279.

Weichbrodt, R. (1911). Über die Entstehung von Grössenideen. *Arch. Psychiat.*, 57:241–267.

4

BOOK REVIEW

Heinz Werner, *Comparative Psychology
of Mental Development*[1]

Rapaport took the job of reviewing books very seriously, devoting much care and effort to it. Since his
reviews often gave him an opportunity to discuss matters that he did not elaborate elsewhere, most of them
have been included in this volume. They show clearly
that it was not necessarily the book itself which attracted him, but the opportunity to discuss a topic of
central interest to himself, and that three topics were
of perennial importance to him: thought processes,
the general theory of psychoanalysis, and the relation
of psychoanalytic theory to the rest of psychology
and to science at large—M.M.G.

Since Kant's *Critique of Pure Reason* there were many pros and cons as to
whether we shall ever learn the nature of the world of objects or shall
always remain bound to the world of phenomena—to the world as it ap-

[1] New York: Harper, 1940.

First published in The Journal of Genetic Psychology, *59:429–434, 1941.*

pears to us. It was inevitable that psychologists adopt now this, then the other philosophical view. The progress of psychological research, however, followed a consistent line. It asked how we perceive, how we act, etc.; because perceiving, reasoning, remembering, and acting reflect how the world of living beings is built. Psychology came into the possession of a steadily increasing number of data showing that the world of each individual human being differs from that of others—and that these worlds of "normal" human beings generally differ from the worlds of the feeble-minded, the brain-injured, the psychotic, etc., as well as from that of the human child. Again the worlds of human beings, including all varieties, differ from those of animals, which, in their turn, differ among themselves. Every living creature experiences its world differently, the active extreme of this being man's research and the passive extreme the vegetative passive existence of plant-like animals—depending on the psychophysical organization of the animal. Experiences (percepts, thoughts, feelings, memories) are active products of the organism and are structuralized in accordance with the structure of the experiencing animal. The philosophical conclusions from this ever-increasing body of data have not been drawn as yet since this body of data is scattered in studies of the feeble-minded, of abnormal psychology, neuro-psychiatry, animal psychology, ethnopsychology, child psychology, anthropology, etc. Heinz Werner is the first to attempt a systematization of these data. The work in which he attempted to give us a synopsis of these data is scholarly, reliable, and meticulous. While the last German edition of his work was somewhat interpretive, the present American edition appears to the reviewer somewhat to lean in the opposite direction—it is all-too factual, avoiding interpretations whenever possible. The opinions concerning this method of presentation will probably be divided, and the majority of the readers will no doubt hail the factual seriousness of the book. All will probably agree, however, that it is a pioneer work of admirable maturity.

When replacing philosophical speculation concerning the nature of human knowledge by the results of psychological observation and experiment, developmental psychology revolutionizes epistemology which, in turn, is the basis of the methodology of any science. Heinz Werner's book is to be regarded as a distinguished contribution in this direction. Although not directly concerned in this book with these general problems he has nevertheless organized his material with a fine scientific sense so as to shed light on the development of the concepts underlying scientific endeavor, namely on space, time, and causality, as they exist on different developmental levels and levels of pathological primitivization. It was the spirit of the twentieth century that impressed upon science a relativistic character as reflected in relativistic physics, Freudian psychodynamics, and Marxian economics. As in modern physics, space and time are subject to the principle of relativity, so do they become in modern psychology, as the material collected by Heinz Werner amply demonstrates that their nature is dependent on the developmental level of the living organism by whose experience time, space, and causality are created. This relativistic tendency expressed by the gestalt psychological and organismic teachings, which maintained the interdependence of organism and environment as well as the interdependence of function and total organism, gains a fuller expression in the discoveries of developmental psychology. Functions hitherto mostly regarded as objective reflections of the outside world, or as unique to the human mind, appear relativized in the light of the discoveries of developmental psychology which unearthed the corresponding functions of other developmental levels of living organisms. In this light, Heinz Werner's contribution gains specific significance.

All through the presentation of this unusual wealth of data, Werner remains true to the organismic point of view. Functions are explained in terms of the total organism to which they belong; characteristics of a function are considered as its aspects; and attempts at piecemeal description of these characteristics as elements forming a function are being systematically discouraged. Though this method of thinking is a typically dynamic one, Werner's main concern remains the structure of the different functions on different developmental levels. Similar to Goldstein and the gestalt psychologists, with the possible exception of Lewin, his main concern is so prevalently determined by the aim to build a dynamic morphology of perceiving, thinking, and acting, that the emotional dynamics of the personality are all but disregarded. Werner shows us the levels of structuralization of the different functions. We learn from him that there is a meaningful lawfulness and even a dynamic lawfulness implied in the structuralization of these functional levels. He shows us that the different functional levels are not possessed exclusively by a group of living creatures but that even in the civilized human being of our times, the different lower functional levels are coexistent with the highest ones. He shows us that the lower functional levels cannot be considered immediate historical predecessors of the higher levels, though they may be analogous to these predecessors. However, we hear from him nothing about the relation of these different structural levels to the development of the dynamics of the personality as discovered by psychiatric and especially psychoanalytic investigations. The organism is considered as a whole, the functions are dealt with as an aspect of the life of the organism. Even the problem of personality organization is dealt with, but no developmental theory of personality dynamics is touched upon. Neither the text nor the index has reference to psychosexual development, to the unconscious, to the work of Freud. This is perhaps the only gross lack of this unusually rich, well-rounded, and broad-minded presentation. This lack, however, is not merely a formal one. It has bearing on the present state of developmental psychology as well as on the nature of organismic psychology in general. Organismic psychology is an important step toward the integration into a meaningful whole of the functions which were earlier considered isolated entities. It is in many respects a successful attempt. It remains, however, shy of having a personality theory that could account for the development of the dynamics of personality of which the developmental levels of functional structures are only expressions. Neither organismic psychology nor the even younger organismic developmental psychology has arrived at a personality theory. Viewed from this angle, this important lack of Heinz Werner's presentation is perhaps a merit rather than an omission. He reflected truly the state of the science the results of which have been first systematized by him. An attempt at integrating it with personality theory would not have been in keeping with the true state of affairs. Neither organismic psychology in general nor organismic developmental psychology in particular has arrived at a personality theory, nor has psychiatric and psychoanalytic research been able to instigate such research and to develop a theory that would explain the dependence upon developmental levels of personality dynamics of the developmental levels of perceptual, motor, thought, and action structures. Werner has nevertheless integrated a body of data without the systematization of which fruitful progress could probably not be expected on either side. It is to be hoped that Werner's presentation will be a powerful stimulation for both sides to reach a common point of understanding through factual investigations, or through interpretation of already secured data.

In the last few years clinical psychology has developed methods of investigating and diagnosing personality. Examples of these methods, called "projective techniques," are the Rorschach, the Szondi, the Thematic Apperception, etc., tests, play, drawing, clay modeling, etc., techniques. The concept-formation tests have similar features and the intelligence tests, when evaluated qualitatively, have some kindred implications. These means, evolved on the basis of empirical findings, have been recently used to study human development. Their usefulness in developmental investigations—even as crude empirical tools—is a well-nigh established fact. The theoretical unification of the empirical findings has, however, not been attempted as yet. The material Werner has systematized sheds light in many respects upon the empirical data obtained with these techniques. The clinical psychologist and the student of human development using these "techniques" will gain appreciable help by viewing his material in the light of the knowledge offered by Heinz Werner's book. As L. K. Frank put it, projective techniques open a path into the "private world" of the individual—whether healthy or afflicted. It is in the study of this private world, in which rudiments of earlier developmental levels survive and become discoverable, that the knowledge gathered and systematized by Werner may achieve great practical importance. To clinicians and investigators of development this book should prove to be inspiring.

Werner shows us that the nature of perceptions, concepts, mode of thinking, etc., varies qualitatively on different developmental levels. He writes:

"It is one of the most important tasks of developmental psychology to show that the advanced form of thinking characteristic of Western civilization is only one form among many, and that more primitive forms are not so much lacking in logic as based on logic of a different kind. . . . neither illogical nor 'pre-logical.' It is simply logical in another, self-contained sense" (pp. 15–16). *Perception* on lower developmental levels is shown to be "physiognomic," animistic, the meaning of the percepts being received as a subjective impression rather than an objective cognition. *Space* is being subjectively created around the human body and its natural directions and organized as a localization of action. *Time* conception is created by natural happening and human action and thus is discontinuous, concretistic, having frequently a purely egocentric character. *Causality* is conceived as creation by action of the causal conditions. *Thinking* on lower developmental levels is shown to be diffuse and concretistic at the same time with concepts varying between qualitative configurational, concrete individual, and concrete-schematic abstractions. Perception on primitive levels is affect-ruled; thinking and causality are magical. Whether the emotional experience on these levels differs from ours remains an open question. The author's silence concerning this point makes it probable that no such difference is assumed. The great problem not yet solved and hardly even clearly stated in developmental psychology is just how these affects and emotions which rule the primitive physiognomic perception create the first concepts of space, time, and causality, constitute the essence of magical thinking, and assume the rôle they play in the civilized human being of the Western world. The crystallization of "objective" space, time, and logic, the receding of the affective realm to positions relatively remote from the objective realms, as well as the eventual interaction of the two, are the great problems of developmental psychology. For an attack on these problems the systematizing work of Heinz Werner will prove an indispensable preparation. It is, however, probable that the methods and discoveries of psychoanalytic research, which already have given us some insight into the interaction of reality and primitive animistic thinking ruled by wishes or affects, will likewise prove indispensable.

Psychology has a long history; the science of psychology, however, is very young. If psychology be the science striving to discover the laws of human behavior, developmental psychology is not one of its branches but its main stem. Scientific understanding is genetic understanding and genetic understanding is the discovery of the laws of development. Discoveries from the different fields of psychological observation converge into a picture of development. In those which do not yet do so (e.g., many discoveries in the field of perception), developmental studies will follow and reveal much about the nature of these perceptual phenomena.

Heinz Werner's truly compendious work is a first attempt to show that the different fields of psychology become really integrated only when viewed from the developmental point of view. The careful reader will be confronted with a multiplicity of problems to be solved and with points where an experimental decision is indispensable, easily possible, but not yet made. Werner's book is an inspiring invitation to a vast field of manifold experimental possibilities.

5

TELEOLOGY AND THE EMOTIONS

WITH ALDEN O. WEBER

I

In a recent article Professor M. C. Nahm (1939), defending what he characterizes as an amplified version of the James theory of the emotions, argues that teleological principles are required in any adequate definition of the emotions. Mechanistic principles may account for the physiological basis of emotional experience (Nahm, 1939, p. 461), it is maintained, but if we are to define the total experience, which includes a certain conscious content, we must go beyond the mechanistic hypothesis and regard the emotions as directed toward certain ends. He proposes to reveal the "epistemological core" of the problem of the emotions with the evident intention of indicating the lines which the development of the theory of the emotions should follow. It is the aim of this paper to scrutinize the general problem of the emotions in the light of Mr. Nahm's arguments and to consider specifically: (1) the alleged teleological implications of the problem, (2) the statement of the problem of the emotions as it is given in Mr. Nahm's paper, and (3) the present state of research as it may be relevant to the question whether Mr. Nahm's presentation makes for philosophical clarity or methodological advancement in science.

First published in Philosophy of Science, *8:69–82, 1941. Copyright ©, 1941, The Williams & Wilkins Company, Baltimore, Md. 21202, U.S.A.*

80

II

What Mr. Nahm means by teleology is not entirely clear. Historically the term has been subject to a considerable ambiguity, but there appear to be at least three main senses in which it has commonly been used, two of which merge into each other. There is in the first place what may be called the descriptive sense, a loose, not very well-defined sense in which the term is regarded as synonymous with "purposive" or "having a purpose." It is intended as nothing more than a description of a common mental attitude in which some plan is projected for the future, or, in biological terms, as a description of a process, the causes of which are not yet clear, in the light of its obvious results. The term in this sense asserts no particular view of the nature of the processes involved, being consonant with mechanistic associationism or even extreme forms of behaviorism, and posits, further, no particular view of causality which requires us to suppose that there is a determination of processes beyond what is given in any set of conditions. If teleology meant nothing more than this, there is no reason why every scientist should not be a teleologist. It must be clear, therefore, that when the term is used as a principle of explanation, it is not used in this sense.

In the second sense the term is taken to mean that the goal or end toward which a process is directed is itself a determinant of the process. Thus on the teleological hypothesis so defined, the character of the process is determined by that which is as yet unrealized, i.e., the end or goal. Expressed in nontemporal terms, this same idea is conveyed by saying that there is some informing principle or entelechy above and beyond what is actually given and that this entelechy is a determinant of the nature of the thing. It is the mysterious "life-principle," according to the vitalist, which differentiates living organisms from inorganic things. It is this entelechy or formal principle which transcends the elements taken in their relations that causes the thing to be what it is and determines the process in the realization of its end. Teleology in this sense implies more than means to an end. It indicates that the means exists for *the sake of* the end, for without the end the means would not be what it is.

The third sense, which may be called the metaphysical sense, is nothing more than a systematic extension of this same principle to the entire universe. Reality is conceived to be a hierarchy of ends, exhibiting varying degrees of systematic completeness and tending toward a single end, which thus to the extent to which all other things are instruments in its service determines their existence and character—the "one far-off divine event to which the whole creation moves." The classic example of teleology in this sense is the Aristotelian theology of the Middle Ages.

Now it must be clear that if by teleology Mr. Nahm means to say something about the way in which emotional experience is determined, he must use the term in some sense other than the descriptive sense. He must regard the teleological character of the emotions as an explanation of the particular way in which these states are brought about. No one would deny that in psychology, for instance, there are such attitudes as those described as "having a purpose" or "seeing a means toward an end." But these descriptive phrases of common psychological attitudes do not entail the assumption that the end toward which an organism moves is itself a determinant or cause of that action. At our present state of knowledge purposive behavior is explicable in terms of the individual's drive mechanisms and past experience, being a projection into the future of an ideational content related to these. It was in accordance with this conception of purposive behavior, for example, that Tolman (1932) was especially concerned to show the rôle of motives in the purposive activity of animals. Explanations of relatively complicated forms of goal-directed behavior have been given by Lewin in terms of needs and tensions, the functions of which have been described in topological and vectorial terms (Lewin, 1935, 1936). On this view there is no need to assume any of the mysterious principles of the vitalist or the entelechist. In much of what Mr. Nahm has to say about the purposive character of the emotions there is nothing incompatible with the working hypotheses of empirical science, and teleology is thus reduced to little more than a name for the fact that empirical science has not as yet explained everything about the emotions. But surely by teleology Mr. Nahm means to suggest more than the fact that we do not now know all there is to be known about the emotions: "The teleological or vitalistic hypothesis of emotion attempts a definition of the emotional experience in terms of goal, end or function assumed to be involved, without reference to the *type-of-act*" (1939, p. 461).

It seems clear enough that Mr. Nahm is not inclined to apply the concept of teleology universally as a metaphysical principle, for he does not feel called upon to defend the *"finalisme théologique"* into which a universal extension of the principle would appear inevitably to lead (1939, p. 473 n.). Thus it seems that the sense in which Mr. Nahm uses the term teleology is nearest to the second of the three senses that have been enumerated. It must be observed that his usage is not altogether free from ambiguity and that he is inclined to see in teleology, even when it appears in the first sense (as, for instance, in Cannon's writings), his own concept of teleology. It is therefore not surprising that he points out in his discussion of Cannon that the notion is not applied consequently.

The issues which are controversial for mechanism and vitalism have been so often resuscitated [1] that it would be difficult and perhaps profitless to attempt to deal with all of them in these few pages. The central, and perhaps ultimately the only, question with which we are concerned is this: Precisely what does Mr. Nahm's discussion add to our knowledge of the

[1] An extensive discussion pertinent to the issues here discussed is given in J. H. Woodger (1929).

emotions? It is the task of philosophical analysis to clarify the underlying problems of the several sciences in order to help in the solution of these problems. If philosophical analysis is not carried out in a spirit which is sympathetic toward the methods and aims of science, it confuses and obscures the issues and only makes the problems of science more difficult of solution.

We have now to inquire into the grounds which Mr. Nahm adduces in support of his contention that teleological principles must be introduced into an adequate definition of the emotions. The main argument which he cites in support of his teleological thesis follows that of Kant: Because of the nature of the organization of certain complex phenomena in the natural order, it is necessary to supplement mechanistic principles by postulating teleological conceptions. There are certain limits beyond which mechanistic principles of explanation cannot go, so that it becomes necessary, if we are to understand these more complex phenomena, to introduce the concept of purpose to account for these higher forms of organization.[2]

This argument is, both historically and logically, entirely negative and wholly lacking in conclusive force. The fact that there are complicated phenomena, particularly in the biological world, which have as yet failed to yield to analysis in nonteleological terms does not constitute a refutation in principle of the mechanistic hypothesis.[3] Only when it can be shown that certain phenomena require principles of explanation which are incompatible with the fundamental assumptions of the mechanistic hypothesis will the mechanistic hypothesis be demonstrated to be inadequate or false. One of the historically embarrassing facts which the proponents of vitalism and teleology in general have had to face is the constant invasion, on the part of experimental investigations revealing causal relations, of those spheres of scientific investigation which the teleologists had relegated to themselves on the ground that they were intelligible in teleological terms alone (Ber-

---

[2] What the significance of the Kantian doctrine of teleology in scientific terms is and what its relevance to the procedure of science may therefore be are somewhat puzzling questions, mainly because the Kantian system is more than an empiricism. It is accordingly sometimes difficult to see where scientific empiricism leaves off and where critical metaphysics begins. Kant's view that teleology is a regulative rather than a constitutive principle, for example, raises the question whether the notion has any meaning in empirical terms. A similar question arises in connection with Kant's belief that the apparent opposition between mechanism and teleology is reconciled at a higher level of insight than that of which the empirical mind is capable.

[3] Whether it is possible to amplify and amend the mechanistic hypothesis in such a way as to meet the objections posed by the vitalists or whether the further postulates of the organismic hypothesis are required is a question which would take us beyond the limits of this paper. It is important to observe, however, that in any case the hypothesis must be stated in terms that lend themselves to empirical testing. Mr. Nahm's argument at this point is based on the questionable assumption that the inadequacy of the mechanistic hypothesis implies the truth of the supplementary vitalistic hypothesis. The possibility of another alternative is ignored.

talanffy, 1933, pp. 30 f.). The history of modern science has been little more than the history of the substitution of problems and explanations in the quantitative terms of empirical science for older explanations in terms of purpose, entelechies, "life-principles," etc. Science as it is known today had its beginning in those times when the teleological principles of Aristotle, which formed the basis of science in the Middle Ages, were replaced by principles which implied a denial of the purposive character of the universe.

In its attempts at explanation vitalism introduces a mysterious "life-principle" or entelechy to which are attributed certain characteristics of the organism. Were this vitalistic principle nothing more than a name for a problem, there would at times be justification for its introduction. But the vitalist regards it as more than a name for a problem; he makes the mistake of attributing explanatory efficacy to it and thereby violates the canons of empirical science. For it is an axiom of the method of empirical science that explanation must always be given in terms of experienceable entities rather than in terms of mysterious forces for which we can have no experimental evidence.[4] Phenomena must be explained in terms of forces and entities immanent in the observable phenomena themselves. Such concepts as those of a vital principle, purpose (in the strict vitalistic sense), or entelechy are, as in their very nature unverifiable, scientifically meaningless; or they are but names of problems. Thus the general notion of vitalism is not calculated to help in carrying out the business of science. In its lack of concreteness and in its essential unverifiability the vitalistic hypothesis is conducive only to scientific apathy and indifference and contributes nothing to the furtherance of research in the field. It is the point of view of those who prefer darkness to the light.

III

After having thus discussed the general argument for teleology, we may now go on to consider the specific and more concrete arguments advanced to justify the introduction of teleological principles into the theory of emotions. Mr. Nahm regards his own theory as basically an amplification of James's theory. After summing up the theory of James in three points, he states that "implied in the three propositions and in what has already been written of James' theory are two modes of definition, the one primarily concerned with the physiological and neurological basis for their reaction, the other primarily concerned with the end or purpose subserved by the reaction" (1939, p. 461). Unfortunately, it is not at all clear how this conclusion follows from his three points quoted from James, and there is no explicit reference to "what has already been written" to inform the reader

[4] What is the difference in operational terms between entelechy, the phlogiston theory, and the "purposiveness" of emotions?

precisely what the author had in mind. There are, however, two possible explanations of what Mr. Nahm had in mind. The first concerns the first part of his second quotation, where James refers to the "total situation" and to the "instinctive reaction on that one of the elements which strikes us for the time being as most vitally important." In this quotation "total situation" and "most vitally important" might be interpreted to signify something teleological in character. But a reference to the context from which these quotations were taken makes it clear that such an interpretation misrepresents James's position. In that part of "The Physical Basis of Emotion" (1894, p. 518) from which the quotation was taken, James considers Worcester's observation that a bear has different effects on us when in a cage, when in chains, and when loose in the woods. According to the latter, it is a feeling factor, the expectation of being eaten, and not the perception of the bear, which excites the movements of fear. The quotation cited was part of James's answer to this objection. A part of this passage which is not quoted by Mr. Nahm, however, causes James to appear to be more mechanistic than vitalistic:

> A reply to these objections is the easiest thing in the world if one only remembers the force of association in psychology. "Objects" are certainly the primitive arousers of instinctive reflex movements. But they take their place *as experience goes on,* as elements in total situations, the other suggestions of which may prompt to movements of an entirely different sort [1894, p. 518; italics ours].

Mr. Nahm appears to have misunderstood James's position in favor of his own argument; this becomes clearer when further statements of James are considered.[5]

James uses the term "teleological" several times in his writings on the emotions, once to warn against unwarranted extensions of the concept to emotional experience (1890, Vol. 2, p. 483). For him it signifies ordinarily a means to an end, but it never implies that the means exists for the sake of the end in the sense that the means would not exist if it were the case that the end did not exist. James denies that metaphysical teleology is implied in his system when he says that his theory has no philosophical implications (1894, p. 522). Quite the contrary is the case, he points out. There are many instances of emotional expression which appear to have served no useful purpose, being "the purely mechanical results of the way in which our nervous centers are framed" (1890, Vol. 2, p. 484), and others that are entirely accidental. The conception of instrumentality here postulated is as mechanistic as Darwinism itself: Events occur in a causal series; the effects may or may not be useful in the struggle for existence. The events are not

---

[5] Listed in the index of *The Principles of Psychology* (1890), under the heading "Teleology," is the topic "its barrenness in the natural sciences," which indicates well enough James's general attitude toward teleology in natural science.

determined to fit into a design or plan, and their nature is therefore not determined by the end they serve. The sole principle which decides that certain effects (and with them their causes) shall survive is that of natural selection. Now if teleology means nothing more than this, namely, that every cause is the means to an end, its effect, then there is nothing in it which the mechanist does not himself assert, for a denial that there are means to certain ends is a denial of the principle of causality itself. But teleology and vitalism, as representing points of view distinct from mechanism, intend to assert more than this: They maintain in general the subservience of means to end,[6] the determination of things by that toward which they tend; and, in biology, the introduction of a mysterious "life-principle" which transforms matter into living organisms.

The other point Mr. Nahm might have had in mind is suggested in the latter part of the second quotation and in the third quotation, namely, the connection of the emotions with the instincts.[7] The instincts, as inherited, purposeful reactions, might well serve as prototypes of teleological reaction. Now, quite apart from the issue implied in the third quotation, that emotions are "weakened *repetitions of movements which* formerly *were of utility*,"[8] the main issue in this formulation of the problem lies in the nature of instinctive behavior. Mr. Nahm quotes Bernard, but makes no attempt to cope with the latter's nonteleological theory of instincts. If, instead of insisting that instincts and emotions are alike purposive in nature, Mr. Nahm had tried to ascertain what the present status of the problem of the instincts in the light of experimental investigation is, what he has to say might have been stated in terms which lend themselves to further experimental research on the nature of the emotions. But his insistence on the basically teleological character of instincts and emotions only makes it more difficult to understand what is useless and purposeless in them.

Modern research on the problem of instincts by Müller, Lorenz, and others has taught us that even instincts yield to empirical research more information than merely the dubious fact of their "purposefulness." Thus Lorenz in a lucid ornithological essay has been able to show that the instincts are not necessarily inborn in their full-fledged form and that in a certain sense they are adaptive and thus "purposeful," while in another sense they are rigid and thus entirely "purposeless" (Lorenz, 1935). In an investigation of the social instincts of birds, particularly with reference to the rôle of the comrade in the life of birds, he was able to show that, while certain birds, especially autophagous species, will attach themselves from the very

---

[6] Aristotle, *Physics,* 199ᵃ 15-ᵇ4; ᵇ15–28.

[7] This interpretation is supported by his later extended discussion of the relation between these, which constitutes in effect an argument for the purposive character of the emotions based on the alleged purposive character of the instincts and the intimate connection between instincts and emotions (Nahm, 1939, p. 478).

[8] Nahm (1939, p. 461). "Formerly" is italicized in the original passage.

beginning only to grown-up individuals of their own species, others, e.g., the gray goose, have a sensitive period after coming out of the egg, during which the first subject seen becomes the subject of attachment. If this happens to be a human being, they will be attached to individuals of the human species. After the very short sensitive period is over, the attachment becomes unchangeable. Thus it is seen that this instinct has in certain species an innate "imprinted parent-image," while in other species this image is acquired in a sensitive period, and, far from being purposeful, is determined by the accident of a first meeting. In the light of instances of this latter kind, it seems clear that instincts are best understood, not as directed purposively, but in terms of their genetic antecedents, particularly as these are revealed in the variations that occur in the life history of the different species. If the assumption is made that all instinctive behavior is purposive, these negative instances become unintelligible; if, on the other hand, it is assumed that the explanation of this kind of behavior is to be sought in the genetic conditions which determine this behavior, new light is thrown on the whole problem of instincts and on the problem of the emotions to the extent to which the two are interrelated.

IV

Mr. Nahm's arguments against the theories of Cannon and Dumas likewise fail to justify the assumption of teleological principles. Mr. Nahm's principal criticism of Cannon is that he is inconsequent: Although Cannon writes about "usefulness" and "preparation for emergency action," he fails to come to a teleological theory. Cannon's failure to follow through consistently the implications of his position is for Mr. Nahm especially obvious in his distinction between "emotional behavior" and "emotional experience." This distinction, however, shows only that Cannon used the term "useful" in a purely descriptive sense and discarded it when it was no longer "useful" for purposes of description. This was the case when, for example, it was found that, "in normal conditions the bodily changes, though well marked, do not provoke emotion" (Cannon, 1927, p. 114). Although he criticizes the experimental evidence adduced by Sherrington and Cannon, there is no reference to the important pathological material which gives evidence regarding the rôle of the hypothalamus in human emotions included in Cannon's book and in Bard's (1934) summary of the research on the emotions. Cannon's theory can hardly be criticized without taking into account this body of evidence.

In his criticism of the physiological theories of Dumas and Piéron, Mr. Nahm confuses behaviorism and mechanism. What his criticism of Dumas and Piéron really comes to is that in their introduction into their description of the emotional state of such terms as "joy," "sadness," etc., they have exceeded the limits of strict reflexology, which denies the significance of such subjective aspects. But this is a criticism of behaviorism rather than of mechanism, and in identifying the two, Mr. Nahm has overlooked an important distinction: Mechanism implies a certain conception of causation, while behaviorism, in its strict formulation, is a psychological doctrine which denies the reality of consciousness. Now it is, of course, historically true that the mechanistic hypothesis as it was developed in physics issued in a behavioristic psychology, the reason being that mental events as they are defined in the Cartesian dualism are incapable of expression in spatiotemporal terms. The difficulty of accounting for psychophysical interaction, together with the amenability of physical events to formulation in spatiotemporal terms, was in a large part responsible for the behavioristic emphasis which later had the effect of denying the reality of consciousness.[9] Yet from the mechanistic hypothesis of Descartes there stemmed another psychology quite different from the behaviorism which was the result of the physicalistic emphasis: English associationism, from the time of Locke until the time of the Mills, attempted a development, on the mental side of the mind-body dualism, of a psychology analogous to mechanistic physics on the side of matter. The whole history of English associationism, then, is testimony to the fact that the mechanistic hypothesis does not necessarily imply a behavioristic psychology.

What Mr. Nahm is really criticizing is behaviorism rather than the mechanistic hypothesis as such. And with his rejection of behaviorism as inadequate because of its denial of the fact of consciousness there must be agreement, for an abundance of evidence, derived in large part from the literature of psychopathology, makes it clear that psychical mechanisms play a determining rôle in emotional experience.[10] But while there is agreement with Mr. Nahm's argument in so far as it is a criticism of behaviorism, it must be pointed out that his argument proceeds to an improper conclusion: What his argument has shown is that in its denial of the fact of consciousness behaviorism fails to take account of an important aspect of emotional experience. It does not at all show that there is some end or purpose subserved, for it has not been established that consciousness in itself is teleological in character.

V

James's theory is a contribution of lasting historical significance. As against the claims of Wundtian structuralism, in which the emotions were regarded as a special kind of mental element amenable to analysis in purely intro-

---

[9] Descartes was not, as Mr. Nahm implies on p. 473, a behaviorist, at least as far as human psychology is concerned, for in his dual-substance theory Descartes insisted upon the reality of *res cogitans*. Animals alone were true automata; in human beings there is an interaction between mind and body.

[10] The reference here is especially to the psychoanalytic literature.

spective terms, James maintained that the character of emotional experience can be revealed only through an investigation of relations between subjective factors and bodily processes. It is not the particular form which he gave to this argument, but rather the argument itself, that makes James's contribution an important one (see Angell, 1916, p. 261). Physiological and anatomical research into the bodily conditions of emotional experience has today gone far beyond the physiological and anatomical conceptions in terms of which James formulated his theory; at the same time there has been a parallel advance in psychology and psychiatry. Head (1920), Cannon (1929), Papez (1937, 1939), and others have in recent years shown the importance of central factors in the genesis of emotional experience, so that it is now clear not only that the integration of emotional behavior is effected in the hypothalamus but also more than probable that hypothalamic activity is intimately connected with the psychological aspects of the emotions. Other recent research has shown the intimate connection between the instincts and the emotions pointed out by James in the mechanisms of the central nervous system. Grinker, for instance, writes:

> As a cephalic representative of the autonomic nervous system, the hypothalamus has to do with energies of visceral origin which are the forces of the instincts.
>
> . . . To achieve these slower adaptive responses the hypothalamus became subordinated to higher newer cortical centers by inhibitory processes emanating therefrom. . . .
>
> However, in turn the hypothalamus influences activity within the cortex or ego. Its drives are synonymous with id demands or necessities of the instincts [1939, pp. 44–45].

In the recent psychological literature, Lund (1939, pp. 11–14) argues for the view that the emotions have to be considered as an integration of mental, somatic, and visceral variables together with the variables of the stimulus situation. In the literature of psychoanalysis the emotions are considered as derivatives of drives (Jones, 1923). Their bodily as well as their feeling symptoms are regarded as the expression of conflicting drive cathexes (Federn, 1933; Kulovesi, 1931). In the field of psychiatry McKinney suggests that emotions be defined as modifications of the organism's energy in conflict (1930, p. 46).

Thus our present understanding of emotional experience has been made possible through the first statement, by James and Lange, of the thesis that certain bodily processes are integral to the emotional experience. But whatever the importance of James in this respect may be, it is certain that his importance for the theory of emotions is not based on any advocacy of a vitalistic or teleological principle. James's importance derives from the fact that his statement of the problem was such as to make possible the development of this further research on the problem of emotions by showing the integration of emotional expression and feeling and the common source of both.

REFERENCES

Angell, J. R. (1916). A Reconsideration of James's Theory of Emotion in the Light of Recent Criticisms. *Psychol. Rev.*, 23:251–262.

Bard, P. (1934). Emotion: I. The Neuro-Humoral Basis of Emotional Reactions. In *A Handbook of General Experimental Psychology*. Worcester: Clark University Press, pp. 264–311.

Bertalanffy, L. von (1933). *Modern Theories of Development: An Introduction to Theoretical Biology*. New York: Oxford University Press.

Cannon, W. B. (1927). The James-Lange Theory of Emotions: A Critical Examination and an Alternative Theory. *Amer. J. Psychol.*, 39:106–124.

———— (1929). *Bodily Changes in Pain, Hunger, Fear and Rage*, 2nd. ed. New York: Appleton.

Federn, P. (1933). Das Ichbesetzung bei den Fehlleistungen. *Imago*, 19:312–338, 433–455.

Grinker, R. R. (1939). Hypothalamic Functions in Psychosomatic Interrelations. *Psychosom. Med.*, 1:19–47.

Head, H. (1920). *Studies in Neurology*, 2 vols. London: Frowde.

James, W. (1890). *The Principles of Psychology*, 2 vols. New York: Holt.

———— (1894). The Physical Basis of Emotion. *Psychol. Rev.*, 1:516–529.

Jones, E. (1923). Classification of the Instincts. *Papers on Psycho-Analysis*, 4th ed. Baltimore: Wood, 1938, pp. 196–202.

Kulovesi, Y. (1931). Psychoanalytische Bemerkungen zur James-Langeschen Affekttheorie. *Imago*, 17:392–398.

Lewin, K. (1935). *A Dynamic Theory of Personality*. New York: McGraw-Hill.

———— (1936). *Principles of Topological Psychology*. New York: McGraw-Hill.

Lorenz, K. (1935). Companionship in Bird Life. In *Instinctive Behavior*, ed. & tr. C. Schiller. New York: International Universities Press, 1957, pp. 83–128.

Lund, F. H. (1939). *Emotions: Their Psychological, Physiological and Educative Implications*. New York: Ronald Press.

McKinney, J. M. (1930). What Shall We Choose to Call Emotions? *J. Nerv. Ment. Dis.*, 72:46–64.

Nahm, M. C. (1939). The Philosophical Implications of Some Theories of Emotion. *Phil. Sci.*, 6:458–486.

Papez, J. W. (1937). A Proposed Mechanism of Emotion. *Arch. Neurol. Psychiat.*, 38:725–743.

———— (1939). Cerebral Mechanisms. *J. Nerv. Ment. Dis.*, 89:145–159.

Tolman, E. C. (1932). *Purposive Behavior in Animals and Men*. New York: Century.

Woodger, J. H. (1929). *Biological Principles*. New York: Harcourt, Brace.

6

PRINCIPLES UNDERLYING
PROJECTIVE TECHNIQUES

I propose to discuss the hypotheses underlying projective techniques. I shall discuss the necessary and sufficient conditions which should be fulfilled by a method to justify its being called a projective technique. Then I shall discuss the hierarchic interrelations of several projective techniques with reference to the levels of personality they reflect and with reference to the conscious or unconscious, latent or overt personality trends they indicate.

I

Projective techniques are a relatively young tool in clinical practice. Their underlying principle is, however, identical with that of the case history, considered indispensable for all clinical work. A case history is taken on the assumption that from it the personality of the subject, his characteristic adjustment or maladjustment, may be inferred, and that based on it, a clinical diagnosis or prognosis may be made.

In other words, the life history is a projective reflection of the personality but by no means a projective technique. Further examples of the principle underlying projective techniques, such as are found in analyzing works

Opening address, Round-Table Conference on Projective Techniques, 1941 meetings of the American Psychological Association. First published in Character and Personality, *10:213–219, 1942.*

of art or facial expression, cannot be dealt with here. I propose to call this principle underlying projective techniques "the projective hypothesis." We are concerned here not with general applications of the projective hypothesis but with the scientific formulation of it which renders the commonly accepted idea a means of scientific and clinical investigation. The projective hypothesis may be formulated as follows: All behavior manifestations of the human being, including the least and the most significant, are revealing and expressive of his personality, by which we mean that individual principle of which he is the carrier. This formulation of the projective hypothesis implies a specific definition of the term "behavior," which includes all of the following aspects: (a) behavior historically viewed in the life history; (b) behavior statically viewed as reflected in the environment with which the subject surrounds himself, such as the furniture of his house, the clothes he wears, etc.; (c) bodily behavior, or the patterns of voluntary, habitual, and expressive movements; (d) internal behavior, including percepts, fantasies, thoughts. This formulation of the projective hypothesis expresses only the *necessary conditions* implied in the application of a projective technique. It does not state, however, the *sufficient criteria,* which when fulfilled justify our applying the procedure as a "projective technique."

What then are the *sufficient* criteria? It appears that there are many realms of human behavior whose relation to "personality" is remote. This remoteness may be due to one of two factors: to cultural evolution resulting in the development of a hierarchy of functions, or to the conventionalizing effect of social patterns in our civilization (Rapaport and Brown, 1942). Out of these follows one of the sufficient criteria: *The realm of behavior to which the projective technique is applied should not be a conventionalized one nor one remote from the core of the personality.* Four other sufficient criteria issue from a comparison of clinical observations with projective techniques. The advantage of projective techniques over the subjectivity of clinical observation lies in that they are applied to a realm of behavior which allows: (a) *easy objective observation;* (b) *easy and objective registration;* (c) *systematization or scoring of the material obtained so as to permit direct intra- and interindividual comparison;* and (d) *the significance of the test and test reactions is unknown to the subject.* To facilitate the application of these four criteria to choosing the subject matter for a projective technique, we shall discuss two problems: first, that which we shall call "the methods of projection," and second, the interrelation between clinical observation and projective techniques. We shall proceed to discuss two methods of projection: that of "organization" and that of "choice."

In our everyday life we distinguish different kinds of people by their dress, by their living quarters and its furnishings. In terms of the projective hypothesis, such judgments imply that people express themselves through their dress and the furnishings of their living quarters. How can we explain that a man's hat or the furnishings of his house express him? It is through the choices he makes when buying his hat and the furnishings of his house that they achieve this expressive significance. It may be argued that the assembly or, in other words, the *organization* of these choices is expressive of the person. Nevertheless, we maintain that the character of the expression is here determined by these *acts of choice*. This becomes more obvious when contrasted with the process of organization.

When confronted with a Rorschach inkblot (Rorschach, 1932; Rorschach and Oberholzer, 1924) the subject faces something new, something to which *he* has to give meaning by organizing it. The process of organization proceeds from those features of the inkblot which induce in the subject a meaning. Then the subject turns back to the inkblot to assemble and organize more of its features to fit this meaning, but by doing so he modifies the meaning itself to fit these other features of the blot. This process of organization continues in an interplay between meaning and objective features of the stimulus, mutually modifying each other, and issues in the verbal response of the subject. This process is usually a silent one, but becomes overt in certain compulsion neurotics who verbalize the entire process in their test response.

It might be argued that we deal here with a choice between the parts of an inkblot, i.e., between the meanings these parts suggest; the process of organization discussed here is, however, a more intricate one than this. Choice and organization may shade into each other, but by making a distinction between the two we gain insight into the nature of projection. For this reason in the examples given we considered the dominant function only: the function of choice in the first example and that of organization in the second. If the material elicits socially or phylogenetically patterned behavior, the function of choice predominates; if the material is unorganized or unfamiliar, the function of organization becomes predominant. A comparison of Schmidl-Waehner's drawing technique (1942) with the Rorschach Test will make this distinction more obvious. While the subject matter for interpretation in Schmidl-Waehner's drawing technique is the choice made by the subject between different kinds of drawing material (the choice of shape and kind of paper, the choice between variously colored crayons, chalks, paints, etc., the choice of colors), the subject matter for interpretation in the Rorschach Test is the influence of colors, shadings, forms, etc., on the subject's organizing of percepts.

The value of distinguishing between the processes of organization and choice becomes more obvious when applied to the Thematic Apperception Test (Murray, 1937; Masserman and Balken, 1939, 1940). It will be readily seen that the interpretation of the Thematic Apperception Test has two aspects (Rapaport, 1942): one involves a choice, the other an organization process: A choice process is involved in deciding with whom to identify the pictured figures, and a choice selects from all the actions allowed for by the pictures those actions which then, organizing the person's strivings and obstacles chosen, create the sequence of events and the outcome of the story.

While the choices made reflect the outstanding figures and acts of the subject's life-space, the organization produced reflects his strivings, hopes, frustrations, and achievements.

The B. R. L. Sorting Test (Rapaport and Brown, 1942; Weigl, 1941) and the Szondi Test (Rapaport, 1941) are examples of the choice function. In the B. R. L. Sorting Test the subject is to choose from among a number of objects the ones which "belong with" a given sample object. However, the possible choices the material can elicit are so strongly patterned by conventional concepts of our civilization that the test reveals only one aspect of the subject's mental functioning, namely, his concept formation. It appears to be a general rule that the more patterned the knowledge of and attitude toward a given material, the more limited the choice processes become, thus narrowing the interpretation of results to only one aspect of mental functioning. Since, however, the more disorganized subject adheres less to conventional patterns, the test tends to reveal projectively the depressive's narrow and the schizophrenic's enlarged concept-basis. In the Szondi Test the subject must choose in six series, each consisting of eight photographs of persons, the two most liked and the two most disliked pictures. Like and dislike of facial features are apparently an extremely individual matter, and the choices made from among the eight pictures (which are those of a homosexual, a sadistic murderer, an epileptic, a hysteric, a catatonic, a paranoiac, a depressive, and a manic) seem to be as revealing of the person's character as is, for instance, the Rorschach Test.[1]

The Rorschach Test and the Hanfmann-Kasanin (1936) Concept Formation Test are examples of the organizing function. The process of organization in the Rorschach Test has already been discussed. In the Hanfmann-Kasanin Test the subject must organize twenty-two blocks differing in shape, height, width, and color into four internally consistent groups. As in the Rorschach Test, organizing proceeds from any feature of the blocks, and on its basis the grouping is attempted. Failure of the attempt or a clue given by the examiner initiates a modification of the grouping principle; further modifications are made until the correct solution is reached. Since the material here is not so indefinite as that of the Rorschach Test, this is a concept-formation test, in which, however, the organizing process is present and allows for observation of the personality in action, its resources in solving problems, its reaction to help, failure, frustration, and success.

For those working with projective techniques it is useful to be aware of the processes of organization and of choice inherent in these techniques, for the projectively obtained material is empirical material the proper understanding of which requires general psychological knowledge. We cannot elaborate on the dynamics of organization and of choice processes; however, most of the workers using projective techniques are probably aware of the rôle of tensions and stresses in the field underlying organization proc-

[1] [See Chapter 3, n. 17—Ed.]

esses and of the dialectic processes present in choice situations where the thing most desired may be chosen or may be avoided depending on the existing conditions.

Having discussed the methods of projection, we shall now consider the interrelation of projective techniques and clinical observation. The observation of outstanding behavior manifestations does not yield an objective set of data; first, because a subjective selection is made from the infinite number of details of the behavior; second, because a description by the examiner of the behavior is necessarily an interpretation. A projective technique, however, since it investigates a limited realm of behavior, yields the full description of an unfettered response, and is subject to no interpretive selection. Thus it must employ a material on which the subject's action yields to easy observation and to full objective description. The material obtained by a projective technique should yield to scoring or to a schematic description and should allow for direct inter- and intraindividual comparison as well as interpretation in terms of a personality theory. Thus we compare sets of schematized data, not interpretations. Most workers in the field will agree that, while the Rorschach and Szondi tests do fulfill these requirements, the other projective techniques need improvement in this respect.

II

The projective hypothesis and the criteria discussed create a hierarchy ranging from those techniques which fulfill more or less strictly the necessary and sufficient requirements, such as the Rorschach, Szondi, and the Thematic Apperception tests, to those concept-formation and intelligence tests to which the projective principle may be profitably applied; the transition is a very fluid one. At present we are unable to define the position in this hierarchy of the projective methods used in therapeutic work. Graphology, painting, drawing, finger painting, clay modeling, and play techniques seem to fall between the two extremes just mentioned.

The study of projective techniques implies yet another hierarchic problem pertaining to the level of personality structure to which the projectively obtained data refer. Thus, in our experience, the data obtained by the Thematic Apperception Test do not usually allow for a clinical diagnostic differentiation, but they do reveal the strivings and *identifications* of the subject. The Szondi Test reveals the distribution of the basic drives of the personality rather than a clinical category, and the dynamics thus diagnosed pertain to the deep levels of personality rather than to action and intellection. In the Rorschach Test, by which both diagnostic category and personality description are usually obtained, there are some cases in which the clinical diagnosis is questionable (as in extremely rich protocols, replete with rare details, with fabulationlike scenes, movement and color responses), other cases in which the personality description is questionable (as in the meager protocols of many psychotics and of certain neurotics), and still other cases in which neither personality description nor clinical diagnosis is possible since the test reflects only a temporary state or attitude (as in purely anatomical or purely descriptive protocols). The Szondi Test reflects the interrelation of basic drives; the Rorschach Test usually yields, except for its contents and symbols, a dynamic scheme of the personality; the Thematic Apperception Test furnishes the concrete contents of the dynamics.

A third problem of hierarchy is that of determining whether a tendency indicated by the material obtained is conscious or unconscious, overt or latent. A good example of this is seen in the various interpretations given of the bleeding thumb in the Thematic Apperception Test. My experience has been that overtly aggressive patients see the thumb and explain it in a horror story; people with well-balanced aggressions see and describe it in an objective manner, and people with aggressions which are strong but countermanded and latent are inclined to refuse interpretation or even to misinterpret the picture. In general I am satisfied with this empirical finding but do not know whether similar interpretive principles can be applied to the exaggerated, objective, or rejecting stories given to sex, crime, and other pictures. To distinguish between conscious or unconscious and between latent or overt qualities in the strivings indicated or avoided by the subject is a serious and still unsolved problem in the Thematic Apperception Test. In this respect the Rorschach Test is much more explored, but it still presents many problems. For instance, from the Rorschach record as a whole one can infer whether the "impulsive affectivity" indicated by pure color response finds its expression in behavior, in thinking, or in somatic equivalents, but the principles underlying these inferences are as yet not clear. The number of examples could and should be increased; I am aware, for instance, that I have not done justice to the projective techniques used in therapy; however, my practical experience is limited to the tests discussed.

In conclusion, I should like to suggest that the worker using projective techniques strive to use several simultaneously in order to establish out of their interrelations the levels of personality to which they refer.

SUMMARY

(1) The "projective hypothesis" underlying projective techniques and applicable to behavior in general has been discussed. (2) The "methods of projection" were shown to be that of organization and that of choice: the dynamics of organization and choice processes has been discussed and illustrated. The criteria on the basis of which a method can be called a projective technique have been discussed. (3) The hierarchic relation of different projective techniques has been described and illustrated, and it has been shown that the hierarchic arrangement of the tests depends upon the degree

to which they meet the criteria discussed and upon the level of personality to which they refer.

REFERENCES

Hanfmann, E., & Kasanin, J. (1936). A Method for the Study of Concept Formation. *J. Psychol.,* 3:521–540.

Masserman, J. H., & Balken, E. R. (1939). The Psychoanalytic and Psychiatric Significance of Phantasy. *Psychoanal. Rev.,* 26:343–379, 535–549.

Masserman, J. H., & Balken, E. R. (1940). The Language of Phantasy: III. The Language of the Phantasies of Patients with Conversion Hysteria, Anxiety State, and Obsessive-Compulsive Neuroses. *J. Psychol.,* 10:75–86.

Murray, H. A. (1937). Techniques for a Systematic Investigation of Fantasy. *J. Psychol.,* 3:115–143.

Rapaport, D. (1941). The Szondi Test. *Bull. Menninger Clin.,* 5:33–39.

——— (1942). The Thematic Apperception Test; Qualitative Results of a Study of 250 Psychotic, Neurotic, and Normal Subjects. Paper read at the meetings of the Midwestern Psychological Association.

———, & Brown, J. F. (1942). Concept Formation and Personality Research. Unpublished ms.

Rorschach, H. (1932). *Psychodiagnostik.* Bern: Hans Huber.

———, & Oberholzer, E. (1924). The Application of the Interpretation of Form to Psychoanalysis. *J. Nerv. Ment. Dis.,* 60:225–248, 359–379.

Schmidl-Waehner, T. (1942). Formal Criteria for the Analysis of Children's Drawings. *Amer. J. Orthopsychiat.,* 12:95–104.

Weigl, E. (1941). On the Psychology of So-called Processes of Abstraction. *J. Abnorm. Soc. Psychol.,* 36:3–33.

7

POETRY

Since the early years of adolescence I have found the reading and remembering of poetry a most heartening habit. I find it rather difficult to tell why I enjoy reading poetry so much. Is it because my mother used to read poems to me in leisurely hours and would quote an appropriate line whenever possible? Or is it because my teachers read poems to us with an enthusiasm suggesting that they were putting before us the greatest treasures not only of the past, but also the greatest treasures of their heart? Or is it because I always found it hard to express myself and in poetry I find expressions great men coined for feelings similar to mine? I do not know the answer. I know, however, that in great sorrow or great joy, in the long hours of expectancy and in the hours of letdown, after days of tension, in tiredness and in voluntary repose, I reach for poetry. In humiliation I like to read expressions of humbleness, in hours of pride those of self-reliance, in hours of fantasy and planning those of great dreams and proud undertaking.

I like to read what I already know well. I greet these poems as old friends and they always present the same unsuspected surprises that old friends offer—a thus-far undiscovered hidden meaning, a turn of rhythm I had not before observed. I read new poems, too, but always with some inner reluctance.

Nearly all the poems I am really enthusiastic about were handed to me

Reprinted with permission from The Bulletin of the Menninger Clinic, *6:87–88. Copyright 1942 by the Menninger Foundation.*

by good friends. They frequently mean to me what these friends embodied to me. They remind me of these friends, of the intimate hours of happy discourse we had, much as a quaint memento reminds one of the friend who sent it.

I remember certain poems when the mood or meaning of a situation is such that their lines give it expression, an expression often so deep and miraculously coined that I myself could never have given it utterance. Later these lines are charged with the moods and meanings of the situations in which I remember them. They become for me depositories of my own past.

I enjoy reading poetry to others and I like to hear it read or recited well. I like even to mumble it to myself, enjoying the rhythm, the music of it.

Though an illustration carries with it the danger of becoming a confession, still it seems necessary to give one. A phrase of Faust was a companion to me for many years.

> The spirit-world no closures fasten;
> Thy sense is shut, thy heart is dead;
> Disciple, up; untiring, hasten
> To bathe thy breast in morning-red:
>> GOETHE: *Faust*. Monologue, Scene I.

These words meant and still mean much to me. The first line warns and encourages me whenever doubt and skepticism take hold of me, whenever I am thwarted by difficulty of understanding in solving a problem. The second line gives the reason for my lack of understanding and is always a powerful prompting. It tells me to wake up, to open my senses, to enliven my heart if I would understand. It always aids me to shake off the inertia that takes hold of one after failure. The other two lines tell me to face the facts and again submerge myself in action. Then only—not in painful speculation—will I reach the solution.

Mereschkowsky, the Russian biographer, once wrote a series of short biographies of great men and called it *Eternal Companions of My Travels*. In this sense these lines are my companions in many travels. In this sense much of poetry may be a companion to people who crave secure, wise, unfaltering companionship in the long, hard, and tedious travels of life.

Does reading poetry have an objective, psychological value also, or is this all merely my subjective reaction to it? I certainly cannot be an objective judge of this question. I believe, however, that in a time when the meaningful magnificence of human expression and the dignity of human interrelations have become so deeply undervalued, poetry can give to those who desire these things a real satisfaction otherwise denied in everyday life.

8

THE HISTORY OF THE
AWAKENING OF INSIGHT

What is insight? I do not believe that a satisfactory, concise answer to this question can be given at the present state of our knowledge. In particular do I not believe that a definition which would cover what is commonly called insight has as yet been developed. In general, however, one might state that the human being, wherever he turns, is confronted with appearances and that the world of physical happening as well as that of conscious psychological happening all seem to be such appearances. Underlying these appearances, we assume, are processes. It seems that every glance beyond the appearances, into the processes assumed to underlie them, is what we generally call insight. It can be objected that such a definition does not take into account the possibility that such insight may be true or false. This objection is sustained, and I should like to suggest that the transition between true and false insight, as well as between partial and full insight, is a fluid one and is perhaps what makes for the great difficulty in gaining insight into the nature of insight. We probably consider both the partial and false "insights" of the old philosophers or naturalists to be insights, while we would be loath to consider as insights the statements of a paranoiac.

Before going any further in the discussion of insight, I would like to

Presented June 10, 1942, at the Menninger Foundation. This paper is published here for the first time.

attempt to build a link between the problem of insight and the problem of ego psychology. Let me attempt this by presenting an example of what Dr. Ernst Lewy (1941) termed "the return of repression" to show that an attempt to lose insight may elucidate the nature of insight in the psychological sense. The example is a long passage from Karen Horney's *New Ways in Psychoanalysis* (1939). I chose this example not only because it is, as Dr. Geleerd recently pointed out to me, an excellent example of the return of repression, but also because this return of repression takes advantage of the weakest link in psychoanalytic theory, namely the lack of a sufficiently developed ego psychology. With these points in mind, I ask you to bear with me through this long quotation.

In *New Ways in Psychoanalysis,* Horney wrote:

> Chronic neurotics give the impression of having no say in their lives. . . . This is most conspicuous with the compulsion neurosis but is roughly true for all severe neuroses, not to speak of psychoses. Freud's metaphor of the rider who, though thinking he guides the horse, is taken where it wants to go, appears to be a good description of the neurotic "ego."
>
> Such observations in neuroses do not, however, permit the conclusion that the "ego" in general is merely a modified part of the instincts. This is not conclusive even for neuroses. Assuming that to a large extent a neurotic's pity for others is transformed sadism or externalized self-pity, this does not prove that some part of sympathy for others is not "genuine." * . . . In my opinion, however, there may be "genuineness" which can be dissolved neither by Freud's resort to instincts nor by the relativists' resort to social valuations and conditioning [pp. 185–186].
>
> . . . in his concept of the "ego" Freud denies—and on the basis of the libido theory must deny—that there are any judgments or feelings which are not dissolvable into more elemental "instinctual" units. In general his concept means that on theoretical grounds any judgments about people or causes must be regarded as rationalizations of "deeper" emotional motivations, that any critical stand toward a theory must be viewed as an ultimately emotional resistance. It means that theoretically there is no liking or disliking of people, no sympathy, no generosity, no feeling of justice, no devotion to a cause, which is not in the last analysis essentially determined by libidinal or destructive drives.
>
> The denial that mental faculties may exist in their own right fosters insecurity of judgment; for example, it may lead analyzed people not

---

* "Genuine" in this context means that the feelings—or judgments—in question do not permit further analysis into allegedly instinctual components; it combines the meaning of elemental and spontaneous. [K.H.]

to take a stand toward anything without making the reservation that probably their judgment is merely an expression of unconscious preferences or dislikes. . . .

Another consequence is that it promotes uncertainty about feelings and thus involves the danger of rendering them shallow. A more or less conscious awareness of "it is only because" will easily jeopardize the spontaneity and the depth of emotional experiences. Hence the frequent impression that although an analyzed individual is better adapted he has become "less of a real person," or, as one might say, less alive.

The observation of such effects as these is sometimes used to perpetuate the time-honored fallacy that too much awareness makes a person futilely "introspective." . . . it is merely dogmatic to assert . . . that a judgment cannot be simply the expression of what one holds to be right or wrong, that one cannot be devoted to a cause because one is convinced of its value, that friendliness cannot be a direct expression of good human relationships.

It is often regretted in psychoanalytical literature that we know little about the "ego" in comparison with our extensive knowledge concerning the "id." This deficiency is attributed to the historical development of psychoanalysis, which led first to an elaborate study of the "id." The hope is expressed that just as elaborate a knowledge of the "ego" will follow in time, but this hope is likely to be disappointed. The theory of instincts, as propounded by Freud, leaves no more scope, no more life to the "ego" than is indicated above. Only by abandoning the theory of instincts can we learn something about the "ego," but then it will be a different phenomenon from the one Freud has in mind [pp. 187–189].

I am not going to give in to the temptation to defend Freudian theory against Horney. This is not the place for it nor does the theory need it—I am assuming the Freudian presupposition. The important point in this quotation is that Horney restores the "appearance" to a "genuine" existence and tries to get away from the insight into the processes underlying it. Fromm makes the same attempt in *Escape from Freedom,* in his discussion of the "nongenuineness" of Luther's faith.[1] I again refrain from the tempta-

---

[1] "Luther's doctrine of faith as an indubitable subjective experience of one's own salvation may at first glance strike one as an extreme contradiction to the intense feeling of doubt which was characteristic for his personality and his teachings up to 1518. Yet, psychologically, this change from doubt to certainty, far from being contradictory, has a causal relation. We must remember what has been said about the nature of this doubt: it was not the rational doubt which is rooted in the freedom of thinking and which dares to question established views. It was the irrational doubt which springs from the isolation and powerlessness of an individual whose attitude toward the world is one of anxiety and hatred. This irrational doubt can never be

tion to demonstrate the essentially antiscientific character of such attempts to substitute an appearance for the underlying process by claiming that the appearance is "genuine." I will point out, however, that an attempt to consider as a "time-honored fallacy" that "too much awareness" makes "a person futilely 'introspective' " is full of danger and moreover contradicted by Horney just before she attempted it, when she says:

> Another consequence is that it promotes uncertainty about feelings and thus involves the danger of rendering them shallow. A more or less conscious awareness of "it is only because" will easily jeopardize the spontaneity and the depth of emotional experiences. Hence the frequent impression that although an analyzed individual is better adapted he has become "less of a real person," or as one might say, less alive.

This is not, however, merely a time-honored fallacy. It is a historical fact which gave birth to the idea of the "vanity of vanities" of the Bible. In the book of Ecclesiastes we read: "For in much wisdom is much grief: and he that increaseth knowledge increaseth sorrow." It is the fact that gave birth to Greek sophistry and skepticism, to the "methodical doubt" of Descartes, to post-Kantian classical German philosophy, and to many other such episodes in the history of philosophy.

Upon discovering that there are processes underlying appearances, the human being can no longer rely on the verity of appearances: doubt and uncertainty become his lot. The birth pains of new insights are the historical basis for the tremendous reactionary forces handicapping the development of scientific insight into the system of processes underlying phenomena. Such insight becomes a closed system which replaces to a certain extent the world of appearances by merging with it and giving it a new meaning; it

---

cured by rational answers; it can only disappear if the individual becomes an integral part of a meaningful world. If this does not happen, as it did not happen with Luther and the middle class which he represented, the doubt can only be silenced, driven underground, so to speak, and this can be done by some formula which promises absolute certainty. *The compulsive quest for certainty,* as we find with Luther, *is not the expression of genuine faith but is rooted in the need to conquer the unbearable doubt.* Luther's solution is one which we find present in many individuals today, who do not think in theological terms: namely to find certainty by elimination of the isolated individual self, by becoming an instrument in the hands of an overwhelmingly strong power outside of the individual. For Luther this power was God and in unqualified submission he sought certainty. But although he thus succeeded in silencing his doubts to some extent, they never really disappeared; up to his last day he had attacks of doubt which he had to conquer by renewed efforts toward submission. Psychologically, faith has two entirely different meanings. It can be the expression of an inner relatedness to mankind and affirmation of life; or it can be a reaction formation against a fundamental feeling of doubt, rooted in the isolation of the individual and his negative attitude toward life. Luther's faith had that compensatory quality" (Fromm, 1941, pp. 77–78).

remains the mother of doubt. But let me not follow this trend of thought further. Let me merely state that we will have to return to the very beginnings of systematized, logical thinking, namely, to Greek philosophy, to learn more about how human thinking behaved when first faced with the contradiction of appearances and the processes underlying them, which is the situation calling for insight. This is the first justification for involving Greek philosophy in these considerations. A further scrutiny of Karen Horney's quoted passages will, however, yield further justification.

Horney attacks Freudian ego psychology, believing that without assuming a "genuineness" of ego experiences there cannot be an ego psychology. It is in this connection that the issue of "genuineness" needs to be discussed further. Is it true that the molecular laws of physics became "ungenuine" when the electronic nature of matter was discovered? Did the latter in turn become "ungenuine" on Schrödinger's bold theoretical discovery that the behavior of matter can be represented in terms of a wave theory? I am sure that you will agree with me when I answer these questions with an emphatic "no." Ego experiences and functions do not become less genuine when their relation to the unconscious and the instincts is discovered. It is here that the return of repression begins to operate, and the chance for it to operate is provided by the fact that we do not know quite enough about the genetic dependence of ego functions on id functions. The attention recently concentrated on defense mechanisms and ego analysis affirms rather than contradicts the great need for further work in this field. The gap in our knowledge of ego psychology becomes clearer, however, if we envisage how little we know about the relation of the so-called normal thought processes of everyday life and logic to unconscious processes.

The terms in which we talk about psychological processes pertaining to the id and the ego were coined by Freud. He called them "primary and secondary processes." I hope that I am not being extravagant when I state that we appear to know infinitely more about the primary process than about the secondary process. If one scans *The Interpretation of Dreams,* or *The Psychopathology of Everyday Life,* or, for that matter, the "Papers on Metapsychology" or *The Ego and the Id,* one finds a systematic treatment of the different mechanisms, such as condensation, displacement, etc., of the primary process, while the secondary process is dealt with summarily as the logical, purposeful, and reality-adapted one. Neither the genetic relation of this secondary process to the primary process, nor the mechanisms of its operation, nor again the relation of purpose to wish, have been traced clearly. Freud made only two suggestions toward the explanation of the secondary process. One relates to the fact of consciousness, which is explained as being due to the hypercathexis attached to a given idea. The other relates to the verbal traces of the preconscious, an association with such traces apparently being necessary for an idea to become conscious. But the relationship of such hypercathexis and such verbal traces is not clarified.

Thus while we have much knowledge developed by psychoanalysis concerning the psychology of the unconscious and a rather rich knowledge of the psychology of perceptual processes revealed by general psychology, the psychology of thinking has been but little attacked in either psychoanalysis or general psychology. It is true that the psychology of thinking has been dealt with in ethnopsychological studies and comparative and developmental psychological studies. These studies, however, showed the similarity of primitive, childish, and deteriorated psychic function to the primary process, and the great unknowns here too are the psychological processes and mechanisms underlying what is called "logical thinking." This may be elucidated if one turns to the ancient problems of philosophy. It is probably safe to assert that, of these problems, the interrelation of body and mind, the interrelation of mechanics and dynamics, and the interrelation of atomistic and holistic conceptions of the world are the ones in the foreground of our present-day scientific discussion. These are the ones which color and to a certain extent determine our scientific frame of mind. Sometimes a fourth is added, namely, the problem of the absolute or relative character of the experienced world, which is one of the underlying considerations in our appraising the world of the patient as a world individual and unique to him and independent of what we know or imagine the world to be. Rarely, however, do we confront all the implications of this latter view. These implications may be brought into sharper relief by using the formulation of Leibnitz. Leibnitz's philosophy was centered on an endeavor to understand how it is possible that the logically deducible truths contained in the human mind, deducible without immediate recourse to reality, can make us understand the nature of reality; or as he formulated it, "What is the relation of *vérité du fait* to *vérité de la raison*." There is probably no doubt in the mind of any one of us that *vérité de la raison* develops in the course of the child's growth as reality testing progresses; that its development is instituted, directed, and shaped by the constant influence of reality. But just how that happens, and why *vérité de la raison* crystallizes into those laws which we call laws of logic or dialectics, are the great unanswered questions. Hume thought that there is no idea in our minds without a corresponding original perception, that the laws of nature we conceive of are not due to causality inherent in the world but to the associations created in our minds between events that occur contiguously or successively, and that the strength of the laws is the strength of the association of ideas. Consequently he considered that no causal laws but only probabilities exist in this world. Kant reformulated Hume's thesis in his *Prolegomena to Any Future Metaphysics* in what he called a Copernican turn, maintaining that Hume forgot about general ideas and relations and missed the fact that the incoming percepts are organized and synthesized according to the inherent laws of "pure" reason. According to him, space and time are but modes of our apperception, and causality, finiteness, infiniteness, etc., are categories of pure reason. He thus maintained that the "thing in itself" remains forever beyond our reach, and what we cognize is merely the percept of it, apperceived in terms of our modes of apperception and synthesized according to the categories of pure reason. Accordingly, employing logical-philosophical, not psychological, terms, Kant became the first to recognize that our mentation is a synthesis between our autonomous psychological functioning and incoming stimuli. Thus the ancient problem of epistemology, or in other words, the problem of the nature of knowledge, or again in other words, the problem of our view of reality, or again in other words, the relation of the individual and his world, was formulated in logical-philosophical terms. Psychoanalysis taught another formulation of the same thing in terms of the psychology of instincts and wishes. One might say that psychoanalysis revealed the relativity of our view of the world in terms of the psychology of the id, while Kant revealed the same thing in terms of the psychology of thinking, that is, through a logical, philosophical analysis of thinking. Unhumble as it may seem, I would like to venture the suggestion that one of the royal roads toward a psychoanalytic psychology of thinking may lead through the discovery of the psychogenesis of the modes of apperception and the categories of pure reason which Kant postulated as the autonomous logical functions accounting for our view of our world. The scope of this suggestion may perhaps be better appraised if we remember that Freud, in "Formulations Regarding the Two Principles in Mental Functioning" (1911), clearly envisaged the emergence of the reality principle from the pleasure-pain principle, and indicated the change of function taking place, but he did not give a genetic analysis nor a description of the anatomy of the change taking place. Thus we read in Freud:

> In the situation I am considering, whatever was thought of (desired) was simply imagined in an hallucinatory form, as still happens to-day with our dream-thoughts every night. This attempt at satisfaction by means of hallucination was abandoned only in consequence of the absence of the expected gratification, because of the disappointment experienced. Instead, the mental apparatus had to decide to form a conception of the real circumstances in the outer world and to exert itself to alter them. A new principle of mental functioning was thus introduced; what was conceived of was no longer that which was pleasant, but that which was real, even if it should be unpleasant. This institution of the *reality-principle* proved a momentous step [p. 14].
>
> In place of repression, which excluded from cathexis as productive of "pain" some of the emerging ideas, there developed an impartial *passing of judgement,* which had to decide whether a particular idea was true or false, that is, was in agreement with reality or not; decision was determined by comparison with the memory-traces of reality. . . .
>
> Restraint of motor discharge (of action) had now become neces-

sary, and was provided by means of the process of *thought,* which was developed from ideation. Thought was endowed with qualities which made it possible for the mental apparatus to support increased tension during a delay in the process of discharge. It is essentially an experimental way of acting, accompanied by displacement of smaller quantities of cathexis together with less expenditure (discharge) of them. For this purpose conversion of free cathexis into "bound" cathexes was imperative, and this was brought about by means of raising the level of the whole cathectic process. It is probable that thinking was originally unconscious, in so far as it rose above mere ideation and turned to the relations between the object-impressions, and that it became endowed with further qualities which were perceptible to consciousness only through its connection with the memory-traces of words [pp. 15–16].

In suggesting the need for a psychological analysis of the modes of apperception and of the categories of the "pure-reason" laws of logic, we also come to the problem of the meaning of the usual principles of logic first formulated by Aristotle, such as the principles of "identity," "contradiction," and the "excluded third." [2] One could go further, and suggest the need for a psychological analysis of the Socratic method of dichotomy, or the dialectic method of Heraclitus.

One may summarize that in the course of the history of philosophy, the usual features of our everyday thinking have been crystallized into definite scientific philosophical methods and principles of thinking, and that if one wants to understand our thinking—an eminently significant part of our ego functions—one may utilize the psychological analysis of the principles mentioned above.

Let me return now to the problem of insight. I believe it is safe to assert that in the history of philosophy the awakening of insight was accompanied by the negation of "appearance" and followed by doubt and skepticism, which in turn were followed by attempts to suppress the insight in one way or another. Let us take the early Greek philosophy which crystallized man's awakening awareness that his reasoning tells him something different from what his senses show him. The Milesian philosophers—Thales, Anaximander, and Anaximenes—as well as Heraclitus of Ephesus, attempted to show that appearances are derived from one single underlying existence and happening. This was water for Thales, the *infinite*—an abstract archprinciple from which everything derives by differentiation—for Anaximander, air for Anaximenes, fire for Heraclitus. While these philosophers taught a genesis of appearances from these archmatters, the Eleatic school conceived of appearances as "nonexistent," or as we might say, as "mere" appearances, while the existing is the *one,* the truth, what is grasped by the mind only and

[2] [Although Rapaport always spoke of the "excluded third," the more usual English rendering of the term is "excluded middle"—Ed.]

not by the senses. It was merely a step from this negation to sophistry and skepticism. There the world of appearances was no longer denied with the bold one-sidedness of the Eleatic school. Protagoras' *homo mensura* principle, according to which "man is the measure of all things—of the existence of existing things as well as of the nonexistence of nonexisting things"—did not deny the existence of appearances or claim the existence of a true material world; it put the measuring rod for existence into the individual person. The consequences were devastating in every respect: doubt penetrated every cranny of thought. Gorgias claimed that nothing exists, and if anything did exist, it could not be cognized, and even if anything could be cognized, such knowledge would be incommunicable. The consequences in social philosophy were a glorification and justification of the right of the strongest. The search for truth was abandoned and its place was taken by the sophistic art of persuasion. One is taken aback by the extreme similarity of this situation to that of Weimar and Nazi Germany—only the ancient half of the comparison appears to be incomparably nobler. Plato and Aristotle made momentous attempts to reconcile the appearance with the underlying process, the testimony of the senses with that of the mind. It is curious to see how Plato hypothesized a *sensus communis,* a "common" sense which synthesizes the sense experiences and makes them meaningful, and simultaneously assumed the existence of *anamnesis,* namely the perceiving of memories from earlier lives of the individual to explain the origin of thinking and the validity of its results. It is curious to see that the greatest empiricist of ancient times, Aristotle, is the one who formulated the first general table of categories (there was an incomplete Pythagorean one before his) describing the terms in which the human mind conceives of the world: substance, quality, quantity, relation, space, time, position, possession, action, and passivity. Their attempts—though of tremendous later consequence—were overruled by the Hellenistic school of philosophy which more or less completely abandoned insight already gained. Similar historical events led to Descartes's philosophy of doubt, and from Kant's insight to the Hegel-Fichte-Schelling type of German idealism.

After every one of these insights had been exposed to testing and, by virtue of systematic exploration, became an accepted principle of scientific thinking, its doubt-producing value decreased but the fight changed its scene and is still ever going on. Apparently its current scene is where the drama of the unconscious determination of conscious processes is reviewed by scientists. We have already seen Horney's attempt to get away from the Freudian insight. It is a good example of the fact that insight once gained can easily be lost—a fact well known from occurrences in the usual therapeutic procedure. There an attempt is made to exploit the insight, develop it into knowledge by linking it with all that relates to it in the patient's problems. Historically, every attempt to lose an insight sets a great task to those championing that insight: to investigate, explore, and fill in—in terms of the insight—the gap through which came the flood that threatens to bury the insight which was won by so hard a struggle. In our case, this gap is the psychology of the ego in general and the psychology of thinking in particular.

Let us return to the problem of the psychology of thinking. Just as in primitive thinking, so too in the Greek philosophers do we find many ideas and modes of thought resembling primary processes (for instance, Thales' statement that the magnet has a soul because it attracts iron), especially when we scrutinize their religious and moral ideas. My aim, however, is not to enumerate these; we would prefer to see the beginnings of so-called systematic thinking which attempts to explain nature. In attempting to find these beginnings, we are soon forced to exclude not only purely magical ideas but another body of statements also, namely those containing pure observations, for instance, Anaximander's observation of the circular path of the sun. The nature of thinking becomes clearer where the human being expresses his ideas about the unobservable, where his thinking acts just as it does when he organizes a Rorschach inkblot. If we center our attention on functions which are presuppositions of observation inherent in the first steps of systematic thinking, we find that the most central idea is that everything is derived from one common archmatter. This is certainly not an observation of fact, and no longer merely a magical idea. Monism is apparently one of the first inherent characteristics of systematic thinking. Water, air, fire, each may have been empirically chosen to be the single basis of the world, but that the world is built from one single matter was probably nothing empirical, and if Anaximander refrained from linking the single principle out of which the world is built with any empirically known matter, he gave further proof to this contention. The constant change of Heraclitus and the unchangeability of Parmenides are more abstract empirical forms given to the nonempirical idea of monism.

I cannot enumerate all the ideas the Greeks had which can be discerned to be not of empirical origin but to be inherent logical forms of systematic thinking at its very beginnings. It is important, however, to note what Gomperz, one of the greatest historians of Greek philosophy, stated very clearly: "Here it may almost be said that inexperience was the mother of wisdom." He recognized the nature of that part of old Greek wisdom which I have been describing. Let me enumerate just a few modern ideas whose counterparts are present in ancient Greek philosophy, though the empirical material on whose basis these theoretical ideas have been conceived in our time was obviously unavailable to Greek thinkers. For instance, the cornerstones of modern chemistry, the existence of elements and the indestructibility of matter, were clearly stated by the Greeks. And the theory of evolution was expressed in the idea that a human being could not have been created as such and had developed from animals living in the sea. I am aware of the plausible objection that the Greeks might have meant something entirely different from what we read into their statements today. This is quite possible and one might even add that all these statements are known to us in fragmentary form and not in their original context. I would like to plead, however, against underestimating the significance of these statements. They came from a people among whose fragments we read sentences like the following: ·

"Those who are awake have one world in common; those who are asleep retire every one to a private world of his own."

"We ought not to act and speak like men asleep."

"Man's character is his fate."

"I have sought to understand myself."

"Much learning does not teach wisdom, else would it have taught Hesiod and Pythagoras, Xenophanes, too, and Hecataeus."

"You could not discover the boundaries of the soul though you tried every path, so deep does its reason reach down."

The Pythagoreans were the first to attempt to crystallize into "categories" what seemed to them to be inherent forms of thinking. Here are their ten pairs of categories: (1) limited—unlimited; (2) even—odd; (3) one —many; (4) right—left; (5) man—woman; (6) resting—moving; (7) straight—curved; (8) lightness—darkness; (9) good—bad; (10) square—rectangular.

The one-sidedness of this table of categories was determined by the presupposition that the basis of everything in the world is the number. We have already seen the categories of Aristotle. Although more inclusive, they too were one-sided, inasmuch as they were influenced by grammatical-logical considerations. But if one realizes that these two tables of categories, as well as the other basic ideas of logic, are extremely similar to categories developed by more recent philosophers, one cannot help recognizing the significance of most of them. For instance Descartes, the great empiricist, the genius of mathematics and physics, who in his youth rejected anything which did not fit his empiricism, recognized certain innate ideas in his posthumously published *Rules for the Direction of the Mind,* and these ideas were the following: the cause, the simple, the universal, the one, the equal, the similar, the straight line. Kant's categories also show similarities: universe, multitude, unit; reality, negation, limitation; substance and attribute, cause and effect, community and interaction; possibility and impossibility, existence and nonexistence; necessary and incidental. How we can derive these general inherent ideas of ordered thinking, and possibly many others, out of primary processes, and what their relation is to defense mechanisms of the ego and to its emotional make-up, are questions about which I do not propose to speculate, tempting though some of them may be. My aim is only to point out that it is not the primary processes alone which are inborn equipment of the human organism. There appear to exist inherent forms of thinking which are prerequisites of and organizing principles of conscious experiencing. In other words, they are as characteristic of conscious thinking as is the primary process of the unconscious. There is, however, a very significant difference between the two. As early as psychological processes in the infant become amenable to any observations, the primary process appears to be present. The inherent principles of conscious thinking, however, appear to develop in a prolonged process of maturation. Perhaps, though, even this distinction is not really sharp: Both may be subject to a process of maturation. If so, it is very probable that the maturation processes of the two overlap.

Having arrived at the end of these loosely organized ideas, I have to ask myself whether it was not superfluous to burden this presentation with the discussion of two such apparently disparate topics as insight and ego psychology. I would like to answer by stating that one of the essential implications of my discussion is that the problem of insight may be reformulated in terms other than those I have used thus far. The ego is a realm of appearances, but it can turn back upon itself and upon the id in trying to discover that realm of processes out of which it has developed in the course of phylogenesis as well as ontogenesis. While our initial definition of insight implied only a general concept of insight designating every understanding of appearances in terms of processes underlying them, now we have arrived at a more specific description of psychological insight. Its significant difference from the more general concept of insight is that in it the relation between appearances and processes is not investigated by an external third agent, but human thinking as a realm of appearances turns back upon itself and tries to unearth the processes underlying itself. I assume that it can be stated without further explanation that without the existence of many human individuals, interpersonal relations, changing interpersonal relations, and changing society, neither the possibility of nor the necessity for such insight would exist. This is the point Dr. Knight and I championed in connection with Dr. Carl Tillman's paper[3] when the problem of insight was discussed at the beginning of this year. At that time it was stated that insight is a concept which is relative to the society in which it occurs. Now, while sustaining this view, I would like to add one point about its limitation. In the concept of insight, the degree of trueness or falseness, as well as of wholeness or partness, is what has reference to the social background, inasmuch as it is the society which gives the occasion for insight. This consider-

[3] [Unpublished paper presented to the staff of the Menninger Foundation—Ed.]

ation also sheds some light on the only true nucleus of the contention of those psychiatrists (ranging from Stekel to Schilder) who claim that psychiatric disorders are social disorders.

In this paper I have conceived of psychological insight as a turning upon itself and the processes underlying it, and have attempted to clarify the inherent characteristics of thinking, or, in other words, of the secondary process, by enumerating some of its most naked, early, Greek forms where its nature was least hidden by empirical observations. The essence of this paper is the suggestion that the nature of insight will be better understood when the mechanisms of the secondary process are better known; I suggested that the escape from psychoanalytic insight has been facilitated by the lack of such knowledge about ego psychology in general and the psychology of thinking in particular; I suggested that one of the royal roads toward a psychology of thinking lies in discovering the psychological processes that brought about the laws of logic and the different categories of human thinking suggested by the Pythagoreans, Aristotle, Descartes, Kant, and others.

REFERENCES

Freud, S. (1911). Formulations Regarding the Two Principles in Mental Functioning. *Collected Papers,* 4:13–21. New York: Basic Books, 1959.

Fromm, E. (1941). *Escape from Freedom.* New York: Farrar & Rinehart.

Horney, K. (1939). *New Ways in Psychoanalysis.* New York: Norton.

Lewy, E. (1941). The Return of the Repression. *Bull. Menninger Clin.,* 5:47–55.

9

A CASE OF AMNESIA AND

ITS BEARING ON THE

THEORY OF MEMORY

WITH MERTON M. GILL

THE PROBLEM

Memory is one of the fields of psychology in the exploration of which much effort has been expended, and yet it is a field in which we remain remote from an understanding of the function as it really operates in everyday life. The laws of frequency of repetition, time decrement, retroactive and associative inhibition, primacy-recency, and many others do not suffice for understanding the memory function as encountered in everyday life. Yet the warning of Janet (1901) that "illness analyzes memory better than do psychologists" has remained relatively unheeded and but little attention has been paid to the psychopathology of memory by experimental psychologists. Psychiatrists, being clinicians, have observed and described many spectacular memory disturbances, such as amnesias, loss of personal identity, paramnesias, pseudoamnesias, Korsakoff syndrome, and the like, but,

Paper read at the 1942 meetings of the Eastern Psychological Association, Providence, R.I. First published in Character and Personality, *11:166–172, 1942. Spanish translation published in* Merton M. Gill and David Rapaport, Aportaciones a la Téoria y Técnica Psicoanalítica. *Asociación Psicoanalítica Mexicana, A.C., 1962, pp. 260–268.*

lacking theoretical zeal, they have not been concerned with the theoretical implications of their accumulated treasures. Of the many historical and theoretical reasons why an inclusive memory theory has not as yet been evolved only two will be mentioned here. The first is the lack of recognition that the concept "memory" is but an abstraction and that "memory" in everyday life is but *one aspect of our thought processes*. The second is the disregard of the pathological memory phenomena. These two factors have had a paralyzing effect on experimental and theoretical attack directed toward understanding the memory function.

The term amnesia refers to many conditions in which wholesale forgetting is the outstanding symptom. The lack of careful delineation of the period which is forgotten, as contrasted with the period over which the forgetting persists, makes for much confusion. In retrograde amnesia one who has normally experienced and remembered a period of his life suddenly forgets all the events of this period. In anterograde amnesia one continuously forgets immediately experienced events. Distinguished from these amnesias are the fugues, and loss of personal identity. The transition between these two is obscure in the relatively small literature on the subject. A further complicating circumstance is that these states are frequently denoted "somnambulic states." A person in a fugue state does not know of his previous life, name, and the like. But neither does he realize this, living under a new identity, nor does he become conspicuous to people who did not know him in his former state. In contrast to this, loss of personal identity is a state in which the person is aware of the fact that he does not know who he is, where he comes from, and so forth. It is known that fugues are sometimes followed by loss of personal identity, but it is probable that such states come about also without preceding fugues. The awakening from states of fugue and from loss of personal identity is usually followed by an amnesia for the period of the fugue or loss. (The relation of these states to multiple personalities is another intriguing but as yet unsolved problem.)[1] The case to be reported here unites features of fugue states and of "loss of personal identity."

THE INCIDENT

Mr. X is a 31-year-old employee of a small manufacturing company owned by his father-in-law. In childhood and adolescence he worked hard trying to fulfill the ideal of "independence" taught him by his father. Later he worked for the concern by which his father was employed. Shortly thereafter he was married and was soon induced by his father-in-law, who lived in another part of the country, to work for him. Against his better judgment

[1] For sources of literature and material concerning the clinical varieties of amnesia and for a discussion of the nature and interrelation of these varieties, see Rapaport (1942, Chapter 7).

and his own father's wish, he did so and was chagrined to find himself in a minor, poorly paid position, but was unable to declare his dissatisfaction. A growing family and poor budgetary sense soon plunged him into debt from which he was periodically extricated by his father-in-law at his wife's intervention but with violence to his ideals of independence and manliness. On the weekend before the onset of the amnesia, having fallen into a serious financial difficulty, he drove with his family to the nearby city in which his father-in-law lived, with the intention of asking for a loan. He could not bring himself to ask for the money, so on Sunday afternoon he set out for home, his mission unfulfilled. He was preoccupied with thoughts of finding a new job to make more money.

It was then that a loss of personal identity began to set in, so that by the time he reached home he did not know who he was, did not recognize his wife or children, and spoke only of finding a new job. The next morning he was taken to his office but recognized no one. He was brought to the hospital that afternoon with the statement that he was being taken to a new job. For the first twenty-four hours in the hospital he falsified reality in terms of his belief that he was working—the physician was the boss, the rooms were offices, the noises were those of machinery, the other patients were other employees, and so forth. This period was also marked by anterograde amnesia in that any data contrary to his falsification of reality, such as his introduction to another physician on the ward, for example, were immediately forgotten.

On Tuesday evening he dozed off in a chair and awakened soon thereafter with a recovery of personal identity, calling for his wife and children urging them to hurry to get ready for the trip back home. He thought it was four o'clock Sunday. He did not know where he was nor how he had got there. He was given orienting data. The next day he remembered everything up to Sunday at four o'clock and retained all impressions occurring subsequent to Tuesday evening but remembered nothing of the period between.

Thursday afternoon he was read the story of Pygmalion, and he repeated it.[2]

On Friday morning, while repeating this story at the request of the exam-

---

[2] The text of this story as read to the patient is the following: A young man worked years to carve a white marble statue of a beautiful girl. She grew prettier day by day. He began to love the statue so well that one day he said to it: "I would give everything in the world if you would be alive and be my wife." Just then the clock struck twelve, and the cold stone began to grow warm, the cheeks red, the hair brown, the lips to move. She stepped down, and he had his wish. They lived happily together for years, and three beautiful children were born. One day he was very tired, and grew so angry, though without cause, that he struck her. She wept, kissed each child and her husband, stepped back upon the pedestal, and slowly grew cold, pale, and stiff, closed her eyes, and when the clock struck midnight she was a statue of pure white marble as she had been years before, and could not hear the sobs of her husband and children.

iner, he suddenly fell into a brief trancelike state and began to recall in consecutive fashion the experiences beginning with the preceding Sunday afternoon. These experiences were recounted, however, in terms of the misidentifications as directed by the delusion of being at work, and were also marked by his inability to identify places and people encountered in the period of the loss of personal identity and normally familiar to him (e.g., in recounting his experiences with his wife he was unable to identify her as such, but spoke of her as a strange woman). At this time he recalled that on Sunday afternoon he had had suicidal thoughts.

The next day he said that if he had listened to his wife he would not be in his present position. He explained that he remembered that shortly after leaving his father-in-law's home on Sunday afternoon his wife had suggested that they turn back and that she talk to her father. The memory of this fact he had persistently disclaimed in previous questioning. This, then, was the first memory of the period of loss of personal identity which was recounted with the presence of personal identity. From then on he progressively related the events of the forgotten period, in terms of personal identity and with a recognition of the misidentifications and delusion. Efforts to make the patient skip a period in recounting the story resulted in a return to description without personal identity—as though the penetration of the memories by personal identity could take place only in a temporally consecutive manner.

We will now try to reconstruct in brief the psychogenesis of Mr. X's illness. He found himself in a situation full of contradictions. His ideal of manliness compelled him to take care of his family, but it also barred the only way possible in reality, namely, obtaining help from his father-in-law. Suicidal thoughts were rejected. Apparently the only way out he could see was to find a new job and earn more money. But his obligations were so pressing that this solution was not really possible. He therefore had to lose recognition of all the data that could have revealed to him that this solution was unsatisfactory and this was possible only through the "loss of personal identity." The period of this loss was in turn forgotten when personal identity was recovered.

THEORETICAL INTERPRETATION

This case of amnesia has several bearings on the general theory of memory. The necessarily brief presentation can do no more than to demonstrate a general pattern, and allows for no more than the formulation of a few hypotheses. There are three problems of memory theory concerning which hypotheses may be set up in reference to this case: (1) personal identity and its relation to memory; (2) the rôle of strivings in memory organization; (3) the problem of communication of traces.

(1) It has long been known that memories have a personal relevance.

W. Stern (1930) emphasized this specifically and Claparède (1911) coined the concept "moité," translated "me-ness." It was implied that without such "me-ness" memory becomes either logically deducible knowledge or else the material becomes altogether unavailable for recall. The amnesic states called loss of personal identity seemed to bear out this contention inasmuch as mere impersonal knowledge and habits were found to be retained in spite of the loss of personal identity, while memory material of personal relevance appeared to be lost together with the personal identity. What this "me-ness" or personal identity was remained a moot question. The case reported above allows for some interpretation of it. Mr. X, in his period of loss of personal identity, was possessed by a single idea, "I am out to find a job." This single idea together with the striving it expressed seem to have replaced all his usual strivings, which we usually call personality, and his introspective knowledge of them, which we usually call awareness of one's self. We mentioned above that the striving to find a job replaced the conflicting, unacceptable, and realistically impossible strivings of Mr. X. Thus it may be hypothesized that "moité" or "me-ness" of a memory involves the striving that delivers the memory into consciousness, and that "personal identity" is the setting of all the strivings characteristic of an individual, which determine and deliver the thoughts and memories which enter consciousness. When a striving becomes unacceptable the pertinent memories lose their "me-ness." When a set of such strivings becomes unacceptable or in other words is repressed, the usual "personal identity" which they constitute disappears and a state of "loss of personal identity" results. This state usually is characterized by a single striving replacing all the conflicting ones. This, however, brings us to our second problem, the organization of memory functioning by strivings.

(2) As early as thirty years ago Müller-Freienfels (1913) maintained that words and ideas are merely the clothing, the form of expression chosen by feelings, attitudes, or strivings. Bartlett's (1932) experiments showed that reproduction is essentially production in an attempt to justify an attitude. Freudian psychology explains memory errors and forgetting as resulting from the influence of unconscious strivings (Freud, 1901). The evidence for such theories in the case of Mr. X is this: In the state of loss of personal identity every percept was assimilated, distorted, and later remembered in the sense of the single striving that ruled that state. The later penetration of the memories of this period by personal identity was not really a recovery of memories, but rather an entire recasting of experiences in terms of the patient's personal identity. The recovery of his memories, in a sense, took place through a reliving of his disease. The recall of the Pygmalion story apparently reawakened in him the conflict situation that was present at the time of onset of the loss of personal identity. The brief trance state which appeared and which can be equated with the period of loss of personal identity once again was dominated by the solution: "I must find a

new job"; so that now the memories of the period dominated by this striving could once again enter consciousness. Thus we see that the memories which were lost with the disappearance of a striving were regained when the striving returned.

(3) Our third problem is that of the communication of traces. Gestalt psychologists, and especially Koffka (1935), explained remembering and recognition by the communication of the present process with a memory trace of the previous process now to be remembered. Koffka maintained that such a communication, though frequently brought about by attitudes of the ego, may occur in the trace field, independently of ego attitudes. In our case the story of Pygmalion was chosen for its similarity to the patient's problem situation. Yet reading and immediate recall of the story did not elicit any observable reaction. When, however, a day had passed and the subject was again asked to reproduce the story, an emotional reaction was elicited which issued in the recall of the events of the forgotten period.[3] It is crucial that the emotional reaction *preceded* the recall of the forgotten material; the patient stated that first he had to cry though he didn't know why, then he remembered his suicidal thoughts, and only then did the revival of the memories begin. It must be stressed that a day elapsed between the initial statement and this emotionally significant delayed recall of the story. In this period, just as in Wulf's (1922) experiment with the autonomous changes of figures, the communication and integration of the trace of the story with the pertinent psychic material came about only after a lapse of time. But not the mere communication of traces with a lapse of time is sufficient to initiate recall. It appears that something more is needed—namely, an identical striving or affect pervading two traces—or in other words, communication of traces implies penetration of them by identical attitudes and strivings.

SUMMARY

A case of "loss of personal identity" is reported, in the course of which were observed part of the period of loss, the period in which the events of this "loss" were forgotten, and the experimentally precipitated recovery of this forgotten period. The following theoretical hypotheses were discussed on the basis of this case: that memory organization and delivery of memories into consciousness are effected by strivings, affects, attitudes; that "personal identity" is the setting of the strivings, affects, and attitudes of the individual; that its loss comes about when too many of these strivings become contradictory to each other and become replaced by a single striving; and finally that communication of traces responsible for recognition and recall takes place when the attitudes, affects, and strivings underlying the communicating traces are similar.

[3] In this connection, see also H. Lundholm's theory of functional amnesia (1932).

REFERENCES

Bartlett, F. C. (1932). *Remembering: A Study in Experimental and Social Psychology.* Cambridge: Cambridge University Press.

Claparède, E. (1911). Recognition and "Me-ness." In *Organization and Pathology of Thought,* ed. & tr. D. Rapaport. New York: Columbia University Press, 1951, pp. 58–75.

Freud, S. (1901). The Psychopathology of Everyday Life, tr. A. A. Brill. *The Basic Writings.* New York: Modern Library, 1938, pp. 33–178.

Janet, P. (1901). *The Mental State of Hystericals.* New York: Putnam.

Koffka, K. (1935). *Principles of Gestalt Psychology.* New York: Harcourt, Brace.

Lundholm, H. (1932). The Riddle of Functional Amnesia. *J. Abnorm. Soc. Psychol.,* 26:355–366.

Müller-Freienfels, R. (1913). Der Einfluss der Gefühle und motorischen Faktoren auf Assoziation und Denken. *Arch. Psychol.,* 27:381–430.

Rapaport, D. (1942). *Emotions and Memory.* Baltimore: Williams & Wilkins.

Stern, W. (1930). Personalistik der Erinnerung. *Z. Psychol.,* 118:350–381.

Wulf, F. (1922). Beiträge zur Psychologie der Gestalt: Über die Veränderung von Vorstellungen. *Psychol. Forsch.,* 1:333–373.

I O

EMOTIONS AND MEMORY

Psychological theory has often disregarded in the past and still often disregards certain fields of psychological phenomena. We can hardly enumerate here how the investigations of personality were long left to the writer of belles-lettres or to the historian, how the investigation of many psychological phenomena is still left to the linguist, or how the investigation of many psychological problems is left to the psychiatrist and anthropologist. In the following we shall see that a similar compartmentalization exists in the field of memory phenomena. Theories of the Ebbinghaus type view memory as a specific function which can be investigated by experiments in learning and by testing the retention of learned material. This view implies the assumption that the simpler and more nonsensical the material, the more accurately and truthfully the laws of memory functioning will show themselves in the experiment. These theories disregard the fact that memory phenomena (imprinting, retention, recall, recognition) occur not only in the setting of purposeful learning, but also *continuously* in everyday life, and that in fact all psychic processes imply one phase or another of memory functioning. They therefore neglect the investigation of memory phenomena in their natural setting as well as of pathological memory phenomena. Janet aptly said:

Paper read in the Psychology Section, 1941 Dallas meetings of the American Association for the Advancement of Science. First published in The Psychological Review, *50:234–243, 1943.*

> The psychologists in their descriptions admit of no other elementary phenomena of memory than conservation and reproduction. We think that they are wrong, and that disease decomposes and analyses memory better than psychology [1901, p. 102].

The problems of amnesias and paramnesias, the Korsakoff syndrome, etc., have remained in the psychiatrist's domain. Hypnotic memory phenomena have been left to the hypnotists' care. Everyday forgettings, slips of tongue, and the universal amnesia for the greater part of childhood experiences were a no-man's-land until Freud and other psychoanalysts became interested in these phenomena. There have been significant discoveries made in these fields, but these discoveries have never been integrated or consolidated along the lines of general psychological findings or of theories of memory. Of the few attempts at integration, those of the psychologists Ray (1937) and Sears (1936), in the 1930's, remained a mere beginning, while those of the psychiatrists Gillespie (1937) and Schilder (Abeles and Schilder, 1935) cannot boast of much better results. The fact that memory is but one of many aspects of our thought processes and not an independent function was not made sufficiently clear in these attempts, nor was experimentation sufficient to clarify the laws governing either the normal functioning of that aspect of our thought processes which we are accustomed to call memory or its disturbances.

In the following we shall attempt to describe the progress made by experimentation and clinical observation toward a new understanding of the memory processes.

In the experimental field the main headway toward an understanding of the functioning of memory in everyday life was made through investigating *the influence of context and of attitude on learning and memory.* Usually the contexts used were well delimited, in contrast to everyday life where usually no delimitation exists. Also the attitudes were conscious and formulated in verbal-logical terms, while in everyday life no such formulation can be found and attitudes are usually affect bound. The rôle of the context in these experiments was to constitute a similar or a heterogeneous background either of which could be *meaningful* or *meaningless.* The contexts of everyday life, however, play the pianoforte of attitudes which they elicit, or, rather, interact with, thus *determining* and *organizing*—not merely *facilitating* or *inhibiting*—imprinting and recall. The attitudes usually investigated were "like-dislike," and "pleasantness-unpleasantness" of the learned material and of its context. Other attitudes were elicited by reward and punishment, by obscene, religious, etc., connotations of the learned material. It was assumed that in the experimental situation these attitudes were subject to interindividual agreement. In everyday life, however, attitudes are subjective matters varying with individuals and depending upon a wide range of personal constellations running the gamut from intellectual judgmentlike attitudes to affective, instinctive strivings deeply rooted in the personality of the subject. These experiments frequently claimed to have demonstrated the influence of emotions on memory or to have proved or disproved the Freudian theory of repression. Though these claims were unwarranted, the experiments at least kept alive the problem of a more general theory of memory.

As long as memory experimentation was essentially based on the Wundt-Ebbinghaus presuppositions or on the frame of reference of conditioned response, the attempts to investigate the functioning of memory as one aspect of the thought processes of everyday life were, as we have just described, generally limited to experimentation on contexts and attitudes.

A new attack on the field of memory, designed to approach memory function as it exists in everyday life, was started by Ach, according to whom associations and memory revival obey not only the law of strength of associative bonds but also that of a "determining tendency." Lewin (1926), disagreeing as to the nature of this tendency and its relation to the associative bonds, showed the central significance for learning and memory of a specific type of attitude he called "readiness to reproduce," or "readiness to rhyme." On the basis of this finding he later developed the theory of tension systems, according to which a decision, an intention, etc., corresponds to a psychic tension system which becomes discharged only when the decision or intention is carried out. If the memory of the objectives of these decisions or intentions is also dependent on these tension systems, they will be better when the intention has not yet been carried out than after it has been. Zeigarnik's (1927) often verified experiments proved that this deduction was correct.

Thus, experimental proof was offered concerning a phenomenon frequently observed in everyday life. The main deficiency of the Lewinian experiments was that they did not make quite clear just which of the many memories pertaining to an interrupted task, that is to say, to a tense psychic system, have an advantage in remembering. The experiment dealt merely with the remembering of the names of the interrupted tasks—while in everyday life the tension systems exert an influence on many related psychic contents. Thus, their relation to the functions of everyday life still remains questionable, though some experiments on substitute activities appear to attack the problem mentioned.

Whereas in order to study "normal" memory functioning, general experimental psychology investigated context and attitude, and Lewinian psychology investigated the link between memory and tense psychic systems, gestalt psychology investigated the issue of "meaning." The classical and the conditioned-response type of memory experiments used nonsense material for the most part. Gestalt psychology attempted to show that the memorizing of any material, even that of nonsense syllables, utilizes an organizing process by which some kind of structure, or in other words, a "meaning," is given to the material. But the gestalt psychologists unfortunately restricted their investigations to *logical* meaningfulness. They showed that reproductive memory function is most similar to what happens in everyday life when it deals with meaningful material, in the reproduction of which it essentially acts as problem solving or productive thinking does. Certainly, our everyday thinking and that aspect of it which we are accustomed to call memory are penetrated by logical meaningfulness; but if one were to try to represent our thinking and memory functions as satisfying merely *logical* meaningfulness, he would soon have to call the logically flawless reasoning of the paranoiac "sane," because he would neglect the *affectively* meaningful factors which lead to the paranoiac's deluded presuppositions on which his logic is built. The logical meaningfulness that gestalt psychology came to investigate is one of the most important aspects of memory functioning, but it must not be forgotten that it is only one aspect among many.

Bartlett's (1932) experimental attack on the everyday function of memory may be considered a bridge to clinical observations on memory. He experimented mainly with the reproduction of stories and interpreted his results as showing that the core of reproduction is always an attitude, an emotional-affective tendency, and that *re*production is essentially *production* around this core: an attempt to justify and to convey this attitude. His experimental results corroborated views expressed previously by theoretical psychologists such as the personalist W. Stern, or the kinesthetist R. Müller-Freienfels. Contrary to such conceptions of memory functioning as those of Ebbinghaus, Wundt, and G. E. Müller according to which an idea in consciousness is followed by that idea having the strongest associative bond to it, what actually happens in the memory function of everyday life corresponds to the finding of Bartlett: an attitude, an affective or emotional striving, expresses itself by reviving and organizing memory traces.

The available clinical observations on memory functioning can be grouped from either the point of view of subject matter or that of method. As regards subject matter, we may distinguish between normal and abnormal memory phenomena. Clearly, the study of memory functioning pertains to the organization of memories, of which organization memory-distortion and forgetting are examples. As regards method, there were the mere clinical observations as distinguished from clinically oriented experiments, only the latter of which can justifiably be called controlled observations of the memory function in general and of the gross pathology of memory.

The greatest mass of observations concerning memory function was accumulated by the psychoanalytic school. These observations were crystallized into several concepts, such as parapraxis (Freud, 1901), repression (Jones, 1923), and primary mechanisms (Freud, 1900; Lewin, 1935, pp. 243–247). The theory of parapraxes, of which everyday forgetting is only an example, maintains that slips of the tongue and slips of memory as well as forgetting are due to an unconscious striving interfering with the tendency to revival of the memory in question. The theory of repression maintains that a striving which would be painful to consciousness is therefore kept out of consciousness and that memories connected with the striving become themselves unconscious, that is to say, are "forgotten," but can be recovered under proper conditions; in other words, there is a tendency to avoid the awakening of pain through memory. The theory of primary mechanisms maintains that ideas can replace each other, can merge with each other, and can be displaced to express and yet through distortion to conceal basic strivings of the person. These theories have found some experimental substantiation in the experiments on substitution conducted by the pupils of Lewin (1935), in the experiments of Bartlett (1932), and in experiments to be referred to later on.

The observations concerning the pathology of memory are so manifold that they can hardly be summarized here. The main bearing on memory theory of the investigations on retro- and anterograde amnesias, multiple personalities with alternating systems of memory, loss of personal identity or fugue states, and the Korsakoff syndrome may be summed up as follows (Rapaport, 1942):

First, the investigations on loss of personal identity and fugue states show that attached to memories there is a personal sign, an attitude of personal identification, which if lost or withdrawn from a whole period of experiences results in an amnesia of a particular type (loss of personal identity or fugue state). It probably plays a rôle also in the difference between accumulated knowledge of impersonal character and the memory of personal experiences and is an important factor in recognition. In multiple personalities, two or more systems of such attitudes of personal identity are probably responsible for the reciprocal systematic amnesias. This personal sign, or attitude of personal identity, is a link to Bartlett's experimental results as well as to those results of Lewin which maintain that attitudes or affective tendencies are the essential factors in recall.

Second, the investigations on the Korsakoff syndrome show that memories have a "temporal sign" the loss of which causes impairment of remembering in everyday life and peculiar reduplicating paramnesias and amnesias, although at the same time, learning and immediate recall may be relatively intact. The memories emerge inappropriately and may emerge incidentally, but are unavailable at the proper moment. Such a factor of temporalization probably plays an important rôle also in the difference between knowing, remembering, and recognizing, and may probably underlie the phenomenon of "déjà vu." Although the relation of the loss of temporal sign to the affective disturbance present in the Korsakoff syndrome has not yet finally been clarified, it appears probable that the disturbance of temporalization is related to a disturbance of the dynamics of the strivings of the individual.

Third, the investigations on amnesias by means of relearning experiments show saving, while common hypnotic as well as drug-hypnotic experiments show recall. These facts demonstrate that in functional and even in organic amnesias traces of earlier experiences are not simply lost; rather, they are unavailable for recall. Thus the Ribot law—so widely accepted as explaining memory loss—which maintains that the more labile recent memories and not the old and well-entrenched ones are lost, becomes invalidated. It probably will have to be replaced by a law to the effect that memory traces have an architectonic in which the attitudes link earlier traces to later ones and that when these attitudes are withdrawn they necessarily follow this architectonic rather than a temporal sequence.

The clinically oriented experiments have attempted to show how individuality, personal strivings, unconscious motives, and typical psychiatric conditions influence memory material. We refer here mainly to three types of experiments, (1) story reproductions, (2) reproductions of drawings, and (3) hypnotic experiments.

Of the first group, the pioneer experiments of Köppen and Kutzinski (1910) showed the memory distortions typical for different psychiatric categories. These were followed up by many investigators inquiring into more individual characteristics of memory changes, and showing how symbolic, condensing, and concealing distortions of memories come about. More recent experiments, like those of Despert (1938), show how fairy tales heard in childhood are changed by organizing memory to fit the needs of the individual recalling them.

The experiments of the second group leaned partly on the gestalt-psychological experiments of Wulf (1922) on changes of drawings in reproduction. It was shown that in cases of brain disease and of functional psychoses the reproduced figures degenerated to more primitive forms (Bender, 1938). Other experiments of this group, like those of Pötzl (1917), Malamud (1934), etc., showed that in tachystoscopically presented pictures, parts painful to the subjects are omitted in the immediate recall.

In experiments of the third group, of which Erickson's (1939) experiment is an example, strivings and tendencies were implanted into the subject by posthypnotic suggestion. By demonstrating that attitudes and strivings assert themselves by organizing memories, these experiments verified the basic rôle of attitudes and strivings in memory functioning. The memory organization they bring about to express themselves is one in which the Freudian mechanisms of symbolism, condensation, and displacement, the dynamics of trace systems of gestalt psychology, as well as the influence of contexts and attitudes, are all interwoven.

What then is the field a new theory of memory would have to embrace and what are the main lines along which such a new theory can be crystallized?

A new theory of memory will have to embrace not only the problems of rote learning and those of meaningful learning, but also the problems of memory functioning in everyday thought processes (of which logical thinking in problem solving is only a special case), and the phenomena of memory pathology.

The main lines along which such a theory may crystallize are the following:

(1) Remembering and forgetting are essentially emergence and non-emergence in consciousness, that is to say, expressions of whether a content is available or unavailable for emergence in consciousness;

(2) Forgetting as a result of decay may or may not exist—in either case it is of negligible importance. Rather, the essential fact is that dynamic factors cause memories either to be delivered into consciousness or to be prevented from emerging there;

(3) Drives, strivings, motives, needs, affects, emotions, tension systems, determining tendencies, attitudes, mental sets, etc., are names for the different dynamic factors responsible for the organization of memories. This organization may result in the facilitation or inhibition of reproduction or may result in transformation, distortion, symbolical substitution, condensation, or displacement of memories. A theory that purports to explain the memory phenomena of everyday life as an aspect of thought processes can only be built on the basis of investigations that reveal the relation of these dynamic factors to the phenomena of memory organization.

REFERENCES

Abeles, M., & Schilder, P. (1935). Psychogenetic Loss of Personal Identity: Amnesia. *Arch. Neurol. Psychiat.*, 34:587–604.

Bartlett, F. C. (1932). *Remembering: A Study in Experimental and Social Psychology*. Cambridge: Cambridge University Press.

Bender, L. (1938). A Visual Motor Gestalt Test and Its Clinical Use. *Res. Monogr. Amer. Orthopsychiat. Assn.*, No. 3.

Despert, J. L. (1938). *Emotional Problems in Children*. Utica, N. Y.: State Hospitals Press.

Erickson, M. H. (1939). Experimental Demonstration of the Psychopathology of Everyday Life. *Psychoanal. Quart.*, 8:338–353.

Freud, S. (1900). The Interpretation of Dreams, tr. A. A. Brill. *The Basic Writings*. New York: Modern Library, 1938, pp. 179–549.

——— (1901). The Psychopathology of Everyday Life, tr. A. A. Brill. *The Basic Writings*. New York: Modern Library, 1938, pp. 33–178.

Gillespie, R. D. (1937). Amnesia. *Arch. Neurol. Psychiat.*, 37:748–764.

Janet, P. (1901). *The Mental State of Hystericals*. New York: Putnam.

Jones, E. (1923). *Papers on Psycho-Analysis*, 3rd ed. New York: Wood.

Köppen, M., & Kutzinski, A. (1910). *Systematische Beobachtungen über die Wiedergabe kleiner Erzählungen durch Geisteskranke*. Berlin: Karger.

Lewin, K. (1926). *Vorsatz, Wille und Bedürfnis*. [Intention, Will and Need. In *Organization and Pathology of Thought*, ed. & tr. D. Rapaport. New York: Columbia University Press, 1951, pp. 95–153.] *Vorbemerkungen über die psychischen Kräfte und Energien und über die Struktur der Seele.* Berlin: Springer.

———— (1935). *A Dynamic Theory of Personality.* New York: McGraw-Hill.

Malamud, W. (1934). Dream Analysis: Its Application in Therapy and Research in Nervous and Mental Disease. *Arch. Neurol. Psychiat.,* 31:356–372.

Pötzl, O. (1917). The Relationship between Experimentally Induced Dream Images and Indirect Vision. *Psychol. Issues,* 7:41–120, 1960.

Rapaport, D. (1942). *Emotions and Memory.* Baltimore: Williams & Wilkins.

Ray, W. S. (1937). The Relationship of Retroactive Inhibition, Retrograde Amnesia, and the Loss of Recent Memory. *Psychol. Rev.,* 44:339–345.

Sears, R. R. (1936). Functional Abnormalities of Memory with Special Reference to Amnesia. *Psychol. Bull.* 33:229–274.

Wulf, F. (1922). Beiträge zur Psychologie der Gestalt: Über die Veränderung von Vorstellungen. *Psychol. Forsch.,* 1:333–373.

Zeigarnik, B. (1927). Über das Behalten von erledigten und unerledigten Handlungen. *Psychol. Forsch.,* 9:1–85.

I I

BOOK REVIEW

George Katona, *Organizing and
Memorizing: Studies in the Psychology
of Learning and Teaching*[1]

I

Psychologists interested in the problems of education will heartily welcome
and read with relief Katona's book. At a time when the attention of
teachers and educators is averted from the subject matter and absorbed
either in "conditioning" rather than learning or in the welfare and adjustment of the pupil, Katona daringly undertakes to analyze the process of
learning in reference to the subject matter and method of teaching. Though
it is hard to judge developments we ourselves witness, the question may be
seriously raised whether or not the relative sterility of experiments on learning, which for so long have constituted the central subject matter of educational psychology, was one of the main factors influencing educators to lean
over to the other side and become absorbed in the problem of the adjustment of the pupil rather than in his acquiring knowledge, tradition, civilization, and culture—the roots by means of which he becomes an organic part

[1] New York: Columbia University Press, 1940.

First published in The Journal of General Psychology, *28:149–157, 1943.*

of the community into which he is born. Katona's work certainly shows that experimentation on learning need not be sterile for educational practice. The present reviewer would interpret the practical bearing for education of Katona's book as follows: good teaching is meaningful teaching, that which makes the subject matter meaningful for the student and which enables him to use the things he has learned; good teaching can be done only by the teacher who "lives" in his subject matter and for whom that subject matter is meaningful.

Although we regard Katona's contribution as significant for theoretical psychology, we believe that the field of learning and memory is only partially embraced by his theory inasmuch as a theory of learning and memory cannot be considered satisfactory unless it gives an account of the rôle of affective factors. Katona justifies his avoiding these problems by stating that he—in accordance with requirements of scientific logic—dealt with the *simple* case and attempted to establish the *general* laws inherent in all learning. He admits that

> The psychology of learning is certainly the most important cue to our knowledge of memory, but there are memory phenomena which are not encompassed by an investigation of learning alone [p. 306].

These other phenomena of memory are, however, neglected in favor of the *simple* case and *general* law. The affective factor of memory function is relegated to the realm of individual or contextual differences or to that of attitudes and settings. There is even a hypothesis ventured that the attitudes may be the result—not the determiners—of the particular organization present.

To the present reviewer, educational and theoretical psychology suffer from two diametrically opposite handicaps. Educational psychology, on the one hand, sold out its goods and went in for "emotional" factors lock, stock, and barrel; it is in need of educational research which will make it aware of the fact that meaningful teaching, one that analyzes its subject matter, is what prepares people to be able to learn and think. Katona made a valuable contribution in this respect. Theoretical psychology, on the other hand, is still far from recognizing and experimentally as well as theoretically evaluating the influence of emotions on memory and learning. It is still sold on theories which are far from accounting for reality, for the functioning of living, feeling human beings—in our case for the learning and remembering of human beings, who have interests, strivings, conflicts, feelings. This realm has not been tackled by Katona's work.

II

Every psychologist has had to read and learn much in his own as well as in related fields and to reflect on the ease or difficulty of learning. Paradoxically, the subject matter of these reflections has rarely been subjected to experimental scrutiny. It is an agreeable surprise in Katona's book that the familiar reflections are attacked experimentally. Katona shows us *how* a meaningful learning method (learning through understanding) is superior to meaningless memorizing. He shows us that repetition gives mainly a chance to organize, to "understand," the material, and is not the *cause* of retention. He shows that the organization and understanding of the material may come about either slowly or rapidly—sometimes after only one perception. He shows us that knowledge through "understanding" of a material survives much better and is much more flexible at application than that of a rote-learned material. Katona attributes these differences to a different type of memory trace which he calls "structural" as opposed to "individual." These concepts are a logical development of Köhler and Koffka's "trace theory" and constitute the most original of Katona's many contributions. They give the first systematic answer to the disquieting question of those antagonistic to any trace theory (Stern, Wheeler, Bartlett): If there are traces left of an experience, why is a story heard reproduced in entirely different words? The concept of "structural trace" appears to be a valuable contribution to the development of the psychology of thinking, though much is yet to be learned about the nature of the "structural trace." For example, the common experience of the crystallization of understanding, in other words, of the structural trace, in the course of memorizing needs explanation. Katona opens the way by emphasizing the fluid transition between learning by memorizing and learning by understanding. It must be explained how application of a principle to different contexts, or the familiarization with the same material from different points of view, results in a more rapid learning by understanding, that is, in a rather rapid formation of structural traces. We must also explain how the meaning of the structural trace develops out of different materials as their "logical product."

Katona makes it clear that in his view learning and remembering are essentially organizing processes. We must ask, if such autonomous organization takes place, how can we expect that the product of these processes reflects truly the nature of our environment? Hence the question is: How can the meaningful organization into perception of material obtained through the senses, and the meaningful organization of the traces of these perceptions into memories, and finally, the meaningful organization of these perceptions and memories into thought processes, become an adequate representation of reality and how can it guide us to an accurate prediction of reality and on to appropriate action? That the inner logic of the mind and its appraisal of meaningfulness can no more do this alone than blind trial and error or the mere frequency of recurrence of events could do it was clearly indicated in the futile outcome of the attempts of rationalistic philosophy to solve this riddle. The relation of meaningfulness and blind empirics—in other words, the relation of structural and individual trace, or again in other terms the relation of autonomous and automatic (mechanic) activity of our minds—remains unsolved. We probably have to do with some kind of interaction of the two, where inborn equipment, affective development, strivings, and testing of reality to direct the strivings must all have significant determining rôles—the "logical meaningfulness" being only of partial significance.

III

In the center of Katona's theory of learning stands the concept of "meaningfulness." Katona handles this problem most of the time experimentally and empirically. One could almost say that he defines meaningfulness out of characteristics of retention and reproduction.

> What characterizes the learning results which are due to finding a principle embracing the entire subject matter?
> 1. *Retention* lasts for a long period of time. Forgetting does not begin immediately after the memorizing period and does not accelerate within a few hours as is commonly asserted; the curve of retention seems to run quite differently.
> 2. Learning is possible without *repetition* of the series. No repetition of the series was necessary when the principle was discovered by the subject (or when it was told to the subject), although without knowledge of the principle repetition was necessary.
> 3. The answers of Class 3 [the group to which the meaning of the material was taught] were given with greater *certainty* than those of Classes 1 and 2. When the experimenter, in later tests, suggested that the fifth number should be 3 instead of 1, members of Class 3, sure that he was wrong, refused to modify their statement.
> 4. "Reproduction" is not necessarily the exact repetition of all the items; transpositions and altered order may also reveal effects of the learning period. The *variability* and flexibility of reproduction, however, are not unlimited. Their range, which is dependent on the principle, will have to be studied [pp. 13–14].

> The interrelations discovered by Class 3 are distinguished from other possible relations as follows: (*a*) the relations comprise consistently the entire series, and (*b*) the whole or its principle determines its parts. The second quality indicates the main difference between the grouping by Class 3 and the other forms of grouping. If one part is missing, it can be *derived* from the other parts on the basis of

the principle of the whole. Knowledge of the principle enables one to construct the individual items. There is no arbitrary connection between two neighbors, but they complement each other by inner necessity [p. 15].

These observations help us to characterize the process of reproduction on the part of the "meaningful learners." The subjects proceeded to discover or to construct the solution, and the preceding training helped them in doing so. Reproduction was not at all similar to a door bursting open, because a button has been pressed—it did not consist of the presentation of an ever-ready response to the appropriate stimulus. It was more like the processes of discovery, of problem solving, and of construction. Remembering can here be best characterized as a rediscovery—a *reconstruction*. The effect of learning was ability to reconstruct [p. 43].

Further on he assumes the existence of structural traces acting for the survival or retention of principles of meanings.

Hypothesis I: Traces referring to specific items of past experience and those connected with and derived from the whole-character of a process can be distinguished from each other. We shall call the first "individual traces," the latter "structural traces."

Hypothesis II: Individual traces are characterized by a certain degree of fixation and rigidity, while structural traces are more readily adaptable and flexible.

Hypothesis III: The formation of individual traces is usually a long and strenuous process, while under certain conditions understanding may lead quickly and with less effort to the formation of structural traces.

Hypothesis IV: Structural traces persist longer than individual traces, which vanish soon unless reinforced [pp. 194–195].

This extremely adroit manner of handling the issue of "meaning" could be used even for an operational definition of it. However, Katona does not advance any such definition so strange to the spirit of gestalt psychology. He defines meaningfulness in terms of Wertheimer as "requiredness," "inner necessity."

The definition of "meaningful" on which our use of that term is based is to be found in Wertheimer . . . He states that meaningful behavior, meaningful completion, meaningful prediction, and so forth, require a unity in which the place of each part is not arbitrarily formed, but in which existence and quality of the parts are determined by the structure of the whole [p. 233 n.].

Passing up trivial objections against such concepts—that they are metaphysical or vitalistic—one is confronted by an extremely serious problem.

In the quotations given, and generally in Katona's experimental material, the subject matter is either directly arithmetical-mathematical or one which can be dealt with in such terms. The problems implied are the following:

(1) Is it true that the material of all learning implies principles, relations, in other words, "meaningfulness" of this kind?

(2) Is it true that "meaningfulness" or relevancy is always of this logical, mathematical, intellectual type?

(3) What is meant by this "meaningfulness"; what is its philogenesis; its ontogenesis?

As far as the first problem goes, Katona certainly renders a good service to psychology when showing that memory function is but one-sidedly represented by the laws of frequency of repetition, and to educational psychology when showing that besides massed repetition there are other methods of learning, better and more efficient. What would, however, his advice be for the teaching of geography, where most of the data do not admit of the discovery of clear-cut principles such as those discovered by the subjects in the numbers and puzzles of his experiments? This example is brought forth, not to militate against his finding concerning the rule of "meaningfulness" and "relations," but to indicate that the nature of "meaningfulness" and of "relations" is not necessarily of the type of "principles." We would like to go even further and state that "meaningfulness" and "relations" are mostly not of the intellectual type of "principles." Let us take, for instance, the learning of history; the massed data of years, names, geographic locations, and events do not yield "discoverable principles" and remain most frequently meaningless for the student. Such data are the only objective material of history; they can be linked up with narratives of various types. The narratives in Nazi Germany will be different from those in this country; the latter again will differ from those in England. They will be different when written for scientists, for the general public, or for adolescents, and still more so when narrated by a good teacher who knows his pupils. All the narratives will attempt to make the data of history "meaningful" to their audience. This frame of reference and thus this "meaningfulness" is, however, a subjective one, varying according to groups and even according to individuals. It does not have the character of "principles," and is penetrated by affects, emotions, attitudes, interests, and so on. The aim of this argument is not to contradict Katona's results but to call attention to the fact that they are very specified results which need extension in the terms indicated above.

The second problem appears to be rooted in the general tendency of gestalt psychology to consider the human being to be a rational, intellectual being. No wonder that the examples in Katona's book are arithmetical and that even when he discusses attitudes (and this point will be taken up later in these pages) they turn out to be intellectual tendencies and the tentative hypothesis is made that they are the result of the process of organization rather than the determiners of this process. The impressive honesty and the regard for the human being expressed in this psychology compels the understanding psychologist to respectful admiration. It does not compel him, however, to forget that such a view of the human being and of his psychology is one-sided. The discovery and exploration of the rational, meaningful, and lawful in psychic happening in a period penetrated by the blind passivity of statistical probability and of arbitrary bonds cannot be overestimated. Neither can be underestimated the danger of the intellectual one-sidedness issuing in the dissipation of the genuinely *psychological* in favor of the *logical*. What is the relation of logic and of arithmetic to psychology? The human being of the Western civilization developed a type of logic different from that of primitives (see Heinz Werner), different from that of mystics (see Cassirer), different from that prevailing in dreams (see Freud), or in the thinking of mentally disordered human beings (see Bleuler, Freud, Jung). It is only in this logic that the axioms of identity, of contradiction, and of the excluded third [2] are valid, while in the other types of logic they do not have either validity or meaning. This logic developed by the Western civilization is a psychologically intriguing problem in itself; its "internal necessity" forced Leibnitz to assume two unconnected fields of truth, that of "vérité du fait" and that of "vérité de la raison." However, Hume denied the existence of a realm corresponding to "vérité de la raison" and maintained that the knowledge of facts and relations is derived from experience by virtue of the frequency of the occurrence of events. Kant, in what he called a "Copernican turn," reversed Hume's assertions and attributed our knowledge of relations and rules to the nature of the "pure reason." It is probable that gestalt psychology and modern nonmechanistic psychology find themselves nearer the Kantian way of thinking than to the vitalistlike philosophy of Leibnitz or the purely mechanistic philosophy of Hume. This way of thinking maintains that the human mind performs an autonomous activity, not a mechanical one as maintained by mechanists. I do think, however, that we have to ask whether this autonomous activity of the mind is solely expressed in its logical ordering of the material of experience. The logical ordering of the material of experience according to the concepts of space, time, causality, etc., belongs to what the psychoanalyst would call functions of reality testing. Mathematical-arithmetical relations are but part of the highly developed superstructure of such reality testing. The action and reaction of the human being of our civilization are, however, not ruled solely by this reality testing. Meaningfulness, relevance, and relations in our world of experiences are not merely logical.

At this point the third problem raised above becomes pertinent. Instinctive, affective, interest-motivated actions and reactions are based on meaningfulness, relevance, and relations other than logical. Accordingly, perception, retention, and recall of material and its organization in either of these

[2] [See Chapter 8, n. 2—Ed.]

three phases are not ruled solely by logical principles but by "psycho-logical" ones as well. It is true that to learn material that yields to logical principles is more efficient by principles than by massed rote learning; however, in most cases the material of learning yields to entirely different types of meaningfulness and relevance. What Katona proved for logical principles appears to hold also for these other types of meanings, relations, relevances; they also appear to create structural traces. A historical figure presented by a teacher to adolescents as a hero, a fighter for ideas relevant to these adolescents and connected with historical facts expressing what the hero stands and fights for, is an example of a type of teaching tending to create a structural trace of a historical pattern. The teacher necessarily will have to take care of making one historical pattern sharply distinct from the other, because isolation is as important a principle of the retention and recall of this type of material as it was in Katona's experiments.

The reaction of animals is acknowledgedly also meaningful and not the result of a reflex automatism. But what is the meaning of "meaningfulness" in animals? Lorenz describes that the stork will feed its young only in response to their alternately opening and closing their mouths. This is apparently the sign which elicits the feeding activity of the mother stork. This sign is meaningful for her while the mere presence of her young is not, or at least not as a stimulus for feeding activity. What is the nature of this meaningfulness? As far as we know it is inborn, inherited, instinctive in its character. What is the nature of the meaningfulness of facial expression of emotions? Is there any meaningfulness of the intellectual logical type inherent to them? As far as one can see at present the names emotion and affect denote just the fact that their meaningfulness is not of the intellectual kind.

It is perhaps superfluous to mass further examples. It appears that meaningfulness, relevance, etc., are not one homogeneous concept of intellectual character but exist on every level of the hierarchy of psychic existence from the automatonlike instinctive to the intellectual logical levels. How it should be defined in view of its enormous complexity is a difficult problem. It may be suggested that meaningfulness or principle be defined in the manner in which the "distinguished path" is defined in the systems of geometry.

IV

For the theoretical psychologist, for the investigator of memory and learning, as well as for the educator and educational psychologist, this book has much material and many thought-provoking implications. One need not agree 100 per cent with gestalt psychology in order to find this book useful; one need not ask whether its statistics are sufficiently sophisticated in order to grasp the implications of the experimental work which attacks central problems of present-day theoretical and educational psychology.

12

THE PSYCHOANALYTIC CONCEPT
OF MEMORY AND ITS
RELATION TO RECENT
MEMORY THEORIES

WITH ERNST LEWY

This relatively early paper is derived from Rapaport's studies in *Emotions and Memory* (1942) and adumbrates the experimental studies of attention cathexis and structure formation on which he was engaged when he died. In addition to summarizing Freud's views on memory functioning, it attempts to bring together academic psychological and psychoanalytic views of memory, to make suggestions for experimental work, and to distinguish memory distortions and "normal" memory functioning. But a comparison of this paper with later ones shows how much more sophisticated and precise Rapaport's theoretical studies grew.

Read before the Topeka Psychoanalytic Society on February 28, 1942. First published in The Psychoanalytic Quarterly, *13:16–42, 1944.*

In this paper he does not make a careful distinction between Freud's views as they developed and changed chronologically, as shown for example in his juxtaposing Freud's views from the time of the topographic theory (in the sense of defining the psychic systems in terms of their relation to consciousness) and the later structural theory (p. 144), though he actually uses the term "topographic" as equivalent to structural (pp. 140, 143, 144). He uses the concept *Pcpt.-Cs.* in the context of *The Interpretation of Dreams* of 1900 (p. 147), though in that work Freud clearly distinguished *Pcpt.* and *Cs.*, saying that the two sense organs were similar in "being susceptible to excitation by qualities, but incapable of retaining traces of alterations—that is to say, as having no memory" (*Standard Ed.,* Vol. 5, p. 615) and that excitations flowed into the *Cs.* both from the systems *Pcpt.* directed to the external world and from the interior of the psychic apparatus itself (p. 616). Not until later did Freud unfortunately obliterate the distinction between these ego apparatuses by lumping them together as *Pcpt.-Cs.,* as in "A Metapsychological Supplement to the Theory of Dreams" (*Standard Ed.,* Vol. 14, p. 232) and *Beyond the Pleasure Principle* (*Standard Ed.,* Vol. 18, p. 24, where Strachey comments on the change in an editorial note). Furthermore, Rapaport three times mistranslates *Bw.* as *Pcpt.-Cs.* (pp. 149–150), though this does not really affect his argument. There remains at this point the unresolved problem of the distinction between the displaceable energy of the drives and the displaceable energy at the disposal of *Cs.* (or *Pcpt.-Cs.* as Rapaport mistranslated) which Rapaport already here proposed to resolve with the Freudian concept of "hypercathexis" (p. 150). (See the discussion of the distinction between the German *"frei"* and *"mobil"* for the two kinds of displaceable energy in Gill [1963, p. 14].) Rapaport already here referred almost explicitly to *Cs.* as an apparatus of the ego (p. 150) and later spelled out clearly the development of the concept *Cs.* in Freud's writings.

Rapaport in this paper also failed to distinguish sharply enough between *Ucs.* and *Pcs.,* writing, for example (p. 140), that "the memory systems belong to the system called Unconscious," though Freud clearly stated in *The Interpretation of Dreams,* to which Rapaport is referring, that memories were both *Ucs.* and *Pcs.,* though only from the *Pcs.* were they accessible to consciousness (*Standard Ed.,* Vol. 5, p. 541). Rapaport should have said only that "our memories . . . are in themselves unconscious" (p. 539) rather than writing of the "system called Unconscious."

Despite Rapaport's de-emphasis of the *Pcs.,* he saw the importance of distinguishing between instinctual strivings and their derivatives (p. 148) and calls the "relationships of these derivatives to the original drives . . . one of the least understood chapters of metapsychology" (p. 148). Hence he somewhat ambiguously formulated that "not only the primary but also the secondary process is instigated and dominated by derivatives of instinctual forces" (p. 148). Despite the accumulation of clinical knowledge, one wonders how much the concepts of neutralization and sublimation have really elucidated this "chapter of metapsychology." It is true that Rapaport apparently did not yet know Hartmann's concept of secondary autonomy, which enables one to conceive of impulses arising in the ego as well as in the id, though it had already appeared in German in his *Ego Psychology and the Problem of Adaptation,* which Rapaport later translated (Hartmann, 1939).

Furthermore, in this paper Rapaport speaks of the primary and secondary processes in a one-to-one relationship to unconsciousness and consciousness respectively (p. 147), though in his later monograph, *The Structure of Psychoanalytic Theory,* he was to write: "The relationship of Conscious vs. Unconscious to primary vs. secondary processes is not, however, a one-to-one coordination" (1959, p. 46, n. 7) and "All behaviors have both primary-process and secondary-process aspects, though one or the other may predominate" (p. 50). Even in this paper, however, in his reference to dreams and hallucinations (p. 146) there is a hint of the exceptions to the ordinarily unconscious character of primary-process organized material and the ordinarily potentially conscious character of secondary-process organized material. Primary-process organized material may be conscious, as in hallucinations, and apparently secondary-process organized material may remain inaccessible to consciousness, as in certain repressed fantasies, though it is true that the secondary-process character of the latter is a façade, like the secondary revision of dreams. It was these discrepancies which played an important rôle in leading Freud to give up the relationship to consciousness as a criterion of systems and to his proposing the structural systems, id, ego, and superego, instead. I have discussed these latter issues in *Topography and Systems in Psychoanalytic Theory* (1963), the major portion of which was written in the course of continuing correspondence and discussions with Rapaport.

I have taken the liberty of using abbreviations for systems as Freud ordinarily did instead of spelling them out as the originally published version of this paper did, and I have changed several references and translations which were in error and which I feared might mislead the reader, but which would be too cumbersome and not important enough to detail— M.M.G.

In recent years both psychoanalysts and academic psychologists have felt that a closer collaboration is necessary and possible. Some psychologists (Lewin, 1937) have come to a fuller appreciation of the achievements of psychoanalysis in certain fields which were neglected by academic psychology. On the other hand, many psychoanalysts have seen that, although the facts on which psychoanalytic theory is built are well substantiated, certain concepts in the theory itself need clarification and that in this task collaboration with general psychologists, who are interested in more precise definitions of concepts, would be of benefit. This paper is an attempt at such a collaboration.

No concept appears more important or suitable as the subject of a joint investigation by psychoanalysis and psychology than that of memory. Aside from the general importance of the function of memory for psychic life, it assumes a central position in psychoanalytic theory and practice. In the earlier publications of Freud, the *Studies in Hysteria* and the "Five Lectures," we encounter the view that "the hysteric suffers from reminiscences." The daily work of the analyst is constantly directed toward obtaining the memories of his patients. Our theoretical understanding of the psychic processes is to a great extent based on an understanding of the forces and processes bringing about the emergence or the repression of reminiscences.

The ever-present use of the concept of memory in psychoanalytic theory implies a specific theory of the memory function, but such a theory has never been presented in a systematic way. Neither in Freud's writings nor in any other psychoanalytic publication do we find a coherent presentation of the facts and hypotheses which psychoanalysis has to offer about memory. The ideas pertaining to this specific sector of psychoanalytic theory are scattered over nearly all the works of Freud, appearing as by-products of the investigation of various phenomena, and need to be gathered and pieced together. However, before doing this, we must attempt to describe the psychoanalytic conceptions of that part of the mental apparatus the activity of which is called the memory function.

First we must gain an idea of the memory apparatus in a topographical sense. We shall see later that, in order to do justice to the dynamic nature of memory function, it will be necessary to rearrange the view we have obtained although the very nature of our attempt will make it impossible to keep the two approaches entirely apart.

In "A Note upon the 'Mystic Writing Pad,'" Freud stated that our mental apparatus "has an unlimited receptive capacity for new perceptions and nevertheless lays down permanent—even though not unalterable—memory traces of them," and that this unusual capacity has "to be divided between two different systems (or organs of the mental apparatus)" (1925, p. 470). According to this view, we possess one system, *Pcpt.-Cs.*, which receives perceptions from the outside, but retains no permanent trace of them, so that it can react like a clean sheet to every new perception; and another, the "mnemonic system," that preserves permanent traces of the excitations which have been received. Freud expressed the difference between these two systems in *Beyond the Pleasure Principle* by saying that consciousness arises in the perceptual system instead of the memory traces (1920, p. 28). The implication appears to be that the phenomenon of consciousness, instead of the formation of permanent memory traces, occurs in the perceptual system; whereas in the mnemonic systems, in which permanent traces come about, the phenomenon of consciousness does not occur. Earlier, in *The Interpretation of Dreams* (1900), Freud maintained that the memory systems belong to the system called Unconscious, which implies that the memory systems lack the quality of consciousness. Furthermore he stated that

. . . we conceive of the psychic apparatus as a compound instrument, the component parts of which we shall call *instances,* or, for the sake of clearness, *systems.* We shall then anticipate that these systems may perhaps maintain a constant spatial orientation to one another, very much as do the different and successive systems of lenses of a telescope. Strictly speaking, there is no need to assume an actual spatial arrangement of the psychic system. It will be enough for our purposes

if a definite sequence is established, so that in certain psychic events
the system will be traversed by the excitation in a definite temporal
order [1900, p. 488].

The afore-mentioned "mystic writing pad" is another simile by which Freud
pictured memory. He compared the deeper located wax slab of this mystic
writing pad to the memory systems and the thin sheet of wax paper, which
is brought in contact with the wax slab in the act of writing, to the perception system. The thin sheet does not retain any trace of the impressions
made upon it, whereas the wax slab shows the permanent traces left in it by
the impression. The impressions act through the medium of the thin wax
paper without leaving any imprint on it, just as perceptions pass through the
perception system without leaving any trace. It receives stimuli from outside itself, which means not only from the outside world but also from
within. These stimuli may or may not become conscious even though the
excitation leaves permanent traces in the memory systems. Thus the quality
of consciousness is not one of the characteristics of these memory systems.
On the contrary, memories which are altogether prevented from becoming
conscious are proven to be the most tenaciously retained and the least
changeable.

Freud wrote:

> The first thing that strikes us is the fact that the apparatus com-
> posed of ψ-systems has a direction. All our psychic activities proceed
> from (inner or outer) stimuli and terminate in innervations. We thus
> ascribe to the apparatus a sensory and a motor end; at the sensory end
> we find a system which receives the perceptions, and at the motor end
> another which opens the sluices of motility. The psychic process gen-
> erally runs from the perceptive end to the motor end [1900, p. 488].

He then elaborated on the place of memory function in this arrangement:

> The percepts that come to us leave in our psychic apparatus a trace,
> which we may call a *memory-trace*. The function related to this
> memory-trace we call "the memory." . . . We assume that an initial
> system of this [psychic] apparatus receives the stimuli of perception
> but retains nothing of them—that is, it has no memory; and that be-
> hind this there lies a second system, which transforms the momentary
> excitation of the first into lasting traces [1900, p. 489].

According to Freud, it is impossible to state with certainty the nature of the
permanent modification of perceptive stimuli into what we call memory
trace. In keeping with the scientific state of affairs at the time when he wrote
Beyond the Pleasure Principle, which was published in 1920, he surmised
that the diminution of the resistance, which supposedly has to be overcome
by the excitation when it passes from one element to the other, produces

permanent traces in the sense of creating a path (*Bahnung*) between the two elements (1920, pp. 29–30).

On further investigation it becomes clear that our percepts are connected with one another in our memory. According to Freud this makes it necessary to assume the existence of a plurality of memory systems. Memory traces in the memory systems are associated and linked with each other according to certain factors such as the simultaneity of their occurrence, their similarity, etc. Even in his early work Freud was greatly impressed by the orderly fashion in which the memory material presented itself to his investigation.[1] He discussed his early experiences with regard to the organization of the memory material in "The Psychotherapy of Hysteria" (Breuer and Freud, 1893–95, Chapter 4) in which he described a triple stratification of the memory material, namely, that of a temporal sequence, that of a concentric organization around the traumatic event, and that following the thought content.[2]

---

[1] It was perhaps his early technique which was especially apt to produce this effect. By using the modern psychoanalytic technique one can hardly expect the material to emerge in a well-organized form, although undoubtedly, by piecing it together, one finally obtains a complete view of its organization.

[2] "The first and strongest impression which one gains from such an analysis is surely the fact that the pathogenic psychic material . . . still lies ready in some manner and, what is more, in proper and good order" (pp. 216–217).

"The psychic material of such hysteria presents itself as a multidimensional formation of at least *triple stratification*. . . . First of all there is a nucleus of such reminiscences (either experiences or mental streams) in which the traumatic moment culminated, or in which the pathogenic idea has found its purest formation. Around this *nucleus* we often find an incredibly rich mass of other memory material which we have to elaborate in the analysis in the triple arrangement mentioned before. In the first place, there is an unmistakable *linear chronological* arrangement, which takes place within every individual theme. As an example of this, I can only cite the arrangement in Breuer's analysis of Anna O. The theme is that of becoming deaf, of not hearing, which then becomes differentiated according to seven determinants, and under each heading there were from ten to one hundred single reminiscences in chronological order. It reads like an abstract from an orderly kept archive" (pp. 217–218).

"The grouping of similar reminiscences in a multiplicity of linear stratifications, as represented in a bundle of documents, in a package, etc., I have designated as the formation of a *theme*. These themes now show a second form of arrangement. I cannot express it differently than by saying that they are *concentrically stratified around the pathogenic nucleus*. It is not difficult to say what determines these strata, and according to what decreasing or increasing magnitude this arrangement follows. They are *layers of equal resistance* tending towards the nucleus, *accompanied by zones of similar alteration of consciousness* into which the individual themes extend. The most peripheral layers contain those reminiscences (or fascicles) of the different themes, which can readily be recalled and which were always perfectly conscious. The deeper one penetrates the more difficult it becomes to recognize the emerging reminiscences, until one strikes those near the nucleus which the patient disavows, even at the reproduction" (p. 218).

"We must now mention the third and most essential arrangement concerning which a general statement can hardly be made. It is the arrangement according to the con-

Now let us turn our attention from the topographical to the dynamic presentation of the memory processes. With the division of the mental apparatus into the systems *Pcpt.-Cs.* and *Ucs.,* Freud first attempted to do justice to the phenomenon of consciousness in a static rather than in a dynamic fashion by assuming that consciousness is a characteristic of certain parts of the mental apparatus. The one quasi locality in the mind, the system *Pcpt.-Cs.,* is characterized by its quality or at least potential quality of consciousness; the other quasi locality, the system *Ucs.,* is characterized by its absolute lack of consciousness. As pointed out by Freud in his paper, "The Unconscious" (1915b, pp. 108–109), this presentation of the problem necessitated the assumption that certain psychic entities are recorded twice somewhere within the mind. We may, for instance, talk of a memory and suppose that this memory at a certain time is unconscious. It would then be located in the system *Ucs.* When this memory becomes conscious, it would mean that it would also have to be present in the system *Pcpt.-Cs.* This notion was given up by Freud because of its incompatibility with a dynamic view of the functioning of the mental apparatus. Thus he wrote:

> [We must assume] *two kinds of processes or courses taken by excitation.*[3] . . . Let us now try to correct certain views which may have taken a misconceived form as long as we regarded the two systems, in the crudest and most obvious sense, as two localities within the psychic apparatus—views which have left a precipitate in the terms "repression" and "penetration." Thus, when we say that an unconscious thought strives for translation into the preconscious in order subsequently to penetrate through to consciousness, we do not mean that a second idea has to be formed, in a new locality, like a paraphrase, as it were, whilst the original persists by its side; and similarly, when we speak of penetration into consciousness, we wish carefully to detach from this notion any idea of a change of locality. When we say that a preconscious idea is repressed and subsequently absorbed by the unconscious, we might be tempted by these images, borrowed from the idea of a struggle for a particular territory, to assume that an arrangement is really broken up in the one psychic locality and replaced by a new one in the other locality. For these comparisons we will substitute a description which would seem to correspond more closely to the real estate of affairs; we will say that an energic cathexis is shifted to or withdrawn from a certain arrangement . . . Here again we replace a

---

tent of thought, the connection which reaches the nucleus through the logical threads, which might in each case correspond to a special, irregular, and manifoldly devious road. This arrangement has a dynamic character in contradistinction to both morphological stratifications mentioned before" (pp. 218–219).

[3] The "two kinds of processes" refers to the "primary" and "secondary" processes, the former referring to the unconscious, the latter to the conscious thought processes. See below, p. 147.

topographical mode of representation by a dynamic one; it is not the psychic formation that appears to us as the mobile element, but its innervation [1900, pp. 540–541].

In the exposition of this dynamic point of view Freud designed the theoretical tripartition of the psychic apparatus into the id, the ego, and the superego. In *The Ego and the Id* (1923), Freud reviewed the meaning of the terms "conscious," "preconscious," and "unconscious," and then stated that it became evident that these distinctions were inadequate explanations of the observable clinical facts. The dynamic approach yielded a new structural picture of the personality and clarified the following facts: it is unsatisfactory to define a neurosis as a conflict between the conscious and the unconscious or to identify the *Ucs.* with repressed material. A part of the ego is also unconscious and a part of the *Ucs.* is not repressed material. Thus the concept of unconsciousness has to be understood as a mere quality of psychic phenomena, a quality of many meanings, to be sure, but not identical with the statically defined psychic system *Ucs.* as it was originally conceived. From that time on the structural division into the id, the ego, and the superego took the place of the division into the systems *Ucs.* and *Pcpt.-Cs.* with consciousness a potential quality within the ego.

When we attempt to express what we know about the phenomenon of consciousness in reference to memory functioning in terms of this new conception, it becomes obvious that this can only be done by using the dynamic concept of cathexis in which cathexis is the amount of psychic energy attached to psychic contents. Freud distinguished three aspects of the metapsychological analysis of psychic material, topographical, dynamic, and economic. When the rôle of cathexes in memory function is considered the economic aspect appears. The act of becoming conscious is conceived of as occurring when a surplus of cathexis (hypercathexis) becomes attached to a memory trace.

It has been mentioned before that the deposition of memory traces seems to follow certain patterns of organization which determine the revival of memories. This is reflected in Freud's assumption of the structure of the memory systems, based on the principles of similarity, simultaneity, etc. Although the purposeful revival of memories is not explained by either of these principles, they appear to operate in "normal," everyday revivals. Yet, as we know, the revival of memory traces does not occur unhampered, but is sometimes delayed, replaced by other emerging memories, or even blocked entirely. The observation of these facts and a study of the rôle memory plays in such phenomena as fantasies and dreams led to the discovery and investigation of further factors which exert their influence on memory traces.

We find a description of these factors, in other words, of some of the vicissitudes of the memory traces, in *The Psychopathology of Everyday*

Life: "The memory material succumbs in general to two influences, condensation and distortion" (1901, p. 174 n.). Freud, distinguishing between the emotional and the indifferent parts of the memory material, described the function of distortion and condensation in memory organization as follows:

> Distortion . . . directs itself above all against the affective remnants of memory traces which maintain a more resistive attitude towards condensation. The traces which have grown indifferent, merge into a process of condensation without opposition; in addition, it may be observed that tendencies of distortion also feed on the indifferent material . . . these processes of condensation and distortion continue for long periods, during which all fresh experiences act upon the transformation of the memory content . . . [1901, p. 174 n.].

Forgetting, another vicissitude of the memory traces, is discussed by Freud as follows:

> It is quite probable that in forgetting, there can really be no question of a direct function of time. From the repressed memory traces, it can be verified that they suffer no changes even in the longest periods. . . . The most important, as well as the most peculiar character of psychic fixation consists in the fact that all impressions are, on the one hand, retained in the same form as they were received, and also in the forms that they have assumed in their further development. . . . By virtue of this theory, every former state of the memory content may thus be restored, even though all original relations have long been replaced by newer ones [1901, pp. 174 n.–175 n.].

How are we to understand this state of affairs? Is it that different traces of the same memory content in its different states are preserved and can be revived? Or is it that the trace is influenced by other traces and strivings and becomes entangled with these and can again be disentangled by the procedure of free association? A definite answer to this problem can hardly be given at present. The difficulties are pointed out by Freud: "The fact is that a survival of all the early stages alongside the final form is only possible in the mind, and that it is impossible for us to represent a phenomenon of this type in visual terms" (1930, p. 20). We may attempt to come to a better understanding by applying our knowledge of dream work to this problem. Just as the latent dream thought can be inferred from the dream content, so the original memories may be recaptured from the network of the later forms in which they are embedded and by which they are influenced, without assuming the existence of several traces.[4]

[4] In *The Problem of Anxiety* (1926) Freud discussed the vicissitudes of repressed instinctual strivings. This discussion can be interpreted as supporting the above considerations and may contribute to a better understanding of the point in question, even though it does not directly pertain to the problem of memory: "The answer

The fact that memory yields to distorting and suppressive influences was the basis for the notion that memory traces usually succumb to the destructive influence of time. In *Civilization and Its Discontents* (1930), Freud stated again that psychoanalysis relinquished the idea that forgetting means destruction of the memory trace and that rather we now lean toward the opposite assumption. His formulation, which seems to be more cautious than the one we just quoted from *The Psychopathology of Everyday Life,* reads as follows: "Perhaps we ought to be content with the assertion that what is past in the mind *can* survive and need not necessarily perish" (1930, p. 20). For the purpose of a working hypothesis in investigating the dynamics of memory function it is therefore worth while to assume that nothing is lost of the memory traces, but that the familiar disturbances of memory are brought about by the interference of certain psychic forces. In other words, it can be assumed that we may gain more insight if we apply the same deliberate neglect to the effect of sheer time on memory that Freud applied to the influence of heredity in investigating the neuroses.

The nature of memory organization, of memory distortions, and of the possibility of restoring memories of original experiences may be somewhat elucidated by referring to the distinction Freud made between "memory images" and "perceptual images." The perceptual image is obviously the trace of an original and simple sensory perception, whereas the memory image is a more complex unit which probably contains all the qualities a perception acquires when it becomes embodied into the individual's psychic life—the spatial and temporal relations in which it participates, and the strivings, affects, and moods prevalent at the time it was being perceived. As a result of this process some sensory impressions remain unconscious.[5] Thus what Freud called "perceptual images" should perhaps more exactly be called "sensory images."

In normal thinking we seem to use memory images rather than perceptual images. Only in certain states, such as dreams and hallucinations, which are more or less alien to the normal waking conditions, are the perceptual images revived.

In addition to these we also find verbal images deposited in the memory

---

appears obvious and certain: The old repressed desires must still persist in the unconscious, since we find their lineal descendants, the symptoms, still active. But this answer is inadequate; it does not make it possible to distinguish between the two possibilities that, on the one hand, the old desire now operates only through its descendants, to which it has transferred all its cathectic energy, or, on the other hand, that the desire itself persists in addition. If it was its destiny to be expended in the cathexis of its descendants, there remains the third possibility that in the course of the neurosis the wish was reactivated through regression, so out of accord with the present may it be" (p. 109 n.).

[5] We know from our everyday experience (Pötzl [1917] was able to show it experimentally) that not only memory but also perception is selective.

systems.[6] Their significance in memory functioning will be discussed below.

These processes, which we have recognized as factors in memory organization, belong to the primary process, that kind of process which is characteristic of the system Unconscious, in contradistinction to the secondary process which is the kind of thinking we consciously use.

According to psychoanalytic theory, the primary process is the only one tolerated by the system *Ucs.;* that which results in the system *Pcpt.-Cs.* under inhibiting influences is the secondary process. Freud wrote:

> The primary process strives for discharge of the excitation in order to establish with the quantity of excitation thus collected an *identity of perception;* the secondary process has abandoned this intention, and has adopted instead the aim of *an identity of thought.* [In other words all] thinking is merely a detour from the memory of gratification . . . to the identical cathexis of the same memory, which is to be reached once more by the path of motor experience [1900, p. 535].

In the dreaming state (induced by the wish of the sleeper to sleep), the mental apparatus is shut off from outside stimulation and is deprived of its ability to effect changes in the outside world by means of motility. The process of excitation consequently goes in a direction different from that in normal waking activity. Instead of proceeding from the memory images toward the motility systems, the process follows a regressive path which leads toward the original perceptual or sensory images. These are cathected and function in a hallucinatory capacity. This process, which uses the mechanisms of displacement, condensation, and symbolization, is directed by wishes which we also may describe as cathexes stemming from drives.

The course followed by what we call "normal logical thinking" in the waking state is different in that it goes on within the system *Pcpt.-Cs.* and is not subject to the mechanisms of the primary process. The system *Pcpt.-Cs.* prevents the result for which the primary process strives, namely the free discharge of instinctual tension. Instead, it operates with small quantities of mental energy, thereby using a vast treasure of stored-up memories in the service of the purposive idea whose aim is to achieve gratification by changing and dominating the outside world through planned action.

The primary process uses the available memory images only in part or only in their original form as perception (sensory) images.

Thus we see that the actual driving forces that motivate and shape the vicissitudes of the memory traces are instinctual strivings, wishes, and at-

[6] With regard to their nature, Freud said: "Verbal residues are derived primarily from auditory perceptions . . . The visual components of verbal images are secondary, acquired through reading, and may to begin with be left on one side; so may the sensori-motor images of words . . . The essence of a word is after all the memory-trace . . . that has been heard" (1923, p. 22).

titudes. These forces operate on the pain-pleasure principle. It is of course to be remembered that not only the primary but also the secondary process is instigated and dominated by derivatives of instinctual forces. The relationship of these derivatives to the original drives is one of the least understood chapters of metapsychology.

This theory of the vicissitudes of memory traces is also applicable to the phenomena of everyday psychopathology. In *The Psychopathology of Everyday Life* (1901, p. 174 n.) Freud showed that the condensation, distortion, and repression of recent memories are also ruled by the pain-pleasure principle. He wrote, *"The forgetting in all cases is proved to be founded on a motive of displeasure"* (p. 96), and "the motive of forgetting is always an unwillingness to recall something which may evoke painful feelings" (p. 175). In the second quotation the basic idea is expressed in such a way as to suggest that disturbances like forgetting are not due simply to the tendency to forget unpleasant memories, as is often erroneously assumed, but to the wish to avoid the recollection of anything which may in some way give rise to conflict.

We know that those memories which are likely to evoke painful feelings are repressed by the psychic censorship which is seen at work in what has been termed resistance and defense. The ideas which are connected associatively with these repressed memories are either forgotten, or if the attempt to forget them is unsuccessful, distorted. Here, as in dreams, the memory material is changed and rearranged by the primary process in accordance with the drives ruling it. The rôle of these drives, or strivings, is as important in dreaming as in waking thinking.

We know that no new thoughts are formed in dreams, that all the dream can do is to utilize given memory material. In the dream the mind "does not think, calculate, or judge at all, but limits itself to the work of transformation" and "thoughts must be exclusively or predominantly reproduced in the material of visual and acoustic memory-traces . . ." (1900, p. 467).

Let us now turn to the concept of repression. When Freud wrote *The Interpretation of Dreams* he believed that repressed memory traces are characterized by the withdrawal of cathexis from them. This explanation proved unsatisfactory and it was necessary to assume that a countercathexis is essential in keeping repressed ideas unconscious.

In his paper, "Repression" (1915a), Freud wrote that a common characteristic of the mechanisms of repression is the withdrawal of the energy cathexis. However, in the same paper we encounter an amplification and, in a way, a modification of this theory. He pointed out that, at least in compulsion neuroses, the withdrawal of the energy cathexis is effected by a reaction formation which involves "intensifying an antithesis" (p. 96). This is the germ of the concept of countercathexis.

This idea is developed in "The Unconscious" (1915b) in the following passages:

But this process of withdrawal of libido does not suffice to make comprehensible to us another characteristic of repression. . . .

What we are looking for, therefore, is another process . . . and this other process we can only find in the assumption of an *anticathexis,* by means of which the system Pcs guards itself against the intrusion of the unconscious idea [pp. 113–114].

Further elaboration of this theory is found in *The Problem of Anxiety:*

. . . from the uninterrupted character of the instinctual impulse there arises the demand on the ego to insure its defense by an unremitting expenditure of effort. This action for the protection of the repression is what we experience, in the course of our therapeutic efforts, as *resistance.* Resistance presupposes what I have termed *anticathexis* [1926, p. 1934].

In "The Unconscious," repeating ideas previously expressed in *The Interpretation of Dreams,* Freud maintained that the conscious idea comprises both "the concrete idea plus the verbal idea corresponding to it, whilst the unconscious idea is that of the thing alone" (1915b, p. 134). The system *Ucs.* contains object cathexes, while the system *Pcs.* contains verbal traces. It requires a hypercathexis to link the object image with a verbal trace and to make its emergence into consciousness possible.

The relationship of hypercathexis to verbal images and to the theory of free and bound cathexes is of paramount importance in the transition from the primary to the secondary process. In *Beyond the Pleasure Principle* we read:

It may be assumed that the excitation has, in its transmission from one element to another, to overcome a resistance, and that this diminution of the resistance itself lays down the permanent trace of the excitation (a path): in system Bw. there would no longer exist any such resistance to transmission from one element to another. We may associate with this conception Breuer's distinction between quiescent (bound) and free-moving "investment-energy" in the elements of the psychic systems; the elements of the system *Pcpt.-Cs.* would then convey no 'bound' energy, only free energy capable of discharge. In my opinion, however, it is better for the present to express oneself as to these conditions in the least committal way. At any rate by these speculations we should have brought the origin of consciousness into a certain connection with the position of the system *Pcpt.-Cs.* and with the peculiarities of the excitation process to be ascribed to this [1920, pp. 29–30].

. . . we have to do with two ways in which a system may be filled with energy, so that a distinction has to be made between a "charging" of the psychic systems (or its elements) that is free-flowing and striv-

ing to be discharged and one that is quiescent. Perhaps we may admit
the conjecture that the binding of the energy streaming into the
psychic apparatus consists in a translating of it from the free-flowing
to the quiescent state [p. 36].

Since the excitations of instincts all affect the unconscious systems,
it is scarcely an innovation to say that they follow the lines of the
primary process, and little more so to identify the psychic primary
process with the freely mobile charge, the secondary process with
changes in Breuer's bound or tonic charge [p. 42].

The issue of free and bound cathexes is one of the least clear points of
metapsychology. In the first passage just quoted it is maintained that the
system *Pcpt.-Cs.* conveys no "bound" cathexis but only "free energy capable of discharge," while the second and third passages maintain that energy
may be either free flowing and striving to be discharged (a condition apparently fulfilled in the unconscious, in other words, in the primary process),
or quiescent. Thus, according to one, cathexes are unbound in the secondary; according to the other, they are unbound in the primary process. This
contradiction could be resolved as follows: in the unconscious the energies
of instinctual strivings are free cathexes which may shift freely from one
instinct representation (idea) to another. The freedom of cathexes in the
secondary process, however, appears to refer to the fact that there appear to
be psychic energies at the disposal of the ego which do not carry the characteristics of the instinctual source from which they were derived. Thus, they
appear to be free moving. The relation of these latter energies to the hypercathexis necessary in linking an idea with a verbal trace so that it can enter
consciousness is probably a direct one, but one nowhere discussed in psychoanalytic literature.

Here it is necessary to consider the important fact that memories have
two aspects, ideational and emotional. Freud dealt explicitly with the problem of the difference between the vicissitudes of these two components,
especially in reference to the phenomena of isolation and *la belle indiffér-
ence*. In *The Ego and the Id* we read:

> We then come to speak, in a condensed and not entirely correct man-
> ner, of "unconscious feeling," keeping up an analogy with unconscious
> ideas which is not altogether justifiable. Actually the difference is that,
> whereas with Ucs *ideas* connecting-links must be forged before they
> can be brought into the Cs, with *feelings,* which are themselves trans-
> mitted directly, there is no necessity for this. In other words: the dis-
> tinction between Cs and Pcs has no meaning where feelings are con-
> cerned; the Pcs here falls out of account, and feelings are either
> conscious or unconscious. Even when they are connected with verbal
> images, their becoming conscious is not due to that circumstance, but
> they become so directly [1923, p. 26].

Although this passage was published in 1923, it appears to be less satisfactory from a dynamic point of view than one in "The Unconscious," published in 1915, in which Freud said: "The whole difference arises from the fact that ideas are cathexes—ultimately of memory-traces—whilst affects and emotions correspond with processes of discharge, the final expression of which is perceived as feeling" (1915b, p. 111). He answered the question of the fate of affect-laden ideas which become unconscious by saying, "there are no unconscious affects in the sense in which there are unconscious ideas," and, more clearly, "the unconscious idea continues, after repression, . . . in the system Ucs, whilst to the unconscious affect there corresponds in the same system only a potential disposition which is prevented from developing further" (1915b, p. 111).

Let us again summarize the theory of how memories become conscious in terms of cathexes. Memory traces are unconscious in themselves but they can be made conscious by a certain amount of psychic cathexis. "The act of becoming conscious depends upon a definite psychic function—attention—being brought to bear" (1900, p. 529). We have to assume that in the process of becoming conscious an additional amount of cathexis has been given the memory traces which

> . . . seems to be available only in a determinate quantity . . . [This] certain quantity of excitation, which we call "cathectic energy," is displaced from a purposive idea along the association paths selected by this directing idea. . . . The train of thought cathected by some aim becomes able under certain conditions to attract the attention of consciousness, and by the mediation of consciousness it then receives *"hyper-cathexis"* [1900, p. 529].

No such additional cathexis is put on a train of thought which is without interest at the time.

This process seems to point to a necessary participation of the ego because the "certain quantity of excitation," called attention, which is put by a purposive idea onto a memory trace, or a conglomerate of memory traces, belongs to the ego. In *The Problem of Anxiety* Freud explicitly stated that "The ego controls the entrance into consciousness . . ." (1926, p. 26).

"It is such hypercathexes, we may suppose, that bring about higher organization in the mind and make it possible for the primary process to be succeeded by the secondary process which dominates Pcs" (1915b, p. 134).

In summary we can now state that the memory apparatus operates as follows: the driving force which puts the apparatus in motion is always an instinctual striving, a wish. This wish strives for free discharge as long as it is unconscious and operates in the mode of the primary process. In this state the cathexis, stemming from the wish, attaches itself to various available memory traces suitable to the expression of this wish. These cathected memory traces become organized according to the mechanisms of the primary process because the pathways leading through secondary elaboration to motility are barred in the dream state and in conditions characterized by repression. In this way the underlying striving discharges its cathexis freely, either in the form of a dream or of a neurotic symptom. If, however, the wish is in harmony with the set of strivings and attitudes which we designate as the ego and superego and if it succeeds in attracting attention and the energy of hypercathexis, then it is admitted to the elaboration by the secondary process which operates under the guidance of directing purposive ideas. The cathexis of the striving is then transferred to purposefully selected memory traces and the result of this selection finally appears in the form called logical, realistic thinking.

In the light of our present-day knowledge we look upon this functioning of the secondary process as belonging to what we call ego functions. It is this part of what we regard as a product of the integrating function of the ego which becomes manifest in the action of the secondary process. It inhibits the free discharge of instinctual tension and suspends it until the testing and planning processes are finished. It transforms the short-term affect tension which strives for quick, but, as far as reality is concerned, ineffectual relief, into a long-term tension capable of sustaining a realistically effective and useful effort. The mechanisms of this function are not nearly as clear to us as are those of the primary process and are in need of further investigation.[7]

Thus far we have attempted to show that the psychoanalytic theory of memory is based on the view that memory traces are used by psychic forces which find expression through them. We have also seen that the modes in which strivings make use of memory material vary significantly among such phenomena as everyday remembering, dreams, and remembering childhood experiences.

Now we shall turn to the memory theories of academic psychology and its concepts regarding the rôle of strivings in memory organization and functioning.

The multiplicity of memory phenomena and mechanisms revealed by psychoanalysis represents a realm unknown to experimental psychology which has instead studied the quantitative relationships between learning and retention, such as the relationship of the number of repetitions in learning to the amount of material retained and the effect of the elapsed time between learning and recall on the amount of material that can be recalled. Psychoanalysis did not contribute directly to the development of the theory of memory dealing with the phenomena of learning because it was more concerned with the pathological phenomena of memory. Experimental psychology in turn has remained aloof from both the vital memory phenomena encountered in everyday life and those revealed by psychoanalysis. It has

[7] See also in this connection Freud (1920, p. 42) and Hendrick (1942, p. 55).

left unanswered the question of how things are remembered when they are needed and how they are frequently forgotten in spite of the fact that they are needed and in defiance of the laws of memory arrived at experimentally. Thus, though these laws of memory maintain that the more frequently repeated material is better retained, often an event encountered only once becomes "unforgettable," or "memorable," while familiar facts encountered perhaps a thousand times may suddenly be forgotten. Between the two extremes of experimental psychology and psychoanalysis, in other words between the memory theories of rote learning and those of motivated remembering and forgetting, everyday memory function has remained a stepchild and will come into its own only through an approximation of these extremes. Recent developments in experimental psychology, such as the "trace theory" of gestalt psychology (Koffka, 1935) and the theory of "tension systems" of Lewinian psychology (Lewin, 1935), are in the direction of such as approximation.

The trace theory hypothesizes that one may infer the characteristics of the physiological processes underlying the memory functions from an experimental investigation of the relevant psychological processes. In other words the nature of the physiological processes occurring in the brain when a memory is deposited as a trace, those occurring while a trace is retained and transformed in the course of time, and those occurring when the memory is reproduced in consciousness, can all be established by psychological experiments. It is maintained that the physiological processes corresponding to a conscious experience leave traces which have properties similar to quasi-stationary electrochemical potential changes, inasmuch as their intensity decreases in time to a certain degree, and they tend to change toward a form of "least resistance," or as the gestaltists call it, toward a "good form." The tendency of the traces to change can best be seen in the merging of "similar" traces to form an "aggregate" trace. The common features of the component traces become pronounced and the temporal, spatial, and affective characteristics giving the single trace its individuality are lost. When a stimulation or experience, and consequently the corresponding trace, is dissimilar to the rest of the traces—or in terms of the gestaltists, is "isolated"—its individual survival becomes more probable. This theory of memory, since it attempts to understand the fate of the individual memory by inquiring into its relation to other memories, explains more than does the classical theory of memory based on frequency and time decrement. It also is similar to the Freudian theory of memory which as we saw is also based on the interaction of memories, rather than on frequency and time loss. However, what is meant here by similar and dissimilar traces remains a problem. The gestaltists talk about "structural" similarity and expose themselves to severe criticism by appearing to advance a circular reasoning, explaining that similar traces form aggregates, and aggregates are trace systems formed by similar traces, i.e., good gestalt in terms of the direction in which a trace changes, and the trace changes in terms of good gestalt. We believe that the reason for the circularity is that gestalt psychologists have not investigated memory phenomena of personal importance, such as those investigated by psychoanalysis, because in them similarity may be defined without circularity, in terms of the identical drives, affects, strivings, and attitudes which a given content expresses and to the satisfaction of which it contributes.

The concept of similarity has yet another rôle in gestalt psychology. Remembering is described by gestalt psychology as follows: a process is set off by a recent stimulation and this "communicates" with the trace of an experience which is thereupon remembered. This function appears to be easily explained in ordinary recognition in which the recent process is similar to the old one with whose trace it communicates. However, if memories are revived in the course of a thought process, it is difficult to see why those particular traces which are actually revived communicate with the process. Koffka sensed this difficulty and saw that the problem of forgetting, or the "noncommunication" of traces and process, also needed specific explanation. Toward this end he employed a new concept, the "attitude" (Koffka, 1935, pp. 520 ff.). He explained that a trace must be conceived as consisting of two parts, one registering what is being experienced and the other registering the attitude of the ego toward what is experienced. This dichotomy may sound strange to the psychoanalyst and is certainly artificial, but in the field of experimental psychology it is a great step forward toward views more meaningful to the psychoanalyst. It is then conceived that the attitude is at least partly responsible for the communication between process and trace.

To make the concept of attitude more concrete, Koffka adopted the findings of Lewin and his pupils (1935, p. 14) who showed in carefully controlled experiments that if a subject abides by instructions and thus sets up an intention to do a task, upon being interrupted in carrying out that task, he will make attempts to resume it. They hypothesized that such intentions create psychic "tension systems" which strive toward discharge and prompt resumption of the interrupted tasks. The concept of psychic events in terms of a tendency to diminish or discharge tension is one which the psychoanalyst considers his own and thus Lewin's efforts may be considered as experimental explorations in a field of everyday actions along those lines which are of interest to the psychoanalyst. Similar experiments showed that memories of interrupted activities, in which tense psychic systems remain undischarged, are better retained than memories of completed activities (Zeigarnik, 1927; see also Lewin, 1935, pp. 243–247). However, in cases where the interruption of activities is attended by the experience of failure, though there appears to be no reason to assume that the corresponding tension system has been discharged, the memories of the interrupted task are less well retained than those of the uninterrupted ones. The frequently made inference that repression has been here directly demonstrated experimentally should be avoided because only statistical probability vouches for it. It can be safely pointed out, however, that we have memory theories here in which tensions striving for discharge and conditions preventing discharge are considered as underlying memory functioning. In this sense they are analogous to the psychoanalytic theory of memory even though they are established by investigating conscious levels of memory functioning alone.

Let us return to the attitudes and their rôle in the trace theory. Koffka adopted the theory that these attitudes are tensions (in the Lewinian sense) connected with the traces—particularly the ego portion of the trace which preserves the memory of the ego's attitude toward the experience. These attitudes are responsible for linking the memory traces and processes and thus also for the revival of memories. An English psychologist, Bartlett, who is close to the gestalt position, showed experimentally that the attitude or affective setting is the responsible factor in memory revival. He wrote:

> . . . the main conditions for the occurrence of images appear to be found in their affective setting. This functions as an "attitude," and the attitude is best described as an orientation of the agent towards the image. . . . If, then, as in specific recall, we are called upon to justify the image, we do so by constructing, or reconstructing, its setting. Thereupon the attitude acquires rationalisation . . . [1932, p. 303].

The detailed experimental evidence put forth by Lewin, Koffka, and Bartlett cannot be surveyed here. The important point seems to be that these memory theories, derived from experimentation, show a tendency to coincide. They agree that in becoming conscious of a memory, psychic tensions, attitudes, affective settings—in other words, directed and specific psychic forces—play a predominant rôle. It is true that Koffka was not at all sure whether this is necessarily true for all remembering. It is true that the nature of Lewin's tensions and their relation to the sources of psychic energy have never been really clarified. Finally, it is true that neither Lewin nor Bartlett coupled their theory with a trace theory of memory. Nevertheless, these three variants of experimentally derived memory theories show a striking parallel to the psychoanalytic theory of memory which is essentially a theory in which deposited traces of experiences are organized by strivings which endeavor to find their expression through them. It should not be forgotten, however, that these experiments were made with material of an intellectual nature and not with material of vital personal relevance like that dealt with by psychoanalysis. Thus while the memory theory of psychoanalysis showed us the unconscious dynamics of memory functioning, these experimentally derived theories arrived at structurally similar theories by investigating the memory function of the level of the secondary processes. This is a result which we would theoretically hardly expect, since in the secondary process, logic and purposive ideas seem to replace driving force.

Still, instincts and drives—the factors supplying the propelling power of memory material—apparently become perceptible even at the level of the normal secondary process and not only as wishes in dreams where the secondary process functions only in part.

Before these results can be fully evaluated and exploited by psychoanalytic psychology, the nature of the hypercathexes in their relation to verbal images during the process of bringing memories into consciousness, and the relation of bound to free cathexes, must be further clarified by psychoanalysis.

One more discovery of gestalt psychology, formulated by G. Katona (1940), should be discussed here. Objections were raised against the trace theory on the grounds that a story may be reproduced in words altogether different from the original. Katona showed experimentally that traces are retained, not only of the individual sensory impressions constituting an experience, but also of the structure of the *meaning* of the experience. The significance of this finding cannot be overestimated by psychoanalysts because it is an experimental simile of what we know as dream representation and symbolic representation. In symbolic representation the structure and meaning also remain constant while the form varies. Naturally, the structure of the meaning of gestalt psychology is intellectually conceived and is thus only a distant parallel to the constant content of dream and symbol.[8] Nevertheless it indicates how one may think of these processes in a more concrete form which is at the same time more amenable to experiment. Herbert Silberer's (1909) observations on hypnagogic hallucinations also belong to this realm of phenomena in that the structure of thoughts remained unchanged and was merely translated into visual hallucinatory images.

Are these experimental parallels to the psychoanalytic theory of memory

---

[8] [There seems something scrambled and forced about this simile. Katona speaks of two issues: the preservation of the individual traces and the deposition of a trace of the structure of the meaning of an experience, and implies a third, the expression of the same meaning by different contents. The contents then may vary while the meaning remains constant. The authors seem at first to relate variable content and constant meaning to symbolization. But they also seem to refer to dream representation and symbols as though they are the same. A more precise analogy would be that while manifest dream contents may vary, their latent meaning may be the same and that certain dream symbols seem to have a constant unconscious meaning (though this is not invariable since what seems a symbol may have specific meanings as revealed in the associations of the individual dreamer) and that symbols of different content may turn out to have the same unconscious meaning. Freud pointed out that symbols in dreams are often not associated to, so that their meaning has to be inferred, and that the realms for which symbols are employed are relatively few, encompassing the basic concerns of mankind such as sex, siblings, parents, birth, and death. It is possible that "symbolization" is used here by the authors more in the general sense of indirect representation than in the technical sense of dream symbols with a constant unconscious meaning—Ed.]

of any use to psychoanalysts and to psychoanalytic theory? We believe that they may be useful in several ways. What do we gain if we consider the mechanisms of the psychoanalytic theory, described in the first part of this paper, as phenomena of the organization of memory traces by strivings? First of all we carry on Freud's effort to divest these mechanisms of their abstract and, at the same time, anthropomorphic (or perhaps egomorphic[9]) character. They become processes that operate through memory traces and their study becomes the study of memory organization. It is probable, for instance, that the primary mechanisms will be recognized as different degrees of the same process. When we imagine a striving that finds a memory of an early experience in which a similar striving found gratification, it can be seen that it will use the traces of this memory to express itself. This would be, however, only the expression of a similar striving and thus to express its specificity the striving must also use other memory traces which will express this specificity. In this way the first memory trace will be combined with another or others. If a compound memory trace is used, its alterations by other traces will appear as its distortions, while if many traces contribute equally to the expression of the striving or wish, the product will appear as a composite picture—a condensation. Naturally, the same process could be described differently by considering every part of these composite formations as the contributions of various partial wishes so that the balance, the compromise, of these wishes would be the resulting composite revived memory.[10]

By considering these mechanisms as memory phenomena we also bring them into a relationship which frequently eludes us when we view them singly.

To conceive of a phenomenon as belonging to an integrated whole is also the prerequisite of experimental exploration. The disadvantages of the lack of such an integration are seen in those psychological experiments that set out to prove or to disprove the theory of repression by investigating whether the memory material of a pleasant or of an unpleasant connotation is better retained. A greater amount of recalled pleasant material was considered proof of the theory of repression and vice versa. What was often overlooked

[9] See Weiss (1935, p. 402).
[10] [The formulation that the "primary mechanisms will be recognized as different degrees of the same process" may very well be wrong in that displacement and condensation may be quite different processes, despite the fact that they both serve the economic function of discharging as great an amount of drive energy as possible (". . . the whole stress is laid on making the cathectic energy mobile and capable of discharge . . ." [The Interpretation of Dreams, *Standard Edition*, Vol. 5, p. 597]). The discussion of "distortions" (displacement) and condensations seems relatively nondynamic and fails to stress adequately the rôle of conflict (censorship). For a discussion of these issues see the forthcoming paper by the editor on the primary process to appear in a collection of essays dedicated to Rapaport and edited by Robert R. Holt as a volume in *Psychological Issues*, No. 18/19—Ed.]

was that what is consciously unpleasant is not necessarily repressed but that distortion, displacement, and condensation may occur instead. Viewing these mechanisms as forms of memory organization will prevent such errors and will make the field more amenable to experimental exploration.

REFERENCES

Bartlett, F. C. (1932). *Remembering: A Study in Experimental and Social Psychology.* Cambridge: Cambridge University Press.

Breuer, J., & Freud, S. (1893–95). *Studies in Hysteria.* New York: Nerv. Ment. Dis. Publ. Co., 1936, pp. 190–232.

Freud, S. (1900). The Interpretation of Dreams, tr. A. A. Brill. *The Basic Writings.* New York: Modern Library, 1938, pp. 179–549.

———— (1901). The Psychopathology of Everyday Life, tr. A. A. Brill. *The Basic Writings.* New York: Modern Library, 1938, pp. 33–178.

———— (1915a). Repression. *Collected Papers,* 4:84–97. New York: Basic Books, 1959.

———— (1915b). The Unconscious. *Collected Papers,* 4:98–136. New York: Basic Books, 1959.

———— (1920). *Beyond the Pleasure Principle,* tr. C. J. M. Hubback. London: International Psycho-Analytical Press, 1922.

———— (1923). *The Ego and the Id,* tr. J. Riviere. London: Hogarth Press, 1927.

———— (1925 [1924]). A Note upon the "Mystic Writing-Pad." *Int. J. Psycho-Anal.,* 21:469–474, 1940.

———— (1926 [1925]). *The Problem of Anxiety,* tr. H. A. Bunker. New York: Psychoanalytic Quarterly & Norton, 1936.

———— (1930 [1929]). *Civilization and Its Discontents,* tr. J. Riviere. New York: Jonathan Cape, 1930.

Gill, M. M. (1963). Topography and Systems in Psychoanalytic Theory. *Psychol. Issues,* No. 10.

Hartmann, H. (1939). *Ego Psychology and the Problem of Adaptation,* tr. D. Rapaport. New York: International Universities Press, 1958.

Hendrick, I. (1942). Instinct and the Ego during Infancy. *Psychoanal. Quart.,* 11:33–58.

Katona, G. (1940). *Organizing and Memorizing: Studies in the Psychology of Learning and Teaching.* New York: Columbia University Press.

Koffka, K. (1935). *Principles of Gestalt Psychology.* New York: Harcourt, Brace.

Lewin, K. (1935). *A Dynamic Theory of Personality.* New York: McGraw-Hill.

———— (1937). Psychoanalysis and Topological Psychology. *Bull. Menninger Clin.,* 1:202–212.

Ovsiankina, M. (1928). Die Wiederaufnahme unterbrochener Handlungen. *Psychol. Forsch.,* 11:302–389.

Pötzl, O. (1917). The Relationship between Experimentally Induced Dream Images and Indirect Vision. *Psychol. Issues,* 7:41–120, 1960.

Rapaport, D. (1942). *Emotions and Memory*. Baltimore: Williams & Wilkins.

——— (1959). The Structure of Psychoanalytic Theory: A Systematizing Attempt. *Psychol. Issues,* No. 6, 1960.

Silberer, H. (1909). Report on a Method of Eliciting and Observing Certain Symbolic Hallucination-Phenomena. In *Organization and Pathology of Thought,* ed. & tr. D. Rapaport. New York: Columbia University Press, 1951, pp. 195–207.

Weiss, E. (1935). Todestrieb und Masochismus. *Imago,* 21:393–411.

Zeigarnik, B. (1927). Über das Behalten von erledigten und unerledigten Handlungen. *Psychol. Forsch.,* 9:1–85.

13

THE PSYCHOLOGIST IN THE

PRIVATE MENTAL HOSPITAL

This paper will deal with (1) the present status of the clinical psychologist in the private mental hospital; (2) the training of psychologists for work in the private mental hospital. In addition, the future situation of the psychologist in the private mental hospital and the general problem of training will be touched upon.

I

In order to survey the existing situation the author sent a questionnaire to eighteen leading private institutions.[1] Eight questionnaires were returned.[2] The responses may be summed up as follows:

First published in The Journal of Consulting Psychology, *8:298–301, 1944.*

---

[1] The following questions were asked: (1) How many psychologists are employed in your institution? What are their titles and standings? (2) What is the status of the psychologist, with or without experience, upon entering the employ of your institution? What provision for advancement is there? (3) What are the duties of the psychologists in your institution? (Testing: What is the nature of the test reports? Are they used for stating an I.Q. or other numerical test results, or, are they also clinical diagnoses? What tests are used? Therapy: What type of therapy, if any, is being done by psychologists?) (4) What kind of training and educational facilities do you have for psychologists in your institution? (5) What kind of research activities do psychol-

(1) One institution employs a part-time psychologist who is also an instructor in neuropsychiatry at a university; one institution had a psychologist until a year ago, when she left for a college teaching job; two institutions have never had a psychologist, and in one of these, "the members of the staff do what psychological work they wish to do with their own patients"; four institutions occasionally use the psychologist of nearby child guidance clinics "for intelligence tests" and "occasional Rorschach studies."

(2) The attitude toward clinical psychology appears favorable in these answers. The reasons given for not employing psychologists are: "we just never got around to it, we hope the time will come"; "cannot find one"; "we get all we need from the guidance-clinic psychologist." In one institution where psychiatrists do the psychological testing the chief of staff used to be a psychologist, and the answer stresses that training is given in testing methods. Whenever mention is made of the status of the psychologist, it is stressed that he is accorded status equivalent to that of the psychiatrist.

(3) No therapeutic work (except in one case, some child-guidance counseling) is done by the psychologist, and in only one institution has there been any research carried on in clinical psychology.

It is not known whether the eight returned questionnaires constitute a representative sample or why the other institutions did not answer. The replies seem to indicate that although the attitude toward clinical psychologists is favorable, they are rarely employed; although testing is favorably looked upon, its use is limited; although the professional status of the psychologist is recognized, his work does not include therapy and research.

To analyze in detail the possible reasons for the situation so scantily represented by these returns does not appear profitable. Perhaps the author's personal experiences in seeing a department of psychology grow up in a private mental hospital may contribute to the clarification of the situation.[3]

---

ogists conduct in your institution? (6) What is the relationship of the psychologist to the psychiatric staff? Does he have a regular standing on the staff of the hospital? (7) Additional comments about the psychologist's personal feeling concerning his status, opportunities, and limitations in his work?

[2] I am grateful for their kind cooperation to the John Sealy Hospital of Galveston, Texas; the Westbrook Sanitorium of Richmond, Va.; Chestnut Lodge of Rockville, Md.; the Butler Hospital of Providence, R. I.; the Wauwatosa Sanitarium of Milwaukee, Wis.; the Bishop Clarkson Memorial Hospital of Omaha, Neb.; the McLean Hospital of Belmont, Mass.; and Tratelja Farms of Diamond Point, N. Y.

[3] The department of psychology of the institution with which the author is affiliated [The Menninger Foundation] employs at present [1944] two staff psychologists, one assistant psychologist, one research assistant, and offers, in addition, two full-year internships and one summer internship.

II

For many years this institution employed one psychologist; now part time, now full time. Originally the psychologist worked mostly at the school for problem children (Southard School) of the institution—not only giving various standard tests, but also teaching and helping out with administration and with attending to children. Later, with the advent of tests of personality (Rorschach) and experimental work in personality (Lewin), the clinic itself became interested in having patients tested and research carried on. The attitude was: "Let us see how that can help us." At first the test reports spoke a strange language, and it was more the interest in the "new," the possible promise of research results, and finally the custom over the country of having some tests done—at least for the I.Q.'s—that kept a psychologist employed in a hospital.

The first changes occurred when the psychological test reports began to speak largely in terms familiar to psychiatrists. Later the psychiatrists became familiar with some of the specific "test" terms used in the reports. Thus they had for the first time a chance to check whether the tests could indicate the same things as clinical observation; whether the tests could in some instances help them to make up their minds about a case; whether the tests could uncover some pathology missed by observation; and even whether in some instances the tests could be correct even though contradictory to their findings. When afterwards some research—partly in validation of tests, and partly in clinical problems—started, the door for new personnel and growth of the department was opened. Thus it appears that the development of the department hinged on: (a) the psychologist learning the facts, problems, theory, and terminology of the psychiatrist and developing his own knowledge of testing procedures so as to be able to have clinically useful findings and to be able to express those in a manner meaningful to the psychiatrist; (b) the attack, through research, upon problems of immediate clinical interest; (c) the educating of the psychiatrists to accept, understand, and use the data of testing, as well as the acquainting of them—in terms useful to them—with the systematic ways of looking at psychological phenomena as developed by some "schools" of psychology. To the possible implications of this development for the training of clinical psychologists we shall return later on.

III

Let us turn, however, to another facet of this development. This institution always had a great number of applications from young psychologists who wanted to "intern" at the school for problem children of the institution, to learn how to deal with such children. What these people had in the backs of their minds was mostly to learn psychotherapy. For many years they were accepted. *In principle,* there was nothing wrong with this; *in practice,* it was all wrong. In principle, here were the sick children, and opportunity was given to be with them (tutoring, playing, attending)—a golden opportunity for a theoretically well-grounded person to gather experience and to take steps toward learning how to help such children. In practice, a private mental institution is not a professional school, and even though a few courses were given, they did not provide adequate training; the young interns generally did not have the background to profit from their experience, they had to work hard, and they usually felt exploited. Therefore these internships were discontinued and a door through which some young psychologists hoped to enter the practice of psychotherapy was shut.

The problem growing out of these experiences is: how can a psychologist become a psychotherapist? Most of the people we saw trying to become psychotherapists—there were exceptions—had the urge to learn, some even had the intuitive talent it takes, but none had the background it takes, and none had clearly recognized that there is still no paved way for a psychologist to become a psychotherapist.

Many psychologists feel that psychiatrists *do not want* psychologists to practice psychotherapy; some even say, "They don't like competition." The actual situation is probably that in some cases opposition stems from ignorance and intolerance, and in others it comes from knowing only too well what the training to be a psychotherapist requires and how few of the psychologists have it.

Notwithstanding all this, two psychologists made their way in the practice of psychotherapy in our institution. To begin with, they accepted jobs other than therapy; they showed their mettle, accepted instruction, attempted to learn what the psychiatrist learns, accepted and still accept supervision of experienced psychiatrists, and thus created a place for themselves.

It is the author's opinion—though he is not a psychotherapist—that one does not become a psychotherapist merely by taking courses—and certainly not the type of courses available at present—nor by thinking that anyone with good common sense and clear reasoning can counsel "maladjusted" people, nor by disclaiming the need for psychiatric information and attempting to apply to the "treatment" of maladjusted people the principles of a school of psychology which never investigated the nature of maladjustments. That psychiatry is a discipline in change does not justify a psychologist's not studying the facts and relationships it has discovered. We are usually proud of our "scientific" training; but though it may help toward clearer thinking in the study of human maladjustment, such training is worthless in practice without clinical psychiatric experience.

IV

The future rôle of the private mental hospitals was recently analyzed by Allen Gregg with great penetration.[4] He showed that hospital care is becoming a community responsibility and only those private hospitals will survive which have research and educational programs—in both these ways *furthering progress*. For research and education the private mental hospital needs the well-trained and pioneering clinical psychologist. The place of the psychologist both in research and education can best be established if he learns the problems, needs, language, and theory of the psychiatrist, because, first, these embody the problems he is to cope with, and, second, it is the psychiatrist with whom he must collaborate in this endeavor. If the psychologist has something to offer—and the author believes that such is the case—he will have to learn how to make his contribution meaningful to the ones he offers it to.

The possible implications of the experience of the author for the training of clinical psychologists may be summed up as follows: (a) first of all, more studying, and in *all* fields and schools of psychology, because the problems in the clinical field—and even in testing alone—are so manifold that all that has been discovered by psychological research can and should be put to use in understanding and solving these problems; (b) more and varied experience with people; (c) a new attitude toward tests, aiming not at measures in "objective" (numerical) terms, but rather at obtaining qualitative as well as quantitative indications which are meaningful in terms of a theory of adjustment and maladjustment; (d) for psychotherapy aspirants special courses should be set up for the teaching of modern psychiatry.

There is great need for psychotherapists—but only for well-equipped and competent ones.

V

Finally, we may raise again the question: Why do the private mental hospitals have scarcely any psychologists?

To the author it appears that the present trend in psychiatry as a discipline-in-change is to accept clinical psychology and to pay at least lip service to such acceptance—a breach in the previous forbidding solid wall. It is merely a breach, however, and essentially the resistance is still great. This resistance is supported by the fact that neither has clinical psychology succeeded in developing an educational program for clinical psychologists worthy of respect and confidence, nor have clinical psychologists done sufficient pioneering into the field to "sell" their discipline and themselves. These are the two great tasks challenging clinical psychology today.

[4] Address to the centennial meeting of the American Psychiatric Association, Philadelphia, May 1944.

14

THE SCIENTIFIC METHODOLOGY
OF PSYCHOANALYSIS

Rapaport gave two series of lectures on the subject of methodology. The first series (1944) was left in a quite polished, if colloquial, unpublished form, while the second series (1948) existed only in the form of an unedited transcript. Although the two series covered much the same ground, some material from 1948 has been incorporated into the 1944 manuscript in the version that follows; all such additions are enclosed in brackets.

Rapaport's own view of these lectures is indicated in the following excerpt from a letter of June 3, 1949, to Gardner Murphy, to whom he had sent a copy of the 1944 series:

Though I do feel that I was trying to wrestle with some real problems in those six lectures I was amazed that you found anything to enjoy in them. . . . To publish? I feel that my thinking about this matter is, at the moment, much more in a chaos than it was at

---

Series of six lectures presented at the Menninger Foundation in 1944. Published here for the first time.

165

the time of the six [1944] lectures and the three [1948] lectures, and I don't know how many years it will have to wait until the dust will settle and I might feel reasonably honest to publish anything about it. In the meanwhile I have tried not a methodological but an epistemological attack on the problem but I'm afraid even of that I don't have a manuscript: it was mixed up with lectures on the Seventh Chapter of The Interpretation of Dreams. *The only thing I have left from it is the little paper I mentioned to you dealing with "Dynamic Psychology and Kantian Epistemology" [see Chapter 23]. Then again I made an attack on it from the point of view of conceptual models [a version of which is included in this volume as Chapter 34]. . . . Maybe the day will come when I can put together the methodological, the epistemological, and the conceptual treatment of these issues. That day, however, seems to me right now very far off. Frankly, the more I fool around with these things the more ignorant do I find myself.*

The justification for publishing this material is its unusual and stimulating approach, which leads to many interesting, even if not completely carried through, ideas. There is much that is debatable here, but I believe such debates would be worth while. I have not attempted to specify my own doubts, nor have I eliminated repetitions, because I feel that the reader would prefer to formulate his own doubts, and that the varying nuances in the repetitions may bring him to a clearer idea of just what Rapaport meant. My only changes in the text have been minor stylistic ones—M.M.G.

LECTURE NO. 1

The topic I would like to put before you has hardly ever been treated in the psychoanalytic literature. More than that, scientific method and what it is and what it is not, scientific methodology and what it is and what it is not, are not fixed issues.

[I believe that something like what we are attempting here—a methodological analysis—is indispensable. It will have to be done before we get very far into a really systematic psychoanalytic psychology. That I am quite sure of. I believe that that is true for any science and we can be quite sure that on that score we are not wasting our time. If you ask me whether I am anywhere near as sure of what I will specifically suggest concerning psychoanalysis in this regard, I would emphatically say "no."]

The discussions will inevitably have to deal with abstractions. I feel some reluctance about this because I am myself too fond of abstractions, too ready to linger among them and enjoy them for their own sake. In order to keep within one framework I will not be in a position to discuss psychoanalytic facts in any detail. I will have to take for granted an orientation concerning them.

This first part of my presentation, then, will be devoted to methodology and its relation to psychoanalysis. You will find that for a while my remarks will seem introductory and you may consider that they are unimportant and will be elaborated on later. To me these introductory remarks, though necessarily fragmentary, will treat of matters of the greatest importance; I might say, *the* important things, and maybe all the rest is not important.

The concepts of science, psychoanalysis, methodology, require explanations. I shall make a statement about each. These statements, though they cannot claim to be definitions, have importance in creating the attitude desirable for our endeavor. First, a word about science. Science is only too often looked upon as a tool of prediction. In one of his epigrams, the German poet Schiller says that "to some people science is the goddess and to others the cow that gives the milk." The cow that gives the milk! No attitude toward science can be stranger to us! We should realize that science is not just a tool to make life easier in terms of bathtubs and refrigerators, but that science is *man's key to the understanding of nature*. Not that we disparage practical values. But the place of science must be consistent with our view of art, poetry, and other activities of no material gain: it must remain the tool of our search for the original lawfulness of nature. However, if science be reduced to a set of probable propositions, that is to say, if we look down on nature as something about which we learn what is more likely to occur in it and what is less likely to occur in it, if science be reduced to the rôle of manipulating nature, then there is no need to work out a methodology of science. This issue alone could take up not five but twenty-five lectures and discussions. I would merely like to offer this initial consideration.

Now for the second concept in the title: methodology. It is the question of what kind of methods does the science of psychoanalysis use; methods not merely of prediction but of pursuing laws, unchanging laws of what we call psychic existence and which we presuppose to exist. Since this brings us to what are psychoanalysis and psychology, I shall discuss these concepts first, and methodology afterward.

There are many views concerning psychoanalysis. I shall give the Freudian view, incorporated in the Introduction to the "Five Lectures on Psychoanalysis"—Freud's lectures at Clark University—as paraphrased by Ives Hendrick:

> The term "psychoanalysis" is properly used in the following ways:
> 1. to designate *empirical observations* on those determinants of human personality and behaviour which are not disclosed by the investigation of rational thought and motivation (either by introspection or by direct study of another);
> 2. to describe the special *technique* of Freud for the demonstration and study of these unconscious mental events and for the treatment of personality problems and neurotic symptoms; and
> 3. to signify that theoretical system of psychology which consists in the abstraction of these observations and the inductive inferences made from them [1939, p. 3].

First, psychoanalysis is a method of investigation of psychic life, a method of observation. Second, psychoanalysis is a treatment technique. Third, the term psychoanalysis pertains to a theory. It is very difficult to treat the methodology of something which is three things. I cannot forego reflecting upon just what claims are made by psychiatrists concerning these three things. Freud strove to build up something called a psychoanalytic psychology (metapsychology); he strove, with the psychoanalytic technique of observation and therapy, to build up a system of theoretical tenets of psychology. A look at Hartmann's *Ego Psychology and the Problem of Adaptation* (1939) will show that Hartmann, and before him Schilder, thought it possible to build a system of psychology entirely on psychoanalytic principles.

There is a claim that psychoanalysis is to explain psychic life or that it should be built so as to yield a theory explaining psychic functioning in general, not just psychological phenomena encountered in the therapeutic setting. To make this somewhat more plausible, I shall enumerate some of the things psychoanalysis has been called upon to explain. A human being sleeps, wakes, eats, copulates, excretes, moves, grows, rests, breathes, dies. He also dreams, daydreams, fantasies, thinks, learns, remembers, reasons. And another list—he washes, dresses, puts on make-up, amuses himself in the most varied ways imaginable, uses gadgets. He has feelings, ambitions, attitudes, expressive movements, moods, perceptions, sensations. He does a multitude of things through the sensory organs. Now, this is a rough and sketchy grouping of human functions. This list is incomplete. It would take weeks or months to complete and so group these things that no contradictions or omissions could be found. It is the interrelationships of these that psychology is to explain. Now, what you see on the blackboard represents the theoretical constructs of psychoanalysis which have to explain all these things:

Instincts	*Quality*	*Points of View*	*Genetic View*
(libido)	Conscious	Economic ————	Oral I ⎞ Phases of
Origin	Preconscious	Pleasure-pain principle——	➤Oral II ⎟
Object	Unconscious	Nirvana principle	➤Anal I ⎬ libido
Aim		Reality principle	Anal II ⎟
(strength)		Dynamic	Genital ⎠ development
Oedipus complex		Erotic instincts	
		Destructive instincts	
		Topographic	
		Id	
		Ego	
		Superego	

Meaning			
Interpretation			
(*Frame of reference*)		*Basic Phenomena*	*Methods*
Childhood		Transference	Free association
Actual reality		of affects	Dream analysis
Transference situation		of conflicts	Analysis of defense
		Resistance	(transference and
		of repression	resistance)
		of need	Interpretation
		for sickness and suffering	
		Symbolism	
		Defense mechanisms	
		Sublimation	

This shows a sharp contrast between phenomena and explanatory constructs, a contrast that is always encountered when psychoanalysis is dealt with as a psychology.

[You know very well that there are psychological methods of observation other than the psychoanalytic. Take one in gross contrast—you all know that the method of conditioned response also claims to make observations on psychology, not only on animals but on human beings. It is also a method; the patient isn't put on the couch but rather tied in the Pavlov frame. It is obvious that on the Pavlov frame you will be able to learn many things about certain kinds of adaptations—how somebody adapts to something. You may learn something about how long an adaptation is retained, you may learn about discriminations, what discriminations are made by this person or by this animal. You can learn about both animals and human beings. On the couch you usually learn only about human beings. It is very likely that on the couch you won't accumulate reliable observations concerning the type of discriminations you will learn about when working with the observational method of the Pavlov frame.

Let's take another example, not so far removed. Take the method of association theory, which budding psychoanalysts are always quick to identify with their own theories because they too have to do with associations. In its crudest form, association theory maintains that there is a mechanism of associations, that things which often occur together in space or in temporal sequence are tied to each other, and if one comes to mind the other is dragged after by the bond of this frequent occurrence together. That too is a method of observation: it is observed how certain things are together in the person's time and space experience, and from the observations of that contiguity all mental functions—thinking, learning, discriminating, perceiving, orienting in a space which has depth—can be derived. Much of that can never be derived on the couch. But someone who works with the assumption of frequency, of contiguity, will never understand many things which those who use the couch know very well and see very often. What, for instance? That somebody could never forget something he saw only once. There is no place for this in an observation system in which everything depends on observing how things occur together, and yet it is a system of observation, a possible system, a system that has been used, some die-hards are still using it. Another thing which they will never understand because there is no place for it: *déjà vu:* a situation which you encounter is suddenly something which you have felt before, seen before, encountered before, experienced before. In explaining this the associationists have just never gotten to first base. For the psychoanalyst it will mean that this experience has something to do with the internal setting, with a feeling that overwhelms the person at that moment and was also overwhelming at another time when the actual outside experiences were quite different. Here you see another example of how the method of observation determines what you get, what you don't get, what you can understand and what you can't, what you can handle theoretically and what you can't. The method used determines what you get as observations and determines the theories you build upon them.]

Probably this all sounds disconnected, but I shall fill in the gaps as we go along. I felt that I had to throw this contrast before you at this point because it is one of the first things that hits the eye when one tries to deal with the methodology of psychoanalysis.

Now to the concept of methodology. I thought it simplest to state first that a science always uses techniques. When you look for a system in these techniques, when you try to create a theory describing their interrelationships, what you do is to describe the method of that science. If you then investigate these methods which you have inferred, what you treat of is methodology. If you discuss all the possible arguments about what free association should or should not be, you are discussing technique; such a discussion clarifies methods. If you place the method called free association beside the other methods of this discipline to trace its relationships to them, then you are exploring methodology. [Let me warn you that 90 per cent of the time, when you read the word "methodology" in the literature, what the authors really mean is not what methodology is. What they mean is a treatise on technique and that radically differs from methodology because if you go to a course on technique what you get indoctrination in or lectured to about is what you should and shouldn't do. Methodological treatment of something means that you investigate what consequences adopting this method has for the material to be obtained and what kind of consequences it has for the theory that must be built to encompass, to make understandable, to unify these observations. In other words, if you are taught to do this and that in psychoanalysis, interpret at this time and don't interpret at that, let the resistance mount and confront it thus and thus, recognize resistance by this and that, once obtained and interpreted, material must be worked through—these are rules of procedure, of scientific discipline, that is, they are techniques. If you start asking the question, Once having started to use this type of technique, what empirical material will be obtained in consequence and what will be immediately dependent on the method itself? you are asking a truly methodological question. Methodology tries to establish (1) how much of the material that is obtained is determined by the method used. How the selection of the observational material depends upon the method used. (2) How the theory can be predicted in advance without empirical observation. Whether this method, once applied, can hope to encompass this material. Whether the method, even though applicable to the subject matter in question, is not misapplied to it and is a telescope that is pointed here instead of being pointed there. You could paraphrase all this by saying that the first question is whether one doesn't shout into a room and hear only himself and not what is in the room. And about the selection of material, you could ask whether this thing he threw into the room is such that only part of what is in the room will modify the reverberation. In other words, the method he employs will yield in return only material which has been affected by that part of the room which responds to the method. The material obtained is thus selected and one cannot conclude that one knows all about the room. To decide whether a microscope or a telescope should be looked through, or whether the telescope should be pointed here or there, is methodology. There is a fundamental difference between methodology and method or technique.]

This may seem too abstract. I can dwell upon it only long enough to give an illustration of why it is worth while to investigate methods. My example will have to oversimplify the issue. In a group of children, adolescents, or grownups, I will say, "If I cut ten apples into six pieces each, how many pieces are there going to be?" Some will give right answers, some wrong ones. If I then establish what methods each used to get the results, I shall be investigating method. Some people will say they simply took the apples to another room, cut them up, and counted the pieces. Some will say, "Each apple has six pieces so you have ten times six apples." Or, "Each apple having six pieces, numbered one to six, there will be ten sets of six pieces." Children will say, "I guessed it." Now, some of the people giving these explanations will give the wrong answer; an occasional child who "guessed it" will give the right answer. Thus, neither good nor bad *results* will tell you whether the *method* used is correct. The problem implied here is this: if you can get the same result when using different methods, the result is correct; if a method obeys the rules of scientific method, it is likely to be correct. So much for the question of what methodology is.

Now I would like to offer some nonlogical and nonreasoning considerations concerning methodology. There are two contrasting ways one may feel about methodology after having tried it for a while. One is an extreme pride in the consistency of human thinking and one's own thinking; the other is an absolute despair about the hopelessness of human endeavor, because methodology will always show the circularity of human reasoning and a basic inability to penetrate the laws of nature. The first book ever written on methodology was Descartes's *Discourse of Method*. Originally I planned to read you a few sentences of it to show how, in that one discourse, deep despair about the futility of systematic thinking is mixed with the highest pride in it.

I would like to give a more detailed consideration to the procedure, or reasoning, called methodology.

CONSIDERATION NO. 1: SCIENCE OBSERVING ITSELF

If I am in a state of "observing myself," my state can be described as turning back upon myself, or bending back upon myself, and describing myself. But I can afterward bend back upon my various *observations* and scrutinize their relationships to each other and to myself. Thus, we know that Freud's results in *The Interpretation of Dreams* (1900) were arrived at by integrating his observations on himself with what he saw in other people. The human being has the peculiar quality of being able to observe himself and then to bend back upon his observations and make a theory. He can explore observations, explore observations of observations, etc., and make theories about that. There is no end to it. It is most peculiar, most frightening, most enchanting.

So far I have been describing some psychological phenomena. But the coin has another side; it has to do with methodology. The bending back of science upon itself to see scientific interrelationships between its own constructs and theories—that is methodology. I would like to give an illustration. It may seem superfluous to most of you; but if it makes the issue clearer to even one person, I will not regret having spent time on it. Even an army has theories: it calls them plans. These plans are usually divided into two parts called strategy and tactics. Tactics deals with the elements necessary for more or less localized operations; strategy is the interrelationships of all these operations. Since these are known concepts, I propose that anything that is method and technique be called the tactics of a science, and anything that is methodology be called the strategy of a science. Just as individual differences among the soldiers described in history made some masters of tactics, others masters of strategy, individual differences between scientists make some masters of scientific disciplines, others masters of the methodological disciplines. Individual differences are apparently so prominent and so profound that they seem to prohibit the uniting in one and the same person of the strategic and tactical genius of science. This is why human beings, if they are strategists, tend to underestimate tactics, and vice versa: this underestimation pertains not only to persons and their activities, but unfortunately to the scientific disciplines themselves. Much of the disrepute of psychoanalysis among psychologists, and academically trained people in general, is this mutual contempt of the strategist and the tactician.

CONSIDERATION NO. 2: GRASPING THE DYNAMICS OF A SCIENCE

I will now take up a point which seems to me of considerable importance. With it I hope to elucidate the significance of methodology from still another point of view. When a book is published in your scientific field, attacking tenets of that science with proofs, considerations, etc., your ability to judge the merits of those facts and considerations depends on your knowledge of the structure of your field. Let us imagine that you are a physicist and that this is the day Einstein publishes his treatise on the special theory of relativity. If you are not aware of the structure of your science, the publication must shake you to your very toes because it spells a revamping of the whole theory of physics. You would *have* to take a stand against it because it threatens all previous practical procedures. But if you are aware of the relationship of those tenets of physics which were attacked by Einstein to those tenets of physics which he did not touch, then you realize that the latter remain exactly the same as long as you remain in the realm of velocities that do not approximate the velocity of light. This example shows that if you know how a new theory fits into a science as a whole, you will be able to judge that new theory correctly. Thus, if Horney or Fromm publish a book, Rado or Alexander make a speech, disclaiming a certain tenet of psychoanalysis, you will be able to judge the argument correctly *only* if you know the position of that tenet within psychoanalytic theory. You will judge it correctly *only* if you know whether that tenet is fundamental to the whole theory, or fundamental to the systematic relationship between parts of the theory, or just an unimportant appendage of it.

Methodological analysis is the tool that shows which concepts depend on others, which are fundamental and which can be altered without damage to the whole. Or, defined in terms of strategy and tactics, a general has a good strategic plan if he knows exactly which positions must be held at any cost, and which others can be given up without touching the original plan. Good strategy in science means methodology; methodology means the hierarchical arrangement of concepts and theories making clear which concepts are built on which others, which are basic and which are subsidiary. Even for the practical man of today, whose science is exposed to attacks and revisions which he is supposed to assimilate or reject, some methodological thinking is indispensable.

CONSIDERATION NO. 3: METHODOLOGY'S PROCEDURE

Next I shall talk about what methodology does. As a rule, it does three things. The first is to scrutinize the material a science deals with: its nature, its peculiarities, and the avenues of approach to it. In psychology the avenue of approach to psychological phenomena is crucial, and will be the topic of the next lecture. Here the Freudian approach has overthrown all the others, such as those which once investigated human beings like astral bodies, where behavior is the subject matter of investigation; or those which dealt with sensory perceptual behavior. The Freudian revolution pointed to subjective experiences as the avenue to the subject matter of psychology. The first thing methodology does, then, is to ask: What is the subject matter and what are the avenues of approach to it?

The second thing it asks is more difficult: What are the hypotheses and concepts underlying the science? In other words, what are the initial hypotheses this science takes for granted and manipulates? Or, again, what are its theoretical constructs?

[In other sciences the manner in which methods determine theories was always discovered when someone, usually after a considerable time, sat down and tried to figure out what are the tacit assumptions that the method implies. It is not very clear what the method does to our thinking until one asks about the tacit assumptions upon which the whole reasoning of the science is built. The search after the tacit assumptions usually led to formulations called postulates, axioms, hypotheses, definitions, and other such terms. You know that as far as we know it was not until after some 500 years of geometry that Euclid for the first time presented geometry in a systematic way, and at the head of his presentation he put three brief sections. The first section he called Definitions, the second he called Postulates, and the third he called Axioms. At that time they already knew more than the average man of our civilization knows. Euclid concluded that if he wanted to make systematic all that people before him or his contemporaries or he had done in geometry, he had to demand that five things be taken for granted, that they be assumed to be true. These are they: (1) That from any point to any other point a straight line should be able to be drawn. We usually don't stop at such a simple thing. It is obvious. You draw it. But if you want to make a geometry you have to make that simple assumption.

(2) Any limited line should be able to be continued in its own direction without ceasing. (3) That around any center a circle with any radius should be able to be drawn. (4) That all right angles be equal to each other. That all sounds self-understood, but in so far as it is self-understood, it is a tacit assumption of geometry. (5) That two lines transected by a third line should meet when continued if the inner angles formed by the intersecting line are less than two right angles. That is the famous fifth postulate around which the storms were raging. It seems very obvious, but it is far less obvious than the other four.

Another set of assumptions more of you will know. They are the three Newtonian assumptions about mechanics. (1) If no force is acting on a body, then the body remains at a state of rest or in uniform movement. (2) If a force is acting on a body, the change of movement or acceleration is in the same direction as the force and is proportionate with that force. (3) That action is equal to reaction and their directions are diametrically opposite. You see, the latter three are not so obvious to everybody, yet to a physicist they are commonplaces.

Let me dwell on the geometric postulates. To draw a sharp line between what is axiom and what is postulate is an unprofitable business, is more or less quibbling for our purposes here. If one says that the five Euclidean postulates are self-understood, the question is, how many such self-understood things do you have to have before you can build the whole business? How many such do you have to introduce which are not self-understood? To build a set of postulates is just to find out what are the minimum primary assumptions that you have to make in order to make sensible, meaningful, the whole building of a science. One more historical word before we abandon the five postulates. The fifth postulate worried everybody for 2,000 years. Why? Because it didn't seem as simple and as obvious as the others. It probably didn't seem as obvious to you either. People tried to solve it, deduce it from the others, prove it. They didn't succeed. The famous Lagrange was said to have been the last who was allowed to present a thesis on it to the Academie Française. When he arrived, he started his sentence, thought a bit, said, "I have changed my mind," and left. From then on they didn't accept any more new attempts to prove it. I am trying to indicate to you the importance people attached to issues like this. What was the end of the issue? Around the beginning of the last century, a Russian, a German, and a Hungarian more or less simultaneously (the Hungarian claiming priority) reversed this and said, what if the postulate were not assumed? What would then result? (You remember in *Peter and the Wolf* —and what if Peter had not caught the wolf?) And a new, very marvelous world of geometry shot up. A geometry that is absolutely different from though coordinate to the geometry Euclid built. In other words, these self-understood things are puzzlers, we have to ferret them out, find them, because it is quite possible that if we take one away or add one, a building arises which is very different. What methodological scrutiny does, then, is not merely tell us that this method can be useful here but not there, or that this method does such selection, has such limitations, but it actually can break through limitations and get through to new methods. This much about the need to ferret out postulates, and this much about how if you ferret out what the tacit implications of a method are, you may get to assumptions that change the whole structure you are building.

I would like to shift the scene and bring up another issue concerning the material of these postulates. That issue is quite important, as you will see later in our psychological considerations. The issue is simply a logical one. If you say that all men are mortals and that Socrates is a man, you deduce from that that Socrates is a mortal. Actually, you have not added anything to your knowledge. Propositions which have this nature are called analytic propositions, because you arrive at the conclusion by analyzing Socrates, discovering in him the property human, and therefore know, without adding anything, that he also has the attribute mortal. Now it was discovered that there are propositions of a very different kind. These propositions were particularly exciting, because to understand what mathematics is about was rather impossible without them. Just a sentence about it: Mathematics usually uses the method of deduction, and one would assume therefore that once you have the fundamental axioms or postulates of mathematics, whatever they may be, all the rest will yield themselves purely deductively. Once you assume that something is equal to itself, that contains all mathematics and everybody who can deduce—and we are all more or less capable of that—should be able to know all there is to mathematics because it is all contained in that. Actually, the situation is not like that. Most of us don't encompass all of mathematics, nor is it true that mathematics can always be deduced. Take, for example, the fifth postulate, that two lines transected by a third should meet when continued if the sum of the two inner angles is less than two right angles. Kant called this type of statement an a priori synthetic statement. Time forbids going into all that this means. A priori means, for example, that the statement about the circle seems to you a priori true. You can't prove it, but it seems true. It is synthetic because the subject of this sentence does not imply its predicate, and in this it differs radically from the syllogism concerning Socrates, in which it was implied in Socrates that he is a man and you know it in advance. But by analysis of no part of the concept circle can you deduce that it should be able to be drawn with any radius around any given point. The existence and validity of these a priori synthetic theses were never understood until Kant. Leibnitz did not understand them, and gave a very funny formulation. He asked, how is it possible that we can reason something out and there is truth in our reasoning, and in the meanwhile there are happenings in the world which have their own truth, and that these two show some kind of similarity? That is an a priori thesis in a different form. You a priori perceive that something seems to be correct, and you can then find it in reality.

The Kantian explanation of the existence of these was that experience is so integrated in the human mind—what he called pure reason—as to be consistent and yield laws. These laws imply the experience which is being integrated by us between the laws or categories of pure reason and the forms of our sensibility, namely time and space. I know that this is abstruse, yet this all belongs here because the question is, what are those fundamental experiences and what are our integrating principles by which these are so integrated that we no longer recognize how we did it, take them as self-evident truths, imply them in our methods, build theories by them, and when we go at the theories we discover that we have implied a number of self-evident truths as if they had been given to us by the deity. Kant knew they were not given by a deity. Kant knew they were works of something going on in human beings, in human nature. Notice that at this point we are implying that hunches and methods are human hunches and human methods that determine and limit our possibilities of knowledge, because in all of them a human being with a certain mode of thought gets hold of a corner of the world of reality and forms it so as to allow prediction and allow communication between human beings. In this respect the mode of Kantian thinking is not very different from the one which is characteristic of psychoanalytic thinking, but the premises are very different and the levels on which he described it were very different.]

The main things methodology wants to know about the hypotheses and concepts of a science are: (1) Their necessity. (2) Their existence. (3) Their sufficiency. What is necessity? If you are observing human beings and can find no explanation for a number of things occurring in them, you will have to state that it seems *necessary* to assume the existence of an unconscious psychological life. As for existence, you have to offer proof of the existence of what you assume, and give some kind of demonstration of it. Now what is sufficiency? In science, as in life, a thing that seems necessary doesn't always exist, and even when it does, it may not be sufficient. Thus, when it is necessary to assume an unconscious psychological life to explain certain phenomena, this assumption may not suffice to explain all phenomena. You may have to find something more in the conscious subjective experience. You may have to make some other corollaries to the proposition of the unconscious. Hartmann suggested that that something is biological. Psychoanalysis had to make the corollaries that it is not merely unconscious but psychologically unconscious, that it is brought forth by biological nature, that parts of it were once conscious experiences. Necessity, existence, and sufficiency are the three properties of a science that methodology investigates to create a hierarchy of theoretical constructs.

The third thing methodology does is the most complicated of all. We will have to come back to it later.

I want to give some examples of what methodology does. What I am going to allude to is well known to psychoanalysts. A woman sent to a neighbor to borrow her clothesline. The neighbor sent back the message, "I am drying flour on it." The woman came over and said, "One doesn't dry flour on a clothesline." The neighbor's answer was, "If I don't want to lend it to you, I can dry flour on it." If I want to wrong you, though you may be ever so good, I will wrong you anyway. If you have an initial hypothesis, you will get out of things only your initial hypothesis. If you shout into an empty room, you will get back only your own sound, because there is nothing else to get from there. The meaning of this is: If you start out with a basic assumption, you may collect observations and a hundred proofs, but finally you will come out with something that you could have deduced from your hypothesis without any observations. This does not necessarily prove that your hypothesis is incorrect; it just means that it is not scientifically waterproof. The fact that something was a priori predicted without empirical evidence does not mean that it was false. If I am convinced that another person is a son of a bitch, I will prove that he is one; that does not prove that he isn't one. [In other words, if I in anger call someone a fool and therefore assume that the other *isn't* a fool, I make a fool of myself.]

The task of methodology then is to scrutinize what are the consequences of initial hypotheses that are independent of observation. Many of these consequences may be borne out in the course of human observation. It may be that the kinds of hypotheses we are able to make are limited by our own psychological structure. Otherwise, people would never have gotten the idea that the shortest distance between two points is a straight line—which is not true. The task, then, of methodology is a very complicated one—to see *how* theoretical constructs depend upon original assumptions, and to see whether these constructs are in accordance with observations. Similarly, original assumptions and hypotheses may, and do, lead to a complete picture of the world. Psychologists, psychiatrists, and psychoanalysts have a picture of the world peculiar to them. Methodology shows how that picture depends on their original hypotheses. In the second lecture I will try to collect just a few samples of the constructs of psychoanalysis and elucidate some of their hierarchical relationships.

LECTURE NO. 2

My present topic concerns the difficulties facing a scientific methodology of psychoanalysis. I believe that the main difficulty, or the main root of all difficulties, in building a scientific methodology of psychoanalysis is that the claims of psychoanalysis are so sweeping as to allow the psychoanalyst who remains within what he calls his method to scrutinize every kind of ideational product for its psychological origins. We know that psychoanalysts scrutinize any kind of art work; the literature gives quite a bit of evidence of that. Certainly works of literature, art or not art, are being scrutinized by psychoanalysis; also political theories. Though it is not very frequent to find physical and chemical theories scrutinized in the psychoanalytic literature, there are traces of this, and within the framework of the psychoanalytic method there is considerable justification for scrutinizing any and every kind of theory. Zilboorg scrutinized psychiatry and methods of psychiatric thinking, as reflected in the history of psychiatric thinking, with the psychoanalytic method. He maintained that the very idea of localizing the psychic functions in the head is just human arrogance, and later characterized it as a result of the historical development of our psychological functions. Psychoanalysis which is a part of psychiatry can scrutinize psychiatry with the methods of psychoanalysis. It has scrutinized physical theories too. Rado (1922) was bold enough to do that, although I don't believe that methodological analysis would accept his scrutiny. The claims of psychoanalysis are so enormous that they include scrutiny of any kind of methodology, because any person who thinks about methodology does so with his psyche, and psychological functions can be scrutinized by psychoanalytic methods. One can again "bend back upon" methodology with methods of psychoanalysis and investigate why its analyses were done, how they were done, and what conclusions were reached. The prime difficulty in building any kind of scientific methodology of psychoanalysis appears to be rooted in this situation. Methodology is a bending back by the scientist upon his own science, exploring his own methods. You are dealing here with a science which claims that it can bend back upon any kind of science or thought product. It is like being in an elevator with mirrors on two opposite sides. You look into one and see yourself looking at yourself in the other, and so on into infinity. It sounds very discouraging, but I believe methodological endeavor is always burdened with such discouraging features.

I would like to make two or three more specific points to show how this leads to difficulties. As you know, all sciences are anthropomorphic at the beginning, and all of them attempt to get away from this feature. Every science we know started as an anthropomorphic science: the human being judged phenomena happening in him, around him, etc., as if they were happening to him because this was the only way he could get an understanding or "sympathy" with them. This is how the concept of "forces" came about: on the basis of his own experience, he knows that something can be made to happen by him if he uses force. Physics has developed to the point where it claims that it now excludes all anthropomorphism. A popularizing book by Eddington, *Science and New Pathways,* can be read even by those who know nothing about physics, and it goes into the highest of physics. Eddington endeavors to show that to obtain the data physical theory is built on, all one needs to presuppose is a tiny bit of retina to be able to read a scale with a pointer; anything that cannot be thus established does not have any place in physics. Thus, all that is necessary for physics is a small bit of sensory function which tests only the coincidence of the pointer with one of the lines on the scale.

Is this kind of ideal of science a general ideal for science, and for psychological science too? This question seems to be of considerable significance. Murray of Harvard wrote some time ago:

> Figurative language, such as I am using here, is widely condemned as rank anthropomorphism, but what sin could be more pardonable than this when talking about *men*—not about vegetables, minerals, and sewing machines? Anyhow, such talk is pragmatically effective in deal- ing with most patients; and hence by this token scientific. Technical language, on the other hand, is ineffective and therefore "illogical" in the Paretian sense. For this reason, emotive speech will always have its place—resistant to certain poisons in "scientific" psychology— even after it is found that some complex of chemicals is mostly re- sponsible for the rebel in us, another for the pacifist, still another for the lecher [1940, p. 161].

Rado deals with the same point much less eruditely and in much less liter- ary language. Rado tries to prove that the principle of causality is an an- thropomorphic postulate, and ends his argument like this: "Determinism has, to be sure, proved to be a truly anthropomorphic postulate. However, our mental life is an exquisitely anthropomorphic object of research; it is anthropos himself. In the pre-psychoanalytical era we met with enough de- terring examples of psychologies that approached the study of man's mental life with premises far removed from humanity" (1922, p. 700). In reading these two texts to you my aim was to restate more concretely the point I tried to make when I called attention to the fact that psychoanalysis in its methodology suffers from the difficulty that you can bend back upon it and ask, Are such methodological considerations justifiable? Perhaps they are anthropomorphically made, and if they are, is it correct or incorrect to make them? What is more anthropomorphic—to accept anthropomorphic science or to purge science of anthropomorphism?

I would like to pursue the point further. When you work out a methodol- ogy you use logic as your tool. Note the next difficulty—psychoanalysis in most of its pursuits uses a type of thinking which has to be characterized not as "logical" but rather as "psycho-logical." The rule or laws we accept as prevailing in the functioning of the unconscious are not logical rules but ones that may be called prelogical—psychological. Though one could ob- ject that this refers only to the method that is used by psychoanalysis, and that the methodology of psychoanalysis can be free from it, the fact remains that thus far methodologies have been built about methods that are "logi- cal," and now we are trying to work out a methodology of methods that are not "logical." Here "logical" designates that system of ideas referring to our system of conscious thinking which originated with Socrates, was later systematized by Aristotle, reached its peak in Kant, and has recently been modified by non-Aristotelian logicians. What remains out of the whole consideration is that you are trying to apply a logical system of methodology to something that is itself not necessarily approachable by logic but rather, as Alexander put it, by a logic of affects, by "psycho-logic," or at least by another kind of logic. Our tools, the tools of psychoanalysis, are just very different from those used in the other sciences—that is, different from logic, which is the tool of methodology.

The last difficulty, which is much more technical and practical, is the question, The methods of what are to be investigated? Psychoanalysis has a method which is used in the so-called psychoanalytic constellation in the psychoanalytic hour. Some psychiatrists use it in the discussion of papers by other psychiatrists, and some people abuse it as a parlor game in the evening. Usually we consider the latter use either "shop talk" or bad manners. But it is not facetious to ask, Is it the same method which is being used in the actual psychoanalytic situation and in poking fun at your adversaries in a local or national meeting and when you use it in the evening as teasing? Is the psychoanalytic method as applied to everyday phenomena identical to what occurs in the psychoanalytic situation? There is no doubt that in the early psychoanalytic writings the cleavage was sharp: the psychoanalytic method proper takes place in the psychoanalytic situation; all the other uses are merely analogies which are fruitful and inspiring to other sciences. Psychoanalytic analyses of art and literature will indicate at the very beginning that an "as if" analysis is being made. It is a question whether the psychoanalytic method that is being investigated to build a scientific methodology is the one that occurs in the psychoanalytic hour or the one by which the psychoanalyst has attempted to encroach upon and to inspire other fields of science, or come to the help of other sciences, depending upon the point of view. The sciences in question are mainly anthropology and sociology. Peculiarly enough, the psychoanalysts who were interested in these more "practical" sciences very quickly forgot the "as if" character of their analyses. One more possibility about the methodology of what is being investigated concerns the claim, which I have already discussed, that psychoanalysis is a psychology that makes general assumptions about psychological life, behavior in general, the conscious and unconscious, active and passive behavior of human beings. In this case the methodology in question would be that of a full-fledged psychology, not one of a treatment procedure or one of helpfulness to other sciences.

Lack of clarity about these possibilities for a methodology is one of the main difficulties in the way of methodology. In the whole psychoanalytic literature there are only three or four papers about methodology, showing that these difficulties have led to an avoidance of the issue. There are, after all, only a few things that a good psychoanalyst will not try his hand at, because the tool is very powerful, because one may try one's hand at anything, and because the fields in question are really virgin fields.

LECTURE NO. 3

The topic for today is how the methods the psychoanalyst applies predetermine his concepts, that is to say, the concepts or conceptual framework called psychoanalysis. In order to discuss this we first have to fix in our minds two features of the psychoanalytic procedure, both of which are rooted in the simple fact that what psychoanalysis deals with is the "psyche." Psychoanalysis is a psychology: it deals with the psyche. Two consequences issue from this. Discussion of either will lead to a few concepts which may be entirely new and unfamiliar, but there is nothing particularly complicated about them. The first point about any investigation concerning psychology is, How does the subject matter of psychology relate to the subject matter of all other sciences? In other words, what is the position of psychology among other sciences? There are two main assumptions, or two points of view, concerning this question. One point of view says that psychology is radically different from all other sciences because its subject matter, unlike that of other sciences, is available by immediate or direct experience. The subject matter of the other sciences is not so given; it exists outside of the subject. The other point of view is the opposite of this, and says that there is no difference between the subject matter of psychology and the subject matter of any other science. It maintains that all "reality" is conveyed to us by or represented to us in our consciousness, that it is out of the material appearing in consciousness that, with different manipulations, we arrive at distinctions in it which become the subject matters of physics, chemistry, anthropology, etc. I suggest that we adopt for the purposes of the present discussion, without finally deciding the issues, the first point of view.[1] The reasons are in the following argument. The two points of view really are answers to two different questions. If we take the question to be: What is the nature of our knowledge or information about the subject matters of different sciences, among them that of psychology?, that is to say, if we were asking a question about the nature of our knowledge (in other words, an epistemological question), then we would be justified in making a distinction between the subject matter of psychology and the subject matters of other sciences, and we reach the first point of view. But if we take the question to be about the methods of sciences, that is to say, the methods by which human beings in their conscious experience try to discover the continuity between these different parts of their conscious experience and the methods according to which the continuity or discontinuity of the conscious experience is subdivided into the subject matters of different sciences, then no distinction between the subject matters of sciences can be made, and we reach the second point of view. If in our consciousness we find

[1] This point of view is in harmony with the general psychoanalytic frame of reference in which we are not interested in the actual happenings in "reality" but in the *experiences* of the subject concerning that reality.

that a certain matter is yellow, that when we manipulate it in a certain way it turns green, and that by no kind of manipulation of our retina or our body will that change from yellow into green occur, then we have observed a continuity relationship between the conscious experiences of green and yellow and what was likely a chemical manipulation, and have started to delimit a subject matter of science. This continuity would be independent of our own psychological state. Such are the guides by which we delimit the borders of sciences from the point of view of method.

I would like to point out that this discussion has an intimate relationship to the discussion of last time concerning the difficulties of psychoanalytic methodology. I discussed four different difficulties, all of which really issue from a misunderstanding of what is being dealt with, epistemology or methodology. From a methodological point of view, any discussion starts with the representation of the world in consciousness. From an epistemological point of view, there are grave differences between the different types of conscious contents.

The first consideration I would like to call to your attention is, What are the consequences of the nature of the subject for method and theory? What does every science do with its subject matter? What does physics do? Physics sees movements, changes, processes, and attempts to create generalizations about these changes, processes, etc. It starts with the conscious content, which is empirical, and proceeds toward theory—causal theory—toward something which isn't given empirically. The electron is not given empirically; waves of light are not given empirically. They are inferences, theoretical constructs. What does psychology do? Psychology starts out with a lot of conscious experiences, and what it has to come to, if it is to be a science, is something which isn't conscious experience but a theoretical construct. The superego isn't a conscious experience. Conscious experience is certain behavior of human beings. The censor isn't a conscious experience, not even if it seems similar to some conscious experiences we have when we experience shame or attempt to keep a secret. The misrecognition of the rôle of constructs in psychology, and the demand often heard that they be "empirical," are misunderstandings of the nature of science. I would like to call your attention to a statement in Kardiner's "Psychoanalysis and Psychology." He discusses the structure of psychoanalysis, and comes to a criticism of the concept of instincts: "The concept instinct suffered from the disadvantage that it could not be treated in the same empirical manner as sensation and reflex . . . this fact that the basic unit was not directly observable but had to be inferred or assumed created a serious handicap" (1941, p. 236). So Kardiner wants a concept which is a conscious experience, a demand that is contrary to the procedure of any science and contrary to the essence of scientific endeavor itself.

Let me now turn to the consequences of the fact that the subject matter of psychoanalysis is the psyche. The subject matter psyche is a part of all

the subject matters represented in our consciousness which become the subject matters of the different sciences. Out of that fact issues the first consequence: that the next step of every science is to go beyond this subject
matter, beyond the phenomena which are presented to us in consciousness.
We have to go beyond them and create something which is by definition
different from the experience itself, from the conscious content itself. Many
of the confusions of psychoanalysts concerning their own theory and many
of other people's misunderstandings of the psychoanalytic theory issue from
lack of clarity on this point.

The next question is, To what extent will the concepts to be created be
independent of the methods by which we segregate that subject matter
which we call psyche from other subject matters, and to what extent will
these concepts issue from the nature of that subject matter which we call
psyche?

The next point to be considered is of a very different nature. The fact is
that, inasmuch as the subject matter is given in consciousness and it is the
psyche, this psyche is distinguished from all the other subject matters by the
fact that though the subject's information about it is just like his information about the subject matter of other sciences, it has parts which have
reference to the present and others which have reference to the past. If we
get down to eliciting information about psychological experiences, we get
statements about the subject's past. This is the main alley—the so-called
clinical method—used in the exploration of the subject matter that we call
psyche. Psychiatry and psychoanalysis both approach the "psyche" by asking for information from the patient about himself. This method, the clinical method, is *the* main alley used by psychoanalysis. Even if you are dealing with a dream you ask for information about the past, even if seemingly
not about a very remote past. You thus adopt a method that asks about the
past, goes to the past for information. It does so of necessity because it is
tapping a reservoir where apparently anything that is a "statement" now
was an experience once.

If someone tells you something and you ask him why he thinks that, the
only place in himself for him to turn for an explanation is to his past, or to
"logic" which in turn is a crystallization of his past. The clinical method,
dealing with the subject of experience as the object of investigation by making him the subject of questioning, leads inevitably to explanations by the
past.

The adoption of the clinical method itself implies a great series of consequences. [When the psychoanalyst started out to make his psychoanalytic
theory, he started out with a method in which two people were together and
one asked the other, by implication at least, to tell about himself. Implicit in
it also was the assumption that it is good for you to tell about yourself. Also
implicitly assumed was that everything which comes to mind should be told
without reservation, also assumed was that not only is it good for you but it

will explain something. All these implicit assumptions. If you really stop to think about it, you will see that there are these silent assumptions in the whole psychoanalytic theory. But these things still come to our mind at times. Some of the implications do not come to our minds and it is on some of these that I would like to dwell.]

These consequences can be more clearly seen if we define two types of science, ideographic and nomothetic. "Ideographic" means that you describe, you paint a picture of an idea; "nomothetic" means that you state laws. In other words, you can do two things with a phenomenon; you can describe it or try to get at its laws. History is the classical example of ideographic science, physics of nomothetic science. History describes phenomena and tries to describe the relationships by analysis, by massing data from the past. Physics elicits phenomena, observes phenomena, varies conditions, and thus establishes the main variables and their relationships to one another, which then are referred to as physical laws. Thus sciences which deal with phenomena that are unique, singular, once-occurring, of necessity become ideographic. In history nothing repeats itself. In the human individual an experience is never repeated. Sciences which deal with subject matters in which occurrences recur in relatively identical form and/or can be relatively well reproduced experimentally, become nomothetic sciences. I cannot discuss here more exactly what the nature of the differences between the two types of sciences is. Nevertheless, it should be stated that these differences are not so rigid as they may seem. One stone is not like the next; but we have laws which sufficiently cover the mode of "free fall" of any stone. Differences in the *major* conditions of a "free fall" are easily established. Physical forces are considered independent; physics is built on the thesis of independence of forces. If one force pulls in one direction and another one in another, the object will arrive at the same place it would arrive if first one and then the other force operated. But in history, if an additional force is present things happen differently. If another person and I are sitting in a room we may come to an exchange of ideas we would not reach if a third person were there, though a dialogue of mine or his with that third person might have led to an identical exchange of ideas. In a historical situation there is no independence of forces. That is to say, here we have two distinct types of science, though there is no sharp cleavage but rather a continuous transition; all sciences rank somewhere in between the ideographic and nomothetic extremes. Attempts have been made in the past to make history into a nomothetic science. The most heroic of these was made in the Renaissance by Giambattista Vico, in his *Scienza Nuova*. There is a huge German literature about ideographic science (*Geisteswissenschaft*—sciences of "spirit" as contrasted with sciences of "nature"). The main point is that where psychology stands in this clash of methods is quite a question. Why? Because it shares with the ideographic sciences two different basic facts: the historical-clinical method, and the fact that the phenomena dealt with are unique, singular, and once-occurring. There is, however, sufficient justification for attempting to build a nomothetic (i.e., natural) science of psychology. There are conditions under which variations of the same psychological phenomenon occur, and these variations can be investigated, referred to the variables in the conditions in which they occurred, and "laws" or "rules" can be inferred and used for prediction. Psychoanalysis is a natural science; it is meant to be the natural science of the psyche.

What are the consequences of adopting a clinical or historical method? Let us turn for a moment to a very different field of information. Every primitive (or, as they are referred to recently, preliterate) tribe or group of people attempts to explain its own history. One of these attempts is the Old Testament. You realize where this attempt led: it led to the beginning, to the Creation: Genesis. Now that is no accident; the same thing is true in every mythology: in trying to describe their history, sooner or later all peoples get down to an explanation of the beginning of the world. The historical, clinical method, that is to say, a method which gives ideographic descriptions of happenings and relationships of these happenings, leads to a "regression" [2] in time, sooner or later to the birth of the world. This is independent of the question whether or not the psychoanalytic theory of psychosexual genesis is correct, independent of the question whether or not our explaining late maladjustment by childhood trauma is correct. The clinical method that psychoanalysis adopted inevitably leads to the finding of causes for events in the early history of the individual. This historical "regression" follows from the nature of the "clinical-historical" method. It does not vouch for the validity of the results it obtains. Such vouchers can be obtained only from empirical observation. Both the validity and the limitations of all methods can be found only in the empirical material. What methodological investigation shows is the nature of the consequences of the method used: in this case, thus far only the inevitability of historical "regression."

Where do empirics come in? We can demonstrate that in the history of psychoanalysis. There is a book, *The Trauma of Birth,* by Rank (1924). At one point in psychoanalytic history most psychoanalysts were tempted to assume that the final explanation of neuroses lay in the "trauma of birth." This is merely an example of where, by virtue of its nature and continuity, the clinical method inevitably has to lead. The psychoanalytic theory of the present time has stopped quite a bit short of the "trauma of birth" in the historical "regression" because of empirical findings that place the emphasis on oral, anal, and oedipal experiences. Some people want to follow blindly the historical method to before birth, to intrauterine experiences and

---

[2] The term "regression" is used here in the philosophical sense (as in Leibnitz's proof of "the impossibility of infinite regression") and without any relation to the psychological connotation of the term. It connotes merely "causally folding back upon."

even beyond that. Empirically, however, the link here becomes biological rather than psychological. This is the nature of the method we are using: the examples show the dangers of the method we are using. The only criterion for stopping short of such conclusions as I have referred to is empirics, which will show, for instance, that one of the crucial points is not at birth but at the oedipal situation, another at the oral phase, sucking and all that is connected with it.

I would like to point out three concepts which are immediate consequences of the historical-clinical method in psychoanalysis. These are the concepts of psychic continuity, meaning, and determinism. Let me briefly discuss these three. Psychoanalysis deals with the psyche, it adopts the clinical method, it wants to be the natural science of the psyche. It has to come to certain considerations of lawfulness. If one historical event in the psychic life is to have anything to do with another, it has to be assumed that there is a psychic continuity. This seems to be one of the basic postulates of psychoanalysis. It appears reasonably certain that if the basic method of a psychology were based on conditioned and unconditioned reflexes, we would not have any kind of hypothesis of continuity of psychological happenings because the continuity we would have to presume would be a biological continuity, from the reflex as a biological phenomenon to the conditioned response as an epiphenomenon, and it would not be necessary to presume any kind of continuity of these psychological "epiphenomena." Let's suppose there is a hand movement that is conditioned, and a foot movement that is conditioned. There wouldn't have to be any kind of continuity presumed between the two corresponding subjective conscious experiences. It is the historical-clinical approach, then, that demands our looking upon psychic happening as a continuity or, in other words, our building our psychological theory on the assumption of psychic continuity.

[Let me state this idea in another way. When you tell somebody implicitly that it will be good for him if he talks and tells everything, also that it will explain something to us, you imply that whatever comes to his mind will have a continuity, which continuity will lead to those things for which he came to you. There is no sense in telling him that it is good for him and will explain things and relieve things unless it is assumed, tacitly implied, that all he will say belongs to a continuum, is tied together, is also tied to what ails him, and that what ails him will yield to this process—the conception of psychological continuity, I believe, is the fundamental assumption psychoanalysis makes. But let's play the game out. Earlier I said that if I assume the fifth postulate is not true, if I assume that the opposite is true, what will happen? What if we talk about psychology in terms of conditioned reflex? Let's suppose that I condition your eyelid to react to a certain set of stimulations, and condition your hand to another set of stimulations, etc. Even if we allow that there is an integration in the nervous system, if I want to learn about eyelid responses that I observe twenty-five years later, I will have to go back to a neurological connection. I can't say to my patient that I can arrive at this by following his ideas. If you wanted to assume that you can get to that trouble through chains of ideas, you would then have to presume that the integrative action of nerves is something which always results in an ideational representative. Even if it is only five or six years later— for instance, if it is an integration that came about before puberty, and, as is so often the case, became disorganized in puberty—you would have to assume a new ideational concomitant of the now disorganized integration. You come to an impossibly complex theory. Let me throw it into relief in another way. Let's suppose somebody has a bacterial disease. You can't get to the source of it by following up the ideas of the patient, because the disease does not have a psychological representation in its etiology. I don't mean to be grotesque about it, but you see what is in question. Here is another illustration. Let's suppose a stone falls on somebody's head. Though we talk much about people who are accident prone, it just so happens that there are stones which fall on nonaccident-prone people. Or again, I am not sure whether much of what we talk about as psychosomatic problems will sooner or later prove to be not approachable psychologically. You already know how much of it you can cure and how much you can't cure. Because there are things to which no ideational chains lead. When functional diseases structuralize, a structural lesion comes about. Then even if you arrest the process by relieving the psychological tension, you don't change the structural damage that has been done because there are no psychological chains leading to that damage. This is the negative meaning of psychological continuity. What this shows is where it doesn't go, where it doesn't reach, actually where you can't hope to go with it; your postulates show you some of the limitations of your method, namely, that as far as psychology goes one of its postulates is that a thread leads to all that is psychological or psychoanalytic, but there are limitations.]

It appears that meaning is one of the concepts of psychoanalysis that we use and misuse more often than others. What do we mean by meaning? We ask about a dream, "What is the meaning of it?" What do we mean? I submit that we mean, "How does that dream fit into the psychic continuity of the individual who dreamed it?" We don't imply anything else in our query about "meaning," as far as I can see. The concept of "meaning" would then be a corollary of the concept of "continuity." In this sense, there is no "meaning" in a reflex action because there is no psychic continuity.

[In other words, meaning is not really a new postulate; it has the silent implication of psychological continuity. The concept of the meaning of a symptom or an idea or a symbol or a dream brings it into a certain place in the psychological continuity. Thus, by trying to clarify another concept, we see that we could also have made an entirely different approach to the issue of continuity.]

Maybe I shouldn't have discussed these three concepts in this sequence but should have talked about determinism first. I couldn't because there is no definite intrinsic sequence or hierarchic relationship between the concepts of psychic continuity, meaning, and determinism. Determinism implies that we presuppose that within the psychological sphere there is a causal determination of any one happening by others, that nothing in psychic happening is accidental, which in a sense implies psychic continuity. In another sense, determinism is merely a corollary of psychic continuity. "Continuity" as a postulate is implicit in all ideographic science, while determinism is a distinctive characteristic of nomothetic science. If you presuppose that in psychic life everything is determined and nothing is accidental, then you have merely said that you want to build a science, that is to say, a nomothetic science, and nothing else. [What form determinism takes is a specific postulate. Here it takes the form of psychological continuity, that is to say, there is lawfulness if you know psychological function as an emergent level of development. If there is a new set of emergent laws, psychoanalysis says there is a thoroughgoing determinism and a continuity. Psychological continuity is actually the form a thoroughgoing determinism takes in psychological material when investigated by the clinical method. You don't have to go back to physiological laws to have an understanding of what the interrelationships here are. That is the meaning of thoroughgoing psychological determinism, that is to say, fatigue won't account for a slip of tongue, the slip of tongue is accounted for by psychological continuity. There are somatic interrelationships, but they act only in so far as there are psychological dynamics which take the opportunity. The postulate of psychological continuity could well be replaced by thoroughgoing psychological determinism. Freud is not very specific in *The Psychopathology of Everyday Life* (1901) and *The Interpretation of Dreams* (1900) about what is the specific psychological form of determinism, namely, what we talked about here as psychological continuity. You will notice later on another feature of determinism which is characteristic of psychology, what is called overdeterminism, but about that later on. Another of the implicit implications of the method, as you will see, leads to overdeterminism quite independently of the empirical findings, whatever they may be. If you really want to define thoroughgoing psychological determinism, one ingredient will be continuity, and at least one of the other ingredients will be overdeterminism, so one has to go a little bit slowly when one talks about thoroughgoing determinism in psychology.] The consequence of our method, the clinical-historical method, for our theory is that the theory is of necessity built on the concepts of psychic continuity and meaning, and the effort to create a nomothetic science leads to the postulate of determinism.

[And perhaps I should have pointed out that the concept of conflict is fundamental to the method itself, quite before any empirical findings, because of the wish to communicate in order to get well and the inability to communicate, and to find, through that part of the psychological continuity which is at the beginning of treatment accessible in consciousness, the psychological event or experience or series of constellations which underlie the symptom or disease or trouble. That itself is the fundamental basis for all that you call conflict.]

What is the next theoretical consequence of the method? I suggest that there are two: the concept of instinct and the concept of the unconscious. Out of the postulation of determinism immediately issues the concept of instinct, out of that of psychic continuity the concept of unconscious. Why? Because, if you follow your historical "regression" further and further, what you get down to is the biologically given body. Inasmuch as psychoanalysis wants to be a natural science, it has to take care of the natural relationships of the psyche. For that, the psyche cannot be construed as existing in thin air. Psychoanalysis adopted the biological attitude: without biological function, no psychological function. It is from the body that what we call psychological function emerges. Thus, if you presume determinism and if you want to have a psyche that isn't existing in thin air, isn't an undefined formless nonentity, you have to presume that this psychological happening is built on biological happening. This is the reason why the concept of instinct is indispensable. That is to say, if you carry the clinical method to its last consequences and still want to maintain that the psyche isn't something which exists somewhere in the metaphysical spheres, you have to arrive at a concept which links the biological and psychological spheres. In the meantime, if you stick to the postulate of determinism, then your link can only be a deterministic-causal link. If you want the biological sphere as the origin of psychological functioning, assuming that there is a determinism working, then you arrive at a definition of instinct: it is a link to the biological, and it is the final causal determiner of the psychological happening. You don't, however, have any further qualification of the instinct concept as yet. [But I believe it can be shown that the instinct concept implies, among other things, a concept of energy. Let's not forget the time in which this method was first used, and the fact that the first cases on which it was used were in the main hysterialike cases. They were cases of gross hysterical symptoms for which people sought neurological explanations. What was the consequence for the theory of the fact that Freud began with this material? You know what kind of case he saw. With his method of continuity he had to presume that it led to somatic avenues. Inevitably, in this clinical setting, out of the postulate of continuity there had to come a concept fundamental to the whole theory, which must be a borderline concept between the somatic and the psychological. If you add to that that fundamental concepts are energy concepts, it is clear that he had to come out with an energy concept which is a borderline concept of psyche and soma. He gave that the name instinct.]

To go back to the very first argument I offered about methodology: I stated that what we want to find out is what we can drop out of a systematic theory without losing any of its main tenets, and what is the indispensable cornerstone without which the whole structure collapses. In today's argument I attempted to show that because psychoanalysis is built on the clinical method, instinct is one of its indispensable theoretical constructs. What isn't inevitably settled by adopting the clinical method itself is the number and kinds of instincts we are to assume. As yet, we are still free to choose how many instincts to adopt to form our theory around.

The concept of the unconscious is indispensable by definition. Experience shows that conscious experiences do not themselves show a continuity. Starting with the adoption of the clinical method, we came to a hypothesis of psychic continuity. If we are to abide by this hypothesis, since conscious experience appears empirically discontinuous and the nature of science demands going beyond the *phenomenal*—what is here the *conscious*—we have to assume something beyond the *conscious*. Thus the concept of the unconscious is just like the concept of instinct, a consequence of the method and postulates thus far adopted. [To state the issue again, what we call continuity is a very funny continuity. It is a discontinuous continuity. In other words, once the continuity proposition is maintained and the actual discontinuity is observed, you have obviously made an assumption somewhere which isn't explicit but which of necessity leads to the concept unconscious, to a concept of some variant of psychological continuity which fills up the gaps of apparent discontinuity. Out of the logic of the situation, out of the clinical setting as the method of investigation, the concept unconscious issues without any kind of observation. That we have good empirical evidence for it is an entirely different question.]

Thus far, we see that when you start with a clinical method with a nomothetic aim, you get a deterministic science, a science which presumes psychic continuity, a science which implies historical regression, postulates a link to the biological sphere demanding a concept of instinct, and leads to a concept of an unconscious.[3] The clinical method itself, however, does not imply anything about the laws that operate in the unconscious, nor about what kind of instincts we are to adopt as constructs. [Does what I have asserted so far concerning the clinical situation hold for other disciplines besides psychoanalysis, other theories besides psychoanalysis, also using

[3] [In 1948, Rapaport said: "I have dealt with issues of emphasis on the past, issues of instincts, issues of psychological continuity, issues of the unconscious, and issues of meaning. That is to say, I have actually dealt with only five concepts, trying to indicate how they are silent implications of the clinical method. I hope that at least some of these, in the long run, when the material has been studied thoroughly, will be included in the minimal number of postulates or silent, tacit assumptions to which we will boil down that apparatus with which this science deals." Determinism is not mentioned in this list, as it was in the 1944 list, but that is probably because he saw psychological continuity as the form which determinism takes in psychological material—Ed.]

the clinical method? As a matter of fact, psychiatry in general uses that method, and as a matter of fact, in psychiatry in general the idea of the unconscious was easily accepted, much more so than many other specific psychoanalytic tenets. Every psychiatrist today talks about the unconscious, all talk most of the time about instincts, or drives, or urges. Even if they start shouting against instincts, they introduce them as urges or drives or I don't know what. The same holds more or less for meaning and the same holds in a half-hearted way for psychological continuity. Obviously, for all questioning methods, the past is the reference point; that is why it was so easily accepted. Most psychiatrists do ask for a history and do talk about the past, even if they do not go very far for reasons I shall discuss later.]

LECTURE NO. 4

In the last seminar I attempted to show that the three postulates of continuity, meaning, and determinism and the concepts of instinct and the unconscious are direct consequences of adopting the clinical-historical method. They cannot be abandoned without shaking the whole theoretical structure of psychoanalysis because they are rooted not in empirics but in the method itself as it is used for investigation. I would like to devote the first part of this presentation to making a few amendments. In the second part of the seminar I will discuss the more specifically psychoanalytic method, that is to say, what in the clinical method adopted by psychoanalysis is specifically psychoanalytic. I shall also attempt to trace these specifically psychoanalytic methods to their consequences for the theory of psychoanalysis.

The first amendment I would like to make to the last presentation is to enlarge upon one point. It is maintained that the concept of instinct and the concept of unconscious are direct consequences of the clinical method adopted, and you understand that the clinical method is the clinical method at large, characterized by asking for information about psychological behavior, by the question, "What do you think that means?" or "What do you think is the cause of that?" The clinical method is to be contrasted, for example, to the experimental method. Though the concepts of instinct and the unconscious are direct consequences of the adoption of the clinical method, it has to be kept clearly in mind that this does not imply anything specific about the concept of instinct other than what we discussed last time when we discussed instinct as the link between the biological and the psychological functioning; it does not imply anything specific about the unconscious other than that it is the "filler-upper" of the apparent discontinuity of those conscious contents which are segregated as those which are to be the subject matter of psychological investigation.

Let me be somewhat more explicit. Concerning what is nothing implied? Nothing is implied concerning the instinct theory itself. Nothing is implied about how many instincts there are going to be, that is to say, how many we are to adopt to obtain a satisfactory theory. Nothing is implied that would oblige us to adopt an instinct theory which gives every instinct the triad of attributes—origin, object, and aim—which instincts have in Freud's instinct theory. It is not implied that the instincts should or should not be the erotic and destructive instincts, libidinal and ego instincts, life and death instincts. Nor is anything implied concerning the unconscious other than what was mentioned above. What isn't implied? Nothing is implied about whether the unconscious is to have the same or different "rules of the game" —usually referred to as *logic*—as the conscious has. If the unconscious is to have a different set of "rules of the game" from the conscious, the rules which in fact we call the laws of the primary process (a term referring to the laws of functioning of the unconscious processes), these laws are not predetermined by the clinical method of investigation. Or again, what we know from the psychoanalytic theory about parts of the *superego* being unconscious, about part of the *ego* being unconscious, and the *id* constituting the main bulk of what we call the unconscious, is not predictable from the clinical method.[4]

A psychoanalyst would have to stick to only the postulates of continuity, meaning, and determinism, and the concepts of instinct and the unconscious, if he doesn't adopt specific psychoanalytic methods in addition to the general clinical methods.

I would like to follow up one more consequence of the adoption of the clinical method, not because there are not hundreds of consequences of various importance, many of them more eminent than this one, but because this one is so intriguing to me and because it seems to me that its discussion may prove particularly revealing. Furthermore, other examples I will bring up later in other connections will have an immediate connection with this one. I said that determinism and continuity in psychic life are immediate consequences of the adoption of the clinical method. I would like to endeavor to show that the concept of projection, which seems so specific to psychoanalysis and which we experience in everyday life in various connections, is a direct consequence of the postulates of continuity and determinism in psychic life.

You may ask, Why do you play this game of logical deductions? My answer is: All that was said last time is really a thinking through of our discipline and has the aim of saving us from the embarrassment of having to think over again and again, if and when the discipline or parts of it are attacked by reformists, whether the tenet that is being scrutinized is dispensable or indispensable for the whole of the theoretical structure.

Let me turn then to the concept of projection. Everything in psychological life is determined, not arbitrary, not accidental, not "spontaneous."

---

[4] The importance of clarifying what is and what is not implied in a method of investigation can easily be assessed if one considers the danger of "discoveries" which are merely statements of what were introduced as latent assumptions to begin with.

[Let me talk about the simple use of the term "project" in the phrase projective method, projective techniques of testing. Let me substitute a simple example instead: Somebody says "What a beautiful day it is," and you say "Now isn't that funny. I found this day rather a disconcerting day." And you may add, "Aren't you projecting?" You know that this is how we talk about things. Let me add a few more general things such as what one considers good or bad, nice or ugly, or the values one attributes to things—esthetic values, moral values, etc. In a way these are all such that somebody else can say "You are just projecting. You like it, so you call it beautiful. It fulfills a need of yours and you say it is good or it clashes with some needs of yours and you say it is awful." And if somebody is a dinner-table analyst he will immediately jump on the person and say "You are projecting." Well, you all know that this is how you use the term. If after this example, which was a broadening of what we call projective techniques, I come back to projective techniques, I can illustrate my point by telling you something that happened to me when I was first looking for a job in this country. I went to an old-time analyst, who asked what kind of things I could do, and among other things I said I knew how to do Rorschachs. He said, "Oh, that's nothing. I can take anybody's hat, see how it is crumpled, and tell you what kind of guy he is." That is true, too. There is something about crumpling a hat or wearing it cockily, or pulled down, that tells you something about the kind of person the wearer is. What is that? Now one thing it certainly isn't—it isn't the defense mechanism projection, attributing one's own affect to another person. It is rather this forming or describing of the environment in terms of something inside one's self. Well, this kind of projection corresponds very much to what one calls in the movies a projector, namely, if things go through the projector it makes the screen look like something.]

Now let us take a percept, the most common percept, a visual impression. Let us take this chair that is being perceived by me right now. Let us suppose that this chair exists somewhere outside myself, that is, has an objective existence, and I have a perception of it. Let us realize that there seems to be a contradiction here, in that on the one hand we presuppose continuity and determinism in psychic life and on the other consider the percept of the chair to be determined by the chair's existing in outside "reality." The contradiction becomes clearer if we consider the percept in relation to the continuity of psychic life. We then have two ways out. We can give up the postulate of psychic continuity and say that perceptions that come in "from the outside," from "existing things," do not belong to that continuity; then we break up this continuity altogether, because a great part of our psychic life deals with such perceptions, and thus we abandon the original postulate that followed from the adoption of the clinical method. What is the other way out? We can say: Whether the chair does or does not exist in the outside world is absolutely irrelevant. What we deal with is *the chair as experienced* by us, and that experience *is an integral part* of our psychic life's continuity. Then the postulate of psychic continuity holds before as well as after this perceptual experience. What would this mean? The consequence is this: In psychoanalysis we cannot speak about objects existing in the outside world, but speak of objects only in so far as they are experienced by us. That is to say, if we have a percept of a chair, it is not considered to be the chair that is outside of ourselves somewhere, but to be the chair experienced by us, determined by the continuity of all our other experiences, by the continuity of our psychic life. How do these perceptions fit into our psyches? They will have different "meanings," will "fit" differently into the psyches of different people.

[As long as the chair is in my experience, it has to fit my psychological continuity. How? By my attributing meanings to it. It could be, for instance, an empty chair; for me, this one here at the moment could be a chair in which somebody sat the last time I was here. This kind of meaning of the chair is more subtle than that in its physical conformity the chair is something different for me than for anyone else. The meaning of the chair is different for every single person, because in each person it is experienced in a different psychological continuity. Therefore, it is no surprise that every piece of the world and every different time of our experiencing of the world has its own characteristic imprint on that world, and that is what we mean by this first type of projection. I tried to describe its roots in the postulate of psychological continuity.]

How does this view of objects differ from the general concept of "projection"? As we see the chair, the chair appears to be in the outside world; but we have just established that it belongs in the continuity of our inside world, and that the percept not only obeys the laws of physics but also all the laws of the perceiver's psychic continuity. Here we have the general pattern of "projection." When one deals with a patient, one doesn't ask whether an event happened or not. One asks how the experience reported fits into the individual's psychic continuity; what meaning does it have? One deals with these ideas as projections.

Here no further specific psychoanalytic methods and theories of psychoanalysis were necessary for arriving at the basic pattern of projection. The concept of projection is amplified and made more specific in many other senses in the further elaboration of psychoanalytic theories. It must not be forgotten, however, that the basic pattern of projection issues from the adoption of the clinical method.

This allows for two inferences. First, why is it so much easier for general psychiatrists and psychologists to accept the theory of projection than many other psychoanalytic theories? Conjectures concerning this could be made on the basis of this relationship of projection to the clinical method.

The second is that the world the analyst lives in, in his psychoanalytic work, is basically determined by this type of general scheme of projection, and it ought to be clear to us that this does not follow out of the empirical discovery of the specifically psychoanalytic mechanisms of projection as seen in cases of paranoia, but is the implicit scheme of projection as seen in the issue just discussed.

I will now go on to the second part of today's presentation, a discussion of the specifically analytic methods. Though there may be many such methods, I thought that the proper procedure would be to single out the three which appear to be the most characteristic. I would think that the first in importance of these specifically psychoanalytic methods is the psychoanalytic constellation: a stable relationship of two people. I will refer to this in the following as the "interpersonal relationship." This seems to be the most distinctive feature of the psychoanalytic method. You could ask me, Why isn't that simply a corollary of the clinical-historical method? Because the clinical-historical method can simply go to the records of history; the clinical method can operate with a questionnaire. The stabilized "interpersonal relationship" characteristic of the "psychoanalytic constellation" is a specifically psychoanalytic method if it is carried to its last consequences. The psychiatric interview also creates an interpersonal relationship, but it does not carry it to its last consequences; the situation is similar in any interview technique.

Inasmuch as there are many other procedures which seem to imply interpersonal relationships, from now on when I use the phrase interpersonal relationship I will mean the relationship between the analyst and analysand. About the other procedures which seem to be "interpersonal relationships" I will endeavor to show that they are "pseudointerpersonal relationships" in this specific sense of the phrase, because they do not carry the interpersonal relationship to its last consequences as psychoanalysis does. My task will be to investigate the consequences that issue for the theory from this "interpersonal relationship" and to see what it means to drive this "interpersonal relationship" to its "last consequences."

The second distinctive feature of the psychoanalytic method proper seems to me to be the method of free association, and the third the method of dream interpretation. One might say with complete justification that this triad of specific psychoanalytic methods, used within the framework common to all clinical-historical methods, distinguishes psychoanalysis from the other clinical-historical methods. One could argue that other features of the specifically psychoanalytic method are equally important. I do not propose to contend that these are the *only* distinctly psychoanalytic methods. I do not feel that I have proved this to myself. Nevertheless, I submit that they have a sufficient claim to importance so that a demonstration of the points in question can be attempted on them without exposing ourselves to the danger of neglecting too much, and at present this is the utmost that we can strive for. One might argue that if we include the free association method, we should include the analysis of resistance as its historical counterpart. I feel, however, that it will be more systematic to deal with the analysis of defense mechanisms under the "interpersonal relationship." One might argue that dream interpretation is parallel to the method of analysis of memories in general, of infantile and screen memories, and to the analysis of repressions, but all these can be dealt with in relation to defense mechanisms, and as I have already stated, I feel that these should be taken up in the discussion of the interpersonal relationship. May I also submit that a common denominator, but at the same time the dividing characteristic, of these three just enumerated mainstays of the psychoanalytic method can be given as follows: Psychoanalysis as a unique method postulates psychic continuity, it investigates this continuity in the so-called "psychoanalytic constellation," in which this continuity expresses itself in the method which I referred to as the "interpersonal relationship." The two other main methods here mentioned—dream interpretation and free association—also issue out of the general postulation of psychic continuity. To see this clearly, let us for a moment fix before our eyes the nature of dreams and the nature of free association. Aren't they the two phenomena of psychic experience which appear at first glance to be most exempt from obeying any kind of rule of psychic continuity? Aren't they those psychic phenomena which appear at first inspection to be the most alien to the continuity of psychic life? But introspection will easily and quickly show that processes which on first inspection appear to be so continuous and logical immediately reveal great gaps. In a logical chain of reasoning representing the sequence of ideas which led us to a discovery, impressive or unimpressive as the discovery may be, we soon discover that between the steps of logical reasoning, between the different stages of that discovery, there are deep gaps. If we confront another person with the necessity for reasoning out a simple arithmetical task of which he knows everything, we find to our surprise the gap of his being unable to mobilize, at the proper moment, the proper knowledge that he has. There is something lacking in between two steps which prevents him from bringing up the needed knowledge, and this something, if present, is still not part of the apparent continuity of conscious experience. In introspection, continuous conscious experience reveals its gaps, and psychoanalysis adopted the methods of free association and dream analysis in the hope that the *apparently* noncontinuous may yield material which fills in the gaps in the *apparently* continuous conscious experience. The three main methods of psychoanalysis are tied together, and also distinguished from each other, by their relation to the postulate of psychic continuity.

In the time left, I would like to take up only one thing about the method of "interpersonal relationship" or "psychoanalytic constellation." Note that in the psychoanalytic constellation two people are present. The presence of these two people leads, as reflection on your own experience will show, to a threefold rôle of the person who is being investigated. He is someone who wants or does not want to cooperate; he is someone who is to yield material to the other person and cannot. The "cannot" usually refers to the id.[5] His wanting to cooperate, wanting to yield material, is referred to as identification, and you talk about this as the rôle of the superego that an analyst assumes. You may talk about the person who does or does not want to cooperate as the ego. It is hard to make this threefold rôle clear without a lengthy discussion. It is important, however, to realize that in any conversation we carry on such a threefold rôle, first calculating our own and second our partner's stand, and third by our being determined in these calculations by our own unconscious stand. Peculiarly enough, we find many triads of concepts, trichotomies, in the psychoanalytic theory.

Let me give another trichotomy which may be only an analogy or may be something more. Consider for a moment the situation of an artist, a sculptor, when he is trying to carve something out of marble. I take this example not because the situation is similar in aim or content to the psychoanalytic constellation, but rather because its pattern resembles a pattern which we encounter in the method of "interpersonal relationship." If an artist is carving a statue, there are three factors present in the situation. Let us first of all consider the marble. As you know, marble is a material which has veins, and you cannot cut marble just any old way. You have to go with those veins, and any arbitrary effort to cut a stone just the way you want it must lead to disaster, that is, the chips will fall in a way that you don't want them to fall, and you won't get your form. You can't do violence to marble. Not only is marble a hard material which resists, but its resistance is not amorphous: it follows certain rules of structure. These structural laws of the marble, then, are the first factor present in the situation. The second factor is given in the man who makes the statue: there is the degree to which he knows the rules of the marble and how to handle his chisel. The third factor is given in the creative imagination of the artist in general and in the specific dream that the artist is about to put into marble in particular. These three factors were very finely integrated in the great sculptor, Rodin. Rodin's Nymph is a statue in which the figure really emerges out of the marble background as if it had always been there and the sculptor had only to brush away the marble covering it with his hand to bring it to light. It was all there in the crude marble when it was brought to his atelier. It may sound as if I am driving this comparison and play with ideas too far, but please note that a trichotomy is given in the very encounter of the human being with raw material, and even more so is it given in the encounter of two human beings.

Is there any empirical necessity for assuming any trichotomies in psychic functioning, or are these trichotomies merely direct consequences of the clinical setup and the psychoanalytic constellation in which our investigation takes place? I have not gone so far as to be able to demonstrate that

[5] If the reference is made not to the "censor" but to the unconscious id contents.

these trichotomies are due merely to the method of investigation. Note that, besides the ego-id-superego, similar triads are set up concerning instincts—instincts have an origin, an object, and an aim—and this triad also appears to follow the pattern of "interpersonal relationship." It comes from somewhere which is unknown to consciousness (origin), goes somewhere (object), and has an aim which can be referable to the conscious aims of the person who experiences the conscious derivatives of these instincts. Couldn't the triad of qualities of experiencing—conscious, preconscious, and unconscious—also be referable to the same basic constellation? Couldn't the threefold meanings of any dream—childhood, actual life situation, and transference meaning—also be referable to the situation determined by the method of investigation itself? By no means do I maintain that the analogies I have described here can claim any stringency of the type I urged when talking about the five mainstays of the psychoanalytic theory that result from adopting the clinical method. Nevertheless, throughout the structure of the psychoanalytic theory triads of concepts seem to crop up with a kind of "inevitability." I do not believe that this discussion of the problem of triads has even scratched the surface of the issue; it has merely pointed out an intriguing and unsolved problem. It is not my job nor within my abilities to solve this problem properly, but I feel that the very fact of talking about the psychoanalytic constellation obliges one to try to draw attention to the fact that there appears to be within this "constellation" itself a triadic structure which may have more to do with the triadic concepts of psychoanalysis than meets the eye. The fact that a triadic theoretical structure crops up again and again does not have to imply that the theory formation is wrong. Just as in my former illustration, calling someone in anger a son of a bitch does not mean that he is not one just because it is discovered that he was called one in anger. He may well be a son of a bitch, though my calling him one without having established the fact does not make him a son of a bitch. Similarly, the triads of concepts in psychoanalytic theory may be a direct consequence of the method of "interpersonal relationship," and still may be "good" theory adequately representing the interrelationships of the phenomena in question.

LECTURE NO. 5

I would like to turn now to the question left open in our last discussion. What does it mean to carry the "method of interpersonal relationship" to its last consequences? To obtain any answer to that question, I believe that we once more have to focus our attention upon the interpersonal relationship that is present in two people's contact. In the psychoanalytic constellation this is the analyst's and the analysand's contact. In this constellation the give-and-take is relatively vivid. I don't mean a situation which has deteriorated to the analyst's telling the analysand that "then I went to Harvard," or one which has deteriorated into an uninterrupted flow of stuff from the patient, which can be reciting Milton's "Paradise Lost" where the analyst doesn't see any place to pitch in, or a steady repetition of one motif which when interrupted just produces the same thing again. These are the two extremes into which the "method of interpersonal relationship" may deteriorate. If the "method of interpersonal relationship" is carried to its last consequences, it will never be satisfied with these deteriorative forms.[6] That is to say, these forms do not imply "carrying to the last consequences" because something isn't carried to its last consequences if it deteriorates in the beginning. A child born dead doesn't have a life history. Let me make the point more concrete. If someone listens to a patient for an hour and then preaches to him for four hours, he uses a clinical method and certainly creates an interpersonal relationship, and there is necessarily some give-and-take present; but this certainly isn't carried to its last consequences. On the other hand, if you let a person talk as is done in the Catholic confession, that is a clinical method, too, but it is not a carrying of the "interpersonal relationship" to its last consequences. The extremes of the forms this method can take are thus staked out. The method in its full form implies a relatively free give-and-take. It is obvious that this free give-and-take in the "method of interpersonal relationship" is identical in its form of appearance with conversation. It is not identical, though, with a deteriorated conversation in which both sides say something about the weather, not with a "conversation" which consists of somebody's lecturing, not with one where somebody is undergoing an examination. It is not to these deteriorated forms of conversation, but to conversation at its best, that the "method of interpersonal relationship" is here compared, though the deteriorated forms of both show some striking parallels.

Let us consider, then, the nature of conversation. I have heard it said that if you meet an old friend from your school days you immediately revert to the same old form of contact you had with him, and talk as you talked in the old days. From my own experiences, it seems to me that in only a few instances when I have met someone 10 or 15 years afterwards was I able to recapture the old contact altogether, not to speak of the fact that it never occurred instantly. Maybe I am merely describing a personal difficulty of my own here; but analyzing the conditions under which recapturing such a relationship occurs will be something independent of a personal difficulty and will yield some information of more than personal validity.

---

[6] It will be obvious that psychotherapy in its usual form, Coué's autosuggestive method, DuBois's method of "persuasion," as well as hypnosis operating with direct therapeutic suggestions should be considered "deteriorative forms" only from the point of view of the "method of interpersonal relationship"—which does not vitiate the possibility of their usefulness as independent methods. Whether hypnoanalysis is or is not a procedure which can carry the "method of interpersonal relationship" to its last consequences remains to be proved. [There is some evidence that if the attempt is made, there are important repercussions on hypnotizability—Ed.]

What finally happened was always that both of us demonstrated that a number of "common premises" had survived in some way or other over the period during which we were parted. A demonstration of such "common premises" had to be present before real conversation could be reinstated. What does the idea of "common premises" mean? I would say that in a very superficial way it means that you can trust the other person and the other person can trust you; it means the showing of having something which is good enough and extensive enough so that whatever has happened in those 10 or 15 years, whatever horrible thing you have done, you can still be accepted by the other by virtue of those so-called common premises. One cannot talk to another person without reservations, one cannot build a "conversation"—in the specific meaning of the word—if one is not sure that the other person will accept one in spite of all that an unrestrained and sincere exchange would lead to. This is a basic problem in everyday conversation: if you cannot communicate whatever you come to without the fear of losing the other person's acceptance of you, either you become insincere and lose it anyway, or you have to exclude certain fields from your conversation; and when you start excluding one field, another soon gets excluded, and then a third, and finally what remains is the weather. Surely you don't expect me to tell you that this is a rigid dividing line, that either there is a conversation or there is not. There are transitional forms; but conversation in its last consequences appears to follow the pattern I have tried to describe. It is no accident that the analysts who have written on the psychoanalytic method—H. Hartmann, I. Hermann, and S. Bernfeld—all stress that the specific prerequisite of the psychoanalytic constellation is a "mood of confidence," a special mood that belongs to it. This is Hermann's term; the others used different terms, but I think this term expresses their meaning too. A mood of confidence is present, it underlies even the sharpest phases of resistance, and is broken only when the patient leaves the psychoanalytic constellation.

It may seem that I have left the original problem I started out to tackle, the problem of what it means to carry the "method of interpersonal relationship" to its last consequences. We saw what it means to carry conversation to its last consequences, at least we saw a part of it. Let me add one more part. Let us suppose that a person is proud. When you have a conversation with that person, at what moment will he be ready to discuss matters which may cut into his pride? Only when he knows that he has at least as good a defense in you of what he defends with his pride as he has in himself. Thus, if you can demonstrate such basic premises which guarantee to the other person that you will not reject him, then he can give up his own defending of himself and as a consequence the field of conversation enlarges. Bernfeld would represent these issues by speaking about secrets; he would speak about resistance to giving up a secret and about confession as the result of the removal of the resistance. You don't need to couch them in terms of repression-resistance-interpretation-understanding-meaning; these are analogous representations of the same issue.

What does it mean, then, to carry the method of interpersonal relationship to its last consequences? It doesn't mean anything more, I believe, than carrying conversation to its last consequences, but in order to demonstrate that more clearly I would like to talk about something quite unrelated for a moment. When we discuss the question of the psychoanalytic constellation, we have to warn ourselves of a difficulty that I mentioned once previously. This difficulty is the temptation to mix up terms denoting empirical observations with those denoting theoretical constructs. Note that, e.g., transference and resistance are not empirical observations, though transference and resistance are terms which you can apply to describe empirical observations. The fact is, however, that the terms transference and resistance in psychoanalytic theory are not designed to describe empirical observations; they are concepts, which condense a set of dynamic variations of phenomena into a theoretical construction. We nevertheless use the phrase, "the patient showed resistance today," referring to a phenomenon. In the present context I shall use these terms as explanatory constructs and not as descriptive terms, e.g., the term resistance will refer to a mechanism which will be considered explanatory of any phenomena which it is advisable to treat in terms of resistance.

Returning to the question I have repeated again and again, What does it mean to carry the method of interpersonal relationship to its last consequences? It means that the person who handles the relationship, in our case the analyst, takes responsibility for attempting to eliminate "any and all" obstacles that are present in the interpersonal relationship, and does not stop short of eliminating any whose elimination seems necessary. How does this differ from the techniques which do not carry the interpersonal relationship to the last consequences? If and when the interpersonal relationship refers merely to and takes responsibility merely for one segment of the person's problem (either one symptom or one syndrome or the "neurosis"), and is not ready to concern itself if necessary with the character problem which underlies any of these, it remains short of carrying the method to its last consequences. We must realize that this destination just arrived at looks very arbitrary. The phrase "if necessary" seems to indicate this arbitrariness, yet "carrying the method to its last consequences" implies just this open-door attitude: to go from the symptom to the dynamics of a neurosis, from these dynamics to their root in the character problem—if necessary. So I would refuse to give any definition further than saying that to carry the method of interpersonal relationship to its last consequences means to keep the door open, by means of the method of interpersonal relationship, to the roots of the disturbance in question or the phenomena in question, to wherever these roots lead. It will be obvious that what usually happens in psychiatric practice does not leave these doors open. Now you could ask about Horney's method, Does it carry the interpersonal relationship to its last consequences? And you would note that there the consequences to which the method is carried are the problems of anxiety or aggression. There is a certain point where they stop short, and no effort is made to go further. This is, however, merely a superficial illustration of the point in question, without doing justice to the complexity of the problem connected with Horney's method.

[In the clinical situation, psychoanalytic or otherwise, two people are involved. More important, there is somebody who communicates, something that is communicated, and somebody to whom it is communicated. That is true for any clinical constellation, but there is one feature in which the psychoanalytic constellation differs radically from all the other clinical situations. What it is becomes clearer if one reformulates that threefold link between communicator, subject matter of communication, and to whom the communication is directed, as follows: something which urges for expression, what is being expressed, and to whom it is expressed. If you formulate it that way you very soon discover that the first problem is, why isn't it always expressed, why isn't it always communicated? If you raise that question, it quickly becomes clear that the purpose of the psychoanalytic situation is to discover why it isn't communicated, or why it cannot be communicated, and to eliminate the obstacle and make it communicable; once that is seen, then the radical difference between all the other clinical methods and the psychoanalytic method becomes very clear. If you place the emphasis on companionship in a therapy, two people being together, then you are not interested in what techniques have to be used in order to advance the communication; you are not even interested that there be any communication. It is left up to the patient whether he cares or does not care to communicate. You rely on the being together of the two people to do something for the patient. In suppressive psychotherapy—I am using terms only for purposes of illustration—and in many others, you are not involved in the question of what are the obstacles to communication and how are they to be eliminated. But that question is one of the fundamental and specific implications of the psychoanalytic method. What is the history of this formulation? Under hypnosis people suddenly could tell what ailed them with a resulting catharsis and relief from the symptom. Freud set out to find another method in which in a so-called rational way the same effect could be achieved and in which what hypnosis eliminates as an obstacle—I am giving history, not my opinion—can be systematically lifted step by step. This is the fundamental difference between a clinical situation in general and the psychoanalytic constellation. The method is aimed at discovering and eliminating the obstacles to communication. By communication, I don't mean verbal communication alone, I also mean all that goes with it, affective communication, etc. Something more could probably be derived if we knew how to talk about affect communication. I do not intend to leave it out, but

I can't get specific because I don't know how. If I knew how to make something specific out of the affective, I would, and it would be a gain.

A closely related issue is the problem of nonverbal communication. We have talked about communication in general and have not distinguished between verbal and nonverbal communication. I could be nasty and say you thought I was talking about verbal communication because we are accustomed to think about that and don't know how to talk about nonverbal communication. I don't mean to imply that gesture or related phenomena do not belong in the psychic continuity. You will find a number of discussions of such things as a patient pulling down her skirt or a patient blushing, and if you search the literature for a theoretical discussion of what the system of relationships there is, you will find that we don't have a good system of relationships. The problem of expressive movements in general we deal with intuitively. We don't have theoretical assumptions for what their meaning is.

I would say about nonverbal communication that you have to work it through the verbal communication until it becomes a real experience. Just what do we mean by that? We all know what we mean, but do we know how to talk about it? I don't. We don't know how, theoretically, to fit nonverbal communication into the psychological continuity, but when we see an isolated symptom we know what has happened. I don't say that such communication doesn't belong to psychological continuity. I am saying that the theory by which we should encompass it by postulates is not clear.

Once you talk about obstacles to communication you imply conflict. Conflict is implied from the method. And I talked not about communication in words—obstacles to verbal communication—but about obstacles in the way of any communication. If I could be specific and distinguish among affect communication, verbal communication, and nonverbal communication, I would be very much happier than I am about it. I don't know what to make of it.

In this respect, then, the psychoanalytic method differs radically from the clinical method in general. I don't know any stringent and scientific expression for what I am trying to say. It seems that by driving the method of interpersonal relationship, the three-linked chain, to its last consequences, by not relenting in the effort to eliminate the obstacles to communication, the psychoanalytic method differs from the clinical method in general.]

There is another aspect of this method of interpersonal relationship on which I want to focus for a moment, in the hope that it will give us added understanding of the method. The two people who are present in the psychoanalytic situation each appear in the world of the other: the analysand exists for the analyst as a part of the analyst's own world, and the analyst exists for the analysand as a part of the analysand's world. The same considerations are valid as those connected with the "chair." That is to say, for the purposes of our discussion, the problem of an "objective existence" has to be discounted as meaningless. For our investigation, the "existence" of the analyst is meaningful merely in terms of the world of the analysand, and the existence of the analysand is meaningful merely in terms of the world of the analyst. Even if the analyst makes efforts to see the place of the patient in the patient's own world, this "own world" of the patient's is a world that the analyst conceives of in terms of his own world.

One of the consequences of this state of affairs for the technique of psychoanalysis is the problem of whether or not patients should be analyzed by analysts who have backgrounds of a similar general nature. These are, however, problems of psychoanalytic technique, of method more than of methodology. I am mentioning them to give an example which will help to delimit the field of methodological investigation from others as much as possible.

What are the consequences of the just discussed feature of the psychoanalytic constellation ("method of interpersonal relationship") for psychoanalytic theory? This is the methodological problem here. The concepts of transference, resistance, identification, and more specifically those of father-, mother-, brother-, and sister-transference, are direct consequences of the just discussed implications of the method.

At this point one might ask, isn't there transference and identification in everyday life? And one would have to answer, surely there are transference phenomena, that is to say, there are different kinds of phenomena that look analogous to transference. But transference as defined here is not a phenomenon; it is a theoretical explanatory construct issuing from the method of interpersonal relationship, adopted and employed by psychoanalytic theory. In this method each of the two people who are sitting together assumes, by virtue of existing in the other's world, properties of the other's world and attributes properties of his own world to the other person, e.g., if the properties for a big looming figure in the analysand's world are father properties, the analyst can have only those properties in the eyes (in the world) of the analysand. All the consequences of this situation are attributed to the mechanism which is referred to by the theoretical construct of "transference" and/or by the one called "identification," whatever kind of identification it may be. And because these are mechanisms inferred from the "psychoanalytic constellation" and not phenomena, one has to be very cautious in drawing any conclusions to be considered more than analogies concerning phenomena of everyday life which are similar to the phenomena explained in the psychoanalytic constellation by the construct "transference." [7]

---

[7] The importance of "appearing and existing in the world of the other" is quite different in everyday life and in the psychoanalytic situation. In everyday life we operate as if we all were in a world that is objectively existing and common to us. But the more consistently the "method of interpersonal relationship" is carried to its last consequences, the more the private world of the individual becomes accepted, and the further away we get from the significance of the objectively existing world.

Two methodological conclusions then are dealt with here. One concerns the nature of "transference" and its source in the method adopted; the other is the distinction between transference as a mechanism and transference phenomena as encountered in the psychoanalytic treatment and its analogies encountered in everyday life. At this point the concept of "projection," which I discussed in relation to the general clinical method, takes on a different character. It appears in the form of "identification." The person of the analyst appearing in the world of the analysand is identified with other people from his earlier life, or with himself, and the propensities of these people are projected upon him.[8]

Thus at this point we have a set of new concepts issuing from the specific character of the method of "interpersonal relationship" adopted by psychoanalysis. Let us look, however, at another aspect of the method to gain further information concerning the consequences of the "psychoanalytic constellation." Between the two people who are together in the constellation there is a continuous exchange to which, in so far as the analysand is concerned, you can apply the basic postulate of psychic continuity. Applying that postulate, we must conclude that whatever material the analysand offers, there must be behind it, underlying it, unrevealed links which make for the continuousness of the apparently discontinuous. These underlying links are of two kinds. First, there is *how* he prevents himself from communicating; second, there is *what* he prevents himself from communicating. The former is the defenses he offers, the latter is the unconscious material. One could trace this further, and demonstrate that the distinction between the material which one prevents oneself from communicating and the methods by which one prevents oneself from communicating is forced upon us by the method of "interpersonal relationship." Thus, we see again in the method adopted the reasons for the formation of theory, and as long as one wants to go through with this method to the last consequences one cannot get away from this form of theory, from the distinction discussed here, either. Horney really was the one who, possibly somewhat earlier than Anna Freud, pushed the investigation of defense mechanisms to the fore, justifiably so, because the psychoanalytic method allows and obliges the analyst to investigate both the unconscious material the patient prevents himself from communicating and the defense mechanisms by which he chooses to prevent, or to get by without such communication.[9]

[8] This concept of "projection" is still not identical with the one commonly used in psychoanalytic parlance, but is nearer to it than the "projection" concept discussed in connection with the perception of a chair. I shall later come to the discussion of the concept of projection proper.

[9] [By 1948 Rapaport had some second thoughts about the psychoanalytic situation as an interpersonal relationship and a "group of two," saying:

"I discussed the issue of 'the group of two' in great detail in the six lectures I gave in 1944. I would not now deal with it with the arguments I dealt with it in 1944 because I now have many more doubts about what I think about it than I did at that time"; and "How far psychoanalytic theory is or is not a theory of interpersonal

[I would like to call attention to the fact that the concepts which we call defenses are all derived from the conceptual scheme in which the center is

---

relationships is a question. I don't say that it is not at all one, but how far is a very ticklish question. If you think through the implications of such an issue as the postulate of continuity, I am sure you will find that there is where the dog is buried." He amplified these thoughts as follows:

"If I investigate the relationship of two people, an interpersonal relationship, with a certain method, it is quite possible that the method that I adopt will tell me nothing about the interpersonal relationship. Or it may tell me only something about it. For instance, when the psychoanalytic method investigates an interpersonal relationship different from the one between analyst and analysand, it may come out learning about the relationship of one person to his image of the other person and then learn about the other person's relationship to his image of the one person, and nothing, or hardly anything, about the interpersonal interaction. That is, by the way, a point that Sullivan drove so hard with little success, but the point seems to be an important one, a good one."

"Here is the patient and here is the analyst, and the injunction is that there is a psychological continuity. The patient is told that if he talks he will find out what the meaning of his symptom is, he will get to what ails him. The patient is supposed to subsume everything that occurs to him into this continuity, including the analyst. The concept transference is again a direct derivative of the method; the specific form it takes we have to establish by empirical investigation. But the fact that the analyst is to be a part of the psychological continuity is demanded of the patient to begin with. It is clear that when you tell the patient that everything he will think forms a continuity that means that what he says to the analyst or thinks about him belongs to the continuity. Let's not talk about an analyst, let's talk about a chair. There is the chair. You perceive it, you see it, that conception is part of the psychological continuity, has to conform with it. You know about the chair only in so far as it is in the psychological continuity. It does not have a meaning for you as long as you assume it is something outside and in that respect the concept of continuity does two things. It destroys your naïve awareness that there is an outside world obviously existing. The chair is a different chair for one sitting on it, one who looks at it, because it is integrated into that psychological continuity which is the patient's world. We all have a private world in which every object of the so-called reality has a specific meaning with which it is or becomes a part of our psychological continuity. In other words, the silent implications for psychoanalytic theory of the injunction 'tell me all and we will get to the root of this matter' is that all objects of the outside world—animate, inanimate, human, inhuman objects—are for the individual just figures in his dream, as in *Alice in Wonderland,* where they say 'Don't wake her up because we are all in her dream and if you wake her up we will all disappear.' If one wanted to be very exact one would say that this is one of the epistemological implications of psychoanalytic theory. In general, one would also say that it is a solipsistic implication; but I don't want to discuss that question. The chair therefore is fitted into this psychological continuity and has its existence for that person in that sense. The analyst has his meaning also only in that psychological continuity. Quite apart from what he is in reality, he means what is transferred upon him of the affects, feelings, images, etc., of the person whom he is analyzing.

"But—to turn more directly to the interpersonal issue—the other principle of the conceptual structure of psychoanalysis is that this bipolarity of the situation—patient and doctor—is also a basis for conceptualization. A contradiction grows out of it which is difficult to bridge. The contradiction is that this bipolarity is not a real bipolarity because the analyst is a part of the continuum. It is a difficult situation which leads to many complexities"—Ed.]

difficulties of communication. While the other concepts we have discussed so far were all derived quite independent of the analyst out of the psychological continuity, the concept of defense is derived from the conceptual scheme me and him, analyst and patient. One of the difficulties of integrating ego psychology and id psychology is based on these two different points of departure for forming concepts. I know that I am not very lucid about this point. I would like to recapitulate once more: when we started out to discuss concepts, the five concepts I discussed were derived more or less out of psychological continuity, while the concept defense pertains to the difficulty of communication derived from this analyst-patient relationship. Consequently you have two points of departure for concepts. The concepts pertaining to the unconscious issue from a different feature of the method than those pertaining to defenses. I submit that the difficulties of our integration of ego psychology and id psychology are at least in part dependent upon this different source of forming concepts.

Let me turn to another issue relating to defense which will illustrate another distinction in the source of concepts—namely those deriving from methodological considerations and those deriving from the empirical subject matter of psychoanalysis. I have suggested that the concept of defense arises from difficulty of communication in an interpersonal situation. But it has been suggested in psychoanalytic theory and stressed by Anna Freud that defenses function against instinctual danger, prevent the psychic apparatus from being flooded by instinctual impulses, defend the ego against the id. From the point of view of the technique and the internal consistency of the theory formation, this is a logical conclusion. It is absolutely correct that as far as psychoanalytic theory is concerned, defense is against instinct. But it is a very different thing if you take the defense concept historically, go back to what Freud has to say about defenses in terms of resistance. Where you first hear about defense you see very clearly that it is derived out of the interpersonal situation. "He resists me." This does not contradict the view that defense is against instinct. These are two radically different points of view. When it is found out what relation this business or resistance and defenses has to the psychological apparatus, to the subject matter of this science, to the empirical material, these concepts have a very different place than when you ask what relation they have to the method. Methodology asks what is the relationship of a concept to the technique, to the methods used. The relationship of defenses to the methods used is that in the method used it is communication and the difficulty of communication from which these concepts are derived; but as far as the psychic apparatus is concerned, these defenses are defenses against instinct. The distinction is between what issues out of the method and what issues out of the empirical data of the subject matter. If one centers upon the psychic apparatus, centers on the psychoanalytic theory which describes how the psyche works and gives a set of rules about how to deal with it, one is not altogether naïve about the subject matter, but already implies some knowledge of it. Even though the method itself always has some reference to the subject matter, still you can divide pretty clearly the subject matter and its influence from what you shout into the empty room, that is, the method. From the latter point of view, the defenses originate from the issue of difficulty of communication. When you look upon the matter from the point of view of the furnishings of the room, then you have to formulate it in terms of defense against instinct. When it is empirical material you are dealing with, that is no longer the concern of methodology. The first thing methodology asks is: What is a consequence of a method of observation for the theory without the subject matter having much to say about it? I admit that a few assumptions concerning the subject matter always creep in, but in this series of lectures I am trying to show how little one has to assume concerning the subject matter to derive certain basic psychoanalytic concepts. I am also trying to indicate where the specificity of a concept is not derived from a method alone but is somehow a result of the mating of the method and the empirical material.

You could ask, "Why do we need methodology when it can't get to some important, fundamental psychoanalytic consideration?" My answer would be this. You can see very clearly that this methodological consideration indicates that if you are using the psychoanalytic method then you are centering upon difficulties of communication. Other methods which don't dwell on those difficulties of communication are not psychoanalytic methods. Once your method eliminates that, there is no way to talk about defenses, no way to get to them empirically. If a counseling method starts to talk about defenses it will be dealing in stolen goods, because there is no way to get to these concepts without a method which dwells on difficulties of communication.]

In a method of interpersonal relationship, efforts to get away from dealing with either the content material or the method chosen to avoid communicating it result in methods which do not carry the method of "interpersonal relationship" to its last consequences.

May I make an aside and call your attention to an intriguing possibility here for investigating why defense mechanisms were explored and brought into the literature later than was the content material. I am sure you will see these possibilities without my dwelling on them.

I would like to turn to another aspect of this "interpersonal relationship," one which appears quite different from the three aspects I have already described. We are dealing here with a method of "interpersonal relationship," the next of kin of which is conversation. One of the prime postulates underlying it is that of psychic continuity. Doesn't it necessarily follow that such a method, if it wants to find the material with which the gaps in continuity can be filled in, will turn to those materials which in "conversation" are usually the avoided ones, the gaps? Isn't it of necessity that it will start to think about what the kinds of topics are that do not come up in conversation, what are those aspects of life that are not brought into usual conversation? You will remember that in discussing the clinical method I pointed out that the concept of instinct is an inevitable consequence of the clinical method itself. What kind of instinct we have to adopt as an explanatory concept, however, is not determined by adopting the clinical method. But if we adopt the method of interpersonal relationship together with the postulate of psychic continuity, we will immediately be obliged to look for those topics which are usually not present in conversation, and adopt instincts as explanatory concepts; the ideational derivatives are referable to the topics around which conversation usually becomes discontinuous. These are, obviously, sex and aggression.

Note that this reasoning is very similar to the reasoning we followed concerning the method of dream interpretation and free association: to them, where the "continuity" was to all appearances absent, did we turn to find the material which would make for the continuity of the *apparently* continuous conscious thought process. You will remember our discussing that if we adopted the method of investigating reflexes, conditioned and unconditioned reflexes, instead of a clinical method, we would not come to the postulate of psychic continuity. I would like to make another such thought experiment, of seeing whether in another type of psychology we would necessarily have to consider the kind of thing which is hush-hush in everyday conversation to be the derivative of the instincts which are to be adopted as the explanatory dynamic principles of psychic life. Let us suppose it were not "conversation" or the "method of interpersonal relationship" with which we started out, but a biological method. In such a case, all the functions of the psyche would be attributed to the brain, and to explain not yet understood psychic functions we would turn to not yet explored biological functions of the brain. This really is happening. When no gross anomalies of the brain were found to explain mental disorder, physiologists turned to brain metabolism at large, then to anoxia, anoxemia, and finally to oxygen potentials. A similar process occurred in relation to the electrical propensities of brain functioning. The tendency is always to go into what is not yet known, in a sense into the "hush-hush," but it can be "hush-hush" in any field. If we started out with a biological interpretation, we would certainly not get to an instinct theory in which the derivatives of the instincts are the "hush-hush" material of everyday conversation. Again this may all sound very farfetched, but it should demonstrate the fact that by taking your method as it is, you define your concepts, and by following these up you see at least some of the specific requirements for the instinct you are to adopt. It should be such that its derivatives are the greatest "taboos" in life. Obviously the continuity of psychic existence itself compels you to go to the tabooed material and it specifies what was not specified in the clinical method, which demanded only adopting instinct as an explanatory construct.

If we observe all this, then we will gain an inkling of why psychoanalytic psychiatry has had a delayed development full of difficulties. As soon as you get to the psychoses the method of "interpersonal relationship" encounters difficulties; it becomes difficult to apply because of the condition of the patient. Where the method doesn't fully apply, the explanatory concepts dependent on it cannot be expected to be easily applicable either.

LECTURE NO. 6

I have discussed that there seem to be three methods specific to psychoanalysis: (1) the "psychoanalytic constellation" itself, (2) the method of free association, and (3) the method of dream interpretation. There are two more things about the psychoanalytic constellation that I think should be briefly discussed. One of them pertains to the defense mechanisms of the ego, and the other to the concept of overdetermination.

The analogy with conversation made it relatively clear, I hope, that there are two different materials that are not part of the apparent continuity of the psychological processes taking place in the "interpersonal relationship," and these are, first, the preconscious content the patient attempts to prevent himself from communicating and, second, the methods by which he prevents himself from communicating. These methods, which are usually referred to in psychoanalysis as "defense mechanisms," follow the same kinds of patterns that could very easily be shown to be present in everyday conversation. An example of this is the manner in which, in everyday conversation, we usually give the idea itself without communicating our essential affects about it, the way a painful topic is split into parts and interspersed in the conversation so that only the skillful converser or an FBI man could tell what the real feeling is. I don't think it would be useful to draw further parallels, because by doing so we would be tempted to stretch an analogy too far. The one defense mechanism which I would like to discuss further is projection. You remember that I considered the percept of a chair as something like a projection because the postulate of psychic continuity demands that whatever the source of the percept is, it conform to the psychological setting of the perceiver. Thus, it is not the chair existing in the outer world but the impression that it makes on us that we refer to as "chair." The percept of the chair is dependent on the place it has in the psychic continuity of every single individual perceiving it; thus, the "chair" bears marks of this "continuum" which are, so to speak, projected upon it. Later on we came to see another form of "projection" when we discussed the analyst's existence solely in the analysand's world and there we realized that this "big looming" person in the analysand's world has to take on those properties which belong to a "big looming" person in the world of the analysand, whether those be the properties of the father figure, mother figure, etc. Note that in these cases, with the chair and with the analyst who is in the "interpersonal relationship," the place they (namely, the chair, the analyst, etc.) take in the perceiver's world is in a sense determined by the set of properties which is being transferred, with all the affective and emotional connotations, onto the percept in the process of its being "fitted" into the psychic continuity of the perceiver.

[Let me discuss the second kind of projection in other words. There are certain people toward whom we assume a very peculiar attitude, as if what they say has to be true, what they express must be benevolence. To others we act as though what they say must be bad, as though they exude malevolence. You find it even more peculiar when you see that person whom you consider someone whose dictum has to be taken in relation to another person to whom he takes a submissive attitude, or takes a child's rôle. Then you feel either like a grandchild and happy, or you don't want to be a grandchild to that person and are unhappy.

As before, the dinner-table analyst's dicta can tell us something. When we say, isn't he a magnificent, nice, kind man, our dinner-table analyst will say either "You have developed quite a transference to him," or "Good God, you are projecting, that's the worst son of a bitch I ever met." It is a naughty habit, but it is being done all the time. What is the meaning of it? The meaning is that in a very peculiar way we are prone to do not only what I described earlier as the first kind of projection—namely that when I am in a good mood, everything looks good, or as the old-time analyst put it, I make my hat conform to myself—but I do a less wholesale thing too. I take people and make them conform to a certain pattern for myself. It is something more specific, because not everything is seen as good. Furthermore, it doesn't vary readily with time, but has a relatively great stability. But this stability holds only for a particular area of one's life, and there may be great variations from one area to another. William James knew that and was therefore very much inclined to disclaim the existence of any kind of fixed personality. He said, "I have a dinner-table personality; I have a study personality; I have a personality for my children; another for my wife." It was not so crazy as it sounds, because people relate to us in exactly this way, and since we aim to please—all of us aim to please part of the time— we do have this kind of variation. Let us forget for the moment the question of how we comply with what people do to us, because that is not important in this connection. What is important in this kind of projection is that a certain very specific set of attributes is given to another person. It happens not only in the psychoanalytic situation but in everyday life too. Some time ago people disposed of this kind of projection by saying "He just doesn't know people." But we have learned to recognize such behavior as not a misjudgment but as a peculiar kind of thing which our literature calls projection. It was learned from the psychoanalytic situation, in which two people were sitting together and it was noticed that one person plays out on the other the relationships he had with people, that he attributes to that other person all kinds of attributes of people from the past. It is the same story in this respect as Freud described in regard to the psychopathology of everyday life. Whereas the phenomena he dealt with were earlier considered just incidental mistakes, he discovered and described their causal relationships for the first time.

This second kind of projection presupposes the fundamental insight into the existence of communication between two people in which the communication channels open are those which allow the playing out on this other person—the therapist—of attitudes previously held toward people. It is a different level of method. It is not merely the method of psychiatry, "Tell me something; it will be all right"; it is "Tell me something and then through your telling and action it will become clear what relationships you will develop to me because they are the relationships you were able to have to people in the past."]

Note how different the situation is if the "projection" dealt with is "projection" conceived as a defense mechanism. What takes place in "projective" defense, unlike perceptive and identifying projection, is not the transfer of a full set of attitudes, but a very different procedure. Let us remind ourselves of the simplest formula of paranoid projection: "I don't love him. I hate him. Because he hates me." Here the hate against the disappointing love object is projected upon the love object; an affective attitude is transferred from the paranoid person's self onto one figure of his *own* world.[10] In other words, as long as the unconscious material that the subject prevents himself from communicating is "projected," its full contents are thrown upon, projected upon, the figures, chair, analyst, of the subject's world; while in the procedure of preventing himself from communicating (defense mechanism), an affect or a set of affects is transferred, "projected" from the self onto part of the subject's world. In this case it is not a matter of letting someone who is a part of your world have the properties of an imago; it is rather attributing something which belongs to your self to a part of your world other than the self.[11] Thus, the final concept of "projection" (that of "projection" as a defense mechanism) is arrived at only if we search for how a person by "projection" prevents himself from seeing and communicating latent contents. The difference is principally between the two conceptions of projection. If it is a parent image that I see in some people and I behave accordingly, then the discovering of that parent image as the governor of my behavior is the task of the analyst, is a search for content material. That content material was never the self's own property, it

[10] It should be kept in mind that the person who is made a persecutor by the projection exists for the paranoid person in *his* world.
[11] For the psychoanalyst (and for that matter, for the gestalt and topological psychologist also) the world of the individual is an intrapsychic world in which all the objects have their existence; the person's self has just as much a place in this world as the other objects.

was the property of certain objects in his world. But his affect "I hate him" is the self's property. The discovery of the origin of the affect connected with the experience "he persecutes me" is not a search for an unconscious content, but rather a search for the method by which he prevents himself from seeing and communicating that "I don't love him, I hate him" which in turn is the "denial" (another defense mechanism) of the content "I love him."

[The third projection is thus understandable on another level of method entirely. I have already dwelt on the question of the fundamental difference between the clinical and psychoanalytic method and tried to characterize the psychoanalytic method as centering on obstacles of communication and attempting to circumvent and lift them. When you center on these you are at the psychoanalytic method proper, and that is the very point at which the defense mechanisms come in. In this kind of projection, what is being implied is "I am not communicating; I am not telling what I feel, not even by denying or reversing. I am only telling you what I see in the other; it is the other who hates me." What I feel is not communicable even by reaction formation but only by experiencing it as an outside happening: "I observe that they hate me." It is on the third level of method that this becomes palpable to us.

In our work and literature we use the term "projection" pretty crudely and indiscriminately. Analysis of the method shows us that there are at least three different concepts of projection, and once again reveals the value of methodological study. I want to emphasize the many transitions between the types of projection. I chose these three because they are quite distinct. In the first, the essential thing is that a person lives in a private world of his own in which everything bears the imprint of his world. More specifically than that, he has organizing principles which make the world appear the way it does to him. But, because interpersonal relationships are usually highly specific, these organizing principles have isolated, specific foci, namely, the people to whom he had important relationships, and these foci remain as archaic residues and do not influence the organization of his whole world. Even more specific archaic residues are those in which a specific striving and a corresponding affect become so isolated that they cannot be communicated at all, and have to be disowned and projected into the outside. In the first kind generalized organizing principles are externalized, in the second an identification figure is externalized, while in the third it is an impulse with its corresponding affect which is externalized.]

This is all the discussion of this problem our time allows. My purpose was to show how the concept of "projection" develops and changes its form of appearance in accordance with the method we are using. We followed the forms it took when merely the clinical method and its corollary, the postulate of psychic continuity, were presumed. We saw its character when, beyond the "clinical method," the method of "interpersonal relationship" was also postulated, and finally, we saw it in its full form when in the latter method the differentiation between "material prevented from communication" and "method of preventing communication" was made.

There is another amendment to last week's discussion. The discussion concerned mostly the methods by which one prevents oneself from communication. The issue of overdetermination I want to discuss pertains more to the "content the communication of which is prevented." I will endeavor to show that the concept of overdetermination issues directly out of the fact that we use the method of interpersonal relationship as the method of investigation. Let us suppose that there was an experience in childhood which was psychologically determined and an integral part of the psychic continuity at that time, and that today it emerges again, as a memory or as a re-experiencing in the "analytic constellation." Its emergence in the analytic situation will be embedded in the psychic continuity of the "analytic constellation." Thus, this experience will be part of the psychic continuity of the subject in two different senses. The situation I am describing will be very clear to those of you who have worked with hypnosis and have seen such a thing as a person reliving and relating a childhood event of falling from a high chair, and saying, "I am falling; catch me, Doctor, catch me!" Here the emotional and actual experience is relived intertwined with the "interpersonal relationship" to the doctor existing here and now. The method used itself inevitably leads to it; as long as there is an interpersonal relationship and you use the clinical method of recovering the past, these methods imply that the past continuum of psychic events is made to re-emerge by the lever of the "interpersonal relationship." Overdetermination is not a magic coincidence of many motives; it is rather a direct consequence of the method of investigation used by psychoanalysis. If you say, "I use a clinical method," you already have a theory formation implying dual determination, though not necessarily overdetermination. Why? Because in all clinical methods events have two references—one being to some original childhood events, and the other to the meaning of the events in the context of the actual life situation. But since the psychoanalytic method carries the method of interpersonal relationship to its final consequences, in it events have not only these two meanings but also have reference to the transference relationship. All these three overlap again and again, and this is how the concept of overdetermination becomes indispensable in the theory.

[You have at least three different levels of continuity and on each of these levels there is, if you please to call it so, causality or determination. The picture you get is even more complicated if you realize another feature of the psychological continuum, namely one which we have not talked about here—the fact that we are ruled by two principles, a reality principle and a pleasure principle. The actions which we undertake, the solution which is made, are always such as to try either by compromise or by a lucky chance to fulfill both principles. It is a very long road to come from methodology to these two levels, but there again overdetermination becomes just as clear as on the three different levels of continuity. When you talk about overdetermination you are not talking about a psychological indeterminacy, but about something which is a direct consequence of our method of going at psychological events, because the meaning of an event is the psychological continuity into which it fits, and these continuities are always multiple. In other words, when you are faced with the question of what is prior, what is the main determinant, there is no answer. It is a question of which of these various levels of continuity now play such a rôle that the patient can be brought, without too much anxiety, to understand better the event under discussion. There is no primary determinant, and if somebody claims that the issue of reality is primary, surely that is not true; that is only one level of the continuity of meaning. There are several levels, and if you neglect them, so much the worse for you.] With this method of investigation, by the logic of the method itself, you cannot build any type of theory except one that implies overdetermination.

I will now turn to a brief discussion of the methods of free association and dreams. The question is, first of all, in what way was the theory formation of psychoanalysis influenced by the method of free association? I earlier proposed that while the adoption of a clinical method forced us to adopt a concept of unconscious as an explanatory construct, it left us free in determining the nature of the concept of "unconscious" we are to choose and in adopting the rules of unconscious processes. Adopting the method of free association, however, binds us, to a far-reaching degree, in respect to what kind of rules, what type of logic, there are in the unconscious. For example, if one idea follows another in a chain of free associations, the analyst will assume *post hoc ergo propter hoc* (after it thus because of it). I believe that this rule goes without an explanation. What is the justification for psychoanalysis taking such a stand? Perhaps the *propter* is somewhat too narrow a term, because frequently the causal relationship just referred to is reversed like this: "The cause of it, therefore after it." At any rate, if the method of free association is used in the hope that it will fill in the gaps of the apparently continuous but really discontinuous logical reasoning or thinking, the assumption of *post hoc ergo propter hoc* becomes indispensable. If free association as practiced shows that its material becomes meaningful by making such assumptions, we have the right to consider the rule *post hoc ergo propter hoc* as a part of the "logic of the unconscious." [12] Note that an analyst doesn't proceed arbitrarily in so reasoning; he merely proceeds on the assumption that the next idea emerging is in some kind of essential relation to the preceding one.

Let me turn to another example: Somebody brings a dream, or an idea

---

[12] These rules are usually referred to as the Freudian mechanisms, or the mechanisms of the primary process, in contradistinction to the secondary process, that is to say, the rules of logical thinking.

which burdens him, to his analytic hour, and the analyst asks him what is the most striking thing to him in that dream or idea, and the patient answers, "This is it," pointing out the part which strikes him the most. The analyst may say, "Never mind the rest; just tell me your associations to this one thing," and if the patient is surprised the analyst may explain, "This part accounts for the whole thing." Now this is a very exaggerated example, and frequently the most important and explanatory part of an idea or dream is the least obviously striking one. In any case, the analyst has adopted a *pars pro toto* (the part stands for the whole) logic. Thus, in the free-association chain, *post hoc ergo propter hoc* and *pars pro toto* are apparently rather general rules. Let us remind ourselves that these are the abhorrent examples our logic teachers gave us in school to show us how not to think. In the logic of free association, in the logic of the unconscious, they have as eminent a place as the rules of the syllogism have in ordered thinking. We might as well make up our minds that the exploration of the rules of free association gives some of the specific rules of the theoretical construct of the unconscious, which latter has been forced on us by the method we adopted. If we come to dreams, we will meet some more of these rules.

There is one more outstanding consequence of the "free-association method" that needs to be discussed. In psychoanalysis it not infrequently happens that at the end of the hour the analyst, who has been silent for the better part of the hour, declares: "Would you please note that you started with this, and despite many diversions came back to this again and again? You talked about one thing all the time, and what you said about it boils down to just about this." The analyst thus points out the fact that a chain of associations represented one single impulse. This is again a simplification, because usually several impulses interact in such a chain of associations. However, it must become clear from the nature of the chains of free associations, if analyzed properly, that psychoanalysis theoretically has to assume that any idea which comes into consciousness is pushed into it as a derivative or representation of strivings, impulses, drives, instincts. Otherwise, the method of free association and its use would be meaningless. If you adopt this method, you adopt with it the hypothesis that every idea coming into consciousness is a derivative, or in other words an ideational representative, of some instinctual force. This hypothesis is merely an implication of the method. Inevitable also will be the conclusion that even rational thought processes are in some way or other derivatives of similar sources. What gives them the apparent continuity and lets them abide by the rules of the secondary process looms as a large question, but there cannot be any doubt that by adopting the method you adopt the hypothesis that *all* thoughts are pushed into consciousness as representatives of some kind of impulse. It will be remembered that the postulate of instinct itself, in a nonspecific form, issued from the clinical method. But only here, on this point, do we learn that the specifically psychoanalytic method stipulates that the instincts to be adopted as explanatory constructs must be so conceived as to have ideational representations or derivatives in consciousness of the type discussed above.[13] It should also be noted that this consequence of the free-association method is the justification for the two basic rules of psychoanalysis, that is to say, the basic rule of frankness on the part of the patient and freely hovering attention on the part of the doctor.

There is, however, another point connected with free association that seems to me of such great significance that I have to devote some time to it. Let us take the impossible case, that Dr. G. and Dr. H. come in here five minutes apart and one reports that his patient had a dream about a horse, and the other also reports that his patient had a dream about a horse. We will be very much surprised by the coincidence. But let us go back to the problem of free association. Let us suppose that a stone is falling in front of me, and that I had a set of ideas going on when the stone went by, and the falling stone gets incorporated into the chain which goes on afterwards. The chain is remembered and repeated to an analyst. Let us suppose the analyst looks at what happened in the chain after the stone fell and tries to construct a *post hoc ergo propter hoc* explanation. That is permissible. But how about looking at what happened in the chain before the stone fell, and constructing a *post hoc ergo propter hoc* explanation for the stone falling from the preceding ideas of the subject? That is not permissible, because continuity is only psychic continuity, while the physical world is discontinuous. The fact is that any surprise about coincidence is usually a consequence of lack of scrutiny whether the coincidence is in a medium which is continuous or discontinuous. Let us suppose I left my key at home and it suddenly occurs to me that I left it at home; that is a physical happening, but it is in my psychic continuity. If a stone is falling, I am thinking what I please, but it is in my psychic continuity. Either I presume mind reading, or I have to stick to what is a cell of psychic continuity. I can read some minds; sometimes my unconscious can read them out of minute, consciously imperceptible signs. But all this kind of mind reading belongs to and complies with the rules of psychic continuity. If, however, coincidences occur in discontinuous cells, and one is forced to overstep the assumptions of continuity and assume the possibility of delving into the unknown by telepathy too, as for example, if someone reports that he had a dream and wrote the dream down, and that what was in the dream happened to him afterward, then one must ask oneself whether there isn't another rule besides the rule of psychic continuity. The hope of investigating telepathic phenomena by psychoanalytic technique is a vague dream for the time being, because psychoanalytic method implies the postulate of individual psy-

[13] [The rôle of instinct implied here would now be modified by the concepts of ego autonomy, both primary and secondary, as well as by considerations of the relation to reality—Ed.]

chic continuity without providing for the understanding of events that occur in noncontinuous cells, or that occur in cells of another type of continuity such as are presumed to occur in telepathy and in extrasensory perception.

About dreams and dream interpretation, I would like to make the following points: First, an additional set of rules of the unconscious is implied by our adopting the method of dream interpretation. Thus, for instance, in the dream ideas are represented visually, and if we consider dreams to be representations of happenings, inasmuch as happenings always involve space and time, we first of all get to the rules of space and time in the unconscious, which are not revealed by the free-association method. We thus learn that in the unconscious, as represented in the dream, "side by side" means "following in sequence," that apparently occurrence in sequence refers to causality. Then you get, apparently, to some kind of relationship like this: instead of causality, you have sequence of occurrence, instead of sequence in time you have coexistence in space, instead of space relationships you have plane relationships. This additional set of rules is imposed upon us by dream interpretation. A systematic further exploration would show that symbolism, displacement, condensation, etc., are also necessary theoretical corollaries of the method of dream interpretation.

One more comparative consideration will be in place. It appears that the rules of the unconscious imposed upon us by the free-association method are more easily accepted by psychiatrists than those imposed by dream interpretation. A question frequently raised concerning dreams is, Do we experience the dream in the moment that we awake, or does it go along in the nighttime? The question cannot be answered directly. For the majority of people one might say that the dream as it presents itself to them is the dream which is present when they awake. That is to say, the dream is all in the continuum of the so-called conscious process and has all the gaps that conscious processes imply. If looked at closely, dreams are also a part of the conscious thought process, but look more gappy, more inconsistent, than conscious processes in general. Then we take our hypothesis of psychic continuity and apply it to the dream, and it is thereby that we arrive at the basic hypothesis of dream interpretation. The applying of the continuity hypothesis says that what you get in a dream is only the manifest gappy content, and the latent dream thought is something different and still has to be figured out, by filling up the gaps of the manifest content. In that sense, one might say that the method of dream analysis is nothing but an extension and application of the postulate of psychic continuity, as practiced in any skillful conversation as well as in the free-association method. As a matter of fact, we learned these relations first from dream interpretation; the postulate of psychic continuity was first applied to dreams, yielding differing latent and manifest material. Later we learned that it can be applied to any kind of continuity in everyday thinking. There are three theoretical consequences of the method of interpretation of dreams: (1) I can slip over the very first and most commonplace point, that the method of dream interpretation assumes that a dream has to fulfill a wish because, in the theoretical structure of psychoanalysis, it plays the same rôle as the one just described about the impulses delivering ideas into consciousness in connection with the free-association method. (2) The method of dream interpretation demonstrates the relationship and meaning of "manifest" and "latent" in reference to the psychic continuity. (3) The method of dream interpretation reveals unconscious mechanisms to us.

What I wanted to point out to you in these lectures is that it appears that all the main theoretical constructs of psychoanalysis can be reasonably brought into a relatively direct connection with the methods adopted. Note, however, that not a word has been said here about the pleasure-pain principle, etc. It is my impression that in the coming about of these "principles" so many methods, so many features of the psychoanalytic method, interact that it would be very hard to trace any one of them to one single source. This is all I can sum up in this short hour.

REFERENCES

Freud, S. (1900). The Interpretation of Dreams, tr. A. A. Brill. *The Basic Writings*. New York: Modern Library, 1938, pp. 179–549.
———— (1901). The Psychopathology of Everyday Life, tr. A. A. Brill. *The Basic Writings*. New York: Modern Library, 1938, pp. 33–178.
Hartmann, H. (1939). *Ego Psychology and the Problem of Adaptation,* tr. D. Rapaport. New York: International Universities Press, 1958.
Kardiner, A. (1941). Psychoanalysis and Psychology. A Comparison of Methods and Objectives. *Philos. Sci.,* 8:233–254.
Murray, H. A. (1940). What Should Psychologists Do about Psychoanalysis? *J. Abnorm. Soc. Psychol.,* 35:150–175.
Rado, S. (1922). The Course of Natural Science in the Light of Psychoanalysis. *Psychoanal. Quart.,* 1:683–700, 1932.
Rank, O. (1924). *The Trauma of Birth.* New York: Harcourt, Brace, 1929.

I5

PRINCIPLES UNDERLYING
NONPROJECTIVE TESTS
OF PERSONALITY

INTRODUCTION

This discussion will consist of four sections. In each of the first three sections, we shall make an assumption of principle underlying nonprojective tests of personality and examine our reasons for that assumption.

Our *first* assumption is that there are, on the one hand, active, *nonstationary*, psychological functions; and, on the other hand, *quasi-stationary* functions. It is these *quasi-stationary functions* which are tapped by nonprojective tests. This term, quasi-stationary, will be clarified in the course of discussion.

Our *second* assumption is that nonprojective tests of personality are to be so constructed that their parts correspond to these quasi-stationary psychological functions and are to be so construed as to allow for comparison of these quasi-stationary functions with each other in the individual and against the norm of their interrelationship in the total population.

Our *third* assumption is that it is necessary to have a definite concept and theory of the quasi-stationary functions underlying the achievements on nonprojective tests, in order that these tests become efficacious tools for evaluating adjustment and maladjustment.

First published in Annals of the New York Academy of Sciences, *46:643–652, 1946.*

In the fourth section we shall discuss very briefly the relationship between the motivating forces of the personality, the nonstationary functions, and the quasi-stationary functions; and advance the thesis that the quasi-stationary functions really reveal the mode of control of basic drives and impulses.

I

The simplest distinction between projective and nonprojective tests of personality is that, in projective tests, we infer the subject's personality make-up from his responses to unstructured material, while in nonprojective tests we infer it from structured material. The term *structured* refers to a clear and unequivocal meaning, the term *unstructured* refers to an unclear, equivocal material to which the subject gives meaning. To put it simply, in projective tests, the subject does not know what reaction is expected of him; in nonprojective tests, he knows clearly. This simple statement is, however, misleading. To be correct, it would need many modifications. For instance, one would have to state that, in the projective Rorschach Test, there is no unequivocal, socially accepted, logically exclusive, and one-to-one verifiable reaction; while, in a nonprojective test, such as an intelligence-test item asking, "What is the capital of Italy?," there is a definite, expected reaction which can be verified, and concerning which there is a definite and logically indisputable agreement. In other words, one could say that the nonprojective tests measure the subject's reaction to, knowledge of, and compliance with, general agreement. The projective tests do not have such standardization. But even this formulation has weaknesses in its reference to both the projective and the nonprojective tests. First of all, the projective tests also establish "popular" trends and even expected norms, the differentiations from which constitute diagnostic indications. Second, the nonprojective tests do not *all* ask for statements concerning which verifiability, social agreement, and logical necessity are all present. For instance, such a question as that in Bell's Inventory, "Do you feel tired most of the time?," is one the verifiability of which is of a different order than the verifiability of the capital of Italy. Social agreement on the response can be had only with great difficulty, would be of questionable value, and no logical necessity would be attached to it.

There are other difficulties in our simple formulation of the difference between projective and nonprojective tests. The subject may know that, on an intelligence test, he is expected to give a definite, factually correct answer, or that, on a questionnaire, he is expected to give a statement of fact; but on the projective test also, the average subject, in general, assumes the same. Furthermore, in both kinds of test, the individual response (concerning the *meaning* of which the subject may have some very definite ideas) derives its *significance* for the examiner not from itself, but rather from its statistical relationship to other responses of the subject and to response patterns of the general population. If we then exclude those tests which are mere questionnaires, replacing other modes of quest for information of which the subject is consciously in possession, the differences between projective and nonprojective tests of personality appear to dwindle.

At this point, it would seem that this paper, which set out to state the principles underlying nonprojective techniques of personality appraisal, has become a funeral march to the tune of which the nonprojective techniques are to be buried in the mass grave of projective procedures. So let us state explicitly that the original definition—that projective tests deal with unstructured, while nonprojective tests deal with structured, material—does hold true and has far-reaching consequences. In the projective test, the subject organizes or structures an unstructured material and, in this structuring, reveals his own psychological structure. In the nonprojective tests, the responses are usually not those which bring about structuring; but the totality of responses, when compared with the trend of responses of large populations, proves to have a structure also reflecting the subject's personality structure. It is as though, in the projective tests, the conclusions are drawn from the manifestations of the *active functioning* of the subject, while in the nonprojective tests, the conclusions are drawn from the patterns of his *conventional* responses. To be specific: In a test like the Rorschach, we see perceptual and associative processes at work in new creation, and we must infer their nature from their work. In a test like Similarities in the Bellevue Scale, we see the subject's verbal concepts; in Comprehension, his formal judgment; both crystallized, both quasi-stationary, and both born in the course of a long history of active, associative, creative work. They are so stationary that their function character frequently eludes us altogether. Both the active functioning of a personality and its crystallizations in the interrelationships of the quasi-stationary structures, such as judgment and verbal concepts, are revealing of the personality. The attacks of the projective and nonprojective techniques of personality appraisal differ from each other, in so far as the projective attack attempts to tap the active principle of the personality, while the nonprojective attack is aimed at the personality's quasi-stationary structures. *Thus, the first assumption underlying nonprojective techniques is that there are, on the one hand, active, nonstationary psychological functions; and, on the other hand, quasi-stationary functions.*

II

Let us now consider more closely these quasi-stationary psychological functions we have referred to. Under different conditions, our motives and desires may choose different pathways and may be modified and altered, and take devious courses toward their goals; and thus they will appear as nonstationary psychological functions. But, if we want to account for any inter-personal understanding and agreement, we must assume stationary struc-tures in our psychological life, or within that segment of it to which we refer as intellect. Now, we may look upon intellect as a storehouse of static as-sets, or static liabilities, or we may look upon it as comprising various abili-ties that are being used by our motives and wishes whenever expedient. Thus, for instance, one may think of verbal concepts simply as static assets possessed by an individual, or as tools once acquired and used when expe-dient. However, if we realize that we create concepts steadily (the scientist does it in all of his moves, and so does the man in the street in many of his moves), we shall find it nonsensical to consider our crystallized verbal concepts as something different from our active concept-creating activities. Rather, we shall see verbal concepts as sediments, crystallized quasi-stationary forms of these active concept-creating functions. The transition between the active, nonstationary functions and the quasi-stationary ones appears to be fluid and continuous. In other words, the more the conditions calling for use of concepts can be met by verbal concepts already formed and crystallized (we call these acquired), the more we are entitled to speak about a quasi-stationary function being at work. Underlying it, however, there appears to be a function with few stationary characteristics—a func-tion which is flexible and modifiable, and, thus, is related to the mode of functioning of man's motives and desires. Obviously, we must assume that the quasi-stationary function, represented by verbal concepts, is not the only quasi-stationary function of our psychological make-up.

Let us here turn from our consideration of these quasi-stationary func-tions, and focus again on their relationship to personality appraisal. If it is assumed that these quasi-stationary functions have been created by active nonstationary functions, then the wealth, stability, accuracy, etc., of these quasi-stationary functions, as demonstrated in the test achievements, must reflect the strength and the development of the active functions, as well as the encroachments of maladjustment upon them. If, then, the wealth and stability of these quasi-stationary functions can be compared with each other in terms of the test achievements, we should obtain a picture of the relationship of the wealth and strength of the different active functions un-derlying these "tools." In our work on personality evaluation by means of intelligence and concept-formation tests, we found that the relationships thus assessed are characteristic for different types of personality develop-ment. Therefore, from the intercomparison of the performance or achieve-ment of the quasi-stationary functions, inferences can be drawn as to the active functions underlying them; and from the inferred relationships of underlying functions, inferences can be drawn as to the type of personality, or type of encroachment upon personality development, characteristic of a subject.

However, this is easier said than done. An achievement, usually, does not imply a single quasi-stationary function, but many of them; and from this fact certain consequences ensue. (1) It is advisable to consider these quasi-stationary functions as aspects of, that is, as our mode of looking upon, our psychological functioning, rather than as something that has its own independent, actual existence. Thus, in our work, we found that memory, concept formation, attention, concentration, anticipation are some of the quasi-stationary functions we had to postulate as aspects of our psychological functioning. (The precise meaning of these concepts, as used here, is discussed in our volumes. *Diagnostic Psychological Testing* [Rapaport, Gill, and Schafer, 1945–46]). When, in the Similarities test on the Bellevue Scale, the question is asked: "In what way are a dog and a lion similar?" there can be no doubt that the subject must first of all *"attend"* to the question itself; must make a correct *anticipation,* in order not to come out with a statement of the opposites, or with descriptions of the dog and of the lion, instead of a common denominator of the two; that he implicitly performs a *memory function* in correctly invoking the characteristics of dogs and lions; yet, though attending, anticipating, and remembering are all involved, the preponderant function remains one of verbal concept formation. Such clear preponderance, however, is by no means the usual case. (2) Another consequence is that it is difficult, therefore, to determine how many, and which, are these quasi-stationary functions. In working with the Bellevue Scale, we had to assume the existence of such quasi-stationary functions as concept formation, memory, the triad of attention-concentration-anticipation, visual organization, and visual-motor coordination.

Whether or not the dividing line between these quasi-stationary functions and the nonstationary functions, here discussed, follows the dividing line of ego and id in the psychoanalytic sense, is a moot question. It is quite possible that the line dividing the ego and id, and that dividing the conscious and not conscious parts of the ego, will be drawn more sharply if and when the relationship between the basic motivating forces, the nonstationary functions, and the quasi-stationary functions is better understood. This does not imply that projective tests explore the id directly. It is clear only that these quasi-stationary functions have much to do with the ego, and exploring them is an important part of what is called ego psychology. It is the issue of the exploration of the psychology of the thought processes. *Thus, our second assumption underlying nonprojective techniques of personality appraisal is that nonprojective tests of personality are to be so constructed that their parts correspond to quasi-stationary psychological functions; and they are to be so construed that they allow for comparison of these quasi-stationary functions with each other, within the individual and against the norm for this relationship, in the total population; because only out of the relative strength of these functions shall we perceive the variants of developmental conditions characteristic for the personality.* A corollary of this assumption is that nonprojective tests of personality are to be based on definite assumptions as to the functions underlying responses to their different parts. Therefore, nonprojective personality tests are a tool, not only of diagnosis, but also of exploration of the psychology of thinking.

III

My discussion, thus far, has referred to, and been based on, intelligence and concept-formation tests, used as nonprojective tests of personality. Even admitting the validity of these considerations and assumptions for these tests, it might still be objected that we have not demonstrated, or even suggested, why these assumptions should be valid for all nonprojective tests of personality. The objection is sustained, and no claim is made here as to the general validity of these considerations and assumptions. Nevertheless, it will be worth while to examine whether or not we can cite further considerations making it advisable to keep these assumptions seriously in mind as applicable to other nonprojective tests of personality.

It might be argued that, in order to construct a successful nonprojective test of personality, it is not necessary to have any kind of theory or assumptions as to quasi-stationary or other functions underlying test responses. It might be argued that, by giving a sufficiently large and varied set of questions to a sufficiently wide normal population, which has sufficiently large and well-defined neurotic and psychotic subgroups of all important varieties, one will be able to find sets of questions the responses to which will reliably differentiate all the major groups, as well as all the subgroups from each other. Such an argument I could support with a series of data concerning such successes. All these data, however, have one or more of the following three features in common: (1) The application of the tests was successful in limited groups, which in age, background, and education were highly similar to the standardization group. (2) The differentiations afforded by the tests were few and gross, that is to say, they sought to segregate successful or nonsuccessful students; they stated, "he is all right," or "there is something wrong with him"; they attempted to differentiate psychotics, neurotics, and normals; and, perhaps, attempted a further bidivision, in the psychotic range, by differentiating affective and schizophrenic psychoses. (3) The tests pertained to one very specific aspect of the personality (as, for instance, vocational interest), and the successful tests among these used homogeneous sets of questions.

The data which these tests thus afforded to support the contention that statistical procedures alone are sufficient really pull the last bit of ground out from under this contention, and prove that, in the long run, this statistically safeguarded dream of machinelike personality assessment is a hopeless illusion. What chemist would agree to use chemical tests which will detect acidity only if it occurs under certain definite conditions, and particularly only under the same conditions under which it has already been seen in the past? A test is testing only if, *under new conditions,* it can detect the old and known elements (in chemistry) or relationships (in chemistry and in psychology). Conditions are always new, even in our inorganic world; more so, in our organic world; and, most of all, in our psychological world. Tests are useful and of general validity only if they are not limited to specific conditions, but are, in themselves, able to cope with variations of conditions, and either lead to a detection of the entity or relationship that is being sought, or indicate specifically the other testing procedures to be applied under the changed conditions.

The two concepts of testing here contrasted are not merely the contrast of two testing procedures; they are expressions of two diametrically opposed views of science and of the world. They are expressions of the contrast between mechanical, statistical, atomistic, pragmatic views and functional, dynamic, organismic views. For the atomistic view, science is a matter of probabilities, theories are illusions, and, instead of theories, correlation coefficients assume the rôle of the demigod. For the organismic view, science is a search for functional relationships and laws; the keystones of science are hypotheses, in terms of which data and observations can be systematized; and statistics, the most important crucial testing tool of the validity of these hypotheses, remains merely a *tool.* This view of science does not expect statistics to take care of thinking, or to reveal relationships. It does not trust statistics more than human experience and intuition. It relies on statistics only to check, test, systematize, verify, cleanse, and build into communicable form what is given in human experience.

Let us return to the three conditions which we found operating in successful nonprojective tests built upon the purely statistical approach: (1) that the groups tested must be limited and similar to the standardization groups; or (2) that the differentiations are few and gross; or (3) that the tests utilize homogeneous sets of questions. On the first two points, we may ask, "How is it that statistically designed procedures will work, to some extent, even for limited groups, and yield even gross differentiations?" Cultural patterning, and its tremendous impact upon personality structure, supplies the answer. The situation is somewhat different as regards the third point, the homogeneous structure of the tests. To illustrate: In a test like Bell's Adjustment Inventory, one finds a question like "Has it been necessary for you to have frequent medical attention?" together with a question like "Do you get angry easily?" One question asks for a statement of fact, the other asks for a subjective appraisal of one's subjective experience, both as to degree and as to frequency. Inventories, questionnaires, and other nonprojective tests of personality are generally inclined to mix indiscriminately questions pertaining to different levels of the personality, and in these circumstances responses will be based on very different quasi-stationary functions of the individual. In a test like the Vocational Interest Test of Strong, we do not find such mixtures. We find, rather, several well-defined, structured sets of questions, all essentially similar to each other, asking for preferences in vocations, in amusements, in activity, in people, in styles of living, in school subjects; though, regrettably, we also find a group of subjective, self-rating items. The explanation of the efficacy of this test is based, in our appraisal, on this consistent (for the most part) uniformity of the questions. The questions pertain to interests. Interests, also, are apparently quasi-stationary functions of personality, although we know as yet very little about their dependence upon total character structure. Thorough personality studies, incorporating this very successful Strong test, may reveal to us those nonstationary functions which underlie interest formation. They may reveal to us what the variants of the quasi-stationary functions called interests are, and what is their systematic place in psychological functioning. It is quite possible that, sooner or later, if we explore many other such quasi-stationary functions, we shall have ways to reconstruct the relationship between these and those underlying interest formation. From these relationships, we shall obtain more clear-cut pictures as to the quasi-stationary structure of the individual personality. At this point, nonprojective testing of personality will be as efficacious as, or more efficacious than, projective testing of personality as it is at present. There is little doubt in the author's mind that, for educational and vocational advice, for counseling, and for industrial testing, the significance of nonprojective tests of personality is greater than one can perceive for the projective personality tests extant. How projective and nonprojective tests will complement each other is a question to be answered in the future, on the basis of factual findings. *Our third assumption underlying intelligence and concept-formation tests used as nonprojective tests of personality* (and which recommends itself to be applied to *all* nonprojective tests of personality appraisal) *is the necessity of having a definite concept and theory of the quasi-stationary functions underlying the reactions and achievements on these tests.* A corollary to this assumption is that it is desirable that the questions or problems of these tests be homogeneous, or that the test consist of internally homogeneous item groups. In this way, they will each tap different quasi-stationary functions, or different variants of a quasi-stationary function, and render them subject to comparison. Out of these comparisons, characteristic patterns of quasi-stationary functions can be derived, and the relationship of these patterns to specfic types of personality developments and maladjustment may be inferred.

IV

Let us consider, finally, the nature of quasi-stationary functions, and their relationship to the nonstationary functions. We have already stated that it is both expedient and in accord with our experience and analyzed data to conceive of these quasi-stationary functions as crystallized sediments of nonstationary functions, intimately related to motivating forces of the personality. How should we conceive of the relationship of the nonstationary and the quasi-stationary functions to these motivating forces? It will not be possible for me to adduce evidence, within the limits of this paper, to substantiate the view of this relationship to which we adhere in our studies. Therefore, I shall make only a brief statement of it.

Drives or motivating forces of an individual may undergo, in the course of his development, different vicissitudes. These vicissitudes will mold what we refer to as his personality. They may lead to the attitude well characterized by the motto of the proverbial three monkeys, "I hear no evil; see no evil; speak no evil." It has become a custom to refer to the fate of drives resulting in such a motto as "repression" and "inhibition." Since everything in the world of perception and action may bring danger, the field of action, as well as that of perceptual intake (attention), becomes limited. Here we see, then, a vicissitude of the drives expressing itself in quasi-stationary forms. The quasi-stationary functions underlying information and the function of attention become seriously limited. Another vicissitude of drives is seen when the threatening danger is responded to by alertness keyed to the highest pitch and is ever-present. It is the custom to refer to the results of this vicissitude as "obsessiveness" or "compulsive meticulousness." The function of attention becomes overemphasized; the quasi-stationary function underlying information works intensively and extensively; verbal concepts become sharp and rigid.

These examples are given to illustrate the thesis that the quasi-stationary functions discussed here really reveal *the mode of control of drives and impulses,* of the fundamental motives of all psychological life. We as yet have few, if any, reliably direct measures of the native strength of these drives and impulses, and what little we know qualitatively about personality structure refers mainly to their mode of control. Thus, one can justifiably state that, for the time being, we distinguish one personality from another by reference to these different types of mode of control. Nonprojective tests of personality dealing with the quasi-stationary functions discussed above make these modes of control (or rather the crystallized results of such modes of control) palpable and testable.

REFERENCE

Rapaport, D., Gill, M. M., & Schafer, R. (1945–46). *Diagnostic Psychological Testing,* 2 vols. Chicago: Year Book Publishers.

16

THE PSYCHOLOGICAL INTERNSHIP
TRAINING PROGRAM OF
THE MENNINGER CLINIC

WITH ROY SCHAFER

Internship training programs are relatively new on the psychological scene. Consequently any specific internship program bears an experimental character, as well as the earmarks of the conditions within the institution in which it developed. To present a description of an internship training program has therefore a great merit and yet involves a serious danger. The merit is that the various experimental attempts and methods growing out of different settings can be described and thereby be made public property to be applied or avoided by others. The danger implied is that an attempt at a clear description tends to simplify and to represent experimental procedures as goods ready for sale. The description presented here represents our program and its development, and argues for a number of procedures which seem to us inevitable *in our setting*. Our plea to the reader is to distinguish what seemed necessary to us from what may appear to be valid for internship programs in general.

First published in The Journal of Consulting Psychology, *10:216–220, 1946.*

I

The first internships at the Menninger Clinic were offered at the Southard School for Maladjusted Children in January, 1935. They afforded board and room and minimum pocket money; they allowed the intern some time to commute to the University of Kansas to attend courses toward a graduate degree. The interns worked virtually as attendants to the children of the school and their "training" consisted of the opportunity to be with problem children and to hear the discussion of the psychiatrists and other therapists concerning cases. They were given some opportunity to attend staff seminars and some opportunity to administer a few tests. In the later years of this arrangement (1940–41) an attempt was made to give more systematic courses in testing, and in the psychology of personality, thinking, and memory in relation to clinical work. More systematic attempts were also made to allow the interns to do some research under supervision. Though such provisions had been made earlier they were relatively unsystematic.

The experience with this type of internship was very unsatisfactory. The young psychologists felt dissatisfied with the attendant rôle. The administrators of the school felt that they had to put in too much time in supervision and instruction and had to allow too much time for university attendance and courses at the Menninger Clinic. The internships were not economically self-sustaining. Furthermore, since these young psychologists did not intend to stay with the school and since the school had no provisions for retaining them, their training could not be conceived of as an investment that would pay for itself by the greater efficiency of the interns during a second year of residency. The conclusion was inevitable: the internships were discontinued and we were left with the knowledge that (1) a private institution cannot afford to take interns and allow them simultaneously to work toward a degree; (2) psychological interns should not be placed in positions of which the main substance is getting acquainted with patients in the rôle of attendant.

II

After a lag of about a year a new internship program was started. This program was based on the following plan:

(1) The internship was intended to give intensive training in clinical-psychological procedures which at our institution meant primarily psychological testing;

(2) The internship was to be set up so that the institution would take a full economic loss during the first half-year, with the hope (a) that in the second half-year the intern would be able to contribute to the psychological work of the institution on the basis of the experience and instruction of the first half-year; (b) that a few of the interns would prove to be proficient

enough in their work to be retained for a second year, in which partly by their work and partly by research participation they would bring returns on the initial investment; (c) finally, that from these interns, with the expansion of the psychology department, a group of psychologists carrying the responsibility for routine testing and research might develop. In the past few years, the program based on the above conception expanded from one internship position to four.

III

In the course of the four years in which this internship program has been in operation the following routine has developed which may be presented as our present program. The custom has evolved of asking the interns to familiarize themselves with the research and publications of the clinic staff, particularly Karl Menninger's *The Human Mind* (1937); the volumes of the *Bulletin of the Menninger Clinic;* and the collected papers of the staff. With respect to the tests routinely used in our clinic, the intern first is required to cover the rather complete reprint collection pertaining to one of the tests, at the same time observing administrations of that test by seniors of the psychology department. This is followed up by the intern's covering the publications and research material of the department concerning that test, and also by reviewing all the current records of that test that have been given in the routine work of the department. These readings are followed by a discussion of the literature, either at departmental meetings or with one of the seniors of the department. Following such discussions the intern is expected to administer the test to from 10 to 20 cases at the local state hospital, following which his scoring and diagnostic analysis of each of his test records are discussed with one of the seniors of the department. In this period the intern is also expected to analyze the records of tests administered by other members of the department and to submit for criticism written reports of his analyses to those members of the department who are responsible for the cases in question. The course of work on this first test culminates in the intern's administering it to patients of this clinic with one of the seniors of the department observing; afterward the senior discusses with the intern his procedure, difficulties, and mistakes. After from five to ten such observation periods the intern is usually considered proficient enough to administer the test independently.

The entire procedure is repeated for all the tests routinely used in the department.[1] The standard sequence is for the intern to master first intelligence tests; second, tests of concept formation; third, tests of ideational content (word association, Thematic Apperception) and finally, the Rorschach Test. The prevailing emphasis throughout is awareness of inter- and intraindividual variability of thought organization. The underlying assump-

[1] For the routine battery, see Rapaport, Gill, and Schafer (1945).

tion we attempt to instill in the intern is that the individual will generally indicate his pathology as well as his characteristic dealing with affects, anxiety, fantasy, etc., through the medium of the thought processes required by psychological tests. This assumption has been discussed elsewhere as the projective hypothesis.

At about the time when the intern has already covered the tests of intelligence and tests of concept formation, but not yet the tests of personality and ideational content, he is expected to read a number of textbooks of clinical psychiatry and abnormal psychology. The books in question are the following: Kraepelin's *Lectures on Clinical Psychiatry* (1913), Bleuler's *Textbook of Psychiatry* (1918), White's *Outlines of Psychiatry* (1935), Henderson and Gillespie's *A Textbook of Psychiatry* (1927), McDougall's *Outline of Abnormal Psychology* (1926), Maslow and Mittelmann's *Principles of Abnormal Psychology* (1941), and MacCurdy's *The Psychology of Emotion* (1925). The more energetic and able students are expected to cover more books of this type, the less promising ones read only a few.

These routine procedures are the mainstay of the internship training and are systematically required and carried through. The rest of the training is mostly less systematic and is less stressed, even though parts of it have been carried through consistently for all interns recently.

The internship training program also includes the following features:

(1) A course of weekly one-hour lectures on psychological testing. In the course of a year these lectures cover all the tests used routinely, covering their practice and theory and the pertinent clinical and theoretical psychological information which facilitates their use. Reference is also made to tests not routinely administered.

(2) A daily one-hour conference of the entire psychology department, at which either current cases presenting difficult diagnostic problems are discussed in advance of final decision, or cases are discussed in which staff conferences have brought out a discrepancy between the clinical picture and the reported psychological-test conclusions. These departmental conferences also include discussion of all kinds of practical and theoretical problems pertaining to the work of the department, and presentation of ideas as well as reports on the work of members of the department and interns.

(3) Over a period of one-quarter to three-quarters of a year, two or three half-days a week are spent by the interns in the Recreational Therapy Department where they have an opportunity to see the patients in their everyday life in the sanitarium. Interns are expected to report to the departmental conference synoptic pictures of the clinical material, testing data, and observations of the patients with whom they have had most contact.

(4) When the interns reach a stage where they can competently administer all the routine tests, they are expected independently to analyze and report complete cases, discussing their reports with the seniors of the de-

partment. Whenever the intern has given more than three tests to one patient, he is admitted to the clinical staff conference at which all the pertinent data concerning that patient are presented and discussed, and the patient's diagnosis, prognosis, and treatment recommendations are decided.

(5) The interns are required to attend the weekly staff seminar of the Menninger Clinic at which reports of work and research of the staff members or important relevant reviews of new work or books are presented. At frequent intervals guest lecturers from all parts of the country describe their work and research in psychology, psychiatry, and allied fields, as well as in any other field of common interest to the group.

(6) Some of the interns are given opportunity to familiarize themselves with the infant testing and with the occasional vocational testing of the department.

(7) Under supervision some of the interns are given an opportunity to go to nursery schools, kindergartens, grade schools, or high schools to do some research of their own, mostly in developmental studies utilizing different test procedures.

(8) Some interns are given opportunity to assist and participate in research projects conducted in the institution.

Thus these features of the training program are intended to supplement routine test administration by requiring the intern to learn how to synthesize the indications of a *battery* of tests as well as how to synthesize clinical observations and reports with the test results; further, the consistent emphasis on research is intended to make the intern aware of the complexities and unsolved problems in clinical-psychological thinking.

No training in the techniques of interview, counseling, and therapy is given to the interns. It is felt that the lack of training in interview technique is an actual deficiency of the program since only indirectly—through hearing at staff conferences the reports of interviews done by psychiatrists and social workers—do the interns learn about interviewing. Since, however, the major part of the case-history interview is done by the social worker in this institution, it has not thus far proved expedient to enlarge the training of the psychological intern to cover this field. Plans, however, are afoot to cope with this deficiency.

The lack of training in counseling and psychotherapy is not considered a simple deficiency in this institution. It is felt that only a thorough acquaintance with the workings of a psychological clinic and with clinical procedures is an adequate basis for later training in counseling and therapy. There is no barrier of principle raised against a psychologist who after his internship training indicates a leaning toward therapy. As a matter of fact, there are precedents of psychologists becoming therapists at this institution. However, the intern must have demonstrated at the end of his training period that he has achieved sufficient theoretical orientation and clinical acumen to warrant an attempt at training for therapy. In fact, the same principle holds in the training of resident psychiatrists. The road of obtaining training as a therapist is not routinely an open highway here, but is a matter of demonstrating individual initiative and acumen.

A few particular problems of internship training related to the academic preparation brought by the interns to the clinical setting must be mentioned here:

(1) Academic university courses are too remote from everyday clinical work; hence the beginning intern is unfamiliar with the workings of different kinds of psychiatric clinics and requires a period of orientation, losing valuable time.

(2) Training in testing at universities appears to take too little account of the qualitative analysis of test results, and thus considerable time must be spent in detailed supervision of administration and principles of analysis.

(3) Problems (1) and (2) are related to a third, namely, that the status of clinical psychology is not presented in academic courses, so that the intern must be made aware of the confusions, uncharted areas, and contributions currently existing after he has begun his training.

(4) Departments of psychology in universities tend to be too one-sided in their theoretical emphases: an awareness of the essential contributions to method and knowledge made by gestalt psychology, psychoanalysis, field theory, behaviorism, and other schools of thought is a necessary background for the intern. This background constitutes a set of concepts which he can bring to bear on grasping and organizing clinical-psychological data.

Even though the interns are encouraged by the atmosphere and by direct advice to study psychoanalytic literature, gestalt-psychological literature, field-theoretical literature, comparative psychological literature, and even though in discussions of research many methodological and epistemological considerations are taken up and philosophical, epistemological interests are stimulated, it is felt that all these subjects are unsatisfactorily covered in our present internship training program. There are plans afoot to enlarge and further systematize this program by joining forces with a university and with the training program in clinical psychology of the Veterans Administration, since a broader program will allow for much more systematic course work in these fields as well as in fields allied to clinical psychology, such as cultural anthropology and sociology.

REFERENCES

Bleuler, E. (1918). *Textbook of Psychiatry*, tr. A. A. Brill. New York: Macmillan, 1924.

Henderson, D. K., & Gillespie, R. D. (1927). *A Textbook of Psychiatry*. Oxford: Oxford University Press.

Kraepelin, E. (1913). *Lectures on Clinical Psychiatry*. London: Ballière, Tindall & Cox.

MacCurdy, J. T. (1925). *The Psychology of Emotion, Morbid and Normal.*
    New York: Harcourt, Brace.
McDougall, W. (1926). *Outline of Abnormal Psychology.* New York: Scribner.
Maslow, A. H., & Mittelmann, B. (1941). *Principles of Abnormal Psychology.*
    New York: Harper.
Menninger, K. (1937). *The Human Mind,* 2nd ed. New York: Knopf.
Rapaport, D., Gill, M. M., & Schafer, R. (1945). *Diagnostic Psychological
    Testing,* Vol. I. Chicago: Year Book Publishers.
White, W. A. (1935). *Outlines of Psychiatry,* 14th ed. Washington: Nerv.
    Ment. Dis. Publ. Co.

I7

THE FUTURE OF RESEARCH IN
CLINICAL PSYCHOLOGY
AND PSYCHIATRY

Though Rapaport was most widely known as a
scholar, he had strong propensities toward social and
political activism, which he deliberately inhibited
after his early years of political activity (see editor's
obituary). He showed thereby, despite his many and
diverse interests, the rare capacity to act on the
knowledge that, even for the gifted, excellence and
precision demand relatively exclusive and single-
minded devotion to one path. He knew that he was
sacrificing certain intense personal drives, and it is to
his sacrifice that we owe the high quality of his psychoanalytic writings. But he did not lose perspective,
and continued to be intensely concerned with social
and political issues. Unfortunately, he did not write
much about them. But we do have from him papers
such as this one, his "Discussion at Mass Communi-

Excerpt from the annual report of the Director of the Research Department of the
Menninger Foundation to the Board of Trustees for the fiscal year 1945–46. First published in The American Psychologist, 2:167–172, 1947.

cations Seminar" (Chapter 42), a "Memorandum on Group Theory" (Chapter 46), and "The Study of Kibbutz Education and Its Bearing on the Theory of Development" (Chapter 56)—M.M.G.

We have been and still are bombarded in our daily newspapers and in our professional journals with statements of the tremendous need in the community for psychiatric service. We have been made keenly aware of the fact that our present psychiatric facilities and personnel are totally inadequate to handle the actual size of the psychiatric problem in the community. I shall dwell on this issue only briefly. The long waiting list in our Department of Clinical Services at the Menninger Clinic proves the point. Good documentary evidence can be obtained from data of the Veterans Administration, which absorbed into its services a great part of the psychiatrists and clinical psychologists available in this country and still finds most of its installations understaffed.

The tremendous demand for psychiatric education has also been hammered at us in the last few years with penetrating power. Documentary evidence for this can be had in the number of applicants we have had to reject in our schools. Further evidence for this is the fact that the Veterans Administration is working on setting up still more centers for the education of psychiatrists and psychologists. Would it not seem correct then to say that in times of such great need for actual services for training, research is a superfluous luxury? Let me quote to you a passage from Raymond B. Fosdick's (President, Rockefeller Foundation) Morton Memorial Lecture:

> I talked the other day at Lake Success with one of the high officials of the United Nations. "The chief thing we lack at the present time," he said, "is knowledge, tested knowledge. We seem to have to guess our way along."

If I understand it correctly, the United Nations official was complaining that the time is past when political art could solve the problems of international relations. The problems have grown so tremendous and complex that tested *knowledge* is necessary instead of the *art* of "guessing our way along." Psychiatry and clinical psychology are in the stage in which there is a great discrepancy between the meagerness of teachable tested knowledge on the one hand and the richness of our experience and versatility in the clinical art on the other. I certainly do not assume that dealing with people, with human beings, will not always retain to some extent the character of art. Nor do I assume that therapy will not always be to some extent dependent on the individual ingenuity, the individual art of the therapist. How should I think otherwise when even the application of well-tested tools, well-tested knowledge of machines, requires the individual ingenuity of the mechanic? The crux of the matter is whether we shall have well-tested tools, well-tested knowledge, applied with clinical ingenuity, or whether all shall be left, as it is grossly at present, to the ingenuity of the individual therapist.

It is the job of research, and research alone, to produce tested knowledge that can be used *with* the art of the clinician. The question could be raised: Is it possible that clinicians in their clinical work produce this tested knowledge? The atmosphere of the Hippocratic oath, the importance to the clinician to discharge his duties to the patients first, is inimical to research. Add to this the present-day never-ending stream of patients and there is no room left for contemplation, no peace for theoretical, systematic clarification. We have seen these years a stream of ingenious, topflight clinicians lecture in our institution, from all over the country and even from overseas. I believe that it was our overwhelming impression that—excepting a very few like the late Otto Fenichel—systematizing ingenuity was not a part of these clinicians' equipment. On the other hand, the academic men who lectured here showed that the clinical immediacy of the problems and the formation of concepts in terms meaningful and useful to clinicians were more or less missing in their thinking. The task therefore is the creation of a research atmosphere within the clinical setting which will introduce academically trained people to clinical problems and induce clinical people to clear theoretical systematic thinking. Only this coupling can assure substantial development in psychiatry and clinical psychology. This development, however, will not take place if academically trained people coming into the clinical setting are only introduced into its hectic character, its restlessness, its lack of peace. Nor are clinicians going to be induced to theoretical thinking simply by living side by side with academic people. Only the creation of an island of peaceful work in the clinical setting, within which sufficient time for contemplation is given, will make such a marriage fruitful.

I have raised the question whether or not, at this time of great demand for psychiatric services and for psychiatric education, research should be considered a dispensable luxury. After the foregoing considerations my answer would be that it is clinical services and teaching, in so far as they deplete all our sources of research personnel and finances, that should be considered at this time luxuries, rather than research.

However, without clinical practice, clinical psychological and psychiatric research would tend to become sterile. Without teaching, it would become divorced from the responsibility and the possibility of self-perpetuation by raising new researchers. If it were not for these facts, one would want to recommend that the most able psychiatrists and clinical psychologists be withdrawn altogether by some means from practice and teaching to be cloistered for research.

If we turn, however, from this enlightening paradox to the confused and confusing reality, we find, besides the fact of tremendous need for service and training, further facts which deserve our serious consideration. I believe that in charting the course of our research it is our responsibility to take stock of the major factors which are influencing psychiatric and clinical psychological research in the country. I feel that together with formulating our own research plans we have to formulate also general principles for which all of us will stand in the various responsible positions in our respective professions and in American life. Without effective work on this broader plane we stand little chance to realize our own research plans.

There seem to be four major factors that have decisive influence at present upon the future of research in psychiatry and clinical psychology: (1) the distribution of talent, (2) public awareness of the need for research, (3) the National Mental Health Act, and (4) the private foundations. Let me take these one by one.

Psychiatric and clinical-psychological talent at present is thinly spread all over the country. Some years ago Gregg (1941) already clearly recognized one of the factors responsible for this thin spread. He concluded that the greatest single enemy of medical research is the competition of private practice with its great earning opportunities and lure for the able and self-assertive man. If we consider in addition that the Veterans Administration has opened a large number of positions—compared with the number of available psychiatrists and clinical psychologists—and that with the increasing need for teaching, new departments of psychiatry and schools of clinical psychology have opened up, we have plentiful explanations for this spreading thin and diverting from research of psychiatric and clinical-psychological talent. Further, we find that able young psychiatrists and clinical psychologists, the future promise for psychiatric and clinical-psychological research, are now absorbed by institutions and universities in high teaching and administrative positions. These men who were slated in our minds for research are now casting around for more people to add to their departments or are now engaged in creating private clinics. They do all this with the pipe dream that when they find enough people to man their respective institutions they will have opportunity for research. Yet we know very well the facts of clinical practice and education: the need for therapy is insatiable; there come always new and more patients; the demands of education go beyond all bounds because a professional discipline which is grossly an art can only be taught by precept. The energies of teachers and clinicians are all absorbed by these tasks. I believe that there are two things that can be done: first, we must build up professional public opinion which will build up dams against the lures of private practice by giving recognition and standing to people in research and not merely, as it has been done so far, to people who write papers. Professional standing, professional respect and reward for people in painstaking, systematizing work has to be enhanced in order to make the positions for such work attractive. Still along the same lines, the main institutions responsible for the thin spread of the professional talent have to strive to concentrate talented men in a few chosen places and enable them to devote themselves freely to research work. We know that the Veterans Administration has provided generously for research finances through direct grants as well as through grants to the National Research Council. We have to say to the Veterans Administration that money alone will not do it. First, research talent will not arise without concentration of able people in a few places. Second, research positions have to fulfill two criteria: they must be financially attractive and have tenure, and they must not be linked with a demand for immediate production. Research does not flourish if it has to deliver the goods immediately. Good thinking is not characterized by the ability to produce immediately, though good thinking can in real need be called upon for immediate production. Physics and chemistry which rose to the national emergency in the course of the war did not do so merely because of pressure but rather because many years of painstaking preparation made their thinking sufficiently good to rise to real need. Pressure alone would never have done it; pressure alone will never do it.

The second major factor that has a decisive influence upon psychiatry's future is public awareness of the need for psychiatric and clinical psychological research. Psychiatry and clinical psychology have been oversold. A discipline whose earning power is great and which in addition is oversold is in danger that its needs will not be seen. That is particularly true of research needs. That this is not merely a theoretical speculation is clearly shown by the fact that even the planned appropriations of the National Mental Health Act, which are monumental compared with research finances we have had so far for psychiatry and clinical psychology, do not come up to the advertised or even the actual size of the psychiatric problem. The other danger in the psychiatric and clinical-psychological position is the great public demand—due to overselling—for the application of psychiatry and psychology in industry, in personnel relations, and in social and political affairs. Psychiatrists and psychologists were only too tempted to hear these demands. Yet the fact is that well-tested knowledge is not extant and psychiatrists and psychologists are—to use Fosdick's words—"guessing their way along." I would suggest that we let others "guess their way along" even if with the help of psychological insight we would be able to guess 10 per cent, 20 per cent, or 30 per cent better. We certainly could not do any better than that. It should be hammered into psychiatric and psychological as well as into the more general public consciousness that psychiatrists and clinical psychologists must be left to cope with the patients and with the enormous expanse of research problems and not run to try to solve the ills of the world right away. We have to discipline ourselves and let first things come first. Surely, we would want to contribute to the solution of the world's problems, to bridging the gap that came about when technological progress outstripped development of our interpersonal, social, and international relations. However, we will be best able to do that if we, for the time being, resign ourselves as professionals to establish further the science of our own profession and take stands on the social, political, and international affairs only as individuals, acting on our own personal responsibility. Public consciousness has to be influenced, however, in another respect also. In our whole huge country all the research professors in psychiatry can be counted on the fingers of one hand. Researchers hardly have tenure. They are hoping to become regular professors, research professorships being scarce, and when they achieve this hope they are weighed down with duties of education, and research aims are relegated at best to minor importance. This is true also where research is connected with clinical work; there practical duties lure away from research and militate against systematic thinking, while propagating artistic-intuitive thinking. We must build up a public consciousness which will value long-range thinking, which will not reward its thinkers—as Cannon put it—with deanships, a reward of a Trojan-horse character.

Our civilization underestimates leisure. It fails to distinguish it from idleness, and thereby cuts a rich source of power and inventiveness of imagination and creativeness. I believe I speak with the authority of the best of researchers of this country when I say that we will have to educate our public by rising as knights in defense of leisure, leisure for the researcher and thinker, leisure institutionally created and protected. We will have to do this by providing finances and positions, by protecting ourselves from premature social application, by creating groups of people who can fertilize the thinking of each other instead of spreading our talents very thinly.

The third major factor in psychiatry's future is the National Mental Health Act. The existence of this Act is a great step ahead. We must not forget, however, that research is not the sole purpose of this Act and that within its functioning the relative emphasis may be either on supporting services, or education, or research. So the considerations here advanced concerning the relative importance of these should hold for the National Mental Health Act also. Research will be fostered by it primarily only if the general consciousness concerning need for research is foremost in the psychiatric and clinical-psychological community as well as in the broader community. As to the problem of research proper within the Mental Health Act, a series of considerations deserves our attention. Foundations that have supported psychiatric research in the past have contributed little to the firm grounding of psychiatric research in general and to the security, tenure, and leisure of the researcher. They supported isolated researches in psychiatry and even in clinical psychology, but the general air was that these researches are to be undertaken in order to "deliver the goods" within a given range of time. Most of these have been short-range grants and guaranteed no tenure. The researcher's security therefore depended upon his carrying another job as well. This, of necessity, took his leisure away. There have been only very few exceptions to this rule. Now the National Mental Health Act will not be in a position to endow research institutions or to create continuous fellowships or research positions in places other than the National Mental Health Institute. It should, therefore, be vigorously pointed out to the administrators of the National Mental Health Act that they will contribute to building up psychiatric and clinical-psychological research and to determining its policy for the country by giving long-range grants. These, however, will depend upon annual appropriations by Congress. What other safeguards could be sought within the functioning of the National Mental Health Act for the continuity of psychiatric and psychological research? The only one, I believe, is that the administration of this Act support researches formulated in general terms. That is, not to support mainly researches concerning isolated bits of problems carried on mainly by isolated investigators but rather to support groups of investigators who attack general problems without binding themselves to obtain specific results with specific methods. I have in mind researches like those conducted in schizophrenia at Worcester State Hospital where the grant was given for any investigations their changing team of investigators cared to undertake and was in the position to undertake in the field of schizophrenia. Similarly, I have in mind broadly defined research projects, leaving it up to the team and its changing interests, facilities, and opportunities to define what they will be doing. Thereby the project would not terminate when an isolated attack seems to have exhausted its usefulness or when an investigator leaves, but will be continued whether or not one attack seems to have survived its usefulness.

Another problem pertaining to the Mental Health Act is that its existence does and will influence profoundly the attitude and relationship of private foundations to psychiatry. We already know of two foundations which have suspended allocating funds to psychiatric research, delaying decision until after the policies of the National Mental Health Act have been established. This imposes an added responsibility upon administrators of the Mental Health Act.

Still another problem is the National Mental Health Institute planned in the bill setting up the Foundation. It is not certain whether in the present precarious personnel situation such an institute will actually play a positive or a negative rôle in the development of psychiatric and clinical-psychological research. Since, however, years will pass between the bill, the appropriation, the erection of the building, and the selection of the personnel, it is premature to judge the significance of such an Institute.

Now about private foundations. Grants for psychiatric and psychological research will be supplied by the National Mental Health Act and probably in such amounts and to so many places that, considering the present shortage of research personnel, no justified demands on such money will remain unfulfilled. What will be the function of private foundations in the field of psychiatry and psychology? I believe that it is the job of the administrators of the National Mental Health Act and of all people who think of the future of psychiatric research to state clearly that at present the tasks of the various foundations supporting psychiatric and psychological research are: to endow institutions for psychiatric and psychological research and to endow research professorships, and to secure the opportunity for professionals of attainment and reputation to spend years away from their usual professional pursuits in institutions of research in psychiatry with traditions different from their own. It will be the job of all of us to indicate the limitations of a federally supported research and to point out that where these limitations start, as indicated above, there the rôle of the private foundations begins.[1]

.   .   .[2]

The field is wide open; in spite of the advancements of the last 50 years, little of all these problems has been settled definitely and it is our job to contribute directly with our research and indirectly with our influencing psychiatric, psychological, and general public consciousness to the solution of these problems. Somehow it is hard to escape the impression that we are late and the time is flying: research is the fat of the land on which practice and teaching live—we must act vigorously to replenish this fat of the land.

REFERENCE

Gregg, A. (1941). *The Furtherance of Medical Research.* New Haven: Yale University Press.

[1] [A few of Rapaport's statements need comment in the light of the 19 years that have passed since he made them. Continuous fellowships and research positions in places other than the National Mental Health Institute were in fact established by NIMH. Groups of investigators approaching problems in general terms have been supported by NIMH, as Rapaport hoped, but it remains to be proved that the results of such investigations entirely justify his faith in them. Private foundation support of mental-health and psychiatric research has not ended as a result of governmental support, though the lines of their respective rôles still remain blurred—Ed.]

[2] [Here Rapaport described in detail the research projects in progress at the Menninger Foundation in 1947, the difficulties attending them, and plans for future research. Since this material is not only parochial but obsolete, the passage has been omitted—Ed.]

18

THE NEW RÔLE OF PSYCHOLOGICAL TESTING IN PSYCHIATRY

WITH KARL A. MENNINGER AND ROY SCHAFER

It is common knowledge that the systematization of psychiatric nosology was begun by Kraepelin, but it is unfortunately not commonly appreciated that the cradle for this systematization was built in the psychological laboratory of Wundt. The journal *Psychologische Arbeiten,* published by Kraepelin, as well as Kraepelin's own volumes, particularly *Manic-Depressive Insanity and Paranoia,* bear witness to the fact that Kraepelin observed fundamental differences in the basic psychological functions of different types of psychiatric cases and hoped that it would prove possible to distinguish between them by means of psychological laboratory experiments. Perception, attention, consciousness, memory, retention, train of ideas (the thought process), associations, inhibition, mental efficiency, mood, pressure of activity and speech, degree of excitability—these were some of the functions Kraepelin considered fundamental.

However, although it was Kraepelin who envisaged these psychological functions as fundamental, he did not proceed to organize them into a consistent framework from the point of view of psychopathology or psychology

Read at the 102nd annual meeting of the American Psychiatric Association, Chicago, Illinois, May 27–30, 1946. First published in The American Journal of Psychiatry, *103:473–476, 1947.*

proper. The list just cited confuses functions with phenomena (e.g., attention as a function and inhibition as a phenomenon); it also includes functions not clearly distinguished from one another (e.g., memory and retention). Further, the so-called "fundamental" psychological functions as listed by Kraepelin include many symptoms, such as hallucinations and delusions.

Bleuler, the other fountainhead of modern psychiatry, was much more clear-sighted in this respect. In his rarely read and untranslated volume *Dementia Praecox, or the Group of Schizophrenias*[1] he distinguished the fundamental or *primary* symptoms of schizophrenia from its secondary symptoms. As primary symptoms he included the association disturbances, the affect disturbances, and the ambivalence, with corollary disturbances in perception and apperception, orientation, memory, consciousness, motility, reality appraisal, attention, and will; and as the *secondary* symptoms he listed sensory illusions, delusions, catalepsy, stupor, negativism, mannerisms, hyperactivity, automatism, echopraxia, impulsive acts, confusion, twilight states, deliria, and fugues. According to him, the primary symptoms precede the secondary ones in time—often by a considerable period—hence he considered the early detection of these primary symptoms to be the prime diagnostic task in schizophrenia. Bleuler relied partly on the word-association experiment and partly on the interview to establish the presence or absence of such primary symptoms. Like Kraepelin, he hoped that psychological experimentation would become the tool for detecting disordered functioning before gross and overt mental disorder develops.

We are therefore justified in asking what progress has been made to date in the wake of the initial ideas of these two thinkers. The balance sheet one can draw up from modern textbooks of psychiatry indeed provides a disappointing answer. Interest in psychological functions (in the sense quoted above from Kraepelin and Bleuler) did not increase; in fact it *decreased*. There seem to be two good reasons for this. The reasons lie in the retardations in the development of psychiatry on the one hand and in those of psychology on the other.

On the side of psychiatry, for a long time the prevalent nosology was arbitrary and not based on the etiology of the disorders, and therefore any differential diagnostic technique was doomed to failure. Psychological experiment could be no more useful than the framework in which it was applied. Interest in psychiatry subsequently, and to some extent consequently, shifted to the etiology of mental disorder and the new emphasis fell partly on neuropathology and partly on psychopathology of psychoanalytic orientation.

On the side of psychology, it must be remembered that the laboratory of Wundt, whence Kraepelin's work emerged, was also the cradle of experimental psychology. Psychology was at its very beginnings. The functions

---

[1] [An English translation was published in 1950—Ed.]

and phenomena it proposed to investigate were not yet well defined. How could these ill-defined functions have been the basis for sound diagnostic differentiations, even if they had been applied to etiologically clear nosological entities? They were not applied, however, and the result was discouragement, reflected in the literature by futile, unsystematic attempts and by loss of interest.

The integrating of the efforts of psychiatry and psychology had to be postponed until more etiological clarity had been achieved in psychiatry and more theoretical maturity had been reached in psychology. Thus, the ways of the two disciplines, once so closely linked, parted. The distance between them grew particularly great when psychiatry's interest in dynamics and etiology became all-absorbing, e.g., in psychoanalysis; and when psychology's paramount interest became theoretical, e.g., in gestalt psychology.

In the meantime, however, psychological testing, issuing from a cradle different from the common Wundtian cradle, developed on its own and served as a temporary liaison between psychology and psychiatry. It was first confined to intelligence testing, later to aptitude testing and to the questionnaire method of personality testing. Yet, all the while, it again and again used the association experiment and, under the fructifying influence of dynamic psychiatry, it also developed what is commonly called projective testing.

Today, psychological testing has reached an unparalleled development in this country and has proved that it is here to stay. Yet for a long while it suffered under the same handicaps which doomed to failure the early attempts at joining the efforts of psychiatry and psychology. It set out first to appraise intelligence before the concept intelligence was systematically understood. In the absence of systematic understanding, pragmatic application, always handy, was the result. In general, intelligence tests were applied only to make pragmatic distinctions between degrees of mental ability and efficiency. This remained the case until recently, even though for the last 35 years efforts were also made to study the qualitative relationships between different parts of intelligence-test performance and different types of adjustments and maladjustments, as well as the qualitative relationships between different types of responses on the word-association test and different types of disorders. These efforts of psychological testing were also handicapped, as indicated above, by the continuing lack of nosological clarity in psychiatry, and also by the fact that validation of diagnostic indicators was precluded by the conflicting and inconsistent diagnostic criteria used in state hospitals, the usual source of cases for research. An additional handicap was the statistical-pragmatic construction of intelligence tests, without a theoretical orientation. As a matter of fact, even most of the currently popular projective tests were developed as pragmatic procedures (excepting perhaps the play techniques, which were based on the concept of the projection mechanism and which used psychoanalytic interpretive principles).

The Rorschach Test and the Thematic Apperception Test developed without theoretical clarity as to the processes involved in producing the responses and as to the laws governing the relationship between response and personality make-up. Yet old-timers in clinics well knew that there are qualitative relationships between test performance and specific diagnosis, and had hunches as to how the development of a story or response comes about differently in different types of people and in different types of sick people. This knowledge, however, remained either anecdotally or not at all recorded. So the Kraepelin-Bleuler heritage, the idea that changes in psychological functions or their relationships is characteristic and therefore diagnostic of different types of disorders, remained all but forgotten even with the advent of general interest in testing.

Psychiatry, however, has begun to approach greater etiological clarity—even though it is far from having solved its nosological problems. Similarly, psychology has grown out of its mechanistic childhood boots; and its developmental, comparative, and experimental, as well as theoretical, achievements set at least a baseline against which evaluation of efficiency of functioning can be made. In psychological testing new advances have been made, not only in the sense of developing more, new, bigger, and better testing procedures, but also in the sense that interest has arisen in the functions that go into achievements or reactions on different tests.

Therefore the time appears to be ripe once again to raise the Kraepelinian and Bleulerian questions: what psychological functions are selectively impaired in different mental disorders; and can we, and how are we to, establish the presence or absence of the primary symptoms of mental disorder before the gross, secondary symptoms are clinically conspicuous?

Diagnostic psychological testing can help answer these questions, motivated as it now is to approach every case with these questions in the back of its mind. It has the advantage over clinical observation in that it has completely-recorded segments of the patient's behavior at its disposal, and through the study, scoring, and evaluation of these segments it makes possible quantitative inter- and intraindividual comparison of those psychological functions which go into producing the various achievements and reactions on the several tests. Clinical observation, in contrast, never has isolated segments of behavior nor has it had quantifiable behavior at its disposal. For example, a notation of impairment of both judgment and attention based on direct observation or case history is at best only a gross estimate, and does not allow for a decision as to which of the two functions is the more impaired. But only such relative assessment of impairment or retention of psychological functions can serve as an objectification of what Kraepelin already observed: that specific impairments are characteristic of specific mental disorders. Furthermore, fine interindividual comparisons of impairments cannot be made from clinical observation: who would be ready to say which is the poorer of two poor judgments made in two different settings by two different people? Or who will be or is able to judge without tests like the association test or Rorschach Test the presence of a fundamental but early associative disorder, distinguishing the products of such an associative disorder from genuine originality of thought and wealth of idiosyncratic memories?

In today's clinical psychology a variety of new intelligence tests (particularly the Bellevue Scale) and concept-formation tests (particularly those of Goldstein), as well as the Rorschach Test and its parallel series; the Thematic Apperception Test, and the various quantifiable play and other projective procedures all serve to eludicate assets and impairments in various psychological functions. And modern psychiatry's trend toward a loosening of nosological rigidity allows for more reliable comparison of varieties of mental disorders in regard to the characteristically impaired psychological functions in each. Furthermore, the ever-increasing interest of dynamic psychiatry in ego psychology and defense mechanisms opens a way for psychiatry to understand assets of everyday psychological functioning and to compare these with assets seen in test achievements. Finally, the theoretical developments of psychology allow for exploring the specific nature of these functions, which, by their impairments or by their being outstanding assets of the individual, reflect the character or the disorder make-up, the defense mechanisms or their breakdown, used by the individual to cope with his conflicts.

It appears that the following interlocking sequence is fundamentally important for the test assessment of patients in adjustment and maladjustment: certain patterns of defense mechanisms are adopted and these determine specific strengths and weaknesses in psychological functioning which then become characteristic of the adjustment of the personality; with the onset of maladjustment, an exaggeration or breakdown in these strengths and weaknesses characteristic for that maladjustment occurs which can be measured; this leads to a diagnostic differentiation.

For the psychological examiner the interlocking sequence should be, first, knowledge of the dynamic etiology of the mental disorder as productive of specific defenses or their breakdown; second, the theoretical knowledge of the psychological functions which are related to specific defenses or their breakdown; and finally, the knowledge of tests of the psychological functions.

The systematic and intelligent use of tests in psychiatry should yield extremely fruitful results. The employment of these test methods should not only lead to a greater proportion of correct and timely diagnoses, but in addition they can be utilized in an experimental way to investigate an important aspect of ego psychology, namely, the nature of human thinking.

As a practical matter this is now working out as follows: Psychological testing has revealed the presence of a schizophrenic process in many patients, while clinical evidence of schizophrenic tendencies is faint or absent.

To put it another way, the psychologist is discovering schizophrenia or "potential" schizophrenia or "latent" schizophrenia in patients who are not suspected of being classifiable as schizophrenic according to old concepts and who have puzzled the psychiatrist diagnostically and therapeutically. This is not happening in a few cases, but in a considerable number of cases, enough to make us suspect that the vast majority of persons in whom a "schizophrenic process" is present are not easily recognizable as such without specific testing. It may be, indeed, that it is only the exceptional schizophrenic who comes to the psychiatric hospital for treatment, and it may be, again, that many persons whom we have called "alcoholic addicts," "psychopathic personalities," "intractable neuroses," and so on, must be viewed in a very different diagnostic (and therefore therapeutic) light. If so, our present nosological systems and many of our notions about "typical" clinical pictures are going to have to be radically revised. It may be that we shall have to look more sharply for certain traits of negativism, incongruity, impracticality, and so on, and less searchingly for such gross manifestations of dereism as hallucinations and ideas of reference.

This is only one of the modifications in psychiatry which collaboration with modern psychological testing techniques is bringing about. The better the cooperation between psychologists and psychiatrists, the better founded will be the development of new nosological concepts, the more accurate and more timely our diagnoses, and the more specifically directed our treatment.

19

SOME REQUIREMENTS FOR A
CLINICALLY USEFUL
THEORY OF MEMORY

> This paper was the last of a series of twelve lectures, entitled "To What End Psychology?," given at the Menninger School of Psychiatry in the late 1940's. The lectures were designed as an introduction to psychology for psychiatrists, and, as such, were both elementary and general. Therefore, and also because they have suffered somewhat from the passage of time, the series as a whole has not been included in this volume. No. 10 was originally published in 1947 and is reprinted as Chapter 20. The present paper is published here because of its intrinsic merit and because it is still useful today—M.M.G.

In my original outline I planned to spend one or two lectures on the problems psychiatry poses to its basic science, psychology. As I wrote out these lectures, working from hour to hour, I was left with only one lecture of the twelve for this topic. After some thought I decided that it would probably be best if I limited myself to one problem and demonstrated on it how

This paper, written in 1947, is published here for the first time.

psychiatry poses problems for psychology. I hope that this example will also show how the intention to pose problems for solution can enrich psychiatry and how the problems, once posed, promise to enrich psychology also.

I

First, I should like to make a few ad hoc assumptions, making it clear in advance that these assumptions are merely to simplify the argument and we need not necessarily attribute any validity to them otherwise.

First, let us assume that psychopathological phenomena, or phenomena of abnormal psychology, and psychological phenomena in normals are not two different classes, but parts of the same continuum. Second, let us assume that every theory of memory implies a theory of learning and vice versa. Third, let us assume that the memory theories of classical associationism, of conditioned reflex, of the Yale-type conditioned response, of gestalt psychology, of Lewin as far as he had one, of Skinner, Guthrie, Sir Henry Head, and Bartlett, all hold different parts of the same elephant—memory—and that therefore we need not engage here in a dispute with them.

II

Next, let us review a few clinical findings.

(1) AMNESIA

In the textbooks two kinds of amnesia are usually mentioned, retrograde and anterograde. More recently a third type was added which Abeles and Schilder called "loss of personal identity." I have had the opportunity to study a dozen or so cases of amnesia representing all three types. In retrograde amnesia, all that has happened either in the patient's life or in a discrete period preceding a certain event is forgotten. In anterograde amnesia, all that was experienced after a certain event is no longer retained. In cases of "loss of personal identity" the patients forget only what pertains to their personal identity, while information on and memory of things more or less impersonal remain intact. I may mention that the cases of "loss of personal identity" and retrograde amnesia that I have studied or read of gave some rather good evidence that the short-lived retrograde amnesia usually covers periods of "loss of personal identity." What do these three types of amnesia mean for memory theory? Since all three may occur in psychogenic and reversible forms, the state of affairs is relatively transparent. Two requirements for a memory theory issue from it:

(a) It is required that a memory theory account for a memory organization that is amenable to a massive, total, retrograde forgetting of life events and amenable to forgetting only of memories directly pertaining to personal identity. To use a weak simile: it is as if a rock split both along a horizontal plane and along the root system of a tree growing in it. This requirement would become much more complex and specific if consideration were given to multiple personalities and to the phenomena described in Freud's *The Psychopathology of Everyday Life,* etc.

(b) It is required that a memory theory be so structured as to account for the forgetting of past experiences and also for the inability to retain experiences progressively encountered. Actually, German psychiatry and to some extent German psychology had terms to distinguish the two— *Merkfähigkeit* and *Erinnerungsfähigkeit*—ability of notation and ability of recall. Neither German psychiatry nor German psychology made an attempt to clarify these concepts and their theoretical implications.

(2) WORD ASSOCIATION TEST

For further clinical data, let us turn to the Association Experiment, or Word Association Test, and see what bearing it may have on memory theory. In the association experiment, when a certain response word to the same stimulus is very frequently given by subjects, we speak of a "popular response." It has been known since Kent and Rosanoff's work—and my own published work has emphatically confirmed it—that there is a strong general tendency in normals as well as in psychiatric patients to give such "popular responses." We found in a normal population 60 per cent, in a neurotic population 53 per cent, in a psychotic population 43 per cent popular responses. It is also well known that the most common disturbance in the association experiment is delayed response. At times, however, prolonged response time is followed by a standard response or in the extreme by no response. Many subjects report a blank in the period of delay, and yet subsequent clinical examination shows that the stimulus word itself touched upon a central problem of the subject. There are other types of association disturbances. One of these is where the subject's response is by no means a standard response word; rather, it reveals a central problem of his. While he may or may not be aware of this, subsequent clinical examination will show that even the stimulus word itself was related to this central problem. In yet another association disturbance the subject may respond with a word which neither for him nor for the examiner appears to have anything to do with the stimulus word, nor does the clinical examination always discover the relationship. Such a response is called a "distant response." When extreme, or repeatedly present in one record, it is usually an indicator of some degree of schizoid trend or schizophrenic disorder. But what does all this have to do with memory theory? I believe we can assume that the first word brought to the mind by a stimulus word is one closely associated with it in the person's memory organization. How is that organization constituted if it usually brings forth "popular responses" while in association disturbances it brings forth either responses of great affective-personal significance, or responses which conspicuously deviate from the "popular responses," sometimes to the point of being bizarre? It is as if memory were so organized that the handiest response words are a matter of high social agreement; it is as if it were so organized that where important emotional problems are touched, the popular agreement breaks down and a personally significant response breaks through; finally, it appears to be so organized that in far-reaching fundamental disturbances of the personality, the links responsible for popular agreement are more or less abandoned. Therefore, it should be required:

(a) That memory theory account for the far-reaching agreement in different people as to what words are most intimately linked with a given stimulus word;

(b) That it account for the mode in which affects interfere with the popular response;

(c) That it account for disturbances where apparently no specific affect interferes, yet the principle of social agreement seems discarded.

(3) INTELLIGENCE TESTING

Let us now turn to data derived from intelligence testing to see what we find there of import for memory theory.

Let us first compare three subtests that have to do with memory: Information, Digit Span, and Story Recall. As we all know, an information test calls for isolated bits of information ranging from "Who is the President of the U.S.?" through "Who discovered the North Pole?" to "What is the Apocrypha?" Digit Span asks for a repetition forward and backward of ever-increasing series of numbers called out by the examiner. Story Recall asks for the repetition of a one-paragraph story immediately following reading by the examiner and also after a 10- to 15-minute delay.

When equated scores for these three subtests are available, the discrepancies between them are brought sharply into relief, and we find cases with great intrapersonal discrepancies both in psychiatric populations and in "normal" groups. A few patterns of these discrepancies should be mentioned here. If these three tests are given in a battery of tests, we are likely to find cases in which the scores on both Information and Story Recall are at least average, while the person gets a low score on Digit Span. This pattern is common for a great part of the normal population. Very common for psychiatric populations is the pattern: Information and Story Recall, far superior to most of the other subtests of the battery, Digit Span, profoundly lowered. In a normal population a group of cases will show an average performance on Information and Story Recall with Digit Span far above that. So far our examples have centered on Digit Span. If we focus on Information, we will find cases—both normal and neurotic—where Information alone will be below the Story Recall and below that person's average performance, and cases where Digit Span and Information will be below both Story Recall and the person's average. Statistical findings appear to indicate that these last groups are related to the clinical syndrome of hysteria in which repression is one of the outstanding defense mechanisms. Finally, if we center our attention on Story Recall, we will find cases— mainly in the psychotic population—where Story Recall is profoundly impaired while Information is intact and Digit Span may or may not be impaired and may even be far above the person's average.

What are the inferences one may draw for memory theory from these clinical data? With some complacency one obviously could settle this matter by maintaining that these differences have long been known to us, and simply say: Information is the piecemeal recall of remote memories, Story Recall is the immediate and delayed recall of meaningful material, and Digit Span is the immediate recall of rote or nonsense memory material. This is, however, like the explanation in Molière of why opium produces sleep—"Because there is in it sleep-producing power"—and a close look at the literature of immediate, delayed, and remote recall, and of rote, piecemeal, and meaningful memory material will show that our knowledge of their relationships is minimal. The gestalt psychologists' efforts notwithstanding, our present techniques of experimentation, our present constructs of memory theory, do not facilitate but rather prohibit clarifying their relationships.

I believe that out of these data the following requirements for memory theory issue:

(a) It is required that memory theory be so structured as to account for the relationships between immediate, delayed, and remote recall as well as for the relationships between memory for rote, piecemeal, and meaningful material. In passing, one might mention that the problems of incidental memory, reminiscence, and oblivescence are related to this point.

(b) It is required that memory theory take cognizance of and account for the individual differences in various forms of recall and for various types of memory material; it should consider the study of these individual differences as one of the highways toward building an adequate theory of memory.

(c) It is required that memory theory clarify the concept of memory so as to account for the discrepancies seen in clinical findings. It is particularly urgent to clarify whether we should conceive of memory as one among many functions of the organism, or as a "capacity" having certain rules of mobilization of its own. If memory is one function among many, the following situation obtains: since no complete functional independence can be envisaged in the human organism, the memory function would never be completely isolable experimentally and a study of it would require the simultaneous study of the other functions interacting with it. If memory is a "capacity," then I am afraid memory theory will have to deny that it is obliged to account for the clinical phenomena here discussed.

Clinical experience with each one of these three tests raises still further questions in regard to memory theory.

(1) Let me discuss Information. I have mentioned that the pattern of Information score being lower than a person's average score on the other tests of a battery is statistically associated with hysterical traits of personality make-up or hysterical features of maladjustment. Now it is well known that one of the operating mechanisms in such personality make-ups and/or maladjustments is clinically referred to as "repression." Freud demonstrated repression mainly on clinical examples of the forgetting of specific events, data, and relationships, and on the massive oblivescence of childhood events. The former are elusive for experimental investigation. A memory has to be related to *fundamental* attitudes and strivings unacceptable to the ego, otherwise its elimination from memory cannot justifiably be considered repression. To manipulate or elicit in the laboratory such fundamental strivings and attitudes has proved to be difficult. Most experimentalists therefore took the easy path and misinterpreted repression to mean the "forgetting of the unpleasant." What relation that has to repression is hard to describe briefly. Several years ago I wrote a monograph, *Emotions and Memory* (1942), devoted to a critical analysis of the pertinent evidence, experimental and otherwise. In the clinical material of psychological testing, however, we find a new kind of evidence, a new avenue of exploration. This evidence seems to indicate that repression not only refers to isolated events related to unacceptable strivings, but may become a general characteristic of memory organization with the result that memory organization limits generally the assimilation of material of experience, resulting in a limited store of knowledge and information. I believe that from here, again, several requirements issue for a memory theory:

(a) It is required that memory theory be so structured as to account for phenomena of repression in both of the following forms: where it eliminates isolated memories related to fundamental strivings unacceptable to the ego, and where it so influences memory organization that assimilation of experiential material into information and knowledge becomes generally impeded.

(b) It is required that memory theory differentiate between structural and affective regulation in memory. That is to say, it should account for what would be called in clinical parlance the ego psychology of memory—for instance, the general restriction on assimilating information—and it should also account for what would be called the id psychology of memory—for instance, the repression of specific affectively important and personally unacceptable memories. It should account for the clinical finding that in certain types of personality make-up and disorder, the accumulation of

e.g., aggressive feelings, becomes extremely strong, or where control of aggressions is rigid) they distort the story content even where the meaning structure is retained. The affect will then distort the story content, exaggerate its destructive details, or erase them directly. The more profound the maladjustment, the stronger the sway affect has on recall; thus the standard story of a flood may become a fire, a hailstorm, an iceberg rushing in on a town. Here a disturbance of the frame of reference combines with an affective organization of memory, the latter taking the place of memory frames of reference. I believe that the following consequences issue from this:

(a) It is required that memory theory be so structured as to account for both the logical meaning structure and the affective meaning structure of the material, which normally intertwine but in certain conditions may become separated.

(b) It is required that memory theory be so structured as to account for the relationship between meaning structure and content details.

(c) It is required that memory theory account for both improvement and impairment of recall after repetition.

III

Now that I have surveyed a segment of clinical data pertinent to memory theory, I must make several admissions. First, I have avoided burdening this argument with references to Selz, Ach, Marbe, and many others who are now all but forgotten, but who saw many of the problems here referred to. Second, I realize that I have given no answers, but only raised questions. In self-defense, I want to remind you that I did not undertake to do anything else. Third, to achieve the latter would have required much more space and much more complex an argument. I was tempted to say I did not want to burden you with it—the truth is, I don't feel I am prepared to cope with it. To attempt to cover the field more completely would require a discussion of the memory implications of other tests, for instance the Rorschach and the Thematic Apperception Tests, and of other conditions such as confusional states, organic disorders, e.g., the Korsakoff syndrome, and experience with toxicosis and drugs in general. All this would necessitate so many ad hoc assumptions for the creating of a common ground for discussion that I felt disinclined to embark on it.

To end this presentation I can say only this: Memory experimentation appears to have reached an impasse, a blind alley, or let us say, a point of diminishing returns. Clinical observation and statistical data issuing from psychological tests put new concrete questions to experimental psychology, and offer new horizons for theory formation. Out of the latter, productive experimentation could issue. With this presentation I wanted to call your attention to concrete problems posed by clinical observation. They are a challenge to the reductive ingenuity of the experimenter.

I wanted to show that psychological test data can be used for more than a gross correlational analysis of achievement and molecular clinical behavior—as Brunswik would put it, I suppose. It is not the sole use of test data to establish their statistical association with clinical syndromes. In fact, diagnostic psychological testing as we know it today does not and cannot work that way. It presupposes understanding of the psychological functions underlying test performance; it presupposes knowledge of the dynamics of adjustment and maladjustment; it requires knowledge about the vicissitudes of various psychological functions under various dynamic conditions of adjustment and maladjustment. It requires all this to enable us to reconstruct from patterns of achievement the status of the functions implied in achievement, to infer from these the prevailing dynamic conditions of adjustment and maladjustment, and to conclude—in turn—from these the clinical status of the patient. Putting it in Brunswik's terms, test data are amenable to, and in fact demand, a treatment in terms of "mediationalism" and "geneticism."

Psychologists—academic or clinical—are critical, often even scornful, of the type of empirical data-collecting and theory-making prevalent in psychiatry. To be critical, however, imposes responsibilities. The status of knowledge concerning adjustment and maladjustment is precarious indeed and needs study. The password of such study is: the laws of psychological functioning are indivisible; they are the same in adjustment and maladjustment. And theory formation must take this into account. To my mind, the solution lies in the experimenter's becoming familiar with the data of the clinic. These will indicate how he must formulate his theories if they are to bear on our understanding of psychopathology.

REFERENCE

Rapaport, D. (1942). *Emotions and Memory*. Baltimore: Williams & Wilkins.

20

PSYCHOLOGICAL TESTING:

ITS PRACTICAL AND ITS

HEURISTIC SIGNIFICANCE

I will have to divide my presentation into two parts. The first part will deal with psychological testing and its practical significance. In this part I intend to give you a description of psychological testing as I see it and its clinical role as we practice it. The second part will deal with the heuristic significance of psychological testing. In that part I would like to present some investigations in psychological testing that pertain to ego psychology.

I

The best way to obtain a perspective of psychological testing is to consider our clinical psychiatric tools, disregarding for the moment the psychoanalytic technique. Case history and observation-interview are the time-honored tools of clinical psychiatry. Psychological testing originated when Simon and Binet grew dissatisfied with the subjective character of judging mental retardation in children from the case history and from observation. They wanted to have objective measures. They opened an era of striving for objectivity, for the measurement of intellectual capacities. This striving for objectivity generalized fast, particularly when it reached this country and

First published in Samiksa, *1:245–262, 1947.*

spread to other areas of psychological endeavor. Intelligence quotients were supplemented by personality quotients, educational quotients, adjustment quotients, etc. As usual with a bona fide trend, it went to extremes which may nowadays seem ludicrous. Such development, however, always carries in itself the seed of its opposite. Quantitative observations started to pile up. It was noticed that in the various parts of the intelligence test performance subjects showed striking discrepancies, failing on some parts while achieving high scores on others. It was noticed that *qualitative* peculiarities of thinking are observable in these tests. On the negative side, it was noticed that the numerical measures obtained, the various quotients themselves, far from leading to the hoped-for complete understanding of the person, led to utter confusion and sterility.

In the meantime subjective methods, like graphology and physiognomy, were not stamped out by this striving for objectivity, nor was the judgment of people by body build. As to the trend of development issuing from Kraepelin's observations that specific disturbances of intelligence, will, attention, memory, thinking, etc., are present in various psychiatric disorders, and from Bleuler's observation that the association disturbance is the primary symptom of schizophrenia—this trend was arrested by the striving for objectivity but not forgotten. It has lived in rudimentary form in psychiatric clinics.

Striving for objectivity was in its heyday in this country when Rorschach first published his test, and still going strong when play techniques inspired and developed by psychoanalysis made their first appearance. Striving for objectivity had strong foundations in associationistic psychology and the psychology of conditioned response. But, by the time of the thirties, the wings of these psychologies were pretty badly broken by the attacks of gestalt psychology, Lewinian psychology, and the first effects of psychoanalysis on psychology. By 1933, the first year of the influx of European psychologists to this country, the first battles of breaking the hegemony of spurious objectivity were already won by Gordon Allport, Gardner Murphy, and others.

The Rorschach Test and its use spread like wildfire. Projective techniques of all kinds, drawing, painting, finger painting, the visual-motor gestalt test issuing from gestalt psychological experimentation, concept-formation tests issuing from Gelb and Goldstein's investigations in the brain injured, play techniques, psychodrama, and many others showed a luxuriant growth. Murray's new projective technique, the Thematic Apperception Test, came to stay and to rival the Rorschach Test in stability and importance. Objectivity in intelligence testing was the staunchest die-hard. Finally, observations on the discrepancies of an individual's achievements on various parts of an intelligence test jelled when the Wechsler-Bellevue Intelligence Scale, the parts of which are homogeneous items groups, made these discrepancies startlingly obvious. Intraindividual discrepancies drew interest and the correspondence of these discrepancies in functional efficacy to personality make-up and pathology have begun to be explored.

A new picture of testing emerged. A new-found objectivity of qualitative exploration grew up. This testing was no longer the establishment of a numerical score of one or another attribute of a person with occasional qualitative observations in the testing situation. This testing became the laboratory attached to the psychiatric clinic. The clinician gathered material by interview, by historical material obtained from relatives and from the patient, and by observations on the patient in the interpersonal situation between the patient and himself. He organized this material to yield a diagnosis and to reconstruct out of the patient's past performance and present behavior his make-up and the nature of his trouble. The psychological tester did not use case history, did not assess interpersonal relationships. Rather he conceived of the individual as a unit who carries deposited within the confines of his skin all that his life history made him to be; the psychologist considered his test a controlled situation for the purpose of eliciting information extant within the confines of the skin of the individual. He had to make the general assumption that anything and everything an individual does is characteristic of his make-up and maladjustment (if any). As these characteristics are covered up by much conventional material, modern tests try to create situations in which the subject does not know the meaning of his reactions and thus minimize the appearance of the conventional, crystallized patterns of social convenience that would cover up what is idiosyncratic and individual. The Rorschach Test achieves this by presenting unorganized inkblots. The Thematic Apperception Test achieves it by presenting photographs of ambiguous, indefinite situations. These and similar unstructured but standard situations became the basis of the projective tests. The standardization and the careful choice of situations was necessary in order to obtain material which is amenable to scoring in terms of formal characteristics. By formal characteristics we mean that not *what* the patient says or does but rather *how* he says it, *how* he does it is important. This *how* can be scored and put into formal categories the patient is not aware of and does not command. These are some formal characteristics: on the Rorschach Test some people are inclined to respond to details of the card, others to the whole of the card, again others to tiny details of it; some persons will react to the form of the cards, others to their colors, and again others to their shadings. Scoring on the basis of such formal characteristics allows for counting the responses. Counting allows for direct comparison of intrapersonal discrepancies in efficacy of functions and for interpersonal comparison of achievements. Thereby similarities and differences in personality make-up and diagnostic categories could be expressed more or less in patterns of numerical scores.

Thus, the cornerstones of present-day diagnostic testing are: (1) to confront the patient with an unstructured situation to eliminate his use of conventional responses; (2) to confront him with a standardized situation, that is to say, one which is the same for all subjects and at the same time one in which his total reaction can be recorded, in contrast to the clinical situation in which the total behavior of the individual can never be recorded; (3) to choose testing situations so that they yield responses amenable to scoring on formal characteristics; and finally, (4) to use a scoring that is expressible in numerical terms and allows for inter- and intrapersonal comparisons.

These inter- and intrapersonal comparisons on the various tests led to findings characteristic of various types of personality make-up and various types of pathology. Let us not forget, however, that they led to these in the hands of people who knew about personality make-up and clinical nosological categories as well as testing. These comparisons led not to single scores characteristic of this or that type of personality or disorder. We all know that if they had led to such single characteristic scores, they would have been just as spuriously objective as were the original intelligence quotients. Rather, they led to indices referring to the kinds of inclinations and characteristics present in the subject. These indices formed patterns. There are as many such patterns as there are people. A pattern may conform with one commonly seen in this or that type of personality or disorder; but it is always unique, and to reconstruct the individual personality it is not enough to state which standard pattern this individual resembles most, but it is necessary to state in what ways he deviates from that standard pattern and to state specifically what is his personality which is his alone and unlike anyone else's on earth.

It was discovered that tests, though objective in that they record a totality of a behavior sample—which clinical observation, which always must make selections, never can—and objective in that in them the behavior sample recorded can be objectively classified into scoring categories, and objective in the sense that the scores can be numerically expressed, making direct "interpersonal comparison" possible, are not going to do the work of diagnosing automatically like a machine or like the I.Q. intelligence tester. It became clear that, to handle tests, it is necessary to have people who understand clinical syndromes and clinically observed character make-ups, who have a well-grounded dynamic understanding of these, and who approach the patterns of test indices on the basis of this dynamic understanding. With such an approach, the tester can reconstruct a meaningful picture of the patient's character and maladjustment. When this recognition was reached—and one must sadly admit that it has not yet been reached by all clinical psychologists—the last door was shut on the spurious objectivity that sired all testing procedures.

Diagnostic testing thus emerged as the laboratory of a new kind of objective method of clinical psychiatry. Besides anamnesis, good medical practice requires laboratory findings. With the advent of diagnostic testing, psychiatry began to avail itself of a set of tools for similar practice. This beginning is reaping its fruits. It is not uncommon to see that children, to all appearances feeble-minded, are revealed by the tests as psychotic, or severely neurotic. It is not infrequent in cases of multiple obsessions to discover by the tests a masked schizophrenic process. Particularly where there is no time for exhaustive history taking and contact with relatives, psychological tests offer significant safeguards.

For a follow-up during treatment and for checking the clinical assessment of treatment results, tests are proving more and more to be an indispensable tool. It is quite possible that only the further development and spread of their use will bring us out of the shameful situation that no consistent objective studies of therapeutic techniques and their results have ever been conducted.

II

But this leads me to the second part of my paper, the heuristic value of psychological tests. I would like to make two brief introductions.

What we see most immediately reflected in all our tests is the thought organization of the subject. Whatever else we infer from the tests is read from the peculiarities of the subject's thought organization indicating his type of control of impulses or the encroachment of impulses on his thought organization. Thus, a theory of psychological testing implies a fundamental theory of thought organization. This, however, is obviously a part of ego psychology.

Our deficiencies in developing an ego psychology, and particularly a psychology of thinking, are greatly responsible for the confusion that ensued whenever a group seceded from the psychoanalytic fold. Actually the majority of these groups promulgated a common-sense psychology of environmentalism, tacitly disclaiming all obligation of psychoanalysis to build either a systematic metapsychology or an ego psychology. It we had a systematic ego psychology, the environmentalist fallacy could be easily unmasked as unpsychological.

The explorations in the psychology of thinking made necessary and possible by psychological testing contribute to building such a systematic ego psychology. In the rest of this presentation I shall try to demonstrate in what way this is accomplished.

The shift of emphasis in psychoanalytic theory and practice from exclusive interest in unconscious content to mechanisms of defense spelled the beginnings of a psychoanalytic ego psychology. At first psychoanalysis kept clear of problems of the ego. There were reasons for this. Psychoanalysis was the first psychology which carried into the field of exploration of the psyche the general scientific requirement that the subject matter of science be divested of conscious qualities, or as is customary to refer to them, secondary qualities. No wonder, then, that it had to keep away from the ego,

which at first was conceived of as the system *Pcpt.-Cs.* Discoveries showing
the existence of unconscious parts of the ego paved the way for psychoanalysis to make the ego the subject matter of its investigations. Ego psychology, however, is a late child of psychoanalysis and has still great limitations
in many respects. Our knowledge of the intellect, organization of thought
processes, adaptation to environment, sublimation and integration achievements, all of which are ego functions, is pitifully scanty in contrast to what
we know of the mechanisms of the unconscious and the defenses of the ego.
Usually the assumption is made that the ego develops out of the id. So far
very few phases of this development have been isolated or demonstrated
with any degree of clarity. As a matter of fact, Heinz Hartmann lucidly
demonstrated that sooner or later empirical evidence may force us to assume that potential ego characteristics are native and that the choice of
defense mechanisms is constitutionally performed.[1]

If the ego psychology of psychoanalysis were a well-developed explanatory theory extending over all ego functions, it would be altogether unwarranted to expect a contribution to it from results of psychological tests,
which are themselves tools developed in a very haphazard fashion. In the
present state of affairs, however, any contribution to systematizing the phenomena of the intellect and of thought processes should be highly welcome,
because only a phenomenological systematization of the field can pave the
way to theoretical systematization. In this presentation I shall restrict myself to the relationship of a few results of intelligence testing to ego psychology.

First, however, some considerations on ego organization.

INSTINCT AND INTELLECT

I would like to start out with a few quotations. Anna Freud wrote (1936,
p. 178):

> This intellectualization of instinctual life, the attempt to lay hold on
> the instinctual processes by connecting them with ideas which can be
> dealt with in consciousness, is one of the most general, earliest and
> most necessary acquirements of the human ego. We regard it not as an
> activity of the ego but as one of its indispensable components.

Heinz Hartmann (1939, p. 13)[2] writes somewhat more concretely: ". . .
some of the relationships between the instinctual drives and *mental devel-*

---

[1] [Rapaport ultimately, on both theoretical and empirical grounds, definitely abandoned
the older assumption of the ego's development from the id in favor of the "undif-
ferentiated-phase" theory of Hartmann (1939) and Hartmann, Kris, and Loewenstein
(1946), which stresses the automonous, independent roots of the developing ego. See,
e.g., Rapaport (1960)—Ed.]

[2] [This paper was written before either of Rapaport's translations of Hartmann (1939)
were published. Quotations from Rapaport's final, 1958, translation have been substituted for the quotations originally given—Ed.]

opment are well known. We know how conflicts and taboos involving instinctual drives may hamper intellectual development, temporarily or permanently." On the other hand, we learn from Anna Freud that in puberty intellectualization serves as a defense against instinctual dangers, intellectualization being an attempt to control the instincts by indirect means. It is in this sense that she says (1936, p. 179): ". . . instinctual danger makes human beings intelligent." We have the right to raise the question: On what does it depend that just this and not any other mode of instinct control is being chosen, in other words, on what does it depend that here more and there less intellectualization comes about? Evidence derived from intelligence testing cannot decide the question here raised; not only that, but the question cannot be decided until we know what this "more or less" of intellectualization means and where it occurs. To the solution of the latter problem, intelligence testing can and has already made some contributions.

The following data are taken from intelligence-test results of some 200 clinical cases falling into 18 clinical classifications and 54 normal control cases of whom 32 were found well adjusted, 17 somewhat maladjusted, and 5 definitely maladjusted. The 200 patients were consecutive cases at our Clinic, the control cases of Kansas farm background. Thus we may expect an initial difference between intelligence quotients to the advantage of the clinical population. Let us see the data. The average I.Q. of the well-adjusted group was 118, that of the rest of the control group only 110. We have to conclude that maladjustment impairs the I.Q. Thus our clinical cases, even though originally of a richer cultural background, being maladjusted, would have to approach the I.Q. of the control.

Let us see the I.Q. distribution in the clinical group. The schizophrenic groups ranged in average between 90 and 100, paranoid states averaged 118, and the preschizophrenics ranged from 118 to 123. The latter were cases in which a schizophrenic process is masked by an obsessive façade. The averages for our depressive groups were not much different from the schizophrenics. The neurotic groups averaged from 107 to 119; among them the obsessive-compulsives 118. The anxiety and depression group— that is, compulsive personalities decompensating into a state of anxiety and depression—averaged 119, while the hysterics averaged 113 and the neurasthenias 107. In short, the clinical groups having an I.Q. equal to or more than the well-adjusted control group were: obsessive-compulsives, anxious and depressed compulsives, schizophrenics with an obsessive façade, and the paranoid states. It needs no special discussion that by nosological definition these are the groups which libidinize thought processes, use ideation and thought processes in symptom formation. There, higher I.Q. shows that prior to their breakdown these cases showed more tendency to intellectualizing than the others. Surely, this finding does not decide whether this intellectualization is due to the activity of a defense mechanism alone or to "native intellectual endowment" that is being used by the defense mechanism. That the lowest I.Q.s are obtained in deterioration, depressive psychotic retardation, and neurasthenic sluggishness goes without saying, and adds nothing to ego psychology. The discrepancy between the low average I.Q. of hysterics and high average I.Q. of obsessionals, however, is a meaningful datum.

You could justifiably object: "This isn't new, you said so yourself; besides, these results could have been theoretically predicted out of nosological definitions—what then is the contribution?" The objection is well taken. This is not a contribution, merely a demonstration that intelligence testing can quantify and check theoretical deductions and clinical observations pertinent to ego psychology. Thus the argument remains very general. These I.Q. differences demonstrate that intelligence tests can be used to systematize and quantify phenomena of ego functioning, a task not previously tackled.

Are there any contributions that can be made beyond demonstrating that intelligence testing is a tool for future contributions? There are a few, I believe. To pave our way to these we have to remember that the I.Q.—just like the term intellectualizing in psychoanalytic literature—is a vague generality that may mean a hundred things. Let us examine the concepts intelligence and intellectualization. What the analyst observes in the cases to which he applies the term "intellectualizing" is a steady tendency of the patient to veer away from dealing with his affects, to reasoning, speculating, rationalizing. It is then generally presumed that that person prizes intellectual pursuits. Nevertheless, even a cursory inquiry will show that among such people some are very poor at learning—interested only in their own mental constructions—while others are very good at learning anything and everything but cannot put two and two together for themselves; others again will be good in everything until it comes to arithmetic, or again, others will be no good in any intellectual performance but arithmetic. The situation is similar with the I.Q., e.g., a high I.Q. can be obtained by very high achievements on one or more test items, with the rest average or impaired. Thus emerges the new problem of differential achievement and differential impairment in various partial intelligence functions and their relationship to various types of ego structures and prevalent defense mechanisms.

Let us hear again from Heinz Hartmann; this time on the problem of differential achievement (1939, p. 62):

> . . . we see intellectual achievements as both tools of conflict solving and of rationalizing, and consider them in relation to the demands of the external world and the superego and, of course, in their interaction with other ego functions. The analysis of inhibitions, neuroses, and particularly psychoses, has made us familiar with all degrees of disorder in the various functions of intelligence; and though the severe degrees occur only in psychoses, the milder, mostly temporary and re-

versible, forms are frequent in other mental illnesses. Each of the functions mentioned may be disturbed: selective control, time perspective, reality testing, objectivation, abstraction, ability to delay . . . . and so on. A specific failure of adaptation corresponds to the disturbance of each of these functions.

These sentences reveal that Hartmann, like most other psychoanalysts, knows intellectual disturbances only in relationship to his own yardstick, that is to say, in relation to the ego, id, and superego, but not in terms of thought processes, not in reference to the relation of the partial thought functions to each other and their significance in everyday adaptation and functioning. This critique means only to point out a neglected frame of reference which psychoanalysis must take account of if ego psychology is to overcome its limitations. This critique does no imply that psychological testing can right now solve the problem or do any more than contribute a step to the understanding of differential attainment and differential impairment in thought processes.

First, what can psychological testing find out about differential achievement? If we look at the average Vocabulary scores of our clinical and control groups, we find the highest average scores are attained in the same four groups that have the highest I.Q.s: paranoid states $13°5$, overideational preschizophrenics $14°6$, anxiety and depression $13°4$, and obsessive-compulsives $13°4$. Of the rest of the groups, only the neurotic depressives and the normal control average more than 12 on Vocabulary.

Now let us take another test: to find a missing part in a drawing requires mainly concentration. When we examine the four neurotic groups on this score, we find that the obsessive-compulsive and the anxiety and depression groups do most poorly. To put together jigsaw pieces of a figure of a man, of a face, and of a hand, is a function requiring mainly visual-motor coordination. Of the psychotic groups, the paranoid states and the overideational preschizophrenics are among the poorest here.

Let us not now raise the question whether these findings were predictable, nor the question of their significance for ego psychology. For the time being let us be satisfied that intelligence tests can be the tools not merely of differentiating intellectualizing and not-intellectualizing types of disorders, but also the tools of spotting other differential attainment and impairment.

Let me call your attention to the fact that within the sphere of thought functioning we have here distinguished between visual organization, motor performance, and verbal attainment. These three are means at the disposal of the ego, the functional relationship of which to those ego functions which have been explored by psychoanalysis has not been as yet established. This is to show that by thus making such differentiations, psychological testing puts new problems before psychoanalytical ego psychology—problems which have so far evaded solution.

One more consideration. Hartmann attempted to differentiate between conflictful and conflict-free ego spheres and functions. He attempted to show that psychoanalytic ego psychology dealt with ego functions expressing conflict, reaction formations to conflict, or defenses against conflict. He pointed to the possibility that some of the conflict-free ego functions may be innate, here mentioning simple perceptual functions; to the possibility that ego functions which came about as defenses or reaction formations may become independent structures. The latter may be activated by instincts but their course of functioning is crystallized and is independent from these instincts that set them off. Hartmann writes (1939, p. 26):

> An attitude which arose originally in the service of defense against an instinctual drive may, in the course of time, become an independent structure, in which case the instinctual drive merely triggers this automatized apparatus . . . , but, as long as the automatization is not controverted, does not determine the details of its action.

In the light of these considerations on the ego, let us again compare the Vocabulary-score averages. We will find that in the four intellectualizing clinical groups vocabulary must belong to a conflict-free sphere, since it is not impaired by the maladjustment. In the schizophrenics, whether paranoid or unclassified, whether acute, chronic, or deteriorated, this is not the case. It may or may not be justified to link up this finding with Freud's suggestion that verbal images in the schizophrenic process are cathected as if they were objects when the schizophrenic withdraws his object cathexes.

DIFFERENTIAL ACHIEVEMENT NO. 1: *Information and Comprehension*

Let us turn our attention to another differential of functions which may be more directly fruitful theoretically. The Bellevue Scale has a group of items called Comprehension which contains questions like: What would you do in a movie fire, with a letter found in the street, when lost in a forest, and questions on why taxes, laws, marriage licenses, etc., are necessary. It is obvious that these questions pertain to judgment. These judgments, like all judgments in life, may more or less deteriorate into mere verbal stereotypes. Another group of items in the Bellevue Scale calls for simple information, ranging from the name of the President of the United States to the meaning of the word Apocrypha. Inasmuch as the Bellevue scores were established for a sample of the average population, it will be no surprise that our normal subjects showed little difference between their judgment and information scores, similarly with the neurotics. In all schizophenic and related groups, information scores are much higher than judgment scores. While information in the schizophrenic remains a more or less conflict-free sphere, judgment belongs in a definitely conflictful sphere.

Let us now compare the judgment and information scores of the hysteriform neurotic groups on the one hand and the obsessional-like neurotic groups on the other hand. In the three hysteriform groups it is judgment that is better retained; in the two obsessive groups it is information. Since information depends on memory functions, it must suffer whenever repression impairs memory, as is assumed to be the case in hysterics. Similarly, in obsessive rumination, judgment must succumb to the manifold possibilities that are being ruminated. Formulated from the point of view of a theoretical ego psychology: judgment in hysterics, but information-memory function in obsessives, are conflict-free ego functions, and conversely, judgment in obsessives but information memory in hysterics are conflictful ego functions. At this point I would like to point out that this is a contribution to ego psychology, because here expectations on the basis of general conceptions of ego psychology, such as repression in hysteria, doubt in obsessionals, have been demonstrated actually to occur. Furthermore, it has been demonstrated that repression and doubt do not manifest themselves only on specific single ideas, but in certain clinical conditions become so generalized as to determine the character of the thought organization of the subject belonging to this category.

The relationships of test results discussed here are merely samples of the types of contribution to ego psychology that can be expected from intelligence testing. It is my firm belief that in the final analysis all such relationships will be amenable to discussion in terms of ego psychology. The last example I would like to give here is somewhat more involved. For that, its significance may prove greater.

Since the tests to be discussed refer to the functions of attention and concentration, and since these are related to the problem of cathexes, I will have to ask you to bear with me again through some restatements of a few general ideas of ego psychology and through a somewhat involved consideration of test materials.

In *The Ego and the Id* we read: ". . . the ego is that part of the id which has been modified by the direct influence of the external world acting through the Pcpt-Cs . . . the ego has the task of bringing the influence of the external world to bear upon the id . . ." (Freud, 1923, pp. 29–30). It is in a sense a buffer between the demands of the instincts and the demands of reality. In "Formulations Regarding the Two Principles in Mental Functioning" (Freud, 1911), we read that by means of thought processes the ego obtains a delay of motor discharge. In other words, the thought process arises in the period of delay between the emergence of the impulse and its actual motor discharge. Obviously one could conceive of the thought process as coming about during the delay of discharge of the instinctual impulse and being energized by the impulse in that delay. This points to a possibility Heinz Hartmann foresaw. May I requote (1939, p. 26):

An attitude which arose originally in the service of defense against an instinctual drive may, in the course of time, become an independent

structure, in which case the instinctual drive merely triggers this automatized apparatus . . . , but, as long as the automatization is not
controverted, does not determine the details of its action.[3]

The rôle of the impulse, then, would be a selective one, determining only
which of the relatively autonomous thought mechanisms be activated. Ego
psychology does have some further knowledge about the nature of these
thought processes. We know that the cathexes of instinct representations
are counteracted by countercathexes of the ego, thus preventing them from
entering consciousness. Furthermore, it is assumed that in order to enter
consciousness the countercathexes must be withdrawn and the representations have to be given hypercathexes by the ego; this appears to be equivalent to the representations becoming linked to verbal images of the preconscious. It is relatively easy to understand the cathexes of the representations
as derived from the instincts which are the sources of psychic energy, and
which originate in the biological sphere. It is much less easy to conceive of
the countercathexes and the hypercathexes. We could visualize their origin
in two ways. We could assume countercathexis to mean that the ego uses
energies derived from instincts to keep another instinct from entering its
ideational representation into consciousness. Or, we could picture the ego
in its development becoming independent of the id, not only as a structure
but also as a dynamic entity having at its disposal energies divested of their
original instinctual character. Indeed, psychoanalytic literature speaks
about ego energies as "desexualized libido." The fact is, however, that
though psychoanalytic literature could be interpreted as leaning toward the
second one of these views, the question is by no means settled. It is quite
possible that both types of processes here assumed occur actually.

Let us turn now to results on the Digit Span and Arithmetic subtests. In
Digit Span the subject is to repeat forward and backward ever-lengthening
series of numbers called out by the examiner. In the past psychologists
considered such performance to be a feat of memory. Empirical and theoretical evidence can be adduced that memory is not the main function underlying performance on Digit Span. Without now adducing the evidence,
let us assume that it would point up Digit Span as a test of attention. This
concept is used here as one closely related to, if not identical with, what the
analyst calls evenly hovering attention, that is to say, a free receptivity
and/or productivity that remains effortless. Let us now turn to the other
test in question, Arithmetic. Its items are simple addition, subtraction,
multiplication, and division. We can presuppose that the patterns of
thought structures necessary to solve these problems are present in adult
people of our civilization. All they have to do is to call upon these structures at their command, that is to say, to concentrate on them. This is

[3] [Rapaport is clearly subsuming "thought processes" under Hartmann's "attitude" and
"apparatus"—Ed.]

usually not an effortless but a voluntary and selective process. Attention is effortless and nonselective, concentration effortful and selective. Attention and concentration then are the two concepts with which we shall now deal.

Let us see the statistical results on these two tests. The statistical data show, first of all, that in normals, neurotics, and depressives, performance is better in Arithmetic, while in the schizophrenias performance is better on Digit Span. Could these findings mean that schizophrenics cannot make the voluntary effort necessary for concentration because their egos do not command sufficient energies independent of instinctual impulses? Similarly, could insufficiency of free effortless intake, that is to say, of attention, of the neurotics mean that they do not possess sufficient free ego energies to keep disturbing affects, anxieties, and impulses out of consciousness? Is it possible that the neurotic still has sufficient ego energies to compensate with voluntary concentration for what effortless attention cannot do, besieged as it is by impulses, affects, and anxieties? It is probably clear to you that this picture again corresponds to Hartmann's conflictful and conflict-free spheres of the ego. Attention, the ability for effortless intake, is conceived of as a corollary of a well-protected ego. Impaired attention, with concentration compensating, is a corollary of an ego encroached upon by impulses, affects, and anxieties, but still able to maintain a reasonable level of efficiency. It will also be clear that attention and concentration both refer to sustained contact with the outside world; hence the schizophrenic's impairment of concentration would correspond more or less to giving up that contact.

To test these hypotheses at least partially, we turn to the affect which is relatively easy to spot, which is relatively stable, and the interference of which with effective contact to the outside world is well known, namely anxiety. The psychiatrist collaborating on the study divided our normal control groups into anxious and nonanxious subjects. We compared their scores on Digit Span and found that the anxious group had a Digit Span very much poorer than that of the nonanxious group. The difference was so great that, according to statistics, such a difference could be due to chance only in 2 to 5 cases in a hundred. In other words, we found that anxiety entering consciousness disturbs "attention." Inasmuch as we already have seen that in schizophrenia Digit Span tends to score high, we had to raise the question: Is this due to the fact that one of the aims of the schizophrenic process is to free the patient of anxiety?

To answer this question our psychiatrist divided the controls into schizoid and nonschizoid groups. The schizoid group was found to have a much higher Digit Span score than the nonschizoid. The difference between the schizoid and nonschizoid groups was so great that according to the statistics only 5 to 10 times in a hundred could it be due to chance. The next step we undertook was to divide our anxious group into schizoid and nonschizoid. We found that the anxious *nonschizoid* controls tended to have an extremely low Digit Span score, the anxious *schizoid* controls tended to have an unusually high one. The difference was so great that, according to the statistics, in only 2 cases out of a hundred could it be due to chance. Accordingly, we excluded from our anxious and nonanxious groups the schizoid controls. We found that the anxious nonschizoid group tended to have a very low Digit Span score, while the nonanxious nonschizoid group tended to have a good average Digit Span score. The difference between *these* two groups was so great that it could have been due to chance only in 1 or 2 cases out of a hundred. Please recall that the groups anxious and nonanxious—when they included the schizoid cases—showed a statistically less reliable difference of only 2.5 per cent. Thus for ego psychology one may conclude that the relationship between attention and concentration as measured by these tests may be characteristic of different ego organizations; one may conclude that the impairment of attention is indicative of the encroachment of anxiety upon thought organization, an exception being the schizoid organization, where thought processes, and maybe even the ego, are so organized that anxieties do not encroach upon the attention function. One may further conclude that concentration and its efficiency indicate the degree of relative intactness of the ego; the breaking down of concentration, that is to say, its impairment in relation to other functions—particularly in relation to attention—appears to be an indicator of the total defenselessness of the ego.

Our investigations did not reach the point where the relationship of the concepts concentration and attention to cathexes and hypercathexes could be more than vaguely indicated. Nevertheless, the difference in ego organization in regard to the influence on attention of anxiety in the schizoid vs. nonschizoid ego organizations appears to be a finding which cannot be interpreted away.

These were samples of the type of material offered by intelligence testing which raise the problems of ego psychology in an objective and quantitative form. It is true that only rationalization, intellectualization, repression, and cathexes, that is to say, only a small sector of the problems of ego psychology, have been here brought into relationship with intelligence-test results. However, there exist other kinds of tests, and the relationships they tap also bear directly on other ego functions, and their relation to thought organization. However, our time limitations do not allow us to enter upon a discussion of these now.

REFERENCES

Freud, A. (1936). *The Ego and the Mechanisms of Defence.* New York: International Universities Press, 1946.
Freud, S. (1911). Formulations Regarding the Two Principles in Mental Functioning. *Collected Papers,* 4:13–21. New York: Basic Books, 1959.

———— (1923). *The Ego and the Id,* tr. J. Riviere. London: Hogarth Press, 1927.

Hartmann, H. (1939). *Ego Psychology and the Problem of Adaptation,* tr. D. Rapaport. New York: International Universities Press, 1958.

————, Kris, E., & Loewenstein, R. M. (1946). Comments on the Formation of Psychic Structure. *Psychoanal. Study Child,* 2:11–38. New York: International Universities Press.

Rapaport, D. (1960). Psychoanalysis as a Developmental Psychology. *This volume,* Chapter 64.

21

TECHNOLOGICAL GROWTH AND THE
PSYCHOLOGY OF MAN

May I introduce my paper with the admission that to my knowledge psychology has no explanation for the relationship between technological growth and the psychology of man. Lagrange is reputed to have appeared before the Académie Française to read a paper proving Euclid's fifth postulate. After mounting the rostrum, he thought for a while, said, "Gentlemen, I have changed my mind," and departed. Lacking such courage, I shall proceed to state the unsolved problems in the relationship between technological growth and the psychology of man.

There are two sets of questions which may be raised, the first set dealing with genetic relationships, the second with evaluative relationships. The first set is: In what way does technological growth *issue* from the psychology of man? In what way does technological growth *influence* the psychology of man? Has the *mode of issuance* of technological growth from the psychology of man changed since the first advent of technological growth in human history? Has the *manner of influence* of technological growth on the psychology of man changed in the same period?

The second set of questions is of a more pragmatic and evaluative nature: Is technological growth advantageous or deleterious in its effect on the

Paper delivered at the Round Table on The Impact of Technology on Society, 1946 meetings of the American Association for the Advancement of Science. First published in Psychiatry, *10:253–259, 1947.*

psychology of man? Can technological growth be so organized and directed as to avoid its deleterious effects on human nature and foster its advantageous ones? Or will it be necessary to call a halt to technological progress in order to safeguard a stable equilibrium of the psychology of man? Within the social structure in which we live, what can be done about the advantageous or deleterious features of technological growth or about technological growth at large?

I shall now take these questions one by one and attempt to collect what contributions psychology can make toward answering each, keeping in mind throughout that no final answers are to be expected here.

First, in what way does technological growth issue from the psychology of man? Much has been said and written about the alloplastic achievements of man.[1] It has been pointed out that some alloplastic achievements are made by subhuman mammals, particularly monkeys. The *genesis* of alloplastic achievements has been observed for the most part in monkeys as, for instance, in Köhler's chimpanzee observations. Historically the *issuance* of the using of tools from the *human* psychological make-up—the first step in technological progress—is unobservable and unobserved; and only inferences from subhuman, preliterate, and child observations shed some light on it. Thus, the attack on the origin of technology must remain an indirect one. It may be helpful therefore to consider it in the light of our understanding of the genesis of planful human action.

According to Freud there is reason to believe that the psychological apparatus fundamentally subserves the purpose of removal of excitation from the organism. Action originates when either internal stimulation—that is to say, needs—or external stimuli bring the organism into a state of excitation, and removal of this excitation or tension is sought by either satisfying the need or extinguishing the external stimulation. But the need-satisfying object is not always immediately available, nor are the means to remove or extinguish the outside stimulation. When such a situation arises, action toward these ends must be postponed until the means to achieve these ends have been found. The tension set up by the excitation therefore is not at once discharged, since only part of it is used for what might be called tentative or experimental action to find the means toward the end. Delay of action may also be necessitated by the experience of danger that might attend discharge of tension by immediate action. We further learn from Freud that the tentative action in the period of delay is directed by thinking and often altogether replaced by it. Thinking in turn is directed by the memory of the satisfying object—or as Freud formulates it: "All thinking is merely a detour from the memory of gratification." In other words, all ac-

---

[1] The term "alloplastic" is used here in contradistinction to "autoplastic" and designates nonsomatic developments in adjustment comprising tools, techniques, and technology at large.

tion in the final analysis is rooted in the tension set up by internal need or external stimulation.

How are we to fit into this setting those means referred to at large as tools or technology? They apparently are instruments used by man as means toward his ends. Accordingly, we should find them characterized by economy of expenditure of energy and attended by least danger to the organism. Obviously, from this point of view, tools and therefore technology at large are to be considered alloplastic achievements of the human being in relation to his environment, without necessarily having the connotation of being tools purposefully directed toward the conquest of nature. Yet we should be warned not to make too sharp a distinction here. The man who achieves the success of satisfying his needs, whether he be preliterate or the "civilized" man of the twentieth century, feels himself a conqueror—so much so that if he does not succeed in satisfying his needs, he will pretend satisfaction if he can at least be a conqueror.

Ernest Mach in his renowned *History of Mechanics* has been able to demonstrate that the applications of fundamental principles of mechanics, for example, the lever principle, far preceded and even later eluded theoretical consideration. They must thus be considered empirical and not theoretical advancements—unwitting alloplastic adjustments rather than thought-out developments.

I shall not now pursue further the problem of how technological progress is rooted in the psychology of man but turn to the question of how technological growth *influenced* the psychology of man. What psychology has discovered in this respect is in a way anticipated and summarized rather clearly in the thesis of Hegel: "Man, in so far as he acts on nature to change it, changes his own nature." The man who delayed his action did so in search of tools wherewith to reach in a least dangerous but most economic way the objects satisfying his needs. When he found a technique or a tool, he became a man different from the one who had only to reach out to find his satisfaction in a lush world—although it should be noted that even there he had to reach out. The man using a tool to obtain his ends becomes not only a man who is satisfied but a man who is a tool-user. His memory of the use of tools has changed the spatial organization of his psychological world, since it has changed the spatial relationship between himself and the gratifying object. A late derivative of this type of change is that of our world-picture—as mentally experienced—because of the increased speed of vehicles that we use. The tool-using man is a new man: his thought processes are changed. In them is present not only the hallucinatorily vivid memory of gratification which, it must be presumed, always arises with the action-prompting tension, but also the memory of the detour from the direct path to the gratifying object. His field of consciousness is no longer structured by the bipolarity of need and need-gratifying object. New matter restructuring this field, namely, tools, appears in the field of consciousness as new memories, and, instead of a bipolar field, a multipolar field with an appropriate structure of lines of force emerges. Man, in acting on nature to change it, has changed his own nature. In the period of delay of action, tool-using changes the theme "need → need-satisfying object" into a new pattern—"need → tools → need-satisfying object"—which again allows for further variations, and each new variation for new ones again. Mach's *History of Mechanics* is a living documentation of how the *experiential* discovery of the principles of mechanics forced man to mold his thought processes—or theories, if one prefers—so as to be able to encompass the successful alloplastic adjustments he unwittingly made. Historically, thought and theory formation *followed* the experiential alloplastic adjustments; thus the latter were the prime movers of the development of thought!

It may be said that the Freudian concept of the genesis of action, inferred from analyses of psychopathological data, has insufficient substantiation from its own sources. However, educational psychology, developmental psychology, and anthropology offer abundant data to support these views as well as Hegel's thesis. One of the facts pertinent here is that educational psychology had to conclude that human beings learn and retain best, not from books or teachings, but from first-hand experience, and our school system should be adapted to this conclusion. To apply himself creatively in a field, a person must come to grips with the field in first-hand observation. That is, he must allow himself to be influenced, his thought patterns to be formed, by the realities of that field. Only in this way will his knowledge cease to be sterile, activating in him fundamental thought patterns flexible enough for creative variability in the course of further experience, and enabling him to capture and interpret *new* variations and interrelationships of phenomena which are not yet part of the body of knowledge he has been taught. In other words, educational psychology has learned that good teaching means exposing people to phenomena and allowing them to develop in themselves thought patterns to account for them. Second-hand knowledge may enable one to repeat operations that one was taught, but it will be insufficient when it is applied to new variations and new situations.

In allowing man to cut more and more varied pathways through nature toward the gratifying object, the use of tools allowed man also to develop in himself thought patterns relevant to more and more varied relationships in nature. Technological advance, therefore, by serving the enrichment of thought patterns in man, became one of the primary movers of the development of human thought, which *is* humanity. Again we are courting the danger of overestimating technology. It will be good therefore to warn ourselves that technology was by no means the only moving force in this development. At least one other powerful motor of human development should be mentioned; one probably far more powerful than technology. I am speaking of society: social interaction.

We next come to the question: Has the mode of issuance of technological growth from the psychology of man changed in human history? To clarify the contribution of psychology to this problem, we must consider a more specific facet of the issuance of technology from human psychological make-up. It has often been maintained that tools are extensions of organs of the human body. There is much reason to believe that in the beginning of technology this actually was the case. But the relationship that obtains between the first stick used and the human hand, or the first flint knife and the human tooth, should be distinguished from the relationship between the human eye and the microscope. They are similar in that the microscope, the stick, and the flint are intended to do what the human eye, hand, and tooth cannot do or can do only with difficulty. However, the use of the human eye and the use of the microscope are linked by a long chain of human thought with manifold abstractions and conclusions, many of which had little to do with the human eye and its efficacy; whereas the thought processes and experiences linking the hand and the stick, the flint and the tooth, were concrete connections. In the course of technological progress, a definite and far-reaching change took place in the relation between technological growth and the psychology of man. The mode in which tool-using first issued from the psychology of man is different from the mode in which technology issues in our time.

Technological growth which started as an alloplastic adjustment transformed human thinking. It stimulated the development of thought patterns which served originally to indicate to man, in the course of delay of action, which tools would be useful in a given situation to achieve his ends. With the increased wealth of thought patterns, *thinking obtained an autonomous status;* and man, who started with exploring the world he lived in, found a new segment of the world to explore—namely, the realm of his own thought patterns, developed in him in the course of his search for the most economic and least dangerous pathways leading to his ends. Out of the exploration of thinking itself—to which the discovery of all our scientific as well as psychological theories belongs—a new possibility for technological growth arose. The immediate need leading to sheer alloplastic achievements no longer is the prime mover of technological discovery. The search stimulated by needs is replaced by scientific investigation—that is to say, by systematic search for human thought patterns which are able to encompass new and ever new segments of nature.

It might be objected here that the procedure Ehrlich followed in discovering Salvarsan was a systematic search to answer a definite need, and thus not different qualitatively from the original alloplastic achievements. Yet we seem to have a testimonial of Ehrlich's thinking which would contradict such an explanation. Ehrlich apparently thought that if Metchnikoff viewed phagocytes as cells which eat up enemy bacteria, why should he not be able to find a bullet with which to shoot at these enemies? It would seem that a leading thought pattern—familiar in other fields of thought—played as much a part in Ehrlich's endeavor as did the attempted alloplastic answer to a need. A much simpler instance is the present dispute concerning "basic research" versus "applied research" that clarifies how technological growth no longer issues mainly out of alloplastic adjustments to prevailing needs. It was clearly expressed in Vannevar Bush's (1945) report to the President, *Science, the Endless Frontier*—which was in other ways unsatisfactory and even objectionable—that free exploration of nature, basic research, is the only sound fundament from which future technological growth may issue, and that mere pragmatic application of basic knowledge already possessed will only deplete our fund of basic knowledge and amount to an arrest of technological growth. This view patently demonstrates the change that has taken place in the relation between the psychology of man and technological growth. I should like to repeat here a formulation concerning basic research which I gave in a discussion of Vannevar Bush's report:

> A favorable atmosphere for basic research is an atmosphere in which the maturing thinker is permitted not to be abashed by his dreams and is given the opportunity to assemble intellectual equipment to hew out of reality a segment in such a way that his hewing becomes charting of an unknown territory; and in the course of this his dream progresses from being a "pipe dream" to being the thought pattern underlying the laws in terms of which our understanding of the newly charted territory is patterned. What are laws anyway? They are *our* mode of understanding nature—in communicable terms. Events of nature *are not* communicable; thought patterns *are* communicable. Each segment of nature we know was "discovered" by us when a unique individual and unique part of nature met. The uniqueness of the individual is always that in him certain thought patterns— more or less dormant in others—were amenable as daydreams in consciousness, and these thought patterns were apt to capture the pattern of interrelationships in a unique segment of nature. Since thought patterns are common to all humanity, though they may remain latent in most of us, the meeting of the unique individual and the unique segment of nature makes the patterns of that segment of nature communicable to humanity—and a conquest of nature has been made. The fostering of individual uniqueness therefore—paradoxically—is the fundamental prerequisite for the communicable conquest of nature for the collective of humanity.

Direct contact with matter and phenomena is still the main prerequisite of scientific advancement—just as it was in the days when technological growth was nothing but alloplastic adjustment—but this advancement does not nowadays issue from the pressing need which is commonly expressible to all humans; rather it results from an encompassment of not yet charted segments of nature amenable only to specific individuals in whom suitable thought patterns have developed. Through it a segment of nature of which humanity in general is not immediately aware can become our common possession.

I shall depart from this topic to consider a controversy in psychoanalytic anthropology, which is pertinent here. The old school of psychoanalytic anthropology, noticing a correlation between habitual techniques of child rearing in preliterate tribes and the dominant ideas of the preliterate group, concluded that the ideas are derived from the infancy situations. For technology this would mean that all tools and techniques, and the thought patterns composed in them, are merely "projections" of the objects and goals of infantile fantasy, and technology at large nothing but projection of magical wishes. Erik Homburger Erikson, in a recent analysis of his observations on the Sioux and Yurok, sharply attacks such views and points out the influence of the dominant ideas of the group on the infant-rearing procedures as one of the basic self-regulating mechanisms of a culture which keeps itself in harmony with its conditions of living and its technology. Keeping in mind these views of Erikson will help us to grasp the point he makes concerning the changed mode of issuance of technological growth from the psychology of man:

> Primitive tribes have a direct relation to the sources and means of production. Their techniques are extensions of the human body, their magic is a projection of body concepts. Children in these groups participate in technical and in magic pursuits; body and environment, childhood and culture may be full of dangers, but they are all one world. The expansiveness of civilization, its stratification and specialization make it impossible for children to include in their ego synthesis more than a section or sections of their society. Machines, far from remaining an extension of the body, destine whole classes to be extensions of machinery; magic becomes secondary, serving intermediate links only; and childhood, in some classes, becomes a separate segment of life with its own folklore. Neuroses, we find, are unconscious attempts to adjust to the heterogeneous present with the magic means of a homogeneous past. But individual neuroses are only parts of collective ones. It may well be, for example, that such mechanical child training as western civilization has developed during the last few decades, harbors an unconscious magic attempt to master machines by becoming more like them, comparable to the Sioux' identification with the buffalo, the Yurok's with the river and the salmon [1945, p. 345].

Erikson's formulation leads us to the next question: Has the manner of influence of technological growth on the psychology of man changed with its *mode of issuance?* Very little can be said on this point in a positive manner. Erikson's formulation—"Machines, far from remaining an extension of the body, destine whole classes to be extensions of machinery . . . such mechanical child training as western civilization has developed during the last few decades, harbors an unconscious magic attempt to master machines by becoming more like them, comparable to the Sioux' identification with the buffalo, the Yurok's with the river and the salmon"—suggests that technology stepped between nature and man, and man, instead of developing a rich manifold of thought patterns in interaction with nature, became limited to interaction with small segments of nature; and even with those small segments, his interaction occurs through the means of technology, and a limited, one-sided development takes place, short of what one would want to consider humanistic—if not human. Some people refer to this development as the "curse of civilization." A Chicago educator described it thus: "We are teaching more and more about less and less." The laborious efforts at developing hobbies as a haven in a world of impatience whose tempo is dictated by cars, streamliners, and airplanes testifies to the alienation of man from nature that has taken place.

In trying to answer this last question I find myself in the midst of the second set of questions which I designated as evaluative.

The first of these questions—Is technological growth advantageous or deleterious in its effect on the psychology of man?—might be justifiably designated by scientists as a meaningless question. Technology is here to stay. Luddite wreckers did not destroy it. Rousseau's slogan "back to nature" did not deter humans' relentless efforts to explore their own thought patterns, and to try themselves on ever new raw material, to hew a meaning out of its shapelessness and to apply it to bettering human life. It seems justified to use Nietzsche's phrase "beyond good and evil" in describing the process of technological growth and its effect on the psychology of man.

The last question now appears more meaningful—Can technological growth be so organized and directed as to avoid its deleterious and foster its advantageous effects on human nature?—especially if we rephrase it to read: Can technological growth be so used as to lead not only to the conquest of nature but to the happiness of man, so directed as to promote further technological growth and not to nurturing its doom on its own breasts? Obviously the answer to these questions at the present state of our knowledge is a confession of creed and not a scientific conclusion; yet some postulates may be laid down with reasonable safety. If technological growth is not to lead to its own doom, we must take cognizance of the fact that only the meeting of a unique individual and a unique segment of nature makes the patterns inherent to that segment of nature communicable to humanity and usable in the course of technological growth. Therefore, we must create a system of education with opportunities for study for all. Our system of education must forestall early specialization. We must bring up generations in which the efforts of the greatest possible number of people will be used for exploring and harnessing nature toward the end of the happiness of man. Otherwise technology will lead more and more to specialization and mechanization of human thinking, to complacency, with Frigidaires and

Maytags, and to technical skill and abolishment of incentive to wrestle with nature for new conquests. Obviously, what is needed is not only free education for all, not only broad education without early specialization, but also freedom of basic research without pressure toward application, and freedom of scientific communication without restrictive patents and restrictive security regulations.

I am keenly aware that all this does not answer the query as to the happiness of man and its relation to technological growth. It should be pointed out that the comforts provided by technological growth and the complacency in which they result are often mistakenly thought to lead to the happiness of man. All thinking human beings know that this is the hoax of our century. And we know that technological change—and with it the changing conditions of our society and the attendant insecurities—leads to insecure parents with inconsistent parental behavior, and so to young people growing up with no stable ideal to share with their society, in blind aimlessness; and we know this to be one of the most potent factors leading to the unhappiness of man; yet we have no remedy for it. It does seem that the transitory period we are living in, with its extremely rapid social change often blamed on technology, is one of the basic sources of human unhappiness; yet it is not technology alone which makes for instability of social conditions and lack of ideals. In fact, we should envisage a society in which the ideals and aims remain sufficiently stable to allow bringing up secure children in the light of such ideals and aims without curtailing technological progress. A society with stable ideals as a substantial basis for education will be able to absorb and utilize in the furtherance of human happiness even the most rapid technological progress. I presume that it will be the sociologist's job to theoretically map out the structure of such a society. But it will be the business of all of us to shoulder the responsibility for building it.

REFERENCES

Bush, V. (1945). *Science, the Endless Frontier*. Washington: U.S. Government Printing Office.
Erikson, E. H. (1945). Childhood and Tradition in Two American Indian Tribes. *Psychoanal. Study Child,* 1:319–350. New York: International Universities Press.

22

IN MEMORIAM

Kurt Lewin

Kurt Lewin died. Many, many have read these words without an inkling of how much human riches, how much of the history of psychology of the last 35 years, and last, but not least, how much deep-rooted Jewish feeling passed away with him.

Kurt Lewin was already a psychologist of great renown when he came to this country from Germany over a decade ago. In this country he became one of the most sought-for teachers of psychology and one of the most outstanding psychologists, one who exerted more influence upon the development of present-day American psychology than any other single person.

Kurt Lewin came to psychology with interests in epistemology, scientific methodology, and the comparative study of sciences. He had made significant contributions in these fields. He appeared in the field of psychology at a time when the first big clashes between associationist psychology and gestalt psychology were taking place. The mechanistic and atomistic thinking of associationist psychology was clashing with the dynamic-holistic psychology of gestalt. The interests of both sides in this struggle were centered on perceptual organization and problems of learning. The human being himself was not the center of these disputes. In the background another new

First published in Youth and Nation, *April 1947, pp. 18–20.*

dynamic psychology, that of psychoanalysis, was developing. In psycho-analysis the human being himself, his motivations, his feelings and affects were the center of interest. But this new psychology was founded on clinical grounds, on observation and not experimentation. Kurt Lewin was the first to carry the problems of motivation, affect, and will into the laboratory. After a fundamental, experimental attack which disproved the contentions of associationist psychology on its own grounds, namely in learning and association, he clarified in a series of theoretical papers the reorientation psychology needed. In these papers he laid the outlines of new experimental methods and set the framework of what he called "the psychology of affect and action." These papers were followed by a series of experimental inves-tigations on affect and action by Lewin and his students. Actions and affects were for the first time elicited in a laboratory, they were investigated and their dynamics revealed. Resumption of interrupted tasks, memory for in-terrupted tasks, substitute discharge of tensions set up by task interrup-tions, satiation through repetitive action, anger as a dynamic phenome-non, level of aspiration, etc., were the subjects of the experimental investi-gations that issued from Lewin's laboratory.

At about the time he came to this country, there was a sudden apparent change in Lewin's interest. Actually this was an expression of and—as it were—a closing summary of ideas worked out before. While pursuing his early interests in scientific method, he was searching for ways which would make it possible to quantify, or otherwise to represent in a mathematically treatable form, psychological events. He soon found that the promise for objective, mathematically treatable representation of psychological hap-penings lies not in metric mathematics but rather in the nonmetric topologi-cal methods. His volumes on the measurement of psychological forces and topological and vector psychology represent this apparent turn of interest. *A Dynamic Theory of Personality* presents his conclusions from the experi-mental investigations of affect and action to the English-reading public.

In the next series of experimental investigations with his students, the problems of the previous experimentations were again taken up but they were enriched partly with the topological frame of reference he had devel-oped, and partly by interest in problems to which psychoanalysis called attention. Frustration, regression, but also problems like rigidity, decision, etc., took the center of his field of interest. These studies were published from the Iowa Child Welfare Station at which he worked.

However, a survey of his papers and lectures given in this country shows that another undercurrent was working in him while he developed the im-portant theoretical and experimental ideas just referred to. This other cur-rent manifested itself in deep concern with the world's tragic events. The problems of psychological differences between nations, the problems of mi-norities, the problems of discrimination, and foremost among the rest, the problem of anti-Semitism loomed large on Lewin's horizon. He took a lion's share in the development of the Society for the Psychological Study of Social Issues; he initiated experimental investigations in the analysis of "authoritarian," "democratic," and "laissez faire" social organizations; he became interested in leadership training which he considered the fundamental need of democratic society if it is to survive. When war came, he became interested in investigating the conditions of efficient production and experimented with improvement of production methods to expedite war production. When the food problem and food shortages came, he worked experimentally in exploring the nature of food habits, and the methods of changing food habits, contributing thereby to the promotion of rational nutrition methods at a time of shortage of usual food materials.

All these interests and investigations led up to Lewin's last major change of direction. He became more and more convinced that psychology must explore how groups form their opinions and how formation of group opinion can be kept free from prejudice. He deeply believed that groups, if they are well informed, will, if left to their own decisions and not manipulated, find democratic and progressive decisions. He became interested, therefore, in community interrelationships and in minority-majority interrelationships and devoted the last few years of his life to organizing an institute of group dynamics devoted to the exploration of how groups work together in forming their opinions, in helping to adjust the group members, and in finding methods of promoting good relationships within the subgroups in the group. In many a conversation he told me that it was his dream that such a group dynamics institute would extend its workings as far as group therapy of psychiatric cases.

There can be little doubt that this final idea was the red thread of Lewin's whole life. There can be little doubt that he gave all he had for it. There can be no doubt that he was deeply aware of the responsibility the scientist has to society; and there can be no doubt that his identification with his people, with Jewry, and his deep devotion to the idea of contributing something to change the tragic fate of his people was the final driving force behind his thinking. He knew it and would talk about it.

One does not understand Kurt Lewin if one does not know the kind of man he was. It can be seriously doubted that there is any man on the present psychological scene who had as many pupils all over the world (from Soviet Russia to many a corner of this country and all over Europe) who have remained as devoted to their teacher as Kurt Lewin's pupils have. They may have disagreed with the turns he took, they may not have followed him, but the ties remained. In each of his turns of interest he inspired, stimulated, set to work more people than any other psychologist on the present scene. He induced thought wherever he went. With his mode of thinking, he prompted people not to stop at a thought, but to do something about it by trying to verify it and to realize it. In his endless vitality and vitalizing power was already apparent what he came to profess in the last few years: psychology has to act!

Whenever he met someone who had worked with one of his students or who had met one of his students, his eyes would light up in talking about the person whether it was an outstanding person or not. His eyes would light up even if he heard about a good student of another man who might be a coming man on the psychological scene. His eyes would light up whenever any new, daring venture in psychology or any serious consistent work in the field was mentioned or reported. You found him in the Society for the Psychological Study of Social Issues; he had his own group which met year by year to discuss the developments in topological psychology; you found him trying to bridge the gap between psychology and psychoanalysis; you found him arranging discussions between psychologists and sociologists, promoting cooperation of psychology, psychoanalysis, anthropology, and sociology; you saw him in the movement for the "Unity of Science." There is hardly an important part of the American psychological scene with which he was not connected.

My teacher was a pupil of Kurt Lewin. I came to him with a letter from my teacher and after that time I found him always interested in whatever I was doing. He was ready to see me wherever he was, and however busy he was, in Boston, in Iowa, in Chicago, and in New York. He knew that I had lived in Eretz Yisrael. He would always ask me about what I heard from Eretz Yisrael. He would always tell me what his children wrote to him from the Eretz—he had children there. He would talk with a sigh and with a far-away look and one gathered from what he said that somehow he felt that our place should be there. He would say that once he was to go to teach at the Hebrew University and then would add sadly, "but it did not work out." Then he would say, "We can do here many things . . ."

Kurt Lewin was about to achieve what he wanted. At the Massachusetts Institute of Technology he found the opportunity to build up an Institute of Group Dynamics. He built it up and worked with the Jewish Congress sponsored Community Relationships Council on manifold researches in group relationships. It was at this point that his death came.

One may disagree with some of Lewin's psychological conclusions; one may reject his ideas as to the role and responsibilities of psychology on the social scene; one must not forget, however, that dialectical thinking knows that science centering on social issues—with whatever premises—becomes of its own movement revealing of the internal contradictions of society and thereby becomes an ally of progress. But leaving this aside, Lewin's deep sincerity, his genuine modesty, his intolerance for all humbug, his powerful convictions, and human-Jewish warmth engendered deep respect and love for this knight of science.

23

DYNAMIC PSYCHOLOGY AND
KANTIAN EPISTEMOLOGY

Though Rapaport never published this paper, clearly regarding it as only a beginning in grappling with large and complex issues, he nevertheless did include it in the bibliographies to several of his other papers. His doctorate was on a psychological-philosophical topic—the history of the association concept from Bacon through Kant—and he wrote a later paper, summarizing the thesis and carrying the history further (see Ch. 1). It was decided to publish the present paper because it at least shows the trend of his thinking and may be stimulating to those who might wish to pursue the topic further, as well as because psychologists and psychoanalysts tend to ignore the philosophical matrix from which their disciplines sprang and therefore rarely deal explicitly with or are aware of the epistemological assumptions which they perforce use. In *Organization and Pathology of Thought* (1951), Rapaport in a number of places dealt ex-

Paper presented at the Staff Seminar of the Menninger Foundation School of Clinical Psychology, January 1947. First published in Journal of the History of the Behavioral Sciences, *2:192–199, 1966.* © *1966 by Psychology Press, Inc.*

plicitly with the relations between epistemology and
psychology, including the subject of the present paper
(see esp. pp. 721–723)—M.M.G.

I

According to Runes' *Dictionary of Philosophy,* epistemology is that branch
of philosophy which investigates the origin of, structure of, validity of, and
methods for ascertaining knowledge. I know of no dictionary from which I
can take a definition of "dynamic psychology," and I am therefore forced to
improvise one. Dynamic psychology is not a branch of psychology but,
rather, the most advanced stage of development of the psychology which
investigates the interrelationships of the individual and his environment,
attempting to do justice both to the forces which impinge upon the individual and to the physiological and psychological (conscious and unconscious)
forces and regulative mechanisms which determine the individual's functioning within this environment.

Epistemology is interested in the various possible modes of acquiring
generally valid knowledge concerning nature. Dynamic psychology is interested in the relationship of the human subject to nature, that is to say, to his
environment. The quest for valid knowledge of nature common to all human subjects and the quest for the laws governing the various possible relationships of the human subject to nature are, respectively, the avowed purposes of these two sciences.

Theoretically, dynamic psychology presupposes an epistemology, because it aims at gaining valid knowledge and therefore it presupposes the
principles of acquiring valid knowledge. Practically, from the point of view
of empirical science, epistemology in its striving to establish the principles
of gaining valid knowledge is merely a part of the striving of dynamic
psychology, namely a part of the quest for the laws of the interrelationships
between the human subject and his environment. In other words, the search
for generally valid knowledge of the human subject concerning nature is
merely one of the various relationships the human subject enters with his
environment.

Thus, epistemological investigation may be of two different kinds: first,
philosophical, in the sense of investigating the fundamentals of acquisition
of knowledge in various sciences for their implied presuppositions and for
the validity of these presuppositions; and second, psychological, in the
sense of investigating genetically the development of the methods and forms
of "knowing" in the ontogeny of individual human subjects. The first of
these approaches is the classical philosophical approach, *aprioristic* (and
this term will be later discussed) in character; the second, more recent in
origin, is the one dubbed the psychologistic approach, which is eminently
empirical in character. Vehement struggles between the *aprioristic* and the

psychologistic approaches to epistemology have taken place in the past. It is probably safe to say that the psychologistic, genetic, empirical analysis of "knowledge" is an indispensable part of dynamic psychology. It seems to me, however, that such genetic analysis will never obviate the *aprioristic* philosophical analysis of the conditions of gaining generally valid knowledge once these conditions have come about, whatever genetic analysis may reveal about the development leading to the prevalence of these conditions in the mature specimen of the species Homo sapiens.

So much as a preface to refresh our minds about the implications of the concepts embodied in the title of this paper.

II

Like all branches of philosophy, epistemology has had many schools. The two major antithetical poles among these schools were those of idealism and materialism. The most poignant expressions of the epistemology of these two extremes are to be found in the rationalist versus empiricist epistemologies. According to Runes' *Dictionary of Philosophy,* the epistemology of empiricism maintains that the sole source of knowledge is experience; no knowledge is possible independent of experience. Empiricist epistemology may take the form of denial that any knowledge can be obtained *a priori,* that is to say, denial that there are universal and necessary truths. Rationalist epistemology relies on reason as the source of genuine knowledge, and here the criterion of validity is not sensory but intellectual and deductive. That is, rationalist epistemology may take the form of denial that sensory data, or empirical data in general, give any new valid knowledge. Empiricists capitalize on the fact that the method of our science is empirical, while rationalists capitalize on the fact that we rely on rules of our own reasoning (of whatever origin they may be) to yield verifiable and valid conclusions even about material which is not yet completely empirically known to us.

A similar though not so pervasive division of views exists in psychology too. I am referring to the split between the psychologists who view the human being as primarily dependent upon his environment and the stimulation coming from it, for whom the theory of learning is the answer to all—well, almost all—problems of psychology, and whose position in this respect could well be compared to the position of an empiricist epistemology, and those psychologists who are mainly interested in the rules of functioning *inherent* in the psychological subject, for whom the organizing methods of the psychic apparatus have primacy over all experience and learning, and for whom the organizing principles (gestalt, emotions, unconscious processes, etc.) actually determine the evaluation and assimilation of all experience. Thorndike's "trial and error" versus Köhler's "a-ha," Pavlov's and Hull's conditioned response versus Freud's unconscious instinctual strivings, the associationistic principles of older perception psychology versus

Wertheimer's gestalt principles, are examples of contrasting empiricist-environmental and inherent-intrapsychic principles.

Kantian transcendentalism in epistemology and what is called "dynamic psychology" in psychology have attempted to bridge the gap between these two views. My aim in this paper will be to point up some fundamental similarities in these two attempts, or, more correctly, to point up some fundamental similarities in the points of view rather than in the achievements of these two attempts. My purpose in doing so is to demonstrate that familiarity wtih Kantian epistemology may contribute to developing felicitous systems of constructs and theories for the dynamic psychology which we see abuilding before our eyes and in the building of which we are ourselves involved.

III

Let us first review the mode of thinking called Kantian transcendentalism, which was designed to bridge the gap between empiricism and rationalism. Radical rationalism often led to extremes. One of the most instructive of these extremes is the one called solipsism. The rationalists, impressed by the fact that logical reasoning led to true conclusions while appearances in the empirical world were often fluid, misleading, and deceptive, and only reducible to valid invariables by operations of reason, tended to assume that the only valid reality is the reality of reason. Such thinking, when pursued consistently, led to a denial of the existence of the outside world, to the assumption that only the world of reason exists. If, in addition, difficulties in communication between one individual as a carrier of reason and other individuals were also encountered by the rationalist, he tended to reduce all objects and humans to an existence solely in his own (*ipse*) subjective world of reason. For the solipsist, what exists is his own reason alone: the world is a creation of this reason. Not all rationalists went to this length, however. The most reasonable formulation of the problem of rationalism is the one set forth by Leibnitz, even though his answer to the problem, namely the theory of monads, is a rather extreme one. Leibnitz raised the question as follows: how is it possible that the laws of reason do somehow apply to the laws of fact, or in other words, that the laws of reason do correspond to laws of nature? One could put it in a more pedestrian way, as follows: how is it possible that in one's thinking one can come to conclusions which prove to be true in nature? Generally put, the question reads: what is the relationship between *vérité de la raison* and *vérité du fait*? As already stated, the radical rationalistic answer was that there are no laws of the external world, there is no external world, all of it is within man's reason, and therefore a distinction between nature and reason is only an illusion.

The empiricist's point of view was probably most sharply stated by

Hume. He maintained that all that there is in the mind comes into it through experience, through the senses. Since, however, experience—empirical observation—is changeable and fluctuating, it can teach only how things are or may be, not how things must be. Therefore Hume insisted that the necessity which the rationalist attaches to the laws of reason, i.e., logic, cannot derive from experience. What then is the nature of this logical necessity? asked Hume. His answer was that it is a mere illusion and "nothing but a long habit of accepting something as true because it occurred regularly enough and of mistaking subjective necessity of associative connection as objective law of nature." In other words, Hume maintained that the logical necessity of reason is nothing but an illusion created by the associative habit of our psychological make-up. Hume maintained that events which occur simultaneously or in sequence often enough become attached to each other and give us the illusion of the necessity of this connection, that is, of a "causal" connection. Hume thus became the father of associationistic psychology and of pragmatic philosophy for which not inherent natural laws, but probabilities for the recurrence of phenomena—derived from sufficiently frequent contiguous appearances of these phenomena—are the basis of our knowledge about the world.

How did Kant reconcile these two contradictory views? I cannot attempt to recapitulate his reasoning step by step in the short time that is at my disposal. I shall resign myself to representing the views he arrived at. The easiest way of approaching a description of these views is first to remind ourselves that Kant made a sharp cleavage between, on the one hand, "appearances," namely the things of the world as they present themselves in our "sensibility" (by which Kant meant roughly what we would today call perception), and on the other hand, the "the thing in itself," the real world, about which we do not know anything directly, but only through our "sensibility."

The next step Kant took was the analysis of the three types of statements we can make concerning nature. The first type of statement, for instance "all bodies are extended," is characterized by the fact that the predicate of the statement does not add anything to our knowledge about the subject of the statement; that is, it is by definition that objects are extended. This statement merely analyzes the concept of the subject of the statement: it is an analytic judgment. Such judgments are always correct, always have general validity. The second type of statement, for instance "all bodies consist of atoms," is one in which the predicate says something new about the subject of the statement. It increases our knowledge about the subject. This statement reflects empirical discovery. It does not imply, however, that we will never discover a body which does not consist of atoms; it is valid only for the cases in which it has already been investigated and empirically found to be true. Such statements which increase our knowledge are called synthetic statements, and inasmuch as they are made after an empirical investigation, they are referred to as *a posteriori* synthetic statements. The third type of statement, for example "a straight line is the shortest distance between two points," presupposes that the line is subsumed under the concept of quantity: as in the phrase "the shortest." Analysis of similar statements shows that they all presuppose general concepts under which the subject of the statement is automatically subsumed by our—as we would say today—"thinking," or as Kant expressed himself, "pure reason." He also found that if we omit all empirical observations concerning bodies and their alterations from our conception of these bodies, the concepts of space and time still remain with us. In other words, from studying the nature of these *a priori* synthetic statements, Kant found that over and beyond the empirical material in the mind there are general conceptions present in it which are partly like time and space—which he designated "forms of apperception"—and partly like "causality," "quantity," etc., which he designated "categories of pure reason" and to which we automatically refer all "appearances." He therefore inferred that while we do not know anything about "the thing in itself," the "appearances" are integrated by our sensibility and pure reason in terms of these "forms of apperception" and "categories of pure reason." By becoming integrated with these, "appearances" become "experiences" lending themselves to statements of *a priori* synthetic character, and in this way it becomes possible for us to reach generally valid conclusions about them. In Kant's own words: "This is therefore the result of all our foregoing inquiries: all *a priori* synthetic principles are nothing more than principles of possible experience, and can never be referred to anything more than mere appearances, and can only represent either that which makes experience generally possible or else that which as it is derived from these principles must always be capable of being represented in some possible experience," and he concludes, "the understanding does not derive its laws from, but prescribes them to nature."

If we want to put this too into pedestrian terms, we could say that Kant discovered that in our minds we have principles according to which incoming stimulation is organized and interpreted. He inferred that this mode of fundamental organization of incoming stimulation turns stimulation into experience and thereby makes it amenable to valid empirical science. He also inferred that these general principles of organization are applied only to "appearances" and never to "the thing in itself." Finally, he inferred that the automatic application of these general principles of integration to incoming stimulation by pure reason, that is to say by our thinking, makes it possible to make valid predictions for future "appearances" that may present themselves to our minds. He concluded that this is the basis of the possibility of man's attaining generally valid knowledge. Instead of the random probability of Hume, dependent on subjective associations (in the psychological sense) of contiguous events, a picture of a lawful universe emerges, a universe which is ordered and amenable to systematic exploration owing to the presence of the lawgiver, the mind. In other words, the Kantian view is one in which sciences are *our* mode of viewing the world, and not discoveries of laws that exist in the "outside world in itself" which, according to Kant, is not accessible to us.

IV

The Kantian theory of knowledge can be summarized in the following statements: knowledge is possible only about "appearances" and never about "the thing in itself"; *a priori* synthetic statements are possible only because of the synthesis of perceptions by "pure mind" by means of its "forms of apperception" and "categories"; and generally valid knowledge is possible only because it is the "forms of apperception" and "categories" of "pure mind" that *a priori* organize the world of "appearances" with which our knowledge concerns itself.

Are there such general statements in which the fundamentals of dynamic psychology can be summarized? I have abstracted the Kantian views from the *Critique of Pure Reason* and the *Prolegomena to Any Future Metaphysics*. I do not know any place to extract the fundamentals of dynamic psychology from. I have to undertake the premature attempt to summarize what I would consider the fundamentals of dynamic psychology to date. I can think of only four phrases which are general enough to be considered as representing fundamental points of view in dynamic psychology: (1) "the private world of the individual"; (2) "the organism as a whole" (or, generalized, "the psychosomatic-environmental unity"); (3) "unconscious determination" (implying instinctual, physiological, and hereditary determinations); and (4) "the functional autonomy of the ego."

Let us take these one by one.

(1) *"The private world of the individual"* implies that the individual experiences his world according to his own lights, which are in turn products of his own history and situation. This formulation is agreed upon by all the various schools of dynamic psychology, by the projective tester, by the Lewinian psychologist, by the psychoanalyst, etc. Dynamic psychology implies that the world of the individual is organized according to the organizing principles of the individual. Note the similarity of this conception to the Kantian formulation that "pure reason" has its own synthesizing "categories" and "forms of apperception," and can know only about "appearances" which are synthesized *a priori* in terms of these, never about "the thing in itself."

(2) *"The organism as a whole"* and its generalization, "the psychosomatic-environmental unity" (where environment implies, in accordance with Erikson's suggestion, the historical-traditional roots of the environment), have a no less intimate relation to Kantian epistemology than has the first principle, although this relation is less easily demonstrable.

I believe it is correct to say that we arrived at the necessity for thinking in terms of a psychosomatic-environmental unity owing to the fiasco of our having thought in terms of isolated somatic, psychic, and environmental approaches. Yet I submit that even today we continue to think in the three isolated terms, only feebly trying to link them up. Would it not be more revealing to say that the three approaches are three different ways of ours, of human beings, to look at what we refer to as the functioning human body, three ways which are inherent in our nature? I submit that much confusion would be eliminated if we talked only about three different ways of looking at the phenomenon in question, rather than talking about inter-actions between environment, psyche, and soma. I believe much confusion would be avoided if we admitted to ourselves that we are striving to de-scribe all phenomena of the functioning human body in terms of each of these three aspects which grow out of our own nature; and if we also ad-mitted to ourselves that for the time being we will always look at each phenomenon of the human body in terms of that aspect from which its description is most feasible at the time, without giving up the hope that sooner or later it will be possible to describe it in terms of the other aspects also. To look upon our various modes of approach to the functioning hu-man body as the possible approaches anchored in and given by our own nature is looking upon them from a point of view which is in accord with Kantian transcendentalism.

(3) *"Unconscious determination"* implies, from the point of view of various schools of dynamic psychology, either unconscious determination without any further specification, or instinctual determination, or, driven further, physiological and even hereditary determination of personality make-up as well as of individual action and thought. The chain of uncon-scious, instinctual, physiological, hereditary came about as an attempt at further- and further-reaching causal reduction. At the moment we are not interested in the details of the history of this chain nor in established knowl-edge about it, but only in the general assumption of unconscious determina-tion itself. We want to note that stable individual characteristics as well as passing actions—and among the passing ones are "purposive" actions, "aimless" actions, expressive movements, physiological expressions, feel-ings, thoughts—are without exception referred by dynamic psychology to the unconscious determining stratum. This principle is apparently a direct expression of the characteristic of our thinking which is commonly called "causality" and apparently represents a necessary dimension, or in Kantian terms a necessary "category," under which we subsume all observations, all impressions, or, in Kantian terms, all appearances. It is an application of the principle of causality in the specific conditions which prevail when the subject matter called "psyche" is investigated. And by the principle of causality here I do not mean the scientific principle of causality which is a postulate of all science, but rather the Kantian category of "causality"

which is apparently a necessary referent of all apperception. Much acrimony in the discussion of the unconscious, the id, instinctual determination, etc., would be eliminated if we could look upon these as steps in the search for the most simple formulation of one of the referents of all apperception, namely, causality.

(4) Finally, *"the functional autonomy of the ego"* implies that we recognize a relatively independently functioning organization which, though having developed out of the id, once having come about has relative autonomy from the id; which, though unconsciously determined, still has regulative power over this determination; which, though it represents the impingements of the environment, integrates these impingements according to its own organizing principles and, vice versa, while it integrates the environmental stimulation according to its own principles, still takes cognizance of these stimulations and their constellations. It is also implied that the ego is the actor of the thought processes, and this latter implication is the one which is most important when we scrutinize the fundamentals of dynamic psychology in relation to Kantian transcendentalism. This assumption of the relative functional autonomy of the ego is the basis on which, regardless of developmental considerations, we can search for general principles, such as the Kantian "categories" and "forms of apperception," that hold sway in the ego's ordered thought processes directed at the acquisition of valid knowledge. Even though we may make genetic investigations of the development of our space concept, time concept, causality concept, quality concept, quantity concept—all the general concepts to be found in the Kantian table of categories, and also others not to be found there—the findings concerning the development of these concepts cannot encroach upon the general validity of these categories and integrating principles of goal-directed, ordered thinking prevailing in the ego and aimed at the acquisition of valid knowledge.

Here again we are apparently confronted with tendencies inherent in our human nature. In the principle of *unconscious determination* we see our inherent tendency to reduce structure and phenomena causally; in the principle of the *functional autonomy of the ego* we note an opposite inherent tendency, according to which whatever emerges through development is considered as a closed system, with rules and interrelationships of its own which are amenable to investigation in themselves. It is very important to recognize that here two avenues of investigation, both inherent in our own nature, allow two different approaches to a subject matter, in this case the ego. It would be ill-advised indeed if we tried to bypass either of these in our striving to gain valid knowledge. Human beings do not have so many avenues to knowledge that some can be bypassed lightly, and it is important that we recognize those avenues which are given in our nature and use them *all,* instead of starting fights amongst ourselves about whether genetic reduction or exploration or autonomous units is the valid way of ascertaining knowledge. Both avenues are inherent in the nature of our thinking; thus both are valid. Knowledge is the product of our minds' methods of organizing stimulation into experience and our reflecting upon this experience and further organizing it into more global units. In this endeavor, our becoming aware of our organizing tendencies is crucial.

V

I had hoped to be able to give a systematic application of the ideas which I have tried to expound, but as I worked on this presentation I realized that this would be premature and ill-advised. I would like to draw attention to only two implications of the foregoing. (1) Kantian transcendentalism gives two warnings: (a) that in working at science we have the right and obligation to strive for and expect to capture laws in nature, including human nature, instead of merely hoping to arrive at the probabilities of the pragmatist and operationalist; and (b) that whatever laws we derive will be valid laws, but they should be recognized as our—the human being's—mode of looking upon nature, including our own nature, and the several different ways of looking at nature should all be utilized and looked upon synoptically. (2) The second implication that deserves our attention is that the exploration of thought processes, so crucial a part of ego psychology, demands that we become aware of the principles of integration of experience by the mind. Our discovery of these principles of integration may be aided and abetted by Kant's valiant attempt to discover such principles, but it certainly is aided by the tendency of dynamic psychology to assume a functional autonomy of the ego, which forcefully calls attention to the fact that there may be structural laws of the ego and of thought organization which, although genetically derived from unconscious determining sources, yet have a definite autonomy.

REFERENCE

Rapaport, D., ed. & tr. (1951). *Organization and Pathology of Thought.* New York: Columbia University Press.

24

DISCUSSION IN "THE PSYCHOLOGIST
IN THE CLINIC SETTING"
ROUND TABLE

Why should a round table on "The Psychologist in the Clinic Setting" start with a discussion of the scientific basis of clinical psychology? Indeed, when Dr. Beck asked me to be the first discussant in this round table I asked myself: "What can he have in mind with this topic for an opener?" True to diagnostic habit, I spurned the simple way and did not ask him about it. I tried to reason it out and this is what I arrived at: The need for clinical help is so great that a situation arose in which "everything goes"; thus clinical psychology has become vastly oversold. We live, as it were, in a fool's paradise where haphazardness does not backfire, whether it is the haphazardness of pragmatic practice lacking theoretical background, or poor practice issuing out of ignorance, or outright malpractice. Such a time is time for soul searching; it is the time where the cry for establishing the scientific basis of our practice should be raised so high as to reach the sky.

Not that we need be ashamed of our achievements. We have developed many tools that work; we have many good men in our ranks who have broad experience and can be relied upon to face complex situations skillfully and who prove helpful. In fact, we acquitted ourselves well against

First published in The American Journal of Orthopsychiatry, *18:493–497, 1948. Copyright the American Orthopsychiatric Association, Inc.; reproduced by permission.*

severe odds in the war years. It must be said that what we accomplished was accomplished under most unfavorable conditions. Until a short while ago, clinical psychology and clinical psychologists had no home for their investigations in the academic halls of their academic psychologist brethren and had one in only a few of the psychiatric institutions. This, however, is not all that must be said.

It is true that our scientific conscience must be disturbed by the huge discrepancy between "tested knowledge" and admiration of what "seems to work" or what "gets by." It is true that it is very practical to protect ourselves against quacks and against the lunatic and ignorant fringe to establish the respectability of our profession. That is to say, we have yet to make clinical psychology an exact science and an established profession.

The fact that clinical psychology is at present on a seller's market makes these tasks both difficult and imperative. Difficult, because this seller's market, sustained partly by the huge demand for psychiatric-psychological help and partly by the fact that in the postwar era people can pay for such help, is a natural breeding ground for quacks. Imperative, because "boom" conditions put the means within our reach, and because in a crisis the boom town of clinical psychology is likely to turn into a ghost town.

The adverse conditions of our routine clinical and investigative work in the past are relieved for the moment, a change that imposes on us new responsibilities. We can no longer be satisfied with tools that "work" and practitioners who "get by." We must not forget that we are responsible for having allowed clinical psychology to be oversold, a fact that imposes on us the responsibility to catch up with this overselling by producing "the goods" through clarifying and fortifying the scientific fundamentals of clinical psychology. If we are not successful in doing so, then the next economic crisis, or the wave of disappointment in psychiatric-psychological help, inevitable if not based on sound "tested knowledge," will leave clinical psychology exposed as naked and lacking sound foundations. It will leave hungry the great mass of people who are attracted into clinical psychology. And I mean hungry in the very concrete sense of the word. Clinical psychology has about 2,000 practitioners or would-be practitioners at present. It is on the verge of becoming a profession, or else it is on the verge of receding into ignominious oblivion! This is the juncture at which it is vital to scrutinize the conditions which make a discipline a profession, and which make its practitioners know their interests. To my mind, there are two tasks before us. The first is to organize as a profession. What this means and how it should be done, I cannot go into here. Second, we must scrutinize the scientific foundations of our discipline and make up our minds to use the time left to crystallize these bases and amend them with as feverish a devotion as we can summon.

Let us now scan the status of the scientific foundations of clinical psychology. Our field of routine, as well as of research, can grossly be divided into two major realms: testing and therapy. For the sake of simplicity I shall omit the middle ground of interview and observation which, depending on their purpose, can be subsumed either under testing or under therapy.

What is the present scientific theoretical foundation of our testing work? It consists of the theories of sampling, test construction, standardization, and validation. Without attempting to underestimate the advances made in these fields, I submit that all these are statistical theory rather than psychological theory. The psychological theory that could serve as a basis for testing work exists only in rudiments in the theories of ego psychology and defense mechanisms, in some advancements of topological and gestalt psychology, in some achievements of developmental psychology and cultural anthropology.

But these advancements, bearing on a theory of thought organization and on control of motility and action, have hardly been brought to bear upon the problems of testing. Psychological testing is a pragmatic procedure, protected by a thin veneer of statistical respectability and hardly in touch with the psychological reality of the problems it tackles. It is true that some advancements in the psychology of personality have been brought to bear upon our testing problems. Particularly, the achievements of dynamic psychiatry in personality appraisal have become somewhat useful in testing.

If we look closer, what an awkward sight presents itself to our eyes! Not that the hypotheses and findings of this dynamic psychiatry have been explored and tests developed to probe into the entities held crucial by dynamic psychiatric theory. Rather, some tests have incidentally been used in modern clinical settings and the dynamic psychiatric theory of these clinical settings forced itself upon the testers because it pointed to a more useful understanding of the tests. To develop testing procedures on the basis of the theories of dynamic psychiatry is a job that is ahead of us. The job of exploring *thought processes* underlying various thought products, the job of exploring the methods of control of motility and action underlying various forms of motor expression and action has barely been started, even though it is *the* task that must be tackled before a solid scientific foundation of our testing work will be available to us as a guarantee of continuity of our discipline. This picture of our situation in testing is not a rosy one, but an enormous challenge it is.

The picture of psychotherapy and its scientific foundations is no brighter. A therapy without a theory of maladjustment, implying in turn a theory of personality, is a therapy without scientific foundation. True enough, in therapy the personality of the therapist, his understanding and empathy, are one-half of the game. However, fundamental understanding of what personality is, how it relates to the rest of what we know in psychology, and how maladjustment and mental disorder come about, are fundamental requirements for a scientific therapy—a therapy which is not merely pragmatic, but can be systematically taught; which does not depend mostly, but only partly, on the therapist's personality and ability to empathize with his patient. The only school of therapy which has attempted systematically to build a theory of personality, and link it with some of our knowledge about human beings, is psychoanalysis. Even this school of therapy, which excels in this respect, failed to integrate into its fund of knowledge and theory much of what is known in psychology. The completion of this job awaits the clinical psychologist.

To date, however, psychologists have learned very little about this school of psychotherapy and about psychoanalysis in general. Not even the advancements this school made in scientific therapy have been taken seriously enough by psychologists. It must be taken very seriously and kept in mind that any psychotherapeutic procedure which does not explain its therapeutic steps in terms of a theory of maladjustment which is an integral part of a theory of personality, in turn closely tied up with the rest of our psychological knowledge, can only be a pragmatic therapy. In this case pragmatic therapy means one that has only one justification: results. These results can be related solely to the therapeutic procedure—a situation which Molière so pointedly characterizes when he has the doctor explain how opium produces sleep: *Quia est in ita vis dormitiva*—"because there is in it sleep-producing power." A scientific psychotherapy is one which is backed by a theory of personality to which the steps of the psychotherapeutic procedure, as well as the status of the patient before and after therapy, can be reduced. Only such a reduction to a theoretical framework will enable us to evaluate psychotherapeutic procedures and psychotherapeutic results. If this argument does not suffice to indicate the requisite scientific basis of therapy and its evaluation, then let me invite you to search our literature for systematic evaluations of psychotherapy. Their absence in the literature will show clearly that there is something fundamentally wrong about evaluating psychotherapy.

One more consideration which applies both to testing and to therapy, and perhaps to all clinical research. It seems that so far we have been either smugly satisfied with unsatisfactory applications of research techniques of experimental psychology, or just stumbled around without definite technique or design. Even the idea that clinical research may need a new methodology is as yet scarcely recognized.

The consolation that all these problems are debits not only on our ledger, but also on that of psychiatry, social work, and to some extent, psychoanalysis, does not make the burden of our responsibility any lighter.

The general question with which we are dealing is the significance of theory for our science. For long we have been following a purely pragmatic line of approach, asking always only, "What works?" The necessity of the hour is that the pragmatistic approach be forgotten and replaced by live theory-building, uniting all the fields of psychological knowledge with those of personality, thought organization, and control of motility and action. If we do not apply ourselves to this task, we will be caught flat-footed by our conscience. As we get older our pragmatic results will no longer satisfy our conscience. We will be scorned by the younger generation of our profession because we will have nothing systematic to teach. And finally, we may get caught by an economic crisis showing us up in our *actual* present state.

25

BOOK REVIEW

Jean-Paul Sartre, *The Psychology of Imagination*[1]

Many will be disconcerted by the loud jacket, narrow margins, crowded pages, and the typographical errors of this book. The translation is confusing and the translator's name and the date of original publication are not given. Even without these handicaps the book would make difficult reading, for Sartre mixes the terminologies of psychology, philosophy of phenomenology, introspective account, and metaphysics. Familiarity with any of these terminologies is of no help to the reader for the upshot is a terminology which is strictly Sartre, with small islands here and there creating a false sense of familiarity. Factually incorrect or, at least, questionable information is not infrequently presented as "the truth" (e.g., p. 46 on the Müller-Lyer phenomenon; p. 52 on entoptic phenomena and hypnagogic reverie; p. 62 on the motor basis of attention; p. 213 on schizophrenia; p. 215 on hallucinations).

And yet the reader who persists through the jungle of terminology, and all other obstacles, may find some rewards. Sartre calls attention to the forgotten insights of Husserl, Meinong, and Brentano. Many of his observa-

[1] New York: Philosophical Library, 1948.

First published in The Psychoanalytic Quarterly, *18:389–390, 1949.*

tions of subtleties of conscious experiences, awaiting explanation by dynamic psychology, are still totally disregarded in its recent literature. We are reminded that contents of images in consciousness may be "posited as existing," "not posited as existing," "posited as nonexisting," "posited as assumed," "posited as present," "posited as absent," etc. From the point of view of the psychoanalyst, these describe fine shadings of reality testing and judgment, opening a broad and enticing vista of phenomena yet to be studied by psychoanalytic ego psychology. Since Paul Schilder's *Die Psychologie der progressiven Paralyse* and *Seele und Leben,* psychoanalytic theorizing has paid precious little attention to these important subtleties.

An introspective analysis of "perceiving consciousness," "imaging consciousness," etc., leads Sartre to the assumption that these are different forms of consciousness. By carrying introspection to a fine point, he approaches the very conclusion toward which recent empirical investigations are leading us (see Lewin, 1949; Brenman, 1949): between waking and dream consciousness there is an unbroken continuum of forms of consciousness distinguishable by the degree of reflection and by the balance of voluntary effort versus "spontaneity" present. Sartre writes: "Every consciousness posits its object, but each does so in its own way. Perception, for instance, posits its object as existing. The image also includes an act of belief, or a positional act [act of positing]. This act can assume four forms and no more: it can posit the object as nonexistent, or as absent, or as existing elsewhere; it can also 'neutralize' itself, that is, not posit its object as existing" (p. 16).

Gems of observation and insight hidden in a thicket! The question is only who will find it worth his while to seek them out.

REFERENCES

Brenman, M. (1949). Dreams and Hypnosis. *Psychoanal. Quart.,* 18:455–465.
Lewin, B. D. (1949). Mania and Sleep. *Psychoanal. Quart.,* 18:419–433.

26

BOOK REVIEW

Jean-Paul Sartre, *The Emotions.*
Outline of a Theory[1]

This book has the loud jacket and poor translation of its sister volume, *The Psychology of Imagination,* but its printing is agreeable to the eye and its conception more ordered. The author attempts to sketch a phenomenological theory of emotions. He gives a blistering critique of positivist academic psychology, a justifiable criticism of James's and Janet's theory of emotion, and uses the investigations of Lewin and Dembo on anger as the basis for his theory.

His discussion of psychoanalysis acknowledges that "psychoanalytic psychology has certainly been the first to put the emphasis on the signification of psychic facts" (pp. 41–49). Yet he rejects psychoanalytic theory because in it the signification is that of something extraconscious and thus it contradicts the Cartesian *"cogito ergo sum"* which is Sartre's *sine qua non.* Beyond these generalities his discussion reveals no familiarity whatsoever with the psychoanalytic theory of emotions.

The premise of Sartre's theory of emotion is: ". . . a phenomenological description of emotion will bring to light the essential structure of consciousness, since an emotion is precisely a consciousness. And conversely, a

[1] New York: Philosophical Library, 1948.

First published in The Psychoanalytic Quarterly, *18:390–392, 1949.*

problem arises which the psychologist does not even suspect; can types of consciousness be conceived which would not include emotion among their possibilities, or must we see in it an indispensable structure of consciousness?" (p. 15). Haughty and commonplace as this may sound, it remains a fact that "varieties of emotional experience as conscious experience" have so far been insufficiently explored (this is particularly obvious for anxiety). That even the psychoanalytic theory of emotions (not to say anything about the other theories of emotional experience) is but a series of fragments[2] is partly due to the lack of such phenomenological groundwork.

The salient points of Sartre's theory of emotions are:

> Fear is not originally conscious of being afraid any more than perception of this book is consciousness of perceiving the book. Emotional consciousness is at first unreflective [p. 50];
> . . . emotion is a certain way of apprehending the world [p. 52];
> . . . they [emotions] represent a particular subterfuge, a special trick, each one of them being a different means of eluding a difficulty [p. 32];
> It [emotion] is a transformation of the world. When the paths traced out become too difficult, or when we see no path, we can no longer live in so urgent and difficult a world. All the ways are barred. However, we must act. So we try to change the world, that is, to live as if the connection between things and their potentialities were not ruled by deterministic processes, but by magic. Let it be clearly understood that this is not a game; we are driven against a wall, and we throw ourselves into this new attitude with all the strength we can muster. Let it also be understood that this attempt is not conscious of being such, for it would then be the object of a reflection [pp. 58–59].

Sartre's conclusions are derived partly by aprioristic speculation and partly by introspective inspection of consciousness, handicapped by an utter disregard for and by an aprioristic rejection of unconscious determination. Nevertheless, they call attention to important facts. They stand in stark contrast to the conception of emotions as physiological processes, disorganized responses, etc., prevailing in academic psychology. They show a parallel to psychoanalytic conceptions of emotions in that they emphasize the primordial magical aspect of emotional experience. In Freud's theory, when immediate discharge is delayed (1911, p. 16) the arising instinct representations have a qualitative aspect (cathected memory trace) and a quantitative aspect (the charge of affect), and their discharge becomes manifest as emotional expression and emotion felt (1915). Dembo's conception of emotions, Sartre's model, also refers emotions to difficulties which by delaying action prevent the discharge of tension. Just like the psychoanalytical theory, Sartre's theory too refuses to relegate emotions to physiological or

[2] For a summary of these fragments see Rapaport (1942, pp. 28–33).

neurological analogies and insists that they be psychologically described and accounted for.

It is regrettable that what Sartre calls an outline of a theory is in the main a bit of speculation and a few worth-while pointers for phenomenological observation not yet exploited for the theory of emotion. A theory it is not.

Sartre makes it too easy for us not to notice a worth-while point or to notice it only to say that we have known it all the time.

REFERENCES

Freud, S. (1911). Formulations Regarding the Two Principles in Mental Functioning. *Collected Papers*, 4:13–21. New York: Basic Books, 1959.
———— (1915). Repression. *Collected Papers*, 4:84–97. New York: Basic Books, 1959.
Rapaport, D. (1942). *Emotions and Memory*. Baltimore: Williams & Wilkins.

27

BOOK REVIEW

Clyde Kluckhohn and Henry A. Murray, Editors, *Personality in Nature, Society, and Culture*[1]

This is a rich source book reflecting our knowledge, our ignorance, and our disagreements about the interrelationships of society and personality. Many would insist nowadays that to speak of an "interrelationship" in this context is misleading, since in speaking of personality and society one refers merely to two aspects of a unitary process. The volume is timely, for we do not possess as yet the particulars of tested knowledge to substantiate such sweeping conclusions on general principles. One of the great merits of this volume is that it brings into relief the gaps of such cohesive, tested knowledge.

Even though the volume avowedly did not strive to attain completeness (p. xiii), it reflects a great variety of theories, approaches, methods, and findings. Its lack of conscious bias in selection offers much food for thought, not only to the layman and the student, but to all who are involved in the study of either personality or society. There is some attempt at integrating the contradictory views of the various contributors by the "Introduction,"

[1] New York: Alfred A. Knopf, 1948.

First published in The Psychoanalytic Quarterly, *18:525–528, 1949.*

by the chapters "A Conception of Personality" and "The Determinants of Personality Formation," by the introductions to each section and to each contribution by the editors.

The views of the editors are most clearly presented by the following:

> Some anthropologists have tended too much to view personality simply as the product of special cultural conditions, particularly the patterns for the training of children. Some psychiatrists have, on the other hand, presented over-simple formulations which derived culture patterns almost wholly from the projection, sublimation, or symbolization of various unconscious dynamisms in individuals. Today there is increasing realization that both of these viewpoints must be modified and merged with other factors in wider abstractions [p. 161].

The psychoanalyst reading this volume will be gratified to notice not only the contributions of analysts (Alexander, Erikson, Fromm, Greenacre, Levy, Waelder), but also that hardly any of the other contributions fails to show the impact of psychoanalytic findings and thinking. He will, however, probably find the volume wanting because "projection, sublimation, or symbolization of various unconscious dynamisms in individuals" are not given their due share of attention. He will, let us hope, notice with humility and curiosity that there are many problems of human behavior for the understanding of which knowledge other than psychoanalysis is needed, and that such knowledge will broaden his theoretical and perhaps even his practical horizons. He will almost certainly realize that his instinct theory must be sharpened and clarified, so that it have its due impact—which at present is in abeyance—on social-psychological and anthropological thinking. He will also find that the development of psychoanalytic ego psychology will be greatly enhanced by regard for the facts and methods collected in this volume and, on the other hand, that the field covered by it stands to gain greatly by the achievements of psychoanalytic ego psychology.[2]

The recently published related volumes are Newcomb, Hartley, et al., *Readings in Social Psychology* (1947) and Róheim's *Psychoanalysis and the Social Sciences* (1947). The three volumes provide a rather rounded picture of the field. Even so, since the Róheim volume is not intended as a source book, the representation of the psychoanalytic contribution remains lopsided. A source book of the psychoanalytic contribution to social sciences and an assay of the bearing of psychoanalysis on social science is yet to be written.

These days developments in genetics are about to root out the last vestige of the nature-nurture dichotomy (Sonneborn, 1949) and developments in the theory of evolution are about to redefine the organism-environment relationship (Simpson, 1949). New patterns of thinking deriving from biol-

---

[2] See, e.g., Erikson's paper, "Childhood and Tradition in Two American Indian Tribes," familiar to us from *The Psychoanalytic Study of the Child* (1945).

ogy are becoming available for assaying our knowledge of the personality-society interrelationship, and for designing methods of attack on its problems. It is good that we are given these source books now. It is likely that in a few years the situation in the field—that was never quite consolidated—will become again so fluid that no one will be in the position to give such interim assays as they do. Yet it is regrettable that instinct phenomena and instinct theory of animal psychology (Uexküll, Lorenz, Wheeler, Tinbergen) and of psychoanalysis hardly entered Kluckhohn and Murray's selection. The chances are that the new synthesis to come will draw on these more heavily. Kluckhohn and Murray's best intent to the contrary notwithstanding, their source book and their own introductory chapters are still heavily slanted to the environmentalist side. Heinz Hartmann's *Ego Psychology and the Problem of Adaptation* (1939) could well have served to balance the picture given—at least in part.

The imbalance is well reflected in the listing of the "determinants of personality formation": (1) constitutional determinants; (2) group membership determinants; (3) rôle determinants; (4) situational determinants. The instinct-drive-unconscious determination of personality development is underplayed (pp. 38 ff.), even though the theoretical necessity of accepting the "concept of need, drive or vectorial force," and the concept of "tension reduction" are stressed (pp. 14–15). Consequently myth, legend, and superstition, the time-honored fields in which the integration of unconscious individual and social dynamics can be relatively readily studied, are little regarded in the selection. True, such studies usually slant the issue in the other direction, but that is no reason to omit them from an assay in which nearly each contribution has a slant of its own.

The title of the volume promises that "personality in culture" will also be treated in it. The topics science, art, and religion, the usual referents of the term "culture," are, however, hardly treated at all in this volume. Is this the editors' omission, or lack of research material available? Probably the latter. It is amazing that most of what we know about the personalities who become culture creators, and about culture as a builder of personality, is derived from belles-lettres and biographies. The psychoanalytic contributions to these problems, though varied and many, are not systematic and are concerned more with the individual personality or art product than with culture as such. But even here Freud's *Civilization and Its Discontents* and *The Future of an Illusion* are exceptions.

The Kluckhohn-Murray volume is "must reading" for the psychoanalyst. It will set his sights to the tasks that will have to be fulfilled before an integrated theory of the personality in its social setting can arise.

REFERENCES

Erikson, E. H. (1945). Childhood and Tradition in Two American Indian Tribes. *Psychoanal. Study Child,* 1:319–350. New York: International Universities Press. Also (revised) in *Personality in Nature, Society, and Culture,* ed. C. Kluckhohn & H. A. Murray. New York: Knopf, 1948, pp. 176–203.

Hartmann, H. (1939). *Ego Psychology and the Problem of Adaptation,* tr. D. Rapaport. New York: International Universities Press, 1958.

Newcomb, T. M., Hartley, E. L., et al. (1947). *Readings in Social Psychology.* New York: Holt.

Róheim, G., ed. (1947). *Psychoanalysis and the Social Sciences.* New York: International Universities Press.

Simpson, G. G. (1949). *The Meaning of Evolution.* New Haven: Yale University Press, 1952.

Sonneborn, T. M. (1949). Beyond the Gene. *Amer. Sci.,* 37:33–59.

28

ON THE PSYCHOANALYTIC
THEORY OF THINKING

I

The aim of this paper is to piece together what the science of psychoanalysis has taught us concerning thinking.

Such an attempt is fraught with inevitable difficulties. First, it is of necessity incomplete: there is more to cover than time allows. Second, psychoanalytic writing on thinking is fragmentary and belongs to various stages of the development of psychoanalysis; consequently, it requires interpretation and speculative completion. Presenting it therefore invites the time-worn critique; what is good in it is not new and what is new is not good. Third, the psychoanalytic theory of thinking is a part of metapsychology—which, dealing as it does with abstractions and being several steps removed from immediate therapeutic concern, remains the least familiar and to many the least palatable part of psychoanalytic theory. Fourth, the psychology of thinking is in the main ego psychology; and since psychoanalytic ego psychology itself is still in the early phases of its evolution, it does not offer a

First published in The International Journal of Psycho-Analysis, *31:161–170, 1950. Reprinted in Robert P. Knight and Cyrus R. Friedman, eds.,* Psychoanalytic Psychiatry and Psychology, Clinical and Theoretical Papers, *Austen Riggs Center, Volume 1. New York: International Universities Press, 1954, pp. 259–273. Spanish translation published in Merton M. Gill and David Rapaport,* Aportaciones a la Téoria y Técnica Psicoanalítica. *Asociación Psicoanalítica Mexicana, A.C., 1962, pp. 97–117.*

313

solid framework for the psychology of thinking. In fact, some of the future development of other aspects of ego psychology will depend on developments in the psychology of thinking. Fifth, the psychoanalytic psychology of thinking cannot be a bridge between psychoanalysis and a solidly built academic theory of thinking because the latter likewise is still fragmentary. Yet the psychoanalytic theory of thinking cannot disregard the important beginnings that have been made in academic psychology.

In so far as my attempt fails, I believe it is that the task exceeds my ability. The necessity and feasibility of the task should not be doubted: we need a crystallization of the psychoanalytic theory of thinking from its fragments; this theory must be cast as an indispensable part of psychoanalytic ego psychology; it can be formulated only in metapsychological terms considering the genetic, structural, dynamic, and economic points of view.[1] And last, but not least, it must extend into the field of the academic theory of thinking to congelate the beginnings of the dynamic understanding of thinking to be found there.

II

For the psychoanalyst it must be clear that the point of departure in understanding thinking is that the thought process is motivated by the instinctual drives. It will be remembered that Freud (1900, p. 535) maintained that all thinking is a detour from the direct path toward gratification. Since Freud used the word "ideation" for the products of the primary thought process and "thinking" for those of the secondary process (1911, p. 16), it is clear that he regards the detour as motivated by instinctual drives as much as is the direct path, the secondary process as much as is the primary (1900, p. 536). To understand Freud's view of the secondary process, we shall have to review first the dynamics of the primary process.

We will first give Freud's view of the state of affairs as it is assumed to exist prior to the development of ideation and the primary process. The construction is, of course, only a schema. When the potential energy of an instinctual drive rises to a certain critical point—and the object of the drive

[1] [It will clarify Rapaport's views on the metapsychological points of view as expressed in this paper to refer to his later conception. In "The Points of View and Assumptions of Metapsychology" (Chapter 62), five metapsychological points of view are defined: dynamic, economic, structural, genetic, and adaptive. It will be seen in the summary of the present paper (pp. 325–326) that he actually uses these five points of view, though the "dynamic" is not separately labeled or discussed, and he refers to the adaptive as the "biological," clearly its forerunner. While he also employs a "topographic" point of view here, it is clear that he meant by it only the relation of a mental content to consciousness; he agreed with the conclusions of my "Topography and Systems in Psychoanalytic Theory" (Gill, 1963) that a topographic *point of view* should not be employed, but that, rather, "topographic" should be used for a lower, descriptive level of abstraction, specifically the relation of content to consciousness —Ed.]

is present—the sluices of motility open and the discharge of tension takes place (Freud, 1915a, pp. 60–66; 1900, pp. 508–509; 1911, p. 14). This can be stated in other words by saying that when a tension, usually referred to as a "need," reaches a certain intensity and the need-satisfying object is present, discharge of tension takes place. From the point of view of the dynamics of instinctual drives this process is called gratification (Freud, 1900, pp. 509, 533–534). From the point of view of the regulation of psychic energy distribution the process is subsumed under the concept of the pleasure principle (Freud, 1920, pp. 1, 82). From the point of view of energy dynamics in general the process reveals the fundamental tendency of all energy, namely that toward even distribution. From what Freud would have called the biological point of view, this process is the direct discharge or gratification discharge of cathexes, requiring as a condition of discharge and deriving its biological usefulness from the presence of the need-satisfy-ing object (Freud, 1900, pp. 533–534). As we shall see later, the secondary process requires the fulfillment of considerably more complex conditions before discharge can take place, and its biological usefulness is charac-terized by experimental action with small quantities of energy. The dis-tinction between the two is epitomized by Freud in the contrasting concepts of gratification discharge and action (Freud, 1911, p. 16; 1900, pp. 533–534).

So far we have described the concepts related to the process of the pri-mordial gratification discharge. Freud's concept is that ideation arises only when this process is interfered with. When the need tension rises to the point where discharge should take place but the need-satisfying object is not present, the discharge is delayed. During this externally imposed delay begin the changes which are to have such far-reaching significance for the development of the psychic apparatus. Here is the beginning of the detour on the road toward gratification (Freud, 1911, p. 14; 1900, pp. 508–510, 533).

There are two main effects of this delay. One can be observed; the other must be reconstructed. The observed effect is generalized undifferentiated restlessness which Freud views as the discharge of the drive tension into the soma, this discharge substituting for the direct gratification discharge. This discharge into the soma Freud conceptualizes as affect discharge and con-siders it the archetype of all affective behavior. A later formulation of affect discharge contrasts it with motor action. The latter is an attempt to change the external environment, to re-establish safe conditions of gratification; while the affect discharge is directed at changing the internal somatic rather than the external environment (Freud, 1911, p. 16; 1915c, p. 111, espe-cially footnote; 1900, p. 511).

The second effect of the delay of discharge, an effect which is a construc-tion rather than an observation, is the emergence of a hallucinatory image of the need-satisfying object when tension rises to the point where discharge should take place but the need-satisfying object is not present. The hallucinatory image is the archetype of thought. Its appearance in consciousness is determined by the drive tension; it is the fundamental element in the primary process; it represents that special case of the pleasure principle which is conceptualized as wish fulfillment (Freud, 1900, pp. 509, 533). In the absence of the need-satisfying object the alternative of the hallucinatory revival of the original gratification is chosen. Concerning the rôle of this hallucinatory image in the primary process and the other characteristics of the primary process we will say more later.

The biological utility of this hallucinatory image is difficult to discern. It is an abortive effort at discharge. It provides neither the gratification of direct discharge nor the advantages of experimenting with small quantities of energy. From the economic point of view—or to put it otherwise, the point of view of cathectic dynamics—the emergence of the hallucinatory image of the need-satisfying object is possible only because of the mobile character of the drive energies or cathexes. It is because the cathexes are mobile that they can be displaced from the perception of the need-satisfying object to the memory trace of this object, thus imparting to the memory trace an intensity which makes it hallucinatorily vivid (Freud, 1900, pp. 492–493, 531, 533–534; 1920, pp. 34–36).

From the point of view of the instinctual drive the hallucinatory image is an instinct representation since its emergence in consciousness indicates that the need tension arising from the instinctual drive has mounted to the point at which it is seeking discharge. From the point of view of memory theory the appearance of the memory of a need-satisfying object in the hallucinatory form in consciousness indicates that the memory is cathected by, that is to say, charged with the energy of the instinctual drive (Freud, 1915b, p. 91; 1915c, p. 111).[2] Clearly instinct representation and cathected memory trace are two different conceptualizations of a state of a memory or idea. The study of the hallucinations of psychotics, the descriptions of illusions of people on the brink of starvation or dehydration, and the analysis of hypnagogic and dream hallucinations are the empirical data from which these retrospective reconstructions have been derived. Out of these, and particularly out of the study of hallucinatory deliria (Meynert's amentia), we may derive empirical evidence to show that the hallucinatory image does not provide by its momentary appearance more than a minute opportunity for discharge. If the hallucinatory attempt at gratification becomes continuous, as in hallucinatory deliria, death results by exhaustion (Freud, 1917, p. 145; 1900, pp. 509, 533). The transition from these highly cathected hallucinatory images to memory traces cathected by minute amounts of energy is the transition from the primary to the secondary process. The conditions of this transition will be discussed in further detail below.

[2] See also Lewin (1935, pp. 175 ff.) on "valence" (*Aufforderungscharacter*).

From the genetic point of view a more complete description of the hallucinatory image must be made, and from it important conclusions may be derived concerning the primary process. From developmental psychology we know that the original experience of the need-satisfying object is a diffuse undifferentiated experience in which visual, acoustic, tactile, thermal, cutaneous, kinesthetic, and other stimulations are fused. Discrete objects do not as yet exist, and thus the need-satisfying object itself is not differentiated from the context in which it appears nor even from the experiences immediately preceding or following it (Werner, 1926; see also Hartmann, Kris, and Loewenstein, 1946).

It is this diffuse global image of the need-satisfying object which is pushed into consciousness when instinctual tension mounts. In the course of development this diffuse image differentiates into discrete objects and experiences, all of which are still related to instinctual drives in the same fashion as was the original undifferentiated image of the need-satisfying object. Thus we find a multitude of instinct representations replacing the original undifferentiated instinct representation, any of which are mutually interchangeable since their essential meaning is that they are representations of the instinctual drive. From the point of view of the theory of thinking and the theory of memory we have here what may be called a drive organization of memories. Empirically we observe such organization even after the establishment of the secondary process. For instance, when we trace the unconscious sources of slips of the tongue (as Freud did in *The Psychopathology of Everyday Life,* 1901) we find that the free associations to the slip map out for us single examples of such drive-organized memory systems. Similar observations can be made in selective amnesias or in fugues (Freud, 1901; Rapaport, 1942).

Within such systems of drive organizations of memories the mobile drive cathexes can be freely displaced. The equivalence of all memories within such a system makes possible the condensation of any number of such instinct representations into a composite one of heightened energic cathexis, since the composite combines the cathexes of the separate representations. Such condensations are familiar to all of us from the study of dreams.

We see that this description of the evolution of the hallucinatory image makes plausible the nature and origins of the mechanisms of the primary process (Freud, 1900, pp. 492–493, 467, 531).

From the topographic point of view we must note that the hallucinatory image is the archetype of consciousness and that intense drive cathexes may, under certain conditions, be alone responsible for making an idea conscious. Later on we shall see that the most common form of consciousness, as encountered in secondary-process thinking, is from the point of view of cathectic dynamics quite different (Freud, 1911, p. 14). Yet we are already warned here that consciousness is not a single genotype but rather a phenotype which may have various genetic and causal roots. Consciousness during dreaming, for instance—like that of the hallucinatory image—is one in which the intensely concentrated drive cathexes make for consciousness. The necessary concentration of cathexes is obtained by the primary-process mechanisms of condensation and displacement. Dream consciousness also seems feasible in the main only in conjunction with visual images serving as instinct representations. The state of consciousness referred to as dream consciousness is thus in the main motivated by drive cathexes and carries in the main the character of visual imagery as its major formal characteristic. The latter Freud expressed in the theory of dreams by the concept of "regard for representability" (1900, pp. 485–486).

III

So far we have sketched the psychoanalytic conception of the primary process. We found it working with mobile cathexes, regulated by the pleasure principle, striving toward direct gratification discharge. We have seen the emergence during the period of delay of discharge of hallucinatory images of need-satisfying objects. Pursuing the fate of these images into the early course of development, we have seen how two of the mechanisms of the primary process, condensation and displacement, follow, as it were, of necessity (Freud, 1900, pp. 525 ff.). Our next task is to reconstruct the conditions under which the secondary process arises.

From the structural point of view, the emergence of the secondary process is one aspect of early ego development in its differentiation from the id (Freud, 1911; 1923, pp. 29–30; 1900, p. 536). In psychoanalytic writing the discussion of early ego development is most frequently dealt with in terms of introjection and identifications. These aspects of ego development, though certainly of fundamental significance for the theory of both normal and pathological thinking, we shall have to bypass here (Freud, 1923, pp. 36 ff.). The aspects of early ego development with which we shall deal are rather those of the first structuralization of the control of impulse—the prototype of defense—and the development of reality testing (Fenichel, 1945, pp. 144 ff.).

The primary process aimed at direct discharge of cathexes, and when circumstances delayed such discharge substituted for it wish fulfillment in the form of hallucinatory revival of the need-satisfying object. The secondary process converts this involuntary delay due to external circumstances into an internally controlled delay (Freud, 1911, p. 16), assuring postponement of discharge until external reality conditions have been found suitable for discharge. We know that this detour as often as not implies not only search for suitable conditions in reality but also motor action designed to change reality so as to make it more suitable (Freud, 1900, pp. 533–534). The core of this change from the primary to the secondary process appears to be the change in the character of delay. The delay to begin with was due to external circumstances and is turned into an ability to delay, into an internal control. Thus is a necessity made a virtue.

From the point of view of cathectic dynamics, some aspects of this change in the character of delay are familiar to us from the theory of repression. While repression proper—or as it is sometimes called, "afterexpulsion"—can be conceived of dynamically in terms of the withdrawal of conscious and preconscious cathexes, the study of the conditions of primal repression necessitates the assumption of countercathexes which expresses the dynamic implication of the change in the character of delay (Freud, 1915c, pp. 113–114; 1911, p. 16). With the introduction of the concept of countercathexes, psychoanalytic theory introduced the fundamental concept of impulse controls, which is central to our conception of the structure of the ego. Little is known about the nature of the process by which these countercathexes arise. It is possible that their precursors are to be found in what Freud referred to as "the stimulus barrier" (1920, pp. 30 ff.; 1925a; see also Bergman and Escalona, 1949) or in what Hartmann referred to as "maturation of organic control structures" (1939).[3] Be that as it may, we are not lacking analogies in energy-organization processes that can make the emergence of such control organizations as countercathexes plausible (Freud, 1900, p. 537). It is a rather common occurrence for energy distributions which usually strive for discharge, when they are prevented from doing so, to structuralize to prevent or regulate their own discharge.

From the structural point of view these countercathexes set the fundamental pattern for ego controls, and their emergence is thus one of the crucial steps in ego development. Though Freud's conception of them seems to be closely tied up with the theory of repression, it will be well to remember that their significance is far broader than would be implied by the current use of the concept repression. The earlier concept of repression as Freud used it in the period between 1910 and 1915 was a global one, including all defensive processes of the ego. It seems probable that all defenses are varieties of countercathectic organizations.[4] It therefore becomes clear that the controlled delay described above is the prototype of defense. It will also be worthy of note that in these countercathexes we see the prototype of the energies that become bound in the structuralizing process of ego development and thus become the energies at the disposal of the ego (Freud, 1923, pp. 64–65; 1920, pp. 34–36).

While this process of structuralizing is progressing, the primary drive or-

[3] [This phrase antedates both of Rapaport's published translations of Hartmann (1939). While Hartmann does not explicitly speak of "control" structures, he clearly implies this and their position as precursors of defense. See Hartmann (1939, pp. 50–51; 1950, p. 83)—Ed.]

[4] See particularly Freud (1915c, p. 119) concerning "negation" and compare with his "Negation" (1925b). A general comparison of Freud (1915b) and (1915c) on the one hand, and Freud (1926) and A. Freud (1936) on the other, illustrates this point. See also Fenichel (1945).

ganization of memories also undergoes significant alterations. The establishment of delays and controls results in the development of partial drives (Freud, 1905, pp. 593 ff., 597 ff., 614 ff.; 1915a, pp. 65 ff.; Abraham, 1927). The progressive differentiation of the objects of these partial drives, coupled with the enrichment by experience of the range of instinct representations organized in closed systems of drive representations, results in overlapping systems in which, depending on its context, an idea or object may be a representation of any of several drives. Thus the exclusive equivalence of ideas in terms of the drive around which they are organized breaks down and transitions and equivalences between the several systems of drive organizations of memory become feasible. A particular idea is no longer dependent upon the mounting tension of a single drive for its emergence in consciousness. The cathexis of a particular idea is no longer exclusively referable to a single drive. This change paves the way for the new organization of memories replacing the drive organization of memories. In this new organization, known to us from the experimental investigations of Bartlett and others, conceptual, temporal, and spatial belongingness organizes ideas into memory frames of reference. These conceptual, spatial, and temporal frames of reference develop in the course of experience and thus correspond to the relationship patterns of reality (Freud, 1911, p. 16; Bartlett, 1932; Koffka, 1935, pp. 607–614; Gillespie, 1937).

The setting for the secondary process is thus prepared in the countercathexes at the disposal of the ego and in the new memory frames of reference replacing drive organizations of memories (see Rapaport, 1942). Besides the results of motor behavior which differentiate what is external from what is internal (Freud, 1917, pp. 148–149), it is in these new memory frames of reference that we find the first safeguards for reality testing (Freud, 1900, pp. 488–492, especially p. 490). Yet we must consider this transition process from at least one more vantage point to obtain a clearer picture of the operation of the reality principle and of the process of reality testing.

IV

Freud assumes that in the primitive undifferentiated phase of development, in which no differentiated objects as yet exist, there are two qualities in terms of which internal tension becomes conscious. These are pain and pleasure, the former related to mounting tension, the latter to discharge (Freud, 1900, pp. 545, 546; 1920, p. 2). The hallucinatory images of the need-satisfying objects introduce additional new conscious qualities (Freud, 1911, p. 15; 1900, pp. 529, 546). The primitive ideation is still regulated, however, by the pleasure-pain signals arising from the tension inside the psychic apparatus. In the secondary process the organism achieves, by means of the new conscious qualities, a relative liberation from

the exclusive rule of these pleasure-pain signals. These new conscious qualities ultimately make up what we refer to as "thoughts." Their prototype is
the hallucinatory image, itself genetically derived from perception. How is
this relative liberation from pleasure-pain signals achieved?

We have already seen that the instinct representation has two aspects—a
quantitative and a qualitative one (Freud, 1915b, p. 91; 1915c, p. 111; see
also Brierley, 1937, and Glover, 1939). The quantitative one is the affect
charge that discharges into the interior of the somatic apparatus, resulting
in affect expression or somatic changes of affective origin; the qualitative
one is the idea, the cathected memory trace. Both of these serve both as
indicators of and safety valves for mounting drive tension. The quantitative
aspect serves especially the safety-valve function and the qualitative serves
especially the function of indicator. But both partake of both rôles. Freud
was forced to distinguish between these two aspects of instinct representation by observations of hysterical and obsessional conditions. In hysteria
the quantitative (affective) aspect of instinct representation is emphasized,
while in obsessional conditions it is the qualitative (ideational) aspect
which is prominent (Freud, 1915b, pp. 93 ff.).

Genetically it is clear that this differentiation into two aspects does not
begin before the controlling countercathectic energy distributions and their
structuralization develop. In hallucinatory ideation the two aspects are still
indivisible. The differentiation of these two aspects of instinct representation is the prototype of the defense mechanisms of isolation and intellectualization (Freud, 1926, pp. 55–57; 1915c, pp. 133–136).[5] The controlling
countercathectic energy distributions, once arisen, differentiate affective
and ideational instinct representations and thus liberate the new conscious
qualities of ideation from the rule of affective pleasure-pain regulation. In
this way the new organization of ideas in terms of memory frames of reference can give orientation to reality relationships relatively unencroached
upon by intrapsychic pleasure-pain regulations. Thus emerges the reality
principle, and thus reality testing by means of memory traces cathected by
minute amounts of energy—that is to say, experimental action with minute
cathexes (Freud, 1900, pp. 533–534)—becomes possible.

V

The emergence of countercathectic energy distributions, their structuralization, the new organization of memory frames of reference, and the reality
principle set the stage for the secondary process. A further understanding of
the operation of the secondary process may be derived by following the
topographic conditions and the corresponding cathectic dynamics that arise
with the emergence of these ego organizations and structures.

[5] Yet it is conceivable that a constitutional potentiality, determining what should prevail after the differentiation has taken place, is present from the beginning.

The little that is known of the cathectic dynamics of the secondary process derives from our understanding of "afterexpulsion"—that is to say, of repression proper (Freud, 1915b, pp. 86–87). It is conceived that repression proper begins with the withdrawal of the cathexes of the conscious and preconscious systems from the ideas to be repressed (Freud, 1915c, pp. 112–113). This is then followed by countercathexis of these ideas in order to prevent their continuous re-emergence and the continuous struggle and anxiety which would otherwise ensue (Freud, 1915b, pp. 89–90; 1915c, pp. 113–114). These cathexes of the preconscious and conscious are referred to either as "attention" cathexes or hypercathexes (Freud, 1915c, pp. 124–127, 133–134; 1917, pp. 148–150; 1900, pp. 529, 546). In another context we are familiar with them as delibidinized or sublimated energies (Freud, 1923, pp. 62–65; Rapaport, 1947; see also Rapaport, Gill, and Schafer, 1945). In general it may be formulated that these are energies divested of the hallmarks of their instinctual origin even though their instinctual origin as such is not called into question. We have seen how countercathexes arose with the beginnings of the emergence of ego structure in the form of controls of drives. It may be conjectured that with the further development of ego structuring these countercathectic energies become available to the ego for uses other than those of countercathexis (Freud, 1915c, pp. 113–114). Another way in which we can form a conception of the nature of these conscious cathexes of the ego is the following: the energy distribution of instinctual drives regulated by the pleasure principle is overlaid in the course of development by a superimposed countercathectic energy distribution. These two energy distributions together establish a new field of forces. The ego cathexes may be conceived of as those energy exchanges that take place within this new field of forces.[6]

It is conceived that only a determinate—that is to say, a limited—amount of such energy is available to the ego. Therefore, once this energy is employed in hypercathexis to make conscious an idea or a group of ideas, it must of necessity be withdrawn from other ideas. Thereby these other ideas, though capable of becoming conscious, remain nonconscious or, as we are accustomed to say, preconscious. This function of conscious cathexes is the dynamic process of attention (Freud, 1900, p. 529).

This does not, however, tell the whole story of consciousness and attention. First of all we pointed out that intense drive cathexes of ideas—as in hallucinations—may in themselves make an idea conscious, though this is a different kind of consciousness from the usual one. Second, when the drive cathexis of an idea mounts and the drive and its ideational representation are not countercathected, the increasing drive cathexis will attract attention to cathexes of consciousness (Freud, 1900, p. 529). Third, Freud postulated that these hypercathexes link the instinct representations or instinct

---

[6] Compare, however, Hartmann (1950, pp. 85–90), and Hartmann, Kris, and Loewenstein (1949).

derivatives with verbal images and thus achieve their becoming conscious (Freud, 1923, pp. 21 ff.; 1900, p. 546; 1915c, pp. 133 ff.).[7] Fourth, it became necessary to assume a censorship—that is to say, a controlling energy distribution—not only at the point of transition between unconscious and preconscious where the countercathexes discussed above are distributed, but also at the point of transition between preconscious and conscious (Freud, 1915c, pp. 123–127). The need for this assumption derives from observations of daydreams and fantasies which have a different form of existence in the preconscious from those ideas which, though fully capable of becoming conscious, are not at a given moment cathected by attention (see Kris, 1950). Therefore, fifth, for an idea to become conscious it must pass the censorship between preconscious and conscious—expressed otherwise, there must be no countercathectic energy distributions against it as it passes from preconscious to conscious.[8]

VI

Here we arrive at the uncharted, hardly touched areas of the psychoanalytic theory of thinking. Thus what follows can be only recounting of problems and conjectures and nothing more.

We have already seen that the nature of "consciousness" of hallucinatory images is dynamically radically different from the usual consciousness of ideas. We have no reason to assume theoretically that these are the only two kinds of consciousness possible. Observation and experience, on the other hand, suggest that there is a group of such states of consciousness ranging between the hallucinatory consciousness characteristic of the dream and waking consciousness. Examples of such states of consciousness and the workers whose names are most closely identified with their study are the following: hypnagogic states, Silberer; Korsakoff patients, Hartmann; paresis, Schilder; amentia, Meynert, Schilder, and Hartmann; fugues and amnesias, Janet (see Rapaport, 1942, 1951a). In a recent exploratory study with more or less continuous recording of the dreams, reveries, and thought productions through the nights of several weeks, I believe I have observed a more or less continuous series of such states of consciousness which seemed to me distinguishable from each other by the formal characteristics of their mode of thinking (Rapaport, 1951b). The differences in cathectic dynamics between these states of consciousness and the forms of the thought processes determined by them are so far unknown. A field of exploration lies wide open here, and a huge gap in our theory of thinking awaits bridg-

---

[7] Compare, however, Freud (1940, pp. 41–46).

[8] [It will be seen that, in the discussion of topography in this section, though Rapaport speaks only once explicitly of "conscious and preconscious systems," he had not yet reached complete clarity on the use of "topographic" to mean only the relation of content to consciousness—Ed.]

ing. For the present, cathectic dynamics and thought processes can be dealt with by us only by means of the dichotomy between primary process and secondary process. It is not impossible that a study of the phenomena of this gap referred to will break down this dichotomy and replace it by gradual transitions (see Hartmann, 1950).

For the present, psychoanalytic theory is forced to assume two kinds of censorship, one between unconscious and preconscious and one between preconscious and conscious. In 1927 Jones expressed the idea that it is probable that censorship is distributed in a more diversified—or, as he put it, "streamlined"—fashion throughout the psychic apparatus (Jones, 1948). Theoretically we have no good reason to assume that the same process by which the original countercathectic energy distribution arose is not repeated over and over again in the course of development of the ego structure. Every countercathecting energy distribution can give rise to a new energy distribution, the delays of discharges within which structuralize to give rise to a new countercathecting energy distribution and so forth *ad infinitum*. In fact, the observations of conscious thought processes may give some support to such an assumption. In the acquisition of a new set of abstract concepts, there is a struggle characterized by occasional falling back upon the concrete data from which the abstractions were derived. When the acquisition is complete there is an energy-saving and ease of operation which makes the new set of concepts well conceived of as a hypercathectic organization. It seems clear that there is an intrinsic relationship between this set of problems related to censorship, countercathectic and hypercathectic energy distributions on the one hand, and the above-discussed problems of variants of thought processes in different states of consciousness on the other.

Another intriguing problem of the secondary process is that of the character of ego cathexes. Are these all independent and undirected energies that the ego can manipulate freely, or are they directed energies whose use remains more or less determined by their instinctual origin (see Hartmann, 1939, 1950)? An approach to this problem must remain mindful of the great influence that attitudes, conscious strivings, opinions, biases, and so forth can exert on an individual's thought organization (see Murphy, 1947, pp. 362 ff.; Sherif and Cantril, 1945–46; Klein and Schlesinger, 1949; Tolman, 1949). There is even experimental evidence to show that conscious strivings may give rise to thought formations showing some resemblance to those produced by primary processes. Müller, Ach, and others have observed such thought formations and labeled them "apperceptive fusions" (Rapaport, 1951a). The theoretical question such observations pose is this: Is it necessary to assume every time such an attitude or striving organizes conscious thought in a fashion not consistent with the laws of the secondary process that instinctual drives have asserted themselves, as they do, for instance, in slips of the tongue? Two alternate hypotheses to this assumption are possible: first, it could be assumed, as Kris has demonstrated for poetic creation and the comic, that in these thought organizations the ego makes use of the primary process for its purposes (Kris, 1944), or second, it could be assumed that every countercathectic organization of energies gives rise to a new set of forces which, though derivatives of the original instinctual drives, have a degree of independence from them. At this stage of the game no decision among these three hypotheses is possible. It is, however, probable that the last hypothesis, since it implies relatively independent ego forces, will prove more consistent with our present theory formation, dominated as it is by our interest in exploring the extent of the independence of the ego as a dynamic structure.[9]

To summarize: *Genetically,* the thought process is conceived of as arising in the form of hallucinatory images and ideas of drive objects, or hallucinatory wish fulfillments, and to develop into a process of detour on the way toward gratification. Genetically, therefore, we distinguish primary and secondary processes. The former strive for full immediate discharge of tensions, operate with mobile cathexes, and stand under the regulation of the pleasure principle. On the basis of the equivalence of all ideas which are representations of the same drive, the primary process employs condensation, displacement, and other mechanisms in pursuing its aims of tension discharge. The secondary process operates with small amounts of bound cathexes, and allows no discharge before experimental action with these small amounts has proved that the action is likely to decrease tension; it assumes equivalences not in terms of representations of the same drive, but in terms of reality relations and meaning, being regulated by the reality principle.

Topographically, thought processes may be either unconscious (primary processes), or preconscious and conscious (secondary processes). This parallelism of unconscious and primary, on the one hand, and preconscious-conscious and secondary on the other, is somewhat arbitrary, since the ego may use primary processes too for its purposes as in wit, inspiration, etc., by hypercathecting them (see Kris). There are, however, at this point problems of cathectic dynamics which await future clarification. The criteria for distinguishing these so-called topographical concepts are achieved in psychoanalytic metapsychology more or less exclusively in terms of differential characteristics of cathectic processes.

Structurally, the emergence and development of thought processes is one aspect of the emergence and development of the ego, and thought processes are integral parts of ego processes. They are an outstanding aspect and instrument of reality testing subserving the reality principle. The interesting and important problems of the role of thought processes in the synthetic and differentiation processes of the ego have not been discussed. Nor have we touched on the relationship of thought processes to skills, motor abili-

[9] Compare Allport (1937, pp. 191–211) on "functional autonomy."

ties, etc., i.e., to the whole field of problems Hartmann referred to as the conflict-free ego sphere.

Economically, we have traced the development of cathectic (energy) distributions. We have followed the development from mobile to bound cathexes and clarified the concepts of countercathexes, hypercathexes, attention cathexes, and delibidinized or sublimated energies. We have attempted to show how the development of systems of control of cathexes by systems of energies of a higher cathectic level though of lesser intensity comes about. We have dwelt on the functions of consciousness and attention and defined both in terms of cathectic dynamics.

Finally, we have shown that *from the biological point of view* thinking is experimental action with small amounts of energy. Thinking explores the possible pathways of action to find the one of least resistance, least danger, and greatest directness, while preserving almost intact the energy necessary for motor action. This formulation integrates the biological advantage of thinking into the psychoanalytic theory of thinking.

REFERENCES

Abraham, K. (1927). *Selected Papers.* London: Hogarth Press, 1948.
Allport, G. W. (1937). *Personality.* New York: Holt.
Bartlett, F. C. (1932). *Remembering: A Study in Experimental and Social Psychology.* Cambridge: Cambridge University Press.
Bergman, P., & Escalona, S. (1949). Unusual Sensitivities in Very Young Children. *Psychoanal. Study Child,* 3/4:333–352. New York: International Universities Press.
Brierley, M. (1937). Affects in Theory and Practice. *Int. J. Psycho-Anal.,* 18:256–268.
Fenichel, O. (1945). *The Psychoanalytic Theory of Neurosis.* New York: Norton.
Freud, A. (1936). *The Ego and the Mechanisms of Defence.* New York: International Universities Press, 1946.
Freud, S. (1900). The Interpretation of Dreams, tr. A. A. Brill. *The Basic Writings.* New York: Modern Library, 1938, pp. 179–549.
———— (1901). *The Psychopathology of Everyday Life,* tr. A. A. Brill. New York: Macmillan, 1948.
———— (1905). Three Contributions to the Theory of Sex, tr. A. A. Brill. *The Basic Writings.* New York: Modern Library, 1938, pp. 551–629.
———— (1911). Formulations Regarding the Two Principles in Mental Functioning. *Collected Papers,* 4:13–21. New York: Basic Books, 1959.
———— (1915a). Instincts and Their Vicissitudes. *Collected Papers,* 4:60–83. New York: Basic Books, 1959.
———— (1915b). Repression. *Collected Papers,* 4:84–97. New York: Basic Books, 1959.
———— (1915c). The Unconscious. *Collected Papers,* 4:98–136. New York: Basic Books, 1959.

——— (1917 [1915]). Metapsychological Supplement to the Theory of Dreams. *Collected Papers,* 4:137–151. New York: Basic Books, 1959.

——— (1920). *Beyond the Pleasure Principle,* tr. C. J. M. Hubback. London: Hogarth Press, 1948.

——— (1923). *The Ego and the Id,* tr. J. Riviere. London: Hogarth Press, 1947.

——— (1925a [1924]). A Note upon the "Mystic Writing-Pad." *Collected Papers,* 5:175–180. New York: Basic Books, 1959.

——— (1925b). Negation. *Collected Papers,* 5:181–185. New York: Basic Books, 1959.

——— (1926 [1925]). *The Problem of Anxiety,* tr. H. A. Bunker. New York: Psychoanalytic Quarterly & Norton, 1936.

——— (1940 [1938]). *An Outline of Psychoanalysis,* tr. J. Strachey. New York: Norton, 1949.

Gill, M. M. (1963). Topography and Systems in Psychoanalytic Theory. *Psychol. Issues,* No. 10.

Gillespie, R. D. (1937). Amnesia. *Arch. Neurol. Psychiat.,* 37:748–764.

Glover, E. (1939). The Psycho-Analysis of Affects. *Int. J. Psycho-Anal.,* 20:299–307.

Hartmann, H. (1939). *Ego Psychology and the Problem of Adaptation,* tr. D. Rapaport. New York: International Universities Press, 1958. Also in (abridged) Rapaport (1951a). pp. 362–396.

——— (1950). Comments on the Psychoanalytic Theory of the Ego. *Psychoanal. Study Child,* 5:74–96. New York: International Universities Press.

———, Kris, E., & Loewenstein, R. M. (1946). Comments on the Formation of Psychic Structure. *Psychoanal. Study Child,* 2:11–38. New York: International Universities Press.

———, Kris, E., & Loewenstein, R. M. (1949). Notes on the Theory of Aggression. *Psychoanal. Study Child,* 3/4:9–36. New York: International Universities Press.

Jones, E. (1948). *Papers on Psycho-Analysis,* 5th ed. Baltimore: Williams & Wilkins.

Klein, G. S., & Schlesinger, H. (1949). Where Is the Perceiver in Perceptual Theory? *J. Pers.,* 18:32–47.

Koffka, K. (1935). *Principles of Gestalt Psychology.* New York: Harcourt, Brace.

Kris, E. (1944). Approaches to Art. In *Psychoanalysis Today,* 2nd ed., ed. S. Lorand. New York: International Universities Press, pp. 354–370.

——— (1950). On Preconscious Mental Processes. *Psychoanalytic Explorations in Art.* New York: International Universities Press, 1952, pp. 303–318.

Lewin, K. (1935). *A Dynamic Theory of Personality.* New York: McGraw-Hill.

Murphy, G. (1947). *Personality.* New York: Harper.

Rapaport, D. (1942). *Emotions and Memory,* 2nd unaltered ed. New York: International Universities Press, 1950.

——— (1947). Psychological Testing: Its Practical and Its Heuristic Significance. *This volume,* Chapter 20.

——— ed. & tr. (1951a). *Organization and Pathology of Thought.* New York: Columbia University Press.

——— (1951). States of Consciousness: A Psychopathological and Psychodynamic View. *This volume,* Chapter 33.

———, Gill, M. M., & Schafer, R. (1945). *Diagnostic Psychological Testing,* Vol. I. Chicago: Year Book Publishers.

Sherif, M., & Cantril, H. (1945–46). The Psychology of "Attitudes." *Psychol. Rev.,* 52:295–319; 53:1–24.

Tolman, E. C. (1949). There Is More Than One Kind of Learning. *Psychol. Rev.,* 56:144–155.

Werner, H. (1926). *Comparative Psychology of Mental Development.* New York: Harper, 1940.

29

BOOK REVIEW

Norbert Wiener, *Cybernetics, or
Control and Communication in the
Animal and the Machine*[1]

This book, which deals with principles believed to be common to all self-regulating (homeostatic) mechanisms—"in the flesh and in the metal"—is difficult reading. The mathematics of Chapters II, III, and IV is heavy; the connection between the chapters is very loose; there is no index; the printing and proofing are poor; and last but not least, the content and language are extremely uneven.

It is hard to perceive to whom this book is addressed. If it were addressed to scientists other than mathematicians and physicists, Chapters II, III, and IV certainly should have been given a more didactic and explanatory treatment, and the other chapters would have required more than the passing familiarity with other sciences revealed by Wiener's comments on psychology, psychoanalysis, and psychiatry. One of Dr. Wiener's main practical propositions is (pp. 8–9) that the "boundary regions of science . . . offer the richest opportunities"; and that, for example, in the border region of physiology and mathematics "ten physiologists ignorant of mathematics will get precisely as far as one physiologist ignorant of mathemat-

[1] New York: Wiley, 1948.

First published in The Psychoanalytic Quarterly, *19:598–603, 1950.*

ics," and therefore "proper exploration of these blank spaces on the map of science could only be made by a team of scientists, each a specialist in his own field, but each possessing a thoroughly sound and trained acquaintance with the fields of his neighbors." Judging by this book the thesis has serious limitations. The aid of teams of other scientists will be of little use where psychology, psychoanalysis, and psychiatry did not push their own discoveries near enough to the boundaries of the other sciences. Before that has occurred, even as eager a scientist as Dr. Wiener will be in the position to choose only those bits of information which seem to him to fit his cybernetic scheme, instead of discovering those which both reflect the true nature of the psychological subject matter and may gain clarification by "cybernetic" ideas. Indeed, immersing one's self in a subject matter to discover its nature is not a team job, and the team job can at best follow it. Dr. Wiener, with his nearly Leibnitzian catholicity of interests, constitutes a one-man team; and his achievement shows that the total effect cannot be better than the weakest link in the chain, which is in this case—in contrast to the undoubtedly excellent mathematics—psychology, psychiatry, and psychoanalysis. Yet, several ideas in this volume may prove of real relevance to the mental sciences in general, and to psychoanalysis in particular.

Students of psychoanalytic ego psychology will be particularly interested in Wiener's discussion of the difference between power- and communication-engineering (pp. 53–54). He characterizes the 19th-century conception of the organism as one in which "All the fundamental notions are those associated with energy . . . The engineering of the body is a branch of power engineering." He argues that ". . . we are coming to realize that the body is very far from a conservative [closed] system," that is, one for which the basic laws of thermodynamics hold, and he concludes:

> The electronic tube has shown us that a system with an outside source of energy, almost all of which is wasted, may be a very effective agency for performing desired operations, especially if it is worked at a low energy level. . . . the neurons . . . do their work under much the same conditions as vacuum tubes . . . the bookkeeping which is most essential to describe their function is not one of energy. . . . the newer study of automata, whether in the metal or in the flesh, is a branch of communication engineering, and its cardinal notions are those of message, amount of disturbance or "noise" . . . quantity of information, coding technique, and so on.
>
> In such a theory, we deal with automata effectively coupled to the external world, not merely by their energy flow, their metabolism, but also by a flow of impressions, of incoming messages, and of the actions of outgoing messages.

The student of ego psychology will probably be reminded here of one of Freud's earliest reconstructions of the conditions of the secondary process (1900, pp. 533–534):

To change the outer world appropriately by means of motility requires the accumulation of a large total of experiences in the memory-systems, as well as a manifold consolidation of the relations which are evoked in this memory-material by various directing ideas. . . . The activity of the . . . [secondary process] . . . tentatively sending forth cathexes [charges] and retracting them, needs on the one hand full command over all memory-material, but on the other hand it would be a superfluous expenditure of energy were it to send along the individual thought-paths large quantities of cathexis, which would then flow away to no purpose and thus diminish the quantity needed for changing the outer world. Out of a regard for purposiveness, therefore, I postulate that the second system succeeds in maintaining the greater part of the energic cathexes in a state of rest, and in using only a small portion for its operations of displacement. The mechanics of these processes is entirely unknown to me; anyone who seriously wishes to follow up these ideas must address himself to the physical analogies, and find some way of getting a picture of the sequence of motions which ensues on the excitation of the neurones. Here I do no more than hold fast to the idea that the activity of the first system aims at *the free outflow of the quantities of excitation,* and that the second system, by means of the cathexes emanating from it, affects an *inhibition* of this outflow, a transformation into dormant cathexis, probably with a rise of potential. . . . After the second system has completed its work of experimental thought, it removes the inhibition and damming up of the excitations and allows them to flow off into motility.

The student of ego psychology will probably feel that this is not simply a matter of the power engineering of the drives or of the communication engineering of the secondary process and the ego, but rather one of the complex process of binding cathexes (energies), which makes the dynamics of thought (experimental action) a combination of power- and communication-engineering. He will probably be tempted to drop a note to Dr. Wiener calling this to his attention, and supporting it with the argument that "in the flesh" information and communication arise only when motivation for them is present.

Yet the student of ego psychology will be grateful to know that considerations parallel to his exist in other fields. He will feel stimulated by the idea that treatment of psychic processes in terms of communication and information alone is conceivable. He will probably be reminded of Sullivan's (1944) concepts of "channels of communication" and "consensual validation," Bernfeld's (1934) concept of the "effects of secret," and will thus be made more alert to the tasks ahead of him, and to the role of the psychology of thinking in meeting them.

Students of the nature of psychic structure will be interested in the formulation describing information as negative entropy (pp. 71–72 and Chapter III). They will probably be reminded of the pleasure principle and its general formulation in terms of entropy, that is, in terms of elimination of tension, or the tendency toward the lowest feasible potential differences. They will be mindful that the development of psychic structure in one of its major aspects is a delay, a postponement, of the discharges directly regulated by the pleasure principle, and that thought arises as a product of this delay. They will wonder whether the parallel between thought and delay of entropic discharge (directed by the pleasure principle) on the one hand, and information and negative entropy on the other, is merely a neat analogy or something fundamental, and what they can begin with it. Some of them will also be reminded of the recently rising interest in the physical nature of biological organisms and the role in it of the concepts "negative entropy" and "open systems for which the classical law of entropy does not hold"— recalling Schrödinger's (1945), Bertalanffy's (1950), and Brillouin's (1949) recent contributions.

Let me mention a third point of general interest. The concept of feedback is central to all self-regulating "automata." The simplest model of the concept is Watt's steam-engine governor: two balls attached to pendulum rods swinging on opposite sides of a shaft rotated by steam pressure; as the pressure rises the centrifugal action lifts the balls and thereby regulates the intake valves and lowers the pressure. Wiener, applying the principle to the organism, writes:

> . . . for effective action on the outer world, it is not only essential that we possess good effectors, but that the performance of these effectors be properly monitored back to the central nervous system, and that the readings of these monitors be properly combined with the other information coming in from the sense organs to produce a properly proportioned output to the effectors [p. 114].

He gives the ataxia of tabetic and Parkinson patients as examples of the failure of such monitoring feedback, and provides thereby a provocative and probably promising new pattern for thinking about certain neurological problems. But such feedback processes are characteristic of all detour behavior described as thought processes. On the way toward the discovery and conquest of the need-gratifying object, detours are made, and these detours are governed both by the need (and its derivatives) and the realities encountered. While the goal is sustained in the course of the detour, the momentary direction, the preferred path, is determined by "feedback" of information. Indeed, in wish-fulfilling hallucinations it is the lack, or minimization, of feedback from the external world which permits the direct and naked emergence of the wish in its hallucinatory form. The thought disorder of the schizophrenic—both its concrete-literal and its overgeneralizing form—is amenable to description in terms of such disturbed feedback processes. The phenomena to which this concept of feedback refers are familiar to the observations and theory of psychoanalysis. It is, however, probably correct to say that the concept, once deliberately applied, may bring definite clarification, even discovery, to all psychological—including psychoanalytic —thinking.

About Chapter VII, "Cybernetics and Psychopathology," and the two passages (pp. 152–153, 173–174) devoted to psychoanalysis, the less said the better.

Chapter VI, on "Gestalt," with its discussion of McCulloch's work on an auditory reading device for the blind, is exciting and provocative. It cannot be discussed here because of the complexity of its central concept, scanning; this is regrettable since it seems to offer analogies to the phenomena of "symbolism" and "indirect representation" in dreams and in psychopathological processes.

It is regrettable that Wiener's important and provocative ideas are all but lost in the mathematics, rambling, and poor bookmaking of this volume; yet the few who struggle through at least the nonmathematical chapters, and cut through to the essentials, will bring away new patterns of thinking probably applicable to the theory of the psyche and its pathology. And what are we more in need of these days?

REFERENCES

Bernfeld, S. (1934). Die Gestalttheorie. *Imago,* 20:32–77.

Bertalanffy, L. von (1950). The Theory of Open Systems in Physics and Biology. *Science,* 111:23–29.

Brillouin, L. (1949). Life, Thermodynamics, and Cybernetics. *Amer. Sci.,* 37:554–568.

Freud, S. (1900). The Interpretation of Dreams. *The Basic Writings,* tr. A. A. Brill. New York: Modern Library, 1938, pp. 179–549.

Schrödinger, E. (1945). *What Is Life?* New York: Macmillan.

Sullivan, H. S. (1944). The Language of Schizophrenia. In *Language and Thought in Schizophrenia,* ed. J. S. Kasanin. Berkeley: University of California Press, pp. 4–16.

30

THE THEORETICAL IMPLICATIONS
OF DIAGNOSTIC
TESTING PROCEDURES

I. THE PRACTICAL NEED FOR DIAGNOSTIC
PSYCHOLOGICAL TESTING AND ITS FOUNDATIONS
IN THE THEORY OF PSYCHIATRY

Diagnostic psychological testing operates with two very general tacit assumptions: (1) psychiatric practice needs the aid of diagnostic testing devices; (2) the theory of diagnostic testing and that of psychiatry are somehow in harmony. The time has come to make these two assumptions explicit and to reinvestigate them. This section will, in the main, deal with the first assumption, while the next section will treat of the second assumption.

(1) WHAT IS THE NATURE OF PSYCHIATRY'S NEED FOR DIAGNOSTIC
TESTING?

The answer to this question usually pivots around the key word of *objectivity*. Psychiatry, like all other clinical disciplines—the usual argument

First published in Congrès International de Psychiatrie, *2:241–271. Paris: Hermann, 1950. Reprinted in Robert P. Knight and Cyrus R. Friedman, eds.,* Psychoanalytic Psychiatry and Psychology, Clinical and Theoretical Papers, *Austen Riggs Center, Volume I. New York: International Universities Press, 1954, pp. 173–195.*

runs—needs *objective,* laboratory procedures to supplement its clinical methods which imply subjective experience and judgment, and would, without such objective subsidiaries, be akin to an art. This argument usually marshals the historical evidence that Binet introduced the first psychological test in order to objectify the adjudgment of feeble-mindedness.

To be able to pass on this argument we must evaluate the nature of the *objectivity* of psychological tests. Let us compare them with the time-honored methods of clinical psychiatry: case history and psychiatric examination. The data of the latter are selections from a very extensive manifold of data. In giving a case history patient and informants alike introduce selection: an unconscious one rooted in the organization of their memory, an involuntary one rooted in the limitations of their knowledge, and also a deliberate selection rooted partly in judgments based on their attitudes and partly in intentions to conceal which may be based on a great variety of dynamic conditions. In the clinical examination the psychiatrist exercises further selection: from among the infinite details of the patient's behavior he selects what he considers significant. As a consequence of such selections, different case histories are likely to contain different categories of data. Therefore, no point-to-point comparison is ever possible of the data of case histories or of clinical examinations. Another consequence of this selection and lack of comparability is that quantification of data is hardly ever possible, and therefore an organization of those data into a meaningful whole, so as to yield a nosological and personality diagnosis and prognosis and treatment recommendations, of necessity involves further subjective selection and judgment based on the insight, knowledge, and experience of the examining psychiatrist.

We shall not dwell on those features of case history and psychiatric examination which have made them the powerful and important tools they are. Rather, we shall scrutinize diagnostic psychological testing to see whether it is free of the subjective selection factors just described. Only to the extent to which it is free of such selection is it an *objective* contribution to the evaluation of the patient. We shall first establish the degree and kind of this objectivity and then raise the question: where does it get us?

Diagnostic psychological tests record a limited behavior segment. Once the behavior segment to be tested is predetermined, no further selection takes place. Good diagnostic tests select behavior segments which can be well delimited so as to make a relatively complete recording of this behavior segment possible. Thus the first advantage, the first gain in objectivity, of diagnostic tests over clinical procedures is the completeness of recording of a behavior segment.

The second gain issues from the first: the same categories of reaction are obtained from all patients, making direct comparisons of the recorded data possible. Such comparisons are made interindividually and intraindividually: we compare, on the one hand, different individuals' performances and, on the other hand, different aspects of a single individual's performance. But this gain is not as general as the first one. The various tests reach different psychodynamic strata in different subjects. Thus, the directly comparable material may be very meager and/or much unique and uncomparable material may also make its appearance.

The third gain in objectivity arises from these two: since the categories of data obtained from various subjects are delimited and mostly comparable, quantification, that is scoring, is possible. This does not imply, however, that full quantification or any consistent scoring is always feasible. The Thematic Apperception Test is a good example that not even in a very useful diagnostic test is consistent scoring always possible. In the main, diagnostic psychological testing attempts to select behavior segments in which the possibilities of scoring and quantification are maximal, as in the Rorschach Test and the Wechsler-Bellevue Scale. Where this is achieved the organization of the test data gathered is freed of the subjectivity inherent to the organization of clinical data even if the examiner is guided by a definite theoretical point of view.

With this, however, the gain in objectivity of tests ends. Though the objectivity thus gained supports the examiner in the final analysis of his organized material, in establishing diagnosis, personality description, prognosis, and recommendations, he uses subjective judgment based as much on his experience, theoretical knowledge, and insight as on the objective data. It has become customary among psychodiagnosticians to describe this state of affairs as follows: the diagnostician must consider the total configuration of the data rather than the single score.

This review of the objectivity of diagnostic tests demonstrates, I believe, that although there is in diagnostic testing a definite gain of objectivity over case history and clinical examination, the general statement that diagnostic psychological tests are objective laboratory tools of psychiatry is true only in a limited sense.

The issue of objectivity is, however, incompletely treated if we disregard the price paid for the gain in objectivity and the dangers that lie in the stress on objectivity. Let us, therefore, dwell on these before evaluating the need for psychological tests in clinical practice. We have seen that gain in objectivity is attained by preselecting limited behavior segments. Here is the first price we pay for objectivity: no limited segment of behavior can be counted upon to reveal all the dynamic conditions underlying total behavior of every subject. To counteract this limitation we have come to the well-founded conclusion that batteries of tests, rather than single tests, should be used. Also we attempt to test such behavior segments as will make the data obtained maximally revealing of the personality. When all this is said and weighed, the fact remains that we have paid for objectivity in the limitations of the behavior base on which we build our evaluations. It is on this realization that the practical postulate of all clinical diagnostic testing and even much of the research use of diagnostic tests must be based. This practical postulate is: *since clinical methods obtain a broad but unsystematic behavior sample, while testing procedures obtain a narrow but systematic one, sound clinical practice will always use both, each to offset the disadvantages of the other.* The stress on objectivity exacts yet another sacrifice in the form of a widespread self-deception. Many psychodiagnosticians forget the limitations of test objectivity and allow themselves to believe that the concepts designed to express relationships obtaining in test data describe relationships actually existing in the psyche: the thousand-headed Hydra of reification begins to lurk everywhere. I have seen testers making their tests the sole criteria of psychiatric diagnosis and I have seen psychiatrists accepting this unquestioningly with a desperate "grasping at the last straw," to which we are often driven when contemplating the unsettled state of psychiatric nosology. Yet worse than the attitude of these testers and psychiatrists was the one expressed to me by an academic psychologist of world renown: "Why don't you forget about these antiquated categories of psychiatry, and group your test data as they fall and establish on their basis your own nosology?" This is the more dangerous since it is usually the more sensible diagnostician who falls into this pit, the rest sticking to isolated scores and interpreting them with the help of texts used as dreambooks. Indeed only a small step divides this reification from the supreme theoretical task of diagnostic testing. The full significance of diagnostic testing is approached when relationships between test data are studied, the rationale of the processes underlying them is inferred, and then this rationale is fitted into a unitary theory of psychodynamics and psychopathology. Reifying the relationships obtaining between test data merely short-circuits this arduous endeavor.

These dangers are not very different from that greatest danger which the stress on objectivity holds. The simplest way to put this danger is to call it: all hopes pinned on factor analysis. The message of this hopeless hope is this: gather any set of test data, factor them, and then you will know how many factors underlie the variance in the data at hand. There are some people who actually believe that the number and kinds of factors so obtained will exactly correspond to psychologically meaningful dynamic factors. The spirit of this kind of thinking implies: (a) a despair over, or a lack of comprehension of, the complexity of psychodynamics; (b) the hope that the excellent ancillary research tool of statistics can do the bulk of our thinking for us and can largely replace psychological understanding; (c) the false assumption that statistics can do something for us *before* we have learned enough about the subject matter to raise questions which are psychologically meaningful and statistically answerable. The last five decades have taught us that psychological phenomena are overdetermined by a hierarchy of motivating factors; clinical experience has shown that in most psychodynamic phenomena of crucial importance no independence of factors can be assumed—as would be a requirement of factor analysis. All this passes unnoticed with the apostles of factor-analytic salvation.

Then, in view of these limitations, what service can testing render to clinical psychiatry?

Psychiatry is a young scientific discipline, although the past of psychiatric practice is long. It befits us to keep in mind the youth of psychiatry as a scientific discipline, lest we overlook the disarray which characterizes its etiology and nosology. The latter are indeed in a permanent flux, to say the least. We have but few definitely established disease entities. Under such conditions even the limited objectivity of diagnostic tests is greatly needed. Psychodiagnostic tests can make an important contribution if only their limitations are not forgotten and if they are used to clarify clinical findings rather than to replace them.

(2) WHERE ARE THE FOUNDATIONS OF DIAGNOSTIC TESTING
IN THE THEORY OF PSYCHIATRY?

Over and above this entirely pragmatic need of clinical psychiatry for diagnostic psychological testing there is a need for it which, though no less practical, is amenable to formulation in less pragmatic and more conceptual terms. This need was stated in germinal form by Kraepelin and by Bleuler. Kraepelin attempted to systematize disturbances of attention, concentration, memory, etc., in various disorders. Bleuler maintained that the primary symptom of schizophrenia is an association disorder. Both stressed the need to find diagnostic criteria in the comparison of disordered and intact thought functions. Both (Kraepelin more, Bleuler less implicitly) hoped to find in this realm—which I propose to call "thought organization" —steadily present and unchanging symptoms of mental disorder. They hoped that this realm would yield a basis for the diagnosis, particularly for an early diagnosis, of mental disorder more reliable than the louder and more obvious symptoms. The latter are unreliable since they may be absent, or useless since they may appear only in the advanced forms of the disorders, or again intractable to scientific analysis, since when present they impede or sever further communication with the patient, barring one of the major avenues for the exploration of their nature. Psychodiagnostic testing in its advanced forms comes, at least in part, to fill this need stated already by Kraepelin and Bleuler. What underlies the performance on psychodiagnostic tests, and therefore the data they furnish, is the thought process. Thought processes precede the responses to the problems of the Bellevue Scale, the Rorschach Test, the Thematic Apperception Test, etc., etc.[1]

---

[1] It is true that this conception of thought processes is extremely broad if we include such tests as the Mira (1943) Myokinetic Test, the Digit-Symbol Test of the Bellevue Scale, and the drawing tests (Luria, 1932; Machover, 1949). All processes preparatory to action become thought processes. This broad formulation may prove inexpedient and superfluous when, for instance, the psychology of motility and sensorimotor coordination shall have been explored. It must be noted that this formulation hardly

Diagnostic tests reopened avenues of exploration of thought processes for diagnostic purposes which Kraepelin and Bleuler opened several decades ago. In the lull between their time and ours, direct connections between psychodynamics, particularly id dynamics, and clinical symptomatology and nosology were the focus of interest. Only in the course of the last two decades did clinical and therapeutic interest shift to the relation between ego dynamics, along with id dynamics and clinical symptomatology. Only when the influence of this shift in emphasis reached testing did the rationale of psychodiagnostic tests begin to bud. The beginnings made by Kraepelin and Bleuler had to wait for the growth of an ego psychology before a more systematic approach to disorders of thinking and to the organization of thinking, both parts of ego psychology, could develop. Clinical investigation reconstructs the patient's psychodynamics, that is to say, it reconstructs the id-ego-superego relationship out of observed or reported behavior; diagnostic psychological testing reconstructs this relationship from the organization of thought processes it infers from test data. The inferences from test data regarding thought processes are based on the rationale of the tests. The inferences from thought processes regarding personality organization are founded on the fact that the development of thought organization is an integral part of and concomitant with the development of personality organization which it thus reflects. Since both clinical and test studies have serious limitations, they need each other's supplementation.

Neither the usual clinical methods nor our testing devices are, however, merely pragmatic tools. They are—like all tools in a new science—also research tools with which to broaden our understanding of the pathology which is our subject matter. Diagnostic tests, whether alone or in relation to the usual clinical procedures, open up the broad and uncharted field of thought organization, the exploration of which is indispensable if we are to cut pathways into the still junglelike state of pathology.

II. THE SPECIFIC THEORETICAL FOUNDATIONS OF DIAGNOSTIC PSYCHOLOGICAL TESTING IN THE THEORY OF DYNAMIC PSYCHOLOGY AND PSYCHIATRY

We shall discuss here three salient theoretical assumptions on which diagnostic psychological testing is based: (1) every behavior segment bears the imprint of the organization of the behaving personality, and permits—if felicitously chosen—of reconstruction of the specific organizing principles

---

applies to graphology, for instance, which may be surmised to draw its inferences from "frozen," "structuralized" characteristics of actions, the building of which was originally greatly influenced by thought processes, but which in the course of development attained a relatively independent structural existence.

of that personality; (2) pathology is always an exacerbation, that is, decompensation, of trends existing in the adjusted personality, hence fundamentally diagnosis is always personality diagnosis; (3) the theory of diagnostic personality tests deals with the rationale of how, by what processes, the organizing principles of the personality and their pathological alterations are carried over into test performance.

(1) THE RELATION OF BEHAVIOR SEGMENTS TO PERSONALITY ORGANIZATION

The responses to the Rorschach Test, the stories on the Thematic Apperception Test, the answers to the Wechsler-Bellevue Scale items, the reaction words on the Association Test (Schafer, 1945), the sortings on the Goldstein-Scheerer Object-Sorting Test (1941), the incomplete phrases in a sentence-completion test (Stein, 1947), the drawings on the Draw-A-Person Test (Machover, 1949), etc., are each a behavior segment. *It is assumed that these behavior segments bear the imprint of the organization of the subject's personality, and therefore it is expected that the test performance will be revealing of that personality. Indeed, dynamic psychology and psychiatry assume a thoroughgoing determinism of all behavior segments.* Massive evidence supporting this general assumption was offered by Freud (1901) for a whole array of behavior segments: the forgetting of proper names, foreign words, order of words, impressions and resolutions; childhood and screen memories; slips of the tongue and of the pen; faulty, symptomatic, and chance actions, etc. He offered equally massive evidence for dreams (1900) and symptoms (1905–18). The evidence for a variety of other behavior segments, though abundant, has never been systematically collected and remains scattered in psychoanalytic and psychological literature in the form of incidental observations; the evidence for yet others has been organized in a manner which stresses general lawfulness more than pertinence to individual personality organization, as is the case of wit (Freud, 1905), superstitions, religious phenomena (Freud, 1913, 1927), etc. Diagnostic psychological tests founded on this assumption of determinism in all individual productions are perforce the tool of choice for the empirical exploration and demonstration of its general validity. Psychodiagnostics has already made some contributions to answering the question: how does personality organization express itself in the various segments of behavior?

The assumption having been stated in its broadest form, two reservations qualifying its generality must be made. First, the assumption is meaningless unless the concept *behavior segment* is defined, either generally or from case to case. A general definition does not seem feasible at this time. What we know so far is this: any arbitrarily delineated part of behavior is not a behavior segment. We have already pointed out that in order to serve as the basis of a diagnostic test, a behavior segment must be well-enough segregated to be fully recordable. It must have a degree of self-containedness, or "closure" (as gestalt psychology puts it): it must be a relatively well-segregated whole. One of the most difficult tasks in designing and studying diagnostic tests lies in establishing what constitutes such a whole (Koffka, 1935). Behavior, like any other continuity, is divisible into infinitely many elements. But the elements obtained by arbitrary division do not contain the *meaning* of the behavior. An outstretched arm does not necessarily reveal the meaning of the behavior which it is part of. In turn, the meaning of broad segments of behavior is often hard to determine because of the overlapping of meaning in it. Those segments of behavior which are wholes, in that they have a self-contained *meaning* but which they would lose if further subdivided, are units of behavior. Gestalt psychology calls these molar behavior units, in contrast to the molecular units obtained by subdivisions disregarding meaningfulness. Thus, one of the principles underlying diagnostic testing is a gestalt principle: *behavior segments are molar, not molecular, entities. Molecular behavior segments need not correspond to specific personality dynamics underlying them; molar behavior segments which are to be revealing of personality—must.*

The second reservation rests on the fact that behavior segments vary in the degree to which they are revealing of personality organization, and that they reflect various sides of it. The degrees and kinds of expressiveness of behavior segments will be further discussed in Section III. Here we shall dwell only on a few of their aspects.

We usually assume that a behavior segment, if it is to be revealing of personality organization, must fulfill the following criteria:

(a) It must be unknown to and therefore not consciously manipulable by the subject. This is an important criterion, but one requiring extensive qualification. Thus, in intelligence tests the subject does have an idea of what the examiner is after; but this ceases to be true as soon as an analysis of the pattern of subscores (scatter analysis) is introduced into the treatment of the test results. In contrast, in the Thematic Apperception Test we expect that the subject does not know what the examiner is after; it turns out that on this test the subject withholds much information, precisely because of his suspicions and embarrassment concerning what the examiner, to his mind, is after. This state of affairs becomes increasingly prevalent as public "information" on the nature and setting of these tests spreads. There is an urgent need to study the import for the selection of test-behavior segments of the fact that test objectives may not be wholly unknown to the subject. Yet it is already clear that the concept "unknown to the subject" has lost its absolute character. Lewin's demonstration (1927) that objective standard experimental conditions do not exist in psychological experiments is thus reaffirmed.

(b) The subject matter of tests should be unstructured in order to allow maximal expression of the structuring principles of the individual personality. This principle has been realized to a great extent in the Rorschach inkblots which allow the manifestation of individual perceptual-associative organizing patterns to a striking extent: it is our best single diagnostic tool. In a sense, the principle of using unstructured material as the subject matter of tests has been derived from the striking success of the Rorschach Test.

But this criterion of unstructuredness also necessitates reservations. Rorschach himself, as well as workers using Stern's cloud pictures (1937), noted that inkblots altogether lacking structure (i.e., without any articulation and symmetry) are less conducive to responses than the slightly structured material of the Rorschach inkblots. Evidence is accumulating to show that a considerable segment of the population finds even these inkblots too little structured. True enough, this segment of the population thereby reveals itself in the test as inhibited, rigid, or depressed in the extreme, or of considerable intellectual poverty. This is, however, all that the test reveals about them; the rich revelations expected from the unstructured character of the test material are not forthcoming.

The significance of the criterion of unstructuredness is also considerably qualified by all those tests which present well-structured material for the choice of the subject, such as Sorting Tests (Goldstein and Scheerer, 1941; Rapaport, Gill, and Schafer, 1945–46) of concept formation which have proven themselves clinically, and the Szondi Test (Deri, 1949) which has yet to prove its clinical value. In these tests the material and sometimes (e.g., in the Sorting Tests) even the task is well-structured, yet the choice patterns of the subjects show an amazing variability. In these tests unstructuredness or multiple possibility of structuring lies not in the stimulus material, and often not even in the task, but rather in the intrapsychic choice possibilities. Similar is the situation in structured drawing tests, ranging from the Draw-A-Person Test (Machover, 1949) to the Bender Visual Motor Gestalt Test (1938), in contrast to finger painting and free drawing and painting procedures (Schmidl-Waehner, 1942).

Further qualifications issue from experience with intelligence tests amenable to scatter-pattern analysis. In these, test material and task are mostly highly structured. However, the pattern of achievements can vary in the extreme, and since it reflects the balance of development or efficiency of various intellectual functions, it allows important inferences to be drawn concerning personality organization.

The concept of "unstructured material" has become relative. A hierarchy of structuring principles emerges; these principles not only organize unstructured material, but also bring structured material into ever more embracing organization. We are facing the issue of a hierarchy of substructures so well known from gestalt psychology.

(c) Moreover, the desirable behavior segment should be an overt reaction to standard stimuli, and the subject's introspections regarding that reaction should also be obtainable. For instance, we know the meaning of blocking on the fourth Rorschach card only from the objective conformation of the card and from the reactions of many patients to it. The meaning of a friendship story on the Thematic Apperception Test picture representing a choking scene is familiar to us only because we are familiar with the picture to which it refers. Just any literary product or an interpretation of passing clouds will not serve as a behavior segment on which a test can be built; such would share in the difficulties of case history and clinical examination. Hence, the criterion of standard test stimuli with which the psychodiagnostician can be thoroughly familiar.

The requirement that both test reaction and introspective report be obtainable has its foundation in Lewin's (1922) early studies which reintroduced introspection, previously fallen into disrepute, as a method of psychological exploration. He demonstrated first that stimuli and reactions must often necessarily remain indeterminate of meaning if no report is available of how they are subjectively experienced; and second that introspections can serve as a basis of systematic theoretical inference only if their stimulus and reaction referents are known. Therefore, Lewin demanded the simultaneous use of behavioral and introspective evidence. In most of our tests we obtain introspective material by *inquiry*. In some of our tests the verbal responses include introspective material. The utilization of the introspective reports from both sources requires utmost skill and theoretical clarity, since dealing with these always contains the danger of breaking through the unity of the behavior segment. For instance, inquiring into a T.A.T. story of a severely schizoid patient may easily elicit fantasies originating on a different dynamic level than the T.A.T. fantasies themselves. As a rule the meaning of the fantasies so elicited is of a different order than that of the T.A.T. stories, hence not interpretable in the same fashion. Including them unwittingly in the T.A.T. interpretation is a mistake which amounts to breaking down the segregation of the T.A.T. behavior sample. The behavior segment in turn will often not be a self-contained whole unless supplemented by introspective material.

(d) The criteria of sharp segregation of the behavior segment, of scorability and quantifiability, have already been mentioned.

Space does not allow us to pursue further criteria of behavior sample selection. It is clear, however, that criteria so far discussed are closely interwoven with fundamental principles of dynamic psychology and require thoroughgoing further exploration.

(2) PERSONALITY ORGANIZATION AND PATHOLOGY

The assumption that psychopathology is an exacerbation, that is, decompensation, of personality patterns existing already in the adjusted personality is common to dynamic psychiatry and psychodiagnostics. As such it is just as much an aid to diagnosis as a source of the most flagrant kinds of misdiagnoses, for both clinical and test-diagnostic methods. How often would, in the present-day psychiatric clinic, an eccentric be diagnosed an ambulatory schizophrenic or simply a schizophrenic? Indeed, it is likely that many of the eccentrics the *belles-lettres* describe would, on examination, display a schizophrenic process. Yet these eccentrics, at least many of them, do find a social niche (for instance, that of the eccentric) and do not have to be hospitalized. Their adjustment may be deviant and precarious but an adjustment nevertheless. Yet clinical examination is somewhat less likely to disregard this fact, almost certainly overlooked by diagnostic testing. At least, it will always be difficult to tell by tests which of these precarious adjustments will or will not hold up. Pathology is a decompensation of adaptations and adjustments also, therefore various forms of existence and adaptation that are made possible by society within the patient's immediate and broader environment become crucial in evaluating pathology for adaptation possibility and prognosis. These, however, cannot be read out of tests. Hence, the practical requirement: test diagnoses must always be viewed in the context of the total picture of clinical and social diagnosis.

But not only the social picture and its relevance for drawing the line between personality and pathology may be missed in tests. The struggles of an obsessional adjustment, which the clinician may be able to adjudge correctly on the basis of life-history data, may appear on the tests as an obsessional decompensation. Those clinically very elusive entities which we label reality testing, ego strength, adaptation, etc., may also be missed, or not yet grasped, by tests. This is not all a disadvantage. Where the clinician is misled to see ego strength in protracted efforts to hold on "by the teeth" or to see intact reality testing in intellectualizing, or is generally unable to penetrate a well-maintained façade, the tests will be almost certain to unmask these. Yet again, in transitional periods, such as adolescence, the upheaval in a schizoid youngster may well appear on the tests like an incipient schizophrenia, while complete investigation will prove it but a rearrangement of balances—even if one fraught with dangers. In turn, the danger signals appearing in adolescence, easily overlooked by clinical examination alone, are soon spotted by tests. It is likely that some of these shortcomings of the tests are due to our present lack of grasp of their indications. Our emphasis here is, however, on their inherent theoretical limitations.

The relativity of the concepts of normality, adjustment, mental health, adaptation, are fundamental theoretical problems for dynamic psychiatry and psychopathology. Heinz Hartmann put this succinctly when he branded conflict-free normality an illusion. The studies in normality by Jones (1931), Hartmann (1939), Hacker (1945), Glover (1932), etc., are all contributions to this fundamental theoretical and practical problem of psychodiagnostics. Diagnostic psychological testing, which has brought more so-called well-adjusted people under personality study than any other method of investigation, has contributed effectively to unmasking the concept of happy, carefree normality. It is paying a price, however, by having to be constantly on guard not to mistake personality organizations within the normal range for decompensations, i.e., for pathology.

Psychodiagnostics is surer to avoid this pitfall by using both unstructured tests revealing more the organization and conflict patterns of personality, and structured tests revealing more the strength of socialization and adaptation. However, "structuredness"—as we have shown—is not purely a matter of tests materials; thus this distinction depends greatly on the individual patient's psychodynamics, which latter may even render it entirely spurious.

One of the tasks with which psychodiagnostics has only begun to cope, and in coping with which it may make its greatest contributions to the theory of psychodynamics and psychopathology, is the study of how to distinguish latent from overt, repressed from latent, controlled from decompensated trends of personality, by means of test indicators. The simultaneous use of behavior samples of varied degrees of structuredness and social compliance is an indispensable prerequisite for such investigations.

(3) PSYCHODYNAMICS AND THE RATIONALE OF THE PROCESSES UNDERLYING TEST PERFORMANCE

An example may elucidate this issue. Psychodynamically we may describe a schizophrenic as a *regressed* person, one who has withdrawn from reality, etc. On the tests we may describe him as a person who contaminates, whose concept formation becomes overabstract (loose) and/or overconcrete. The theoretical question is: what is the connection between regression (libidinal regression, ego regression, withdrawal of object cathexis, etc.) on the one hand, and the change to contaminations and to conceptual disorder on the other? In order to find this connection, "intervening variables" must be introduced between schizophrenic behavior and its psychodynamic explanation on the one hand, and test performance on the other. Broadly stated, these intervening variables are thought processes. To build this bridge we have studied, and will yet have to study further, two aspects of the thought process—concept formation with its disorders and perception with its associative elaboration and its contaminative disorders. The exploration of the relation of these thought processes to normal psychodynamics is the next step, followed by exploring how pathological processes take the form of regressive disorganization in behavior and the form of contamination and conceptual disorder in test performance. Therefore, the essentials of the theory of psychodiagnostic testing rest upon the rationale of the processes underlying test performance, that is, broadly speaking, upon the general theory of thought processes.

The theory of thought processes is one of the least explored realms of both psychoanalysis and academic psychology. In the latter, the beginnings made by Ach, Marbe, Claparède, Bühler, Lewin, and Bartlett have scarcely been followed up. In the former, the beginnings made by Freud in Chapter

VII of *The Interpretation of Dreams* (1900), "Formulations Regarding the Two Principles in Mental Functioning" (1911), "Repression" (1915a), "The Unconscious" (1915b), and "Negation" (1925) have been read little and pursued even less. The theory of thought processes is, however, not only the foundation of psychodiagnostic tests but also a vast domain of theory in which psychodiagnostic tests are the tools of choice for empirical exploration. The major dimensions of thought organization (see Rapaport, Gill, and Schafer, 1945–46, pp. 385 ff., and Schafer, 1945), memory, concept formation, attention, concentration, anticipation, as well as perception and its associative elaboration and sensorimotor coordination, all can and need to be explored by the methodology of test investigation. This methodology permits exploration of (1) the normative kind; (2) the kind which uses pathology to elucidate normal conditions; (3) the kind which uses inter- and intraindividual comparisons of the functional efficiency of various processes to establish the pattern of functioning characteristic for the individual, and corresponding to his individual psychopathology and adjustment. In all these studies the concepts evolved in developmental psychology, such as those of H. Werner and J. Piaget, the concepts developed by psychoanalysis, those developed by gestalt psychology in general, and by Lewin in particular, all must be brought to bear.

It goes without saying that such investigations involve all the methodological difficulties and problems which have been met by research in dynamic clinical psychology and dynamic psychiatry. Therefore, the methodological considerations put forth by Lewin (1927), Brunswik (1947), Gill and Brenman (1947, 1948), Klein (1949), and Schafer (1949), will all be relevant to them.

III. A THEORETICAL SYNOPSIS OF PSYCHODIAGNOSTIC TESTS

No attempt will be made here at a survey of any degree of completeness. Actually our purpose is not to survey testing devices but to assay certain theoretical problems implicit to them. Recent surveys of testing procedures will be found in Sargent (1945), White (1944), Bell (1948), Rapaport, Gill, and Schafer (1945–46), and Rosenzweig (1949).

It became customary among psychodiagnosticians to distinguish between projective (Frank, 1948; Rapaport, 1942b) and nonprojective tests (Roe, 1946; Rapaport, 1946). The Rorschach Test, the Thematic Apperception Test, Make-A-Picture Story (Schneidman, 1948), the Word Association (Schafer, 1945), and Sentence-Completion Tests (Stein, 1947), the Szondi Test (Deri, 1949), the Draw-A-Person Test (Machover, 1949), the House-Tree-Person Test (Machover, 1949), the Picture-Frustration Test (Rosenzweig, 1945), graphology, and kindred diagnostic devices and methods are presumably projective tests. Their little-standardized or unstandardized relatives, construction tests such as the Mosaic Test (Wertham and Golden, 1941) and World Test (Bolgar and Fisher, 1947), play techniques, free painting, drawing, finger-painting test, etc., are called projective techniques. Intelligence tests and their performance-test varieties, personality inventories, questionnaires and schedules, tests of concept formation, and the like, are presumably nonprojective tests.

The distinction between projective and nonprojective tests is apparently based on the "structured" vs. "unstructured" character of test material and problem situation. In other words, this distinction implies sharply differing expectations of the two types of tests. In nonprojective tests the questions asked or the tasks set have a unique and verifiable answer or solution. For instance, the intelligence-test question, "Who is the president of the United States?" has an answer verifiable by public record; a Block Design task has a solution verifiable by the preprinted design. In projective tests an objectively verifiable single answer is lacking: the subject's answer will correspond to an intrapsychic determiner rather than to an external criterion of validity. For instance, the red blotches on top of the second Rorschach card may be seen as a thumb, a head and cap, red clown's hat, flames, blood, etc., but whichever choice is made is expected to correspond to an intrapsychic criterion. We have already argued that no such sharp distinction does obtain for any test. To reinforce this reservation we might add that projective tests too elicit responses which approximate "objective verifiability," whereas responses to nonprojective tests may have some projective characteristics. All projective tests elicit responses of the type called *popular* on the Rorschach Test (so-called because of the high popular agreement on them indicated by their frequency). Again, in nonprojective-test items the response itself, as well as its verbalization, may bring to the fore intrapsychically determined reactions. For instance, the question, "What should you do if while sitting in the movies you were the first person to discover a fire?" which has a one-to-one verifiable answer may elicit, "Shout fire," or "Sneak out before anyone else notices it," etc. In other words, test responses are always determined both by the stimulus and the intrapsychic organizing factors. Thus, the prevalence of one or the other determines the phenomenal character of the test.

The difficulties of the projective vs. nonprojective dichotomy are not exhausted by these reservations. The concept of projection is itself unclear, and with it the meaning of this dichotomy must also remain so, awaiting systematic exploration. The psychoanalytic concept of projection, from which the term "projective techniques" derives, has its unclarities. The relationship between various forms of projection has not been clarified by psychoanalysis, though clinically a variety of phenomena have been so labeled: (1) the externalization by which the infant attempts to make everything displeasurable external, and everything pleasurable internal—the genetic prototype of projection; (2) the paranoid projection by which an instinctual impulse is externalized, that is, projected upon the object[2]—the mechanism underlying paranoid delusions and erotomania; (3) the phobic projection by which an internal danger is externalized—the underlying mechanism which, along with other determinants, turns, for instance, fear of the father into an animal phobia; (4) the externalizations of feelings and attitudes described as transference and identification phenomena. The projection concept of projective techniques further confounds this unclarity. Any organizing of the external world according to a principle of organization of the subject's "private world" is considered projection. From this vantage point then all the nonprojective tests, in so far as they reflect something about the personality, should be considered projective.

Far from being disheartening, this confusion indicates that we are on the threshold of a rich virginal and most promising realm of investigation. From what can be gleaned so far it is clear that the varieties of mechanisms which we subsume at present under the concept "projection" differ appreciably from each other. The systematic exploration of these differences promises to show us that the world of the human being is molded not by a single set of intrapsychic forces or organizing principles but rather by a whole hierarchy of these. This hierarchy ranges from the diffuse instinctual organizing principles to well-organized systems of values and attitudes (Rapaport, 1942b). In fact, the experiments of the last decade on the subjective determiners of perception furnish independent evidence to this effect (Murphy, 1947; Schafer and Murphy, 1943; Levine, Chein, and Murphy, 1942; Bruner and Goodman, 1947; Bruner and Postman, 1948; Bruner, Postman, and McGinnies, 1948). Furthermore, we have indications that forces working on various hierarchic levels use different organizing principles and executive mechanisms in molding the world of our experience. The mechanisms of expression corresponding to the various levels of this hierarchy on the Rorschach Test may be crudely illustrated as follows: (a) an impulse may manifest itself in content, for instance, in responses replete with aggressive or sexual material; (b) an impulse may manifest itself in symbolic content, for instance, in responses having obviously symbolic content (snake, sword, drill, to the top of Card VI), given to those parts of the blots prone to draw sexual responses; (c) impulses may be expressed by formal characteristics of specific responses, for instance, by vague, pure color, or pure chiaroscuro responses to inkblots, or to those parts of them, which usually elicit responses pertaining to certain impulses; (d) impulses may be expressed by formal characteristics of the responses in general, for instance—where impulse control crumbles—by vagueness, pure color, and pure chiaroscuro as the prevalent mode of response, or—where impulse control becomes extremely rigid—by pure form as the prevalent mode of response or by an extreme dearth of responses. These are but a sample of

[2] This formulation grossly oversimplifies the mechanism of paranoid projection. See Fenichel (1945).

the mechanisms of expression on the various hierarchic levels of motivation. The total picture is infinitely more complex not only because there are many more of these, but also because the hierarchic levels of motivation and their mechanisms appear mostly simultaneously even in a single test and certainly in the various tests of a single individual. Schafer's (1948) diagnostic studies are replete with examples illustrating this point.

Lest we feel that we have entered the limbo of speculative theorizing it will be useful to remind ourselves that Piaget (1927, 1936), in his studies on the development of intelligence and thinking, has in a sense forecast the problems and theoretical possibilities we are encountering. For instance, the hierarchy of developmental levels of causality described in his longitudinal studies corresponds to the hierarchical levels psychopathology discovered in its cross-sectional investigations (see Werner, 1926).

The dichotomy projective tests vs. nonprojective tests is admittedly somewhat arbitrary, yet we will do well to retain it until empirical exploration brings more refined differentiation. This dichotomy will serve us well as a reminder that some tests give us information by exposing the subject to slightly structured material, eliciting little socialized reactions, while others will expose the subject to structured material, eliciting the subject's patterns of socialized reactions. It will clarify this point to realize that the primitive and fundamental forms of organizing our world, which lie at the base of the hierarchy discussed above, are impulse-determined. They disregard both the objectivity and the relativity of the real world. One of the fundamental aspects of psychological development is the erection of impulse controls. These controls arise progressively in hierarchical layering, and to each of these layers there seems to correspond a manner of organizing experience. To every advance in impulse control corresponds a step ahead toward an increased regard for the real world in the manner of organizing experience. This increased regard expresses itself in a realization of the objectivity of the world experienced and in a realization of the relativity of its appearance. Ultimately this relativity requires the recognition of the point of view of the other fellow, that is, socialization. Thus, one aspect of the hierarchy of levels of personality organization is increasing socialization. The more standard and familiar a stimulus situation, the greater the likelihood that the reaction to it will be on a more socialized level of the hierarchy. The less structured the stimulus situation, the greater the likelihood that it will bring into play idiosyncratic, little-socialized modes of reaction. The organization of little-socialized reactions, as well as the individual patterning of socialized reactions, are equally revealing of the personality organization, though of different aspects of it. In a previous study (1946) I attempted to characterize this difference by assuming that projective tests tend to elicit functions and organizing principles corresponding to fundamental motivations, while nonprojective tests elicit quasi-stationary functions inherent to thought organization which transform generalized principles of personality organization into organizing principles of thinking. It is in line with the recent trend in psychological theory formation to assume that in the course of psychological development general motivating forces differentiate into specifically structured quasi-autonomous partial motivations which become quasi-stationary characteristics of the individual personality organization.

We can decrease the structuredness of a test setting by a great variety of means; e.g., (1) presenting little-structured material (Rorschach, tautophone [Shakow, 1938]); (2) making the task indefinite (Thematic Apperception); (3) time pressure (Association Test, tachistoscopic presentation); (4) overcrowding the stimulus field (Sorting Tests); (5) increasing the time intervals (delayed recall); (6) sensory interference (Jung's [1906] distraction experiment); (7) altering the subject's needs (hunger, thirst, sleep deprivation, and other frustration states); (8) altering the subject's state of consciousness (hypnosis, hypnagogic states, sleep states, drug states). Yet we have so far not explored these thoroughly and certainly have not used them systematically as means to investigate the hierarchy of structuring.

It goes without saying that the exploration of the issues just touched upon is impossible without systematic theoretical assumptions of the type we have come to label the "rationale" of tests. Amassing and statistical processing of test records without systematic theorizing will do us no good. It is clear that we are faced with a realm containing much crucial information about human nature. We shall wring this information from nature only if we dare ask many questions, formulate many hypotheses, in the hope that some among them will fetch the answer. Data collecting around the shaky framework of our present-day nosology alone raise no such questions.

It is also clear that our primary need of the moment is not the introduction of new testing procedures but the systematic theoretical exploration by means of clinical observation and experiment of the tests we already have. Experimental investigations of the type Hanfmann, Stein, and Bruner (1947) have conducted tachistoscopically analyzing Rorschach responses are particularly promising beginnings in this direction.

IV. PROSPECTS

What are the next tasks of diagnostic psychological testing in regard to the theory of dynamic psychology and psychiatry? What are the prospects for new psychological devices based on present psychological and psychiatric theory?

(1) THEORETICAL TASKS

We have stressed the exploration of the testing procedures we already possess as against the designing of new procedures. Here we must make a reservation for the case where new tests are designed to cope with *specific* clinical problems, and where in the course of designing and validating the tests, theoretical exploration of clinical problems is also attempted. We do not need new tests designed to differentiate various nosological entities. Of these we have so many that we have been unable to establish their rationale adequately. We do, however, need new tests designed with a definite rationale, which will contribute to a general systematic theory of test rationale and thereby also to building a rationale for our already available tests.

I shall give three examples to illustrate the theoretical tasks and possibilities of psychodiagnostic testing for present-day psychological and psychiatric theory.

R. Schafer has undertaken an investigation of the orality-passivity problem by means of a variety of testing procedures. By means of the techniques of immediate and delayed recall, association of words and of images, tachistoscopic perception, etc., and using materials of orally significant character, he is studying a group of subjects with a great variety of problems of passivity. Such an investigation promises many kinds of yields: (1) It may be expected to shed light on the orality-passivity-dependence relationship derived by psychoanalysis from clinical and therapeutic observation. In this respect the study is an exploration of a global relationship which is still in need of systematization, though many specific varieties of it are well known. (2) It may yield data on a variety of thought functions (association, memory, perception, etc.), showing the degree to which and the form in which a certain type of motivation (oral-passive dependence) penetrates them and becomes manifest through them. In this respect the study is an investigation of thought functions as carriers and media of expression of a certain kind of motivation. (3) As a test investigation it may be expected to yield information as to the clinical meaning of various manifestations of orality in tests, and as to the most promising special procedures for the clinical evaluation of the role of oral passivity.

For our second example we may consider the striking differences between recall of recently learned meaningful material, of information learned in the past, and of immediate recall of nonsense or digit-span material. Rapaport et al. (Rapaport, Gill, and Schafer, 1945–46; Schafer and Rapaport, 1944; Rapaport, 1947) attempted to establish a rationale explaining these differences. As their point of departure they took the cathectic theory of consciousness and attention of psychoanalysis. According to this theory percepts and memories become conscious if they attain attention cathexis (energy charge). This energy cathexis is at the disposal of the ego, is divested of the hallmarks of its instinctual origin, is available only in a determinate quantity, and serves not only the function of consciousness (as hypercathexis) but also the function of keeping impulses, ideas, and affects out of consciousness (as countercathexis). Consequently, where surging impulses and anxieties have to be constantly kept at bay, such cathexis should be scarcely available to bring ideas into consciousness. The Digit-Span subtest of the Bellevue Scale, and the other tests mentioned, were studied on the assumption that this cathectic theory may elucidate the striking discrepancies of performance on them. Though these investigators achieved some success in linking their test findings to this segment of psychoanalytic theory, the exploitation of both the cathectic theory of psychoanalysis and the intra- and interindividual discrepancies between recall of past and recent meaningful and nonsense material has hardly begun. Here again both existing and new test methods will be required to substantiate and qualify or else replace the rationale Rapaport et al. offer. A well-founded rationale of the relationships involved would be important for the theory of thinking and the rationale of testing; but it would also give us a toehold in the realm of those most crucial and most elusive entities called ego strength, will, etc., since these phenomena are closely linked with the energies the ego has at its disposal and with the conditions which limit the uses to which the ego can put these energies.[3]

We shall use G. Klein's and Schlesinger's (1949) recent studies for our third example. They demonstrated individual differences apparently related to personality characteristics in fundamental perceptual processes, such as flicker-fusion. If this finding holds up under further scrutiny we shall have not only an entirely new range of potential psychological testing procedures, close to the realm of physiological processes such as are tapped, for instance, by the electroencephalograph, but also a theoretical orientation point for the clarification of the relationship between personality organization and the perceptual apparatuses used by the functioning personality.

(2) PRACTICAL POSSIBILITIES

The preceding section amply demonstrates that theoretical tasks and practical possibilities are indivisible. This holds in clinical medicine also where efforts at developing new tests led and still lead to a better and better understanding of pathology and etiology. Yet in this section we shall take up a few instances in which available theoretical formulations may help us in designing radically new tests, which in turn may evaluate and systematize those theoretical assumptions.

One of the main assumptions of psychoanalytic psychology is that in the final analysis all controlling and inhibiting organizations within the psychic apparatus serve the purpose of controlling the sluices of motility in order to prevent prohibited impulses from obtaining hold of and directing motility. The study of the control of motility should, therefore, play a crucial role in our evaluation of personality. Yet tests dealing with motility mostly stress

---

[3] For a discussion of these issues, see Knight (1946).

[The theory of attention cathexis remained one of Rapaport's paramount interests; for the experimental approach to it on which he was embarking at the end of his life, see Rapaport (1959, 1960). See also Paul (1959) and Schwartz and Rouse (1961), whose studies were carried out under Rapaport's guidance—Ed.]

motor skills and aptitudes and at best visual-motor coordination. With the exception of the experiments of Luria (1932) and some abortive studies in graphology, motility has remained a more or less virgin field of psychodynamic and psychodiagnostic exploration. It is an area which well deserves the concentration of our ingenuity. Some pathways toward it were opened by Mira (1943), by the Visual Motor Gestalt Test (Bender, 1938), and by the Draw-A-Person Test (Machover, 1949).

Closely related to the problem of motility is the problem of emotional expression. According to our present assumptions emotional expression is a discharge channel for pent-up tension (Rapaport, 1942a). However, our studies of emotional expression mostly failed, partly because of the difficulty in eliciting "genuine" affects, and partly because even if "genuine" affects were elicited, as in Dembo's (1931) and similar experiments, attention was focused mainly on their effect on general behavior or on intellectual performance. While much systematic test exploration is yet to be done even in these areas, it is possible that we shall reach an understanding of expressive movements more readily by studying the intra- and interindividual differences in stereotyped modes of expression, that is, frozen expressive movements: the handshake, the smile, the position of the fingers and the palm when the instruction is to place the hand on the table, etc., etc.

In summary: the theory of diagnostic psychological tests is in its infancy. The nosological disarray of psychiatry exaggerates the realistically great need for diagnostic psychological tests to a point where dangerously smug satisfaction is encouraged with what has been achieved by psychodiagnostics. Psychodiagnostics, clinical psychology, and psychiatry can ill afford such self-satisfaction. Dynamic psychology and psychiatry have a powerful tool in the methods of psychodiagnostics; they have already raised disquieting and far-reaching questions, and if assiduously applied, may bring answers of crucial significance. Psychodiagnostics, both as a clinical method and as a tool of scientific investigation, needs a systematic rationale which is first of all a systematic theory of thought organization and second, the embedding of this theory into the general theory of psychodynamics.

REFERENCES

Bell, J. E. (1948). *Projective Techniques*. New York: Longmans, Green.

Bender, L. (1938). A Visual Motor Gestalt Test and Its Clinical Use. *Res. Monogr. Amer. Orthopsychiat. Assn.*, No. 3.

Bolgar, H., & Fisher, L. K. (1947). Personality Projection in the World Test. *Amer. J. Orthopsychiat.*, 17:117–128.

Bruner, J. S., & Goodman, C. C. (1947). Value and Need as Organizing Factors in Perception. *J. Abnorm. Soc. Psychol.*, 42:33–44.

———, & Postman, L. (1948). Symbolic Value as an Organizing Factor in Perception. *J. Soc. Psychol.*, 27:203–208.

————, Postman, L., & McGinnies, E. (1948). Personal Values as Selective Factors in Perception. *J. Abnorm. Soc. Psychol.*, 43:142–154.

Brunswik, E. (1947). *Systematic and Representative Design of Psychological Experiments.* Berkeley: University of California Press.

Dembo, T. (1931). Der Ärger als dynamisches Problem. *Psychol. Forsch.*, 15:1–144.

Deri, S. (1949). *Introduction to the Szondi Test; Theory and Practice.* New York: Grune & Stratton.

Fenichel, O. (1945). *The Psychoanalytic Theory of Neurosis.* New York: Norton.

Frank, L. K. (1948). *Projective Methods.* Springfield, Ill.: Charles Thomas.

Freud, S. (1900). The Interpretation of Dreams, tr. A. A. Brill. *The Basic Writings.* New York: Modern Library, 1938, pp. 179–549.

———— (1901). *The Psychopathology of Everyday Life,* tr. A. A. Brill. New York: Macmillan, 1948.

———— (1905). Wit and Its Relation to the Unconscious, tr. A. A. Brill. *The Basic Writings.* New York: Modern Library, 1938, pp. 631–803.

———— (1905–18 [1901–14]). Case Histories. *Collected Papers,* 3:1–605. New York: Basic Books, 1959.

———— (1911). Formulations Regarding the Two Principles in Mental Functioning. *Collected Papers,* 4:13–21. New York: Basic Books, 1959.

———— (1913 [1912–13]). Totem and Taboo, tr. A. A. Brill. *The Basic Writings.* New York: Modern Library, 1938, pp. 805–930.

———— (1915a). Repression. *Collected Papers,* 4:84–97. New York: Basic Books, 1959.

———— (1915b). The Unconscious. *Collected Papers,* 4:98–136. New York: Basic Books, 1959.

———— (1925). Negation. *Collected Papers,* 5:181–185. New York: Basic Books, 1959.

———— (1927). *The Future of an Illusion,* tr. W. D. Robson-Scott. New York: Liveright, 1949.

Gill, M. M., & Brenman, M. (1947). Problems in Clinical Research: Round Table 1946. *Amer. J. Orthopsychiat.,* 17:215–222.

————, & Brenman, M. (1948). Research in Psychotherapy: Round Table 1947. *Amer. J. Orthopsychiat.,* 18:100–110.

Glover, E. (1932). Medico-psychological Aspects of Normality. *Brit. J. Psychol.,* 23:152–166.

Goldstein, K., & Scheerer, M. (1941). Abstract and Concrete Behavior; an Experimental Study with Special Tests. *Psychol. Monogr.,* 53, No. 2.

Hacker, F. J. (1945). The Concept of Normality and Its Practical Significance. *Amer. J. Orthopsychiat.,* 15:47–64.

Hanfmann, E., Stein, M. I., & Bruner, J. S. (1947). Personality Factors in the Temporal Development of Perceptual Organization—A Methodological Note. *Amer. Psychol.,* 2:284–285.

Hartmann, H. (1939). Psycho-Analysis and the Concept of Health. *Int. J. Psycho-Anal.,* 20:308–321.

Jones, E. (1931). The Concept of a Normal Mind. *Papers on Psycho-Analysis,* 5th ed. Baltimore: Williams & Wilkins, 1948, pp. 201–216.

Jung, C. G. (1906). *Studies in Word Association*. New York: Moffat, Yard, 1919.

Klein, G. S. (1949). Adaptive Properties of Sensory Functioning: Some Postulates and Hypotheses. *Bull. Menninger Clin.,* 13:16–23.

———, & Schlesinger, H. (1949). Where Is the Perceiver in Perceptual Theory? *J. Pers.,* 18:32–47.

Knight, R. P. (1946). Determinism, "Freedom," and Psychotherapy. *Psychiatry,* 9:251–262. Also in *Psychoanalytic Psychiatry and Psychology, Clinical and Theoretical Papers,* Austen Riggs Center, Vol. I, ed. R. P. Knight & C. R. Friedman. New York: International Universities Press, 1954, pp. 365–381.

Koffka, K. (1935). *Principles of Gestalt Psychology*. New York: Harcourt, Brace.

Levine, R., Chein, I., & Murphy, G. (1942). The Relation of the Intensity of a Need to the Amount of Perceptual Distortion: A Preliminary Report. *J. Psychol.,* 13:283–293.

Lewin, K. (1922). Das Problem der Willensmessung und das Grundgesetz der Assoziation. *Psychol. Forsch.,* 1:191–302, 2:65–140.

——— (1927). Gesetz und Experiment in der Psychologie. *Symposion,* 1:375–421.

Luria, A. R. (1932). *The Nature of Human Conflicts*. New York: Liveright.

Machover, K. (1949). *Personality Projection in the Drawing of the Human Figure*. Springfield, Ill.: Charles C Thomas.

Mira, E. (1943). *Psychiatry in War*. New York: Norton.

Murphy, G. (1947). *Personality*. New York: Harper.

Paul, I. H. (1959). Studies in Remembering: The Reproduction of Connected and Extended Verbal Material. *Psychol. Issues,* No. 2.

Piaget, J. (1927). *The Child's Conception of Physical Causality*. London: Kegan, 1930.

——— (1936). The Biological Problem of Intelligence. In *Organization and Pathology of Thought,* ed. & tr. D. Rapaport. New York: Columbia University Press, 1951, pp. 176–192.

Rapaport, D. (1942a). *Emotions and Memory,* 2nd unaltered ed. New York: International Universities Press, 1950.

——— (1942b). Principles Underlying Projective Techniques. *This volume,* Chapter 6.

——— (1946). Principles Underlying Nonprojective Tests of Personality. *This volume,* Chapter 15.

——— (1947). Psychological Testing: Its Practical and Its Heuristic Significance. *This volume,* Chapter 20.

——— (1959). The Theory of Attention Cathexis. *This volume,* Chapter 61.

——— (1960). On the Psychoanalytic Theory of Motivation. *This volume,* Chapter 65.

———, Gill, M. M., & Schafer, R. (1945–46). *Diagnostic Psychological Testing,* 2 vols. Chicago: Year Book Publishers.

Roe, A., ed. (1946). Non-projective Personality Tests. *Ann. N. Y. Acad. Sci.,* 46:531–678.

Rosenzweig, S. (1945). The Picture-Association Method and Its Application in a Study of Reactions to Frustration. *J. Pers.,* 14:3–23.

—— (1949). Available Methods for Studying Personality. *J. Psychol.,* 28:345–368.

Sargent, H. (1945). Projective Methods: Their Origins, Theory, and Application in Personality Research. *Psychol. Bull.,* 42:257–293.

Schafer, R. (1945). A Study of Thought Processes in a Word Association Test. *Character & Pers.,* 13:212–227.

—— (1948). *The Clinical Application of Psychological Tests.* New York: International Universities Press.

—— (1949). Psychological Tests in Clinical Research. *J. Consult. Psychol.,* 13:328–334. Also in *Psychoanalytic Psychiatry and Psychology, Clinical and Theoretical Papers,* Austen Riggs Center, Vol. I, ed. R. P. Knight and C. R. Friedman. New York: International Universities Press, 1954, pp. 204–212.

——, & Murphy, G. (1943). The Role of Autism in a Visual Figure-Ground Relationship. *J. Exp. Psychol.,* 32:335–343.

——, & Rapaport, D. (1944). The Scatter: In Diagnostic Intelligence Testing. *Character & Pers.,* 12:275–284.

Schmidl-Waehner, T. (1942). Formal Criteria for the Analysis of Children's Drawings. *Amer. J. Orthopsychiat.,* 12:95–104.

Schneidman, E. S. (1948). Schizophrenia and the *MAPS* Test. *Genet. Psychol. Monogr.,* 38:145–223.

Schwartz, F., & Rouse, R. O. (1961). The Activation and Recovery of Associations. *Psychol. Issues,* No. 9.

Shakow, D. (1938). Schizophrenic and Normal Profiles of Response to an Auditory Apperceptive Test. *Psychol. Bull.,* 35:647.

Stein, M. I. (1947). The Use of a Sentence Completion Test for the Diagnosis of Personality. *J. Clin. Psychol.,* 3:47–56.

Stern, W. (1937). Cloud Pictures: A New Method for Testing Imagination. *Character & Pers.,* 6:132–146.

Werner, H. (1926). *Comparative Psychology of Mental Development.* New York: Harper, 1940.

Wertham, F., & Golden, L. (1941). A Differential-Diagnosis Method of Interpreting Mosaics and Colored Block Designs. *Amer. J. Psychiat.,* 98:124–131.

White, R. W. (1944). Interpretation of Imaginative Productions. In *Personality and the Behavior Disorders,* ed. J. McV. Hunt. New York: Ronald Press, pp. 214–251.

3 1

THE AUTONOMY OF THE EGO

In attempting to understand and to encompass theoretically the nature of thought processes, the problem of the autonomy of the ego recurs more often than any other. Even though much of what I present in describing this problem will not be original, or new, or even clearly related to the theory of thought processes, yet I feel that these considerations are not only indispensable postulates for a psychoanalytic theory of thinking (Rapaport, 1950), but are also of paramount importance both in general and in therapeutic research.

I

A story from the Talmud [1] illustrates some of the fundamental issues encountered by psychoanalytic ego psychology. There was an Eastern king who heard about Moses. He heard that Moses was a leader of men, a good man, a wise man, and he wished to meet him. But Moses, busy wandering forty years in the desert, couldn't come. So the king sent his painters to Moses and they brought back a picture of him. The king called his phrenol-

[1] [See Chapter 57, n. 6—Ed.]

Presented at a seminar of the Menninger School of Psychiatry, Winter Veterans Administration Hospital, June 1950. First published in Bulletin of the Menninger Clinic, *15:113–123. Copyright 1951 by the Menninger Foundation. Reprinted in Robert P. Knight and Cyrus R. Friedman, eds.,* Psychoanalytic Psychiatry and Psychology, Clinical and Theoretical Papers, *Austen Riggs Center, Volume I. New York: International Universities Press, 1954, pp. 248–258.*

ogists and astrologists and asked them, "What kind of man is this?" They went into a huddle and came out with a report which read: This is a cruel, greedy, self-seeking, dishonest man. The king was puzzled. He said, "Either my painters do not know how to paint or there is no such science as astrology or phrenology." To decide this dilemma, he went to see Moses and after seeing him he cried out, "There is no such science as astrology, or phrenology." When Moses heard this he was surprised and asked the king what he meant. The king explained, but Moses only shook his head and said, "No. Your phrenologists and astrologists are right. That's what I was made of! I fought against it and that's how I became what I am."

This story is a good allegory of the first encounter of psychoanalysis with ego psychology. It speaks of the recognition that there are other things to a human being besides the drives. Psychoanalysis at first assumed that these other things were defensive structures which were born of conflict (Freud, 1894, 1896, 1926; A. Freud, 1936). But ego psychology did not stop at this point. Let us raise a few questions about the Moses story and see what kind of problems ego psychology had to face afterward.

First, what does it mean: "I fought against it?" On the "fought" we can easily agree: that means *conflict*. But what conflicted? The old conception which prevailed before the advent of ego psychology (Freud, 1923) was a conflict of drives with the censor. After the concept of the ego was already coined, it was assumed that the ego and the id conflicted, and yet we learn that the ego itself was born out of conflict (Freud, 1923, p. 36). So the first problem that budding ego psychology met was: How are the participants of the conflict to be conceived of? This is one of the points I propose to discuss.

The second question is: If he "fought against it" and became what he was, what happened to that which he "was made of"? Did it vanish? The Bible says that Moses was not quite the holy man without spot. When he was told to touch the rock, he hit it. He acted as if *he* were doing the wonders and not the Lord. When he descended from Mount Sinai, after communing with the Lord, and saw the golden calf and the erring of his people, he went into a violent rage and broke the Tablets.

This much is already clear: even though Moses, by his struggle, became somebody very different from the stuff he "was made of," in moments of strain that grandiose, competitive, raging, immodest stuff of which he was made, and which the astrologists and phrenologists saw in his features, made its appearance in his behavior. We realize that this is how it always happens in psychological life. So we need not be concerned that we may be accused of forgetting, like Horney, the persistence underneath of what the struggle seems to have conquered, when we speak of what someone became by a struggle against his impulses, that is, when we deal with the *function* of the ego. We do not forget, even if our emphasis is on the ego, that Moses was not altogether "holy" though he fought against the "unholy" things within him which we nowadays call impulses and drives.

There is yet a third question: How is it possible for the ego to let something that it has conquered come through, as it did in the case of Moses in the Tablets and the rock episodes?

II

Before discussing these three points, I will raise yet another consideration. When psychoanalysis was young, and people did not read all Freud had to say about psychic life, for instance Chapter VII of *The Interpretation of Dreams* (1900), or the "Papers on Metapsychology" (1911–1917), the impression was that he conceived of psychic life as an ever-seething cauldron, that strivings clashed continuously with each other without mitigation, in a perpetual revolution, and every time something happened in consciousness or behavior it issued from a new equilibrium reached by clashing drives. In borderline and psychotic patients we observe at times a state which, in a mild form, resembles this conception. I needn't remind you how consuming, devastating, and paralyzing such states are. Yet such was the early psychoanalytic conception—not Freud's conception, but certainly Stekel's (1924) and others'.

Adler, and later Horney and others, tried to get away from this conception of the seething cauldron, and gave their attention to the adaptive and social functions of the ego. They came to do so in part by virtue of the carefulness of their observations, which showed them the relative stability of the defensive, adaptive, and social motivations of man, a field of observations which was at the beginning outside of the sharp focus of psychoanalytic study. But they did so in part as a result of the carelessness of their understanding of Freud's psychoanalysis, which was by no means just a conception of the seething cauldron, but had, in its concepts of resistance, defense, and secondary process, the nucleus of an ego psychology. In revolt against the conception of the seething cauldron, they did not note these. They proceeded to build anew, rejecting the drive psychology of psychoanalysis, which they equated with the conception of the seething cauldron.

The seething-cauldron concept and the concept which wants to get away altogether from the beasts that struggle down under somewhere, this thesis and antithesis, found a synthesis in psychoanalytic ego psychology, which recognizes the id forces as well as the new organization, the ego, which is pitted against them. This organization has a certain degree of constancy and reliability: it cannot and need not be created totally anew in every clash of id forces with each other, with reality, or with it. The nature and degree of this constancy and reliability, or as we have come to refer to it, this autonomy,[2] is the subject of this paper.

An emergent organization is one which has laws of its own, distinct from those of the elements which constitute it: such as, for example, the social group when viewed in relation to the individuals composing it. Such emer-

[2] The concept was formulated by Heinz Hartmann (1939).

gent organizations partly control, and are partly controlled by, the underlying organizations from which they emerged. In the study of organic matter, in that of the nature of man, and in that of society, we encounter at every step such emergent organizations.

Let me give you an example which, though it disregards many social realities, yet contains a true, though oversimplified, moral. Suppose that twenty of us should land on a desert island. At first we would all try to do all the jobs, mutual assistance and good will running rampant. But since the nature of man is what it is, quarrels would start and some people would begin to stake out their claims. It might begin with the question, "Who should do the dirty jobs, and who the others?" And then, "Which is a dirty job and which isn't?" A division of labor would sooner or later, of necessity, be established, and once a division of labor has come into existence it is very hard to change. Why? Because the people who have been at a certain labor for a while will know best what and where the tools for it are, and they will know most about that work. There will be symbols and status attached to the work and workers as time goes on. A society will have slowly formed in which, over and above the original mutual good will which prevailed at and soon after the landing and over and above the personal predilections and aversions, a new set of rules—a division of labor and know-how and symbols representing these—takes precedence. These rules and divisions become perpetuated by the children perceiving their own parents' occupations and preoccupations, by their hearing about "do's" and "don't's." Thus develops a social structure which is relatively independent of the original good will, of the original competitions, and is often even contrary to these.

This is a very superficial simile of a society's birth. But there is a true core in it: the so emerging organization has a considerable degree of independence from the individuals who are the members and even originators of it! Social groups constitute themselves thus so that they may survive for generations. People are born and people die, but roles and rules remain. Suddenly after generations, internal, economic, and other forces may break this framework of autonomy and a revolution is at hand. The psychological apparatus, too, is such an arrangement of emergent organizations. Understanding the personalities of individual participants does not explain a social happening. Similarly, the understanding of a person's drives, drive conflicts, and drive vicissitudes alone will not make his personality, nor even necessarily his pathology, understandable. We have good evidence for this in the many unsuccessful attempts at creating a psychiatric nosology based on drive vicissitudes.[3]

Another sort of supporting evidence comes from the diagnostic evalua-

[3] Dr. Karl Menninger and his associates arrived, after many attempts to build a nosology on drive vicissitudes, at a nosology free of such interest [Menninger, Mayman, and Pruyser, 1963].

tions of the patient made by analysts of exclusively psychoanalytic training. These evaluations were usually based on a free-association interview which revealed how well the patient could free associate, and what drive constellations and overt behavior he displayed—but little or nothing was, as a rule, learned from it about the patient's personality as a whole, his strength, assets, and prognosis. Without an orientation toward—and without technical skill for—the understanding of psychic structure, the knowledge of drives and conflicts cannot give a rounded picture of the personality. A psychological theory in terms of energy distributions, lacking structural concepts, does not make a psychology. This is why even before *The Ego and the Id* (1923), Freud in his "Papers on Metapsychology" (1911–1917) insisted that without simultaneous understanding of the dynamics, topography, and economy of a psychological event, there is no full understanding of it.

Similarly, Fritz Heider has pointed out that one of the major weaknesses of the dynamic psychology of Kurt Lewin is that it has no structural concepts. This holds for other systems of psychology also, for example, Tolman's and particularly for the Yale school's (Hull, Dollard, Sears, Doob, Miller). Regrettably, psychoanalysts attempting to make a liaison with psychology, and psychologists attempting to make liaison with psychoanalysis, appear to forget that a viable psychology must have both energy-dynamic and structural concepts. Striking examples of this obliviousness are: Thomas French's (1933) paper on the relation of conditioned reflex and psychoanalysis, Masserman's (1946) theory, O. H. Mowrer and Clyde Kluckhohn's (1944) paper on the relation of learning theory and psychoanalysis.

III

Our first question as to the nature of the autonomy of the ego was: If the ego grows on conflict, how are we to conceive of the participants of this original conflict? Note the circularity: the ego is both born out of the conflict, and party to the conflict. How can we explain this seeming contradiction? The answer can be seen in the study of infants, in the individual differences between infants, which are present from the very beginning of development, suggesting inborn personality determinants *in nuce* (Escalona and Leitch, 1951). It may be seen in one of Freud's last papers, "Analysis Terminable and Interminable" (1937), in which he directly postulates inborn, inherited ego factors. It can be seen also when we consider that after all psychology has found some general laws of perception, memory, and learning which show some interindividual consistency. Let us forget for a moment that we would want to restudy these three functions from the point of view of psychoanalytic ego psychology, and that in recent studies these interindividually consistent laws have yielded individual differences and gained a new meaning (Klein, 1949; Klein and Schlesinger, 1949). Whatever interindividual consistency there is in these functions shows that these apparatuses of perception, memory, and motility are inborn and characteristic of the species and the biological individual before they become expressive of conflict and experience. Memory, perception, and motility have already been existing and functioning before conflict ever occurred. Here then we see apparatuses which antedate conflict, and become the core of ego development. Indeed we know that these apparatuses may remain, in many cases, outside of conflict later on also. It is thus that a patient on the verge of psychosis, totally helpless to deal with his problems, and torn in every respect, may nevertheless display on the couch, or in the interview, or in testing, an amazingly accurate memory, or sensitive perception, or perfection of motility.

It was Heinz Hartmann (1939) who gave the first systematic evaluation of the rôle of these apparatuses in ego development. He labeled the autonomy of these apparatuses "primary autonomy." The functions which are at any given time outside of the range of conflict he conceptualized as belonging to the conflict-free ego sphere. From the rôle of this primary autonomy in ego development, he concluded that our usual conception that the id preexists the ego is inadequate, that there must be a period in human individual development in which what will later be the ego, and what will later be the id, coexist, as yet undifferentiated from each other; and that it is by the differentiation from an initial undifferentiated phase that both the ego and the id arise (Hartmann, Kris, and Loewenstein, 1946; Hartmann, 1948).

Psychologists concerned with the psychology of development, and biologists concerned with instincts, had recognized something like this much before Hartmann. Indeed, rereading material like that summarized by Heinz Werner (1926) clearly suggests an initial undifferentiated phase in which percepts are physiognomic, concepts are syncretic, and experience is diffuse. Biologists, on the other hand, have recognized that domestication alters instinct behavior. The rigid coordination of drive tension and goal, so clear, for example, in insects, is lost in the course of domestication (Lorenz, 1935; Thorpe, 1948). It was again Hartmann (1939, 1948) who clarified this issue, concluding that in the human individual, drives are not as adaptive and reality-attuned as they are in the animal; the id is reality-distant, while animal instincts are primary guarantees of survival by virtue of the strict coordination of drive tension and drive object.

The inborn ego apparatuses, and their integration into the ego—which, just like the id, develops from an originally undifferentiated matrix by differentiation—provide the way out of the paradox described above. Yet, without an additional consideration, the answer to the question, "What conflicted with the drives?" may not be clear. We must remember that the motor, perceptual, and memory apparatuses, as well as other inborn apparatuses such as those of affect expression, stimulus barrier, etc., have definite thresholds which are their *structural characteristics*. These *structural characteristics* will set limits to the discharge of drive tension, that is, to the pleasure principle, even when the need-satisfying object is present, and even before drive discharge is prevented by the absence of the need-satisfying object. The very nature of structure will always prevent total discharge of tension. The existence of inborn structural elements in the undifferentiated phase may be what precipitates developmentally the differentiation of it into the ego and the id. The developing ego then integrates these structural apparatuses and re-represents their discharge-limiting and -regulating function in forms usually described as defenses. These are the foundations of the primary autonomy of the ego (cf. Piaget, 1936).

IV

There is, however, more to ego autonomy, and to get a closer view of this "more," and get closer to the answer to our second question, let us turn to Freud's (1900, 1911) model of primitive psychic function. According to this model, when drive tension rises and the need-satisfying object is absent, instead of the tension discharge which would occur were the need-satisfying object—say the breast—present, a new distribution of tensions—that is, energies—occurs. We describe this new energy distribution by saying that the drive which cannot be satisfied is repressed. Metapsychologically we formulate repression thus: a countercathexis is pitted against the cathexis (energy charge) of the repressed drive.

This is not only a model of instinct vicissitude, but also one of the development of the ego. The countercathexis reflects a reality fact: the unavailability of the need-satisfying object. The model thus represents the internalization of reality, which is one of the crucial characteristics and functions of the ego. This internalization is not only a modification of the distribution of drive cathexes by the impact of reality, but also a crucial step in the development of thought organization. Instead of drive discharge, prevented first by the absence of the object and later by repression, there arise on the one hand, affect discharge observed as affect expression, on the other, ideational representations, in the form of wish-fulfilling, hallucinatory images. In the illusions of people on the verge of starvation or dehydration, and in the hallucinations of schizophrenics, we have phenomena substantiating the heuristic value of this model.

Reality is then internalized and represented in the psychic apparatus not only by the countercathexis of repression, but also by the arising ideational representation, and indirectly even by the affect discharge. The countercathexis of repression is only one of the countercathectic energy distributions which arise in this fashion. Every defense mechanism we observe corresponds to such a countercathectic energy distribution. Each of these is a new apparatus of the ego, added to the already discussed inborn ego apparatuses. They, arising in the course of the differentiation process of the ego and the id from the undifferentiated phase, also serve to control drive discharge. These defensive apparatuses come to our attention in the form of motivations of behavior, such as denial, avoidance, altruism, honesty, etc. These motivating forces, too, are relatively autonomous, and constitute what "more" there is besides inborn autonomous apparatuses to ego autonomy. They are what Moses referred to in the story saying: "That's how I became what I am."

To demonstrate to ourselves the autonomy of these defensive apparatuses (secondary autonomy), let us take another look at their development. There was a clash between drive-need and reality. Out of this clash arose controlling apparatuses. Some of these, once they arose as emergent organizations, became relatively independent from the source of their origin. How do we know? We know that in our therapeutic work we encounter defenses which we do not manage to break down even in many years of analysis. You could counter this with, "That is no proof. More and better analysis would have penetrated these!" Possibly. But the very fact of difficulty in analysis bespeaks relative autonomy.

But there is more telling evidence for this autonomy than the pragmatic consideration just advanced. We have known from reconstructions in psychoanalysis for many years that many altruistic, aesthetic, and antiviolence motivations are somehow related to reaction formations against impulses of the anal-sadistic phase. Anna Freud reported [4] that they observed in their Hampstead Nurseries that children who displayed, in a particularly blatant fashion, behavior characteristic of the anal-sadistic phase, became later on very benign, nice youngsters, with a keen liking for people and animals, and with a sharp aversion to cruelty. We have all seen, clinically, people similar to the youngsters Anna Freud observed, and saw that though we could analyze the reaction formation and its interferences with adjustment, altruism as a motivating *value*—though it arose as a reaction formation or an altruistic denial—need not be lost, and is mostly not lost, in successful analyses.

To generalize this point: what came about as a result of conflict sooner or later may become independent of the conflict, may become relatively autonomous. This becomes particularly clear in studying thought processes: the developing independence of the secondary process from the primary one is not completely reversed even in many of the major schizophrenic thought disorders, but mostly persists side by side with the breaking-through primary process. This is probably what gave the "split" impression to early observers of schizophrenia, including Bleuler. I do not believe that any prolonged study of thought in various psychiatric disorders can leave anyone without the strongest impression that the secondary process once established shows such persistence against the onslaughts of conflict, and

[4] In a meeting at the Austen Riggs Foundation, Stockbridge, Massachusetts, April 1950.

against the return of the repressed primary process, that it can be understood in no other way but by assuming that this is not due only to those apparatuses involved in thought (perception, memory) which have primary autonomy, but also to the persisting autonomy of apparatuses which have attained secondary autonomy (Hartmann, 1939).

But here we have come to the answer to our second question. While it is true that apparatuses of primary autonomy tend to *remain* such and to persist in the conflict-free ego sphere, and while defensive apparatuses born of conflict may become autonomous, and may function in the conflict-free sphere, and tend to retain their autonomy against the onslaught of conflict —nevertheless secondary and even primary autonomy is *relative,* and these apparatuses, too, may and do get involved or reinvolved in conflict. To give an extreme example: motility, in spite of its primary autonomy, is involved in conflict in all hysterical motor disorders and schizophrenic motor mannerisms.

In other words, we have to conclude that the autonomy of the ego we are talking about, though it is a most impressive guarantee of independence from instinctual drives, of reality testing, and of social adaptation, is only relative, and may appear so impressive only because without it we would be entirely at the mercy of our impulses. Yet there are in every one of us some functions and structures the autonomy of which proves irreversible in the course of our life history. Such persisting autonomy seen in a case history can be crucial in establishing the prognosis in severe schizophrenics and character disorders, provided that the basically guarded prognosis is not replaced but only modified thereby.

V

Superimposed on the original drive cathexes, new organizations of energy arise which, owing to processes of binding or neutralization, do not abide any more by the rule of the primary process, which is tension-level-lowering discharge at all costs. That is, the pleasure principle is superseded by the reality principle, by postponement of discharge, by detour, by experimental operation with small quantities of energy. These processes of binding or neutralization which progressively transform the discharge-bent drive energy to a system-bound form seem to play a crucial role in the development of defensive apparatuses (secondary autonomy) and their motivations. Keeping this in mind, let us see whether we can obtain some kind of an answer to our third question about the occasional failure of the ego to bind the forbidden impulses.

To make my point concrete I want to refer to a group of borderline cases, all of whom survived, as it were, on counterphobic defenses. Reckless wild tricks, fearlessness, apparent self-sufficiency, rebelliousness, denial of needs (including need for help), contempt and hate for all who show "weakness," were outstanding characteristics of them all. They were "independent" in the extreme, because they wished and feared dependence in the extreme. In some of these I have seen the dire effects of a direct interpretation of the aggressive meaning of their "independence," in the form of catatonic excitement. I have seen some of them run away when overactive therapy brought positive transference prematurely to a head, thus bringing on an overwhelming threat to their independence. I have seen some of them, however, where a profound respect for the independence and dignity of man permeated the therapeutic atmosphere and where the analysis of the counterphobic defense was extremely gradual and did not call into question independence as a value and motivation. The autonomy of the value motivation was not attacked when the conflict-involved counterphobic defense was analyzed. In some cases therapeutic failure may be due to a lack of autonomy of the "independence striving" as a value motivation, it being just one subordinate aspect of the conflict expressed in the counterphobic defense; in others it may be due to the therapist's neglect to distinguish between the autonomous value-motivation aspect and the conflict-laden, defensive aspect of the same psychic formation.

The tentative answer to the third of the questions raised is: that autonomy, particularly secondary autonomy, is always relative, and the onslaught of drive motivations, especially when unchecked by therapeutic help or when aided by overzealous therapeutic moves, may reverse autonomy and bring about a regressed, psychotic state in which the patient is, to a far-reaching extent, at the mercy of his drive impulses. The higher-level autonomous motivations are, as it were, dissolved, and the allies the therapist usually counts on—spontaneity and synthesis—are absent. Thus we can see that the issue of ego autonomy is not merely a theoretical problem but also a practical one of therapy, particularly in borderline and psychotic cases.

What was conquered by Moses in his struggle lurks there, always ready to make an attempt to recoup its old ground. If it succeeds—we are faced with a psychosis. This recoup is rarely complete—all ego autonomy is hardly ever suspended—yet a sufficient part of this autonomy may be dissolved to warn us that the therapist of such a borderline case should respect and foster all autonomous ego functions to avoid their crumbling.

REFERENCES

Escalona, S., & Leitch, M. (1951). Some Problems in Infant Psychology. Address to the Topeka Psychoanalytic Society, January 1951.
French, T. M. (1933). Interrelations between Psychoanalysis and the Experimental Work of Pavlov. *Amer. J. Psychiat.*, 12:1165–1203.
Freud, A. (1936). *The Ego and the Mechanisms of Defence.* New York: International Universities Press, 1946.

Freud, S. (1894). The Defence Neuro-Psychoses. *Collected Papers,* 1:59–75. New York: Basic Books, 1959.

———— (1896). Further Remarks on the Defence Neuro-Psychoses. *Collected Papers,* 1:155–182. New York: Basic Books, 1959.

———— (1900). The Interpretation of Dreams, tr. A. A. Brill. *The Basic Writings.* New York: Modern Library, 1938, pp. 179–549.

———— (1911). Formulations Regarding the Two Principles in Mental Functioning. *Collected Papers,* 4:13–21. New York: Basic Books, 1959.

———— (1911–17 [1911–15]). Papers on Metapsychology. *Collected Papers,* 4:13–170. New York: Basic Books, 1959.

———— (1923). *The Ego and the Id,* tr. J. Riviere. London: Hogarth Press, 1947.

———— (1926 [1925]). *The Problem of Anxiety,* tr. H. A. Bunker. New York: Psychoanalytic Quarterly & Norton, 1936.

———— (1937). Analysis Terminable and Interminable. *Collected Papers,* 5:316–357. New York: Basic Books, 1959.

Hartmann, H. (1939). Ego Psychology and the Problem of Adaptation. In (abridged) Rapaport (1951), pp. 362–396.

———— (1948). Comments on the Psychoanalytic Theory of Instinctual Drives. *Psychoanal. Quart.,* 17:368–388.

————, Kris, E., & Loewenstein, R. M. (1946). Comments on the Formation of Psychic Structure. *Psychoanal. Study Child,* 2:11–38. New York: International Universities Press.

Klein, G. S. (1949). Adaptive Properties of Sensory Functioning: Some Postulates and Hypotheses. *Bull. Menninger Clin.,* 13:16–23.

————, & Schlesinger, H. (1949). Where Is the Perceiver in Perceptual Theory? *J. Pers.,* 18:32–47.

Lorenz, K. (1935). Companionship in Bird Life. In *Instinctive Behavior,* ed. & tr. C. Schiller. New York: International Universities Press, 1957, pp. 83–128.

Masserman, J. H. (1946). *Principles of Dynamic Psychiatry.* Philadelphia: Saunders.

Menninger, K. A., Mayman, M., & Pruyser, P. (1963). *The Vital Balance.* New York: Viking Press.

Mowrer, O. H., & Kluckhohn, C. (1944). Dynamic Theory of Personality. In *Personality and the Behavior Disorders,* Vol. I, ed. J. McV. Hunt. New York: Ronald Press, 1944, pp. 69–135.

Piaget, J. (1936). The Biological Problem of Intelligence. In Rapaport (1951), pp. 176–192.

Rapaport, D. (1950). On the Psychoanalytic Theory of Thinking. *This volume,* Chapter 28.

————, ed. & tr. (1951). *Organization and Pathology of Thought.* New York: Columbia University Press.

Stekel, W. (1924). The Polyphony of Thought. In Rapaport (1951), pp. 311–314.

Thorpe, W. H. (1948). The Modern Concept of Instinctive Behaviour. *Bull. Animal Behav.,* 7:1–12.

Werner, H. (1926). *Comparative Psychology of Mental Development.* New York: Harper, 1940.

32

PAUL SCHILDER'S CONTRIBUTION
TO THE THEORY
OF THOUGHT PROCESSES

Ladies and Gentlemen,

I feel awed and privileged to be here to give your Schilder Memorial Address—awed by the task of sketching Schilder's contribution to the theory of thinking, and privileged by the opportunity offered. Let me hasten to say that it is due to Dr. Lauretta Bender, and the chance by which she discovered that I am familiar with and have studied most of Schilder's writings, have become involved in them and, through them, in the man Paul Schilder. I became acquainted with Schilder's writings in the course of my studies on the psychology of thought, over the last fifteen years. I am delighted to have the opportunity to talk about Paul Schilder.

Let me tell you why by way of a story: there was once a king who was entertaining another one. And since he was the king who had originated the idea that a king should have a cabinet, he introduced his cabinet to his guest. The guest asked who was the most important member of the cabinet. The king pointed to one so far not introduced. "And what is his portfolio?"

Schilder Memorial Address given to the Schilder Society, New York, January 18, 1951. First published in The International Journal of Psycho-Analysis, *32:291–301, 1951. Reprinted as Appendix to Paul Schilder,* Medical Psychology, *trans. D. Rapaport. New York: International Universities Press, 1953, pp. 340–356.*

asked the guest. "Oh, he is the Minister without Portfolio"—and seeing the bewilderment of his guest, he added, "He knows what the rest of them are doing, and tells me about it." That is how I feel about Paul Schilder. Indeed there is hardly any area of psychiatric and psychological problems which Schilder did not recognize, tackle, and illuminate; scarcely a syndrome which he did not study, whether schizophrenia, mania, depression, aphasia, amentia, paresis, or Korsakoff; hardly a function which he did not explore, whether memory, perception, consciousness, motility, language. Few indeed are the problems with which he did not deal, whether they pertain to the form varieties of conscious experience, psychosomatic relationships, neuro-psychological interrelations, epistemological foundations of our relation to reality, or the nature of man's socialization; and exceptional the psychiatric phenomenon or symptom which he did not describe, whether depersonalization, *déjà vu,* or body image. His was an encyclopedic mind—he was a psychiatric polyhistor in our time.

I would like to discuss three topics. First, I would like to demonstrate that it is worth while for psychiatrists to be concerned with the theory of thinking, indeed that the theory of thinking is in a way a measuring rod of the status of the theory of psychiatry. Second, I would like to discuss some of the salient contributions of Schilder to the theory of thinking, demonstrating that in many ways he pointed ahead to theoretical developments which we have only recently reached, and to much that is yet to be reached. Finally, I would like to discuss the present state of psychiatric theory—characterized as it is by competing factions—to establish Schilder's position in this picture, in the hope of contributing something to the understanding of the role of the individual scientist and of the meaning of factions in the development of a science.

I

Let us then turn to the theory of thought processes. What is the basic paradox with which any broad theory of thinking has to cope? Excepting a few "die-hards," all agree that human behavior, and thus human thought also, is motivated by fundamental needs, drives, or instincts, if you prefer. Yet human thought so motivated is adapted to the reality of objects and society. How to reconcile the motivatedness with the social, as well as objective, reality adaptedness of thought, is the basic paradox faced by the psychology of thinking. Indeed, this is the question faced by every psychiatrist treating every patient. But in therapy the patient's own synthetic forces, as well as the psychiatrist's intuition, steadily cope with this problem and prevent it from emerging in stark nakedness. In theoretically treating this problem no such merciful disguises obtain; the stark nakedness of the problem becomes threatening and the paradox has been faced by only a few giants. Freud saw it clearly. He described those thought processes which prevail when primary, unconscious motivation exerts its effects directly, as for instance in dreams. He discerned and described their mechanisms, such as condensation, displacement, substitution, symbolization, and labeled them the primary process. He saw clearly that in everyday life, superimposed over the thinking organized in terms of the primary process, a different kind of thinking obtains which abides by the laws of logic and is adapted to social and objective reality—this he labeled the secondary process. He devoted incomparably more interest to the exploration of the primary process than to that of the secondary process, and it may seem that he solved the paradox by erecting a dichotomy (see Rapaport, 1950). Actually, in Chapter VII of *The Interpretation of Dreams* (1900), in *Wit and Its Relation to the Unconscious* (1905), and in the papers "Formulations Regarding the Two Principles in Mental Functioning" (1911), "Repression" (1915a), "The Unconscious" (1915b), and "Negation" (1925), he laid down the cornerstones for the exploration of the secondary process, and indicated that he did not regard the dichotomy as hard and fast. Not only was this little noted, but two decades after the first publication of *The Interpretation of Dreams* we find Freud complaining in a footnote to a new edition that, even as regards the primary process, people were concerned mainly with rules of thumb for finding the latent dream thought in the manifest dream content, and utterly disregarded the dream work by which the latent thought is translated into the manifest content—that is, the primary process. He reiterated that the dream was primarily a thought process. He was aware of the fact that his followers became interested, to the exclusion of almost everything else, in the content of thought (see Freud, 1900, pp. 466–467).

Here then is the first demonstration of how the theory of thinking becomes a measuring rod of the status of psychiatric theory: lack of interest in theoretical foundations is early expressed by disregard of thought processes in favor of thought content. The central role of the theory of thinking in psychiatric theory becomes more generally clear if we call to mind that, for instance, the obsessional person is one with a certain personality organization and drive dynamics, but that the obsessive compulsive activity, characterological or symptomatic, is prepared for by thought processes which are interposed between the personality organization and drive dynamics on the one hand and the obsessive compulsive behavior or symptoms on the other. And this also holds for other kinds of personality structures and their expression in behavior. Personality organization and drive dynamics translate themselves into behavior and symptoms through thought processes, and indeed the psychiatrist in his everyday work deals with these mediating processes rather than directly with the symptom or directly with the personality. Direct dealing with the symptom we usually regard with healthy skepticism, and as for dealing directly with the personality, we do not even know how to go about it. While content often serves as a reliable guide to the relation of symptom and dynamics, fundamentally only the dynamics, economics, and topography of the thought processes give full information as to what is going on. Our intuition may in everyday practice make concern with the formal characteristics of thought processes unnecessary, but disregard of them will certainly leave us out on a limb when confronted with theoretical claims such as those of Sullivan or Fromm—in one word, the culturalists who, having become involved with the rôle of culture in personality organization and pathology, claim for it the crucial and exclusive position in personality development. What they disregard is again that without the understanding of the mediating processes, which are thought processes—in the broad sense in which I use this term here (Rapaport, 1951a)—there is no understanding of sociocultural impact, and that without understanding of motivation and mediation there is no understanding of socialization. Psychoanalysts often retreat from facing the paradox of motivation vs. socialization and reality adaptation of thinking to an exclusive concern with basic motivation and thought content as its indicator. The culturalists also retreat from facing this basic paradox of the theory of thinking, to an exclusive concern with socialization and adaptation, and the derivative motivations corresponding to these. We can make clear the error of the culturalists only if we do not make the opposite error of considering thought and behavior only in its motivated and not in its adaptive and socialized aspect as well.

II

Let me turn now to Schilder's contribution to the theory of thinking to show that he did not make either kind of retreat. Schilder faced squarely the question of how thought can be both motivated and adaptive-socialized, which is tantamount to the question of what is the relationship between the primary and secondary processes. He saw clearly that primary-process phenomena, such as are encountered in dreams, free association, schizophrenic and other pathology of thought, are also present in the course of normal thinking. We know that Freud was aware of this when he wrote:

> The tendency of the thinking process must always be to free itself more and more from exclusive regulation by the pleasure-principle . . . but we are aware that this . . . is seldom completely successful . . . and that our thinking always remains liable to falsification by the intervention of the pleasure-principle [1900, p. 536].

Schilder, however, went further and demonstrated in various studies summarized in his paper, "On the Development of Thoughts" (1920), that thought formations seen in thought disorders appear in normal thinking as preliminary phases of problem solving, remembering, etc. Thus he arrived at the bold generalization that every thought of the human individual undergoes a development before it becomes conscious in its final form. He asserted that this development proceeds from indefinite to definite forms, passing through associatively related ideas, and that in the early phases of this development, imagery is more prevalent, and personal affective influences—that is, primary-process mechanisms—play a greater role than in the later phases of the development, which are increasingly object- and reality-oriented. Accordingly, he considered the pathological forms of thought to result when these processes of thought development come to a premature close, bringing to consciousness forms which are normally only preliminary phases of thought development instead of completed thoughts. He also inferred from his observations that even when such thought developments reach completion, imagelike and affect-distorted preliminary developmental forms may come into consciousness alongside the completed thought. It is clear—and Schilder said so—that this conception was based on the idea that ontogenesis recapitulates phylogenesis, a pattern so prevalent in the thinking of the beginning of this century. We need not discuss here the validity of this bold assumption. Some aspects of it have been borne out by recent empirical investigations; see, for example, R. Schafer (1945). Schilder, however—unlike Stekel, who offered a similar conception in his "The Polyphony of Thought" (1924)—was not satisfied with this solution. Indeed, this conception of thought development would imply that whenever any thought comes to consciousness it is preceded by a battle of the Titans, enacted by all our fundamental impulses, reaching down to and shaking the foundations of our psychological existence, only to give birth to a meek mouse of an idea. Schilder had to get away from this conception, and he did. He studied with great care an array of thought disorders; aphasia, agnosia, Meynert's amentia, paretic and other dementias, schizophrenia, and neuroses. He came to the surprising finding that in all of these disorders the same fundamental forms of thought disorder were present (1930). He described these in great detail, and in summary stated that they all boil down to this fact: the whole cannot be differentiated into parts, and the parts cannot be integrated into a whole. What then is the distinctive character of each of these disorders? he asked. The answer which he gave was this: the psychic apparatus is so built that its central core of impulse dynamics is surrounded by means-layers which serve it in expressing and executing the impulses. The layer of perception and verbalization is the one farthest removed from the central core. It has an autonomous synthetic function of its own, which is the one affected in aphasic and agnosic disorders. The perceptual material synthetically integrated by this means-layer of the psyche serves as raw material for the apperceptive means-layer, which integrates it on another level establishing the object relationships of the percepts. This integrative, synthetic function is the one affected in Meynert's amentia. The material thus integrated in turn serves as the raw material of another means-layer of the psyche which integrates and evaluates it conceptually. This is the synthetic function affected in dementia. The process of final, personal integration in terms of drives—operating by methods we would call the mechanisms of the primary process—is laid bare in dream work, in neurotic symptoms, and schizophrenic thought disorders. Everywhere the pattern of the thought disorder is the same, but its substratum in each disorder is a different one of these means-layers (see Schilder, 1930, pp. 566–568, 577–580). This conception, however vulnerable, and in parts outdated by more recent explorations, contains factual discoveries and theoretical assumptions which have only recently been approximated by psychoanalytic ego psychology, through the studies of Nunberg (1931), Hartmann (1939), and Hartmann, Kris, and Loewenstein (1946). It implies the assumption of ego apparatuses which have a relative autonomy and serve drive dynamics as an integral apparatus (see Rapaport, 1951b). It implies the recognition of synthetic functions layered over each other in a hierarchic series. It implies also the recognition that the secondary process is not as a whole juxtaposed to the primary process, but that there is a whole series of levels on each of which derivative motivations, progressively further removed from the basic drive, bring about primary-processlike phenomena, counteracted or replaced by more and more successfully socialized and reality-adapted secondary-process phenomena (see Kris, 1950; Rapaport, 1951a, Part VII). To show more concretely Schilder's insight, let me present to you his discussion of the relation of common slips of the tongue to the parapraxes of aphasics. We all remember Freud's discussion of the nature of parapraxes: that if, when robbed of my pocketbook in a dark street, I complain to the police that darkness robbed me of my money, I am mistaken, because darkness provided only the occasion for the robbery. Similarly—he continued—we are mistaken when we attribute slips of the tongue to fatigue, which gives only the occasion for impulses to break through in the form of slips of the tongue (see Freud, 1901, esp. p. 50). In discussing aphasic parapraxes, Schilder shows that they are not specifically related to repressed impulses as are our common slips of the tongue. The synthetic function inherent in the process of verbalization is itself affected in aphasia by organic damage, and therefore the parapraxes are diffuse and not impulse-specific. Yet we know that when an aphasic becomes excited his parapraxes also become more pronounced and specific, even though the disorder is otherwise diffuse. In turn, with normal people, the more fatigue and other general factors interfere with the effectiveness of the synthetic function of verbalization, the more occasion is given for the impulse to do its slip-producing work. Indeed the relationship between diffuse thought disorder and specific impulse interference with autonomous psychic apparatuses is nowhere in our literature presented with the lucidity of Schilder's discussion (see also Schilder, 1930, pp. 565–566). Not even in the Silberer-Jones controversy (see Nachmansohn, 1925, esp. pp. 283–284, n. 81), which had the same core, did it attain such clarity. Silberer (1912) claimed that the hypnagogic state by its very nature, owing to its low energy level, is conducive to symbolization, while Jones (1916) insisted that only repressed impulses are symbol-producing. Whatever the final fate of Schilder's theoretical construction may be, he did point out with unforgettable clarity the fact that thought disorders do become diffuse and generalized, that it is rather the exception for them to be specific and traceable to single impulse dynamics, as are common slips of the tongue, and that there is a fluid transition between the dynamics of a diffuse and an impulse-specific thought disorder.

Schilder, having recognized the fluid transition between the primary and secondary processes, the multiple layering of synthetic and controlling energy distributions—which Hartmann, Kris, and Loewenstein (1949) recently described as the progressive neutralization or binding of drive cathexes—proceeded to create a conception of the thought process in keeping with the conception of autonomous means-layers, or as recent psychoanalytic ego psychology would put it: in keeping with the conception of autonomous ego apparatuses (see Schilder, 1924, pp. 56, 72, 104–105). I shall choose four salient points to sketch Schilder's conception.

III

To outline Schilder's view of the thought process, I shall attempt to sketch his conception of the motivation of thought processes, of the nature of concepts, of anticipations, and of judgment.

Motivations. Our task would be easy if Schilder had anywhere directly expressed himself concerning the nature of the motivating forces of the thought process, but it would have been quite unlike him to do so. We must not forget that, though a man of insatiable thirst for facts and unceasing urge to make sense of these facts by hunch and theory, Schilder was not a systematizer. There can be no question that instincts, drives, and libido were to his mind the ultimate motivators of psychic events. There can be no question that he was aware of their rôle at every point of the way. But when it came to the motivations of thought processes, we hear him talk about tasks, goals, determining tendencies, readiness, attitudes (*Einstellungen*), intentions, interests, strivings, affects, drive orientations, instead of drives. In other words, as soon as he began to talk about motivations of thought processes other than the pure primary thought process, his terminology was other than that of libido, drive, or instinct. This much is obvious to anyone who studies his writings. From here on it takes work—at times arduous work—to discover what he means. One has to wander from his *Brain and Personality* (1931) to the "Studies Concerning the Psychology and Symptomatology of General Paresis" (1930), and from there to his *Mind: Perception and Thought* (1942), and painstakingly piece together Schilder's concept that the motivations of thought form a hierarchy, all deriving from the fundamental drives, all having an autonomy, that is, capable of exerting their motivating role, once they are stimulated either by more fundamental motivations or by perceptions from the external world. Thus, not only do the means layers of the psyche have a hierarchy, but so do the motivations of thought. This conception may remind one of the more recent—or let us say neo-Freudian—conceptions, in which defensive structures and the energies related to them are considered to be basic motivations of human behavior, as in Horney and Fromm. The difference is only that Schilder never forgets, or lets us forget, that higher-level motivations derive from the more fundamental ones, even though he remains keenly aware of the relative autonomy of the former (see Schilder, 1924, pp. 197 ff.).

Schilder conceived of the role of motivations in thinking as follows. An impulse—which to begin with implies an object-directedness—is checked (or as Freud would have put it: delayed in discharge), either by another impulse or by structural characteristics of the psyche. Such checking, braking-effect, or delay gives rise to thought which in itself is both an indicator of the lack of fulfillment of the impulse and a carrier of the undischarged tension. Thoughts so arising develop from an indistinct, imageless, and wordless form into more distinct imagelike and verbal forms, by being again and again modified by other similarly developing thoughts and structural obstacles. Thus thoughts, being resultants of both impulses and of delaying influences, express not only the original impulse and its object, but also these intrapsychic and the objective delaying influences; they become progressively more reality adapted, point the way to the object in reality, and so fulfill the original aim of the impulse (see Schilder, 1924, pp. 190 ff.). What is not fulfilled by the diffuse, imageless thought is fulfilled by the discrete image, what is not fulfilled by the discrete image comes closer to fulfillment by the process of verbalization, and what is not fulfilled even by the verbalized thought is experienced by us as meaning; and this final residue points directly to the object of the impulse and cannot be fulfilled except by the action on the object toward which the impulse was originally directed (see Schilder, 1930, pp. 528–530). Thus Schilder carried a long way further what Freud sensed and expressed when he wrote: thought is experimental action with small quantities of energy (1911, p. 16).

Concepts (see Schilder, 1930, pp. 528–529; also Schilder, 1920, pp. 515–518). This still was not specific enough for Schilder; he was not satisfied with the realization that the process of thought can be initiated by motivation from any level of the motivational hierarchy, either by intrapsychic or external perceptions, nor with the implied recognition of the relative autonomy of the levels of motivation. He seems to have reasoned: if thought leading to action can be initiated on any of the autonomous levels of motivation, then thought itself must also have relatively autonomous building stones (Schilder, 1923). These he found first of all in concepts. He was aware that ethnopsychology argues that primitive concepts are action concepts, that is, for a dog trained to jump on a chair the verbal signal "chair" means something to jump up and crouch down on, and anything that can be so acted on is subsumed under the primitive concept "chair." In one word, he was aware that primitive concepts refer to things-of-action (see Werner, 1948). He maintained that in order to act one has to have stable objects. In a world of constant change, lacking stability, in a world of piecemeal perception without synthetic integration, no action (that is, intentional action) is possible. He was aware that this is one of the fundamental implications of obsessive and schizophrenic doubt, indecision, and inactivity. This then is where concepts come in: they extract out of the world of objects the most constant and reliable features, and provide thereby reliable orientations and objects for action. Indeed, he insisted that concepts which guarantee us the stability of objects are in essence but action-readiness directed toward specific objects (Schilder, 1930, p. 529). Furthermore, he maintained that to be successful, action requires insight into object relationships, and realized that effective concepts do indeed comprise such insight (pp. 522–524). He knew that concepts do not have to be given birth to again and again, every time they come up in our thinking, but once they come about they are at our disposal as ready-made parts, apparatuses of our thinking. They are an expression of, and serve as a guarantee for, the autonomy of the secondary process. He was also aware, however, that in the course of our thinking these concepts undergo progressive growth and remolding; though they appear ready-made, relatively stable, even quite rigid in some people (for example, feeble-minded; Schilder, 1930, pp. 562 ff.), in others—and at certain times in most people—they can become fluid again. He saw that in creative thinking they are resolved at times even into complete fluidity, only to be reborn from a battle of Titans in an entirely new form, in that of new artistic or scientific invention. He knew that concepts have a constancy, an autonomy, but he knew also that this autonomy is only relative, and creative processes can dissolve it and rebuild it again more richly (see Schilder, 1924, pp. 122 ff.). He conceived of every concept as surrounded by a halo of connected associations which he termed "the sphere," and believed that it is in these spheres that motivations of any level find concepts to orient them toward finding their object in reality, and lead them to action and discharge on these objects; and also that it is within these spheres that concepts are remolded in the course of intellectual growth as well as in the heat of creative invention (see Schilder, 1920, pp. 515–518; also 1924, pp. 330 ff.).

Anticipations. But Schilder was not satisfied with inserting concepts and their spheres as autonomous apparatuses to explain the relation and transition between the primary and secondary processes. He observed that motivations imply as expectancies the objects toward which they are directed. This expectancy begins even with the drive in the sense that drive discharge becomes possible only in the presence of its satisfying object (see Schilder, 1924, pp. 168 ff.). Freud showed this and Schilder never forgot it. He also learned from the experiments of Selz that in the course of thought processes directed toward problem solving, schematic expectations of the solution precede the solution itself (Schilder, 1930, pp. 537–539). It is no surprise that Schilder knew Selz, who delivered one of the first decisive blows at conventional academic association psychology, for he knew this conventional psychology as well as gestalt psychology and Lewin. Indeed with the exception of only a few psychoanalysts who are our contemporaries, he may be described as the psychiatrist most broadly versed in the psychological literature. For these expectations accompanying any and all motivation, he adapted from Selz the concept of anticipation patterns. Thought does not develop merely from the clash, or delay, of motivations by the structural hierarchy of the psychic apparatus, nor by these motivations using crystallized concepts to guide them to action; but motivations carry with them, to a greater or lesser degree, structuralized anticipation patterns which guide them in selecting the proper concepts (see Schilder, 1920, pp. 507–509; also 1942, pp. 271, 324–325, and 1930, pp. 532–537). These anticipations, like concepts, are again, as it were, relatively autonomous apparatuses in the service of the thought process. If we talk about selectiveness in memory, in perception, in thought, we are referring to the effect of these anticipations. It is clear from Schilder's writing that he was guided in his formulation of the rôle of anticipations by Bleuler's description of hysterical mechanisms as "occasional apparatuses," but it is also clear that he went far beyond Bleuler in perceiving the significance of such apparatuses (see Schilder, 1931, pp. 68–70; 1924, p. 144; also Hartmann, 1939, pp. 392–396). Again it is clear that though such anticipations may and do come about anew in creative as well as in everyday productive thinking, many of them, once crystallized, stay with us and guarantee the reality adaptedness of the thought process and the socially shared character of communication (see Schilder, 1918, pp. 45 ff.). For instance, if I now say the word "although," I have elicited in all of you the anticipation that I will follow this word "although" with two coordinate and antithetic sentences. Indeed all the conjunctions of the language are verbal expressions of such highly structuralized (automatized) and socially shared anticipations, which, as we know, do not exist in such primordial forms of thought as for instance the dream (Schilder, 1942, p. 261).

The conception of structuralization, automatization, of apparatuses implicit in Schilder's view of concepts and anticipations was explicitly and systematically put forth by Hartmann (1939). This conception proved in Hartmann's treatment to be an inevitable cornerstone in the systematic theory of psychoanalytic ego psychology.

Judgment. Finally let me discuss Schilder's concept of judgment. It is clear that in both "Formulations Regarding the Two Principles in Mental Functioning" (1911) and "Negation" (1925) Freud had set the concept of judgment in the center of the function of reality testing; yet he left the formal characteristics of this function unexplored. Schilder studied the function in various thought disorders and demonstrated that judgment, when functioning in relation to action, consists of a matching of the percept of the object to be acted on and the result of the action, with the anticipation and the concept of the object to which the motivation was directed. He also demonstrated that judgment, when functioning in relation to thought, consists in a matching of the anticipation pattern accompanying the motivation with the memory associations of the sphere through which the thought development had passed. In other words, passing through the various associations of the sphere, judgment matches the various associations met with by the anticipation pattern implicit to the motivation (see Schilder, 1930, pp. 532–537).

These conceptions alone would seem to be important contributions. Yet Schilder went further. Merlan (1945, 1949) and Bernfeld (1951) recently reported evidence that Freud had studied with Brentano and was familiar with act psychology and with the philosophy of phenomenology. Indeed, those who did text-critical work on Freud's writings have been anticipating something like this, since traces suggestive of Brentano's influence are again and again encountered in Freud's writings (see particularly 1917). But here is the difference between Freud and Schilder. Freud digested whatever in Brentano and phenomenology fitted his purpose and his thinking. Schilder studied these and set out deliberately to apply their thinking to psychiatric research (see Schilder, 1914, 1923). Their thinking fitted in well with his great interest in describing pathological phenomena. Applying act psychology to the issues of reality testing led him to see that human thinking and consciousness are such that we are capable of having ideas in our consciousness as specific memories, as facts of general knowledge, as daydreams, as future expectations, as facts, as assumed, doubted, certain, etc. He showed that it is useful to subsume all these as form-varieties of the function of judgment, and that without these forms of conscious experience implied in judgment, the refinement of reality testing, that is, the function of the reality principle, would be altogether crude and far short of the stage it has reached (see Schilder, 1924, pp. 124 ff.). Schilder's awareness of these forms of conscious experience is so far-reaching that at times he gives the impression of assuming that these varieties of conscious experience generalize into autonomous states of consciousness, of which there again exists a broad, but hierarchically ordered, variety. To my mind, the understanding of the phenomena of transition between the waking and the dream state, and of many pathological conditions (for example, fugues, amnesias, schizophrenic blockings, etc.), is not possible without making some such assumption (see Schilder, 1924, pp. 105, 269–270; and 1931, pp. 11–13). But let me resist the temptation, so great at this point (see Rapaport, 1951c), which would lead me away from what are certainly Schilder's ideas, to where my own would inevitably, if imperceptibly, creep in.

IV

Now that I have attempted to sketch the nature of Schilder's contribution to the theory of thinking, I feel I have delayed long enough in presenting Schilder's two fundamental points of departure, which he held with an intensity amounting to articles of faith, and the validity of which he endeavored to demonstrate in multifarious ways. These two fundamental premises are:

First: human thinking is directed toward an existing world of objects, and without assuming the existence of such a world of objects, no theory of thinking can be built (see Schilder, 1924, pp. 56 ff.; 1930, pp. 519–527). Clearly this is an epistemological stand, and you may wonder why psychiatrists should be bored with the tedious nonsense of philosophizing, and you may ask who anyhow would doubt such a simple fact. Yet the thinkers of Western civilization, from Heraclitus to Schopenhauer, have struggled for 2,500 years with this issue and offered many contradictory solutions to it. In psychoanalytic writing also there has been a good deal of confusion about it (see Hermann, 1924, 1929). When thinking is considered only in its motivated aspects, and not in its reality-adaptive and socialized aspects as well, what we perceive may indeed appear as mere projection of the objects of our motivation. Schilder insisted early, just as did Freud in his last writings (1926, 1937), that human psychic life is not a product of conflicts only. It is Hartmann's (1939) merit to have formulated this issue systematically: we are born with apparatuses—those of memory, perception, musculature, etc.—which exist before the ego and id have become differentiated, and which are integrated after this differentiation into the ego, and then subserve its functions. Hartmann realized that these inherited apparatuses potentially guarantee reality adaptation—providing that maturation and integration take place relatively unhampered. Schilder stated his epistemological stand as early as 1923 (*Seele und Leben*), and though never advanced to the level of the formulations of Hartmann, the spirit of this epistemological stand permeated all his writings. Projection is indeed a fundamental corollary of the basic motivated nature of thought, and without projection and introjection the formation of the ego, the differentiation of the "me" and the "not-me" is hardly conceivable to those who grew up on Freud's "Metapsychological Supplement to the Theory of Dreams" (1917), and *Beyond the Pleasure Principle* (1926). Yet neither projection nor introjection are conceivable without the perceptual and motor apparatuses, these preformed and inherited guarantees of human adaptation. Reality adaptation is not a late acquisition in man's ontogenesis: it is also his fundamental inherited potentiality, though its unfolding occurs in the course of ontogenesis, and is contingent upon the conditions and conflicts of ontogenesis (see Hartmann, 1948). Schilder was right, and present-day psychoanalytic ego psychology came to the same conclusion: without this postulate, psychological life is not understandable. If an illusion to the contrary could be sustained in any other area of psychology, a consistent attempt at building a theory of thinking would certainly break such an illusion to bits.

The *second* basic premise of Schilder was that socialization, just like reality directedness, is not an acquisition of thinking or human psychological life, but a basic implication of it.[1] He endeavored to demonstrate this on drive actions and expressive movements, showing that these forms of behavior are already directed to an audience, are communications. He linked language to expressive movements, tracing thus its fundamentally socialized character (Schilder, 1930, pp. 524 ff.). He stressed that the very motivations of thought and the corresponding anticipations and concepts imply, to begin with, the socialized character of man, and though experience, learning, and the corresponding development of the higher levels of motivation, anticipation, and conceptual abstraction lead to more and more adequate reality and socially shared (socialized) forms of thought, socialization is not just acquired but lies in the very nature of human psychic organization. Here again Schilder did not break the continuity between drive and primary process on the one hand, and experience, learning, cultural influence, socialization, and secondary process on the other, but rather insisted that there is a continuous development from the one to the other, and that socialization and secondary process cannot be understood without realizing the basically, even if only potentially, socialized implications of the fundamental motivations, and of the thought forms of the primary process that pertain to them. Though deeply interested in all the matters so dear to the heart of the present-day, so-called culturalist, schools of psychoanalysis, he could not afford to forget the fundamental motivations in favor of the higher-level defensive and adaptive motivations to which these schools resorted as ultimate explanatory principles of behavior.

It is curious to see how the environmentalist and culturalist thinking pushes *learning* into the foreground of psychological interest, and how it is inclined to accept conditioned-reflex and conditioned-response theories of learning. Schilder, however, though he was fully cognizant of and deeply interested in conditioning, saw and stated clearly the fallacy of such a procedure (see Schilder, 1924, pp. 152 ff.). He argued: though we see complex motor mechanisms built up on simple reflex mechanisms, it would be a mistake here, as elsewhere, to start with the analysis of the simplest forms. Obviously he had Coghill and Minkowski in mind. The simple reflex mechanisms are crystallizations of previous global and undifferentiated proc-

[1] See, e.g., Schilder (1942, p. 244): "The body image as well as the object are built by continuous interchange with other human beings; they are therefore socialized. Socialization is thus a fundamental form of human experience." See also Schilder (1942, p. 261) and Piaget (1937).

esses. So do habits automatize into relatively stable occasional apparatuses from undifferentiated flexible and goal-seeking processes (see Schilder, 1931, pp. 65–71). The understanding of habits becomes possible, therefore, only on the basis of an understanding of those automatization processes, which are the fate of many complex psychological dynamisms. This is a crucial point which has in academic psychology been most clearly perceived by Kurt Lewin (1926, especially pp. 129–130, 141–143), and in psychoanalytic ego psychology by Heinz Hartmann (1939).

The two points of departure of Schilder's psychiatric thinking in general, and of his theory of thinking in particular, are the belief in the basic directedness of all psychological processes toward objects of an existing reality, and the belief in the basically socialized character of the human psychic apparatus—which matures in the course of experience and learning, but is not created by them.

V

Schilder is the "Minister without Portfolio," and the Minister without Portfolio is supposed to tell us about what all the rest are doing. Let us then ask: What does he tell us about all the rest?

As you can see from the scattered comments I have made about Freud's theory of thinking, Freud centered on the issue of the fundamental motivation of thought, and though he opened up the problems of the theory of thinking in many directions beyond this fundamental interest, he had to pay for his systematic singleness of purpose by doing little exploration of the adaptive and socialized nature of thought. On the other hand, we see how the interest in adaptation, culture, societal influences, results in centering much of contemporary psychoanalytic interest upon defenses, values, socialization, and learning, and we know how the psychoanalysts so interested —for instance, Horney, Fromm, and Sullivan—pay for this interest. They lose contact with, and in fact have to turn forcibly against, what we have learned of the basically motivated nature of man's behavior and thought.

I am sure you are by now asking yourselves, "Was Schilder the only man who did not pay anything, since he could see all of it?"

This is certainly not the impression I would want to give you. This encyclopedic mind, this psychiatric polyhistor of our time, paid dearly for his discarding the claim to any portfolio. He never developed systematically any of the infinitely rich observations and countless hunches he developed in well-nigh all fields of psychiatric interest. Unresting and fruitful, he spread his effort all around, sowing rich seed without being interested in a definitive harvest. And so it happens that the full scope of his contribution has been hardly assessed, and that his writing is often so difficult to read.

So it is in the development of science. For every achievement we pay dearly by turning away and indeed cutting ourselves away from other possibilities and facts. No individual and no school can encompass the riches of phenomena in any science, and even less so in the science of man, with which we are concerned. I believe the "Minister without Portfolio" tells us that none of us can behold all aspects of man at once, and the one who attempts to do that will give a rich and intuitive but scattered picture. He makes it easier for us to understand why, in exploring cultural influence in personality development, one is prone to forget basic motivation by showing us that a high price has to be paid, by every one of us, for what we would discover.

This price is determined by what our interest centers on, and our interest in turn flows from our character and personal proclivities. It is a different person with partly different values who is possessed with the discovery of basic motivation, from the one who finds defensive and socializing motives to be the ultimate ones. So with Schilder too: personal proclivities, values, and urges ultimately determined the choice of the price he paid. Let us, however, not ask what the personal proclivities of Schilder were that shaped the character of his scientific creativity; let us rather honor the man, so rare in our time, who sowed seeds richly and was little concerned with the harvest.

REFERENCES

Bernfeld, S. (1951). Turning Points in Freud's Life. Lecture at Yale University, Department of Neuropsychiatry, April.
Freud, S. (1900). The Interpretation of Dreams, tr. A. A. Brill. *The Basic Writings.* New York: Modern Library, 1938, pp. 179–549.
———— (1901). *The Psychopathology of Everyday Life,* tr. A. A. Brill. New York: Macmillan, 1914.
———— (1905). Wit and Its Relation to the Unconscious, tr. A. A. Brill. *The Basic Writings.* New York: Modern Library, 1938, pp. 631–803.
———— (1911). Formulations Regarding the Two Principles in Mental Functioning. *Collected Papers,* 4:13–21. New York: Basic Books, 1959.
———— (1915a). Repression. *Collected Papers,* 4:84–97. New York: Basic Books, 1959.
———— (1915b). The Unconscious. *Collected Papers,* 4:98–136. New York: Basic Books, 1959.
———— (1917 [1915]). Metapsychological Supplement to the Theory of Dreams. *Collected Papers,* 4:137–151. New York: Basic Books, 1959.
———— (1920). *Beyond the Pleasure Principle,* tr. C. J. M. Hubback. London: Hogarth Press, 1948.
———— (1925). Negation. *Collected Papers,* 5:181–185. New York: Basic Books, 1959.
———— (1926 [1925]). *The Problem of Anxiety,* tr. H. A. Bunker. New York: Psychoanalytic Quarterly & Norton, 1936.
———— (1937). Analysis Terminable and Interminable. *Collected Papers.* 5:316–357. **New York: Basic Books, 1959.**

Hartmann, H. (1939). Ego Psychology and the Problem of Adaptation. In (abridged) Rapaport (1951a), pp. 362–396.

———— (1948). Comments on the Psychoanalytic Theory of Instinctual Drives. *Psychoanal. Quart.,* 17:368–388.

————, Kris, E., & Loewenstein, R. M. (1946). Comments on the Formation of Psychic Structure. *Psychoanal. Study Child,* 2:11–38. New York: International Universities Press.

————, Kris, E., & Loewenstein, R. M. (1949). Notes on the Theory of Aggression. *Psychoanal. Study Child,* 3/4:9–36. New York: International Universities Press.

Hermann, I. (1924). *Psychoanalyse und Logik.* Wien: Internationaler Psychoanalytischer Verlag.

———— (1929). *Das Ich und das Denken.* Wien: Internationaler Psychoanalytischer Verlag.

Jones, E. (1916). The Theory of Symbolism. *Papers on Psycho-Analysis,* 5th ed. Baltimore: Williams & Wilkins, 1948, pp. 87–144.

Kris, E. (1950). On Preconscious Mental Processes. In Rapaport (1951a), pp. 474–493.

Lewin, K. (1926). Intention, Will and Need. In Rapaport (1951a), pp. 95–153.

Merlan, P. (1945). Brentano and Freud. *J. Hist. Ideas,* 6:375–377.

———— (1949). Brentano and Freud—A Sequel. *J. Hist. Ideas,* 10:451.

Nachmansohn, M. (1925). Concerning Experimentally Produced Dreams. In Rapaport (1951a), pp. 257–287.

Nunberg, H. (1931). The Synthetic Function of the Ego. *Practice and Theory of Psychoanalysis.* New York: Nerv. Ment. Dis. Publ. Co., 1948, pp. 120–136.

Piaget, J. (1937). Principal Factors Determining Intellectual Evolution from Childhood to Adult Life. In Rapaport (1951a), pp. 154–175.

Rapaport, D. (1950). On the Psychoanalytic Theory of Thinking. *This volume,* Chapter 28.

———— ed. & tr. (1951a). *Organization and Pathology of Thought.* New York: Columbia University Press.

———— (1951b). The Autonomy of the Ego. *This volume,* Chapter 31.

———— (1951c). States of Consciousness: A Psychopathological and Psychodynamic View. *This volume,* Chapter 33.

Schafer, R. (1945). A Study of Thought Processes in a Word Association Test. *Character & Pers.,* 13:212–227.

Schilder, P. (1914). *Selbstbewusstsein und Persönlichkeitsbewusstsein.* Berlin: Springer.

———— (1918). *Wahn und Erkenntnis.* Berlin: Springer.

———— (1920). On the Development of Thoughts. In Rapaport (1951a), pp. 497–518.

———— (1923). *Seele und Leben.* Berlin: Springer.

———— (1924). *Medical Psychology,* ed. & tr. D. Rapaport. New York: International Universities Press, 1953.

———— (1930). Studies Concerning the Psychology and Symptomatology of General Paresis. In Rapaport (1951a), pp. 519–580.

———— (1931). *Brain and Personality,* 2nd ed. New York: International Universities Press, 1951.

———— (1942). *Mind: Perception and Thought in Their Constructive Aspects.* New York: Columbia University Press.

Silberer, H. (1912). On Symbol-Formation. In Rapaport (1951a), pp. 208–233.

Stekel, W. (1924). The Polyphony of Thought. In Rapaport (1951a), pp. 311–314.

Werner, H. (1948). *Comparative Psychology of Mental Development,* rev. ed. New York: Follett.

33

STATES OF CONSCIOUSNESS

A Psychopathological and
Psychodynamic View

I would like to try to present a psychopathological—or if you prefer, psychodynamic—point of view concerning the referent of this very vague term, consciousness. I will make some introductory remarks to link my presentation to last time's discussions.

Dr. Barry and I had a talk this morning, and it seems that we both felt that the difficulties we were beset by last time centered around the alternatives: Are we here to define consciousness?, or, Are we here to put together a lot of phenomena and try to figure out from them what we mean by consciousness? Well, I certainly do not have the answer. I do believe, however, that I can point to some difficulties the clinician encounters in discussing phenomena of consciousness with scientists working in other disciplines.

The first of these difficulties, I feel, is that the concept or term "consciousness" is a rather discredited one. For the last 30 years we have all been made accustomed by behaviorism to look upon consciousness as a highly unreliable phenomenon, a very subjective matter, which, like a siren, can sing beautiful songs, and brings those who listen to it onto the rocks. I believe that the clinician would comment: yes, that is so, if you listen to it

First published in Problems of Consciousness, *Transactions of the Second Conference, March 19–20, 1951. New York: Josiah Macy, Jr. Foundation, 1951, pp. 18–57.*

385

with unprepared ears. However, if you can approach consciousness with systematic methods of science—if I may take the hallowed word on unchaste lips—then it can become a fundamental avenue for the exploration of human nature.

It so happens that part of the information about human nature is presented to us in conscious experience in a certain kind of code. Let us leave aside for the moment what that code is. A salient part of information concerning human nature is presented to us in the introspection of the human being, in his conscious experience—that is, in his reports of these—and in no other way. The question is how to decipher that code. Now, this is not a new situation for the scientist. For instance, the phenomenon light also was, to begin with, presented to our unaided sense organs, that is, to the subjective conscious experience of the human being. At that point "light" was a descriptive term and not yet a concept.

Then the physicist went at it. He discovered the varieties of the referent of this term "light." He disentangled the formal characteristics of these varieties, for instance, their intensity, frequency, etc. Thus this term "light," which was to begin with a descriptive term, changed into a concept of clear definition, subsuming the multitude of varieties, some of which had, others of which had not before been considered light phenomena. It may be similarly feasible for us to start out with this subjective experience called "consciousness," refer to its varieties by the descriptive term consciousness, and by a study of these varieties turn it into a scientifically usable concept. Actually, I believe that psychoanalysis has already made considerable strides in just this direction. Others may not agree with this evaluation. But since that is a matter of judging certain kinds of data and relationships, I would like to describe today some of the variants and varieties of conscious experience, in order to see whether the study of these allows us to accept that concept of consciousness which is accepted by at least some psychodynamic theorists.

A second difficulty one of my ilk encounters in such a discussion group as this becomes obvious in the discussion of the relationship of certain forms of conscious experience to physiological and biochemical phenomena. I am thinking, for example, of Dr. Hoagland's and, in part, of Dr. Kleitman's presentations. The issues they brought forth were stimulating to me, yet there is some uneasiness attending such stimulation. I asked Dr. Barry this morning whether there are propositions in embryology which are considered valid though they cannot be expressed in terms of physiology, biochemistry or, for that matter, nuclear physics. If I understood Dr. Barry correctly, his answer was, "Sure there are." The plea of psychodynamics is: accord psychology the same right the embryologist accords to himself; the right to start out with a description of psychological phenomena, to search for functional dependencies within the confines of the psychological phenomena, and to wait and see whether these functional dependencies, once clarified, can be reduced to (let us put it crudely) organic terms.

If we attempt such reduction prematurely we may find that we have torn a set of phenomena out of its context, out of the whole of which it is a subordinate part. Since it may happen that only the whole of this set and its relationships can possibly be reduced to organic terms, a premature attempt at reduction will be useless and misleading.

After this introduction, I would like to indicate just what I am going to talk about.

Psychodynamic theory considers consciousness one of the human being's means of adaptation to his reality. It considers consciousness a function of the ego or, if you please, an apparatus in the service of the ego.

Let us for a moment assume that consciousness is somehow a superordinate sense organ: what happens on the receptors, and much of what happens intrapsychically, is relayed to it, and is re-represented by it in a certain code (see Freud, 1900, pp. 540–549). From the point of view of this "superordinate sense organ" both the intrapsychic happenings and those on the receptor, constitute an "external world." I believe that it is useful to make this experiment of looking on consciousness in this fashion: it permits us to see the curious phenomena of consciousness one encounters in the psychological clinic from a different angle than the customary one.

Now, an illustration to make this way of viewing consciousness plausible. According to our present knowledge, in the state of sleep very little of what impinges on the receptors is relayed to this "sense organ" consciousness. But dreams seem to testify that quite a bit of what happens intrapsychically is relayed to it. While certain sensory stimulations that impinge in the course of sleep on the sense organs are relayed to consciousness and are incorporated into the dream, the fact remains that certainly far less is so relayed and incorporated than what comes to consciousness in the waking state of the stimulation that impinged upon the sense organs (see Schrötter, 1911). I remind you of this differential selectiveness of waking and dream consciousness to indicate both the organized and selective character of consciousness which is conducive to describing it as a "sense organ" and the variability of its organization and selectivity. It is worth pointing out that the manner of re-representation in dream consciousness differs from that in waking consciousness.

So much to indicate the angle from which I will here approach the phenomena of consciousness.

Now as for my presentation: I will give three examples of variants of consciousness in order to make plausible some crude generalizations that can be made clinically about consciousness. I have chosen for this purpose (a) a case of amnesia of the sort called "loss of personal identity"; (b) some observations I have made of dreams, hypnagogic reveries, daydreams, and thoughts of my own; (c) some well-known observations on Korsakoff's syndrome.

The type of amnesia I would like to discuss was first systematically described in the literature by Abeles and Schilder (1935) under the name of loss of personal identity. Since then, Gill and I (1942; Rapaport, 1942), Geleerd, Hacker, and I (1945), and most extensively Fisher (1945, 1947; Fisher and Joseph, 1949), have studied and written about it. A simple case illustration is this: a man is found at the Hudson walking up and down in a strange fashion. A policeman is called and the man cannot identify himself, shows great bewilderment, and complains of a terrible headache. He is brought to a hospital where study establishes that he has no memory of any relevance to his personal identity, and he is aware of this fact and bewildered by it. For ten days all attempts with hypnosis and barbiturates do not avail in trying to break through this condition. On the tenth day a sodium amytal interview brings back his memories and awareness of personal identity, and reveals that he is unemployed, that he had a violent quarrel with his wife, and that he remembers nothing that happened between leaving his home after the quarrel and being approached by the policeman at the Hudson. Two weeks later the memory of this period too is recovered in a barbiturate interview: in the eight hours, he was walking the streets in a daze, full of gnawing uneasiness and guilt, and felt he must end it all; he was scarcely aware of the path he took to the Hudson, nor of any thoughts, but only of his daze, guilt, and the wish to end it all.

Thus the development of this case so far had two major phases: in the first phase, which lasted eight hours, the patient was dazed, possessed and driven by the sole experience of guilt and wish to end it all; the loss of personal identity had already occurred but he was not aware of it. The second phase, which was to last ten days, began when the policeman approached him and he suddenly became aware that he had lost his personal identity. Gill and I (1942) have pointed out the biphasic character of this development in certain amnesias; Gill noted the difference between the *loss of personal identity* of the first phase, and the *awareness of loss of identity* of the second phase. We noted the fugue character of the first phase and the amnesia for it, once the awareness of the loss of personal identity emerged. Restudying the literature of fugues and amnesias I (1942) found evidence to suggest that states of awareness of loss of identity are usually preceded by a fugue characterized by a loss of, or change of, personal identity without awareness of it, and in turn fugues are frequently followed by a period of awareness of loss of personal identity. These inferences were corroborated by Fisher (1945; Fisher and Joseph, 1949) on a series of consecutive cases in the Second World War.

Concerning the first phase, the fugue phase, or phase of loss of personal identity, the following points are of importance here: (1) it may be guided by a single central idea or wish to the exclusion from awareness of everything else, in which case the person is usually somewhat dazed, soon becomes conspicuous, is challenged, then becomes aware of his state of loss of identity, and the fugue phase proves of short duration; (2) the fugue state may be guided by a complex set of ideas, by a whole fantasy, which is normally unconscious; in which case a change of personal identity takes place—a point particularly stressed by Fisher. The person in such a state may remain altogether inconspicuous and the state may last as long as years. But this way of putting it certainly overstates the role of external interference with the fugue, understates the significance of the internal stability of a state of consciousness organized around a wish-fantasy, and certainly grossly underestimates the extent to which the wish-fantasy and the reality cues can be merely two aspects of one indivisible unity. —These two varieties of fugue are closely parallel with the two types of somnambulism discerned by Pierre Janet (1907): the monoideic and polyideic forms of somnambulism. Indeed the analogy does not seem purely formal, and the monoideic fugue does show features common with sleepwalking: its daze, its lack of capacity for reflection, etc. In turn, polyideic fugues—or in our terms, the states of changed personal identity—show a close relation to cases of multiple personality. (3) There are cases in which the fugue phase reduces to a short syncope, and the disorder consists of amnesia for the contents of the syncope and of the subsequent awareness of loss of personal identity.

No recent investigator of any of these conditions failed to recognize that all these states are closely related to dreams, in that they all act out an unconscious wish, just as the dream expresses one in symbolic form. That the dream was a next of kind was apparently easy to recognize. The difficulty lay rather, on the one hand, in determining what the specific differences were between the dream state and these states, and, on the other, among these various states. The state of sleep was held responsible for the form of expression of the wish in the dream. But the specific conditions for the expression of unconscious wishes in these other forms were not so readily discernible. I shall not, however, dwell on what psychoanalysis has helped us to learn about the dynamics of these specific conditions; our interest here lies rather in discerning their import for the study of consciousness.

Risking the danger of being considered facetious, I should like to relate a brief story from Popper-Lynkeus' *Phantasien eines Realisten* (1899). In this story the maiden of Corinth, who is adored and coveted by all men, becomes very disturbed because one man is unmoved by her charms and pays no attention to her. She requests to see him and asks him what gives him the strength to resist her powers, which no other man could ever withstand. His answer is: I am immune to the lure of women because I can image to myself how I would feel five minutes after having surrendered to their charms. Now I believe that this story is not just inappropriately facetious, but brings into focus something about the elusive experience of consciousness.

"Passion is blind," we are wont to say; and we mean that it admits of no reflection, consideration, or regard for circumstances and consequences.

Let us put it thus: it tends to obliterate our awareness of ideas and percepts other than those of the object of the passion. It strives to attain its object, brooking no interference, tolerating no delay or detour which circumspective reflection would recommend.

Now the fugue does the same: it acts out a wish in a more or less undisguised form. More or less undisguised—this phrase is made of rubber, because actually these wishes are so primitive that except for patricides, matricides, and rapes committed in fugues (and these are relatively rare), the fugue actions are usually highly symbolic actions which execute many strivings at once, in varying degrees of disguise. For example, the man in our example—so the psychiatric study showed—was motivated both by a rage implying murderous wishes toward his wife, and by guilt implying the wish for self-punishment. The suicidal form the wish for self-punishment took was also a violent blow to the wife who would then be bereft of the relief money which was her source of livelihood. This imperious impulse excludes awareness of everything else, and the fugue is therefore a loss of awareness of personal identity: most checks on impulses are suspended, and with these, awareness is also gone. Awareness, reflectiveness, appears to be a matter of the existence and effectiveness of controls over impulses.

Let me come to the second phase, the phase of awareness of loss of identity. Noteworthy are the following points: (a) the patient appears normal; in first approximation his sensorium and consciousness are unclouded and his thinking and memory good; (b) however, he has no recollection of anything pertaining to his personal identity, and he is aware of this fact and will show bewilderment and discomfort over it of individually varying degrees of intensity; (c) but closer study shows not only that his memory has selective gaps excluding cues to his personal identity, but that his current perception is also similarly selective—and in this sense his awareness now, though strikingly broader and superior in efficacy to that of the first phase, is still very limited. At times this limitation is of such extent that he does not recognize the need to stay in the hospital, and believes that he can get along by himself.

The problems we encounter here are similar to those so common in psychiatric experience: illnesses with and without the awareness of illness. The *"belle indifference"* of hysterics, the lack of illness awareness in many schizophrenias and in most paranoid disorders, in contrast to the illness awareness and suffering of most neurotics, all seem to belong to this context. Furthermore, the inability of people in depression—and of many in other types of distress—to envisage a time when they will be free of their suffering, is also a type of limitation of awareness that pertains to this context. Nor are we so-called "normals" free of occasional—to understate the issue—frames of mind in which we are unable to conceive of how we will ever be free of a presently plaguing distress: this is characteristic of certain kinds of physical pain experiences also.

In this second phase of amnesia all that was in consciousness in the first phase is gone, and awareness of personal identity is lost just as in the first phase, but awareness of this loss and of impersonal knowledge and thought is now feasible. We understand readily that impersonal knowledge will be available, and thinking feasible, once the imperious impulse is again under control, is banned. So we assume that impulse controls abandoned in the first phase were re-established. But what about the loss of personal identity —how are we to understand that? And what about the awareness of it that exists? The assumption that offers itself—and is supported by manifold clinical observations and by theory—is that the re-established impulse controls are brittle, and awareness of personal identity might easily revive the conflict which just recently ended in a breakdown of these controls. Therefore, conditions are created which forestall this danger, eliminate awareness of personal identity, demobilize by rigid control not only the impulse but whatever might serve as a stimulant to it, and as a noxious agent to the solidity of the re-established controls. I imagine that the biologists and physiologists in our group will not find it hard to suggest analogous biological processes subsequent to an organic injury. The often prolonged duration of this second phase itself seems to bear on, and on closer study may even bear out, this assumption. The fact that even after recovery of personal identity, the patient remains amnesic for the fugue period also appears to support the assumption. Indeed there is evidence to show that without recovery of the amnesia for the fugue state the patient is prone to produce other symptoms (conversions), and even a new fugue and loss of personal identity.

But this state of affairs shows that the control of impulses is not the only condition of awareness, nor (Rapaport, 1942) lack of such control the only limitation to awareness. True, once the impulse is not riding free of most controls, awareness of impersonal knowledge becomes possible, and even an awareness of the loss of personal identity emerges. But overcontrol eliminating an important segment—that pertaining to personal identity—of past experience, implying a demobilization of the motivations that would otherwise bring it to consciousness, limits awareness—as we have pointed out— to a dangerous degree. Thus not only the breakdown of controls, but excessively extensive and rigid control of motivations also limits awareness.

I have indicated, on the side, that states of loss of personal identity, as well as states of awareness of loss of personal identity, have many shadings and variants. I have also indicated that both are related to other psychopathological states and psychopathological and psychological phenomena which display yet other varieties of awareness. The first task for a scientific analysis of a phenomenon is to find the varieties of a phenomenon—as manifest forms of a dependent, or several dependent variables—from which we usually hope to infer the independent variables underlying them. Our considerations of amnesias and related phenomena seem to have provided us with a range of varieties of awareness—or of states of consciousness, if you like—and may thus be considered a first step in an effort toward clarifying the concept and functional relationships of consciousness and states of consciousness.

Would it be correct to suggest that our considerations did more than just collect a range of varieties of awareness? I do not know. I must admit that to my mind they did; moreover, I confess to the belief that to those steeped in clinical experience, and in the implicit postulates imposed by such work, it would. My doubts pertain to this point: I am not sure whether we are yet equipped to put the points I have in mind into forms required by the usual procedures of scientific inference. But in this respect I feel that where the usual methods would be paralyzing to inference, it is better to forget about them for the time being and recognize that other sciences too had their preliminary phases of development, and did not spring as ordered systems of inference from the blue, like Pallas from the head of Zeus: our science too is entitled to a productive, if not exact, phase rather than being doomed forever to sterile exactitude irrelevant to the phenomena studied.

I should like to submit that the material on amnesias suggests that:

(1) These varieties of awareness depend on impulses and their control as independent variables.

(2) The functional dependence in question is one in which maximal awareness correlates with optimal control of impulses, while both excessive lack of and excessive extent of controls correlate with limitations of awareness.

(3) The awareness and its varieties are only one of the characteristics of consciousness, and we have limited ourselves only to these, having touched only tangentially on thought content, thought form, reflectiveness, subjective experience of clarity, relation to reality, and not at all on other characteristic relationships of consciousness. Furthermore, even these forms of awareness were treated only in a gross fashion. Thus the functional relationships suggested must not be considered sufficient to account for all the varieties of awareness in particular, and certainly not for those of consciousness in general.

Let me now turn to the second example and present some details and some inferences from self-observation of hypnagogic hallucinations, reveries, and dreams which I have recorded. I do this with some uneasiness, both because of the feeling of extravagance of this kind of observation and the pitfalls attending it. The methodology of observations in which the object is at the same time the subject has never been worked out and thus the procedure is not in good repute. What I did was to train myself to rouse at night as much as possible after each dream, reverie, and hypnagogic hallucination, to record them. The state in which I recorded was one of drowsiness; I recorded in the dark, remaining in the supine position in which I aroused, and transcribed the record the next morning, in so far as I was able to: at times these records are unreadable. Writing under these conditions becomes to a considerable extent automatic: at times one knows and records that just a moment before one had been writing something and knows not what. The hand writes without any subjectively experienced decision or intent—just as one observes it sometimes in subjects doing automatic writing in hypnosis or otherwise.

One word about the reason for my undertaking such observations. For years I have studied varieties of thought processes. One of the puzzles I encountered was the—to my knowledge—common experience that in the course of ordered, and even problem-solving, thinking, there suddenly intrude apparently irrelevant memory images of past experiences. Psychoanalytic experience strongly suggests that these are not irrelevant but rather belong to the preparatory process of thought. My repeated attempts to clarify their role were unsuccessful, particularly because I could not gather a representative sample of them either from subjects or from my own experience. In self-observation the conscious intent to observe interfered. So I sought to make recordings under conditions in which *will, intention,* etc., seem to play a lesser role than in full waking consciousness. This then is how I came to make such recordings (cf. Varendonck, 1921).

I have only two sets of such recordings: one covering a period of seven weeks, the other a period of one week, more or less continuously. I consider these only preliminary explorations.[1] I would like to describe now what these records seem to add up to and then give one example from this material to illustrate a point. The study of these records shows that (1) they contain thought fragments which do not seem to differ from waking thought; (2) they contain segments about which I noted while recording that they are just like the daydreams into which I occasionally drift off, interrupting my regular work, in the daytime, and their character—as recorded—bears this out; (3) they contain material which is introduced by comments to the effect that I am unable to continue recording, sleepiness is catching up with me. I am apparently "falling off" to sleep, but I "come to" soon and record what passed while "falling off." These are usually called reveries or some of them "hypnagogic hallucinations." They vary greatly in length, and in character, some of them are like dreams, some quite unlike dreams; (4) these records contain dreams, but these also vary greatly in character: some of them are accompanied by the awareness that "this is just a dream," others seem quite "real." For the sake of tracing the continuity of these phenomena I would like to remind you of those dreams of schizophrenic and borderline schizophrenic cases which seem to the patient, even after awakening, to have been realities. Such I did not find in my recordings: I did find some, however, the mood or feeling of which lingered with me after awakening for a shorter or longer while.

These four kinds of experiences in the record are not vouched for only by

[1] [Rapaport never reported any further recordings of this kind—Ed.]

the subjectively experienced similarity to the waking, daydream, reverie, and dream experiences. There are other parameters which also appear to distinguish them.

First of all, in progressing from waking thought to dream the reflective awareness decreases. It is a commonplace that waking consciousness is characterized both by being aware of a content and by the possibility of becoming aware of the fact of this awareness. This is what I call here reflective awareness. Now, in the common dream there is no—or little—such possibility present: where there is some of it preserved, the dream is of the sort in which we are aware that "this is just a dream." The daydreams and reveries too have many varieties in this respect. They range from those which are so automatically recorded that there is no more trace of them than the awareness that there was an experience, to those which are clearly recognized to be translations into the language of the reverie or daydream of the thought at which the "falling off" began. An example of this is when I, while recording a dream, cannot remember the continuation of it and begin frantically to search for it. I become tense, "fall off," and the reverie I record is, "I am in a labyrinth, I search for a door, I can't find it, but I know if I find it, I will have the continuation of the dream."

There is here a continuum ranging from waking thought to dream—and in the progression toward the dream the reflective awareness, the awareness of awareness, progressively fades out. There are situations where there is definitely no reflective awareness, and others in which there is a very clear awareness of being aware of something happening.

Second, we have another rather vague parameter: the ability *to exert effort, to will.* The more closely the dream state is approximated, the less it is possible to exert voluntary effort. One of the indicators of this is in those notes which show that in such states close to the dreaming state the recording becomes extremely effortful and reveries of the content, "This is not important material, it need not be recorded," crop up. It is worth mentioning that Varendonck (1921) has also noted and reported this phenomenon.

Third, and most clearly, the differences between these states show up in the formal characteristics of thought, that is, in the form in which intrapsychic and external perceptions are represented in these various forms of consciousness.

There are many such formal characteristics of thought in which these forms of consciousness differ, and I will mention here only a few outstanding ones:

(a) The closer the thought to the waking form the more verbalized it is; the closer it is to the dream form the more visual imagery becomes its medium. I do not mean to imply that there is no visual imagery involved in waking thought, nor that there is no verbalization in dream thoughts: both are common, yet the preponderances are so striking that—well, it is one of those cases where you don't need a chi-square. I did not obtain a correlation coefficient either. This is not, however, the only formal characteristic of thought.

(b) As one proceeds from the waking toward the dream forms of thought, one finds that in the waking form the thought is explicit, in the dream forms it becomes implicative.

May I give an example of what I mean by implicative. This in a fragment of a dream: I am somewhere with my father and the record says, "I know he is now satisfied with me." And the record adds, "I do not know how I knew that: there was no external expression on him to show that."

This is an implicit experience. Such implicative forms are common in dreams while they are rare or absent in waking forms of thought.

(c) One set of the outstanding formal characteristics of waking thought is what we call logic. In dream thought its place is taken by forms like *pars pro toto, post hoc ergo propter hoc,* "What holds for the little, holds the more so for the big"—that is, by participatory (Lévy-Bruhl, 1923), syncretic (Piaget, 1927), animistic (Freud, 1913, especially pp. 865 ff.) forms; the so-called dream mechanisms, or mechanisms of the primary process: condensation, displacement, substitution, prevail here (Freud, 1900; see also Rapaport, 1950). It is not that we do not find in waking thought such aberrations of logic (e.g., wishful thinking, poetic expression, etc.), nor is the dream free of waking logic, as represented by "secondary elaboration" (see Freud, 1900, pp. 455–467), but progressing from the waking state to the dream state, the rôle of logic becomes less, and that of the above-mentioned forms increasingly greater.

I am implying that we are dealing here with continuous transitions where one cannot draw any hard and fast dividing lines. I cannot say that up to here these are hypnagogic hallucinations and here begin the daydreams, because I have records where daydreams shade in the middle into such hallucinations, to become at the end again like daydreams. In other words, what was described by Freud as the contrast between the primary and the secondary processes is clearly there in these observations, but with a continuous transition between these two forms. It is always a question of more or less.

By the way—just for the sake of those who might wonder—it so happens that Freud was aware of this (1900, pp. 536, 459).

(d) There are also definite changes of syntax as one progresses toward the dream state. It seems that the conjunctions tend to fall out more and more, and the position usually accorded to what is syntactically important in a sentence tends to be taken by what is psychologically outstanding (compare Vigotsky, 1939).

Let me not dwell further on these parameters. It is late. Let me give one example. I hope it will illustrate some of the differences between the varieties of consciousness. In this example I have been recording a dream I just had. I am halfway with my recording, when partly sleepiness and partly a re-experiencing of the tension of the dream becomes intolerable and I "fall off" into a reverie. The reverie retranslates into its language partly the tension state I experienced while recording and partly the dream content I was recording. I would like to anticipate an objection: it could be argued that this last assertion is arbitrary and misuses a chance analogy between a dream and an experience that took place while recording it on the one hand, and a reverie succeeding these on the other. This is an argument hard to refute. Those experienced in working with dreams will not be concerned with this argument. To those not so experienced I can only say that if this were a singular observation, their argument would have some weight. But I found over a score of such sequences in the records I am discussing.

The record of the dream begins as follows: I am going to an examination at the University. I am supposed to be there at eight o'clock. It is five minutes of eight and I am afraid I will be late to the examination. I arrive at the main door. The University seems strange, it is not like my Alma Mater, so I do not know where to go for the examination and my tension that I will be late mounts. I go to the janitor to find out where my examination is to take place. I ask the janitor. He begins to stutter in a most terrible way (my question and his stuttering are "implicit" only) and I get more and more tense—to a point where I feel like bursting. The recording of the dream is interrupted at this point and the continuation of the dream, which is of no importance to us here, follows later in the record.

First I dreamt the dream to the end. Then I aroused myself to a state just awake enough to scribble. I recorded the dream up to the point described above. The record indicates at that point that I felt extremely tense. I "fell off," the dream recording was interrupted and an interpolated reverie occurred, which is reflected in the record as follows: first there came in the record a series of words, or letter combinations which sounded like distorted Latin, Greek, Hebraic, Arabic words. These were followed by the comment: "I do not understand." Then: "A father in a monastery, panting, says to his son, 'I am so glad you got in before they shut the door.'" The distorted foreign words were verbal images; the rest partly visual, partly verbal. After this the record of the dream is resumed and completed.

What happened? At the point of the highest tension I could not maintain the level of consciousness necessary for recording (reflective remembering and motor action). I "fell off." The tension was related to the fear that in the dream expressed itself in the danger of being delayed by the janitor's stuttering from arriving at the examination, which in turn was represented in the reverie by the garbled, foreign sounding words, which I could no more understand than the stuttering of the janitor. The rest of the hypnagogic reverie re-represents the dream wish in a simplified fashion, in the form language of the reverie: a father says to his son in a monastery, "I am so glad that you got in." This wish fulfillment occurs on the level on which the manifest content of the dream expressed the fear. Only the "father," "son," and "monastery" carry distant vestiges of the latent dream thought and wish which are clear in the here omitted ending of the dream.

The example shows a translation of subjective tension as well as of dream content and thought into hypnagogic reverie. Though for brevity's sake and other reasons many details of the dream are here omitted, the increased rôle of verbalization and explicitness in reverie are illustrated; the difference in the formal characteristics of thought is most obvious in the image of the University which simultaneously *is* and *is not* my Alma Mater (the rule of the excluded third [2] is here suspended).

Another example: I have "lost" a dream after which I have just awoken. I am making a great effort to find it and I still have its feeling tone with me. In the effort I get very tense and "fall off." In the reverie that follows I see something like a linear wave advancing in its own line direction. I feel that it must reach a certain (ill-defined) point in the water and it depends on the effort I am making whether it will get there. (I am exerting great effort.)

Similar observations were made and reported previously by Silberer, around 1910 and 1911.

For curiosity's sake, I would like to mention that in states very close to dream states, at times the record takes on the form of a conversation between two parts of a multiple personality (cf. Prince, 1921, especially Chapter XVIII, and Erickson and Kubie, 1939, 1940). There are six examples of this in the records I obtained. What generalizations can one make about such observations? When there is no, or a decreased amount of, external stimulation available or admitted to consciousness, the internal motivations come more and more to expression in consciousness. Paralleling the degree to which external stimulations are admitted to consciousness, we find form varieties of consciousness differing from each other in decreasing availability of reflective awareness, verbalization, syntax, logic, explicitness, and effort.

Well, the two examples I have given so far, I believe, have both shown some varieties of reflective awareness. In the first example the emphasis was on gross, directly observable varieties of awareness: fugues (loss of personal identity *without* awareness of this); loss of personal identity *with* awareness of this; retrograde amnesia for the fugues. The second example dealt with more subtle varieties of consciousness and focused on several parameters, particularly on the varieties of formal characteristics of thought, that go with these varieties of consciousness.

The third example will center on yet another, and in some ways, even more subtle, set of variations of consciousness. I came to label these *varieties of conscious experience*. I will set out from an example of pathology to illustrate these. The Korsakoff syndrome is usually considered to be characterized by progressive forgetting of recent experiences (anterograde amnesia), confabulations, and emotional lability (Korsakoff, 1890, 1891;

[2] [See Chapter 8, n. 2—Ed.]

Bonhöffer, 1901; Rapaport, 1942). It was originally considered to be the psychological concomitant of polyneuritis due to chronic alcoholism. In the last four decades it has become clear that it may accompany almost any condition associated with organic brain damage: it was found as a sequel or concomitant of traumatic brain injury, strangulation, carbon-monoxide poisoning, general paresis, senility, etc. The picture of the syndrome also changed in this period, except in the minds of our textbook writers. This change is mentioned here because the main features of the syndrome I shall describe are not in the textbooks.

Pick (1915), Grünthal (1923), Bürger (1927), Betlheim and Hartmann (1924), Hartmann (1930), Schilder (1925, 1930), Bürger-Prinz and Kaila (1930) have described the phenomena I shall discuss and my own studies have borne out what they described and suggested.

If we give a Korsakoff patient stories to recall, more likely than not we will find that some of these stories he will recall as happenings belonging to his own life experience (Betlheim and Hartmann, 1924). At the least we will encounter—in our inquiry into this or that detail of the stories—responses like this: "I do not know—I wasn't there" (Bürger-Prinz and Kaila, 1930). These responses indicate that the patient took the story, if not for his personal experience, then at least for a historical event and not for the material of a memory test.

In their recall of stories, as well as in their conversation, we find them "confabulating," that is, "making up" as they go along, parts of the story, or parts of the events or facts they are relating (Schilder, 1930; Bürger-Prinz and Kaila, 1930). Their recall and conversation are studded with fragments which impress one—and duly so—as if fragments of their daydreams had replaced parts of what they were about, but were unable, to recall or to converse about (Schilder, 1930). The German literature called this *"Verlegenheitsconfabulation"* (confabulations of embarrassment): "memory" not supplying the next step in recall or conversation, "fancy" steps in and provides a replacement. Moreover, the patient—once he has created such a confabulation—is likely to perseverate with it and to regard his momentary brain child as fully real (Bürger-Prinz and Kaila, 1930).

But these phenomena are not exclusive to Korsakoff cases, though they are characteristic of them and striking in them. Pick (1915) reports similar observations on normal people emerging from ether anesthesia. It is a known fact that cases of the disorder pseudologia fantastica do actually believe their fancies to be realities. It is also known that some of us "normal people" are prone to do, and under certain conditions all of us are capable of doing, what the foot soldier of the fable did who spoke so often about his fancied horse that finally he was convinced that he was a hussar.

There is a similarity between these phenomena and the Wolf-Gibson type of experiment. The completion of broken figures, however, seems to abide by a simple set of rules: the completion tends either to closure, or to "Prägnanz," or to similarity with something known before. The theoretical explanation of these—in gestalt psychology—is based on the isomorphism hypothesis (Koffka, 1935). Now the "completions" to which we referred here as confabulations have a wish fulfillment of a sort present in all daydreams as their content. Schilder (1930) has demonstrated this particularly. The similarity on the observational level does not seem so obvious as soon as we come to the explanatory level.

These examples taken from, or related to, the phenomena of the Korsakoff syndrome lead us to a new set of characteristics of consciousness. This set of characteristics was well known to the act psychology of Brentano (1874) and its successors, as well as to the phenomenological philosophy of Husserl (1921), Meinong (1902, 1914), etc. At present some existentialist philosophers make of it a poorly understood chapter of their metaphysics (see Sartre, 1948; Rapaport, 1949). The characteristics in question are these: we can be aware of a door as a percept, as a memory of one, as a thought, as a general knowledge, as pure imagery, as a dream or daydream image, as an illusion, as a delusion, as a "déjà vu" phenomenon, and—so as not to stretch this enumeration too long—as various combinations and degrees of certainty of each of these.

Furthermore, an idea we have in our consciousness may be experienced by us as a fact, an assumption, as something false that is negated, as something doubted, as something hoped for, etc. These infinitely multitudinous and infinitely subtle varieties of conscious experience play a decisive rôle in the ability of our thinking to orient us correctly in the infinitely complex and changing reality we are facing. Let us remind ourselves how when we studied a foreign language and had not yet assimilated those turns of it which are evocative of some of these varieties of conscious experience, we were lost in deciding whether what we were reading was a fact, a memory, or an opinion. I remember clearly my own difficulties with the Latin *oratio recta* and *oratio obliqua* (direct and indirect discourse) of 30 years ago. Let us also remind ourselves that the difference between a sense of humor and the lack of it depends proximally on whether the appropriate variety of conscious experience can be mobilized by the person, or whether he will take it all "seriously."

Schilder (1930) has shown that these varieties of conscious experience play a crucial rôle in the function of judgment. "Poor judgment," the clinical phrase that describes a form of pathology so characteristic of most psychiatric conditions of gross organic etiology (Rapaport, Gill, and Schafer, 1945), results at least in part from an impoverishment of the range of varieties of conscious experience that can be evoked, and upon an unreliability of the coordination of reality changes with varieties of conscious experience evoked by them. It is demonstrable that these varieties of conscious experience lie at the core of the functions Freud described by the concepts *reality principle, reality testing,* and judgment in "Formulations Regarding the

Two Principles in Mental Functioning" (1911). Freud had demonstrated that one crucial aspect of mental development may be conceptualized as a progressive transition from what he called the primary process to the secondary process, the former being characterized by the striving for immediate, even if hallucinatory, gratification of needs, the latter by delay of such gratification, detour from the direct, dangerous, or hallucinatory path to a search for the possibility of gratification in reality. He formulated: the primary process abides by the pleasure principle, the secondary process by the reality principle. The primary process operates by condensations, displacements, symbolizations, tolerates contradictions, as, for example, in dreams; while secondary-process thought operates more or less by logic, syntax, the rule of the excluded third, the law of contradictions. The development of the varieties of conscious experience here discussed is a salient part of the development of the secondary process abiding by the reality principle (see Freud, 1900; Rapaport, 1950).

Pick (1915), Grünthal (1923), and Schilder (1930) demonstrated that the Korsakoff patient, once he has a content in consciousness, cannot bring into consciousness other knowledge contrary to or modifying it; that his thinking is—as it were—linear, without side streams that would amplify, correct, modify, negate it. That is, however, just what varieties of conscious experience do automatically in our thinking. Let us also realize that in the fugues it is this very modification, correction, amplification, that does not occur.

To complicate matters, let us realize that one of the implications of Pick's, Grünthal's, and Schilder's views, as well as of the conception of varieties of conscious experience, is that consciousness has qualitative varieties of reflectiveness. The pathological linearity of thinking these authors describe is in essence a description of an awareness, the content of which is not reflected against and modified by reflection against other thoughts. In turn the varieties of conscious experience indeed imply a reflecting of the content of consciousness against various organized, not necessarily conscious, contexts. It is always worth noting that most of these varieties of consciousness have a whole range of degrees of certainty with which they may appear.

Consciousness from the point of view of the clinician is not a mere descriptive term. I have given three illustrations of the great variability of the phenomenon of consciousness. The question is: Can we reduce these varieties to a common denominator? So far, I believe, only one general attempt has been made to that end. It was the attempt made by Freud in Chapter VII of *The Interpretation of Dreams* (1900). Freud's theory may be summed up as follows (Rapaport, 1950; Lewy and Rapaport, 1944).

All psychological happening is motivated, that is, ultimately it serves the purpose of diminishing a tension. The quantity of the tension in question is termed cathexis (charge). Drives, needs, strivings, interests, are terms to describe such cathexes, their origins, and their direction, that is, the goal object on which these cathexes can be discharged.

There is some evidence to show that early in ontogeny when the drive cathexis cannot be discharged, because the drive object is not present, a hallucinatory image of previous discharge situations (gratifications) arises. This is the primitive prototype of all conscious experience. It corresponds to the drive cathecting of the memory trace of gratification. In the adult when dreaming, when in dire deprivation (starvation, dehydration), when sick (delusions, hallucinations), or when in special states (drugs, hypnosis), etc., this primitive prototypic form of conscious experience appears again. One of the salient characteristics of this form of conscious experience is that something intrapsychic (the goal of motivation) appears in consciousness as if it were a perception of external reality. Another salient feature of it is that the perceptions (and thoughts) which become thus conscious do not abide by logic but by a prelogic (such as that described by the dream mechanisms: condensation, displacement, substitution, symbolization, etc.), based on the syncretic, diffuse, and undifferentiated character of primitive perception (and memory trace; Werner, 1926). In fugues we see one manifestation of this type of consciousness: the drive need is imperious and the ideas expressing it monopolize consciousness.

Later on in ontogeny, the delay of drive discharge does not result in hallucinatory ideation monopolizing consciousness. Intrapsychic controls develop, and not only the object of the drive but objects which lead in reality to the gratifying object, or facilitate getting to it, also enter consciousness (Rapaport, 1951b). *Delay* of discharge and *detour* from the direct path to gratification become possible (Freud, 1911). This is a slow, gradual development, which parallels the differentiation of external perception and is to a great extent dependent on it. This development establishes a harmonious relationship and unity between the consciousness of external perception and the consciousness of the gratifying objects and those leading toward it. The cathexes which originally were drive cathexes become bound in the organizations controlling drive discharge. They no longer press for instantaneous discharge. The function of delay has given rise to delaying structures. The controlled motivations are still directed toward discharging their cathexes. But they can be delayed in doing so. The controlling structures have cathexes bound up in them. These cathexes, termed hypercathexes or attention cathexes, now play a crucial rôle in relation to consciousness (Rapaport, 1951a, Part VII). The "sense organ" consciousness regulates the distribution of these attention cathexes. Without a cathecting by these, ideas do not become conscious. The study of the phenomena of repression has amply demonstrated this. The attention cathexes are allocated to external perceptions and to memory traces and thereby these become conscious. A drive tension which rises to discharge-threshold intensity will attract attention cathexis, will spread to memories of objects and experiences related to the drive object. The relationships themselves thus become conscious and through them an experiment (we call it a thought process) occurs which establishes the best avenue to the goal (gratification). The drive discharge is in the meanwhile delayed until this experiment is completed, then "the sluices of motility are opened"—as it were—and discharging action guided by the completed thought process takes place (Freud, 1900, 1915a, 1915b).

The gradual development from thought as "hallucinatory gratification" to thought as "experimental action" reflects the gradual development from monoideic consciousness of the drive gratification to polyideic consciousness of the relation of perceived external reality, internal need, and memories of past experiences. The gradual development corresponds to varieties or forms of consciousness in which various balances are struck between perception of internal and external reality, in which internal experience is to various (ever-decreasing) degrees experienced as external reality, and in which internal and external perception (thought and perception of reality) are differentiated with increasing clarity. Correspondingly, the thought forms consciously experienced change gradually from prelogical to logical, from syncretic to abstract, from idiosyncratic to socialized (Werner, 1926). (The rôle of interpersonal relationships, communication, and socialization in this process is grossly underplayed here for the sake of simplicity of presentation; Rapaport, 1951a). This gradual development is reflected in those forms of conscious experience which I have described in reporting on the preliminary studies of my recordings of dreams, reveries, daydreams, etc.

When thought has reached the differentiation where it appears as experimental action, exploring reality for the safest and most feasible path toward gratification, it has attained a complex organization of safeguards guaranteeing a correct appraisal of reality and a sharp distinction of wish and reality, certainty and uncertainty, etc. It is this complex organization that is reflected in those varieties of conscious experience which I have described above in connection with the Korsakoff syndrome, in which these safeguards are to a considerable extent put out of action by the pathological process.

REFERENCES

Abeles, M., & Schilder, P. (1935). Psychogenetic Loss of Personal Identity: Amnesia. *Arch. Neurol. Psychiat.,* 34:587–604.

Betlheim, S., & Hartmann, H. (1924). On Parapraxes in the Korsakoff Psychosis. In *Organization and Pathology of Thought,* ed. & tr. D. Rapaport. New York: Columbia University Press, 1951, pp. 288–307.

Bonhöffer, K. (1901). *Die akuten Geisteskrankheiten der Gewohnheitstrinker.* Jena: Fischer.

Brentano, F. (1874). *Psychologie vom empirischen Standpunkte.* Leipzig: Dunker & Humbolt.

Bürger, H. (1927). Zur Psychologie des amnestischen Symptomenkomplexes. *Arch. Psychiat. Nervenk.,* 81:348–352.

Bürger-Prinz, H., & Kaila, M. (1930). On the Structure of the Amnesic Syndrome. In *Organization and Pathology of Thought,* ed. & tr. D. Rapaport. New York: Columbia University Press, 1951, pp. 650–686.

Erickson, M. H., & Kubie, L. S. (1939). The Permanent Relief of an Obsessional Phobia by Means of Communications with an Unsuspected Dual Personality. *Psychoanal. Quart.,* 8:471–509.

———, & Kubie, L. S. (1940). The Translation of the Cryptic Automatic Writing of One Hypnotic Subject by Another in a Trance-like Dissociated State. *Psychoanal. Quart.,* 9:51–63.

Fisher, C. (1945). Amnesic States in War Neuroses: The Psychogenesis of Fugues. *Psychoanal. Quart.,* 14:437–468.

——— (1947). The Psychogenesis of Fugue States. *Amer. J. Psychother.,* 1:211–220.

———, & Joseph, E. (1949). Fugue with Awareness of Loss of Personal Identity. *Psychoanal. Quart.,* 18:480–493.

Freud, S. (1900). The Interpretation of Dreams, tr. A. A. Brill. *The Basic Writings.* New York: Modern Library, 1938, pp. 179–549.

——— (1911). Formulations Regarding the Two Principles in Mental Functioning. *Collected Papers,* 4:13–21. New York: Basic Books, 1959.

——— (1913 [1912–13]). Totem and Taboo, tr. A. A. Brill. *The Basic Writings.* New York: Modern Library, 1938, pp. 805–930.

——— (1915a). Repression. *Collected Papers,* 4:84–97. New York: Basic Books, 1959.

——— (1915b). The Unconscious. *Collected Papers,* 4:98–136. New York: Basic Books, 1959.

Geleerd, E., Hacker, F., & Rapaport, D. (1945). Contribution to the Study of Amnesia and Allied Conditions. *Psychoanal. Quart.,* 14:199–220.

Gill, M. M., & Rapaport, D. (1942). A Case of Amnesia and Its Bearing on the Theory of Memory. *This volume,* Chapter 9.

Grünthal, E. (1923). Zur Kenntnis der Psychopathologie des Korsakowschen Symptomenkomplexes. *Monatschr. Psychiat. Neurol.,* 53:89–132.

Hartmann, H. (1930). Gedächtnis und Lustprinzip. Untersuchungen an Korsakoffkranken. *Z. Neurol. Psychiat.,* 126:496–519.

Husserl, E. (1921). *Logische Untersuchungen,* 2 vols. Halle: Niemeyer.

Janet, P. (1907). *The Major Symptoms of Hysteria.* London: Macmillan.

Koffka, K. (1935). *Principles of Gestalt Psychology.* New York: Harcourt, Brace.

Korsakoff, S. (1890). Über eine besondere Form psychischer Stoerung. *Arch. Psychiat.,* 21:669–704.

——— (1891). Erinnerungstaeuschungen (Pseudoreminiszenzen) bei polyneuritischer Psychose. *Allg. Z Psychiat. Neurol.,* 47:390–410.

Lévy-Bruhl, L. (1923). *Primitive Mentality.* London: Allen & Unwin.

Lewy, E., & Rapaport, D. (1944). The Psychoanalytic Concept of Memory and Its Relation to Recent Memory Theories. *This volume,* Chapter 12.

Meinong, A. (1902). Über Annahmen. *Z. Psychol.,* Suppl. Vol. 2. Leipzig: Barth.

———— (1914). *Gesammelte Abhandlungen. I. Abhandlungen zur Psychologie.* Leipzig: Barth.

Piaget, J. (1927). *The Child's Conception of Physical Causality.* London: Kegan, 1930.

Pick, A. (1915). Beiträge zur Pathologie des Denkverlaufes beim Korsakoff. *Z. Neurol. Psychiat.,* 28:344–383.

Popper-Lynkeus, J. (1899). *Phantasien eines Realisten.* Dresden: Carl Reissner, 1922.

Prince, M. (1921). *The Unconscious,* rev. ed. New York: Macmillan.

Rapaport, D. (1942). *Emotions and Memory,* 2nd unaltered ed. New York: International Universities Press, 1950.

———— (1949). Review of Jean-Paul Sartre, *The Psychology of Imagination. This volume,* Chapter 25.

———— (1950). On the Psychoanalytic Theory of Thinking. *This volume,* Chapter 28.

———— ed & tr. (1951a). *Organization and Pathology of Thought.* New York: Columbia University Press.

———— (1951b). Paul Schilder's Contribution to the Theory of Thought Processes. *This volume,* Chapter 32.

———— Gill, M. M., & Schafer, R. (1945). *Diagnostic Psychological Testing,* Vol. I. Chicago: Year Book Publishers.

Sartre, J.-P. (1948). *The Psychology of Imagination.* New York: Philosophical Library.

Schilder, P. (1925). *Introduction to a Psychoanalytic Psychiatry.* New York: Nerv. Ment. Dis. Monogr. Series, No. 50, 1928.

———— (1930). Studies Concerning the Psychology and Symptomatology of General Paresis. In *Organization and Pathology of Thought,* ed. & tr. D. Rapaport. New York: Columbia University Press, 1951, pp. 519–580.

Schrötter, K. (1911). Experimental Dreams. In *Organization and Pathology of Thought,* ed. & tr. D. Rapaport. New York: Columbia University Press, 1951, pp. 234–248.

Silberer, H. (1909). Report on a Method of Eliciting and Observing Certain Symbolic Hallucination-Phenomena. In *Organization and Pathology of Thought,* ed. & tr. D. Rapaport. New York: Columbia University Press, 1951, pp. 195–207.

———— (1912a). On Symbol-Formation. In *Organization and Pathology of Thought,* ed. & tr. D. Rapaport. New York: Columbia University Press, 1951, pp. 208–233.

———— (1912b). Symbolik des Erwachens und Schwellensymbolik überhaupt. *Jhb. Psychoanal. Psychopath. Forsch.,* 3:621–660.

Varendonck, J. (1921). The Psychology of Daydreams. In (abridged) *Organization and Pathology of Thought,* ed. & tr. D. Rapaport. New York: Columbia University Press, 1951, pp. 451–473.

Vigotsky, L. S. (1939). Thought and Speech. *Psychiatry,* 2:29–54.

Werner, H. (1926). *Comparative Psychology of Mental Development.* New York: Harper, 1940.

34

THE CONCEPTUAL MODEL
OF PSYCHOANALYSIS

I. ON SOME PROPOSED MODELS

The building of conceptual models is again in the center of the psychologist's theoretical interests. It appears that psychologists are losing confidence in the last vestiges of the association model, and in the conditioning model which for so long has been dominant. Allport's (1935–47), Krech's (1949, 1950a, 1950b, 1951), and Stagner's (1951) papers, and Hebb's (1949) volume, suggest that this loss of confidence derives from the ever-broadening impact of observations—mainly clinical—pertaining to motivations; the models seem to be incapable of comprehending the increasingly embarrassing richness of motivational data.

We may infer this of the gestalt model of Prägnanz-closure (Koffka, 1935), with its Köhler corollary of isomorphism (Köhler, 1923), since Krech and Hebb find it necessary to introduce a thoroughgoing neural model to account for motivational data; the Lewinian tension-system model

First published in Journal of Personality, 20:56–81, 1951. Reprinted in George S. Klein and David Krech, eds., Theoretical Models in Psychology. Durham, N. C.: Duke University Press, 1952, pp. 56–81; and in Robert P. Knight and Cyrus R. Friedman, eds., Psychoanalytic Psychiatry and Psychology, Clinical and Theoretical Papers, Austen Riggs Center, Volume I. New York: International Universities Press, 1954, pp. 221–247. Spanish translation published in Merton M. Gill and David Rapaport, Aportaciones a la Teoría y Técnica Psicoanalítica. Asociación Psicoanalítica Mexicana, A.C., 1962, pp. 58–96.

(Lewin, 1926, 1935) and its hodological-space corollary (Lewin, 1936, 1938), even though specifically designed for such data, is found unsatisfactory by Krech (1949) in his crusade for a neural model; it is of little importance to Hebb's (1949) theory.

Allport (1947) attacks what he calls the genetic model, which is apparently both the conditioning model and the infant model of psychoanalysis; he argues justly—at least *prima facie*—that the motivations of rat and infant lack what is most characteristic in human motivation, and to encompass this he introduces what might be called the intention model. This conception—leaning considerably on Brentano's (1874) act psychology—falls short of becoming a model, at least to my understanding, though it demonstrates vividly what is *not* encompassed by other models. Of similar portent is his attack on Boring (1946) as a proponent of the machine model. The machine model too has many new advocates in this day of cybernetics (Wiener, 1949; Frank, 1948; Brillouin, 1949; Förster, 1949): it is just possible that part of the impetus for model building derives from the threat of the modern Frankenstein monsters, the calculators.

Krech and Stagner alike refer motivated behavior to dynamic systems of some sort, and recognize that definite hierarchic relationships of these systems must be hypothesized if they are to serve as the explanatory constructs of behavior. Krech and Stagner differ, however, in that while the latter speaks of homeostatic systems in general, the former refers to neural systems in particular; the latter relates to these systems as if they were fairly well understood, the former as if their exploration were only beginning; the latter seems to speak—at least by implication—of "closed systems," while the former speaks definitely and with emphasis of "open systems" (Bertalanffy, 1950; Brillouin, 1949); the latter seems to imply a conditioning theory of learning as a subordinate theory, the former does not. I forego discussing here Hebb's (1949) position in these respects, because it would require extensive treatment.

This cursory discussion of a few papers dealing with conceptual models for psychological theory brings out the fact that we have:

(1) both a complacency with (Stagner), and a dissatisfaction with (Krech), psychological models;

(2) both an eclectic complacency with the conditioning model (Stagner), and a determined rejection of it (Allport);

(3) both a determined demand for a psychological and human model, however vague (Allport), and an equally determined demand for a purely neural model (Krech), for the hypothetical constructs of psychology;

(4) both a partial neural model which does not embrace motivational phenomena (Köhler), and an imperious neural model which is intended to do away with the cognition-motivation dichotomy (Krech);

(5) both a determined rejection of the machine model (Allport), and a vigorous and in many ways potentially fruitful pursuit of it (Wiener; McCulloch and Pitts, 1947);

(6) attacks on the purely psychological models of psychoanalysis (Lewin) on the grounds that they are either not "neural" enough (Krech) or not "human" enough (Allport);

(7) both models which treat the dynamic substratum of human behavior as "closed" thermodynamic systems (Stagner), and models which, considering this method not sufficiently up-to-date, treat it as "open" thermodynamic systems (Krech). (For the distinction see Bertalanffy, Brillouin, etc.) The disagreements between the model makers dwarf all their agreements—except one: that model making is necessary.

II. FAVORING A PURELY PSYCHOLOGICAL MODEL

I am not embarking on the task of creating a new model, but only of spelling out the psychoanalytic one, which to my knowledge has never been explicitly done. Nevertheless, I feel obliged to state my belief as to its position in relation to other models.

The psychoanalytic model is a purely psychological one, yet to my mind is sufficiently flexible to meet the requirements the others were created to meet. I should not like to be misunderstood on this point. I am not implying that psychoanalysis has the answers to all psychological questions, nor that its answers to the questions it has tackled so far are necessarily correct, nor that it has no limitations in regard to quantitative treatment. I am asserting only that the conceptual model implicit to psychoanalysis is sufficiently broad and flexible to embrace on the one hand those realms of psychological phenomena which other models effectively conceptualize, and on the other those realms which have remained intractable to them.

This I realize is a grandiose claim, and I do not expect to substantiate it in this presentation; the purpose of this essay—as I understand it—is to present models. My purpose is to call the reader's attention to the fact that the model to be presented has such a claim. I am not the first to advance it: Hartmann (1939) and others have stated it more explicitly than they have the model itself.

The only point which I wish to discuss in this connection is the purely psychological character of the model to be presented, since recently Tolman (1949), Hebb, and Krech have gone to bat for neural models and against purely psychological ones.

It is becoming the vogue to invoke physicists in discussing conceptual models for psychology. They are invoked on "open systems," on "feedback" mechanisms, but rarely on their attempts to deal with biological issues.

Recently several physicists (e.g., Schrödinger, 1945; Delbrueck, 1949) have concerned themselves with biology. They have pointed out that biological events, unlike those of physics, are time-bound and historical, and therefore cannot be treated with the usual methods of physics. They have concluded that the study of biological phenomena may necessitate new physical concepts. Delbrueck has suggested that to account for the biological realm of observations we may have to sacrifice our demand for description in quantum-theoretical terms, just as in accounting for the behavior of the atom we had to sacrifice our demand for exact determination of the locus and/or momentum of the individual electron. They have stressed that biological phenomena can be expressed—and already have been, as in genetics—by valid biological laws despite our ignorance of the underlying and mediating physicochemical processes. Actually, these views expressed by physicists are quite like the arguments of molar behaviorists, and seem to hold for psychology also.

Putting it more directly, I feel that psychological observations should be integrated on their own terms and by constructs built on the basis of psychological models. Whether the results so reached can or cannot be directly related to a neural substratum is an important question, and, as such, a subject matter for empirical exploration. But first a theory which embraces the psychological observations on hand must be evolved, and so far no model has provided a conceptual framework which does not disregard many areas of existing observation.

For these reasons, I am interested in the purely psychological model of psychoanalysis.

III. CONCERNING THE PSYCHOANALYTIC MODEL

The psychoanalytic model is intended to account for both those processes characteristic of the developing individual, and those characteristic of the mature one (Hartmann and Kris, 1945). Therefore it is easiest presented dichotomously: first the primary model, and then the secondary model which—so to speak—arises from it. The dichotomy is a matter of presentation, and the transition between the processes each half describes is fluid. The primary model is as necessary to account for many normal and pathological processes in the adult (dreams, illusions, hallucinations) as for the processes of early psychological development. Actually, it could be said that the primary model is merely an abortive form of the secondary one, and the two are an indivisible unity, linking together phenomena qualitatively as diverse as infantile rage and intentional, value-regulated, goal-seeking adult behavior.

The psychoanalytic model is intended to account for all the phenomena traditionally categorized trichotomously under the headings: conation, cognition, affection. This model considers the phenomena so segregated to be merely aspects of a unitary process. Nevertheless, available language and custom make it convenient to use this terminology, and in so far as it is used here it is meant to refer not to three kinds of processes, but to aspects of a unitary process. This is particularly important since it will be convenient to discuss the psychoanalytic model in terms of this trichotomy, and if the unity here suggested is not kept in mind the impression may be that the conative model is the basic one, with the cognitive and affective ones only subsidiary. Actually they form a unity in which none is conceivable without the others.

The presentation to follow will be in six main sections, three presenting the primary models of conation, cognition, and affection, and three presenting the secondary models.

The psychoanalytic model proper, however, embraces all six in a unity. Without attempting to explain here, I will state it (see Diagram A).

Diagram A
THE PSYCHOANALYTIC MODEL

$$\text{Need} \longrightarrow \left\{ \begin{array}{l} \text{Need-Satisfying Object} \\ \text{and/or Delay} \end{array} \right\} \longrightarrow \left\{ \begin{array}{l} \text{Need Gratification and/or} \\ \text{Affect Discharge and/or} \\ \text{Ideation (of Goals and Means)} \end{array} \right\}$$

IV. A PRIMITIVE MODEL OF CONATION

I submit that the primary psychoanalytic model of conation derives from the following behavior sequence observed in the infant:

> *restlessness* → *appearance of breast and sucking* → *subsidence of* *restlessness* (Freud, 1900, esp. pp. 508–509, and 1911, esp. p. 14).

Restlessness is conceptualized as tension, and this in turn is conceived as having its source in a drive; breast and sucking are conceptualized as tension-lowering means and activity, and are related to the drive as its object and discharge; subsidence of restlessness is conceptualized as tension subsidence, and is related to the drive as its gratification.

Another specifically psychoanalytic conceptualization of this basic observational model is the generalization of tension as *pain,* and of tension subsidence as *pleasure;* the direction implicit to the model is conceptualized as the pain-pleasure principle, or simply as the pleasure principle. Here pleasure and pain are concepts, and need not coincide with subjective experience (e.g., Freud, 1920, esp. pp. 1–7). In this entire conceptual structure, the drive is that which is usually conceptualized in psychological literature as *motivation.* The pleasure principle is then the conceptual expression of the directional aspect of this motivation.

Yet another conceptualization of the observational model—though not specifically psychoanalytic—generalizes tension as *disequilibrium;* breast and sucking as means and activity directed at *restoring equilibrium;* subsidence of tension as *equilibrium restored.*

The historical connection of the specifically psychoanalytic conceptualizations to Fechner and Helmholtz, and of the equilibrium conception to Cannon's homeostasis, cannot be traced here.

From the point of view of psychoanalysis this model is that of discharge activity; from the general psychological point of view, this is *the conative model.* Our next step is to demonstrate that the conceptual model of psychoanalysis derives cognition and affection from the same observational model.

Before turning to the cognitive and affective models, I should like to consider the nature and status of such an observational model. To serve as an effective one it is not necessary that the observational sequence be of general validity, that is, always be present in its entirety whenever any part of it is observed. Indeed, it is not necessary that such a model be based on an *observational* sequence; it can well be based on a hypothetical construction, so long as it systematically coordinates the constructs to be used and holds out the hope that a realm of phenomena can rather completely be referred back to it.

At this point the question arises: what does "refer back to it" mean? It means that verifiable deductions from the model and from the concepts must be possible: this is the portent of the hypothetico-deductive method. Is it necessary that these deductions be expressible in quantitative terms, and verifiable experimentally? It would seem that this is desirable, but often neither possible nor necessary. Delbrueck (1949) wrote of evolution theory: "[It is] not one proved by decisive experiments, but one that has become more and more inescapable through centuries of accumulated evidence," and he added that at the time of Darwin the theory could not even be put forth in any precise terms. Thus, for the time being, the breadth of relevant observations embraced by the model, and the experiential evidence which directly supports it, must determine the choice of model. There is sufficient experience to show that the more rigorous, quantitative, and experimentally predictive a model is, the narrower is the range of psychological phenomena for which it has any relevance. The model so far discussed may be represented by Diagram B.

Diagram B
A DISCHARGE-ACTION (CONATIVE) MODEL

Observational Sequence	Restlessness ⟶ Breast and Sucking ⟶ Subsidence of Restlessness
1° Abstraction	Tension ⟶ { Tension-Lowering Means and Activity } ⟶ Subsidence of Tension
2° Abstraction (Psychoanalytic)	Pain ⟶ { Pleasure-Gaining Means and Activity } ⟶ Pleasure
3° Abstraction (Psychoanalytic)	Drive ⟶ { Drive Object and Drive Discharge } ⟶ Gratification
4° Abstraction	Disequilibrium ⟶ { Equilibrium-Restoring Means and Activity } ⟶ Equilibrium Restored
5° Partial Abstraction (The Direction of the Model)	⟶ Pleasure Principle (Directional Aspect of Motivation) ⟶

A further conceptualization, usually termed in the psychoanalytic literature as the economic one, may be added: the tension is conceptualized quasi-quantitatively as the drive cathexis (charge); the tension-lowering object as the cathected object; the tension-lowering activity as the activity discharging the cathexis; the tension subsidence as the state after the cathexis has been discharged.

V. A PRIMITIVE MODEL OF COGNITION

Let us now take the observational model and assume that the drive cathexis has mounted to a point where discharge would take place if the drive object were present. Now let the drive object be absent, and discharge thus delayed. Let us then assume that under such conditions a hallucinatory image of the memory of the gratification arises (Freud, 1900, esp. pp. 508–509, and 1911, esp. p. 14), and the following model is arrived at (see Diagram C). Since this is a model, it could well stand as hypothesized above: its fate

Diagram C

Drive ⟶ { Absence of Drive Object: } ⟶ { Hallucinatory Image of the
          { Delay of Discharge   } { Memory of Gratification

depends on its usefulness. However, the concepts within this model will not necessarily be identical with those in the discharge-activity model, unless it is demonstrable that, when drive discharge is delayed, under certain conditions the hallucination phenomena do actually arise. In psychoanalytic literature the model has been derived from the study of precisely such phenomena, particularly dreams. Observations reported by persons who have been on the brink of death by starvation or dehydration, as well as observations on toxic hallucinoses (Meynert's amentia), schizophrenic hallucinations, illusions of normals, daydreams, and so on, further demonstrate that such hallucination phenomena do occur. (See Bleuler, 1912; Murphy, 1947, esp. pp. 362–390; also Bruner and Krech, 1949, esp. Bruner and Postman, 1949, and Klein and Schlesinger, 1949; Blake and Ramsey, 1951, esp. Bruner, 1951, and Klein, 1951).

Thus, all that is assumed here is that the sequence *restlessness → absence of breast → hallucinatory image* occurs *in infancy*. It is irrelevant for the model whether or not it does occur, so the indirect evidence which makes such an assumption plausible will not be discussed here. But since comparative psychological evidence indicates that infantile perception is diffuse and syncretic (Werner, 1926), the infantile memory of gratification must be conceived as an experience which contains in an undifferentiated form the somatic spatial and temporal context of the drive object, of the discharge action, and of the gratification. Actually, study of adult dreams, illusions, and hallucinations demonstrates that in them also the gratification situation is represented by means which can be justifiably labeled syncretic: these means are conceptualized as the Freudian mechanisms of condensation, displacement, substitution, symbolization, etc. (Freud, 1900, esp. pp. 320–396).

The model is further generalized by assuming that hallucination arises when the memory trace attains full drive cathexis (see Diagram D).

Diagram D

Drive Cathexis Reaches } ──► Delay of Discharge ──► { Hallucinatory Drive Cathexis
Discharge Point }   of the Memory Trace of
                                                     the Gratification Situation

The drive cathexis is also conceptualized as mobile cathexis: it obeys the pleasure principle in striving for direct discharge; when discharge is not feasible it cathects the memory trace of past discharge (gratification) situation(s); if this is not directly feasible, then, by condensation of various partial memories of gratification, or by displacement to one of them, sufficient cathexis is concentrated to raise to hallucinatory vividness the memory trace of the condensation product, or of that memory trace to which displacement occurred (Freud, 1900, esp. pp. 485–497). The entirety of the processes which strive for direct discharge, using mobile cathexes and the mechanisms described, is conceptualized as the *primary process* (Freud, 1900, esp. 525–540). The model: drive cathexis → delay of discharge → hallucinatory gratification is in psychoanalytic terms the model of ideation; in general psychological terms, it is the model of primary cognition. The direction implicit to it is analogous to the pleasure principle in the model of discharge activity. In the present model it is usually conceptualized as wish fulfillment.

These considerations may be condensed into Diagram E.

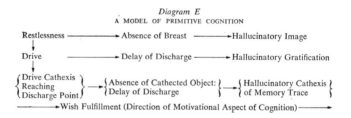

Diagram E
A MODEL OF PRIMITIVE COGNITION

This hallucinatory form of cognition differs from the usual forms of conscious thought in that it does not permit reflection and, in contrast to thought, is as imperious as the drive action: we encounter it in obsessions, hallucinations, monoideic and polyideic fugues, and dreams (Rapaport, 1951d). This type of cognition is conceptualized in psychoanalytic literature as ideation, the single contents as ideas or drive representations. The thought organization of this primitive cognition is termed primary-process thinking: it abides by wish fulfillment and the syncretic mechanisms (condensation, displacement, substitution, symbolization), uses sensory (particularly visual) memories, and thus is usually bereft of conjunctions and causal, temporal, and other relationships.

This primitive form of cognition and its conformity with the model proposed above has been abundantly documented in Piaget's work (1931, 1936), and in the material concerning the comparative psychology of development which H. Werner (1926) has integrated. It goes without saying that I have discussed this form of cognition here mainly in its conative relations, and have not attempted to enter the realm of its subtle complexities.

VI. A PRIMITIVE MODEL OF AFFECTS

Let us return again to the situation in which drive cathexis has mounted to the point where it would discharge, were the drive object present. Assume the drive object to be absent. This is always in fact the first phase of the discharge-activity model, when, before the object appears and activity can take place on it, restlessness prevails. It is this restlessness on which we shall focus our attention now. When the need-satisfying object is absent— or not yet present—the mounting tension may be indicated both by restlessness and by a hallucinatory image of the gratification. We have already seen that the hallucination is conceptualized as drive representation. Should the restlessness also be so conceptualized? It is, in psychoanalytic theory (Freud, 1915a, esp. p. 91, 1915b, esp. p. 111, 1900, esp. p. 521). The drive representation has two aspects: (1) the qualitative one, the idea, which is ultimately the cathected memory trace; (2) the quantitative one, termed the "charge of affect," which comes to expression in those motor and secretory discharge processes which become observable in affect expression. Both the cathexis of the memory trace and the cathexis conceptualized as "charge of affect" are only a fragment of the drive cathexis which has accumulated to the point of discharge. The usual relation between the magnitudes of these three divisions of cathexis, inferred from a variety of observations, appears to be as indicated in Diagram F. It should be remembered, however, that we are still within the framework of the primary model, and all these cathexes are, in their quality and origin, drive cathexes.

Diagram F

Drive Cathexis > Affect-Charge Cathexis > Hallucinatory Cathexis of Memory Trace

The distinction between the two kinds of drive representations is necessitated not only by the need to account for the "restlessness" in the observational model, but also by other empirical observations. For instance, while in hysteria the ideational representation of the drive may be in abeyance (repressed), affect expression—in the form of hysterical affect storm or symptom—will take its place; in obsessional neurosis the ideational representation may remain conscious (obsessional idea), but the affect will usually be in abeyance (repressed or displaced).

This state of affairs may be expressed as follows (see Diagram G). Hallucinatory idea and restlessness, memory-trace cathexis and affect discharge, are both indicators of and safety valves for mounting drive tension. But they *do not* discharge, as a rule, more than a small fragment of the drive cathexis (Brierley, 1937).

Diagram G

$$\text{Drive} \longrightarrow \text{Delay of Discharge} \longrightarrow \text{Drive Representation} \diagdown \begin{array}{l}\text{Cathected Memory Trace (Idea)} \\ \text{Affect-Charge Cathexis} \\ \text{(Affect Discharge: Affect Expression)}\end{array}$$

It is noteworthy that the segregated cathexis conceptualized as "affect charge" strives for immediate discharge as much as does the drive cathexis itself: it is subject to the pleasure principle (Freud, 1900, esp. pp. 535–536). *A primary model of affect* is outlined in Diagram H.

Diagram H
A PRIMARY MODEL OF AFFECT

$$\text{Drive} \left[\begin{array}{l} \text{Drive Cathexis} \\ \text{Affect Charge} \rightarrow \left\{ \begin{array}{l}\text{Affect Discharge (Behavior)} \\ \text{Observed or Physiologically Measured}\end{array} \right\} \rightarrow \text{Affect (Subjectively Felt)} \\ \text{Cathexis of} \\ \text{Memory Trace (Idea)} \end{array} \right.$$

I shall not dwell on the relation of this model to the James-Lange or Cannon theory, and will refer merely to my discussion of the issue in *Emotions and Memory* (1942a). The segregation of affect charge from the drive cathexis proper, and its discharge as affect expression, assumes that drive discharge is not immediately feasible. This seems to imply a drive-inhibition (conflict) theory of affect. Indeed, to some extent it does. But I shall not dwell on this either, except to point out that such a conception goes back to Spinoza and even earlier, and to refer to MacCurdy's (1925) and my own treatment of this issue (Rapaport, 1942a).

I wish to add that drive discharge may be not feasible, or only incompletely feasible, simply because of the structure of the somatic and psychic organization, and not only because of absence of object or presence of conflict. Here we reach the point where a relation between the segregation of the affect charge and the organic discharge thresholds seems to be suggested. Affect charge would then be defined as that amount of the drive cathexis which can be discharged through the motor and secretory channels of affect expression. Evidence seems to indicate that this amount attains a relative segregation from the rest of the drive cathexis in the course of normal development. Thus, in the discharge thresholds and in this segregation, we encounter—even in the primitive tension-discharge models—structures which maintain rather than discharge tension, and processes due to such tension maintenance (Hartmann, 1939; Hartmann, Kris, and Loewenstein, 1946). This again cannot be discussed further here.

Thus conation, cognition, and affection—at least in their primitive forms —are derived here from the same observational model. Without entering on the controversy concerning affect and motivation recently opened by Leeper (1948), I mention it to bring into relief how unclear even the most conscientious of current psychological thinking is as to the relation of motivation and affect.

VII. CONCERNING PRIMARY AND SECONDARY MODELS

The primary models of action, thought, and affect dealt with the dynamics and economics of cathexes; that is, in their main features they were tension-discharge models. I could have said that these models were stated in terms of energy distributions. The intent to keep the models purely psychological —and the wish not to be faced here with the question, "Do you mean $\frac{1}{2}mv^2$ when you say energy?"—accounts for the term cathexis. Yet I cannot forego saying that these cathexes do seem to behave in the way energy distributions do (see Rapaport, 1950).

Besides being tension-discharge models, these primitive models did imply certain structural givens: the constitutionally given coordination of drive and drive object, the existence of some sort of memory traces, the discharge thresholds and channels of motility and of secretion (Hartmann, 1939; Hartmann, Kris, and Loewenstein, 1946). Yet they dealt pre-eminently with cathectic dynamics. Now it is obvious that human behavior is not produced from moment to moment in a Battle of Titans of drive cathexes, any more than the human body is produced from moment to moment by metabolic and other processes: only when studied together do function and structure, in their well-known interpenetration, yield the approximate picture we have of the organism. The structures of the psychic apparatus were considered in these primary models, but by implication. Fritz Heider has pointed out that one of the salient shortcomings of Lewin's dynamic psychology was that it centered on tensions (dynamics) to the virtual exclusion of structure—on the processes of tension discharge only, to the neglect of those of tension maintenance. Allport (1946) has rightly insisted that the demonstration of the genetic (onto- or phylogenetic) continuity of motivations accounts neither for the complexity and uniqueness of the adult's motivational structure, nor for the functional autonomy of his motives. Allport seems to consider that a consistent theory, embracing both those phenomena which demand the postulation of the primary model and those which demand models implying functional autonomy, is not feasible. This is precisely what psychoanalytic ego psychology is, and I shall endeavor to present it here (Freud, 1926; Hartmann, 1939; Rapaport, 1951a, esp. pp. 689–730, and 1951b). Our next task is to center on structure formation, and to present those forms of the psychoanalytic model which include structure. It is inevitable that these models—dealing with far more complex relationships—be even more schematic than the primitive models.

I should like to interpolate that—for reasons that lie beyond the scope of this paper—I will not deal here with the relevance or irrelevance of this model to phenomena which are variously referred to as those of conscience, ego ideal, superego, etc.

VIII. A SECONDARY MODEL OF CONATION

Let us return to the situation in which drive tension has risen to a point close to the discharge threshold, with the drive object absent. This hypothetical situation implies the existence of threshold structures, and serves also as a reference point of further structure formation.

The empirical study of motivations shows that besides (a) the motivations which strive for direct discharge and do not tolerate delay, and are conceptualized as drives, there are (b) motivations which are repressed, that is, cut off from direct discharge, as well as (c) motivations which are neither repressed nor undelayably discharge-bent, but amenable, in various degrees, to postponement of discharge. On the one hand, the drives which have succumbed to the process of repression, or to other defensive operations, may or may not manifest themselves indirectly as altered forms of motivation. On the other hand, the drives which have become amenable to postponement of discharge appear as new forms of motivation. Both sorts of motivations—those deriving from repression of, and those deriving from control of, drives—are usually referred to as derivative motivations and are rarely distinguished carefully. The nature of the process of repression and other defenses, and the nature of motivations arising from them, are relatively well understood; but the process by which the other type of derivative motivations arises has been little explored (Freud, 1915b; Rapaport, 1951a, esp. pp. 689–730).

Let us now concern ourselves with repression (Freud, 1915a). We have seen that the drive abides by the pleasure principle: it strives for direct and complete discharge, to re-establish equilibrium. If the drive object proves "unreliable"—that is, if it is not available regularly within a limited time of delay—then re-establishment of equilibrium by discharge is not possible, and a new method for re-establishing it develops: the organism acts as though the disequilibrium did not exist. In this it follows, on the one hand, the pattern set by the pre-existing discharge threshold; on the other, it actually raises these discharge thresholds by erecting new barriers against discharge. This is achieved by the process of repression (I shall forego treating here of the other defenses) which is conceptualized as follows: against the accumulated drive cathexes, other cathexes—countercathexes—are pitted, establishing an equilibrium on, so to speak, a higher level of "potential." Once such a countercathecting (repression) has come about, no discharge occurs, even when the drive object is present. Indeed, the ideational representation, and even the perception, of the object is usually barred from consciousness by repression. A variety of observations suggests that the countercathexis derives from the very drive cathexis whose discharge it prevents. The countercathectic distribution so established appears to behave as though it has a *relative* functional autonomy. The concept "functional autonomy" is used here in Allport's (1937) sense. The term "relative" indicates a modification of this concept: the degree to which the countercathectic distribution increases or decreases with—that is, remains dependent upon—the changing intensities of the repressed drive varies from person to person, in time and with situations, and ranges from apparently total independence to that total dependence which becomes manifest in neurotic and psychotic breakdowns (Rapaport, 1951b). The particular importance of this point lies in the fact that countercathectic distributions, just like cathectic distributions, manifest themselves as motivations of behavior: often, in the case of repression, simply as avoidance motivations; in the case of reaction formation, as motivations diametrically opposite to the original drive motivation, etc. (Hartmann, 1939; Freud, 1926, and 1915a, esp. pp. 92–97). Allport is certainly right that such reaction formations are autonomous motivations once they are established, and may even definitely resist change by psychoanalysis (Allport, 1946, p. 165); but clinical observation amply shows that the opposite is just as often the case, that psychoanalysis can do away with a motivation of reaction-formation character by uncovering its genetic origins and making this form of defense superfluous.

It must be added that these motivations may be just as imperious as the drives themselves, or may be more amenable to delay and detour in reaching their ends. It seems that the degree of relative autonomy is indicated by the degree of such imperiousness. It also should be noted that in the course of normal development these motivations become themselves subject to defensive and delaying controls just as did the drives. The hierarchic layering of defenses is an empirical datum. It is partly by the hierarchic repetition of this process of defense-structure formation that drives are "tamed" into adult motives; and it is mostly the failure at one point or another of this taming process that gives rise to neurotic, psychotic, or character disturbances.

Turning now to the second kind of derivative motivations, we find that they differ in several salient points from repressed drives: (a) delay does not result in the organism's treating them as nonexistent; (b) fortuitous delay is replaced in them by a capability of being delayed in discharge, of being controlled; (c) unlike the repressed drives they are not changed into their opposite, or turned back on the subject, etc., but are discharged when the drive object again becomes available (Freud, 1900, esp. pp. 525–540, and 1911). The process by which these derivative motivations come about is not well understood. It may be conceptualized either as a consequence of repression or as an independent process. In the former case, it would be assumed that the countercathexes which work in repression affect the other drives also, though not in repressing them but in controlling their discharge. In the latter case, it would be assumed that the discharge threshold becomes modifiable by an arrangement which deploys and withdraws countercathexes in accordance with the availability or unavailability of the drive object (Freud, 1900, esp. pp. 533–536, and 1915b, esp. pp. 120–127). Clinical observation suggests that there is no sharp dichotomy between these two kinds of derivative motivations, but rather that they shade imperceptibly into each other. It also strongly suggests that both the controlling and defensive processes are reapplied to the emerging "tamed" motivations, building a hierarchic series and perpetuating the process of taming; this results in motivations which are increasingly amenable to delay and detour en route to their goal, and in the rise of vicarious subgoals; thus their goal is altered from need satisfaction (tension reduction), to tension maintenance, reality appraisal, and socialization.

This process of "taming" will be more clearly viewed if we keep in mind that these derivative motivations arise from cathectic distributions which alter the drive's discharge thresholds. In effect, these alterations of discharge thresholds are intrapsychic representations of facts of external reality: that is, they modify the drive discharge in the direction of tension maintenance, to discharge only in conformity with reality (Rapaport, 1951a, esp. pp. 723–726).

Though the evidence suggests a hierarchic layering of these "taming" processes, it also suggests strongly an interpenetration of the various layers, resulting in an immense complexity of interrelationships. From the point of view of psychoanalysis, this is the genetic history of the rise of ego motivations from drive motivations; mobile drive cathexes abiding by the pleasure principle—that is, discharge bent—are in part transformed into "bound" cathexes (partly employed in the discharge-controlling structures, and partly limited by them in discharge) amenable to delay of discharge and available to the ego for deployment, for which the pleasure principle no longer fully holds, but yields in part to the reality principle (Kris, 1950, esp. pp. 485–491). From the point of view of general psychology, this is the genetic history of the relationships between basic needs on the one hand, and on the other, strivings, interests, attitudes, opinions, preferences, sets—that is, between the varieties of observed motivations (Allport, 1935; Gibson, 1941). It might be worth noting that K. Lewin's theory of the dependence of quasi needs on genuine needs implies such a hierarchic conception, and his theory of the dynamic independence of quasi needs implies the conception of relative functional autonomy (Lewin, 1926).

The structures here discussed provide for the possibility of delay of discharge, and for both the possibility and means (reality-adapted motivations) of finding in reality the object which permits discharge. The totality of such structures is conceptualized as the ego, while the congeries of immediately discharge-directed drives is conceptualized as the id (Hartmann, 1939, 1948; Hartmann, Kris, and Loewenstein, 1946). The processes amenable to delay and abiding by the reality principle are conceptualized in psychoanalysis as the secondary process; those abiding by the pleasure principle as the primary process. The above characterization of motivations shows that the ego and id are limiting concepts, and that the processes and structures corresponding to them interpenetrate. It is notable that the secondary process does not dispense with the pleasure principle, but rather modifies it, postpones it, and partially executes it (Freud, 1911).

Thus, all motivated actions share the tension-reducing character of drive actions. Simultaneously, however, they are also consequences of those tension-maintaining structures and processes which prevent direct drive action, and give rise to the derivative motivations of action. Indeed, it seems that in a sense all motivated actions—except drive actions—serve in part to sustain these tension-maintaining structures, to prevent their being swept away by mounting drive tensions. In psychoses, both functional and organic, and in extreme reality situations, these structures fail to a greater or lesser degree (Freud, 1920; Rapaport, 1951b).

In drives, delay of discharge—except when effected by constitutional discharge thresholds—is fortuitous, in that the environment enforces it; in derivative motivations, delay is guaranteed by internalized—psychological—structures.

The concept of detour has not been defined here. Yet from the studies of Lewin (1926) and Tolman (1932, esp. Chapters 11 and 12), as well as from clinical observation (French, 1941), one aspect of detour can be readily adduced. Objects other than the need-satisfying or valent object—encountered or sought out in the period of delay—attain secondary valence if action on them will lead to the valent object's becoming available in reality. In other words, means to reach the end object attain part valences of the end object. This state of affairs represents one of the differences between the "mobile cathexes" of the primary process and the "bound cathexes" of the secondary process. While the "mobile" drive cathexes can be displaced only from one drive representation to another, the "bound" or neutralized cathexes can be displaced to anything that serves as a *means* toward the attainment of the object in reality (Freud, 1900, esp. pp. 533–536, and 1915b, esp. pp. 120–127).

The claim that all actions are motivated—that is, cathected by need, and directed toward need-satisfying objects and discharge of need cathexis—may be questioned on the ground that means actions, habits, and so on, do not conform with this pattern. Lewin's (1926, esp. pp. 129–130, 141–143) conception of *ossification,* and Hartmann's (1939, esp. pp. 375, 392–396) similar conception of *automatization,* cope with this objection; they show that means actions and habits are not built in the elementalistic fashion of conditioned responses, but are automatized, skeletal, and structuralized forms of originally need-gratifying (motivated) actions. Schilder (1931, esp. pp. 65–71; see also Rapaport, 1951c) has discussed this issue in similar terms.

These structuralized means, with which human motivation and action are so invariably intertwined and implemented, are also part and parcel of that cohesive organization of psychological processes and structures which—as was indicated above—is conceptualized as the ego. Let us remind ourselves

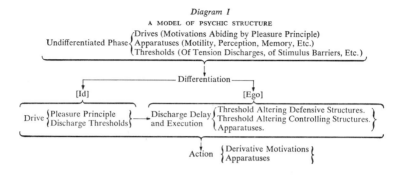

Diagram I

A MODEL OF PSYCHIC STRUCTURE

Undifferentiated Phase
{ Drives (Motivations Abiding by Pleasure Principle)
  Apparatuses (Motility, Perception, Memory, Etc.)
  Thresholds (Of Tension Discharges, of Stimulus Barriers, Etc.) }

——————— Differentiation ———————

[Id]   [Ego]

Drive { Pleasure Principle
        Discharge Thresholds }   Discharge Delay
                                  and Execution { Threshold Altering Defensive Structures.
                                                  Threshold Altering Controlling Structures.
                                                  Apparatuses. }

Action { Derivative Motivations
         Apparatuses }

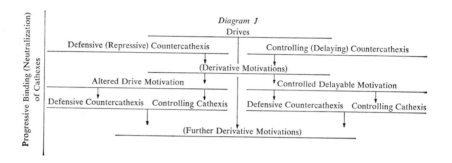

Diagram J

Drives

Defensive (Repressive) Countercathexis   Controlling (Delaying) Countercathexis

(Derivative Motivations)

Altered Drive Motivation   Controlled Delayable Motivation

Defensive Countercathexis   Controlling Cathexis   Defensive Countercathexis   Controlling Cathexis

(Further Derivative Motivations)

Progressive Binding (Neutralization) of Cathexes

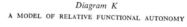

Diagram K

A MODEL OF RELATIVE FUNCTIONAL AUTONOMY

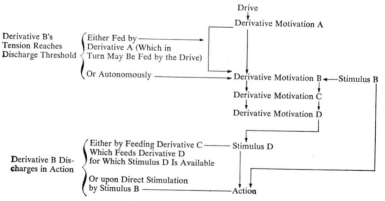

Drive

Derivative Motivation A

Derivative B's
Tension Reaches
Discharge Threshold { Either Fed by
                      Derivative A (Which in
                      Turn May Be Fed by the Drive)

                      Or Autonomously ————→ Derivative Motivation B ◄——Stimulus B

Derivative Motivation C

Derivative Motivation D

Derivative B Dis-
charges in Action { Either by Feeding Derivative C —— Stimulus D
                    Which Feeds Derivative D
                    for Which Stimulus D Is Available

                    Or upon Direct Stimulation
                    by Stimulus B ———————— Action }

that such structures as the memory, the perceptual, and the motor apparatuses, and the various perceptual and discharge thresholds of the organism, are also integrated within this cohesive organization. It is assumed also that these apparatuses exist before the differentiation of the ego from the id, and serve as nuclei of this process (Hartmann, 1939, 1948; Hartmann, Kris, and Loewenstein, 1946; Rapaport, 1951a, esp. pp. 689–730). It is possible that psychologies founded on phenomena of associative memory, perception, motility, may be integrated into a psychology built on the model described, but this cannot be pursued here.

In order to arrive at the secondary model of action, we must first sketch a model of psychic structure (see Diagram I).

Implicit to this model is a model of hierarchy of motivations and controls (see Diagram J). It will be useful to represent the conception of relative functional autonomy also in the form of a schema and for this purpose the motivational hierarchy will be presented in an arbitrarily simplified linear form. A model of relative functional autonomy is outlined in Diagram K. The stimulus here does not create a "drive," but merely triggers the discharge of the drive tension which is close to threshold intensity.

Thus we arrive at the secondary model of action in which the motive, here designated as need, may be any derivative motivation. What appears in the above model as discharge by triggering further derivative motivations, or delay of discharge until Stimulus B has been found, appears in this model as structuralized delay and detour.

For a secondary model of action see Diagram L. Both the considerable range of variability of the object and consummatory action possible within this model, and the phenomenon of their "fixation" (narrow range), are familiar from psychoanalytic investigations and Lewin's experimental studies (1926, esp. pp. 126–132; Rapaport, 1951a, esp. 705–708, 714–718).

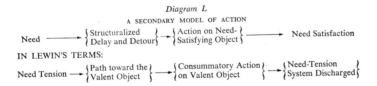

Diagram L
A SECONDARY MODEL OF ACTION

Need ⟶ {Structuralized Delay and Detour} → {Action on Need-Satisfying Object} ⟶ Need Satisfaction

IN LEWIN'S TERMS:

Need Tension ⟶ {Path toward the Valent Object} ⟶ {Consummatory Action on Valent Object} ⟶ {Need-Tension System Discharged}

In the course of development of that type of action which is conceptualized by the secondary model, its ascendance over that conceptualized by the primary model does not do away with the latter, which we actually observe under special normal or pathological conditions (Bleuler, 1912; Murphy, 1947, esp. pp. 362–390; Bruner and Krech, 1949, esp. Bruner and Postman, 1949; Klein and Schlesinger, 1949; Blake and Ramsey, 1951, esp. Bruner, 1951, and Klein, 1951). A good example is the somnambule's actions, or those of a person in a monoideic fugue (Rapaport, 1951b).

IX. A SECONDARY MODEL OF COGNITION

It is readily seen that the primary model of cognition, i.e., *drive cathexis* →
delay of discharge → *drive cathexis of the memory trace,* implies a specific
set of conditions under which an idea becomes conscious. It should be
pointed out that it implies also a form of memory organization, concept
formation, and anticipation (see Rapaport, Gill, and Schafer, 1945–46,
esp. pp. 385–389).

In the primary model, consciousness depends upon the drive cathexis of
the idea (Rapaport, 1950, and 1951a, esp. pp. 689–730). Memory traces
are raised to consciousness only in so far as they are drive representations,
that is, are associatively related to the situation of gratification; but any
memory that is so related can substitute for any other one. Analysis of free
associations, slips of the tongue, and dreams, shows that memories in the
primary process are organized around drives, as their representations. This
is conceptualized as the drive organization of memories. Concepts—that is,
the belongingness of objects—in the primary process are therefore drive
centered, and thus of the character described by H. Werner (1926) as
"things of action" and "physiognomic percepts," or "affective concepts."
We may add that the "logic" of the primary process is of the sort Lévy-
Bruhl described as "participation," Domarus as "paralogic," etc. Anticipations in the primary process appear to reflect the specific relation of the
drive and its object: the drive can be said to anticipate its object, since
without it no discharge is attained.

In the secondary process, consciousness does not depend merely upon
drive cathexis (Freud, 1900, esp. pp. 540–549, and 1915b, esp.
112–127). Even ideas which have drive cathexis, without countercathexis,
may fail to become conscious when other contents command attention: in
such cases, the status of the idea is conceptualized as preconscious. Consciousness of both intrapsychic and external stimuli is dependent upon the
allotment of *attention cathexis* (hypercathexis). Here consciousness is not
a descriptive term but a concept; it is conceived of as a superordinate sense
organ—as such, an apparatus of the ego—which has a determinate amount
of bound (neutralized) cathexes at its disposal. Unlike the drive cathexis,
this attention cathexis can be commanded by any external as well as intrapsychic stimulus. Thus, to attain consciousness here does not depend upon
drive cathexis alone, and may not depend on it at all; further, in full consciousness the relationships of the thought which is conscious are also conscious, or at any rate amenable to consciousness (preconscious) (Rapaport, 1950, 1951a, esp. pp. 698–699, and 1951d). This is not the case with
ideas brought to consciousness by drive cathexes.

The drive organization of memories has also yielded to a different organization. We know from Bartlett's studies (1932) that organization in terms
of higher-level derivative motivations (interests, attitudes, etc.) is charac-

teristic for the secondary process; we also know from studies in problem solving that abstract conceptual organization is also one of its characteristics. We formulate: the drive organization of memories of the primary model yields in the secondary model to a memory organization in terms of frames of reference. Here equivalence is not defined by what can equally serve as drive representation, but rather by what can equally enhance the chances to discover the object in reality—or so change reality that the object becomes available (Freud, 1900, esp. pp. 533–536, and 1915b, esp. pp. 120–127; Rapaport, 1951a, esp. pp. 710–712).

In the primary process, concept formation (Rapaport, 1951a, esp. pp. 708–710) of the physiognomic and "thing of action" types indicated the belongingness of objects only in terms of drive representation or potentiality in promising "pleasure" or "pain"; in the secondary process, this yields to abstract concepts expressing the most general commonalities of the objects of reality (Freud, 1900, esp. pp. 545–546; Schilder, 1920, esp. p. 515; Bleuler, 1911, esp. pp. 641 ff.).

The primitive forms of logic based on physiognomic concepts—such as paralogic, participation, animism (magic), *post hoc ergo propter hoc, pars pro toto*—are replaced by a logic founded on abstract concepts, which is organized in terms of the categories space, time, and causality, and employs deductive, inductive, and dialectic forms of reasoning (Werner, 1926).

The primitive form of anticipation—wherein a drive tension anticipates the drive object as its sole condition of discharge—develops into complex forms of anticipation which express the range of objects and ideas compatible with sets of simultaneously existing motivations, defenses, reality possibilities and limitations. The most highly developed forms of these are anticipations codified in the language—that is, in communicated thought— in the form of the conjunctions (though, however, if, etc.) which arouse in us general syntactic and specific content anticipation (Rapaport, 1951a, esp. pp. 712–714, and 1951c; Varendonck, 1921, esp. pp. 461, 466–467).

The juxtaposition of these extreme forms of consciousness, memory organization, concept formation, logic, and anticipation, indicates only descriptively the change in the role and nature of thought for which the secondary model of cognition must account. The change itself is characterized in the psychoanalytic literature (Rapaport, 1950) as follows:

(1) ideation (hallucinatory drive representation) is an indicator and safety-discharge valve of drive tension; it changes into thought, which is experimental action with small cathectic quantities;

(2) ideation uses representations of a drive; it changes into thought, which has available to it—ideally—all memory traces and their relations, for orientation in reality;

(3) ideation is partial discharge, and as such compelling; it changes into thought, which is amenable to delay, detour, and vicarious function;

(4) ideation uses drive cathexes; it changes into thought, which uses neutralized cathexes.

These extremes, however, are connected by a quasi-continuous series of transitory forms (Rapaport, 1951a, esp. pp. 689–730). The development of these transitory forms of cognition is most directly familiar to us from Piaget's (1931, 1936) various investigations and from Werner's (1926) systematizing work. In psychoanalysis, both clinical material and the studies of Susan Isaacs (1930) demonstrate it. This development appears to parallel closely the development of the hierarchy of motivations and defenses discussed above, and is particularly dependent upon (a) delay possibility, without which no motive-representing thought arises; (b) neutralization of cathexes, without which the motive-representing thought cannot be raised to consciousness except when the motive tension has reached threshold intensity.

Here too, just as we have seen in regard to action, a relative functional autonomy obtains: a thought may be aroused as a response by a stimulus setting off any appropriate derivative motivation, without relation to any motivation more basic. And just as in action, the thought may directly arouse other thoughts, and so seek the object of the motivation by using neutralized cathexes; or it may set off further derivative motivations, and indirectly through them other thoughts, and so seek the object.

There is here an additional point which cannot be bypassed. The memorial connections, the conceptual belongingness, and the anticipations which have once arisen in the interplay of motivations and in the quest for the object which satisfies simultaneously several effective motives (overdetermination), are not lost with the progress of psychological development; rather, by again and again recurring in approximately similar situations, they become structuralized (Hartmann: "automatized"; Lewin: "ossified") and available as fixed tools, quasi-stationary apparatuses, for use in the thought process. The more or less idiosyncratic sets and instrumental attitudes (Allport, 1935), as well as the conjunctions of the language—of so high an order of social agreement—are such ossified anticipations. The "popular responses" on association and other projective tests are such automatized memorial and conceptual connections (Rapaport, 1942b, 1946). The thought forms of general syntax and logic also develop thus. In contrast to the conditioning conception, we have here a conception in which the simple automatic connections are simplified automatizations of complex interactions of motivations. The derivative motivations—as we have seen—come about as modifications of more basic motivations by the internalization of environmental limitations. The development of the fixed structures of thought amounts similarly to internalization of environmental conditions, and thus guarantees the reality adaptedness and socialized character of thought. The role of communication in this process is salient, but cannot be discussed here. Piaget's studies and the clinical studies of identification provide the initial material for conceptualizing the role of communication (interpersonal relationship) in the development of reality adaptation and socialization. The processes referred to here are usually treated under the heading of "learning." But the conventional theories of learning usually disregard both the motivational and the structure-creating aspects of these processes (Rapaport, 1951a, esp. pp. 723–728).

In the ascendance of the secondary process over the primary, the latter, together with the transitory forms between the two, survives and manifests itself—though modified—in wishful thinking, daydreams, dreams, etc., under normal conditions; in illusions, preoccupations, hypnotic phenomena, etc., under extreme conditions; and in delusions, hallucinations, obsessions, pseudo memories, etc., under pathological conditions.

In order to present the secondary model of cognition we must first sketch Diagram M.

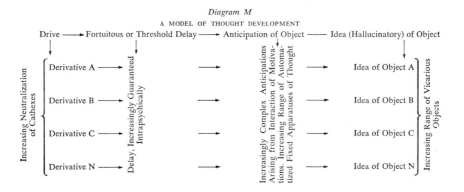

Diagram M

A MODEL OF THOUGHT DEVELOPMENT

Drive ⟶ Fortuitous or Threshold Delay ⟶ Anticipation of Object —— Idea (Hallucinatory) of Object

We may now sketch Diagram N.

Diagram N

A SECONDARY MODEL OF COGNITION

{ Need (Any Derivative Motivation)

{ Delay of Discharge Guaranteed
{ by Intrapsychic Regulations

(Setting off of Further Derivative Needs [E.g., Quasi Needs (Lewin)]
{ or Directly Initiating a Thought Process (Using Neutralized Cathexes
{ and Taking Detours through Conceptually and Memorially Related
{ Thoughts) Regulated by Means of Automatized Anticipations, Concepts,
(and Memorial Connections Relevant to the Need.

(Thought Process Development, Using Ever-Narrowing Anticipations and
{ Conceptually Related Ideas as Means to the End of Reaching, in Reality,
(the Need-Satisfying Object or the Pathways Leading to It.

{ Consciousness of the Object and of the Ways to Reach It in Reality.

X. A SECONDARY MODEL OF AFFECTS

Space permits only a perfunctory treatment of the secondary model of affects.

The observational facts for which a secondary model of affects must account are in the main clinical. They comprise the continuum ranging from elemental discharges (e.g., joy and rage) through mild conscious experiences of feeling tone (e.g., pleasantness and unpleasantness) to "cold affects" which hardly differ from the intellectual experience that a given feeling would be appropriate (Rapaport, 1942a). The model must also account for the fact that this continuum is by no means as simple and linear as it may seem. Elemental affect discharges comprise expressive movements, visceral and secretory processes, emotion felt, and consciousness of the relation to a stimulus; but in each of the various forms of affect any of these constituents, or any combination of them, may be absent. The model should also account for the observational fact that affects can become chronic either in their totality (e.g., in some forms of anxiety), or in their physiological concomitants (e.g., in functional hypertension), or in their feeling tone (e.g., in moods), or in their expressive movements (e.g., in the stereotyped frozen smiles or angrily set jaws, or in individually characteristic postures; see Freud, 1926, and Landauer, 1938). Furthermore, it must account for the histrionic affects, the "as if" affects which are subjectively experienced as "not genuine," the affects which are excessively indulged in, as seen in schizoid personalities and disorders. Finally, of the many other varieties of affects to be accounted for, we might mention those involved in the experience of wit or humor (Freud, 1927; Kris, 1938).

First, the secondary model of affects conceptualizes the continuum referred to above as affect forms related to the delay in discharge of derivative motivations. As with drives, so with these derivative motivations there appear affect discharges which serve as safety valves and indicators of their increasing tension. *Second,* it conceptualizes the absence of the various components of affects as the result of their having succumbed to repression, isolation, or displacement. *Third,* it conceptualizes the chronicity of affects, or of certain of their components, as the result of the segregation, autonomy, and automatization of their affect charge; this charge can be triggered either momentarily by derivative motivations, or continuously by processes other than the threshold intensity of the motivation corresponding to it. This is the case in anxiety, where the ego plays the triggering rôle (Freud, 1926), and in guilt and depression (Landauer, 1938), where it is played by the superego—a structure which here remains undefined. *Finally,* it may be mentioned that, under specific conditions, the affect-charge cathexes may play a motivational rôle. This, however, is by no means so general that it would make tenable Leeper's and Duffy's attempts at offering a motivational theory of affects. The essential relation of affect to motivation is that the affect charge is a part of the motivational cathexis, i.e., constitutes as much of the motivational cathexis as can find discharge through the motor and secretory channels proper to affect discharge.

Since this treatment is perfunctory, and does not meet many of the issues and theories customarily presented in discussions of affects, the model I present here is even more sketchy than the others presented above (see Diagram O).

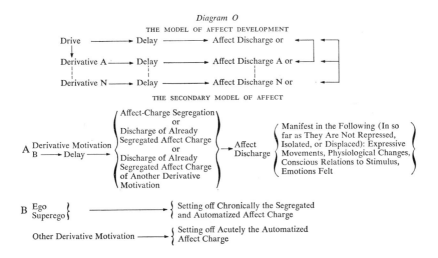

Diagram O

THE MODEL OF AFFECT DEVELOPMENT

Drive ⟶ Delay ⟶ Affect Discharge or ◄⟶

Derivative A ⟶ Delay ⟶ Affect Discharge A or ◄⟶

Derivative N ⟶ Delay ⟶ Affect Discharge N or ◄⟶

THE SECONDARY MODEL OF AFFECT

A Derivative Motivation
B ⟶ Delay ⟶
{ Affect-Charge Segregation
or
Discharge of Already Segregated Affect Charge
or
Discharge of Already Segregated Affect Charge of Another Derivative Motivation }
⟶ Affect Discharge
{ Manifest in the Following (In so far as They Are Not Repressed, Isolated, or Displaced): Expressive Movements, Physiological Changes, Conscious Relations to Stimulus, Emotions Felt }

B Ego }
Superego }
⟶ { Setting off Chronically the Segregated and Automatized Affect Charge

Other Derivative Motivation ⟶ { Setting off Acutely the Automatized Affect Charge

XI. CONCLUSION

The model presented here is characterized by the following features:

(1) it does away with the arbitrary segregation of conation, cognition, and affection;

(2) it has the scope to do away with the arbitrary segregation of memory, association, imagination, etc., conceptualizing them as various aspects of thought organization;

(3) it has the potentiality to integrate within its framework the motor and the perceptual processes—which was hardly hinted at in the present sketch;

(4) it takes account of motivation (function) as well as structure;

(5) its crucial concepts—delay and detour—may serve as a bridge between the extremes of animal psychological observations and cybernetic, goal-seeking, feedback mechanisms;

(6) its pervasively motivational character implies Allport's "intention" and Brentano's "intentionality";

(7) it is genetically oriented, and thus capable of encompassing developmental and comparative psychological phenomena;

(8) it has grown out of clinical ground, and thus can account for psychopathological obscrvations;

(9) it is a purely psychological model, cast to systematize psychological data—observational and introspective—no matter how remote from any neurologically or physiologically tangible phenomena. Yet it does not exclude the hope that, in the distant future, the gap may considerably narrow between these psychologically systematized observations and those neurologically and physiologically systematized.

REFERENCES

Allport, G. W. (1935). Attitudes. In *A Handbook of Social Psychology,* ed. C. Murchison. Worcester: Clark University Press, pp. 798–844.

——— (1935–47). *The Nature of Personality: Selected Papers.* Cambridge, Mass.: Addison-Wesley Press, 1950.

——— (1937). *Personality.* New York: Holt.

——— (1946). Geneticism vs. Ego-Structure in Theories of Personality. In Allport (1935–47), pp. 158–169.

——— (1947). Scientific Models and Human Morals. In Allport (1935–47), pp. 187–197.

Bartlett, F. C. (1932). *Remembering: A Study in Experimental and Social Psychology.* Cambridge: Cambridge University Press.

Bertalanffy, L. von (1950). The Theory of Open Systems in Physics and Biology. *Science,* 11:23–29.

Blake, R. R., & Ramsey, G. V., eds. (1951). *Perception: An Approach to Personality.* New York: Ronald Press.

Bleuler, E. (1911). The Basic Symptoms of Schizophrenia. In Rapaport (1951a), pp. 581–649.

——— (1912). Autistic Thinking. In Rapaport (1951a), pp. 399–437.

Boring, E. G. (1946). Mind and Mechanism. *Amer. J. Psychol.,* 59:173–192.

Brentano, F. (1874). *Psychologie vom empirischen Standpunkte.* Leipzig: Dunker & Humbolt.

Brierley, M. (1937). Affects in Theory and Practice. *Int. J. Psycho-Anal.,* 18:256–268.

Brillouin, L. (1949). Life, Thermodynamics, and Cybernetics. *Amer. Sci.,* 37:554–568.

Bruner, J. S. (1951). Personality Dynamics and the Process of Perceiving. In Blake & Ramsey (1951), pp. 121–147.

———, & Krech, D., eds. (1949). *Perception and Personality, a Symposium.* Durham, N. C.: Duke University Press, 1950.

———, & Postman, L. (1949). Perception, Cognition, and Behavior. In Bruner & Krech (1949), pp. 14–31.

Delbrueck, M. (1949). A Physicist Looks at Biology. *Trans. Conn. Acad. Arts Sci.,* 38:173–190.

Förster, H. von, ed. (1950), *Cybernetics. Circular Causal, and Feedback Mechanisms in Biological and Social Systems,* Transactions of the Sixth Conference, March 24–25, 1949, New York, N. Y. New York: Josiah Macy, Jr. Foundation.

Frank, L. (1948). Foreword: Teleological Mechanisms. *Ann. N. Y. Acad. Sci.,* 50:189–196.

French, T. M. (1941). Goal, Mechanism and Integrative Field. *Psychosom. Med.,* 3:226–252.

Freud, S. (1900). The Interpretation of Dreams, tr. A. A. Brill. *The Basic Writings.* New York: Modern Library, 1938, pp. 179–549.

——— (1911). Formulations Regarding the Two Principles in Mental Functioning. *Collected Papers,* 4:13–21. New York: Basic Books, 1959.

——— (1915a). Repression. *Collected Papers,* 4:84–97. New York: Basic Books, 1959.

——— (1915b). The Unconscious. *Collected Papers,* 4:98–136. New York: Basic Books, 1959.

——— (1920). *Beyond the Pleasure Principle,* tr. C. J. M. Hubback. London: Hogarth Press, 1948.

——— (1926 [1925]). *The Problem of Anxiety,* tr. H. A. Bunker. New York: Psychoanalytic Quarterly & Norton, 1936.

——— (1927). Humour. *Collected Papers,* 5:215–221. New York: Basic Books, 1959.

Gibson, J. J. (1941). A Critical Review of the Concept of Set in Contemporary Experimental Psychology. *Psychol. Bull.,* 38:781–817.

Hartmann, H. (1939). Ego Psychology and the Problem of Adaptation. In (abridged) Rapaport (1951a), pp. 362–396.

——— (1948). Comments on the Psychoanalytic Theory of Instinctual Drives. *Psychoanal. Quart.,* 17:368–388.

———, & Kris, E. (1945). The Genetic Approach in Psychoanalysis. *Psychoanal. Study Child,* 1:11–30. New York: International Universities Press.

———, Kris, E., & Loewenstein, R. M. (1946). Comments on the Formation of Psychic Structure. *Psychoanal. Study Child,* 2:11–38. New York: International Universities Press.

Hebb, D. O. (1949). *The Organization of Behavior; A Neuropsychological Theory.* New York: Wiley.

Isaacs, S. (1930). *Intellectual Growth in Young Children.* London: Routledge & Sons.

Klein, G. S. (1951). The Personal World through Perception. In Blake & Ramsey (1951), pp. 328–355.

———, & Schlesinger, H. (1949). Where Is the Perceiver in Perceptual Theory? In Bruner & Krech, eds. (1949), pp. 32–47.

Köhler, W. (1923). Zur Theorie des Sukzessivvergleichs und der Zeitfehler. *Psychol. Forsch.,* 4:115–175.

Koffka, K. (1935). *Principles of Gestalt Psychology.* New York: Harcourt, Brace.

Krech, D. (1949). Notes toward a Psychological Theory. *J. Pers.,* 18:66–87.

——— (1950a). Dynamic Systems, Psychological Fields, and Hypothetical Constructs. *Psychol. Rev.,* 57:283–290.

———— (1950b). Dynamic Systems as Open Neurological Systems. *Psychol. Rev.*, 57:345–361.

———— (1951). Cognition and Motivation in Psychological Theory. In *Current Trends in Psychology.* Pittsburgh: University of Pittsburgh Press, pp. 111–139.

Kris, E. (1938). Ego Development and the Comic. *Psychoanalytic Explorations in Art.* New York: International Universities Press, 1952, pp. 204–216.

———— (1950). On Preconscious Mental Processes. In Rapaport (1951a), pp. 474–493.

Landauer, K. (1938). Affects, Passions and Temperament. *Int. J. Psycho-Anal.*, 19:388–415.

Leeper, R. W. (1948). A Motivational Theory of Emotion to Replace "Emotion as Disorganized Response." *Psychol. Rev.*, 55:5–21.

Lewin, K. (1926). Intention, Will and Need. In Rapaport (1951a), pp. 95–153.

———— (1935). *A Dynamic Theory of Personality.* New York: McGraw-Hill.

———— (1936). *Principles of Topological Psychology.* New York: McGraw-Hill.

———— (1938). The Conceptual Representation and Measurement of Psychological Forces. *Contr. Psychol. Theory,* 1, No. 4 (reprint, 1948).

MacCurdy, J. T. (1925). *The Psychology of Emotion, Morbid and Normal.* New York: Harcourt, Brace.

McCulloch, W., & Pitts, W. (1947). How We Know Universals. The Perception of Auditory and Visual Forms. *Bull. Math. Biophysics,* 9:127–147.

Murphy, G. (1947). *Personality.* New York: Harper.

Piaget, J. (1931). Children's Philosophies. In *A Handbook of Child Psychology,* ed. C. Murchison. Worcester: Clark University Press, pp. 377–391.

———— (1936). The Biological Problem of Intelligence. In Rapaport (1951a), pp. 176–192.

Rapaport, D. (1942a). *Emotions and Memory,* 2nd unaltered ed. New York: International Universities Press, 1950.

———— (1942b). Principles Underlying Projective Techniques. *This volume,* Chapter 6.

———— (1946). Principles Underlying Nonprojective Tests of Personality. *This volume,* Chapter 15.

———— (1950). On the Psychoanalytic Theory of Thinking. *This volume,* Chapter 28.

————, ed. & tr. (1951a). *Organization and Pathology of Thought.* New York: Columbia University Press.

———— (1951b). The Autonomy of the Ego. *This volume,* Chapter 31.

———— (1951c). Paul Schilder's Contribution to the Theory of Thought Processes. *This volume,* Chapter 32.

———— (1951d). States of Consciousness: A Psychopathological and Psychodynamic View. *This volume,* Chapter 33.

————, Gill, M. M., & Schafer, R. (1945–46). *Diagnostic Psychological Testing,* 2 vols. Chicago: Year Book Publishers.

Schilder, P. (1920). On the Development of Thoughts. In Rapaport (1951a), pp. 497–518.

———— (1931). *Brain and Personality,* 2nd ed. New York: International Universities Press, 1951.

Schrödinger, E. (1945). *What Is Life?* New York: Macmillan.

Stagner, R. (1951). Homeostasis as a Unifying Concept in Personality Theory. *Psychol. Rev.*, 58:5–17.

Tolman, E. C. (1932). *Purposive Behavior in Animals and Men.* Berkeley: University of California Press, 1949.

——— (1949). The Psychology of Social Learning. *J. Soc. Issues Suppl. Ser.*, No. 3.

Varendonck, J. (1921). The Psychology of Daydreams. In (abridged) Rapaport (1951a), pp. 451–473.

Werner, H. (1926). *Comparative Psychology of Mental Development.* New York: Harper, 1940.

Wiener, N. (1949). *Cybernetics, or Control and Communication in the Animal and the Machine.* New York: Wiley.

35

ON THE ORGANIZATION OF
THOUGHT PROCESSES
Implications for Psychiatry

I

When we study a patient, whether we interview or test him, we are dealing with the products of his thought processes. The mediating processes through which personality structure or dynamics express themselves in symptoms or behavior are thought processes. Obsessional character structure results in a limitation or inability to act. The mediating link between the two, however, is a variety of thought organization which is characterized by "doubt." It appears plausible that enhanced knowledge of thought processes should prove useful for both psychiatric understanding and therapy.

The first salient issue about thought processes is the distinction between the contents and the formal characteristics of thought. Condensation, displacement, indirect and visual representation, for example, are salient formal characteristics of the dream as a thought process, though there are many other such characteristics.

Though the understanding of contents is sufficient for everyday commu-

Lecture presented at the Connecticut State Hospital in 1951. Published here for the first time.

nication and for many needs of diagnostic and therapeutic practice, it is insufficient for a fundamental understanding of personality and thought processes. Consideration of contents will have to be supplemented and reinterpreted into formal characteristics of the thought process.

The first impact of psychoanalysis on psychiatry centered attention on content, and led to a neglect of formal characteristics. The projective techniques which, for instance, in the Rorschach Test, at first centered paramount interest on formal characteristics, are only too often invaded nowadays by overwhelming consideration of contents. On the other hand, the studies published by Kasanin (1944) in *Language and Thought in Schizophrenia* center on formal characteristics, and the scatter or pattern analysis of intelligence-test results is also an avenue for studying these.

II

Another salient issue of thought organization is that of the primary versus the secondary thought processes and their motivations. Freud assumed that the primary process operates with *drive energies* which strive for immediate discharge, while the secondary process operates with bound energies, secondary-process thought being "experimental action" with minute amounts of energies (cathexes). More recent studies by Kris (1950), and by Hartmann, Kris, and Loewenstein (1949), lead to the assumption that there is a continuous transition between drive and bound energies, between the primary and secondary processes. Binding or neutralization of cathexes is progressive and never quite complete. If it were, everyday thinking would always be strictly logical and never wishful. In turn, not even dreams and delusions are totally without logical ordering—or as Freud (1900) put it, secondary elaboration; or as Nunberg (1931) put it, synthesis. In these, bound cathexes already play some rôle.

Let us, following Kris (1950), take daydreams for our point of departure. They fall roughly into two categories. In one of these we correct a past mistake and/or prepare for a future performance, exploring the various avenues of behavior for the various contingencies. This kind of daydream is experimental action, though it does not follow the laws of logic as closely as does realistic thinking. It is wishful throughout, though the intervening realistic judgment will interrupt it wherever the wishes come too close to obliterating reality obstacles or considerations. In the other category we find daydreams which have nothing to do with future performance, which are not preparations for such, which are substitutes for rather than preparations for action. According to Kris's assumption, these varieties of daydream indicate that in them cathexes of various degrees of neutralization play the motivating force, with corresponding degrees of tendency to immediate discharge in imagery versus degree to which they can be delayed and so made preparations for action. Thus instead of a dichotomy—either primary or secondary process, either operation with displacement, condensation, substitution, symbolization, etc., or logical orderedness and no such Freudian mechanisms—we have a continuity of more or less of these. This understanding should prove useful in the study of various psychiatric syndromes where the usual case is that delusions and other symptoms, abiding by Freudian mechanisms, exist side by side with fragments of logical and ordered thinking. This understanding should also be helpful in interpreting why condensation, displacement, substitution, etc., phenomena are observed in experiments like those of Bruner (McClelland's, Lazarus', as well as Murphy and his students' experiments too have such implications) (see Rapaport, 1951, p. 399, n. 2, and pp. 404–405, n. 17), where not drive motivations but relatively high-level motivations such as attitudes, values, opinions, interests, appear to operate by means of such Freudian mechanisms. It seems that for now we are justified in formulating the following exploratory assumptions: (1) there is a whole hierarchy of motivations deriving from basic drives by means of a process of neutralization; (2) these motivations differ from each other in the degree to which they exert their effect in thought and action by means of Freudian mechanisms, or forms of ordered logical thought, but *all* motivations may under certain conditions use some of either thought forms.

III

Yet another important issue is the relation of the theory of thinking to prevailing theories of learning. Its importance is increased by attempts like those of Maier (1949) and Masserman (1943) to draw inferences about psychodynamics from experimental neuroses of animals, and by attempts to derive principles of psychodynamics and psychotherapy from learning experiments, like those of Mowrer (1950), Mowrer and Kluckhohn (1944), and Dollard and Miller (1950).

What is the basic problem a theory of thinking has to cope with? It is the paradox that thinking is, on the one hand, motivated behavior and, on the other, adapted to reality and socialized to communication. In its primitive basic form of hallucinatory wish fulfillment it is expressive only of drive needs; in its most highly developed forms it is science reflecting physical reality with high accuracy, art expressing emotion with great sensitivity, and interpersonal communication conveying meanings with the optimal freedom from ambiguity. In between there are all other forms of thought, some more expressive of intrapsychic need, others more reflecting of reality. Accordingly, there is a whole hierarchy of forms of thought ranging from drive representations to reality-adequate thought. On all these levels thought is motivated—a point I have discussed in the previous section of my presentation.

But what about learning theory? It seems to me that it is fair to say that it purports to deal with the acquisition of reality-adequate responses. There was a time, that of classical association theory, when the acquisition of such responses was not considered a motivated process, but a matter of contiguity associations. After Ach's (1905) studies of determining tendencies, after Thorndike's "law of effect" (1913, 1927), after Lewin's studies in readinesses and quasi needs (1922, 1926), this is no longer the case, and academic learning theory, too, for instance that of Yale, speaks of "drives" as motives of learning. Yet the fact remains that learning theory purports to solve the question of how in man reality-adequate thought is acquired, which we must remember is thought motivated by the furthest derivatives of the fundamental motivations in the hierarchy of motivations.

Once it is clear that learning theory purports to deal primarily with this one aspect of thought organization, various fallacies of present-day learning theory become obvious:

(1) In so far as it uses animal experiments to test its assumptions it deals, on the one hand, with organisms whose motivational organization is so different from the complexity of that of the social animal, man, that the application of its results to man is more than questionable; on the other hand, with motivations so basic that the applicability of the results to higher-level motivations must be called into question.

(2) In so far as it studies achievements which are acquired by repeated performance it disregards those human "acquisitions" that occur on a single performance, which learning theory mentions only under the heading of "incidental learning" and which incidentally seem to provide the avenue for the organization of the major part of human knowledge.

(3) In so far as learning theory in a sense still takes conditioned reflex and habit as the model of its theory, it forgets that reflexes evolve (as demonstrated by Coghill and Minkowski) out of global, undifferentiated motor patterns, and that habits come about as automatizations of motivated problem solutions directed at finding an object that will satisfy the motivating need. These automatizations, however, seem to vary with the hierarchic level of the motivation in question, and only studies within the framework of a hierarchic theory of motives promise a broad understanding of habits and conditioned responses as thought organizations.

(4) In so far as learning theory attempts to become a comprehensive theory to explain psychodynamics and psychotherapy, it lacks perspective since it attempts to generalize the scanty knowledge gained on remote derivative motivations to the entire psychic organization including basic drives. In essence, it tries to generalize from reality-adapted thought (or response) to need-expressing thought (or response). Such an attitude neglects laboriously acquired clinical knowledge.

(5) In so far as learning theory considers itself a theory of all acquisition of thought (or response) it fails to recognize that acquisition is not always ad hoc, particularly not that form of it which is called problem solving, but

rather that it progressively builds autonomous apparatuses which are then available not only for simple reacquisition but also in the production of new responses. Concepts, anticipations, sensorimotor sets, are the minimum of categories of such autonomous apparatuses used in thinking, and in that particular form of it which is called learning. Once acquired, these are available to the motivations seeking reality-adequate expression. There are others yet to be discovered.

(6) Learning theory, in so far as it did not rest content to remain a limited segment of animal psychology (Uexküll, Tinbergen, and Lorenz showed it to be a limited segment of it indeed), failed to recognize that only as a part of a general theory of thought organization, built on the principles that thought is motivated behavior whose motivations are hierarchically layered, and that the corresponding hierarchy of thought forms becomes progressively less need expressive and progressively more reality reflecting, can it meaningfully survive.

Surely I have here lumped together all the learning theories, yet that of Tolman (particularly recently), that of Lewin, and that of gestalt are less implicated in these fallacies than others.

IV

Another facet of the theory of thinking of interest to the clinician is the relation of thought organization to the varieties of conscious experience.

The subtleties of our conscious experience include, among other things, distinctions between internal and external perception, remembered event and fancy, fact and assumption, memory and percept, hope and actuality, certainty and doubt, and infinite shadings of many others. These conscious experiences reflect the refinement of the function which we are accustomed to label judgment, or reality testing. In various pathological conditions there are many different kinds of failure of such distinctions. A considerable body of knowledge is extant about the drive background and content of such varieties of conscious experience as myth, *déjà vu,* illusions, hallucinations, confabulations—but the formal characteristics of these varieties of conscious experience have so far been little explored, though such exploration would get into the anatomy of the function of reality testing.

V

Let me finally bring up one more issue which I would like to label as the relation of thought organization and state of consciousness.

In the case of a transitory illusion, a specific drive constellation of wish and fear is projected for an instant into the external world with illusionary intensity. It is a momentary variation of the mode of conscious experience, explainable in terms of a specific drive constellation. In the case of loss of personal identity, there is also a changed drive constellation. But in the latter the change of conscious experience is not momentary; indeed, a variant of conscious experience persisting for several days may come about, within the framework of which many of the usual variations—though limited by the framework in range—of conscious experience may appear. Nor is *all* the mass of behavior readily explainable in terms of the known dynamic constellation itself: it is rather that once the dynamic constellation has resulted in a loss of personal identity, individual behavior items are explainable within the situation so created. That is, they depend only indirectly upon the drive constellation, but not directly and specifically on a drive impulse.

A similar relation obtains—as Schilder described particularly clearly (1930; Rapaport, 1951, p. 288, n. 2)—between everyday slips of the tongue and the massive verbal parapraxes of aphasics. A slip of the tongue may be precipitated by tiredness of the apparatus, yet it is always traceable to a specific drive. The parapraxes of aphasics are always due to the interference of an organic trauma with the apparatus, though occasionally they may be drive specific.

Bleuler, Jung, Abraham, and others demonstrated that schizophrenic thinking reveals the same "complex" determination as that discovered by Freud in hysteria and dreams. What they (excepting for Bleuler) did not ask themselves was: Is all of schizophrenic thought pathology really explainable in terms of "complex effects," that is, in terms of the Freudian mechanisms of the primary process (displacement, condensation, substitution, symbolization, etc.)? What they asked but had not found an answer to was: Why do these effects seem to be so overwhelming in schizophrenia, as compared to hysteria? Jung (1907) made the assumption that an "X toxin" is responsible for this; Abraham (1908), that a difference in "psychosexual constitution" is responsible; Bleuler (1911), that a "disruption of associations of organic etiology" is responsible. Yet many schizophrenic symptoms, such as blocking, perseveration, mannerisms, literalness of concepts, etc., have no direct equivalent or explanation in terms of Freudian mechanisms, and cannot be traced to a specific drive. In fact, paralogical forms of schizophrenic thought which have equivalents in Freudian mechanisms—for example, the use of a part to represent the whole—are commonly present in such diffuse and luxuriant form that they no longer show "complex" or "drive" specificity, that is, they cannot be traced to a drive as their cause, as can a condensation in a common slip of the tongue. There are reasons to make the assumption that it is the totality of a schizophrenic's mode of thought, as a form of thought organization, which is the consequence of a given drive constellation, and unlike common slips of tongue, the single specific forms of schizophrenic thought cannot be traced to a specific complex or drive. Thus the state of affairs would be similar to what we have just suggested for the "loss of personal identity."

I have come to label these states, which are characterized by a specific form of thought organization with intrinsic rules of its own, which as a whole, but not in their specific characteristics, are traceable to a constellation of drive dynamics, as states of consciousness. One of the reasons for the label is that the first such states I encountered were the normal, the daydream, the hypnagogic, the dream, and that of schizophrenic confusion, in each of which a different quality seems to inhere to the consciousness of experiencing. You may want to note that these states of consciousness have a relatively stable character as compared to the phenomena I described above as "varieties of conscious experience."

Some time ago I trained myself to arouse at night sufficiently to be able to record my dreams, hypnagogic reveries, daydreams, and thoughts. Preliminary study of these records appears to show that:

(1) There is a continuum of states of consciousness between waking and dreaming.

(2) They differ from each other in the kind and extent of reflective awareness possible in them.

(3) They differ in the extent of voluntary effort possible in them.

(4) They differ in the form of thought organization prevailing in them, inasmuch as: (a) the closer the state is to the dream state, the more pictorial and implicative thought becomes; (b) the closer the state is to waking, the more verbal and explicit it is; (c) in progressing from the latter to the former, sentence structure changes from an emphasis on the syntactically important to an emphasis on the psychologically important; (d) the rôle of the subject becomes more diffuse in this progression, and somewhere along the line experiences resembling those of multiple personalities are encountered.

If these considerations and observations were to be borne out, a new and exciting vista would open for exploration, holding out much promise for penetrating into some of the so-far impregnable secrets of schizophrenic and other thought disorders.

I have attempted to indicate that what the theory of thinking concerns itself with may be of clinical relevance, importance, and use. If what I presented was a mosaic of broken bits, it was because the theory of thinking is still in its infancy.

REFERENCES

Abraham, K. (1908). The Psycho-Sexual Differences between Hysteria and Dementia Praecox. *Selected Papers*. London: Hogarth Press, 1927, pp. 64–79.
Ach, N. (1905). Determining Tendencies: Awareness. In Rapaport (1951), pp. 15–38.

Bleuler, E. (1911). The Basic Symptoms of Schizophrenia. In Rapaport (1951), pp. 581–649.

Dollard, J., & Miller, N. E. (1950). *Personality and Psychotherapy: An Analysis in Terms of Learning, Thinking, and Culture*. New York: McGraw-Hill.

Freud, S. (1900). The Interpretation of Dreams, tr. A. A. Brill. *The Basic Writings*. New York: Modern Library, 1938, pp. 179–549.

Hartmann, H., Kris, E., & Loewenstein, R. M. (1949). Notes on the Theory of Aggression. *Psychoanal. Study Child*, 3/4:9–36. New York: International Universities Press.

Jung, C. G. (1907). *The Psychology of Dementia Praecox*. New York: Nervous and Mental Disease Publishing Co., 1944.

Kasanin, J. S., ed. (1944). *Language and Thought in Schizophrenia*. Berkeley: University of California Press.

Kris, E. (1950). On Preconscious Mental Processes. In Rapaport (1951), pp. 474–493.

Lewin, K. (1922). Das Problem der Willensmessung und der Assoziation. *Psychol. Forsch.*, 1:191–302; 2:65–140.

———— (1926). Intention, Will and Need. In Rapaport (1951), pp. 95–153.

Maier, N. R. F. (1949). *Frustration: the Study of Behavior without a Goal*. New York: McGraw-Hill.

Masserman, J. H. (1943). *Behavior and Neurosis: An Experimental Psychoanalytic Approach to Psychobiologic Principles*. Chicago: University of Chicago Press.

Mowrer, O. H. (1950). *Learning Theory and Personality Dynamics*. New York: Ronald Press.

————, & Kluckhohn, C. (1944). Dynamic Theory of Personality. In *Personality and the Behavior Disorders*, Vol. I, ed. J. McV. Hunt. New York: Ronald Press, pp. 69–135.

Nunberg, H. (1931). The Synthetic Function of the Ego. In *Practice and Theory of Psychoanalysis*. New York: Nervous and Mental Disease Publishing Co., 1948, pp. 120–136.

Rapaport, D., ed. & tr. (1951). *Organization and Pathology of Thought*. New York: Columbia University Press.

Schilder, P. (1930). Studies Concerning the Psychology and Symptomatology of General Paresis. In Rapaport (1951), pp. 519–580.

Thorndike, E. L. (1913). *Educational Psychology*, Vol. I. *The Original Nature of Man*. New York: Teachers College, Columbia University.

———— (1927). The Law of Effect. *Amer. J. Psychol.*, 39:212–222.

36

INTERPERSONAL RELATIONSHIPS,
COMMUNICATION, AND
PSYCHODYNAMICS

In 1951, as seen in this paper, in his discussion at a seminar on mass communications (see Ch. 42), and in *Organization and Pathology of Thought,* also published in 1951, Rapaport used the concept of "channels of communication." He was clearly searching for a structural concept to identify an important aspect of interpersonal communication. Though it may be only a name for a congeries of interpersonal attitudes and relationships, the concept might be valuable if further developed. Rapaport himself, however, never followed it through.

I

Permit me to open with a personal reminiscence which may shed some light on our topic of tonight. When I was a little boy my parents were in the habit of rubbing into me the brilliance, charm, and affectionateness of a girl

Presented at the Menninger Foundation, Topeka, Kansas, February 1951. This paper is published here for the first time.

cousin of mine. I hated every bit of it, and the girl every inch. Over thirty years passed, we are good friends now, the bitterness and the memories have faded. Yet one still stands out: it proved to be my first encounter with the issue of communication. My parents, gloating, envious, and with an air of, "This is the kind of thing you ought to produce," bade me listen to a letter this cousin wrote to her absent father. It said: "I want to write 'I love you,' but if *you* read it, it will mean to you that 'You love me'; so—for you to get me right—I have to write, 'You love me.'" —To me this seemed terribly bright, despicably so—and I felt it was all affected. Yet it also puzzled me so much as never to be forgotten again. Translated into adult language, the essence of the quandary it left me in would read: is communication really this descriptive? Do I have to translate what I think in my language into the other person's language for him to understand it? —I imagine many of you will already have come to the conclusion that this must be a screen memory, condensing and hiding experiences in interpersonal relationships, in socialization, in thought, in communication, and other matters as well. May I plead not to have to continue on that path any further?

II

Let me offer a clinical example which may lead us further into the topic which I hope is opened up by this reminiscence. This example is lifted from a group control seminar of several years ago. The therapist was treating the young wife of an up-and-coming young businessman in the international trade. She was a borderline case, surviving on counterphobic mechanisms, globe-trotting, and independence. He was a hard-driving softie who hoped soon to slacken the pace. He was Jewish, and married her over the protest of his Orthodox family in the hope that she would join the synagogue; she was not interested in doing so. Soon after the marriage she showed decompensation phenomena, without becoming acutely psychotic, and was hospitalized. Her husband left soon after this on a series of business trips to last many months. The therapy progressed at an extremely slow pace: every feeling that arose for the therapist amounted to a threat to her independence, self-sufficiency, and the counterphobic defenses that held her together in the face of a continuous danger of far-reaching paranoid decompensation. Denial of feelings toward the therapist on the one hand, acting out and a consuming preoccupation with divorce and resuming a globe-trotting life on the other, were the outstanding trends. The therapy was well into its second year of frustrations for the patient, therapist, and husband, when the latter returned to the Midwest for a prolonged stay with his wife. In preparation for his arrival, the patient's feelings toward the therapist were intensified, as were the fear of becoming dependent on him, the fear of the marriage, the preoccupation with divorce, and guilt toward the husband.

Once the husband arrived, the patient's next maneuver was driven by this guilt and dread of becoming dependent on the therapist: she took flight from the therapist to the husband. This was at the moment in keeping with her counterphobic needs. On the one hand, the husband returning with business success did not seem to be as weak a softie, promising no protection, as he had in the period after marriage; on the other hand, he was by no means as strong and formidable as the therapist appeared to her now, when her powerful needs of dependence were pushing her toward him. She attempted to suppress her competitive, contemptuous feeling toward the husband; the marriage bonds, usually so intolerable to her counterphobic attitudes, she experienced as less constraining in comparison to the overwhelming dependency needs which arose in her relation to her therapist: she was beginning, in her own mind, to make a "go" of the marriage.

What was the husband's frame of mind? He had originally hoped that his wife would soon join him in his business sojourns. His urging letters to this effect, and his inhibited character made it probable that he did not enjoy his second bachelorhood. There was evidence that he was time and again sufficiently exasperated to ask himself whether this marriage could ever be made a go of, yet this inclination seemed to be counterbalanced both by his prodigious sense of duty and by his stubborn determination not to have to face his family's "I told you so's," which seemed buttressed by his traditional attitude to marriage. On arrival, his precariously balanced ambivalence was perpetuated: the positive gained support in his wife's attempts at making a go of it, the negative side in the obvious symptoms of illness and in no termination of therapy being in sight.

At this point the therapist saw the husband and made a mistake clearly motivated by countertransference attitudes. It is the anatomy of the communications comprising the mistake that I want to interest you in here, and the case data so far presented serve merely to set the stage for these communications.

In the interview, the husband complained bitterly about the patient's being difficult, inquired angrily when the therapy could be expected to end, asked when his wife would be well enough to consent to go through with the religious marriage ceremony in the synagogue, and related that if he had known she was this sick, he would never have married her. The therapist, who did not forewarn the husband that he would do so, gave the patient next day a full account of this conversation.

The group control session clearly demonstrated that the therapist responded as a matter of uncontrolled countertransference in the following fashion: (a) as an expression of anger in response to the patient's angrily abandoning him in favor of her husband, just after her transference feelings for the first time became available to analysis; (b) as an expression of anger in response to the angry inquiries of the husband whom he unconsciously experienced as a rival on several levels; (c) as an expression of resentment against the patient's counterphobic move in attempting to make a go of her marriage, which he rationalized by his reality judgment that this marriage was doomed—a judgment which in itself may have been justified, according to the control group. The control group also felt that the account given to the wife was a betrayal of the husband's confidence.

Let us now agree for tonight on three definitions of terms:

(1) Whenever a person can communicate a certain type of feeling or thought, we will speak of the *existence of a channel of communication* pertaining to that type of content.

(2) Whenever channels of communication exist for a certain type of feeling or thought, and these can be communicated to a certain person, we will speak of *an open channel of communication,* while when these cannot be communicated to a certain person, we will speak of *a closed channel of communication.*

(3) When information, which for one reason or another is intolerable, is sent through a channel of communication, we will speak of *a channel of communication being clogged up.*

Let us be clearly aware that these definitions pertain to well-known clinical facts, well accounted for—for most of our clinical purposes—by the concepts of repression (resistance), denial, isolation, and other defense mechanisms. If I propose these definitions it is to explore: (a) whether they allow us to take a look at these defenses from another angle, namely, that of interpersonal interaction and communication, rather than intrapsychic dynamics; (b) whether they would afford a conceptual tool to deal systematically with some aspects of human relationships (and therapeutic technique), which we have managed (or mismanaged, as in the present case) so far only intuitively, because the systematic treatment by means of the concepts of defense proved too cumbersome; (c) whether the slogan "science of interpersonal relationships," which is becoming a fetish and a battle cry of many who would revise psychoanalytic theory, could not be boiled down to its actual content of psychodynamics by means of some such conceptual equivalence as the one that would obtain between defenses and "channels of communication" as here defined.

I do not know the answers to these questions, and thus I merely submit the material for your consideration.

Let us then return to our threesome.

The husband, partly repeating a pattern that once obtained between him and his father, partly imitating—apparently on the basis of competitive identification—the pattern that was supposed to obtain between the therapist and his wife, lapsed into a "confessional" frame of mind in the interview with the therapist. His channels of communication for anger toward the therapist, as well as for anger toward his wife, were open. Now it is clear that the channel of communication to his wife of his anger toward her was not open at the same time. I do not speak here, however, of channels for subverbal and indirect symptomatic communications. It seems that his needs to preserve the marriage, to live up to his duties toward the person for whom he had assumed responsibility, to save face with his family whose advice and sentiments he had flouted, must have closed the channels of communication for his anger to his wife, lest he shoot his bolt prematurely. However, the patterns of the confessional which were activated in this feminine man in the conference with the therapist gave him the opportunity for venting his angers, and channels of communication opened, not only for the angers toward the therapist but also for those toward the wife. The psycho-dynamics of this spreading are too obvious to dwell on.

Now as for the wife: her channels of communication of anger toward the husband were closed, though more safely to the husband than to the therapist, who still heard some criticisms of him. Again, we are not talking of the symptomatic and unconscious channels which in her precarious state were certainly less safely closed than those of her husband. The reasons why those channels of communication were closed are rather clear: fear of dependence on the therapist, and guilt over her anger toward the husband adding up to an attempt to make a go of the marriage, accompanied by a closing of those channels of communication which would militate against the success of this attempt. The consequence of these channels of communication being closed is clear too: a minimization of those messages which could have contributed to opening the husband's channels of communication of his anger toward her.

Clearly the husband did not mean his communication of his anger toward her to reach her, nor had she been preparing to precipitate or receive such communications from him, although she did keep some channel open to give to and receive such communications from her therapist. This wife and husband had closed their channels of communication for their mutual angers, they had, as it were, turned these channels away from each other. These channels proved, however, to be open toward the therapist; they were turned, as it were, toward him. His ill-advised account connected these channels, which were meant to be closed and averted from each other. The immediate consequences were a closing of the wife's channel of communication to the therapist of her anger toward the husband, and an opening of the channel for anger toward the husband to him, the channels of goodwill closing. The further consequences are of no interest to us here.

We might reflect that whenever we follow our usual rule for dealing with relatives of borderline cases, namely, whenever after the work-up period we make it clear to them that whatever they tell us will be relayed to the patient, we not only protect the patient, making it clear to him that we are "on his side" and will not be partners to any "plot against them," we also carry out a much more complex operation. We protect the relatives' confidences by warning them not to communicate anything that they would not want to be relayed to the patient, or by which their relation to the patient might be jeopardized. We also protect the patient in several ways on another level: first, by preventing inadvertent jeopardizing by the relatives of whatever relationships exist between them; second, by helping the relatives to keep their own defenses up we prevent their losing control over their angers, fears, impatience, etc., toward the patient, and this is of crucial importance, because what they, by letting their defenses down, communicate to us may crystallize, particularly if we mismanage it, into a new and undesirable stand toward the patient. While in the patient what comes to the fore when defenses are given up is handled therapeutically, for the relatives this is not the case.

III

In everyday life, channels of communication are highly stable; we take it for granted that we talk or do not talk about certain topics and in certain veins to certain people, to our mates, children, friends, acquaintances, strangers. This very stability makes these channels of communication little noticed. Yet even in everyday life they do come to our notice in certain situations. Siegfried Bernfeld discussed one of these in a remarkable paper, in which he dwelt, among other things, on the psychology of secrets. He pointed out that when a person harbors a secret from another, communication between the two is likely to break down, because—to word it in my terms—the channels of communication related to those of the secret will become closed too, protecting, as it were, the secret. Another situation in which the role of channels of communication is directly experienced in everyday life is this: A is a friend of both B and C. Something personally important has happened to him, and he wants to relay it to both of them separately. He goes first to B, with whom he is more intimate, and intends to see C later. To B he usually relates his subjective experiences also, to C mainly the events; the first is a relationship of direct intimacy, the second a bond of unspoken understanding. Now he finds C with B, and the situation becomes embarrassing. If he talks as he usually does to B, C will certainly find it undignified and forward; if he talks as he usually does to C, C may find even that too personal in the presence of B, and B may not understand either why he has to talk about it at all, or, if so, why in such impersonal terms. So he may find himself searching for a neutral topic, or he may fasten his seatbelt and weather it out listening to the other two. Luckily, natures of little rigidity may manage, provided their friends too are sufficiently flexible, to make communications to which their usual channels of communication with both B and C are passable. In a slightly different situation, where B and C are neither close friends of A nor close acquaintances of each other, such double communication may well shade into double talk.

IV

One aspect of what I have attempted to convey by these examples may be boiled down theoretically to the following: we are familiar with processes which are, to begin with, occasional occurrences, but, once they have repeated themselves, often become stabilized and generalized. In fact, our conception of the development of many neurotic symptoms follows this pattern. We conceive of the development of inhibited characters as a stabilization and generalization of repressions. Observation of this pattern prompted Bleuler to describe hysterical symptoms as "occasional apparatuses" which, once established, perpetuate themselves autonomously until they are broken down. This is how we conceive of the development of habits from complex, goal-directed processes; indeed, it appears that it is thus that functions create or modify structure. Kretschmer (1922) referred to this process by his concept of "formular abbreviation." Schilder spoke of it as one of the fundamental mechanisms of the organism in his *Brain and Personality* (1931), and many other writings. Hartmann (1939) described the process by the concept of "automatization." In my discussion of "The Autonomy of the Ego" (1951) I presented considerations, partly those of Hartmann, which apply to the autonomy of these automatized, structuralized processes.

I would like to submit that the phenomena I have referred to here tonight as "channels of communication" are highly stable in everyday life, and being so stable, they too must have undergone automatization and structuralization. If so, they must abide by autonomous rules of their own. Some of these rules are implicit in the definitions themselves, others in the examples I have given. Some of these we are familiar with from the mechanisms of defense. I am not prepared to go any further on these lines at present; I would like to point out, however, that people who can talk only shop, or can talk only about the weather, that people who can talk only to people with whom they have been long acquainted, that people who need another person to spark-plug their conversation, etc., are good examples of how rigidly fixed and limited channels of communication do become.

I should like to point out that in psychoanalysis and psychotherapy, many of the problems of technique boil down to problems of channels of communication: how to use existing ones? how to open new ones? how to respect closed ones? how not to clog up open ones? how to clean out clogged ones? I should like to point out also that psychoanalysis and psychotherapy in general are not the ideal locus to observe the great stability and autonomy of channels of communication. First, because in a therapy that is going well the therapist is intuitive and senses which channels are open and which closed, what would open wider and what would clog up communication, and last but not least, unconscious channels of communication are used in abundance. Second, because in therapy that is going well communication channels are created, undone, opened, reopened, closed, clogged, cleaned, combined, etc., so that they appear highly unstable rather than stable.

However, in dealing within a hospital setting with interrelationships of patients, of patient and personnel, with relatives, the stability and autonomous rules of the channels of communication can be well observed. At another time I should like to give examples of these out of our current experience with the interaction of our patients at Riggs. But even in therapy proper with extremely rigid, inhibited, and borderline cases, where communication channels are likely to go dry, we struggle at first and often for long with the problem of finding and securing communication channels rather than with interpreting defenses or content.

V

There is, however, another aspect of these channels of communication, the theoretical consideration of which we cannot bypass.

Freud, both in "The Unconscious" (1915) and in *Beyond the Pleasure Principle* (1920), discussed the nature of what he called at that time the system *Pcpt.-Cs.* He noted that consciousness as a sense organ receives stimulation from both external and intrapsychic perception. He pointed out that while contents of intraspsychic perception have to pass both the censorship between the *Ucs.* and *Pcs.*, and that between the *Pcs.* and *Cs.*, contents of external perception do not run this gamut in becoming conscious. That Freud was cognizant of the fact of selective perception, and of Pötzl's (1917) work on the function of repression in perception, makes this formulation the more significant.

If we now consider what was so emphatically brought home to us by Freud in Chapter VII of *The Interpretation of Dreams* (1900)—that for the purpose of reality testing it is necessary that memory traces of objects and their relationships be available to consciousness—then the advantage external perception has over the intrapsychic in coming to consciousness attains new significance. To say "new significance" is actually a crude overstatement, since it is this differential ease in the coming to consciousness of external perception that all rational, interpretive therapy exploits. The clarification, integration, and interpretation, by the therapist to the patient, presents to the patient's external perception what he could not quite bring to his consciousness by intrapsychic perception.

We may conclude that it is this differential ease of external perception which gives communication not only in therapy but in psychic life in general the important role it actually has. Let us not for a moment forget that the confessional (which is not just a Catholic institution), the confidential talk to parents, teachers, family doctors, friends, are older institutions of mental hygiene than they are of formal psychotherapy. At the minimum, external perception can provide memory traces of objects and relationships to serve reality testing when the memory traces of the prior experiences of these are not available to intrapsychic perception due to the censorships, or in other terms, due to repression or other defenses. But human communication is the most varied, rich, and condensed source of external perceptions, and therefore its role in safeguarding the reality principle, the secondary process, and reality testing cannot be overestimated. My experience with deteriorated schizophrenics tells an eloquent tale of the effect of communication on reality testing.

But it does not do to assess the significance of communication for psychological dynamics at this minimal level. A more adequate appraisal seems to offer itself if we start out from the process of repression. It is the psychoanalytic conception that the primal repression of a drive is followed by the after-expulsion (repression proper) of its ideational representations from consciousness. Indeed, ideas which attain an even remote association with such drive representations succumb to repression. We know that under usual conditions it is the recently acquired or the disused ideas which so succumb to repression. Ideas that are well-integrated into close networks of relationships with ideas amenable to consciousness are less likely to share this fate. Thus communication, continuously re-presenting ideas and fitting them into ever-new relationships, militates against repression. The same goes for most of the other mechanisms of defense also, but this is a topic which I cannot enter today.

Thus, while it has always been clear that defenses can limit and cut down communications by destroying channels of communication, closing them or causing them to be clogged up, we must now add just as clearly that communication, keeping channels of communication open (and it seems to be one of their rules that disuse tends to make them close up or cease to exist), limits the spread of defenses and their effect on channels of communication and consciousness. Here again we must remind ourselves that though we tend to think mostly in terms of verbal, conscious communications, we are talking about the nonverbal and unconscious communications also.

VI

I realize fully that what I have said is not new, and that probably most of it, if not all of it, can be expressed in our customary psychoanalytic terms. The terms I used were not meant to replace any of the customary ones, but rather to supplement them if it should turn out that some problems of interpersonal relations in general, or therapeutic relationships or techniques in particular, would be more easily dealt with conceptually, or would become less obscure, through the use of these terms as conceptual tools.

To me it seems that Sullivan, Fromm, Horney, etc., and the others who speak so much about interpersonal relations and the role of cultural influences in psychological development have called attention to facts which psychoanalysis has not so far been sufficiently interested in, and which psychoanalytic theory has not always clearly encompassed. It seems to me, however, that they have not done much more than call attention to these— and depreciate the significance of many of those facts psychoanalysis has encompassed theoretically. I believe that their insistences have channeled much therapeutic intuition into a good direction—warning against purely id-psychological dogmatism. Yet theoretically psychoanalytic ego psychology has done more than they have, and Erikson, I believe, has succeeded in showing many avenues through which psychoanalysis—id psychology and ego psychology together—may begin to encompass the neglected areas of ego development, socialization processes, and the processes of cultural influence. I wonder whether a concept of channels of communication as here proposed, if taken seriously, could not serve as a concrete avenue to the study of the psychodynamics of interpersonal relations, for the study of which the only major concepts we have so far are those of transference and identification, and the great interest in which, displayed by the culturalists, has resulted in only phenomenological demonstrations and descriptions with some small degree of systematization, but not in theoretical systematization.

Let me close by reminding you of what Schilder said about socialization (1924): socialization is not an acquisition of man, he does not learn it in the course of his lifetime. It is a fundamental implication of his nature: it unfolds as he matures, but it is there from the beginning. Communication is the quintessence of socialization; it would be surprising if it were not guaranteed by autonomous stable arrangements and had to be again and again re-established in battles of Titans, drives, and defenses, in each of the partners to the communication. I believe there are such rather stable arrangements guaranteeing communication. I suggested for them tonight the term "channels of communication," and attempted to indicate where and how I seem to see them.

REFERENCES

Freud, S. (1900). The Interpretation of Dreams, tr. A. A. Brill. *The Basic Writings.* New York: Modern Library, 1938, pp. 179–549.
——— (1915). The Unconscious. *Collected Papers,* 4:98–136. New York: Basic Books, 1959.
——— (1920). *Beyond the Pleasure Principle,* tr. C. J. M. Hubback. London: Hogarth Press, 1948.
Hartmann, H. (1939). *Ego Psychology and the Problem of Adaptation,* tr. D. Rapaport. New York: International Universities Press, 1958.
Kretschmer, E. (1922). *Medizinische Psychologie.* Leipzig: Thième.
Pötzl, O. (1917). The Relationship between Experimentally Induced Dream Images and Indirect Vision. *Psychol. Issues,* 7:41–120, 1960.
Rapaport, D. (1951). The Autonomy of the Ego. *This volume,* Chapter 31.
Schilder, P. (1924). *Medical Psychology,* ed. & tr. D. Rapaport. New York: International Universities Press, 1953.
——— (1931). *Brain and Personality,* 2nd ed. New York: International Universities Press, 1951.

37

BOOK REVIEW

O. Hobart Mowrer, *Learning Theory and Personality Dynamics*[1]

I

This sizable volume is a collection of twenty-four papers, sixteen of which have been previously published (1939 to 1949); some of those previously unpublished are "little more than a collection of work-notes" (p. 617). The papers divide into twelve on learning theory and twelve on personality dynamics. Introductory notes and footnotes are intended to give unity to the divergent topics and changing views. The bookmaking job is excellent. The over-all effect—enhanced rather than mitigated by the notes—is disjointed and repetitious. One cannot help asking: Why has the author—who obviously has no difficulty with writing—chosen to reprint rather than to give a unified and economic presentation?

The first group of papers presents a new learning theory, the second a new theory of personality dynamics, neurosis, and therapy. There is an effort to base the latter theory on the former, implying an awareness of the need to overcome the present disjointedness of psychology. The uses Mowrer sees for the volume are: (a) reference work; (b) textbook or text

[1] New York: Ronald Press, 1950.

First published in The Journal of Abnormal and Social Psychology, *47:137–142, 1952.*

supplement on learning theory, language, personality, or psychotherapy; (c) possible guide to persons in neighboring sciences in interdisciplinary research (p. vii). This reviewer cannot but be awed by the ambitiousness of the undertaking, and filled with uneasiness that a collection of papers is to serve as its vehicle. Another uneasiness, too, must be admitted. The author asserts that

> Today it is by no means uncommon to find psychologists who are equally versed and interested in laboratory research and in psychotherapy or other clinical work and who move freely, both in their thinking and in their activities, from one to the other [p. v].

This reviewer does not belong to the group described; moreover, he has yet to encounter a publication rooted in learning theory which meets clinical problems on their own ground.

II

According to Mowrer, there are two kinds of learning: conditioning and problem solving. His "conditioning" is akin to Pavlov's, in that it depends on contiguity of onset of stimulation and consists of stimulus substitution; but it is unlike Pavlov's in that it accounts only for the "learning of secondary drives." His "problem solving" is akin to Hull's reinforcement learning, in that it abides by the law of effect; it depends on the termination of the drive once the response has occurred; and it consists of response substitution. The secondary drives learned by conditioning also abide by the law of effect. It is unlike Hull's reinforcement learning in that the secondary drives are acquired by conditioning. Mowrer formulates, "solution learning is problem solving, drive reducing, pleasure giving, whereas sign learning, or conditioning, is often—perhaps always—problem making" (p. 5).

The scrutiny of this theory *qua* learning theory must be left to learning theorists. Only four points crucial to personality dynamics will be discussed: insight, maturation, structuralization, and the relation to psychoanalysis.

Insight. Cognitive theories of learning discuss thought processes—central to psychodynamics, psychopathology, and therapy—under the heading of *insight.* Mowrer's treatment of insight and thought processes, therefore, may well serve as an index of the integration of learning and personality dynamics he achieved.

Hilgard (1948) in his survey of learning theories concludes that, "A strong case can be made for the . . . view that blind learning is not the prototype of all learning" (p. 207), and "Watching a child learn to brush its teeth . . . makes most of our learning principles inadequate" (p. 237). Hebb (1949) writes: "The failure of psychology to handle thought adequately . . . has been the essential weakness of modern psychological theory . . ." (p. xvi). Mowrer, however, equates a strikingly faster "blind learning" of his experimental group of rats with insight, which he interprets in terms of "problem solving" and secondary drives (p. 322). He does not face, but rather explains away, the problem of insight: ". . . insight learning is not learning at all . . . but a kind of higher activity—or complex habit—that utilizes the results of learning but is not learning itself" (pp. 6–7). Thought processes are mentioned only once: they too are "important intervening variables" (p. 198 n.).

Maturation. A basic implication of both developmental psychology (Werner, 1926) and psychoanalysis is the dependence of motivations, behavior, and thought upon maturation processes. "Fixation" means interference with a maturation process. Mowrer does speak of fixation. Does his learning theory take account of maturation?

Piaget (1923, 1927) has analyzed the maturation of thought and language forms and investigated the maturation of "sensorimotor intelligence" into "abstract intelligence" (1936a, 1936b, 1937). Hilgard (1948) indicated that a maturation theory of learning is still an open possibility. Hebb (1949) found "early" and "later" learning qualitatively different, the former being associative, the latter conceptual. But neither Mowrer's "conditioning" nor his "problem solving" is specific to the early phases of development: learning involving primary drives always operates by "problem solving"; conditioning—by which secondary drives are established—occurs concurrently. Mowrer could argue that early learning is dominated by primary, later learning by secondary drives; but with Mowrer, learning— whether it involves primary or secondary drives—operates by the law of effect, and therefore this difference makes no difference.

According to Mowrer, everything is learned (except primary drives); therefore he has no use for maturation. Even perceptions and emotions are considered learned ("conditioned"), their inborn mechanisms are disregarded (e.g., pp. 199, 211), and a "guilt theory of anxiety" flouting the genetic relation of anxiety to fear is proposed. A reflection of Mowrer's disregard of psychological maturation is,

> By and large, the solutions to individual problems involve the central nervous system and the skeletal musculature, whereas the solutions to social problems involve the autonomic nervous system and the organs which mediate emotional responses [p. 240].

Structure formation. Most learning theories have one structural concept: habit. Habits are *structures* in the sense that—according to some learning theories—they are the products of learning, and once established they are used to meet situations *without* a process of learning. With few exceptions, S-R learning theories have no other structural concepts, and therefore reduce everything to habits or to learning processes (reinforcement). Psychoanalytic theory (Freud, 1923) and Allport's (1935–47) ego psychology require for the understanding of human psychodynamics further structural concepts (see Rapaport, 1951a, 1951b). The familiar structural concepts of psychoanalysis are: id, ego, superego. Mowrer uses these concepts. Does his learning theory have a place for such structural concepts?

In so far as Mowrer's theory centers on secondary drives, regarding them as motivations attuned to reality, it implies these as structural concepts, and is in harmony with the clinical observations and theory of a hierarchy of motivations: drives, defensive motivations, defense-modified drives, defenses against these, etc. (Rapaport, 1951a, 1951b). While for ego psychology the derivative motivations, once established, have a "functional autonomy," Mowrer's negative view of Allport's "functional autonomy" (pp. 23–24, 424, 508, 693) suggests that he is not concerned with the structural implications of such motivations.

Mowrer does see some of the limitations of a learning theory that lacks structural concepts: "What the law of effect *does not* tell us is what . . . organisms will learn or do if they perform actions which are followed by consequences . . . both rewarding and punishing . . . both immediate and remote. The investigation of these problems takes us into . . . ego psychology" (pp. 206–207). He introduces the structural concept "ego," yet he also maintains that "it should not be supposed that there is any discontinuity between the fundamental laws of learning . . . at the lower levels of behavior and the generalizations that . . . hold best at the higher levels" (p. 198). More explicitly, "We know a good deal about both the genesis and nature of the emotions, and I see no advantage in separating ourselves from this knowledge by speaking of ego-involvement instead of emotional arousal" (p. 205). Mowrer does see the complex situations which defy reduction to the law of effect, yet he cannot give up the hope of reduction ("no discontinuity," "emotional arousal") and consequently he does not face the problem of structure. His term "ego" is empty: there is no discussion in this volume of ego functions (for definition, see p. 586).

The superego (conscience) is treated in a curious tripartite way: (a) it seems to be an autonomous structure when its role in neuroses is discussed (pp. 517–530); (b) yet it is reduced to products of conditioning which operate as secondary drives (Chapter 21); (c) or it disappears into a simple or ego-enforced compliance with external authority (e.g., pp. 462 ff., 540, 614).

Of the more subtle structures involved in thought processes (anticipations, concepts, syntax, logic, etc.) only anticipations are discussed, but they are put out of the way as emotions, i.e., secondary drives. Not even structures of the order of Bartlett's (1932) memory schemata, or Piaget's (1936a) sensorimotor and abstract schemata are introduced.

Relation to psychoanalysis. Psychoanalytic theory distinguishes primary and secondary processes (Freud, 1900; Rapaport, 1950). The primary processes abide by the pleasure principle—striving for immediate discharge—and use the associative mechanisms of condensation, displacement, substitution, symbolization, etc. (as seen in dreams, fantasies, hallucinations, etc.). The secondary processes abide by the reality principle—delay of discharge, experimental action, i.e., thought, detour activities—and use the mechanisms of ordered thought (concepts, logic), and purposive action (Freud, 1915a, 1915b, 1925; Rapaport, 1950). The transition between primary and secondary processes is continuous, though in the course of it new structures arise.

Mowrer states that "problem solving" corresponds to the pleasure principle and "conditioning" to the reality principle (e.g., pp. 5–6, 10, 239). Is this so? Mowrer's "conditioning" ("emotion learning") operates by contiguity association and its products (secondary drives) by the law of effect (pleasure principle?), whereas Freud's reality principle operates primarily by those cognitive principles for which there is no place in Mowrer's system. For Mowrer, "problem solving" dominates adult adaptive behavior, while for Freud the sway of the pleasure principle is limited in adults by the reality principle. This kind of misunderstanding may disturb the reader and reviewer. For a science of psychology, however, it is irrelevant: Mowrer's concepts need by no means correspond to Freud's—if they advance us. But that is just what the above comparison calls into question: Mowrer—except for his conception of socialization by means of the conditioning of secondary drives—disregards even the problems raised by the concept of reality principle.

III

Mowrer presents his personality dynamics in a running engagement with psychoanalytic theories, accepting, disregarding, rejecting, and modifying them variously. What this does to the rest of the psychoanalytic theory, and the observations it is founded on, is rarely considered. He justifies these alterations by reference to "the best-established principles . . . of learning" (p. 525), to clinical evidence which, except for three fragments, is not quoted, and occasionally to what may be considered a *Weltanschauung,* philosophy, or religion (e.g., Chapter 20, or p. 538).

The relation between learning theory and psychodynamics is nowhere systematically presented, and what there is of it appears to be conjectural. In fact, one of Mowrer's merits is the awareness that rat experiments are but "experimental analogues" (p. 368), "to demonstrate a principle, in its . . . least ambiguous form" and then "to return to . . . human behavior with improved understanding" (p. 428). But that's just the rub: neither Mowrer nor anybody else has demonstrated whether and how that can be done. Thus the learning theorist, an exacting scientist in his own realm, goes fancy-free in applying what he learned from his rats: e.g., discussing his experiment on preparatory set, Mowrer suddenly discovered,

"This is probably the dynamics of 'masochism'" (p. 33 n.). Many academic psychologists consider psychoanalytic theory as a wild flight of fancy and overlook its orderly relation to clinical observation. Freed from experimental caution and not bound by case material, they will treat clinical theory with a degree of unwarranted "freedom." But this does not entitle us to reject a priori what Mowrer has to say. In the clinical domain an arbitrary presentation may contain important insights.

Mowrer's views may be discussed under four headings: (1) superego in neuroses; (2) the nature of anxiety; (3) therapy; (4) evaluation of psychoanalysis.

(1) SUPEREGO IN NEUROSES

Mowrer reports that according to psychoanalysis neurosis is due to the repression of the id by the ego-superego alliance, and contends per contra that it is due to the repression of the superego by the id-ego alliance. He argues that the basic problem (paradox) of neurosis—its simultaneous self-perpetuating and self-defeating character—is not solved by Freud's theory, but is solved by his.

The neurotic paradox. In his discussion of identification Mowrer attempts to reduce the superego to a set of learned motives: ". . . the fears and loyalties which constitute the basic stuff of conscience are probably acquired . . . [by] conditioning" (p. 614). Consequently, according to Mowrer, Freud's "over-severe superego" explains the self-perpetuating character of neurosis by a *"learning excess"* and goes counter to "one of the best-established principles . . . that all learning tends to undergo extinction unless . . . reinforced" (p. 525). Mowrer explains neurosis as a *"learning deficit"* (p. 525), as "ignorance rather than illness" (p. 521), "Because of resistances which the infantile ego sets up against the socializing forces and . . . later . . . against . . . the superego, the ego remains immature, asocial, id-dominated" (p. 525). This argument is confusing: (a) On page 492, Mowrer reports that psychoanalysis explains the self-perpetuating character of neurosis by its gratifying of id wishes, and its self-defeating character by the punishing superego; here Mowrer condemns psychoanalysis because—according to him—it explains self-perpetuation by an oversevere superego. (b) Is it not—to use Mowrer's expression—"question begging" to explain "learning deficit" by "resistances of the infantile ego"? Does this formulation not reintroduce through the back door the question which it was to settle, namely, the relation of id-ego-superego to each other?

The superego. According to Mowrer, neurotics suffer not from repression but from immaturities. Their fixations are not "libidinal" but "moral": having *"persisted* in a strategy of secrecy, deception, and dissociation" (p. 361), "the neurotic distrusts, spurns, and represses conscience" (p. 516). People become neurotic "not because of what they would do but cannot, but because of what they have done and would that they had not" (p. 515).

Consequently, "the neurotic character lies much closer to the criminal character than we have commonly thought" (p. 516). Mowrer's arguments correctly imply that: (a) the unconscious superego and the unconscious sense
of guilt are indispensable clinical concepts; (b) pre-World War I psychoanalysis did not account for phenomena pertaining to these; (c) many analysts and psychiatrists still do not pay sufficient attention in their therapeutic work and writings to these, and to the values and loyalties of man. How
should one explain, however, Mowrer's ignoring that: (a) the projection of
the unconscious superego in delusions was discussed by Freud as early as
1911;[2] (b) the concepts of unconscious sense of guilt and unconscious
superego were introduced by Freud in *The Ego and the Id* in 1923 (p. 75)
and became accepted and central conceptions of psychoanalysis (e.g.,
1933); his assertions ("deception," "criminal," etc.), since he does not
present clinical evidence for them, may be understood as calling the neurotic a "sinner" or "gold-bricker."

Mowrer propounds a superego-centered psychology, as early analysts
(e.g., Stekel) did an id-centered psychology, or as Adler did an ego-envi-
ronment-centered psychology. The difference: Mowrer appears late and
does not offer clinical evidence. There is place for a stress on the superego,
unconscious guilt, values, etc., in clinical practice, theory, and research, but
it is too late in the game to find a simple solution for neuroses.

(2) THE NATURE OF ANXIETY

According to Mowrer,

> Freud's theory holds that anxiety comes from evil wishes, from acts
> which the individual would commit if he dared. *The alternative view
> here proposed is that anxiety comes . . . from acts which he has
> committed but wishes that he had not. It is . . . a "guilt theory" of
> anxiety rather than an "impulse theory"* [p. 537];
> . . . the one holds that anxiety arises from repression that has been
> turned toward the *id;* . . . the other . . . that . . . [it] arises from
> repression . . . turned toward the *superego* [p. 537].

Yet he also maintains—though anxiety is his favorite secondary drive—
that "fear is a 'conditioned reaction,' anxiety is 'unconditioned,' primitive,
reflexive" (p. 551). As for the role of anxiety in neuroses,

> In terms of modern learning theory, anxiety is the *problem* and the
> symptom is the "habit" or *solution* . . . As we have seen in earlier
> sections, this hypothesis brilliantly accounts for a wide variety of so-
> called "addictions," "vices," and common "bad habits" [p. 546].

[2] [Rapaport was presumably referring to Freud's paper on Schreber (Freud, 1911;
see, e.g., pp. 66, 77–78), although Freud did not use the term "superego" at that
time—Ed.]

(The present reviewer did not discover these accounts.)

A transformation of repressed "moral force and guilt" (p. 539) into anxiety is a silk purse made of a sow's ear, as was Freud's transformation of repressed libido into anxiety, to which Mowrer's theory is admittedly similar (p. 539). What is wrong with it is this: (a) Guilt and anxiety are affects. They can displace each other when the underlying dynamic conditions change but they cannot be transformed into each other. This sort of realization led Freud to develop his later (1926) theory of anxiety of which Mowrer gives but a perfunctory account. (b) Psychoanalysis made us familiar with superego anxiety: it is a signal of the ego that a superego punishment will follow if the id and ego processes impending are not stopped. This, however, is *not* a transformation of guilt. (c) How anxiety can be a transformation of repressed guilt, *and* "unconditioned," *and* a conditioned secondary drive is hard to see.

To support his theory Mowrer invokes—instead of clinical evidence— King David the Psalmist, Kirkegaard, and Poe. The sensitive discussion of Poe is perhaps the best part of the book, but it demonstrates only the role of unconscious guilt, and proves nothing about the guilt theory of anxiety (see p. 619). Critical analysis of intuitive writing is one thing, but to use the poet's opinion to confirm one's own is another. To have King David pronounce on the theory of guilt and anxiety is bad enough, but this use of Kirkegaard is worse.

> "Dreaming spirit" may at first seem but a vague, poetic metaphor; but . . . for Kirkegaard "spirit" was equivalent to what "superego" was for Freud. And if we translate "dreaming" to mean "sleeping," "dormant," or "repressed," we arrive at the statement: Dread is a consequence or manifestation of a repressed superego [p. 544].

Mowrer's final argument for his theory:

> . . . it brings scientific anxiety theory into fundamental agreement with the implicit assumptions of the great religions of the world concerning anxiety, namely, that it is a product . . . not of over-restraint and inhibition, but of irresponsibility, guilt, and immaturity [p. 538].

Is it the task of psychology to *understand* religions and their great influence on man, or to reach a "fundamental agreement" with their teaching?

(3) THERAPY

Mowrer maintains that according to Freud "the task of psychotherapy is to help the patient move in the direction opposite to that in which the parents tried—and supposedly succeeded only too well—to take him" (pp. 10–11), because "he regarded the superego as a more or less archaic relic of childhood and . . . traditions, values, and morality . . . , as . . .

carryovers from early stages . . . of the race" (p. 527). Mowrer contends that "a neurotic can be cured only if he 'opens his heart' to the great moral teachings and emotional values of his society" (p. 526), because "traditions and social values represent some of our strongest guides to psychological and social reality" (p. 528). Mowrer speaks of "the Freudian imputation that anxiety is an imposter—foreign, unfriendly, and destructive" (p. 540) and in contrast maintains that "psychotherapy must involve acceptance of the essential friendliness and helpfulness of anxiety, which, under such management, will eventually again become ordinary guilt and moral fear, to which realistic readjustments and new learning can occur" (pp. 539–540). Finally, according to Mowrer, "Psychotherapy, if sound, ought . . . to generate a philosophy of life . . . preventive as well as . . . corrective" (p. 9) and psychoanalysis "actually aggravated . . . the very conditions it is supposed to correct" (one of Mowrer's authorities on this is Msg. Fulton J. Sheen, p. 564).

I will not demonstrate how slanted this statement of Freud's view of therapy is. If Mowrer maintained only that Freud was much concerned with the pathogenic influence of society, culture, and religion on man, but little concerned with their positive role in ego and superego development, he would be right. If Mowrer implied that some psychoanalysts still treat patients as though they were living in a social, cultural, and religious vacuum, and as though social, cultural, and religious values were only noxious rationalizations—he would still make a contribution. Freud lived and worked in a late Victorian society in which a homogeneous social, cultural, educational, and religious support of ego and superego development was taken for granted and escaped scientific analysis. Our society does not provide such homogeneous support and this may be one of the reasons that the clinical picture of isolated neuroses has yielded its pre-eminence to character disorders and that besides the pathogenic rôle of id repression, that of ego weakness and that of warping of the superego have also come into relief. But Mowrer has gone much further, and the panacea he offers reflects this clearly. It amounts to an attempt to turn back the clock: tradition, religion, sense of duty, acceptance of social demands is the cure-all.

There are several things wrong with these premises and conclusions: (a) Anna Freud (1936), and in her wake, psychoanalytic ego psychology (e.g., Hartmann, 1939; Erikson, 1950), have studied the positive rôle of society and culture in ego and superego development. (b) If norms, duty, religion, could play the rôle in our changing society which Mowrer recommends as a remedy, there would be no need of a remedy (Mowrer's or others') to begin with. (c) There is the possible implication that education and therapy could become the means to enforce the individual's compliance with society (the state?), and on the end of that road looms Orwell's *Nineteen Eighty-Four*. For who is to declare what are to be "stable truths" the compliance with which is Mowrer's salvation of the individual? The task of the ego is to synthesize and reconcile id impulses, superego commands, and reality demands. Therapy's task is to facilitate this and thus make id-impulse gratification, ego-interest pursuit, achievements and life style consistent with values (ego ideal, superego) possible. Most of the time therapy achieves only some of these and only to some degree sufficient to make life worth living for the patient, and the ego's synthetic forces are relied on to expand these gains further. Thus, it is quite possible for an intuitive therapist to achieve results in the way Mowrer points. But both personality theory and flexible therapy take into account more than the one facet of human personality Mowrer happened to center on.

(4) EVALUATION OF PSYCHOANALYSIS

Some of the less than adequate statements of psychoanalytic theory have been mentioned; there are many others. The most striking misstatements seem to arise from Mowrer's dating Freud's writings by their English publication dates. Thus *The Interpretation of Dreams* is 1920 instead of 1900; *Three Contributions to the Theory of Sex* 1916 instead of 1905; *Totem and Taboo* 1918 instead of 1913; *The Ego and the Id* 1935 instead of 1923; *The Problem of Anxiety* 1936 instead of 1926. "Mourning and Melancholia" appears both under its correct and its English publication date. No wonder that Freud's early theories loom large on Mowrer's horizon.

IV

It is probably not fair to Mowrer to suggest that the origin of his theory is a wish for the return of the times of obedience to strong social norms, an obedience which would be guaranteed by a "conditioned" superego, and by drive-reduction learning dependent on social reward. Yet these are the leitmotifs of his theory.

REFERENCES

Allport, G. W. (1935–47). *The Nature of Personality: Selected Papers.* Cambridge, Mass.: Addison-Wesley Press, 1950.
Bartlett, F. C. (1932). *Remembering: A Study in Experimental and Social Psychology.* Cambridge: Cambridge University Press.
Erikson, E. H. (1950). *Childhood and Society.* New York: Norton.
Freud, A. (1936). *The Ego and the Mechanisms of Defence.* New York: International Universities Press, 1946.
Freud, S. (1900). *The Interpretation of Dreams,* tr. A. A. Brill. New York: Macmillan, 1913.
——— (1911). Psycho-Analytic Notes on an Autobiographical Account of a Case of Paranoia (Dementia Paranoides). *Standard Edition,* 12:3–82. London: Hogarth Press, 1958.

———— (1915a). Repression. *Collected Papers,* 4:84–97. New York: Basic Books, 1959.

———— (1915b). The Unconscious. *Collected Papers,* 4:98–136. New York: Basic Books, 1959.

———— (1923). *The Ego and the Id,* tr. J. Riviere. London: Hogarth Press, 1947.

———— (1925). Negation. *Collected Papers,* 5:181–185. New York: Basic Books, 1959.

———— (1926 [1925]). *The Problem of Anxiety,* tr. H. A. Bunker. New York: Psychoanalytic Quarterly & Norton, 1936.

———— (1933). *New Introductory Lectures on Psycho-Analysis,* tr. W. J. H. Sprott. New York: Norton.

Hartmann, H. (1939). Ego Psychology and the Problem of Adaptation. In *Organization and Pathology of Thought,* ed. & tr. D. Rapaport. New York: Columbia University Press, 1951, pp. 362–396.

Hebb, D. O. (1949). *The Organization of Behavior; A Neuropsychological Theory.* New York: Wiley.

Hilgard, E. R. (1948). *Theories of Learning.* New York: Appleton-Century-Crofts.

Piaget, J. (1923). *The Language and Thought of the Child,* 2nd ed. London: Routledge, 1932.

———— (1927). *The Child's Conception of Physical Causality.* London: Kegan, 1930.

———— (1936a). *The Origins of Intelligence in Children,* 2nd ed. New York: International Universities Press, 1952.

———— (1936b). The Biological Problem of Intelligence. In *Organization and Pathology of Thought,* ed. & tr. D. Rapaport. New York: Columbia University Press, 1951, pp. 176–192.

———— (1937). Principal Factors Determining Intellectual Evolution from Childhood to Adult Life. In *Organization and Pathology of Thought,* ed. & tr. D. Rapaport. New York: Columbia University Press, 1951, pp. 154–175.

Rapaport, D. (1950). On the Psychoanalytic Theory of Thinking. *This volume,* Chapter 28.

———— (1951a). Toward a Theory of Thinking. In *Organization and Pathology of Thought,* ed. & tr. D. Rapaport. New York: Columbia University Press, pp. 689–730.

———— (1951b). The Conceptual Model of Psychoanalysis. *This volume,* Chapter 34.

Werner, H. (1926). *Comparative Psychology of Mental Development.* New York: Harper, 1940.

38

PROJECTIVE TECHNIQUES AND
THE THEORY OF THINKING

Let me take the liberty to characterize for a moment, in a fashion some will consider caricature, the achievements of the big I.Q. testing movement. Where did it get us with its pragmatism and famous operational definition: intelligence is what intelligence tests measure? It helped us in solving some practical problems in a rather crude fashion, and it taught us a lot of statistics. Except for those who have put their faith into the robot of factor analysis, nobody believes that it taught us anything about the *nature of the mind;* and except for the clinician who thinks in terms of *pattern analysis, item analysis,* and *verbalization analysis,* nobody seems even to hope that it can teach us more.

I believe that this state of affairs is due to the absence of theoretical analysis as to how these tests work and how they fail. Theory of testing, the *rationale,* is lagging far behind the practical use of tests by rule of thumb. This holds not only for intelligence tests but for projective tests also. One is deluged by what may be considered evidence for this, if one works in an institution to which the referring physicians relay test reports. The phrases

Extract of a lecture to the Southern California Regional Division of the Society for Projective Techniques, February 15, 1951. First published in Journal of Projective Techniques, *16:269–275, 1952. Reprinted in Robert P. Knight and Cyrus R. Friedman, eds.,* Psychoanalytic Psychiatry and Psychology, Clinical and Theoretical Papers, Austen Riggs Center, Volume I. New York: International Universities Press, 1954, *pp. 196–203.*

of Rorschach, Klopfer, Beck, and *Diagnostic Psychological Testing* (Rapaport, Gill, and Schafer, 1945–46) are, in most of these reports, dished up in more or less of a hash. I would like to suggest that this, too, is a consequence partly of a lack of effective theory of tests and partly of fragmentary theories. By fragmentary theories I mean that the Rorschach has some theory, the TAT has some, the Szondi has some, etc., but they all have hardly more in common than vague references to psychoanalytic ideas—and even from among these ideas the different tests theories choose different ones. When reading them I am reminded of the Hungarian Count waiting for his wife's delivery. As he was pacing the floor, the nurse brought in the surprise: the triplets his wife had just delivered. The Count stopped his pacing, with finger on temple considered them for a while, and then pointed at the middle one saying, "I choose this one." But for us there is no choice; it is clear that we must find a unitary theory for all tests. True, there was a time in physics in which the theory of electricity had nothing to do with that of light, or magnetism, or heat, or mechanics—but let us not forget that in those days the unity of nature was by no means as obvious as it is today, and let us admit that the phenomena tapped by the Rorschach and the TAT are not as far from each other as are light and sound!

It is my belief that a sufficiently broad theory of thinking can be formulated to encompass the rationale and phenomena of all tests. This does not mean that there is such a theory of thinking extant more than in traces and fragments (Rapaport, 1942b, 1950, 1951a, 1951b). *The way to get a theory behind testing is to use and study tests so as to contribute to a theory of thinking, then the theory of thinking will increasingly contribute to the theory of testing* (Rapaport, 1942a, 1946, 1947).

Tonight I should like to take up four points which are in need of and amenable to such work. The points I have chosen are: *Projection, Motivations of selective perception, Fixed tools of thought,* and *Varieties of conscious experience.*

PROJECTION

When we use the term projection, as for instance in "projective testing," we actually mean externalization, and not just the defense mechanism of projection described by Freud. We certainly do not mean the mechanism of paranoid projection: I love him—but that is too dangerous; so I hate him—this tension is intolerable; therefore, it is rather that he hates me—so I am justified in hating him. This sequence contains the reversal into the opposite of an impulse, as well as the externalization of the result (Freud, 1911). Nor do we mean the infantile prototype of projection which plays such a fundamental role in the differentiation of the "me" and "not-me": everything that is pleasurable must belong to the infantile ego and is, therefore, "introjected," and everything that is painful, tension producing, must belong to the external world and is, therefore, projected (Freud, 1917). Nor even do we mean by projection just the phenomena of transference in which the revived attitudes toward the parents (or other important figures in one's life) are directed wholesale toward the therapist and make him appear in the patient's eyes as possessing the attributes of one parent or the other or both (Freud, 1912). What we mean by projection in the phrase "projective techniques" is rather what L. K. Frank (1939, 1948) expressed and what I would like to paraphrase as follows: each individual has a private world which is structured according to the organizing principles of his personality, and projective testing studies these organizing principles by inducing the subject to bring them to bear upon more or less unstructured material, incorporating it into his private world. One could argue that there is a salient difference between the psychoanalytic and this concept of projection, in that the former has as its core the externalization of a specific tension, while the core of the latter is merely the organization of perception and production in terms of intrapsychic organizing principles. One could, however, argue also the other way around; there is no difference in principle between the two, organizing principles are always strains and stresses within the personality, and bringing them to bear on the world of percepts or productions amounts always to partially ridding oneself of these strains and stresses; furthermore, phenomena subsumed under the psychoanalytic conception of projection are not so homogeneous either: paranoid projection, infantile projection, projection in transference phenomena are rather a graduated continuum which becomes progressively more general, extending from the externalization of a specific type of tension in paranoid projections, to that of any kind of tension in infantile projection, to that of a whole system of attitudes and tensions in transference phenomena, to where it imperceptibly shades into the externalization in the form of a "private world" defined by the organizing principles of one's personality.

Both arguments have much to support them. Yet both seem to neglect one point: the organizing principles of personality are neither a sum (or as Wertheimer would have put it: *Und-Summe*), therefore not a congeries of tensions of the sort which are involved in paranoid projections, nor are they one homogeneous entity. The referents of the concept "projection" Frank talks about are no more homogeneous than those of the psychoanalytic concept. The organizing principles are not merely strains and stresses of the same character as the tensions involved in projection, but they are also—at least part of them—structures, or structuralized tensions. It seems that we are dealing here with a continuum of externalizations, somewhere along which externalizations of structural organizing principles, referable to structuralized tensions, also come into play. We are dealing here, in part at least, with the problem of the relation of function and structure. Such a conception seems to be implicit in G. Allport's (1935) distinction between motivating and instrumental attitudes. In my discussion of nonprojective tests

(Rapaport, 1946) I have pointed toward such a distinction. It seems that the kinds of projection that are implicit in our projective techniques are manifold, and one of our urgent tasks is to observe, describe, systematize, and theoretically evaluate these differences in kind. There is no theory of thinking nor a theory of projective techniques conceivable without the clarification of the hierarchy of these externalization functions we call projection.

There is a radical difference between those externalization—or if you prefer, projection—processes which fill a Rorschach record with towers, power drills, swords, or torn, mutilated, crumbling things, and those which result in an overwhelming number of responses of the small detail, or the unusually sharp form variety. Similarly, there are differences in principle between those externalization processes which result in scatter patterns of the Bellevue and those resulting in the contents of the TAT.

The sensitive clinician knows and respects these differences intuitively. The good teacher of clinical psychology instills a sense for these in his students. In the long run intuition will always remain our guide in clinical work. But the science of psychodynamics and the theory of testing is a different matter. There we need systematic knowledge of the varieties of these externalization processes and of their relation to each other. Here a broad field of observation and systematic exploration opens, one which is of more fundamental importance than the now fashionable effort of inventing new projective tests or new indicators in the old ones.

MOTIVATIONS OF SELECTIVE PERCEPTION

Let me now turn to another topic of import both for projective techniques and for the theory of thinking, which at first sight may not differ much from that of the varieties of externalization just discussed.

Let us take the TAT for our point of departure. You will all remember TAT records in which noble sentiments, values of altruism, tender feelings for human beings, animals, and objects, and compassion with suffering prevailed and appeared as the motivating forces of the behaviors in the stories. I am equally sure that you all remember records in which the characters were moved by strivings toward rational goals, realistic interests. Then again, there are those records which are permeated by gloom, despondency, fright, and other feelings; sometimes these remain pure descriptions, at others these feelings and moods are presented as the motivations of behavior. And there are records—mostly those of psychotic patients—where rage and craving, retaliation and hunger, appear as motivations. It goes without saying that the average record contains, as a rule, some of all these varieties and is not as extreme as any of the schematic examples I mentioned. Yet these extreme examples bring into relief an issue crucial for both projective techniques and for the theory of thinking. We take it for granted that all thought is motivated behavior, and these examples drive it home that the motivation we are considering is not homogeneous but is rather a whole hierarchy of motivations. Is this so new? No—in a way it is not. We have been accustomed to consider the *value, "altruism,"* to derive as a reaction formation from certain forms of aggression, so we are aware that it is a derivative motivation (A. Freud, 1936). What has not been so clear to us is that it can become a relatively autonomous motivation even though it was born as a reaction formation. Nor was it clear to us that motivations arrange themselves in a hierarchy at the base of which there are the basic drive motivations, and advancing upward we find progressively more controlled, more easily delayed, more socially shared, and reality-attuned motivations. The study of thought processes makes it necessary to assume such a hierarchy of motivations, in fact, present-day psychoanalytic ego psychology seems also to point toward the necessity of such an assumption (Hartmann, 1939; Kris, 1950; Rapaport, 1951b).

The view of motivations that seems to shape up is this: whenever a basic drive motivation meets reality obstacles or intrapsychic structural obstacles, a controlling organization is established which will regulate the drive discharge and modify the drive itself, giving rise to a derivative motivation. Such derivative motivations again are subject to the same fate. Thus arises a hierarchy of motivations in the process of building which the motivations also diversify. The higher-level the motivation, the more effectively it is controlled. As far as thought organization is concerned, wherever motivations are at work they will tend toward discharge. They will, to some extent, abide by the pleasure principle. Even in logical, ordered thinking we discover traces of it and call it wishful thinking. But the higher-level derivative motivations will be more amenable to delay and less productive of condensations, displacements, and symbolizations so characteristic of the thought organization motivated by primary drives, as are, for example, dreams. In turn, thought organization corresponding to the higher-level motivations will abide more by reality-adequate logic.

But at this point our understanding of the organizing rôle in thought processes of these motivations of various hierarchic levels stops, and again a broad field is open for exploration. These motivations organize thought in highly specific fashions, the description of which seems to be by no means exhausted by saying that in some more, in others less, primary-process mechanisms are at play. We know but little about these organizations.

FIXED TOOLS OF THOUGHT

Another topic I selected for discussion is that of *fixed tools of thought vs. processes of thought.* To illustrate what I mean, let us consider two different tests of concept formation. In a test like the Hanfmann-Kasanin (1942) the patient is asked to create a new concept. In such tests as Similarities and

Differences, the effective use of already existing concepts is tested. Obviously the difference is not as sharp as it may seem: in the H-K too, concepts already in existence are used in creating the new one and in the Similarities and Differences too, concepts are often remolded before being put to use (Rapaport, Gill, and Schafer, 1945–46; Schafer, 1948).

At any rate, though thinking is a motivated process, not every element of thought is given birth anew every time by the motivation. There are quasi-stable fixed building stones to thought which are used, but not created anew, by the motivation forming the thought and expressing itself through the thought. The more structured a test, the more such quasi-stable formations or—as I will refer to these—quasi-stationary processes, will play a rôle in it (Rapaport, 1946).

Concepts, anticipations, certain kinds of memories are all such quasi-stationary means of thought (Rapaport, Gill, and Schafer, 1945–46; Rapaport, 1951a). This is important to keep in mind because genuine motivational theories of thought, problem-solving theories as well as purely learning theories of it, are equally prone to become oblivious of these, all being inclined to discount structure and to be concerned only with the process.

The more structured the tests become, the more structuralized—quasi-stationary—tools of the thought process are involved in the test responses elicited; and consequently the more structured a test the more the pattern of all the responses, rather than the content or anything else intrinsic to the single response, reveals the distinctive aspects of the individual's psychological make-up (Rapaport, 1946).

The links between conative and cognitive processes—between need-expressing and reality-reflecting thought—are quasi-stable structures, which must be, but have not been, systematically studied.

VARIETIES OF CONSCIOUS EXPERIENCE

The last topic I have chosen for discussion tonight is that of the varieties of conscious experience as an aspect of thought organization, and as a significant feature of responses given to projective tests. It is a commonly known fact—Brentano's (1874) act psychology focused on it and so does existentialism (Sartre, 1948; see also Rapaport, 1949) of today for the better or for the worse—that contents of consciousness can be experienced variously: as memories, as illusions in the present, as perceptions, as hallucinations, as wishes for the future, as thoughts, as facts of various degrees of certainty, as assumptions, as something doubted, etc. It is also known that these varieties of conscious experience are closely interrelated with the function of judgment and thus with reality testing. These varieties of conscious experience indeed give evidence that there is continuously at work a preconscious function which automatically sorts out our experiences so as to orient us whether what we experience is an external or intrapsychic perception—an actual sense perception or an illusion; a memory or a product of imagination; and what status it has within these categories—an actual object or a picture of one, the memory of an event or the memory of a fantasy.

Now you all know the Rorschach and the TAT records of people who restrict themselves to a few obvious responses and a brief factual story, which is hardly more than a description of the TAT picture. These are the people who are surprised when asked whether they could give any more responses or elaborate on the story: they declare emphatically that they have told you all that is there. They may even ask you whether you want them to "invent" something. But if you say "yes" it turns out that they are incapable of that. These are usually people with extremely limiting and rigid controls on intrapsychic perception—who, therefore, experience whatever they perceive as *the* external reality. You are, I am sure, familiar also with records in which there are no rigid and limiting controls, and yet whatever is seen assumes a reality existence. I have in mind those borderline and schizophrenic records in which the most fantastic and gruesome combinations of percepts are given as responses, with an air of certainty that the card is a painting which they accurately perceive. In turn there are those people whose every response states explicitly that *they* are making the blot by means of their imagination into what it is. Some of these people are again extremely rigid and we usually find it mildly amusing when they give a popular response with an air of hesitance, stressing that they consider this popular response a wild stretching of imagination, and they act as though they were sticking their necks out entirely too far. Others of them—and these again are usually schizophrenic—state with a full assurance what the blot is, though at the same time they will explain the response by the physiological processes that take place in the brain, or the physical processes which occur between the card and the retina.

These are but a few examples of the varieties of conscious experience encountered in the course of projective testing. I, Gill, and Schafer (1945–46) have labeled these "increased distance from the card" and "loss of distance from the card," and described many other varieties of these. We have pointed out that they have their parallels in association-test reactions, which we labeled close and distant reactions (Rapaport, Gill, and Schafer, 1945–46; Schafer, 1945). We have also pointed out that self-references in TAT stories or on Comprehension or other Bellevue items or in the association test also indicate "loss of distance."

We must realize that in all these and other comparable responses we are dealing with indicators of varieties of conscious experience, which in turn indicate on the one hand the degree and kind of intactness of the patient's reality testing and loyalty to reality and on the other hand the price paid in the form of restrictions of intrapsychic observation in order to fend against violation of reality.

The varieties of externalization, the hierarchy of motivations, the quasi-stationary structures of the thought process, and the varieties of conscious experience are only a few examples of the many issues which could well serve as points of departure for systematic studies to lead toward unification of the rationales of the various tests into one systematic theory of thinking.

REFERENCES

Allport, G. W. (1935). Attitudes. In *A Handbook of Social Psychology,* ed. C. Murchison. Worcester: Clark University Press, pp. 798–844.

Brentano, F. (1874). *Psychologie vom empirischen Standpunkte.* Leipzig: Dunker & Humbolt.

Frank, L. K. (1939). Projective Methods for the Study of Personality. *J. Psychol.,* 8:389–413.

——— (1948). *Projective Methods.* Springfield, Ill.: Charles C Thomas.

Freud, A. (1936). *The Ego and the Mechanisms of Defence.* New York: International Universities Press, 1946.

Freud, S. (1911). Psycho-analytic Notes upon an Autobiographical Account of a Case of Paranoia (Dementia Paranoides). *Collected Papers,* 3:387–470. New York: Basic Books, 1959.

——— (1912). The Dynamics of the Transference. *Collected Papers,* 2:312–322. New York: Basic Books, 1959.

——— (1917 [1915]). Metapsychological Supplement to the Theory of Dreams. *Collected Papers,* 4:137–151. New York: Basic Books, 1959.

Hanfmann, E., & Kasanin, J. (1942). *Conceptual Thinking in Schizophrenia.* New York: Nervous and Mental Disease Publishing Co.

Hartmann, H. (1939). Ego Psychology and the Problem of Adaptation. In (abridged) Rapaport (1951b), pp. 362–396.

Kris, E. (1950). On Preconscious Mental Processes. *Psychoanalytic Explorations in Art.* New York: International Universities Press, 1952, pp. 303–318. Also in Rapaport (1951b), pp. 474–493.

Rapaport, D. (1942a). Principles Underlying Projective Techniques. *This volume,* Chapter 6.

——— (1942b). *Emotions and Memory,* 2nd unaltered ed. New York: International Universities Press, 1950.

——— (1946). Principles Underlying Nonprojective Tests of Personality. *This volume,* Chapter 15.

——— (1947). Psychological Testing: Its Practical and Its Heuristic Significance. *This volume,* Chapter 20.

——— (1949). Review of Jean-Paul Sartre, *The Psychology of Imagination. This volume,* Chapter 25.

——— (1950). On the Psychoanalytic Theory of Thinking. *This volume,* Chapter 28.

——— (1951a). Paul Schilder's Contribution to the Theory of Thought Processes. *This volume,* Chapter 32.

——— ed. & tr. (1951b). *Organization and Pathology of Thought.* New York: Columbia University Press.

———— Gill, M. M., & Schafer, R. (1945–46). *Diagnostic Psychological Testing,* 2 vols. Chicago: Year Book Publishers.

Sartre, J.-P. (1948). *The Psychology of Imagination.* New York: Philosophical Library.

Schafer, R. (1945). A Study of Thought Processes in a Word Association Test. *Character & Pers.,* 13:212–227.

———— (1948). *The Clinical Application of Psychological Tests.* New York: International Universities Press.

39

BOOK REVIEW

Edwin G. Boring, *A History of Experimental Psychology*[1]

Both those who believe that psychoanalysis is to become the core of an all-embracing psychology and those who expect it to find its position within the rest of psychology will welcome this volume. The first will find in it much with which an all-embracing psychology has to cope, the latter an orientation about the remote and recent past of the scientific neighbors among whom it will have to find a place.

Boring's volume is not just a history of experimental psychology, but also of its matrix—general psychology. Flugel (1933), Zilboorg (1941), and even Woodworth (1948) tackle only fragments of what this volume encompasses, and only Murphy (1949) compares with it. Many will prefer Murphy to Boring. Murphy devotes 45 per cent of his volume to most recent issues and developments, 10 per cent to psychoanalysis, and speaks about psychoanalysis and psychology in terms we like to hear. Boring spends, in this second edition, only 20 per cent on recent developments and only 6 per cent on *all* dynamic psychologies, and is by no means a partisan of dynamic psychology. Yet Boring's is a remarkable book and in many ways more instructive to the psychoanalytic reader than Murphy's. First, since

[1] Second edition. New York: Appleton-Century-Crofts, 1950.

First published in The Psychoanalytic Quarterly, *21:123–126, 1952.*

history is not an objective science, if we read it in the version which is close to how our fancy would have it, we are prone to miss too much which a writing of opposite bias would reveal; second, Murphy's emphasis on the recent past obscures somewhat the perspective for the broader design of trends. Finally, the real impact of psychoanalytic theory is more exactingly measured when it passes through the academic die-hard's dissecting scrutiny (even of one as good-humored, bent on attaining objectivity, and suppressing his own bias as Boring in this book) than by the critical appreciation of the dynamic psychologist whose tenets are after all indivisibly interwoven with those of psychoanalysis.

In the first edition, Freud was mentioned only incidentally (four times). He now appears as one of the four big figures of psychology (with Darwin, Helmholtz, and James): "The history of psychology cannot be written in the next three centuries without mention of Freud's name." Psychoanalysis (previously one reference under Stanley Hall) is discussed in eight pages, and with grudging though real respect. Boring—who at Harvard in the Psychology Department is "conservatively" separated from all dynamic psychology, set apart in the Social Relations Department—is stiffened in his conservatism in this writing by an impressive sense of responsibility for history. So it is safe to say that academic psychology at its most conservative is bowing to facts. What are these facts? Has Boring, and those for whom he stands, come to appreciate the method and theory of psychoanalysis? Scarcely.

As I understand it, there are three groups of facts to which he bows. First, he is impressed by the impact of Freud and psychoanalysis on our time; to him that which has such impact belongs to history, and Freud is great "judged by the criterion of . . . persistent posthumous importance" (p. 743). Second, he is impressed by the fact that clinical psychology "works" (pp. 576–577, 741), and he knows that this has to do with dynamics and motivation. Perhaps most important, Boring, who had not a single index reference in his first edition to motivation, now is persuaded that "The psychology of human nature is a motivational psychology, because the prediction and control of behavior is the most important practical thing to know about man as a living, choosing, adapting organism" (p. 693). Motivation is dynamic, and "the principal source of dynamic psychology is, of course, Freud." At this point, unlike most psychoanalysts, he *sees* the historical roots of Freud in Leibnitz, and *knows* of Brentano's influence on Freud (pp. 693, 703). Indeed, it seems that linking Freud through Brentano to Würzburg is one of the factors which makes psychoanalysis in a way palatable, though not digestible, to this gourmand of history. That these dynamic psychologies give him indigestion becomes rather clear when he says, "It seems probable that psychology already has enough language—the Yale language—to make 'motivology' clear" (p. 729). That in that "language" most of the essence of what "motivology" rescued from

Brentano and the phenomenologists is lost is forgotten. With soothing calm Boring adds: "The special vocabularies may belong to the pragmatics of science, not to its semantics, for they seem to be related to group loyalties which stimulate research. Perhaps these languages prevent lethargy in thinking. Certainly they are symptoms of intellectual alertness" (p. 729).

Boring's book abounds in such turns and in striving for objectivity. These are admirable, considering the author's inevitable bias defined by his historical position. Boring is a connoisseur of history; most of his facts have the flavor of firsthand acquaintance, and most of his formulations the earmark of thorough assimilation of his material. This is not so much the case when he writes of dynamic psychologies—but no one can know it all. In his hands figures of psychological history, even though they remain sketches, gain life, and their influence on each other and interaction with their time become tangible.

I wish to give one example of the countless labors of love, so paradoxical and so characteristic of this author and this book. The man who delights in the divorcement of psychology from philosophy and considers it one of its real achievements (p. 742), adds in his second edition five new pages on Kant because "German psychology and physiology do not quite make sense when he was slurred over, even if Wundt did have his master eye fixed on the British school [of philosophy]." The section added is one of penetrating clarity, and the dynamic psychologist reading it will discover—if he has not discovered it for himself before—that the ultimate epistemological foundations of dynamic psychology do not quite make sense without Kant (see Rapaport, 1943).

This, then, is a book which will be enjoyed for its directness, humor, language, and historical sensitivity, which will be admired for its command and usefulness of data, which will prove helpful in orienting the reader to the psychological landscape, even if its bias and historical caution stint in allotting space to psychoanalysis in the panorama.

REFERENCES

Flugel, J. C. (1933). *A Hundred Years of Psychology (1833–1933)*. New York: Macmillan.
Murphy, G. (1949). *Historical Introduction to Modern Psychology*, rev. ed. New York: Harcourt, Brace.
Rapaport, D. (1943). Review of G. Katona, *Organizing and Memorizing: Studies in the Psychology of Learning and Teaching. This volume*, Chapter 11.
Woodworth, R. S. (1948). *Contemporary Schools of Psychology*. New York: Ronald Press.
Zilboorg, G. (1941). *A History of Medical Psychology*. New York: Norton.

40

BOOK REVIEW

William James, *The Principles of Psychology*[1]

This volume is the reprinting of James's famous "longer course," published first in 1890 and not reprinted since 1907. It is not only *the* American classic of psychology but, to this reviewer's mind, is unequaled in breadth and scope in the entire psychological literature.

It is reprinted at just the right time. The hegemony of conditioned response in psychology has been broken. Gestalt psychology, Tolman's purposive behaviorism, Allport's psychology of the personality and the ego and, last but not least, the attacks of physiological psychologists (Lashley, Klüver, Hebb) delivered the decisive blows. The impact of psychoanalysis on psychology—partly through the growth of clinical psychology, though planless and untutored—also did its share. Conditioned-response psychology—"the psychology of the empty organism"—is dead, but it does not seem to take cognizance of the fact. It attempts to rejuvenate itself by a marriage of convenience with psychoanalysis: "you give me the goods, and I'll give you the respectability." And Sears's, Dollard and Miller's, and Mowrer's attempts to this end will be sooner or later recognized as showing that psychoanalysis has to be emasculated before it will fit the conditioning

[1] New York: Dover Publications, 1950.

First published in The Psychoanalytic Quarterly, *21:430–431, 1952.*

robes of academic respectability and that conditioning theory, when trying to adapt itself to clinical reality and psychoanalysis, produces wilder flights of speculation, and more striking disregard for established clinical fact and psychoanalytic theory than any disregard for experimentally established facts and theory built on them to which accusing academic fingers could point in psychoanalysis. The main reason that conditioning theory, though dead, does not lie down is that no broad and bold synthesis has arisen to sweep it aside.

But now James is republished: one of the fathers of American positivism speaks again. Much of what he said may be interpreted as carrying the message: Conditioning? Law of effect? No introspection? Experiments which ask no essential questions of nature? Facts that should speak for themselves and reveal the nature of the mind without theory? This is not what I meant by positivism!

Here is a general psychology which regards psychology in relation to philosophy and epistemology, clearly envisaging that ultimately every psychology depends on the stand it takes in regard to the possibility of attaining knowledge. James rejects the Platonic, as well as the Locke-Hume, solution: neither the "soul" nor the "soulless mechanics of ideas" for him.

Here is a psychology in which pathological phenomena have as much place and are as much regarded as are "normal" phenomena, everyday observations as much as experimental facts, brain- and perceptual-physiology of the time as much as psychological data.

Here is a psychology which, though preoccupied with habit and memory dynamics, centers on the self and on thought defined in the broadest possible sense. James's is a psychology in which the virtues of experiment are extolled, yet self-observation and the comparative method are given a status equal to experiment's.

Here is a psychology which is a positivist's, and yet purposes and goals have as much place in it as do causes, facts of behavior as much place as Brentano's intentionality (i.e., the object directedness of all psychic acts).

For the psychoanalyst, as well as the dynamic psychologist, the republication of James is an important event. If read carefully, it is found to contain a blueprint for a psychology broad enough to have space and place for all that psychoanalysis and academic psychology have discovered to date. It is not a rival of the many psychologies that exist now; it is a view of psychology catholic enough to lead the reader's mind toward a broad synthesis. Perhaps Schilder's *Medical Psychology* (1924) is the only volume since James's which has as broad a synthesizing scope as his, but none, including Schilder's, is as free of the partisanship and premature commitment which limit scope. Though dated in its details, its main lines are still as valid as ever.

REFERENCE

Schilder, P. (1924). *Medical Psychology,* ed. & tr. D. Rapaport. New York: International Universities Press, 1953.

41

ON THE PSYCHOANALYTIC
THEORY OF AFFECTS

I

We do not possess a systematic statement of the psychoanalytic theory of affects.[1] The attempt I shall here make to piece together the existing fragments of this theory encounters two major difficulties. The first is that we have to deal with formulations originating from all three phases of the development of psychoanalysis: the beginning phase in which the theory of catharsis and the theory of psychoanalysis were not as yet sharply separated; the middle phase in which the id was in the center of interest; and the recent phase in which interest is increasingly centered on the ego. The treatment of the formulations of three such disparate origins is the more difficult partly because each of them persists into the later phases, and partly because most of the later formulations are to some extent anticipated in the

---

[1] The term affect in this paper will be used to stand for the terms "emotion" and "feeling" also, since there is no clear distinction in the literature in the use of these terms. For a suggested terminology, see Rapaport (1942, Chapter 2).

First published in The International Journal of Psycho-Analysis, *34:177–198, 1953. Reprinted in Robert P. Knight and Cyrus R. Friedman, eds.,* Psychoanalytic Psychiatry and Psychology, Clinical and Theoretical Papers, *Austen Riggs Center, Volume 1. New York: International Universities Press, 1954, pp. 274–310. Spanish translation published in Merton M. Gill and David Rapaport,* Aportaciones a la Teoría y Técnica Psicoanalítica. *Asociación Psicoanalítica Mexicana, A.C., 1962, pp. 118–169.*

earlier phases. The second difficulty is that the fragments to be put together are only too familiar, and culling them will thus appear to many just as superfluous as their systematization will seem unpalatable and unacceptable officiousness to others.

In view of these difficulties it will be worth while to remind ourselves, before going on to the task set for this paper, that an attempt at systematizing the theory of affects is not merely a theoretical nicety, but has eminent practical importance. Freud (1915b, p. 109) wrote: "If the instinct did not attach itself to an idea or manifest itself as an affective state, we could know nothing about it." Indeed, it goes without saying that in his everyday work the transference affects are the guide of the therapist, and that, though affect storms of abreaction and catharsis are no longer the aims of psychoanalytic therapy, "recall" and "insight" without affective experience do not usually yield therapeutic advance. But it is less obvious how we can explain theoretically that affects serve as such guides and that without them insight is ineffective. We know that when—in therapy in general, and particularly in "working through"—defenses are "undone," affects arise as indicators of the drive discovered and "liberated" from its defense shackles. Freud (1914, p. 376) wrote: "Theoretically one may correlate . . . [working through] with the 'abreaction' of quantities of affect pent-up by repression, without which the hypnotic treatment remained ineffective." We also know that "liberation" of drives in the form of abreaction, i.e., massive affective outburst, is not as a rule therapeutically effective. Fenichel (1935), criticizing Kaiser's resistance analysis, wrote:

> . . . there is a "taking distance" from the affect which seems to me, in contrast to Kaiser, to be desirable. The judging ego of the patient should stand at a distance from its affect and should recognize it as untimely, while remembering its origins affectively. A break-through of affect without such "taking distance" is—as Freud once well put it—"an outright mishap." Kaiser's comment, that "after a 'genuine instinctual break-through' there is nothing left for the analyst to explain or clarify or add to the contents expressed by the patient" makes us suspect that he actually does not recognize this "mishap" for what it is, that he neglects the process of "working through" and does not understand its essential role in the true elimination of repressions, so that he is aiming at a sort of "neo-catharsis" instead of analysis [p. 346].

Anna Freud (1936, p. 42), in discussing the use of mechanisms of defense against affects, points to the importance of the understanding of affects for the technique of child analysis, and her point seems to have a validity beyond the confines of the latter also:

> The analysis and bringing into consciousness of the specific form of this defence against affect—whether it be reversal, displacement or

complete repression—teaches us something of the particular technique adopted by the ego of the child in question and, just like the analysis of resistance, enables us to infer his attitude to his instincts and the nature of his symptom-formation. It is therefore a fact of peculiar importance in child-analysis that, in observing the affective processes, we are largely independent of the child's voluntary co-operation and his truthfulness or untruthfulness in what he tells us. His affects betray themselves against his will.

Clearly, S. Freud, Fenichel, and Anna Freud imply that the liberation of drives from repression is necessarily accompanied by an appearance of affects, and therapy is dependent upon effecting the appearance of these affects in certain forms and handling the emerged affects in certain ways. But we are not so clear theoretically about the relationships between drive and affect implied in these propositions derived from therapeutic experience. Therefore clarification of the theory of affects should be a step toward the theory of psychoanalytic technique and therapy. It might even be asked whether a metapsychological theory of technique and therapy is altogether conceivable before the metapsychological status of affects, which occupy a central position in the processes of therapy, has been clarified.

Their central role in therapy, however, does not exhaust the clinical significance of affects. We have come to label as affect such a wide variety of phenomena that both in diagnostic and therapeutic work we are in danger of being led astray by the term, as long as we lack a systematic view of the relationships of all the phenomena to which we apply it.[2] A brief survey will show the complexity of the situation.

We call affect not only the infant's rage (encountered later on in tantrums and in the destructive outbursts of some catatonics) and the adult's anger accompanied by the corresponding expressive movements and other physiological concomitants, but also the subjective feelings of those well-controlled adults who show little or no affect expression, as well as the anger of overcontrolling compulsive persons who just "know" that they "could be" or "should be" angry. We also call affects those displays which impress the onlooker as histrionic or as affectations, and which certain character types are prone to produce, either in exaggeration of experienced, or as substitutes for not experienced, affects. It is not quite clear how these are related to the "as if" affects of those schizoid personalities described by

---

[2] While all the phenomena discussed below have to do with affects, and are time and again so referred to in the literature, my listing them here does not imply that they are correctly labeled as affects nor that the theory of affects alone must account fully for all of them. Indeed, some of the phenomena to be listed are most complex, and more than the theory of affects will have to be invoked for their explanation. What I imply by listing them here is that they constitute an important problem for the theory of affects also.

Helene Deutsch (1942, p. 123).[3] Nor is their relation clear to those over-sensitive incipient and ambulatory schizophrenics who appear to wallow in their affects, which on closer inspection turn out to be restitution products following a total withdrawal of object cathexes[4]; these patients are affectively moved by anything that seems to promise them the experience of affects, because it proves to them that they are still capable of feeling.[5] Nor is there clarity about the relation of both these latter types to those more crudely obvious schizophrenic affect phenomena termed "flat affect" and "inappropriate affect." We need not dwell on displaced affects, somatic affect equivalents without conscious affect experience, or on the relation of these to conversion symptoms and psychosomatic disorders and all the rest that belong to the chapter of "unconscious emotion"; they have been variously discussed (Fenichel, 1945; Alexander, 1943; Rapaport, 1942). But we must mention the related phenomena of "frozen affects" which find expression—without conscious affect experience—in stereotyped postures, facial expressions, tones of voice, motility, etc., to which Reich (1933) called attention. And we must take notice of such affects as anxiety, guilt, elation, depression, which—in contrast to the momentary affects so far mentioned—may take pathological chronic forms; even more important, they may take characterological chronic forms, as in anxious people, gay people, gloomy people, bashful people, etc. (Landauer, 1938). Furthermore, we must mention a special group of affects, namely those grouped around the experiences of the comic, wit, humor, etc., which are apparently related to a specific kind of saving of cathectic expenditure, rather than to any specific kind of cathectic tension. It is noteworthy that a proclivity to elicit and/or experience such affects may also take a chronic form and structuralize into a character trait (Brenman, 1952). Finally we must mention such specific and complex affective states as apathy, nostalgia, boredom, etc., which are also relatively chronic affect formations (Bibring, 1953).

To make even more glaring the complexity of what a theory of affect must account for, we might add that, on the one hand, neurotic inhibition and ego limitation cuts down the range of intensity and variability of affect experiences; on the other, regression processes bring to the fore unbridled and unmodulated affective attacks in which, while intensity is formidable, range and variability are minimal.

---

[3] ". . . outwardly he conducts his life as if he possessed a complete and sensitive emotional capacity. To him there is no difference between his empty forms and what others actually experience. . . . [this] is no longer an act of repression but a real loss of object cathexis."

[4] Here the subjective experience of lack of affect in depersonalization (Schilder, 1924; Fenichel, 1945) and in certain allied syndromes of organic etiology (Bürger-Prinz and Kaila, 1930; Schilder, 1924) is also relevant.

[5] Compare Federn on narcissistic affect (1936, p. 336).

II

I shall now review the concepts of affect of each of the three phases of the development of psychoanalysis.

The dominant concept of affect of the beginning phase of psychoanalysis, in which no sharp differentiation between the theory of cathartic hypnosis and that of psychoanalysis had as yet occurred, equates affect with the quantity of psychic energy, which was later conceptualized as drive cathexis. But while later the cathexis of affects is distinguished from drive cathexis proper and from bound (ego) cathexes, here affect stands for all of these. Freud (1894, p. 75) wrote:

> . . . among the psychic functions there is something which should be differentiated (*an amount of affect, a sum of excitation*), something having all the attributes of a quantity . . . a something which is capable of increase, decrease, displacement and discharge, and which extends itself over the memory-traces of an idea like an electric charge over the surface of the body [italics added].

Accordingly, the role of affects in symptom formation is that affects prevented from discharge remain on the one hand fixed to the pathogenic idea or fantasy, and on the other find outlet in the innervations of conversion symptoms. Freud (Breuer and Freud, 1893–95, pp. 7–8) wrote: "The ideas which have become pathogenic are preserved with such freshness and affective force because the normal process of absorption by abreaction and by reproduction in a state of unrestrained association is denied them." And Breuer (Breuer and Freud, 1893–95, pp. 151–152) wrote: "The 'hysterical conversion' is then complete, for the original intercerebral excitement of the affect was changed into the process of excitement of the peripheral paths, and the original affective idea no longer evokes the affect, but only the abnormal reflex." Correspondingly, the role of affects in therapy is that the discharge of the dammed-up affect drains the pathogenic idea of its force and influence. Breuer and Freud (1893, pp. 40–41) wrote: "By providing an opportunity for the pent-up affect to discharge itself in words the therapy deprives of its effective power the idea which was not originally abreacted . . ."

Simultaneously the anxiety affect was explained as affect or libido (these terms were at this point still interchangeable) transformed by being repressed. Freud (1895a) wrote:

> . . . an accumulation of excitation is involved . . . anxiety . . . probably represents . . . *the deflection of somatic sexual excitation from the psychical field, and . . . an abnormal use of it, due to this deflection* [p. 97].

> Libido will therefore subside . . . and the excitation will express itself instead subcortically as anxiety [p. 99].

Freud also (1898, p. 227) wrote: ". . . anxiety actually was libido diverted from its usual course."

This concept of affect and anxiety persisted into the second phase of the development of psychoanalysis which, as we shall see, already contains fragments of a more advanced theory of affects and anxiety. Freud (1900, p. 537) wrote: "The fulfilment of these wishes would no longer produce an affect of pleasure, but one of pain; *and it is just this conversion of affect that constitutes the essence of what we call 'repression.'* " Even later Freud (1909, p. 178) wrote:

> When once a state of anxiety establishes itself, the anxiety swallows up all other feelings; with the progress of repression, and the more those ideas which are charged with affect and which have been conscious move down into the unconscious, all affects are capable of being changed into anxiety.

Indeed the use of the term affect as though it were psychic energy (cathexis) in general—aided and abetted by Bleuler's (1912), Jung's (1907), and Schilder's (1920, 1930) usage—persists in psychoanalytic literature to our own day. Academic psychology, psychosomatic medicine, and psychiatry at large lent a hand in perpetuating it and making it general usage, when psychoanalytic theoretical development had long since abandoned it.

Before turning to the affect concept of the next phase in the development of psychoanalysis, we must point out that in *Studies in Hysteria* (published in 1893–95) and in Freud's posthumously published "Project for a Scientific Psychology" (written in 1895 [1895b])—which will not be discussed here—there are already traces of the later conception of affects. For instance, the relation between drive and affect is indicated for the first time, though not theoretically further developed; the affective state of "being in love" is derived from the "sexual instinct." Freud (Breuer and Freud, 1893–95, pp. 145–146) wrote:

> This is glaringly observed in the wonderful phenomenon of being in love . . . [The object] becomes endowed with the whole quantity of excitement set free by the sexual instinct; she becomes . . . an "affective idea." That is, in assuming actuality in consciousness, she sets free the increased excitement which really originates in another source, namely, in the sexual glands.

Even traces of a distinction between disposal of tension by action, by affect, and by binding through the work of thought (association) are already present, though still clouded by the affect terminology. Breuer and Freud (1893, pp. 30–31) wrote:

> The fading of a memory or of its affect depends . . . foremost . . . on whether an energetic reaction (discharge of feeling) supervened on the affective experience or not. By *reaction* we here mean the whole range of voluntary and involuntary reflexes, by which . . .

affects are habitually worked off—from weeping up to an actual act of revenge . . . the reaction . . . to the trauma has a . . . complete "cathartic" effect only if it takes the form of a fully adequate reaction, such as an act of revenge. But man finds a surrogate for such an act in speech . . .

"Abreaction" is, however, not the only kind of solution at the disposal of the normal psychical mechanism . . . the normal man succeeds by means of associations in dissipating the accompanying affect.

III

The second phase of the development of psychoanalytic theory begins with *The Interpretation of Dreams* (1900); it is characterized by the metapsychological systematization of psychoanalytic discoveries in general and by the development of the economic point of view, the theory of cathexes, in particular. It is a familiar fact that, while the dynamic point of view was highly developed by the time this phase of the theory opened, and while the economic point of view was developed in this phase, the structural point of view—the third of the metapsychological triad—was still lagging behind, taking the form of the topographical point of view. Metapsychology as we find it in Freud's main writings devoted to it (1900, Chapter VII, and the "Papers on Metapsychology," 1911–17) is an incomplete theory preparatory to the developing of the structural point of view, the advent of which ushers in ego psychology and completes the formal framework of metapsychology.

The Interpretation of Dreams already breaks sharply with the previous conception of affect as psychic (drive) energy proper, and considers affects to be motor and secretory (discharge) processes which are controlled from the unconscious. Freud (1900, p. 521) wrote: "We here take as our basis a quite definite assumption as to the nature of the development of affect. This is regarded as a motor or secretory function, the key to the innervation of which is to be found in the ideas of the *Ucs.*" But this sharp break was not noted at the time; only well in the third phase of the development of psychoanalysis did Kulovesi (1931) come back to it, noting and attempting to clarify the relation between the James-Lange and the psychoanalytic theories of affects.[6] The break is sharp, the dynamic is no longer that of affects but rather that of the energy (drive cathexis) inherent in wishes. Affects are released by, and are indicators of, unconscious wishes. The complex relation of affects to the other class of indicators (representations) of drives— i.e., ideas—is also considered. Freud (1900, p. 537) wrote:

The memories from which the unconscious wish evokes a liberation of affect have never been accessible to the *Pcs.,* and for that reason this

[6] Note also Landauer (1928).

liberation cannot be inhibited. It is precisely on account of this generation of affect that these ideas are not now accessible even by way of
the preconscious thoughts to which they have transferred the energy of
the wishes connected with them.

And:

> . . . *the ideational contents have undergone displacements and sub-
> stitutions, while the affects have remained unchanged.* No wonder,
> then, that the ideational content which has been altered by dream-
> distortion no longer fits the affect which has remained intact [p. 434].

The realization of the theoretical program forecast in the *Studies in Hysteria*—to differentiate between tension disposal by means of action on the
one hand, and by means of affect discharge on the other—was ushered in
by regarding affects as motor and secretory functions controlled from the
unconscious. But not until eleven years later, in "Formulations Regarding
the Two Principles in Mental Functioning" (1911), did Freud take the next
step, when in delineating the development of the reality principle he formulated that, with its advent, the role of motility changes: while hitherto it
fulfilled, in the main, a safety-valve discharge function for drive tensions
(affect discharge), it now becomes an apparatus used in action designed
to alter reality. This view coordinates affect discharge with the pleasure
principle and with alteration of the internal environment, and contrasts it
with action, which it coordinates with the reality principle and with the
alteration of the external environment so as to make the drive object ultimately available. Affect discharge is then the short cut to tension decrease,
while action is the realistic detour toward it. Freud (1911, p. 16) wrote:

> A new function was now entrusted to motor discharge, which under
> the supremacy of the pleasure-principle had served to unburden the
> mental apparatus of accretions of stimuli, and in carrying out this task
> had sent innervations into the interior of the body (mien, expressions
> of affect); it was now employed in the appropriate alteration of real-
> ity. It was converted into *action*.

Freud (1915b, p. 111 n.) returned to this point to clarify further:

> Affectivity manifests itself essentially in motor (*i.e.* secretory and
> circulatory) discharge resulting in an (internal) alteration of the sub-
> ject's own body without reference to the outer world; motility, in ac-
> tions designed to effect changes in the outer world.

The tension which is diminished by affect discharge is that of drives.
More specifically, affect expression is the final outcome of the discharge of
a specific part of drive cathexes, termed "affect charge." "Affect charge"
and "ideas" are both drive representations; they had to be theoretically

distinguished because their fate under repression is different. They may both be repressed, as in severely inhibiting hysterical neuroses; ideas may be repressed while affects remain amenable to consciousness, as in hysterias characterized by affect outbursts; or ideas (or their derivatives) may remain amenable to consciousness while affects are repressed, displaced, or isolated from them, as in obsessional neuroses. Freud (1915a, p. 91) wrote:

> In our discussion hitherto we have dealt with the repression of an instinct-presentation, and by that we understood an idea or group of ideas which is cathected with a definite amount of the mental energy (libido, interest) pertaining to an instinct. Now clinical observation forces us further to dissect something that hitherto we have conceived of as a single entity, for it shows us that beside the idea there is something else, another presentation of the instinct to be considered, and that this other element undergoes a repression which may be quite different from that of the idea. We have adopted the term *charge of affect* for this other element in the mental presentation; it represents that part of the instinct which has become detached from the idea, and finds proportionate expression, according to its quantity, in processes which become observable to perception as affects. From this point on, in describing a case of repression, we must follow up the fate of the idea which undergoes repression separately from that of the instinctual energy attached to the idea.

In comparing the two kinds of drive representations, Freud points out that affect expression and affect experience are related to discharge of cathexes; ideas, to cathecting of memory traces. He makes this distinction to explain that ideas when repressed—when their cathexis is withdrawn, or when they are countercathected—persist as actualities (as memory traces) while affects when repressed (decathected or countercathected) persist only as potentialities. Freud (1915b, p. 111) wrote:

> The whole difference arises from the fact that ideas are cathexes—ultimately of memory-traces—whilst affects and emotions correspond with processes of discharge, the final expression of which is perceived as feeling. In the present state of our knowledge of affects and emotions we cannot express this difference more clearly.

I believe that here Freud as yet lacked the observations which could have indicated to him (as they did to him as well as to Brierley and Jacobson later) that discharge thresholds of drives and affects are indispensable concepts of an affect theory. But such thresholds heightened (presumably by countercathexes) to attain repression of affect would render the repressed "affect charge" just as actual as memory traces render unconscious ideas. Freud's conception here shows the limitations of a pure discharge theory of affects which has no place in it for threshold structures.

In this discharge theory, all affects, including the anxiety affect, are partial vicissitudes of drives. Thus, though the earlier "toxic" or "transformation" theory of anxiety still persists, it no longer implies that undischarged affects can be transformed into anxiety, but only that repressed drive cathexis can be so transformed. Freud (1915a, pp. 91–92) wrote:

> The fate of the quantitative factor in the instinct-presentation may be one of three, as we see by a cursory survey of the observations made through psycho-analysis: either the instinct is altogether suppressed, so that no trace of it is found, or it appears in the guise of an affect of a particular qualitative tone, or it is transformed into anxiety. With the two last possibilities we are obliged to focus our attention upon the *transformation* into *affects,* and especially into *anxiety,* of the mental energy belonging to the *instincts,* this being a new possible vicissitude undergone by an instinct.

Let us now fit this theory into the psychoanalytic model of psychic processes. This model [7] is formed on the following observational (or hypothetical) sequence: the restlessness of the hungry infant → the appearance of the mother, i.e., breast, and sucking → subsidence of restlessness. We conceptualize this sequence as: drive tension → appearance of, and action on, drive object → gratification. In the absence of the drive object, restlessness will persist and/or a hallucinatory image of past gratification will appear. We conceptualize the restlessness as *expression* of affect and refer it to an "affect charge," that is, to a part of the drive cathexis which would be discharged if the drive object were present and drive action on it could take place. We conceptualize the hallucinatory gratification as *idea,* and refer it to the drive cathecting of the memory traces of past gratification situations. Idea and affect charge are both conceptualized as *drive representations,* safety valves of drive tensions. The quantitative relations that appear to obtain are: drive cathexis > affect charge > cathexis of memory trace.

It seems to be assumed that if drive action—discharge of drive cathexes —were possible, no separating off of a cathectic amount in the form of affect charge, or disposal of it in the form of affect discharge, would take place. This proposition contains on the one hand a crucial implication for the theory of affect and on the other a factual fallacy. The *implication for theory* may be formulated as the "conflict theory" of affects. The *fallacy* lies in the untenable assumption of immediate and complete discharge by drive action. Let us discuss these, keeping in mind that our framework at this moment is that of drive cathexes and drive representations, that is, mobile cathexes and primary processes. In other words, we are still considering that hypothetical state of affairs which is supposed to obtain before definitive ego formation, before the establishment of bound cathexes and secondary processes, before the internalization of the *delay* of drive discharge and

---

[7] Freud (1900, Chapter VII, pp. 508–509; 1911, p. 14). See also Rapaport (1951a, Part VII; and 1951b).

of the *detour* behavior toward the drive object, and before they become guaranteed by psychic structure formation, that is, before the familiar, advanced, defensive and adaptive mechanisms are established. Or, in other terms, we are considering the state of affairs in which the pleasure principle is supposed to hold full sway before the establishment of the reality principle.

The "conflict theory" of affects. The major implication of the affect theory of the second phase of psychoanalysis is that affect expression is the outcome of the discharge of part of the accumulated drive cathexes when direct discharge in drive action *cannot* take place. This conception of affects was already forecast by Spinoza (1901, p. 129): "By emotions (*affectus*) I understand the modification of the body by which the power in action of the body is increased or diminished, aided or restrained and at the same time the ideas of these modifications," and by Dewey (1894–95): "When there is no inhibition there is no overflow and no affect."

The psychologist Drever (1917) saw the necessity for such a conflict (for him, "obstacle") theory of affect, but realized its insufficiencies for the explanation of continuous pleasurable affects.

One of the finest Anglo-Saxon psychiatric observers and thinkers, Mac-Curdy, influenced by psychoanalysis, by his studies of circular psychoses, and by the theories of James, Lange, Dewey, Cannon, McDougall, etc., stated this conception in 1925—before Freud's *The Problem of Anxiety*—and concluded that affects are products of conflict. He wrote (1925, p. 65): "[Affects] . . . appear both objectively and subjectively when instinct is aroused but not in operation as such. The function of emotion is to warn oneself or others of the nature of behavior that is likely to develop." In the psychoanalytic literature too—though only after *The Problem of Anxiety*—we find a tendency to state the conflict theory of affects explicitly. Landauer (1938, p. 390) interpreted Freud's *The Problem of Anxiety* to imply such a conflict theory. He wrote:

> The affective process is not a simple response to a stimulus . . .
> there are at work at least two directly conflicting tendencies . . .
> Freud thinks that we must assume in all affects an inherited compromise of this sort between conflicting tendencies . . . the affects are
> inherited hysterical attacks.

In a discussion of the state of affairs obtaining *after* definitive ego formation, after *delay* of drive discharge has been internalized—that is, after drives and discharge-controlling structures clash intrapsychically—such a conflict theory would be a matter of course for us;[8] it seems less obvious at this point, where drives conflict with reality—i.e., where the absence of the drive object is what prevents drive action. Several considerations recom-

[8] Federn's affect theory (1936, pp. 337 ff.), which is part of his ego psychology, also implies such a conflict theory.

mend themselves at this point: (1) To consider affects, which derive from the clash between mounting drive tension and the reality absence of the drive object, as a prototype of conflict (namely, of that conflict which gives rise to affect discharge) has a precedent in our theorizing: the derivation of anxiety from reality danger. Freud (1926, p. 116) wrote: ". . . instinctual demands often become an (internal) danger only because . . . their gratification would bring about an external danger . . ." (2) In discussing the concept of "unconscious affects" Freud inferred from his observations that the "affect-charge" cathexis is *not* segregated in a persisting fashion from drive cathexes proper; when repression (or other defense?) blocks its discharge it has—unlike the idea—no actual unconscious existence but only a potential one, in that when the discharge channels are unblocked affect discharge again serves as a safety valve to mounting drive tension. Freud wrote (1915b, pp. 110–111):

> . . . we apply the term 'unconscious' to those affects that are restored when we undo the work of repression. So . . . the use of the [term] . . . is logical; but a comparison of the unconscious affect with the unconscious idea reveals the significant difference that the unconscious idea continues, after repression, as an actual formation in the system Ucs, whilst to the unconscious affect there corresponds in the same system only a potential disposition which is prevented from developing further.

Thus in this conception "affect charge" would be defined simply as that amount of drive cathexis which the constitutional nature—that is, thresholds—of the affect discharge channels (motor, secretory, etc.) permits them to carry off. This is a pure "dynamic theory" in which affects are always created *de novo* (see Freud, 1926, pp. 19–20). It will be discussed later whether or not such a conception can be sustained for the state of affairs that obtains after discharge controls and delay are internalized and become the preventers of drive discharge—that is, whether or not "affect charge" remains always an unsegregated and *ad hoc* discharged part of drive cathexis even when, with the advancement of psychic development, structuralization of other psychic functions becomes the typical form. It is clear here, however, that in this phase of his theorizing Freud considered affect discharge a dynamic product (that of the conflict between mounting tension and discharge-preventing reality) and saw only its direction as determined by inborn discharge avenues. A consideration of these discharge avenues leads to the *factual fallacy* mentioned above.

The *fallacy* in question seems not to vitiate the core of the "conflict theory," but only to point up its limitations. It is a fallacy inherent in a purely dynamic—i.e., drive cathexis—theory of affect. To bring this into sharp relief, let us remind ourselves that the stress we have put in our discussion on inborn discharge channels of affects is in part "borrowed" from Freud's

The Problem of Anxiety (1926, pp. 70–71, 117), that is, from the third phase of the development of psychoanalytic theory. In the second phase, motor and secretory channels are neither treated with a stress on their inborn character, nor built into the theory. The very existence of inborn discharge channels raises several questions: Does discharge in drive action not itself have channels and thresholds? Or in other words: To what point (threshold) must drive tension mount before discharge in action becomes imperative? Do inborn drive-discharge thresholds—as structures—prevent drive discharge before the absence of the drive object in reality prevents it, and thus before defenses—or more generally: internalized delay mechanisms —prevent it? Is it possible that such drive-discharge thresholds (disposition to frustration tolerance?) have decisive influence on how the experience of the absence of the drive object will affect psychic structure formation? Does the relation of affect-discharge thresholds to drive-discharge thresholds explain why drive action too (e.g., sexual intercourse, cf. Jacobson, 1951)—and not only its delay—is accompanied by affect discharge and affect experience? Does the relation of these two kinds of thresholds to each other influence decisively the development of controlling and defensive structures? These questions lead into the most obscure and least explored areas of psychic organization to which we refer by such terms as "disposition to anxiety," "constitutional intensity of drives" (Reich, 1933; Freud, 1937), etc. There are but a few facts known which are relevant to these questions:

(1) Affect discharge can and does occur not only when the drive object is absent, but also before the drive tension has reached the point where its discharge is imperative, and even parallel with actual drive discharge. These familiar phenomena cannot be explained by the dynamic—i.e., conflict— theory of affects. They indicate that a conflict and drive-safety-valve (dynamic-economic) theory of affect is insufficient and has to be supplemented by a structural theory, which must take into consideration affect-discharge and drive-discharge thresholds[9] (cf. Jacobson, 1951, 1953).

(2) It seems that we can conceive of two kinds of such thresholds: inborn ones (Freud's [1920, 1925] "stimulus barrier" is of this type), and defensive countercathexes (repression is of this type). It is possible that a structural theory will explain the relations between drives and affects— pointed to in the questions above and in (1)—by the conflict of thresholds of defensive and controlling organizations of countercathexes with discharge-bent drive tensions for which affects serve as safety valves and indicators. It is, however, just as—indeed even more—possible that such a structural theory will have to take *inborn* discharge-thresholds also into consideration. In doing so it would have a precedent in Hartmann's treat-

---

[9] It is not implied here that consideration of thresholds will alone make the theory a structural one, nor that a structural theory considering thresholds is necessarily an adequate theory of affects.

ment of memory, motility, perceptual organs, as ego apparatuses: that is, structures which unlike some other ego structures do not grow from conflict, and are in this sense "autonomous"; being innate they are pre-existent to the differentiation of the ego and the id from their undifferentiated matrix, and become—once the ego is fully developed—apparatuses in the service of the ego. Thus drive- and affect-discharge thresholds would be added to the so-far familiar list of those inborn apparatuses which have primary autonomy from conflict (though these, too, like other such apparatuses, may become secondarily involved in conflict).

(3) These considerations are not pure theoretical niceties: there are clinical phenomena necessitating some such assumption. (a) The psychosomatic symptoms appearing in the first days of life, such as infantile eczema, inclination to colic, and also the early manifest individual differences, e.g., of hypo- and hypermotility, suggest the crucial role of differential thresholds in channeling the discharge of tensions into specific, individually varying directions (Escalona and Leitch, 1951). (b) The observations of autistic disorders of infancy and childhood (Kanner, 1944; Putnam, 1948; Mahler, 1949; Bergman and Escalona, 1949) show hypersensitivities and affect phenomena which are relevant in this context. Bergman and Escalona (1949) felt that their observations could be explained by assuming that the discharge thresholds are low in these cases, giving rise to high sensitivity, with the result that a precocious, partial, and uneven ego development sets in, in order—as it were—to establish new and higher thresholds to compensate for the low inborn thresholds.

Summing up: The affect theory of the second phase of the development of psychoanalysis is a *cathectic (economic) theory* in that affect discharge (affect expression and affect felt) is a discharge of a definite part of the accumulated drive cathexis, termed *affect charge*. It is a *dynamic theory* in that affect charge is discharged as a safety-valve function when discharge of drive cathexes by drive action meets opposition ("conflict"). It is, however, also a *topographical theory* in that *affect charge* is conceptualized as a drive representation of the same order as the *idea*.[10] It contains also traces of a *structural theory*, in that it stresses the importance of discharge channels by characterizing affect expression as discharge into the interior of the body, in contrast to action which is discharge into the external reality. As a structural theory it is quite unsatisfactory, in that it deals exclusively with primary affects carrying fully mobile drive cathexes which strive to discharge with full intensity. This theory remains an id theory of affects, not exploring their relation to, and function in the service of, the ego and its role in the development and release of the broad range and variety of "tamed" affects (Freud, 1937; Fcnichel, 1941, 1945). It was left to the

---

[10] [The use of "topographical" here is unclear. Rapaport probably wanted to emphasize that since affect charge is conceptualized as a *drive representation,* just as is idea, it is a *psychic* and not a somatic concept—Ed.]

third phase of the development of psychoanalytic theory to make the first systematic moves toward coping with these problems, partly with the aid of the budding concepts of the structural point of view and ego psychology, which were available for the first time, and partly as a means and a by-product of its attempts to develop these very concepts.

IV

The discussion of the affect theory of the third phase of psychoanalytic theory must begin with the admission that here too the development of affect theory has remained scanty, and received little attention; the beginnings we do possess have not been made very explicit, and are even less integrated with the rest of the theory than were the previous affect theories. The discussion of this third affect theory is even more difficult than that of the first two, because it presupposes a metapsychological theory of psychoanalysis complemented by the structural point of view (absorbing the topographical one), a systematic presentation of which is simply not extant.[11] Hartmann's (1939, 1951), Hartmann, Kris, and Loewenstein's (1946, 1949), and my own (1951a, 1951b) efforts to develop such a systematic presentation remain incomplete; they will not be reviewed here, since the more incomplete a theory, the less it lends itself to concise restatement.

Though the systematic status of this third theory is still deplorable, its roots go back to *The Interpretation of Dreams* (1900). There the conversion theory of affects (particularly of anxiety) still persists in the framework of the cathectic (second phase) theory. Freud wrote (1900, p. 521):

> . . . the suppression of the *Ucs.* becomes necessary . . . [because] if the movement of ideas in the *Ucs.* were allowed to run its course, it would develop an affect which originally had the character of pleasure, but which, since the process of *repression,* bears the character of pain.

Nevertheless, traces of the third theory of affects already appear. Even then Freud recognized that one of the concomitants of the development of the secondary process and reality testing is the "taming" of affects to the point of changing them into signals, though he was also cognizant of the fact that this process is never crowned by complete success.

> Thought must concern itself with the connecting-paths between ideas without allowing itself to be misled by their intensities. But it is obvious that condensations of ideas and intermediate or compromise-formations are obstacles to the attainment of [this] . . . Such procedures are, therefore, carefully avoided in our secondary thinking. It

[11] [The closest approach to such a systematic presentation is Rapaport's own later monograph, "The Structure of Psychoanalytic Theory: A Systematizing Attempt" (1959)—Ed.]

will readily be seen, moreover, that the pain-principle, although at other times it *provides the thought-process with its most important clues,* may also put difficulties in its way in the pursuit of identity of thought. Hence, the tendency of the thinking process must always be to free itself more and more from exclusive regulation by the pain-principle, and *to restrict the development of affect through the work of thought to the very minimum which remains effective as a signal. . . .* But . . . this refinement is seldom completely successful, even in normal psychic life, and . . . our thinking always remains liable to falsification by the intervention of the pain-principle [1900, pp. 535–536; italics added].

Thus affects appear here as "most important clues" and "signals" of the secondary process, but also as "falsifiers" of it, since this "refinement is seldom completely successful," and therefore actually—to use Fenichel's term—affects of all degrees of "taming" appear in consciousness.

Furthermore, defenses directed against affects (in the example below: reaction formation) are already noted and attributed to the "secondary system" [12] which binds cathexes—that is, delays and regulates discharge, instead of directly discharging mobile cathexes. Defense against affects is a part of the complex structural view of affects, and will be further discussed below. Freud wrote (1900, p. 537): ". . . such a conversion of affect occurs in the course of development (one need only think of the emergence of disgust . . .), and . . . is connected with the activity of the secondary system."

It is in accord with this that in *The Interpretation of Dreams,* and even more in "The Unconscious" (1915b), there are indications of the conception that it is not repression which gives rise to anxiety (affect) but rather anxiety which is a motive of repression. Freud (1915b, p. 110) wrote: ". . . to suppress the development of affect is the true aim of repression and . . . its work does not terminate if this aim is not achieved."

But let us turn now from these predecessors to the third phase of the theory. *The Ego and the Id,* which officially ushers in the third phase of psychoanalytic theory, contains a simile which paraphrases well the portent of the third phase of the theory of affects also; it forecasts the view that, owing to structure development, processes which are originally related to the conflicts of the id recur and involve higher levels of psychic structure. Freud (1923, p. 53) wrote: "The struggle which once raged in the deepest strata of the mind . . . is now carried on in a higher region, like the Battle of the Huns which in Kaulbach's painting is being fought out in the sky." Otherwise, we find in *The Ego and the Id* little about affects in general, but much about guilt and unconscious guilt. I cannot discuss the complex issue of guilt here, since it would lead us far afield. I will restrict myself to point-

[12] This point was then taken up first by Grüninger (1917).

ing out—crudely simplifying matters—that Freud represents the guilt affect as arising from a conflict of the ego with the superego; and that his discussion of "unconscious guilt" again implies the conception of defense against affects. Thus a structural conflict theory of affects is already forecast here, and so is a hierarchic layering of affects. But at the same time Freud holds fast to the previous drive theory of affects, though he has to invoke the death instinct to do so. He writes (1923, p. 77):

> If we turn to melancholia first, we find that the excessively strong super-ego which has obtained a hold upon consciousness rages against the ego with merciless fury, as if it had taken possession of the whole of the sadism available in the person concerned. . . . the destructive component had entrenched itself in the super-ego and turned against the ego. What is now holding sway in the super-ego is, as it were, a pure culture of the death-instinct . . .

This conception of the guilt affect[13] was further extended, in regard to both its origin in conflict and its multiple layering, by Jones in his "Fear, Guilt and Hate" (1929), which already makes use of Freud's major contribution to the third phase of affect theory, i.e., *The Problem of Anxiety* (1926). It is to my knowledge the first study of affects in the literature to make use of this advance in affect theory. Jones shows that fear, hate, and guilt are multiple-layered, in that any one of them may appear not only under the basic dynamic conditions which usually give rise to it, but also as an outcome of defense against any of the others. This conception implies, besides the conflict origin of these "secondary affects" and their hierarchic layering, the concept of defense against affects. Regrettably, Jones makes no clear distinction between the defense against the underlying drives and the defense against the affects; nor does he point up that these three affects are, even in their basic forms, of different orders of complexity (and thus imply even before the "secondary defense" a hierarchic order) in the ascending sequence: fear, hate, guilt—although in the adult individual there are fears, hates, and guilts of equivalent orders of complexity also. Jones (1929, p. 317) wrote in his summary:

> . . . I called attention to the various layers of secondary defence that covered the three attitudes of fear, hate and guilt, and pointed out that the defences themselves constituted a sort of "return of the repressed." We have seen how deep must be the primary layers of these three

---

[13] Federn (1929, 1936) presents a different theory of guilt and of affects in general. His theory is not only the earliest but also the most extensive attempt to develop a theory of affects which takes the structural point of view into account, and most of the problems and phenomena of affects touched on in the contributions here discussed are noted and tackled in it; I will not discuss it here because its idiosyncratic character and terminology divide it from the mainstream of psychoanalytic thinking, and make its presentation (short of a most extensive review) impossible.

emotional attitudes, and also that two stages can be distinguished in the development of each of them. The relationship of the secondary layers would appear to be somewhat as follows. Any one of these primary attitudes may prove to be unendurable, and so secondary defensive reactions are in turn developed, these being derived, as was just indicated, from one of the other attributes. Thus a secondary hate may be developed as a means of coping with either fear or guilt, a secondary fear attitude ("signal" anxiety) as a means of coping with guilty hate, or rather the dangers that this brings, and occasionally even a secondary guilt as a means of coping with the other two. These secondary reactions are therefore of a regressive nature, and they subserve the same defensive function as all other regressions.

As we see, Jones leaves it rather indefinite whether these secondary affects are *the* defenses pitted against the primary ones, or whether they issue from the defenses that are brought to bear. This type of uncertainty—implying also the uncertainty of distinction between defenses against drives and those against affects to be touched on below—is characteristic for the psychoanalytic theory of both defenses and affects.

After this excursion on guilt, for the sake of which we have broken the chronological order, we come to Freud's *The Problem of Anxiety* (1926), which by its treatment of anxiety and defenses ushered in ego psychology, gave substance to the program of the structural approach presented in *The Ego and the Id,* and constitutes the most important advance of the third phase of psychoanalytic theory in regard to the theory of affects.

In the first theory, affects were equated with drive cathexes; in the second theory, they appeared as drive representations, serving as safety valves for drive cathexes the discharge of which was prevented; in the third theory they appear as ego functions, and as such are no longer safety valves but are used as signals by the ego. Freud wrote:

> Anxiety . . . [like any] affective state . . . can . . . be experienced only by the ego [1926, p. 80].
> [Anxiety is] not to be explained on an economic basis;[14] is not created *de novo* in repression, but is reproduced as an affective state . . . [1926, p. 20].

This is then a structural view of affects. "Affect charge" if prevented from discharge does not become merely "potential," as was asserted in the discussion of "unconscious emotion"; it is structuralized and thus it can be reproduced as a signal without its "economic basis," i.e., without "affect discharge" actually taking place. The ego, which before the affect was "tamed" into a signal endured it passively, now produces it actively.

[14] That is, the affect is no longer a cathectic discharge process; it does not serve as a safety valve for drive tension damned up by repression.

Brierley's (1937) was the first attempt to state the ego theory of affects here implied. She did this partly by stressing the role of affects in the interplay between internal and external reality, and partly by insisting that affects are tension, rather than discharge, phenomena. Basically, however, she persisted with the second (cathectic) theory. She wrote (1937, p. 259):

> All our modern conceptions of the relation of anxiety to symptom-formation and of its rôle in development contradict the idea that affect is itself a discharge and support the view that it is a tension-phenomenon impelling to discharge either in the outer or the inner world. . . . Affects which appear to arise spontaneously always have unconscious stimuli and, in practice, we find affectivity tends to be high where frustration, particularly internal frustration, is marked.

In considering affects as tension phenomena and in bringing up the question of thresholds, she touches on issues crucial to the structural approach, but she does not make the transition from the cathectic to the signal theory. She wrote (1937, pp. 259–260):

> The conception of affects as tension-phenomena is, of course, in line with Freud's earliest formulations of the working of the psychic apparatus and the pleasure-pain principle . . . [*The Interpretation of Dreams*]. On the quantitative side we have, I think, to conceive of some threshold above which instinct-tension becomes appreciable as affect, and of a higher threshold, which may be attained either by the strength of the stimulus itself or by damming due to frustration, above which affect becomes intolerable and necessitates some immediate discharge, either outwards or inwards.

Brierley's viewing of affects as tension phenomena is certainly in keeping with the general conception of ego psychology: the ego, the secondary process, strives on the one hand to bind mobile cathexes, and on the other to control and delay their discharge. But even in terms of the cathectic (second) theory one might consider affects as tension phenomena, as phenomena of drive tension mounting to threshold intensity; though—since this theory is concerned with mobile cathexes and deals with the safety-valve role of affects—this distinction of tension *versus* discharge has little theoretical meaning in it. However, it has much theoretical meaning on the level of the third, the ego theory, of affects. Yet it is possible that a *pure* tension concept of affect (Brierley's is not quite that: note again the quote from pp. 259–260) empties out the baby with the bath water, by laying the foundations of an ego theory of affects at the price of disregarding the indispensable elements of the superseded id theory. Indeed Landauer (1938) and Fenichel (1941) referred to genetic (developmental) observations, showing how massive affect discharge recedes with maturation, and thus began to lay the foundations of a theory which takes both the discharge and tension aspects of affect into consideration. Landauer (1938) wrote:

> Thus it is really only in children that we see affective attacks in an approximately pure form. But we see too how phylogenetically older affects are overlaid by others more recent and more complicated, which in their turn become obsolete and are gradually surmounted. Thus in a new-born baby fright can still be very easily and extensively mobilized, especially in the form of starting. It is only gradually that fright is increasingly pushed aside by anxiety [pp. 396–397].
>
> I have described anxiety as a secondary hysterical attack, which serves as a means of escape from the primary hysterical attack of fright. The affects of gaiety and sadness have been evolved as a means of escape from despair; they have absorbed the latter affect and amalgamated it with many other tendencies. In melancholic and manic seizures the two affects become to a large extent disintegrated and then certain characteristic features of despair become prominent [p. 401].

Fenichel described the role of increasing ego mastery in the decreasing discharge character and increasing tension character of affects during the course of development, as well as the consequences in affect phenomena of pathological impairments of ego mastery. Just as ideation is tamed into "trying out" experimental action in thought, so, according to him, affect discharge is tamed into anticipatory signals in the service of the ego. Fenichel (1941, 217–218) wrote:

> . . . children and "neurotic personalities," i.e., persons with many repressions, and therefore greater tensions, in general have more frequent emotional spells than normal adults. It is obvious that the normal adult does not lack emotions. But he does not have overwhelming emotional spells. Apparently the ego's increasing strength enables it somehow to get the upper hand of the affects at the moment when they arise. The ego is no longer overwhelmed by something alien to it, but it senses when this alien something begins to develop and simultaneously upon this recognition it re-establishes its mastery, binding the affects, using them for its purposes—"taming" them, as it were. To be sure, even the most adult ego can do this only to a certain degree. Too much excitement is emotionally upsetting for everyone. Thus we see that the first stage, in which the ego is weak and the affects dominant, is followed by a second in which the ego is strong and has learned to use the affects for its purposes. But a third state is always possible in which once more an elemental affect may overwhelm the organism.

Furthermore, Fenichel (1945, p. 43) wrote:

> When the child learns to control his motility, purposeful actions gradually take the place of mere discharge reactions; the child can

now prolong the time between stimulus and reaction and achieve a certain tolerance of tension. The characteristic capacity for "trying out" that is thus acquired changes the ego's relation to its affects. Affects are originally archaic discharge syndromes that supplant voluntary actions under certain exciting conditions. Now the growing ego learns to "tame" affects and to use them for its own anticipating purposes . . .

Indeed, the very fact that Freud in *The Problem of Anxiety* envisaged two forms of anxiety production—on the one hand, anxiety issuing from economic conditions, i.e., as safety-valve drive discharge, and on the other, anxiety being issued by the ego as a signal (pp. 108–109)—already foreshadows Landauer's and Fenichel's views.

Most recently Jacobson (1951, 1953) has criticized sharply both the tension and the discharge theory of affects. She argued justly:

> MacCurdy [1925] and even Brierley [1937] and Rapaport [1942][15] seem to ignore . . . that not only all normal ego functions, but particularly direct instinct gratifications, such as the sexual act or eating, are accompanied by intensive affective expression [1951].

Analyzing the course of the pleasure experience in orgasm, she concluded that (a) the orgastic experience includes alternating increases of tension and partial discharges accompanying the rise of tension to a climax and its drop after the climax; (b) the affect experience corresponds neither to tension nor to discharge per se, but rather to the change (increase or decrease) in tension. Thus hers, too, is a combined tension and discharge theory of affect. But this theory leaves us with the questions: (a) Does it not limit itself to considering only the conscious experience of affect? (b) Does it not equate the concepts of pleasure-pain as defined in the pleasure principle with subjectively experienced affect? But more about this later. Jacobson (1951) wrote:

> If what we perceive as feelings is not "tension"—in contradistinction to "discharge"—but the flux of mobile psychic energy released, the changes in the level of tension—or in the amount of excitation, respectively—above a certain threshold, then Brierley's tension concept would become more meaningful, but her argument against the discharge idea would be senseless, because what we would "feel" would be the rises as well as the drops of tension in the course of a discharge process.

[15] Jacobson's criticism applies to my discussion in *Emotions and Memory* (1942), which at the time failed to consider the structural ego-psychological issues. See, however, my discussions in *Organization and Pathology of Thought* (1951a) and in "The Conceptual Model of Psychoanalysis" (1951b).

The recent closely reasoned and stimulating paper by M. Schur (1953) concerning the theory of anxiety centers also on this discharge versus signal (tension) dichotomy, and proposes a theory to resolve it. His theory—as I see it—stresses that the ego is always passive in anxiety experiences, and that anxiety is always a regression phenomenon. He therefore negates the "signal theory" and explains the role of the ego in anxiety by means of Kris's (1950) concept of "regression in the service of the ego." Though Schur's theory appears to have a primarily id-psychological slant, actually it touches on the least clear, yet central issues of the ego psychology of affects, and it treats of ego aspects of the anxiety and affect problem not heretofore discussed in the literature.

But let us return to the affect theory of *The Problem of Anxiety,* to outline further features of it. Freud takes cognizance there of the innate factors in affect formation.[16] He characterizes affects as congenital hysterical attacks and suggests that even the obscure phobias of early childhood are remnants of congenital equipment commonly observed in animals. Freud (1926, p. 71) wrote:

> For we hold that other affects as well are reproductions of past experiences of a character vital to the organism, experiences possibly even antedating the individual; and we draw a comparison between these, as universal, specific, congenital hysterical attacks, and the seizures of the hysterical neurosis, later and individually acquired, the genesis and significance of which as memory symbols have been made clearly manifest by analysis. It would of course be most desirable to be able to demonstrate the validity of this conception for a number of other affects, but at the present time we are far from being in a position to do this.

and further (1926, p. 117):

> The enigmatic phobias of early childhood deserve mention once again at this point. Certain of them—the fear of being alone, of the dark, of strangers—we can understand as reactions to the danger of object loss; with regard to others—fear of small animals, thunderstorms, etc.—there is the possibility that they represent the atrophied remnants of an innate preparedness against reality dangers such as is so well developed in other animals. It is the part of this archaic heritage having to do with object loss which alone has utility for man. If such childhood phobias become fixed, grow more intense, and persist into a later period of life, analysis demonstrates that their content has become connected with instinctual demands, has become the representative of internal dangers also.

---

[16] In doing so, he returns to a conception already expressed in *Studies in Hysteria* (Breuer and Freud, 1893–95), according to which hysterical attacks are abnormal expressions of affects.

Thus Freud's ego theory of affects implies the recognition of the innate character of some basic affect-discharge channels, and even the innate character of their thresholds and of their relation to releasing stimuli. It seems safe to assert that any theory of affects which implies the structural point of view will consider these innate aspects of affects as its point of departure. But Freud's theory also shows how these innate structures are to be embedded into the rest of the theory. These preformed affect-discharge channels are made use of for safety-valve discharge by a whole series of conflicted drives on various levels of structure formation in the course of development. In the case of anxiety, for instance, the series of conflicts has the common denominator of helplessness, and some of the situations in which conflicts leading to helplessness use anxiety as a safety valve are: birth, separation from the mother, castration threat, etc. Furthermore, Freud points up that these inborn discharge channels and thresholds—as well as new ones formed in the course of development—come progressively, with advancing psychic structure formation, under the control of the ego. Freud (1926, pp. 114–115) wrote:

> The danger situation is the recognized, remembered and anticipated situation of helplessness. Anxiety is the original reaction to helplessness in the traumatic situation, which is later reproduced as a call for help in the danger situation. The ego, which has experienced the trauma passively, now actively repeats an attenuated reproduction of it with the idea of taking into its own hands the directing of its course.

And further (1926, pp. 108–109):

> The anxiety felt in the process of birth now became the prototype of an affective state which was obliged to share the fate of other affects. It was reproduced either automatically in situations which were analogous to that of its origin and as an inexpedient type of reaction, after having been an appropriate one in the initial situation of danger; or else the ego acquired control over this affect and reproduced it itself, making use of it as a warning of danger and as a means of rousing into action the pleasure-pain mechanism. . . . To anxiety in later life were thus attributed two modes of origin: the one involuntary, automatic, economically justified whenever there arose a situation of danger analogous to birth; the other, produced by the ego when such a situation merely threatened, in order to procure its avoidance.

Fenichel (1945, pp. 133–134) states some aspects of this view of the development of affects concisely:

> This triple stratification of anxiety may be summarized in a short table:

ANXIETY

(1)	Trauma	Anxiety automatic and unspecific
(2)	Danger	Anxiety in the service of the ego, affect created by anticipation, controlled and used as a warning signal
(3)	Panic[17]	Ego control fails, affect becomes overwhelming, regression to state (1); anxiety spell in anxiety hysteria

The same triple stratification of anxiety will be found again in all other affects.

While as a schema this triple stratification appears to be correct, in actuality there is a fluid transition between the three; Fenichel's emphasis on ego control also seems to imply that there are transitions of all shades between these three strata, depending on the availability of the synthetizing forces of the ego (and these, of course, vary in the course of individual development, show interindividual variations, and fluctuate in the adult individual also). On the one hand, there occur normally, even at sustained ego control, automatic affect phenomena; on the other, affect attacks due to pathological failing of ego controls have many shades short of panic. This, too, seems to be the implication of Fenichel's phrase concerning the ego's "taming" of affects. One facet of this process is described in Jones's discussion of the various layers of hate, fear, and guilt affects, and of their relation to defensive operations. Further light is thrown on it by the process of binding of affects by processes of thought, pointed out already by Breuer and Freud. They (1893, p. 31) wrote: " 'Abreaction' is . . . not the only . . . solution . . . the normal man succeeds by means of associations in dissipating the accompanying affect." This process of binding affects by processes of thought is elucidated in Freud's description of the work of mourning. He (1917, p. 154) wrote:

> The task is now carried through bit by bit, under great expense of time and cathectic energy, while all the time the existence of the lost object is continued in the mind. Each single one of the memories and hopes which bound the libido to the object is brought up and hypercathected, and the detachment of the libido from it accomplished. Why this process of carrying out the behest of reality bit by bit, which is in the nature of a compromise, should be so extraordinarily painful is not at all easy to explain in terms of mental economics. It is worth noting that this pain seems natural to us. The fact is, however, that

[17] Fenichel (1934a) liked to use the analogy that panic occurs when the drive tension is excessive, and thus the anxiety signal acts like a lighted match in a powder keg.

when the work of mourning is completed the ego becomes free and uninhibited again.

Glover's characterization of certain obsessional systems, too, seems to be relevant to elucidate this process of binding. Indeed, it seems to link "binding" and "taming" of affects, and to suggest that their end products are variable and modulated affects instead of massive affect attacks. Glover (1935, p. 137) wrote:

> . . . we see that apparently complicated rituals . . . provide an ever more complicated meshwork of conceptual systems through which affect may pass in a finely divided state. When . . . these rituals are interfered with we observe once more the existence of massive affects.

Fenichel's and Anna Freud's discussions of defenses against affects elucidate this taming process. Fenichel's discussion (1934a) of defense against anxiety, and of anxiety as a motive of defense, is a particularly instructive analysis of the hierarchic layering of gradually tamed affects. Anna Freud's (1936) discussion centers on the relation between defenses against drives and defenses against affects, and states sharply the relative independence of these two. She wrote (pp. 34–35):

> We know that the fate of the affect associated with an instinctual demand is not simply identical with that of its ideational representative. Obviously, however, one and the same ego can have at its disposal only a limited number of possible means of defence. At particular periods in life and according to its own specific structure the individual ego selects now one defensive method now another—it may be repression displacement, reversal, etc.—and these it can employ both in its conflict with the instincts and in its defence against the liberation of affect. If we know how a particular patient seeks to defend himself against the emergence of his instinctual impulses, i.e. what is the nature of his habitual ego-resistances, we can form an idea of his probable attitude towards his own unwelcome affects. If, in another patient, particular forms of affect-transformation are strongly in evidence, such as complete suppression of emotion, denial, etc., we shall not be surprised if he adopts the same methods of defence against his instinctual impulses and his free associations. It is the same ego, and in all its conflicts it is more or less consistent in using every means which it has at its command.

Fenichel pursues further Anna Freud's distinction between defenses against drives and defenses against affects; his treatment of blocking, postponement, displacement, equivalents, reaction formations, change of quality, isolation, projection, and introjection, and the varieties of defenses against guilt (1941; 1945, pp. 161 ff.) appears to be singular in the literature. Yet even this discussion leaves the concept of "defense against affects" with some of the same lack of clarity as Jones's (1929) contribution left it with. (a) Fenichel speaks of defenses against affects as "primitive defenses," a phrase suggesting a relation to "prestages of defense." "Prestages of defense" in turn seems at least in part to imply for Fenichel (1945) inborn mechanisms; it certainly implies for Hartmann (1939) such inborn mechanisms of "primary autonomy" which determine the subsequent choice of defense mechanisms used against drives. If these "primitive defenses" against affects are indeed to be so understood, then they must be closely linked to, or identical with, the thresholds and other propensities of inborn affect discharge-channels. (b) Fenichel does not shut the door on interpreting "defense against affects" as defense against the drive impulse which gave rise to them; though (c) in the main he seems—in agreement with Anna Freud—to suggest that signal affect just like thought, and affect charge just like ideas, and all of these just like drives, are subject to defensive operations. It is possible that this lack of clarity arises because all these three forms of defense are extant and used on the various levels of the motivational and structural hierarchy in all kinds of complex combinations.

Landauer pointed out another aspect of the "taming of affects," namely their changing their "attack" character to one of a continuous state, and attributed it to continuous superego stimulation, as Freud did for grief (1917), guilt (1923), and certain forms of anxiety (1926). Landauer (1938, p. 389) wrote:

> Are the affects really reactions? In children we still see them as such. But in later life anxiety is apparently continuous in the anxious-minded, the pessimist is permanently melancholy and the cheerful man consistently buoyant. How does an isolated reaction become a continuous state? Freud has solved this problem in the theory of the affects by demonstrating the function of the super-ego in their release. He illustrated his remarks chiefly from the example of anxiety.

Landauer expressed the conception of continuous affect stimulation in a different way also, implying—as did Jones (1929)—a conception of hierarchic layering of affects arising from defensive operations, directed against more basic affects. Landauer (1938, p. 402) wrote:

> Some of the affects have been relegated to subordinate egos, whilst the ego-in-chief addresses itself to reality in a manner at once reasonable and good, affectionate and defensive. These affects have gradually become shut off, have dwindled into mere reflexes. But the converse process may take place and super-affects be formed. Thus there arises embarrassment, i.e. fear of shame, and prudence, i.e. fear of anxiety. Since a prohibited affect threatens to return again and again,

the super-affect, once formed, seems to be continuously present. A mood or a certain type of temperament is created. The commonest super-affect is certainly anxiety, but there are quite a number of other super-affects. Embarrassment may mean not only that we fear shame but that we are ashamed of fear. Next to anxiety sadness is, I think, the commonest super-affect. Since it may bring about a real loss of love or, later, forestalling the condemnation of the super-ego, an endopsychic loss of love, sadness becomes itself an occasion for sadness.

While Landauer's terminology (subordinate egos, superaffects) is not easy to follow and his documentation is insufficient, he certainly points more than any other psychoanalytic author—excepting perhaps Flugel (1948)—to the need to explain continuous affects which take the form of structuralized affective states and even of character traits. Flugel (1948)—like Drever—notes the insufficiencies of a purely dynamic conflict theory of affect for the explanation of sustained pleasurable affects, and advances a theory of hierarchically layered derivative needs to explain these. Landauer's suggestion that continuous affects are to be explained by continuous stimulation by one of the three structural divisions of the psyche seems to fit certain cases (e.g., certain forms of sadness and guilt). But studies of boredom (Fenichel, 1934b; Greenson, 1953), apathy (Greenson, 1949), teasing (Sperling, 1953), Freud's (1927) discussion of humor, Kris's (1936, 1938, 1939) various papers on the comic, and particularly Bibring's (1953) discussion of depression and Brenman's (1952) discussion of teasing, suggest that in general such affective states are too complex to be so accounted for, and though they are ego reactions or ego states, yet in them ego, id, and superego contributions are integrated into complex quasi-stable substructures.[18]

The attempt to develop a definitive psychoanalytic theory of affects has culminated in two attempts at a classification of affects. The first of these, Glover's (1939, p. 300), brought the great variety and complexity of affect phenomena most clearly to the fore:

> . . . affective phenomena call for a greater variety of approaches than any other mental manifestation. This is borne out by the fact that affects can be classified in a great variety of ways. They can be described in crude qualitative terms, e.g. of subjective pleasure or "pain",

---

[18] By this comparison I do not imply that Landauer's superaffects, moods, affect attitudes crystallized into character traits, apathy, etc., are of the same order of complexity. I mean only that all these, though they must be dealt with by a theory of affects, are complex integrated formations which cannot be accounted for by an affect theory alone. Kris's contributions are well known, thus only his theory of the affective reaction to the becoming conscious of daydreams (1950) should be particularly pointed to. Bibring's (1953) and Brenman's (1952) contributions are, however, little known, and the reader's attention is called to their far-reaching implications for the extension of the structural point of view in general and that of the theory of affective states in particular. It would lead too far afield to discuss them here.

or labelled descriptively according to the predominant ideational system associated with them in consciousness. They can be classified by reference to the instinct or component instinct from which they are derived, or they can be considered as either "fixed" or "labile." They can be divided into primary affects and secondary affects, more precisely into "positive" and "reactive" affects, or they can be considered as tension and discharge phenomena. Finally, they can be grouped as simple or compound ("mixed" and/or "fused") affects.

Otherwise, however, Glover's theory failed to pass from the second (cathectic) to the third (signal) level of affect theory, and remained—as Jacobson (1951) implied in her discussion of it—a fragmentary drive theory without significant application of the structural point of view. The second of these classifications implying an affect theory—Jacobson's—is founded on the structural point of view and succeeds in restating the "conflict theory" of affects in structural terms. In this theory, affects arise from tensions in the id or ego, or from tensions between id and ego, or ego and superego. Jacobson (1951) wrote:

> We may consider replacing . . . [Glover's] with a classification that employs our current structural concepts. Even though all affects are ego experiences and develop in the ego, one of their qualitative determinants must be the site of the underlying energetic tension by which they have been induced and which may arise anywhere within the psychic organization. Practically, certain affects have always been characterized in this way; guilt feelings, for instance, are commonly defined as arising from a tension between ego and superego. There is no reason why we should not introduce this kind of classification for affect types in general. Thus we might distinguish:
>
> (1) simple and compound affects arising from intrasystemic tension:
>   (a) affects that represent instinctual drives proper, i.e., that arise directly from tensions in the id (e.g., sexual excitement, rage);
>   (b) affects that develop directly from tensions in the ego[19] (e.g., fear of reality and physical pain, as well as components of the more enduring feelings and feeling attitudes, such as object love and hate or thing interest);
> (2) simple and compound affects induced by intersystemic tensions:
>   (a) affects induced by tensions between the ego and the id (e.g., fear of the id, components of disgust, shame, and pity);
>   (b) affects induced by tensions between ego and superego (e.g., guilt feelings, components of depression).

As will be noticed, I have not included tensions between ego and reality. These represent "conflict," that is, affective responses to reality.

---

[19] Federn (1936) has dealt with these extensively and, indeed, has attempted to reduce all affects to this category.

The underlying energetic psychic tension can only arise within the psychic organization and not between it and the outside world. (This is another example of the prevailing lack of distinction between affective and energetic processes.)

The problems Jacobson's theory leaves us with are these: (a) One wonders whether or not her structural theory is achieved at a price of disregarding some of the insights (drive representation, affect charge, affect discharge) of Freud's previous drive theory of affects without which an affect theory cannot be complete, since it would disregard the hierarchic continuum discussed above. (b) One is left uncertain whether her treatment of pleasure and pain (referred to earlier in this paper) means to subsume pleasure and pain as affects, and if so, whether or not so doing disregards the fact that in the conception of the *"pleasure-pain principle" pleasure* and *pain* are *neither affects* subjectively felt nor "affect charges," *but concepts* the referent of which is the process of discharge regulation; the various phases of this may or may not be experienced as pleasure or pain, and if they are so experienced, they *are not just pleasure or pain in general but specific qualities of pleasure and pain.*[20] (c) It is difficult to be sure whether or not Jacobson, by limiting her discussion to the conscious subjective experience of affect, has neglected affect discharge and affect equivalents, for which it is hard to account without incorporating the second (the cathectic) theory into the definitive one. An affect theory centered on the conscious experience of affects runs into yet another difficulty: the very act of becoming conscious is dependent on a complex balance involving more than just the affect process (cf. Kris, 1950; and Brenman, 1952). (d) One wonders whether in its classificatory simplicity it may not preclude a theoretical accounting of the many shades and varieties of affects arising in the taming process, as well as those varieties of continuous "affective states" which we referred to above and which appear to be quasi-stable formations integrating complex id, ego, and superego contributions and their shifting balances into something like a substructure. In passing, it may be mentioned that the structural point of view does not seem to stop at the analysis of ego, id, superego factors; it enters upon the study of structuralization within each of these, as well as upon the study of structuralization of functions uniting components from all (Hartmann, 1939; Kris, 1950; Brenman, 1952).

V

The complexity of the phenomena and of the theoretical implications of affects which I have attempted to unfold here in the fashion of a review makes a definitive formulation of an up-to-date psychoanalytic theory of

---

[20] The same difficulty is particularly clear in a paper by Jelgersma (1921) dealing with the psychoanalytic theory of feelings.

affects certainly ill-advised, if not impossible. Yet I should like to sketch the outlines of a theory as it seems to emerge from this review, because even though necessarily characterized by gaps and assumptions easily proved to be unwarranted, it will give us one possible interpretation of where we stand and thus may facilitate orientation for future observation and theorizing.

The following outline of a theory attempts to integrate the affect theories of the second and third phase, and uses some contributions from the theory of the first phase.

(1) Affects use—to begin with—inborn channels and thresholds of discharge. These may be considered apparatuses pre-existing the differentiation of ego and id from their undifferentiated matrix (Hartmann, Kris, and Loewenstein, 1946). This is the referent of the phrase "affects are inherited hysterical attacks." In this respect affects are common properties of the species, and this may have to do with the roots of their social role in communication and empathy (Schilder, 1924). Yet even in this respect there are already at birth great interindividual differences (Bergman and Escalona, 1949; Escalona and Leitch, 1951) which seem to have to do with what develops into a "predisposition to anxiety" and into various affect equivalents in psychosomatic pathology, as well as into various "frozen affects" taking the form of character traits (Reich, 1933).

(2) At the reconstructed hypothetical stage (see above) where the pleasure principle holds full sway, drive (mobile) cathexes strive for immediate discharge; affects arise as safety-valve functions when drive discharge by drive action is not possible because of the absence of the drive object in reality. This stage is hypothetical because drive tension, too, has thresholds and before these are reached no discharge occurs; thus these set limits to the full success of the pleasure principle, i.e., they prevent a completely tensionless state. At this stage affects appear as discharge phenomena of a part (a determinate quantity) of drive cathexis, which is conceptualized as "affect charge" and is probably determined by the amount of cathexis the various inborn affect-discharge channels can carry.

(3) "Affect charge" and "idea" are drive representations, both still operating with mobile cathexes, abiding by the pleasure principle. Affect discharges are massive affect storms, which discharge into the interior of the body through secretory and motor innervations, instead of discharging in action onto the drive object.

(4) The general development of psychic structure begins with innate discharge-regulating thresholds, is fostered by delays of discharge enforced by reality conditions, and progresses by internalization of the delay of discharge caused by reality, establishing an *ability to delay*. This ability is achieved by defenses (countercathectic energy distributions), which may be regarded as alterations of discharge thresholds. The damming up of drives by defenses makes for more intensive and more varied use of the affect-discharge channels and of the corresponding "affect charges."

The establishment of countercathectic energy distributions, however, has other crucial consequences. It gives rise to varied derivative and partial drives (the latter particularly in conjunction with somatic maturation), some of which arise as modifications of the drives defended against, others as modifications of drives to which the countercathectic energy distributions generalized (that is, spread or were displaced), others as motivating forces originating from the countercathectic energy distributions themselves (see Rapaport, 1951a, pp. 699–701). These all have their thresholds of discharge, and when prevented from discharging by reality conditions or by the countercathectic energy distributions which developed as internalizations of these reality conditions, they apparently use and modify the thresholds of the existing affect-discharge channels. This process is repeated variously for the derivative and partial motivations also in the course of development, giving rise to a hierarchy of motivations ranging from drives to interests and preferences. This process is apparently synonymous with that of binding (Freud, 1900; see also Rapaport, 1951b) and/or neutralization (Hartmann, Kris, and Loewenstein, 1949) of mobile cathexes. Another aspect of this process is the development of the secondary thought process from the primary one, that of experimental action in thought by means of small amounts of bound (neutralized) cathexes and memory traces, from hallucinatory gratification by means of drive-cathecting of memory traces to perceptual (hallucinatory) intensity (see Freud, 1911; also Rapaport, 1951a). The drive-representing idea tends to become reality-representing thought. Drive discharge is delayed and becomes action using thought as preparation, and the tension damned up by delay is discharged through the safety valve of affect discharge. But affects do not remain inborn discharge channels used by dammed-up drives as safety valves; they too partake in the development sketched: they become progressively tamed. This is achieved by various means: (a) At each level of the motivational hierarchy the derivative motivations use affects as safety-valve discharge channels, but the cathexes of these motivations are more and more neutralized with the ascent of the hierarchy; consequently the cathexes of the affect charges too become less and less peremptory, and the affect discharges less automatic and massive. (b) It appears that not only are the discharge thresholds of the drive derivatives and of the affects altered with the ascent of the hierarchy, but also new, more complex, and subtle affect discharge-channels are created with general maturation, ascending hierarchy, and psychic structure formation. (c) Furthermore, affect charges themselves also seem to become subject to defensive countercathecting, that is, to direct modification of their discharge thresholds.

(5) This hierarchic development has a dual outcome: (a) On the one hand, since various drives and derivative drives (motivations) from all levels of the hierarchy remain effective in psychic life, we find in the normal adult also affect phenomena of quite mobile cathexes, akin to massive affect at-

tacks, just as we find in his conscious thought primary-process phenomena, too. (b) On the other hand we find affects of highly neutralized cathexes, which serve as signals and means of reality testing for orientation to both external reality (danger) and internal reality (drive inundation). The continuum of affects extends in all shadings from massive affect attacks to mere signals and even signals of signals (Fenichel, 1934a). The development of the motivational and affect hierarchy is one aspect of structure formation and ego development. In the course of it the ego, which originally endured affects passively, obtains control of them and comes to release them in tamed forms of anticipatory signals. Massive affect attacks may come about either owing to weakening of ego control or with the "consent" of the ego as "regressions in the service of the ego" (Kris, 1950). Schur (1953) suggests that affect signals too are such "regressions in the service of the ego." To be sure, there are great differences within the normal range as to which end of the affect continuum, and which qualities of affect within it, are emphasized in the individual. On the whole, the less rich the hierarchic development of controlling countercathectic energy distributions, the less the variability and modulation and the greater the intensity of massive affect outburst; the less flexible and more excessively rigid these controls, the more meager both in intensity, variability, and modulation affects become; and, as so often in life phenomena, the optimum is not the maximum. Rich and modulated affect life appears to be the indicator of a "strong ego."

(6) "Affect charge" if discharged may arouse further tensions. To prevent the development of these, the underlying drive as well as the "affect charge" must be defended against. Thus affects (e.g., anxiety) become motives of defense (Fenichel, 1945). It appears that otherwise also, under special conditions, affect charge as energy quantity may come to play the role of motivation. But these conditions are not well understood and it is not certain that, if understood, they cannot be accounted for by assuming that the drive underlying the affect rather than the affect itself acts as the motivation. Should this way out not prove feasible, we are faced with a return—true, only a limited and partial one—of the first phase of affect theory, in the framework of the third-phase theory.

(7) The development of the ascending hierarchy of motivations appears to be one aspect of psychic structure formation, id-ego-superego differentiation. On each level of the hierarchy the conflict of discharge-bent cathexes with innate thresholds, or with reality (absent object), or with countercathexes, is the *dynamic aspect* of affect formation. The *economic aspect* of affect formation is the partial discharge of motivational cathexes of ever-increasing neutralization. The *structural aspect* and the *adaptive aspect*[21] of affect formation are more complex.

21 The "adaptive aspect" is not of the same order as the dynamic, economic, and structural. Actually it may be regarded as part of the structural aspect. It is here

(8) *Structurally* the integration of the ascending motivational systems into id, ego, and superego amounts to the creation of mutually controlling systems of organization, continuous conflicts among which also give rise to tensions and to their discharge, i.e., to affects which may thus become continuous. This is what Landauer (1938) and Jacobson (1951, 1953) conceptualized, following Freud's (1923, 1926) lead. But such enduring affective states are mostly not outcomes of a conflict within one, or between two, of the three institutions; rather they often come about as integrations of complex balances and conflicts of components from all three major structural divisions of the psyche. The closer study of these complex affect states and of their chronic characterological forms (see, e.g., Brenman, 1952) may lead to an important advancement of the structural point of view.

(9) From the *point of view of adaptation:* On the one hand, affects seem to start even in human beings to some extent—and certainly in animals—as what Hartmann called states of adaptedness: that is, the affect-discharge apparatus has a limited attunement to certain external reality stimuli, such as is seen in startle (Landis and Hunt, 1939) and smile (Spitz and Wolf, 1946). On the other hand, affects as signals are just as indispensable a means of reality testing as thoughts. Indeed, they are more indispensable for reality testing in all except successfully intellectualizing and obsessional characters. Reality testing without the contribution of affect signal readily changes into obsessional or paranoid magic. The expelled affect signal returns through the back door: there is no warning of the impending affect formation which may therefore, unimpeded, appear as mobile cathexis and disturber of the secondary process.

VI

The theory of affects, the bare outlines of which seem to emerge, integrates three components: *inborn affect-discharge channels* and discharge thresholds of drive cathexes; the use of these inborn channels as safety valves and indicators of drive tension, the modification of their thresholds by drives and derivative motivations prevented from drive action, and the formation thereby of *the drive representation termed affect charge;* and the progressive "taming" and advancing ego control, in the course of psychic structure formation, of the affects which are thereby turned into *affect signals* released by the ego.

---

separated and singled out thus because of its singular importance, which has already been stressed by Hartmann (1939). [Rapaport subsequently changed his mind on this point; see "A Theoretical Analysis of the Superego Concept" (Chapter 55), "The Points of View and Assumptions of Metapsychology" (Chapter 62), and "The Structure of Psychoanalytic Theory: A Systematizing Attempt" (1959). The issue is still debated, and Glover (1961, p. 98 n. 8) has argued against considering adaptive as of the same order as dynamic, economic, and structural—Ed.]

REFERENCES

Alexander, F. (1943). Fundamental Concepts of Psychosomatic Research: Psychogenesis, Conversion, Specificity. *Psychosom. Med.,* 5:205–210.

Bergman, P., & Escalona, S. (1949). Unusual Sensitivities in Very Young Children. *Psychoanal. Study Child,* 3/4:333–352. New York: International Universities Press.

Bibring, E. (1953). The Mechanism of Depression. In *Affective Disorders,* ed. P. Greenacre. New York: International Universities Press, 1953, pp. 13–48.

Bleuler, E. (1912). Affectivity, Suggestibility, Paranoia. *State Hosp. Bull.,* 4:481–601.

Brenman, M. (1952). On Teasing and Being Teased: And the Problem of "Moral Masochism." *Psychoanal. Study Child,* 7:264–285. New York: International Universities Press.

Breuer, J., & Freud, S. (1893). On the Psychical Mechanism of Hysterical Phenomena. *Collected Papers,* 1:24–41. London: Hogarth Press, 1948.

Breuer, J., & Freud, S. (1893–95). *Studies in Hysteria.* New York: Nerv. Ment. Dis. Monogr. Series No. 61, 1937.

Brierley, M. (1937). Affects in Theory and Practice. *Int. J. Psycho-Anal.,* 18:256–268.

Bürger-Prinz, H., & Kaila, M. (1930). On the Structure of the Amnesic Syndrome. In Rapaport (1951a), pp. 650–686.

Deutsch, H. (1942). Some Forms of Emotional Disturbance and Their Relationship to Schizophrenia. *Yearb. Psychoanal.,* 1:121–136. New York: International Universities Press, 1945.

Dewey, J. (1894–95). The Theory of Emotion. *Psychol. Rev.,* 1:553–569; 2:13–32.

Drever, J. (1917). *Instinct in Man.* Cambridge: Cambridge University Press.

Escalona, S., & Leitch, M. (1951). Progress Report: Early Phases of Personality Development. A Non-normative Study of Infant Behavior. Report to the U.S. Public Health Service, Project MH-27.

Federn, P. (1929). The Ego as Object and Subject in Narcissism. *Ego Psychology and the Psychoses.* New York: Basic Books, 1952, pp. 283–322.

——— (1936). On the Distinction between Healthy and Pathological Narcissism. *Ego Psychology and the Psychoses.* New York: Basic Books, 1952, pp. 323–364.

Fenichel, O. (1934a). Defense against Anxiety, Particularly by Libidinization. *Collected Papers,* 1:303–317. New York: Norton, 1953.

——— (1934b). On the Psychology of Boredom. *Collected Papers,* 1:292–302. New York: Norton, 1953. Also in Rapaport (1951a), pp. 349–361.

——— (1935). Concerning the Theory of Psychoanalytic Technique. *Collected Papers,* 1:332–348. New York: Norton, 1953.

——— (1941). The Ego and the Affects. *Collected Papers,* 2:215–227. New York: Norton, 1954.

——— (1945). *The Psychoanalytic Theory of Neurosis.* New York: Norton.

Flugel, J. (1948). "L'Appetit Vient en Mangeant": Some Reflexions on the Self-sustaining Tendencies. *Brit. J. Psychol.,* 38:171–190.

Freud, A. (1936). *The Ego and the Mechanisms of Defence.* New York: International Universities Press, 1946.

Freud, S. (1894). The Defence Neuro-Psychoses. *Collected Papers,* 1:59–75. New York: Basic Books, 1959.

———— (1895a [1894]). The Justification for Detaching from Neurasthenia a Particular Syndrome: The Anxiety-Neurosis. *Collected Papers,* 1:76–106. New York: Basic Books, 1959.

———— (1895b). Project for a Scientific Psychology. *The Origins of Psychoanalysis: Letters to Wilhelm Fliess, Drafts and Notes, 1887–1902.* New York: Basic Books, 1954, pp. 347–445.

———— (1898). Sexuality in the Aetiology of the Neuroses. *Collected Papers,* 1:220–248. New York: Basic Books, 1959.

———— (1900). The Interpretation of Dreams, tr. A. A. Brill. *The Basic Writings.* New York: Modern Library, 1938, pp. 179–549.

———— (1909). Analysis of a Phobia in a Five-Year-Old Boy. *Collected Papers,* 3:149–289. New York: Basic Books, 1959.

———— (1911). Formulations Regarding the Two Principles in Mental Functioning. *Collected Papers,* 4:13–21. New York: Basic Books, 1959.

———— (1911–17 [1911–15]). Papers on Metapsychology. *Collected Papers,* 4:13–170. New York: Basic Books, 1959.

———— (1914). Further Recommendations in the Technique of Psycho-Analysis. Recollection, Repetition and Working Through. *Collected Papers,* 2:366–376. New York: Basic Books, 1959.

———— (1915a). Repression. *Collected Papers,* 4:84–97. New York: Basic Books, 1959.

———— (1915b). The Unconscious. *Collected Papers,* 4:98–136. New York: Basic Books, 1959.

———— (1917 [1915]). Mourning and Melancholia. *Collected Papers,* 4:152–170. New York: Basic Books, 1959.

———— (1920). *Beyond the Pleasure Principle,* tr. C. J. M. Hubback. London: Hogarth Press, 1948.

———— (1923). *The Ego and the Id,* tr. J. Riviere. London: Hogarth Press, 1947.

———— (1925 [1924]). A Note upon the "Mystic Writing-Pad." *Collected Papers,* 5:175–180. New York: Basic Books, 1959.

———— (1926 [1925]). *The Problem of Anxiety,* tr. H. A. Bunker [second printing]. New York: Psychoanalytic Quarterly & Norton, 1936.

———— (1927). Humour. *Collected Papers,* 5:215–221. New York: Basic Books, 1959.

———— (1937). Analysis Terminable and Interminable. *Collected Papers,* 5:316–357. New York: Basic Books, 1959.

Glover, E. (1935). A Developmental Study of the Obsessional Neurosis. *Int. J. Psycho-Anal.,* 16:131–144.

———— (1939). The Psycho-Analysis of Affects. *Int. J. Psycho-Anal.,* 20:299–307.

———— (1961). Some Recent Trends in Psychoanalytic Theory. *Psychoanal. Quart.,* 30:86–107.

Greenson, R. R. (1949). The Psychology of Apathy. *Psychoanal. Quart.,* 18:290–302.

———— (1953). On Boredom. *J. Amer. Psychoanal. Assn.*, 1:7–21.

Grüninger, U. (1917). *Zum Problem der Affektverschiebung.* Zurich: Buchdruckerei des Schweizerischen Grütlivereins.

Hartmann, H. (1939). Ego Psychology and the Problem of Adaptation. In (abridged) Rapaport (1951a), pp. 362–396.

———— (1951). Technical Implications of Ego Psychology. *Psychoanal. Quart.*, 20:31–43.

————, Kris, E., & Loewenstein, R. M. (1946). Comments on the Formation of Psychic Structure. *Psychoanal. Study Child*, 2:11–38. New York: International Universities Press.

————, Kris, E., & Lowenstein, R. M. (1949). Notes on the Theory of Aggression. *Psychoanal. Study Child*, 3/4:9–36. New York: International Universities Press.

Jacobson, E. (1951). The Psychoanalytic Theory of Affects. Unpublished ms.

———— (1953). The Affects and Their Pleasure-Unpleasure Qualities in Relation to the Psychic Discharge Processes. In *Drives, Affects, Behavior*, ed. R. M. Loewenstein. New York: International Universities Press, pp. 38–66.

Jelgersma, G. (1921). Psychoanalytischer Beitrag zur Theorie des Gefühles. *Int. Z. Psychoanal.*, 7:1–8.

Jones, E. (1929). Fear, Guilt and Hate. *Papers on Psycho-Analysis*, 5th ed. Baltimore: Williams & Wilkins, 1948, pp. 304–319.

Jung, C. G. (1907). *The Psychology of Dementia Praecox.* New York: Nervous and Mental Disease Publishing Co., 1944.

Kanner, L. (1944). Early Infantile Autism. *J. Pediat.*, 25:211–217.

Kris, E. (1932–52). *Psychoanalytic Explorations in Art.* New York: International Universities Press, 1952.

———— (1936). The Psychology of Caricature. In Kris (1932–52), pp. 173–188.

———— (1938). Ego Development and the Comic. In Kris (1932–52), pp. 204–216.

———— (1939). Laughter as an Expressive Process. In Kris (1932–52), pp. 217–239.

———— (1950). On Preconscious Mental Processes. In Kris (1932–52), pp. 303–318.

Kulovesi, Y. (1931). Psychoanalytische Bemerkungen zur James-Langeschen Affekttheorie. *Imago*, 17:392–398.

Landauer, K. (1928). Die Gemültsbewegungen oder Affekte. In *Das psychoanalytische Volksbuch*, 2 (pt. 1), ed. P. Federn & H. Meng. Stuttgart: Hyppokrates-Verlag, pp. 136–151.

———— (1938). Affects, Passions and Temperament. *Int. J. Psycho-Anal.*, 19:388–415.

Landis, C., & Hunt, W. A. (1939). *The Startle Pattern.* New York: Farrar & Rinehart.

MacCurdy, J. T. (1925). *The Psychology of Emotion, Morbid and Normal.* New York: Harcourt, Brace.

Mahler, M. S. (1949). Remarks on Psychoanalysis with Psychotic Children. *Quart. J. Child Behav.*, 1:18–21.

————, Ross, J. R., Jr., & De Fries, Z. (1949). Clinical Studies in Benign and

Malignant Cases of Childhood Psychosis (Schizophrenia-like). *Amer. J. Orthopsychiat.,* 19:295–305.

Putnam, M. C. (1948). Case Study of an Atypical Two-and-a-Half-Year-Old. *Amer. J. Orthopsychiat.,* 18:1–30.

Rapaport, D. (1942). *Emotions and Memory,* 2nd unaltered ed. New York: International Universities Press, 1950.

———, ed. & tr. (1951a). *Organization and Pathology of Thought.* New York: Columbia University Press.

——— (1951b). The Conceptual Model of Psychoanalysis. *This volume,* Chapter 34.

——— (1959). The Structure of Psychoanalytic Theory: A Systematizing Attempt. *Psychol. Issues,* No. 6, 1960.

Reich, W. (1933). *Charakteranalyse.* Vienna: Selbstverlag des Verfassers.

Schilder, P. (1920). On the Development of Thoughts. In Rapaport (1951a), pp. 497–518.

——— (1924). *Medical Psychology,* ed. & tr. D. Rapaport. New York: International Universities Press, 1953.

——— (1930). Studies Concerning the Psychology and Symptomatology of General Paresis. In Rapaport (1951a), pp. 519–580.

Schur, M. (1953). The Ego in Anxiety. In *Drives, Affects, Behavior,* ed. R. M. Loewenstein. New York: International Universities Press, pp. 67–103.

Sperling, S. J. (1953). On the Psychodynamics of Teasing. *J. Amer. Psychoanal. Assn.,* 1:458–483.

Spinoza, B. de (1901). *Improvement of the Understanding, Ethics, and Correspondence.* New York: Willey.

Spitz, R. A., & Wolf, K. M. (1946). The Smiling Response: A Contribution to the Ontogenesis of Social Relations. *Genet. Psychol. Monogr.,* 34:57–125.

42

DISCUSSION AT MASS
COMMUNICATIONS
SEMINAR

It is with considerable hesitation that I make any comment in this discussion, since the little I know about communication derives from face-to-face communication, or from the effects of communication on the individual, while you are interested in communications to masses.

I am a psychologist, who is interested in thinking, and therefore involved in the question: How is thought communicated?

You people are concerned with very practical things and want to get to practical conclusions. Consequently, it is very difficult for me to talk, because I have nothing practical to say. Indeed I have to conclude from my thinking about communication that I do not know what its nature is, that I do not know what it is we are talking about.

Let me indicate what kind of problems I feel I and other people who work with the types of material I work with are up against, in studying communication.

(1) In hypnotic experiments, or psychotherapy conducted in hypnosis, thoughts and feelings are conveyed between the participants in a way which

Presented at a meeting sponsored by the Viking Fund, New York, May 11–13, 1951.
First published in Hortense Powdermaker, ed., Proceedings. *New York: Wenner-Gren*
Foundation, 1953, pp. 121–128.

is different from that observed in nonhypnotic experiments and psychotherapy. Communications are different. But we do not know how to conceptualize this difference: Should it be conceptualized as a difference of degree or of quality? Should it be conceptualized as a consequence of the changed state of consciousness of the hypnotized person? Or should the change of the state of consciousness be regarded as the consequence of "use of different channels of communication"? Or should both of these be conceptualized as functions of a change of interpersonal relationship? Or should all these be regarded as equally valid alternative descriptions—from different aspects—of a unitary process?

(2) The situation of psychological testing might serve as another example. Usually when we communicate to a person, for instance by a cartoon or a poster, we present him with a situation which is relatively well defined, and we assume that his responses are relatively predictable, just as we can usually predict what the other person will answer us when we tell him something in a cocktail-party situation. In the situation of psychological testing, the communication I, the examiner, make, presents the person with a variety of situations ranging from well-structured ones to quite unstructured ones, upsetting the anticipations and predictability we usually have for a cocktail-party conversation: in the testing situation, for the most part, the usual cocktail-party escape routine—the "Let's talk about the weather" and the rest—is closed. The lesson from the testing situation is that our naïve reliance on what we used to consider the unequivocal definition of poster, slogan, and other communications, is shattered: we can't believe any more that our communication simply implies our intent and nothing else, and that the other's understanding of the communication will be identical with our intent.

The question is, "What then is communication?" Obviously I don't know. I came to learn something about communication, to get a set of concepts which I could apply to the phenomena I observe, to bring some unity into them.

Incidentally, before I go on I would like to say something about the humanists. I think that the humanists, particularly the critics, have taught us something about communication, even if one thinks only about such recent writings of Empson's (1949) study of ambiguities, or the recent revival in Cleanth Brooks's (1939) writing of the concern with the Elizabethan conception of irony. Those are indeed studies in communication. They investigate what happens when artistic communication relies highly on multiple meaning, or ambiguity and irony.

(3) Getting back to the problem: I would like to ask you to come along with me in my attempt to play with a few ideas. A friend of mine, a very fine psychologist, once gave us a puzzle. His name is Fritz Heider—probably one of the outstanding thinkers in psychology alive. The puzzle was as follows: What is it you can give without losing? The answer to the conun-

drum is: Information. That's very neat, but the trouble is simply that it isn't true. Yet I always thought that this conundrum somehow comes somewhere near to the core of the communication problem.[1]

Obviously this point is of anecdotal character and as unworthy of the ears of statistically minded people as anything can be, but bear with me and let me spin on from there. Why isn't it true that information is something we can give without losing it? For instance, we all know the type of jealous teacher who wants to have every idea of his appear under his name, who forces all his students to use the thoughts he communicates to them and to publish them in their theses with his name as senior author on them. Such teachers will be very jealous of the communications they make and very stingy with any communication the publication of which under their name is unguaranteed. They act as though they would lose the information they communicate. Priority fights, plagiarism suits, and patents too are evidence that information may or may not have a unique rôle amongst goods: it may or may not be something given without being lost.

Clinically one sees this even more clearly. We have patients who cannot give us information without feeling that they have lost something. As a matter of fact there are extreme cases where perfectly conscious material cannot be communicated lest the patient afterward feel bereft of everything he ever possessed—his security, his self-respect, and indeed his self. I do not like to enter into descriptions of clinical cases: I have in mind cases friends of mine and I have treated and in particular a case of Dr. Hanna Fenichel's. My point is (1) that the thesis, "You give information without losing it," is not generally valid; (2) that this peculiarity of information has to be regarded in studying the nature of communication.

Now, permit me to invite you to take a look from this vantage point at what happens when you communicate—let us say through mass media—to people who are bereft of riches and well-being. I believe that you can easily lose something in doing that. Why? What comes to my mind suddenly is a book I haven't thought of for several years. It was one of the earliest books to come out of Russia after the revolution. I don't remember the name of the author; the title was *Chocolate*. It tells of a man who, through his wife's doings, gets into a tough spot. He is some kind of commissar, and she accepts some kind of presents from a black marketeer. In prison he has a dream which prompts him not to defend himself; plead guilty and take the death punishment, as the only way out. He dreams, against the background of a rising brown field and dark overcast sky, of a huge peasant plowing

---

[1] Since the time of this discussion I have come across a paper by Brillouin (1950) who, starting out with Wiener's generalization of entropy to information and definition of information as negentropy, formulates that while in the course of communication *absolute information* is lost in getting to the receiver, it is not lost at the transmitter, and that *distributed information* is indeed dependent on the number of receivers and may be many times greater than the absolute information.

over the hill. The picture is one you don't forget even after twenty-five years. He goes up to the peasant and tells him that the Communists are his comrades, that he is his comrade, and offers to help him plow. And he helps. However, once, as he leans over, a piece of chocolate covered in tinfoil drops out of his pocket. The peasant points at it and shouts, "You! You were telling me you came to help me; but my children and I hunger, while you have chocolate in your pocket!" Awakened, the commissar feels that, however he would explain that he is innocent, he could not communicate that to *the people*. The only true communication of the Communist Party's honesty would be to punish him by death: so he confesses and dies.

I do not know how to draw the theoretical conclusions from this. But I mean (a) the chocolate was a communication which amounted to a loss to the transmitter; (b) that false confession and consequent death were the only feasible effective communications left. In communication we can lose by giving away something that we did not want to give away, and we can lose by clogging up our channel of communication to others, stopping others from listening to us. The victor in communicating to the vanquished, the "haves" communicating to the "have nots," the idealist avant-garde communicating to the "masses," is particularly liable to fall into such pits.

(4) Here is another thing which puzzles one who studies thinking, and which has some bearing on communication. It's nothing new, you all know it; yet there is nothing about thinking I've found more puzzling in fifteen or sixteen years of study: I read a book, and I understand it. But could I have written it? No! As a matter of fact, there are books in which, at every step, I can predict what will come, but could I have written them?

I had my first experience of this when my mathematics professor stood at the blackboard in the midst of a deduction and asked us, "What is the next step? Where do we go from here?" I wanted so bad to be able to make the next step! You know how a youngster, an adolescent, feels about these things. I could not. Then he wrote it on the board, and it was so obvious that I could have kicked myself.

What is this peculiar thing about thinking that we can passively follow, understand, what we cannot ourselves actively produce? You will ask, "What does this have to do with communication?" It is the same kind of thing Dr. Lazarsfeld talks about or Dr. Northrop talks about. The question is, "What is there in a person which can be mobilized, which he would not spontaneously bring forth, and what are the means by which we can mobilize it?"

It seems to me that the prerequisite for the discovery of these means is the realization and exploration of the duality of thinking, that what can be passively followed by it is not necessarily actively produced or pursued by it. I believe that this is one of the important messages which somebody concerned with thinking has for those who are concerned with the study of communication.

I would like to make here a little detour to Dr. Lazarsfeld's point about his investigations showing that Western stories sell best in the woolly West, that old people like to read about the old, young about the young, towns-people about townspeople, etc. I believe Dr. Northrop made the point that this may be a question of choosing the symbols which are appropriate to your population, and whatever statistical measures you use, the results obtained reflect the symbols available.

For my money the explanation of this finding might be something very different. It may be that we are dealing with the old story that "you get out of it just as much as you put into it." I mean this: if you have systematically trained a population to react to mass propaganda, or mass communication, you cannot expect to get from them anything else but a response to mass communication. When we shout into an empty room, and expect to hear anything else but our own echo—we are crazy. If standardized magazines, Book-of-the-Month clubs, movies, radios, television, buy only stuff which they expect the public to like, then the public, fed on this material, will soon consider "good" what is being fed to it thus. Let me sharpen this point by relating an experience. An acquaintance of mine who survived a concentration camp wrote a book about the psychological portent of what he observed. I called a publisher's attention to the manuscript, suggesting that he might be interested in publishing it. The answer I received was, "Our public does not want to hear any more about these things: it wants to forget them." Knowing that this publisher was one in Europe before, I took the liberty of pointing out to him that the publisher's job used to be conceived, not as one focused on pleasing his public, but as one focused on educating it. As long as those in control of mass-communication media abide by the slogan "We aim to please," I do not know what—if anything—the meaning of our statistics on the reading preferences of their audiences is. I remember that as children we were interested more in the stories of explorers of and adventurers in far-off lands than in books or journals describing life in the Hungarian peasant town we grew up in. Is it a fair question to ask: What has changed?

That's the same story as the discrepancy between the behavior of animals at Yale and the behavior of animals in the field. If you put an animal into a Pavlov frame or into a maze, then you are going to get responses which are appropriate to the Pavlov frame: impoverished and polarized behavior. If Benjamin in Denver takes the rats and handles them, befriends them every day, they quit acting according to the Yale S-R theory expectations. That's all there is to it. How can you expect anything else?

Let me attempt—if you can bear with me for another few minutes—to elaborate on some implications of this last point I made.

(5) If we were to choose a single psychological discovery which has become commonly accepted in these last few decades, I believe we could agree that it is Freud's discovery that basic drives are at the foundation of

all human psychological processes. Yet in the course of the development of psychological and psychoanalytic knowledge, this discovery proved to be only a partial explanation of human behavior. We have learned that no dynamics of forces alone can explain what a human being does. We know from biology, and from social studies also, that functions, once established, structuralize, i.e., they form steady states which are resistive to change. In psychological life too we find such automatized functions, which do not have to be created anew, which behave as structures. The most common ones of these are known under the names ego, superego, but grammar, syntax, logic, as well as concepts, anticipations, and organized bodies of knowledge, whether about abstractions or material matters, also belong here.

What does this have to do with our topic? To come back to our topic I have to depart from it further first. We have learned that it is impossible to conceive of every human action as the outcome of a battle of basic drives. Early psychoanalysis thought differently: in its conception, when a stimulus came in all the instincts went into a battle with each other, all the mountains went into labor to produce—a little mouse—an action be it as insignificant as it may. It is impossible to conceive that for every thought that comes to our mind all our instincts, drives, have to go into battle. Our drives have long since come to certain kinds of quasi-stable equilibria, and these equilibria formed structures which produce—to the extent to which they do indeed produce—or are the stuff out of which are produced, our thoughts.

I have mentioned some of these structures. We have learned, for instance, that concepts are such structures. We know that infants' concepts are diffuse, syncretic, and concrete. Only when development reaches a certain point do concepts become abstract: abstract concepts have a long genetic history. But once abstract concepts have come about they are ready-made tools and are used as such by our motivations. Such structures, such automatized functions, such ready-made tools, are ubiquitous in psychological life. I would like to suggest—and here I am returning to our topic—that not only concepts, anticipations, memorial organizations are ubiquitous and genetically established structures and tools of the thought process. It seems to me hard to conceive that the functions of communication would not give rise to such structures; it seems to me inconceivable that a function as variable and rich as communication would have to create its forms every time anew, and would not be structurally guaranteed. Let me propose that we assume for the moment that the function of communication too has ready-made, structuralized tools at its disposal, progressively formed in the course of the ontogenetic history of the individual. Let us furthermore give the name of channels of communication to one set of such hypothetical structures. Our assumption implies that communication does not depend alone on the familiar sensorimotor means for intake and output of communication, but that these are organized into a series of alternatively possible communication channels for output and input. Let us note that we are usually absorbed in the contents of the communications we receive and give, and hardly ever concerned with the varieties of channels through which they are sent to us and received by us or sent by us and received by others, that is, with the channels that are available to the human being for output or intake of communication. We do not study these, though we do seem to have intuitive knowledge of them. Each of us, talking to his wife, knows when he can tell her good news and get a rise out of her, tell her bad news and not get fussed at, make a request and not be refused. Indeed, the individual husband knows those communication areas in which a topic known to both of them cannot be communicated by him but only by his wife, if communication in general is not to break down between them temporarily. May I suggest for this phenomenon the term "one-way channel of communication"? And may I use the phrase: communication which disregards the one-way character of a channel of communication clogs it up? Such one-way channels are not specific to wife and husband; they are present in all human relations. There are certain things which a speaker will expect his audience to say or to indicate nonverbally before he will go on to the heart of the matter he is to discuss. He will have to have a certain response before he can make his demand on his audience—before he can declare just what he is "selling."

There are yet other propensities of these hypothesized communication channels, but I cannot discuss them here. I would like only to state the status of these hypothetical channels of communication in the terminology of psychoanalytic ego psychology. They would appear as ego apparatuses of the sort which are produced in the course of development, and which seem to be autonomous, in the sense in which defenses are autonomous, or ego structures are in general autonomous, in relation to id or drive dynamics. That is: they are not created anew every time by basic drive motivations but are rather only used by them as well as by the ego and its motivations as ready-made tools. The clinical opportunity for observation of channels of communication is ample, but no concepts are available to systematize these observations.

(6) I would like to make one final point. There is a real danger in transposing directly individual psychological concepts to group and mass phenomena. Why is there a danger? Let me take identification and projection for examples. Identification is a loose concept which can be defined in many ways. One of the common definitions is: "Those ego changes, by which characteristics of the object which have been perceived previously become propensities or characteristics of the subject, of the ego, are identification processes." In contrast, projection processes are those ego changes by which propensities or characteristics of the subject are made not to be perceived as such, but rather as the propensities or characteristics of the object.

These definitions are suitable for the theory of psychotherapy. But are they of use when you describe the behavior of an audience or of a member of it and ask, "Is this identification?" It is a good question, and I don't know the answer. Let me tell you why. I have to ask myself: "Does this audience reaction really amount to an ego change—as implied in the above definition of identification?" Some psychoanalysts will be quick to answer this question in the negative and to explain that the ego changes in identification and projection are based on id processes, and therefore belong to the psychoanalyst's domain and method of observation and are not applicable to data gathered by methods of study of mass communication. Though this view seems to me rash, and I could not subscribe to it, yet the connection between method of observation and concepts which it points up certainly deserves noting.

My point is different. We have learned from H. Jackson that in the course of development fundamental processes are represented and re-represented again and again. This seems to me to be the case with identification too; it is continuously re-represented on ego levels also by processes which are homologous, if you please, with identification as defined above. But for that matter, all motivations are homologous with drive motivations. For that matter, all defensive operations are homologous with fundamental defensive operations.

They are homologous all the way through, and, as fate would have it, we know relatively much about the id processes, but we have hardly ever explored how the whole hierarchy of homologous ego-processes differs from them. I think that if you want to use such concepts as identification or projection in describing audience response, you will need to ask the question: "What is the genetic history by which this process which seems to be homologous with identification derives from identification?" If this is too cumbersome, then—"Call it armadillo and let it alone." But to use these concepts without such genetic study involves the danger of unwarranted application of individual psychological concepts, id concepts. Our literature is cluttered with that. Psychologists and sociologists really went whole hog in using these terms—and not without some justification, but at a disregard for the hierarchic derivation relationship between the phenomena observed and these id-psychological concepts.

SUMMATION

As I understand it, several participants in this discussion, being involved in the practical pursuit of directing mass communication media, came with the expectation that they would get here scientific information as to how to plan movies, or other mass communications, to convey the information and instill the attitudes it is their job to convey to, and instill in, other people.

Now it is my impression that the tremendous impact French culture has had on Europe since the seventeenth century was exerted through various cultural achievements. But neither classic French drama nor the Encyclopedia was planned and executed with the purpose of affecting Europe. They grew out of the French life of the time and their effect shows that Europe was ready for and receptive to them. I do not believe that this growth from, and attunedness to, existing conditions could be replaced by anything scientists—sociologists, anthropologists, psychologists, communication experts—could, with the best effort and best skill, discover. In other words, I do not believe that we could have predicted that it would be classic French drama and the Encyclopedia that would sell France to Europe. Nor do I believe that if we could have predicted and blueprinted it, we could have found the people who, following our blueprint, could have produced it. I am not sure but what the answer to the prayer of mass communication officers will come from giving opportunity and encouragement to young Japanese, German, and last but not least, American, talent, young authors who have got little chance anyway, in competition with the authorities of Broadway. A cultural impact—I mean one of any depth—cannot come except from cultural communications which themselves have depth. Such, however, are not tooled with the tools of psychology, anthropology, or sociology. They are tooled either by the tools of power creating facts, or by the equally powerful tool—the artist, who is a far more sensitive tool of communication than anything our social sciences have developed. Validity and effectiveness of communication depends, among other things, first on the economy with which it reflects the multiplicity and multiple layering of fact and experience. Empson writing on ambiguity and Brooks writing on irony have shown that the artist's imagination is the means par excellence for creating such communication, for subsuming in symbols the multiplicity of human, individual experience. The sensitive and motivated creative individual rather than the scientific blueprint is the answer to the problems of mass communication media.

If I may, I would like to make one more point. One who studies psychopathology and practices psychotherapy is prone to arrive at the curious idea that the opposite of the communication is the secret, and that the study of the latter may shed important light on the former. This may sound to you like playing with words, because in what sense is there an opposite to a process like communication? Yet the nature of the secret contains the key to many questions of communication, certainly insofar as individual communication is concerned. Those of you interested will profit by reading the pertinent papers by Bernfeld (1941) and Gross (1934).

Now that I have brought up the topic of the secret, let me point out that it is closely related to one of Dr. Kroeber's points. If we want to convey to a people something about ourselves, about the American way of life, how shall we do it? Should we assume that if we tell another people directly all those things which we consider good about ourselves, that that will convey to them what we are, what democracy is—and that it is good? I am tempted to call this a linear approach: "This is what we think about ourselves; it's good, here you have it, come and get it." Or is it more convincing to tell about our good and bad sides both? And if so, should the good and bad always add up to a "happy ending," or can it add up to one of our own "American tragedies"? Is it un-American and dangerous to tell some disagreeable truths about ourselves, or is it more dangerous to tell only nice things and let the disagreeable be told by our opponents? Surely there are no absolutely valid answers to any of these questions. But there is historical precedent against the "linear approach." It is not what historically lasting big organizations did. It is not what the military organizations or the Catholic hierarchy, the historically oldest known organizations, did. They always acted as carriers of a big secret of which the masses got only indications, and into which the individual was slowly inducted with his passing trials and ascending in the hierarchy. Heraclitus, speaking about nature, or about deity, put it clearly 2,500 years ago: "It does not reveal, it does not conceal, it indicates." How to *indicate* without dishonestly *concealing* and without prematurely and destructively *revealing* the secret of one's life one cherishes or dreads, is the great enigma of communication.

REFERENCES

Bernfeld, S. (1941). The Facts of Observation in Psychoanalysis. *J. Psychol.,* 12:289–305.
Brillouin, L. (1950). Thermodynamics and Information Theory. *Amer. Sci.,* 38:594–599.
Brooks, C. (1939). *Modern Poetry and the Tradition.* Chapel Hill: University of North Carolina Press.
Empson, W. (1949). *Seven Types of Ambiguity,* rev. ed. Norfolk, Conn.: New Directions.
Gross, A. A. (1934). The Secret. *Bull. Menninger Clin.,* 15:37–44, 1951.

43

BOOK REVIEW

John Dollard and Neal E. Miller,
Personality and Psychotherapy: An
Analysis in Terms of Learning,
Thinking, and Culture[1]

This is a difficult volume to review, because it is hard to pin down its arguments. This for several reasons. First, it professes to be a collection of hypotheses and to use clinical material only to illustrate, and not to prove anything. Second, it is disarming in its admission of our general ignorance and of the need for further knowledge before a definitive theoretical structure can be built. Third, it is ambiguous in its alternating enthusiasm for and rejection of psychoanalytic premises, concepts, and theories. Its ground in this respect is shifting and therefore difficult to come to grips with. Last but not least, it has been reviewed before by both psychologists and psychiatrists who, unlimited by familiarity either with learning theory or with psychotherapy, hailed it with the starry-eyed enthusiasm of wishful thinking.

There is one fixed point around which this book pivots, and this is learning

[1] New York: McGraw-Hill, 1950.

First published in The American Journal of Orthopsychiatry, *23:204–208, 1953.*
Copyright, the American Orthopsychiatric Association, Inc. Reproduced by permission.

theory. There is also a somewhat less fixed point, namely, the use of learning theory in order to explain phenomena of neurosis and therapy. These two points will be taken here as points of departure.

I

Dollard and Miller suggest that the concepts of drive, cue, response, and reward (reinforcement) are "exceedingly important" for the understanding of all levels of acquired behavior. These concepts readily indicate that this theory of acquired behavior is a learning theory and, more particularly, one of the conditioned-response vintage. The authors guardedly dwell on the question whether these concepts are "essential" or just "important" for the understanding of acquired behavior (pp. 25–26). Nevertheless, their actual argument seems to assume that all behavior can be understood in terms of motivating drives, which elicit responses when the proper cues are present, and that cues and responses are linked to the drive and to each other by the success of the response, which both establishes and reinforces these links.

This theory sounds much like the psychoanalytic theory. At the same time, it appeals much more to "common sense" than the psychoanalytic theory. It is therefore tempting to demonstrate the shortcomings of this theory as a learning theory, and to show up its inadequacy in coping with the phenomena for which psychoanalytic theory was developed. This is, however, neither our task here, nor possible in a brief review. Instead, it should suffice to say that Dollard and Miller may leave their readers with an erroneous impression. They propound this theory of learning as if to say that those aspects of it which they present are well established, though other aspects of it may be still open to question. This is, however, not the case. The battle of cognitive vs. stimulus-response theories of learning is still on. Not long ago Tolman (1949) summarized his studies in an article entitled "There Is More Than One Kind of Learning"; he found that there are eight different kinds. Only recently the neuropsychologist Hebb (1949) has put forth evidence to show that neither the gestalt nor the conditioned-response theories of learning do justice to many fundamental observations concerning learning, and particularly to the observation that early learning in infancy is qualitatively different in character from late learning. None of the learning theories have as yet integrated Piaget's (1945) genetic observations concerning learning. Last but not least, the most recent review of the theories of learning by Hilgard (1948) shows clearly that the many competing theories of learning have so far failed to come to grips with its core problems. Surely, Dollard and Miller are entitled to prefer one theory of learning over all the others. They are certainly entitled to apply the theory of their choosing to the problems of neurosis and psychotherapy. One would wish only that they had made it clear that they were applying the *theory they prefer,* that they had made plain to the psychiatrist, social worker, etc., not versed in learning theory, that the concepts they apply to psychotherapy and neurosis are—to say the least—far from being universally accepted. It would have been desirable if they too, like Kendler (1951)—one of the adherents of this type of learning theory—had spoken out candidly: "In spite of its relative sophistication, S-R reinforcement theory is still basically a primitive formulation. It would be unwise for S-R psychologists to try to 'sell it' for anything more than that" (p. 372). One would also wish the authors had brought to the attention of all who are not versed in the theories of learning that the problems of learning are just as complicated and just as unsolved as the problems of neurosis and psychotherapy. It is certainly to Dollard and Miller's credit that they even attempted to bring the problem of neurosis and the problem of learning to bear on each other. They vitiate their merit, however, by giving the impression that "normal learning" is already understood and that therefore its "laws" can now be applied to "pathological learning." It should be said in their defense, however, that they also stress that much can be learned about learning from patients; patients may oblige us where normals do not have the motivation to let us learn from them.

II

Dollard and Miller are emphatic that their use of clinical material should not be construed as proof or evidence for their hypotheses, but only as concrete illustration of principles (p. 16). Thus we are given a series of principles of learning and a series of illustrations for them from everyday life, as well as from clinical experience. Some of the examples of clinical phenomena are labeled with customary psychiatric or psychoanalytic terms, others with new terms. Surely, this again is a justified endeavor. It is in accord with the commonly accepted scientific procedure of taking concepts which apply to some phenomena and applying them to phenomena in a different realm of observation. The question which always arises in such endeavors is whether this new set of concepts is more parsimonious than the one used heretofore to describe, to explain, and to predict in this realm. Dollard and Miller in general do not attempt to offer any proof that their concepts and theory are preferable to those of psychoanalysis. All they do is express their hope that they are bringing a better conceptual system into the field of neurosis and psychotherapy than the one used heretofore, slip in a few pejorative assertions concerning some common Freudian concepts, and praise their own concepts as superior to the Freudian. They could have argued explicitly and not merely by implication that their theory which was tested in animal and human experiment should also be "more scientific" in the field of neurosis and psychotherapy than the prevailing, experimentally untested theories. Their implicit argument disregards the fact that their theory was developed to account for a very limited range of animal behavior and an even more limited range of human behavior. It is therefore necessary to stress explicitly that no proof is offered by the authors that the conceptual system of psychoanalysis at large is any better or worse for prediction of phenomena of neurosis and psychotherapy than the conceptual system they champion and attempt to illustrate in this volume. There is an old proverb which says, "When the angels came down to earth, they too did eat." When Dollard and Miller came down from the experimental laboratory to clinical material, their treatment of phenomena and their use of concepts is certainly no more rigorous than the psychiatrists' and psychoanalysts' treatment of phenomena and use of concepts. Indeed one may ask whether theirs has as much consistency and rigor as the latter.

III

It would be unfair to Dollard and Miller to apply to their study the yardstick of Freudian theory, even if they do occasionally claim acceptance of this theory. Yet it seems important to point out one relationship between psychoanalysis and their theory. From the beginning one of the outstanding characteristics of psychoanalytic theory has been its distinction between, on the one hand, the *primary processes* which are motivated by basic drives and which in their operation display the so-called Freudian mechanisms (condensation, displacement, symbolization, etc.) and, on the other hand, the *secondary processes* which follow the rules of logic and reality testing. In the course of the development of psychoanalytic theory this distinction developed into the distinction between the ego and the id. The fluid transition between these two types of processes, their interaction in adjustment, creativity, and neurosis, etc., was brought into the framework of psychoanalytic theory. It is one of the merits of Dollard and Miller's theory, as it is of Mowrer's recent theory, that by the distinction between innate and learned drives they attempt to do some justice to the distinction between early and late learning, between primary processes and secondary processes. (Earlier learning theories disregarded this distinction entirely.) This merit is, however, vitiated by the fact that, according to their theories, both innate and learned drives operate by the same reward-reinforcement mechanism. The complexity of clinical phenomena which led to the development of psychoanalytic ego psychology and which also led to Allport's recognition of functional autonomy within the framework of his ego psychology, the phenomena which made it necessary for all ego psychologies to assume that the ego has constitutional foundations of its own, are not even envisaged by these learning theories. Dollard and Miller's "acquired secondary drives" and their single reliance on the reward mechanism of learning cannot come to grips with these complexities, not even if the concept of reward is formulated so broadly as to include social rewards. It is characteristic for Dollard and Miller's presentation that phenomena of concern to psychoanalytic ego psychology are as a rule dealt with tangentially and without apparent awareness of the existence of psychoanalytic ego psychology. This holds for defenses, which are treated only in the sense of "resistance" (pp. 265 ff.), synthetic functions, differentiation functions, as well as "higher mental processes." It appears that Dollard and Miller's understanding of psychoanalysis is in most—if not in all—respects as of 1922, that is, of a date preceding Freud's *The Ego and the Id* (1923) and *The Problem of Anxiety* (1926), as well as Anna Freud's *The Ego and the Mechanisms of Defence* (1936). In this sense these authors are proponents of a peculiar psychoanalytic orthodoxy, which should be as unsatisfactory to any neo-Freudian psychoanalyst or psychiatrist as it is to the psychoanalyst aware of the development in psychoanalytic ego-psychology. The contributions of Horney to our understanding of defenses, of Sullivan to our understanding of the self, of Fromm to our understanding of social and cultural factors, have as little place in the framework of this theory as anything Freud had to say after 1923, and as any of Anna Freud's, Hartmann's, Kris's, E. H. Erikson's, Redl's, and Bettelheim's contributions.

While we are all eager to reach a state where our theories will be not only borne out by clinical experience but also verified by experiment, we have to acknowledge the fact that the reason that our theories are no better than they are is not simply because we are not clever enough to develop rigorous operational concepts, but because our subject matter is complex and we are yet at the beginning of its exploration. Under such handicaps, not even scientists equipped with the methodology of operationalism and with experimental know-how, as Dollard and Miller certainly are, can develop a neat and simple theory for us. Indeed the more they try to make it neat and pat, the more cavalier they become in their disregard of clinical fact.

IV

Finally, I can't help remarking that in an attempt as ambitious as this we could expect somewhat more clinical sophistication than is evident. A single example of the unfortunate combination of lack of clinical understanding with a mechanical application of an inapt theory, so characteristic of this volume, follows.

> *Example of the problem of masturbation.* Masturbation presents a special problem to the therapist because it is a response that frequently occurs and produces a marked reduction in drive but is not the socially most desirable form of sexual adaptation. It is an inferior form of adaptation because it *removes one of the strong rewards from marriage*[2] which seems to provide the best all-round basis for personal adjustment.
>
> If the patient has too much fear to try any heterosexual responses,

2 Italics mine—D. R.

masturbation may be good as the first step toward the goal of normal sexual behavior. When the patient first tries masturbation, the orgasm produced in this way will reward the general attempt to try sexual behavior, help to define the goal, and *give the patient a good chance to discover and extinguish some of his fears of sex.*[2] We will expect this extinction to generalize and tend to weaken the fear motivating the inhibition of heterosexual behavior. On the other hand if the therapist shows any signs of *disapproval*[2] at this stage, he will strengthen the patient's fear, and this fear will tend to generalize to all forms of sexual behavior.

If the therapist *allows*[2] masturbation to become established as more than a transitional habit, it will become so strongly reinforced that it may be hard to abandon. Furthermore it will tend to keep the sex drive so low that the heterosexual responses never can become stronger than their inhibitions. Finally, the patient may be having undesirable phantasies during masturbation. *Associating the strong sexual reward of the orgasm with the cues involved in these phantasies may increase his appetite for childish, perverse, or extramarital sex outlets.*[2]

This theoretical analysis yields several practical suggestions. If possible, it is better for the patient to move directly toward a heterosexual marital adjustment. If the patient's inhibitions are too strong for this to be possible, it may be necessary for the therapist to be *permissive*[2] toward masturbation at first. After masturbation is started, it may be desirable for the therapist to try to *exert some control over the accompanying phantasies and direct them toward the heterosexual marital goal.*[2] Finally, after the patient's inhibitions have been weakened enough so that he will be able to try better responses, it may be necessary *to discourage masturbation by pointing out the ways in which it is an inferior response*[2] [pp. 386–387].

I have to leave it to the reader to judge in what sense this example is consistent with the authors' initial statement:

We have concentrated our analysis on the one type of therapeutic practice with which we are familiar—namely, the Freudian. Even here, we have attempted to analyze only those features of theory and practice that we understand best [p. viii].

REFERENCES

Freud, A. (1936). *The Ego and the Mechanisms of Defence.* New York: International Universities Press, 1946.

Freud, S. (1923). *The Ego and the Id,* tr. J. Riviere. London: Hogarth Press, 1947.

[2] Italics mine—D.R.

———— (1926 [1925]). *The Problem of Anxiety,* tr. H. A. Bunker. New York: Psychoanalytic Quarterly & Norton, 1936.

Hebb, D. O. (1949). *The Organization of Behavior; A Neuropsychological Theory.* New York: Wiley.

Hilgard, E. R. (1948). *Theories of Learning.* New York: Appleton-Century-Crofts.

Kendler, H. H. (1951). Reflections and Confessions of a Reinforcement Theorist. *Psychol. Rev.,* 58:368–374.

Piaget, J. (1945). *Play, Dreams and Imitation in Childhood.* New York: Norton, 1951.

Tolman, E. C. (1949). There Is More Than One Kind of Learning. *Psychol. Rev.,* 56:144–155.

44

SOME METAPSYCHOLOGICAL CONSIDERATIONS CONCERNING ACTIVITY AND PASSIVITY

It may seem surprising that Rapaport never published this paper, since it is obviously in a careful, "finished" form. He even states that he has decided to publish the paper despite difficulties which various people called to his attention in relation to earlier drafts (p. 535). In another paper, "The Theory of Ego Autonomy: A Generalization" (Chapter 57), he said that he did not publish the present paper because his dual models of activity and passivity in relation to drive had yet to be complemented by such models in relation to the external world. Yet he writes here that he has attempted to deal with this issue in part III by a review of the literature. In the last set of seminars he ever delivered, in 1960, he said that he had not

Paper presented at two seminars at the Austen Riggs Center, June 16 and August 11, 1953. Published (in English) in Archivos de Criminología, Neuropsiquiatría Disciplinas Conexas (*Ecuador*), 9:391–449, 1961.

530

published the paper because it failed to explore the relations of activity and passivity to aggression and masochism, which latter two, he suggested, might be a "complex derivative" of activity and passivity. He hints at this relationship in the hitherto unpublished paper on the superego (Chapter 55), and in the seminar he also suggested a link between activity and passivity and the superego.

An exploration of the reasons why this paper was not published would doubtless lead to a recognition of the special importance which issues of activity and passivity played in Rapaport's own life. There is internal evidence of this in the seminar material, and it was evident to anyone who knew Rapaport. To say so is hardly a revelation, however, nor an unseemly invasion of his privacy, since—in his view at least—problems of activity and passivity play an important rôle in everyone's life. What was perhaps special in him was the intricate and subtle layering of activity and passivity, a point he develops so skillfully in the case material in this paper.

But more important than this personal matter would be an effort to indicate something of the extraordinary scope of the concept of activity and passivity in Rapaport's mind, a scope that is not entirely explicit in this paper. For he regarded it as at the very heart of an adequate conceptualization of the human psyche. Look at the list of crucial topics and concepts of psychoanalysis that he felt could be subsumed under and illuminated by the concept of activity and passivity:

(1) Structure formation—lying at the heart of psychic development (the signal theory of anxiety is an illustration and, in Rapaport's view, so are all learning and thinking)—can be viewed as activity. More generally, the issue is that of the relative autonomy of the ego. Several of these points are especially developed here.

(2) Defense formation is only a subheading under structure formation.

(3) The superego may be viewed as an integrate of structures developed to master impulse actively, and the basic distinction between superego and ego may lie in the fact that the superego integrate is more

passive in relation to id than is the ego integrate of structures built in the service of active mastery.

(4) Aggression may be a complex derivative of activity. Masochism is a turning of aggression against the self—and Rapaport also viewed the instinctual vicissitude of turning against the self as subsumable under activity and passivity. He believed that Freud's concept of the death instinct was an attempt to conceptualize the activity and passivity problem.

Is it any wonder that Rapaport sometimes privately said that his insight into activity and passivity was his most original and creative? And, of course, that too has implications for his not having published this paper.

Another noteworthy sidelight is that the paper takes its point of departure from a case he treated himself, under supervision. Rapaport treated very few cases in his career, and disavowed any competence in therapy. Yet this too may be one of the reasons for the nonpublication of this paper. For this man—regarded by many as so brazen—was of course also painfully shy. And that too is no revelation, for how can there be brashness without shyness?

But what of the concept of activity and passivity? It was criticized as too abstract to serve the function he saw for it. But is it really more abstract than the concept of an instinct of aggression—an instinct whose bodily zone has been described no more successfully than by a global reference to the body musculature?

It may be that the concept really is capable of opening a bold new way of conceptualizing the psyche. The purpose of this note is to show its scope in his mind, a scope he revealed only by dark hints— one of his favorite ways of communicating what was closest to his heart—M.M.G.

I. THE PROBLEM

The terms activity and passivity are used with increasing frequency in the psychoanalytic literature. Phrases like passive character, passive-dependent needs, oral-passive wishes, passive-demanding attitude, are ubiquitous, though ill-defined. Another set of phrases referring to activity and passivity has even firmer roots in our literature and theory: activity-passivity as one of the three basic polarities of psychic life, activity-passivity as equivalents or characteristics of masculinity-femininity, turning passivity into activity as one of the methods of drive and reality mastery, passive-receptive mastery often connected with regressive processes, etc. But even in these usages the terms activity and passivity do not seem to be well defined and certainly were never treated in metapsychological (dynamic, economic, and structural) terms. Freud's discussions of the issue I will review below. Hart's (1952) paper on passivity provides a bibliographical orientation in that problem. The treatment of passivity which comes closest to the one here presented is that of Bergler (1949). The only direct treatments of activity I am familiar with are those of Hendrick (1942, 1943a, 1943b) and Erikson (1950). The problem of the so-called specifically feminine passivity I will not discuss in this paper, and will therefore only touch on Freud's (1931) and bypass H. Deutsch's (1944–45) discussions of it. The problems I will deal with are intimately intertwined with the problem of masochism. I will avoid, however, the explicit discussion of this problem. Reference to, and agreement with, Brenman's (1952) recent paper on it is, however, implied.

Before I proceed to outline the plan of this paper, I should like to make some comments on the origins of my interest in the problem, as well as on the scope and form of presentation of the problem.

I encountered the problem which I label here as that of activity and passivity first in connection with thinking and, indeed, the experiences in question were some of the roots from which my interest in thought processes arose. At times there arise in our minds ideas—as it were, spontaneously—and we feel that they are not ours. At times we think thoughts and recognize—or think we recognize—that they are not ours, that we read them here or there, that we learned them from this or that teacher. And conversely, at times a "spontaneously" rising idea appears to us not as a strange obsession nor as "inspired" by an external agency, but as our own intuition, our own hunch, our own brain child; and ideas learned from others appear in new light, new meaning, new productiveness, as our very own. Similarly we may carry on our work with great effort, assiduously collating information, applying our logic at its sharpest and best—and what we arrive at feels like honest hackwork, devoid of all originality. At times, however, the same applying of ourselves results in an edifice which somehow has achieved, to our own feeling, the character of originality. These variants of experience, and the objective originality or unoriginality which may or may not correspond to the accompanying subjective experience, have puzzled me for some decades now and have served—to my understanding—as my first concrete encounters with the problems of passivity and activity.

The human need to shake off the shackles to our imagination of the thinking of predecessors, and the equally powerful human need to resign our own imagination and gain security by dwelling in the arbors of thought planted by the imagination of our predecessors, implies the same problems of activity and passivity and has often led to bitter struggles of orthodoxy and heterodoxy in the course of the history of human thought. The struggle between orthodoxy and heterodoxy in psychoanalytic thought did not belong to the least bitter among these, and thus my preoccupation with the system and history of psychoanalytic thought and theory has again and again aroused my interest in this problem of activity and passivity.

But these experiences were bolstered by others in centering interest on the problem. Knight's (1940) paper on the relationships of aggression, homosexuality, and paranoia, and Gill's (1945) further pursuit of these considerations, played an important rôle for me here. They have shown that the formulation that paranoia is a defense against homosexuality is only one of the possible dynamic sequences; that homosexuality can be a defense against paranoia; that both can be and usually are defenses against aggression. The manifold layering of passivity and activity as defenses against each other was brought home to me there first.[1]

Further experiences of importance were contacts with psychiatrists and psychologists in states of profound pathological distress. The fact that their knowledge about, and awareness of, their state and its prognosis was available to them and yet had no dynamic effect left an indelible impression on me, and I saw this phenomenon in many variants in other patients too later on. While previously I was accustomed to settle this issue as a problem describable in terms of intellectual vs. emotional insight, after the experiences with psychiatrists and psychologists in distress I was—and I still am —inclined to see a broader implication, namely that of activity and passivity, in these phenomena. Indeed, I am inclined to regard the problem of intellectual vs. emotional insight as a special case of passivity vs. activity.

As for the scope of the problem and the form in which I present it here, it may be questioned whether the framework of activity and passivity is indeed a fortunate one to present these issues in: (1) The terms are strongly anchored in everyday use and are descriptive terms in their own right, so that redefining their psychoanalytic use may both lead to confusion and appear internally contradictory. (2) The issue indeed exceeds in several respects the boundaries of the problem of activity and passivity, and, as I note further below, is intimately intertwined with the problem of the autonomy of the ego and with the psychological dynamics underlying the phenomenon of "will." [2]

---

[1] That these considerations were later further bolstered by the writings of Bergler I realized only when this paper was completed. This cryptomnesia—I believe—is justified by Bergler's extremely one-sided treatment of passivity, equating passivity with oral passivity and disregarding the merit of the issue of activity.

[2] These difficulties were pointed out in a discussion of Part II of this paper at a seminar at the Austen Riggs Center, by Drs. Chassell, Howard, Knight, Wheelis, Brenman, E. A. White, and Shapiro, and Mr. Erikson. I am indebted to all of them.

As for the first objection: I recognize the need for the common-sense and clinical use of the terms activity and passivity. I realize and regret the potential confusion in-

In spite of these difficulties, I decided to publish this paper[3] since I felt that I would not, for a considerable time, be in a position to develop a broader treatment of the issue which would be free of these difficulties.

An attempt will be made here (1) to illustrate the problem on a clinical example; (2) to clarify the history and usage of the terms; (3) to clarify in the light of this material the distinction between *regression proper* on the one hand and *regression in the service of the ego* on the other; (4) to present a general metapsychological consideration and an application of the relationships discussed to problems of the theory of thinking.

II. AN ILLUSTRATIVE CASE AND ITS DISCUSSION

The clinical material I am presenting here is taken from a case which has centered my attention on the problem. I shall not present a case history in the proper sense of the word, and I do not intend to prove or even demonstrate anything with this material. My sole purpose in presenting it is to illustrate on an extreme case a variety of phenomena which to my mind are the proper referents of the terms activity and passivity.

A young woman in her early thirties came into therapy after her therapy

---

herent in the dual use of the terms. I do not think, however, that the coining of new terms is called for, and I believe that stating by context or directly whether the descriptive or the explanatory use of the terms is intended should take care of the difficulty.

As for the second objection, I am particularly indebted to Dr. Brenman, who discussed the paper with me at length. Among other things, she suggested that the issue might be done more justice if treated under the general heading of "metapsychological considerations of the freedom of the will." I agree with her, except that I am not ready for such a treatment. See, however, the relevant and related considerations of Knight (1946).

A further difficulty of the here presented conception of activity and passivity was brought home to me at the Riggs Center seminar discussion (particularly by Drs. Wheelis and Knight) and in personal discussion with Heinz Hartmann. They suggested that my treatment defines the concept of ego activity and ego passivity, the biological activity and passivity, that of the total person, that of the id and that of the superego, and finally that in relation to the external world, still remaining separate problems.

As for this third objection: it is possible that in the long run the definition of activity and passivity here presented will prove to be that of ego passivity. It is certainly an ego-psychological definition, though to my mind it deals with intersystemic relationships, with those between ego and id, ego and superego. Whether or not the activity and passivity of the person requires yet a different treatment, I do not know. While I hope it does not, the answer to this question can be given only by future observation and theoretical work. As for applicability of the concepts of activity and passivity to the id and the superego: I am not aware of clinical or theoretical work which would necessitate such an application. But the raising of the question makes it necessary to explore the possibility and necessity of such an application. Finally, activity and passivity in relation to the external world: in Part III, by means of a review of the literature, I have attempted—for better or for worse—to come to grips with this problem.

[3] [See the introduction to this paper—Ed.]

with a young psychiatrist came to an "impasse" resulting in a psychotic break. The initial diagnosis: paranoid-schizophrenic episode in remission in a narcissistic paranoid character. The symptomatology included promiscuity, tantrums (a mixture of hysterical fit, panic state, catatonic excitement), and a readiness for all sorts of somatization and/or conversion reactions.

One of the outstanding characteristics of this patient's difficulties was her utter uncertainty about her illness, and about what was expected of her in the institution and in therapy. She was uncertain whether her hysterical fits, flaccid paralyses, and mutism could or could not be controlled by her— whether they were "put on by her," i.e., whether she was actively producing them, or whether they "came on her without her being able to do anything about them," i.e., whether she was passively suffering them. She was uncertain whether she was expected to show her symptoms or to suppress them —whether she was expected to "let go" passively of her impulses and act out, or whether she was expected to exert active self-control—or in her own words, whether she was expected to "put the lid on." She felt that if she passively "let herself go" she was psychotic, and if she actively "put on controls" she was a pretending psychopath. She was afraid that if she did the former she would be considered too sick to stay in the open setting of the institution and would be sent to a closed hospital and to electric shock; and if she did the latter she would be considered a well person and would have no place at the institution for that reason. She was consequently in constant terror that either way she was deceiving the therapist and the staff, and that by so duping them she would be the only loser.

The red thread that went throughout the course of her therapy was the struggle against becoming completely passive and dependent on the therapist and thereby again psychotic, and the struggle against actively controlling herself and thereby becoming phony and psychopathic.

I shall not discuss here the details of what was learned about the oedipal and preoedipal genetic antecedents of this state of affairs. I will present only a few salient historical facts to give a "feel" of the case: (1) the patient's father was a failure and a paranoid dreamer, who had become a full neurotic invalid (asthma and ulcer) at the height of the child's oedipal involvement with him; (2) the mother—a teacher and the provider for the family —was a prim, intrusive, and lonely woman, who made the patient her confidante and burdened her with all the heavy worries about money and the father's health, as well as her contempt for the father which the patient came to share, at a most early age; (3) the patient was the youngest of eight children, in competition with her next sister who was the father's favorite and with the older of the two boys with whom she competed for being—and whom she displaced as—the mother's confidante; (4) therapy revealed that the patient had had an infantile neurosis with repetitive nightmares, represented later in a rape and castration conception of intercourse, defended against by counterphobic defenses in general and extreme promiscuous sexual behavior in particular. In the latter she took—turning passivity into activity—an active seductive role rather persistently. The preoedipal antecedents of this infantile neurosis will not be discussed here.

I cannot discuss here the course of the therapy either, and will choose only three salient features of it which are relevant to our problem. (1) Competitiveness with the therapist dominated the scene; interpretations were experienced as oral and anal intrusions and the patient experienced her role in therapy as a passive one with which she coped partly by competitive insistence on doing the work of therapy by herself and partly by acting out in analyzing all comers outside the hour. Here too she turned passivity into activity. (2) Her work with the first therapist broke up and ended in a psychotic episode when she responded to the therapist's indicating that they probably could not go on further with a flood of what she called "impressions"—which were schizophrenic pseudo memories of full hallucinatory vividness replete with incestuous, rape, and polymorph-perverse material. In other words, she responded to the threat of losing the therapist with a passive submission, bringing him what she felt he expected—infantile material—and thereby opening the floodgates for a psychotic episode. (3) A continuous struggle over sedation and alcohol attended the course of the therapy. Not before total withdrawal following a severe barbiturate toxicity could the patient even begin to regard my withholding sedation as anything but a deliberate attempt on my part to frustrate her and a sign of my lack of concern for her; nor could she begin to regard her own attempts at controlling her intake of sedation as anything else but a pretense of not being sick or an admission that she was never sick and had only pretended to be.

I believe that this is an extreme case in which the following phenomena, present in less extreme forms and other variations in all patients, and pertaining to activity and passivity, stand out strikingly. In the description of these phenomena the dynamic condition of activity and passivity and the patient's subjective experience of them must be kept apart. While the two often coincide, they must never be unquestioningly equated:

(1) *Passivity* in this case appears as a state in which the ego's controls of or defenses against drives are not used or are in abeyance, and a state in which no or ineffective use is made of the ego apparatus to seek out and to perform the detour activity leading to the drive object in reality. This state of passivity and the wish for it appeared to be somehow ego syntonic, and in the patient's subjective experience at once both "honest" and dangerous; "honest" in that it was experienced as the unquestioned goal of the patient, dangerous in that she felt that it would lead to psychosis, to a locked hospital, shock treatment, lobotomy, annihilation.

(2) *Activity* in this case appears as a state in which the controls and defenses against drives are used, as well as a state in which the available

ego apparatus is used to seek by detour the drive object and thus find gratification in reality. This state appears ego dystonic, and any internal or
external stimulation of it as a demand for compliance. In the patient's subjective experience, activity in this sense was "phony," "psychopathic,"
"dishonest," and self-defeating, as well as dangerous; dishonest and self-
defeating because only that which comes to one without "making a play for
it" by such activity can be experienced as real gratification; and because
such activity itself was experienced as a compliance with the demand,
"Little Tommy Tucker, sing for your supper," or as the patient put it, as
resulting in "a conditional acceptance." Dangerous, because to go on com-
plying would amount to continuing a pretense at being well, by counterphobic maneuvers and by a calculating, scheming existence, i.e., continuing
under ungratified mounting tension; and because such pretense would prevent her being given help and would lead to her discharge as a well person
who had no place in the institution.

   (3) *Activity and passivity*—it must be clear from the outset—are relative concepts. In the beginning of the treatment of this patient, the use of
controls and defenses—what was termed here a state of activity—was in
general (and this is an oversimplified statement of the situation) turned
dynamically into passivity, having been enforced by an "excessively strict"
and "corrupt" superego. This is what corresponded dynamically to the subjective experience of dishonesty and psychopathic phoniness. This is, however, not to say that there were not—even at the beginning of therapy in
and out of the hour—periods in which use of controls and defenses was
experienced as activity. With shifts in the dynamic conditions there were
shifts in the activity-passivity balance. Indeed, one of the features of this
case which compelled attention was these striking dynamic shifts and the
resulting changes in passivity and activity, as well as the corresponding
shifts—or lack of them—in subjective experience. The behavior spontaneously and ego-syntonically displayed one day bore, the next day, all the
earmarks of pretense and ego-dystonic compliance. The shifts in subjective
experience were naturally not always parallel, having been beclouded by
denials, isolations, reaction formations, rationalization, etc. With the progress of therapy there took place a systematic shift that increasingly prevented such turning of activity into passivity.

   Conversely, what was termed here passivity, a state of abeyance or disuse
of defenses, controls, and apparatuses, was at the beginning of the treatment turned into activity dynamically. That is to say, the only activity the
ego was capable of aiming at or performing was to demobilize its defenses
against and controls of impulses. It was this that represented itself in the
subjective experience of the unhampered passive drive discharge as the only
"honest" goal. But here again there were frequent dynamic shifts from the
beginning on, and a systematic shift with the progress of therapy, increasingly preventing such turning of passivity into activity.

   So in a sense—in this illustrative case as well as in general—all activity is also passivity and all passivity is also activity, and only the study of the dynamics of any given situation reveals which is the prevailing or dominant trend, or rather—and more correctly—what the balance of activity and passivity is at any given point.

The question is whether this illustration is, or is not, a good point of departure for conceptualizing the terms activity and passivity, which have become indigenous in the literature without having been defined, i.e., without having been conceptualized. Without committing ourselves to the conclusions we will reach, let us attempt to see what kind of conceptualization we arrive at if we take this illustration for our point of departure.

Let me for the moment envisage the infantile situation and remind ourselves that with Freud (1917) we have come to assume that the first primitive distinction between that which is *inner* and that which is *outer* is made by the infant by motor activity. The stimulation tension that can be escaped by motor activity is *external* and that which cannot be so escaped is *internal*. Let us avoid a discussion of the pertinent issues of the formation of the "pleasure ego" and the introjections and projections, or rather their predecessors, in the fluid, indistinct—or in the adult eye incorrect—boundaries of the body, "me," or "self," in reference to which such terms as "inner" and "outer" would be rather meaningless. Let us rather realize that in relation to what is *at this point* external the infant can be active, but toward much that is at this point internal he cannot. Further below, in reviewing the history of the terms activity and passivity, we shall see that the contrast of the management of internal, as against that of external, stimuli has something to do with passivity and activity, but that his relationship alone, without the considerations here advanced, would lead to an unsatisfactory conceptualization.

The very hypothetical state of affairs resulting in these attempts of the infant which Freud inferred and conceptualized as the effort to establish a purified pleasure ego testifies that the original passive helplessness of the infant arises primarily in relation to the continuous tension of undischarged instinctual drives. Let us add that the discharge of these tensions too may be dynamically passive, i.e., not controlled and synthesized by a cohesive ego. *Thus the model of passivity is a dual one: (a) the helpless-passive experience of tension, and (b) the passive-gratifying tension discharge.*

As for activity, there too we deal with a dual model. Let us remind ourselves that when the drive-gratifying object is absent, and the drive tension has reached threshold intensity, the psychic apparatus—among other measures—tends to heighten the threshold by countercathexes which we variously label either as defenses or as control apparatuses. The establishment of such defensive and controlling countercathectic energy distributions contributes to ego development. The very existence of such defense against and control of impulses is a prerequisite of activity and contrasted to helpless passivity in the face of continuous drive tension. But this is only one facet of the model of activity. To glean the other we have to turn to the process of tension discharge. The discharge of tension takes place through existing apparatuses, some of which are reflex apparatuses to begin with, others of which are not. Both types of apparatuses are progressively integrated into and come under the control of the developing ego. The use of these apparatuses—after their control by the developing ego with the attendant delay of tension discharge is established—amounts to activity as we use the term here. Such activity is usually part and parcel of a detour process subserving the end of reaching the drive object in reality. *Thus the model of activity is also dual: (a) the defense against and/or control of drive tension doing away with passive helplessness in the face of drive demands, and (b) the ego-controlled discharge of tension, through ego apparatuses by detour processes aiming to find the drive object in reality.*

It is from this vantage point that we can get the full meaning of Freud's formulation of the insatiability of infantile drives, namely, that there can be no gratification characterized by complete passivity:

> Childish love knows no bounds, it demands exclusive possession, is satisfied with nothing less than all. But it has a second characteristic: it has no real aim; it is incapable of complete satisfaction and this is the principal reason why it is doomed to end in disappointment and to give place to a hostile attitude. Later on in life, the lack of ultimate gratification may conduce to a different result. This very factor may ensure the undisturbed continuance of the libinal cathexis, as is the case in love-relations inhibited in their aim [1931, p. 259].

In our present-day terms we would add that the thresholds and apparatuses, which are congenital givens just as much as are drives, set limits to passive gratification. Their very existence implies the roots of activity, while their initial ineffective organization is closely tied to the dynamics of passive helplessness. It is thus that complete passivity is a theoretical extrapolation which can never exist in reality, however devoted the mother attending the child may be. The state of affairs Freud describes is combatted only by developing activity.

At the stage of development Freud speaks of, the organism and its environment are as yet an undifferentiated unity. The very existence of internal thresholds and external delays disrupts this unity and leads to the differentiation of the "me" and the "not me" (the first step in reality testing). At one and the same time the first decisive blow to the infant's hypothetical omnipotence and theoretically unlimited gratification is also delivered.[4] Freud's formulation to my mind describes the primordial state of passivity and points out that it carries the kernels of its own disruption. The conse-

---

[4] The adjectives *hypothetical* and *theoretical* are used to indicate that these conceptions are derived from reconstructions, and if one were to be precise one would speak rather of the primordial conditions from which the wishes and ideas of omnipotence and unlimited gratification arise.

quences of this disruption are set out in Erikson's (1950) discussion of "trust" and "basic mistrust" as the polarity dominating the first phase of ego development.

The model of passivity is thus a state of uncontrolled drive demand both in its helplessness in the face of undischargeable tension and in its effortless passive gratification.

The model of activity is thus a state of ego control of drive demand both in its defensive aspect of making drive tension tolerable and in its executive aspect of discharging drive tensions, through detour activity by means of ego apparatuses.

But these models must be further studied to provide a conceptual definition of activity and passivity. Is there no passivity once ego controls are in existence? Since we have seen that our patient's using her controls was compliance, and amounted dynamically to passivity rather than activity, clearly there is passivity even after far-reaching structure development, and clearly not all use of structuralized controls and of ego apparatuses is activity. But can we understand this by means of the models we have presented for passivity and activity?

At this point I would like to advance only one consideration which may shed some light on the conditions, though it is unlikely to settle the problem:

The development of activity as we sketched it appears to be coterminous with the developing autonomy of the ego. Activity appears as the measuring rod of the extent to which the ego as an autonomous agency enters the clash of drive demand and reality and transforms it into intrapsychic conflict. Ego autonomy, the roots of the subjective experience of volition, ability to delay discharge and to undertake detour actions toward the drive object, and activity are somehow closely related.

Assuming that the erection of countercathectic controlling and defensive barriers to drive tension and the use of ego apparatuses in detour actions is the model from which to derive the concept of activity, how does it happen that our patient feels that her use of these is ego alien, is enforced from the outside? Theoretically there are three possibilities for this which we do not (as yet or forever?) know how to distinguish empirically: (a) the drive is too strong; (b) the discharge threshold is too low; (c) there is continued need for external (and later superego) stimulation to maintain the countercathectic barrier.

(a) *The drive is too strong* (see Freud, 1937). The intensity of the drive may be such that the once-established countercathectic energy distribution is insufficient to keep it under control and periodically new demands are made for countercathectic expenditure from those cathexes at the disposal of the ego. Such a state of affairs might well be represented both dynamically and in subjective experience as a compliance with instinctual demands rather than as an active use of cathexes by the ego.

(b) *The discharge threshold is too low* (see Bergman and Escalona,

1949). This possibility, like the first one, is conceived of in terms of the individual's constitution, in the sense that every tension of the organism does have a threshold at which its discharge becomes mandatory. Surely height of threshold and drive intensity are relative to each other and may remain indistinguishable as long as we do not have independent methods to estimate each. Yet it is worth noting that the cases Bergman and Escalona studied seemed to have low thresholds (i.e., high sensitivities). And it is worth considering that countercathectic energy distributions are used—at least early in development—to raise such discharge thresholds. If the thresholds are too low and the constant countercathectic investment available is insufficient, then the same situation arises as in the first case discussed above under (a).

(c) *Continued need for external (or superego) stimulation to maintain countercathexes.* This possibility will be best envisaged if we remind ourselves that in childhood repetition of parental prohibitions and continued discipline are necessary stimulants to the maintenance of certain internal countercathexes, and that in some cases some of these are never internalized and in others they are internalized more as superego injunctions than as ego controls. Persevering need for support from the external world for the maintenance of countercathectic barriers and persevering contribution to their maintenance by an oversevere superego which is not fused with but stands rather sharply divided from the ego may result, both dynamically and in subjective experience, in a state of affairs in which drive control and detour actions are not ego-syntonic activity but rather externally enforced compliance.

In the illustrative case mentioned there was abundant evidence for the presence of the third possibility, with an overeagerness to comply serving as a cloak for acting out, a state of affairs studded with traps for both patient and therapist. But there were some indications—this was more an impression than any clear-cut evidence—of an excessive intensity of drive also. In contrast to this case another borderline case comes to mind, who gave the impression of low thresholds rather than of excessive intensity of drives. This patient had been a musical infant prodigy, whose unusual musical, poetic, linguistic, and general sensitivity bespoke low sensory and discharge thresholds. Her preferred defense was an extreme limitation of action to the point where she could feel sure that what she actually undertook was *her* action, i.e., real activity, and not compliance either with drive demand or external demand. The zeal with which she guarded herself against any compliance, against doing anything for which people might accept her, instead of "accepting her for herself" (for that self that she was so unsure of) was prodigious. Strong evidence for the role played by the oversevere superego, unfused with the ego—our third possibility—was present in the material of this patient too. Whether the difference between the two patients to which I pointed has or does not have anything to do with the apparently excessive intensity of drive in the first and the apparently low thresholds in the second case is an interesting question to which at present there is no answer. The relation of activity and passivity to constitutionally given drive intensity and threshold levels on the one hand, and to the "severity" of the superego on the other, is an open question.

III. THE HISTORY AND USAGE OF THE TERMS ACTIVITY AND PASSIVITY

In order to gain perspective on the conceptualization of activity and passivity here presented, let us review the usage of these terms in the psychoanalytic literature and thus primarily in Freud's writings. This review will revolve primarily around two themes: the meaning of the terms and the processes of turning activity into passivity and passivity into activity. A third theme, that of regression and regression in the service of the ego, I will leave for a later section of this presentation.

While sporadic use of these terms is encountered previous to it, the spirit of Freud's early usage of them is fairly represented in his *Three Essays on the Theory of Sexuality* of 1905. Here activity and passivity appear as two different sexual aims, or rather, as two kinds of aims of instinctual drives. To illustrate we may quote:

> In the perversions which are directed towards looking and being looked at, we come across a very remarkable characteristic with which we shall be still more intensely concerned in the aberration that we shall consider next [sadomasochism]: in these perversions the sexual aim occurs in two forms, an active and a passive one [1905a, p. 36].

The drive of active aim is considered primary and that of passive aim is assumed to arise from it by means of a transformation. Freud wrote:

> . . . it may be doubted at first sight whether . . . [masochism] can ever occur as a primary phenomenon or whether, on the contrary, it may not invariably arise from a transformation of sadism [1905a, p. 37].[5]

Specific body zones correspond to and represent the drives of active and of passive aims; to quote Freud again:

> The *activity* is put into operation by the *instinct for mastery,* through the agency of the somatic musculature; the organ which, more than

[5] In a footnote to this point, originating in the 1920's, Freud indicated that he had changed his views on this matter. We shall discuss this change further below in connection with *Beyond the Pleasure Principle* (1920) and "The Economic Problem in Masochism" (1924).

any other, represents the *passive* sexual aim is the erotogenic mucous membrane of the anus [p. 76];

and

Ever since Jean Jacques Rousseau's *Confessions,* it has been well known to all educationalists that the painful stimulation of the skin of the buttocks is one of the erotogenic roots of the *passive* instinct of cruelty (masochism) [p. 71].

Furthermore, activity and passivity seem to be equated with masculinity and femininity, the former being considered the predecessors of the latter, and indeed it is asserted that biological masculinity and femininity attain psychological meaning only after fusion with activity and passivity respectively; to quote:

. . . masculinity and femininity . . . are combined in bisexuality— a contrast which often has to be replaced in psychoanalysis by that between activity and passivity [p. 38];

and

A second pregenital phase is that of the sadistic-anal organization. Here the opposition between two currents, which runs through all sexual life, is already developed: they cannot yet, however, be described as 'masculine' and 'feminine,' but only as 'active' and 'passive' [p. 76].

And to quote now from a later writing (Freud, 1915a) in order to elucidate the implications of this formulation:

The antithesis of active—passive coalesces later with that of masculine—feminine, which, until this has taken place, has no psychological significance. The fusion of activity with masculinity and passivity with femininity confronts us, indeed, as a biological fact, but it is by no means so invariably complete and exclusive as we are inclined to assume [p. 77].

However, a different train of thought—and one important for our considerations—also appears. It expresses the realization that libido is always "active." Freud wrote:

. . . it would also be possible to maintain that libido is invariably and necessarily of a masculine nature, whether it occurs in men or in women and irrespectively of whether its object is a man or a woman [1905a, pp. 96–97];

and more emphatically, in a footnote added later, he commented:

'Masculine' and 'feminine' are used sometimes in the sense of 1) activity and passivity, sometimes in 2) a biological, and sometimes, again, in 3) a sociological sense. The first of these three meanings is the essential one and the most serviceable in psycho-analysis. When, for instance, libido was described in the text above as being 'masculine,' the word was being used in this sense, for an instinct is always active even when it has a passive aim in view [p. 97].

But this specific assertion is paradoxical. It certainly clarifies that there are no passive drives. But what does it mean to say that there are drives with "passive aims in view"?

For the answer to this question we will have to turn to Freud's "Instincts and Their Vicissitudes" (1915a), written ten years later. The significance of this paper for our present purpose is threefold: (1) it restates the proposition concerning "passive aims" but it also defines the instinctual drive and its aims, thus permitting an answer to the question just raised; (2) it gives a new meaning to activity and passivity; (3) it enters upon a clarification of the conception of turning activity into passivity which as we have seen above was so far taken for granted and not explored. It also introduces the possibility that passivity may precede activity and may even be turned into activity. This discussion has the added import for us that it relies heavily upon the concept of narcissism introduced by Freud a year earlier.

The restatement here of the conclusion of the *Three Essays* reads:

Every instinct is a form of activity; if we speak loosely of passive instincts, we can only mean those whose aim is passive [1915a, p. 65].

How are instincts and instinctual aims defined? The definition of instincts reads:

. . . from a biological point of view, an 'instinct' appears to us as a borderland concept between the mental and the physical, being both the mental representative of the stimuli emanating from within the organism and penetrating to the mind, and at the same time a measure of the demand made upon the energy of the latter in consequence of its connection with the body [p. 64].

The definition of the instinctual aim reads:

The *aim* of an instinct is in every instance satisfaction, which can only be obtained by abolishing the condition of stimulation in the source of the instinct [p. 65].

The instinctual drive then is an energy (cathexis) characterized by the aim of striving for gratification, i.e., immediate discharge. Now the internal contradiction of speaking of passive aims becomes entirely clear. The instinct was recognized before—as quoted—to be always active; but it will not get us around the problem of passivity to attempt to bring passivity in through the instinctual aim: the instinct is always active, precisely because its aim is always discharge. That Freud must have sensed this is shown by the two other attempts to give activity and passivity an—as it were—external anchorage, i.e., one not rooted in the nature of the drive. One of these attempts is anchored in the organ zones, the other in external stimuli. Only after discussing these in brief shall I come to his discussion—which is the core of this paper—of the interrelations between activity and passivity, which to my mind implies a more satisfactory explanation of activity and passivity. This explanation I believe to be consonant with the conception put forth in the previous section of this paper.

Freud's attempt to explain activity and passivity by organ zones reads as follows:

> In the auto-erotic instincts, the part played by the organic source is so decisive that, according to a plausible supposition of P. Federn and L. Jekels,[1] the form and function of the organ determine the activity or passivity of the instinct's aim.
>
> [1] *Zeitschrift,* Bd. I, 1913 [1915a, pp. 75–76].

This formulation has two things wrong with it. *First,* since the aim of all instinctual drives is discharge gratification, the aim can depend neither on the form nor on the function of the organ zone. What could and does depend on the organ zone is the mode of execution of discharge, the kind of *drive action* by which the aim, the gratification, is achieved. *Second,* drive action and its dependence on organ zone could not provide a satisfactory explanation of activity and passivity. Under the heading of the various oral and anal phases and under that of displacement of cathexes from zone to zone and under that of organ language, psychoanalysis has long known that organs permit dual and indeed multiple functions and can take over each other's functions. The broadest formulation of this state of affairs has been given by Erikson (1950), who conceptualized the distinction between the organ zone and the organ mode (e.g., retentive, expulsive, receptive, intrusive) and has shown that these modes can and do become autonomously displaceable. Indeed, there is reason to assume that these modes, having become autonomous and having undergone various vicissitudes, provide some of the salient patterns of the adaptive and the defensive, as well as the action and the thought, organization of the ego. Considering the originally multiple modes organ zones are capable of and considering the displaceability of these modes, to use them for the explanation of activity and passivity becomes unfeasible.[6]

Freud's attempt to anchor the explanation of activity and passivity in the contrast of internal (instinctual) and external stimuli reads as follows:

> The relation of the ego to the outer world is passive in so far as it receives stimuli from it, active when it reacts to these. Its instincts

[6] The point is that the same organ mode on the same organ, as well as on different ones, may in one person subserve activity, in another passivity; moreover, even in the same person an organ mode may subserve activity at one time and passivity at another.

compel it to a quite special degree of activity towards the outside world, so that, if we wished to emphasize the essence of the matter, we might say that the ego-subject is passive in respect of external stimuli, active in virtue of its own instincts [1915a, p. 77].

This formulation is certainly correct in a sense, and one wishes that Dollard and Miller (see Rapaport, 1953a) and Mowrer (see Rapaport, 1952), as well as psychoanalysts captivated by the conditioned-response theory of learning (French, 1933; Masserman, 1946; Hendricks, 1952; Cohen, 1951), would notice it and note that it just will not do to equate, as they do, external stimuli with drives; or at least that if one does equate these, one has a drive concept which has little to do with the psychoanalytic concept of instinctual drive. But as regards the terms activity and passivity, this usage of the terms appears both barely related to any of these usual usages and is in a sense also incorrect.

Let me start with the latter point: the assertion that the ego is passive in receiving stimuli from the outside world represents the photograph-phonograph conception of perceptual processes, a conception that has been totally abandoned even by the most old-fashioned psychologies of our day. It has been replaced by a conception of perception in which active selection and organization of the incoming stimulation is the crucial characteristic. Indeed, the development of this new conception has been ushered in by psychoanalytic discoveries concerning parapraxes and memory functioning (see Lewy and Rapaport, 1944; Rapaport, 1942; also Blake and Ramsey, 1951, and Klein and Schlesinger, 1949). So much for the factual incorrectness of the usage.

As to the irrelevance of the usage of any of the customary meanings of activity and passivity, we can most easily orient ourselves by recalling the fundamental difference between external stimuli and internal drive-tension postulated in the psychoanalytic definition of instinctual drives, namely that *in general* the organism can withdraw from external stimuli, but *in general* it cannot to begin with do so from the continuous stimulation of instinctual drives. The external stimulus creates tension only when it impinges on the organism, and the organism is equipped with reflex means to withdraw actively from it. The internal drive-stimulation cannot be escaped except by discharge, which is possible only when the drive object is present; in the absence of the drive object the organism is helplessly passive in relation to the mounting drive tension and can rid itself of it only by building a complex psychic apparatus by which on the one hand the discharge threshold is heightened and on the other hand finding the drive object becomes possible. Freud wrote:

> We see then how greatly the simple physiological reflex scheme is complicated by the introduction of instincts. External stimuli impose upon the organism the single task of withdrawing itself from their action: this is accomplished by muscular movements . . . Those instinc-

tual stimuli which emanate from within the organism cannot be dealt with by the mechanism. Consequently, they make far higher demands upon the nervous system and compel it to complicated and interdependent activities, which effect such changes in the outer world as enable it to offer satisfaction to the internal source of stimulation; above all, instinctual stimuli oblige the nervous system to renounce its ideal intention of warding off stimuli, for they maintain an incessant and unavoidable afflux of stimulation [1915a, pp. 63–64].

It would seem then that we would be *more nearly correct* if we were to assert that the psychic apparatus (and Freud labels it in this paper often as the ego) is active in relation to the external stimuli and passive in relation to the instinctual drives, than vice versa; I say *more nearly correct* because only as a theoretical abstraction can such a proposition be sustained. In actuality, it has—like all other theoretical abstractions—limitations imposed by conditions to be accounted for by other theoretical abstractions.

Some of these limitations are readily appreciable and deserve to be mentioned here:

(a) In the average case the organism has at its disposal means of preventing extreme mounting of drive tension and of reducing the existing drive tension, both militating against passive helplessness in the face of it: *first,* there is a coordination of mother and child (what Erikson [1950] calls mutuality, and what Schilder [1924] refers to when he asserts that human beings do not just become socialized, but are, as a species, born as social beings; see also Burlingham [1935]) which prevents indefinite absence of the drive object, indefinite delay of discharge, unlimited mounting of tension and helpless passivity; *second,* there are affect discharge channels and there is the hypothetical hallucinatory cathecting of memory traces which serve as safety valves of drive tension and are not dependent for tension reduction upon the presence of the drive object; *third,* there are the structure-building potentialities of the organism which lead to the development of defense and control structures as well as to the binding of drive cathexes in thought and other structures—but these are not so much primordial tension-reducing means but rather the avenues to higher-level structure building to combat passive helplessness. All in all, then, in the average case the passive helplessness of the primitive psychic apparatus in relation to drives is by no means complete. Failure of these factors limiting passive helplessness appears, however, at the root of much pathology.

(b) The other major and obvious limitation pertains to the organism's activity in relation to external stimuli. While the organism is equipped with reflex and other motor means of withdrawing actively from external stimulation, congenital and/or maturational (biological and psychological) failure to develop such apparatuses may doom the organism to passive helplessness in relation to external stimuli. Bergman and Escalona (1949) studied children showing the consequences for ego development of such states of affairs. Moreover, unusual or intense stimuli to handle which no inborn equipment is available, or external conditions preventing withdrawal from external stimulation, may and do make the organism passively helpless in relation to continued external stimulation also. It is indeed possible that this is what Freud (1920) implied in his treatment of traumatic neuroses in *Beyond the Pleasure Principle*. The insufficiency of the *stimulus barrier* he speaks about there may stand for this lack of equipment. It is also possible that the Pavlov frame and the other means of confinement of animals in conditioning experiments which make the animal helplessly passive in relation to external stimulation are responsible for the investigators' equating continued external stimuli and drives, and then arriving at a theory of learning which has little to do with the normal learning process. Finally, it is possible that the effects of long solitary confinement, of concentration camps, and the effects of incessant propaganda (whether in Hitler's Germany or in Orwell's fantasy *Nineteen Eighty-Four*) show that even in adult human individuals, inescapable external stimulation may render the ego passively helpless to external stimulation.

Since models are theoretical constructions and are not supposed to be free of limitations, it would be possible to consider—in spite of the limitations discussed—the archaic relationship of the psychic apparatus to external stimuli as the model of activity and that to internal drive stimulation as the model of passivity. It would thus be possible to formulate that: (1) the psychic apparatus is "active" when it can relate to external stimuli as well as to internal stimulation as the archaic psychic apparatus of this model related to external stimuli; (2) the psychic apparatus is "passive" when it relates to internal drive stimulation as well as to external stimuli as the archaic psychic apparatus of this model related to internal stimuli. It seems to us, however, that while the archaic relation to external stimuli and internal drive stimulation is closely related to activity and passivity, there is no gain in choosing this relation as the model over the model proposed above. Yet it is an open question whether consideration of further pertinent issues or of new observations and findings may or may not prove the model of external stimuli vs. internal drive stimulation to be the more economical of the two.

Let us now return to "Instincts and Their Vicissitudes" after this detour from it which, I believe, led us into the very core of our topic. Let us concern ourselves with its discussion of the instinctual vicissitude of *turning round upon the subject*. This is one of the four instinctual vicissitudes Freud mentions in this paper: reversal into the opposite (love into hate), turning round upon the subject, repression, sublimation. That repression is a defense we know; the status of sublimation—though Bergler (1945) treated it as defense—is still unclear. But it appears that we easily overlook the fact that Freud was inclined to consider all these vicissitudes as defenses or at least prestages of them, and thus as part and parcel of ego development.[7] Freud wrote:

> . . . we approach the more general view that those vicissitudes which consist in the instinct being turned round upon the subject's own ego and undergoing reversal from activity to passivity are dependent upon the narcissistic organization of the ego and bear the stamp of that phase. Perhaps they represent attempts at defence which at higher stages of the development of the ego are effected by other means [1915a, p. 75].

The statement of the defense character and of the dependence upon ego development of this vicissitude is clear in this formulation. But Freud's reference to the dependence of the reversal from activity to passivity upon the narcissistic organization of the ego is in need of elucidation, because it appears to lead again into the heart of the activity and passivity problem.

The reversals from activity into passivity which Freud considers here are those already discussed in *Three Essays* (1905a), namely sadism-masochism and scoptophilia-exhibitionism. In both cases the "active" drive, when for some reason its drive object has to be abandoned, is "turned towards the subject's own person," and thus arises the "passive" drive. The defensive character of this vicissitude to which Freud referred above is obvious here. But at this point we are in 1915, and not in 1905; and Freud had already, in 1914, in "On Narcissism," introduced the concept of narcissism, that of the narcissistic phase of libido development, and that of the narcissistic object choice preceding the libidinal object choice: ". . . to be loved is the aim and the satisfaction in a narcissistic object-choice" (1914, p. 55). While in 1905 the active drive was definitely considered primary, and masochism could be conceived of only as sadism being turned upon the subject, now a "passive" narcissistic orientation is seen to precede genetically an "active" libidinal orientation. "Instincts and Their Vicissitudes" explores scoptophilia from the same angle and conjectures that a similar state of affairs may obtain for sadism also. In summary Freud wrote:

> . . . we can recognize in the scoptophilic instinct a yet earlier stage . . . at the beginning of its activity the scoptophilic instinct is auto-erotic: it has indeed an object, but that object is the subject's own

---

[7] In this sense the paper "Instincts and Their Vicissitudes" is an important and often overlooked link in the history and development of psychoanalytic ego psychology. It bridges the gap between the theoretical discussion of defenses in the 1890's and that in 1926 in *The Problem of Anxiety*. I am not unmindful here of the continuity maintained in the clinical papers of the intervening years, nor of the dynamic and economic —but hardly ever structural—treatment of the defense issue in Chapter VII of *The Interpretation of Dreams* (1900) and the "Papers on Metapsychology" (1911–1917) other than "Instincts and Their Vicissitudes."

body. It is only later that the instinct comes . . . to exchange this object for the analogous one of the body of another . . .

A preliminary stage of this kind is absent in sadism, which from the outset is directed upon an extraneous object, although it might not be altogether unreasonable to regard as such a stage the child's effort to gain control of his own limbs [1915a, pp. 72–73].[8]

We will then not be surprised to find that at this point—1915—Freud drops the previous meanings of activity and passivity and proposes a new and quite general meaning, namely:

. . . our mental life as a whole is governed by *three polarities,* namely, the following antitheses:
Subject (ego)—Object (external world),
Pleasure—Pain,
Active—Passive [pp. 76–77].

Nor will we be surprised to find that Freud describes the necessary persistence side by side and fusion of passive and active forms of integration of drives. Thus, e.g., he clearly formulates that mature genital love is characterized by the coexistence of the tendency to love and the tendency to be loved, both of which arise from the narcissistic passive phase after multiple vicissitudes (1915a, p. 83, and 1914, pp. 56–59).

We may conclude that the introduction of the narcissistic phase permitted Freud to demonstrate that drive actions characterized by "activity" have in this phase a predecessor characterized as it were by "passivity"—by a passive-narcissistic object choice. I would like to summarize (1) that hereby the origin of passivity is linked with a developmental phase in which object and subject coincide, in which active mastery of drive tensions by defense and delayed (i.e., controlled) discharge is not yet possible and the psychic apparatus is passively helpless in the face of such tension; (2) that here the defense is regressive in character; (3) that after the introduction of the death instinct (1920) Freud shows none of the reluctance he displayed above to demonstrate that sadism too has in the narcissistic phase its "passive" predecessor in what he then labeled *primary masochism.* He devoted to this demonstration the paper "The Economic Problem in Masochism" (1924). Here I can only assert—I cannot take space to document— that Freud's demonstration of the point holds up independent of the concept of the "death instinct" and that indeed the very conception of the narcissistic phase (which as a concept is about to yield to Hartmann, Kris, and Loewenstein's [1949] *undifferentiated phase*) makes the death-instinct concept superfluous. The further clinical and theoretical exploration of the sequence primary narcissism—object choice—secondary narcissism, and of the sequence primary masochism—sadism—secondary masochism, and the

[8] See Hartmann, Kris, and Loewenstein, "Notes on the Theory of Aggression" (1949).

problem of passivity in general can be found in Freud's (1931) "Female Sexuality" and in the chapter on "The Psychology of Women" in *New Introductory Lectures on Psycho-Analysis* (1933). I cannot dwell on these papers in detail, though they demonstrate that passivity and activity overlaying each other in alternating layers build a whole hierarchy of drive vicissitudes, i.e., defensive formation;[9] and that the older layers of this hierarchy persist alongside or underneath the newer ones—a point already clear to Freud in "Instincts and Their Vicissitudes":

> . . . [The] earlier active direction always persists side by side with the . . . passive . . . , even when the transformation is . . . extensive [1915a, p. 73].

But there are a few points in these papers that must be mentioned in this context: (1) The first is that in them Freud says explicitly that it is the *mode of gratification* that he speaks of when he used the term aim:

> Psycho-analysis teaches us to manage with a single libido, though its aims, *i.e.* its modes of gratification, are both active and passive [1931, pp. 268–269].

(2) Furthermore, Freud draws the distinction between passivity and inertia:

> One might make an attempt to characterise femininity psychologically by saying that it involves a preference for passive aims. That is naturally not the same as passivity; it may require a good deal of activity to achieve a passive end [1933, p. 157].

Last but not least, (3) we find here Freud's (1931) clear recognition that in the multiple layering of activity and passivity there is no primacy of either:

> . . . there is an antithesis between the attachment to the father and the masculinity-complex—this is the universal antithesis between activity and passivity, masculinity and femininity—but we have no right to assume that only the one is primary, while the other owes its strength merely to the process of defence [1931, p. 272].

We have briefly reviewed the process of activity turning into passivity, and will now turn to the converse process of passivity turning into activity, to show that the literature considers this process one of the methods used to increase the *relative* independence from the pleasure principle and from helpless inundation by drive cathexes, and also an integral part of the development of reality mastery. The literature is extensive, so I will restrict myself to quoting the passages of *Beyond the Pleasure Principle* where Freud (1920) introduced the concept:

[9] For the conception of the hierarchy of defense layering, see particularly Jones (1929), and for a general discussion of hierarchic organization see Rapaport (1953b).

The analysis of a single case of this kind yields no sure conclusion: on impartial consideration one gains the impression that it is from another motive that the child has turned the experience into a game. He was in the first place passive, was overtaken by the experience, but now brings himself in as playing an active part, by repeating the experience as a game in spite of its unpleasing nature. This effort might be ascribed to the impulse to obtain the mastery of a situation (the "power" instinct), which remains independent of any question of whether the recollection was a pleasant one or not. But another interpretation may be attempted. The flinging away of the object so that it is gone might be the gratification of an impulse of revenge suppressed in real life but directed against the mother for going away, and would then have the defiant meaning: "yes, you can go, I don't want you, I am sending you away myself." The same child a year later than my observations used to throw on the floor a toy which displeased him, and to say "Go to the war!" He had been told that his absent father was at the war, and he did not miss him at all, giving the clearest indications that he did not wish to be disturbed in the sole possession of his mother. It is known of other children also that they can give vent to similar hostile feelings by throwing objects away in place of people. Thus one is left in doubt whether the compulsion to work over in psychic life what has made a deep impression, to make oneself fully master of it, can express itself primarily and independently of the pleasure-principle. In the case discussed here, however, the child might have repeated a disagreeable impression in play only because with the repetition was bound up a pleasure gain of a different kind but more direct [pp. 14–15];

and

If a doctor examines a child's throat, or performs a small operation on him, the alarming experience will quite certainly be made the subject of the next game, but in this the pleasure gain from another source is not to be overlooked. In passing from the passivity of experience to the activity of play the child applies to his playfellow the unpleasant occurrence that befell himself and so avenges himself on the person of this proxy [pp. 15–16].

Thus the defensive structure building by turning passivity into activity too seems to need the support of drive impulses in order to come into existence; here too the principle of multiple function holds.

Fenichel's summary of the issue may also be in place here, since it shows clearly that meaning of passivity and activity at which this paper is pointed:

Whenever the organism is flooded with a very large quantity of excitation it attempts to get rid of it by subsequent active repetitions of the situation that induced the excessive excitation. This takes place in the early games of little children . . . [Freud, S., *Beyond the Pleasure Principle;* Waelder, R., "The Psychoanalytic Theory of Play"] and in their dreams as well . . . [Grotjahn, M., "Dream Observations in a Two-Year-Four-Months-Old Baby"]. Between the original flood of excitation and these repetitions there is one fundamental difference: in the original experience the organism was passive; in the case of the repetitions, the organism is active and determines the time and degree of excitation. At first the passive experiences that aroused anxiety are reproduced actively by the child in his play in order to achieve a belated mastery. Later on, the child in his play not only dramatizes the exciting experiences of the past but he also anticipates what he expects to happen in the future [1945, pp. 44–45].

Fenichel also gives a discussion of the various ways in which passivity is turned into activity, but we cannot enter here on a discussion of these. Moreover, Fenichel also clearly points (1945, pp. 53, 119–120, 468) to the fact that both pathological and adequate adaptation may make use of what he calls passive-receptive mastery. To this point we shall return in the next part of this paper, when discussing Kris's concept of "regression in the service of the ego."

I believe that this discussion of the literature shows (1) that a useful concept of activity and passivity will not refer to what appears active or passive to the observer or to the subject, nor to the organ modes receptive vs. intruding, invaginating vs. extruding, etc.; (2) that a useful concept of passivity refers to the helpless condition of inundation by drive cathexes (whether these compel discharge irresistibly, unleash floods of paralyzing anxiety or other affect, or render the psychic apparatus inert by compelling continued expenditure of excessive amounts of cathexes available to the ego for countercathecting, i.e., for defense against them); (3) that a useful concept of activity refers to the control of the ego over drive cathexes, affects, and the discharge effecting drive action. The observational fact that an action coordinated by the ego may still bear marks of passivity, and that refraining from action may bear the marks of activity—in the sense in which activity and passivity are here defined—does not militate against the usefulness of these concepts and will be further discussed in the next part of this paper.

IV. AN APPLICATION: "REGRESSION" VS. "REGRESSION IN THE SERVICE OF THE EGO"

In this section I propose to survey the theoretical position at which I believe we have arrived in the previous sections. This survey will lead us into a consideration of the distinction between regression proper and regression in the service of the ego, to which we have referred repeatedly.

If passivity is defined as helplessness in the face of drive demand, we must realize that theoretically two forms of it should exist, and indeed two such basic forms do exist according to clinical observation. The helplessness in the face of drive demand may take its original hypothesized model form of overwhelming inundation by drive demand in the absence of a possibility for executing drive action, either because of internal stalemate between defenses and drive demands, or because of lack of established executive ego apparatuses for the discharge of the drive in question, or because of absence of a gratifying drive object. The helplessness in the face of drive demands, however, may also take the form of execution of the drive demand in direct or disguised form through ego apparatuses, without the consent of the ego (and superego) and indeed in contradiction to the tendencies of the ego—as it were not by the cooperation but by the paralysis or by the overrunning of ego control. In this sense, behavior both ostensibly "passive" and obstensibly "active" may be "passivity" as here defined.

If activity is defined as the ego's control over drive demands, then here too theoretically two forms of it should exist, and indeed clinical observation does verify this theoretical expectation. On the one hand the ego's control over drive demand may take the form of definitive and effective defense persistently preventing drive action. On the other hand, the ego's control of drive demand may take the form of delaying drive discharge, of inducing experimental action in thought to discover the safest and shortest path in reality toward the drive object, of guiding detour behavior to find the object discovered in thought—on the path discovered in thought—and then of executing a thus ego-integrated action which results in gratification (i.e., drive discharge). Thus in this sense behavior both ostensibly "passive" and ostensibly "active" may amount to "activity" as here defined.[10]

Let us remind ourselves that throughout we have been talking about the dynamic conditions of "activity" and "passivity." In actual clinical observation the conditions are complicated by the subjective experience of the patient, which may not correspond to these dynamics since it may be a product of reaction formation, denial, etc.

Indeed, the situation is further complicated by the clinical observations showing that the process of turning passivity into activity, while ostensibly successful, may or may not result in intrinsic "activity" as the concept is here defined. The compulsive repetition of traumatic experiences follows the pattern of turning passivity into activity, and yet when unsuccessful it results in an ego-dystonic symptom outside of the control of the ego. More-

[10] A particularly interesting situation which further demonstrates the complex overlapping of "activity" and "passivity" obtains in people among whose conditions of gratification the outstanding one is that the drive object present itself adventitiously, spontaneously, i.e., without any activity on the side of the subject. This situation on the face of it seems to imply passivity; yet, since the ego controls and prevents drive action until and executes it when the drive object is encountered, in fact dynamically it often amounts to activity.

over, the clinical illustration which I cited in the beginning of this paper
shows that even when the process of turning passivity into activity successfully masters anxiety by setting up counterphobic defenses, the resulting
counterphobic behavior may prove simply a disguise for the discharge of
the drive tension which is at the root of the anxiety that was counterphobi-
cally mastered. Then, as in the illustrative case, the counterphobic actions
will not be actually under ego control, they will have to the observer a
driven, impulse-ridden character, and in the subject's experience they will
appear dishonest, phony, or even ego dystonic.

But the situation is not different with the process of turning activity into
passivity either. If turning scoptophilia into exhibitionism may be regarded
(as Freud did) as a defensive move implying regression to the narcissistic,
self-observing, passive predecessor of scoptophilia and as a paradigm of the
so varied and frequent passive-regressive defensive maneuvers, then we
may see in it an example of the successful turning of activity into passivity.
Yet activity may be turned into a passivity which is only ostensible, the
actual control of the ego over the drive demand remaining sustained. Kris
subsumed a broad segment of such processes under the concept of *regression in the service of the ego.*[11] The distinction between a turning of activity
into passivity which is successful and amounts to a loss of ego control and
thus to a regression, and one which achieves passivity in appearance but
remains intrinsically activity and thus amounts to a "regression in the service of the ego," is illustrated in Kris's discussion of the difference between
ecstasy and inspiration:

> . . . the driving of the unconscious toward consciousness is experi-
> enced as an intrusion from without—an attitude of a passive nature
> *par excellence.* The decisive difference, however, can be formulated
> more clearly. In ecstasy the process results in an emotional climax
> only; in states of inspiration it leads to active elaboration in creation.
> The process is dominated by the ego and put to its own purposes—for
> sublimation in creative activity [1939, p. 302].

But this state of affairs concerning the "regression in the service of the ego"
will become even clearer in Kris's following more general formulation:

> Topographically, ego regression (primitivization of ego functions)
> occurs not only when the ego is weak—in sleep, in falling asleep, in
> fantasy, in intoxication, and in the psychoses—but also during many
> types of creative processes. This suggested to me years ago that the
> ego may use the primary process and not be only overwhelmed by it.
> . . . This idea was rooted in Freud's explanation of wit . . . [*Wit
> and Its Relation to the Unconscious*] according to which a preconscious
> thought "is entrusted for a moment to unconscious elaboration," and

---

[11] It seems to be an open question whether this concept subsumes all such processes,
and, if it does not, what characterizes those which are not so subsumed.

seemed to account for a variety of creative or other inventive processes. However, the problem of ego regression during creative processes represents only a special problem in a more general area. The general assumption is that under certain conditions the ego regulates regression, and that the integrative functions of the ego include voluntary and temporary withdrawal of cathexis from one area or another to regain improved control (Hartmann . . . [*Ego Psychology and the Problem of Adaptation;* "Psychoanalysis and the Concept of Health"; "On Rational and Irrational Action"]). Our theory of sleep is based upon the assumption of such a withdrawal of cathexis. Sexual functions presuppose similar regressive patterns, and the inability to such suspension of ego control constitutes one of the well-known symptoms of obsessional, compulsive characters.

The clinical observation of creators and the study of introspective reports of experiences during creative activity tend to show that we are faced with a shift in the cathexes of certain ego functions. Thus a frequent distinction is made between an inspirational and an "elaborational" phase in creation. The inspirational phase is characterized by the facility with which id impulses, or their closer derivatives, are received. One might say that countercathectic energies to some extent are withdrawn, and added to the speed, force, or intensity with which the preconscious thoughts are formed. During the "elaborational" phase, the countercathectic barrier may be reinforced, work proceeds slowly, cathexis is directed to other ego functions such as reality testing, formulation, or general purposes of communication. Alternations between the two phases may be rapid, oscillating, or distributed over long stretches of time [1950, pp. 551–552].

Creative experiences vary from those in which the artistic or scientific invention appears in subjective experience as hallucinated, entirely "inspired" from the outside, to those in which it appears in subjective experience as entirely the product of "deliberate effort." Yet the ego integration of the creative product is characteristic of all creative processes, and this ego integration—rather than the subjective experience—is decisive, whether the process in question is one of activity or one of passivity, as here defined.

We are touching at this point upon the dynamic and structural conditions underlying the subjective experience of "will" and "voluntary effort." But this is not the place to do more than just call attention to the point.

V

Activity and passivity thus appear as concepts characterizing the relationship of psychic structure in general and of the ego in particular to instinctual drives and to the motivations deriving from them. The last task I have set myself in this paper is to make an attempt to bring to bear on this view of activity and passivity the theoretical understanding we have of the origin and role of psychic structure in general and thought organization in particular. My hope is that such an attempt may result in some mutual clarification of the psychoanalytic conception of the development of structure and thought on the one hand, and of this conception of activity and passivity on the other.

Let me start out by quoting a few passages from Freud. These passages were written prior to the introduction of the structural point of view; yet to my mind they provide the metapsychological preparation for the structural point of view. Their importance lies in the fact that after having introduced the structural point of view, Freud did not systematically explore its relation to the other two—the dynamic and the economic—points of view, but was preoccupied with clarifying its relation to the topographic point of view which it so to speak replaced. In other words, it was the relation of the systems *Ucs.-Pcs.-Cs.* to the id-ego-superego that preoccupied him. While in Chapter VII of *The Interpretation of Dreams* (1900) and in the "Papers on Metapsychology" (1911–17) he did explore the relation of the systems *Ucs.-Pcs.-Cs.* to the dynamics of instinctual drives and to the economy of cathexes, he gave us hardly any systematic exploration of the relation of the id-ego-superego to the latter. Thus we must start out from the metapsychological considerations which were preparatory to the structural point of view.

Keeping in mind that there is a rough—but *only* rough—parallel between primary vs. secondary processes on the one hand and id processes vs. ego processes on the other, let us recall what Freud meant by the former. The primary process abides by the pleasure principle and strives for direct gratification discharge; its energies are therefore conceived as mobile. On the secondary process, let us have here Freud's (1900) own words:

> . . . I postulate that the second system succeeds in maintaining the greater part of the energic cathexes in a state of rest, and in using only a small portion for its operation of displacement. . . . Here I do no more than hold fast to the idea that the activity of the first ψ-system aims at *the free outflow of the quantities of excitation,* and that the second system, by means of the cathexes emanating from it, effects an *inhibition* of this outflow, a transformation into dormant cathexis, probably with a rise of potential. . . . After the second system has completed its work of experimental thought, it removes the inhibition and damming up of the excitations and allows them to flow off into motility [pp. 533–534].

Let us take note here of the phrase "probably with a rise of potential" and note a similar implication in Freud's (1915b) following two formulations also:

> . . . from the point of view of repression we were obliged to place the censorship which is decisive for consciousness between the systems

> Ucs and Pcs. Now it becomes probable to us that there is a censorship
> between the Pcs and the Cs. But we shall do well not to regard this
> complication as a difficulty, but to assume that to every transition from
> one system to that immediately above it (that is, every advance to a
> higher state of mental organization) there corresponds a new censor-
> ship [p. 124];

and

> . . . the existence of the censorship between the Pcs and the Cs
> teaches us that becoming conscious is no mere act of perception, but
> is probably also a *hyper-cathexis,* a further advance in the mental
> organization [pp. 125–126].

We may take it that "advance in mental organization" means here structure
formation. Clearly we assume that structure formation implies: (a) that
the energic cathexes of drives are controlled by means of lesser amounts of
cathexes of a higher potential; (b) that this control is coterminous with
"censorship"; and (c) that establishment of such controls results in the
availability of an amount of cathexis (hypercathexis) at the disposal of the
structure formed.

Even a cursory glance at Chapter VII of *The Interpretation of Dreams*
shows that the hypercathexes here discussed are conceived as identical with
the attention cathexes the dynamics of which underlies the phenomena of
consciousness. Freud (1900) wrote:

> The train of thought cathected by some aim becomes able under cer-
> tain conditions to attract the attention of consciousness, and by the
> mediation of consciousness it then receives *"hyper-cathexis"* [p. 529];

and

> The act of becoming conscious depends upon a definite psychic func-
> tion—attention—being brought to bear. This seems to be available
> only in a determinate quantity, which may have been diverted from
> the train of thought in question by other aims. Another way in which
> such trains of thought may be withheld from consciousness is the fol-
> lowing: From our conscious reflection we know that, when applying
> our attention, we follow a particular course. But if that course leads us
> to an idea which cannot withstand criticism, we break off and allow
> the cathexis of attention to drop. Now, it would seem that the train of
> thought thus started and abandoned may continue to develop without
> our attention returning to it, unless at some point it attains a specially
> high intensity which compels attention [p. 529].

But we need a still closer view of the process of structure formation. This
Freud provides most clearly in his theory of repression. Having demonstrated that withdrawal of attention cathexes does not suffice to keep ideas

representing drives permanently out of consciousness, nor does it account for the so-called primal repression of what never has been in consciousness, Freud (1915b) advanced the following theory:

> What we are looking for, therefore, is another process which maintains the repression in the first case and, in the second, ensures its being established and continued; and this other process we can only find in the assumption of an *anti-cathexis,* by means of which the system Pcs guards itself against the intrusion of the unconscious idea. We shall see from clinical examples how such an anti-cathexis established in the system Pcs manifests itself. This it is which represents the continuous effort demanded by a primal repression but also guarantees its persistence. The anti-cathexis is the sole mechanism of primal repression; in the case of repression proper ('after-expulsion') there is in addition withdrawal of the preconscious cathexis [i.e., attention cathexis]. It is quite possible that the cathexis withdrawn from the idea is the very one used for anti-cathexis [pp. 113–114].

He thus assumes—to put it in our structural terms—that it is the same supply of cathexes at the disposal of the ego which is used both for hypercathecting and for countercathecting. If we now put together what we heard above about hypercathexis, censorship, and advance in structure development, and what we heard here about countercathecting, it becomes clear that establishment of defensive and controlling countercathectic barriers against drives is a crucial step in structure formation. It raises the cathectic process to a higher energy potential, it uses lesser cathectic amounts,[12] and, once consolidated into a continuous system of defenses and executive apparatuses, it has energies at its disposal—partly those *bound* in the *structure* so created and partly those which are its free reserve (hypercathexes = attention cathexes = neutralized cathexes, more or less divested of the hallmarks of their drive origin). Structure building thus may be conceived of as the internalization of the unavailability of or dangerousness of drive objects and of the reality conditions surrounding them. In keeping with these considerations of the relation of structure formation and cathectic dynamics, the following metapsychological conception of activity and passivity emerges:

(1) Advance in structure formation implies establishment of controlling and/or defensive countercathectic organizations, new censorships, and the becoming available to the new structure (and in broader terms, to the ego) of cathexes which may be used either as hypercathexes for experimental action in thought and detour activity for reaching the drive object in reality, or as countercathexes to reinforce the defensive and/or controlling structures.

---

[12] Probably because of the consolidation of all the countercathectic barriers in the fashion of a continuous defense line with a token manning (countercathexes) and a free reserve (hypercathexes) which can be thrown in as reinforcement on any point.

(2) The controlling and defensive structures themselves work effectively when they consist of small amounts of bound cathexes, leaving most of the energy used in establishing them in a neutralized form at the disposal of the new structure, either as reinforcing countercathexes or as hypercathexes.

(3) When increased drive tension (or superego demand) commandeers a countercathectic disposition of these neutralized cathexes at the disposal of the defensive and/or controlling ego structure, then the dynamic condition prevailing is that of passivity. When the ego can freely dispose of these cathexes at its disposal, the dynamic condition prevailing is that of activity.

(4) Since we conceive of the psychic structure as of a multiply layered hierarchy at each level of which we find controlling and/or defensive structures with corresponding censorship functions and freely available cathexes, these freely available cathexes are of varied degrees of neutralization and the phenomena of activity and passivity are also multiple and varied. Activity in thought may be accompanied by passivity in action, etc.

I will now attempt to give some examples of the application of these concepts to the theory of thinking, continuing some of the considerations touched on in the introduction.

Since it appears that structure formation goes along with cathexes becoming available within the structure formed (hypercathexes), and since on the highest level of structure development these hypercathexes are the attention cathexes which underlie the subjective experiences of consciousness, it will be useful to consider once more the issue of consciousness. (1) A thought may appear in consciousness by virtue of its being the ideational representation of a drive of such intensity that it commands hypercathexis. Examples: hallucinations, obsessional ideas, etc. These are of compelling intensity, and are, under normal and even neurotic conditions, attended by the subjective experience of passivity and are ego dystonic. Or (2) a thought may appear in consciousness as a displacement substitute of the motivating drive, and in this case will be used by the secondary process in the course of its "experimenting at action"—i.e., thinking. Thinking is a detour activity which takes place at considerable distance from the drive as well as from the goal object which is defined both by the motivating drive and the reality situation. In the course of this detour the displacement substitutes assume a rationalized thought-form and serve as indispensable guideposts on the route toward the goal object. Such thought has little compelling intensity and is experienced as ego syntonic. We are familiar with, roughly speaking, two forms of such thought, though these shade imperceptibly into each other. These two forms are: productive, and automatized. For example: (a) the response to the question how much is 2×2 is, in the adult of our civilization, an automatized thought—available as a tool to the thought process; similarly automatized tools are our common concepts, like chair, table, house. Calculus may or may not be such an automatized concept, depending on the individual. The experience of such thoughts is passive yet ego syntonic. (b) The combination of several automatic thoughts, such as $2 \times 2 = 4$, of perceptual cues, of skill with carpenter tools, and of much general information in building, say, a lean-to in a forest, is productive thought. The subjective experience of such thoughts is one of activity and they are ego syntonic. (3) Finally, thought may arise from sensory perception. Freud (1911) wrote:

> The increased significance of external reality heightened the significance also of the sense-organs directed towards that outer world, and of the *consciousness* attached to them; the latter now learned to comprehend the qualities of sense in addition to the qualities of pleasure and 'pain' which hitherto had alone been of interest to it. A special function was instituted which had periodically to search the outer world, in order that its data might be already familiar if an urgent inner need should arise; this function was *attention*. Its activity meets the sense-impressions halfway, instead of awaiting their appearance [p. 15].

Here again some of the thoughts of such origin we can take or leave; others have a compelling, obsessing effect on us. The latter—to our understanding —have triggered some instinctual drive or its derivative. Those which we can take or leave are at a distance from the drives, and the attention cathexis they attracted by virtue of their perceptual intensity or saliency is responsible for their becoming conscious. I shall forgo here discussing sense impressions of such intensity or persistence, or encountered by us under such conditions, that we cannot withdraw ourselves from their encroachment and find ourselves in a helpless passivity in the face of them. We have touched on them briefly before.

We have to dwell, however, for a moment on automatized thoughts. On the one hand such automatized thoughts (and actions—i.e., habits) become easily reinvaded by drives and can become ego alien and dynamically passive, as in automatic writing and parapraxes. Partly they can, while remaining ego syntonic, become dynamically passive when used to conform with defensive operations enforced by drive, superego, or external reality. Automatized thought and action can be dynamically active only when used as a means of productive thought. But here too the situation is quite complex, as is readily seen in creative thinkers. Some creative thinkers will be able to experience (note that we know little here of the dynamics) their product as an active achievement of their own only if it came to them without any subjective sustained active effort; others only if it came through sustained active effort at thinking. In the former the secondary-process-organized thought is too closely linked to id pressure or superego pressure enforcing passivity; in the latter id pressure threatens passivity, and activity cannot (or can little) reside in aspiration and has its abode in its elaboration by organized thinking.

My purpose in giving this sketchy review of varieties of thought is to indicate that on this high level of structure formation, i.e., on that of thought organization, too, we encounter the "polarity" of activity and passivity. I hope that I have given some of the indications—though I have certainly not "proved"—that the polarity phenomena on this level too conform with and can be dealt with by the conception of activity and passivity here proposed: where structure controls drives we find thought phenomena which may be characterized dynamically as activity and may even be accompanied by a subjective experience of activity; where drive imposes itself upon structure we find thought phenomena bearing the dynamic—and perhaps even the subjective experience—earmarks of passivity.

As long as we are at the discussion of thought processes, I would like to call attention to a characteristic of certain thought processes which by analogy may elucidate the nature of structure formation and the problem of activity and passivity. I would like to stress that what follows is an *analogy* and *not an explanatory construction*.

I want to suggest that the process of psychic structure building and that of forming new abstractions—in the course of learning or thinking—are analogous. We saw that defenses are countercathectic energy distributions which by means of lesser intensities (amounts) of cathexes, but such as are on a higher potential, control greater amounts of drive energies.[13] I suggest that abstractions are to the concrete items they subsume as structure is to the drives it controls. Indeed, I suggest that building an abstraction is the erection of a new hypercathectic organization. Such building is *activity* by our present definition and is also experienced subjectively as an active effort. The attention cathexes of the system are concentrated and if they are available in sufficient amounts, an abstraction can come into existence. If the difficulties of the material to be linked together into the abstraction exceed the available attention cathexes, the work of abstracting collapses and has to be started again. Usually fragments of the abstraction persist after the collapse and serve as points of departure for the new attempt. Once the building of the new abstraction has been completed, the attention that was fully absorbed in building it—so much so that any distraction of attention could have brought about a collapse and a loss of that already achieved—becomes again freely available as though no appreciable part of it had been used up in building the abstraction. The new freely available attention relates to the abstraction as to any other object of external or internal perception. That is why the analogy of minute intensity on a high potential seems so appropriate to describe the character of an abstraction once achieved.

But the analogy goes further: individual percepts usually retain their belonging to the external world: we experience them as "out there." They

[13] The analogy here to the cybernetic model, i.e., to the contrast of power- vs. communication-engineering, is noteworthy. See Rapaport (1950).

become internalized only by the abstractive work of the synthetic function of the ego. Note here the analogy between percept vs. abstraction and introject vs. identification. But we are not dealing here with dichotomies: every perception is already an active abstraction—there is no such thing as passive sense perception (see Schilder, 1942). But the perceptual abstraction relates to the conceptual one as the latter does to higher-level abstractions —and so on, more and more ascending in the degree of abstractness, of internalization, of activity, and of theoretical generality.

I believe we have encountered in these considerations a high-level analogue of the hierarchic layering of activity and passivity. It is relevant in this connection that Silberer (1912), in his studies of hypnagogic hallucinations, concluded that *active* thought effort changes into passive hypnagogic visual forms when there is an *insufficiency of attention,* and he adduced observations and views of other investigators to support this conclusion. In my paper on "States of Consciousness" (1951) I presented some evidence from my studies of amnesias, dreams, hypnagogic hallucinations, reveries, daydreams, thoughts, and Korsakoff cases, supporting and generalizing Silberer's conclusion. The material I brought together shows that the progression from waking and ordered thought through reveries to dreams passes through a continuum of ego states with corresponding characteristic states of consciousness, and that with the progression in this continuum there is a progressive decrease of the possibility of voluntary effort, a progressive increase in the passive "givenness" of ideas, an increasingly more direct expression of drive demand and defense, a decreasing use of the secondary-process forms of thought with increasing obviousness of the primary-process mechanisms, a decreasing explicitness of the thought contents which thus become more and more implicative—and these implications are increasingly accepted without evidence or scrutiny (passively).

The evidence I put forth concerning amnesias and Korsakoff cases shows also that drives, when they attain command, make thoughts passively accepted, since active reflection and comparison are in abeyance because contrary or comparable thought contents are not as a rule available in consciousness, or when they are occasionally available they are allowed to stand side by side in unreconciled contradiction, or else—as in the Korsakoff syndrome—such contradictions may be glossed over by superficial syntheses which in clinical parlance justly merit the description *"Verlegenheitskonfabulationen"*—i.e., confabulations rooted in embarrassment.

The relevance and importance of the concepts activity and passivity for thought organization could be illustrated by an endless further array of examples. I will choose only one, in the form of a brief clinical illustration. I hope that this clinical episode, besides shedding some further light on our problem, will also indicate that in discussing activity and passivity we have abstracted merely one aspect of the complex dynamics of psychic processes.

We cannot reduce this complexity to the simple activity-passivity relationship—nor was this the purpose of my presentation. The episode consists of three steps:

(1) A young schizophrenic man begins a therapy hour by expressing hatred toward a man A, whom he otherwise both admires and fears and wishes to become closer friends with. The reason for his hate of A is that A refuses to hate B, whom the patient hates. (2) Then the patient relates a conversation with B in which B called him insensitive, and when the patient expressed to B his fear that B might have gotten this idea through his therapist from me, B plays this to the hilt, asserting that it was so. The patient now proceeds to complain to me in dismay that as long as he was in B's presence he had to believe fully what B said, and that indeed this happens to him in his contact with other people also. (3) I talked with him about both themes and attempted to give him some understanding that any intimacy with A or B amounts, to him, to a fusion with them. Unless A hates B, just as he, the patient, does, there can be no intimacy between them—indeed, when A refuses to hate B, in the patient's mind A fuses with B and is hated by the patient just like B; in turn, while the patient is with B he fuses with him and B's thoughts become his. I then tried to show him that this is just what happens in the infant's world owing to its lack of differentiation. In the course of this conversation the patient suddenly stopped and said: "But I did manage not to believe what B said, even while I was with him. I tried hard to think of you and when I got a clear visual image of you, I thought: 'That's all just B's idea; it isn't true—he is just trying to torture me.' "

I believe this clinical vignette throws some light on the dynamic conditions of passive helpless exposure to contagion by thought. It is the patient's passive-dependent (and devouring) drives that expose him to this contagion, lending uncontested reality value to the ideas of others. Surely, without the structural conditions prevailing in this schizophrenic patient, this would not be possible to such an extent. (But man's reaction to propaganda and Orwell's *Nineteen Eighty-Four* show that *to some extent* the preconditions for such contagion exist in all of us.) The momentary renewal and reinforcement of the process of identification with the therapist—which was one of the main ongoing processes at that time in this therapy—momentarily put an end to this contagion. But what is such an identification if not a structure-building process? Passive contagion yields to active thought—which implies a judging ego function, when structure is reinforced so as to be able to exert control over the drive.

Let me end on this clinical vignette, and on a note stressing that in the individual case the complex relationships of activity and passivity to the general historical vicissitudes of libidinal, aggressive, and structural development cannot be simplified to the formula of activity and passivity. Yet activity-passivity appears to be an important parameter of the drive vs. ego-control balance. The complexity of the state of affairs that gives rise to this parameter will be appreciated if it is kept in mind that even in this simple clinical vignette regression and identification problems enter the picture and that, e.g., we have not even touched on the role of the superego in it. Other cases bring other complexities.

VI

In this paper I have attempted to define activity and passivity as parameters of the control of structure over drive or of the relative lack of such. In other words, I have suggested that activity and passivity are parameters of the relative autonomy of the ego. I have endeavored to present a clinical illustration of varieties of phenomena to which the concepts of activity and passivity pertain. I have tried to give a metapsychological treatment of these concepts, and finally, I have sought to show that the concepts as defined here have important relevance for the psychology of thought processes.

REFERENCES

Bergler, E. (1945). On a Five-Layer Structure in Sublimation. *Psychoanal. Quart.,* 14:76–97.
———— (1949). *The Basic Neurosis: Oral Regression and Psychic Masochism.* New York: Grune & Stratton.
Bergman, P., & Escalona, S. (1949). Unusual Sensitivities in Very Young Children. *Psychoanal. Study Child,* 3/4:333–352. New York: International Universities Press.
Blake, R. R., & Ramsey, G. V., eds. (1951). *Perception: An Approach to Personality.* New York: Ronald Press.
Brenman, M. (1952). On Teasing and Being Teased: And the Problem of "Moral Masochism." *Psychoanal. Study Child,* 7:264–285. New York: International Universities Press.
Burlingham, D. T. (1935). Die Einfühlung des Kleinkindes in die Mutter. *Imago,* 21:429–444.
Cohen, R. A. (1951). Review of J. Dollard and N. E. Miller, *Personality and Psychotherapy. Psychiatry,* 14:352–353.
Deutsch, H. (1944–45). *The Psychology of Women: A Psychoanalytic Interpretation,* 2 vols. New York: Grune & Stratton.
Erikson, E. H. (1950). *Childhood and Society.* New York: Norton.
Federn, P. (1913). Beiträge zur Analyse des Sadismus und Masochismus. I. Die Quellen des Männlichen Sadismus. *Int. Z. Psychoanal.,* 1:29–49.
Fenichel, O. (1945). *The Psychoanalytic Theory of Neurosis.* New York: Norton.
French, T. M. (1933). Interrelations between Psychoanalysis and the Experimental Work of Pavlov. *Amer. J. Psychiat.,* 12:1165–1203.

Freud, S. (1900). The Interpretation of Dreams, tr. A. A. Brill. *The Basic Writings.* New York: Modern Library, 1938, pp. 179–549.

———— (1905a). *Three Essays on the Theory of Sexuality,* tr. J. Strachey. London: Imago, 1949.

———— (1905b). Wit and Its Relation to the Unconscious, tr. A. A. Brill. *The Basic Writings.* New York: Modern Library, 1938, pp. 631–803.

———— (1911). Formulations Regarding the Two Principles in Mental Functioning. *Collected Papers,* 4:13–21. New York: Basic Books, 1959.

———— (1911–17 [1911–15]). Papers on Metapsychology. *Collected Papers,* 4:13–170. New York: Basic Books, 1959.

———— (1914). On Narcissism: An Introduction. *Collected Papers,* 4:30–59. New York: Basic Books, 1959.

———— (1915a). Instincts and Their Vicissitudes. *Collected Papers,* 4:60–83. New York: Basic Books, 1959.

———— (1915b). The Unconscious. *Collected Papers,* 4:98–136. New York: Basic Books, 1959.

———— (1917 [1915]). Metapsychological Supplement to the Theory of Dreams. *Collected Papers,* 4:137–151. New York: Basic Books, 1959.

———— (1920). *Beyond the Pleasure Principle,* tr. C. J. M. Hubback. London: Hogarth Press, 1948.

———— (1924). The Economic Problem in Masochism. *Collected Papers,* 2:255–268. New York: Basic Books, 1959.

———— (1926 [1925]). *The Problem of Anxiety,* tr. H. A. Bunker. New York: Psychoanalytic Quarterly & Norton, 1936.

———— (1931). Female Sexuality. *Collected Papers,* 5:252–272. New York: Basic Books, 1959.

———— (1933). *New Introductory Lectures on Psycho-Analysis,* tr. W. J. H. Sprott. New York: Norton.

———— (1937). Analysis Terminable and Interminable. *Collected Papers,* 5:316–357. New York: Basic Books, 1959.

Gill, M. M. (1945). Paranoia, Homosexuality, and Aggression. Unpublished ms.

Hart, H. H. (1952). The Meaning of Passivity. *Psychiat. Quart.,* 29:595–611, 1955.

Hartmann, H., Kris, E., & Loewenstein, R. M. (1946). Comments on the Formation of Psychic Stucture. *Psychoanal. Study Child,* 2:11–38. New York: International Universities Press.

————, Kris, E., & Loewenstein, R. M. (1949). Notes on the Theory of Aggression. *Psychoanal. Study Child,* 3/4:9–36. New York: International Universities Press.

Hendrick, I. (1942). Instinct and the Ego during Infancy. *Psychoanal. Quart.,* 11:33–58.

———— (1943a). Work and the Pleasure Principle. *Psychoanal. Quart.,* 12:311–329.

———— (1943b). The Discussion of the "Instinct to Master": a Letter to the Editors. *Psychoanal. Quart.,* 12:561–565.

Hendricks, R. C. (1952). Review of J. Dollard and N. E. Miller, *Personality and Psychotherapy. Psychoanal. Quart.,* 21:243–244.

Jekels, L. (1913). Einige Bemerkungen zur Trieblehre. *Int. Z. Psychoanal.,* 1:439–443.

Jones, E. (1929). Fear, Guilt and Hate. *Papers on Psycho-Analysis,* 5th ed. Baltimore: Williams & Wilkins, 1948, pp. 304–319.

Klein, G. S., & Schlesinger, H. (1949). Where Is the Perceiver in Perceptual Theory? *J. Pers.,* 18:32–47.

Knight, R. P. (1940). The Relationship of Latent Homosexuality to the Mechanism of Paranoid Delusions. *Bull. Menninger Clin.,* 4:149–159.

———— (1946). Determinism, "Freedom," and Psychotherapy. *Psychiatry,* 9:251–262.

Kris, E. (1939). On Inspiration. *Psychoanalytic Explorations in Art.* New York: International Universities Press, 1952, pp. 291–302.

———— (1950). On Preconscious Mental Processes. *Psychoanal. Quart.,* 19:540–560.

Lewy, E., & Rapaport, D. (1944). The Psychoanalytic Concept of Memory and Its Relation to Recent Memory Theories. *This volume,* Chapter 12.

Masserman, J. H. (1946). *Principles of Dynamic Psychiatry.* Philadelphia: Saunders.

Rapaport, D. (1942). *Emotions and Memory,* 2nd unaltered ed. New York: International Universities Press, 1950.

———— (1950). Review of N. Wiener, *Cybernetics, or Control and Communication in the Animal and the Machine. This volume,* Chapter 29.

———— (1951). States of Consciousness: A Psychopathological and Psychodynamic View. *This volume,* Chapter 33.

———— (1952). Review of O. H. Mowrer, *Learning Theory and Personality Dynamics. This volume,* Chapter 37.

———— (1953a). Review of J. Dollard and N. E. Miller, *Personality and Psychotherapy: An Analysis in Terms of Learning, Thinking, and Culture. This volume,* Chapter 43.

———— (1953b). On the Psychoanalytic Theory of Affects. *This volume,* Chapter 41.

Schilder, P. (1924). *Medical Psychology,* ed. & tr. D. Rapaport. New York: International Universities Press, 1953.

———— (1942). In Search of Primitive Experience. *Mind: Perception and Thought in Their Constructive Aspects.* New York: Columbia University Press, pp. 3–6.

Silberer, H. (1912). On Symbol-Formation. In *Organization and Pathology on Thought,* ed. & tr. D. Rapaport. New York: Columbia University Press, 1951, pp. 208–233.

45

BOOK REVIEW

Ernst Kris, *Psychoanalytic Explorations in Art* [1]

This volume collects fourteen essays, written by the author over a period of more than twenty years, concerning the nature of art as elucidated by psychoanalytic methods, concepts, and theories. Except for the introductory essay which has been rewritten and considerably expanded, and a hitherto unpublished essay which is added to the third as an appendix, these essays are reproduced largely unchanged. They have, however, been provided with annotated footnotes which give an orientation to the relevant literature of recent years, and to some extent interrelate the essays collected here. The choice of this form of publication unfortunately results in some redundancy and lack of cohesiveness.

Those familiar with the psychoanalytic literature—particularly with the trials and tribulations of the psychoanalytic investigator who wants to shed some light on the nature of art, the artist, the art product, and the effect of art on the audience—will not fail to be impressed with this volume. The very persistence in one field of study—rare in the literature since Freud—is in itself striking. A sustained attempt to do more than decipher the latent meaning of the manifest art product and then relate that meaning to the artist's life is—to say the least—still infrequent. The vigilance and sensitiv-

[1] New York: International Universities Press, 1952.

First published in The International Journal of Psycho-Analysis, *35:362–364, 1954.*

ity with which material is gathered, from such varied fields as ancient biography, aesthetics, art criticism, subjective accounts of artists' experiences, historical accounts of psychotic artists and their products, clinical observations of psychotic artists and their products, psychoanalytic observations and others, have succeeded in culling material for future work and have provided hints for future investigators as to where and how such material may be found.

The merit of Dr. Kris's studies is thrown into relief when set against the background of the major trend of psychoanalytic studies of artists and their works. This major trend, which has become standardized in the decades since Freud's discussions of Leonardo da Vinci and Jensen's *Gradiva,* consists of several more or less parallel running prescriptions:

(1) Study a work of art and infer from it the basic—and omnipresent—wishes and/or conflicts it seems to imply. Assume then that these are unconscious wishes and/or conflicts of the artist, and infer that he had some sort of access to his own unconscious processes and that the audience reacts to his expression of them. Thus, you may assert that you have contributed to the verification of truths discovered by psychoanalysis by means independent from its technique; and that you have contributed to the understanding of the effect of the art work on the audience. Dreams, songs, myths, ambiguities, paradoxes, slips of the tongue and other parapraxes incorporated in the work of art will serve you particularly well in reaching such conclusions.

(2) If you are more thorough you will turn to the life history of the artist, and if you are lucky or undaunted you will find material in it which confirms the inferences concerning wishes and conflicts that you have drawn from the artist's work. If you are especially careful, you will locate the work of art in the life course of your artist and show that his experiences are used in relation to his conflicts and wishes in the same way that day residues are used in relation to the latent thought in dreams. Study of several works of the same artist, set against the background of his life's course, may permit you to make inferences regarding the various ways in which he coped with his conflicts at various points of his life.

(3) If you are bent upon being up to date, you will not be satisfied with searching for wishes and conflicts but, duly equipped with the knowledge about defenses and their multiple layering, you will look for and find those in the work of art. And these too can be confirmed—with luck or sufficient arbitrariness—by the life history. This pursuit is particularly rewarding when the artist conceived his work while in analysis.

(4) But you may be bolder and may want to go beyond Freud (and not only in pursuing the above lines more thoroughly) who thought that we had no means of tackling the core of the artist's genius. Then you will gather evidence as to the basic conflict common to all artists. (The oral conflict is a particularly suitable one, but exhibitionism may do.) In this pursuit you

may or may not want to mix in defensive character-forming processes. At any rate, you must carefully avoid defining your pursuit as "the vocational choice" of the artist, because that might involve you in complex cultural and social considerations which would impede you in establishing connections as time-honored as those between aggression and the vocations of soldiery or butchery, urethral erotism and the vocation of the arsonist or fireman, etc.

Dr. Kris—while he demonstrates in his "Prince Hal's Conflict" that he is master of these techniques—is not satisfied with these tried recipes alone. He drives home the theses that: (1) the problem art poses for psychoanalysis is not that of the commonalities but that of the differences between art work on the one hand and dream and daydream on the other—that is, the problem is that of the form; (2) the problem art poses for psychoanalysis is not just that the art work is a particular expression of, or defense against, wishes and conflicts, but rather what the cathectic economics of this particular expression are.

Thus, he is interested in the dynamics of the experience of artistic invention (Chapters 13, 14) and of the enjoyment of art (Chapters 6, 7, 8), rather than in the relation between the lives and the works of artists. He studies the style rather than the content of the art work, and the communicative rather than the self-expressive characteristics of it; to do this he turns to the art of psychotics (Chapters 3, 4, 5) and to criticism; that is, the study of style (Chapter 10) in which he finds the equivalents, for his purpose, of "the missing links" for the student of evolution.

But these points do not exhaust the merits of this volume. The persistent attempt to gather material is accompanied by an equal persistence in formulating assumptions and theories to account for the material. And this is the crux of the matter: Kris's theories, at one and the same time, are both steeped in what might be called id psychology and are building stones for present-day psychoanalytic ego psychology. Our understanding of art is still scanty, and the question *how much* Kris's contributions have advanced it will be debated for some time. What will probably not be debated is this: Kris has advanced our understanding of art. He alone has shown persistently that the demonstration of the expression of various id tendencies and defenses in works of art does not *per se* explain art, and that an oral complex *per se* does not explain an artist. Furthermore he has pointed to and used new approaches to the understanding of art. In doing so he has developed new conceptual means and these have proved to be both contributions to ego psychology and introductions of ego psychology into the study of art.

What are the main theses developed by Kris?

(1) The artist's "repressions" are more flexible than those of other people. Artists have easier access to "id material" and also are able to subject this material to an ego synthesis.

(2) Art developed from magic action into a form of communication. In psychotic artists, art regresses from communication to magical action.

(3) Artistic invention or inspiration is a temporary "regression in the service of the ego," that is, an ego-controlled regression, after which the material which has become available to the artist, and which abides by the rules of the primary process, is subjected to synthetic elaboration by the secondary process.

(4) Artistic creativity is fundamentally a passive (regressive) inspirational process; but it also implies active elaboration of the passively attained material.

(5) The concepts of "bound energies," "neutralized energies," and sublimations are not synonymous, and all three are necessary for the conceptual representation of creative activity and of the audience's reaction to its product.

Since several of these essays have not been available in English until now, and since the various materials Kris treats of attain quite a different significance once they can be surveyed synoptically, and, finally, since the literature of ego psychology is extremely fragmentary and scattered, this volume fulfills a real need. Yet this reviewer cannot forgo an expression of regret that we have not been given a unified presentation of all this material and of the theoretical views which inform it. The introductory essay on "Approaches to Art" and the final one "On Preconscious Mental Processes" present the author's views to a considerable extent, but they do not give what would be offered by a systematic presentation, even if much more condensed than the present volume.

The reason for forgoing a systematic representation of this material may be conjectured: our psychoanalytic understanding of art is limited and a systematic presentation of explorations toward it might seem premature. The author is keenly aware of these limitations, and indeed one of the merits of this volume is that it does not hesitate to point out the gaps in our knowledge. He reminds us that so far we have no way of approaching an understanding of the genius; that so far we have no real understanding of the "vocational choice" of the artist; that a psychology of style is simply nonexistent; that the exploration of the dependence of the work of art on society, culture, and contemporary setting has as yet barely begun. If a critic may be permitted to bring solace, I would say this situation might well be remedied by the study of, and the psychoanalytic re-evaluation of, literary and art criticism and what it has discovered about style, an avenue just barely opened by Kris (Chapter 10); and by the application of the approach Ginsburg, Ginzberg et al. have opened to vocational choice and of the ego-psychological concepts Erikson has developed for the treatment of complex psychosocial phenomena.

The psychoanalytic investigator and student is given, in this volume, a collection of one of the sources of the concepts and thinking of present-day ego psychology. The broad range of materials for sources of, avenues to, problems in, and concepts for art by psychoanalysis, collected in this volume, is more likely to stimulate explorations in the psychology of art and to set the contemporary standard for it than any other contribution since Freud's early work.

46

MEMORANDUM ON
GROUP THEORY

> This memorandum was addressed to the group-research project team of the Austen Riggs Center, to which Rapaport was a consultant. Although clearly not intended for publication, it is included here not only for its intrinsic merit as a statement about group processes, but because it is the only generalized statement Rapaport ever wrote on a topic which interested him greatly and which—despite his disclaimer—he obviously had thought a great deal about. His interest in these matters was doubtless related to his political activity in his earlier years and his continuing concern with social processes—M.M.G.

I wish I knew enough about group dynamics to formulate a cohesive statement of those theoretical propositions of group dynamics which are relevant to our problem. Regrettably, I have no such knowledge. Thus, I will speak about groups and problems as I understand them.

As I see it, there are several general questions implied in our problems: I. What is a group and how can it be characterized? II. How do groups change and how can changes in them be induced? III. How do group changes affect individuals and how do individual changes affect the group?

Written in August and September 1954. Published here for the first time.

I. WHAT IS A GROUP AND HOW CAN IT BE CHARACTERIZED?

What is a group? It seems to me that this question is equivalent to: In what way does a number of people incidentally met differ from a group? It seems to me that the difference, while it usually appears to be qualitative, is actually quantitative and relative. A Scout Troup is a group as compared to the people in a bus between Stockbridge and Pittsfield. Clearly, if dispersed, the Scout Troop will regather, while the bus group may never do so. The former has well-known bylaws, the latter does not seem to have them. But: note the relative constancy of the people boarding the bus at 7:00 A.M. or 8:00 A.M.; note also that there is an unwritten code of bus behavior which, when broken, is resented. The difference is rather that

(A) The forces that gather the Scout Troop are apparently more uniform and formalized than those individual aims of locomotion which gather the bus population. (Note, however, that the common Scout goal covers a great variety of individual activations, and the individual aims of locomotion of the bus travelers at 7:00 A.M. are also expressible by and large by the common denominator "going to work.")

(B) The Scout rules are more specific and explicit than the bus-traveler ethos.

Note also that if the bus gets stranded in a flood, its travelers immediately become a somewhat more tightly knit group: mutually reassuring, commiserating, supply sharing, escape planning, etc. They may, indeed, if the emergency lasts long enough, form lasting relationships and get together for anniversary meetings.

Groups are thus characterized by forces that hold them together, which may be more internal to the group or may be more restraining forces confining the group members together:

1° *The degree and quality of cohesiveness (and permanence) is thus one of the salient characteristics of the group.* (Quality here refers to internal and restraining forces only.)

Scouts, as well as bus travelers, abide by a code of behavior. This code may be of various degrees of explicitness and implicitness, specificity or generality, may be exclusive to the kind of group or be part of a more general code.

2° *The explicitness versus implicitness, specificity versus generality, the exclusive ownership of versus the derivativeness from a more general one of the* GROUP CODE *is a salient characteristic of a group.*

The Scouts have a Troop leader, the bus travelers have a driver. These provide leadership, are guardians of the code, but the former's rôle is more variegated than the latter's. In both Scout and traveling groups spontaneous leadership may arise.

3° *Leadership (spontaneous and/or pre-established) quality and extent (versatility of the rôle) is a salient characteristic of a group.*

4° *A group is also characterized by a common past which may or may not be formalized by institutions and tradition.*

(Some people's customary place on the bus may be respected; it is neighbors who usually speak to each other, etc.; in comparison, Scouts have highly formalized and institutionalized traditions.)

5° *A group may also be characterized by its structure: subdivisions, hierarchic relations, channels of communication, etc.*

(The military and the Scouts have elaborate structures of this sort, the bus population has hardly any.)

5a° *Group structure yields further group characteristics such as structure flexibility; rôles conferred; leader-group relations.*

(In a discussion group with changes of topic, the rôles and leader-group relations may change flexibly, while in an army there are few such change possibilities: the rise in the hierarchy itself is prescribed in its route, with high structural hurdles provided for enlisted men, for non-West Pointers, etc.)

6° *Group goals and partaking in the pertinent information also characterize groups.*

(This implies the characteristic degree of the predominance of group goals over individual goals. All people come to groups and stay in them by their individual motivations, but these motivations may be totally unconscious and rationalized as individual goals which are parts of the group goal; or they may be partly conscious alongside the group goal; or they may be predominant and the belonging to the group and the avowal of the group goal may be regarded, openly or surreptitiously, as simply a means to reach the goal of the individual. All combinations of these forms are possible.)

7° *A group is also characterized by a give-and-take balance:*

what the individual is *expected* to give and what *needs* of his are fulfilled (by the group and/or its other members).

7a° *The group may also be characterized by the balance of renunciations and gratifications demanded and afforded.*

(This point implies group code issues (2°), relationships of individual and group goals (6°), as well as "give-and-take" issues (7°).)

8° *A group is further characterized by its relation to other groups and to society at large.*

((a) The degree of overlapping versus exclusiveness of membership: Early Christians demanded renunciation of family, while an Elk group favors overlapping membership; (b) The degree to which a group is open or closed: the survivors of the G.A.R. versus a Great Books Club—although the latter too has a degree of closedness; (c) Degree of coordinateness and subordinateness: management versus an employee group is an example of subordination, voluntary social-service organizations and religious organizations one of coordination. A state hospital staff and the state welfare group is an example of subordination, the Riggs staff and the state welfare group one of coordination; (d) A common affliction or a common asset serving as a criterion for membership, as, e.g., our patient group versus our therapy staff, a blind group versus an inventor's society—in both the asset or liability is transformed into some kind of group goal. These problems and characteristics are related to 1°, the cohesiveness issue).

9° *Group morale also characterizes a group.*

(See in this respect the discussions concerning morale and responsibility in the research records.)

10° *A group is further characterized by the output of activity,*

and within that output by the balance between two kinds of activity: activity which amounts to a locomotion toward the avowed dominant group goal and activity which ranges from locomotion toward subsidiary goals to apparently random locomotion arising—so to speak—from the mere fact of living and belonging to the group. (The Riggs staff group meets for its staff conferences as a matter of locomotion toward its goal, but it meets for a Christmas party as a matter of living in a group—the same for playing pingpong and gathering for lunch as activities.)

11° *A group is also characterized by techniques possessed for achieving group decisions.*

E.g., a Quaker group has definite procedures, other groups adopt parliamentary procedures, others again are closer to a "leaderless group" type of procedure. What can be "lobbied" in advance and by whom, and what cannot, and who cannot lobby or buttonhole others outside of meeting; what cannot be spoken of (or by whom) at all; what cannot be spoken of in a meeting (or by whom) but can outside—all these are techniques of assuring that group decisions will be reachable but will be reached only about matters which should be subject to group decisions. Obviously these points are all closely related to 5° and 6°, but differ from those in that only part of what this present *group characteristic* includes is actually structuralized in the sense of 5°. E.g., in our patient group meetings the therapist can make a variety of interventions which would be impossible in a parliamentary group: the technique of calling attention to a subjective motivation taking the place of objective consideration is an accepted one and may rule the former out of court. The present point is also related to the issue of unwritten (unformalized) tradition, touched on in 4°.

II. HOW DO GROUPS CHANGE AND HOW CAN CHANGES IN THEM BE INDUCED?

Some of the characteristics of groups enumerated in I. show that changes can occur in groups. Some of these characteristics are amenable to direct manipulation (independent variables); the change of others may come about only as a consequence of changes induced in the former (dependent variables).

This situation is complicated by the fact that the dichotomy of independent versus dependent variables is not one which can be made in abstracto by inspecting the variables, nor once and for all empirically by demonstrating the manipulability of some and the dependence of the other variables. Groups not being isolated from their setting, not being independent from their history and tradition, the manipulability of any variable depends on the conditions. Indeed, it is possible that any characteristic (as a variable) will become manipulable (independent) under certain conditions, and conversely that any characteristic may, under certain conditions, become unmanipulable (dependent). For instance, the morale of a successful group is not encroached upon by attacks upon it, while the morale of a failing group is so encroached upon. The cohesiveness of a bus-traveling group between Stockbridge and Pittsfield can hardly be increased unless they are stranded in a flood, or with the passing of time (i.e., events taking place do increase, within certain limits, the cohesiveness of the group). The characteristics enumerated were: 1° Cohesiveness; 2° Quality of group code; 3° Leadership quality; 4° Traditions; 5° Structure; 5a° Structure flexibility, rôles conferred, leadership atmosphere; 6° Group goals and their cognitive representation; 7° Give-and-take balance; 7a° Renunciation and gratification balance; 8° The relationships of the group; 9° Group morale; 10° Action output; 11° Decision techniques. Moreover, we have to keep in mind that some of these group characteristics, even when the conditions are propitious, change in different ways than do others. (A) Some, such as structures, can be directly changed by decision: e.g., new subdivisions may be introduced by group decision (but even these may or may not "take"). (B) Other changes are such that the group decision can be only of a "we intend" character. This is a self-induced mandate. (C) There are yet other characteristics, e.g., morale, concerning which "intending" them is a symbolic ritual, like holy water. Certain actions tend to maintain them, others to ruin them.

(A) Under favorable conditions the following group characteristics can be changed by group decision: 5° Structure; 8° The relations of the group; this is also possible, less definitely, with 6° Group goals, and parts of 5a°, particularly with rôles conferred, and with some aspects of 2° Group code, and some of 11° Decision techniques. Similarly, in other groups subdivisions, changes of lines of communication, relationships with other groups, are very often introduced by group decisions, though the same may also come about insidiously and spontaneously as a result of procedures seeking their simplest and most effective form. It should be noted, however, that the introduction of such clearly feasible (whenever they are feasible) structural changes does not guarantee that these will "take" and will not become vestigial, empty forms. Such structures must be means of execution of actions which have energy sources behind them. If they do not become such, then the introduction of such structures by decision will have no consequences, will bring about no changes in the other group characteristics, and thus the difference introduced by the change will not make any difference.

Since structures and liaisons are far more tangible and concrete matters (and even they may not "take" when introduced), it stands to reason that though certain group goals, rôles, codes, and techniques may be introduced by group decision, they will be even more subject to the question "Will it take?" Thus, a therapy group may adopt by decision the goal of taking young and promising patients, but it is only partially in their hands to do so. They can exclude older ones, but whether they get young people will depend on their successes with young people, and upon the spread of these successes as their reputation. Moreover, only with experience will they sharpen their judgment and obtain good criteria for the selection of "promising" patients. But thus success and reputation and young patients will come only with time, though the formal group goal was stated clearly. Indeed, this stated group goal may remain an empty statement owing to overriding financial pressures which will force exceptions as to both age and promise. Rôles may similarly be created, e.g., a chairman of a committee, but if the need for the work of the committee peters out, or the person on whom the rôle is conferred does not have the energy to use or find means to take care of the need, the rôle will decay into an empty title. Similarly, the parliamentary rules deteriorate into an empty force in a small club which has no need for such elaborate techniques. In turn, informal free discussion as a technique (leaderless group technique) may break down into a free-for-all confusion if this technique is introduced without preparation, even though it was by group decision that it was introduced. Rôles, goals, techniques, "take" either if they correspond to powerful needs and are obvious answers to this need and there are no adverse dynamic factors opposing them, or if they are carefully and with sufficient time nursed to fit the situation and are proved to be the feasible and sufficient answer to the need. This point is particularly important to spell out more clearly: certain changes remain formal—even if they do fit the group situation and bring about appropriate characteristics for the group—until they come into harmony with other dynamic factors and characteristics of the group. (Such as: the selection or self-selection of the proper person for the rôle can take place, that is, the group becomes ready to allot one of its powers to the filling of the rôle.)

(B) Group decision can imply only the intending of such changes as: 10° Action output; 7° Give-and-take balance; 7a° Renunciation-gratification balance (the same holds for most aspects of 6°, 5a°, 2°, and 11°, which I have just discussed), since these have a temporal course in which they develop and express themselves; thus they cannot be established once and for all. Some aspects of these, therefore, will always appear rather as dependent than as independent variables in such a study as ours.

(C) Group decisions cannot be made about direct induction of changes in such characteristics as: 4° Traditions; 9° Group morale. These—as well as some aspects of the characteristics discussed in (A) and (B) above—can change only indirectly as the other characteristics directly amenable to change by manipulation (and by actual events in the group and in the environment of the group) are changing or are changed. Thus, these characteristics will appear as dependent variables in a study like ours. I would like to stress again that I am trying here only to stake out certain relationships and destinations, without any intention of making the enumerations or the differentiations either complete or precise. To achieve these, further careful conceptual analysis is necessary, and ultimately only empirical study will bring a progressive completeness and increasing precision.

III. HOW DO GROUP CHANGES AFFECT INDIVIDUALS AND HOW DO INDIVIDUAL CHANGES AFFECT GROUPS?

The title of this section does not clearly express or cover what this section should sketch. While I. dealt with group characteristics and II. dealt with their manipulability, or rather the degree of their amenability to change, so far three crucial issues pertaining to groups have not been discussed: (A) The conceptualization of the relationship between individual and group (genetic and structural [1] points of view); (B) The mediation processes in groups, e.g., the mediation between group goal and group action (adaptive point of view); (C) The interaction of forces and the disposition of energies in the group (dynamic and economic points of view).

(A) The conceptualization of the relationship between individual and group (genetic and structural points of view).

(1) Individual genetic proposition: Erikson's theory of society's creating institutions so as to make developing individuals into its own members,

---

[1] [Here and elsewhere in this memorandum, the naming of the points of view has been changed to conform to the definitions in the later article by Rapaport and Gill (Chapter 62)—Ed.]

so as to harness their unfolding energies into the service of the goals and development of society, and so that the exercise of institutionalized behavior toward these developing members fulfills the needs of and regulates the behavior appropriate to the life phase of the mature member, is the ontogenetic background of these considerations.

(2) Group genetic proposition: The development of a group consists in the development of structures and mediation processes (and others?) maintaining the group unchanged, and at the same time structures and mediation processes (and others?) which make it possible for the group to undergo such changes as are necessary for its survival and/or optimal function. Among these the structures and mediating processes pertaining to the admission, initiation, and assimilation of new members play a specific rôle.

(3) Structural propositions:

1° The group processes take place in and through the individuals who, at the given time, constitute the membership of the group.

2° The group is not, however, a *congeries* of the individuals who at any given time constitute the membership of the group, but rather represents the fact that these individuals are in a characteristic relationship to each other determined by the group's structure, tradition, cohesiveness, and other characteristics, as well as by the characteristics of the individuals' pregroup relationships and history within the group.

3° The group goal (as well as other group characteristics) may be represented either (a) structurally, or (b) in certain individuals (spontaneous leadership), or (c) in the public consciousness of the whole membership, or in any combination of these.

(a) The predominant structural representation usually becomes ossified and shows maximal resistance to change.

(b) Groups in which at various points various leaders can emerge spontaneously, who are able, because of their personal proclivities, to see and state what is, in a given situation, the direction and the means of locomotion toward the group goal, are of optimal flexibility and of greatest survival power.

(c) The public consciousness is generalized usually only at the beginning and at crisis points of a group—e.g., in militant groups.

4° The forces (and the energy distributions they arise from) which determine a group's locomotion are of three kinds:

(a) Those arising from individual motivations (individual forces);

(b) Those which arise from the relationships of the individuals determined by the characteristics of the group (intragroup forces);

(c) Those which arise from the relationship of the group to other groups or to its environment in general (intergroup forces).

5° Group locomotion and locomotion within the group are probably in general determined (overdetermined) simultaneously by individual, intra-, and intergroup forces.

While it is probable that a variety of relative dominance relationships may obtain between these three types of forces, it appears that one such relationship has a salient rôle in group processes. This is that relationship in which intergroup forces play a selector rôle over intragroup forces, and intragroup forces a selector rôle over individual forces. (In a nation which is to survive in a crisis, usually that party comes to rule which advocated a policy practicable within the given international situation.)

(B) The mediation processes in groups (adaptive point of view).

1° The point this section is to make will probably come into view most easily if we reconsider the distinctions made in II. between various group characteristics in regard to the degree of their direct amenability to change. II.(C) points out that 4° Traditions and 9° Group Morale are least amenable to such change (under average conditions). Therefore, it will be clear that building or changing traditions and morale will have to occur by creating or changing group characteristics which are more amenable to direct change. It will be obvious that here mediating processes will take place which, under favorable conditions, will result in the development or change of traditions or morale. It will also be obvious that, in a group of any permanence, structures (routine procedures, organizational divisions, divisions of labor, rôles, watchdog positions, symbols, etc.) will also be created which will assume a perpetual mediating rôle.

2° But the concept of mediation can readily be elucidated from another vantage point also. Let us assume that changes take place in the environment of the group, that is, the intergroup relations change, and that this change is of vital importance to the group. How will the group take cognizance of these changes and how will it react to them? Clearly, the individual would take cognizance of them through his senses and would react in behavior (including speech), but here too there is a mediation question, from perceiving to evaluating and from evaluating to deciding and from deciding to acting. The group too has sense organs: in some groups these are of the "ambassador" or spy type, in others of the watchdog or patrol type, in yet others there is no such division of labor and all group members' sense organs are involved, with the addition that the information obtained goes either by a division of labor to a functionary of the group, or without such division of labor to the group when and as assembled. The same is true of the executive function, where there may also be a greater or lesser degree of division of labor. At any rate, we see that various institutions serve to mediate information to the group and execution of action by the group. The mediation is thus a matter of the formation of structures and structuralized procedures in the long run, though it may be a step-by-step decision of the total group in the course of the development of the group.

3° Just as an individual is not always conscious of his goals, interests, etc., the group's goals, interests, and other characteristics are not as a rule constantly represented in all the individual members' consciousness. Either institutions (the memory man of the Indian tribe) or individual initiative will ensure that these goals, interests, etc., are taken care of automatically or are brought to the consciousness of the whole membership for group decision about group action toward the goal or in safeguarding group interest. This topographic[2] consideration too brings into relief the issue of mediation. Expressed in common-sense terms: in groups it is not enough to state what end condition, result, achievement, morale, goal, would be desirable, nor is it enough to convince all members of this desirability. Crucially important seems to be the social invention which makes the group locomote toward what is desirable. To convince a group membership that the group needs money is only a preliminary. To design a social technique by which they will contribute it from their own pockets in painless and feasible installments, or by which they can earn it or acquire it in a way which is feasible, is the solution. To say that our patients should accept more responsibility is pious preaching and a sentiment just as laudible as "we are all against sin"; the crux of the matter is to design social inventions which make responsibility-taking feasible and necessary. These social inventions will have the character of mediating processes and structures. Thus, while it is true that consciousness of group goals is an essential ingredient of many group characteristics guaranteeing survival, consciousness of these alone may be of no more positive value in the group than is the consciousness to the obsessional patient of all the possibilities amongst which he cannot choose. Consciousness and conscious intending will not transform a group characteristic not amenable to direct change: that will take new mediating social inventions.

(C) The interaction of forces and the disposition of energies in the group (dynamic and economic points of view). Structural propositions 4° and 5° anticipated some of the economic and even some of the dynamic propositions, but here we will have to restate them and introduce further such propositions:

Economic proposition 1°

We distinguish energies originating intraindividually, intragroup, and intergroup.

Economic proposition 2°

Moreover, it will probably be necessary to distinguish among the intraindividual energies those which are only channeled (id forces?) from those which are induced by intra- and intergroup potential differences. (Individual drives which happen to be in the direction of group locomotion versus ego energies mobilized by decisions under the influence of the group.)

Economic proposition 3°

It will probably also be necessary to distinguish among intragroup energies which are:

2 ["Topographic" here apparently refers to "relationship to consciousness" as later clarified by Rapaport and Gill (Chapter 62; Gill, 1963). Rapaport goes on to discuss the bearing of the topographic consideration on an adaptive issue and the structuralization of the solution of such an issue—Ed.]

(1) potential differences between individual and group or subgroup;

(2) potential differences between subgroups;

(3) potential differences between subgroup and group (examples: (a) dominance struggle of a leader; (b) rivalry of subgroups; (c) rebellion or separation of a subgroup).

Economic proposition 4°

Finally, it will probably be necessary to distinguish among the intergroup energies which are:

(1) potential differences between the group and its environment at large;

(2) potential differences between the group and a certain other group or a specific set of other groups.

Dynamic proposition 1°

One of the crucial interactions of the individual, intragroup, and intergroup forces is that in which the intergroup forces act as selectors of intragroup and/or individual forces, and the intragroup forces act as selectors of individual forces. (This selector function is a subject matter for empirical exploration. The way it seems to work is that the selector force does not itself cause the locomotion but rather uses the selected forces to cause it, somehow neutralizing the other forces [from among which the selected force was singled out] which would tend to prevent locomotion or to promote locomotions in other directions. E.g., the Gestapo used selected elements in various concentration camps to run "internal" governments in the direction of maximal mutual debasement of the inmates.)

Dynamic proposition 2°

Selector forces can also induce forces in the organization over which they act as selectors. Such induction is conceived in the sense of electrical induction: no new energies are created in the group; existing group energy is so reorganized as to manifest itself as force and become usable for work, that is, action. The induced energy will be referred to here as surplus energy supply, and energies at the disposal of the ego will be considered as an example of this, in contrast to the id drives discussed in Dynamic proposition 1°. It is assumed that a group has, besides the energies necessary for locomotion toward the group goal, surplus energy too for other functions such as those which raise group morale without being locomotion toward a group goal. This is conceived parallel to the individual's having energies for hobbies also, and not only for indispensable life-goal pursuits.[3]

Dynamic proposition 3°

It is probable that in conceptualizing group action we will have to conceive of it as always occurring through individual actions and thus always

[3] [One might well question the restriction of "surplus" energy to ego energy. Perhaps Rapaport considered it a logical conclusion in the light of the peremptory nature of id energy, which presumably *must* be discharged, and in that sense cannot be "surplus" or "unused"—Ed.]

involving individual energies. If so, then the concepts of selector and inductor forces, as well as those of selected and induced forces, would have a central rôle in the theory of group action, and the conceptions of selection and induction would appear as central dynamic concepts of the theory of group action.

Dynamic proposition 4°

Conflict in the group arises (a phenomenology of the manifestations of conflict within the group does not so far exist; I am taking here the stand that a lack of declaration or of locomotion toward the group goal, as well as all other forms of disruption of group function not otherwise explained, are results of conflict) from two main sources: (1) clash between and combination of individual, intragroup, and intergroup including selected and induced forces; (2) clash between structure and forces. Keeping in mind that structures too may serve as selectors (e.g., any time-honored social institution will rally individuals of conservative bent to its support against its attackers), we can see one form in which structure and forces clash. It seems that some dynamic constellation like this underlies the great survival value of institutions and traditions.

Dynamic proposition 5°

One of the crucial dynamic conflicts within the group is the clash of the institutionalized rôle with the individual force of the person who fills the rôle. In such cases the individual may fall from his general rôle of group member, violate the group code; or he may fall from his special rôle and thus discredit and/or misuse his office.

REFERENCE

Gill, M. M. (1963), Topography and Systems in Psychoanalytic Theory. *Psychol. Issues,* No. 10.

47

CLINICAL IMPLICATIONS OF EGO PSYCHOLOGY

> Although Rapaport dealt with theory in a far more
> sophisticated way in his published papers, this hith-
> erto unpublished lecture is presented here because it
> makes so clear the relevance of theory to specific
> clinical problems—a relevance that is not always
> apparent in his more theoretical writings. It also illus-
> trates Rapaport's facility in adapting his presentation
> to circumstances, his ability to simplify without undue
> distortion—M.M.G.

I assume that in talking about ego psychology here I can take it for granted
that it is familiar to most of you and therefore I will discuss mainly some
clinical implications. However, I would like to spend the first third of my
presentation on certain concepts of ego psychology, so that I can afterward
talk more easily about things clinically important. What is ego psychology?
In general, it is a term used in contrast to and complementary to id psychology. The great discovery of psychoanalysis was a thoroughgoing psychic determinism in all behavior. This consideration of motivation had a huge im-

*Presented at the staff conference of the Mental Hygiene Clinic, Veterans Administra-
tion, Los Angeles, California, March 4, 1954. This paper is published here for the
first time.*

pact upon psychiatry, psychology, and clinical psychology. In the course of the search for the motivation of behavior, we forgot or neglected for a long time our interest in matters not motivational. In the amoeba, whatever motivating state exists is going to create pseudopods. It will reach out, pull in, etc. But it has a nucleus which does not change with motivation. Human behavior has many features comparable to the nucleus of the amoeba: for instance, what we today call inborn ego apparatuses, namely, motility, perception, memory, and the threshold apparatuses. The latter define the point at which the organism is ready to discharge a certain tension. My first point, then, is that ego psychology deals with the apparatuses we use in reaching the goal of a motivation. However, this is not all ego psychology has come to represent.

Again we have to look back on what we have learned from psychoanalysis and what has become commonplace in psychiatry, psychology, etc.; namely, if a human being behaved in a certain way we have been looking first of all for his motivation and have come to disregard the fact that behavior is determined not only by unconscious motivation but also certain reality conditions. For example, a cigar can be just a cigar and not primarily a penis symbol. We are infected with a kind of thinking: something peculiar a patient does is immediately interpreted in terms of dynamics, to the neglect of environmental conditions. It is a difficult job to create concepts which take account both of intrapsychological motivations and reality adaptation. How difficult this is will be clear to you if you consider for a moment the aims of treatment. What is the aim of psychological treatment? Is it to liberate an individual from his defenses? We all would agree that liberation from crippling defenses is the aim of our work. In the meantime, however, there is also something we keep in the back of our minds, and some of us may even keep it in the foreground: the patient needs to find his place in society and lead a useful, productive life. What is our goal? Is it liberation of the person or is it fitting him into something? This is a kind of choice which probably should not be made by us. Maybe it could be compared with the choice of the young Hungarian nobleman who was waiting for his wife to deliver. As he was waiting the nurse came and brought out triplets. He put his finger to his nose, pondered, and finally said, pointing to the one in the center, "I'll choose this one." Should we lay down the law and say to the patient, "You've got to quit doing rebellious things and be a good boy?" Maybe the patient's only way to survive is to be rebellious and the only way he can serve as a useful person is to be a very sick, reckless person and the way in which to give him help is to help him feel reasonably comfortable as a reckless, rebellious person. Once you start out that way you are all involved in the problem of social adaptation the way Adler, Horney, etc., were and the danger is that you may begin to forget the intrapsychic determination. The balance between understanding unconscious motivation and finding the social niche into which a person fits is not essentially a paradox, but people have chosen to do either one or the other instead of trying, as present psychoanalysis tries, to reach a synthesis. The problem of adaptation versus the problem of freedom from crippling defenses is a problem of ego psychology.

I would now like to proceed to some points in ego psychology which have direct clinical relevance. I will first present a concept termed by Hartmann "preparedness for an average expectable environment" and labeled "mutuality" by Erikson. Its significance and clinical relevance is in shedding new light on the mother-child relationship. What is preparedness for an average expectable environment? Erikson and Hartmann attempt to collate evidence that the human infant is born so that it is prepared to be able to survive in an average expectable environment. That is, the mother has a receiving apparatus for the signals of the infant; the infant has a receiving apparatus for certain nonverbal signals of the mother; and from the beginning on there exists a mutual relationship by which the infant steers the mother and the mother steers the infant. Inherent in this concept is the idea that it speaks of an evolutionary product, of one which is guaranteed by evolution for this creature, man, who has the longest dependency period of all creatures. His helplessness has evolutionary advantages only because of certain mutual steering devices of mother and child by which this helplessness can be managed. This might seem to be a very abstract concept. What does it have to do with the clinic? You all, I am sure, have heard about the "schizophrenogenic mother," the mother who makes her child schizophrenic. Such concepts as those of Erikson and Hartmann demonstrate that this is an inadequate concept. This is important because if the concept of the schizophrenogenic mother is canceled out, then our outlook on the illness changes and therapeutic work becomes somewhat more hopeful. I would like to try to show you in what sense the concept of mutuality militates against the concept of the "schizophrenogenic mother." If the relationship is mutual, then the relationship between the mother and child is relative and neither party can be blamed. Once you start with this assumption, you hit on clinical evidence which was not noticed around Washington, where the concept of the schizophrenogenic mother was born. The infant who later becomes schizophrenic often displays very early a certain lack of response to signals. Clinically we see these children later as borderline schizophrenics who do not give you any indication of whether they like what you are doing or not. In that type of case, which is called the autistic or schizophrenic child, there is apparently from the very beginning some kind of lack of mutuality, lack of signal giving and receiving. This deficiency then comes into the hands of a mother who herself may have difficulties of some sort. She reacts to his deficit with rejection and guilt, and thereby perpetuates it. It is easy to forget that it is partly the child who made the mother like that and that it is hard to be a mother to such a child. This is an ego-psychological issue for three different reasons: (1) It deals with the apparatuses, namely, the threshold for signal giving and receiving. (2) It deals with the very first adaptation, and it deals with preadaptation on which all other adaptations are built. (3) As the therapist, you will deal with these patients not by approaching this type of problem in terms of motivation but in terms of the problem of re-establishing a human relationship in which the lack of ability to give signals is going to be re-encountered and re-evaluated, in which the desire to give adequate signals may arise for the first time in such a patient's life. No interpretations are going to bridge the original gap in equipment, yet this gap is not irremediable. It certainly is remediable with schizophrenics who before they became schizophrenic had some achievements, and it is remediable even in some autistic children who never developed the requisite thresholds and signals. All of us as children had, in some respects, weak signals. Our thresholds varied greatly, and our mothers, having met our deficiencies, helped us slowly to develop adequate thresholds and helped us to develop a mutual relationship, out of which later in life trust could develop instead of leaving us in a condition of lack of mutuality, the hotbed of mistrust as a fundamental ego tendency. Even before Hartmann and Erikson, Paul Schilder had pointed out that man does not "become socialized" from being first an "egotistic" little wild animal, as the period of enlightenment and even psychoanalysis thought. Schilder asserted that man is a social being from the word go. This is something important to keep in mind when working with a schizophrenic, because if you had to make him into a social being by your work with him, at some point you would give up, unless your megalomanic ideas about yourself are unlimited. Unless you know that he has it in him and you need only to discover and to liberate it, the courage which is necessary to stick it out with a schizophrenic cannot be had. Even this fundamental, primitive, and really remote ego-psychological concept thus has considerable clinical relevance.

Now I would like to pick up another concept, Freud's definition of the ego in *The Ego and the Id* (1923). The first definition that Freud gave of the ego, and the most general one, was that the ego is "a cohesive[1] organization of mental processes" (1923, p. 15). This definition distinguishes the ego from the id, which is not a cohesive organization; drives coexist in it side by side. The superego is not a cohesive organization either. It collaborates with the id in what it is intending and punishes the ego for its intentions. Maybe you know the story about the little boy going toward the candy jar. Before he got there, there was a great clap of thunder and the boy looked up and said, "Good God, isn't one even permitted to think of it?" I suggest that the superego does that in an even more extreme way. The boy would not even have to be sure he was going after the candy; just some slight yearnings and

---

[1] [Both here and elsewhere Rapaport quotes Freud as defining the ego as a *"cohesive"* organization, whereas both the Riviere and *Standard Edition* translations say *"coherent"* organization. Apparently Rapaport felt that "cohesive" better expressed the idea of a *unity,* and we will let his usage stand where it appears, for Freud did speak of the "tendency to unity, which is . . . characteristic of the ego" (1923, p. 64) —Ed.]

punishment would already be there. On the other hand, there is a fluid transition between the ego and the superego in what we call the ego ideal. So the superego is not cohesive either. This definition thus counterdistinguishes the ego from the other structures in the psychic apparatus. Is this all it is supposed to do for us? No, this definition implies quite a bit more. If it is a cohesive organization, then it should be capable of keeping various of its aspects coordinated. It indeed does so, through what we call the synthetic function of the ego. What is this synthetic function and what is its clinical relevance? I will try to give an example. Suppose that among the few ideas I have introduced so far, one is relatively new to some of you here. Let us assume that I tried to present that relatively new idea so that it should not come out of the clear blue sky. But even then the connections in which I presented it were only in my mind and did not yet have a place in your own thought organization. After a while, however, if you are struck by one such idea, it will lodge safely and securely among other ideas you have in your mind. It is not my job to put it in place in your mind. If you had to place it by an effort, listening would be a most difficult job. Actually, neither my nor your special effort places a new idea in its place in your thought organization. It is done quasi-automatically by the synthetic function. The new idea is put together with old ideas rather automatically. True, we can do a deliberate and effortful job of thinking at times, but most of us, most of the time, rely on the synthetic function of the ego in general, and in particular on that aspect of this function which works in thought organization to put things together for us. We say it "fell into place" and we understood. This may not happen while we listen, but maybe not until later; the beginnings, however, are there. The speaker tries to bring the material in and move it into position for that function to grab it and put it into place. What is the clinical relevance of this? First of all, it is relevant in relation to the long-standing discussion of the dynamics of the effect of our most important therapeutic tool, namely interpretation. How does it help? An interpretation brings into a new relationship the existing conflicts and defenses and then leaves it to the synthetic function of the ego to do its job on it. If the interpretation did not take, you work it through, over and over again, applying it with the patient to ever new areas. It is like a big stone which is lodged heavily in a stream. You are trying to get the dirt from around it and start rolling it, leaving it to the stream to lodge it in a place where it will not be an obstacle but an advantage. With schizophrenics we know that unless we bring about a situation where synthetic forces can work again, the job cannot be done, because it cannot be done by the therapist alone. To achieve this is often not a job of interpretation but a job of a different sort, that of creating a relationship that can free sufficient energies with which synthetic forces can begin to work. A knowledge that you can rely on the synthetic forces to come into play sooner or later is actually what can keep you working at psychotherapy with the schizophrenic or even with the neurotic.

I would like to turn now to a third problem, that of autonomy. What is autonomy? First of all, it means that the sensory apparatuses, the motor apparatuses, the memory apparatuses, and the threshold apparatuses are not born out of conflict. These are ego apparatuses, the most important use of which is in searching for the drive object in reality. If one assumes that ego apparatuses are, from the beginning, part of the psychic organization, then the old psychoanalytic conception that ego is born out of id does not hold up. It becomes necessary to assume, as Hartmann indeed does, that the ego and the id both emerge by differentiation from a common undifferentiated matrix. These primary ego apparatuses pre-exist conflict and enter the conflict as independent factors. Although they may be drawn into conflict, they are autonomous from the beginning. But there is also another type of autonomy: if, in the course of an instinctual conflict, new structures, for example defenses, are created, these defenses may persist after the conflict that gave rise to them has long since subsided. They become independent from the original conflict and become secondarily autonomous apparatuses. They become ready-made tools to cope with all kinds of tasks of executive, conflictual, or adaptive nature. Language is a good example. There may be a question about any autonomous apparatus or ready-made tool of behavior, about whether it is a primary, ready-made tool pre-existing the differentiation of ego and id, or is only acquired in the course of the battle of life and then becomes detached from its instinctual, conflictual source of origin.

There is one specific issue of autonomy on which I would like to dwell further. Suppose a person developed a certain defense; for example he cannot show, or even experience, his aggressions. He leans over backward and is oversweet, with a great inclination to be very helpful to all comers. "No, I am not aggressive at all, I am most accommodating." He aims to please. Suppose you analyze that person. Does it mean this person then must quit being a helpful and serviceable human being and become an aggressive bastard? Is this an inescapable implication of therapy? Luckily, human nature is not that way. An autonomy once achieved survives. That is why Koestler is wrong when, in his *Arrival and Departure*, he has his hero arrive on an island as an honest radical and depart from it after being analyzed as a smug Philistine. Man does not happen to be made that way. What is the clinical relevance of this? It is that in a schizophrenic the structures that have been built up in the course of the development of his personality have not been obliterated by his illness. They go into disuse, they become unreachable—just as your sense of humor may be lost for a time when you are in a disagreeable position but returns to you later—but they are not destroyed. Sometimes when we are with a bore, we find ourselves to be just as big a bore as our counterpart. You know the situation, don't you? Does it mean that we have lost all the structure we have achieved, all the knowledge, all the interest? We do not lose them, they have just become unusable. The same for the schizophrenic patient: his structures just become unavailable to him and your job as the therapist is to help rediscover them. This is what we help them to get at and not something strange that belongs to somebody else. Dynamically as well as therapeutically, this autonomy is of the greatest significance. It is easy to see what is wrong in our patients but a lot more difficult to see what is right, what is preserved. To learn to look for what is preserved is of great importance and is the point driven home to us by the conception of autonomy: whatever was once achieved is never lost. Any achievement noted anywhere in the case history, any valid perception, any single bit of knowledge, any differentiated feeling, any success, indicate to us that somewhere there was once something that can serve again as a nucleus of a new departure, providing we can reach it, free the synthetic forces, and progress from there to further self-discoveries of the best in the patient's essential social nature. This is the point no patient fully expects and that many of us do not fully appreciate in ourselves: there are persevering secondary autonomous structures and there is a basic sociability, and there are primary autonomous ego apparatuses even in our sickest patients.

The last point I would like to dwell on is the issue of identity. I have indicated already that the social adaptation that man makes is outside of our ken while we are hunting only for motivations. The explanation of social adaptation has not been part of our psychoanalytic teachings for a long while. While Adler, Kardiner, Fromm, Horney, and Sullivan were very interested in this adaptation problem, they forgot to deal with the problem of unconscious motivation. The problem arises: What kind of concept can one develop by which both adaptation and unconscious motivation can be dealt with simultaneously? In order to be able to talk about concepts I will dwell on Erikson's concept of identity. Let us assume that to begin with there is a loose ego organization holding together the various thresholds and the apparatuses of motility, perception, memory, etc. As instinctual development progresses, we reach the point where this ego organization has to cope with thoughts, approvals, disapprovals, etc. All of these will impinge on this ego organization and alter it. There will remain a continuity between the original, loose ego organization and the later, more differentiated ones. For this continuity we do not have an agreed term. Sullivan talked about "self." But he used this term for the ego also, while it does not replace the "ego." In the eight stages of man, Erikson attempts to represent both the alterations in ego organization coming about in the course of libido development and the constant features of ego organization and their developmental phases. Hartmann and Loewenstein too speak of autonomous ego development, but Erikson's eight phases are the only consistent attempt to characterize the autonomous course of ego development. To come closer to the clarification of this point, let us turn to another definition Freud gives of the ego in *The Ego and the Id* (1923). According to this definition, the ego is the precipitate of identifications with abandoned objects (p. 36). The point is that in order to sever a relationship to a drive object, we reinstate it in our internal world by identification. Indeed, you know people tell you, "You are just like papa"; you put your coat on the way he does, you spit the way he does, etc. But what of the continuity of ego development? Do a person's identifications simply remain a congeries of all these identifications? According to Erikson, in the course of development the synthetic functions of the ego jell all these identifications into one unity. They do not remain disparate parts within us, such as father, grandfather, Uncle Sam, etc.; they are turned into one unity. It is similar to what happens in the course of studies; when you have studied books by various authors your knowledge of psychology is that of the authors, but you are not going to keep each of their thoughts and principles separate very long. Sooner or later they will yield to a unity: your own view of psychology will jell out of them. Similarly the identity jells together all identifications. Erikson was able to demonstrate that in puberty and adolescence there is not only a recrudescence of the various impulses of earlier libido-developmental phases, but also of identifications which were made in the periods in which they were prevalent. They are revived and pass review. Indeed, these and many new identifications which are made are then jelled into one unity: the identity. But these identifications, their social-role, vocational-role, etc., components, acquired skills and expectations, are so jelled into an identity as to guarantee the person a niche in society compatible with his expectations and self-respect. In other words, you find here in Erikson's concept a flowing together of three different conceptual strains. (1) From id psychology the dynamics of identification. (2) From ego psychology the dynamics of synthesis. (3) From social psychology the dynamics of fitting into a social niche, social role. You can see that here we are dealing with concepts integrating these three strains. This I believe is the core and the most lasting merit of Erikson's contribution.

The clinical significance of this is great. In our society, young adulthood is prolonged and reaches well into the 30s, which is later than—to my knowledge—has ever been the case before in history. Because of this, finding an identity and a definite choice of occupation becomes necessary and is made possible by a social moratorium, that is, by society's acceptance of experimentation. This does not explain the dynamics and I am not endeavoring to go into that now. We do know, however, that what the adolescent and young adult are struggling for is to unify identifications and a lot of roles so as to find the niche that fits them, and thus to gain recognition which will guarantee self-respect. Our first rule in therapy is to interpret what is readily available. This struggle for identity and role definition is usually the most obvious and readily available material in young adulthood.

REFERENCE

Freud, S. (1923). *The Ego and the Id,* tr. J. Riviere. London: Hogarth Press, 1927.

48

PRESENT-DAY EGO PSYCHOLOGY

I. OBJECTIVE

The aim of this paper is to assess the position of Hartmann's and Erikson's contributions in the framework of psychoanalytic ego psychology. The pursuit of this aim encounters obstacles other than its intrinsic difficulties. For one thing, there are no generally agreed-upon answers to the questions: What is psychoanalytic ego psychology? What is Hartmann's contribution? What is Erikson's contribution? For another, we cannot count on a common level of familiarity with either of these in any audience. A third point is that our strong opinions on some of these at times outstrip our familiarity with them.

Therefore, let me—at the risk of repeating common knowledge—give a rough sketch of the history of ego psychology.

II. THE DEVELOPMENT OF EGO PSYCHOLOGY: A SKETCH

Freud's first theory of neuroses—in the 1890's—pivoted around trauma, reality, ego, social morality, defenses, and undischarged affect. The trauma was assumed to be an actual reality event that the ego found incompatible with its own and its society's norms. Therefore, the ego defended itself

Lecture given to the San Francisco Psychoanalytic Society, January 9, 1956. This paper is published here for the first time.

against the memory of the trauma, thereby bottling up the attendant "affect," which then found its expression in neurotic symptoms. If this theory could have been sustained, the doors to the exploration of the ego's relation to reality, of the ego's norms, of their relation to social norms, and of the ego's defensive activities, would have been wide open. The theory collapsed, however, under the impact of the discovery that the seduction trauma was not, as a rule, a reality, but a fantasy.

The Interpretation of Dreams (1900) presented Freud's new theory, which pivoted around the wish giving rise to the fantasy, i.e., around the instinctual impulse. In this theory the ego became a shadowy entity represented in the main by the censorship, which as an intrapsychic agency comprised an indistinguishable mixture of both the ego's own and its society's norms; the ego's relationship to reality was represented by the secondary process, about which *The Interpretation of Dreams* had little to say, in contrast to the wealth of its propositions about the primary process; the ego's defensive activities lost their differentiation and merged into the concept of repression. It would be historically incorrect to say that this theory did not advance ego psychology. Yet it *is* correct to say that in it the focus of interest shifted to the drives, and the development of libido theory magnified this shift still further. The interest shifted to the newly discovered "endogenous" determining factors of human behavior (instinctual drive, libido development, unconscious wish, etc.) and away from the "exogenous" (reality) factors.

Not until "Formulations Regarding the Two Principles in Mental Functioning" (1911) and the "Papers on Metapsychology" (1911–17) introduced by it, do we again find an awakening interest in the functions of the ego and in reality. These papers constitute, among other things, a systematic expansion of the concept of the secondary process in the same metapsychological terms in which it was advanced in Chapter VII of *The Interpretation of Dreams*. The primary process's pleasure principle now attained its parallel in the reality principle regulating the secondary processes. The reality-testing process, by which the reality principle was assumed to operate, acquired specific mechanisms: delay of impulse, consciousness, attention, conceptual organization of memory (i.e., notation), and judgment, all of which turned the ideation of the primary process into thought (i.e., experiment with small cathectic amounts) and drive discharge (i.e., use of musculature) into action. Moreover, consideration of defenses also returned, partly in the form of instinctual vicissitudes (turning upon the self, turning into the opposite, repression, and sublimation), and partly in the form of specific mechanisms of repression. Finally, the detailed exploration of repression and of the relationships between the systems *Ucs., Pcs.,* and *Cs.* in these papers amounted to the exploration of the cathectic dynamics and economics of the ego, and to a metapsychological preparation for the structural conception. All this time, however, the ego and reality remained shadowy entities and only a vague impression of the mutability of instinctual drives by reality vicissitudes attested to their presence.

Then came the 1920's: *The Ego and the Id* (1923) and *The Problem of Anxiety* (1926). While the structural concept of the ego was born in the struggle with the problem of the unconscious sense of guilt as a by-product of the structural conception of the superego, the fact is that it *was* born and again came into the forefront. The form in which it did so is significant. Freud wrote that the relationship to reality is crucial to the ego (1923, p. 48); that the ego is organized around the system *Pcpt.-Cs.* (pp. 27, 29); that the ego is first and foremost a body ego (p. 31); that the ego is a precipitate of abandoned objects and that the abandonment involves an identification (p. 36); that the ego is a cohesive[1] organization of mental processes (p. 15). It should also be mentioned that the new structural concept of the ego implied its unconscious defense and resistance functions, as well as a mechanism by which the ego acquires energies of its own by desexualizing libido. Yet as a witness that this concept of the ego is still one within a context in which drives are the only crucial and ultimate determiners of behavior, the ego is characterized by Freud as a driver who can direct the horse (the id) only where the horse wants to go.

But by the time *The Problem of Anxiety* was published (1926), this had changed radically. The ego appears as an independent agent of great power and authority. It represses the instinctual impulses and has a rich equipment for defending itself against them, namely the mechanisms of defense and the warning signals. How was this change accounted for? The ego, according to this theory, acts under the influence of external reality. It is first of all the role of external reality that has changed. The instinctual danger is reduced to the reality danger that would be met were the instinctual demands acted upon. Ultimately anxiety is on the one hand an inborn reaction, and on the other hand the fear of the danger situation to which it was congenitally or had become ontogenetically attached. Originally this reality danger is the helplessness resulting from loss of the objects (the caretaking person, e.g., mother); later on it is the loss of the love of the object, and later yet the loss of the penis, etc. In these realities the ego has a powerful ally against the instincts and, far from being at their mercy, appears as a structure equipped to anticipate the mounting demand of the instinct and the consequent reality danger. Moreover, the anxiety which the ego originally suffered passively is now at its command to be used actively as a signal for the mobilization of the ego's defensive structures, and for the reinforcement of them by countercathectic use of the cathexes which the ego as a structure has at its disposal. Indeed, since the anxiety signal works by making use of the pleasure principle, the ego now is making active use of processes governed by that principle, to which it was heretofore the passive subject. We should add that the ego here is no longer only *defined* as a

[1] [See Editor's footnote 1, Chapter 47—Ed.]

cohesive organization, but a synthetic function by which this cohesive organization is achieved is also described.

The major effect of *The Ego and the Id* on clinical thinking with regard to the ego was to center attention on its origin in identifications. The main effect of *The Problem of Anxiety* was also to center attention on the ego defenses. The ego's relation to reality, which was implicit in both, remained in the background, and the change in the status of the ego implicit in the latter remained grossly disregarded, even though A. Freud's work did perpetuate all the above-discussed trends of *The Problem of Anxiety*.

This was the situation when there appeared, in the late 1930's, Hartmann's *Ego Psychology and the Problem of Adaptation* (1939), and Erikson's first analyses of play configurations (1937, 1940a), observations on the Sioux Indians (1939), and "Problems of Infancy and Early Childhood" (1940b). In trying to place the contributions of Hartmann and Erikson in the framework of ego psychology, we meet an additional difficulty. Hartmann stated his views in a truly monumental paper (1939), which, however, implies and indicates far more than it states. His later papers spelled out only some of these implications, while adding further elaborations. Erikson, however, groped his way slowly and only his relatively recent volume (*Childhood and Society,* 1950a) provides a more systematic presentation of his views.

III. THE CONTEMPORARY CONTEXT

The main stream of the development of psychoanalytic ego psychology, cursorily sketched above, was not the only relevant context of these contributions. It is worth recalling the date of a few publications which reflect significant preoccupations of the period, though they scarcely affected the contributions here discussed: Horney, *The Neurotic Personality of Our Time* (1937); Sullivan, "Psychiatry: Introduction to the Study of Interpersonal Relations" (1938); Horney, *New Ways in Psychoanalysis* (1939); Kardiner, *The Individual and His Society* (1939). The significant preoccupations of the time were the relationship of psychoanalysis to sociology, anthropology, and psychology. All of these Hartmann shared with Schilder, and Erikson (at Harvard and at Yale) must also have experienced their impact.

These preoccupations raised for psychoanalytic theory the problem: How can psychoanalysis, a theory centered on endogenous explanatory concepts (drive, etc.), give an account of processes which have a palpably exogenous (stimulus) character, such as the impact of social institutions and traditions on man, or, more generally, all the adaptations made by man to his environment? There were four principal possibilities (and innumerable transitory forms): (1) psychoanalysis is limited to those phenomena which can be explained in terms of a drive theory; the rest is the business of sociology, anthropology, etc.; (2) psychoanalysis and its endogenous explanatory principles are omnipotent and will replace anthropology and sociology; (3) a direct relation can and must be created between psychoanalysis as it exists at present and these other disciplines *as they exist* at present, even at the price of jettisoning some of the knowledge psychoanalysis acquired by means of its endogenous explanatory principles; (4) psychoanalysis must be further developed as a theory so that it can meet these disciplines on their own grounds, to their mutual enrichment.

Did psychoanalysis have the conceptual means for such a development? The answers to this question are bound to vary. Those who consider ego psychology a legitimate and successful extension of psychoanalysis will answer with an unqualified "yes," and those of the opposite view, with an unqualified "no." I prefer to answer "yes and no," and to demonstrate how Erikson's and Hartmann's contributions arose from this "yes and no."

First let us consider those conceptual means of psychoanalysis which were available for use in such a development. The above sketch shows that by 1926 psychoanalysis had an ego concept which permitted it not to consider every human behavior, and particularly every response to impinging exogenous stimulation, as determined by endogenous drive principles. The ego was recognized as a rather powerful agent. Reality was no longer regarded as only clashing with the unconscious wish, but also as an agent which, in support of the ego, had a major role in the stability of the psychic apparatus. The ego was assumed to have at its disposal an inborn apparatus, namely, the discharge channels of the fear affect. It was no longer considered a mere equilibrium between endogenous and exogenous forces, but a relatively independent structure.

In centering on ego psychology, however, it is easy to overlook yet other and more deeply rooted conceptions of psychoanalysis that served as firm foundations in the development with which we are here concerned. After all, were not the endopsychic explanatory principles of psychoanalysis (the drives) defined in terms of their objects? Indeed, the outstanding characteristic of drives was that without the presence of certain real objects, no gratification of them was possible. Thus an a priori coordination of endogenous and exogenous factors was built into the drive concept. Moreover, was not psychoanalysis always centrally concerned with the impact of certain social-environmental events upon the endogenous factors? Were not weaning, toilet training, and particularly the oedipal constellation, social events?

But here we reach the point where psychoanalysis did not yet have the concepts necessary for the development here discussed. Surely object relations were always conceived of as reality relations, and weaning, toilet training, and the oedipal constellation were considered crucial social or, if you prefer, interpersonal transactions. Surely psychoanalysis was never merely a nativistic theory. Experience with reality, and particularly social reality, has always played a salient role in it. In this sense it was a genetic theory and a revolution against the psychiatry of the nineteenth century,

particularly against its emphasis on constitution as the central etiological factor of mental disorder. If so, what concepts were missing? Were
not the difficulties merely in the historical emphasis on the fantasy, wish,
and drive described above, which limited the concern for reality? Was not
the difficulty merely the fault of a group of die-hards who took only one
part of the theory, disregarding the environmental-social factors? Both
points seem to have their grain of truth, but the difficulty was more deeply
rooted, namely, in the incompatibility of some of the concepts of the second
and third phase of psychoanalytic theory with an unlimited exploration of
social and reality relations, and in the lack of certain concepts necessary for
such unlimited exploration.

Freud's (1933) thesis, "Where id was, there shall ego be" (p. 112), illustrates the situation. Even as late as 1933 he considered that the ego originates by differentiation out of the id as a superficies under the impact of the
conflict between id and reality. Such an ego could only cushion new id-
environment clashes and could at best serve his three masters, but could not
guarantee either the continuity of the integrated personality or the historical
continuity of human institutions and traditions. These continuities had to be
considered either as imposed by reality, or as guaranteed by the drives and
the (racial) superego, or else as dynamic equilibria achieved again and
again in every individual's instinct-reality struggle. In this conception the
ego originated from conflict, and reality was meaningful only in so far as it
conflicted with the drives. This theory had no concepts to account for non-
conflict experience, nor for any reciprocal adaptive relationship of the psychological organism to the social and geographic environment.

IV. EGO AND ADAPTEDNESS: INBORN OR FOISTED ON ID

It is at this point that Erikson and Hartmann begin to hammer out the
outlines of a new theory which expands the psychoanalytic theory without
jettisoning any essentials of it.

Erikson (1939) wrote:

> . . . the fetus undergoes an epigenetic development, i.e., a step-by-
> step growth of organ systems, each of which dominates the organiza-
> tion of a particular stage: Only the "proper rate" of growth and the
> "proper sequence" of such differently organized stages *guarantee the
> birth of a being properly adaptable to the extrauterine world.*
>
> In considering the ways in which a child gradually is made a typical
> member of a cultural unit into which he is born, it seems worth while
> to emphasize this evolutionary principle of epigenesis which governs
> the unfolding before birth of the organic basis for all behavior and
> continues after birth to govern the *unfolding of an individual's social*

potentialities in the successive encounters of impulse systems and cultural realities [pp. 131–132; italics added].

Hartmann (1939) wrote:

> In his prolonged helplessness the human child is dependent on the family, that is, on a social structure which fulfills here—as elsewhere—"biological" functions also. . . .
>
> The processes of adaptation are influenced both by constitution and external environment, and more directly determined by the ontogenetic phase of the organism [pp. 29–30].
>
> Strictly speaking, the normal newborn human and his average expectable environment are adapted to each other from the very first moment [p. 51].

Thus we find here the following concerted assertions complementary to the usual psychoanalytic propositions: (1) Man is born adapted to an average expectable environment. (2) This adaptedness implies potentialities for further adaptation processes. (3) Both the initial adaptedness and adaptation processes imply the relation to social structure. However, Erikson's stress is already on issues like "epigenetic continuity" and "cultural unit," while Hartmann's emphasis is conceptual: average expectable environment, state of adaptedness, processes of adaptation. At any rate, the new thesis is: the environment does not foist adaptation upon the id; adaptedness of the organism to the average expectable environment is a primary given.

V. THE INBORN EGO APPARATUSES AND ADAPTATIONS

The next question is: How is adaptedness given?

On this point Hartmann is programmatic and conceptually explicit, while Erikson slowly abstracts from his observations and becomes clinically specific rather than conceptually precise.

Hartmann (1939) wrote:

> . . . though the ego certainly does grow on conflicts, these are not the only roots of ego development. . . .
>
> Not every adaptation to the environment, or every learning and maturation process, is a conflict. I refer to the development *outside of conflict* of perception, intention, object comprehension, thinking, language, recall-phenomena, productivity, to the well-known phases of motor development, grasping, crawling, walking, and to the maturation and learning processes implicit in all these and many others [p. 8].
>
> The newborn infant is not wholly a creature of drives; he has inborn apparatuses (perceptual and protective mechanisms) which appropriately perform a part of those functions which, after the differentiation

of ego and id, we attribute to the ego. A state of adaptedness exists before the intentional processes of adaptation begin [p. 49].

. . . these apparatuses, somatic and mental, influence the development and the functions of the ego . . . we maintain that these apparatuses constitute one of the roots of the ego. . . . These components of *"ego constitution"* deserve our attention just as much as the components of drive constitution [p. 101].

No instinctual drive in man guarantees adaptation in and of itself, yet on the average the whole ensemble of instinctual drives, ego functions, ego apparatuses, and the principles of regulation, as they meet the average expectable environmental conditions, do have survival value. Of these elements, the function of the ego apparatuses . . . is "objectively" the most purposive [p. 46].

. . . we assume that adaptation . . . is guaranteed, in both its grosser and finer aspects, on the one hand by man's primary equipment and the maturation of his apparatuses, and on the other hand by those ego-regulated actions which (using this equipment) counteract the disturbances in, and actively improve the person's relationship to, the environment [pp. 24–25].

Hartmann (1939, 1948) concluded that while in animals adaptation is guaranteed by instincts, in man the instinctual drives are alienated from the environment, and the ego is the guarantee, the organ, of adaptedness as well as adaptation. Moreover, with Kris and Loewenstein (1946) he later drew the conclusion that the ego does not develop from the id under the impact of reality, but rather both id and ego differentiate in the course of maturation and development from a common undifferentiated matrix that already contains the inborn ego apparatuses which guarantee adaptedness and adaptation.

Erikson (1940b) remains at first on the level of generality in his epigenetic theme, and, speaking of the child's approaches to his environment and their changes in the course of development, he comments: ". . . in the sequence of these habits the child merely obeys, and on the whole can be trusted to obey inner laws of development, namely those laws which in the prenatal period had formed one organ after another, and now (as these organs search out reality) create one behavior item after another" (p. 717).

This is a maturational-epigenetic conception not alone of libido development, but also of *organs* and behaviors which guarantee adaptation. In Erikson's observations and conception, libido development on the one hand and organ and behavior development on the other hand are two aspects of the indivisible epigenetic process. Indeed his representation of these two aspects appears like a concrete and specific version of the Hartmann, Kris, and Loewenstein conception of the differentiation of the ego and the id from an undifferentiated phase; Erikson (1937) wrote:

The organ-modes, then, are the common spatial modalities peculiar to the appearance of the pregenital impulses throughout their range of manifestation . . .

. . . Pregenitality not only teaches all the patterns of emotional relationship, it also offers all the spatial modalities of experience [p. 178].

The impulses are developed and, as it were, trained at their zones of origin during the (overlapping) stages of child development characterized by the general tendency to *incorporation* (oral-respiratory, nutritional, sensory-tactual), retentive-eliminative *discrimination* (muscular, anal-urethral), and *intrusion* (motor, phallic-urethral). In the course of phylogenetic and ontogenetic development the organ-modes are estranged (because overdue or precocious) from their original zones and can be observed as seeking new manifestations: the organism offers a limited range of safe displacements in habits and minor symptoms; reality allows for certain systems of projections; society accepts the expression through action of a number of character traits [p. 185].

For Erikson the organ modes, as for Hartmann the apparatuses, are the form in which adaptedness and adaptation possibilities are given from the beginning on. But Erikson, since he is clinically specific and leans theoretically on libido development, describes the organ modes first, as it were, in the "undifferentiated phase," in their close relation to libidinal zones. When he characterizes the first phase of ego development dominated by the inborn mutual steering apparatuses of the infant and the caretaking person (e.g., mother) by the term *mutuality phase,* he speaks more directly about these inborn guarantees of adaptation: "His inborn and more or less co-ordinated ability to take in by mouth meets the breast's and the mother's and the society's more or less co-ordinated ability and intention to feed him and to welcome him" (1950a, p. 67).

Again we see agreements in the two views: (1) There are independent sources of ego development: inborn apparatuses and organ modes respectively. (2) The ego and the id emerge from a common undifferentiated matrix. (3) These initial givens of ego development are pre-existing adaptations to the environment in general and to the family and society in particular. These agreements are the more significant since one of these views arose in this country and one in Vienna. One was derived from clinical psychoanalytic work with children (particularly from the analysis of their play configurations) and from the study of two Indian tribes, while the other was derived as much from studies in psychopathology at large as from psychoanalytic work with adults, but chiefly from theoretical considerations in which the systematic relationship of psychoanalysis to psychopathology at large, to psychology, to sociology, and to the philosophy of values played a very great role.

But again we also find differences: Hartmann is intent on theoretical and systematic clarity in recasting old and casting new psychoanalytic concepts (the undifferentiated phase, the innate guarantees of adaptation, the family as a social structure, the inborn ego apparatuses, etc.) and avoids becoming specific in regard to motivations, apparatuses, and the steps of ego-id differentiation. Unlike Hartmann, Erikson does not sharpen his over-all conception into clear-cut concepts, but he is quite specific on the phases of epigenesis, on organ modes as apparatuses, as well as on their actual role in adaptedness and adaptation to society. This contrast becomes even clearer in Hartmann's and Erikson's conceptions of the course of the adaptation process, i.e., in their conception of ego development. I will separate the discussion of their conceptions into one on ego development proper and one on the role of society in this development. This separation is both arbitrary and difficult to carry out: indeed our point is that ego development is inconceivable outside the reciprocal relations with society, and the influence of society on the psychic apparatus is inconceivable without an integrative ego. Yet for the sake of clarity we are constrained to take up the two aspects of this reciprocal relation one after the other.

VI. EGO DEVELOPMENT

Hartmann's (1939) view of ego development is fairly represented by quoting him thus: ". . . to develop the ego psychology begun by Freud, . . . [we must] investigate those functions of the ego which cannot be derived from the instinctual drives. These functions belong to the realm which we term . . . *autonomous ego-development*" (p. 101); ". . . . autonomous ego development is one of the prerequisites of all reality relations . . ." (p. 107).

In speaking about maturation of apparatuses he comments (1950): "We have to assume that differences in the timing . . . of their growth enter into the picture of ego development as a partly independent variable: e.g., the timing of the appearance of grasping, of walking, of the motor aspect of speech" (p. 80).

Hartmann, however close he comes in his concern about maturation and its timing to the epigenetic conception, neither reaches nor explores it. He does make it amply clear, however, that without an autonomous ego development no stable reality relations are conceivable. Like Ferenczi previously, Hartmann sees the core of ego development in the advancements of the secondary process, but he knows much about other forms of ego functions and in his conception the secondary process is not simply imposed by reality but is built upon previously given foundations of adaptedness. Thus Hartmann is in the position to raise and to propose answers to several systematically crucial questions of ego development: (1) Are there, besides inborn autonomous apparatuses, other guarantees for the ego's autonomy from drives, and for autonomous ego development? (2) If there are, what is the process by which they arise? (3) If the ego is autonomous from drives, whence does it derive the energy which it has at its disposal? Hartmann's answers are: there are apparatuses of secondary autonomy; the development of these implies a "change of function" and "automatization"; and the ego has at its disposal cathexes of various degrees of neutralization.

I will take these points one by one in detail, because while Hartmann's conception of autonomous ego development is not clinically concrete, these concepts he advanced go a long way toward establishing the possibility, the means, and the place for encompassing within psychoanalytic metapsychology the observed phenomenological continuity of ego development.

APPARATUSES OF SECONDARY AUTONOMY

> Through . . . a "change of function," what started in a situation of conflict may secondarily become part of the non-conflictual sphere . . . Many aims, attitudes, interests, structures of the ego have originated in this way (see also G. Allport . . .). What developed as an outcome of defense against an instinctual drive may grow into a . . . more or less structured function. It may come to serve different functions, like adjustment,[2] organization and so on. To give you one example: every reactive character formation, originating in defense against the drives, will gradually take over a wealth of other functions in the framework of the ego . . . the results of this development may be rather stable, or even irreversible in most normal conditions . . . [1950, p. 81].
> Some . . . [defense mechanisms] may be modeled after . . . instinctual behavior: introjection . . . probably exists as a form of instinct gratification before it is used in the service of defense. . . . characteristics of the primary process [may be used as defenses], as in displacement [p. 82].

Thus Hartmann shows that by a change of function, a drive (primary-process) mechanism can turn into a defense, a defense mechanism into a means of adaptation: the drive or conflict involved may become part of the conflict-free sphere. He goes further and proposes that such changes of function amount to structure formations and may set new goals, i.e., establish new motivations:

> An attitude which arose originally in the service of defense against an instinctual drive may, in the course of time, become an independent structure, in which case the instinctual drive merely triggers this automatized apparatus . . . , but, as long as the automatization is not controverted, does not determine the details of its action. Such an ap-

2 [In this context, Rapaport would have interpreted "adjustment" to mean "adaptation," between which two terms he carefully distinguished, seeing the former as a relatively passive conformity and the latter as a more active resolution of a reality problem —Ed.]

paratus may, as a relatively independent structure, come to serve other functions (adaptation, synthesis, etc.); it may also—and this is genetically of even broader significance—through a change of function turn from a means into a goal in its own right [1939, p. 26].

It is in these secondarily autonomous structures and motivations that Hartmann finds further guarantees of ego autonomy and autonomous development. Next he is faced with the problem: What process brings these structures about?

THE FORMATION OF STRUCTURES OF SECONDARY AUTONOMY

Hartmann (1939) wrote:

I will discuss first the motor apparatuses. In adults they are organized for certain achievements. In well-established achievements . . . the integration of the somatic systems involved in the action is automatized, and so is the integration of the individual mental acts involved in it. With increasing exercise of the action its intermediate steps disappear from consciousness. To explain this Kretschmer . . . proposed a law of "formular abbreviation" [pp. 87–88].

Not only motor behavior, but perception and thinking, too, show *automatization*. Exercise automatizes methods of problem-solving just as much as it does walking, speech, or writing. . . .

The place of these automatisms in the mental topography is the *preconscious* . . . the term "automatism" here is applied only to the somatic and preconscious ego apparatuses . . . [pp. 88–90].

In using automatisms we apply means which already exist, which we need not create anew at every occasion, and consequently the means-end relations in some areas are, so to speak, "not subject to argument." . . . These apparatuses achieve what we expect of any apparatus: they facilitate the transformation and the saving of energy [p. 91].

Automatization is thus proposed as the process by which apparatus structures are built, and by which the "change of function," detaching them from their original anchorages and turning them into secondarily autonomous ego structures, is accomplished. These explanatory assumptions of Hartmann's are so farsighted that they can well encompass the relevant considerations of psychologists, as well as Erikson's estrangement of the organ modes from their zone of origin. These assumptions, however, raise the question of the origin and characteristics of the energy by which these apparatuses work.

NEUTRALIZED CATHEXES

. . . we assume that once . . . [the ego] is formed it disposes of independent psychic energy, which is just to restate . . . [that] the

ego . . . [is] a separate psychic system. This is not meant to imply
that . . . the process of transformation of instinctual into neutralized
energy comes to an end; this is a continuous process [Hartmann,
1950, p. 87].

Hartmann indicates that the paradigm of neutralization is the process
described by Freud (1923): the identifications built up as structures in the
ego in the wake of object loss, on the pattern of the object, are invested with
id energy, which thus comes to be at the disposal of the ego. Hartmann
(1950, 1955) implies that all sublimations and desexualizations may follow this pattern, and extends this to the neutralization of aggressive energies also. Moreover, he suggests that neutralized energies may originate not
only in this manner secondarily, but may also have an independent source
in the ego apparatuses of primary autonomy. Finally, Hartmann's above
formulation that the automatized apparatuses "facilitate the transformation
and saving of energy" and Freud's suggestion that it is the identification
structures of the ego which bring about neutralization, suggest that the
structure formation by which apparatuses of secondary autonomy are built
and the process of energy neutralization may be closely related to each
other.

Hartmann (1950), in discussing those motivations which are termed ego
interests, wrote:

> The source of the neutralized energy with which the ego interests oper-
> ate seems not to be confined to the energy of those instinctual strivings
> out of which or against which they have developed; other neutralized
> energy may be at their disposal. This is actually implied in thinking of
> them as sharing the characteristics of the ego as a functionally and
> energically partly independent system. We may state that many of
> them (in different degrees) appear to belong to the field of secondary
> autonomy [p. 92].

Hartmann (1950), and also Kris (1950), conceive of energies of various
degrees of neutralization.

Thus Hartmann succeeded in conceptualizing the prerequisites of continuous and undisturbed reality relations. They are: the autonomy of the ego,
primary and secondary autonomous apparatuses of the ego, the process of
automatization as the means of secondary structure-formation, and the neutralized energies which the ego has at its disposal.

We turn now to Erikson's conception of ego development. Here we do
not find the conceptual metapsychological systematizing concern which
dominated Hartmann's contribution. We have already seen that, to begin
with, the epigenetic principle stands in the center of Erikson's conceptual
stage. If we had not noted that his epigenetic concern was with organs in

general and not only with the erotogenic zones, and if we had not sensed that his concern pertained not so much to the erogenous zones themselves as to their modes—which he subsumed together with the modes of the other organs under the concept of organ mode—we might have come to the conclusion that epigenesis was just a fancy word for libido development.

Such a conclusion would have missed Erikson's point. His interest in the organ modes originated in the study of children's play constructions in child analysis and in experimental situations. He was impressed by the fact that the child's bodily (autocosmic) play, toy (microcosmic) play, as well as his (macrocosmic) play with the objects and persons of the adult world, are all patterned (configured) on the organ modes in epigenetic ascendancy (developmental crisis), or involved in a conflict (pathological crisis) (1937, p. 170). The observations showing the general organizing rôle of these modes throughout the life space of the child had a great impact on Erikson's thinking. The patterning of the child's space and time organization by these organ modes made a particularly lasting impression on Erikson the artist. As early as 1937, in discussing M. Klein's interpretations, he wrote:

> Encountering in himself a system of incalculable and truly "unspeakable" forces, the child seeks a counterpart for his inner experience in the unverbalized world of mechanisms and mute organisms. As projections of a being which is absorbed in the experiences of growth, differentiation, and objectivation, they are not as yet systematically described. Their psychological importance *certainly goes beyond sexual symbolism in its narrower sense* [p. 167; italics added].

Clearly the epigenesis Erikson speaks of is not simply libido development. Yet at this point his theory takes the form of an epigenetic chart of libido development, and only the emphasis on the organ modes of the erogenous zones reveals the trend. The epigenetic chart presents, on its diagonal, the ascendant phases: the first oral phase with its incorporative mode; the second one with its biting mode; the anal phase with its retentive and expulsive modes; the phallic phase with its intrusive mode. The horizontal axis represents the epigenetic plan: the sequence of mode ascendancies. The vertical axis represents time. The positions above the diagonal represent the phase-specific ascendant mode's predecessors in, and contributions to, the previous phases. And the positions below the diagonal represent for each ascendant mode its successor in, and contribution to, subsequent phases. Erikson (1937) points out that the zone is surrendered in the course of development but not the mode, and indicates that the modes continue to be used by the child in shaping his ever-expanding relations to reality in general, and society in particular (p. 162). This is not Abraham's oral, anal, phallic character conception in a new form. Here the contributions from a libidinal phase do not *produce* discrete ego equivalents but enter a continuous organized ego development, the epigenetic ground plan of which is realized through the rhythm and succession of phase-specific ascendancies. What is the ground plan and what is the nature of the phases? At this point Erikson cannot yet answer these questions. So far he has discerned only the epigenetic continuity and sequence of the organ modes as distinct from, though related to, psychosexual epigenesis.

This theoretical position, however, soon changes in the wake of Erikson's observations on the Sioux (1939) and Yurok (1943), which enable him to show how the society and its education enter the epigenetic ground plan by "systematically designed educative measures," how each phase of the ground plan of the individual's life cycle both prepares for the later phases and interlocks with various phases of the life cycle of other individuals and with the institutional structure of the society. These demonstrations in turn show Erikson that such an interlocking of the individual's epigenesis with that of others and with societal structure requires a new conception of epigenesis. It must be one in which maturational phase and social response mutually presuppose each other. It is a psychosocial epigenesis, of which mode epigenesis and psychosexual epigenesis are only specific aspects. These demonstrations also made it clear to him that a concept mediating between organ mode and social organization must be found, by means of which the isomorphism between macrospheric and autospheric events can be explained.

He advanced the mediating concept of "social modality" and succeeded in demonstrating that organ modes, in the course of development, turn into social modalities when the social environment provides the opportunities and the approval. For example, the social modalities of "holding" and "letting pass" are derived from the retentive and expulsive modes when the social attitudes centering around retention and expulsion are favorable. Similarly, the social modality of "being on the make" is derived from the intrusive mode of the locomotor phallic phase. Moreover, Erikson showed that these social modalities are effective in as abstract and general aspects of mental life as the spatial and temporal framework of experience.

He also succeeded in discerning the sequence of psychosocial epigenetic phases and in characterizing them by the achievements and failures specific to them. He distinguished eight phases, spanning the whole life cycle. These are familiar to us by now. Listed by their characteristic achievements and failures, they are: trust vs. basic mistrust (encompassing the oral phases), autonomy vs. shame and doubt (encompassing the anal phase), initiative vs. guilt (encompassing the phallic phase), industry vs. inferiority (encompassing latency and early puberty), identity vs. rôle diffusion (encompassing late puberty, adolescence, and the beginning of young adulthood); intimacy vs. isolation (encompassing young adulthood); generativity vs. stagnation (encompassing mature adulthood); and integrity vs. despair (encompassing the last phase of the life cycle—from the onset of old age).

Are these not simply descriptive terms to characterize the outcome of libido-development crises and their solutions? The answer is "no," and the reasons for it are the following: (1) These phase characteristics and their observed dynamics show both continuity and further development when psychosexual development has supposedly reached its final genital form. (2) While the sequence and phases of this epigenetic ground plan are universal, the forms the phases take and the solutions they reach vary from society to society and from family to family. The differences in these solutions are explainable in terms of this psychosocial epigenesis which includes libido epigenesis, but not in terms of libido epigenesis alone. (3) It sheds light on the dynamics of phenomena which, as a rule, remain outside of the scope of psychoanalytic study: psychoses, vocational choice, etc.

Actually, the full import of Erikson's observations and theorizing cannot be assessed without discussing the role of society in ego development. Before doing this, however, let us take stock.

We have seen that Hartmann, in his conception of ego development, elaborated the metapsychological foundation of psychoanalysis so as to accommodate the facts of ego development within it, and to account for them on the basis of it. He was concerned in particular with elaborating the concept of the secondary process, which was the major conceptual representation of the ego in Freud's second theory. He also explored the reality relationships, gave them a conceptual cast, and thus provided a framework for the observations on ego-environment relations within the broader ego psychology abuilding. Erikson's conception of ego development, on the other hand, arose from his effort to account for his observations, and was concerned with the elaboration of the epigenetic view already implicit in the theory of libido development. He extended the epigenetic conception so as to accommodate not only the continuity of drive development, but the continuity of ego development, as well as to encompass the reciprocal relations of the psychological organism and its environment. In the course of these elaborations he introduced the concept of *organ mode* as a link between the libido aspect and ego aspect of epigenesis; and the concept of *social modality* as a link between the ego aspect and the psychosocial aspect of epigenesis.

In spite of differences in emphasis, Hartmann's and Erikson's theoretical contributions are complementary rather than antithetical. In their details, these conceptions are frequently even congruent. Hartmann's concepts of primary and secondary autonomous apparatuses include Erikson's concept of organ modes. Indeed, Erikson's characterization of the development of organ modes as an estrangement of the modes from their zones of origin parallels Hartmann's characterization of the ego-id differentiation. Hartmann considers sublimation a result of secondarily autonomous structure-building, while Erikson demonstrates that the divorcement of organ modes from their zone of origin results in sublimation products. But it is still unclear how broad a segment of secondarily autonomous structures is derived

from organ modes, and what is the nature and origin of other such structures (e.g., defense and control), that is, it is unclear how much broader the
concept of autonomous apparatuses is than the concept of organ modes.

Now we are ready to turn to Hartmann's and Erikson's conceptions of
the rôle of society in ego development.

VII. THE RÔLE OF SOCIETY

Clearly this discussion cannot but retrace the steps of the preceding one. Its
thesis is that human beings are social beings from the very first moment,
and that the reciprocal relation with society is part and parcel of epigenesis,
and thus of ego development.

Hartmann (1939) wrote:

> In his prolonged helplessness the human child is dependent on the
> family, that is, on a social structure which fulfills here—as else-
> where—"biological" functions also. . . . The fact . . . that for the
> small child *the external world is a strong ally against his instinctual
> drives,*[3] is also related to the extensive parental care.
>   . . . Man does not come to terms with his environment anew in
> every generation; his relation to the environment is guaranteed by—
> besides the factors of heredity—an evolution peculiar to man, namely,
> the influence of tradition and the survival of the works of man. . . .
> man lives, so to speak, in past generations as well as in his own. Thus
> arises a network of identifications and ideal-formations which is of
> great significance for the forms and ways of adaptation. . . .
>   . . . the task of man to adapt to man is present from the very begin-
> ning of life. . . . Man not only adapts to the community but also ac-
> tively participates in creating the conditions to which he must adapt.
> . . . the crucial adaptation man has to make is to the social structure,
> and his collaboration in building it . . . . the structure of society, the
> process of division of labor, and the social focus of the individual . . .
> codetermine the possibilities of adaptation and also regulate in part
> the elaboration of instinctual drives and the development of the ego.
> The structure of society decides (particularly—but not exclusively—
> through its effect on education) which forms of behavior shall have
> the greatest adaptive chance. . . . We may describe the fact that the
> social structure determines, at least in part, the adaptive chances of a
> particular form of behavior, by the term *social compliance,* coined in
> analogy to "somatic compliance." Social compliance is a special form
> of the environmental "compliance" which is implied by the concept of
> adaptation [pp. 29–31].

Hartmann, who assumes that ego development is determined by constitution (of both the ego and the id), drive development, and environment,

[3] Italics added.

does not consider society as simply a restraining agent which imposes ego development on the id. He sees adaptation as a reciprocal relationship between the organism and its environment, in which on one side the ego is the organ of adaptation, and on the other society meets the ego by "environmental compliance." Moreover, the organism adapts to a society to which it is preadapted, and which has already been molded by itself and by its predecessors. Clinically these considerations may be illustrated by the well-known fact that a patient's picture of his environment as hostile and persecutory need not be entirely—and may not be at all—a projection. His environment may actually be what he describes it to be, and indeed may have come about in part as a matter of "social compliance" to the patient who "provoked" this. It is possible that the patient may unconsciously have perceived, to begin with, the environment's potentialities for such compliance.

It would seem that Hartmann has fully overcome the limits—imposed by its endogenous explanatory principle—on early psychoanalytic theory's treatment of the rôle of society in psychic development. Indeed, Hartmann and Kris (1945) speak out quite clearly and with few reservations on this in their interpretation of Freud's view:

> . . . Freud clearly stresses the existence of two aspects. He refers to the biological aspect when he states that in tracing an individual's life history we describe some processes that were bound to occur [even if] under alternative conditions . . . [they would have followed] alternative pathways. The other aspect, with far more momentous consequences, concerns the importance of the environment; the object of psychoanalytic observation is according to Freud not the individual in splendid isolation; it is part of a world. Psychoanalysis does not claim to explain human behavior only as a result of drives and fantasies; human behavior is directed toward a world of men and things. The approach of psychoanalysis *in many cases* includes the structure of this world in its scope; and in this sense psychoanalysis is applied Social Science (Hartmann, 1944) . . . a child's "experience," is in psychoanalysis viewed both in relation to the child's biological growth and in its relation to the world around it, a distinction that proves its value, if applied over a long period of observation [pp. 25–26; italics added].

In these last phrases there seems to be no distance between Hartmann and Erikson. Hartmann's clear sight and sure hand in molding concepts are again apparent. So is his lack of concrete specificity. On these issues this lack of specificity turns, in his later writings, into formulations which are either reservations about or reversals of his stand on the rôle of society in the epigenesis of the ego.

In arguing against those anthropologists and "environmentalist" psychoanalysts who fail to realize that the basic modes of psychological functioning cannot show national differences, and after giving a summary of the basic modes of psychological functioning discovered by psychoanalysis, Hartmann, Kris, and Loewenstein rightly assert: "What these assumptions describe is relatively independent of environmental conditions in the same sense as physiological processes are. That does not mean that the processes envisaged appear under all observable or conceivable conditions in the same intensity and/or frequency" (1951, p. 11).

Clearly, anything that is to be accepted as a basic psychological process will not change from the Basutos to the Navahos, and if it were discovered that it did so change, it could no longer be accepted as a basic psychological process. Only those whose view of psychic life is a pure "nurture" view—a Humian view—will fail to recognize any such processes. For the rest of us, Hartmann, Kris, and Loewenstein are right. We are on the quest of such basic processes.

But when Hartmann, Kris, and Loewenstein (1951) begin to discuss "national character differences" it becomes difficult to agree with their view:

> We should like to state . . . that the analyst is likely to be less impressed by the facts and the range of differences in everyday behavior than the anthropologist [p. 18] . . . [the] differences of behavior which are likely to strike the outside observer may be less relevant to purposes of explanation [p. 19].
>
> The development of the doctor-patient relationship during analytic work may illustrate another aspect of the point we want to make. There is little doubt that the way in which the initial contact between the Frenchman, the Englishman, the New Yorker, the Bostonian and the psychoanalyst is established covers wide ranges, e.g., from curiosity to restraint, familiarity to suspicion; certain of these attitudes are more frequent in one group than in another. However, as soon as this superficial and initial contact develops into transference, the differences appear to be much more limited: they concern the way in which the patient reacts preconsciously to his experience of transference, to the modes of verbal expression or rationalization, but according to our clinical experience no significant difference exists in the formation of transference—positive or negative—or in its intensity, structure or essential manifestations [pp. 19–20].

These assertions do not seem congruent with Hartmann's above view of the rôle of society in ego development. If tradition, mores, upbringing, etc., are different in one society than in another, and different in one sociogeographic-economic unit than in another, and if these factors codetermine both ego development and the fate of drives, then there should be—even on the couch—essential differences between the Boston Brahmin and the Texas oilman. Either social differences make an essential difference or they do not. We cannot have it both ways. If they do make such a difference, that difference will also be essential on the couch. If they do not make an essential difference, then why speak of psychoanalysis as an applied social science? A difference that does not make a difference is no difference. I do not mean to imply that the "studies in national character" have discovered these differences. There are various reasons for assuming that, *at best,* they have touched on some of them. But it is hard to know which, if any, of the differences they have found are essential. However, I do mean to imply that the quest for "national character" cannot yet be considered systematically and theoretically unjustified. It would seem that here Hartmann, Kris, and Loewenstein—Homer too nodded at times—either overextended what should be considered psychologically basic and universal, or else prejudged what *can or cannot* be observed in *and* out of psychoanalysis. It is clear that we have before us a problem subject to empirical decision. This attempt to decide it theoretically does not seem justified, and suggests that Hartmann may no longer hold the view on the rôle of society in ego development that he held in 1939. One is reminded here that in the introduction of his major opus (1939) Hartmann wrote:

> . . . other ego functions and the process of coming to terms with the environment . . . did not become the subject matter of research until a later stage of our science. . . . I believe it is an empirical fact that these functions are less decisive for the understanding and treatment of pathology . . . than the psychology of the conflicts which are at the root of every neurosis [p. 7].
>
> It is probable that the study of this conflict-free ego sphere, though it is certainly not without technical significance (for instance, in the analysis of resistance), will in general contribute less to psychoanalytic technique than the study of conflicts and defenses [p. 9].

Hartmann's belief does not seem to be borne out by the present weight of evidence coming from the treatment of psychoses, borderline cases, and autistic children, from the psychoanalyses of character disorders, and even from analyses at large. Beliefs, assumptions, predictions, whether right or wrong, advance the development of science. The Hartmann, Kris, and Loewenstein assertion quoted above is a different matter: it neither seems consistent with Hartmann's view of society's rôle in the development of psychic life, nor does it leave the door open for empirical decisions.

Erikson's conception of the rôle of society in ego development is very different. He tackles the problem unconcerned about the theoretical and systematic possibility of treating, within the framework of psychoanalysis, ego development and society's rôle in it. He is certainly unconcerned with metapsychological issues, and in the beginning even seemingly unaware that he is dealing with ego-psychological issues. Since at first libido theory—and the epigenetic principle it implies—is central to his thinking, he does not

even question whether or not his study of the "configurations" in play behavior is legitimate psychoanalytic exploration.

The empirical starting point toward his theories is at first at a considerable distance from ego psychology, as well as from the rôle of society.
Introducing the report of his first findings (1937), he wrote:

> We tend to neglect the characteristic which most clearly differentiates
> play from the world of psychological data communicated to us by
> means of language, namely, the manifestation of an experience in ac-
> tual space, in the dynamic relationship of shapes, sizes, distances—in
> what we may call *spatial configurations* [pp. 139–140].

His observations soon show him, however, that the play configurations
are molded by organ modes which constitute an "organ language," and that
these organ modes provide not only all the patterns of autospheric behavior, but also most—if not all—patterns of microspheric behavior, and many
of the crucial patterns of macrospheric behavior. It is from this point that
he comes to the crucial—for us here particularly—recognition that organ
modes are methods of dealing with the environment, as well as the infant's
first spatial, temporal, and social modes of relating. For example, in characterizing the first phase of libidinal and organ-mode epigenesis (incorpora-
tive-oral phase) Erikson (1937) wrote:

> . . . at this stage *social behavior* also expresses expectant readiness
> to receive, as is obvious in the rhythm of waiting, crying, drinking,
> sleeping. Reactions to stimuli which require more than the holding on
> with mouth and hands to what has been *offered by the environment*
> remain diffuse and uncoördinated [p. 179; italics added].

Though the first inklings of the rôle of society are here, Erikson still
heavily emphasizes the continuity of the oral dominance in the first epigenetic phase with the embryonic cephalocaudal growth tendencies, the integral unity of the incorporative mode with the oral phase of libido development.

These points are by no means dropped after the observations on the
Sioux and on the Yurok, yet the emphasis changes. It is hard to find a
quotation in Erikson's first Sioux or Yurok papers which conveys the
change of emphasis with the sense of validity which the many details of
concrete observation give. Erikson makes it plausible, for instance, that the
contrast between the Sioux's cradle-board and the unlimited and prolonged
gratification in nursing, and the contrast between this unlimited gratification
and the frustration imposed to prevent the teething infant from biting the
mother-breast, constitute social interventions with the epigenetic rhythm
and particularly with the organ-mode epigenesis, in such a fashion that the
so-modified epigenesis adapts the growing child to rôles, behaviors, cere-
monies, pursuits, and values for which there is a definite place in Sioux

society and its life. For lack of space I cannot quote the details but only a general statement. Erikson (1939) wrote:

> Educational environment, by choosing a focus for its interference with the unfolding set of given human elements [i.e. mode epigenesis], by timing this interference, and regulating its intensity, accelerates and inhibits the child's impulse systems in such a way that the final outcome represents what is felt to be—and often is temporarily—the optimum configuration of given human impulses under certain natural and historic conditions. In thus creating "anthropological" variations of man, instinctive education apparently uses, systematically although unconsciously, the same possibilities for modification which become more spectacularly obvious in the abnormal deviations brought about by deficiency or accident [p. 133].

While "impulses" here are still in the foreground, in the paper on the Yurok (1943) the rôle of society attains an equally prominent place, and the concept of an integrating and integrated ego appears for the first time. Erikson (1943) wrote:

> We expect the human child to bring into life personality potentialities, that is, a variety of potential trait configurations based on the organism *and* [4] the organization in time and space of its basic needs. The potentialities are limited by (1) the evolutionary state of the organism . . . ; (2) the laws of psychological displacement which say that in a human being only a limited and delineated impulse-modification is tolerable (libido economy). Child training, under the influence of an integrated and integrating cultural ego, systematically narrows the number of these potentialities by creating hypertrophies and atrophies, the integration of which is the *cultural* trait configuration characterizing all members of the group. It does so by utilizing that basic polarity of human childhood which makes child care and child training necessary, namely the initial helplessness and prolonged dependence on the one hand, and insatiable desire for independence, mastery and investigation on the other. Concentrating on a few areas of the child's infantile interests, child training develops and thus channels or suppresses them, blocking repression and encouraging sublimation: thus it creates a specific ontogenetic trauma . . . The areas of special educational pressure . . . remain arsenals of strong and conflicting impulses and determine the cultural trait configuration, as well as the nature of individual variations [p. 292].

This clear formulation of the rôle of the society in ego development does not yet reflect how deeply Erikson's conception of it is rooted in the epigenesis of the organ modes which he studied in play configurations. Moreover,

[4] Italics added.

compared with Hartmann's views of the same period, these formulations may sound like libido theory devoid of ego-psychological considerations. The phrase "integrated and integrating ego" should warn us against accepting this impression even if it contains more than just a grain of truth. Yet Erikson's study of the relations between organ modes, behavior modalities, and social ways, traditions, and institutions at this point already amounted to an intrinsically ego-psychological intent, though the author could have claimed with Molière: "I didn't know that all my life I had been speaking prose."

In 1945, however, when synthesizing his observations on the Sioux and the Yurok, Erikson became aware of the theoretical necessity for an explicit ego concept for integrating the organ-mode and modal-configuration conceptions on the one hand, and social tradition, institutions, and economy on the other. Erikson (1945) wrote:

> . . . clinical descriptions, i.e. the description of one or several successive segments of a historical process defines every item of human behavior according to at least three kinds of organization:
>
> (1) The biological one, which reflects the nature of the human organism as a space-time organization of mammalian organ-systems (evolution, epigenesis, pregenitality),
>
> (2) The social one, which reflects the fact that human organisms are organized into geographic-historical units,
>
> (3) The ego-principle, reflecting the synthesis of experience and the resulting defensive and creative mastery (ego development).
>
> None of these principles can "cause" a human event; but no human event is explained except by an investigation that pursues the Gestalten evoked by each principle in constant relativity to the two others [pp. 345–346].

Here Erikson not only arrives at an ego-psychological formulation from his original libido-developmental outset, but also achieves a metapsychological conception requiring the simultaneous analysis of every behavior from several points of view. His first and third organization principles grossly correspond to the classic triad of metapsychological points of view (dynamic, economic, and structural) and seem to include the genetic point of view discussed earlier in this paper. His second principle announces an additional point of view, the social-environmental one, which—though implied—was not explicitly stated by Hartmann. Erikson's formulation of the social-environmental point of view served as one of the points of departure for an investigation in which Gill and I restudied the points of view of metapsychology, and concluded that metapsychology must be supplemented by such a point of view. We labeled it the adaptive point of view (Rapaport and Gill, 1959). Hartmann's initial formulations are the major background and Erikson's above-quoted thesis is the first explicit statement of this point of view. Prior to this, this point of view did permeate Schilder's, and did animate Horney's, Sullivan's, and Kardiner's bold—if lopsided—endeavors.

Erikson is now prepared to face the questions: What is the relationship between the ego of the individual and his society? and, What kind of ego concept is called for to aid the exploration of this relationship? He begins by questioning one of the classic definitions of the ego: "The individual is not merely the sum-total of his childhood identifications" (1945, p. 349). and thus paves his way from an ego conception which is an aggregate of identifications to one which is a "configuration." To express this configuration he coins the term "ego identity." Empirically this concept leans on the observed group identity of primitive societies, and upon the observation that the majority of individual identities are homogeneous with it.

This conception of ego identity serves Erikson in his effort to integrate the somatic, libidinal, ego, and societal contributions to epigenesis. Erikson's (1946) first attempt to define it sheds light on the rôle of the societal factor in particular:

> A child who has just found himself able to walk seems not only driven to repeat and to perfect the act of walking by libidinal pleasure in the sense of Freud's locomotor erotism; or by the need for mastery in the sense of Ives Hendrick's work principle; he also becomes aware of the new status and stature of "he who can walk", with whatever connotation this happens to have in the coordinates of his culture's life plan—be it "he who will go far", or "he who will be upright", or "he who might go too far". To be "one who can walk" becomes one of the many steps in child development which through the coincidence of physical mastery and cultural meaning, of functional pleasure and social recognition, contribute to a more realistic self-esteem. By no means only a narcissistic corroboration of infantile omnipotence (that can be had more cheaply), this self-esteem grows to be a conviction that the ego is learning effective steps toward a tangible collective future, that it is developing into a defined ego within a social reality. *This sense I wish to call ego-identity.* I shall try to clarify it as a subjective experience and as a dynamic fact, as a group psychological phenomenon and . . . as a subject for clinical investigation [pp. 362–363; italics added].

The relationship between the organ modes and social life is implied but not explicitly stated in this formulation. Erikson outlines a program (pp. 381–382) which is to trace the epigenesis of the ego that prepares "the final establishment of a dominant positive ego-identity in adolescence" (p. 383). This program's first realizations appear in "Growth and Crises of the 'Healthy Personality' " (1950b) and in *Childhood and Society* (1950a), which trace the phases of the *psychosocial epigenesis.* Each phase of this epigenesis has the task of integrating those aspects of somatic maturation, organ mode, libido development, social modality, and relation to social institutions which are phase specific.

Again, we cannot go into all the details and will choose for our example the first phase of epigenesis. Erikson (1950b) wrote, concerning the mutual relationship of the newborn and his "society":

> . . . the . . . baby's weakness gives him power; out of his very dependence and weakness he makes signs to which his environment . . . is peculiarly sensitive. A baby's presence exerts a consistent and persistent domination over the outer and inner lives of every member of a household. Because these members must reorient themselves to accommodate his presence, they must also grow as individuals and as a group. It is as true to say that babies control and bring up their families as it is to say the converse. A family can bring up a baby only by being brought up by him. His growth consists of a series of challenges to them to serve his newly developing potentialities for social interaction [p. 189].

These formulations read as though Erikson's intent were to translate into concrete observations the theoretical propositions coined by Hartmann: "The newborn human and his . . . environment are adapted to each other from the very first moment" (1939, p. 51), and "man adapts to an environment which has already been molded by . . . himself" (p. 31).

To make Erikson's (1950b) conception of the integration within an epigenetic phase more concrete, I will assemble here a set of his statements concerning the various aspects of the first phase of epigenesis. I hope that this procedure will make his conception of the rôle of society in ego development particularly clear.

The inborn apparatus—organ mode: "To . . . [the newborn] the mouth is the focus of a general first approach to life—the *incorporative* approach" (p. 191).

The instinctual need: ". . . this stage is therefore usually referred to as the 'oral' stage. Yet it is clear that, in addition to the overwhelming need for food, a baby is, or soon becomes, receptive in many other respects" (p. 191).

"Mutuality," the first phase of psychosocial epigenesis: "At this point he lives through, and loves with, his mouth; and the mother lives through, and loves with, her breasts. . . . [an] accomplishment . . . dependent on her development as a woman; on her unconscious attitude toward the child; on the way she has lived through pregnancy and delivery; on her and her community's attitude toward the act of nursing—and on the response of the newborn" (p. 191).

The incorporative mode in behavior: "As he is willing and able to suck on appropriate objects and to swallow whatever appropriate fluids they emit, he is soon also willing and able to 'take in' with his eyes whatever enters his visual field. His tactual senses, too, seem to 'take in' what feels good. In this sense, then, one could speak of an *'incorporative stage,'* one in which he is, relatively speaking, receptive to what he is being offered" (p. 191).

Social modality: "The simplest and the earliest social modality is *'to get,'* not in the sense of 'go and get,' but in that of receiving and accepting what is given . . ." (p. 192).

Social modality and the rôle of society in mutuality: ". . . this sounds easier than it is. For the groping and unstable newborn's organism learns this modality only as he learns to regulate his readiness to get with the methods of a mother who, in turn, will permit him to coordinate his means of getting as she develops and coordinates her means of giving" (p. 192).

The mutuality phase as a preparation for later phases of psychosocial epigenesis: "The mutuality of relaxation thus developed is of prime importance for the first experience of friendly otherness . . . in thus *getting what is given,* and in learning to *get somebody to do* for him what he wishes to have done, the baby also develops the necessary groundwork to *get to be* the giver . . ." (p. 192).

Erikson (1950a) shows then that whatever type of *giver* the social traditions (and individual development) make the mother, the child becomes a corresponding *type of giver;* and that the *type of giving* in question has a crucial place in the forms, mores, traditions, way of life, and structure of his society:

> We have concentrated on the configurations with which these two tribes try to synthesize their concepts and their ideals in a coherent design for living. This design makes them efficient in their primitive ways of technology and magic and saves them from individual anxiety . . . the anxiety among the Plains hunters over emasculation and immobilization, among the Pacific fishermen over being left without provisions. To accomplish this a primitive culture seems to do two things: it gives specific meanings to early bodily and interpersonal experience so as to create the right combination of organ modes and the proper emphasis on social modalities; it carefully and systematically channelizes throughout the intricate pattern of its daily life the energies thus provoked and deflected; and it gives consistent supernatural meaning to the infantile anxieties which it has exploited by such provocation.
>
> . . . In order to create people who will function effectively as the bulk of the people, as energetic leaders, or as useful deviants, . . . [each] culture must strive for what we vaguely call a "strong ego" in its majority or at least in its dominant minority—i.e., an individual core firm and flexible enough to reconcile the necessary contradictions

in any human organization, to integrate individual differences, and above all to emerge from a long and unavoidably fearful infancy with a sense of identity and an idea of integrity [pp. 159–160].

Throughout the eight phases of epigenesis which he specifies, Erikson (1950b, 1956) demonstrates ever-expanding integrations and relations between society and ego development analogous to those characterized above.

In studying their views on the rôle of society in ego development, we have again found a basic accord between Erikson and Hartmann: (1) While there are innate structural and motivational givens for the development of the ego, and (2) while a maturational epigenetic plan regulates ego development, and (3) while this epigenetic plan involves sequences of basic psychological processes which are independent of the specific environment in which the development takes place, (4) the development of the ego, which is the organ of adaptation of man, consists of a series of readaptations which are reciprocal relations between the ego and the social and geographical environment.

We have, however, encountered again the persisting difference between Hartmann's systematic and theoretical bent and Erikson's inclination to proceed from observations by progressive generalizations. Moreover, we have found a new and probably crucial divergence between their views. Hartmann seems inclined to regard much of what is describable as id process as basic psychological process, unalterable by environmental influences, and thereby to curtail the range of *significant* individual and group differences of societal (exogenous) origin. For Erikson, an explanation of behavior involves a psychosocial (or adaptational) point of view also, consequently according to him in principle every behavior implies societal influences. How significant or insignificant for the explanation of the behavior this social (adaptational) aspect of it is remains—according to Erikson—a matter for empirical decision.

This divergence between Hartmann and Erikson is illustrated by their stand on sublimation. Hartmann's recent paper (1955) subsumes sublimations in general under neutralizations, and establishes the necessity of assuming neutralization of aggressive drives also. Hartmann's formulations establish the position of sublimation in the framework of metapsychology. Surprisingly, the paper contains no intimation of the adaptive rôle of sublimation, or of the rôle of society in sublimation and neutralization processes. Conversely, the rôle of society in sublimations is a central point with Erikson (1950a): "Most successful sublimations are . . . part and parcel of cultural trends and become unrecognizable as . . . [drive] derivatives" (p. 58). His discussion of *common, special,* and *unique meanings* (pp. 191–192) demonstrates the crucial role of society in the development of the "neutralized" *common meanings.*

It would be satisfying to continue here with a comparison between Hartmann's (1939, 1947) contributions on the rôle of values, and Erikson's (1954, 1956) contributions on the origin and nature of ideologies; with that between Hartmann's self-concept (1950, 1955) and Erikson's identity concept (1946, 1950a, 1950b, 1956). In these, as well as in yet other contributions, Hartmann and Erikson, starting from different vantage points, arrive at convergent problems and even formulations. Regrettably, such further comparisons would be premature at this time since, except for certain aspects of Erikson's identity concept, these issues are still insufficiently worked out.

VIII. CONCLUSION

We might conclude that the convergence and the complementarity (rather than congruence) of Hartmann's and Erikson's contributions both widen the scope of present-day ego psychology and provide it with a stability which it would not otherwise have. The development of theory must proceed always both by the scrutiny and systematic expansion of the existing theory to accommodate new problem areas, and by inductive generalizations guided mainly by the study of the subject matter. Ego psychology has not as yet welded together Erikson's and Hartmann's contributions. This paper has attempted to demonstrate that the possibility of doing so is present both in the concepts and in the observed relationships at the disposal of ego psychology.

REFERENCES

Erikson, E. H. (1937). Configurations in Play—Clinical Notes. *Psychoanal. Quart.,* 6:139–214.

———— (1939). Observations on Sioux Education. *J. Psychol.,* 7:101–156.

———— (1940a). Studies in the Interpretation of Play: 1. Clinical Observations of Play Disruption in Young Children. *Genet. Psychol. Monogr.,* 22:557–671.

———— (1940b). Problems of Infancy and Early Childhood. In *Cyclopedia of Medicine.* Philadelphia: Davis, pp. 714–730.

———— (1943). Observations on the Yurok: Childhood and World Image. *Univ. Cal. Publ. Amer. Archaeol. Ethnol.,* 35:257–302.

———— (1945). Childhood and Tradition in Two American Indian Tribes. *Psychoanal. Study Child,* 1:319–350. New York: International Universities Press. Also (revised) in *Personality in Nature, Society, and Culture,* ed. C. Kluckhohn & H. A. Murray. New York: Knopf, 1948, pp. 176–203.

———— (1946). Ego Development and Historical Change. *Psychoanal. Study Child,* 2:359–396. New York: International Universities Press.

———— (1950a). *Childhood and Society.* New York: Norton.

———— (1950b). Growth and Crises of the "Healthy Personality." In *Personality in Nature, Society, and Culture,* 2nd ed., ed. C. Kluckhohn & H. A. Murray. New York: Knopf, 1953, pp. 185–225.

———— (1954). Wholeness and Totality. In *Totalitarianism,* ed. C. J. Friedrich. Cambridge: Harvard University Press, pp. 156–171.

———— (1956). The Problem of Ego Identity. *J. Amer. Psychoanal. Assn.,* 4:56–121.

Freud, S. (1900). The Interpretation of Dreams. *Standard Edition,* 4 & 5. London: Hogarth Press, 1953.

———— (1911). Formulations Regarding the Two Principles in Mental Functioning. *Collected Papers,* 4:13–21. New York: Basic Books, 1959.

———— (1911–17 [1911–15]). Papers on Metapsychology. *Collected Papers,* 4:13–170. New York: Basic Books, 1959.

———— (1923). *The Ego and the Id,* tr. J. Riviere. London: Hogarth Press, 1947.

———— (1926 [1925]). *The Problem of Anxiety,* tr. H. A. Bunker. New York: Psychoanalytic Quarterly & Norton, 1936.

———— (1933). *New Introductory Lectures on Psycho-Analysis,* tr. W. J. H. Sprott. New York: Norton.

Hartmann, H. (1939). *Ego Psychology and the Problem of Adaptation,* tr. D. Rapaport. New York: International Universities Press, 1958.

———— (1944). Psychoanalysis and Sociology. In *Psychoanalysis Today,* ed. S. Lorand. New York: International Universities Press, pp. 326–341.

———— (1947). On Rational and Irrational Action. In *Psychoanalysis and the Social Sciences,* ed. G. Roheim, 1:359–392. New York: International Universities Press.

———— (1948). Comments on the Psychoanalytic Theory of Instinctual Drives. *Psychoanal. Quart.,* 17:368–388.

———— (1950). Comments on the Psychoanalytic Theory of the Ego. *Psychoanal. Study Child,* 5:74–96. New York: International Universities Press.

———— (1955). Notes on the Theory of Sublimation. *Psychoanal. Study Child,* 10:9–29. New York: International Universities Press.

————, & Kris, E. (1945). The Genetic Approach in Psychoanalysis. *Psychoanal. Study Child,* 1:11–30. New York: International Universities Press.

————, Kris, E., & Loewenstein, R. M. (1946). Comments on the Formation of Psychic Structure. *Psychoanal. Study Child,* 2:11–38. New York: International Universities Press.

————, Kris, E., & Loewenstein, R. M. (1951). Some Psychoanalytic Comments on "Culture and Personality." In *Psychoanalysis and Culture,* ed. G. B. Wilbur & W. Muensterberger. New York: International Universities Press, pp. 3–31.

Horney, K. (1937). *The Neurotic Personality of Our Time.* New York: Norton.

———— (1939). *New Ways in Psychoanalysis.* New York: Norton.

Kardiner, A. (1939). *The Individual and His Society.* New York: Columbia University Press.

Kris, E. (1950). On Preconscious Mental Processes. In *Organization and Pathology of Thought,* ed. & tr. D. Rapaport. New York: Columbia University Press, 1951, pp. 474–493.

Rapaport, D., & Gill, M. M. (1959). The Points of View and Assumptions of Metapsychology. *This volume,* Chapter 62.

Sullivan, H. S. (1938). Psychiatry: Introduction to the Study of Interpersonal Relations. *Psychiatry,* 1:121–134.

49

BOOK REVIEW

Donald M. Johnson, *The Psychology of Thought and Judgment*[1]

This volume's aim is to organize present knowledge and to serve as a guide to future research (p. x) in the psychology of thinking and judgment. The program is limited to experimental evidence, excluding "infrahuman problem solving, autistic thought and fantasy, and developmental trends" (pp. ix f.). It includes, however, as a novelty, material from the study of individual differences in abilities and of judgment.

The extensive material covered (746 references), the emphasis on method (including the discussion of a broad variety), and the novelties mentioned (including some "structural" considerations), are the book's assets.

On the debit side: this volume has no point of view, and its organization is arbitrary, unbalanced, repetitious, and disjointed. (Five of its chapters are preparatory, pp. 1–145; five are devoted to the topic proper, pp. 146–389; and three more hang on.) Neither chapters nor volume have summary or conclusions. The triple-layered, unnumbered subdivision of chapters throughout 500 small and rather crowded pages prevents easy orientation, and the table of contents gives only chapter pages and first-order

[1] New York: Harper, 1955.

First published in Contemporary Psychology, *1:134–136, 1956.*

subdivisions. The writing is dull, uneven, and at times downright poor, studded with the dubious ornaments of chapter mottoes ("Seeing is believing") and inflated pronouncements ("This volume is concerned with the most sophisticated, abstract, civilized and specialized things that people do.")

The book invites comparison with several recent publications on thinking: Hebb (1949), Humphrey (1951), Vinacke (1952), and chapters in several recent textbooks (Helson's *Theoretical Foundations,* 1951; Stevens's *Handbook,* 1951; Osgood's *Method and Theory,* 1953; Woodworth and Schlosberg's *Experimental Psychology,* 1954). Piaget's six (1932, 1936, 1937, 1941, 1945, 1947) recently translated volumes and the present reviewer's source book (1951) fall outside its stated program.

Hebb's volume has a central point of view ("Thought . . . [is a] process that is not fully controlled by environmental stimulation and yet cooperates closely with the stimulation," p. xvi) developed into a theory by carefully marshaled evidence. Humphrey's is a judicious, penetrating, analytic volume which traces several major historical problems of the psychology of thinking and adduces evidence only to reach, or to point toward, a decision on them. Vinacke's tidy survey is neither exhaustive nor particularly penetrating, nor without gaps. Yet, not limited by a point of view or to experimental evidence, it freely follows the rambling outlines of the field. The scope of the textbook chapters is limited, centering mostly on problem solving (insight-learning controversy) or concept formation or both.

The present volume has neither a selective point of view, nor a problem-centered analysis, nor tidiness and broad range; and, while it too defines thinking as problem solving and deals both with the learning-insight controversy and concept formation, these are not its main arteries nor are they brought into sharp relief.

What then is the vision from which this volume arises?

The new emphasis on judgment and individual differences points to the answer. The vision seems to come from "applied psychology," from the construction and study of judgment scales and mental tests. The references to the author's publications attest to this (they cluster in the chapters on judgment). The psychology of thinking is used here to link the author's major interests. The search for just such links has always been a fertile source of new insights in science. Here too it leads to important conclusions: (1) the psychology of judgment is part of the psychology of thinking; (2) the isolation of the experimental psychology of thinking from the psychology of individual differences in ability is detrimental ("a tragedy") to the field: "One of the major purposes of the present work is an integration of these two streams of progress" (p. 44).

This vision, however, this attempt at double integration, fails to inspire or to shape the volume. Instead of providing a pervasive point of view, it merely adds more data. Instead of lending a cohesive form, it adds isolated sections and chapters. It brings no integration of the psychology of thinking. In fact, the psychology of thinking presented here looks like a hastily contrived vehicle for the author's diverse interests.

To draw the line between making value judgments and becoming judgmental is always precarious. In writing about books and in judging relatively new ventures it becomes more so. Treating the psychology of thinking as a unified field and including "individual differences" and judgment in it, are new ventures. Thus this failure at integration is perhaps understandable and forgivable. Not to recognize the validity of the vision as a human achievement would be unfair, as it would be not to acknowledge that the juxtaposition of experimental results and individual differences, as well as of problem solving and judgment, is food for thought. If the selection of this food is undiscriminating and its preparation unpalatable, at least we can appreciate the prodigious work of compilation and the few threads which tie the "individual difference" sections to the "experimental" ones (e.g., pp. 83 and 92).

But it is hard to overlook the disregard of organic and functional pathology, particularly Scheerer's (1946) and Hebb's contributions. Both made a definite attempt to link differences in individual ability to the psychology of thinking. Rapaport, Gill, and Schafer's *Diagnostic Psychological Testing* (1945–46)—whatever shortcomings it had—also made such a deliberate attempt. Consideration of these might have saved the volume from the overwhelmingly statistical view of "individual differences." Pathology is nature's experiment—it often isolates variables of which the experimenter had not even dreamt. As for factor analysis: is following statistics to identify the factors isolated a "better" method than using experiment or statistics or both to test assumptions derived from observation? Or is there any evidence that it is easier to build a bridge between a factorial study of individual differences and the experimental psychology of thinking than between the latter and experimental study of individual differences? (Cf. Lewin, 1927, 1935; Klein, 1954; Klein and Schlesinger, 1949.)

On the positive side, we can appreciate the volume's stress on the instruments of thought that do not in themselves solve problems but are indispensable for problem solving and thinking (pp. 126 ff., pp. 222 ff.). In this light the discussion of vocabulary and of the relations between words, concepts and their relations, and of search models, gains a new and instructive emphasis which derives mostly from tests (of association, of concept formation). There is an awareness here (p. 228) that thinking is made possible by the fixed units at its disposal. (Otherwise it would become a croquet game with flamingoes for mallets and hedgehogs for balls.)

But again our appreciation is marred.

These instruments and their relations are presented as the contents and arrangements of a storehouse (p. 128). There is no reference to Bartlett (1932), whose schema concept was an attempt to deal with such instruments of thought, combatting the inadequacies of storehouse conceptions. The repeated—but unexplained—phrases "wheels-within-wheels character of thinking" and "retroflex character of judgment" do not make up for these inadequacies.

The origin and function of these instrumental structures are relegated here to the psychology of learning and skills (p. 222). But can learning theory account for the survival and utilization of these instrumental structures, not to speak of their remolding in the course of utilization? While Hilgard (1948) is not quite sure and Mowrer (1950) and Dollard and Miller (1950) take great pains to explain how learning theory might do so, this volume takes the positive answer for granted: but a theory of thinking cannot take this for granted. Thinking is not possible without fixed units; yet it is equally impossible to explain the remolding of these units in the course of the thought process without also attributing flexibility to them. The ability concepts *rigidity* and *flexibility* (pp. 212 ff.) do not provide a specific explanation and there is no mention here of any theory which does attempt to meet this problem (e.g., Hebb's "assemblies" and "phase sequences," or Piaget's work of the last twenty years).

Yet the book's stress on these long-neglected instrumental structures is important. Dr. Johnson points out that psychoanalysis was not interested in them (p. 13). Noting reinforcement theory's similar lack, in contrast to Gordon Allport's persistent interest and that of the workers in psychoanalytic ego psychology, could have provided an opportunity to explore the fate of thinking, buffeted as it has been between motivational and structural theories. It might even have shed light on the revival of this interest within reinforcement theory (e.g., Osgood, 1953, 1957) and outside it (e.g., Bruner, 1957; Klein, 1954, Klein and Schlesinger, 1949) under the influence of ego psychology and information theory.

With reduced expectations we can appreciate the inclusion of the psychology of judgment in the psychology of thinking. We note the awareness that the degree of similarity between judgments in life and judgments in the laboratory "is unknown" (p. 282), and that the judgments studied are unidimensional (p. 328). We share the hope that the general principles arrived at will have some applicability to life's judgments (p. 282). We read with interest the assertion that the experimental problem of judgment and the ability termed "good judgment" are related (p. 318).

But beyond these points our appreciation diminishes:

Judgment appears here as one of the three "principal thought processes: . . . preparation, production and judgment" (p. 51), as though the meaning—if any—of the "wheels-within-wheels character of thinking" (p. 284) did not imply that the selection of means and directions involves judgments at *every* point of thinking.

Judgment here is "a kind of problem the solution to which is a response in one of several categories [*yes* or *no, high* or *low,* p. 292] prepared in advance of the judgment" (p. 284). Though we hear that judges at times prepare new categories in the course of thinking, the impression is overwhelming that we learn about judges acting on the applied psychologist's scales, rather than about judgments made in the course of thinking. How man comes by and uses (deliberately or unwittingly) apparently unidimensional scales of values and magnitudes, is a striking instance of the instrumental-structure problem (cf. Piaget)—but this matter is not explicit in the volume, nor is it the sole problem of judgment.

Judgment here is "by definition . . . not an automatic reflex" (p. 325). How proudly—or blindly—"rationalistic" can a statement be? How logical: thinking has a "preparation" and a "production" phase and it culminates in a judgment which settles matters, presumably deliberately (p. 282). A lost driver makes a judgment and, "set thusly, his preparation has eliminated cross-country travel . . . spending the night on the road," etc. Some will say, "What a pity that life is not so simple"; others will say, "What luck that it is not so boring." Surely judgment can be defined to exclude everything "automatic" (e.g., by relegating it to habit) and to do away with the judgment versus inclination problem. But will the generalizations derived be relevant to life?

Judgment is a part of the psychology of thinking, because every proposition about judgments states *how* the thought process cooperates with stimulation—to use Hebb's phrase—and every proposition about "good judgment" states *how well* it cooperates. Propositions of the first kind apply to every (not only to the consummatory) phase of thinking; propositions of the second kind are relative to the personality of the thinker.

Yet even this compilation and juxtaposition may prove helpful at a time when the average psychologist pays no more attention to what Brentano, Meinong, Bühler, Freud, Schilder, Lewin, and Piaget contributed to this problem than does the present volume.

The five chapters discussing the volume's stated plan (p. 51) divide into one on preparation, two on production, and two on judgment. Is this veritable Procrustean bed the price paid for including, but failing to integrate, judgment and individual differences? Or is there more to it?

The relation of reason and fact is not simpler in psychology than in any other field: that which is logical is by no means always psychological. This volume's avowed interest is in "the most abstract and civilized things people do," and it takes these things to be problem solving and judgment (p. 20). It deliberately excludes "autistic thought, fantasy, and developmental trends," and by default it excludes pathology, ethnopsychology, wit, humor, and the like, all of which link rational thought to its irrational matrix (Freud, Lévy-Bruhl, H. Werner, Piaget; and for still others see the reviewer's source book [Rapaport, 1951]). It is no surprise that it treats thinking as a logical pursuit within an arbitrary logical framework. The treatment of motivation seems to be of the same "logical" cast. Motivations are notoriously the sources of the illogical in thinking (cf. Descartes,

Hume). In this volume they get short shrift. "Physiological" motives are discarded and "social" motives accepted for thought; then "extrinsic motives" are discarded in favor of "intrinsic" ones (pp. 56 ff.). Those familiar with the difficulties of motivation theories in accounting for the logic of thinking, and conversant with both Allport's attempts and those of the workers in psychoanalytic ego psychology to meet this difficulty, will follow these shifts with sympathy if not without apprehension. But when "intrinsic" motivations too are more or less abandoned and "The Dynamics of Thought" is discussed mainly in terms of sets (disregarding Allport's [1935] and Gibson's [1941] warnings), then it seems to be clear that motivations and the illogical just had to be eliminated. With them goes the, so far, most promising avenue of linking thought to personality and of keeping the door open for the understanding of pathology, dreams, projective techniques, and the like. The thinking *person* is reduced to an aggregate of "abilities." Behind this conception there lies something far worse and more deadening than partisanship for one trend of "applied psychology": it seems to be the product of narrowing specialization.

Even if this assessment of the vision, its validity, and its execution is correct, it fails to resolve a lingering uneasiness.

How is a volume on thinking—published under the most reputable auspices—possible without touching on the essence of the contributions made by Lewin, H. Werner, Tolman, Brunswik, Piaget, and without mentioning Silberer, Schilder, Lashley, Heider, Hebb? How can such a volume ignore the ancestry of the psychology of thinking and judgment to the point that it contains (among the 746) less than a dozen foreign-language references?

Scrutiny of the volume alone is unlikely to answer these questions. There must be a social factor at work: something in the atmosphere of our psychological science that is, to say the least, coresponsible. Although this is not the place to diagnose this "something," an example of its self-perpetuating character may well be pointed out: will graduate students fed on such a treatment of the past and of the foreign-language literature take the Ph.D.'s historical and language requirements for anything more than a formality?

REFERENCES

Allport, G. W. (1935). Attitudes. In *A Handbook of Social Psychology,* ed C. Murchison. Worcester: Clark University Press, pp. 798–844.
Bartlett, F. C. (1932). *Remembering: A Study in Experimental and Social Psychology.* Cambridge: Cambridge University Press.
Bruner, J. S. (1957). Going Beyond the Information Given. In *Contemporary Approaches to Cognition,* J. S. Bruner et al. Cambridge: Harvard University Press, pp. 41–69.
Dollard, J., & Miller, N. E. (1950). *Personality and Psychotherapy: An Analysis in Terms of Learning, Thinking, and Culture.* New York: McGraw-Hill.

Gibson, J. J. (1941). A Critical Review of the Concept of Set in Contemporary Experimental Psychology. *Psychol. Bull.,* 38: 781–817.

Hebb, D. O. (1949). *The Organization of Behavior; A Neuropsychological Theory.* New York: Wiley.

Helson, H., ed. (1951). *Theoretical Foundations of Psychology.* New York: Van Nostrand.

Hilgard, E. R. (1948). *Theories of Learning.* New York: Appleton-Century-Crofts.

Humphrey, G. (1951). *Thinking: An Introduction to Its Experimental Psychology.* New York: Wiley.

Klein, G. S. (1954). Need and Regulation. In *Nebraska Symposium on Motivation, 1954,* ed. M. R. Jones. Lincoln: University of Nebraska Press, pp. 224–274.

———, & Schlesinger, H. (1949). Where Is the Perceiver in Perceptual Theory? *J. Pers.,* 18:32–47.

Lewin, K. (1927). Gesetz und Experiment in der Psychologie. *Symposion,* 1:375–421.

——— (1935). *A Dynamic Theory of Personality.* New York: McGraw-Hill.

Mowrer, O. H. (1950). *Learning Theory and Personality Dynamics.* New York: Ronald Press.

Osgood, C. E. (1953). *Method and Theory in Experimental Psychology.* New York: Oxford University Press.

——— (1957). A Behavioristic Analysis of Perception and Language as Cognitive Phenomena. In *Contemporary Approaches to Cognition,* J. S. Bruner et al. Cambridge: Harvard University Press, pp. 75–118.

Piaget, J. (1932). *The Moral Judgment of the Child.* Glencoe, Ill.: Free Press, 1948.

——— (1936). *The Origins of Intelligence in Children,* 2nd ed. New York: International Universities Press, 1952.

——— (1937). *The Construction of Reality in the Child.* New York: Basic Books, 1954.

——— (1941). *The Child's Conception of Number.* London: Routledge & Kegan Paul, 1952.

——— (1945). *Play, Dreams and Imitation in Childhood.* New York: Norton, 1951.

——— (1947). *The Psychology of Intelligence.* New York: Harcourt, Brace, 1950.

Rapaport, D., ed. & tr. (1951). *Organization and Pathology of Thought.* New York: Columbia University Press.

———, Gill, M. M., & Schafer, R. (1945–46). *Diagnostic Psychological Testing,* 2 vols. Chicago: Year Book Publishers.

Scheerer, M. (1946). Problems of Performance Analysis in the Study of Personality. *Ann. N. Y. Acad. Sci.,* 46:653–675.

Stevens, S. S., ed. (1951). *Handbook of Experimental Psychology.* New York: Wiley.

Vinacke, W. E. (1952). *The Psychology of Thinking.* New York: McGraw-Hill.

Woodworth, R. S., & Schlosberg, H. (1954). *Experimental Psychology.* New York: Holt.

50

COGNITIVE STRUCTURES

I

The relation of cognition to personality is usually treated in terms of motivations. In this paper I shall dwell on another, usually neglected, ingredient of cognition that seems to play a crucial rôle in the relationship between cognition and personality: namely, *cognitive structures*. By cognitive structures I mean both those quasi-permanent means which cognitive processes use and do not have to create *de novo* each time and those quasi-permanent organizations of such means that are the framework for the individual's cognitive processes. I shall present three sets of clinical observations and discuss them so as to bring into relief the rôle of cognitive structures in them. But I shall resist the temptation to present a clinical theory of cognition.[1] I shall try to avoid clinical and psychoanalytic terminology as much

[1] Cf. Rapaport (1950, 1951a, 1952a), as well as the "Rationale" sections of Rapaport, Gill, and Schafer (1945–46), particularly Part Three, Chapter I. By avoiding clinical theory, I may give the impression in the following that the clinician's only contribution to the theory of cognition is his observations. This is not so. Psychoanalytic theory has not only drawn attention to the phenomena to be described here, but has also offered concepts and theories to explain them. I am deliberately neglecting these theories here. The interested reader will turn to Freud (1900, Chapter VII; 1911, 1915a, 1915b), Schilder (1920, 1924, 1930), and Hartmann (1939), and will find further references in my own writings referred to above (see also Piaget, 1931).

Reprinted with permission of the publishers from Jerome S. Bruner et al., Contemporary Approaches to Cognition: A symposium held at the University of Colorado, 1955, *pp. 157–200. Cambridge, Mass.: Harvard University Press. Copyright, 1957, by the President and Fellows of Harvard College.*

as possible, and shall choose the rôle of the naturalist who describes and sorts out phenomena observed *in vivo,* in contrast to the experimenter, whose precise knowledge tested *in vitro* is so often at a great distance from anything *in vivo.*

Before turning to clinical observations, it seems necessary to set down some of the general assumptions concerning cognition underlying the discussions to follow. First, a theory of cognition that is broad enough to have clinical relevance must account (a) for man's ways of gaining information about his environment as well as about his needs and other motivations; and (b) for man's ways of organizing the information he has obtained so that it will serve him in controlling and/or fulfilling his needs, and in coping with his environment (see Rapaport, 1950, 1951b). Second, the subject matter of a theory of cognition should include: conscious and unconscious, perceptual and memorial, imaginary and veridical, self-expressive and reality-representing, dreamlike and waking, ordered and freely wandering, productive and reproductive, normal and abnormal cognition (see Rapaport, 1951a). Third, a theory of cognition must deal both with the processes underlying cognition and with the effects of cognitions on man's behavior. Fourth, a theory of cognition must assume that cognitive processes create some of their components *de novo,* while others are ready-made tools available to them. For instance, a cognitive process may create a new concept but will also use old ones; and the new concept and the method of creating it may crystallize into tools that will be at the disposal of subsequent cognitive processes. For the moment, it is a moot question whether this transformation, apparently characteristic of our thought processes, of a function into a quasi-permanent tool (see Hartmann [1939], and note also the parallel to Allport's [1935–47] conception of "functional autonomy"), can or cannot be accounted for by the familiar principles of existing learning theories (see Rapaport, 1952b, 1953).

Fifth, a theory of cognition must also assume that both the cognitions and the tools of cognition that emerge from cognitive processes are organized in some quasi-permanent and orderly fashion in the mind.

Clearly these last two assumptions pertain directly to the cognitive structures we are concerned with, and here I would like to give a few orienting illustrations.

Memory organizations are perhaps the most common cognitive structures. The classical investigations of memory dwelt primarily on its organizations in terms of spatial and temporal contiguity; early Freudian psychology (Freud, 1901) primarily on its organizations in terms of drives; Bartlett (1932) in his conception of schemata, on its organizations in terms of interests and affects. Both the Socratic method of diaschisis and the results of association tests suggest that there is also a conceptual organization[2] of

[2] I am using the antithesis of drive organization versus conceptual organization as I used it in *Organization and Pathology of Thought* (1951a). The choice of the terms

memories: the majority of the popular (most frequent) association-test responses are conceptually related to the stimulus, and these responses constitute about 60 per cent of all the responses of normal subjects in our sample (Rapaport, Gill, and Schafer, 1945–46; Schafer, 1945).

But memory organizations are not the only cognitive organizations (see Schilder, 1924, 1930, and Rapaport, 1951d). Grammar and syntax reflect a great many cognitive organizations. Let us take the modes as our second example. The conditional mode[3] arises rather late in the child's cognitive development. Once it has appeared, its tool or means character is clear, and both our grammar and our sustained capacity to carry on and/or fall back on thought and behavior based on suspended premises show that this tool of thought is an enduring organization.

We shall choose styles as a third example of cognitive organizations. I do not mean merely styles of written prose but cognitive styles in general, including styles of perceiving, conversing, dreaming, and so on. Styles, as cognitive organizations, show striking interindividual differences (see Klein and Schlesinger, 1949, 1951; Holzman, 1954). Not that there are no interindividual differences in memory organizations and grammatic-syntactic organizations, too, but these organizations are present in some form, or to some extent, in all members of the species. This is not so with styles. Understatement, for instance, is a familiar style, which in some people becomes a major tool shaping most of their cognitive processes, but may be conspicuously absent[4] in other people. My assistant, Dr. I. H. Paul, is on the track of such style organizations. His experimental subjects tend to use images and ellipses to the same extent in their recall of a story told to them as in a story that they produce around a given theme. The correlation coefficients (which are around .5 and are highly reliable) suggest that the tendencies to use ellipses and images are styles that differ interindividually but are stable intraindividually (see Paul, 1959).

I would like to touch on one more problem concerning cognitive tools or

---

is not felicitous. Drive organization is conceptual, too, in the broad sense in which conceptual organization means equivalence organization, and in the narrow sense of physiognomic concepts (Werner, 1926). Conceptual organization, as I use the term, denotes the equivalence organizations akin to those of logical concepts. The transition between the latter and drive organizations (for example, in terms of physiognomic concepts) appears to be continuous, while my discussion of the antithesis is restricted to the two extreme ends of this continuum.

[3] Erikson (1950) has described other types of mode organizations of behavior and cognition that originate in body modes in general or in the modes of "erotogenic zones" in particular.

[4] The choice of the examples of cognitive organizations here and later may appear to be random and may convey the impression that these organizations form a random assembly. This does not seem to be the case. There is considerable evidence that these organizations are related to each other in that they form multiple complex hierarchies. See Rapaport (1942, 1951a).

means. I have used these terms to designate the ready availability (as against *ad hoc* production) of certain cognitive forms, but I have also implied their usefulness as means to an end. It is obvious that a memory or a concept is a means or tool of cognition; each is one of the means by which we orient ourselves in a problem situation. But it is not so evident how broader cognitive organizations, such as styles, are means or tools of the cognitive process. Let me clarify the point by citing an experiment made by George Klein (1954). He used a thirsty and a nonthirsty group of subjects and exposed them to a great number of cognitive (mostly perceptual) tasks and stimuli which involved themes related to thirst. The "new look" expectation would have been that the thirsty subjects would react differently to these tasks and stimuli from the nonthirsty ones. The results of the experiment did not bear out this simple expectation. However, both the thirsty and the nonthirsty groups were themselves composed of two groups of subjects, each representing a perceptual style. Klein called one of these styles "control by constriction," the other "flexible control." In the analysis of the data in terms of this fourfold design (thirsty—flexible control, thirsty—control by constriction, nonthirsty—flexible control, nonthirsty—control by constriction) significant differences emerged. It appears that thirst did influence cognition, but this influence was different in the subjects with flexible controls from influence in those controlling by constriction. Thus, these styles seem to direct or channel the influence of needs or drives, or at least to reflect preferred modes of directing and channeling. This is a familiar situation in clinical practice: the form and direction of drive discharge is coordinated with, if not limited and selected by, defensive organizations. An aggressive impulse defended against by reaction formation may find expression in excessive altruism; one defended against by projection may find expression in self-protective and provocative maneuvers (see Schafer, 1954). This does not mean that style and defense organization are identical, but it does imply that, in the main, both are tools of cognition, used primarily in its dealings with the internal needs of the organism.

A distinction between cognitive processes on the one hand and the structured (patterned and persisting) tools of cognition and their organizations on the other can probably be made by the criterion of rates of change: the processes may be defined as showing a high rate of change, the tools and their organization as showing a low one. In other words, the processes are temporary and unique, the tools and their organizations permanent and typical.

II

Let me begin with a typical example taken from my studies of amnesia (see Rapaport, 1942, 1951c; Gill and Rapaport, 1942; Geleerd, Hacker, and Rapaport, 1945). An unemployed man leaves his home after a violent quarrel with his wife. Eight hours later he is picked up by a policeman at the Hudson River, a three-quarter-hour's walking distance from his home, his behavior suggesting suicidal intent. Brought to the hospital, he seems quite unaware of his personal identity. This condition lasts ten days and terminates when, in a sodium-amytal interview, he recalls the quarrel with his wife. However, now that he has recovered the awareness of his personal identity, it becomes clear that he has no memory of those eight hours that elapsed between his leaving home and his being picked up by the policeman. Two weeks later, in another amytal interview, he recollects this period also, and describes that during those eight hours he was consumed with rage, guilt, and the idea, "I must end it all." He thought of nothing else and walked the streets scarcely aware of them, barely able to orient himself toward the "end": the Hudson River. A study of the case shows three phases.

(a) *The first eight hours:* the patient's conscious cognition is largely limited to the single idea, "I must end it all," and to the concomitant affects. The patient is apparently incapable of ordered cognition, unaware of his personal identity, but also unaware of this incapacity; Gill and I (1942; Rapaport, 1942) found in a number of such cases that patients in this phase are, as a rule, not yet aware of this loss of awareness of their personal identity. Fisher's studies (1945, 1947; Fisher and Joseph, 1949) corroborate this finding. Janet (1901) described such states as monoideic and polyideic somnambulisms; others (Stengel, 1941; Rapaport, 1942) have called them fugues.

(b) *The subsequent ten days:* the patient's ordered everyday behavior and test performance show that he is capable of ordered cognition in general, but that he cannot cognize anything pertaining to his personal identity. Thus he has no awareness of his personal identity. But in the encounter with the policeman he becomes aware—and from then on he remains aware—of his lack of awareness. He shows a certain bewilderment, which increases as he tries to think about his personal identity. This bewilderment is hard to define, though it is distinct from the daze that characterized his behavior at the Hudson River. This phase and its characteristics were first described by Abeles and Schilder (1935).

(c) *The final two weeks:* the patient appears capable of all cognitive activities except those pertaining to the first phase, which had been characterized by the loss of awareness of personal identity without an awareness of this loss. This third phase is akin to the familiar retroactive functional amnesias, except for the fact that in this case the period blotted out by the amnesia was itself a special state and this condition, though frequent, is not a necessary part of functional retroactive amnesia (see Rapaport, 1942).

Gill and I (1942; Rapaport, 1942) have found that this sequence and these characteristics of the three phases are typical for such amnesias. Fisher's studies (1945, 1947; Fisher and Joseph, 1949) corroborated our findings. We should note that the cognitive processes in each of these phases are sharply distinct from each other as well as from normal cognitive processes. While the clinical study of this case, and kindred cases, shows that the basic drive motivations underlying the crucial cognitive phenomena of each of the three phases are identical [5] (in this case it is the murderous hostility directed toward the wife), the cognitive contents of the three phases are different. Thus, the first relationship—actually a commonplace one—suggested by this clinical observation is that the basic motivation does not unequivocally determine the cognitive content or, for that matter, the cognitive form.

An inspection of the cognitive contents of these three phases reveals the cohesive character of what can or cannot be cognized in them. By "cohesive" I mean that the contents that are cognized (likewise those excluded from cognition) are not a random assembly, but are selected and held together by discernible unifying principles. The question arises: do the cohesive cognitive contents, which either monopolize cognition or are excluded from cognition in one of the phases of this disorder, correspond to organizations existing in normal psychological functioning?

Let us consider the first and third phases together. What was cognized in the former and uncognizable in the latter were all cognitive contents related to the motivation represented by the phrase "I must end it all." This motivation was the aggressive drive that became directed toward the self, and was of such intensity that it excluded all cognitions except some that were relevant to its goal. Thus we are dealing with a cognitive organization centered around a drive.

Do we have any evidence that such cognitive organizations or structures exist in normal psychological life? Bartlett (1932) proposed the concept of "schemata" to designate enduring memory organizations as he conceived of them. According to him, these schemata are, to begin with, organized around the special senses, later on probably also around appetites or instinctive tendencies, and still later also around interests, attitudes, and ideals. Bartlett wrote:

> . . . because there is . . . notable *overlap* of material dealt with by different 'schemata,' the latter themselves are normally *interconnected,* organised together and display, just as do the appetites, instinctive tendencies, interests and ideals which build them up, in order of predominance among themselves [p. 212; italics added].

[5] I am not implying here that the total motivational constellations of these three phases are identical, nor even that the total motivational constellations of their crucial cognitive phenomena are identical. Under total motivational constellation we subsume also the motivations of defense, control, ego interest, etc., which are obviously at variance in these three phases. All I assert is that the basic drive motivation involved is identical for the "single motif cognition" in the first phase, for the exclusion from cognition of all that pertains to personal identity in the second phase, and for the amnesia in the third phase for the time span of the first phase.

Would it be far-fetched to suggest that Bartlett observed, in his studies of normal remembering in "overlapping" and "interconnected" forms, cognitive organizations centered around drives[6] of the very type that pathology shows us here in a skeletonized, isolated form?

I want to refer to further observations supporting this suggestion. When in everyday life an interest, or appetite, or affect becomes overwhelmingly strong, it tends to shed its "overlap" and "interconnection" with other interests and appetites. It predominates and even monopolizes, and shows up in the subject's preoccupation with it to the point that he becomes temporarily incapable of cognizing (perceiving and/or thinking about) anything not pertaining to it. Grief and shame, the thought of the beloved or the problem about to be solved, all may grow to this point. We accept these states as normal since, unlike the first phase of our amnesia case, which they resemble, they are not attended by a loss of personal identity and are readily reversible. But we justly characterize people in these states as "obsessed" by their interest or appetite. We encounter the pathological counterpart of these normal preoccupations in obsessional neurotics. In their obsessive preoccupations we find the same limitation of cognition as in the first phase of amnesia and in normal preoccupation, but on the one hand the condition is not readily reversible, and on the other there is no loss of personal identity. However, pathological obsessive preoccupations increasing in intensity lead to obsessional deliria (see Freud, 1909), the cognitive character of which is the same as that of the first phase of amnesia: cognition is limited and awareness of personal identity lost, without an awareness of this loss being present. The normal extreme preoccupation with an interest or appetite—to use Bartlett's terms—does produce cognitive conditions and conditions of awareness that appear to be a transition from normal cognition to that of the first phase of amnesia.

We may add that the analyses of slips of the tongue (Freud, 1901), as well as the study of slips of the tongue experimentally produced by means of posthypnotic suggestion (Erickson, 1939; Erickson and Erickson, 1941), also support the assumption that such drive organizations of cognitions exist in normal psychic life.[7]

Clinically it is easy to show that these drive organizations of memory, by making available as directional indicators both the memories of gratifying

[6] In terms of clinical theory, Bartlett's appetites and instinctive tendencies are probably high-level derivatives of drives. There are cognitive organizations that pertain to and center around these derivatives. Since these derivative motivations are not as peremptory (discharge oriented) as the basic drives, the cognitive organizations corresponding to them shade more readily into the conceptual organization of memory (see Rapaport, 1951a). This conceptual organization was for the most part ignored by Bartlett in his study.

[7] It seems that the experiments of Murphy and his pupils (Murphy, 1947), as well as some of the "new look" experiments in perception (Bruner and Postman, 1947; Bruner and Goodman, 1947), have been concerned with some such motivational organization of perception.

objects and gratifications and their contexts, subserve the search for need satisfiers.[8] Bartlett too seems to imply something of this sort when he maintains that the very factors that build the schemata organize the recall, which he regards as a construction "made largely on the basis of . . . [an] attitude, and its general effect is that of a justification of the attitude" (1932, p. 207).

Let us now consider the second phase of our amnesia case, where cognitions pertaining to the subject's personal identity were not possible though the subject was keenly aware of and bewildered by this loss. The observation implies a loss of cognizability that is not arbitrary but is organized around the subject's personal identity. Is there any evidence that such an organization of cognitions exists in the normally functioning person?

Let us again turn to Bartlett (1932).

While he takes pains to dissociate himself from any "substantial, unitary self, lurking behind experience"—as I would also—he nevertheless has this to say:

> . . . memory, in its full sense, always contains a peculiarly personal reference. . . . [because] the 'schemata' and the appetites, instinctive tendencies, attitudes, interests and ideals which build them up display an order of predominance among themselves. . . . [and] this order remains relatively persistent for a given organism [p. 308].

But what if this order of predominance is disturbed, as in our case of amnesia? Should we then infer that the "personal reference" becomes interfered with and the cognitions particularly related to it become unavailable? Bartlett has nothing to say about loss of personal identity, but he does refer to a related pathological phenomenon: depersonalization. In depersonalization the cognition of personal identity is not lost but is devoid of conviction, of feeling. Correspondingly, though objects are perceived and recognized they appear strange, and though thoughts are developed there is no conviction about them nor familiarity with them.[9] Bartlett refers to this condition as follows:

> . . . the mechanism of adult human memory demands an organisation of 'schemata' depending upon an interplay of appetites, instincts, interests and ideals peculiar to any given subject. Thus if, as in some

[8] See Schilder (1920) and Rapaport (1951d). The drive organizations subserve the search for need satisfiers primarily by means of signals indicating which need is to be satisfied, in other words by making the need cognizable. They are far less serviceable for cognizing the satisfying object (not to speak of the realistically attainable object). There are two reasons for this. First, these organizations are not based on a hierarchic stratification of cognitions but rather on their equivalence as drive representations. Second, the so-called primary-process mechanisms prevail in these organizations. But we cannot pursue this point here.

[9] The experience of depersonalization is akin to the experience of something familiar in a strange context or in a stressful situation. Reports of examination experiences often contain examples of both. See p. 650 below.

pathological cases, these active organising sources of the 'schemata' get cut off from one another, the peculiar personal attributes of what is remembered fail to appear [1932, p. 213].

I could advance further strong evidence from psychopathology for the assumption of a cognitive organization around personal identity. For instance, I have demonstrated in my study and survey (Rapaport, 1942; Rapaport and Erickson, 1942) of alternating multiple personalities that the experiences acquired by such a person in one state are not, as a rule, available to cognition in his other state or states (see also Freud, 1923, pp. 38–39). I could also advance further evidence (though it is rather weak) for this assumption by referring to the rôle of the identification figures in such projective tests as the T.A.T., and by reference to the relation between identity and memories in hypnotic age regression. Claparède's (1911) "me-ness" (*moüté*) concept and the observations he based it on are certainly relevant, and so are some of the theoretical and experimental contributions on ego involvement (Allport, 1935–47), as well as Koffka's (1935) theory of the "core" of the memory trace, which—in contradistinction to the "shaft" of it—communicates with the "ego" and involves its "attitudes" in recall. However, none of these proves the point. "Personal identity"—as we know from E. Erikson's (1956) studies[10]—reflects a complex and high-level integration of behavior which is difficult to pin down when it works normally but which produces dramatic pathological effects when impaired.

I would like to mention two more points before we leave this observation.

The first relationship suggested by the three phases of this case of amnesia is the lack of a one-to-one relation between basic motivation and cognition. Comparing the three phases, the clinician would say that the controls that the personality exercises over drives are usually such that their interference with cognition is imperceptible and takes the form of individual proclivity. In the first phase a drive broke through these controls and interfered with the cognizing of all but its own representations. In the second phase the controls were re-established but—apparently as a precautionary measure—they became so widespread that they interfered extensively with cognition. In the third phase this excessive control was scaled down—it became limited to the drive itself—but, since the drive interfered with cognition in the first phase, its control could not but interfere with it too, and so it prevented the cognition of the experiences of the first phase. If we take this crude clinical description (crude this time in terms of clinical theory) at its face value, we note that there are yet other organizations—controls

---

10 My equating of Erikson's identity concept with that of "personal identity" requires explanation. I hope that Erikson will soon publish the study of a case that has shed considerable light on the relationship of these two concepts. [So far, Erikson has not published this case study. But see Erikson (1956, pp. 130–131)—Ed.]

and defenses—to be taken into account here along with drive organizations, since they too have a powerful regulating control over cognition (see Schafer, 1954). Clinical observation attests to the great permanence of these controlling and defensive organizations. Indeed, the clinician is so impressed by their permanence that he refers to them as structures, and to their mode of function as mechanisms (Freud, 1926; A. Freud, 1936).

Finally, a point about awareness or, as we usually refer to it, consciousness. In our usual state of consciousness we can become aware of our awareness. I assume that Bartlett (1932) meant something similar when he spoke of the organism's ability "to turn round upon its own 'schemata'" (p. 208). In our three phases of amnesia we have three different forms of consciousness, which I characterized crudely as normal in the third phase, bewildered in the second, dazed in the first. Significantly enough, these gross characteristics are paralleled by the corresponding varieties of awareness of personal identity: in the third phase there is an awareness of identity with an unhampered potentiality to become aware of this fact; in the second phase there is a loss of awareness of personal identity with the awareness of this loss; in the first phase there is a loss of awareness of identity without awareness of this loss. Moreover, this constriction of awareness is paralleled by a progressive constriction of the range of feasible cognition.

The question arises whether the narrowing of consciousness is but an epiphenomenon accompanying the narrowing range of cognitions, or whether consciousness has a function of its own in normal as well as narrowed ranges of cognition. In either case it deserves to be taken out of limbo and to be restudied: in the first case as an index of the cognitive range, in the second as an organization subserving cognition. Indeed, clinical theory has been treating consciousness as an organization[11] through all the years in which most of experimental psychology used it as the generic term for deceptive and useless introspections. I hope that the observations I shall next present will lend support to the following theses: (1) consciousness can be usefully treated as an organization subserving cognition; (2) consciousness is not a unitary phenomenon but one that has a whole range of varieties, each corresponding to a different cognitive organization.

Before turning to these observations, however, I would like to quote Bartlett on the first point and Hebb on the second.

Bartlett wrote (1932):

> . . . the organism discovers how to turn round upon its own 'schemata', or, in other words, it becomes conscious [p. 208];

and

> . . . one of the great functions of images in mental life . . . [is] to pick items out of 'schemata', and to rid the organism of over-determina-

---

[11] See Freud (1900), Chapter VII, particularly its last section; Silberer (1912), also Rapaport (1951c) and (1951a), particularly the survey of the clinical conception of consciousness in my footnotes.

tion by the last preceding member of a given series. I would like to hold that this, too, could not occur except through the medium of consciousness. Again I wish I knew precisely how it is brought about [p. 209]. [This theory] . . . gives to consciousness a definite function other than the mere fact of being aware [p. 214].

(See Oldfield and Zangwill [1942] both on Bartlett's more recent views and for a critique of these views.)

Hebb (1949) accounts for the enduring organization of memory in terms of hypothetical closed neural circuits, which are organized into assemblies, which in turn are organized into phase sequences. He links consciousness to the degree of complexity of these memorial-conceptual cognitive organizations when he writes: "Consciousness then is to be identified theoretically with a certain degree of complexity of phase sequence in which both central and sensory facilitations merge . . ." (p. 145). This implies that consciousness is not an all-or-nothing phenomenon. Hebb spells it out: ". . . the distinction is not between discrete, unrelated states but between the extremes of a continuum" (p. 144).

It is worth noting that Bartlett, while attributing to consciousness a definite function besides awareness, speaks about it as a unitary phenomenon, while Hebb, seeing consciousness as a continuum of many variations, does not attribute any definite function to it.

The observation to which we now turn will, I hope, bring into relief a number of varieties of consciousness in addition to those discussed so far, and may make it plausible that the varieties of consciousness can, and probably should, be treated as relatively enduring organizations that perform definite functions.

III

This observation I take from a study in which I attempted night by night, over a prolonged period, to arouse myself after every thought experience just enough to be able to record the experience and its content. The record contains thought experiences ranging from dreams through intermediary forms like hypnagogic hallucinations, reveries, daydreams, to ordered waking thoughts.[12] I cannot discuss here the preparations for this recording, nor its precise conditions, nor even the many obvious and less obvious methodological pitfalls inherent in such a study (see Rapaport, 1951c).

At one point the record shows the following behavior. First, I had a dream, aroused myself after it, but could not "find" the dream. I made efforts to "capture" it. In the course of these efforts I noted that I was "slip-

---

[12] See Brenman (1949), also Schafer (1954). The examples mentioned here do not exhaust the varieties of cognitive experiences. For instance, they do not touch on the various forms of waking imagery, e.g., the form described by Hanawalt (1954) and observed by me also, both in waking and reverie.

ping" into sleep again and told myself I must keep awake until I had "captured" and recorded the dream. Second, I did doze off and saw two "pinwaves"[13] approaching each other, at a small angle, in a dark sea, and made an effort to make them meet. Third, I fell asleep again and dreamed. The dream was: I am going to an examination at the University. I am . . . to be there . . . at eight. It is five . . . of eight. I am afraid I will be late . . . I arrive at the main door. The University is strange, it is not like my Alma Mater[14] . . . I do not know where to go . . . My fear that I will be late mounts . . . I ask the janitor . . . He begins to stutter in a most terrible way . . . I become more and more tense . . . I feel like bursting . . . Fourth, at this point the record of the dream broke off: I "fell off" and had a new experience. The record of this begins with a series of distorted words, some of which sound like Latin, others like Greek, Hebrew, or Arabic, followed by the comment: "I do not understand." This in turn is followed by: "A father in a monastery, panting, says to his son, 'I am so glad you got in before they shut the door.' "

I want to suggest that the four phases of this observation treat the same cognitive motif with different cognitive means, at different levels of awareness.[15] Such "translations" of thoughts from waking cognition into dream cognition have been observed by Freud (1900) and others (Schrötter, 1911; Roffenstein, 1924; Nachmansohn, 1925), from waking cognition into daydream cognition by Varendonck (1921), from waking cognition into hypnagogic hallucinations by Silberer (1909, 1912) and others (Froeschels, 1949). My records contain examples of translation to and from a variety of distinguishable forms of cognition. The one I have chosen to present here contains the greatest number of translations of one theme in my records. May I add here that I transcribed all my records on the day following my taking them and, in doing so, I separately recorded additional observations as my memory supplied them.

The common cognitive motif of the four phases is set out in the first phase. It is the struggle to maintain consciousness until the dream is "captured"; but it also has the connotation[16] of a struggle between tired incapac-

---

[13] "Pin-waves" is the word in the record. Actually the visual image was of two points progressing on straight lines at a small angle, leaving a very narrow wake behind them.

[14] The "strange"-ness of the University and the "it is not like my Alma Mater" were only "implicit" in the dream experience and only the recording brings them out explicitly. In other words, the knowledge that this *was* my Alma Mater and the fact that it did not look like my Alma Mater stood juxtaposed without being experienced as a contradiction.

[15] In the following, when I discuss these four different cognitive means by which the same motif is expressed in this observation, I will treat these observations only on the level of their *manifest form,* unless I specify otherwise. By manifest form I mean what in the theory of dreams is called *manifest content* in contrast to *latent thought.*

[16] It is worth noting here that waking cognition is not free of connotations though, as we shall see below, in comparison with other forms of cognition it appears to be.

ity and ambition or duty. In other words, it is the antithesis: I must—I cannot.

The first phase I should like to describe as one of more or less waking consciousness and of waking cognition, which is, however, not particularly ordered and certainly not disciplined and logical. In the full waking state the experience of "slipping" is either absent or successfully countered by "effort," while my record of this phase shows that I felt I was waging a losing battle. However, I was aware of my slipping awareness, and, according to these records, such awareness of awareness appears to be a good criterion of the waking state. The thought content is that of waking cognition, in that it sets out the struggle with reasonable clarity, though it proposes no means of winning it, as ordered logical thought usually does in these records.

One more characteristic of this phase is noteworthy: I am aware of a "feel" of the lost dream and "reach" for it in my own thoughts: my consciousness turns back upon itself (see Piaget, 1950, also the mathematician Gonseth, 1926). My "self," my own thoughts, my dream, my goal, my sleepiness, are all fairly well differentiated, even though my "reaching" for the dream is indistinct. Such differentiation too is, according to these records, a persistent characteristic of waking cognition in contradistinction to other forms of cognition. (See Lewin [1935] as well as Werner [1926] on differentiation in relation to the development of cognition; also Brenman, Gill, and Knight [1952], and Brenman [1951].)

The second phase I should like to describe as a hypnagogic hallucination of the sort Silberer (1909) studied and described as a thought form characteristic of the transition from waking to sleep in which either the subjective state of the dozing-off person, or the pattern of his dozing-off thought, or the content of it is translated into imagery (see Isakower, 1938). My records contain many of these. The most striking ones, like the one presented here, are related to the main obstacle to this sort of study—namely, the search for fading thought experiences and the struggle against sleep—and take various forms: watching somebody trying to find a way out of a labyrinth; seeing somebody going toward a door only to discover that it is not a door but a shadow; following somebody's increasingly frantic approach toward a door as the door slowly shuts, and so on. Against this background one of the pin-waves of the second phase appears to represent my consciousness, the other the dream to be "captured." The small angle, implying that the meeting point is far away, and perhaps the "dark sea" too, translate the "feel" of a losing battle into this form of cognition.[17] The effort needs no translation.

What then are the characteristics of this state and this form of cognition? The cognition is first of all characterized by the predominance of visual imagery, absent in the first phase except for a vague directional image in

[17] See Erikson (1954) on the effect of the dream investigator's purpose on his dreams.

"reaching" for the dream.[18] Indeed, my records indicate a progressive increase of imagery from waking thought toward dream thought. This translation into images, however, also does away with the clear differentiations of the first phase: there is nothing here like the "turning back upon the dream" in the first phase. Dream and consciousness are leveled, equalized, both being represented by "pin-waves." [19] Yet some differentiation is still left: I myself am an observer of the scene and not a part of it as is usual in dreams. However, this self is a very peculiar observer, one who can make an effort to promote the process he is observing.

Here two further characteristics of the hypnagogic state emerge, one that it shares with daydreams and the other that it shares with dreams. My rôle, as an observer with a preserved awareness of personal identity and yet with the ability to influence the events, is characteristic of daydreams. The daydreamer can doctor up, interrupt, and restart his daydream[20] but while he, as the observer, retains awareness of his personal identity, he also usually appears as a figure in the daydream (Varendonck, 1921). The characteristic this hypnagogic hallucination shares with dreams is this: I, as an observer of the two "pin-waves," felt that I was exerting an effort to make them meet, but my ability to do so and the means by which I was doing so remained unstated, or, in other words, "implicit." Now, according to these records, "implicit knowledge" is characteristic of dreams and diminishes as waking thought is approached. For instance, in dreams one figure "knows" what the other figures feel, though nothing may be said and no expressive movement observed. I do not mean that we do not have such "implicit" cognitions in our waking state, but they are less frequent and we experience them with reservations as subjective impressions rather than with conviction as factual knowledge, or else we are called "psychic," or accused of projection. In dreams we rarely find such reservations and realize only on recording them, as I did, that what we "knew for certain" in the dream had no evidential grounds whatever. But then you may counter that you know psychologists whose "scientific beliefs" make them suspect of living in a continuous dream of this sort. With this I shall not take issue.

I must add here that in hypnagogic hallucinations the subject does not always remain an outside observer with a preserved awareness of personal identity. In those hypnagogic hallucinations in which the subject's personal identity is not preserved there are other features distinguishing the illusions from dreams.

[18] See Bühler (1908) for such directional images and note the relation of these observations to the "imageless thought" controversy.

[19] Concerning "leveling" see Rapaport (1951a, p. 625 n.).

[20] There are people who at times do resume a dream that has been interrupted by their awakening. Some people at times do intend to dream about a definite theme and succeed in doing so. I have even encountered a few reports of dreams which the dreamer restarted and brought to an ending different from the original. But such "manipulations" are quite infrequent in dreams, while they are common in daydreams.

The third phase will be readily recognized as a dream, even though I did not report its continuation for reasons of privacy.

The dream cognition of the common theme may be paraphrased as follows: I am trying to find the "test," and I am trying to pass the "test," but I am hampered by the unfamiliarity of what should be familiar and by "inarticulateness" (i.e., stuttering). This paraphrase shows that here the original theme has taken on additional connotations (see footnote 16). But those familiar with the nature of dreams distinguish between manifest dream content and latent dream thought, and will recognize that this translation of the theme is merely a translation into the manifest dream content. If the theme has already picked up additional connotations in the manifest dream content, the latent dream thought adds further connotations, which expose the subjective meaning in my life pattern of the struggle between capacity and limitations on the one hand, duty and ambition on the other. Those familiar with dreams will also recognize that in this dream our common theme was used in the way day residues of undischarged tension are usually used by dreams.

One of the salient characteristics of dream cognition is, thus, that it takes its departure from day residues of undischarged tension, and translates them into imagery that indicates, in an "implicit" fashion, the connotations of and place in the dreamer's scheme of life of the theme (i.e., day residue) that has been translated.[21] This abundance of connotations in dream cognition contrasts sharply with the waking cognitive function of the first phase, though people do use allusions and connotative designations in waking thought also. How does dream cognition bring about these multiple connotations of its imagery? It does so by use of a variety of mechanisms (see Freud, 1900; Werner, 1926). It *condenses,* for example, when it represents in a single image "my Alma Mater," which the building definitely *is* to me in the dream, and a definitely strange building. It uses *displacement* and produces multiple images when it represents my "losing" the dream of the first phase—a dream which was mine and which I nevertheless did not know—on the one hand by my *unfamiliar* Alma Mater and on the other by the examination I *may not get to.* Moreover, it displaces or *projects* my tired incapacity and inarticulateness onto a stuttering janitor. It uses *substitutions* and *symbols* also, but I believe you will permit me to stop at this point.

These mechanisms are absent in the waking cognition of the first phase. While a detailed analysis of the second phase would show that they are present there, by and large the study of my records—and of dreams in general—indicates that the mechanisms illustrated here (as well as imagery and multiple connotations) are a predominant characteristic in dream cog-

---

[21] See my commentary (1951a) on Schrötter's (1911), Roffenstein's (1924), and Nachmansohn's (1925) hypnotically suggested dreams. See also Pötzl (1917) and Fisher (1954, 1956).

nition, and diminish as we proceed through hypnagogic hallucination, reverie, and daydream toward waking cognition. Let me add that the form of awareness is also characteristic of the dream. In this dream I had no awareness of my personal identity and the awareness of the figure who represented me in the dream[22] appeared to be filled with the idea, "I must get there—I won't," much as our amnesia patient was with his "I must end it all" in the first phase of his illness. While there are dreams during which some awareness of one's personal identity is represented by the feeling and thought that "this is just a dream," they are the exception rather than the rule, both in records of my dreams and in other people's dreams which I have collected.

Finally, let me mention that my questioning of the janitor and his stuttering were only "implicit" in the dream. I "knew" that I asked and that he "stuttered" in answer, but there were no words. I have indicated before that his "implicitness" is characteristic of dream cognition and diminishes as waking thought is approached.

In general, a multitude of connotations—usually mercifully hidden from our waking cognition by defensive and controlling organizations—are "recruited" (to use Hebb's term) to the dream theme by dream cognition. Dream cognition achieves this "recruitment"—which enriches, as it were, the themes of our waking thought—by means of mechanisms that in other forms of cognition are more or less proscribed. The free use of these mechanisms is characteristic of dream cognition, which shares it only with symptom-forming processes and with psychotic thought disorders (see Freud, 1915a, 1915b). Yet all cognitive forms make some use of or show some intrusion of these mechanisms. For example, they are obviously used in poetry and in the arts in general (see Empson, 1949; Brooks, 1939; and Kris, 1932–52).

Let us now turn to the fourth phase of our observation. I shall call it a reverie.[23] The term "reverie" is often used as a synonym for daydream. I, however, shall use it to mean a state of consciousness and a form of cognition midway between those of daydream and hypnagogic hallucination.

[22] I am referring to the figure "I" in the dream. Actually, since the dream is a form of cognition, all the figures in it are the dreamer's thoughts and thus all represent him, or rather various aspects of his inner world. Lewis Carroll has put it thus: " 'He is dreaming now,' said Tweedledee: 'and what do you think he's dreaming about?' —Alice said: 'Nobody can guess that.' —'Why about you!' Tweedledee exclaimed . . . 'And if he left off dreaming about you where do you suppose you'd be?' —'Where I am now, of course,' said Alice. —'Not you!' Tweedledee retorted contemptuously. *'You'd be nowhere. Why, you're only a sort of thing in his dream!'* [Italics added.] —'If that there King was to wake,' added Tweedledum, 'you'd go out—bang!—just like a candle!' 'I shouldn't!' Alice exclaimed indignantly. 'Besides, if *I'm* only a sort of thing in his dream, what are *you* . . .?' 'Ditto,' said Tweedledum. —'Ditto, ditto!' cried Tweedledee" (*Through the Looking-Glass*).
[23] For a survey of a variety of kindred phenomena see Brenman (1949). Freud (1900) also noted a variety of "dream" that is akin to these.

I hope that the discussion that follows here will justify this distinction.

I would like to suggest that the reverie of this fourth phase translates our theme to the form of a wish fulfillment. The father's words, "I am so glad that you got in before they shut the door," as well as the fact that he says this "panting," implies that there *was* a question—"Will he get in, or will he not?"—which is our theme. But this form of cognition places the struggle in the past and makes the present a "happy ending." This aspect of reverie cognition is akin to the wish fulfillment of daydreams (Varendonck, 1921). Who of us has not fancied a glorious reception by his teacher, beloved, or parent, after some equally fancied great deed? This very feature is one of the distinctions between reverie cognition and dream cognition. In the latter, past and future are expressed only by "implication" (Freud, 1900; Spielrein, 1923). What are the other characteristics that distinguish reverie cognition from dream cognition? To answer this question I must explain a bit further the reverie of the fourth phase. In this cognitive experience, as in phase two, I was an observer. I *heard* the distorted words, I *saw* the monastery with a chain across the gate; then I *saw* the father speaking to the son and panting. But it was *I* who interjected after the distorted words: "I don't understand." The facts that I, as a person, was outside the scene and made a comment, and the explicit presence of verbalization, distinguish this fourth phase from dream cognition.[24] My records show that as one progresses from waking- to dream-cognition the use of verbalization decreases. Not that there is *no* explicit verbalization in dreams, but it is rare, and, as a rule, it is a repetition of a familiar or recently heard phrase, as Freud (1900) noted.

Let us note that this reverie arose when, in the course of recording the dream of the third phase, I reached the stuttering of the janitor and—as my supplementary record shows—I again experienced, while recording, the mounting tension. It appears that the distorted words translate into reverie cognition the janitor's stuttering—which, to put it colloquially, was "all Greek to me"—as well as my inability to capture the lost dream of the first phase. Moreover, it appears that the re-experienced tension was translated into the dream by the "panting" of the father.

However, the reverie cognition also shows features that contrast sharply with the waking cognition of the first phase and are akin to those of the dream. The abundance of visual imagery is obviously one of these features, the connotative-recruiting is another. The appearance of the father, of the monastery, and of the "they" who shut the doors, is the most obvious set of features of this sort, locating the meaning of the struggle of capacity and inability with duty and ambition, in the pattern of my life. The details of the

[24] There are also dreams in which the person representing the dreamer is on the sidelines as a mere observer. While this is not quite the same as the reverie observer's rôle, it does point up that these distinguishing characteristics refer to differences in frequency and are not qualitative all-or-nothing distinctions.

visual imagery imply further connotations and reveal the mechanisms by which the recruiting and multiple connotations were brought about. I shall not dwell on these here.

While we have always known that in general we can distinguish our thoughts, daydreams, and dreams from each other, I hope I have demonstrated that these as well as other forms of cognition can be distinguished from each other by objective criteria.[25] The criteria that I found were: use of visual imagery, use of verbalization, awareness of awareness (implying the ability to turn round upon the content or state of consciousness), explicitness versus implicitness, differentiation, recruiting-connotative enrichment by means of the mechanisms of condensation, displacement, and so on. There are still others to which I could not refer in this brief compass without recourse to clinical terminology and theory.[26]

In connection with the dream of the third phase, I have referred to controlling and defensive organizations, but I have refrained from discussing motivations. The motivations involved here range from high-level derivative motivations, such as duty, to basic drives. Our compass, the conceptual means to which I have limited myself here, and—last but not least—personal considerations, prevent me from entering upon these.

I feel that this demonstration of a variety of distinguishable forms of cognition—if sustained by further observations—is a demonstration of cognitive organizations other than those I discussed in my introduction and in the first observation I presented. These cognitive organizations, just like those involved in the three phases of the case of amnesia, are accompanied by varieties of awareness (that is, consciousness) that appear to be specific to them (see pp. 635–636). This suggests that varieties of consciousness are themselves organized means of cognition.[27] It also seems to support the contention that we are dealing here with quasi-stable cognitive organizations that use[28] different tools or mechanisms of cognition, and are themselves organized means of cognition.

[25] These criteria, as indicated before, are not qualitative distinctions, but rather quantitative parameters.

[26] Psychoanalytic theory subsumes these criteria under the generic concept "primary process" to distinguish them from the criteria of the goal-directed, ordered, and logical forms of thought, which in turn are subsumed under the generic concept, "secondary process" (see Freud, 1900, Chapter VII, and Rapaport, 1951a, Part VII).

[27] I cannot pursue this point here. A further demonstration that it is advantageous to treat varieties of consciousness not as epiphenomena of cognition, but rather as cognitive organizations integrating certain cognitive forms, would require the conceptual means of clinical (psychoanalytic) theory. See Rapaport (1951c).

[28] Here, as elsewhere in this paper, the term "use" requires some clarification. I am indebted to Dr. George Klein for pointing this out to me. What I mean is that the assemblies of cognitive forms (here called tools) are not random, but rather constitute a cohesive quasi-stable organization (here called cognitive organization). In this sense there is no justification for the term "use." The relationship in question is that of the whole to its parts and vice versa: the whole *is* the relationship system of its

IV

Now I shall turn to some observations on certain forms of schizophrenic pathology of thought. I am taking these partly from our studies in diagnostic testing (Rapaport, Gill, and Schafer, 1945–46, Vol. II) and partly from observations of pathology of thought in the course of psychotherapy. (See Bleuler, 1911, 1912, 1922, my footnote commentary on them in Rapaport, 1951a, and also Kasanin, 1944.)

I presented the first observation, on amnesia, to illustrate some cognitive organizations—which subserve the integration of cognition—laid bare, as it were, by pathology. I presented the second observation to demonstrate some further cognitive organizations, characteristic of special states such as dreams, reveries, and so on. In the examples to follow, I should like to spotlight other cognitive organizations by focusing on the forms of cognition that arise when the schizophrenic process disrupts such organizations so that their integrative function fails.

Observation A. Schizophrenic patients reporting their dreams comment at times: "When I awoke I was not sure whether I dreamed it or it really did happen." At other times they report: "As I woke up this morning, for a while I was uncertain whether I was awake or dreaming."

Observation B. (1) A schizophrenic patient's response to the seventh Rorschach card is: "Six sharks." The examiner inquires: "What makes it look like that?" The patient's answer: "Because yesterday I read *The Raft.*"

(2) A schizophrenic patient's response to the first Rorschach card: "A histological plate." Inquiry: "What makes it look like that?" Answer: "The sensation obtaining between light and one's eyes."

(3) A schizophrenic patient's response to a part of the sixth Rorschach card: "A vaginal smear containing gonococci." Inquiry: "What makes it look like that?" Answer: "The ink makes it look like that."

Observation C. A young schizophrenic patient describes to his therapist a conversation with another young patient, in relation to whom he displays a variety of feelings, ideas, and impulses which he cannot consciously admit in relation to his therapist. The conversation is the last of a series of similar

---

parts and the parts are defined by their place in the whole. To spell this out concretely: we recognize a cognitive organization by the cognitive forms used, and the significance of any single cognitive form (since it can appear in many cognitive organizations) derives from the cognitive organization within which it appears. But there *is* a sense in which the term "use" is justified. The cognitive organizations give form to contents that in turn express the motivations, intentions, etc., of the organism. The cognitive forms (tools) may therefore be said to be *used* in this form-giving and -expressing process. Dr. Klein raises the further question: "Who uses whom?" Indeed, there are observations necessitating the assumption that this "utilization" process can also work in the reverse direction. This, however, leads to the complex problems to which Allport's (1935–47) concept of "functional autonomy" and Hartmann's (1939) concept of "ego autonomy" refer, and these I cannot pursue further here.

ones. The patient tells the other patient that he feels intellectually inferior, indeed he thinks he may be a moron. The other obligingly agrees. Our patient now—as in earlier conversations—suddenly experiences the other's words as gospel truth, and indeed as his own thought and conviction. All he can and does ask from the other is: "How did you find it out?" The other again obliges, saying that he heard it from his therapist, who is the friend of our patient's therapist, who had heard it from our patient. Our patient experiences this also as "true." But at this point suddenly something dramatic happened which the patient recounted as follows: "I saw you telling his therapist that I am a moron, and in the moment I saw you I *knew* that this was not my thought but something I just heard, something he tried to put over on me, something that was not true."

First, let me state that none of these observations is exceptional or unique in the clinician's experience (see Arieti, 1955; and footnote 9, this chapter) or in my records. Second, I would like to suggest that all these observations have in common one feature that may be crudely characterized as pertaining to an impairment of a "frame of reference" or of its use. I choose the term "frame of reference" here only because it is well worn (for a different interpretation, see Helson, 1951, particularly pp. 379 ff.). Otherwise, however, it is a catchall whose contents are heterogeneous and will have to be sorted out sooner or later. Most cognitive organizations have at one time or another been referred to as "frames of reference."

In observation A, the "frames of reference" of *waking-* and *dreaming-*cognition blur. In observation C, the "frames of reference" of that which is cognized as *"only a thought"* and of that which is cognized as *true* shade into each other. In each of the three B observations, the psychological-perceptual "frame of reference" is left for another one, which in B (1) is the psychological-memorial, in B (2) the physiological-perceptual, and in B (3) the realistic-artifactual "frame of reference." I shall explain these terms later.

Let us take these observations one by one.

Observation A implies that in schizophrenic pathology dreams may appear to be waking experiences and waking experiences may appear to be dreams. It is no explanation to say simply that the discrimination between waking- and dream-cognition fails here because the schizophrenic's experience is dreamlike anyway; *first,* because it restates rather than explains the phenomenon; *second,* because the expression "the schizophrenic's experience is dreamlike" is a meaningless generality; *third,* because the very patients who report such experiences have dreams which they can discriminate from waking, and the very fact of their report—that is, their awareness of this—shows not an absence but a blurring of discrimination between waking- and dream-cognition.

But what is it in these experiences that can and has to be discriminated— is it their cognitive contents or is it something else? I attempted to demonstrate above by comparing the translations of a single theme into the "language" of four different cognitive organizations that dream cognition, waking cognition, and so on, are distinguishable and cohesive cognitive organizations. This might suggest that the different contents, through which the common theme is expressed in the various cognitive organizations, are the means by which we distinguish these organizations. Therefore, let me present an example in which the manifest cognitive content is the same both in waking- and in dream-cognition, though the theme it represents may be different in each.[29] A young male patient reports two experiences: in the first experience he fell asleep with the light on and saw a bus boy come to his room, but afterwards he could not recall whether he actually woke up and saw the bus boy come in or whether he dreamed it. In the second experience he was more certain that he was actually asleep and dreamed that he was awake and saw the bus boy walk into his room. The content of these two experiences is identical and indistinguishable from waking experience. The first experience is to be compared not only with the second more or less definite dream experience, but also with those dreams, familiar to the clinician, whose manifest content is indistinguishable from an actual and repeated experience of the subject, who nevertheless readily recognizes it as a dream. Thus it seems that what can be and is to be identified as waking- or dream-cognition is not the cognitive content but something that transcends the content. This does not prove, but may lend further plausibility to, the contention that dream cognition and waking cognition each form subjectively and objectively distinguishable cohesive cognitive organizations.

How does this observation relate to normal phenomena?

First of all, neurotic and "normal" people also have such experiences. Some of us always arise with a dreamy feeling, others carry the moods and affects of their dreams into the waking state, and yet others experience the uncertainty: "Was it really just a dream?" But unlike the schizophrenic's uncertainty, ours is passing and is either characterologically anchored so that we are accustomed to it and not alarmed by it, or else it is related to particularly intense motivations.[30]

Second, the question arises, How do we usually distinguish our dream experience from a waking one? We do have dreams that seem to us to be entirely real, but these are rare and usually arouse us from our sleep. We also have dreams during which we can "tell" ourselves that "this is just a

---

[29] I borrow this example from Dr. Peter Wolff.

[30] An example: a young man—who was not a psychiatric patient either before or after this incident of many years ago—made a "clean break" with a girl friend. The night following this event he "saw" the girl standing at his bedside and shouted at her, "I told you. You must not come here again." Throughout the experience he felt he was awake and only when roused to full waking by his own voice did he realize the nature of his experience.

dream." [31] In these we retain to some extent the awareness of our personal identity and our rôle as the observer of the scene. Such dreams are rare, however. Usually the distinction between dream and waking experience is far subtler: as a rule we experience the dream, while we are dreaming it, as a reality in which we participate, and yet we experience it with a "belief of reality" (see Freud, 1917a; Rapaport, 1952a) different from that which characterizes waking cognition. This subtle difference appears to be of the same order as the difference between visual memory images and the visual images in daydreams. Visual memory images contain many[32] of the spatial, temporal, and personal relationships of the contents that are cognized through them, while the visual images of daydreams tend to contain fewer or none at all.[33] All of us have had images of the "castle in Spain," or "the prancing steed," which, unlike memory images, carried no indications of their origins. You may also remember the strangeness of some of the images aroused in you by "La Belle Dame sans Merci," or "Kubla Khan." The process that strips visual memory images of their relational (spatial, temporal, personal) characteristics and turns them into the visual images of imagination is probably similar to that which turns the contents of personal experience into the sort of impersonal information that intelligence tests measure.[34] Be that as it may, the "belief of reality" of waking cognition seems to depend partly on the availability of spatial, temporal, and similar

[31] A rather complicated variant of this is the dream in which the content of the subject's dream is that he is dreaming.

[32] Such relationships have been conceptualized variously in terms of schemata (Bartlett, 1932), recruitment (Hebb, 1949), as well as in terms of registration in various memory systems (Freud, 1900). See also Schafer (1945).

[33] This is not a hard and fast distinction. Daydreams too may have visual images rich in memorial connotations.

[34] There is a parallel here also to the relation between deliberate problem-solving behavior and habituated motor behavior. Hartmann's (1939) "automatization" concept appears relevant to these relationships. A perceptual image, upon having been perceived, enters a variety of relations and its content is thereby enriched. The full memorial image is in this sense rich in characteristics. These very relationships, however, also exert a selective effect on the raw material of *perception,* and lay the groundwork for transforming it into a concept that is impoverished in characteristics. Both the enrichment and the impoverishment processes begin with these relationships. The product of the first is the memory laden with the relational characteristics of the experience, as well as with those of prior and subsequent related experiences; the memories the therapist deals with tend to be of this sort. The product of the second is the *concept* held generally and divested of the relational earmarks of its origin. Knowledge, and information in general, is an intermediary station—albeit frequently a final stop for many—on the way to the concept. Hebb (1949) describes concept formation in a manner which is, to my mind, analogous with the one described here. The question may arise how it is that daydream and dream images, which are so laden with personal relevance, are characterized here as "impoverished." Actually, it is the impoverishment in memorial-relational characteristics that makes the image amenable to the process that lends it multiple connotations (see p. 645 above). As a rule, only the day residues of the dream retain their relational characteristics.

characteristics and partly on a type of consciousness—awareness of awareness—which if necessary can turn round on these characteristics, and these
may well be the factors that distinguish the "belief of reality" of the waking
state from that of dream cognition. Let us remember that we usually become aware of the multiple connotations of dream cognition only when we
turn round upon the dream in the subsequent waking state, equipped
with the technique of dream interpretation.

The clinician subsumes the distinctions here discussed under the heading
of reality testing (see Freud, 1911). But to academic psychology also,
these distinctions are familiar from Brentano's act psychology (Brentano,
1874, 1911, 1928; Meinong, 1902), according to which the organism is
not passive in its cognitive experiences, and therefore the cognitive *act* is to
be distinguished and studied apart from the cognitive *content*. The cognitive
act was termed "intention" by Brentano. Perception, thought, imagination,
and so on, may all have the same cognitive content, yet their intentional act
is different. Generalizing from Brentano's view, we might say that we can
"intend" a table by perceptual, memorial, conceptual, hallucinatory, or
dream intentions (see Rapaport, 1951a, 1952a). These differences in intention will then be assumed to lend, or will fail to lend, or will lend a
certain quality of "belief of reality" to the cognized content. It goes without
saying that most of these distinctions are readily made by us in subjective
experience; but it also should go without saying that these distinctions are
indispensable tools for orientation in reality. Perceptual intentions distinguish objects that are present from absent ones, which cannot be perceptu-
ally intended. Perceptual intention, therefore, indicates that the object is
present and can be approached by a more or less direct route. Other kinds
of intentions are no less important: they make it possible to intend the
absent object and to discover its memorial-historical, contextual, and conceptual relations, and thereby enable us to find these objects in reality by
way of a detour (see Freud, 1900, Chapter VII; Schilder, 1920, 1930;
Rapaport, 1950, 1951d).

It seems feasible to define the concept of intention so as to make it independent of its act-psychological trappings and to link certain varieties of
intent with certain cognitive organizations. Our discrimination between the
seen and the dreamed, the remembered and the imagined, is so stable that it
would seem to be more justifiable to assume that this stability is vouchsafed
by relatively stable cognitive organizations and intentions pertaining to
them, than to assume that this stability is achieved by *ad hoc* discriminatory
judgments made from occasion to occasion (Schilder, 1924; Rapaport,
1951d).

Let me now turn to observation B.[35] Our interest in each of the three

[35] These examples are taken from Rapaport, Gill, and Schafer (1945–46), Vol. II,
Appendix II, which contains the full collation of such "deviant verbalizations" of the
patient population discussed in the volume. See also pp. 324–365 of the same volume.

examples centers on the patient's answer to the Rorschach Test inquiry. Most subjects (including patients) have a common understanding of the standard inquiry, "What makes it look like that?" as shown by the fact that they respond to it within the same "frame of reference." I will call it here the *psychological-perceptual frame of reference.* Let me illustrate. Take the response: "A bat." Inquiry: "What makes it look like that?" Answer: "It impressed me as a bat because it had two wings, a body, a head with big ears, and its color was dark gray." This is an explanation in psychological terms since the subject speaks about his impressions and not about un-equivocal facts of reality; moreover, it is also an explanation in perceptual terms since he indicates the features that gave rise to his impression. The question with which the Rorschach cards are presented is also within this "frame of reference": "What does this look like to you?" It asks for a subjective yet still perceptual impression. Subjects vary in their comprehension of the question, as shown by the fact that the responses of some stress the subjective side, those of others the perceptual side. The former tend to give their impressions freely, the latter tend to search for what the inkblot "really represents." These differences of style show intraindividual consistency and have considerable importance in diagnosing personality organization (Rapaport, Gill, and Schafer, 1945–46, Vol. II).

Let us now see how our schizophrenic patients understood the inquiry. In the first example (see Benjamin, 1944) the patient's explanation of his "Six sharks" is: "Because yesterday I read *The Raft.*" Is this a psychological-perceptual explanation? It is a psychological explanation, that is, one in terms of subjective experience, but this subjective experience is in terms of memory rather than perception. While inquiry in terms of the psychological-perceptual "frame of reference" tends to bring forth answers within the same "frame of reference," our patient's answer shifted to the psychological-memorial "frame of reference."

A similar shift occurs in the second example (see Goldstein, 1944, and Cameron, 1944). The patient explains his "histological plate" by "the sensation obtaining between the light and one's eyes." True, without the impact of the light no response to the card could have taken place. But is this a psychological-perceptual explanation? It has something to do with the perceptual, namely, with its physics and physiology, but it contains no trace of the psychologically subjective. The patient shifted from the psychological-perceptual frame of reference of the inquiry to the physiological-perceptual frame of reference of the answer.

The shift in the third example (see above) is in the same direction as the second, only more extreme. The patient explains the "vaginal smear containing gonococci" by "the ink makes it look like that." Again there is no trace of the psychologically subjective in the explanation. It seems to pertain to the "objective cause" of perception, and reflects what as a philosophy would pass as "naïve realism." It could well have come from Piaget's

(1927a, 1931) collection of causal explanations taken from that phase of the child's development which Piaget calls "artificialistic," and in which things happen or are the way they are because they were made by someone to happen or to be that way. Thus, this patient shifted from the psychological-perceptual "frame of reference" to the realistic-artifactual.

I have pointed out that within the psychological-perceptual frame of reference there is room for a wide variety of styles. These patients, however, overstep this frame of reference: the first one does so in the subjective-psychological direction, disregarding perception, while the second and third do so in the perceptual direction; losing sight of their subjectivity, they take their perceptions for objective truth. In these excesses they seem like caricatures of philosophers: the first one a caricature of the idealist-rationalist, the latter two of the pragmatic naïve realist. Psychologists of various beliefs and some sense of humor will discover their own caricatures in these patients. But this comparison should not mislead us: philosophical systems are complex cognitive organizations of a higher order (see Piaget, 1950; Erikson, 1956), showing great qualitative and quantitative differences in interindividual distribution, while the "frames of reference" I discuss here are ubiquitous and, from the beginning of adolescence, belong to our basic psychological equipment.

These are only a few examples of the many fixed "frames of reference" that orient us to the appropriate level of discourse and abstraction and keep us from changing our "realm of discourse." Orientation in our multilayered world of reality would seem rather hopeless without the steering of "frames of reference." Most schizophrenic and many obsessional patients lack this automatic steering. Their attempts to decide from occasion to occasion the level of discourse in which to move results either in shifts of the sort we have seen or in an inability to make a shift when it is appropriate,[36] or in a state of hopeless confusion. Such observations prompt the clinician to attribute structure character to these frames of reference. Problem-solving research is familiar with the normal effects of frames of reference that permit no shifting and hold the subjects in a vise, as well as with those that do not compel any persistence (see Woodworth, 1938, Chapters XXIX and XXX; Duncker, 1945).

I have already indicated that inquiries made in a psychological-perceptual frame of reference draw answers within the same frame of reference. Elsewhere (Rapaport, 1951a; Rapaport, Gill, and Schafer, 1945–46) I have discussed the grounds for considering that relationships of the question-answer variety are mediated by anticipations. I have also pointed out that many such anticipations are structurally guaranteed by linguistic forms, such as conjunctions (but, though, and so on). It seems to me that there is a close relation between anticipations and the type of "frame of

---

[36] See Benjamin (1944). See also Scheerer (1946); many of the considerations advanced in this paper have a close affinity to his point of view.

reference" I have discussed here. Discourse seems to proceed by ever-nar-rowing anticipations and these "frames of reference" seem to form early steps in this narrowing course, while the anticipations that are anchored in specific linguistic forms are later ones.

May I stress that I chose these three examples illustrating "frames of reference" for the simplicity with which they could be presented, and la-beled them *ad hoc*.[37] There is no reason to assume that they or their mal-functions are any more or any less important than the many frames of refer-ence we use, and the malfunctions of which we observe every day. Much—though by no means all—of what the Würzburg School (Ach, 1905; Titchener, 1909) termed *"Einstellung"* and *"Bewusstseinslage,"* as well as what J. Gibson (1941) calls "set," and G. Allport (1935) calls "attitude" (particularly instrumental attitude), show pathological malfunctions simi-lar to those of "frames of reference," and there are reasons to believe that they could be conceptualized as "frames of reference" in the sense of the term used here.

Let us now turn to observation C, concerning the patient who experi-enced the thoughts of another first as "true" and his own, and then suddenly discovered their real nature. If we were to rank the cognitive organizations dealt with in this section, the "frames of reference" would seem the most narrow and specific ones, those related to waking- versus dream-cognition broader and more general, and the ones we are about to discuss the broad-est and most general, and of the same order as the cognitive organization centering around personal identity discussed in the observation on amnesia. The pathology in the present example is related to depersonalization, which we mentioned in the same connection.

On first inspection, our patient's pathology seems to be his lack of dis-crimination between "This I heard," and "This is what I think," and be-tween "It occurred to me," and "It is true." This at first appears to be an impairment of frames of reference. Indeed, the shift from "This I heard" to "This is what I think" is a shift from the hearsay-perceptual to the judging-cognitive "frame of reference"; and the shift from "It occurred to me" to "It is true," a shift from the freely wandering-cognitive to the veridical-cognitive "frame of reference." May I stress again that these are *ad hoc* labels.

But there is more to this than just an impairment of "frame of refer-ence." These shifts in "frame of reference" differ from those of the Ror-schach inquiries: their net effect is to leave the subject open to and at the mercy of the ideas of others, as well as of his own. In clinical parlance, this impairment of "frames of reference" amounts to a weakening of the bound-

---

[37] Dr. George Klein suggests—and I agree—that the specific "frames of reference" treated here might well have been discussed in Heider's (1930; also 1926) terms of "thing" and "medium," since they deal with the mediation of the "thing character" of the object.

ary between the person and his environment. The clinician's retrospective reconstructions (Freud, 1911, 1917a; Schilder, 1935), as well as Piaget's direct observations, suggest that an indistinctness of this boundary is characteristic of early phases of individual development. Moreover, H. Werner (1926) has shown that some weakness—either circumscribed or general—of the boundary between the person and his environment is widespread both in developmental and pathological forms. Indeed, there seems to be a consensus that some weakness or modification of this boundary is one of the underlying ingredients of magical and animistic beliefs and practices (see Lévy-Bruhl, 1923; Freud, 1913; Piaget, 1927b).

It seems then that in this observation the impairment of the frame of reference involves the impairment of that higher-order integration represented by the boundary between that which belongs to the person and that which does not. The circumstances under which integration was restored tend to corroborate this and also tend to connect this higher-order integration with that cognitive organization centered around personal identity which we discussed in connection with the second phase of amnesia. To make this plausible, I have to enter into clinical considerations. The patient in question has not lost awareness of personal identity as our amnesia patient had. He "knows" who he is. He has lost personal identity only in the sense of depersonalization (see Schilder, 1924, pp. 304 ff., and for further sources see my footnotes to the same pages). This depersonalization was a creeping and partial one of which he was scarcely aware before therapy. The patient's failure to distinguish "hearsay" from "thought," and so on, was accordingly also only partial: it was limited to contact with people with whom he formed powerful identifications (see Freud, 1917b, 1923). Indeed, to consider the other's thoughts as "true" and one's own is one aspect of the early phase of any strong identification. Such identifications were sought by our patient in an effort to find a substitute for his personal identity, and as a building stone toward a "new identity." Identity is an integrate of identifications (see Erikson, 1956; Freud, 1923). Dysfunction of personal identity, as in our case of amnesia, as well as its substitution by a single intensive identification, interfere with cognition just as the substitution of a single author's system for the whole of psychology interferes with psychological understanding (see Freud, 1923, pp. 38–39).

I have mentioned that our patient displayed toward the other patient a variety of ideas and impulses which he could not use in relation to his therapist. This both facilitated and hampered his identification with the therapist. But when the therapist's image arose in his mind he suddenly "discovered" a frame of reference other than that of the identification with the other patient, and in this frame of reference he recognized the "hearsay" for what it was.[38] Indeed, he later used the therapist's image as a magic

[38] It is implied that the appearance of the therapist's image was related to the patient's identification with him and that forming this identification was part of the patient's

device to help him distinguish "hearsay" from "own thought," as well as "thought" from "truth." It will be no surprise to you to learn that he also experienced the same difficulties in relation to his therapist. In both cases intensive single identifications usurped the function of identity and left the patient's cognition open and vulnerable in relation to the cognitions of the person with whom he identified.

If you consider that the great achievement of organisms is their relative independence from their environment, then the significance of the integrative organization, and of its impairment, comes into full relief. But the independence from their environment achieved by "open systems"—to use Bertalanffy's (1950) term—is always relative. Similarly, the effectiveness of the integration of cognitions in terms of personal identity, which delineates the person from his environment, is also only relative. I have already indicated that in the widespread magical and animistic beliefs and practices this integration and delineation is fluid. But there are other normal forms that also demonstrate the relativity of this integration. I shall not dwell on the multitude of pertinent hypnotic phenomena and will refer you simply to the studies of Gill and Brenman (Brenman, Gill, and Hacker, 1947; Brenman, Gill, and Knight, 1952). Nor will I discuss the consequences for cognition of the state of "being in love"—they are well known. I should like to mention only that "gullibility" is in many cases—though certainly not in all—a normal and enduring counterpart of the pathological gullibility of our patient. Moreover, when cognition ventures into areas where tested knowledge is meager, or into areas in which the person's information is slight, normal dysfunction akin to this pathology crops up readily.

V

Throughout this paper I have centered on relatively enduring forms in contrast to passing processes. I have suggested that we need concepts of organization- or structure-character to account for all these quasi-stable enduring forms. I am not sure but what the troubles of learning theory are due to its failure—cognitive maps and habit hierarchies to the contrary notwithstanding—to recognize the multitude and variety of these enduring forms. But this criticism may not be fair, and learning theories may simply be reluctant to accord a conceptual status to these relatively enduring forms, on the assumption that these can and must be reduced to a few simple constructs, even if reduction takes a long time. However, the relation of this persistent reducing to the lure of "the psychology of the empty organism" is patent.

My stress upon relatively enduring organization parallels a change of

---

work at reconstituting his identity. It is this background that underlay the effectiveness of the therapist's image in mobilizing the "frame of reference" which had been in abeyance.

emphasis in psychoanalytic theory. The clearest expression of this change is the development of psychoanalytic ego psychology in the last thirty years. Early psychoanalysis laid great stress upon motivations and their gratification processes. Indeed it may be considered the pioneer of the motivational point of view among psychologies. The development of ego psychology *added* an equal stress upon the relatively enduring organizations that not only subserve the defense against and control of these motivations but may give rise to new motivations and may also subserve the adaptation of the organism to its environment. It seems that with this stress on relatively enduring controlling- and means-organizations, psychoanalytic psychology finds itself again in a pioneering rôle.

The specific cognitive organizations or structures that I discussed were meant only as illustrations. My study of these is still in the initial stage and I hold no brief for them, except in so far as they illustrate my general point. Nor for that matter do I hold a brief for any specific psychoanalytic concept that refers to relatively enduring structures. Further study may well replace these concepts. But it cannot abolish the phenomena to which the present structure concepts refer. So far psychoanalysis is the only theory that has attempted to take account of these phenomena. If this theory is weak by the yardstick of academic psychology, the latter has not yet proposed a better one to account for these phenomena and the poet's words may well apply: "Whither we cannot fly, we go limping; the Scripture saith, limping is no sin." [39]

REFERENCES

Abeles, M., & Schilder, P. (1935). Psychogenetic Loss of Personal Identity: Amnesia. *Arch. Neurol. Psychiat.*, 34:587–604.

Ach, N. (1905). *Über die Willenstätigkeit und das Denken*. Göttingen: Vandenhoeck & Ruprecht. In part translated as "Determining Tendencies; Awareness" in Rapaport (1951a), pp. 15–38.

Allport, G. W. (1935). Attitudes. In *A Handbook of Social Psychology*, ed. C. Murchison. Worcester: Clark University Press, pp. 798–844.

———— (1935–47). *The Nature of Personality: Selected Papers*. Cambridge, Mass.: Addison-Wesley Press, 1950.

Arieti, S. (1955). *Interpretation of Schizophrenia*. New York: Brunner.

Bartlett, F. C. (1932). *Remembering: A Study in Experimental and Social Psychology*. Cambridge: Cambridge University Press.

Benjamin, J. D. (1944). A Method for Distinguishing and Evaluating Formal Thinking Disorders in Schizophrenia. In Kasanin (1944), pp. 65–90.

Bertalanffy, L. von (1950). The Theory of Open Systems in Physics and Biology. *Science*, 111:23–29.

[39] Rückert, "Die Makamen des Hariri" (Freud quoted these lines in *Beyond the Pleasure Principle* [1920]).

Bleuler, E. (1911). The Basic Symptoms of Schizophrenia. In Rapaport (1951a), pp. 581–649.

——— (1912). Autistic Thinking. In Rapaport (1951a), pp. 399–437.

——— (1922). Autistic-Undisciplined Thinking. In Rapaport (1951a), pp. 438–450.

Brenman, M. (1949). Dreams and Hypnosis. *Psychoanal. Quart.,* 18:455–465.

——— (1951). The Phenomena of Hypnosis. In *Problems of Consciousness,* Transactions of the First Conference. New York: Josiah Macy, Jr. Foundation, pp. 123–163.

———, Gill, M. M., & Hacker, F. J. (1947), Alterations in the State of the Ego in Hypnosis. *Bull. Menninger Clin.,* 11:60–66.

———, Gill, M. M., & Knight, R. P. (1952), Spontaneous Fluctuations in Depth of Hypnosis and Their Implications for Ego-Function. *Int. J. Psycho-Anal.,* 33:22–33.

Brentano, F. (1874). *Psychologie vom empirischen Standpunkte.* Leipzig: Dunker & Humbolt.

——— (1911). *Von der Klassifikation der psychischen Phänomene.* Leipzig: Dunker & Humbolt.

——— (1928). *Vom sinnlichen und nötischen Bewusstsein.* Leipzig: Felix Meiner.

Brooks, C. (1939). *Modern Poetry and the Tradition.* Chapel Hill: University of North Carolina Press.

Bruner, J. S., & Goodman, C. C. (1947). Value and Need as Organizing Factors in Perception. *J. Abnorm. Soc. Psychol.,* 42:33–44.

———, & Postman, L. (1947). Tension and Tension Release as Organizing Factors in Perception. *J. Pers.,* 15:300–308.

Bühler, K. (1908). On Thought Connections. In Rapaport (1951a), pp. 39–57.

Cameron, N. (1944). Experimental Analysis of Schizophrenic Thinking. In Kasanin (1944), pp. 50–64.

Claparède, E. (1911). Recognition and "Me-ness." In Rapaport (1951a), pp. 58–75.

Duncker, K. (1945). *The Structure and Dynamics of Problem-Solving Processes.* Washington: American Psychological Association.

Empson, W. (1949). *Seven Types of Ambiguity,* rev. ed. Norfolk, Conn.: New Directions.

Erickson, M. H. (1939). Experimental Demonstration of the Psychopathology of Everyday Life. *Psychoanal. Quart.,* 8:338–353.

———, & Erickson, E. M. (1941). Concerning the Nature and Character of Post-Hypnotic Behavior. *J. Gen. Psychol.,* 24:95–133.

Erikson, E. H. (1950). *Childhood and Society.* New York: Norton.

——— (1954). The Dream Specimen of Psychoanalysis. *J. Amer. Psychoanal. Assn.,* 2:5–56.

——— (1956). The Problem of Ego Identity. *Psychol. Issues,* 1:101–164, 1959.

Fisher, C. (1945). Amnesic States in War Neuroses: The Psychogenesis of Fugues. *Psychoanal. Quart.,* 14:437–468.

——— (1947). The Psychogenesis of Fugue States. *Amer. J. Psychother.,* 1:211–220.

——— (1954). Dreams and Perception: The Role of Preconscious and Primary Modes of Perception in Dream Formation. *J. Amer. Psychoanal. Assn.*, 2:389–445.

———— (1956). Dreams, Images, and Perception: A Study of Unconscious-Preconscious Relationships. *J. Amer. Psychoanal. Assn.*, 4:5–48.

————, & Joseph, E. (1949). Fugue with Awareness of Loss of Personal Identity. *Psychoanal. Quart.*, 18:480–493.

Freud, A. (1936). *The Ego and the Mechanisms of Defence.* New York: International Universities Press, 1946.

Freud, S. (1900). The Interpretation of Dreams, tr. A. A. Brill. *The Basic Writings.* New York: Modern Library, 1938, pp. 179–549.

———— (1901). The Psychopathology of Everyday Life, tr. A. A. Brill. *The Basic Writings.* New York: Modern Library, 1938, pp. 33–178.

———— (1909). Notes upon a Case of Obsessional Neurosis. *Collected Papers,* 3:293–383. London: Hogarth Press, 1946.

———— (1911). Formulations Regarding the Two Principles in Mental Functioning. *Collected Papers,* 4:13–21. New York: Basic Books, 1959.

———— (1913 [1912–13]). Totem and Taboo, tr. A. A. Brill. *The Basic Writings.* New York: Modern Library, 1938, pp. 805–930.

———— (1914). On Narcissism: An Introduction. *Collected Papers,* 4:30–59. New York: Basic Books, 1959.

———— (1915a). Repression. *Collected Papers,* 4:84–97. New York: Basic Books, 1959.

———— (1915b). The Unconscious. *Collected Papers,* 4:98–136. New York: Basic Books, 1959.

———— (1917a [1915]). Metapsychological Supplement to the Theory of Dreams. *Collected Papers,* 4:137–151. New York: Basic Books, 1959.

———— (1917b [1915]). Mourning and Melancholia. *Collected Papers,* 4:152–170. New York: Basic Books, 1959.

———— (1920). *Beyond the Pleasure Principle,* tr. C. J. M. Hubback. London: Hogarth Press, 1948.

———— (1923). *The Ego and the Id,* tr. J. Riviere. London: Hogarth Press, 1947.

———— (1926 [1925]). *The Problem of Anxiety,* tr. H. A. Bunker. New York: Psychoanalytic Quarterly & Norton, 1936.

Froeschels, E. (1949). A Peculiar Intermediary State between Waking and Sleeping. *Amer. J. Psychother.*, 3:19–25.

Geleerd, E., Hacker, F., & Rapaport, D. (1945). Contribution to the Study of Amnesia and Allied Conditions. *Psychoanal. Quart.*, 14:199–220.

Gibson, J. J. (1941). A Critical Review of the Concept of Set in Contemporary Experimental Psychology. *Psychol. Bull.*, 38:781–817.

Gill, M. M., & Rapaport, D. (1942). A Case of Amnesia and Its Bearing on the Theory of Memory. *This volume,* Chapter 9.

Goldstein, K. (1944). Methodological Approach to the Study of Schizophrenic Thought Disorder. In Kasanin (1944), pp. 17–40.

Gonseth, F. (1926). *Les Fondements des mathématiques.* Paris: Librairie Scientifique Albert Blanchard.

Hanawalt, N. G. (1954). Recurrent Images: New Instances and a Summary of the Older Ones. *Amer. J. Psychol.*, 67:170–174.

Hartmann, H. (1939). Ego Psychology and the Problem of Adaptation. In (abridged) Rapaport (1951a), pp. 362–396.

Hebb, D. O. (1949). *The Organization of Behavior; A Neuropsychological Theory.* New York: Wiley.

Heider, F. (1926). Thing and Medium. *Psychol. Issues,* 3:1–34, 1959.

———— (1930). The Function of the Perceptual System. *Psychol. Issues,* 3:35–52, 1959.

Helson, H., ed. (1951). *Theoretical Foundations of Psychology.* New York: Van Nostrand.

Henderson, D. K., & Gillespie, R. D. (1927). *A Textbook of Psychiatry.* Oxford: Oxford University Press.

Holzman, P. S. (1954). The Relation of Assimilation Tendencies in Visual, Auditory, and Kinesthetic Time-Error to Cognitive Attitudes of Leveling and Sharpening. *J. Pers.,* 22:375–394.

Isakower, O. (1938). A Contribution to the Pathopsychology of Phenomena Associated with Falling Asleep. *Int. J. Psycho-Anal.,* 19:331–345.

Janet, P. (1901). *The Mental State of Hystericals.* New York: Putnam.

Kasanin, J. S., ed. (1944). *Language and Thought in Schizophrenia.* Berkeley: University of California Press.

Klein, G. S. (1949). Adaptive Properties of Sensory Functioning: Some Postulates and Hypotheses. *Bull. Menninger Clin.,* 13:16–23.

———— (1954). Need and Regulation. In *Nebraska Symposium on Motivation, 1954,* ed. M. R. Jones. Lincoln: University of Nebraska Press, pp. 224–274.

————, & Schlesinger, H. (1949). Where Is the Perceiver in Perceptual Theory? *J. Pers.,* 18:32–47.

————, & Schlesinger, H. (1951). Perceptual Attitudes toward Instability: I. Prediction of Apparent Movement Experiences from Rorschach Responses. *J. Pers.,* 19:289–302.

Koffka, K. (1935). *Principles of Gestalt Psychology.* New York: Harcourt, Brace.

Kris, E. (1932–52). *Psychoanalytic Explorations in Art.* New York: International Universities Press, 1952.

———— (1950). On Preconscious Mental Processes. In Kris (1932–52), pp. 303–318.

Lévy-Bruhl, L. (1923). *Primitive Mentality.* London: Allen & Unwin.

Lewin, K. (1935). *A Dynamic Theory of Personality.* New York: McGraw-Hill.

Meinong, A. (1902). Über Annahmen. *Z. Psychol.,* Suppl. Vol. 2. Leipzig: Barth.

Murphy, G. (1947). *Personality.* New York: Harper.

Nachmansohn, M. (1925). Concerning Experimentally Produced Dreams. In Rapaport (1951a), pp. 257–287.

Oldfield, R. C., & Zangwill, O. L. (1942). Head's Concept of the Schema and Its Application in Contemporary British Psychology, Part III. Bartlett's Theory of Memory. *Brit. J. Psychol.,* 33:113–129.

Paul, I. H. (1959). Studies in Remembering: The Reproduction of Connected and Extended Verbal Material. *Psychol. Issues,* No. 2.

Piaget, J. (1927a). *The Child's Conception of Physical Causality.* London: Kegan, 1930.

——— (1927b). *The Child's Conception of the World*. New York: Harcourt, Brace, 1929.

——— (1931). Children's Philosophies. In *A Handbook of Child Psychology*, ed. C. Murchison. Worcester: Clark University Press, pp. 377–391.

——— (1950). *Introduction à l'épistemologie génétique*, 3 vols. Paris: Presses Universitaires de France.

Pötzl, O. (1917). The Relationship between Experimentally Induced Dream Images and Indirect Vision. *Psychol. Issues*, 7:41–120, 1960.

Rapaport, D. (1942). *Emotions and Memory*, 2nd unaltered ed. New York: International Universities Press, 1950.

——— (1950). On the Psychoanalytic Theory of Thinking. *This volume*, Chapter 28.

———, ed. & tr. (1951a). *Organization and Pathology of Thought*. New York: Columbia University Press.

——— (1951b). The Conceptual Model of Psychoanalysis. *This volume*, Chapter 34.

——— (1951c). States of Consciousness: A Psychopathological and Psychodynamic View. *This volume*, Chapter 33.

——— (1951d). Paul Schilder's Contribution to the Theory of Thought Processes. *This volume*, Chapter 32.

——— (1952a). Projective Techniques and the Theory of Thinking. *This volume*, Chapter 38.

——— (1952b). Review of O. H. Mowrer, *Learning Theory and Personality Dynamics*. *This volume*, Chapter 37.

——— (1953). Review of J. Dollard & N. E. Miller, *Personality and Psychotherapy: An Analysis in Terms of Learning, Thinking, and Culture*. *This volume*, Chapter 43.

———, & Erickson, M. (1942). Multiple Personality. Paper given at the meeting of the American Psychiatric Association.

———, Gill, M. M., & Schafer, R. (1945–46). *Diagnostic Psychological Testing*. 2 vols. Chicago: Year Book Publishers.

Roffenstein, G. (1924). Experiments on Symbolization in Dreams. In Rapaport (1951a), pp. 249–256.

Schafer, R. (1945). A Study of Thought Processes in a Word Association Test. *Character & Pers.*, 13:212–227.

——— (1954). *Psychoanalytic Interpretation in Rorschach Testing*. New York: Grune & Stratton.

Scheerer, M. (1946). Problems of Performance Analysis in the Study of Personality. *Ann. N. Y. Acad. Sci.*, 46:653–675.

Schilder, P. (1920). On the Development of Thoughts. In Rapaport (1951a), pp. 497–518.

——— (1924). *Medical Psychology*, ed. & tr. D. Rapaport. New York: International Universities Press, 1953.

——— (1930). Studies Concerning the Psychology and Symptomatology of General Paresis. In Rapaport (1951a), pp. 519–580.

——— (1935). *The Image and Appearance of the Human Body*. London: Kegan.

Schrötter, K. (1911). Experimental Dreams. In Rapaport (1951a), pp. 234–248.

Silberer, H. (1909). Report on a Method of Eliciting and Observing Certain Symbolic Hallucination-Phenomena. In Rapaport (1951a), pp. 195–207.

———— (1912). On Symbol-Formation. In Rapaport (1951a), pp. 208–233.

Spielrein, S. (1923). Die Zeit im unterschwelligen Seelenleben. *Imago*, 9:300–317.

Stengel, E. (1941). On the Aetiology of the Fugue States. *J. Ment. Sci.*, 87:572–599.

Titchener, E. B. (1909). *Lectures on the Experimental Psychology of the Thought-Processes*. New York: Macmillan.

Varendonck, J. (1921). *The Psychology of Daydreams*. New York: Macmillan. Also (abridged) in Rapaport (1951a), pp. 451–473.

Werner, H. (1926). *Comparative Psychology of Mental Development*. New York: Harper, 1940.

Woodworth, R. S. (1938). *Experimental Psychology*. New York: Holt.

5 1

DISCUSSION

Charles E. Osgood, "A Behavioristic Analysis of Perception and Language as Cognitive Phenomena"

The scope of Dr. Osgood's paper is such that an adequate evaluation of it would require a careful study of his reference points. Since I did not undertake such a study, I will comment on only a few points.

We know from Dr. Osgood's other writings that he is interested in looking into the gap between the stimulus and the response, that he is inclined to pry open the lid of that "little black box," and that he is dissatisfied with a psychology of the empty organism. Here he restates his stand, offering many statements of facts and ideas rarely seen in papers entitled "A Behavioristic Analysis . . ." Perhaps the most striking one is the statement that S-R theories "say little or nothing" about the integration of either sensory or response events, and that "both sensory and motor signals are capable of becoming organized." True, many behaviorists have said something like this. Lashley and Hebb did, and Tolman's cognitive maps, as well as Hull's habit-family hierarchies, are organizations of this sort. But Dr. Osgood seems to go further. He speaks of an experience-determined increase in the *stability* of such integrations, of a transfer to *central programming* of the function of these integrates, of evocative integrations functioning as *units,* of "S-R relations originally organized on the 'voluntary' level . . . becom-[ing] *autonomous integrations,"* and of a syntax of behavior. I believe that the implications of all these statements become particularly clear when Dr. Osgood (like Piaget) lets some of these integrations develop from a *"circular reflex,"* and when he speaks of hierarchies of signs, of instrumental acts, and of mediators, and asserts that "the *availability* of such hierarchies to the mature organism makes possible the tremendous flexibility we observe in behavior." To me all this sounds very much like what Allport is concerned with when he speaks of functional autonomy, and like what psycho-analytic ego psychology calls autonomous structures of the ego. It seems to me that Hebb (the similarities to whose theory Dr. Osgood duly indicates) was involved with the same issues when he took such pains to show how it is that his neural circuits, assemblies, and phase sequences do not "extinguish," though they are not "reinforced." If we take these statements and their terms (integration, structure unit, autonomous integration, hierarchy, availability) at their face value, then we must judge that Dr. Osgood's conception departs considerably from the "habit" conception of behavior phenomena, in which the major—if not the only—guarantee of stability and availability is overlearning.

To my mind, Dr. Osgood's three levels and two stages are one way of taking a forthright stand against the psychology of the empty organism, that is, one way of conceptualizing what goes on in that little black box. They are an attempt to furnish the empty organism. Thus functionalism seems to allow some room for structural considerations, and many an idea that a while ago could have been dismissed as "emergentist" nonsense is lent respectability or conceptual status. I have in mind particularly Dr. Osgood's "units" and "autonomous integrations." I think it would be correct to suggest that S-R theorists refuse to conceptualize many familiar characteristics of cognition which they cannot (or should we say cannot as yet?) reduce to S-R linkages, while Dr. Osgood is ready to conceptualize such characteristics. I think this is a great advance. It seems that even if Dr. Osgood is convinced of the ultimate reducibility of all behavior phenomena to R-R, S-R, and S-S linkages, he still feels that one must take cognizance of the phenomena and of their interrelationships before starting the process of reduction. Indeed, it seems to me that Dr. Osgood implies that whatever the origin of such units, structures, hierarchies, and integrations, and whatever ultimate concepts they might be reducible to, it will not change the fact that they seem to have abiding rôles of their own. But I must not go further; I may be substituting my hopes for Dr. Osgood's intentions.

Let me turn, however, to those points of the paper which I do not consider an advance. Dr. Osgood assumes that he can derive his rather complex furnishings of the "black box" from associative linkages established by frequency. This is disappointing; the integrations, units, and so on, that Dr. Osgood attempts to conceptualize deserve to be conceptualized first of all because they show that stability, availability, etc., of which Dr. Osgood's paper speaks. As I see it, the crux of the issue is this: can an association— or conditioning—theory support such a stability? How do the "structures" in question escape the fate of time decrement or extinction; or, if they do not escape it, whence their stability and availability? How is a relationship established by the vanishing glue of conditioning capable of integrating other "neural events"? Let me put it this way: in every behavior, both the content and the intent must be taken into account. When I grab a paper, I both grab the *paper* and I *grab* the paper, that is, I experience both the paper and my act. While—if we try very hard—we might be able to deal with the contents (here the paper) without an abiding structural point of reference, we cannot do so in dealing with the act (that is, the grabbing, which makes me a grabber). Brentano's acts, Claparède's *moïté,* Head's and Bartlett's schemata, Hebb's phase sequences, in psychoanalytic theory Erikson's "modes," all refer to such stable reference points. The hope of basing this stability of structures on conditioning reminds me of the hope of playing a successful croquet game *à la Alice in Wonderland,* with flamingoes for mallets and hedgehogs for balls. But the associationist croquet game is even more hopeless because it seems to exclude the assumption of a player capable of compensating for the vagaries of his flamingoes and hedgehogs.

It may be appropriate to bring in an epistemological consideration. When we postulate a furnished rather than an empty organism, we shift from a *tabula rasa* conception of the mind to one of a mind that has a nature of its own. Dr. Osgood's structures, units, and hierarchies are steps away from the *tabula rasa* conception. The difference is like that between clay, which can be readily molded, and marble or wood, where you have to go with the grain. In spite of all the furnishings Dr. Osgood has provided it with, his world seems to remain a Humian world, in which behavior is determined by the probability distributions of environmental events, and even the choice of structuralized alternatives is probabilistically regulated. This is particularly striking when Dr. Osgood, in speaking of anticipations in language and illustrating his point by experiments on filling in missing words of sentences, explains the results in probabilistic terms: "At each point in a language message . . . we have a hierarchy of structural alternatives . . . varying in their probabilistic character with the grammatical restrictions in the language as a whole." But there is an alternative explanation of the results of such experiments, according to which the filling of a gap in a sentence is the effect of a series of progressively narrowing anticipations, regulated by "relevance" rather than by probabilistic hierarchy. The results so far do not rule out either of these explanations. What I mean is this: an adaptive organism's behavior is adaptive in that it meshes into environmental probability. Thus probabilistic findings do not necessarily prove that the furnishings of the "little box" are built by the laws of associative frequencies and probability. Max Delbrueck, the biophysicist, has pointed this out. He cautioned the physicist dealing with biological phenomena that adaptive regularities must not be mistaken for laws of nature. The psychological theorists who "follow Hume" seem to me to make this very mistake. They conceive of a mind that has no autonomy. One of the basic problems of psychology as a deterministic science is how to account for the observed relative autonomy of the organism from its environment. I think this is the problem Tolman attempted to solve in his *Purposive Behavior* (1932). Humian conceptions do not account for such observations. While it is difficult to see how associationism of any vintage can account for this relative autonomy, it is incumbent on us not to discount the possibility that it might do so, until it is proven that it cannot. What disquiets me is that Dr. Osgood does not face this issue.

However, let me abandon this epistemological aside and turn to Dr. Osgood's three levels and two stages. I know very little about the nervous system, and thus should tread gingerly here; yet this 2 × 3 seems to be too neat. Studies by Heinz Werner and Piaget in the last twenty years give the impression that the two stages so neatly separated by Dr. Osgood are actually indivisibly intertwined—particularly in the early phases of human ontogeny. Werner's sensory-tonic theory, as well as Piaget's derivation of all "intelligence" from sensorimotor intelligence, raises the question whether or not this sharp separation of "encoding" and "decoding" is simply the intellectual heir to the S-R frame of mind, even if it is much more thoughtful and rich than its parent.

But how about the three levels? Again my limited knowledge of perceptual-neurophysiological facts and theories makes me hesitant. Yet am I altogether mistaken when isomorphism as the first law of the "projection level" reminds me of Hume, Locke, and so on, according to whom clear and simple ideas are valid representations of the objects perceived? Dr. Osgood speaks about Jamesian chaos and about visual images not being things but only signs whose significance must be acquired. Surely this is an advance over the pragmatic, naïve realism of older behaviorism. But is it an entirely mistaken impression that the neat separation among the three levels militates against the study of the very process by which the visual image emerges from the Jamesian chaos and acquires significance? At any rate, the development of the constant object—as described by Piaget in his *Construction of Reality* (1937)—suggests an intertwining of these three levels. Would not also the phenomena of physiognomic perception and the perception-need relationship raise doubts about such a neat and simple progression in "decoding" and "encoding"?

Dr. Osgood's paper is so rich that it might seem ungrateful to point to any lack in it. Yet it seems important to indicate that he has failed to clarify the rôle of motivations in his theory of behavior. He tells us that the rules of operation differ from level to level. Should we nevertheless assume that motivations operate by the same rules—that is, reinforcement—on all levels, except for the projection levels, where they would presumably have no rôle? This lack of clarification of the rôle of motivations is the more striking since Piaget, as well as Hebb, whose goals are in many respects similar to Dr. Osgood's, also gives only a cavalier treatment to motivations. Two questions arise here. Does interest in the relatively permanent tools of cognition and behavior (the furnishings of the black box) diminish the investigator's interest in motivation? Are the conceptual tools appropriate for dealing with structures prohibitive or at least inhibitive of dealing with motivations, and vice versa? May I point out that a similar antithetic relationship seems to have obtained for a long time between the study of motivations and the study of structures in psychoanalysis. But the fact that I raise this matter may rest on a misunderstanding: Dr. Osgood may be taking the S-R motivation theory so much for granted that he feels no need to waste time on any of this. If so, then I should express my feeling that the place of motivations in a structural theory does need clarification.

Let me end by pointing again to advances. In discussing the selection from "the hierarchy of alternatives," Dr. Osgood—even though his major concern pivots around the most "probable" integration—turns finally to "attentional functions," as did Hebb. He asserts with Hull that it is of the essence of representational processes to produce stimuli. To my mind, these conceptions of attention and representation, if carried to their logical conclusion, are steps toward awarding consciousness a conceptual status. We can see the dim outlines of a concept of consciousness as an organization that has integrative and regulative as well as self-regulative functions, such as attention, representation, and stimulus production.

Just a final word: however critical some of us may be of Dr. Osgood's theory, few will fail to appreciate the advance it represents. Moreover, the clarity of its reasoning, the wealth of information it integrates, and, last but not least, the pertinence and ingenuity of the experiments reported in it, command our respect.

REFERENCES

Piaget, J. (1937). *The Construction of Reality in the Child.* New York: Basic Books, 1954.
Tolman, E. C. (1932). *Purposive Behavior in Animals and Men.* Berkeley: University of California Press, 1949.

5²

BOOK REVIEW

Kenneth Mark Colby, *Energy and Structure in Psychoanalysis*[1]

Books on psychoanalysis usually deal with its clinical theory; the most comprehensive one, Fenichel's, indicates this limitation by its title, *The Psychoanalytic Theory of Neurosis* (1945). There exists, however, a fragmentary—yet consistent—general theory of psychoanalysis, which comprises the premises of the special (clinical) theory, the concepts built on it, and the generalizations derived from it. Since this general theory deals with what in Freud's time was *beyond* the scope of academic psychology, and since in relation to the clinical one it is a metatheory, it was named *metapsychology*. It is hardly ever mentioned in books written for nonspecialists; even books written for the specialist seldom do more than touch on it.

In the battle fought over the special theory, the foundations Freud laid for the general theory were scarcely noticed by the antagonists, and its adherents seem to have been too busy to systematize, develop, or use it. Only since the late 1930's has interest in it slowly revived. It is quite possible that the gap between experimental psychology and psychoanalysis, which has remained unbridged in spite of ever-increasing rapprochement, mutual interest, and much earnest work on both sides, is due in part to the undevel-

[1] New York: Ronald Press, 1955.

First published in Science, *125:1152–1153, 1957.*

oped state of the general theory. It has happened before that the integration of two branches of a science was delayed until the theory of one or both reached a sufficient level of generality. Be this as it may, the special (clinical) theory of psychoanalysis remained all but intractable to the methods of experimental psychology, although the weight of amassed observations is such that the validity of the core of this theory can no longer be questioned.

Kenneth Colby's small volume focuses on the general theory. It is directed "not only to psychoanalysts, but to all theoreticians of those fluid borderlands between the psychological, biological, and sociological sciences" (p. v) and calls general attention to those rarely studied writings of Freud which are the major sources of this general theory: the "Project for a Scientific Psychology" (1895), Chapter VII of *The Interpretation of Dreams* (1900), "On Narcissism: An Introduction" (1914), and "The Unconscious" (1915). The book has two further merits. First, it tackles some of the thorniest problems of metapsychology: for example, the relation between energy and structure, and that between thought (meaning) content and function. Colby's treatment of both of these suggests interesting theoretical possibilities. Second, for the few who are conversant with metapsychology, there are many ideas, intuitive perceptions, and hints between the lines.

Considering that this volume has—as it were—no predecessors, it is a bold undertaking. It is to be hoped that it will be read, that it will stimulate specialists to work in metapsychology, and nonspecialists to begin to discover a different aspect of psychoanalysis from that to which they are accustomed.

Yet the volume's importance is matched by its inadequacies. It consists of two parts: one attempts to review Freud's metapsychology and the models it is built on, the other to suggest a different model replacing Freud's.

The weaknesses of the first part are rooted in its being scarcely more than a preparation for the second. The presentation of Freud's metapsychology is, to say the least, incomplete. For example, only two of his "Papers on Metapsychology"—"On Narcissism: An Introduction" (1914) and "The Unconscious" (1915)—are even mentioned. The work of other students of metapsychology fares no better: outstanding ones like Hartmann, Kris, and Loewenstein merit only two references; Hartmann's major study (1939), *Ego Psychology and the Problem of Adaptation,* is not referred to. Ill-informed passages and misunderstandings are embarrassingly frequent. Still, the book gives the impression of serious intent handicapped by lack of tradition rather than by carelessness or malintent.

The principal aim of the book—to replace Freud's outdated and mechanical models with a modern and dynamic one—is not realized. While Freud's theory is mechanical in its trappings and dynamic in its core, Colby's is dynamic in its intent but becomes mechanical in its execution. Yet Colby does introduce the reader to Freud's reflex, tension-reduction, and id-ego-superego models as well as to his own cyclic-circular model. The topographic reflex model represents the course of excitation, in the psychic apparatus, from perceptual stimulation to motor action. The economic tension-reduction (pleasure principle) model represents the tendency of psychological processes to prevent and to reduce tension accumulation. The structural id-ego-superego model is familiar. Colby's own model is an attempt to replace these three models by a single one and to cope more adequately with the problem all these models are designed to solve: the integration of motivations and past experience with current environmental input. It is not possible to discuss here the many cogent points Colby makes in regard to the nature of this integration or to analyze the shortcomings of his treatment of Freud's models or the inadequacies of his own model. The book's main weakness can be revealed, however, by raising the questions: What can we gain by replacing the models of a theory which has not yet been systematized and whose limits of usefulness have not yet been explored? Can one, under these conditions, hope to demonstrate which model is more parsimonious or more powerful? What can be taken as an answer to these questions in Colby's book is singularly weak. And yet, even in this respect there is something to be said for his bold attempt: it might contribute toward weakening an orthodoxy which discourages attempts to take a new look at Freud's theories.

To the specialist, the book as a whole conveys two emphases. It stresses the need for unfettered theoretical speculation and the need to keep in harmony with the conceptions of present-day science (particularly physics). Both these emphases are justified.

But in regard to the first emphasis, Colby fails to show how the empirical data of psychoanalysis can impose discipline on free speculation. This lack will certainly limit the impetus the book can give to systematic theory-building in psychoanalysis, and it may well repel the nonspecialist, leading him to the conclusion that this general theory, just like the special one, lacks that ingredient of cohesion and discipline which makes theories amenable to empirical decision.

The second emphasis consists of frequent references to specific concepts of present-day physics, but no attempt to introduce them systematically to the specialist is made. The nonspecialist in turn may be taken aback, both by the frequency of these references, which may sound to him like lip service, and by the lack of exposition, which may make him wonder how well-digested these concepts of physics are and how relevant the link (or how premature the jump) to psychological concepts is. As an introduction for the nonspecialist, the book founders on an obstacle common to such an attempt in any science: it fails to make the relevance of the theory to observations plausible.

It would be regrettable if, in spite of these shortcomings, this book were not read. What it deals with is at least a possibly—and to my mind, proba-bly—crucial frontier of *psychology's* development into a unified science. Clinical psychoanalysis is in many ways a self-contained specialty, but psychoanalysis at large *is* psychology. It is a psychology built to account for vital phenomena of human behavior not tackled by those theories which arose from experiments. Metapsychology holds the promise that it can bring this psychology to a level of theoretical generality where its unification with experimentally derived theories, or at least its experimental verification, will be possible (see Krech and Klein, 1952; Koch, 1959). Though this promise may prove to be an illusion, still it must be given a try. Colby's book is a contribution toward making such a try possible. Its shortcomings cannot be overlooked, but they can be accepted as reflections of the present state of psychoanalytic metapsychology and of psychology at large.

REFERENCES

Fenichel, O. (1945). *The Psychoanalytic Theory of Neurosis.* New York: Norton.

Freud, S. (1895). Project for a Scientific Psychology. *The Origins of Psychoanalysis: Letters to Wilhelm Fliess, Drafts and Notes, 1887–1902.* New York: Basic Books, 1954, pp. 347–445.

———— (1900). The Interpretation of Dreams. *Standard Edition,* 4 & 5. London: Hogarth Press, 1953.

———— (1914). On Narcissism: An Introduction. *Standard Edition,* 14:73–102. London: Hogarth Press, 1957.

———— (1915). The Unconscious. *Standard Edition,* 14:166–215. London: Hogarth Press, 1957.

Hartmann, H. (1939). *Ego Psychology and the Problem of Adaptation,* tr. D. Rapaport. New York: International Universities Press, 1958.

Koch, S., ed. (1959). *Psychology: A Study of a Science,* 3 vols. New York: McGraw-Hill.

Krech, D., & Klein, G. S., eds. (1952). *Theoretical Models and Personality Theory.* Durham, N. C.: Duke University Press.

53

BOOK REVIEW

Jerome S. Bruner, Jacqueline J. Goodnow, and George A. Austin, *A Study of Thinking*[1]

The psychology of thinking always implies the epistemological problem. How can thought both abide by the laws of the organism, and represent, if only to a limited extent, the laws of the environment? Or in its contemporary form: What is the relation between the need-subserving and the veridical functions of thought? One of the strong points of this volume is that it centers on the veridical function; one of its weaknesses is that it disregards the need-subserving function. The authors are aware of this "choice" and some of its consequences:

> Psychology has been celebrating the role of "emotional factors" and "unconscious drives" in behavior for so long now that man's capacity for rational coping with his world has come to seem like some residual capacity that shows its head only when the irrational lets up. . . . If we have at times portrayed conceptual behavior as perhaps overly logical, we will perhaps be excused on the ground that one excess often breeds its opposite [p. 79].

[1] New York : Wiley, 1956.

First published in Contemporary Psychology, 2:249–252, 1957.

Another consequence (or cause?) of the authors' "excess" is that, its title notwithstanding, the volume deals only with concepts, and, in fact, the experiments reported deal only with "concept attainment" (as distinguished from "concept formation"):

> A word in explanation of this title brings the enterprise to a close. Concept attainment is, to be sure, an aspect of . . . thinking, and in this sense the title justifies itself. But we have also urged a broader view: that virtually all cognitive activity involves and is dependent on the process of categorizing [p. 246].

The volume reports nine new, and discusses several previously published, experiments. Its structure (three introductory chapters—80 pages—and extensive discussions introducing each experiment) leads to a redundancy which does not reduce "cognitive strain." The relation of the Appendix (R. W. Brown: "Language and Categories," 65 pages) to the volume is tenuous (p. 23) and therefore will not be discussed here.

The characteristics of the experimental method used are *information control, externalization,* and the quest for *attainment strategies.* For example, *Material:* an exhibit of cards, each representing a combination of one value of the following attributes: color (green, red, or black); form (square, cross, or circle); number of forms (one, two, or three); number of borders (one, two, or three). *Procedure:*

> We explain to the subject what is meant by a conjunctive concept—a set of the cards that share a certain set of attribute values, such as "all red cards," or "all cards containing red squares and two borders"— and for practice ask the subjects to show us all the exemplars of one sample concept. The subject is then told that we have a concept in mind and that certain cards before him illustrate it, others do not, and that it is his task to determine what this concept is. We will . . . [show] him a card or instance that is illustrative of the concept, a positive instance. His task is to choose cards for testing, one at a time [in any order he chooses], and after each choice we will tell him whether the card is positive or negative. He may hazard an hypothesis [but only one] after any choice of a card, . . . [but] need not do so. He is asked to arrive at the concept as efficiently as possible [p. 83].

Record: The sequence of choices, the hypotheses stated, and occasionally some introspections.

The process studied is called *concept attainment* (but also *classification, categorical inference, problem solving,* etc.): "*Attainment refers to the process of finding predictive defining attributes that distinguish exemplars from nonexemplars of the class one seeks to discriminate*" (p. 22). In contrast, the authors characterize *concept formation* as the sorting of items into "*any* meaningful" class and as "the first step en route to attainment" (p.

22). In addition, we may infer that the study of concept attainment also bypasses the perceptual-abstraction phase of concept formation (p. 136).

The procedure and the definition follow from the requirements of the authors' experimental method: (a) the experimenter must know *the amount of information* conveyed by the instances and their combinations, and the subject must know what he is to expect so that the experimenter can know "to which and to how many . . . attributes the subject is attending" (p. 135); (b) the various theoretically optimal choice sequences (*ideal strategies*) leading to attainment must be inferred from the informational content of the instances; (c) the subject's sequence of choices *externalizes* (makes observable) the process of concept attainment (p. 51); (d) the ideal strategy which is closest to the subject's sequence of choices reveals the subject's "concept attainment strategy."

The attempt to distinguish the phenomena studied from concept formation is justified by the extremely restricted kind of concept formation investigated. The choice of the term *concept attainment* (introduced by Heidbreder [1946, p. 174], whose rigorous but quite different definition is not referred to by the authors) is, however, regrettable. The attempt itself fails for a good reason of which the authors seem to have an inkling: "It is curiously difficult to recapture preconceptual innocence" (p. 50). All concept formation involves "concept attainment," and all "concept attainment" involves the processes of abstraction characteristic of concept formation (see Ach, 1905).

The influence of information theory on this volume (p. viii) takes the form of information control—used effectively by Attneave, Hovland, and others—but also extends (through explanatory instructions) to the control of what the subject attends to. On the face of it this influence appears to be fruitful: one even wonders whether or not such findings as Heidbreder's (1946, p. 192) differential difficulties between the attainment of concrete-object concept, spatial-form concept, and number concepts could be reduced to differences in information content. But can information be controlled when the experiment is not simplified to an extreme? In the present experiments, information control often required presenting the subjects with material and information not usually available to "an intelligent human being" when he "seeks to sort the environment into significant classes of events" (p. viii). Can the link between information control and artificial experimental situations be broken? Or can it be demonstrated that the results of such oversimplified experiments may be generalized to everyday situations? The authors did not sample "real-life situations" (p. 155), nor populations, nor "representative designs" (though they quote Brunswik's *caveat,* p. 68).

As for the authors' confidence in the instructions given to the subject for controlling the information he attends to: it should have been shaken by

Heidbreder's point about "data," "capta," and "facta" (1946, p. 213)—
i.e., from the "givens" subjects "select" and "make" their own.

Information theory certainly has had, and may have in the future, a fertile influence on studies of cognition by stimulating interest in information control. But this is not a direct application of information theory though the authors' emphasis might lead readers to expect (or assume) that it is.

The method of *externalization,* consistently applied here to a cognitive process, is not new in itself. It differs, for instance, from the method of Kurt Lewin's period of "action and affect psychology"—1925 to 1933—only in spurning systematic introspection. The novelty lies in the externalization of *sequences of cognitive steps.*

Extensive temporal segments of behavior have long defied elementalistic treatment. The authors break new ground in using "cognitive strategy," i.e., a temporally extended segment of behavior, as their unit of analysis. While they are aware of this significance of "cognitive strategy" (pp. ix, 243), both their stress on its other aspects and the structure of the volume deaden the impact of their innovation.

The authors stress the rational, veridical, and adaptive aspects of "cognitive strategies." They strive to demonstrate that (a) actual strategies tend to fit one or another of the rationally calculable ideal strategies; (b) the actual strategies serve adaptation by regulating acquisition of information, cognitive strain, and risk. Accordingly, they discuss at length the strategies and "payoff matrices" of game theory and economic theory, the "fit" of actual strategies to these, and the effect of different conditions on the choice and effectiveness of actual strategies.

In contrast to information theory's influence, the theory of games (operation analysis, economic models) furnishes only analogies. One of these is the conception of "strategies." The merit of the "strategies," however, is not this analogy, but the novel unit of analysis they provide. Though, according to the authors, they "limited [themselves] . . . severely in [the] . . . description of some economic models . . . , particularly . . . [of their] more formal properties" and though they claim no more for them than that "They are immensely stimulating to research" (p. 225), the discussion of these theories inflates the volume more than their actual rôle in it would warrant.

The method of externalization itself raises serious questions. All a subject can do at any given point to "externalize" his process of concept attainment is to make a choice. No doubt these choices do represent something about the process. But how much? To what extent do they represent the situation which forces a choice? How much of what the experimenter gets from the subjects did *he* smuggle into the experimental setup? How much does the very procedure of externalization alter the process externalized? It would be too much to expect that a series of experiments answer all these questions. But is it too much to expect that a volume full of leisurely discussion at least raise them?

The ideal strategy of *successive scanning* centers on one hypothesis at a time and chooses instances to test it directly. Though the choices it leads to tend to repeat already available information, they always provide new information as well: thus the strategy regulates risk effectively, but does not provide maximum information economy. Another ideal strategy, *conservative focusing,* centers on a positive instance, demands choices altering only one attribute at a time, separating defining from nondefining attributes with high information economy and good risk regulation. In contrast to successive scanning, it requires no keeping track of the hypotheses tested, since it is guided by the first positive instance. Focusing thus imposes less "cognitive strain" than scanning. These are the "ideal strategies" which frequently "fit" observed strategies.

When subjects work without having the cards before them—that is to say, under increased cognitive strain—the superiority of "focusing" over "scanning" is obvious; but, when they work with randomly distributed (rather than systematically ordered) cards, the preferred strategy is scanning, which in this situation seems to impose the lesser cognitive strain.

Information economy and *risk regulation* are not only borrowed and overlapping concepts, but conceivably reducible to the concept of *cognitive strain,* which seems to be the authors' attempt to objectify that subjectively experienced limitation, to which the "attention span" concept of old and the "attention cathexis" concept of psychoanalysis are addressed. Experimental exploration and quantification of the variable these concepts refer to could provide experimental psychology with a quantitative approach to psychological economy the like of which it has never had, K. Lewin's kindred tension concept notwithstanding. But in their preoccupation with game theory and information theory and more, the authors indicate no awareness of this concept's potential.

> What psychological status shall we afford the construct of a strategy? . . . [It] has, we would say, a kind of middling status. It is not a construct in the grand manner such as *libido* or *habit strength,* for it is in no sense proposed as an "explanation" of the behavior from which it is inferred. At the same time, it is more than a bare account of moves made by an organism. It is, rather, a description of extended sequences of behavior, a description that is also evaluative in the sense that it proposes to consider what the behavior sequence accomplishes for the organism in terms of information getting, conservation of capacity, and risk regulation [p. 241].

A Riddle: What is a "middling" construct, when it is neither an explanation, nor a bare account, but an "evaluative" description which can "propose to consider" something?—What such a "formulation" proposes is that we "call it armadillo and let it alone." [2]

But what *are* cognitive strategies?

For the logic of science they may be either *descriptive terms* or *hypothetical constructs* or *intervening variables,* depending on what their "psychological status" is.

Psychologically they may be either artifacts of the experimental method used, or relatively stable (structuralized) ego functions. Since the volume throws out hints in both directions, let us discuss both possibilities.

(1) The first experiment suggests that subjects persist with "their" strategy as conditions change. If verified, this might mean that "strategies" are structuralized ego functions of the same order as "cognitive styles." If this is so, the authors have kept their hinted promise (pp. viii, 79) and have accomplished a pioneering step in ego psychology. But they had too many obligations to dwell on this possibility, or to mention G. S. Klein's and his associates' related studies of "cognitive styles" (Klein, 1953; Klein, Holzman, and Laskin, 1954), some of which deal with "categorizing strategies" (Gardner, 1953).

(2) The second experiment suggests that subjects change their strategy as the conditions change. This need not contradict the first possibility: subjects may have a variety of "cognitive strategies" and may adaptively shift from one to another. But there are indications that these strategies may be situational artifacts: (a) too many varieties of strategies appear in the other experiments, suggesting that the subjects are captives of the situation's "causal texture"; (b) the authors offer too many *ad hoc* explanations for "deviations" from the ideal strategies (need for confirming redundancy, p. 93; preference for direct tests, p. 94; reliance on familiar forms, p. 111; dislike of disjunctive concepts, pp. 161, 181; reluctance to use negative instances, pp. 168, 181; common form indicates a common cause, p. 181; temporal relation taken for causal relation, p. 189; spread of doubt, p. 200; probability estimate depends on desirability of outcome, pp. 218–220; reluctance to delay decisions, p. 299; change means progress, p. 238; etc.).

Piaget's studies seem to show that at first the infant imitates the adult only when the adult imitates him but later acquires the ability to imitate promiscuously. The difference is like that between *getting what we like* and *liking what we get.* This volume seems to suggest that the "liking what we get" kind of adaptation—"strategies" imposed by the material encountered —is the only rational and veridical mode of thinking. Yet this is far from true. Our rational and veridical adaptation is just as often—or more often —of the "getting what we like" type. Unlike the authors' subjects, we can usually take or leave the problems we are facing, and, even when we *have to* "take" them, we *can* transform them into the kind we "like."

Both these adaptations correspond to ego functions. Experiments study-

[2] [A favorite quotation of Rapaport's, from Kipling's *Just So Stories*—Ed.]

ing the former reflect no more than the ego's capacity to *yield* to the causal texture of the environment and thus the "strategies" they discover will be situational artifacts. Only experiments studying the latter can find autonomous (structuralized) rational and veridical ego functions. The present experiments seem to be of the former kind, and only the *ad hoc* hypotheses advanced to explain "errors" and "deviations" from the ideal strategies seem to reflect both the subjects' attempts to transform the *problems they got* into *problems they like* and some of their autonomous veridical ego functions. These "errors" and "deviations" are related to the rôle of motivations in cognition (several seem to be akin to familiar manifestations of Freud's *primary process*) and might well have given the authors the idea that veridical cognition can hardly be separated from motivations (pp. viii, 15 f., 79).

Man drops a problem—to approach it from a new angle—as often as he pursues it relentlessly. Therein lies that "creativity" to which the authors pay lip service (pp. 7 ff., 232). What we need to know is *in what respect* and *to what extent* can experiments, which prevent both dropping a problem and approaching it anew in the subject's own terms, provide valid information concerning cognitive processes.

The bold, the novel, and the stimulating are drowned in this volume not only by an eclectic tendency to serve too many gods (information theory, game theory, ego psychology, Brunswik's probabilistic ecology, etc.), by an ostentatious erudition, and by catering to what is modish, but also by a curious blend of the forthright, the didactic, the circumstantially cumbersome, the outright repetitious, and the preciously urbane. The authors display an uncannily sure hand at "snatching defeat from victory."

(1) In contrast to the "one-shot experiments" which flood the journals, the authors present a cohesive series of experiments which as a monograph could have provided a paradigm for the whole field. Instead, the experiments are buried in a book in which the very imbalance between them and the discussions necessitates repetitive comments on what the authors *did not* try to do, and what is left to the future and to others. The sharp pioneering edge of the experiments is thus dulled as the authors hedge to forestall criticism.

(2) The redeeming feature of the presentation, the statement of the experiments and results in a continuous narrative rather than in the deadly fashion of our current journals, almost sets an urgently needed example. But this form would require some provision (footnotes or appendices) to acquaint us with the data, their reliability, and the significance of the differences found. Here we have to take all this on faith. While (excepting the statistically minded who do not think in such terms) we have unlimited confidence in the acumen and reliability of psychologists, we still like to be given a chance to think about experiments and to interpret them. This we cannot do if we are given only those figures which support the authors'

ideas. Thus both the statistically-minded and the interpretation-minded psychologist will have grave misgivings about this form of presentation.

(3) The authors have staked out a new area of investigation. But, by attempting to present it as *A Study of Thinking,* they have embroiled themselves in the conceptual problem and in the hopeless attempt to separate "concept attainment" from concept formation. Having discussed the problem of concepts at length, they have left themselves wide open to the criticism that, though they do find space to make offhand remarks about the clinician (pp. 43, 66), they cavalierly disregard all clinical studies of concept formation, several of which (Hanfmann, 1941; Goldstein and Scheerer, 1941; Rapaport, Gill, and Schafer, 1945) are even related to "strategies." Their reference to surveys of the literature (p. 24) does not free them from the obligation—incurred by *their treatment* of the experiments—to come to grips with these clinical studies and with Heidbreder's and Piaget's studies on the nature of conceptualization.

A pioneering experimental report would not entail such obligations, nor would it need to straddle defensively every contemporary fence.

REFERENCES

Ach, N. (1905). Determining Tendencies; Awareness. In *Organization and Pathology of Thought,* ed. & tr. D. Rapaport. New York: Columbia University Press, 1951, pp. 15–38.

Gardner, R. W. (1953). Cognitive Styles in Categorizing Behavior. *J. Pers.,* 22:214–233.

Goldstein, K., & Scheerer, M. (1941). Abstract and Concrete Behavior; An Experimental Study with Special Tests. *Psychol. Monogr.,* 53, No. 2.

Hanfmann, E. (1941). A Study of Personal Patterns in an Intellectual Performance. *Character & Pers.,* 9:315–325.

Heidbreder, E. (1946). The Attainment of Concepts: I. Terminology and Methodology. II. The Problem. *J. Gen. Psychol.,* 35:173–189, 191–223.

Klein, G. S. (1953). The Menninger Foundation Research on Perception and Personality, 1947–1952: A Review. *Bull. Menninger Clin.,* 17:93–99.

———, Holzman, P. S., & Laskin, D. (1954). The Perception Project: Progress Report for 1953–54. *Bull. Menninger Clin.,* 18:260–266.

Rapaport, D., Gill, M. M., & Schafer, R. (1945). *Diagnostic Psychological Testing,* Vol. I. Chicago: Year Book Publishers.

54

LETTER

Response to Robert W. White's Review
of Heinz L. and Rowena R. Ansbacher's
*The Individual Psychology of Alfred
Adler*

> This letter is a fine brief example of Rapaport's schol-
> arship and historical knowledge of the field; it is also
> an example of the vigorous style he often used in
> speaking and teaching but usually toned down in his
> writing—M. M. G.

R. W. White, like "the Little Flower," could say, "I rarely make a mistake,
but when I make one, it's a beaut." In his review (1957) of the Ansbachers' book on Adler, he made it: "In certain respects it is indeed legitimate to
say that Freudian psychology is in process of catching up with Adler" (p.
3).

He bases this "conclusion" on historical data which are half factually,
half interpretationally, incorrect.

(1) White: "Adler wrote of *'safeguarding tendencies'* in 1911, Freud of
defense mechanisms in 1921" (p. 3). The facts: *Studies on Hysteria*

First published in Contemporary Psychology, *2:303–304, 1957.*

(Breuer and Freud, 1893–95, e.g., pp. 122, 147, 214, 235–236, 269, 285) speaks of defense mechanisms, and in the 1890s two other papers deal exclusively with them: "The Defence Neuro-Psychoses" (1894) and "Further Remarks on the Defence Neuro-Psychoses" (1896).

(2) White: "Adler of *the transformation of a drive into its opposite* in 1908, Freud of *reaction formation* in 1915" (p. 3). The facts: (a) this is a "triple beaut": reaction formation is *not* such a transformation (see Freud, 1915, p. 72); (b) reaction formation is described by Freud in the 1896 paper referred to above (pp. 163, 168) and discussed in great detail in 1908 ("Character and Anal Erotism"); (c) the transformation of drive into its opposite is the core of Freud's discussions of sadism and masochism in his *Three Essays* (1905), and its further elaboration in 1915 (pp. 69 ff.) is totally unrelated to Adler's conception.

(3) White: "Adler of *the guiding self-ideal* in 1912, Freud of *the ego-ideal* in 1914" (p. 3). As for the use of the *terms,* White is probably right. But the interpretation is questionable: in the *Studies on Hysteria* (1893–1895) one of the factors of the conflict is again and again described as "the ego['s] . . . repelling force . . . against . . . [an] incompatible idea" (p. 269) and the incompatibility as due to "firmly-rooted complexes of moral ideas" (p. 210).

(4) White: "Adler of *aggressive drives* in 1908, Freud of *the death instinct* not before 1920" (p. 3). Again as to the first appearance of these *terms,* White may be right, though the term *aggressive instinct* was used in *Studies on Hysteria* in the parts by Breuer (1893–95, pp. 201, 246). But the problem of sadism has been Freud's problem at least since the *Three Essays* (1905). His *death instinct* is as dead as a doornail, but the problem of the origin and development of *aggressive drives* is still unsolved. What then would Adler's priority amount to, even if it existed?

In more general terms: (1) In the 1890s Freud developed the foundations for an ego psychology. (2) He turned away from these beginnings around 1897, to center on the investigation of the "unconscious." (3) In 1923 he returned to ego-psychological considerations for reasons connected with "the negative therapeutic reaction." Neither the cause nor the form of this concern had anything to do with Adler's ideas. (4) In 1926 Freud made *the* crucial step toward the development of psychoanalytic ego psychology. In doing so he returned to his concepts of the 1890s—a method of progress characteristic of Freud.

While Freud believed that an ego psychology can be built only upon consolidated knowledge of the "unconscious," Adler thought otherwise. His attempt to build one was bold and often insightful. It contributed much to creating the atmosphere in which the ego psychologies of our day developed, but hardly anything to the *concepts* and *problems* central to present-day psychoanalytic ego psychology. Like so many other pioneers' work, the rôle of his work in the science of psychology amounts to no more than "grease for the wheels of history."

The Ansbachers' and White's gallant efforts cannot retrospectively alter this fate. The fate of theories, like that of people, lies in their character. The character of Adler's contribution was—as White does not seem to realize— that of *ex parte* insights, tied together—as White does realize—by no cohesive theory. This is illustrated by White's comparison of Adler's statements with those of Erikson on the rôle of the mother. White is right: Adler's and Erikson's statements are strikingly similar. But he fails to notice that Erikson's are part and parcel of a developmental theory which is consistent with psychoanalytic theory proper, and which modifies as well as extends it, while Adler's are valuable clinical insights without a theoretical framework which could give them lasting impact.

Is it psychoanalysis or is it history which is still so alien to psychology that in it, instead of facts, predilections guide the judgment even of a man like R. W. White?

REFERENCES

Breuer, J., & Freud, S. (1893–95). Studies on Hysteria. *Standard Edition*, 2. London: Hogarth Press, 1955.

Freud, S. (1894). The Defence Neuro-Psychoses. *Collected Papers*, 1:59–75. New York: Basic Books, 1959.

———— (1896). Further Remarks on the Defence Neuro-Psychoses. *Collected Papers*, 1:155–182. New York: Basic Books, 1959.

———— (1905). Three Essays on the Theory of Sexuality. *Standard Edition*, 7:123–245. London: Hogarth Press, 1953.

———— (1908). Character and Anal Erotism. *Collected Papers*, 2:45–50. New York: Basic Books. 1959.

———— (1915). Instincts and Their Vicissitudes. *Collected Papers*, 4:60–83. New York: Basic Books, 1959.

White, R. W. (1957). Review of *The Individual Psychology of Alfred Adler*, by Heinz L. Ansbacher and Rowena R. Ansbacher. *Contemp. Psychol.*, 2:1–4.

55

A THEORETICAL ANALYSIS

OF THE

SUPEREGO CONCEPT

This draft was written in 1957; Rapaport did not publish it because he was aware that it was unfinished and that he had been unable to resolve some of its obscurities, complexities, and contradictions. He submitted the paper to a number of friends and colleagues who criticized it extensively. Shortly before his death he held a seminar on the superego (with students in the Western New England Institute for Psychoanalysis) in which he dealt with the same problems as this draft and attempted to clarify some of its difficulties. I have included some of the material from that seminar in footnotes, enclosed in brackets, in the hope of making some of the issues and problems of this draft clearer to the reader. This material has been revised only to the extent of making it somewhat less colloquial. I have also added a few footnotes of my own to indicate some of my own views of the issues. These are designed not to resolve the

This paper, written in 1957, is published here for the first time.

issues, which I cannot, but only to clarify what they are. It seemed inappropriate to attempt to incorporate material from the papers on the superego which have appeared in our literature since this draft was written, and in any case I do not believe that they bear very directly on Rapaport's point of view.

In spite of the paper's unfinished condition, I am convinced that it will be a stimulus to the reader. It is clear that the paper not only deals with the superego, but is a statement of Rapaport's ideas, as of 1957, about the major issues of metapsychology with which he hoped to grapple. In fact, the scope of the paper is so broad that it is in effect a theory of structure formation and thus of psychic development, though, as he points out, it deals mainly only with genetic and structural issues. It becomes clear why activity and passivity (Chapter 44) seemed to Rapaport such important concepts, since the distinction between them is an essential basis of his differentiation between ego and superego. At the end of the paper he even hints that this same distinction, with the concept of "turning round upon the self" as a bridge, may lead to a "new conception of the nature and genetic course of the aggressive drive." A paper of such scope must inevitably fail in various ways to resolve the complexities and contradictions with which it deals, but, in Rapaport's hands, it must equally inevitably be a powerful stimulus and aid to those who wrestle with these basic problems of metapsychology—M. M. G.

I

Ever since the introduction of the structural theory by Freud, theoretical interest has centered on ego psychology and neglected the exploration of the superego. This is for good reasons: Freud's writings on the ego provided ample bridgeheads for the systematic clarification not only of the clinical ego theory but also of the general psychoanalytic theory of the ego. This was not the case for the superego. Even the clinical theory—however useful as a guide in practice—has many obscurities, and its general psychoanalytic theory is practically nonexistent. The introduction of the predecessor of the superego in "On Narcissism: An Introduction" (1914), and its exploration in *Group Psychology and the Analysis of the Ego* (1921) and in *The Ego and the Id* (1923) stand in isolation. It did not have the kind of preparation ego psychology had in the early defense papers, in the treatment of the secondary process in Chapter VII of *The Interpretation of Dreams* (1900), nor the kind of continuation it had after *The Ego and the Id* in *Inhibitions, Symptoms and Anxiety* (1926), in the *New Introductory Lectures* (1933), and in several of the late papers. Unfortunately, there is only scattered mention in the literature of the unclarities of the superego concept, and to my knowledge no study exists which spells them out in a concentrated form.

My purposes here are (1) to attempt to state the perplexities which attend this concept, and (2) to advance some considerations which might prove helpful in building a systematic theory of the superego.

II

We conceive of the origin of the superego in the necessity to recapture infantile narcissistic perfection, via incorporating the idealized parent or parents.[1] Clinically, we know what we mean by this proposition. Theoretically, however, this does not seem to be the case, because the concept of narcissism has undergone a change from its introduction to its treatment in *The Ego and the Id* (1923) and from there to Hartmann's and Jacobson's contributions. The ego which in 1914 was assumed to be the original reservoir of all libido yielded this place to the id in 1923. But the corresponding change in the theory of narcissism has not been made, although this theory rested on the primary narcissism of the ego as the reservoir of all libido and the conception of the ego ideal as the means by which, via secondary narcissism, the original narcissistic perfection is recaptured.[2] It is possible that

[1] [First the omnipotence is ascribed to the parents instead of to oneself, and then by an internalization or identification these omnipotent parents are reinstated inside and serve as a substitute for the omnipotence as well as for the narcissistic object, that is, the person. "This ideal ego is now the target of the self-love which was enjoyed in childhood by the actual ego" (Freud, 1914, p. 94).]

[2] [Since the concept of the superego is one of secondary narcissism, it must be regarded as cathected by unsublimated ego libido. But secondary narcissism has been considered a pathogenic factor throughout "On Narcissism" (1914): it determines a certain kind of object choice; is the factor which results in hypochondriacal phenomena; is a factor any excess of which can result in narcissistic neurosis, which today we call psychosis. If you stand on the ground of 1914, you have to make that assumption, and some explanation of why the superego doesn't always work that way has to be found. I can make this point more clearly by referring to Freud's discussion of the difference between idealization and sublimation. Idealization is the same as establishing something as the ego ideal, or as a substitute for it, for that matter. The ego ideal may demand sublimation, but it cannot enforce it. If secondary narcissism, in the form of the establishment of the ego ideal, always led to sublimation—that is, if it were identical to the process Freud described in *The Ego and the Id* (1923)—we would have a simple situation. But Freud warns that this is not so. It is here that Freud's theory of 1914 contained the seeds of its own destruction. If it is true that sublimation always takes place by an identification—the ego offering itself as a love object to the id, thereby capturing cathexes and putting them at the disposal of the

this difficulty can be overcome by linking narcissistic perfection to the earliest phase of development in which id and ego are as yet undifferentiated, and Jacobson—if I understand her rightly—has attempted to do so. But it must be kept in mind that Freud was quite explicit in differentiating the narcissistic phase from the earliest autoerotic phase and thus any attempt of the kind Jacobson made would have to meet Freud's argument. It is also possible that the theory of superego origins as advanced by Freud will not change if we replace—as Hartmann and Jacobson have done and as we probably should—the *ego* by the *self* in this theory. But if this is so, it has yet to be demonstrated. As long as the concept of the self remains murky, such a demonstration is not possible. And the concept is murky: Hartmann equates the self with the person and speaks of the narcissism of the id and superego as well as of the ego.[3] The term "person" so far has no conceptual

---

ego—if this were really narcissism, then why would narcissism cause all the trouble? Why would it be pathological? Why would we observe clinically that there are high ego ideals without sublimated cathexes? If establishment of the ego ideal takes place by identification, and if identification is a means of neutralization, why does Freud have to warn us that establishment of the ego ideal demands but cannot enforce sublimation? According to the mechanism proposed in *The Ego and the Id,* as soon as the ego ideal is established, neutralization is accomplished. Since it is not so, here is the point from which we have recourse to the concept of the self. If the withdrawal of cathexis to the ego results not in secondary narcissism but in sublimation, we have to have something else to which the cathexis is withdrawn. It is true, however, that even in *The Ego and the Id,* Freud at times toys with the idea that withdrawal of cathexis to the ego may result in narcissism. I am trying to point out a contradiction not spelled out in the literature.

Secondary narcissism is withdrawal of the object cathexis in one fashion or another. My point is that this withdrawal cannot be in the fashion that is described in *The Ego and the Id* and still result in secondary narcissism. Sublimation is the building of structures. What is cathected in secondary narcissism, I do not know, but the cathexis has to be withdrawn *not* into something which is part of the ego.]

[3] ["The equivalence of narcissism and libidinal cathexes of the ego was and still is widely used in psychoanalytic literature, but in some passages Freud also refers to it as cathexis of one's own person, of the body, or of the self. In analysis a clear distinction between the terms ego, self and personality is not always made. But a differentiation of these concepts appears essential if we try to look consistently at the problems involved in the light of Freud's structural psychology. But actually, in using the term narcissism, two different sets of opposites often seem to be fused into one. The one refers to the self (one's own person) in contradistinction to the object, the second to the ego (as a psychic system) in contradistinction to other substructures of personality. However, the opposite of object cathexis is not ego cathexis, but cathexis of one's own person, that is self-cathexis; in speaking of self-cathexis we do not imply whether this cathexis is situated in the id, in the ego, or in the superego. This formulation takes into account that we actually do find 'narcissism' in all three psychic systems; but in all these cases there is opposition to (and reciprocity with) object cathexis. It therefore will be clarifying if we define narcissism as the libidinal cathexis not of the ego but of the self" (Hartmann, 1950, pp. 84–85).

So you have here ego narcissism, superego narcissism, and id narcissism. This might be understandable clinically, but what is the theoretical explanation?]

status in psychoanalysis, and the narcissism of the id and superego—which I find clinically meaningful—remains theoretically an enigma. Likewise, Jacobson's concept of the *self*, which is treated mostly as if it were identical with "self-representation," [4] certainly does not enable us to decide whether or not it demands changes in Freud's conception of the origin of the superego.[5] The fact remains that Freud's original conception does account for definite clinical phenomena, that the theoretical underpinning of his conception no longer holds (he himself eliminated some of its foundations, without indicating how the theoretical explanation of his ego-ideal conception should change correspondingly), and finally that Hartmann's and Jacobson's narcissism conceptions, as much as they seem to be clarifying in some respects, do not as yet fill the gap in the theory of the origins of the superego.

[4] ["In a previous paper on depression . . . I introduced for the better metapsychological understanding of such preoedipal, primitive identifications the term 'self-representations,' which Hartmann had also suggested" (Jacobson, 1954, p. 241). Actually Hartmann proposes that "It might also be useful to apply the term self-representation as opposed to object representation" (1950, p. 85), a suggestion which seems reasonable to me. It carries the whole issue into the *inner* world of Hartmann, as distinguished from the *internal* world. Jacobson refers to narcissism as the cathexis of the self-representation, but representations are not what are cathected.]

[5] [The self will have to be given a metapsychological definition before it can be used to clarify the concept of narcissism. I have tried to define it as the set of relationships between the various psychic institutions, but that is only a poor beginning.

What is called the "character" of the ego (Freud, 1923, p. 35) may be a hint at what Erikson later called identity, which may be an approach to what could be defined as the self. It is not certain. There are many unclear problems about it, but the only reasonably elaborated concept we have so far to cover what is again and again called the self by Freud, Jacobson, and Hartmann, is somehow identity. The difficulties concerning it are the problems the self concept always encounters. The self in subjective experience is something which can observe itself. The ego is free of this: the ego is something which functions, it does not observe itself. That is why the topographic systems had to be discarded in favor of the structural systems—because the most important things about the ego are not at all conscious. The self will have to be so defined in the psychological apparatus that it is observable by an ego function which is at the same time defined as a subsidiary organization within the self. The self cannot be simply redefined. It is a concept which has been with man for a long time. Its major characteristic is that it is capable of observing itself. Only a revolutionary new invention could get away from that requirement. The philosophical conundrum of the ages, that the self is something that can observe itself, is a question for psychology to answer. In this answer the self will have to be so formulated within the psychological apparatus that it is amenable to observation, though not necessarily to full inspection, because many parts of it may be, like Erikson's identity, unconscious, indeed ringed around by resistances. But it will also have to be so formulated that the observing function is a subsidiary of the self. I do not drag this point in as a piece of philosophical speculation. It is a problem for psychology, and without facing it the self problem will not be faced.]

III

We conceive of the superego as the "representative of . . . moral restrictions" (Freud, 1933, p. 95), but its precise rôle in enforcing these moral restrictions is not clear. We regard as ego structures the defenses which are the executive mechanisms of the moral restrictions, and as a rule we attribute to the superego only a function of prompting the ego (see Freud, 1923, p. 75)—and it is not the sole prompter at that—to give the anxiety signal mobilizing the defenses. Or to use Schur's (1953) term, we attribute to it a rôle only in influencing the evaluation of the danger situation, not in the reaction to it. The structural theory of psychoanalysis has imposed such a conception upon us. However, in the original form in which the conception was propounded in "On Narcissism: An Introduction" (1914), it was a "censoring agency" (p. 96), and Freud wrote that "we . . . recognize in the ego ideal and in the dynamic utterances of conscience the *dream-censor* as well" (p. 97). If we realize that in *The Interpretation of Dreams* (1900) the term "censorship" stood for all the instinct-restraining factors, it becomes clear that the relationships to defenses of the early and the present conceptions of the superego differ from each other. It might be proposed that the later—structural—conception superseded the earlier one, and that the situation is clear: the superego has nothing directly to do with the defenses, which are ego structures mobilized by the ego on the promptings of the superego, but also on other promptings. This proposition would not be in conformity with much of the literature, among other things not with a formulation Freud gave as late at 1933: "repression is the work of the super-ego—either . . . it does its work on its own account or else . . . the ego does it in obedience to its orders" (1933, p. 98).[6] Nor is this one of those occasions where Homer nodded. This other view of the superego survives side by side with the generally accepted structural conception, and no questions are asked about how the two can be reconciled with each other. One of the reasons for the survival of this older conception is apparent in the study of the predecessors of the superego.[7] Various defenses are recognized as such precursors and genetic components of the superego's struc-

---

[6] [In "On Narcissism" (1914) Freud wrote: "Repression, we have said, proceeds from the ego; we might say with greater precision that it proceeds from the self-respect of the ego" (p. 93). Later self-respect is described as the relationship between ego and ego ideal—so it is this relationship from which repression proceeds. In other words, repression itself is immediately and directly linked to the ego ideal, or, if you prefer, superego, just as it was before 1897.]

[7] [In "On Narcissism" (1914), censorship and conscience or ego ideal are identified directly (p. 96), suggesting that since in present-day theory defense replaces censorship, the superego fulfills functions which we refer to as defense structures. Since the censor is the predecessor both of the superego and of the defenses, the relation between the superego and the defenses must be seriously considered. The concept of defense identifications is the kind of solution I propose for this unsolved relationship.]

ture. Among these, reaction formations (sphincter morality; Ferenczi, Abraham) have always played an eminent rôle. Jones (1947) gave the following general formulation of the nature of the superego's early forms: "We have now traced the super-ego back to . . . [the] pre-moral stage . . . where its main function would seem to be that of a simple barrier against the id impulses . . . At this point it becomes merely one defense among others, though one with a peculiar history. Its special features are due to its formation through introjection of parental objects" (p. 151). If one were inclined to discredit this view as one of Jones's Kleinian "heresies," a study of the literature would quickly dissuade one from so doing. The defense "turning round upon the self" which Freud (1915a) introduced as an "instinctual vicissitude" is homologous in its pattern of function with that of the superego (Freud, 1923, pp. 79–80).[8] Anna Freud (1936) wrote that " 'Identification with the aggressor' "—a defense concept that she introduced into the literature—"represents . . . a preliminary phase of super-ego development" (p. 129). Annie Reich (1954) wrote: "The superego is a complex structure. Most conspicuous . . . is usually the identification with the moral side of the parental personality, which is used for the repression of the oedipal strivings. . . . The instinct-restraining identifications . . . restricting incestuous genitality, become fused with earlier ones directed against pregenital indulgence" (p. 219).

Thus, the relation of the superego to defenses, and through them to the ego, remains unclear.[9] But the last references by means of which I at-

---

[8] [This may be clarified by reviewing the discussion in *The Ego and the Id* (1923) of the replacement of the object cathexis of the mother by identification with her, or by a strengthening of the ancient primary identification with the father. At the root of both of these lies a turning round upon the subject. If the subject offers himself as a love object to the father in identification with the mother, instead of saying, "I hate you; I would like to eliminate you," he says, "No, I don't hate you. I expose myself to all your wrath, even to your sexual attack." Clearly an aggressive impulse is turned round upon the self and the father is viewed as an object in a sadistic sexual relationship. Since this changed dynamic condition is achieved by an identification with the mother, we may conclude that the structure which arises to bring about the turning round upon the subject is an identification structure. Since this identification structure is an oedipal one, it will also enter superego formation. The rôle of the superego, through these identifications, in turning around the aggressive impulse upon the subject, becomes clinically obvious, because in masochism a very cruel superego is always present. The complexities of the concepts of the defusion of instincts and of the death instinct are not necessary to explain this phenomenon. Even in the case of the strengthening of the identification with the father, a reversal is present, but the point is a more subtle one.]

[9] [Are these defensive, repressive structures identical with the ego ideal, or are they only triggered by it? If it could be proved that they are identical, then the theory would become much simpler. Freud equated them in *Totem and Taboo* (1913). He said that whenever it is automatic and self-understood that something is condemned, the consciousness of that is conscience. Obviously, one would have to add to such a formulation the unconscious aspects of conscience.]

tempted to drive this home already involve the concepts of identification and introjection, and it is to these that I will turn now to point up further unclarities of the superego concept.

IV

We conceive of the superego as built of identifications. But this conception too is fraught with theoretical difficulties. First of all, we regard the ego too as a precipitate of identifications with abandoned objects (1923, p. 36) and thus we are in need of a distinction between the identifications which form the ego and those which form the superego. Here again it might be argued that we do have such a clear-cut theoretical distinction: the superego is the heir of the oedipus complex (1923, pp. 47–48), that is to say, it is built of the identification with the oedipal objects.[10] However, this argument runs into more difficulties than any of the others.

First, it was pointed out by Freud that

> behind . . . [the ego ideal] there lies hidden [in man] the first and most important identification of all, the identification with the fa-ther[1]. . .
>
> [1] Perhaps it would be safer to say 'with the parents' (1923, p. 39; see also pp. 68–69).

Indeed, if Melanie Klein's theories made no other positive contribution to our clinical knowledge, they certainly made us aware of the preoedipal identifications which contribute to the development of the superego. Thus such a temporal distinction of ego and superego identifications is not possible.

Second, Freud also suggested that "The super-ego owes its special position in the ego, or in regard to the ego, . . . to the fact that . . . it was the first identification and one which took place while the ego was still feeble" (1923, pp. 68–69), and not only to its being heir of the oedipus complex. But Annie Reich (1954) points out that "We are used to think of earlier identifications as ego identifications; i.e., as identifications which are completely integrated into the ego, and which do not lead to a differentiation within the ego" (p. 219). Apparently, then, no temporal distinction between ego and superego identifications is feasible.[11]

[10] [The observations concerning the history of the superego in the oedipal phase are obviously correct. Fundamentally the superego is more or less established in this phase and is not radically altered thereafter. But this is only a relative truth. In puberty, radical revampings of the superego may spontaneously occur. This is one of the many aspects of adolescence which have not been studied. It is not true that only defensive secondary repression, making unconscious further parts of the superego, occurs at puberty and adolescence. Frequently very radical revampings occur in the wake of finding new ideals. One of the misfortunes of adolescents growing up in this country is that there are very few teachers who are suitable to become ideals.]

[11] [The superego has been described as a representation of the id, while the ego

Third, the concept of identification itself is unclear; in general it is conceived of as a substitute for abandoned objects, but Freud pointed to the superego's origin in "direct and immediate identification . . . [which] takes place earlier than any object-cathexes" (1923, p. 39), and the ego's capacity to make "simultaneous object-cathexis and identification, *i.e.* . . . alteration in character . . . before the object has been given up" (1923, p. 37). Thus regressive replacement of object relation by identification does not distinguish the superego and ego from each other either.

Fourth, this identification conception of the superego runs into still another difficulty of a more recent origin, though not one which Freud failed to envisage. Erikson (1950, 1951, 1956) derived *identity* from identifications and Jacobson (1954) derives the *self* from identifications. Freud, without referring to the self, did anticipate this problem. He wrote:

> If . . . [the ego's object-identifications] obtain the upper hand and become too numerous, unduly intense and incompatible with one another,[12] a pathological outcome will not be far off. It may come to a disruption of the ego in consequence of the individual identifications becoming cut off from one another by resistances; perhaps the secret of the cases of so-called multiple personality is that the various identifications seize possession of consciousness in turn. Even when things do not go so far as this, there remains the question of conflicts between the different identifications into which the ego is split up, conflicts which cannot after all be described as purely pathological [1923, pp. 38–39].

Thus the identifications are called upon to play still a third genetic rôle, and we find no answer to the question whether it is the same identifications which do all of this, and if so, how; or different ones, and if so how they differ. Jacobson's derivation of the self from identifications is particularly perplexing, since it derives the self-representations from identifications, and thus leaves us with the question of the distinction between self and self-representation, identification and object representation: i.e., between structures and contents.

---

identifications are said to be more realistic. How then can the ego identifications be the earlier ones?

Annie Reich (1954) refers to "the instinct-restraining identifications." Then not only the identifications but also the restraints, the defenses, cannot be so easily differentiated between ego and id. This formulation shows that there is a continuity from the primal identification to the oedipal, rather than a jump as one might gather from Freud's writings. This mistake has been repeated by Schafer (1960), and is also implied by Loewald (1962).]

[12] It is worth noting here the reference to intrasystemic conflict, the concept of which has been elaborated by Hartmann (1950).

V

We conceive of the superego also as observing, judging, and punishing the ego. Again, clinically we know quite clearly what we mean by this proposition. Theoretically, however, we are again faced with considerable difficulties when we try to account for these superego functions.

Observation and judgment are, in the structural theory of psychoanalysis, definitely considered as ego functions. Freud's treatment of consciousness as a superordinate sense organ in Chapter VII of *The Intepretation of Dreams* (1900) makes this clear for the observation function: and the "Two Principles" (1911) establishes this for judgment also.[13] The punishing function of the superego has several facets: anxiety, guilt, grief, depression, and self-destructive activity motivated by unconscious guilt. In regard to the superego's rôle in anxiety, we have a reasonably clear theoretical conception. But grief and depression involve all that we have so far found problematical in regard to the superego; though Bibring's contribution (1953) brought us close to a conception of these akin to our anxiety conception, there still remains much to be clarified about the superego's rôle in grief and depression. As for the other aspects of the punishing function, guilt and the consequences of unconscious guilt: of these we have a clinical, but no general theoretical, conception.

In regard to observation and judgment, it could be argued that we should not make an arbitrary and sharp separation between the ego and the superego. Since the latter is but a "differentiating grade" in the ego, there should be no reason why it could not make use of the observation and judging functions of the ego. But such an argument runs into two obstacles. First, though there is no reason to doubt that the superego differentiates from the ego, we assume both clinically and theoretically that they are rather distinct from each other, and this distinctness would disappear if the superego had

---

[13] [If you conceptualize observation as a function of the superordinate sense-organ consciousness, and thus as an ego function belonging to the apparatuses of primary autonomy, what Freud referred to as the observation function would be nothing else but tensions between two systems, as he talks about it repeatedly, tensions leading to guilt, self-reproach, and lowered self-esteem, among other things.

It is also conceivable that the primary autonomous functions may come under the control of a regressively reproduced introject, of a defused identification, just as it is conceivable that in a multiple personality one set of identifications becomes dominant over all the others. The others are isolated (or, if you prefer, repressed or defended against), and this one system of identifications serves as a surrogate ego. But to ascribe observing functions to the superego per se is, I believe, a mistake, as long as the superego is conceived of as a system of structures as *distant* from reality as it is represented to be. Schafer (1960) correctly describes the superego as a representative of reality, but he does so in a context which confuses a historical genetic fact (namely, that the superego is a representative of past authorities) with a dynamic and adaptive fact. He makes it the latter two when he regards it as a structure which directly exerts forces in observing and in acting, rather than influencing action and observation—which are the tasks of the ego—by interstructural relationships.]

direct access to two of the cardinal functions of the ego or duplicated them. Second, if we were to attribute the observation and judgmental functions to the superego as part of the ego, then we would be asserting that the ego is observing itself. This kind of assertion, however, ultimately always leads to the problem of the *self* which I have already touched on, indicating that it is so far an unsolved problem.[14]

VI

Not only the superego's origin in the effort to restore narcissistic perfection and in identifications, nor only its functions of representing moral restrictions and observing, judging, and punishing the ego, are fraught with unsolved theoretical problems. The clinically well-understood proposition that the superego represents to the ego both the standards of society and the id's demands[15] is not yet explained theoretically, nor are its corollaries concerning a "corrupt superego" and a "parasitizing (externalized) superego" so far explained. When I repeatedly said "theoretically unexplained" in the previous pages, I left the statement vague. The time has come to become specific about this point. It does not imply that the specific propositions of the clinical theory which I have discussed so far are necessarily called into question. The clinical theory is based on good observations and orients us in the labyrinth of the patients' productions. It does imply, however, that the present clinical theory of the superego has some discontinuities and even inconsistencies; it has not yet caught up with the changes in the clinical theory's ego psychology, which have been rather rapid in the last three decades. My references to the lack of theoretical explanation mainly apply not to the clinical theory of the superego, but rather to what I call the general

[14] [If the self has an observing function which is a subsidiary of it, then to give the superego also an observing function might complicate the self problem to the point of hopelessness—though it is not certain that it is not hopeless as it stands.]

[15] [What does it mean that the superego is a representative of the id, and that the superego and the id can put the ego into a vise, the id pushing it and the superego punishing it for the very thing to which the id is pushing it? Those identification structures which can be considered representations of the id are defensive structures which are not capable of controlling the id but are controlled by it. This distinction is one aspect of the activity and passivity models I have suggested (1953). In some of these models the defenses are controlled by the id; they passively let the id impulse come through. In other models the defenses are capable of actively controlling the id without a resulting state of intolerable tension. When the id can determine the functioning of a defense or a structure, as is always the case with the earliest identifications, the structure is one which represents the id. This is the same issue discussed in *Inhibitions, Symptoms and Anxiety* (1926), in which is described a transition from a state in which the defenses have to be established against an id impulse after it arises to a state in which the oncoming of the impulse is anticipated and the defense is activated by an anxiety signal. The latter is a prototype of activity, the former a prototype of passivity. If this distinction were applied to superego identifications and to superego structures in general, it would be clearer what is meant by the statement that the superego is a representative of the id.]

theory of psychoanalysis. This general theory is always built by a metapsychological analysis of the propositions of the special or clinical theory. Metapsychology proper consists of the minimal set of basic assumptions underlying all psychoanalytic propositions, and these fall into five groups: dynamic, economic, structural, genetic, and adaptive assumptions. The five metapsychological points of view correspond to these five groups and serve as guides of metapsychological analysis. Metapsychological analysis applied to any set of propositions of psychoanalysis reveals which basic assumptions are and which are not implied in that set of propositions, and thus permits us to discover where any given theory is incomplete or inconsistent or redundant.

Clearly, I am not in a position today to give a metapsychological analysis of the superego concept and of the psychoanalytic propositions pertaining to it. I will therefore restrict myself to a number of considerations which may in the long run promote the possibility of such an analysis.

VII

I should like to begin with the concepts of internalization, incorporation, introjection, and identification. These concepts are used interchangeably in the literature.[16]

Let us start with internalization, which seems to be the most general of them. It is used in two different senses in the literature: first, as an equivalent of any of the other three; second, in the much broader sense in which, for instance, Hartmann uses it (1939) for both phylogenetic and ontogenetic processes as a result of which internal regulation takes over where environmental regulation held sway before, and internal processes replace external action or trial. That the first usage is confusing goes without saying. But the second is not less confusing. It lumps together two disparate things. When we do not perform by trial and error, but use memories and relationships to establish the effective course of action, we certainly operate with products of internalization, in particular with those which Hartmann —if I understand him rightly—has called the "inner world."[17] But when

[16] [Both Schafer (1960) and Loewald (1962) have made suggestions concerning the distinctions and relationships among these which are different from my suggestions, at least at first blush. I believe that my scheme is broader than theirs, but fails to take into account several points they have made.]

[17] [It is important to understand the distinction between the inner world and the internal world. Hartmann described the inner world thus: "In the course of evolution, described here as a process of progressive 'internalization,' there arises a central regulating factor, usually called the 'inner world,' which is interpolated between the receptors and the effectors" (Hartmann, 1939, p. 57). It is the inner world which regulates the orientation in the external world. It is an inner map of the external world. The internal world is the major structures, the identifications, defense structures, ego, id, etc.; they can also be considered internalizations, but they are an internal world. Man's inner map of his world is, however, in the force field of the organization of

our actions or symptoms or postures or preferences are defensive or reveal identifications, then too we have used products of internalization, but these are of a different nature from those internalization products to which I referred by the term "inner world." These defenses and identifications we refer to as structures; indeed, they are major structural determiners of the ego. The "inner world" too is a structure, presumably a structure of the ego, but its elements which are used as representations and relations of representations are not of the same order as the defensive and identification structures. The defense- and identification-creating processes alter the ego (or superego) structure, while those internalization processes which enrich the "inner world" do not as a rule alter the general structure of the ego, though they may become instrumental in setting processes going which do effect an alteration, as in therapy, conversions, etc. This difference often confronts us in the form of contents versus structures and processes, a problem to which Zetzel's (1956) discussion of concept and content is intimately related. Every perception (through any sense organ) may modify the inner world, but not every one can effect a major change of structure. The relationships between inner world and structure formation are complex: (a) the processes which result in structure formation do have representations in the inner world; (b) the structural change (defense and identification) can change the over-all organization of the inner world also; (c) the alterations in the inner world can initiate processes which will result in major structural changes. The relationships between the inner world and the structures and processes of the psychological apparatus at large may be envisaged more sharply if we keep in mind that the inner world contains the representations of the rest (including drives) in so far as these have representations, as well as representations of the external world. These representations are naturally of various degrees of availability and unavailability to consciousness. Earlier I indicated that Jacobson treats the self as if it were identical with self-representation. At this point the difficulty of such a treatment should be clear.

To cope with this welter of complexities it might be desirable to limit the term internalization to those processes which primarily affect the "inner world" or to those aspects of any process which does so—thus separating it from incorporation, introjection, and identification. In regard to the superego this would mean that we would not attribute to it any of the functions of the inner world, because the inner world is a substructure of the ego, which can only *represent* the structures and processes of the superego, id, and of

---

the internal world. The inner map of the outside world has selective omissions and is shaped to the structure of the internal world, that is, of the psychic apparatus. This is an important distinction, which you will not find spelled out.

The relation between the inner world and the internal world is one of the very interesting systematic questions, which may turn out to be the crucial one in the problem of the self.]

the rest of the ego. Naturally it not only represents them but also regulates and modifies them, since it is one of the crucial regulating factors of the ego. It is in this sense that Freud says, in the "Two Principles" (1911): "Thought was endowed with qualities which made it possible for the mental apparatus to support increased tension during a delay in the process of discharge" (p. 16). Thus we would not consider observation and judgment as superego functions. We would rather assume that structural, dynamic, and economic relationships (involving genetic and adaptive considerations) between the ego and superego prompt the observing and judging functions of the ego related to the inner world. It could be argued that the observing and judging functions of the superego were never meant in any other sense. Even so, in the interest of clarity and precision it would have been advantageous to spell out this point.

VIII

Our next task is to clarify the term incorporation. As already indicated, incorporation is used as an alternative term for both introjection and identification. But, just like introjection, it is often used to describe the mechanism which builds the structures we refer to as identifications. Most commonly it is linked to the function of the oral partial drive, both to its preambivalent and ambivalent, reuniting and destructive, forms.[18] It is also commonly used in connection with displaced manifestations of these partial drives, for instance in connection with their displacements to other body zones and functions, like respiration and looking (see Fenichel, 1931, 1935). Erikson has demonstrated that this function-form, or—as he termed it—mode, of the oral drives becomes estranged from its zone of origin, and from the zones to which it gets displaced, to become a behavior and thought modality. As such a modality it is then an ego structure pertaining to the functions of the inner world—both as a mechanism of enriching the inner world and as a mechanism of the functioning of the inner world.

In so far as incorporation remains a mode of the instinctual drives, it is the process by which both introjects and identifications are formed. This already implies a difference between introjects and identifications, though it is yet to be seen whether or not we will find such a difference. In so far as incorporation becomes estranged from its drive origins, it gradually becomes a—or *the?*—mechanism of internalization. We see then a genetic connection between incorporation and internalization: internalization—or at least some internalizations—are higher-order derivatives (neutralized forms) of incorporation. But there is some doubt whether all internalizations originate in this way. It would seem that a significant segment of internalizations

---

[18] [Fenichel (1945, p. 38) states this point more clearly than Freud did in "Instincts and Their Vicissitudes" (1915a). Freud said that sadism is not necessarily destructive in itself, but may rather be a tendency to mastery. Fenichel points out that incorporation per se is not destructive either.]

is guaranteed by the function-form of primary autonomous apparatuses, as innate givens. At any rate, internalization at large and incorporation have no process connection, but only the genetic one that some internalizing processes derive from incorporation processes.[19]

IX

We come now to introjection. Introjection is often used in the very same sense as incorporation, and this is a more justified interchange than any of the others, since introjection is in general defined just as is incorporation, that is, in relation to the oral partial drives. Yet while incorporation is always an instinctual mode, i.e., the form the action of these drives takes, and to my knowledge never used in the sense of defense, introjection is quite generally used as a term denoting a specific defense. In other words, it is possible to assert that the mode of the oral partial drive, that is, incorporation, can undergo a change of function and become a defense mechanism. We have already seen that it can by another change of function become a mechanism, i.e., internalization, which builds the inner world and thus is a mechanism of adaptation. Clearly we are speaking here of clinically familiar relationships, to which Hartmann has repeatedly called attention. It should be mentioned, however, that here much awaits empirical investigation. It is not at all clear whether the instinctual mode incorporation must first change into the defense mechanism introjection before it can change into the adaptive mechanism of internalization. These genetic relationships cannot be established except by observation.[20]

Clearly, the assumption implicit in our theory is that introjects are products of introjection. But here we must raise the question which we should already have asked in relation to incorporation: what is the result of introjection processes? In discussing internalization I have suggested that introjection establishes a structure. But there remains the question: Does it always do so? Does it not at times succeed in destroying the object? Or should we assume that incorporation may or may not do that, but that by introjection we refer to those processes which do not destroy the object but rather re-establish it as a structure?[21] Then again there are those fleeting

---

[19] [Freud (1905, p. 198) called incorporation the prototype of identification. Fenichel (1945, p. 83) similarly wrote: "What was called primary identification . . . [in ego development] is identical with what might be called oral incorporation from the point of view of the instincts." —You see, this is the change of function issue, the double-aspect issue. Loewald too points out repeatedly that incorporation is the instinctual, while identification is the ego, aspect of the same thing. Whether that distinction is sufficient or not, I do not know.]

[20] [Rapaport criticized the present paper for its failure to discuss in detail the issue of "change of function," i.e., that the same phenomenon can have an instinctual, a defensive, and an ego-adaptive aspect—Ed.]

[21] [It is not clear how incorporation—a taking in—can be said to "destroy the object." Perhaps this is shorthand for saying that the incorporation has taken place with a

processes which underlie empathy. Do they establish structure? Again there are a welter of empirical questions which can be answered only by observation.

At any rate, we assume that introjection results in a structural change and not only in the enrichment of the inner world as does incorporation. But here we must also note that the structural change to which we refer as an introject is one which we consider not integrated with the ego or the superego. Presumably introjects may become so integrated. Thus we may consider introjection and introject formation as a process which may lead to integration, in which case we speak about identification; or the resulting introject may stand in isolation, in which case we speak of an introject.[22]

X

Identification is the last in the series of concepts under discussion. We use the term in at least two senses: as a defense mechanism and as a structure-(ego or superego) forming mechanism. As a defense we encounter it in hysterias and as "identification with the aggressor." That both the ego and the superego are built by identifications with abandoned objects is an obvious part of our theory. But it should be noted that identification, according to Freud, is the method par excellence (and he conjectures that it may be the only one) by which drive cathexes can be transformed into ego cathexes. It also should be noted that the earliest identifications are, according to Freud, established prior to object choice, and indeed that identifications can come about simultaneously with object love, that is, prior to abandoning objects. The question then arises, is the process which brings about these identifications also introjection? Moreover, we have to ask ourselves: when we speak of identifications as defenses and about identifications as structures, do we assume that they both come about by an introjection process or that one of them comes about by a different process? If they both come about by introjection, what is the difference between them? Finally, when we talk about identification as a defense, how does that differ from introjection as a defense?

These questions return us to the problem of the superego's relation to defenses in particular and to the ego in general. In order to attempt an answer, we have to clarify the terms in which we expect an answer. We shall therefore use Freud's general psychoanalytic theory of repression as an example to set out from.

---

hostile attitude toward the object representation in the inner world and that the relationship with the object in the external world is "destroyed," that is, terminated—Ed.]
[22] [An ambivalently loved object which is orally introjected does not become part of the ego. According to this definition, it is an error to say that identification takes place in depression. It is rather an introjection that occurs. The internalized object is railed against, the subject calling himself despicable and hateful. Fenichel and others have pointed out that the subject does not act like the lost beloved.]

XI

Freud's theory of repression distinguishes two kinds of repression (primal repression and afterexpulsion) and postulates two mechanisms. The requirement for anything to become conscious and for the execution of any action is a hypercathexis (attention cathexis). The withdrawal of such hypercathexis is one of the mechanisms of repression. But this [alone does not result in repression for it] leaves the representation (or the action impulse) in the condition referred to as preconscious and in a position to attract hypercathexis again. The second mechanism of repression is the countercathecting of the impulse and/or its representation, which prevents the possibility of its attracting hypercathexis. The latter mechanism is that of primal repression, while afterexpulsion applies both mechanisms. Freud stresses that without countercathecting, the result would not be repression but a continuous seesawing of withdrawal and reattracting of hypercathexis, while countercathecting leads to a stable condition, as we are wont to say, to a defense structure which works as a mechanism to prevent resurgence of the impulse and its representations. It is worth noting that the conceptual analysis of the term "structure" shows that when we use the term we mean by it a relatively stable (having a slow rate of change), characteristic configuration that we can abstract from the behavior observed. It should be mentioned that Freud proposed that the countercathexes of which the defense structure is built derive from the impulse countercathected. While Hartmann (1950) proposed that aggressive energy of varying degrees of neutralization contributes to countercathexis even if the warded-off drive was not of an aggressive nature, such difficulties attend this conception that I will here take Freud's proposal as the basis of my discussion. One of the difficulties in question may be briefly mentioned: at the point where primal repression should operate, the genetic conditions are those labeled by the term "undifferentiated phase." [23] That is to say, ego and id, self and external world, are not yet differentiated. It would be inconsistent to assume that at a time when the ego and the id are not yet differentiated, the drives of the id are already differentiated.

The conception of defense formation, then, is the following. When drive impulse has reached threshold intensity and the object is present, drive discharge takes place. There are thus three elements to this prototypical situation: drive, threshold, and object. If the object is absent, the drive cathexis is dammed up and we infer that the threshold must be heightened. It is this threshold heightening to which we refer as defense, inferring that this heightening is achieved by countercathexes. It should be noted that the de-

[23] [What other difficulties Rapaport had in mind I do not know, but it seems clear that Hartmann is referring to afterexpulsion rather than to primal repression, since he speaks of varying degrees of neutralization. Even according to Freud's hypothesis, the countercathexes in primal repression must be derived from undifferentiated energy—Ed.]

fense is thus organized around the threshold, and it is probably this that we refer to when, with Anna Freud, we speak of the ego's fundamental antagonism to drives. If the absence of the object results in intolerable tension or becomes regular, the countercathecting becomes stable in order to eliminate the experience of this tension, in keeping with the pleasure principle. Such stabilization is structure building, i.e., binding of cathexes in structure. Once such a structure is built, part of the originally used countercathexes becomes superfluous and becomes available as hypercathexis. It can be used both as attention cathexis and as countercathexis to reinforce defensive structures.

This model of defense building has one more aspect that is crucial for our considerations. Let us note that the defense structure was established when the object was absent. It thus represents the absence of the object structurally, and it has the object's crucial characteristic, namely that it prevents gratification. Since we do not have a general theory of introjections and identifications comparable to the theory of repression here sketched, it seems advisable to assume that the here sketched characteristic of defense may give us the point of departure for the general theoretical explanation of identifications. If we were to assume, then, that all defense formation is akin to the formation of repression, we could assume that introjection and identification always accompany defense formation.[24] To be sure, this would force on us the obligation to demonstrate the similarity in the basic mechanism of repression and other defense formation. Considering that for several decades repression actually substituted effectively in the clinical theory for all defenses, this would not seem to be an outlandish assumption, even though it might lead us to many new and unexplored relationships

[24] [In the later seminar on the superego, Rapaport indicated that a difficulty is presented here. The statement of the difficulty, as well as of its proposed resolution, are not clear; nevertheless, in the hope that it may at least point to his thinking, I will attempt to state his argument as I understand it. He seems to be asking whether there may not be a contradiction involved in viewing repression as a paradigm of identification, in that in repression the object cathexis is isolated from the remainder of the ego while in identification the structure which takes the place of the object relationship is integrated into the ego (or partly integrated, as in an introjection). His reply seems to be that identifications may be not only with "substantive characteristics" of the object—its actual specific features—but with its "formal characteristics" too, which he describes as its fickleness, unavailability, or dangerousness. Identification with substantive characteristics is what is generally regarded as identification, and Rapaport is apparently arguing that similarity in formal characteristics is also an identification, that the latter is a repression, and that the formal characteristic in which the repression represents a crucial aspect of the object is that it prevents gratification and was erected because the unavailability of the object prevented gratification, as he stressed in the text above. I do not reproduce the original seminar material because I am persuaded that it will not yield any clearer interpretation than the one I have made. The discussion in the text below which points out that defenses *do* become generalized and integrated into the ego is probably a continuation of the argument for the relationship between defense and identification—Ed.]

among defenses. Such assumptions would also raise the question, How then do introjection and identification differ from other defenses? In other words, if introjection and/or identification are always aspects of any defense structure, how does it happen that we speak of them as specific defenses or structures (introjects, identifications)? No complete answer to this question can be even conjectured at this point. But the question has to be raised, since the general theory of the superego depends on a general theory of introjection and identification, which at this point is nonexistent. And a first tentative step—subject to further theoretical analysis and clinical corroboration—can be made.

XII

To make a step toward clarifying the defense-identification relationship, let us return to the model of drive-threshold-object with which we started.

The absence of the object resulted in a damming up of drive cathexis and a heightening of threshold: an establishment of a defense which on further consideration showed itself as a possible structural element of introjection or identification. Let us consider this model further. What are the consequences of the establishment of a defense? First of all, we know that defenses do not, as a rule, remain isolated, but generalize to the other partial drives which they will then control, though not necessarily rigidly defend against. Thus an integration takes place, which Freud discussed in the early sections of *Inhibitions, Symptoms and Anxiety* (1926) when he spoke of defenses and symptoms being integrated by the synthetic function of the ego and invested with ego interest. Indeed, it would seem that at the point of development which is represented by the model, this process of integration is the process of ego (and perhaps superego) differentiation from the undifferentiated matrix.

If we now consider that another consequence of defense development is drive differentiation by means of the development of derivative drives, we will be one step closer to being able to return to considering the theory of the superego. The defense establishment itself results in a new derivative motivation, by which in fact we recognize clinically the presence of defense. Furthermore, we encounter derivative motivations to which we refer as "the return of the repressed." Finally, we find that the generalizing of the defense to other partial drives modifies them also, and the result is further derivative drives. Naturally, these derivative motivations are again subject to defense development of the sort our model represents, and to a new integration with corresponding new motivational development. This process is never-ending and results in the hierarchic arrangement of drives, defense in depth, corresponding affect hierarchy, and progressive neutralization of drive cathexes.[25] This hierarchy is sufficiently familiar from everyday clini-

[25] [It is progressive structure formation which decreases the mobility of cathexes,

cal work to require no further discussion. Freud, in his analysis of the genetics of anxiety (separation, object loss, loss of love of object, castration anxiety, superego, and social anxiety), speaks of one aspect of this hierarchy. Jones (1929) discusses another affective side of the same. Freud's formulation, in "The Unconscious" (1915b), that every advance in structure development involves a new "censorship" and new "hypercathexes," is also relevant to this point. In other words, we find a hierarchy of integrations of defenses and controls which link defenses to each other.

XIII

The question is now, How do defenses, introjects, and identifications differ from one another as structures, if we maintain that all defense development has an element of identification? Let us assume for the moment that when, due to the prevailing fluid dynamic conditions, a defense does not generalize, remains in isolation, we will be faced with the model of the introject. Let us secondly assume that if the generalization and integration of a defense into the developing ego is successful, it may lose its specific character of correspondence to an absent (ungratifying) object. Let us thirdly assume that as defense becomes generalized it may so dominate the integrate that its specific character of correspondence to an absent object becomes characteristic of the level of integration in question, in which case we would speak of an identification and realize that its prerequisite was an introjection implicit in the original defense formation. Let us finally assume that defense-identifications from the various hierarchic levels will also integrate and yield those general structures which we refer to as ego and superego.

The more successful these integrations, the less conspicuous the individual identifications and the more clearly unique the integrate's characteristic configuration, the identity or self.

Actually, clinically this broad and sweeping relation of defense and identifications is not new, though it may strike us as a new way of looking at familiar relationships. The same behavior characteristics which we study as defenses we also study in their relation to the characteristics of the outstanding figures of identification.

XIV

But we are still no further in understanding the relationships of the superego to defenses and the relationships between superego and ego identifications. Perhaps a reconsideration of the relationships of the early levels of integration of defense-identifications to the drives will help us further.

---

turning them from mobile into neutralized cathexes. It is consistent with this formulation to see identifications as performing desexualization and sublimation. Identification is structure formation and therefore a step toward neutralization.]

It will readily be seen that on the early levels of integration the defenses will function primarily in response to the fluctuation of drive intensity, the increase of which will command the investment of hypercathexes to reinforce the countercathexes of the defense structures. In other words, the early hierarchic integration levels will be primarily passive in that they will be regulated by the instinctual drives. How strikingly this differs from the function of the defense integrations of the higher level is most easily assessed by reminding ourselves of Freud's final theory of anxiety. According to this theory, the ego anticipates the rising instinctual tension and actively gives the anxiety signal to mobilize defenses.

If we now also take into consideration Freud's clinically crucial proposition that the superego is not only a representative of general societal and particular parental standards in relation to the ego, but also the representative of the id in relation to the ego, we will be able to make one further tentative step in the general psychoanalytic theory of the superego. Let us conjecture that this just-stated proposition of the clinical theory is equivalent to the theoretical proposition that the lower the level of the hierarchy of integrations we are dealing with, the more it must be assumed to be passive and regulated by the id impulses, and the higher the integration level in the hierarchy the more active its self-regulative rôle.

If we then assume that the ego and the superego are both such structural integrates of defense-identifications, we gain the following picture of their relationships and the relationship of their identifications: the earliest integrations of defense-identifications are part of both the ego and the superego as defense-identification integrates, and are passive in relation to the id. In the course of development, the more active the integrates the less, or the less directly, are they tied into that regulating network of integration to which we refer as the superego, and the more are they integrated and regulated by that network of integration to which we refer as the ego.

If these considerations may be tentatively made the assumptions on which the theory of the ego-superego differentiation rests, then there emerges a relatively clear picture of superego-ego-defense-identification relationships. If we limit ourselves for the moment to the characterization of the ego and superego relationships solely in respect to defenses and identifications, we arrive at the following propositions:

(1) Introjection is one aspect of defense-structure development.

(2) Identifications arise from the integration of defenses. Such structures are to be referred to as defense-identifications.

(3) From this point of view, both the ego and the superego may be considered as integrates of such defense-identifications.

(4) The early defense-identifications contribute to both ego and superego structure, and are characteristically passive in relation to the id impulses. From this point of view, both the ego and the superego may be regarded as controlling networks of such defense-identifications.

(5) In the course of development, with the progressive accretion of hierarchic integration levels of such defense-identifications, the passive regulation of these defense-identification integrates by id impulses abates and their active self-regulation increases. Parallel with this development, the networks controlling these defense-identifications (ego and superego) differentiate. (The causes and mechanism of this differentiation will be briefly indicated below.)

(6) The result of this differentiation is that the superego network does not extend to the higher levels of defense-identification integrates but includes only those which are passively regulated by drive tension and can control the higher levels only through its relation to the ego network. In turn, the ego network includes as archaic levels of its structure the integrates which are passively regulated by drive tension (indeed, regression phenomena show that in regard to them the ego and superego are not yet differentiated), but (short of regressive states) the ego does not regulate these archaic integrations directly, rather only through its relation to the superego.

(7) The differentiation of the ego and the id is not sharp but progressive. It reaches a definitive crystallization with those defense-identifications which arise as a solution of the oedipal conflicts. This point is a separating line between the integrates that are passive and those that are active in relation to the drive tension.[26] The former attain a dominant integration by the superego, the latter a dominant integration by the ego, although these dominances and this separating line are relative.

This conception, though it does not contain much, if anything, new, nevertheless seems to eliminate a number of inconsistencies and obscurities in regard to the ego-superego-defense-identification relationships.

XV

Throughout these last discussions we have limited ourselves to the defense-identification structures, disregarding all other considerations. Yet it is necessary to point out that the experiences which give rise to these structure formations also result in a corresponding enrichment of the inner world by internalizations, the effects of which become the representations of these

---

[26] [Why do not the oedipal identifications become ego structures? If in the course of development two sets of identifications and defense structures are formed, one set integrated more closely with the external environment and the other more immediately controlled by the instinctual impulses, then the intimate connection of the oedipal struggle with the incestuous instinctual impulse is responsible for the integration of the oedipal identifications into the superego set. So too with the prior defenses related to the instinctual impulses, like shame and disgust. The one set of instinctual-drive controlling structures, then, is directly controlled by the impulses, the other by anticipations. This is the main point I tried to make on the distinction between ego and superego in my paper on the superego.]

structures and the motivations (derivative drives) corresponding to them. It should be noted, however, that just as the drive organization of memories yields control in the course of development to the supervening conceptual organization of memories which constitutes a substructure within the ego, the inner world (which encompasses these memory organizations) in the course of development becomes increasingly organized in terms of secondary-process—i.e., ego—regulations and becomes as a whole a crucial agency of ego regulation. It is this development and that of other reality-relationship guaranteeing structures and functions of the ego which—among others—play a crucial rôle in bringing about the ego-superego differentiation we discussed above. It should be stressed here that as a result of these developments and the corresponding ego-superego differentiation, the superego has no control over the ego apparatuses of observing, judging, and action, nor has it independent apparatuses for observing, judging, and action. It is by the interstructural tensions between the ego and the superego that the superego exerts its momentous effects on the ego. These effects are so irrational because the points of contact between the ego and superego at which these tensions arise are—as we are wont to put it—"close to the id" and thus, just like defenses, these tensions pertain to cathexes which have undergone but little neutralization. The ego's observing, judging, and action apparatuses then reflect this interstructural tension in intrastructural ego processes: guilt feelings (which like all feelings are ego processes), self-destructive actions, etc.

XVI

Not even in this tentative and cursory fashion is it possible even to touch on more than a few of the puzzling problems of the conception of the superego. It will have been noted that we centered in the main on the genetic and structural aspects of the problems. Sooner or later we will of course have to come to grips with the dynamic, economic, and adaptive aspects of the superego conception. In the present framework there was no latitude to deal with these. It seems useful, however, to point out that even if there were space and time, the very obscurity of the problems might still prove to be prohibitive. The historical links between the problems of narcissism, masochism, the instinctual vicissitude of "turning round upon the self," the self and identity, the death instinct, the aggressive drive, instinctual-drive fusion and defusion, the superego's turning upon the self, and the energies of the superego form a Gordian knot. It is quite possible that this knot will yield to theoretical discernment only if whoever tackles it is ready to make radical assumptions concerning the nature and origins of the aggressive drive. I believe that the conception of the superego as an integrate and controlling network of defense-identifications, which are relatively passive in relation to the id, i.e., are triggered into function by fluctuations of drive intensity, does permit the clarification of the nature of "turning round upon the self." I also consider it possible that this very clarification may open the avenue to a new conception of the nature and genetic course of the aggressive drive.

REFERENCES

Bibring, E. (1953). The Mechanism of Depression. In *Affective Disorders,* ed. P. Greenacre. New York: International Universities Press, pp. 13–48.

Erikson, E. H. (1950). Growth and Crises of the "Healthy Personality." In *Personality in Nature, Society, and Culture,* 2nd ed., ed. C. Kluckhohn & H. A. Murray. New York: Knopf, 1953, pp. 185–225.

———— (1951). On the Sense of Inner Identity. In *Psychoanalytic Psychiatry and Psychology, Clinical and Theoretical Papers,* Austen Riggs Center, Vol. I, ed. R. P. Knight & C. R. Friedman. New York: International Universities Press, 1954, pp. 351–364.

———— (1956). The Problem of Ego Identity. *J. Amer. Psychoanal. Assn.,* 4:56–121.

Fenichel, O. (1931). Respiratory Introjection. *Collected Papers,* 1:221–240. New York: Norton, 1953.

———— (1935). The Scoptophilic Instinct and Identification. *Collected Papers,* 1:373–397. New York: Norton, 1953.

———— (1945). *The Psychoanalytic Theory of Neurosis.* New York: Norton.

Freud, A. (1936). *The Ego and the Mechanisms of Defence.* New York: International Universities Press, 1946.

Freud, S. (1900). The Interpretation of Dreams. *Standard Edition,* 4 & 5. London: Hogarth Press, 1953.

———— (1905). Three Essays on the Theory of Sexuality. *Standard Edition,* 7:123–245. London: Hogarth Press, 1953.

———— (1911). Formulations Regarding the Two Principles in Mental Functioning. *Collected Papers,* 4:13–21. New York: Basic Books, 1959.

———— (1913 [1912–13]). Totem and Taboo. *Standard Edition,* 13:1–161. London: Hogarth Press, 1955.

———— (1914). On Narcissism: An Introduction. *Standard Edition,* 14:73–102. London: Hogarth Press, 1957.

———— (1915a). Instincts and Their Vicissitudes. *Standard Edition,* 14:117–140. London: Hogarth Press, 1957.

———— (1915b). The Unconscious. *Standard Edition,* 14:166–215. London: Hogarth Press, 1957.

———— (1921). Group Psychology and the Analysis of the Ego. *Standard Edition,* 18:69–143. London: Hogarth Press, 1955.

———— (1923). *The Ego and the Id,* tr. J. Riviere. London: Hogarth Press, 1947.

———— (1926). Inhibitions, Symptoms and Anxiety. *Standard Edition,* 20:87–172. London: Hogarth Press, 1959.

———— (1933). *New Introductory Lectures on Psycho-Analysis,* tr. W. J. H. Sprott. New York: Norton.

Hartmann, H. (1939). *Ego Psychology and the Problem of Adaptation,* tr. D. Rapaport. New York: International Universities Press, 1958.

———— (1950). Comments on the Psychoanalytic Theory of the Ego. *Psychoanal. Study Child,* 5:74–96. New York: International Universities Press.

Jacobson, E. (1954). Contribution to the Metapsychology of Psychotic Identifications. *J. Amer. Psychoanal. Assn.,* 2:239–262.

Jones, E. (1929). Fear, Guilt and Hate. *Papers on Psycho-Analysis,* 5th ed. Baltimore: Williams & Wilkins, 1948, pp. 304–319.

———— (1947). The Genesis of the Super-Ego. *Papers on Psycho-Analysis,* 5th ed. Baltimore: Williams & Wilkins, 1948, pp. 145–152.

Loewald, H. (1962). Internalization, Separation, Mourning, and the Superego. *Psychoanal. Quart.,* 31:483–504.

Rapaport, D. (1953). Some Metapsychological Considerations Concerning Activity and Passivity. *This volume.* Chapter 44.

Reich, A. (1954). Early Identifications as Archaic Elements in the Superego. *J. Amer. Psychoanal. Assn.,* 2:218–238.

Schafer, R. (1960). The Loving and Beloved Superego in Freud's Structural Theory. *Psychoanal. Study Child,* 15:163–188. New York: International Universities Press.

Schur, M. (1953). The Ego in Anxiety. In *Drives, Affects, Behavior,* ed. R. M. Loewenstein. New York: International Universities Press, pp. 67–103.

Zetzel, E. R. (1956). An Approach to the Relation between Concept and Content in Psychoanalytic Theory. *Psychoanal. Study Child,* 11:99–121. New York: International Universities Press.

56

THE STUDY OF KIBBUTZ EDUCATION
AND ITS BEARING ON THE
THEORY OF DEVELOPMENT

I

The upbringing of children in the agricultural collectives in Israel is for the social scientist what an "experiment of nature" is for the natural scientist. The surviving preliterate cultures also furnish such "experiments of nature," but their historical background, their language, and the other communication barriers which exist between them and us, set a limit on what they can teach us about the relationships between instinctual drives, ego, and environment, that is to say, about the relationship between the life of a society and the upbringing and development of children in it. On the other hand, neither the historical conditions which brought about the kibbutz and its method of upbringing nor the communication barriers interfere prohibitively with investigating it. Yet so far only two studies have been published on it: Irvine's (1952), which was limited in time and scope and relied heavily on informants; and Spiro's (1954, 1955, 1956), which was limited

Presented at the Annual Meeting of the American Orthopsychiatric Association, 1957. Published in Hebrew in Ofakim *(Israel), December 1957. First published in English in* The American Journal of Orthopsychiatry, *28:587–597, 1958. Copyright the American Orthopsychiatric Association, Inc. German translation published in* Psyche, *23:353–366, 1958.*

to a single kibbutz and has not yet been fully reported. Besides these, the pertinent literature includes (1) Infield's (1944) and Reifen's (1949) descriptions, which are neither precise nor well documented; (2) Caplan's (1954) discussion (he was apparently connected with Irvine's study) at a Macy Foundation conference which contains only a part of Irvine's material and is neither cohesive nor balanced; (3) Kardiner's brief discussion (1954), which is replete with misinformation and misinterpretation; (4) privately circulated information, from the recently founded "Institute for Research in Collective Education" of the Israeli Kibbutz Organizations, which is in part programmatic and, understandably, at times defensive.

My purpose here is neither to criticize nor to defend, and certainly not to evaluate. For defense there is no need, and for criticism and evaluation the requisite evidence is not yet available. I shall use the meager data we do have in an attempt to expose some of the theoretical questions to the answer of which we may expect a contribution from the study of kibbutz upbringing and of the forms child development takes in it. I have not done any field work in a kibbutz myself, though I lived in one. I have indicated above the sources of the data I shall use. Thus, no responsibility for the accuracy of the data rests with me. To my mind, the problems which I shall discuss below are valid and cardinal irrespective of the specific validity of the available data used to pinpoint them.

II

The kibbutz movement is about 40 years old. It arose from the Zionist-socialist youth movement of Eastern Europe, the main tenets of which were: (a) Zionist ideology; (b) socialist ideology; and (c) the principle of *realization,* i.e., the commitment to translate ideology into action. In keeping with the Zionist tenet, the movement steeped itself in the history of Jewry, in its contemporary cultural, social, economic, and political situation, in the contemporary conditions of Palestine, and in the reviving Hebrew language. In keeping with the socialist tenet, the movement adopted a socialist ideology and explored its ethical, humanistic, social, economic, and political implications, striving to create within itself human relationships based on reason, justice, cooperation, and equality. In keeping with the principle of realization, the members of the movement prepared to go to Palestine, to become people of the soil—in contrast to their East European parents who were intellectuals or merchants or artisans or laborers in industries threatened with extinction by advancing industrialization—and to create on that soil a Hebrew community based on reason, justice, equality, and cooperation.

These are the roots from which the agricultural collectives of present-day Israel grew. The principal tenets, though not unmodified by experience and circumstances, remain: (a) dedication to the building of a Jewish national home; (b) agriculture as the primary economic base of existence; (c) a fraternal community, small enough so that face-to-face contact and familiarity permit the application of the principle "from each according to his abilities and to each according to his needs"; (d) communal life in which a common ideology and practice, decided by the majority, prevails, but where the individual's and minorities' needs are considered as long as these do not clash with the cohesiveness of the community; (e) communal life based on cooperation, equality, justice, and reason, free of competition, private property, exploitation, differences in the status of men and women, and other practices founded on passion or prejudice—religious, moralistic, conventional, or simply thoughtless and unscientific. How fully these ideals have been realized, or to what extent they have become merely lip service divorced from practice, it is not our task to examine.

Thus the kibbutz movement arose as a rebellion against the religious, paternalistic-familial, socioeconomic, and minority life of East European Jewry, much of which is well described by Zborowski and Herzog (1952).

III

What is the upbringing—referred to as "collective education"—which issued from these tenets? The two main characteristics of "collective education" are: (a) The upbringing of the children is the economic as well as the theoretical and ideological responsibility of the community, and not of the individual parents. (b) The upbringing of children by parents in their home is replaced by an upbringing in communal children's houses, where members of the community, trained for this job, are the caretakers and educators.

The leaders of kibbutz education and most observers agree that the objective of "collective education" is to raise a generation which will perpetuate the collective way of life and the ideals it stands for. There is less agreement as to the forces and aims which shaped this education. The divergent views seem to reflect the multitudinous historical, cultural, socioeconomic, traditional, and ideological factors which have shaped collective education in particular and probably shape other forms of education as well.

Let us stop for a moment and consider the theoretical implications. The educational goal of any society is to perpetuate its way of life and ideals. The analysis of the specific conditions which shape a given form of education should reveal *how* and *by what* forces that educational process was shaped in order to achieve that goal. If, for instance, the social conditions in this country usually result in our children having a lot to do with "sitters," and our socioeconomic conditions usually result in our children being taught by teachers who, in relation to their training and to the prevailing wages of labor, are badly underpaid, then these socioeconomic facts are some of the factors which bring about that form of education by which our society perpetuates itself. At first this conclusion may seem arbitrary, particularly to you, many of whom must often have protested against the misuses of "sitters" and against the low wages paid to teachers. But our protests are just as much part of the procedure by which our society creates the form of education by which it perpetuates itself, as the factual conditions and their well-known refractoriness to change. The proof for such assertions should be sought, for instance, in the fact that our society has not yet collapsed, though the teacher's wages and status seem to have been relatively unchanged for several generations.

What are the factors variously assumed to be responsible for the institution of collective education?

Some of the writers mentioned consider the major factor to be the changed rôle of the woman in the collective. If she was to become man's equal and a worker just like him, she had to be freed from household chores. Thus the upbringing of children had to become a job to be performed by those who could do it best or who were available.

To other writers the salient factor seemed to be the rebellion against the patriarchal authority of the East European Jewish father. The pressure of paternal authority was heavy on the Jewish youth of Eastern Europe and bred the determination that their own children should not labor under this burden. This determination seems to be shared by the European immigrant to America also, and may be one of the factors which shapes the upbringing of our children too. This explanation implies that rebels against parental authority do not find it easy to take on the parents' rôle and therefore relegate it to experts.

Still another explanation, mindful of the rationalist ideology of the youth movement and the collectives, attributes a paramount rôle to the wish to prevent the individual parental predilection or pathology from determining the child's upbringing, and to rely rather on up-to-date expert knowledge. Spiro (1956) indicates that this reliance on the expert and this providing of *the best* for the children is a continuation of trends basic to Eastern European Jewish life: reverence for knowledge and reason, and a paramount interest in the future of the child. The kibbutz is a child-centered society in which the children's interest overrides everything except perhaps the cohesiveness of the community and the demands of the farm economy.

Other writers consider collective education a means of dispensing with the institution of the bourgeois family, which results in the patriarchal position of the father-provider, the subordinate position of the mother-housekeeper, the hypocritical morality fostered by the conventions and economics of the marriage bond, and the dependence of upbringing on the will of the parents and particularly on the oppressive authority of the patriarchal father. They stress that the narrow loyalties of the bourgeois family, and its devisive emotional life and interests, are incompatible with communal life.

The last explanation to be mentioned is perhaps the only historically and factually incorrect one: economic need demanded that women, like men, work in the field, and gave rise to this economical, communal, care of children. It is true that the collectives grew up in most adverse economic circumstances which could not help having a determining influence on their form of life and education. This economic influence, however, is mingled with and often overshadowed by the puritanical ethics and ideological intents of the youth movement from which these collectives stemmed, and thus is by no means simple and direct. Factually, it cannot be determined whether collective upbringing is the most economical form of upbringing, because we do not know the cost of upbringing which *these* people would have had to pay if they had not embarked on collective education. What would have happened if Napoleon had *not* been beaten at Waterloo is an unanswerable question. The comparison with the cost of upbringing in cooperative (not communal) settlements seems to show that collective education is the more expensive of the two.

Let us assume, with Erik Erikson (1950a), that in bringing up children, every society confronts each developmental (psychosexual and ego) stage of the child, through its caretaking people and institutions, with the demands of its living conditions, traditions, and attitudes in such a way as to enable and compel the child so to solve the psychosexual and psychosocial crises brought on by development that the solution will bring him a step closer to becoming a viable and effective member of that society. On this assumption, the factors responsible for the existing form of kibbutz upbringing appear as the mediating links between the way of life of this community and the methods it uses to shape new generations to perpetuate it. The uniqueness of collective education lies in, among other things, the fact that these mediating factors could be directly studied, and would not have to be unearthed at a distance of centuries or against the handicap of our own inclination to take our system of upbringing for granted. Such a study may pave the way toward the understanding of Western systems of education and may even begin to show us the ways in which they adjust or can be adjusted to the needs of our changing social conditions. We may even learn to accept the idea that in the upbringing which we gave our children, and in their developmental crises and pathology, we pay the price for our social-technological "achievements." We may cease to be alarmed about our upbringing, or may accept our alarm as an indispensable part of the process of adjustment of upbringing to changing social conditions.

IV

The study of kibbutz education could shed light not only on how social, historical, and economic conditions shape educational institutions, but also on how these institutions of upbringing shape the development of the individual child. Our own form of bringing up children and the changes which are taking place in it give rise to many developmental forms, and some of these alarm us because they seem to be pathological. In addition, our increasing knowledge about psychopathology and psychodynamics, and public consciousness of "mental health," spotlight our children's behavior, doing away with the old privacy of development and education, and we seem to see pathology everywhere. In spite of the contributions toward the understanding of "normal," "healthy" development by Erikson (1950b), and others, we—and the parents—are often bewildered when we have to decide what is pathological and what is developmental. The study of collective education, in which the privacy of familial education is eliminated by factors other than insight and public consciousness, may provide some of the means for deciding whether some of our observations of "problem" behavior are merely developmental, transient though necessary consequences of our changing educational institutions, or pathological outcomes of our failing upbringing.

Let us therefore briefly review the meager information available on the institutions of collective upbringing and on the development of children in the kibbutz.

(1) Collective upbringing begins when the child and the mother return from the hospital to the kibbutz. The infant spends his first year in the "infants' house," in which there may be up to fifteen infants, who, under optimal conditions, are cared for by a *metapelet* and her two aids, all trained for their work. For six weeks the mother does not work; after that she gradually returns to her regular work, though she continues to feed the child on "worktime" until he is weaned (six to eight months), whether the feeding is from the breast or from the bottle. The feeding mothers are usually together at the six feeding times of the four-hour schedule. For the first six months the infant does *not* leave the infants' house, but is visited there by the parents and siblings for an hour in the evening. After six months he is taken to the parents' room for the evening visits. Otherwise the care of the child is entirely entrusted to the *metapelet*.

(2) In general, after the first year the children move to the "toddlers' house," where a new *metapelet* looks after a group of four to six toddlers, taking care of their needs, training in eating and toilet training. The visits with the parents now become two hours long in the evening, and include the whole Sabbath, but remain a time of play, walks, and entertainment. Between the second and third years a nursery teacher enters the toddlers' group; like the *metapelet,* she looks after their physical needs, but is primarily concerned with their social and intellectual development.

(3) At four years of age the children enter kindergarten, and generally move to a new house; the group is enlarged to sixteen to eighteen with a new teacher and *metapelet*. This larger group, though it will change its form of life, will stay together till it enters high school at twelve. Free and super-

vised play, excursions to the farm, arts, group readings, visits with the parents on evenings and holidays, are the children's daily routine; and their care, discipline, and the fostering of group spirit and intellectual development are the responsibility of the *metapelet* and teacher.

(4) A year or two in kindergarten is followed by a "transitional" year, i.e., preparation for grammar school, and with it an hour's work daily in taking care of their house, school, garden, and a few fowl. In the grammar school, teaching is by the project method, and the children have their say in it. The relation to the teacher is informal and passing to the next grade is automatic.

(5) With the twelfth year comes the high school, a male teacher and educator, and membership in the youth movement. The group is enlarged to twenty-five members and includes children from other kibbutzim and from cities. At this point the children begin to work one and a half to three hours a day on the big farm. The curriculum is more like that of a European than of an American high school. Besides the teachers, the educator and the group itself play a major rôle in planning and in the maintenance of discipline.

The effects of this education on development, behavior, and interpersonal relations I shall discuss under three headings: the development of interpersonal relationships; the development of behavior "problems"; and the development of personal effectiveness.

(1) The parents seem to play no less of a rôle in the young child's life than in familial-parental education. The child reacts to their absence, illness, or death *very* strongly, and if the parent (being a *metapelet*) takes care of other children, jealousy is intense; but reactions to the absence or change of the *metapelet* are often just as strong. The anticipation of the visit with the parents is great, but so is the anticipation of returning to the children's house. The disciplinary figure is the *metapelet;* the parents are, in general, permissive figures. The tension between the parents and the disciplining "parent substitutes" seems to result in problems both for the organization of education and for the children in regard to their loyalties, though definitive data on these are not yet available. According to Spiro's questionnaire study (1955), the parent is the person from whom the child can expect praise but not blame. Blame is expected from the *metapelet* and from the group, though praise too is expected from the group and more often so than from the parents. Moreover, when the children enter high school, the attachments to the parents, the frequency of visits, and the intimacies fall off sharply.

The importance of the peer group begins early and steadily increases. In the toddler and nursery-school groups, quick shifts from warm cooperation to angry clashes are common. Yet the peer group early becomes the most important "praising figure," and as the time for high school approaches, the *metaplot* and teachers yield their pre-eminence as the most important blaming figures to the group. The prevalent characteristics of the high-school group are mutual assistance and protection of the weaker members. Identification with the group is strong and is the major source of security. Possessiveness, acquisitiveness, and striving for personal success are minimal, and the striving for excellence is motivated by social responsibility.

(2) The facts concerning behavior problems are even sketchier. Various observers report:

(a) Relative severity of toilet training, and of the problems connected with it. This is attributed partly to the limited time available to the *metapelet,* who therefore deals with the toilet training of the children as a group and not individually. The "difficulties" are also made obvious by the fact that "picking up" children at night is out of the question for practical reasons. The relative severity of training is mitigated by the informedness about prevailing psychological views. The public obviousness of any difficulty may give an exaggerated picture of the incidence of difficulties. No strictly comparable data from other forms of upbringing are extant which could decisively show that the incidence of training difficulties and failures is greater in collective education. Yet reports (particularly Irvine's) of a greater incidence of such difficulties, particularly enuresis, cannot be discounted.

(b) The situation is similar concerning the claims as to a greater incidence of masturbation, nail biting, thumb-sucking, and feeding difficulties.

(c) The reports also seem to suggest a selective neglect of the children at the toddler age, explained by the fact that the *metapelet,* occupied with the household of the toddler house, cannot provide individual care.

(d) High incidence of unmitigated aggression in the toddler and nursery age is also reported. Again, however, there are no reliable comparative data from other types of upbringing, and the public character of collective education, which exhibits rather than conceals these phenomena, cannot be discounted.

Critically inclined observers draw the conclusions:

(a) Collective education, by enforcing separation of the child from the parents, brings these phenomena about, and they should therefore be considered pathological symptoms of the separation.

(b) Mass upbringing, lacking individual care and affection, is responsible for these phenomena, which must therefore be considered pathological.

(c) The multiple parent figures and the division of the sources of affection and discipline are the sources of these phenomena, since they increase the opportunity for conflict, for clashing loyalties, and for frustration, rather than reducing them as kibbutz educators hoped—and at times claimed—they would.

However, the available facts, surveyed above, suggest that collective education involves no *separation* in the customary sense of the word. Tensions in general, divided loyalties and multiple parent figures in particular, are present in all forms of upbringing and may indeed be a necessary part of all except a "hothouse" upbringing. Yet these arguments do not definitely contradict the explanations listed, since there are no objective and exhaustive studies available either to refute or to corroborate these explanations.

All educational systems *have* their tensions. Erikson (1950a) points out that a society shapes the personality types which are viable in it, not only by providing outlets for tensions, but also by building character structure *to maintain and to contain certain tensions*. It is therefore possible that the behavior problems described are forms of developmental crises natural to collective upbringing, rather than pathological symptoms. To what extent these behavior problems are one or the other can be decided only by systematic study of the kibbutz society, of the methods of collective upbringing, and of the development and pathology of the children brought up in it as they attain adulthood. Such studies face the problem of the social relativity of pathology, one of the crucial and unsolved problems of orthopsychiatry. The increasing volume of "pathology" we seem to see in our children requires that we learn to distinguish pathological crises from the developmental crises of normal growth proper to our society and upbringing.

(3) There seems to be agreement that the individuals who grow up in the kibbutz are, in general, adapted to this collective way of life: it is claimed that only 3.1 per cent of these have left it *altogether,* while the lowest percentage of members not brought up in the kibbutz who leave it is *annually* 2.9 per cent. The dissatisfactions which cause Spiro to speak of a crisis in the older generation do not, according to him, touch the younger generation which grew up in collective education.

Observers also seem to agree that the children who, as toddlers, showed such poor eating habits, so much bed wetting, nail biting, aggressiveness (Kardiner [1954] goes so far as to report secondhand that "the law of the jungle prevails among them"), masturbation, motor restlessness, and tantrums, by the time of puberty become cooperative, self-contained, sturdy, responsible individuals. In the ranks of the commandos (Palmach) of the 1948 War of Independence, the majority of whom were recruited from kibbutzim, they acquitted themselves magnificently: the reports claim no incidence of war neuroses among them, describe them as people who readily took responsibility and initiative, and who subordinated personal interest to that of the group to the point of necessary sacrifice.

On the other hand, a tendency to cling to their group or other kibbutz groups when away from the kibbutz, in the army or in occupational training, has been variously interpreted as lack of individuality and independence. However, here again the evidence is inconclusive.

It is also reported that they lack the cultural-intellectual bent of the founding kibbutz generation and the curiosity, speculative bent, and colorfulness of the East European Jew. Some go so far as to describe them as emotionally flat and stolid. Yet the evidence of their art work, their songs and dance, and their agricultural achievements would be hard to reconcile with this sweeping generalization: a study of the actual facts is urgently needed.

The most interesting data pertain to the relationship of the sexes. Since the kibbutz ideology is opposed to all hypocrisy, collective education is coeducational in the full sense of the word. Boys and girls grow up in the same rooms. As toddlers and nursery school children they use the same baths and lavatories, without privacy. This lack of privacy shows a spontaneous devolution; boys and girls spontaneously separate, first in the lavatories and then in the showers. Similar in portent and even more striking is the fact that this education results in exogamy: as a rule, the marriages are *not* between people who have grown up in the same group. A spontaneous "incest" taboo seems to have arisen. Last but not least, it is claimed that not a single case of homosexuality has been encountered amongst the young people of collective upbringing.

Let us assume for the moment that the situation with enuresis, autoerotic manifestations, aggressiveness, and impressions of neglect between the ages of one and six is actually as the most critical reports state it; and that the situation with the young adults' adaptedness, cooperativeness, responsibility, effectiveness is actually as it is stated by the most appreciative reports. On these assumptions we would have to conclude:

(a) We cannot be sure whether our own upbringing, which is hidden by privacy and restraining conditions, has or does not have the same kind and amount of "behavior problems" which become manifest in collective upbringing which lacks such "hiding factors."

(b) It is possible that what we usually regard as "behavior problems" are, in certain types of upbringing, normal phenomena of a development whose outcome is a viable human being adapted to the environment from which that form of upbringing issues.

(c) It is likely that a society, whatever its conscious intentions, more or less inevitably produces a method of upbringing whose crises and difficulties, as well as assets, contribute to the development of human beings adapted to that society.

But these conclusions and their underlying assumptions must be verified by the comparative study of collective and familial upbringing.

V

This survey points up the burning need for systematic studies to lend solid foundations to, or to contradict, the generalizations of the reports so far published. Such systematic studies will have to include historical and factual surveys as well as investigations of attitudes, and sociometric relations as well as diagnostic and follow-up studies. Spiro (1955) is so far the only one who has used some such techniques, showing an appreciation of the problems to which historical studies, interviews, and direct observation alone can give no answer.

The main question to be answered by such systematic studies is: Are the behavior problems reported the natural price (i.e., attributable to developmental crises) that the education for this type of society exacts, or are they pathological symptoms indicating that collective upbringing violates human nature? The two detailed reports agree that the kibbutz is successful in raising generations who can perpetuate its way of life. If their impression is correct, before us lies an education which appears to differ in several ways from ours, which appears to pay a different price for its attempt to raise people fit to live in the society which produced it than the price we pay for our attempts to bring up children to our way of life.

Erikson has shown that the Yurok and the Sioux fostered different kinds of solutions of the common and ubiquitous developmental crises of human development than we do, and thereby raised individuals viable in their life situation and traditional framework, in which the average child brought up in our type of education might not be viable. The study of the kibbutz frame of reference, which should be so much more accessible and comprehensible to us than that of the Indians and other preliterates, may give us a better understanding of the price our education exacts. It may even give us further elaboration of the general relations Erikson infers as obtaining between (a) historical, institutional, and economic realities of societies, (b) practices of upbringing, and (c) forms of individual development. Finally, it may show us that it is inherent in the "human condition" that all societies' education will inevitably exact, and thus all societies will pay, a price—a necessary sacrifice—in the coin of developmental crises and pathology, for their successes in adapting their successive generations to their ways of life.

The scientific problem is not whether collective education is good or bad. Even if that were the question, we would have to ask further, good or bad for whom and for what? The problem is: *What* traditional, historical, organizational, institutional, and economic forces find their unnoted expression in the form of collective education, and *how* do these forms of upbringing induce behavior forms (social modalities) and behavior problems which in their genetic sequence result in individuals who perpetuate the way of life of the kibbutz?

REFERENCES

Caplan, G. (1954). Clinical Observations on the Emotional Life of Children in the Communal Settlements in Israel. In *Problems of Infancy and Childhood: Transactions of the Seventh Conference,* March 23 and 24, 1953, ed. M. S. E. Senn. New York: Josiah Macy, Jr. Foundation, pp. 91–120.
Erikson, E. H. (1950a). *Childhood and Society.* New York: Norton.

———— (1950b). Growth and Crises of the "Healthy Personality." In *Personality in Nature, Society, and Culture,* 2nd ed., ed. C. Kluckhohn & H. A. Murray. New York: Knopf, 1953, pp. 185–225.

Infield, H. F. (1944). *Cooperative Living in Palestine.* New York: Dryden.

Irvine, E. E. (1952). Observations on the Aims and Methods of Child Rearing in Communal Settlements in Israel. *Hum. Relat.,* 5:247–275.

Kardiner, A. (1954). The Roads to Suspicion, Rage, Apathy, and Societal Disintegration. In *Beyond the Germ Theory,* ed. Iago Galdston. New York: Health Education Council, pp. 157–170.

Reifen, D. (1949). Children in Communal Settlements. *New Era,* 30:195–198.

Spiro, M. E. (1954). Is the Family Universal? *Amer. Anthrop.,* 56:839–846.

———— (1955). Education in a Communal Village in Israel. *Amer. J. Orthopsychiat.,* 25:283–292.

———— (1956). *Kibbutz; Venture in Utopia.* Cambridge: Harvard University Press.

Zborowski, M., & Herzog, E. G. (1952). *Life Is with People.* New York: International Universities Press.

57

THE THEORY OF EGO AUTONOMY

A Generalization[1]

My purpose is to bring up to date the summary of the theory of ego autonomy which I presented in 1950 (1951c). This attempt inevitably leads into theoretically little explored regions, where I can do no more than identify issues and point to possible solutions.

To open up the issues, I will contrast the Berkeleian view of man with the Cartesian. In the Berkeleian view, the outside world is the creation of man's imagination. In this solipsistic view, man is totally *independent* of the environment, and totally *dependent* on the forces and images residing within him: he cannot envisage an external world independent of these inner

---

[1] This article leans heavily on the concepts of primary and secondary autonomy introduced by Heinz Hartmann, on the psychosocial point of view introduced by Erik Erikson, and on Merton Gill's theoretical considerations about hypnosis (Gill and Brenman, 1959). The specific references to these authors do not sufficiently reflect how much this article owes them.

Presented to the Topeka Psychoanalytic Institute, December 11, 1956. Spanish translation published in Archivos de Criminología, Neuro-psiquiatría y Disciplinas Conexas *(Ecuador), 5:475–511, 1957, and in Merton M. Gill and David Rapaport,* Aportaciones a la Teoría y Técnica Psicoanalítica. Asociación Psicoanalítica Mexicana, A.C., *1962, pp. 170–200. First published in English in the* Bulletin of the Menninger Clinic, *22:13–35, 1958. (Reprinted with permission; copyright 1958 by the Menninger Foundation.) French translation published in* Revue Française de Psychanalyse, 28:344–370, 1964.

forces. In turn, he need not come to terms with the outside world: since that world is created by forces inherent in man, he is a priori in harmony with it. In the Cartesian world, on the other hand, man is born as a clean slate upon which experience writes. No forces or images exist in man except for those which arise from the impingements of the outside world. In this world, man is totally *dependent* on and in harmony with the outside world. In turn, he is totally *independent* from, i.e., autonomous from, internal forces, which in this conception do not exist.[2]

Observation confirms neither of these views. It shows that while man's behavior *is* determined by drive forces which originate in him, it is not totally at their mercy since it has a certain independence from them. We refer to this independence as *the autonomy of the ego from the id*.[3] The most common observation which necessitated this conception was the responsiveness and relevance of behavior to external reality. But this dependence of behavior on the external world and on experience is not complete either. Man can interpose delay and thought not only between instinctual promptings and action, modifying and even indefinitely postponing drive discharge, he can likewise modify and postpone his reaction to external stimulation. This independence of behavior from external stimulation we will refer to as *the autonomy of the ego from external reality*.[4] Since the ego is never completely independent from the id nor from external reality, we always speak about *relative* autonomy.

I

My previous discussion of autonomy focused on the relative independence of behavior from internal drive forces. *The* great discovery of psychoanalysis was the existence of these unconscious forces. It took quite a while to realize that this discovery does not compel us to embrace a solipsistic theory in

[2] This sketch of Berkeley's and Descartes's views is oversimplified. Neither actually held such an extreme view. For instance, *internal forces* (passions) were conceived of in Descartes's system (see his *Passion de l'Ame*), particularly as interferences with the ordered working of the veridical association mechanism.

[3] This conception was formulated by Hartmann (1939, 1950, 1952). Its roots, however, go back to Freud's treatment of the *secondary process* in Chapter VII of *The Interpretation of Dreams* (1900), in "Formulations Regarding the Two Principles in Mental Functioning" (1911a), and to *The Problem of Anxiety* (1926).

[4] While the psychoanalytic reactions to the theories of the culturalists (Horney, Sullivan, etc.) imply some idea of this sort, to date it has not been explicitly formulated. Note, however, Hartmann (1955): "Once the ego has accumulated a reservoir of neutralized energy of its own, it will—in interaction with the outer and the inner world—develop aims and functions whose cathexis can be derived from this reservoir, which means that they have not always to depend on ad hoc neutralizations. *This gives the ego a comparative independence from immediate outside or inside pressure, a fact that one is used to considering (though usually not in this terminology) as a general trend in human development*" (p. 20; italics added).

which a chimney is primarily a phallic symbol and only secondarily the means for letting smoke out of the house. It was some time before we began to take account of the chimney as a smokestack, because these realistic meanings were not the focus of our early interests (but see Freud, 1911a). However, after psychoanalysis extended its scope to the study of the ego, it became possible and indeed necessary to create conceptual tools to deal with these realistic meanings and their rôle in behavior. This led to the study of the ego's relative autonomy[5] from the id, the guarantee of our relatively even and solid relationship to the outside world.

I tried to illuminate the autonomy of the ego from the id by an old Jewish story[6] in which Moses' portrait was brought to an Oriental king whose astrologers and phrenologists concluded from it that Moses was a cruel, greedy, craven, self-seeking man. The king, who had heard that Moses was a leader, kindly, generous, and bold, was puzzled, and went to visit Moses. On meeting him, he saw that the portrait was good, and said: "My phrenologists and astrologers were wrong." But Moses disagreed: "Your phrenologists and astrologers were right, they saw what I was made of; what they couldn't tell you was that I struggled against all that and so became what I am." In other words, the ego, which arises in the course of life's struggles, can become unlike the original impulses—can be relatively autonomous from them—and can control them.

Now I have another story (Popper-Lynkeus, 1899) to illuminate the autonomy of the ego from external reality.

"A king returned to his capital followed by his victorious army. The band played and his horse, the army, the people, all moved in step with the rhythm. The king, amazed, contemplated the power of music. Suddenly he noticed a man who walked out of step and slowly fell behind. The king, deeply impressed, sent for the man, and told him: 'I never saw a man as strong as you are. The music enthralled everybody except you. Where do you get the strength to resist it?' The man answered, 'I was pondering, and that gave me the strength.' " [7]

In other words, it is possible for man to maintain relative autonomy, i.e.,

---

[5] For the concept of relative autonomy see Rapaport (1951c).

[6] I erroneously attributed it to the Talmud. I learned from the late Dr. Maurice Finkelstein that this form of it stems from the eighteenth century. For its previous history see Ginzberg (1946).

[7] The story actually does not end here. The man tells the king of two even stronger men. " 'The first was so strong that when he wanted it, the sun was only *sun* for him, the moon only *moon,* the wind only *wind,* and the mountain only *mountain,* and they meant nothing else to him.' [The exclusion of "connotative enrichment" is a mechanism of obsessive-compulsive character formation and pathology; see Rapaport, 1957a.] The king asked, 'What happened to this man?' 'He built a high wall around himself,' was the answer. But the second man was even stronger: 'He was equally benign to all people, beautiful or ugly, rich or poor. He gave the best advice to the kings and princes, but they didn't listen. He was thought to be self-seeking: and far across the Gobi Desert, Confucius died, alone, old, and in misery.' "

a degree of independence, from his environment. This relative autonomy of man from his environment is the subject of the following discussion.

Though the conception of the relative autonomy of the ego from the id readjusted the position of the id concept in psychoanalytic theory, it did not dispense with the theory of the id nor did it even alter it radically. Likewise, the theory of the ego's relative autonomy from the environment eliminates neither the theory of the ego's autonomy from the id, nor the theory of the id. In fact, far from being rendered superfluous, our theories of the id, of the ego in general, and of the autonomous ego in particular, may appear in a new light and some of the gaps in our knowledge of them may be bridged by developing the theory of the ego's *relative* autonomy from the environment.

There is actually nothing radically new in what follows. To the medical man, it is a commonplace that nonliving matter cannot escape the impact of its environment and its reactions are strictly (or statistically) predictable, but that organisms can escape such impacts, can avoid responding to them, and when they respond, they can do so in a variety of alternative (vicarious) ways. Man's simultaneous relative dependence on and independence from his environment is an issue well within the biological tradition. While psychoanalytic theory, in general, has had a biological cast from the beginning, this did not extend to its consideration of the environment's rôle in determining behavior (but see Hartmann, 1939, and Erikson, 1950b).

Our task is to seek the answers to two questions: What are the guarantees of the ego's autonomy from the environment? How is the autonomy of the ego from the environment related to the autonomy of the ego from the id?

II

To approach the first question I will review the guarantees of the ego's relative autonomy from the id. That autonomy is guaranteed by ego apparatuses of primary and secondary autonomy.[8]

We no longer assume that the ego arises from the id, but rather that the ego and the id both arise by differentiation from a common undifferentiated matrix (Hartmann, Kris, and Loewenstein, 1946), in which the apparatuses that differentiate into the ego's means of orientation, of reality testing, and of action, are already present. These, termed *apparatuses of primary autonomy,* serve drive gratification and enter conflict as independent ego-factors. They are the memory apparatus, the motor apparatus, the perceptual apparatuses, and the threshold apparatuses (including the drive- and affect-discharge thresholds). They are evolutionary givens which, by virtue of their long history of selection and modification, have become the primary guarantees of the organism's "fitting in" with (adaptedness to) its environment (Hartmann, 1939). In other words, the primary guarantees of the

[8] These concepts were formulated by Hartmann (1950, 1952).

ego's autonomy from the id seem to be the very apparatuses which guarantee the organism's adaptedness to the environment.

The *apparatuses of secondary autonomy* arise either from instinctual modes and vicissitudes, as these become "estranged" (Erikson, 1937) from their instinctual sources, or from defensive structures formed in the process of conflict solution, as these undergo a "change of function" (Hartmann, 1939) and become apparatuses serving adaptation. In other words, the apparatuses of secondary autonomy are not "innate" but arise from "experience." Thus this second guarantee of ego autonomy also involves reality relations. While it is obvious that without relationships to a real external environment we would be solipsistic beings, a long detour was necessary before we could see clearly that the autonomy of the ego from the id—our safeguard against solipsism—is guaranteed by these innate and acquired apparatuses which keep us attuned to our environment.

Now to the guarantees of the ego's autonomy from the environment.

The empiricist *nurture* theories of psychology—association theories and simple Pavlovian conditioning theories—have sought no such guarantees. They shared the Cartesian-Humian world view, which, admitting no guarantees of man's autonomy from his environment, makes him virtually a slave of it. Huxley's *Brave New World* is a caricature of this sort of psychology. Academic psychology's recognition that man is not a passive perceiver and not a blank sheet on which experience can write without restriction implies an autonomy conception (Hebb, 1949; Rapaport, 1957b), but the lack of an explicit autonomy concept was and remains its major impediment. Only a Humian-Cartesian theory can do without a concept of autonomy from the environment, and the validity of such a theory is emphatically contradicted by psychoanalytic observations, which amply demonstrate the survival of pathological behavior forms in defiance of environmental conditions and requirements. In fact, psychoanalytic observations and theory indicate that the instinctual drives are the causal agents and *ultimate guarantees* of the survival of the (pathological and normal) behavior forms which are countermanded by the environment.[9] The evidence amassed by clinical psychoanalysis for this causal rôle of drives in the persistence of all symptoms and many character traits is overwhelming.

There seems to be equally good evidence that cognitive organizations, ego interests, values, ideals, ego identity, and superego influences—all of which are relatively autonomous from the drives—also play a causal rôle in the persistence of many behavior forms. However, since the autonomy of these is secondary, they may be regarded as only *proximal guarantees* of the ego's autonomy from the environment. That the drives (e.g., sex, hunger),

---

[9] Hartmann (1956, p. 44) wrote: "In his stages of rebelliousness the growing individual also rebels against the commonly accepted view of reality. His tendency toward objective knowledge may also muster the help of instinctual drives. However, after having become autonomous, it may reach a considerable amount of stability."

which at peak tension may cause enslavement to the environment, should be the *ultimate guarantees* of the autonomy from the environment is a paradox, which, however—as I will attempt to show later on—can be resolved.

Man's constitutionally given drive equipment appears to be the *ultimate* (primary) *guarantee* of the ego's autonomy from the environment, that is, its safeguard against stimulus-response slavery. But this autonomy too has *proximal* (secondary) *guarantees:* namely, higher-order superego and ego structures as well as the motivations pertaining to them. Like the ego's autonomy from the id, its autonomy from the environment also is only relative.

Thus, while the *ultimate guarantees of the ego's autonomy from the id* are man's constitutionally given apparatuses of reality relatedness, the *ultimate guarantees of the ego's autonomy from the environment* are man's constitutionally given drives.

III

To approach the relationship between the two autonomies, let us examine the conditions which interfere with either or both.

Three examples will illustrate the conditions in which the ego's autonomy from the id is impaired. *First,* there are periods of development in which the drives are intensified and threaten this autonomy of the ego. In puberty, the intensified drives interfere with ego autonomy so extensively that the ego combats them with—among other defenses—intellectualization, which is perhaps the most powerful means of enlisting environmental reality and the apparatuses of memory and thought against the encroachments of the id (A. Freud, 1936). The adolescent's subjectivity, his rebellion against his environment, and his seclusiveness, as well as the converse of these—for instance, his striving for intellectual understanding and objectivity and the quest for all-embracing companionship—indicate the pubertal intensification of id forces and the consequent decrease of the ego's autonomy. The climacteric (both male and female) often involves a similar loss of ego autonomy.

Some recent experiments will serve as the *second* example. Hebb and his students (Bexton, Heron, and Scott, 1954; Heron, Doane, and Scott, 1956; Heron, 1957) put subjects into a soundproof, blacked-out room, in which restraints minimized tactile and kinesthetic sensations. They made two important observations: (a) the subjects experienced autistic fantasies, and a decrease of their ability to pursue ordered sequences of thought; (b) repetitive verbal information given to the subjects—against the background of the stimulus-void—attained such an impact on their minds that some of them came to experience it as "truth" (Rapaport, 1957a), that is, this experience approached delusional intensity and persevered for several weeks. Lilly (1956a, 1956b) carried out a similar experiment, in a blacked-out, soundproof water tank, in which the subject floated free of gravitational, tactile, and kinesthetic stimulation. His findings corroborated Hebb's. Thus stimulus deprivation too is a condition which may interfere with this autonomy.

Our *third* example is the hypnotic state.[10] A common technique of inducing hypnosis is to make the subject concentrate on something and thus in effect to reduce the intake of other external stimulation. The hypnotist further interferes with attention to external stimulation by pouring forth a steady patter. These measures pre-empt the attention cathexes available, and interfere not only with stimulus intake but also with organized, logical, reality-oriented thinking. Thus both the outside and inside sources of signals—which subserve reality orientation and support the ego's autonomy— are blocked. The result—in hypnotizable people—is a regressive state in which the countercathectic barriers differentiating ego and id processes become fluid; images, ideas, and fantasies representing id contents rise to consciousness, and the sense of voluntariness disappears. In the lack of other stimulation which could serve as a comparison, pivot, or means of reality testing, the utterances of the hypnotist attain a great impact, just like the repetitive information droned at the subject in Hebb's room. The reduction of reality relationships to a single interpersonal relationship, in hypnosis, impairs the ego's autonomy from the id.

Disregarding for the moment the subject's increased susceptibility to the information given in Hebb's room and by the hypnotist, we will consider only the interferences with the ego's autonomy from the id in these three examples.

The generally held assumption that ego structures (controls, defenses, as well as the means used in reality testing and action) are stable, and altered only by major disorders, is amply justified by the continuity of character and behavior, as well as by the great "resistance" these structures offer to therapeutic intervention. The very concept "structure" implies a slow rate of change in comparison to processes of drive-tension accumulation and discharge. Yet Hebb's and Lilly's experiments suggest that these structures depend upon stimulation for their stability, or to use Piaget's terms (1936), they require stimulation as nutriment for their maintenance. When such stimulus-nutriment is not available, the effectiveness of these structures in controlling id impulses may be impaired, and some of the ego's autonomy from the id may be surrendered.[11] The example of hypnotic induction seems

---

[10] The starting point of this paper was Merton Gill's and Margaret Brenman's hypnotic work and their discussions of this work with me throughout the 1940's. See also Kubie (1943) and Kubie and Margolin (1942, 1944).

[11] L. Goldberger and R. R. Holt's isolation study indicates that stimulus deprivation results in differential impairments of various structures and in individual subjects. R. R. Holt (personal communication) raises the question whether these findings are compatible with the "nutriment" explanation given here. The explanation of such differences may lie in the "relativity of autonomy," the degree of which, naturally.

to corroborate this inference, and the interference of intensified drives with ego autonomy may be considered as due to drive representations commanding attention and thus pre-empting the attention cathexes necessary for effective intake of stimulus-nutriment (see Freud, 1900, p. 529). The interference of passionate love and deep mourning with the ego's autonomy and reality testing are familiar phenomena, and the work of mourning appears to be the actual process of overcoming the state of absorption which militates against the intake of stimulus-nutriment (Freud, 1917). Without assuming that ego structures (other than those of primary autonomy) need stimulus-nutriment for their autonomous effectiveness and even for their maintenance, the very process of therapy would be inconceivable (see section V).

We have long known this dependence on nutriment of certain structures, e.g., those underlying the conscious superego. When a man pulls up stakes and moves far away where his past is not known, he is subject to temptations: the course of his sea voyage, the mutt he left behind may grow into a Saint Bernard, or the painting by a local amateur which he owned may turn into a Rembrandt. The superego is a persistent structure, but its conscious parts seem to require stimulus-nutriment. In the lack of nutriment it becomes prone to compromise and corruption, and the greater their extent, the more mercilessly does the unconscious superego exact its pound of flesh: the unconscious sense of guilt (Freud, 1923). The maintenance of conscience seems to require the continuous input of the nourishment readily provided by a stable, traditional environment in which the individual is born, grows up, and ends his life; that is, the stimulus of the presence, opinions, and memories of the "others" who have always known him and always will. We seem to choose the social bonds of marriage, friendship, etc., to secure that familiar (paternal, maternal) pattern of stimulation which we need as nutriment for our various superego and ego structures (for example, those which underlie our values and ideologies).[12]

Now, some examples of interference with the ego's autonomy from the environment:

First, I will mention those catatonic conditions of echopraxia, echolalia, and *cerea flexibilitas,* which are the prototypes of surrender of the autonomy from the environment. We view these little-understood disorders as the results of massive blocking of libidinal and aggressive drives. If this is so, it stands to reason that when these ultimate guarantees of the ego's autonomy from the environment are rendered ineffective, the result is stimulus slavery. The literal and concrete thinking of schizophrenics[13] may be considered a milder form of this loss of autonomy.

---

varies from individual to individual and from structure to structure, or in the "internal nutriment."

[12] This is one of the implications of Erikson's (1950a, 1956) psychosocial theory.

[13] See Kasanin (1944), particularly Benjamin's and Goldstein's contributions.

For the *second* example, I take the procedures lumped together under the term "brainwashing." [14] Instead of reviewing the literature, I will discuss Orwell's *Nineteen Eighty-Four* (1949), in which the writer's intuition epitomizes the means used by most "brainwashing" procedures to bring the individual to the point where the ego's autonomy from the environment is surrendered. The aim of these procedures is not just to force a false *confession* of guilt, but also to bring about a *profession* of, or a *conversion* to, a particular view and a *belief* in the "facts" pertaining to it (Lifton, 1956a, 1956b).

In the world of *Nineteen Eighty-Four,* the individual is robbed of his privacy, the environment invades it: whenever the individual is alone he is watched through "telescreens"; whenever he is not driven by his work, he is driven by the "telescreen," which constantly bombards him with information and with instructions which he *must* obey. The language is so simplified that it can convey only factual information and orders; it carries no implications, connotations, allusions, or individual expression. Memory is undermined: when the political alliances of the state change, the books and newspaper files are destroyed and replaced by a revised version which fits the new circumstances. Finally, the fear of unknown but horrible punishment is kept constant. The lack of unobserved privacy coupled with the steady shower of information and orders, the lack of personal expression, the changing records which attack even the continuity vouchsafed by memory, and the mortal fear of punishment, are the means by which the world of *Nineteen Eighty-Four* robs the individual ego of its autonomy and turns the person into an automaton at the command of the environment. *Nineteen Eighty-Four* is an overdrawn caricature of our own world and a good montage of "brainwashing" procedures. The individual rebellion which Orwell describes has its roots in a yearning for tenderness, love, and sex, which —as I suggested above—are *ultimate* guarantees of the ego's autonomy from the environment. *Nineteen Eighty-Four* is fiction, but its implications are corroborated by the evidence available concerning "brainwashing," which indicates that the measures summarized above are potent means for impairing the ego's autonomy from the environment (Lifton, 1956a, 1956b; Rapaport, 1953a).

The *third* example, Bettelheim's paper "Individual and Mass Behavior in Extreme Situations" (1947) (see also Bettelheim, 1943), will stand here for all the literature on concentration camps and on Nazi methods of mass psychology. Its study shows that in concentration camps two overlapping sets of conditions interfere with autonomy from the environment, both of which—though not discussed above—obtain to varying degrees in "brainwashing" situations also.

The first set of conditions includes extreme needfulness (hunger, cold,

[14] R. R. Holt has reviewed the highlights of the pertinent literature in an unpublished paper. A broad survey of this literature is in preparation by S. C. Miller [1962].

etc.) and danger, as well as an attack on the inmates' "identity" (see Erikson, 1956). In extreme needfulness and danger, the drives—which are otherwise the *ultimate guarantees* of this autonomy—endow drive-satisfying objects with a power the effect of which amounts to slavery and surrender of autonomy. The attack on identity (operating through identification with the aggressor, dependence on arbitrary authority akin to the dependence of childhood, and absence of all encomia of status and other supports of identity) impairs the *proximal guarantees* of autonomy.

The second set of conditions includes curtailment of information and stimulation (though less stringent than in Hebb's room), and against the background of this stimulus-void, a steady stream of humiliating, degrading, and guilt-arousing information (akin in its rôle to the repetitive information of the Hebb room and to the hypnotist's patter). The deprivation contributes to the surrender of autonomy both by enhancing needfulness and by providing the background for the steady and overwhelming impact of the environment.

Thus the outstanding conditions which impair the ego's autonomy from the environment are: (1) massive intrapsychic blocking of the instinctual drives which are the *ultimate guarantees* of this autonomy; (2) maximized needfulness, danger, and fear which enlist the drives (usually the guarantees of this autonomy) to prompt surrender of autonomy; (3) lack of privacy, deprivation of stimulus-nutriment, memorial, and verbal supports, all of which seem to be necessary for the maintenance of the structures (thought structures, values, ideologies, identity) which are the *proximal guarantees* of this autonomy; (4) a steady stream of instructions and information which, in the lack of other stimulus-nutriment, attain such power that they have the ego completely at their mercy.[15]

Just as with the guarantees of autonomy from the id, neither the *ultimate* nor the *proximal* guarantees of autonomy from the environment are absolute. Both autonomies require external and/or drive stimulation of a specific intensity and quality for maintenance and effectiveness.[16]

---

[15] Cf. Grünthal's explanation of the Korsakoff thought disorder (Grünthal, 1923; Bürger-Prinz and Kaila, 1930, pp. 659 ff., particularly Rapaport's footnotes).

[16] Independently, both Heinz Hartmann and Bruno Bettelheim (personal communications) pointed out to me that this treatment of the autonomies deals exclusively with the problem of "autonomy from" (i.e., freedom from) drives and environment, while the crucial specific clinical and general psychological problem is that of the "freedom to . . ." implied in these autonomies. I agree with them: the crucial task is the study of the autonomous ego motivations, the ego's methods of setting its goals and the ego's capability to give free reign to and to execute derivative id motivations. My aim in this paper is, however, merely to clarify the elements of the theory of autonomies.

IV

We are now ready to examine the relations between the ego's two autonomies. In hypnotic states (as well as in Hebb's room) both autonomy from the id and from the environment are impaired. How are such impairments related to each other?

A consideration of certain aspects of compulsive and obsessional disorders may serve to clarify the relationships (Freud, 1911b). What follows is only an *ex parte* consideration of these conditions, a supplement to, not a substitute for, the knowledge we have of them. One of the concomitants of obsessive-compulsive conditions is an increased elaboration of the secondary process. This elaboration has two aspects: on the one hand, it provides means for the defenses of intellectualization and isolation; on the other hand, it enables intensified observation and logical analysis to substitute for affective and ideational signals, those natural regulators of judgment and decision which are suppressed by obsessive-compulsive defenses.

Obsessive-compulsive defense thus maximizes the ego's autonomy from the id, but it does so at the cost of an ever-increasing impairment of the ego's autonomy from the environment: the suppression of affective and ideational cues of drive origin renders the ego's judgments and decisions increasingly dependent on external cues. Hence the infirmness of convictions and gullibility of certain obsessive people, but also—as a reaction formation—the blind and rigid clinging to a view once it has been adopted. An extreme form of the obsessive's lack of internal steering is his paralyzing doubt, which may border on the stimulus slavery of the catatonic conditions discussed above. But while the ego's autonomy from the environment is reduced, another development also takes place. The drives and their representations, whose access to motility and consciousness was so strenuously barred, invade "objective" reality by infiltrating the very thought processes and logic which were elaborated to curb them, and succeed in filling the person's perception and thought with magic and animism.

Thus maximizing the ego's autonomy from the id reduces the ego's autonomy from the environment and results in stimulus slavery. Conversely, the reduction of the ego's autonomy from the id (as by the intensification of drives) results in a loss of touch with reality, which amounts to a maximized autonomy from the environment. In turn, maximizing the ego's autonomy from the environment (as in stimulus deprivation) results in a reduction of the ego's autonomy from the id; and the reduction of the ego's autonomy from the environment may result in a maximized autonomy from the id. But can such maximized or minimized autonomy of the ego, either in relation to the id or in relation to the environment, still be considered autonomy in the proper sense of the word?

Let us examine, for instance, stimulus deprivation as maximized autonomy. It is not that the ego's autonomy from the environment reaches its maximum, but rather that the ego has to make do with an environment which provides insufficient stimulus-nutriment for its structures. Stimulus deprivation provides a test of the limits of the ego's autonomy from the environment.[17] Examination of the other instances of "maximized" or "minimized" autonomy leads to similar conclusions.

Yet these extreme instances provide good models for the relationships of the autonomies. They show that the ego's autonomy from the id may be impaired either when its necessary dependence on the environment is excessively increased, or when environmental support is excessively decreased. Likewise, the ego's autonomy from the environment may be impaired when either its necessary independence from or its necessary dependence on the id becomes excessive. Since these autonomies are always relative, their extremes are never reached. Hence, a further implication of the relativity of the autonomies is: only a relative autonomy of the ego from the id—that is, only autonomy within the optimal range—is compatible with a relative— that is, optimal—autonomy of the ego from the environment, and vice versa. This conclusion is consistent with the one reached in our discussion of the autonomy guarantees. Since reality relations guarantee autonomy from the id, excessive autonomy from the environment must impair the autonomy from the id; and since drives are the ultimate guarantees of the autonomy from the environment, an excessive autonomy from the id must impair the autonomy from the environment.

Whether the treatment of these issues in terms of autonomies and their relations is more useful than a treatment in terms of the dependence on (or distance from) id and environment remains to be seen.

V

Do the concepts of ego autonomies and their relationships have any immediate relevance for clinical psychoanalysis and psychotherapy (Gill, 1954)? They seem to be relevant, though it is hard to say whether they capture something new or merely translate something already known into a new language.

The technical conditions of psychoanalysis—the couch, the injunction against "acting out," the psychoanalyst as a blank screen, etc.—involve stimulus deprivation. Psychoanalytic technique explicitly recognizes that a reduction of contact with reality is necessary to permit id derivatives to rise to consciousness. Effective application of this technique brings about a shift in the autonomy balance, increasing autonomy from the environment and decreasing autonomy from the id. Once the theory of autonomy is consolidated, it may become a cornerstone of the theory of psychoanalytic *technique:* there has been a continuous increase in our knowledge of psychoanalytic technique, its applications, and its problems (Fenichel, 1935,

[17] This formulation was suggested by Dr. Stuart C. Miller.

1938–39), but the *theory* of the technique, and particularly its metapsychology, has lagged sadly behind.

The autonomy conceptions also have immediate relevance for the psychotherapy of borderline cases (Knight, 1953a, 1953b). The modifications of psychoanalytic technique for this purpose replaced the couch by the face-to-face situation, the relatively silent psychoanalyst by the participating and supporting psychotherapist, etc., and thus lessened the stimulus deprivation (Eissler, 1950). However, it is still not clear when a borderline case, or a severe neurotic, should or should not be "taken off the couch." We still do not know when stimulus deprivation will tend to overshoot the therapeutically necessary "regression in the service of and under the control of the ego," and lead to pathological regression. But we do know that the relative and reversible reduction of the ego's autonomy from the id—which the technical rules are designed to foster—can get out of hand. How to achieve therapeutically effective insight, while guarding against further regressive, pathological reduction of the ego's autonomy from the id, and against further impairment of the patient's reality relationships, is one of the fundamental problems of the psychotherapy of borderline cases, and perhaps of all therapy.

Psychiatric hospitals for the psychotherapy of borderline and psychotic patients are faced with the problem of organizing the patient's everyday life so as to combat the tendency of hospitalization and of insight-seeking psychotherapy to foster regression (Miller, 1957; Polansky, Miller, and White, 1955). Hospitalization tends to reduce the environmental stimulus-nutriment necessary to those structures which guarantee the ego's autonomy from the id and from the environment. The self-absorption attendant on psychotherapy accentuates this effect of hospitalization. On the other hand, the removal of the patient from his usual surroundings to a hospital, and psychotherapy itself, tend to deprive those defensive structures which have become part and parcel of the patient's pathology of their stimulus-nutriment, and thereby undermine their effectiveness and persistence. (The effect of hospitalization and psychotherapy on the vicious circle of a sado-masochistic symbiosis is an obvious example of this.)

VI

The concept of nutriment is derived from Piaget (1936).[18] According to him, "structures of intelligence" arise by differentiation from constitutionally given sensorimotor coordinations, but require stimulus-nutriment to do so. So far no evidence exists to clarify the relationship between Piaget's structures and those structures which psychoanalytic theory has conceptualized. But since our considerations suggest that psychoanalytic "structures"

18 Note particularly his distinction of this concept from learning theory's "reinforcement" and "practice."

require stimulus-nutriment for their *maintenance* and *effectiveness,* the question arises: does the *development* as well as the maintenance and effectiveness of psychoanalytic "structures" require stimulus-nutriment?

To explore this question, let us consider the differences between the stimuli withdrawn in the various situations discussed. The stimulus-deprivation experiments withdraw that stimulus-nutriment which, conveyed through the senses, is necessary for the maintenance and effectiveness of elementary reality orientation. This nutriment is never directly and massively removed in the psychoanalytic situation, which, though it fosters the voluntary and/or spontaneous renunciation of such nutriment, is really aimed at the nutriment of those structures which underlie proprieties, logical orderliness, defenses, etc. (Freud, 1910–19). Nor do the concentration-camp and brainwashing procedures bank primarily on the withdrawal of this elementary stimulus-nutriment, though they have used that too as an auxiliary technique. The concentration camp removes first of all the nutriment of the structures underlying dignity, self-respect, and identity (Bettelheim, 1943, 1947). The aim of brainwashing is to remove the nutriment for the structures which underlie beliefs, political convictions, ideology, social and personal allegiances, and ultimately identity (Lifton, 1956a, 1956b). These differences point to what psychoanalysis has already discovered about defenses, controls, etc., namely that psychological structures form a complex hierarchy within the psychic apparatus (Rapaport, 1951a). Moreover, these differences suggest that the structures on each hierarchic level may require a different nutriment, ranging from simple, minimally organized sensory stimulations, to those complex experiences which a society provides to maintain, in its individuals, ideological beliefs and identities compatible with that society.

Once the differences in the stimulus-nutriment required for the maintenance of various structures are observed, we begin to see what evidence there is that the structures psychoanalysis deals with require stimulus-nutriment for their *development.* The vicissitudes of instincts and the development of defenses and controls are codetermined by experience, and reconstructions in therapy show that the effectiveness of the experience in question always stems from an antecedent "complementary series" of experiences. Thus the dependence of such structure development upon stimulus-nutriment becomes probable, though our reconstructions of these complementary series usually do not carry us back to simple sensory stimulus-nutriments.

The dependence of such structure development upon stimulus-nutriments has, however, been stated in more specific terms by Erikson. He has shown that the development of the social modalities of behavior proceeds from the organ modes in general and from the modes of erogenous zones in particular, as these become "estranged," i.e., differentiated, from their zone. He has also demonstrated that the occurrence of this differentiation, and the quality of the behavior modality which is its product, are codetermined by the impact of traditions and institutions provided by the society in which the individual develops, and by the social "niches" available in it (Erikson, 1950a, especially Chapters 2, 6, 7; 1950b). Thus Erikson's organ modes and Piaget's sensorimotor coordinations seem to be analogous points of departure for structure development; likewise Erikson's institutions and Piaget's stimuli appear to be analogous nutriments for structure development. Thus, just like Piaget's "intelligence structures," the psychological structures Erikson studied (including such primitive behavior modalities as giving and taking, and as complex ones as value, rôle, ideology, and identity) appear to depend on stimulus-nutriment provided by the environment. Since these structures shade into those customarily discussed by psychoanalysis, the rôle of stimulus-nutriment in structure development may prove ubiquitous.[19] But it should be noted that the nutriment of the structures dealt with by psychoanalysis in general, and by Erikson in particular, is of a highly organized character in contrast to the nutriment of those structures discussed by Piaget.

Erikson has furthermore emphasized that the structure development— termed ego development—here discussed, even though codetermined by drives and environmental stimulus-nutriment, follows a lawful sequence of its own, i.e., it is autonomous. This facet of ego autonomy we have not discussed so far,[20] though it is crucial since if ego development were not autonomous, only *secondary* ego autonomy (derived either from drives or from environmental influences or from *ad hoc* combinations of the two) would be conceivable. Autonomous ego development (its sequence and regulative principles) is a primary guarantee of ego autonomy: it links the apparatuses of secondary autonomy to those of primary autonomy and regulates both the environmental and drive contributions to ego-structure formation.

Before leaving this subject, we must at least touch on the crucial observation that structures can persist and remain effective even when deprived of external stimulus-nutriment. What are the facts and how are they to be explained?

The already-mentioned study by Goldberger and Holt shows that some structures (e.g., "style structures") are relatively little affected by short-term stimulus deprivation and recover rapidly once such deprivation is terminated. Persistence in spite of deprivation is a hallmark of autonomy. Since autonomy is relative, long-range persistence despite deprivation needs further explanation. It is known that people have spent years in solitary confinement without suffering striking impairments of either of the ego au-

---

[19] The literature on "wild" and "autistic" children is pertinent here.
[20] Autonomous ego development has been repeatedly discussed by Hartmann. See also R. Loewenstein (1954). But Erikson was the first to trace its course (1937), and to propose a scheme encompassing its phases (1950a, 1950b).

tonomies, and that people have maintained their ego autonomy in spite of "brainwashing," though of these only a few have survived to tell the tale (Bone, 1957; Weissberg, 1951). There is the familiar figure of the Englishman who, totally isolated from the setting which would provide the natural nutriment for his proprieties, traditions, outlook, and values, maintains these essentially unchanged in the solitude of the jungle or the desert. Last but not least, clinical and therapeutic observation shows that defenses (in the form of both character traits and symptoms) may survive without tangible environmental nourishment, or where the person has to "provoke" nourishment from the environment.[21]

This survival of defense structures without external stimulus-nutriment is understood by psychoanalysis: these structures are maintained, ultimately, by internal (drive) stimulus-nutriment (Freud, 1926). Clinical evidence shows that values, ideologies, and even more complex structures (like identity) too may be maintained by drive-nutriment, to the degree to which they are part of a defensive system. The explanation of the maintenance of such higher-order ego structures in instances of solitary confinement seems at first glance equally obvious: the method of survival seems to be a deliberate application of physical and mental exercise to prevent weakening of ego autonomy and drifting into fearful or wishful daydreaming, or into mindless, empty surrender. This deliberate application has taken various forms: physical exercise, a chronological review of past life, mental arithmetic, solving all sorts of other problems, dictionary-making in several languages, or reviewing other kinds of knowledge.

But what, in these cases, is the intrapsychic source of this deliberate application, which is the *proximal provider* of stimulus-nutriment? We cannot seek this source in the ultimate drive-nutriment because, as we have seen, in extreme deprivation situations, drive-nutriment tends to abet surrender of the autonomy from the environment. Nor would it do to seek the source simply in *ego identity* (Erikson, 1956): though the major attack of such confinements is on ego identity, and stronger ego identities will persist better, to locate the source of stimulus-nutriment *solely* and without further analysis in ego identity would amount to a vicious circle.

The reports of the unscathed survivors of solitary confinement reveal little about the internal source of nutriment. More suggestive are the reports of people whose autonomy from either the id or the environment was on the brink of destruction, but was restored at the last moment by what might be described as a conversion experience (Burney, 1952; Moen, n.d.; Gollwit-

---

[21] "Provocative" and "demanding" behavior may well appear in a different light when treated as quests for stimulus-nutriment. A. Schmale's discussion (unpublished memoranda of the Conferences on Separation, Depression, and Illness, of the Department of Psychiatry, University of Rochester Medical School) of the "object" concept, in relation to the rôle "separation" plays in psychosomatic disorders, may be considered a step toward such a treatment.

zer, Juhn, and Schneider, 1956). While we are far from a full understanding of conversion experiences, what we do know about them, and what we can infer from these reports, points primarily to the superego but also to ego interests and ego identity as the sources of voluntary application.

Tentatively, then, it may be assumed that in certain people strikingly, but probably in all people to some degree, external stimulus-nutriment may be replaced by internal nutriment. This nutriment may take the form of various deliberate activities, whose motivations (i.e., the *ultimate* source of the nourishment) may be drives, superego, ego identity, or ego interests, depending on the structure involved. Hartmann (1950, 1952) made it plausible that we have to assume the existence of intrasystemic conflicts within the ego; likewise it may become necessary to assume intrasystemic cooperation of forces by which one substructure of the ego would give rise to ego forces which, by initiating (motor or thought) activity, would provide stimulus-nutriment to other substructures, enabling them to function and to give rise to their own brand of ego interests, which in turn would initiate activity providing stimulus-nutriment for yet other ego substructures. Indeed, it seems probable that closed circles of such mutually sustaining structures can persist—within those limits which show up ultimately as the *relativity* of autonomy. Since various structures require different external stimulus-nutriment, it is likely that each requires a different kind of internal nutriment also.

VII

This paper has underplayed the id aspects of the phenomena discussed, and has hardly mentioned points showing that this treatment of autonomy is phenomenological and thus incomplete. Yet the concept of autonomy is but one aspect of ego psychology, which in turn—just like id psychology—is only a part of psychoanalytic theory. Metapsychology has also been underplayed, and thus the impression may have arisen that these autonomy considerations are phenomenological in essence and lack a metapsychological foundation. But the concept of ego autonomy *is* amenable to metapsychological analysis (Rapaport, 1951b, 1959).

Classic metapsychology comprises the dynamic, economic, and structural points of view. Gill and I (Rapaport and Gill, 1959) have attempted to demonstrate that this triad must be supplemented by the genetic point of view (which has always been explicit in psychoanalytic theory), and the adaptive point of view (the indispensability of which has become clear in the last two decades). Gill's discussion (Gill and Brenman, 1959) of the metapsychology of regression in general and of hypnotic regression in particular has provided the framework for the metapsychological treatment of the autonomies, and we do have partial metapsychological treatments of the ego's autonomy from the id. My discussion of the hierarchy of derivative drives (motivations) is an implicit treatment of this autonomy from the dynamic and genetic points of view (Rapaport, 1951a, especially Part VII; 1951b); the use of the neutralization concept by Hartmann (1950) and Kris (1950, 1956) has laid the foundation for the treatment of autonomy from the economic point of view. Hartmann's discussions of autonomy, "automatization," and "change of function" (1939), and Kris' discussions of "regression in the service of the ego" (1932–52) are treatments of this autonomy from the structural point of view. Hartmann's conception of adaptation and reality (1956), and Erikson's conception of psychosocial ego-epigenesis (1950a, Chapter 7; 1950b), treat it from the adaptive point of view.

But so far we have no comparable treatments of the ego's autonomy from the environment. This missing link must be provided before the autonomies and their relation to each other can be given a full-scale metapsychological treatment. In an attempt to fill part of this gap, I will review here a so-far-unpublished paper (Rapaport, 1953b) in which I proposed dual conceptual models for activity and passivity.

The *first model of passivity* is the situation of helplessness which ensues when mounting drive tension meets a countercathectic barrier and tension discharge is prevented. The *second model of passivity* is the situation in which the discharge of accumulated drive tension occurs *without* a contribution by the ego. Since drive discharge always involves executive ego apparatuses, the latter situation never exists in reality, but it does exist as a psychological reality in fantasies of wish fulfillment and in therapeutic reconstructions. The *first model of activity* is the discharge of drive tension by means of the ego's control and executive apparatuses. The *second model of activity* is the defensive and/or controlling prevention or postponement of the drive discharge by the ego.

Let us compare the first model of passivity with the second model of activity. The first model of passivity refers to a nonautonomous ego which does not regulate id tension but rather is regulated by it, since the more the drive tension mounts the more unyielding the ego's discharge-barring function becomes. In contrast, the second model of activity refers to a relatively autonomous ego, which controls, postpones, or prevents drive discharge in keeping with the demands of its own organization, but also in view of the state of the whole organism and the reality circumstances. Likewise a comparison of the second model of passivity and the first model of activity shows that the former refers to a nonautonomous ego, that is, to a condition dominated and regulated by drive tension, while the latter refers to an autonomous ego which executes drive discharge in keeping with its controls, but also with regard to the economy of the whole psychic apparatus (or organism), and the reality circumstances.

Now, these models should be complemented by a parallel set representing the passive endurance of and the passive response to external stimulation as well as the active endurance of and the active response to it. It seems that as soon as the "stimulus barriers" and sensory thresholds become insufficient to scale down external stimulation to manageable intensities, psychological —that is, countercathectic—barriers come into play. These in turn seem to be naturally integrated with—and often identical to—the countercathectic barriers which control drive discharge. If these relationships can be conclusively demonstrated, the explanation of the interrelations between the autonomies as well as those between external stimuli and drives will be at hand. The paper referred to did not deal with these latter models of activity and passivity, and was thus incomplete.[22]

If it is realized that the establishment of the "inner world" (Hartmann, 1939) and of representations (of drives as well as of external objects) is a turning of "passive" sensorimotor experience into activity (as Piaget has demonstrated [1936, 1937]; Wolff [1960]); if, furthermore, we keep in mind the clinical facts which show that the turning of passive experience into active performance is at the core of psychological structure development (Freud, 1915, 1920); and finally, if it is noted that the drive and/or stimulus versus structure balance expressed in these conceptions of activity and passivity is at the core of the problems of pathology, then the suggested relation of the ego's autonomies to the conditions of the ego's activity and passivity places the autonomy concepts in the very center of our clinical and metapsychological theory. Moreover, since a metapsychological analysis of activity and passivity appears possible, a way seems to be open to a full-fledged metapsychological treatment of the autonomies.

VIII

Summing up, the organism is endowed by evolution with apparatuses which prepare it for contact with its environment, but its behavior is not a slave of this environment since it is also endowed with drives which rise from its organization, and are the ultimate guarantees against stimulus slavery. In turn, the organism's behavior is not simply the expression of these internal forces, since the very apparatuses through which the organism is in contact with its environment are the ultimate guarantees against drive slavery. These autonomies have proximal guarantees also, in intrapsychic structures. The balance of these mutually controlling factors does not depend on the outcome of their chance interactions, but is controlled by the laws of the epigenetic sequence, termed autonomous ego development.

Both kinds of protective intrapsychic structures are essential components of the ego's structure and organization, and the behavior attributes conceptualized as ego autonomies are characteristics of this ego structure and organization. These structures need nutriment for their development,

[22] Dr. Merton Gill and Dr. A. Wheelis called attention to this deficiency when the paper was first presented.

maintenance, and effectiveness, and their ultimate nutriments are drive stimuli on the one hand and external stimuli on the other. But such nutriment is also provided by other ego structures and by the motivations arising from them, and the more autonomous the ego, the more the nutriment is provided from these internal sources. But this "proportionality" obtains only within an optimal range, since ego autonomy from the id and ego autonomy from the environment mutually guarantee each other only within an optimal range. Maximization or minimization of either disrupts their balance. *Thus these autonomies are always relative.* In terms of the story with which I introduced our problem, the strength which makes a man independent from reality stimulations tends to lead him to build an impenetrable wall around himself.

The ego's autonomy may be defined in terms of ego activity, and impairment of autonomy in terms of ego passivity. The old adage, that freedom is the acceptance of the restraints of the law, returns to us here with renewed significance. The elementary phenomenology from which we started seems to have led us into the very center of metapsychological considerations.

REFERENCES

Bettelheim, B. (1943). Individual and Mass Behavior in Extreme Situations. *J. Abnorm. Soc. Psychol.*, 38:417–452.

———— (1947). The Dynamism of Anti-Semitism in Gentile and Jew. *J. Abnorm. Soc. Psychol.*, 42:153–168.

Bexton, W. H., Heron, W., & Scott, T. H. (1954). Effects of Decreased Variation in the Sensory Environment. *Canad. J. Psychol.*, 8:70–76.

Bone, E. (1957). *Seven Years' Solitary*. New York: Harcourt, Brace.

Bürger-Prinz, H., & Kaila, M. (1930). On the Structure of the Amnesic Syndrome. In Rapaport (1951a), pp. 650–686.

Burney, C. (1952). *Solitary Confinement*. New York: Coward-McCann.

Eissler, K. R. (1950). Ego-Psychological Implications of the Psychoanalytic Treatment of Delinquents. *Psychoanal. Study Child,* 5:97–121. New York: International Universities Press.

Erikson, E. H. (1937). Configurations in Play—Clinical Notes. *Psychoanal. Quart.*, 6:139–214.

———— (1950a). *Childhood and Society*. New York: Norton.

———— (1950b). Growth and Crises of the "Healthy Personality." In *Personality in Nature, Society, and Culture,* 2nd ed., ed. C. Kluckhohn & H. A. Murray. New York: Knopf, 1953, pp. 185–225.

———— (1956). The Problem of Ego Identity. *J. Amer. Psychoanal. Assn.,* 4:56–121.

Fenichel, O. (1935). Concerning the Theory of Psychoanalytic Technique. *Collected Papers,* 1:332–348. New York: Norton, 1953.

———— (1938–39). *Problems of Psychoanalytic Technique*. Albany, N. Y.: Psychoanalytic Quarterly, Inc., 1941.

Freud, A. (1936). *The Ego and the Mechanisms of Defence.* New York: International Universities Press, 1946.

Freud, S. (1900). The Interpretation of Dreams, tr. A. A. Brill. *The Basic Writings.* New York: Modern Library, 1938, pp. 179–549.

———— (1910–19 [1910–18]). Papers on Technique. *Collected Papers,* 2:285–402. New York: Basic Books, 1959.

———— (1911a). Formulations Regarding the Two Principles in Mental Functioning. *Collected Papers,* 4:13–21. New York: Basic Books, 1959.

———— (1911b). Psycho-analytic Notes upon an Autobiographical Account of a Case of Paranoia (Dementia Paranoides). *Collected Papers,* 3:387–470. New York: Basic Books, 1959.

———— (1915). Instincts and Their Vicissitudes. *Collected Papers,* 4:60–83. New York: Basic Books, 1959.

———— (1917 [1915]). Mourning and Melancholia. *Collected Papers,* 4:152–170. New York: Basic Books, 1959.

———— (1920). *Beyond the Pleasure Principle,* tr. C. J. M. Hubback. London: Hogarth Press, 1948.

———— (1923). *The Ego and the Id,* tr. J. Riviere. London: Hogarth Press, 1947.

———— (1926 [1925]). *The Problem of Anxiety,* tr. H. A. Bunker. New York: Psychoanalytic Quarterly & Norton, 1936.

Gill, M. M. (1954). Psychoanalysis and Exploratory Psychotherapy. *J. Amer. Psychoanal. Assn.,* 2:771–797.

————, & Brenman, M. (1959). *Hypnosis and Related States.* New York: International Universities Press.

Ginzberg, L. (1946). *The Legends of the Jews,* Vol. II. Philadelphia: Jewish Publication Society of America.

Gollwitzer, H., et al., eds. (1956). *Dying We Live.* New York: Pantheon.

Grünthal, E. (1923). Zur Kenntnis der Psychopathologie des Korsakowschen Symptomenkomplexes. *Monatschr. Psychiat. Neurol.,* 53:89–132.

Hartmann, H. (1939). *Ego Psychology and the Problem of Adaptation,* tr. D. Rapaport. New York: International Universities Press, 1958. Also (abridged) in Rapaport (1951a), pp. 362–396.

———— (1950). Comments on the Psychoanalytic Theory of the Ego. *Psychoanal. Study Child,* 5:74–96. New York: International Universities Press.

———— (1952). The Mutual Influences in the Development of the Ego and Id. *Psychoanal. Study Child,* 7:9–30. New York: International Universities Press.

———— (1955). Notes on the Theory of Sublimation. *Psychoanal. Study Child,* 10:9–29. New York: International Universities Press.

———— (1956). Notes on the Reality Principle. *Psychoanal. Study Child,* 11:31–53. New York: International Universities Press.

————, Kris, E., & Loewenstein, R. M. (1946). Comments on the Formation of Psychic Structure. *Psychoanal. Study Child,* 2:11–38. New York: International Universities Press.

Hebb, D. O. (1949). *The Organization of Behavior; A Neuropsychological Theory.* New York: Wiley.

Heron, W. (1957). The Pathology of Boredom. *Sci. Amer.,* 196:52–56.

————, Bexton, W. H., & Hebb, D. O. (1953). Cognitive Effects of a Decreased Variation in the Sensory Environment. *Amer. Psychol.,* 8:366.

————, Doane, B. K., & Scott, T. H. (1956). Visual Disturbances after Prolonged Perceptual Isolation. *Canad. J. Psychol.,* 10:13–18.

Kasanin, J. S., ed. (1944). *Language and Thought in Schizophrenia.* Berkeley: University of California Press.

Knight, R. P. (1953a). Borderline States. *Bull. Menninger Clin.,* 17:1–12. Also in Knight & Friedman (1954), pp. 97–109.

———— (1953b). Management and Psychotherapy of the Borderline Schizophrenic Patient. *Bull. Menninger Clin.,* 17:139–150. Also in Knight & Friedman (1954), pp. 110–122.

————, & Friedman, C. R., eds. (1954). *Psychoanalytic Psychiatry and Psychology, Clinical and Theoretical Papers,* Austen Riggs Center, Vol. I. New York: International Universities Press.

Kris, E. (1932–52). *Psychoanalytic Explorations in Art.* New York: International Universities Press, 1952.

———— (1950). On Preconscious Mental Processes. *Psychoanal. Quart.,* 19: 540–560. Also in Kris (1932–52), pp. 303–318. Also in Rapaport (1951a), pp. 474–493.

———— (1956). On Some Vicissitudes of Insight in Psycho-Analysis. *Int. J. Psycho-Anal.,* 37:445–455.

Kubie, L. S. (1943). The Use of Induced Hypnagogic Reveries in the Recovery of Repressed Amnesic Data. *Bull. Menninger Clin.,* 7:172–182.

————, & Margolin, S. (1942). A Physiological Method for the Induction of States of Partial Sleep, and Securing Free Association and Early Memories in Such States. *Trans. Amer. Neurol. Assn.,* 68:136–139.

————, & Margolin, S. (1944). The Process of Hypnotism and the Nature of the Hypnotic State. *Amer. J. Psychiat.,* 100:611–622.

Lifton, R. J. (1956a). Thought Reform of Chinese Intellectuals: A Psychiatric Evaluation. *J. Asian Stud.,* 16:75–88.

———— (1956b). "Thought Reform" of Western Civilians in Chinese Communist Prisons. *Psychiatry,* 19:173–195.

Lilly, J. C. (1965a). Discussion in *Illustrative Strategies for Research on Psychopathology in Mental Health,* Symposium No. 2, June. Group for the Advancement of Psychiatry, Reports and Symposiums, 3:13–20.

———— (1956b). Mental Effects of Reduction of Ordinary Levels of Physical Stimuli on Intact, Healthy Persons. *Psychiat. Res. Reports,* 5:1–9.

Loewenstein, R. M. (1954). Some Remarks on Defences, Autonomous Ego and Psycho-Analytic Technique. *Int. J. Psycho-Anal.,* 35:188–193.

Miller, S. C. (1957). Determinants of the Role-Image of the Patient in a Psychiatric Hospital. In *The Patient and the Mental Hospital,* ed. M. Greenblatt, D. J. Levinson, & R. H. Williams. Glencoe, Ill.: Free Press, pp. 380–401.

———— (1962). Ego-Autonomy in Sensory Deprivation, Isolation, and Stress. *Int. J. Psycho-Anal.,* 43:1–20.

Moen, P. (n.d.). *Peter Moen's Diary.* London: Faber & Faber.

Orwell, G. (1949). *Nineteen Eighty-Four.* New York: Harcourt, Brace.

Piaget, J. (1936). *The Origins of Intelligence in Children,* 2nd ed. New York: International Universities Press, 1952.

—————— (1937). *The Construction of Reality in the Child.* New York: Basic Books, 1954.

Polansky, N. A., Miller, S. C., & White, R. B. (1955). Some Reservations Regarding Group Psychotherapy in Inpatient Psychiatric Treatment. *Group Psychother.,* 8:254–262.

Popper-Lynkeus, J. (1899). Zeichen der Kraft. *Phantasien eines Realisten.* Dresden: Reissner, 1922, pp. 13–14.

Rapaport, D., ed. & tr. (1951a). *Organization and Pathology of Thought.* New York: Columbia University Press.

—————— (1951b). The Conceptual Model of Psychoanalysis. *This volume,* Chapter 34.

—————— (1951c). The Autonomy of the Ego. *This volume,* Chapter 31.

—————— (1953a). Discussion at Mass Communications Seminar. *This volume,* Chapter 42.

—————— (1953b). Some Metapsychological Considerations Concerning Activity and Passivity. *This volume,* Chapter 44.

—————— (1957a). Cognitive Structures. *This volume,* Chapter 50.

—————— (1957b). Discussion of C. E. Osgood, "A Behavioristic Analysis of Perception and Language as Cognitive Phenomena." *This volume,* Chapter 51.

—————— (1959). The Structure of Psychoanalytic Theory: A Systematizing Attempt. In *Psychology: A Study of a Science,* Vol. III, ed. S. Koch. New York: McGraw-Hill, pp. 55–183. Also in *Psychol. Issues,* No. 6, 1960.

——————, & Gill, M. M. (1959). The Points of View and Assumptions of Metapsychology. *This volume,* Chapter 62.

Weissberg, A. (1951). *Accused.* New York: Simon & Schuster.

Wolff, P. H. (1960). The Developmental Psychologies of Jean Piaget and Psychoanalysis. *Psychol. Issues,* No. 5.

58

A HISTORICAL SURVEY OF
PSYCHOANALYTIC
EGO PSYCHOLOGY[1]

If there existed a systematic study of ego psychology, containing a precise definition of the ego and a full listing of ego functions, it would be relatively simple to outline the history of ego psychology. So far no such study has been published, and the survey I intend to give here may be considered as a prerequisite for such a study.

Before beginning our survey it will be worth reminding ourselves that the ego, the id, and the superego are concepts. They are abstractions which refer to certain characteristics of behavior. In contrast to the id, which refers to *peremptory* aspects of behavior, the ego refers to aspects of behavior which are *delayable, bring about delay,* or are themselves *products of delay.* The ego is a general concept: the explanation of those characteristics of behavior to which it refers requires many subsidiary concepts. Ego psychology encompasses all these concepts and its propositions state the relation-

[1] For another survey, see Hartmann (1956).

Condensation of lectures given at the Philadelphia Psychoanalytic Society and at the Department of Psychiatry of the University of Colorado, Denver, in 1954 and 1957. First published in the Bulletin of the Philadelphia Association for Psychoanalysis, *8:105–120, 1958. Reprinted in* Psychological Issues, *1:5–17, 1959. Spanish translation published in Merton M. Gill and David Rapaport,* Aportaciones a la Teoría y Técnica Psicoanalítica. *Asociación Psicoanalítica Mexicana, A.C., 1962, pp. 40–57.*

ships among them. Thus it is the theory of the relationships among the behavioral referents of all these concepts. In addition, however, it includes propositions coordinating ego concepts with the other concepts of psychoanalysis.

The first phase of the history of psychoanalytic ego psychology coincides with Freud's prepsychoanalytic theory; it ends with 1897, the approximate beginning of psychoanalysis proper (Freud, 1887–1902, pp. 215–218). *The second phase,* which ends in 1923, is the development of psychoanalysis proper. *The third phase* begins with the publication of *The Ego and the Id* (1923), and encompasses the development of Freud's ego psychology, which extends to 1937. *The fourth phase* begins with the crucial writings of Anna Freud (1936), Hartmann (1939), Erikson (1937), Horney (1937), Kardiner (1939), Sullivan (1938, 1940), and extends to the present day. The general psychoanalytic psychology of the ego based on the foundations laid by Freud began to evolve in this phase.

THE FOUR PHASES OF THE DEVELOPMENT OF EGO PSYCHOLOGY

THE FIRST PHASE

In the first phase, the main contribution to the development of ego psychology was *the concept of defense.* A subsidiary contribution was the central rôle attributed to *external reality.*

That conception of defense differs from the present concept. Defense was conceived of as directed against the memory and the re-encountering of certain reality experiences (Freud, 1887–1902, pp. 109–115; 1894, 1896; Breuer and Freud, 1893–95). This defense concept and our present one are alike in that both imply that a quantitative factor is dammed up and displaced. But in the early defense conception this quantity was "affect" and not "drive cathexis" (1894, p. 75). They are also alike (Freud, 1915c, pp. 177–178) in that defense, by preventing the recall and re-encounter of a reality experience, forestalls the experience of an unacceptable and thus painful affect (Breuer and Freud, 1893–95, pp. 26–27; Freud, 1894, pp. 61–63).

The crucial difference between the early defense conception and the present one, however, is the setting of the former: a primitive conception of the ego. The term "ego" in the first phase stood either for the "person," or for the "self," or for consciousness (Breuer and Freud, 1893–95, pp. 122–123, 133, 225). The conception was that consciousness is commanded by "the dominant mass of ideas" (p. 116); the memories which are incompatible with this dominant mass of ideas are dissociated from consciousness by defense. Owing to this separation, the affect associated with the memory cannot be dissipated—as it would be normally—over the associative network, and thus is dammed up and turns into anxiety (the toxic theory, Freud, 1895a, pp. 94, 97, 102).

The crucial similarity of this defense conception to our present concept is that reality has a central, though different, rôle in it (cf. Freud, 1887–1902; 1894, 1896; and the third phase below).

THE SECOND PHASE

The theory of the first phase collapsed when Freud discovered that his patients' reports of infantile seduction were not reports of reality experiences but of fantasies (Freud, 1887–1902, pp. 215–218). Consequently, reality experience lost its central position in the theory, and only slowly regained it in the course of the next thirty years. The center of interest shifted to the agent which creates the fantasies and the processes by which this agent works: the discovery of the instinctual drive followed (Freud, 1887–1902, pp. 270–271) and its exploration dominated the second phase (Freud, 1900, 1905). Interest in defenses also declined and the conception distinguishing a variety of defenses was replaced by the global concept of repression (Freud, 1915b). Where defenses retained their individuality they were considered as various mechanisms of repression or as subsequent substitute formations (1915b, pp. 154 ff.). But the centering of interest on instinctual drives had still other effects on the conception of defenses. *First,* some defenses were treated as *instinctual vicissitudes* (1915a, pp. 117, 132). *Second,* the question arose: what is the *repressive* (defensive) *force?* This question was answered by the assumption that repression (defense) is effected by ego instincts (1905; 1914, pp. 77–78; and 1911). Thus in this phase of the theory even crucial ego functions were conceived of in terms of instinctual drives. Yet both of these conceptions contributed to the development of ego psychology: they kept alive the problem of defense mechanisms, and raised the question, "What are the 'ego forces'?" Two more conceptions of this phase are relevant to the development of ego psychology, but since *at this point* they did not directly advance it, they will be only mentioned here: *pleasure vs. reality ego* (1911, pp. 18–19; 1915a, pp. 135–136) and *narcissism* (1914).

However, the outstanding contributions to ego psychology in this phase were the conception of the secondary process (1900, pp. 598–605, 616–617), the conception of the reality principle (1911), and the analysis of the process of repression (1915b, 1915c).

Although the concept of the *secondary process* implied no genetic ego roots independent of the instinctual drives, and was conceived as imposed upon the primary process (i.e., on the instinctual drives) solely by reality experience, it is just as crucial a historical root of ego psychology as the defense conception of the first phase.[2] Although we cannot discuss the sec-

---

[2] Actually, both originate in Freud's neuropsychological theory in the "Project for a Scientific Psychology" (1895b).

ondary process in detail, we must point out that it provided a conception of reality relations (1900, p. 574), and involved a concept of consciousness (pp. 615–616) which was independent of the topographical conception simultaneously introduced (pp. 535–542). Both the concepts of reality relations and of consciousness were crucial for the later structural concept of the ego.

The introduction of *the reality principle* (1911)—though it too implied no ego roots independent from instinctual drives—provided the secondary process with a regulation principle comparable to the pleasure principle of the primary process, and the analysis of its means of functioning (*reality testing*) provided further specifications of the conception of the secondary process (1911, pp. 14–17).

The analysis of the process of repression revealed the insufficiencies and internal contradictions of the topographic conception: the economic conception "easily defeated the topographical one" (1915c, p. 180). Repression proved to be a matter neither of topography nor of ego instincts, but of the withdrawal of hypercathexes[3] and the establishment of permanent countercathexes (pp. 180–181). The discovery in this second phase that these countercathexes are *permanent* and that the resistances which they bring about are *unconscious* (like their antagonists, the instinctual drives, pp. 192–193) anticipated Freud's structural theory of the ego in *The Ego and the Id* (1923) which ushered in the third phase.

THE THIRD PHASE

The Beginning. Freud repeatedly indicated that he expected the theory of the ego to arise from the study of narcissistic neuroses (1915a, p. 125; and 1916–17, pp. 331–332). Yet *The Ego and the Id* and its historical setting suggest that no such new study preceded it and that it may have been written not to clarify the concept of the ego, but, by introducing the concept of the superego, primarily to explain the unconscious sense of guilt and the negative therapeutic reaction.

In *The Ego and the Id* (1923) the ego is introduced as a coherent organization of mental processes (p. 15) which arises from identifications with abandoned objects (pp. 36 ff.), is organized primarily around the system *Pcpt.-Cs.* (pp. 27–28), but also includes the structures which are responsible for resistances and are unconscious (in the same sense as the id is, pp. 16–18), has neutral energies at its disposal (pp. 61–63), and can transform the energies of instinctual drives into energies of its own (pp. 64–65).

Thus in this conception the ego has genetic roots (*Pcpt.-Cs.*) and energies of its own. Consciousness (which in the first phase was more or less equated with the ego, and in the latter part of the second phase—as the system *Cs.*—could account for only a small segment of ego functions) was

[3] [Freud does not explicitly say "hypercathexes," though the inference is reasonable. See my discussion of this point in Gill (1963, p. 109)—Ed.]

scaled down to a mental quality, which—though exclusive to the ego—is only one of the possible qualities of ego functions and structures (pp. 16–18).

Yet this conception of the ego still had significant shortcomings: *first,* though Freud asserted that "in the ego perception plays the part which in the id devolves upon instinct" (p. 30), the ego still appears as a *resultant* of the promptings of id, superego, and reality (pp. 82–83); *second,* the ego is still the helpless rider of the id horse, "obliged to guide it where it wants to go" (p. 30); *third,* although some independent genetic roots are attributed to the ego, it is still assumed to differentiate out of the id; *fourth,* though the ego is viewed genetically, no epigenetic[4] conception of ego development, comparable to that of the phases of libido development, is postulated; *fifth,* even though the structures responsible for resistance are recognized as ego functions, no general theory of the rôle of defensive functions within the ego is developed; *sixth,* though the topographical view of consciousness is dispensed with, the structural conception of consciousness as a superordinate sense organ, developed in the early part of the second phase, is not yet incorporated.[5]

The Culmination. This conception was, however, only the beginning of the third phase, which culminated in Freud's *The Problem of Anxiety* (1926). Here Freud repudiated the conception that the ego is totally subservient to the id (pp. 22–23). The ego autonomously initiates defense by the anxiety signal (pp. 18–19, 86–87), becomes increasingly able, in the course of development, to turn the passively experienced anxiety into a form of active anticipation (pp. 114–115), makes use of the pleasure principle in pursuing its own ends (pp. 18, 80), has a great variety of defenses at its disposal (Chs. IV, V, VI, and pp. 110–112), is ultimately concerned with reality relationships (i.e., adaptation) and therefore curbs instinctual drives when action prompted by them would lead into reality danger (pp. 18, 22, 116).

In this conception Freud finally achieved what he had previously attempted (1911, pp. 13 f.): namely, external reality is brought into the center of the theory (1926, pp. 62, 101, 116), as it was in the first phase, but the central rôle of instinctual drives (p. 87), first established in the second phase, is retained. For the first time a conception of adaptation is implied: this theory of the ego provides a unitary solution for the ego's relations to reality and to instinctual drives. But this conception of adaptation is still limited in that it is developed only in reference to reality dangers.

This conception is the foundation for the concept of the autonomy of the ego, and points to constitutionally given perceptual (1926, p. 18) and affect mechanisms (pp. 71, 75, 90, 117) as roots of this autonomy (pp. 22–23). But it does not yet achieve a concept of ego autonomy.

4 For the concept of epigenesis, see Erikson (1940, 1950a).
5 For an attempt at such an integration, see Rapaport (1951a, 1956, 1957a).

Finally, this theory of the ego implies an epigenetic conception—at least of that aspect of ego development which pertains to anxiety (pp. 88–92)—which involves the turning of the enforced (passive) ego responses into ego-initiated (active) processes (p. 115). But neither this conception of epigenesis nor that of passivity and activity are as yet applied to the development of other ego functions or to ego development in general.

Freud's final conception of the ego includes his concepts of the secondary process and the reality principle (1933, pp. 105–108). He rounded out this final conception in a subsequent paper, making explicit the assumption of inborn ego roots, independent of instinctual drives (1937, pp. 343–344). Freud's implied conception of autonomous synthetic functions of the ego (1926, pp. 26–44) was subsequently made explicit by Nunberg (1931) and Waelder (1930).

The third phase culminated in Anna Freud's volume (1936). By introducing the concept of defense against external stimuli she integrated two of the main themes of this phase: defense and reality relations. By systematizing the concepts of the specific defenses and by investigating the rôle of affects she broadened the foundations which Freud had laid for psychoanalytic ego psychology.

THE FOURTH PHASE

Preliminaries. Psychoanalysis established the first conception of reality relations in terms of the secondary process and in relation to danger situations, but did not generalize it into a concept of adaptation until 1937. Thus the theory of object relations remained outside the scope of psychoanalytic ego psychology, and the psychosocial implications of reality and object relations remained unexplained theoretically.[6] In the late 1930's this gap in psychoanalytic theory apparently became so conspicuous that several simultaneous attempts to bridge it were made.[7] Some of these attempts (Erikson, Hartmann, Kris, and Loewenstein) showed a clear awareness of the foundations which existed in psychoanalysis for a theory of reality relationships in general, and interpersonal (psychosocial) relationships in particular. They also took into account the incipient theory of the ego's autonomous roots, development, and functions implied in Freud's ego psychology. Those attempts (Horney, Kardiner, Sullivan, etc.) which showed no such awareness—though otherwise their contribution to the development of psychoanalytic ego psychology was substantial—cannot be discussed here: they lead far away from the main stream of psychoanalysis. Some of the observations on which they are based have already been accounted for and some of the problems which they raised have already been solved by the recent developments in psychoanalytic ego psychology, which go a long

[6] The "theory" of object relations evolved by Melanie Klein and her followers is not an ego psychology but an id mythology.
[7] An early attempt in this direction was made by Alfred Adler.

way in demonstrating that these problems can be solved without discarding the basic theory of psychoanalysis.

The fourth phase of the development of psychoanalytic ego psychology is dominated by the contributions of Hartmann and Erikson, which are built on and complement the third phase of Freud's theory.

Hartmann and His Collaborators. Hartmann centers on those innate roots of ego development which are independent of instinctual drives; on reality relationships, that is, adaptation; and on the integration of the theory of the secondary process (second phase) with the theory of autonomous defense (third phase).

(1) In the conception of Hartmann, Kris, and Loewenstein, the ego does not develop from the id but both differentiate from a common matrix: the earliest *undifferentiated phase* of postnatal development (Hartmann, 1952; Hartmann, Kris, and Loewenstein, 1946).

(2) Hartmann conceived of the independent roots of ego development as *ego apparatuses of primary autonomy* (motility, perception, memory, etc.) which already exist in the undifferentiated phase and which after differentiation become the ego's major control and executive apparatuses (Hartmann, 1939).

(3) These apparatuses (as well as the coordination which they effect between the instinctual drives and their objects) he recognized as the means of phylogenetically guaranteed coordination to external reality, that is to say, to an *average expectable environment.* He conceptualized this coordination as a *state of adaptedness* which is prior to conflict and not a product of conflict solution, and thus is not wrung from the instinctual drives by the exigencies of reality. Thus he provided a conceptual explanation of the relatively autonomous and adaptive character of the secondary process (1939, 1952).

(4) He recognized that the conflict-born structures and functions of the ego can also attain relative autonomy from the drives. By introducing the concept of *change of function* he offered a conceptual explanation of their observed relative autonomy and termed them *apparatuses of secondary autonomy.* He juxtaposed *processes of adaptation* and *states of adaptedness,* by means of these concepts laid the foundation for the psychoanalytic concept and theory of adaptation, and outlined the first generalized theory of reality relations in psychoanalytic ego psychology.

(5) Hartmann's theory links the concepts *change of function* and *apparatuses of secondary autonomy* (by way of the concepts *automatization* and *neutralization*) to Freud's theories of the secondary process and of (defensive) structure formation by binding of countercathexes. The concepts *automatization* and *automatism* particularize the process of structure formation (Hartmann, 1947). Hartmann's (1950, 1955) and Kris's (1950, 1955) concept of neutralization generalizes Freud's theory of hypercathexes (1900, pp. 593–594, 599–600, 602–603, 617; 1915c, pp. 192,

193–194; and 1923, pp. 61–65), provides at least a partial conceptual answer to the question of the origin of ego energies, and clarifies the relation between *mobile* and *bound* energies by distinguishing the process of *binding* and *neutralization* (Kris, 1950).

(6) The concepts of the apparatuses of primary and secondary autonomy, automatization, and neutralization are the foundation of Hartmann's theory of the ego's relative autonomy from the id, which both generalized and particularized the conception implicit in Freud's theory of anxiety. Hartmann's theory of adaptation, however, does not fully integrate the theories of ego autonomy and reality relationships.[8]

(7) Kris extended the conception of activity and passivity implied in Freud's theory of the third phase, by introducing the concept of *regression in the service of the ego* (Kris, 1932–52). Hartmann made an important step toward generalizing this conception by demonstrating that the ego makes use not only of the highest-order secondary processes and rational regulations, but integrates and makes use both of its own archaic regulations and mechanisms and of the id's regulations and mechanisms (Hartmann, 1939, 1947). This generalization, however, does not include a systematic conception of activity and passivity.[9]

(8) Hartmann (1939) asserted, and Hartmann and Kris (1945) elaborated on, the theoretical necessity of a concept of *autonomous ego development;* Loewenstein (1950) and Kris (1955) demonstrated its clinical necessity. Although Hartmann's concept of secondary autonomy is a powerful tool for building a theory of autonomous ego development, he did not develop such an epigenetic theory.

(9) Hartmann's theory of adaptation includes a generalized theory of reality relations, which stresses the special rôle of social relations (1939; Hartmann and Kris, 1945; Hartmann, Kris, and Loewenstein, 1951). Yet it does not provide a specific and differentiated psychosocial theory.

Erikson. Erikson centers on the epigenesis of the ego (1937, 1940), on the theory of reality relationships (1945), and especially on the elaboration of the theory of the rôle of social reality (1950b), and these are the core of his psychosocial theory of development (1950a), which complements Freud's theory of the third phase and Hartmann's elaboration of it.

(1) Erikson's theory outlines *the sequence of phases* of psychosocial development, and relates these phases to psychosexual epigenesis, thereby laying the groundwork for the study of *ego epigenesis* (1950b). Thus he began to particularize Hartmann's concept of autonomous ego development, which generalized Freud's conception of the development of anxiety.

(2) This sequence of the phases of psychosocial development parallels that of libido development (1950a, Ch. 2) and goes beyond it, spanning *the*

[8] For an attempt at such an integration, see Rapaport (1951b, 1957b).
[9] For an attempt at a systematic conception of activity and passivity, see Rapaport (1953, 1957b).

whole life cycle (Ch. 7). This conception is the first in the history of psychoanalytic theory to encompass those phases of the life cycle which are customarily subsumed under the single concept of genital maturity, and to provide tools for their investigation.

(3) Each phase of the life cycle is characterized by a *phase-specific developmental task* which must be solved in it (1945; 1950a, Ch. 7), though this solution is prepared in the previous phases and is worked out further in subsequent ones (1956). Each phase is described in terms of the extremes of successful and unsuccessful solutions which can be arrived at in it, though in reality the outcome is a balance between these extremes: (1) *basic trust vs. mistrust;* (2) *autonomy vs. shame and doubt;* (3) *initiative vs. guilt;* (4) *industry vs. inferiority;* (5) *identity vs. identity diffusion;* (6) *intimacy vs. isolation;* (7) *generativity vs. stagnation;* (8) *integrity vs. despair.*

(4) Erikson's theory, like Hartmann's adaptation theory, rests on the assumption of an inborn coordination to an average expectable environment. His concept of *mutuality* (1950a) specifies that the crucial coordination is between the developing individual and his human (social) environment, and that this coordination is mutual. The theory postulates a *cogwheeling of the life cycles:* the representatives of society, the caretaking persons, are coordinated to the developing individual by their specific inborn responsiveness to his needs and by phase-specific needs of their own (e.g., generativity).

(5) This theory particularizes Hartmann's theory of reality relations, in that it deals with the ego aspect and the social aspect of object relations. It conceives of the caretaking persons as representatives of their society, as carriers of its institutional, traditional, caretaking patterns, and thus it focuses attention on the fact that *each society meets each phase of the development of its members by institutions (parental care, schools, teachers, occupations, etc.) specific to it, to ensure that the developing individual will be viable in it.* The theory conceives of the sequence of epigenetic phases as universal, and of the typical solutions as varying from society to society (1950b; 1950a, Chs. 3 and 4).

(6) The crucial characteristic of this psychosocial theory of ego development, and of Hartmann's adaptation theory (in contrast to the "culturalist" theories) is that they offer a conceptual explanation of the individual's social development by tracing the unfolding *of the genetically social character of the human individual* in the course of his encounters with the social environment at each phase of his epigenesis. Thus it is not assumed that societal norms are grafted upon the genetically asocial individual by "disciplines" and "socialization," but that the society into which the individual is born makes him its member by influencing *the manner in which* he solves the tasks posed by each phase of his epigenetic development.

(7) Erikson introduces the concepts *organ mode* and *mode epigenesis*

(1937, 1950b) and thereby specifies a major mechanism by which society influences the solution of the phase-specific developmental tasks. These concepts constitute specific instances of Hartmann's concept *change of function*. The modes (inceptive, retentive, intrusive, etc.) in their specific phase of dominance generalize (become displaced) to organs and zones other than those of their origin, and thus can become *estranged* from their origins and can thereafter become autonomous (secondary autonomy). Erikson demonstrates that it is this change of function of these modes which is influenced by the society's caretaking institutions so that those organ modes which correspond to behavior modalities (receiving, taking, giving, letting go, making, etc.) viable in that society undergo a change of function and become ego apparatuses of secondary autonomy, that is, behavior modalities of the individual.

(8) Erikson's theory (like much of Freud's) ranges over phenomenological, specifically clinical psychoanalytic, and general psychoanalytic-psychological propositions, without systematically differentiating among them. Correspondingly, the conceptual status of this theory's terms is so far unclear. To systematize this theory and to clarify the conceptual status of its terms is a task for ego psychology in the future.

(9) Erikson's contributions constitute an organic extension of Freud's theory and they and Hartmann's contributions are consistent with and complementary to each other. Yet Erikson related his theory in an explicit fashion mainly to the concepts of Freud's id psychology, less to the concepts of Freud's ego psychology, and only slightly to Hartmann's theory. Nor did Hartmann attempt to formulate the relation between his and Erikson's theory. Here a task of integration faces ego psychology.

CONCLUSION

This survey is an incomplete outline which traces only the main developments in ego psychology. Even there it understates Anna Freud's and Kris's contributions, neglects the contributions of Bibring and Fenichel, and avoids completely the relationships between the ego and the superego, and those between ego psychology and the technique of psychoanalysis. Moreover, it does not give any account of the contributions concerning self and identity (Erikson, Hartmann, E. Jacobson), values and ideology (Hartmann, Erikson), the psychosocial effects of isolation, deprivation and propaganda (Bettelheim, Erikson, Jacobson, Kris, Rapaport), nor of those arising from the direct observation of child development (Benjamin; Escalona and Leitch; Kris and collaborators; Spitz; K. Wolf), the work with autistic, delinquent, and psychotic children (Bettelheim; Mahler; Rank, Putnam and collaborators; Redl). A survey of these latter contributions, and of my few attempts to which I have referred in footnotes, must await further developments before they can be seen in proper perspective.

REFERENCES

Breuer, J., & Freud, S. (1893–95). Studies on Hysteria. *Standard Edition*, 2. London: Hogarth Press, 1955.

Erikson, E. H. (1937). Configurations in Play—Clinical Notes. *Psychoanal. Quart.*, 6:139–214.

—— (1940). Problems of Infancy and Early Childhood. In *Cyclopedia of Medicine*. Philadelphia: Davis, pp. 714–730. Also in *Outline of Abnormal Psychology*, ed. G. Murphy & A. Bachrach. New York: Modern Library, 1954, pp. 3–36.

—— (1945). Childhood and Tradition in Two American Indian Tribes. *Psychoanal. Study Child*, 1:319–350. Also (revised) in *Personality in Nature, Society, and Culture*, ed. C. Kluckhohn & H. A. Murray. New York: Knopf, 1948, pp. 176–203.

—— (1950a). *Childhood and Society*. New York: Norton.

—— (1950b). Growth and Crises of the "Healthy Personality." In *Personality in Nature, Society, and Culture*, 2nd ed., ed. C. Kluckhohn & H. A. Murray. New York: Knopf, 1953, pp. 185–225.

—— (1956). The Problem of Ego Identity. *J. Amer. Psychoanal. Assn.*, 4:56–121.

Freud, A. (1936). *The Ego and the Mechanisms of Defence*. New York: International Universities Press, 1946.

Freud, S. (1887–1902). *The Origins of Psychoanalysis: Letters to Wilhelm Fliess, Drafts and Notes, 1887–1902*. New York: Basic Books, 1954.

—— (1894). The Defence Neuro-Psychoses. *Collected Papers*, 1:59–75. New York: Basic Books, 1959.

—— (1895a [1894]). The Justification for Detaching from Neurasthenia a Particular Syndrome: The Anxiety-Neurosis. *Collected Papers*, 1:76–106. New York: Basic Books, 1959.

—— (1895b). Project for a Scientific Psychology. In Freud (1887–1902), pp. 347–445.

—— (1896). Further Remarks on the Defence Neuro-Psychoses. *Collected Papers*, 1:155–182. New York: Basic Books, 1959.

—— (1900). The Interpretation of Dreams. *Standard Edition*, 4 & 5. London: Hogarth Press, 1953.

—— (1905). Three Essays on the Theory of Sexuality. *Standard Edition*, 7:123–245. London: Hogarth, 1953.

—— (1911). Formulations Regarding the Two Principles in Mental Functioning. *Collected Papers*, 4:13–21. New York: Basic Books, 1959.

—— (1914). On Narcissism: An Introduction. *Standard Edition*, 14:73–102. London: Hogarth Press, 1957.

—— (1915a). Instincts and Their Vicissitudes. *Standard Edition*, 14:117–140. London: Hogarth Press, 1957.

—— (1915b). Repression. *Standard Edition*, 14:146–158. London: Hogarth Press, 1957.

—— (1915c). The Unconscious. *Standard Edition*, 14:166–215. London: Hogarth Press, 1957.

———— (1916–17 [1915–17]). *A General Introduction to Psychoanalysis,* tr. J. Riviere. New York: Garden City Publishing Co., 1938.

———— (1923). *The Ego and the Id,* tr. J. Riviere. London: Hogarth Press, 1947.

———— (1926 [1925]). *The Problem of Anxiety,* tr. H. A. Bunker. New York: Psychoanalytic Quarterly & Norton, 1936.

———— (1933). Lecture 31: The Anatomy of the Mental Personality. *New Introductory Lectures on Psycho-Analysis,* tr. W. J. H. Sprott. New York: Norton, pp. 82–112.

———— (1937). Analysis Terminable and Interminable. *Collected Papers,* 5:316–357. New York: Basic Books, 1959.

Gill, M. M. (1963). Topography and Systems in Psychoanalytic Theory. *Psychol. Issues,* No. 10.

Hartmann, H. (1939). *Ego Psychology and the Problem of Adaptation,* tr. D. Rapaport. New York: International Universities Press, 1958.

———— (1947). On Rational and Irrational Action. In *Psychoanalysis and the Social Sciences,* ed. G. Róheim, 1:359–392. New York: International Universities Press.

———— (1950). Comments on the Psychoanalytic Theory of the Ego. *Psychoanal. Study Child,* 5:74–96. New York: International Universities Press.

———— (1952). The Mutual Influences in the Development of the Ego and Id. *Psychoanal. Study Child,* 7:9–30. New York: International Universities Press.

———— (1955). Notes on the Theory of Sublimation. *Psychoanal. Study Child,* 10:9–29. New York: International Universities Press.

———— (1956). The Development of the Ego Concept in Freud's Work. *Int. J. Psycho-Anal.,* 37:425–438.

————, & Kris, E. (1945). The Genetic Approach in Psychoanalysis. *Psychoanal. Study Child,* 1:11–30. New York: International Universities Press.

————, Kris, E., & Loewenstein, R. M. (1946). Comments on the Formation of Psychic Structure. *Psychoanal. Study Child,* 2:11–38. New York: International Universities Press.

————, Kris, E., & Loewenstein, R. M. (1951). Some Psychoanalytic Comments on "Culture and Personality." In *Psychoanalysis and Culture,* ed. G. B. Wilbur & W. Muensterberger. New York: International Universities Press, pp. 3–31.

Horney, K. (1937). *The Neurotic Personality of Our Time.* New York: Norton.

Kardiner, A. (1939). *The Individual and His Society: The Psychodynamics of Primitive Social Organization.* New York: Columbia University Press.

Kris, E. (1932–52). *Psychoanalytic Explorations in Art.* New York: International Universities Press, 1952.

———— (1950). On Preconscious Mental Processes. In *Organization and Pathology of Thought,* ed. & tr. D. Rapaport. New York: Columbia University Press, 1951, pp. 474–493. Also in Kris (1932–52), pp. 303–318.

———— (1955). Neutralization and Sublimation: Observations on Young Children. *Psychoanal. Study Child,* 10:30–46. New York: International Universities Press.

Loewenstein, R. M. (1950). Conflict and Autonomous Ego Development during the Phallic Phase. *Psychoanal. Study Child,* 4:47–52. New York: International Universities Press.

Nunberg, H. (1931). The Synthetic Function of the Ego. *Practice and Theory of Psychoanalysis.* New York: International Universities Press, 1955, pp. 120–136.

Rapaport, D. (1951a). States of Consciousness: A Psychopathological and Psychodynamic View. *This volume,* Chapter 33.

——— (1951b). The Autonomy of the Ego. *This volume,* Chapter 31.

——— (1953). Some Metapsychological Considerations Concerning Activity and Passivity. *This volume,* Chapter 44.

——— (1956). The Psychoanalytic Theory of Consciousness and a Study of Dreams. Lecture to the Detroit Psychoanalytic Society, January 14.

——— (1957a). Cognitive Structures. *This volume,* Chapter 50.

——— (1957b). The Theory of Ego Autonomy: A Generalization. *This volume,* Chapter 57.

Sullivan, H. S. (1938). Psychiatry: Introduction to the Study of Interpersonal Relations. *Psychiatry,* 1:121–134.

——— (1940). *Conceptions of Modern Psychiatry.* Washington: William Alanson White Psychiatric Foundation, 1947.

Waelder, R. (1930). The Principle of Multiple Function: Observations on Over-Determination. *Psychoanal. Quart.,* 5:45–62, 1936.

59

EDWARD BIBRING'S THEORY
OF DEPRESSION

I

Edward Bibring was one of the few systematic theoreticians of psychoanalysis. His keen awareness of the complexity of psychoanalytic theory and of the responsibility entailed by every attempt to systematize or amend it explains the fact that the range and scope rather than the volume of his writing give us the measure of his stature as a theoretician. Hence his achievement must be read not only in the lines, but also between the lines of his writing. It is such a reading of his paper on depression that I want to present tonight. Until his literary legacy is published—and perhaps even after that—such studies of his published work must serve us as the means of assessing his theoretical conceptions.

First, a word about his scope and range as a theoretician. As a historian of the theory he gave us the only broad survey of the development of the theory of instinctual drives that we have. As a systematizer he set a standard for such work in his essay on the repetition compulsion. As a critic he provided the first dispassionate analysis of Melanie Klein's theories. His contributions to the clinical theory of therapy you have heard Dr. Anna Freud discuss tonight. As a theory builder he gave us the theory of depression, which is my subject tonight.

Presented at the Bibring Memorial Meeting of the Boston Psychoanalytic Association, April 14, 1959. This paper is published here for the first time.

One of Edward Bibring's central interests was to bring into the present framework of psychoanalytic theory those parts of it which were formulated before the development of the structural approach and present-day ego psychology. Of the solutions he reached he published only his theories of psychotherapy and depression, and even these were written during the struggle with his paralyzing illness. It is hoped that some more of his solutions, or hints about the directions in which he sought solutions, will be gleaned from the study of his files: for instance, a preliminary draft of "The Mechanism of Depression" contains several such hints.

II

The theory Edward Bibring presents in "The Mechanism of Depression" (1953) is deliberately limited to the ego of psychology depression. He wrote: ". . . the conception of depression presented here does not invalidate the accepted theories of the role which orality and aggression play in the various types of depression" (p. 41). Yet his theory points up the inadequacy of the accepted theory. Bibring stated his view as follows: ". . . the oral and aggressive strivings are not as universal in depression as is generally assumed and . . . consequently the theories built on them do not offer sufficient explanation, but require . . . modification" (p. 41).

As we shall see, he relegated to a peripheral rôle the factors which are central to the accepted theory of depression: in his theory they appear as precipitating or complicating factors, and indeed at times even as consequences of that ego state which, according to Bibring, is the essence of depression.

The basic proposition of Bibring's theory is akin to the proposition on which Freud built his structural theory of anxiety. Freud wrote: ". . . the ego is the real seat of anxiety . . . Anxiety is an affective state which can of course be experienced only by the ego" (1926, p. 80). Bibring wrote: "Depression is . . . primarily an ego phenomenon" (1953, p. 40); "[it] represents an affective state" (p. 27). "[Anxiety and depression are] both . . . frequent . . . ego reactions . . . [and since] they cannot be reduced any further, it may be justified to call them basic ego reactions" (p. 34).

Bibring thus set out to explore the structure of depression as an ego state. He used Freud's theory of anxiety, Fenichel's theory of boredom, and some general observations on depersonalization as his points of departure.

How decisive a step this was becomes obvious if we remember that B. D. Lewin's (1950) monograph on elation, for instance, still rests exclusively on id psychology, on the oral triad.

III

Bibring searched the literature of the accepted theory for evidence pertaining to depression as an ego state. Freud had pointed out that both grief and depression involve an inhibition of the ego. Bibring saw this inhibition as a ubiquitous characteristic of the depressive ego state. Abraham (1924) had derived from his clinical observation a concept of primal depression ("primal parathymia"); he found that all subsequent depressive episodes "brought with [them] . . . a state of mind that was an exact replica of . . . [the] primal parathymia" and asserted that "It is this state of mind that we call melancholia" (1924, p. 469). Abraham's observations and formulation indicated to Bibring that the regression in depressions is not simply a regression of the libido to an oral fixation point, but primarily an ego regression to an ego state, implying that the depressive state is not produced *de novo* every time by regression, but is a *reactivation* of a primal state. Here again we see the parallel to Freud's theory of anxiety. Freud wrote: ". . . anxiety is not created *de novo* in repression, but is reproduced as an affective state" (1926, p. 20). Bibring wrote: "Whatever . . . [the precipitating conditions], the mechanism of depression will be the same" (p. 42), and ". . . depression can be defined as the emotional expression . . . of a state of helplessness . . . of the ego, irrespective of what may have caused the breakdown of the mechanisms which established self-esteem" (p. 24). He saw in Fenichel's simple neurotic depressions, in E. Weiss's simple depressions, and in E. Jacobson's mild, blank depression further evidence for the existence of an affective ego state common to and basic to all depressions. The essence of this—as indeed of any—structural conception is that the phenomenon to be explained—in this case depression—is not conceived of as created *de novo* by dynamic factors. Since it is the reactivation of a persisting structure, the fact that it appears in essence unaltered, upon various precipitating conditions and in the most varied dynamic contexts, requires no further explanation. We shall see later that Bibring's structural theory of depression, just like Freud's structural theory of anxiety, involves a signal function.

IV

What are the descriptive characteristics of this basic affective state? According to Freud, depression is characterized by *ego inhibition* and lowered *self-esteem*. Bibring adds to these a third characteristic: *helplessness*. He wrote: ". . . depression represents an affective state, which indicates . . . [the] state of the ego in terms of [lowered self-esteem] helplessness and inhibition of functions" (p. 27).

This formulation raised several problems. First, the various clinical forms of depression had to be explained, and were explained by Bibring as complications of the basic state of depression by those factors which accounted for depression in the commonly accepted theory. Second, since the concept of helplessness had already been used by Freud in the theory of anxiety, Bibring had to clarify the relationship between depression and anxiety. Third, the term self-esteem was not defined explicitly by Freud, nor by anyone else, including Bibring. The central rôle Bibring gave it in his theory leaves us with the necessity to define this term explicitly within the conceptual framework of the psychoanalytic theory, but it also provides an indication of how this defining can be done. We will return to these problems, but first we must consider the genetics and dynamics of the ego state of depression.

V

What are the genetics of this state? Bibring wrote:

> Frequent frustrations of the infant's oral needs may mobilize at first anxiety and anger. If frustration is continued, however, in disregard of the "signals" produced by the infant, the anger will be replaced by feelings of exhaustion, of helplessness and depression. This early self-experience of the infantile ego's helplessness, of its lack of power to provide the vital supplies, is probably the most frequent factor predisposing to depression . . . . the emphasis is not on the oral frustration and subsequent oral fixation, but on the infant's or little child's shock-like experience of and fixation to the feeling of helplessness [pp. 36–37].

By the phase "this early self-experience" Bibring meant the experience of helplessness resulting from frustration of oral needs, and his apparent reservation expressed in the phrase "the infantile ego's helplessness . . . is probably the most frequent fact predisposing to depression" intends to convey that not only the oral but all continued early frustrations are such predisposing factors. His references to Abraham and Erikson corroborate this explanation: "Similar reactions may be established by any severe frustration of the little child's vital needs in and beyond the oral phase, e.g., of the child's needs for affection (Abraham), or by a failure in the child-mother relationship of mutuality (Erikson, 1950)" (pp. 39–40).

What is bold and new in this theory is the assertion that *all* depressions are affective states and as such are *reactivations* of a structured infantile ego state of helplessness. Bibring's conception of the origin of this helplessness is in accord with that of Freud concerning grief in *The Problem of Anxiety*. But Freud does not apply this conception of helplessness to all depressions nor does he imply that grief is the reactivation of a structured state. Freud wrote:

[The infant] is not yet able to distinguish temporary absence from permanent loss; . . . it requires repeated consoling experiences before he learns that . . . a disappearance on his mother's part is usually followed by her reappearance. . . . Thus he is enabled, as it were, to experience longing without an accompaniment of despair.

The situation in which he misses his mother is . . . owing to his miscomprehension . . . a traumatic one if he experiences at that juncture a need which his mother ought to gratify; it changes into a danger situation when this need is not immediate. . . . Loss of love does not yet enter into the situation.

. . . [Subsequently] repeated situations in which gratification was experienced have created out of the mother the object who is the recipient, when a need arises, of an intense cathexis, a cathexis which we may call "longingful." It is to this innovation that the reaction of grief is referable. Grief is therefore the reaction specific to object loss, anxiety to the danger which this object loss entails [1926, pp. 118–119].

It should be re-emphasized that Freud here derives this conception of helplessness from the phenomena of *grief,* while Bibring generalized it to all depressions and—as we shall see—implied that grief is a genetically late, "tamed" reactivation of this helplessness. We might add here that Spitz's observations on the so-called anaclitic depressions seem to support this part of the genetic aspect of Bibring's theory.

VI

Before we pursue further the genetics of this ego state, we must turn first to the experiences which reactivate it in adult life, and then to its dynamics. Bibring wrote:

In all these instances [described], the individuals . . . felt helplessly exposed to superior powers, fatal organic disease, or recurrent neurosis, or to the seemingly inescapable fate of being lonely, isolated, or unloved, or unavoidably confronted with the apparent evidence of being weak, inferior, or a failure. In all instances, the depression accompanied a feeling of being doomed, irrespective of what the conscious or unconscious background of this feeling may have been: in all of them a blow was dealt to the person's self-esteem, on whatever grounds such self-esteem may have been founded [pp. 23–24].

Thus the conditions precipitating the reactivation of this state are those which undermine self-esteem. Here again Bibring is close to Freud's observations, which he quotes:

. . . the melancholiac displays . . . an extraordinary fall in his self-esteem, an impoverishment of his ego on a grand scale [Freud, 1917, p. 155].

The occasions giving rise to melancholia for the most part extend beyond the clear case of a loss by death, and include all those situations of being wounded, hurt, neglected, out of favour, or disappointed . . . [p. 161].

VII

If the crucial dynamic factors of the accepted theory—oral fixation, ambivalence, incorporation, aggression turned round upon the subject—are relegated by Bibring's theory to the peripheral rôle of factors which complicate the basic affective ego state of depression, how are we to understand the dynamics of the reactivation of that state?

Bibring's explanation is based on two assumptions: first, that a blow is dealt to the subject's self-esteem, second, that this occurs while "certain narcissistically significant, i.e., for the self-esteem pertinent, goals and objects are strongly maintained" (p. 24). He formulates: "It is exactly from the tension between these highly charged narcissistic aspirations on the one hand, and the ego's acute awareness of its (real and imaginary) helplessness and incapacity to live up to them on the other hand, that depression results" (pp. 24–25).

He enumerates these aspirations: "(1) the wish to be worthy, to be loved, to be appreciated, not to be inferior or unworthy; (2) the wish to be strong, superior, great, secure, not to be weak and insecure; and (3) the wish to be good, to be loving, not to be aggressive, hateful and destructive" (p. 24).

Protagonists of the accepted theory may argue that all these aspirations are but derivatives of instinctual goals and superego demands; that the conflict is one between the ego and the superego, and involves oral fixation, ambivalence, incorporation, and aggression turned round upon the subject. This argument, however, disregards the core of Bibring's theory. His assumptions that in depression we are faced with an intra-ego conflict and that the dynamic factors of the accepted theory play only a precipitating or complicating rôle, imply that the ego processes involved must be studied and understood in their own right, because the observed commonality of depressions cannot be explained by assuming that depression is created *de novo* every time from the basic ingredients—instinct, superego, etc. This implication of Bibring's theory is also implied by Hartmann and Erikson, and it should be illuminating to cite one of Freud's formulations which also implies it and is directly pertinent to Bibring's theory.

According to Bibring, to be loved and to be loving are among the narcissistic aspirations whose rôle in depressions is crucial. In "Instincts and Their Vicissitudes" Freud defined loving as "the relation of the ego to its sources of pleasure" (1915, p. 78), and he wrote: ". . . the attitudes of love and hate cannot be said to characterize the relations of instincts to their objects, but are reserved for the relations of the ego as a whole to objects" (p. 80).

Thus Bibring's approach to the dynamics of the reactivation of the affective ego state of depression has a precedent in Freud's theorizing. The relationships implied in Freud's formulation have not been explored, and one of the merits of Bibring's theory is that it makes the exploration of them a patent and urgent necessity. The same urgency applies to the necessity of defining self-esteem, and to that of redefining narcissism in ego-psychological terms, since originally it was defined in what we would now call id terms.

Bibring summarized the dynamic aspect of his theory as follows:

> Though the persisting aspirations are of a threefold nature, the *basic mechanism of the resulting depression appears to be essentially the same* . . . depression is primarily not determined by a conflict between the ego on the one hand and the id, or the superego, or the environment on the other hand, but stems primarily from a tension within the ego itself, from an inner-systemic "conflict." Thus depression can be defined as the emotional correlate of a partial or complete collapse of the self-esteem of the ego, since it feels unable to live up to its aspirations . . . [which] are strongly maintained [pp. 25–26].

More generally:

> . . . everything that lowers or paralyzes the ego's self-esteem without changing the narcissistically important aims represents a condition of depression [p. 42].

This conception is in accord with Hartmann's theory of the "intrasystemic conflict" and with Erikson's theory of the crises in psychosocial epigenesis.

VIII

Now we can turn to tracing the fate of the basic depressive state in the course of development.

Bibring's formulation of the epigenesis of narcissistic aspirations is an important step toward specifying the conception of autonomous ego development, which was introduced by Hartmann. It will be worth while to remind ourselves that Freud already implied such a conception in "Formulations Regarding the Two Principles in Mental Functioning":

> . . . the decision as regards the form of subsequent illness (election of neurosis) will depend on the particular phase of ego-development and libido-development in which the inhibition of development has occurred. The chronological characteristics of the two developments, as yet unstudied, their possible variations in speed with respect to each other, thus receive unexpected significance [1911, pp. 19–20].

Bibring formulated the epigenesis of narcissistic aspirations as follows:
The narcissistic aspirations originating on the oral level are: (1) to get

affection; (2) to be loved; (3) to be taken care of; (4) to get supplies. The corresponding defensive needs are: (1) to be independent; (2) to be self-supporting. Depression then follows the discovery of: (1) not being loved; (2) not being independent (p. 27).

The narcissistic aspirations originating on the anal level refer to mastery over the body, over drives, and over objects, and they are: (1) to be good; (2) to be loving; (3) to be clean. The corresponding defensive needs are: (1) not to be hostile; (2) not to be resentful and defiant; (3) not to be dirty. Depression then follows the discovery of: (1) lack of control over libidinal and aggressive impulses; (2) lack of control over objects; (3) feelings of weakness (entailing the former two); (4) feelings of guilt (I will never be good, loving, will always be hateful, hostile, defiant, therefore evil).

The narcissistic aspirations originating on the phallic level refer to the exhibitionistic and sadistic competitive oedipal needs, and they are: (1) to be admired; (2) to be the center of attention; (3) to be strong and victorious. The corresponding defensive needs are: (1) to be modest; (2) to be inconspicuous; (3) to be submissive. Depression follows the discovery of: (1) fear of being defeated; (2) being ridiculed for shortcomings and defeats; (3) impending retaliation.

These steps in the development of narcissistic aspirations correspond to the first three phases of Erikson's psychosocial epigenesis: the aspirations originating on the oral level correspond to Erikson's phase of basic trust vs. mistrust (mutuality); those originating on the anal level to his phase of psychosocial autonomy vs. shame and doubt, and those originating on the phallic level to his phase of initiative vs. guilt.

If these formulations should be found wanting in inclusiveness or exclusiveness, they are as rich and thoughtful a collation of what Freud must have meant when he spoke of ego interests, and what we mean when we speak of them or of values, as any in psychoanalytic writings except Erikson's and possibly Horney's.

These genetic formulations use the concept of narcissistic aspirations and bring sharply into focus the need to redefine the concept of narcissism in structural and particularly ego-psychological terms. Hartmann and subsequently Jacobson have made an attempt to reformulate this concept, assuming that narcissism involves the cathecting of the self-representations rather than the cathecting of the ego. Bibring's formulations seem to require a more radical redefinition of narcissism.

IX

We have here a structural theory which treats depression as the reactivation of a structured state. The universal experiences of grief and sadness, ranging from passing sadness to profound depression, indicate that such an ego state exists in all men. We may infer that individual differences in the rela-

tive ease of and intensity of the reactivation of this state are determined by:
(a) the constitutional tolerance for continued frustration; (b) the severity
and extent of the situations of helplessness in early life; (c) the developmental factors which increase or decrease the relative ease with which this
state is reactivated and modulate its intensity; (d) the kind and severity of
the precipitating conditions. As for the dynamic aspect of this theory: the
depressive ego state is reactivated by an intra-ego conflict. The factors involved in this conflict, however, are not yet precisely defined. As for the
genetic aspect of the theory: the origin of the depressive ego state is clear
and so is the epigenesis of the "narcissistic aspirations" involved.

The economic and adaptive aspects of the theory, however, are not directly treated by Bibring. It is in regard to these aspects that much work is
still ahead of us. I shall not attempt to infer from Bibring's theory the directions this work might take.

X

Freud made several attempts to account for various aspects of the economics of depression.

For instance, he wrote: ". . . the ego's inhibited condition and loss of
interest was fully accounted for by the absorbing work of mourning"
(1917, p. 155). Or for instance:

> The conflict in the ego [meaning at that time the conflict between the
> ego and the superego], which in melancholia is substituted for the
> struggle surging round the object, must act like a painful wound which
> calls out unusually strong anti-cathexes (p. 170).

But Freud also indicated that these assumptions are insufficient and we
need "some insight into the economic conditions, first, of bodily pain, and
then of the mental pain" (p. 170) before we can understand the economics
of depression; and that:

> . . . we do not even know by what economic measures the work of
> mourning is carried through; possibly, however, a conjecture may help
> us here. Reality passes its verdict—that the object no longer exists—
> upon each single one of the memories and hopes through which the
> libido was attached to the lost object, and the ego, confronted as it
> were with the decision whether it will share this fate, is persuaded by
> the sum of narcissistic satisfactions in being alive to sever its attach-
> ment to the non-existent object [p. 166];

and that:

> This character of withdrawing the libido bit by bit is . . . to be as-
> cribed alike to mourning and to melancholia; it is probably sustained

> by the same economic arrangements and serves the same purpose in both [p. 167];

and finally:

> Why this process of carrying out the behest of reality bit by bit . . . should be so extraordinarily painful is not at all easy to explain in terms of mental economics [p. 154].

Though it is clear that the phenomenon from which the economic explanation must start is the inhibition of the ego, the economics of depression is still not understood. Bibring quotes Fenichel's formulation: ". . . the greater percentage of the available mental energy is used up in unconscious conflicts, [and] not enough is left to provide the normal enjoyment of life and vitality" (Bibring, 1953, p. 19). But he finds this statement insufficient to explain depressive inhibition, and proceeds to reconsider the nature of inhibition. He writes:

> Freud (1926) defines inhibition as a "restriction of functions of the ego" and mentions two major causes for such restrictions: either they have been imposed upon the person as a measure of precaution, e.g., to prevent the development of anxiety or feelings of guilt, or brought about as a result of exhaustion of energy of the ego engaged in intense defensive activities [p. 33].

Bibring concludes:

> The inhibition in depression . . . does not fall under either category . . . It is rather due to the fact that certain strivings of the person become meaningless—since the ego appears incapable ever to gratify them [p. 33].

Bibring implies his own explanation in his comparison of depression to anxiety:

> Anxiety as a reaction to (external or internal) danger indicates the ego's desire to survive. The ego, challenged by the danger, mobilizes the signal of anxiety and prepares for fight or flight. In depression, the opposite takes place, the ego is paralyzed because it finds itself incapable to meet the "danger." [In certain instances] . . . depression may follow anxiety, [and then] the mobilization of energy . . . [is] replaced by a decrease of self-reliance [pp. 34–35].

Thus Bibring's search for an economic explanation of depressive inhibition ends in the undefined term "decrease of self-reliance," which, as it stands, is not an economic concept.

Bibring followed his observations and constructions regardless of where they led him, and had the courage to stop where he did. Yet he opened up

new theoretical possibilities. It is to the discussion of these that I will turn
now.

XI

What does it mean that "the ego is paralyzed because it finds itself incapable to meet the 'danger' "? Clearly "paralyzed" refers to the state of helplessness, one of the corollaries of which is the "loss of self-esteem." The
danger is the potential loss of object; the traumatic situation is that of the
loss of object, "helplessness" as Bibring defines it is the persisting state of
loss of object. The anxiety signal anticipates the loss in order to prevent the
reactivation of the traumatic situation, that is, of panic-anxiety. Fluctuations of self-esteem anticipate, and initiate measures to prevent, the reactivation of the state of persisting loss of object, that is, of the state of helplessness involving loss of self-esteem. Thus the relation between fluctuations
of self-esteem and "helplessness" which is accompanied by loss of self-
esteem is similar to the relation between anxiety signal and panic-anxiety.
Fluctuations of self-esteem are then structured, tamed forms of and signals
to anticipate and to preclude reactivation of the state of helplessness.
Yet, according to the accepted theory, fluctuations of self-esteem are the
function of the superego's relation to the ego, just as anxiety was considered, prior to 1926, as a function of repression enforced by the superego. In
1926, however, superego anxiety was recognized as merely one kind of
anxiety and the *repression hence anxiety* relationship was reversed into *anxiety signal hence repression*. Bibring achieves an analogous reversal when
he formulates: ". . . it is our contention, based on clinical observation,
that it is the ego's awareness of its helplessness which in certain cases forces
it to turn the aggression from the object against the self, thus aggravating
and complicating the structure of depression" (p. 41). While in the accepted theory it is assumed that the aggression "turned round upon the
subject" *results* in passivity and helplessness, in Bibring's conception it is
the helplessness which is the *cause* of this "turning round."

Thus Bibring's theory opens two new vistas. One leads us to consider self-
esteem as a signal, that is, an ego function, rather than as an *ad hoc* effect
of the relation between the ego and the superego. The other suggests that
we reconsider the rôle of the ego, and particularly of its helplessness, in the
origin and function of the instinctual vicissitude called turning round upon
the subject.

The first of these, like Freud's structural theory of anxiety and Fenichel's
of guilt (1945, p. 135), leads to a broadening of our conception of the
ego's apparatuses and functions. The second is even more far-reaching: it
seems to go to the very core of the problem of aggression. We know that
"turning round upon the subject" was the basic mechanism Freud used before the "death-instinct theory" to explain the major forms in which aggres-

sion manifests itself. It was in connection with this "turning round upon the subject" that Freud wrote:

> . . . sadism . . . seems to press towards a quite special aim:—the infliction of pain, in addition to subjection and mastery of the object. Now psycho-analysis would seem to show that infliction of pain plays no part in the original aims sought by [sadism] . . . : the sadistic child takes no notice of whether or not it inflicts pain, nor is it part of its purpose to do so. But when once the transformation into masochism has taken place, the experience of pain is very well adapted to serve as a passive masochistic aim . . . Where once the suffering of pain has been experienced as a masochistic aim, it can be carried back into the sadistic situation and result in a sadistic aim of *inflicting pain* . . . [1915, pp. 71–72].

Thus Bibring's view that "turning round upon the subject" is brought about by helplessness calls attention to some of Freud's early formulations, and prompts us to re-evaluate our conception of aggression. Indeed, it may lead to a theory of aggression which is an alternative to those which have so far been proposed, namely Freud's death-instinct theory, Fenichel's frustration-aggression theory, and the Hartmann-Kris-Loewenstein theory of an independent aggressive instinctual drive.

XII

Let us return once more to the relation between helplessness (involving loss of self-esteem) and the simultaneously maintained narcissistic aspirations, noting that their intra-ego conflict assumed by Bibring may have been implied by Freud when he wrote in "Mourning and Melancholia": "A good, capable, conscientious [person] . . . is more likely to fall ill of [this] . . . disease than [one] . . . of whom we too should have nothing good to say" (1917, pp. 156–157).

Fenichel's summary of the accepted view of the fate of self-esteem in depression is:

> . . . a greater or lesser loss of self-esteem is in the foreground. The subjective formula is "I have lost everything; now the world is empty," if the loss of self-esteem is mainly due to a loss of external supplies, or "I have lost everything because I do not deserve anything," if it is mainly due to a loss of internal supplies from the superego [1945, p. 391].

Fenichel's implied definition of supplies reads: "The small child loses self-esteem when he loses love and attains it when he regains love . . . . children . . . need . . . narcissistic supplies of affection . . ." (1945, p. 41).

Though the term *supplies* has never been explicitly defined as a concept, it has become an apparently indispensable term in psychoanalysis, and particularly in the theory of depression. In Bibring's theory, supplies are the goals of narcissistic aspirations (p. 37). This gives them a central rôle in the theory, highlighting the urgent need to define them. Moreover, Bibring's comparison of depression and boredom hints at the direction in which such a definition might be sought by alerting us to the fact that there is a lack of supplies in boredom also. "Stimulus hunger" [1] is Fenichel's term for the immediate consequence of this lack: "Boredom is characterized by the co-existence of a need for activity and activity-inhibition, as well as by stimulus-hunger and dissatisfaction with the available stimuli" (1934, p. 349). Here adequate stimuli are the lacking supplies. Those which are available are either too close to the object of the repressed instinctual drive and thus are resisted, or they are too distant from it and thus hold no interest.

Bibring's juxtaposition of depression and boredom suggests that narcissistic supplies may be a special kind of adequate stimuli and narcissistic aspirations a special kind of stimulus hunger. The implications of this suggestion become clearer if we note that it is the lack of narcissistic supplies which is responsible for the structuralization of that primitive state of helplessness, the reactivation of which is, according to Bibring's theory, the essence of depression.

The conception which emerges if we pursue these implications of Bibring's theory is this: (1) The development of the ego requires the presence of "adequate stimuli," in this case love of objects; when such stimuli are consistently absent a primitive ego state comes into existence, the later reactivation of which is the state of depression. (2) Normal development lowers the intensity of this ego state and its potentiality for reactivation, and limits its reactivation to those reality situations to which grief and sadness are appropriate reactions. (3) Recurrent absence of adequate stimuli in the course of development works against the lowering of the intensity of this ego state and increases the likelihood of its being reactivated, that is to say, establishes a predisposition to depression.

This conception is consonant with present-day ego psychology and also elucidates the economic and the adaptive aspects of Bibring's theory. The rôle of stimulation in the development of ego structure is a crucial implication of the concept of adaptation. At the same time, since psychoanalytic theory explains the effects of stimulation in terms of changes in the distribution of attention cathexes, the rôle of stimulation in ego-structure development, to which I just referred, might well be the starting point for an understanding of the economics of the ego state of depression.

[1] [Also translated as "craving for stimulus" (Fenichel, 1922–36, p. 292)—Ed.]

XIII

This discussion of the structural, genetic, dynamic, economic, and adaptive aspects of Edward Bibring's theory gives us a glimpse of its fertility, but does not exhaust either its implications or the problems it poses. An attempt to trace more of these would require a detailed analysis of those points where Bibring's views shade into other findings and theories of psychoanalytic ego psychology, and is therefore beyond our scope tonight.

Instead, I would like to dwell in closing on three roots of Edward Bibring's theory which are less obvious than the observations and formulations so far discussed.

The first is its root in the technique of psychoanalysis. Bibring wrote:

> From a . . . therapeutic point of view one has to pay attention not only to the dynamic and genetic basis of the persisting narcissistic aspirations, the frustrations of which the ego cannot tolerate, but also the dynamic and genetic conditions which forced the infantile ego to become fixated to feelings of helplessness . . . . [the] major importance [of these feelings of helplessness] in the therapy of depression is obvious.[7]
>
> [7] This is to some degree in agreement with Karen Horney (1945) who stressed the necessity of analyzing not only the "conflicts," but also the hopelessness [p. 43].

This formulation seems to say nothing more than the well-known technical rule that "Analysis must always go on in the layers accessible to the ego at the moment" (Fenichel, 1938–39, p. 44). But it does say more, because it specifies that it is the helplessness, the lack of interest, and the lowered self-esteem which are immediately accessible in depression. It is safe to assume that the clinically observed accessibility of these was one of the roots of Bibring's theory.

A second root of the theory is in Bibring's critique of the English school of psychoanalysis. A study of this critique shows that on the one hand Bibring found some of this school's *observations* on depression sound and, like his own observations, incompatible with the accepted theory of depression; but on the other hand he found this school's *theory* of depression incompatible with psychoanalytic theory proper. It seems that Bibring intended his theory of depression to account for the sound observations of this school *within* the framework of psychoanalytic theory.

Finally, a third root of Bibring's theory seems to be related to the problems raised by the so-called "existential analysis." So far the only evidence for Edward Bibring's interest in and critical attitude toward "existential analysis" is in the memories of those people who discussed the subject with him. Though his interest in phenomenology is obvious in his paper on depression, his interest in existentialism proper is expressed in only a few passages, like: "[Depression] is—essentially—'a human way of reacting to frustration and misery' whenever the ego finds itself in a state of (real or imaginary) helplessness against 'overwhelming odds' " (p. 36). Bibring's intent seems to have been to put the sound observations and psychologically relevant concepts of "existential analysis" into the framework of psychoanalytic ego psychology.

XIV

The measures of a theoretician's stature are the range of his interests; his simultaneous responsiveness to empirical evidence, to theoretical consistency, and to existing alternative theories; his courage to follow his constructions even if they cannot entirely bridge the chasm over which he extends them; and the originality and stimulating power of his thought. By these measures Edward Bibring is one of the few real psychoanalytic theoreticians.

In presenting this discussion of "The Mechanism of Depression"—which I organized on the metapsychological pattern—I intended to demonstrate not only the importance of Edward Bibring's theory of depression, and not only its place in the contemporary developments of psychoanalytic theory. I intended also to reflect the multiplicity of observations, theories, historical and general considerations which Edward Bibring responded to and integrated in his theory of depression.

Our picture of Edward Bibring's achievement would, however, be inadequate if we did not take account of his human achievement, which pervades all the rest. Scientific achievements are human achievements. Psychoanalysts, when looking at a psychological theory as a human achievement, discover its motivation and hence are prone to suspect its objective validity. If this were justified there could be no valid theory: all our theories are the products of motivated human thought. There is little doubt about what provided the immediate motivation for Edward Bibring's theory of depression. He faced the devastating blows of a destructive illness and transformed them into scientific discovery. The motivation of a valid theory need not be different from that of an invalid theory. What they do differ in is the control the theorist has over his motivation. The scientist who develops an invalid theory takes a short cut to the goal of his motivation: he indulges in wishful thinking. The scientist who develops a valid theory takes the detours which are necessary to test and to modify the goals he is motivated to pursue in accordance with observation and existing theory.

Edward Bibring was aware of his motivation and tested it by choosing the detour. His work is a major contribution to psychoanalytic theory and his human achievement is a monument to the power of the human mind.

REFERENCES

Abraham, K. (1924). A Short Study of the Development of the Libido, Viewed in the Light of Mental Disorders. *Selected Papers.* London: Hogarth Press, 1948, pp. 418–501.

Bibring, E. (1953). The Mechanism of Depression. In *Affective Disorders,* ed. P. Greenacre. New York: International Universities Press, pp. 13–48.

Erikson, E. H. (1950). *Childhood and Society.* New York: Norton.

Fenichel, O. (1922–36). *Collected Papers,* Vol. I. New York: Norton, 1953.

—— (1934). On the Psychology of Boredom. In *Organization and Pathology of Thought,* ed. & tr. D. Rapaport. New York: Columbia University Press, 1951, pp. 349–361.

—— (1938–39). *Problems of Psychoanalytic Technique.* Albany, N. Y.: Psychoanalytic Quarterly, Inc., 1941.

—— (1945). *The Psychoanalytic Theory of Neurosis.* New York: Norton.

Freud, S. (1911). Formulations Regarding the Two Principles in Mental Functioning. *Collected Papers,* 4:13–21. New York: Basic Books, 1959.

—— (1915). Instincts and Their Vicissitudes. *Collected Papers,* 4:60–83. New York: Basic Books, 1959.

—— (1917 [1915]). Mourning and Melancholia. *Collected Papers,* 4:152–170. New York: Basic Books, 1959.

—— (1926 [1925]). *The Problem of Anxiety,* tr. H. A. Bunker. New York: Psychoanalytic Quarterly & Norton, 1936.

Horney, K. (1945). *Our Inner Conflicts.* New York: Norton.

Lewin, B. D. (1950). *The Psychoanalysis of Elation.* New York: Norton.

60

IN MEMORIAM

Bela Mittelmann (October 2, 1900–October 4, 1959)

We are gathered for a gesture of parting. To take leave of a man who was part of our lives. We know we are trying the impossible, and yet we know we have done it before. We gather, join in a ritual to attempt the impossible and yet inevitable. We are of a generation which lost its innocence, and many of us are of a profession which is the least innocent of its generation. We know we are gathered for a magical gesture. But we know also that the knowledge which is our pride becomes our bane and shame when, instead of mastering our feelings, it robs us of them. So we gather unashamed to console and to be consoled by the magic gestures of joining together and parting.

We listen to the words of the Bible. To the innocent they bring the promise of the grace and mercy of a heavenly father. But to all of us who will listen, they bring the consoling magic of ancient words of wisdom whispering to the frightened child who still lives in each of us craving for paternal shelter. Bela Mittelmann grew up steeped in the Jewish tradition. He remained true to this tradition, and felt that it contained his roots, that it told him where he belonged. He cherished the magic of the Bible, and his sense

---

Read at the memorial service held on October 7, 1959. Published here for the first time.

774

of belonging to his wandering people was the backdrop against which he lived his life to the end, when he had long since stripped off all comfortable belief in a vigilant almighty father.

But what is the magic we are seeking when we gather here? Magic against what and for what? It is magic to reassure us in the face of the chilling touch of what awaits us all. It is magic against the general loss the poet spoke of: "Every man's death diminishes me, for I am involved in mankind." But for those of us who knew Bela, it is more than that. It is the magic to fight off the impoverishment we have suffered by his loss. And we follow the ancient ritual of enumerating all that he was to us to see whether we can keep some of it alive in ourselves by giving it to others, now that he is no longer here to give it to us.

What should be singled out first of the many things Bela Mittelmann was and gave to us? This choice is difficult. And this difficulty is the first thing about Bela: he was a man of many sides. A tender and warm husband, father, and friend—yet undemanding, not smothering, not excessively attentive. A devoted doctor and psychoanalyst, but not a zealot of his craft, and, however steeped in and successful in his practice, he was always ready for new ventures and always had time to meet people or to go to see something he had just heard about. Though a man of research throughout his general medical, psychiatric, and psychoanalytic practice, in this our age of specialized research designs and teamwork, he was the general practitioner of research who pioneered in new areas with his own eyes and ears his main tools. He even handled his camera himself. He wrote to me once, speaking about his work: "You can get with a jeep where you cannot get with a Rolls Royce." Devoted to psychoanalysis, he did not hesitate to cross the lines into psychosomatic medicine, psychology, and other disciplines, and had the courage to cross and recross the lines of the different schools of psychoanalysis without abandoning the main line or scorning the dissidents. He always taught: in the New York Psychoanalytic Institute, at Cornell, at City College, at Columbia, at Flower, at Bellevue, at Einstein, at Bronx Municipal, at conventions, and through the two editions of his widely used book. But family, practice, research, theory, and teaching even together did not exhaust the varied interests and the indefatigable zest for experience of our slow-moving and soft-spoken friend. He loved the company of people, and many of us gratefully remember that he was as good at getting us to talk and at listening to us as he was at talking himself. But neither his talk nor his interests were limited to the shoptalk he loved. He could listen with equal interest to politics, literature, music, movies, theatre, the shoptalk of scientists in other fields, and everyday things. He and his wife counted among their friends people from a wide variety of professions and occupations. He loved to listen and to learn, and he preferred to learn from hearing rather than from reading. He was an eager listener to and purveyor of information—the information without which in our complex society we would be lost babes in the woods. He loved to hear good stories and to tell them with a bland understatement. And this is still not all: he was a traveler who knew this country, Europe, Israel and its kibbutzim. He was a walker, and for many years an avid tennis player; he was a birdwatcher, a lover of the stage, movies, and music. He knew poetry, and not only his beloved Hungarian poets whom he liked to recite for hours and the German classics, but many of the English and even the newest of them as well. I remember our attempts to make sense of Dylan Thomas whom both of us liked.

And yet, however unlimited his curiosity and zest were, their claim for first place in our image of Bela is contested by his unassuming and undemanding simplicity. It was his undemandingness which kept him free of self-righteousness and self-pity when fighting for what he found to be empirically true against theoretical preconceptions. His simplicity was behind the unself-conscious way in which he wore all the riches of his interests. But how can one man be so many things? Is it just the magic of "de mortuis nil nisi bonum" that makes us think of him thus? Or is it to induce others to speak of us likewise when the hour comes? Or was it because he flirted with all these interests without marrying any of them? I think none of these is the explanation. Bela loved to live, to experience, to know, and he loved to teach and to help. These were more important to him than his ambitions and his wish for success and acceptance. He was neither Pope nor Gray Eminence of any orthodoxy—in his love and devotion to his therapeutic work he did not select the patient for his brand of therapy but searched for the therapy fitting his patient. He was not a theoretician, yet in his work he reached a synthesis of the therapeutic currents of our time. He was not a brilliant speaker, but his real urge to teach opened eyes, sparked thought, and spread understanding. He was not the great discoverer—but his deep curiosity and open eye always led him to discoveries, at least one of which, his study of motility, has the earmarks of brilliance, and all of which are substantial contributions to knowledge, free of false glitter. And if there are more knowledgeable birdwatchers, travelers, connoisseurs of poetry, drama, and music than he, there cannot be many who enjoy these more than he did or who convey to others as much of these as he did.

In our time when, driven by competition or ambition, most of us come to know more and more about less and less, and many cover a lack of general interest and knowledge by one flimsy glitter or another, our quiet, slow-moving friend whose eyes were full of childlike curiosity barely concealed by his half-closed eyelids, remained involved in man, his pursuits, and the world he lives in.

This was the unique color of the man we part from today. And we are much diminished and impaired by losing him because he was interested in us and in what interested us. We felt he could afford this because he had come into his own and was rooted in it. How fatherly this was, and how motherly the unobtrusive form of his interest I do not find the words for.

But it is somewhere around this point that the contradictions of Bela's slow tempo and inexhaustible zest, his widely scattered interests and his solid achievements, his tender caring and his undemandingness, resolve themselves into the harmony we felt around him.

This richness is what he leaves for each of us to choose from, to remember, and to grow on, each according to his own lights. There is nothing we can give him any more—we can give only to those who are still around us; so that when the hour comes for them to part from us, they too can cull sustenance from what we have given them.

As a child I misunderstood the meaning of the ancient Jewish prayer for the dead. Not only did I think that its first words referred to the departed one rather than to a heavenly father, but I also thought it said that the name and memory of the departed should grow and be hallowed in us. This misunderstanding remains my inner understanding of it to this day, and in this understanding I will say from all of us for Bela,

"Yisgadal v'yiskadash sh'mey rabah."

61

THE THEORY OF ATTENTION CATHEXIS

An Economic and Structural Attempt at the Explanation of Cognitive Processes

This manuscript, which was clearly written in haste
and never revised, certainly does not have the form
and precision it would have had if Rapaport had prepared it for publication. It is nevertheless published
here because it is the only comprehensive statement
on attention cathexis which we have by Rapaport,
and is the sweeping blueprint of theory which underlay his program of experimentation on attention
cathexis, interrupted by his death. The work has been
continued by some of his associates, and one of them,
Dr. Fred Schwartz, has kindly helped clarify some
points. I have made a few alterations in the text, but
only concerning points about which it seemed possible to express a little more clearly what Rapaport had
in mind—M. M. G.

This paper, written in 1959, is published here for the first time.

778

I. THE NECESSITY TO DEVELOP SUCH AN ATTEMPT

The adaptive character of the veridical cognitive processes has never been questioned, although the nature of the genetic and contemporary conditions which guarantee this has never been unequivocally clarified. The rôle of primary and secondary autonomy versus the imposition of adaptiveness by the impact of the external world upon the nonveridical primary processes is still an open problem. Indeed, the clarification of the latter problem apparently involves both structural and economic considerations of the sort I am about to treat of here.

The genetic aspect of cognitive processes is a central consideration to psychoanalysis, as well as to developmental psychology in general and Piaget's in particular. Moreover, all the learning theories have been considered by G. Allport and other psychologists to be genetic and reductionist in character, and even though psychoanalysis in essence cannot regard them as genetic since they postulate no interaction between innate givens and experience forming a complementary series, still, even Hartmann and Kris (1945, p. 16) have erroneously considered them as relevant to the explanation of cognitive development. From the genetic point of view the relative rôle in development of structures given in advance and those later acquired is a particularly crucial question. Here too, as with the adaptive consideration, the economic and structural issues which are here my principal concern must be included. Of course both processes and structures are involved in both genetic and adaptive considerations.

· The dynamic attempts at a theory of cognition, which include the S-R theories as well as my attempt in *Emotions and Memory* (1942), may well be considered failures since they did not manage to express cognition and motivation in the same dimensions and thus also failed to give an account of the persistence, that is, nonextinction, of "structures" established by conditioning. It is precisely to account for these that I have repeatedly attempted to formulate an economic and structural conception of cognition by expanding and extrapolating from the Freudian theory of *attention cathexis* (Freud, 1900) and from the Hartmannian conceptions of *automatization* and *secondary autonomy* (Hartmann, 1939).

II. THE TASKS FACING SUCH AN ATTEMPT

First of all, such an attempt is predicated on the proposition that it is necessary to express (quantify) both process and structure variables in terms of a single dimension. That is to say, such an attempt is conceived for the purpose of exploring whether or not structures can be expressed in the dimension of cathexes. In other words, structures are assumed to be cathexes organized under very specific conditions of restriction (binding).

Second, such an attempt is predicated on the proposition that it is necessary to break down the perception-cognition dichotomy. If perception and also "immediate memory" (span) are to be conceived of in terms of attention cathexes, then long-range memory and the learning processes which bring it into existence too must be conceived of in terms of attention cathexes, though the rôle of the already existing structures may be different in one than in the other.

Third, such an attempt is to bridge the gap between those associations which are measured by association tests on the one hand—whose great strength and high stability are attested to both by clinical experience and by experiment—and the associations built in the course of learning experiments and recent experience on the other. The question here is whether the high stability of the former is indeed accountable for in terms of the frequency of contiguous occurrence or reinforcement.

Fourth, such an attempt is to find a variable which accounts for both the trial (work) and achievement (performance) criteria of learning, that is to say, for the individual differences in learning. It may seem that this is an excessive demand since, like *intelligence, learning* too may involve the total genetic history of the individual. But unlike intelligence, learning seems to be a somewhat better defined concept and its customary experimental tests are not so inadequate as the intelligence tests are of *intelligence.* The fact that in an identical number of trials different individuals reach different degrees of achievement, the fact that identical achievements of different individuals require different numbers of trials, and the fact that both in identical numbers of trials and in identical achievements the rate of forgetting (that is, the relative stability of the effect or result of learning) varies from individual to individual, cry out for a new variable (or rather, new variables) which could reduce the chaos of these variations by establishing functional relationships among them.

Fifth, such an attempt should account theoretically for the ubiquitous experience of subjective effort in learning as well as in the forming of abstractions. It is not that effortless learning and sudden insight as bona fide observations should be questioned or disregarded. Indeed, the experiences of effort, effortless acquisition, and sudden insight must be accounted for within the framework of one theory. Nor is it necessary in general that a subjective experience should be a crucial reflection of the processes that underlie a conscious experience of which one aspect is the subjective experience in question. It is rather that on the one hand subjective effort seems to be a very general experience accompanying learning, and on the other this aspect of experience does not seem to be accounted for by the familiar theories of learning.

Sixth, it is possible that such an attempt will find the subjective experience of effort in learning to be explainable by motivations. But these motivations will then have to be distinguished from the motivations that follow the psychoanalytic model of motivations, namely the instinctual drives. These motivations would not have a *spontaneous* rise to threshold intensity and a peremptoriness once that intensity was reached. They would have their origin in instructions and/or encounters with external stimulation (e.g., material to be learned or task to be performed). They may or may not reach threshold (or it would perhaps be better to say: full) intensity before action on the objects has progressed a way. Lewin's (Zeigarnik, 1927; Ovsiankina, 1928) experiments suggest that the intensity of these motivations will abate (leak away) spontaneously with passing time. Moreover, they seem to suggest that, after interruption, these motivations, unlike instinctual drives, do not *seek out* their object but are triggered only by renewed encounter with these objects. (It would be interesting to find out— if an experiment to this effect could be designed—what the effects of the instructions would be if no beginning of task performance—and interruption—occurred.) In this respect, then, these motivations would be akin to Piaget's "desirability" (the only motivational concept which he owns *systematically*) which too is triggered into existence and action by the encounter with objects which, since the schemata are not accommodated to them and have not assimilated them, disequilibrate the schemata, i.e., bring about "desirability." Dr. Peter Wolff and I have used for these motivations the term "short-range forces." How the relationship of the long-range and short-range forces implies the concept of neutralization—and indeed whether or not it implies it—is a problem to be solved, and it is one of the obligations of the following attempt to account for this relationship.

Seventh, since this attempt should apply equally to perception and cognition, the differing fates of what G. Klein (1959) calls focal and incidental perception should also be accounted for by it. The cohesive and synthesized (rationalized) character of the *focally perceived* should be explained by the same variables which explain the fragmented, displaced, and distorted character of the *incidentally perceived*.

III. THE CONCEPTION OF ATTENTION CATHEXIS

(1) Internal and external excitation can become conscious only if it is hypercathected by what will be termed here attention cathexis.

(2) Nothing can be perceived—whether such perception is indicated by the consensually validated consciousness of the perceived or by the symptoms consisting of impingements upon other cognitive experiences—without its being so hypercathected. Thus attention cathecting does not per se guarantee consciousness or the form of conscious appearance of the internal or external excitation.

(3) Internal excitations, i.e., motives and their ideational representations, also require hypercathecting, thus attention cathexis is not equivalent to motivation at large.

(4) Attention cathexis—in first approximation—is available only in a determinate quantity.

(5) This determinate quantity varies with ego states. Drug states, sleep

states, pathological and exceptional states, etc., alter the quantity available. States of anxiety and other states of acute defense diminish it, states of indifference tend to increase it relatively.

(6) Whether there is only one "pool" of this determinate quantity, or whether there are additional reservoirs of it which under certain conditions are mobilizable, is quite unclear so far. Phenomena of concentration and warm-up suggest an explanation by *mobilization*. But it is unclear whether this mobilization should be conceived as: (a) from other reserve pools; (b) from a generally distributed attention cathexis which would be thus "stored" in small quantities in every "representation" (idea); (c) from the single cathectic pool by concentration on a given internal or external excitation; (d) from the single cathectic pool conceived as many small pools which prima facie form one surface but, after the "drainage" of a determinate amount, appear as separated pools the contents of which have to be specifically mobilized; (e) from mobilization due to "natural" replacement; (f) from mobilization due to the process of structure building (to be discussed further below).

(7) Since there is only a determinate quantity of attention cathexis available at any given time, there is competition for it among internal excitations, among external excitations, and between internal and external excitations. This competition results in a complementarity between the attention cathexis of "focal" and "incidental" excitations. There seems to be evidence to show that it also results in diminished availability of attention cathexis for excitations following others, as well as in a "drawing off" of attention cathexis from excitations by subsequent excitations. There also seems to be, however, evidence to show that competition (distraction) under certain conditions increases rather than decreases the attention cathecting of the focal excitation, or at least leaves it undiminished (possibly by an isolation mechanism or in the latter case by a different threshold-heightening process called adaptation in physiology).

(8) Attention cathexis is conceived as psychological energy under highly specialized structural conditions. It is possible that it can be conceived as analogous to a *relatively closed system* under conditions of high entropy, the excitations impinging upon which reduce this high entropy while the system itself tends to reinstate its high level of entropy. From another angle, the whole system might be conceived of as a grid, the changes upon which control the discharge of the low-entropy energies of the whole open system in relation to which it forms a relatively closed system. But in this case the system in question would include not only the *superordinate sense organ consciousness* which operates by the economics of the distribution of attention cathexes, but also the related defensive and stimulus-barrier structures which safeguard the relative closedness of the system.

(9) The attention cathexes—and probably their entropic tendency in particular—are a crucial factor in the synthetic functions of the ego in so

far as they pertain to cognition in general and to conscious cognition in particular.

(10) Attention cathexes are a specialized kind of hypercathexis, and thus a draining of the hypercathectic "pool" should diminish the availability of attention cathexes. Instances of this are: (a) an acute conflict situation or an exacerbation of a chronic one which makes extensive demands on hypercathexes to reinforce or to build defensive structures in an attempt to "solve" the conflict situation (this instance will be further discussed below); (b) since action too (except if highly automatized—a possibility to be discussed further below) is also assumed to require hypercathexes, complex actions making high demands for hypercathecting should also decrease the hypercathectic pool; (c) special states such as sleep, drug states, etc., draining the hypercathectic pool should also decrease the availability of attention cathexes.

(11) Attention cathexes hypercathecting an external or an internal excitation will in general dissipate from that excitation (in keeping with their entropic tendency) in the course of time, unless particular structural conditions prevent such "leakage."

(12) New excitations (both temporally recent and spatially-qualitatively contrasting) will tend to command attention cathexes, probably in part because of the leakage of cathexes from the previous ones and in part because of the rise of excitation thresholds for the previous as well as for the "background" excitations against which they stand out as contrasting.

(13) Other factors being equal, drive representations or other motivation-relevant representations are the more likely to win out in the competition for attention cathexes the stronger the motivation in question is, provided these motivations are not defended against, i.e., are not countercathected.

(14) It is to be assumed from the effect of the synthetic functions observable in dreams, reveries, hallucinations, etc., that some sort of attention cathecting does occur in these states also. The very fact of the existence of these states of *consciousness* points to the same conclusion. The fact that in these states the function of attention cathexes seems to differ from the "normal waking state" function may have its explanation in one or several of the following: (a) attention-cathexis function itself is unchanged, but either the changed relation to external excitation (as in sleep or hypnosis) or the changed relation to internal excitation (as in hallucinosis) explains the changed effect of attention cathecting; (b) more generally, a change of structural conditions (and this would or at least could subsume [a] above) may alter the effect of attention cathecting, though the attention cathexes are not different nor is the cathectic function different from those of "normal waking state"; (c) attention cathexes of differing degrees of neutralization are involved in each of these "states of consciousness"; that is, we would postulate a different attention-cathectic pool for different hierarchic

levels of the psychic structure, with corresponding levels of neutralization; (d) it is possible, however, to assume that both originally neutral and progressively neutralized attention cathexes exist.

(15) The proposition of attention cathexes existing as neutral energies from the first on is a necessary one if Peter Wolff's (1959) observations on infants (showing that [a] from the first hours of life the infant is capable of auditory and visual pursuit, but this pursuit occurs only when the infant is in a state that he labels *alert inactivity,* which he can describe and define operationally by predicting that on exposing moving objects to the infant visual pursuit will ensue [likewise for auditory stimulation]; [b] from the first, states of alert inactivity, alert activity, waking restless states [need states], drowsiness, and sleep states can be discriminated in the infant) are to be explained within the framework of this theory. Moreover, this theory should be able to account for the expansion of the length of time of both alert inactivity and alert activity, and for the contraction of drowsy states, sleep states, and restless states within the day of the infant. It is also to account for the progressively lessening inflexibility and distractibility in states of alert activity.

IV. ATTENTION CATHEXES AND STRUCTURES

(1) It is assumed that structures are activated only by becoming cathected and particularly only when they are also hypercathected: executive structures must be hypercathected even when they are drive cathected in order to execute drive action, and ideational structures must be attention cathected even if they are drive representations, that is, are drive cathected, in order to become conscious.

(2) It is assumed that under conditions of autonomy (with the restriction that such autonomy is always relative) attention cathecting alone may activate structures. But considering the relativity of autonomy, the "motivation"-free activation of structures is a state of affairs which must be considered to obtain only in a first approximation.

(3) It is assumed that fully automatized executive apparatuses may execute drive action without being hypercathected (attention cathected)—as, for instance, in a slip of the tongue—but it is also assumed that such occurrences are only in a first approximation free of being hypercathected (attention cathected) since automatization is never quite complete, just as autonomy is never absolute.

(4) It is assumed that prolonged or repeated attention cathecting of excitations will bring about a reduction of the tendency of cathexes to dissipate from a cathected position, stated in III. (8) and (11). (This dissipation tendency is demonstrated in digit-span tests and measured in the Peterson and Peterson experiment. The reduction of this dissipation tendency is demonstrated in all forgetting curves—decay curves—in that they show a

decay distributed over a longer time span than the Peterson and Peterson (1959) decay curve for immediate [one trial] memory [learning].) But the dissipation reduction by prolonged or repeated cathecting has not so far been measured directly and the modification of the design of the Peterson and Peterson experiment by Peter Schiller is fraught with a systematic flaw, while that by Rapaport appears unwieldy.[1] A measurement of this process is one of the urgent necessities for the theory, and a new access to it must be found or else the Rapaport design must be executed in spite of its unwieldiness.

(5) The reduction of dissipation tendency is termed structuralization or automatization. It is assumed that there are gradations of structuralization (as between a digit series in the digit-span test which is dissipated just as soon as it is repeated, the short-range remembering after cramming, and the long-range remembering labeled, e.g., "knowledge"), but it is not clear whether these gradations should be considered continuous or discrete. This problem will not be solved until much finer measures pertaining to structuralization than those developed in the study of learning become available. Indeed, it is likely that not before the same problem of continuous or discrete gradation is solved for attention cathexes will this problem of structuralization become amenable to investigation.

(6) Structuralization is also termed binding, since it is assumed that structures arise when the dissipation tendency of cathexes is reduced. The cathexes which are thus prevented from dissipating are called bound cathexes, in contrast to displaceable cathexes. But the situation is complicated by the hypothesis that one must distinguish mobile and neutralized cathexes which are both displaceable types of cathexes in contrast to bound cathexes. It is not even clear whether the displaceability of neutralized cathexes is less than that of mobile cathexes, though this does seem to be so. The problem arises because Freud contrasted only displaceable and bound cathexes, failing to distinguish between those structural conditions which reduce the entropic immediate discharge tendency, and thus neutralize cathexes, from those structural conditions which reduce the displaceability of cathexes and thus render them bound. There is a great deal of unclarity about whether or not it should be assumed that mobile cathexes too can be bound (and not only neutralized, e.g., attention cathexes). This is a conceptual problem and the study of defense structures does suggest that in them mobile cathexes may have been bound, i.e., structuralized. But whether or not this is the most economic conceptualization of this point is not at all clear.[2]

---

[1] [This problem has still not been solved. In one experiment, Dr. Schwartz found evidence that structure building decreases cathectic energy available for other (subsequent) mental activity. However, the findings are open to another interpretation, using the concept of automatization—Ed.]

[2] [Rapaport seems to be asking whether mobile (drive) cathexes must first be neutral-

(7) Automatization is assumed to be a structuralization of internal excitations or reactions to external excitations, resulting in a structure which can be activated by excitations other than those whose hypercathecting originally gave rise to the structure in question. These automatized structures are as a rule characterized by a high degree of simplification (in Hebb's [1949] terms all the dispensable—presumably genetically attached—elements are "fractionated" out of them) and particularly all conscious dispensable links are eliminated from them. Thus they lose specificity, gain generality and generalizability. (Erikson's [1937] estrangement of modes from their zonal origin and Hartmann's [1950] instinctual vicissitudes turning first into mechanisms of defense and later into means of adaptation here meet the problems of generalization and transfer of academic psychology and Piaget's coordination of higher-order schemata. Example: the child who is finding it impossible to get the chain out of the match box which is open only ⅛ of an inch, tries, tries, and then begins to open his mouth, close it, open it, and then suddenly for the first time enlarges the opening of the match box with his finger.

(8) Structure building is assumed always to require prolonged or repeated cathecting. That this formulation too is a first approximation is clear from the relative character of the terms "prolonged" and "repeated," and will be discussed further below. The necessity for "prolonged" and "repeated" cathecting is assumed to imply that cathecting by great amounts of cathexis is required as one of the conditions for structure building, that is, for preventing the dissipation tendency of cathexes. Further conditions will be discussed below and probably yet others will have to be sought for. The relevant problems of rate of cathecting and rate of dissipation are crucial, and their empirical assessment is one of the urgent tasks. The problem of rate of cathecting requires new methods of approach. The problem of dissipation rate has been discussed above in connection with the Peterson and Peterson (1959) type of experiments, and the massed versus distributed practice problems are also relevant to it, though the latter bring in new problems, to be discussed in (9).

(9) The natural dissipation rate of cathexes from structures of varying degrees of crystallization (automatization) is assumed to be enhanced by neighboring (preceding or subsequent) structure formation which makes a demand upon the determinate amount (limited quantity) of cathexes available. Our literature studies on retroactive inhibition, Richard O. Rouse's (1959) empirical study of proactive inhibition, our literature studies of incidental learning—particularly Bahrick (1957; Bahrick, Noble, and Fitts, 1954; Bahrick and Shelly, 1958) and Postman (1955)—and Peter Schiller's (1962) experiments in incidental learning are examples in point. But

---

ized and perhaps whether this is a partial reduction of their displaceability which is binding. In other words, can mobile (drive) cathexes be bound directly without an intermediate transformation to neutralized? For the distinction between mobile and neutralized energy in Freud, see Gill (1963, p. 14)—Ed.]

this point is amenable to generalization: structure building will disturb neighboring processes and structures, because it will make a demand on (drain) the available attention cathexes. An example in point is the disturbance in the postcritical series observed in the Townsend-Rapaport experiment, and also the incidental observation of Fred Schwartz concerning the tendency of repeated digits (in digit series longer than 9 items) in our digit-span experiments to "intrude."

(10) It is assumed that another condition for the reduction of the dissipation tendency of cathexes once employed so as to achieve binding, i.e., structure formation (besides the use of it in great quantity), is the relationship building or the existence of a relationship between the excitation that is being hypercathected and other already existing structure or structures. Examples of the rôle in structure building of relationships to existing structures may be found in the learning experiments utilizing Noble's (1952) "m," or the categories used in clustering experiments, or learning experiments using association-strength norms derived from association tests. The process of relationship building is, however, extremely poorly understood and seems to be a much slower process of reducing the dissipation rate.

(11) It is assumed that relations to existing structures mediate the displacement of attention cathexes to structures abuilding. But we do not have clear assumptions distinguishing and deciding between the following possibilities and their relations: (a) the attention cathexes of the "pool" need no such mediation and can by themselves, though at a slow rate, achieve binding; (b) the attention cathexes of the pool achieve by cathecting an excitation only an equivalent of the digit-span test achievement, or perhaps what Rock calls "familiarity," both of which may be extremely fleeting (unless they simply activate already existing structures or change such while activating them) and they suffice quantitatively for this purpose; (c) the attention-cathexis "pool" is sufficient for the function described in (b) only, and additional cathexes from subpools or idea reservoirs (for these see III. [6]) may be mobilized by relationship building. It is possible, however, that this conception of the rôle of relation building or relationships existing between the excitation which is being structuralized and structures already in existence is erroneous, and the relationships tie the invested cathexes (or part of them) into a (relatively) closed system of energy distributions and thereby reduce their dissipation rate.

(12) It is assumed (and implied in the above uses of the term structure) that structures are processes of a slow rate of change (bound cathexes). In keeping with IV. (8) above, structures should be classifiable according to their rate of change and these rates of change will form a transition between processes and structures (whether this is a continuous transition or one of discrete steps is not clear). Indeed, what will appear as a structure in relation to processes of a faster rate of change will appear as a process in relation to structures of a greater degree of stability.

(13) It is assumed that once great amounts of cathexes have been in-

vested and structure building has occurred, only a small amount of the cathexes invested in the course of structure building will be "bound" in the
established structure and the rest of the invested cathexes will be given off.
It is possible to account for the mobilization discussed in IV. (8) and (12)
by assuming that, in the course of learning and perceiving, partial structures
are built and it is the giving off of the cathexes initially invested in them
which will appear as phenomena corresponding to the term "mobilization."
Whether this is an alternative or a complementary assumption in relation to
those referred to above, and which combination of them will account for
the phenomena most adequately and economically, cannot even be guessed
at, at this point.

(14) It is assumed that the structures activated by cathecting retain part
of the cathexes invested upon them and give them off (dissipate them) only
according to a determinate rate corresponding to their structural strength.
This assumption might explain the "recency," "tuning," or priming phenomena Russell (1955), Storms (1958), Postman, and Osgood speak
about.[3] Indeed, if it is considered that motivations command attention cathexes according to their intensity, and if it is assumed that under conditions of high motivation structures will be invested to a high degree with
attention cathexes, it may be that while the usual rate of investment of these
structures with cathexes and the rate of dissipation of these cathexes may
remain characteristic for these structures and dependent upon their
"strength" (stability), nevertheless the actual activation of these structures
and the achievement effects of such activation will not depend on the
"strength" (stability) of these structures but rather on the level of motivation, and therefore no functional relationship between learning and strength
of association will be found, as it was not found by Russell and his pupils
(Russell, 1955) in many instances. The model presented here treats strong
motivation as a condition which can bring about such a state of affairs.
There must exist a variety of other such conditions, and it is possible that
the model given here will encompass them once they are isolated from Russell's, Storms's, etc., material. Similar considerations may apply to backward associations.

(15) It is assumed that structures activated by attention cathecting are
also modified and further stabilized thereby, while structures disused—not
cathected for long periods—lose their degree of stability and cohesiveness.
No assumption can be made so far about whether or not these changes are
accompanied by increase or decrease (respectively) in energy bound in
these structures. Yet this conception is parallel with Piaget's "aliment" conception and with my generalization of it which I termed "stimulus-
nutriment." It is also assumed that "alimented" structures (schemata) do
provide aliment for others; some reasons for this assumption I have mar-
shalled in the paper in which I proposed the just-mentioned generalization
(1957). An intriguing experimental possibility presents itself here if "tun-

[3] [See Schwartz and Rouse (1961) for a detailed discussion of this topic—Ed.]

ing" or "priming" through mediated associations can be demonstrated and the O'Neil experiments (see Russell, 1955) may already even be such demonstrations. The whole problem of mediated generalization is pertinent here.

(16) It is assumed that abstractions are structures in this sense, and indeed automatized structures of a higher order. Higher-order structures of this sort are not well understood. Yet the many analogies between abstractions, schemata, phase sequences (Hebb, 1949), and structures suggest that we are dealing here with different approaches to the same subject matter rather than with mere analogies. My various treatments of defense and identification structures as higher-order structures of great economy and low cathectic requirement are relevant here also, and link this issue to the point discussed in III. (8) above as well as in my review of N. Wiener's *Cybernetics* (Rapaport, 1950). Irving Paul's (1959) schema experiments and his finding on styles in memory function are also relevant here, and possibly also David Elkind's (1961) replications of Piaget's studies of the quantity concept.

V. ATTENTION CATHEXES, STRUCTURES, AND MOTIVATIONS

(1) It is assumed that attention cathexis, just like structure and motivation, is a concept arrived at by abstraction from observations of behavior. Since motivation and structure, just like attention cathexis, conceptualize ubiquitous aspects of behavior, we should not be able to speak of attention cathexes and their function except in relation to structures and motivations.

(2) Yet so little is known about structures, and so much is unknown about motivation, and finally, so much about their function can be understood only in their "interaction" with attention cathexes, that if we were obliged to follow (1) above we would have to contend all the time with three interacting independent variables.

(3) In such situations, science performs an abstraction and attempts to isolate the variables. This is, naturally, feasible only in a first approximation. Abstractions are developed. Inferences are made and then conditions sought under which the variables can, in a first crude approximation, be considered independent.

(4) The postulates and the observations in regard to autonomy permit us to hope that in some learning processes attention cathexes and structures may be studied in isolation from motivations. Naturally the ultimate goal, once the "independent" rules of functioning of attention cathexes are established, is that the rules of their actual functioning in relation to motivation will be investigated. Thus it is a tactical and not a strategic theoretical consideration which leads us to studies under the postulate of independence.

(5) The observations concerning digit span and vigilance experiments

permit us to assume that in them or by means of them (note Peterson and Peterson, 1959) the function of attention cathexes may be studied relatively free of structural restrictions and/or mobilization facilitated by structures, and simultaneously under relatively autonomous conditions, i.e., relatively free of motivational variations. It is to be expected that yet other conditions will be discovered (and corresponding techniques for their exploration) in which the function of attention cathexes can be studied in "independence" of structure and motivation.

(6) However, even these "independence" studies must begin to investigate the structure development by "binding." Both the Townsend-Rapaport preliminary experiment with the "critical series" and the experiment Dr. Schwartz is preparing on the retention of digit series longer than the subject's digit span and in the learning of the same are aimed at this goal (Schwartz and Schiller, research report).[4]

(7) It is intended that the motivational variable too will be studied in relation to attention cathexes and structures in due time. Indeed, the motivational implications of *all* intentional learning will force us not only to study competition for attention cathexes of two different incidental tasks in the absence of intentional tasks, but also to begin varying the motivation both in the way Bahrick (1954; Bahrick, Fitts, and Rankin, 1952) did it and in the way Russell and his pupils (Rosenberg, 1958) varied it to affect incidental learning. Clearly, in this connection both those motivations which Lewin (1922, 1926) termed "readinesses" and those he termed "quasi needs" will have to be studied. Schiller's (research report) pursuit-rotor experiment with the increasing difficulty level of the pursuit task may have automatically introduced a motivational variation which must be studied and isolated.[5]

(8) It is in keeping with this general rationale of isolation that the first stress has been put here on the constancy hypothesis, that is, on the assumption that there is only a determinate amount of attention cathexis available. Clearly this postulate is a working hypothesis prompting the searching out of conditions in which this postulated condition is realized, at least for the purposes of a crude first approximation. The intent is to turn to the variations of the cathectic amount available, after the conditions of quasi constancy and the functional relationships obtaining in it have already been explored. The obvious problem implied in studying structure formation under such conditions of constancy is how to account for the

---

[4] [Dr. Schwartz has completed these and related experiments which showed that providing structure in the series definitely modifies the loss of cathexes by items. This confirms Rapaport's guess that it will be extremely difficult to study attention cathexis in isolation—Ed.]

[5] [Further work by Dr. Schiller strongly suggested that the distribution of attention cathexis was in fact mediated by motivation, which in turn depended upon the difficulty of the intentional task—Ed.]

cathexes that "binding" removes from the cathectic pool. One way to do this is to assume that these amounts are of an order that, in relation to the "pool" and even to the process investments, is either practically infinitesimal (the way three meters are "infinity" in practical optics) or else is theoretically infinitesimal (as in d'Alambert's theorem). Another way to do this is to assume that there is a "physiological" supply rate of the pool of attention cathexes which compensates for the loss of cathexes to structures formed.

(9) The complex conditions of incidental perception (Pötzl, 1917; Fisher, 1954, 1956, 1957; Fisher and Paul, 1959; Klein, 1959; Klein and Holt, 1960) which were boldly attacked combine low levels of cathecting and structuralization with the consequent ready decomposition, recomposition, displacement, fragmentation, distortion, and indirect representation of percepts with motivational and structural conditions which by themselves are likely to bring about or permit (respectively) such vicissitudes of percepts. No doubt many important results have been achieved in these studies and many significant observations made. And yet their full significance may not become explicit until the isolation of these factors discussed here and their quantification have progressed a way.

(10) The structure-motivation relationship has been greatly advanced by the cognitive style and motivation versus control studies of George Klein (1954, 1958; Gardner et al., 1959). His findings have multiple relevance here. *First,* they involve superordinate cognitive structures (styles). *Second,* they necessitate application and expansion of Irving Paul's (1959) findings on memory styles. *Third,* they set the genetic problem of the developmental conditions for such structure formation as one of the eminent tasks for this whole area of investigation.

VI. METAPSYCHOLOGICAL POINTS OF VIEW AND EXPERIMENTAL INVESTIGATIONS

(1) The attempt here undertaken is an application of the Rapaport and Gill systematization of psychoanalytic metapsychology (1959).

(2) In its center stands the attempt to explore whether or not economic concepts which are so far alien to the experimental psychological literature could be applied usefully to attack so far unattacked and/or controversial areas of cognition. (An attempt to apply them to the development, learning, and function of motor skills is also overdue.)

(3) The structural concepts introduced have not been as alien to experimental literature as the economics. Yet they have scarcely been treated as such, and they have certainly never been treated in relation to economic concepts.

(4) The economic concepts pertaining to drive and derivative motivations seemed far less amenable to such an attempt (the ultimate goal of

which may be phrased as the measurement of attention cathexes) than attention cathexes.

(5) The concepts pertaining to the dynamic point of view were not new to the experimental literature. But here we found economic concepts which might bring into an entirely different light what Harlow (1953) called curiosity motive, Bindra (1959) called novelty motive, R. W. White (1959) called competence motivation: all of them, like attention cathexes, are non-paroxysmal and newly triggered into action by the appearance of objects. While the rôle of objects in motivation in general has not stressed this, all drive objects function also by bringing the subthreshold drive intensity to threshold intensity. Yet this is not identical with their rôle in the "motivations" we discussed here, where they bring "exhausted" motivations instantaneously to full threshold intensity.

(6) The genetic problem and concepts did not come much into play here, yet they were touched on where association structures (Kent and Rosanoff, 1910) of enduring stability were mentioned, which should be contrasted with the experimentally developed "learned" associations. The genetic history of these differences is an urgent job for exploration.

(7) The adaptive problem, though only too obvious, did not come in for any elucidation here.

(8) The systematic application to experimental work of the metapsychological points of view seems promising. Metapsychology seems to hold promise beyond the range of psychoanalytic theory. But this is a promise that has yet to be fulfilled.

REFERENCES

Bahrick, H. P. (1954). Incidental Learning under Two Incentive Conditions. *J. Exp. Psychol.,* 47:170–172.

———— (1957). Incidental Learning at Five Stages of Intentional Learning. *J. Exp. Psychol.,* 54:259–261.

————, Fitts, P. M., & Rankin, R. F. (1952). Effect of Incentives upon Reactions to Peripheral Stimuli. *J. Exp. Psychol.,* 44:400–406.

————, Noble, M., & Fitts, P. M. (1954). Extratask Performance as a Measure of Learning a Primary Task. *J. Exp. Psychol.,* 48:298–302.

————, & Shelly, C. (1958). Time Sharing as an Index of Automatization. *J. Exp. Psychol.,* 56:288–293.

Bindra, D. (1959). Stimulus Change, Reactions to Novelty, and Response Decrement. *Psychol. Rev.,* 66:96–103.

Elkind, D. (1961). The Development of Quantitative Thinking: A Systematic Replication of Piaget's Studies. *J. Genet. Psychol.,* 98:37–46.

Erikson, E. H. (1937). Configurations in Play—Clinical Notes. *Psychoanal. Quart.,* 6:139–214.

Fisher, C. (1954). Dreams and Perception: The Role of Preconscious and Primary Modes of Perception in Dream Formation. *J. Amer. Psychoanal. Assn.*, 2:389–445.

—— (1956). Dreams, Images, and Perception: A Study of Unconscious-Preconscious Relationships. *J. Amer. Psychoanal. Assn.*, 4:5–48.

—— (1957). A Study of the Preliminary Stages of the Construction of Dreams and Images. *J. Amer. Psychoanal. Assn.*, 5:5–60.

——, & Paul, I. H. (1959). The Effect of Subliminal Visual Stimulation on Images and Dreams: A Validation Study. *J. Amer. Psychoanal. Assn.*, 7:35–83.

Freud, S. (1900). The Interpretation of Dreams. *Standard Edition*, 4 & 5. London: Hogarth Press, 1953.

Gardner, R. W., et al. (1959). Cognitive Control: A Study of Individual Consistencies in Cognitive Behavior. *Psychol. Issues*, No. 4.

Gill, M. M. (1963). Topography and Systems in Psychoanalytic Theory. *Psychol. Issues*, No. 10.

Harlow, H. F. (1953). Motivation as a Factor in the Acquisition of New Responses. In *Current Theory and Research in Motivation: A Symposium*. Lincoln: University of Nebraska Press, pp. 24–49.

Hartmann, H. (1939). *Ego Psychology and the Problem of Adaptation*, tr. D. Rapaport. New York: International Universities Press, 1958.

—— (1950). Comments on the Psychoanalytic Theory of the Ego. *Psychoanal. Study Child*, 5:74–96. New York: International Universities Press.

——, & Kris, E. (1945). The Genetic Approach in Psychoanalysis. *Psychoanal. Study Child*, 1:11–30. New York: International Universities Press.

Hebb, D. O. (1949). *The Organization of Behavior; A Neuropsychological Theory*. New York: Wiley.

Kent, G. H., & Rosanoff, A. J. (1910). A Study of Association in Insanity. *Amer. J. Insan.*, 67:37–96, 317–390.

Klein, G. S. (1954). Need and Regulation. In *Nebraska Symposium on Motivation, 1954*, ed. M. R. Jones. Lincoln: University of Nebraska Press, pp. 224–274.

—— (1958). Cognitive Control and Motivation. In *Assessment of Human Motives*, ed. G. Lindzey. New York: Rinehart, pp. 87–118.

—— (1959). On Subliminal Activation. *J. Nerv. Ment. Dis.*, 128:293–301.

——, & Holt, R. R. (1960). Problems and Issues in Current Studies of Subliminal Activation. In *Festschrift for Gardner Murphy*, ed. J. G. Peatman & E. L. Hartley. New York: Harper, pp. 75–93.

Lewin, K. (1922). Das Problem der Willensmessung und der Assoziation. *Psychol. Forsch.*, 1:191–302; 2:65–140.

—— (1926). Intention, Will and Need. In *Organization and Pathology of Thought*, ed. & tr. D. Rapaport. New York: Columbia University Press, 1951, pp. 95–153.

Noble, C. E. (1952). An Analysis of Learning. *Psychol. Rev.*, 59:421–430.

Ovsiankina, M. (1928). Die Wiederaufnahme unterbrochener Handlungen. *Psychol. Forsch.*, 11:302–389.

Paul, I. H. (1959). Studies in Remembering: The Reproduction of Connected and Extended Verbal Material. *Psychol. Issues*, No. 2.

Peterson, L. R., & Peterson, M. J. (1959). Short-Term Retention of Individual Verbal Items. *J. Exp. Psychol., 58*:193–198.

Postman, L. (1955). The Analysis of Incidental Learning. In *Associative Processes in Verbal Behavior,* ed. J. J. Jenkins. University of Minnesota, Department of Psychology. Mimeographed, pp. 102–133.

Pötzl, O. (1917). The Relationship between Experimentally Induced Dream Images and Indirect Vision. *Psychol. Issues, 7*:41–120, 1960.

Rapaport, D. (1942). *Emotions and Memory,* 2nd unaltered ed. New York: International Universities Press, 1950.

———— (1950). Review of N. Wiener, *Cybernetics, or Control and Communication in the Animal and the Machine. This volume,* Chapter 29.

———— (1957). The Theory of Ego Autonomy: A Generalization. *This volume,* Chapter 57.

————, & Gill, M. M. (1959). The Points of View and Assumptions of Metapsychology. *This volume,* Chapter 62.

Rosenberg, S. (1958). Motivation, Set, and Number of Trials in Intentional and Incidental Learning. Doctoral dissertation, University of Minnesota.

Rouse, R. O. (1959). Proactive Inhibition as a Function of Degree of Practice on the Two Tasks. Paper presented to the American Psychological Association.

Russell, W. A. (1955). Bi-directional Effects in Word Association. In *Associative Processes in Verbal Behavior,* ed. J. J. Jenkins. Minneapolis: University of Minnesota, Department of Psychology. Mimeographed, pp. 1–11.

Schiller, P. H. (1962). Performance on Two Simultaneous Tasks as a Function of Learning. Doctoral dissertation, Clark University.

———— (research report). Incidental Learning as a Function of Motor Tracking Difficulty.

Schwartz, F., & Rouse, R. O. (1961). The Activation and Recovery of Associations. *Psychol. Issues,* No. 9.

————, & Schiller, P. H. (research report). The Span of Immediate Memory: An Illusive Limit.

Storms, L. H. (1958). Apparent Backward Association: A Situational Effect. *J. Exp. Psychol., 55*:390–395.

White, R. W. (1959). Motivation Reconsidered: The Concept of Competence. *Psychol. Rev., 66*:297–333.

Wolff, P. H. (1959). Observations on Newborn Infants. *Psychosom. Med., 21*: 110–118.

Zeigarnik, B. (1927). Über das Behalten von erledigten und unerledigten Handlungen. *Psychol. Forsch., 9*:1–85.

62

THE POINTS OF VIEW AND
ASSUMPTIONS OF
METAPSYCHOLOGY[1]

WITH MERTON M. GILL

I. ON THE PRESENT STATE OF METAPSYCHOLOGY

Freud first used the term metapsychology to indicate that his psychology deals with what is beyond the realm of conscious experience (1887–1902, p. 246). Later, however, he defined metapsychology as the study of the

[1] The study on which this paper is based was in part supported by a grant of the Ford Foundation in aid of research at the Austen Riggs Center. We are indebted for their suggestions to Drs. C. Fisher, H. Hartmann, R. R. Holt, E. McC. Howard, R. P. Knight, M. Mayman, R. Schafer, J. Schimek, M. Schur, and P. H. Wolff.

After this paper went to press we found a formulation by Edward Glover which parallels the major thesis we present here: "No mental event can be described in terms of instinct alone, of ego-structure alone, or of functional mechanism alone. Even together these three angles [dynamic, structural, economic] of approach are insufficient. Each event should be estimated also in terms of its *developmental* [ge-

Paper presented to the New York Psychoanalytic Society, March 11, 1958. First published in The International Journal of Psycho-Analysis, *40:153–162, 1959. Spanish translation published in Merton M. Gill and David Rapaport,* Aportaciones a la Teoría y Técnica Psicoanalítica. *Asociación Psicoanalítica Mexicana, A.C., 1962, pp. 239–259.*

795

assumptions upon which the system of psychoanalytic theory is based (1917, p. 222). While metapsychological statements are scattered throughout Freud's writings, Chapter VII of *The Interpretation of Dreams,* the "Papers on Metapsychology" (fragments of a never-completed work; see Jones, 1955, pp. 184–187), and the "Addenda" to *The Problem of Anxiety* are our sources for reconstructing Freud's metapsychology.

These sources, however, do not fulfill the program implied in Freud's definition. They do not state systematically that minimal set of assumptions on which the psychoanalytic theory rests. Indeed, in all these sources propositions stating observations, theories, and underlying assumptions are closely interwoven. Systematic studies in metapsychology, however, will have to distinguish between empirical propositions, specific psychoanalytic propositions, propositions of the general psychoanalytic theory, and propositions stating the metapsychological assumptions.[2] In formulating the assumptions which follow here, we have avoided using specific psychoanalytic concepts. We are not yet in a position to present formal definitions of the terms used in stating these assumptions. We are, however, aware that without such definitions a set of assumptions is of limited value and that, indeed, some of the assumptions presented here are little more than covert definitions. Thus the formulation of the definitions will probably modify this statement of the assumptions.

At some point in the development of every science, the assumptions on which it is built must be clarified. Freud meant metapsychology to do just that for psychoanalysis. This justifies our attempt to state explicitly and systematically that body of assumptions which constitutes psychoanalytic metapsychology. We dwell on this justification because from the standpoint of daily clinical practice what follows here may appear to be an unnecessary, sterile, formalistic exercise. Yet a systematization of metapsychology is necessary, if only because the increasing use of the metapsychological points of view in the literature is often at odds with Freud's definitions, without the authors' justifying this or even indicating an awareness of it. Moreover, often only one point of view is made use of,[3] although accord-

---

netic] or regressional significance, and in the last resort should be assessed in relation to environmental factors past and present. The last of these criteria, namely *the relation of the total ego to its environment,* is the most promising of all. It suggests that the most practical (clinical) criterion of weakness or strength should be in terms of *adaptation*" (1943, p. 8).

[2] For instance: *empirical proposition:* around the fourth year of life boys regard their fathers as rivals; *specific psychoanalytic proposition:* the solution of the oedipal situation is a decisive determinant of character formation and pathology; *general psychoanalytic proposition:* structure formation by means of identifications and anticathexes explains theoretically the consequences of the "decline of the oedipus complex"; *metapsychological proposition:* the propositions of the general psychoanalytic theory which explain the oedipal situation and the decline of the oedipus complex involve dynamic, economic, structural, genetic, and adaptive assumptions.

[3] The economic point of view enjoys particular popularity.

ing to Freud a metapsychological analysis is to describe a mental process in all its aspects, i.e., from all the points of view (Freud, 1915b, p. 181).

The three metapsychological points of view formulated by Freud—the dynamic, the topographic, and the economic—will guide us in our attempt to formulate the assumptions upon which the psychoanalytic theory rests. But these very points of view require reassessment.

While the topographical conception of the mental apparatus in terms of the systems *Ucs., Pcs.,* and *Cs.* was superseded by the structural conception in terms of the id, ego, and superego, Freud never explicitly replaced the topographic point of view of metapsychology by a structural one. Though it remains necessary to distinguish between *Ucs., Pcs.,* and *Cs.,* since these distinctions are the observational points of departure for all psychoanalytic theory, the term topographic should not be retained for these, because it still seems to imply that, contrary to Freud's final view, *Ucs., Pcs.,* and *Cs.* are more than psychological qualities (Freud, 1915b, pp. 192–193; 1923, pp. 16–18; 1940, p. 38).[4]

Moreover, while the psychoanalytic theory is undoubtedly a genetic psychology, Freud apparently took this so much for granted that he saw no necessity to formulate a genetic point of view of metapsychology. It could be argued that the genetic point of view is not of the same order of abstraction as the three classical points of view, because every genetic proposition in the theory of psychoanalysis involves dynamic, economic, and structural relationships. But this argument fails to distinguish between psychoanalytic propositions (see p. 796, n. 2) on the one hand and metapsychological points of view and assumptions on the other. Even though in various psychoanalytic propositions one or another metapsychological point of view or assumption may be dominant, *all* psychoanalytic propositions involve *all* metapsychological points of view. Only the assumptions of metapsychology are independent from each other.

Finally, since Hartmann's and Erikson's studies of adaptation, it has become clear that psychoanalytic theory has always implied basic assumptions concerning adaptation, though with varying degrees of emphasis

[4] The readers and discussants of this paper expressed special concern about this point. Therefore we want to stress that we do not question the importance of these so-called "topographical" distinctions as the empirical points of departure of the psychoanalytic theory. However, we deny that they have a metapsychological status, since they are accounted for by dynamic and economic considerations as the sources referred to readily show. We consider this issue at greater length in an extended statement of metapsychology which is in preparation. [The extended discussion of this point is in Gill (1963). In the light of this discussion, we would, in this paragraph, have taken care to use "unconscious," "preconscious," and "conscious," instead of the systemic terms, *"Ucs.," "Pcs.,"* and *"Cs.,"* and would have said that the term "topographic" should be retained to describe the relationship of contents to consciousness. My monograph, which began as a collaboration with Rapaport, is the only part of the "extended statement," referred to here and later, that has been written. It deals with some, but not all, of the issues we intended to write about more fully. See also Rapaport (1959)—Ed.]

(Freud, 1915a, pp. 136, 140). So far, however, we have not had an explicit formulation of these assumptions or of an adaptive point of view in metapsychology. Moreover, there are still some psychoanalysts who refuse to recognize that the psychoanalytic theory does imply adaptive assumptions. They equate adaptation with adjustment, and fear that to take adaptive considerations seriously leads inevitably to the course taken by various schools of psychoanalytic thought who employ their enthusiastic discovery of environmental relationships for the purpose of defensive denial of drive and intrapsychic conflict. These psychoanalysts to the contrary notwithstanding, the question is not whether adaptive considerations form a part of psychoanalysis, but rather: Is the adaptive point of view of the same level of abstraction as the others? can it be considered "metapsychological" at all? [5] or can the adaptive propositions of psychoanalysis be satisfactorily derived from the classical points of view which Freud, in his definition of metapsychology, conceived of in the context of *a mental process* without reference to environmental relations? An adequate discussion of this issue requires an analysis of the relation between behavior and mental process. [6] Here we shall assume that (a) psychoanalysis is a theory concerned with the explanation of those changes which we term behavior; (b) psychoanalysis assumes that all such changes have a psychological explanation (determinism); (c) a system of metapsychology must include the dynamic, economic, structural, genetic, and adaptive points of view.

Metapsychology proper thus consists of propositions stating the minimum (both necessary and sufficient) number of independent assumptions upon which the psychoanalytic theory rests. Metapsychology also includes the points of view which guide the metapsychological analysis of psychoanalytic propositions, both observational and theoretical. Here we will group the assumptions according to the points of view to which they pertain. Since, for the moment, the only test of the necessity, sufficiency, and fruitfulness of such assumptions is the demonstration of their role in familiar psychoanalytic propositions, we shall attempt to give such a demonstration on the propositions of the psychoanalytic theory of affects.

II. POINTS OF VIEW AND ASSUMPTIONS OF METAPSYCHOLOGY

(A) *The Dynamic Point of View*

(1) Definition

The dynamic point of view demands that the psychoanalytic explanation of any psychological phenomenon include propositions concerning the psychological forces involved in the phenomenon.

[5] This question was raised by almost every reader of the early drafts of this paper, and we consider it in the extended statement already referred to.
[6] The extended statement referred to contains such a discussion.

Freud wrote:

Our purpose is not merely to describe and classify the phenomena, but to conceive them as brought about by the play of forces in the mind . . . which work together or against one another. We are endeavouring to attain a *dynamic conception* of mental phenomena [1916–17, p. 60].

(2) The assumptions and their significance

(*a*) *There are psychological forces.*

This assumption underlies, for example, all the propositions concerning drives, ego interests, and conflicts. It is significant because it implies that we can study these forces by psychological methods of observation, without recourse to an organic substrate.

This assumption does not distinguish between conscious and unconscious psychological forces, because that distinction is not an assumption but an inference from empirical observations, and is thus a proposition of the special theory of psychoanalysis but not of metapsychology (Freud, 1914, pp. 16–17).

The application of this assumption to the psychoanalytic theory of affects leads to the formulation of an often implied (A. Freud, 1936) but unstated psychoanalytic proposition: affect—like any other energy discharge—must be conceived of as the work of a psychological force, and thus the introduction of the concept of an affect force—in addition to the concept of drive force—becomes necessary, and this, as we shall see, leads to the formulation of other implied but unstated propositions concerning psychological forces.

(*b*) *Psychological forces are defined by their direction and magnitude.*[7]

This assumption underlies, for example, all the propositions concerning the strength of and the work performed by drives. It is significant because it postulates that in psychoanalysis, as in other sciences, all forces can and should be treated purely in terms of their magnitude and direction, and thus relegates propositions concerning the *qualitative* differences between psychological forces to the special theory of psychoanalysis. Freud wrote: "The simplest and likeliest assumption as to the nature of instincts would seem to be that in itself an instinct is without quality" (1905, p. 168).

The application of this assumption to the theory of affects indicates that the direction of the affect force is determined not by an external goal but by the affect-discharge channels, and that the magnitude of the affect force is determined not only by the magnitude of the drive force but also by the

[7] Quantitative considerations are involved in both the dynamic point of view (magnitude of force) and the economic point of view (quantity of energy), and it is perhaps for this reason that Freud (1915a) did not always distinguish them. For the argument that they are independent of each other in spite of the relationship between the quantity of energy and the magnitude of force, see p. 801 and the more extensive statement referred to.

threshold and capacity of these affect-discharge channels. Thus the application of this assumption leads to a new formulation: there are psychological forces whose direction is determined by goal-objects and whose work changes both the external and the internal environment, and there are psychological forces whose direction is determined by intrapsychic organization and whose work consists of altering the internal environment alone.[8]

(*c*) *The effect of simultaneously acting psychological forces may be the simple resultant of the work of each of these forces.*

This assumption underlies, for example, the propositions concerning conflict, ambivalence, and the relationship of drives in the id. It is significant because it postulates that under certain conditions, certain simultaneously acting psychological forces follow the simple composition law of vectorial addition of forces, and sets for the general theory of psychoanalysis the task of specifying the forces which do so and the conditions under which they do so.

The psychoanalytic propositions concerning ambivalent and mixed affects imply the assumption of the action of some affect-forces in accordance with a simple composition law.

(*d*) *The effect of simultaneously acting psychological forces may not be the simple resultant of the work of each of these forces.*

This assumption underlies, for example, the propositions concerning overdetermination, fusion, defusion, and the integration of pregenital partial drives under genital primacy. It is significant because it postulates that under certain conditions, certain drives acting simultaneously do not follow the simple composition law of vectorial addition and sets for the general psychoanalytic theory the task of specifying the forces which do not do so, the conditions under which they do not do so, and the composition laws which they follow instead. The fact that at present we have no such specifications indicates both the prematurity of this systematization and its heuristic potential: it shows that the concepts of instinct fusion and overdetermination are unclear, and it challenges a re-examination of the observations and the theory pertaining to them.

The psychoanalytic propositions concerning the genesis of discharge and overflow affects from the clash between drive forces and restraining forces (of structure), and those concerning the origins and effects of signal affects, imply the assumption of the action of affect forces according to laws other than that of simple vectorial composition.

(B) *The Economic Point of View*
   (1) Definition
   The economic point of view demands that the psychoanalytic explanation

[8] [This paragraph fails to state that the forces determined by objects are taken for granted—Ed.]

of any psychological phenomenon include propositions concerning the psychological energy involved in the phenomenon.

Freud wrote:

> [The] *economic* [point of view] . . . endeavours to follow out the vicissitudes of amounts of excitation and to arrive at least at some *relative* estimate of their magnitude [1915b, p. 181];

and

> The economic, or, if you prefer, the quantitative factor,[9] . . . is . . . closely bound up with the pleasure-principle . . . [1933, p. 105].

These statements contain not only the formulation of the economic point of view of metapsychology but some of the economic assumptions also.

(2) The assumptions and their significance

(*a*) *There are psychological energies.*

This assumption underlies, for example, all propositions concerning the effects of drive forces, since—by universal definition—the work of a force always expends energy. Its significance is akin to that of the assumption concerning psychological forces: it enables us to study the expenditures, displacements, and transformations of psychological energy, without first having to establish the physiological-biological energy which is its somatic substrate.

The relationship between force and energy stated above may suggest that we should reduce the economic to the dynamic point of view, or *vice versa*. But since forces, which (by definition) have a direction, cannot account for displacements and transformations, and energies which (by definition) are directionless quantities cannot account for directional phenomena, we need —just as physics does—both energy and force concepts.

All psychoanalytic propositions concerning affects imply this first economic assumption, since all affects involve displacement (e.g., discharge) of energy.

(*b*) *Psychological energies follow a law of conservation.*

This assumption underlies, for example, all propositions concerning displacements of cathexes. It is significant because it serves both as a justification and a guide for tracing psychological phenomena to their causal roots: without the assumption of conservation, tracing the fate of cathexes in displacement processes would be meaningless.

The proposition that the amount of drive energy which is discharged in an affect varies directly with the amount of drive energy seeking discharge, and inversely with the amount of drive energy discharged through other channels, implies this economic assumption.

[9] See p. 798, n. 7.

(c) Psychological energies are subject to a law of entropy.

This assumption underlies, for example, all propositions concerning mobile cathexis and primary process: it is the statement of the pleasure principle in general terms. It is significant because it makes superfluous the postulation of a constancy "principle" and a nirvana "principle," since these "principles" represent only the effects of the entropy (pleasure) principle operating under diverse structural conditions.

The conflict theory of affects, which conceives of them as emergency discharges, implies this economic assumption.

(d) Psychological energies are subject to transformations, which increase or decrease their entropic tendency.

This assumption underlies, for example, all propositions concerning neutralization (desexualization, deaggressivization) and binding, as well as deneutralization (sexualization, aggressivization) and mobilization of cathexes. It is significant because it conceptualizes the conditions under which energy does and those under which it does not seem to follow the law of entropy, and thus serves as the foundation for the explanation of the transition from the primary to the secondary process, and of the relationship between energy and structure in psychological phenomena.

The theory of signal affects, and Fenichel's propositions concerning the "taming" of affects, imply this assumption.

(C) *The Structural Point of View*

(1) Definition

The structural point of view demands that the psychoanalytic explanation of any psychological phenomenon include propositions concerning the abiding psychological configurations (structures) involved in the phenomenon.

This definition is our construction. Freud does not give a definition of the structural point of view,[10] and states only the necessity to replace the topographic point of view by the structural one:

> . . . we land in endless confusion and difficulty if we cling to our former way of expressing ourselves and try, for instance, to derive neuroses from a conflict between the conscious and the unconscious. We shall have to substitute for this antithesis another, taken from our understanding of the structural conditions of the mind, namely, the antithesis between the organized ego and what is repressed and dissociated from it [1923, p. 17].

[10] ["Rapaport and I . . . [in "The Points of View and Assumptions of Metapsychology"] were in error in saying that Freud had never defined the structural point of view. We should have referred to his definition of the topographic point of view, which for him was the same thing" (Gill, 1963, p. 54, n. 4). I give a number of quotations there to demonstrate the point—Ed.]

(2) The assumptions and their significance

(*a*) *There are psychological structures.*

This assumption underlies the propositions concerning the id,[11] ego, and superego, those pertaining to the mental mechanisms, Hartmann's (1939) propositions concerning "apparatuses," and Erikson's (1950b) concerning "modes" and "modalities." Its significance is akin to that of psychological forces and psychological energies: it indicates that we are dealing with structures inferred from behavior, regardless of their organic substrate. This assumption implies that Hartmann's motor, sensory, and memory apparatuses are not somatic organs, but rather psychological regulations related to these organs (see Freud, 1900, p. 546).

The propositions concerning affect-discharge channels and thresholds—both inborn and acquired—and those concerning the structural segregation of affect-charge, imply this assumption.

(*b*) *Structures are configurations of a slow rate of change.*

This assumption underlies, for example, all propositions concerning character traits, defences, the "persistence of the past in the present," and those pertaining to fixed formations which are used by psychological processes as means (e.g., concepts, motor executive habits). It is significant because on the one hand it distinguishes structures from processes of a fast rate of change (e.g., discharge and reaccumulation of libido); and on the other it stresses the configurational character of structures and brings into focus the fact that psychological structures are abiding patterns in the flux of processes, from which we infer them.

The propositions asserting that affects are configurations of drive forces, restraining forces, discharge channels, etc., and the clinical propositions concerning the resistiveness to change of predominant, moodlike, and individually characteristic affect forms, imply this assumption.

(*c*) *Structures are configurations within which, between which, and by means of which mental processes take place.*

This assumption underlies, for example, all propositions concerning "interstructural" processes (e.g., conflicts) and "intrastructural" processes (e.g., synthetic function) and means- or executive-apparatuses. It is significant because it implies that the conception of displacements, transformations, and discharges of energy, and the conception of the work of forces, involve structures.

The propositions concerning the origin and role of affects in interstructural conflict, the "intrastructural signal" theory of anxiety, and the propositions concerning the role of affect-discharge channels and thresholds in affect phenomena, imply this structural assumption.

(*d*) *Structures are hierarchically ordered.*

This assumption underlies, for example, all the propositions concerning

11 Though conceived as far less cohesive than the ego, the id too is a structure.

the mutual relations of the id, ego, and superego, and Hartmann's (1939) propositions pertaining to the "rank order of ego functions." It is significant because it is the foundation for the psychoanalytic propositions concerning differentiation (whether resulting in discrete structures which are then coordinated, or in the increased internal articulation of structures), and because it implies that the quality of a process depends upon the level of the structural hierarchy on which it takes place (Rapaport, 1957).

Freud's (1926), Jones's (1929), and Fenichel's (1941) propositions concerning the hierarchy of affects imply this assumption.

(D) *The Genetic Point of View*
  (1) Definition
  The genetic point of view demands that the psychoanalytic explanation of any psychological phenomenon include propositions concerning its psychological origin and development.

Freud does not give a definition of the genetic point of view. However, he does imply it in his statement of the genetic character of psychoanalysis:

> Not every analysis of psychological phenomena deserves the name of psycho-analysis. The latter implies more than the mere analysis of composite phenomena into simpler ones. It consists in tracing back one psychical structure to another which preceded it in time and out of which it developed. . . . Thus from the very first psycho analysis was directed towards tracing developmental processes. It . . . was led . . . to construct a genetic psychology . . . [1913, pp. 182–183].

The genetic point of view is also implied by his concept of the complemental series, which involves both constitutional-maturational and environmental-experiential factors:

> . . . the relation between the two [factors] is a co-operative and not a mutually exclusive one. The constitutional factor must await experiences before it can make itself felt; the accidental factor must have a constitutional basis in order to come into operation. To cover the majority of cases we can picture what has been described as a 'complemental series', in which the diminishing intensity of one factor is balanced by the increasing intensity of the other [1905, pp. 239–240].

Hartmann and Kris have come close to defining the genetic point of view:

> The genetic approach in psychoanalysis does not deal only with anamnestic data, nor does it intend to show only "how the past is contained in the present". Genetic propositions describe why, in past situations of conflict, a specific solution was adopted; why the one was retained and the other dropped, and what causal relation exists between these solutions and later developments [1945, p. 17].

(2) The assumptions and their significance

(*a*) *All psychological phenomena have a psychological origin and development.*

This assumption underlies, for example, all clinical psychoanalytic propositions which are not simply descriptive. It is significant because it distinguishes psychological phenomena from most physical and chemical phenomena, since it implies that psychological phenomena can be understood only by the study of their origin and development. This distinction does not imply that psychological changes are produced by forces other than those acting in the present, but that the forces which are effective in the present and their conditions of action can be inferred only by genetic study. However, autonomous structures and functions, though they too have a psychological history and origin, can be described and their effects can be predicted without reference to their history. Like the assumptions pertaining to psychological forces, energies, and structures, this genetic assumption too predicates that psychological origin and development can be dealt with without recourse to the somatic-physiological substrate. Even the effects of gross somatic changes can be treated in psychological terms.

The clinical propositions concerning the ontogenetic origins and history of affects imply this first genetic assumption.

(*b*) *All psychological phenomena originate in innate givens, which mature according to an epigenetic ground plan.*

This assumption underlies, for example, all the propositions concerning libido development, Hartmann's (1939) concerning autonomous ego development, and Erikson's (1950b) concerning psychosocial epigenesis. It is significant because it amplifies Freud's "constitutional" factor (". . . an individual's first experiences in childhood do not occur only by chance but also correspond to the first activities of his innate or constitutional instinctual dispositions" [1905, p. 183]), and brings into focus the biological-maturational character of psychoanalysis as a science, setting it sharply apart from the learning theories whose emphasis is mainly or solely on experience.[12]

The propositions concerning inborn affect-discharge channels, Freud's theory of the developmental stages of anxiety, and Erikson's theory of the specificity of psychosocial stages for the development of shame and guilt, imply this assumption.

(*c*) *The earlier forms of a psychological phenomenon, though superseded by later forms, remain potentially active.*[13]

---

[12] The question has been raised whether or not this contrasting of psychoanalysis and learning theories is justified: learning theories too speak of biological roots of behavior, such as hunger, thirst, and sex. This contrast rests on the maturational implications of psychoanalysis and on the drive concept of learning theories which includes external stimuli.

[13] Freud wrote: ". . . none of the infantile mental formations perish. All the wishes,

This assumption underlies, for example, all propositions concerning regression, both pathological and in the service of the ego. It is significant because it justifies the use of pathological and exceptional phenomena for the exploration of the origin and development of normal and common phenomena.

Fenichel's (1941), Bibring's (1953), and Schur's (1953) propositions concerning regressive replacements of signal affects by ontogenetically earlier affect forms imply this genetic assumption.

(*d*) *At each point of psychological history the totality of potentially active earlier forms codetermines all subsequent psychological phenomena.*

This assumption underlies, for example, the propositions concerning the integration of previous psychosexual and psychosocial achievements under the primacy of the dominant, i.e., phase-specific, psychosexual and psychosocial tendency. (However, propositions concerning autonomous structures and functions do not imply this assumption.) It is significant because it implies that each integrate is determined by previous solutions (i.e., achievements) and that previous malsolutions may be remedied by subsequent integrations.

This genetic assumption is implied by the propositions of the theory of affects which state that the form and significance of anxiety in a person's life are determined by the methods he has adopted to cope with typical danger situations.

(E) *The Adaptive Point of View*

(1) Definition

The adaptive point of view demands that the psychoanalytic explanation of any psychological phenomenon include propositions concerning its relationship to the environment.

Freud came closer to formulating an adaptive point of view than either a structural [14] or a genetic one: in his "Instincts and Their Vicissitudes," he puts the polarity "ego vs. external reality" on a par with the economic polarity, "pleasure vs. pain" (1915a, p. 140). Nevertheless, only Hartmann's (1939) and Erikson's (1950b) theories made clear the necessity for the explicit formulation of this point of view.[15]

(2) The assumptions and their significance

(*a*) *There exist psychological states of adaptedness and processes of adaptation at every point of life.*

---

instinctual impulses, modes of reaction and attitudes of childhood are still demonstrably present in maturity and in appropriate circumstances can emerge once more" (1913, p. 184).

[14] [See p. 802, n. 10—Ed.]

[15] The contributions involving this point of view made by Horney, Sullivan, etc., are discussed in the extensive systematic statement referred to.

The concept of *adaptedness* is implicit, for instance, in Freud's propositions concerning the coordination between drive and object, and in Hartmann's and Erikson's propositions concerning inborn preparedness for an evolving series of average expectable environments. The concept of *processes of adaptation* is implicit, for instance, in Freud's propositions concerning the progressive shift from the predominance of primary-process to secondary-process functioning in the course of development, and in Hartmann's (1939) and Erikson's (1950b) propositions that each developmental step gives rise to and solves problems in relation to external reality. This assumption is significant because it implies that the human being, just like any other organism, can be understood only in relation to its ecological niche, to which it is fitted by evolution and with which it is in balance or is striving for balance at every point of its life; and because it establishes grounds for distinguishing between adjustment (conformity) and adaptation, since it implies alloplastic as well as autoplastic adaptation processes.

Erikson's (1950a) and Spitz's (1957) propositions concerning inborn affect reactions, and Fenichel's (1941) propositions concerning the taming of affects in the course of development, imply this first adaptive assumption.

(*b*) *The processes of (autoplastic and/or alloplastic) adaptation maintain, restore, and improve the existing states of adaptedness and thereby ensure survival.*

This assumption underlies Freud's proposition that the reality principle subserves the pleasure principle, and is at the core of Hartmann's theory of adaptation and Erikson's theory of psychosocial epigenesis. It is significant because from it can be derived both the propositions which lend psychoanalysis its biological character and those which give it its psychosocial character.

Freud's propositions concerning anxiety as an inborn adaptedness and anxiety signal as a result of adaptation to situations of reality danger imply this second adaptive assumption.

(*c*) *Man adapts to his society—both to the physical and human environments which are its products.*

This assumption underlies, for example, all propositions concerning the role of society's morality in superego development, and Hartmann's (1939) and Erikson's (1950b) propositions pertaining to psychosocial development. It is significant because it lays the groundwork for understanding psychosocial development and for explaining the similarities between the customs of primitive societies and the phenomena of individual pathology in civilized man, without involving the assumption of the inheritance of acquired characteristics.

This assumption is implied in Erikson's (1950a) proposition that the society's affect forms determine what forms of affects its individuals can develop.

(*d*) *Adaptation relationships are mutual: man and environment adapt to each other.*

This assumption underlies, for example, all psychoanalytic formulations concerning the central role in human development of the infant's prolonged helplessness, the critical role the child's various phases of development may play in the parents' pathology or further maturation, and Erikson's propositions concerning mutuality. It is significant because it provides the foundation for the psychological equivalent of biological ecology, as specified, for example, in Erikson's (1950b) formulation of the cogwheeling of the needs of the child and of the caretaking people at each point of development.

The propositions of Erikson (1950a) and Spitz (1957) concerning the dual role of affects in mutuality (dyadic) relationships and those of Schilder (1930) concerning affects as communications, imply this assumption.

III. CONCLUSION

In this paper we have stated and discussed the points of view which guide metapsychological analysis and the assumptions which constitute metapsychology proper.

We repeat the definitions and assumptions here in synoptic form.

The *dynamic* point of view demands that the psychoanalytic explanation of any psychological phenomenon include propositions concerning the psychological forces involved in the phenomenon.

(*a*) There are psychological forces.

(*b*) Psychological forces are defined by their direction and magnitude.

(*c*) The effect of simultaneously acting psychological forces may be the simple resultant of the work of each of these forces.

(*d*) The effect of simultaneously acting psychological forces may not be the simple resultant of the work of each of these forces.

The *economic* point of view demands that the psychoanalytic explanation of any psychological phenomenon include propositions concerning the psychological energy involved in the phenomenon.

(*a*) There are psychological energies.

(*b*) Psychological energies follow a law of conservation.

(*c*) Psychological energies are subject to a law of entropy.

(*d*) Psychological energies are subject to transformations, which increase or decrease their entropic tendency.

The *structural* point of view demands that the psychoanalytic explanation of any psychological phenomenon include propositions concerning the abiding psychological configurations (structures) involved in the phenomenon.

(*a*) There are psychological structures.

(*b*) Structures are configurations of a slow rate of change.

(*c*) Structures are configurations within which, between which, and by means of which mental processes take place.

(*d*) Structures are hierarchically ordered.

The *genetic* point of view demands that the psychoanalytic explanation of any psychological phenomenon include propositions concerning its psychological origin and development.

(*a*) All psychological phenomena have a psychological origin and development.

(*b*) All psychological phenomena originate in innate givens, which mature according to an epigenetic ground plan.

(*c*) The earlier forms of a psychological phenomenon, though superseded by later forms, remain potentially active.

(*d*) At each point of psychological history the totality of potentially active earlier forms codetermines all subsequent psychological phenomena.

The *adaptive* point of view demands that the psychoanalytic explanation of any psychological phenomenon include propositions concerning its relationship to the environment.

(*a*) There exist psychological states of adaptedness and processes of adaptation at every point of life.

(*b*) The processes of (autoplastic and/or alloplastic) adaptation maintain, restore, and improve the existing states of adaptedness and thereby ensure survival.

(*c*) Man adapts to his society—both to the physical and human environments which are its products.

(*d*) Adaptation relationships are mutual: man and environment adapt to each other.

The arguments we have presented for the points of view, however, differ both in kind and in strength from those for the assumptions.

The metapsychological points of view, even if some of the five presented have been formulated as such here for the first time, have a history. Though their use in the literature has been rather haphazard, some experience has accumulated concerning them, and it can be asserted with confidence that these five points of view are necessary and sufficient to a degree which recommends that they should be accepted—for the time being—as the framework of psychoanalytic metapsychology.

The situation is different with the assumptions. It is not yet possible to assess whether all these assumptions are necessary, and whether this set of assumptions is sufficient—when coupled with observational data—to yield the existing body of psychoanalytic propositions. Such an assessment could be achieved only by systematic study, by continuing to subject psychoanalytic propositions to an analysis which would strip away their empirical content and establish whether or not their postulational (nonempirical) implications are accounted for by this set of assumptions. The future development of psychoanalysis as a systematic science may well depend on such continuing efforts to establish the assumptions on which psychoanalytic theory rests.

REFERENCES

Bibring, E. (1953). The Mechanism of Depression. In *Affective Disorders,* ed. P. Greenacre. New York: International Universities Press, pp. 13–48.
Erikson, E. H. (1950a). *Childhood and Society.* New York: Norton.
———— (1950b). Growth and Crises of the "Healthy Personality." In *Personality in Nature, Society, and Culture,* 2nd ed., ed. C. Kluckhohn & H. A. Murray. New York: Knopf, 1953, pp. 185–225.
Fenichel, O. (1941). The Ego and the Affects. *Collected Papers,* 2:215–227. New York: Norton, 1954.
Freud, A. (1936). *The Ego and the Mechanisms of Defence.* New York: International Universities Press, 1946.
Freud, S. (1887–1902). *The Origins of Psychoanalysis: Letters to Wilhelm Fliess, Drafts and Notes, 1887–1902.* New York: Basic Books, 1954.
————(1900). The Interpretation of Dreams. *Standard Edition,* 4 & 5. London: Hogarth Press, 1953.
————(1905). Three Essays on the Theory of Sexuality. *Standard Edition,* 7:123–245. London: Hogarth Press, 1953.
————(1913). The Claims of Psycho-Analysis to Scientific Interest. *Standard Edition,* 13:165–190. London: Hogarth Press, 1955.
————(1914). On the History of the Psycho-Analytic Movement. *Standard Edition,* 14:7–66. London: Hogarth Press, 1957.
————(1915a). Instincts and Their Vicissitudes. *Standard Edition,* 14:117–140. London: Hogarth Press, 1957.
————(1915b). The Unconscious. *Standard Edition,* 14:166–215. London: Hogarth Press, 1957.
————(1916–17 [1915–17]). *A General Introduction to Psychoanalysis,* tr. J. Riviere. New York: Garden City Publishing Co., 1938.
————(1917 [1915]). A Metapsychological Supplement to the Theory of Dreams. *Standard Edition,* 14:222–235. London: Hogarth Press, 1957.
————(1923). *The Ego and the Id,* tr. J. Riviere. London: Hogarth Press, 1947.
————(1926 [1925]). *The Problem of Anxiety,* tr. H. A. Bunker. New York: Psychoanalytic Quarterly & Norton, 1936.
————(1933). *New Introductory Lectures on Psycho-Analysis,* tr. W. J. H. Sprott. New York: Norton.
————(1940 [1938]). *An Outline of Psychoanalysis,* tr. J. Strachey. New York: Norton, 1949.
Gill, M. M. (1963). Topography and Systems in Psychoanalytic Theory. *Psychol. Issues,* No. 10.
Glover, E. (1943). The Concept of Dissociation. *Int. J. Psycho-Anal.,* 24:7–13.

Hartmann, H. (1939). *Ego Psychology and the Problem of Adaptation,* tr. D. Rapaport. New York: International Universities Press, 1958.

————, & Kris, E. (1945). The Genetic Approach in Psychoanalysis. *Psychoanal. Study Child,* 1:11–30. New York: International Universities Press.

Jones, E. (1929). Fear, Guilt and Hate. *Papers on Psycho-Analysis,* 5th ed. Baltimore: Williams & Wilkins, 1948, pp. 304–319.

————(1955). *The Life and Work of Sigmund Freud,* Vol. II. New York: Basic Books.

Rapaport, D. (1957). Cognitive Structures. *This volume,* Chapter 50.

————(1959). The Structure of Psychoanalytic Theory: A Systematizing Attempt. *Psychol. Issues,* No. 6, 1960.

Schilder, P. (1930). Studies Concerning the Psychology and Symptomatology of General Paresis. In *Organization and Pathology of Thought,* ed. & tr. D. Rapaport. New York: Columbia University Press, 1951, pp. 519–580.

Schur, M. (1953). The Ego in Anxiety. In *Drives, Affects, Behavior,* ed. R. M. Loewenstein. New York: International Universities Press, pp. 67–103.

Spitz, R. A. (1957). *No and Yes: On the Genesis of Human Communication.* New York: International Universities Press.

63

OBITUARY

Leo Berman, M.D. (April 13, 1913–December 27, 1958)

Leo Berman was at the time of his death a psychoanalyst engaged in private practice and research; instructor (1950–8) at the Harvard University Medical School; visiting psychiatrist in charge of group work at the Beth Israel Hospital (1952–8); training analyst (1952–8), control analyst (1954–8), Secretary of the Education Committee (1952–7) of the Boston Psychoanalytic Institute; Member of the Editorial Board, *American Journal of Orthopsychiatry* (1954–8); consultant of the Joint Commission on Mental Illness and Health (1956–8). He obtained his medical training at the Univeristy of Basel, Switzerland (M.D., 1937), and his psychoanalytic training at the Boston Psychoanalytic Institute (1941–5).

I

Leo Berman died young in the middle of unfinished work carried on to the last in spite of racking pain. He was not yet generally known outside his own geographical community, the Group for the Advancement of Psychiatry, and group therapy circles, nor had he written much. Yet his work made a lasting impression on his associates, friends, students, and readers of his

First published in The International Journal of Psycho-Analysis, *40:334–338, 1959.*

papers, and contributes to the development of the mainstream of psychoanalytic thought. I am writing about him here not only to express what many of us felt about him as a friend, but also to give voice to the intents that animated his work and life.

Leo Berman and his work are representative of the problems, trends, and aspirations of his generation of psychoanalysts. While his individuality, fierce integrity, courage, and dedication led to a unique synthesis of these problems, trends, and aspirations, his unassuming ways and the untimely interruption of his lifework tend to obscure his contributions to them. The very fact that Leo Berman's work remained uncompleted makes it a more faithful mirror of his generation than any completed lifework could be. Completed work—with the exception of the greatest—usually brings to a head the efforts of past generations, and thus tends to cloud what the current generation's struggle is about.

II

Leo Berman belonged to a generation of psychoanalysts which was steeped in clinical psychiatry. His training and experience included the best and most varied his time had to offer: Bellevue (with Schilder), Butler, Massachusetts General, Army Induction Center work, Cushing VA, Worcester State, Beth Israel (with Grete Bibring); and work with children: Bradley, Judge Baker, Manchester N. H. Child Guidance Clinic. Yet this varied experience did not turn him into an eclectic, and he became a thoroughly grounded analyst, as reflected by his position in the Boston Psychoanalytic Society and Institute.

Psychiatric consultation and hospital service were from first to last an integral part of his workday. In this he represented a goodly part of the Boston psychoanalytic community in which—more than in any other—this is, along with psychoanalytic work proper, part of the pattern of the psychoanalyst's work life.

III

The first psychoanalysts struggled—along with Freud—to deepen and widen psychoanalytic knowledge and its application. Their followers were bent on exegesis, consolidation, and preservation disrupted again and again by the ever-creative Freud's new discoveries, and by dissidents. This phase was followed by the struggle which centered around the development of the ego psychology and social psychology of psychoanalysis and resulted in sharply drawn lines between orthodoxy and dissidence. Leo Berman belonged to the generation of psychoanalysts which grew up as this struggle was abating. This generation of the mainstream of psychoanalysis, imbued with the spirit of a battle won, grew up taking psychoanalysis as an estab lished discipline for granted. In many psychoanalysts this attitude bred complacency in various degrees, in others an unfettered spirit of free search which combined a commitment to the mainstream with a tolerance for productive dissidence. Leo Berman wrote (1957a):

> . . . there seem to be two current trends in theory development in psychoanalysis: the dominant trend is in the direction of refining and elaborating upon the . . . model developed by Freud and the lesser trend seems to be in the direction of searching for different models. I fail to see any inherent conflict in such development. We can anticipate new findings and discoveries based on a variety of theoretical assumptions and time will make it clear which model or models will prove to be most fruitful.

And again:

> Some of us find an answer in orthodoxy, some through a brushing aside of the old, even, if some of the time, our reasons for doing so do not stem from very good understanding of the old. Then there are others of us who recommend changes in theory or technique with explanations that we are still in the mainstream of Freudian thought [1957b, p. 210].

It is clear where Leo Berman stood.

IV

This stand was, indeed, characteristic of him. His intense loyalty took the form of devotion to the historical continuity of the development of psychoanalysis, which in turn included his loyalty to his teachers (e.g., Schilder, the Bibrings), to their ideas, ideals, and the groups which formed around them. Why did these loyalties not turn him, as they did so many others, into a zealot, whose intransigence would freeze any once luminous teaching into rigid rules of practice and doldrums in theory? The explanation lies partly in his teachers, in Schilder's searching, tolerant, yet eclectic and erratic spirit, and in the Bibrings' unself-conscious and unstrained synthesis of the tradition of Vienna with pioneering freedom, but mainly in the fact that his loyalties were to ideas, and his personal loyalties were merely by-products. This made him as loyal to those whom he taught as to those from whom he learned: not only precise in his adherence to the knowledge to which he felt himself heir, but restless and searching when faced with the deficiencies and the ambiguities of this knowledge or of his own understanding. He taught at the Boston Institute, the Harvard Medical School, the Boston University School of Social Work, but chiefly he taught those associated with him in group work. And his teaching drove him to find new understanding, new teachers, and new solutions. In the last few years of his life it led him to a renewed study of psychoanalytic theory.

As a teacher, his demands were as exacting for himself as for his students. There was an aura of integrity around this unself-conscious, unassuming, simple man of ascetic aspect and intensity which commanded intense loyalties, inspiring devotion to work and a thirst for understanding.

V

The generation of psychoanalysts to which Leo Berman belonged matured in the shadow of the economic collapse of 1929, and its social conscience was awakened by it and kept awake by the depression which followed.

The war and the "prosperity" which accompanied and followed were deadening for social conscience; psychiatrists and analysts could—more easily than others—comfort themselves by making the help they gave to suffering men into a salve for their social conscience. Yet this surge of social conscience, however fleeting, had a positive effect on the development of psychoanalytic thinking: the application of psychoanalytic knowledge to psychotherapy—making its fruits available to many to whom psychoanalysis is not available—ceased to be the exception and became common practice.

Leo Berman's social conscience was not put to sleep by prosperity. His was a social conscience in which the rôle of assuaging personal guilt was small, and the rôle of the conviction that intelligence and knowledge can, and therefore must, be applied to assuage suffering was large. With Schilder's and the Bibrings' example before him, he used psychoanalytic psychotherapy where analysis was not feasible or not indicated. But he also believed that new ways had to be found to make psychoanalytic insight useful in the treatment and prevention of suffering. Impressed by Schilder's example, he saw one of these new ways in psychoanalytic group work.

Freud once commented on a paper by Wilhelm Reich: "Reich's presentation has a weak point. It is motivated by therapeutic ambitiousness. This attitude is useless by half for science. It is too tendentious. Free search is enormously hampered by it." This censure applies to many attempts at "brief therapy," but not to all, and certainly not to Berman's, as his critical comments on "brief psychotherapy" show (see 1957b). His dedication to therapy was controlled by his scientific conscience: he conducted his group work as an exploration into psychoanalytic ego psychology and psychoanalytic social psychology. It was from the advances to be achieved in these —and not simply from the therapeutic results—that he expected not only *relief* of suffering but also *prevention* of avoidable misery.

VI

Research by psychoanalysts other than that issuing from psychoanalytic work proper has always been rare. It is still scarce, but the reason for this is no longer what it once was, namely that the problems to be solved could be approached only by means of the psychoanalytic technique itself. The reason now is, to begin with, the psychoanalyst's long, arduous, and expensive clinical training, and later on both his lack of specific research training and the gap between the financial rewards of research and therapeutic work.

Leo Berman belonged to the minority which was not deterred by these heavy odds. What enabled him to take such odds was a particular view of life (including an attitude toward money and comforts) and a wife who shared it. It was not so much that he was indifferent to money and prestige: he disliked the lack of the one and enjoyed the other when it came his way. It was rather that his tastes were ascetic: the home he and his wife (who gave up the practice of psychiatry to raise their five children and to stand by him) created had no unnecessary amenities and luxuries to supplement or replace what they could give each other and their children by their very existence and devotion. Instead of luxuries this home had music (Leo Berman played the violin and his older children the piano), books, and paintings. Though he enjoyed the prestige that his work brought him in the last years, he entered on his research in group methods of therapy and education knowing that this might bring him criticism rather than prestige in his psychoanalytic community. But perhaps "knowing" is the wrong word here. It seems to imply something alien to Leo Berman, who did what his reason and heart told him to do without calculating the cost.

VII

Leo Berman did not leave a systematic statement of the insights to which his work led him, though he spoke about them in various passages in his papers and in conversations. He was struck by the significance of the analyst as a "real" person in the therapeutic situation, and the study of this led him to problems central for the future development of the psychoanalytic psychology of the ego, and of reality relationships.

His experience taught him that the conception of the analyst as a "blank screen" is a fiction, which, however convenient otherwise, prevents the understanding of a great many therapeutic situations. He searched for those factors which "help the patient in his anxious, searching and indispensable evaluation of the analyst as a real person" (1950, p. 158). He did so not only in psychotherapy but in psychoanalysis proper, endeavoring to go beyond both the "blank screen" and the "countertransference" conceptions of the rôle of the psychoanalyst. He wrote:

> Technical expressions such as the aim-inhibited libidinal impulses of the analyst, or the normal residue of countertransference, although pertinent, are not sufficiently inclusive. Actually most analysts' positive feelings for their patients involve a wider range . . . whose totality we shall describe as *dedication* [1949, p. 161].

His experiences showed him that the psychoanalyst forecloses the development of the psychoanalytic theory of reality relations not only when he accepts an exclusive blank-screen or countertransference conception of the therapist's rôle, but also when he blindly relies on the patient's communications about the important persons in his life in the reconstruction of these figures. He wrote:

> We are probably misled by our patients' descriptions of important figures in their lives more often than we realize it, even after they have been in analysis for longer periods. In any case, it would be interesting to make a study of such inferred images by analysts and to test their accuracy [1957a].

Leo Berman knew well (see 1957b) the usual, all-too-ready answers to the disquieting questions which arose from his experience. Whenever he encountered in therapy phenomena which appeared unaccounted for in or contrary to psychoanalytic theory, he asked himself whether he was meeting limitations of his own knowledge or limitations inherent in psychoanalytic theory. But when he felt satisfied that he was observing a limitation of the theory, he spoke out. In others this might have taken remarkable courage; for him it was simply the only way.

He spoke out of experience and not from theoretical speculations. But once he had crystallized what his experience told him, he tried to fathom it theoretically. He saw (1957a) that the focusing of psychoanalytic interest on fantasy life and on the reconstruction of the past resulted in an insufficient concern for reality relationships in both practice and theory. But he considered this an error of emphasis to be remedied, and not an inherent flaw in the theory. In studying these shortcomings of the theory he turned to Hartmann's and Erikson's work for conceptual tools.

VIII

When work is carried on in the spirit of devotion to the continuity of a science, its originality is likely to be hidden rather than displayed, since the investigator who works in this spirit considers what he does to be simply the understanding, the clarification, and the application of the knowledge he is heir to. This was Leo Berman's attitude to his work.

Group work was certainly nothing new when he came to it, and its use in therapy, training, and education was not new either. Group work with a psychoanalytic slant too existed before Berman's, and to many psychoanalysts such an interest as "psychoanalytically oriented group psychotherapies" seemed an alien and unnecessary adventure.

He was convinced that psychoanalytic group psychotherapy "can be approximately as effective [as individual psychoanalytic psychotherapy] in attaining the limited goals which any sound psychoanalytic psychotherapy (apart from regular psychoanalysis) strives for" (1950, p. 161). Therefore

in his work with groups he used all the techniques of psychoanalytic psychotherapy and insisted that psychoanalytic group therapy is not limited to
"offering . . . support on a superficial level, or . . . social intercourse
and a strengthening of ego defenses through an intellectual discussion of
. . . conflicts, defenses, and transference reactions" (1954, p. 423); that
the regressive potential of the group situation must neither be regarded as
its central therapeutic agent, nor be avoided at all costs (1950); that the
neglect or deliberate avoidance of the genetic method of psychoanalysis in
group therapy severely limits its efficacy (1950).

There is one more respect in which he differed from many other group
workers: the standards of training he demanded for the people who were to
work with groups were high. He wrote:

> Current practices . . . suggest that far too many workers are under-
> taking to carry out group psychotherapy without adequate training and
> supervision. The trend toward such practices has been facilitated by the
> lack of active interest in this field on the part of many experienced
> psychiatrists and psychoanalysts [1954, p. 425].

IX

Leo Berman saw the individual therapy situation as a special case of the
group situation (1950). He found that the psychoanalyst who is experienced in the group situation has a better understanding of the reality relationships of those patients whom he treats individually. Indeed, it was his
vision that the solution of many ego-psychological and social-psychological
problems, which would yield new theoretical insights and new techniques
for psychoanalysis and psychotherapy, could be attained by research in
psychoanalytic group work rather than in individual therapy. He specified
several of these outstanding problems.

He pointed out that according to Freud, in mental illness the epinosic
(secondary) gain is not the only contribution of external reality, since the
paranosic (primary) gain too has an "external component" contributed by
reality (1905, p. 43 n.). He stressed that in psychoanalysis the concern with
reality relationships is still centered mainly on the epinosic (secondary)
gain, and that Freud's insight into the rôle of reality in determining the form
of the symptom so that it will attain the primary gain has remained unex-
ploited, though it pinpoints an important problem of the theory of reality
relationships.

He called attention to the fact that psychoanalysis still deals with action
mainly in terms of "acting out," blurring and overusing the concept and
endowing it with a moralistic connotation, so that the psychoanalytic study
and understanding of action proper is badly neglected (1957a).

Berman was aware that these clinical problems which he came upon in his experience converge with those which Hartmann conceptualized. The vision he pursued was to bridge the gap between the internal dynamics of the person which is revealed by psychoanalytic investigation and his every-day actions in his social reality which are directly observed. Since *both* of these seemed to him accessible to observation in the psychoanalytic group therapy situation, he strove to demonstrate that psychoanalytic work with groups is the method by which this gap can be bridged and a psychoanalytic social psychology be built.

X

If this memorial has spoken as much about psychoanalysis in our time as about Leo Berman himself, it should be said that he would have wanted it that way.

REFERENCES

Berman, L. (1949). Counter-transferences and Attitudes of the Analyst in the Therapeutic Process. *Psychiatry*, 12:159–166.
——— (1950). Psychoanalysis and Group Psychotherapy. *Psychoanal. Rev.*, 37:156–163.
——— (1954). Psychoanalysis and the Group. *Amer. J. Orthopsychiat.*, 24:421–425.
——— (1957a). Problems in Working toward an Integration of Individual and Group Psychology. Read before the American Psychoanalytic Association. (Abs. *J. Amer. Psychoanal. Assn.*, 6:121–123, 1958.)
——— (1957b). Some Recent Trends in Psychoanalysis. *Amer. J. Orthopsy-chiat.*, 27:202–211.
Freud, S. (1905 [1901]). Fragment of an Analysis of a Case of Hysteria. *Standard Edition*, 7:7–122. London: Hogarth Press, 1953.

64

PSYCHOANALYSIS AS A
DEVELOPMENTAL
PSYCHOLOGY

For this occasion I have set myself the task of exploring some of the basic
concepts of psychoanalysis as a developmental psychology. I will attempt to
do three things: first, to demonstrate that the core of psychoanalysis as a
developmental psychology is the concept of instinctual drives and drive-
restraining factors; second, to clarify the relation between instinctual drives
and experience; and finally, to reconsider the developmental relation between archaic and ordered forms of thought. For each of these topics I will
present a brief survey of the outstanding relevant theories and discoveries
of present-day nonpsychoanalytic developmental psychology. These surveys will be brief and my choice of examples perforce arbitrary; and, although some of the examples are still controversial, I shall not attempt to
enter on these controversies here to justify my choice.

    Paradoxically, the significance of ego psychology, which is a relatively

*Revision of an address given September 21, 1957, at the presentation of the Freud
statue by the American Psychoanalytic Association to Clark University, to commemo-
rate Freud's only visit and lectures in this country. First published in Bernard Kaplan
and Seymour Wapner, eds.,* Perspectives in Psychological Theory: Essays in Honor of
Heinz Werner. *New York: International Universities Press, 1960, pp. 209–255.*

    *This study was made possible by the Ford Foundation's grant in support of research
at the Austen Riggs Center.*

recent branch of psychoanalysis, for psychoanalysis as a developmental psychology is (owing to the work of Hartmann and particularly Erikson) better understood than the significance of some concepts which have a much longer history in psychoanalysis. I will discuss today some of these older concepts and only where they require it will I touch on ego psychology.

First, however, a few words concerning the concept of development and developmental psychology. In speaking of developmental psychology I refer to those investigations and theories which Werner (1948) surveyed, and not to the "child-study" and "child-development" movement and investigations fashionable in the 1930's and '40's.

Paul Weiss (1939) characterized development as a process of autonomous and progressive differentiation of the somatic organizations which are required for the functioning of the organism, and considered the process to be "determined by *intrinsic* developmental factors quite unrelated to actual functioning" (p. 569). His formulation implies that the development of behavior as seen by the student of organic (as against psychological) development is, on the whole, independent of experience. Weiss writes:

> . . . we must concede to the behavioral system the capacity of being later, secondarily, elaborated into greater detail, higher efficiency, and finer adjustments under the guidance of its actual operation. In order to rate these . . . improvements correctly, one must keep in mind that they compare with the ground-work of organization as the interior decoration of a building compares with its construction [p. 570].

Developmental psychology as a rule uses the term "maturation" to describe those "intrinsic factors" which are prior to and independent of experience, and the term "development" to refer both to these and to their interaction with experience. In the past, attention has only too often been distracted from the rôle of "intrinsic factor" in human behavior by the fact that in human development these intrinsic factors are more flexible than they are in the development of lower organisms, and by the fact that their interaction with experience is far more extensive than what is observed in organic development. In the period when behaviorism dominated psychology, the rôle of experience in development was the focus of interest, and little effort was devoted to the search for maturational factors in human behavior other than those involved in somatic development. Freud's and Heinz Werner's (1948) developmental psychologies did not conform to the trend of this period. Werner searched for the common characteristics of developmental changes, regardless of their experiential content, and defined developmental psychology as follows:

> . . . a discipline which investigates the characteristics common to any behavior in the process of progression or regression, in order to establish both the common pattern of each developmental level and the

relationship between these levels, that is, the direction of mental development [1957].

Clearly his quest was for intrinsic maturational factors.

As for psychoanalysis as a developmental psychology, it is my purpose to demonstrate that its central achievement was the disentangling of an intrinsic maturational factor from the tangle of the progressive changes apparently wrought by experience. I consider such a demonstration the more important since it is this central achievement of Freud's which has been abandoned by all the so-called neo-Freudian schools, whose theories, without exception, lack such an intrinsic factor.

THE CONCEPT OF DRIVE AS THE CORE OF FREUD'S DEVELOPMENTAL THEORY

I shall first briefly sketch Freud's discovery of an intrinsic maturational factor, in order to lay the groundwork for the discussion of this factor and of Freud's genetic method.

Freud's initial discoveries and theory (Breuer and Freud, 1893–95; Freud, 1893–96) were not developmental. His discoveries of traumatic experiences, the unconscious memories and dammed-up affects pertaining to them, and his explanation of these[1] established connections only between experience and subsequent behavior, and involved no intrinsic maturational factors. Hartmann and Kris (1945) characterized such connections as anamnestic, but not genetic in their sense or developmental in our sense.[2] The meaning of these discoveries changed radically when Freud in 1897[3] found that his patients' reports of seduction in infancy referred not to real experiences but to childhood fantasies. The study of these fantasies brought into view something whose impact on behavior is equal to, or even greater than, the impact of external reality. Freud's (1900) account of this factor made internal, psychological reality the subject matter of science for the first time.

Freud conceived of these fantasies as wish fulfillments of instinctual drives, particularly sexual drives, and he generalized this conception into the central proposition of psychoanalytic theory, that innate, progressively maturing, unconscious instinctual drives underlie the conscious and experiential determiners of behavior. With this conception of instinctual drives, Freud postulated an *intrinsic* maturational factor independent of prior expe-

---

[1] Defense against re-experiencing the traumatic situation, e.g., sexual seduction.

[2] "The genetic approach in psychoanalysis does not deal only with anamnestic data, nor does it intend to show only 'how the past is contained in the present.' Genetic propositions describe why, in past situations of conflict, a specific solution was adopted; why the one was retained and the other dropped, and what causal relation exists between these solutions and later developments" (Hartmann and Kris, 1945, p. 17).

[3] This date refers to Draft M (pp. 202–205) and Draft N (pp. 207–210) in Freud (1887–1902).

rience, and thus went beyond the anamnestic relationship between behavior and antecedent experience. The theory of the phases of libido development, which is so often regarded as the core of Freud's developmental theory (1905), is simply the specific theory of the development of this particular instinctual drive, which, considered by itself, can be construed as the progressive alteration of the libidinal drive by experience (see Kardiner, 1939, 1945; and Sullivan, 1953). The significance of the theory of instinctual drives for developmental psychology becomes particularly clear if we contrast this theory with associationist and conditioning theories, the pure forms of which attempt to explain behavior solely in terms of antecedent experience, that is, in terms of learning not organized by and around intrinsic maturational factors.[4]

The method by which Freud arrived at his concept of instinctual drives is also fundamental to his developmental psychology, because it is by that method that he also arrived at the conception of the relation between the intrinsic maturational ("constitutional") and the experiential ("accidental") factors in the determination of behavior. He formulated this relation as follows:

> It is not easy to estimate the relative efficacy of the constitutional and accidental factors. . . . The constitutional factor must await experiences before it can make itself felt; the accidental factor must have a constitutional basis in order to come into operation. To cover the majority of cases we can picture . . . a 'complemental series,' in which the diminishing intensity of one factor is balanced by the increasing intensity of the other [1905, pp. 239–240].

The method—Hartmann and Kris (1945) termed it "the genetic approach" —consists of starting out with a given behavior and situation, and tracing a series of antecedent behaviors, all of which were attempts to solve the same problem posed by the mounting intensity of an instinctual drive, in various situations and at various stages of development. The further back in such a series one goes, the more the relative significance of the experiential (accidental) factor recedes, and the more instinctual drive (the intrinsic maturational factor) and the specific developmental phase in which the problem originally arose and in which the pattern for its ultimate solution was set, become dominant.

The usefulness of the genetic approach for developmental psychology

[4] Some of the reinforcement theorists (e.g., Miller, Dollard, Mowrer) tend to assume that their learning (conditioning) theories are compatible with the psychoanalytic theory and provide it with a learning theory—which it does indeed sorely need. The fact that they have a drive concept seems to suggest that these learning theories are compatible with psychoanalysis. But this is a fallacy: their drive concept is not an intrinsic maturational factor. Moreover, while a psychoanalytic ego psychology has shown (see pp. 825–826, 842 below) that not all behavior can be explained by tension reduction (reinforcement) alone, the sole central principle of these theories is tension reduction. For a discussion of these points, see Rapaport (1952, 1953a).

seems to be limited by the fact that the evidence for its validity comes mainly from the psychoanalytic situation, where the method is complicated by *interpretations*. Freud was aware of these limitations, and wrote:

> The direct observation of children has the disadvantage of working upon data which are easily misunderstandable; psycho-analysis is made difficult by the fact that it can only reach its data, as well as its conclusions, after long détours. But by co-operation the two methods can attain a satisfactory degree of certainty in their findings [1905, p. 201].

In the last decades persistent attempts have been made to carry out what Freud suggested here (Anna Freud and Burlingham, 1943, 1944; Anna Freud and Dann, 1951; Spitz, 1946a, 1946b, 1949; Leitch, 1948; Leitch and Escalona, 1949; Escalona et al., 1952; Kris, 1951, 1955; Benjamin, 1959; P. H. Wolff, 1959; Coleman, Kris, and Provence, 1953; and others). Yet the limitations of the method may not be so formidable as they seem when we consider that Freud developed the genetic approach when he was still using the cathartic technique which involves no interpretations. Be that as it may, the significance of the genetic approach for developmental psychology is not only that it is a method which traces an intrinsic maturational factor—instinctual drive—underlying behavior, but also that it traces the development of a complex unit, namely, "behavior as a problem solution," rather than the development of isolated organs, functions, or abilities. Because the genetic approach can trace the developmental course of complex behaviors, it enabled psychoanalysis to bring the study of personality development within the scope of developmental psychology, a feat not even attempted by any other developmental theory.

The discussion of the instinctual drives as intrinsic maturational factors would be incomplete if I did not mention another closely related discovery of Freud's: the intrinsic factors that restrain instinctual drives. I will discuss these more fully in the last part of this paper, but I want to indicate here that it is this concept that enables psychoanalysis to account for both tension discharge and tension maintenance without explaining either as the consequence of environmental influences alone.

The central rôle of conflict in psychopathology was one of Freud's early discoveries, and it confronted him with the question, What are the conflicting factors? at a time when he still explained behavior by antecedent experience alone (Breuer and Freud, 1893–95), and had not yet arrived at his conception of the instinctual drive. Both of the factors which he designated then as the components of the conflict he conceived of as originating in experience: the affect elicited by experience[5] and the defense mechanisms

---

[5] At this time Freud's (1900, pp. 468, 582) view of affects rested on the James-Lange theory.

resulting from environmental necessity. But when the instinctual drive as an intrinsic maturational factor took the place of affect as one of the factors in the conflict (1900), the question, What is the nature of the other factor? arose again. In regard to this factor Freud wavered: in 1900 and 1911 he believed that it was experiential in nature, while in 1905 and 1914 he saw it as a manifestation of another intrinsic maturational factor. I will quote here only Freud's earliest statement of the latter view, without discussing the ramifications of this conception in present-day psychoanalytic ego psychology:

> It is during [the] . . . period of total or only partial latency that are built up the mental forces which are later to impede the course of the sexual instinct and, like dams, restrict its flow—disgust, feelings of shame and the claims of aesthetic and moral ideals. One gets an impression from civilized children that the construction of these dams is a product of education, and no doubt education has much to do with it. But in reality this development is organically determined and fixed by heredity, and it can occasionally occur without any help at all from education [1905, pp. 177–178].[6]

Freud's ego psychology, which he began to develop in "The Unconscious" (1915b), and continued in 1923, 1926, 1933, and 1937, increasingly implied such an intrinsic restraining factor among the other intrinsic factors in ego development. Anna Freud's (1936) work on defenses, Hartmann's (1939) on adaptation, and Erikson's (1939, 1940) on psychosocial development made this factor more explicit. Finally, Hartmann, Kris, and Loewenstein (1946) arrived at the explicit recognition that the ego in general (and this implies those of its functions which restrain instinctual drives) cannot be derived from the conflict between instinctual drives and reality. They concluded therefore that the assumption that the ego differentiates from the id under the impact of reality is untenable and must be replaced by the assumption that both id and ego differentiate from a common undifferentiated matrix. They further concluded that the ego enters the conflict between id and environment as an independent agent rooted in, among other things, both restraining and adaptive intrinsic maturational factors. The discussion of ego development in general and of the adaptive and other intrinsic maturational factors involved in it are beyond the scope of this paper, yet I want to conclude this section with the most general formulation of the intrinsic maturational factors to be found in psychoanalytic literature. It is Erikson's:

> [In this] sequence . . . the child merely obeys, and on the whole can be trusted to obey inner laws of development, namely those laws which in the prenatal period formed one organ after another, and now

[6] For a parallel statement, see Freud (1900, p. 537).

(as these organs reach out to reality) create one behavior item after another [1940, p. 717].

. . . this evolutionary principle of epigenesis . . . governs the unfolding before birth of the organic basis for all behavior and continues after birth to govern the unfolding of an individual's social potentialities in the successive encounters of impulse systems and cultural realities [1939, pp. 131–132].

I will now briefly survey some observations and some theories other than psychoanalytic which seem to parallel the developmental concepts of psychoanalysis here discussed. The theoretical significance of these similarities is still far from clear. Nor are the observations and theories I will sketch necessarily uncontested. They are presented here partly to show the existence of trends convergent with Freud's conceptions, which stood alone when he advanced them and for a long time thereafter, and partly because some of them seem to have arisen under Freud's influence.

The central implication of the concept of the instinctual drive is that there are certain unlearned appetitive behaviors. The findings obtained by means of the genetic approach show that there exist stages of development determined by intrinsic maturational factors, that these stages are decisive for the effect of experiences encountered during them, and that early experiences are decisive for the whole course of development. The study of the behavior of animals has brought forth many parallel findings. Whether these parallel observations and concepts confirm the basic developmental conceptions of psychoanalysis cannot be unequivocally established at present.

Appetitive behaviors in animals have been observed by Whitman (1919), Heinroth (1910, 1938), and Craig (1918). Lashley (1914, 1938) also studied these, called them instincts, and distinguished them from habits as "prefunctional" (that is, independent of experience), and from reflexes as flexible and complex. Whitman's, Heinroth's, and Craig's observations were systematically followed up by Lorenz (1935, 1937a, 1937b, 1937c, 1942–43), who explained these appetitive behaviors in terms of the concepts of "innate releasing mechanisms" and "reaction-specific energies," which are parallel to the psychoanalytic concept of the instinctual drives as intrinsic maturational factors. Lorenz's work was followed up by a group of investigators who call their discipline ethology, and their findings necessitated, among others, the concept of "innate inhibitory mechanisms" (Thorpe, 1956), which seem to parallel the intrinsic restraining factors of psychoanalysis.

Richter's and Young's studies of appetites followed Katz's exploratory studies on hunger and appetite and Davis's studies on self-selection of diet in the human child. Richter (1941), having destroyed the organ or center for the homeostatic regulation of liquid intake, salinity, temperature, etc., observed appetitive behavior which tended to restore the equilibrium previously apparently maintained by the extirpated organ. He concluded from his observations:

> The results . . . establish the fact that, after the physiological means of maintaining a constant internal environment have been removed, the organism itself makes an effort to attain this end. We may conclude either that the behavior factors take over only after the physiological factors have been eliminated or that in the intact organism they both must function more or less at the same time. In all probability the latter conclusion gives the most accurate description of this situation [pp. 107–108].

Richter termed these behavioral factors "drives." Young (1949) in his experiments demonstrated that in the selection of food, three factors, physiological need, a behavioral factor which he termed *preference* or *hedonic arousal,* and learning usually collaborate and can substitute for each other adaptively, but that any one of them may also conflict with the others and can be experimentally manipulated so that either the preference or the learning will result in unadaptive behavior, i.e., behavior contrary to the physiological needs of the organism. It is hardly necessary to say that such relationships between instinctual drives, physiological needs, and experience in man are clinical commonplaces. These observations, in addition to being parallel to psychoanalytic observation and theory, highlight the fact that "drive" and "preference" are not identical with physiological needs, nor is the principle of tension reduction identical with the homeostatic regulations of the organism, though only too many psychoanalysts and psychologists have gratuitously assumed this to be the case.

Stages of maturation whose sequence is independent of experience and which determine the impact and subsequent effects of the experiences taking place in them have been demonstrated in animals by Scott and Marston (1950), Scott, Fredericson, and Fuller (1951), and others. They designate these stages as "sensitive periods," a term which was introduced by Lorenz (1935) to describe the early and brief period when, in certain species of birds, the objects encountered determine the subsequent social relationships of the individual.[7] The process itself he named "imprinting." Imprinting was observed by Craig (1913, 1914), and others before him, and has since been confirmed for various species of birds and for a few species of mammals (see Beach and Jaynes, 1954). Of these studies the outstanding ones are those of Jaynes (1956, 1957) and Hess (1959).

Freud's proposition that early experiences are of particular significance for later development has other parallels besides the studies of imprinting. Notwithstanding Orlansky's (1949) conclusion that the evidence for Freud's thesis is meager, and the negative results of the replications of

[7] For Lorenz's further observations, see (1957).

Hunt's (1941; Hunt and Willoughby, 1939) "hoarding" studies (e.g., Mc-Kelvey and Marx, 1951), parallel propositions derived from animal experiments have been accumulating in the literature (see Beach and Jaynes, 1954). An early observation by Lashley (1914) is of historical interest, and Levy's pioneering studies (1934, 1935, 1938) should also be mentioned. More recent studies are those of Fredericson (1951), Kahn (1951), Hall and Whiteman (1951), Christie (1952), Kagan and Beach (1953), Thompson and Heron (1954a, 1954b); Bernstein (1952), Scott (1955), Weininger (1956), Levine (1956) (experiments on early handling); Nissen et al. (1951), Riesen (1951) (early sensory and motor deprivation); and Harlow and Zimmermann (1959) ("mothering").

In addition to these observations and concepts, three major theories, those of Piaget, Werner, and Hebb, also show some parallels to Freud's theory. Piaget's concepts are in general radically different from those of psychoanalysis (Piaget, 1956). Nevertheless, both are developmental psychologies, and for this reason a number of parallels exist between them.[8] Two of these are relevant here: first, Piaget (1936, 1937) too assumes an intrinsic maturational factor (the circular reflex and its disequilibrium, i.e., the motivation he terms "desirability"); and second, one of his crucial conceptions is that intelligence develops through a series of stages. Werner's (1948; Werner and Wapner, 1949, 1952) theory of development and his physiognomic, sensoritonic theory of perception and cognition also involve intrinsic maturational factors and a conception of stages (levels) of development. Hebb's (1949) neurological theory of behavior emphasizes the pre-experiential and autonomous activity of the brain, the processes which take place between the stimulus and the response, and the slowness of early learning in contrast to late learning, all of which seem to imply an intrinsic maturational factor and a specific rôle of early development.[9]

To sum up: The core of psychoanalysis as a developmental psychology is the concepts of instinctual drives and restraining factors and the genetic approach, which are in sharp contrast to the agenetic conceptions of behavioristic learning theories and neo-Freudian psychodynamics. These concepts and the basic observations underlying them have parallels in the concepts, observations, and experimental findings of ethology, in the experimental findings concerning appetites, developmental phases, and the effects of early experiences on mature behavior in animals, in Werner's and Piaget's theories of development, and in the developmental aspect of Hebb's neurological theory.

[8] P. H. Wolff's (1960) comparative study of the theories of psychoanalysis and Piaget develops this point.
[9] I. H. Paul's study (1959) sheds further light on the parallel characteristics of Freud's and Hebb's theories.

THE NATURE OF THE INSTINCTUAL DRIVE
AND ITS RELATION TO EXPERIENCE

To clarify the relationship between experience and the instinctual drive, a further examination must be made of the concept of instinctual drive, particularly of the subsidiary concepts of cathexis, zone, aim, and object, because it is by means of these that the psychoanalytic theory unites the intrinsic and the experiential components of psychological development. A brief review of Freud's (1905) theory of psychosexual development will provide the background for this discussion.

Freud outlined his theory of the nature and development of the instinctual drive in *Three Essays on the Theory of Sexuality* (1905), primarily in regard to the sexual instinct. He marshaled evidence concerning the developmental levels, variations, and ecology of sexual behavior: he invoked evidence showing that perversions and inversions can occur in people who are not otherwise maladjusted; that some have been accepted practices in high civilizations; that in situations of deprivation they are practiced by people to whom they are alien otherwise; that most of them appear transiently in infancy and childhood; that they are common contents of the fantasies, practices, and symptoms of neurotic and psychotic patients; and that many of them appear as parts of the play preceding sexual intercourse. Most of this evidence is amply supported by statistical studies of human sexual patterns (Kinsey et al., 1948, 1953) and parallel evidence concerning animals is now also available (Ford and Beach, 1951).

What inferences did Freud draw concerning the *development* of the instinctual drive? He concluded that perversions and inversions correspond to early maturational forms of the sexual instinct which in the usual course of development leave a residue that is later integrated with, and functions under the primacy of, the fully developed genital sexual instinct. If this development is impeded, or if the fully developed sexual drive is interfered with, perversions, inversions, or related symbolic substitute behaviors will arise. The implications of Freud's conclusions are paralleled in Werner's conception of the relationship between genetic levels: ". . . all higher organisms manifest a certain range of operations of genetically different levels . . . the more mature individual compared with the less mature has at his disposal a greater number of developmentally different operations" (1957, pp. 20–21).

What inferences did Freud draw as to the *nature* of the instinctual drive? He concluded that the instinctual drive is a force which expends energy in its work, has a source, an aim, and an object (see also Freud, 1915a). The source is the erotogenic zone (e.g., the mouth in the oral phase) which changes from phase to phase. The aim is the tendency to discharge the accumulated energy of the instinctual drive. The object is both the stimulus which releases the energy-discharging action, and the object toward which the action is directed. If internal restraining factors develop prematurely, or if they are excessively strengthened by experience, or if external conditions prevent discharge, the energy of the instinctual drive is diverted (displaced) into collateral channels or is regressively displaced to an earlier maturational (zonal) position, and will be discharged in the form of a perversion, inversion, or symptom.

The phenomenon of displacement was one of Freud's earliest and most original observations. Freud discovered, as early as 1893, by means of the cathartic method, that the abreaction of dammed-up "affects" results in the disappearance of symptoms which are apparently unrelated to the "affect" in question. It was to explain these discoveries that Freud (1894) first introduced a quantitative concept (affect quantity) into his theory:

> . . . among the psychic functions there is something which should be differentiated (an amount of affect, a sum of excitation), something having all the attributes of a quantity—although we possess no means of measuring it—a something which is capable of increase, decrease, displacement and discharge, and which extends itself over the memory-traces of an idea like an electric charge over the surface of the body [1894, p. 75].

Later on, Freud conceptualized this quantity as cathexis (energy charge), and this concept plays an important rôle in his theory of development. For instance, there are at least two ways of accounting for the shifts in the course of maturation from one erogenous zone as the source of instinctual-drive energy to another. These shifts can be explained by assuming that cathexes are displaced from one zone to another, or by assuming that the erogenous zones mature in sequence, each of them, when matured, becoming a source of cathexes of a specific quality.

The concept of cathexis is crucial for psychoanalysis as a developmental psychology not only in connection with displacement, but in another respect as well. Every theory of human behavior must account for the basic observation that there is a difference between those behaviors which are peremptory—that is, over which the individual has no control [10]—and those which the individual can take or leave. Obsessive ideas and compulsive acts are of the former type; everyday behavior is, by and large, of the latter. This difference is significant for developmental psychology because observation shows that peremptory forms of behavior predominate in the early phases of human development, while voluntary ones predominate in later phases. Psychoanalytic theory accounts for the difference between these two types of behavior, and for the shift from the dominance of peremptory behavior, by

[10] This does not include those behaviors whose initiation the individual does control, but whose manner of execution is automatized and thus beyond his conscious control (see Hartmann, 1939).

the proposition that the peremptory behaviors occur when the tendency of cathexes toward displacement and discharge (a tendency common to all energy) is not extensively curtailed by structural limitations (controls). Conversely, in behaviors subject to the control of the individual, the tendency of cathexes toward displacement and discharge is greatly curtailed by controlling structures. The transition from the former to the latter condition is a process of maturation, which involves both instinctual drives and instinctual-drive restraints. Freud (1900) conceptualized this transition as that from the dominance of the primary to the secondary process. Present-day psychoanalytic theory (Hartmann, 1950, 1952, 1955; Kris, 1950, 1955; Rapaport, 1959) accounts for this transition by the concept of "neutralization of cathexes" in so far as it refers to the displaceable quantity itself, and "structure formation" (Rapaport, 1951) in so far as it refers to the conditions limiting the displacement and discharge of these quantities. Since neutralization of cathexes is one aspect of the development of instinctual drives, and since structure formation—one of the implications of this development—seems to be codetermined by experience (see Rapaport, 1957b, on stimulus nutriment), here we encounter one of the ways in which an intrinsic maturational factor interacts with and is modified by experience.

We must now turn to the concepts of zone and aim. According to Freud,

> . . . in itself an instinct is without quality . . . [it is] a measure of the demand made [by the organism] upon the mind for work. What distinguishes the instincts from one another and endows them with specific qualities is their relation to their somatic sources and to their aims. The source of an instinct is a process of excitation occurring in an organ and the immediate aim of the instinct lies in the removal of this organic stimulus [1905, p. 168].

But if the aim is the universal tendency of all drives toward discharge,[11] how can this aim lend distinctive qualities to different instinctual drives? The answer is that Freud used the term "aim" in two different senses.[12] One of these is the tendency toward discharge; the other becomes clear in, for instance, his discussion of the sexual aim in inversion. He wrote:

> Among men, intercourse *per anum* by no means coincides with inversion; masturbation is quite as frequently their exclusive aim, and it is even true that restrictions of sexual aim—to the point of its being limited to simple outpourings of emotion—are common . . . [1905, pp. 145–146].

Clearly, in this second sense of the term, the aim can be restricted, displaced, and substituted for. This aim is not the universal discharge tendency itself, but something more specific. What is it? Freud's various attempts to

---

11 See pp. 829–830 above.

12 This is particularly striking in "Instincts and Their Vicissitudes" (1915a).

answer this question contain unresolved contradictions.[13] The answer to the question of what endows the instinctual drive with quality, that is to say, what the aim in the second sense is, is, I believe, given by Erikson's concept of instinctual modes (1937, 1950b). Erikson points out that all zones— and, indeed, all functioning organs—have modes, determined by the mechanics of their functioning (e.g., the anus expels and retains), and these modes in turn characterize the discharge action proper to the zone. This amounts to the assumption that the various instinctual drives obtain their distinctive quality from these modes, that is, from the functional patterns of the zones, rather than from energies specific to each zone. The maturational shifts from zone to zone would thus be explained by displacement of cathexes rather than by zonal production of specific cathexes. This explanation would lead to the conception of a central rather than zonal origin of instinctual-drive energy. This conception in turn implies that the instinctual drive differentiates and gains a particular quality when it cathects each zone at the appropriate phase of maturation. The added advantage of this explanation, if it should prove to be empirically tenable and consistent with the rest of the theory, is that it would resolve the unsettled issue of the pluralistic vs. the monistic theory of instinctual drives in favor of the monistic. Ultimately, however, this is an empirical question, and we must be prepared for the possibility that the empirical evidence will require the postulation of a dual (both zonal and central) origin of instinctual-drive energy.

The assumption that the modes are the crucial characteristics of the zones has still other important consequences for psychoanalysis as a developmental psychology. Erikson has demonstrated that these modes and their sequence of ascendancy are not determined by experience. Thus they too are intrinsic maturational factors. However, their fate is codetermined by experience. Any given mode, when it reaches its specific phase of ascendancy, as experience accumulates generalizes to and becomes characteristic of other zones, organs, and behaviors also (e.g., the retentive mode of the anal phase will spread to prehensile behaviors, giving them a grabbing and possessive character). Indeed, this "estrangement" of modes (Erikson, 1937) from their zone progressively changes them from modes of instinctual-drive action into modes available for use in adaptive behavior, and ultimately transforms them into basic thought patterns. Both adaptive behavior and thought patterns are molded by experience and imply that this "estrangement" is codetermined by experience. Moreover, Erikson has also demonstrated that the encounter of these modes with the institutions of a given society shapes and selects those behavior modalities in the individual which are viable in that society (1950b), relegating the others to subordinate rôles or suppressing them altogether. Here again we encounter an interaction between an intrinsic maturational factor and experience.

[13] I have attempted to demonstrate this in some detail in my study of activity and passivity (1953b).

We turn now to the object of the instinctual drive (Freud, 1905, 1915a). On scrutiny, the concept of object proves to be one of Freud's most important conceptual inventions. It is the core of his solution of the problem of the purposiveness of human behavior. The instinctual drive is a force concept, that is, a causal concept, which cannot per se explain the purposiveness of behavior. The proposition that the object is one of the defining characteristics of the instinctual drive implies, however, that this force exerts an effect only when it encounters its object. Thus the instinctual drive is conceived of not as a blind but as a purposively acting force. The coordination of instinctual drive and object is assumed to be innate, i.e., given by evolution. While this coordination is rigid in lower-order animals, it is relatively flexible in man (see Hartmann, 1948), so that experience can modify the gratification of the instinctual drive by the substitution of objects. Thus in the variability of the object of the instinctual drive we again encounter the interaction of an intrinsic maturational factor with experience.

We may conclude that while in the psychoanalytic theory of development the defining characteristics of the instinctual drive, its cathexis, mode, and object, are intrinsic maturational factors, their vicissitudes are codetermined by experience. Thus the psychoanalytic theory of development unites maturational and experiential factors.

I will now review some nonpsychoanalytic parallels to the observations, concepts, and theories discussed in this section. Some of them have already been mentioned, and since parallels to the concepts of mode and object would carry us deep into the literature on learning and into the work of Piaget, I will concentrate on the parallels to the cathectic theory, which are mostly in the literature of ethology.[14] In reviewing these, however, we will also encounter parallels to the concepts of zone, mode, and object.

Lorenz (1937a, 1937b), as we have already seen, introduced two concepts in his study of appetitive behavior: "innate releasing mechanisms" and "reaction-specific energy." It is the latter of these that is of importance here. Lorenz defined it as "energy, specific to one definite activity, [which] is stored up while this activity remains quiescent and [which] is consumed in its discharge" (1950, p. 249). This conception appears to be parallel to the psychoanalytic conception of the zones as the sources of instinctual drive energy. Lorenz's conception of instinct also involved an object, the "releaser" which activates the "innate releasing mechanism." Analyzing experimentally the characteristics of such objects, he and others (Lorenz, 1950; Tinbergen, 1951) discovered that these objects are aggregates of stimuli, only some of which are indispensable for effecting release, and various combinations of which can effect adequate release. The concept of releaser, like Freud's instinctual-drive object, implies some flexibility of the relation between the innate releasing mechanism and the releaser.

14 Schur has explored some of these parallels in his recent papers (1958, 1960).

More recent ethological work, however, has led to a broader conception of the instinct and its relation to the object. Observation and study of the so-called "displacement activities" led at least some ethologists (see Thorpe, 1956) to the assumption of a "drive-specific energy" pertaining to certain groups of innate releasing mechanisms rather than a "reaction-specific energy" pertaining to a single such mechanism. This concept of general drive appears to parallel the conception of the central origin of instinctual-drive energy discussed above.

The displacement activities, named by Armstrong (1947, 1950), were first studied systematically by Tinbergen (1952), who defined them as follows:

> The irrelevancy is found in the fact that although an animal is clearly in fighting motivation, or, in other cases, in mating motivation —in general, when instinct "a" is activated—and although we know by experience that we must except movements belonging to the executive pattern of this instinct "a," we observe movements belonging to the executive pattern of another instinct, "b." The activity seems to be displaced from instinct "b," to which it belongs, to instinct "a" which uses it as if it were a part of its executive pattern [p. 6].

According to Tinbergen, such displacements occur (a) when there is a conflict between antagonistic drives (e.g., birds in a conflict between flight and fight may display, instead of either of these behaviors, a fragment of nesting behavior); (b) when an instinct is aroused but cannot be discharged (e.g., when the sex partner is dilatory, foreplay consisting of fragmentary fighting behavior may occur); (c) when excessive arousal has taken place (e.g., after a bird is flushed but encounters no danger, copulation may occur); (d) when stimulation suddenly ceases (e.g., when the opponent suddenly flees, nesting behavior or copulation may ensue); and (e) as an "afterdischarge" when the drive dies down gradually (e.g., after coition, fighting or nesting behavior may occur).

Tinbergen concluded that (a) displacement activities serve as outlets for residual drive-energy; (b) the behavior patterns used as outlets are those which, for some reason, offer least resistance; (c) displacement activities are usually incomplete forms of the drive activity from which the displacement occurred; and finally (d), on Liddell's evidence, "The fact that displacement activities appear before a neurotic stage is reached . . . indicates that outlet through displacement behavior is a form of defence against neurotic disorder of the central nervous system, enabling it to 'get rid' of the surplus of impulses which would otherwise damage it" (1952, p. 23).

The parallel between the psychoanalytic and ethological concepts of displacement needs no further comment.

But what of the relation between drive and object? I have already discussed the object as a releaser. Another relevant finding of the ethologists (see Lorenz, 1950; Tinbergen, 1952) is that the more the object fits the innate releasing mechanism, the lower the drive tension which it will release, and the higher the tension the less fitting the object need be to effect its release. But[15] ethology has made still other discoveries about the object. I have in mind the already-mentioned process of "imprinting," discovered by Craig (1914). Lorenz (1935, 1937c), who explored and named the phenomenon, concluded that (a) in certain species the objects of the social following instinct and of the sexual instinct are not entirely determined as innate receptory patterns, but must be completed by experience; (b) the limits on what objects can be imprinted are, however, innate, though they vary from species to species; (c) once imprinting has occurred, it is practically unalterable; (d) though imprinting occurs in relation to the social following instinct, it determines the object of the sexual instinct; (e) imprinting occurs only in a well-defined, early sensitive period of the animal's life. Most of these conclusions have been confirmed in rigorously controlled experiments by Jaynes (1956, 1957), Hess (1959), and others (see Beach and Jaynes, 1954).

Imprinting is a remarkable parallel not only to fixation and to the critical, sensitive periods familiar from the study of both libido and ego development (see Erikson, 1950a, 1950b), but also to Freud's (1905, 1914) propositions that (a) libidinal object choice is not specifically determined by the sexual drive in man, and (b) the first objects of the sexual drive are the objects of the self-preservative drive, that is to say, the people who take care of the infant. Thus in both psychoanalytic and ethological theory, experience plays a rôle in determining the choice of object, though psychoanalysis finds the rôle of experience broader than ethology does. This difference is—as Hartmann (1939, 1948) has suggested—probably owing to the difference between the rôle instincts play in the animal's adaptation to reality and the rôle instinctual drives play in man's.

Object attachment and fixation in psychoanalysis and imprinting in ethology refer to processes which create enduring relations between drives and objects. Since the processes which create enduring relationships of any sort are what we have in mind when we speak of learning, the study of imprinting and fixation might well serve as a point of departure for a learning theory relevant to developmental psychology.

To sum up: The crucial factors in the interaction between the instinctual drive and experience are the cathexes (since their displacements can be and are modulated by experience), the modes (since their capacity to become estranged from their zone, to be displaced to other zones, and to be selec-

---

15 Note the analogy to Freud's formulation that "Where the [drive] constitution is a marked one it will perhaps not require the support of actual experiences; while a great shock in real life will perhaps bring about a neurosis even in an average constitution . . . . this view of the relative aetiological importance of what is innate and what is accidentally experienced applies equally in other fields" (1905, p. 171).

tively turned into dominant modalities of behavior can be and is regulated by experience), and the object (because it is subject to substitutions in the course of experience). The literature of ethology provides observations and conceptions which parallel the psychoanalytic observations and conceptions pertaining to the interaction of instinctual drives and experience.

THE DEVELOPMENT OF THINKING

In this attempt to clarify what the basic concepts of psychoanalysis as a developmental psychology are, I have chosen the development of thinking for the third area of discussion, partly because the relationship of the primary to the secondary process which plays a central rôle in it is also crucial for the theory of development in general, and partly because in it we encounter both of the relationships discussed so far (instinctual drives vs. drive-restraining factors, intrinsic maturational vs. experiential factors of development). My purpose in what follows here is to explore the connection between these two relationships in the realm of thinking, and therefore my discussion of the development of thinking will of necessity be a limited one. Even though the development of thinking has many other aspects, I will concentrate only on the relation between the primary and the secondary thought processes. Moreover, though the development of thinking is an integral part of ego development and best discussed in that context, I will avoid a general discussion of its place and rôle in ego development.

The problem of the relation between instinctual drive and experience arose in Freud's studies not only in the form in which I have presented it above, but also in the form of the relation between drive-representing, wish-fulfilling thought and reality-representing adaptive thought. Freud did much to clarify the relationship between these two types of thought process, particularly in regard to the usual dominance of the latter over the former (see especially *The Interpretation of Dreams,* 1900), but many aspects of their relationship, and in particular their maturational and developmental relationship, remained ambiguous. Freud's discussion of this relationship left the general impression that the secondary process arises from the primary under the impact of experience. Yet, as we shall see, this may not be quite what Freud intended.

In *The Interpretation of Dreams* and *The Psychopathology of Everyday Life* (1901), Freud demonstrated the common characteristics of thinking in dreams, pathological states, and childhood. He termed the process responsible for these characteristics the primary process, in contrast to the process responsible for the ordered forms of adult thought which he termed the secondary process. The proposition that the forms of thought characteristic of dreams, pathological states, and childhood show striking common characteristics and thus belong to closely related developmental levels is paralleled by Werner (1948). But Freud's (1900, 1911) assertion that the primary process is the matrix out of which the secondary process arises involves him in contradictions. He wrote (1900):

> The bitter experience of life must have changed this primitive thought-activity into a more expedient secondary one [p. 566].[16]
>
> . . . [the] primitive psychical apparatus . . . [is] regulated by an effort to avoid an accumulation of excitation . . . [and avoids it by] repeating the experience of satisfaction, which involved a diminution of excitation . . . A current of this kind . . . we have termed a 'wish' . . . The first wishing seems to have been a hallucinatory cathecting of the memory of satisfaction. Such hallucinations, however, . . . proved to be inadequate to bring about . . . satisfaction.
>
> A second activity—or, as we put it, the activity of a second system —became necessary, which . . . diverted the excitation arising from the need along a roundabout path which ultimately, by means of voluntary movement, altered the external world in such a way that it became possible to arrive at a real perception of the object of satisfaction [pp. 598–599].
>
> Thought is after all nothing but a substitute for a hallucinatory wish . . . nothing but a wish can set our mental apparatus at work [p. 567].

Finally, he links the secondary process to the restraining factors:

> . . . the *first* . . . system is directed towards securing the *free discharge* of the quantities of excitation, while the *second* system . . . succeeds in *inhibiting* this discharge and in transforming the cathexis into a quiescent one . . . [p. 599].

Clearly, here Freud assumed that the secondary process arises from the primary process owing to "the bitter experience of life," and is motivated by the same wishes as the primary process; so that secondary-process thinking is merely a detour toward the memory of gratification; and although it has a controlling function over the primary process (in suppressing, delaying, and detouring it), it does not contribute anything to the thought process other than what is required by the demands of reality. We may paraphrase this conception as follows: the secondary process is a learned modification of the primary one and no intrinsic maturational factor contributes to its development. But Freud did not consistently carry out the conception just summarized in that he treated the idea of a primordial mental apparatus possessing only a primary process as a theoretical model, rather than as an actuality:

> It is true that, so far as we know, no psychical apparatus exists which possesses a primary process only and that such an apparatus is to that

---

[16] See also Freud (1911, p. 219).

extent a theoretical fiction. But this much is a fact: the primary processes are present in the mental apparatus from the first, while it is only
during the course of life that the secondary processes unfold, and
come to inhibit and overlay the primary ones; it may even be that their
complete domination is not attained until the prime of life [1900, p.
603].

Here we are faced with a difficulty. If a purely primary-process mental
apparatus is a theoretical fiction, then it must be assumed that the secondary process exists from the beginning. But Freud asserts that the secondary
process develops "only during the course of life." If he means that it is not
there in the beginning and arises only from the impact of "the bitter experience of life," then his theory at this point is a purely environmentalistic one,
and contradicts not only his assertion that no pure primary-process psychical apparatus can exist, but his conception of intrinsic maturational restraining factors as well. One obvious way out of this difficulty is to interpret Freud's proposition as follows: rudiments of the secondary process are
present from the beginning but their maturation is slow and dependent on
"the bitter experience of life." This assumption would be consistent with a
developmental theory of thinking.[17] *The Interpretation of Dreams* provides
no grounds for the assumption that this is what he meant, and we can only
conclude that Freud at that time did not perceive the difficulty, and therefore could not resolve it. It seems that when Freud introduced the concept
of the instinctual drive he only partially overcame his early environmentalism,[18] and it is still very much in evidence in his conception of the secondary
process.

A reconsideration of *Totem and Taboo* (1913) will shed further light on
Freud's conception of the secondary process. His discussion of animism as
a theoretical system and of the synthetic function inherent in it came close
to an explicit recognition of an intrinsic maturational factor in the development of the secondary process. Yet Freud did not disentangle the intrinsic
factor but, rather, gave an experiential explanation of the origins of taboos.

In *Totem and Taboo* Freud amassed evidence of the striking correspondence between the magic and animistic conceptions and practices of primitives and compulsion-neurotics (pp. 28–29), and set out to explain these
correspondences. He concluded that the conceptions and practices of primitives and compulsion-neurotics reflect and restrain the same sexual and hostile impulses. Once he had reached this conclusion, he was faced with the
question, Whence the tendency toward this restraint?

In other writings of the same period he explained the restraint in neurotics by the "antithesis between ego-instincts and sexual instincts" (1914, p.

17 With Piaget's in particular; see Wolff (1960).
18 See p. 822.

79). From our present vantage point these ego instincts, like other instinctual drives, would represent an intrinsic maturational factor. In *Totem and Taboo,* however, Freud rejected the possibility that the restraint is exerted by instincts with the argument that if this were the case, no external restraining laws like taboos would be necessary. Freud quotes Frazer in support of his argument:

> 'It is not easy to see why any deep human instinct should need to be reinforced by law. There is no law commanding men to eat and drink or forbidding them to put their hands in the fire. . . . The law only forbids men to do what their instincts incline them to do; what nature itself prohibits and punishes, it would be superfluous for the law to prohibit and punish' [1913, p. 123].

With Wundt, he regarded taboo as "the oldest human unwritten code of laws" (1913, p. 18). Searching for the origin of this law, he arrived, by his method of reconstruction, at the conclusion that these taboos have a historical, experiential origin in the murder of the primal father by his sons, followed by the sons' establishment of rules to prevent the recurrence of such deeds:

> Taboos, we must suppose, are prohibitions of primaeval antiquity which were at some time externally imposed upon a generation of primitive men; they must . . . no doubt have been impressed on them violently by the previous generation [p. 31].

Thus his explanation of the origins of taboo, like his explanation of the secondary process, was environmental, experiential, and not one in terms of an intrinsic maturational factor. But since he assumed that "Unless psychical processes were continued from one generation to another, if each generation were obliged to acquire its attitude to life anew, there would be no progress" (1913, p. 158), he had to explain how these environmentally imposed restrictions were transmitted, and his explanation was Lamarckian:

> A part of the problem seems to be met by the inheritance of psychical dispositions which, however, need to be given some sort of impetus in the life of the individual before they can be roused into actual operation [1913, p. 158].

The difficulties involved in adopting Lamarck's "inheritance of acquired characteristics" are obvious. But this explanation had still other difficulties. Freud himself wondered whether he was making the same mistake which led him, before 1897, to assume the reality of seduction in infancy. He wrote:

> If . . . we inquire among these neurotics to discover what were the deeds which provoked these reactions, we shall be disappointed. We

find no deeds, but only impulses and emotions, set upon evil ends but held back from their achievement. What lie behind the sense of guilt of neurotics are always *psychical* realities and never *factual* ones. . . .

May not the same have been true of primitive men? [1913, p. 159].

A positive answer to this question—a rejection of the assumption of the murder of the primal father as a historical fact—would have opened the way to a generalized conception of the secondary process and of drive restraint in terms of an intrinsic maturational factor, just as the rejection of the historical reality of seduction in infancy led to the conceptualization of the instinctual drive as an intrinsic maturational factor. However, Freud rejected this solution, even though, as we have seen (pp. 824–825) he did have a partial conception of an intrinsic developmental restraining factor.

Nor must we let ourselves be influenced too far in our judgement of primitive men by the analogy of neurotics. There are distinctions, too, which must be borne in mind . . . neurotics are above all *inhibited* in their actions: with them the thought is a complete substitute for the deed. Primitive men, on the other hand, are *uninhibited* . . . the deed . . . is a substitute for the thought. And that is why, without laying claim to any finality of judgement, I think that in the case before us it may safely be assumed that 'in the beginning was the Deed' [1913, p. 161].

Thus we see that here Freud made a decision analogous to the one which he had to revoke in 1897.

But if we shift our attention from Freud's conception of the origins of taboos to his discussion of their nature, we obtain a very different picture of his conception of the origins and nature of the secondary process. Throughout *Totem and Taboo* Freud stressed that taboos are not isolated phenomena but part of a broad system of thought:

The human race . . . [has] in the course of ages developed three such systems of thought—three great pictures of the universe: animistic (or mythological), religious and scientific. Of these, animism . . . is perhaps the one which is most consistent and exhaustive and which gives a truly complete explanation of the nature of the universe [p. 77].

. . . man's first theoretical achievement—the creation of spirits—seems to have arisen from the same source as the first moral restrictions to which he was subjected—the observances of taboo [p. 93].

Thus Freud viewed totem and taboo as integral parts of the animistic theory of the world. The question which now presents itself to us is: how can such an all-embracing system of thought arise from specific prohibitions imposed in ancient times and transmitted by the "inheritance of acquired characteristics"? Freud was aware of this problem:

> . . . we shall have to investigate that system's psychological characteristics . . . For the moment I will only say that the prototype of all such systems is what we have termed the 'secondary revision' of the content of dreams. And we must not forget that, at and after the stage at which systems are constructed, two sets of reasons can be assigned for every psychical event . . . one set belonging to the system and the other set real but unconscious [p. 65].

Thus here Freud places "systems" on the same level as unconscious impulses, refers to them as "reasons" (that is, causal factors), and, as we shall see, attributes to them a function independent from both external environmental pressure and id forces.

> The secondary revision of the product of the dream-work is an admirable example of the nature and pretensions of a system. There is an intellectual function in us which demands unity, connection and intelligibility from any material, whether of perception or thought, that comes within its grasp; and if, as a result of special circumstances, it is unable to establish a true connection, it does not hesitate to fabricate a false one. Systems constructed in this way are known to us not only from dreams, but also from phobias, from obsessive thinking and from delusions. The construction of systems is seen most strikingly in delusional disorders (in paranoia) . . . [p. 95].

Later on—when he had already laid down the foundations of his ego psychology in which thinking was conceived of as a function of the ego and the apparatuses used in thinking as ego apparatuses—Freud (1926) conceptualized these unifying, connecting, rationalizing processes as the synthetic functions of the ego. His reference here to these synthetic functions throws new light on his conception of the secondary process. In *The Interpretation of Dreams* (1900) the main attributes of the secondary process were the instinctual drive-restraining function and reality orientation. In "Formulations on the Two Principles of Mental Functioning" (1911), this reality orientation was elaborated into the reality principle, whose relation to the secondary process was conceived to be analogous to the relation of the pleasure principle to the primary process. The conception of the secondary process changes radically, however, when in *Totem and Taboo* Freud attributes a unifying, connecting, and rationalizing synthetic function to it.[19] Since the synthetic function emerges here as a new function unique to the secondary process, independent of the demands of instinctual drives as well as of those of reality, it is no longer a mere superimposition upon the

[19] In *The Interpretation of Dreams* there were already traces of such a conception, but they were not made explicit.

primary processes by the dire necessities of reality. In the terminology of present-day psychoanalytic ego psychology, we formulate this state of affairs as follows: the secondary process and its synthetic function are autonomous ego functions in relation to both instinctual drives and external stimulation (Rapaport, 1957b). Furthermore, Freud's formulation implies that there are various such synthetic functions which differ from one another: we observe these in, for instance, paranoia, dream, phobias, animism, religion, and science. In my study of states of consciousness (Rapaport, 1957a) I offered independent evidence in support of this proposition.

We may conclude that Freud's study of animism as a theoretical system brought him to the threshold of the discovery of an autonomous synthetic function of the secondary process in addition to the restraining function he had already attributed to it (1900, p. 599). As already mentioned, he finally crossed this threshold in *The Problem of Anxiety* (1926). In "Analysis Terminable and Interminable" (1937) he went further and spoke of innate ego factors in general, not limiting them to the restraining and integrating factors. These beginnings led Hartmann (1939) and Hartmann, Kris, and Loewenstein (1946) to the conclusion that the id and the ego both arise from a common undifferentiated matrix, and that the ego apparatuses of primary autonomy—the psychological apparatuses of motility, perception, and memory—already exist in the undifferentiated phase. I have argued elsewhere (1951) that the discharge thresholds of the instinctual drive too are primarily autonomous apparatuses, and are, in fact, the prototypes of all restraining structures. Hartmann, Kris, and Loewenstein's as well as my own propositions imply that the primary and secondary processes also arise by differentiation from a common matrix and that therefore the rudiments of the secondary process too exist from the beginning—a hypothesis which clarifies Freud's proposition that an organism which operates by primary processes alone does not exist.

We have already discussed some of the relationships[20] which suggest the assumption of an intrinsic maturational restraining factor. We have now encountered a set of considerations which seems to make such an assumption inevitable: (1) the close relation between restraining factors and secondary process; (2) the autonomous character of the secondary process and of the synthetic function, eliminating the possibility that their origins are environmental; (3) the primary autonomous ego apparatuses involved in secondary-process thinking.

My review of *Totem and Taboo* and particularly of the concept of animism has led to two conclusions: First, the secondary process does not simply arise from the primary process under the pressure of environmental necessity, but, like the primary process, arises from an undifferentiated matrix in which its intrinsic maturational restraining and integrating factors

[20] See pp. 824–825 and pp. 836–838.

are already present.[21] Second, animism, which is so striking a form of the primary process in pathological states, preliterates, children, etc., is a "theoretical" system and as such is organized in terms of a synthetic function alien to the primary processes (see Freud, 1915b, p. 119), demonstrating that animistic thought and practices involve secondary processes as well as primary. But if secondary processes are involved in the thinking of primitives just as much as in our everyday, ordered, logical, and scientific thinking, how does our thinking differ from that of primitives? To answer this question we must again go somewhat beyond what Freud had to say. The first answer restates the obvious: the primitive is in his own way no less realistic, logical, and adroit in using his thinking in the service of adaptation than we are.[22] The second answer we have already anticipated: all thought forms involve both primary and secondary processes, but differ from each other in the kind of synthetic function they involve; that is to say, they differ in the degree of dominance the secondary process achieves over the primary. Not even our ordered thinking is free of primary processes. As Freud wrote:

> . . . thinking must aim at freeing itself more and more from exclusive regulation by the unpleasure principle and at restricting the development of affect in thought-activity to the minimum required for acting as a signal. . . . As we well know, however, that aim is seldom attained completely, even in normal mental life, and our thinking always remains exposed to falsification by interference from the unpleasure principle [1900, pp. 602–603].

In arguing that in both the primitive's and our everyday thinking, primary-process forms of thought are integrated by the synthetic function of the secondary process, I have, by implication, equated our wishful thinking and the primary-process forms in the everyday thinking of primitives. But this equation is fallacious. Wishful distortions (e.g., parapraxes) are *intrusions* of primary processes into our secondary-process thinking. The primitive's everyday thinking is not an intrusion into anything: it is subject to a synthetic function and has a secondary-process organization, though this synthesis and organization are by no means so stringent as those of our everyday thinking. The primitive's thinking should be compared only to our own socially sanctioned superstitions, biases, and values, which, although their form often reveals their primary-process origin, are integrated into our secondary-process thinking. The primitive's socially sanctioned animistic thinking, which has its own secondary-process organization, cannot be compared with our "personal" primary processes (e.g., in dreams, halluci-

---

21 See Bergman and Escalona's (1949) observations showing that this process of differentiation misfires in autistic children.
22 Hartmann (1939, 1956) has demonstrated that adaptation to reality is subserved by both rational and irrational processes.

nations, etc.): the primitive too has "personal" primary processes and these are just as much restrained by his secondary processes as are ours by our secondary processes. The secondary processes (of whatever kind) integrate and use primary-process mechanisms, which were originally means of wish fulfillment, as means of adaptation (see Hartmann, 1939; Kris, 1950). It is the primary processes *not* so integrated over which the system of secondary processes exerts its controlling function. Paradoxical as it may sound, one might speak here of a difference between structuralized and nonstructuralized primary-process mechanisms.[23] The essence of this difference seems to be that structuralized primary-process mechanisms integrated by secondary processes are energized by cathexes of greater neutralization than are nonstructuralized primary-process mechanisms.

We may conclude, then, that both the primary processes and the secondary processes involve intrinsic maturational factors. The intrinsic maturational factors involved in the primary processes are related to the instinctual drives, and those involved in the secondary processes are related to instinctual-drive restraints and synthetic functions. We must add, however, that the ontogenetic course of these restraining factors, and their interaction with experience (see Rapaport, 1957b), have been given very little attention so far. It is probable that the study of these relations of restraining factors will center on the problem of structure development and will lead to a learning theory compatible with developmental psychology.

Now, for some parallels to the psychoanalytic conception of the relation between the primary and secondary processes. The first of these is a historical example of the transition from one form of the synthetic function to another, higher one. The second is an example of the various forms the synthetic function takes in the young child. The third is an observational and theoretical parallel to the proposition that the secondary process involves intrinsic maturational factors and its course of development consists of a succession of predetermined stages.

F. M. Cornford, the philosopher, re-examined the thesis that the Greek philosophers of Miletus were the first empirical scientists of the Western world. In *The Unwritten Philosophy* (1950) and *Principium Sapientiae* (1952) he demonstrated that these Greek "scientists" were not empiricists, but dogmatists who took the world explanation contained in the Orphic myths, gave it rational form, and arrived at what appeared to be a theory based on empirical observations. He concluded:

[23] The primary-process mechanisms (displacement, condensation, substitution) are basically means of immediate drive discharge. In this rôle they have a structural characteristic, since the discharge attained through them is slower than a discharge which can take place without them. Nevertheless, they are at best ad hoc, short-lived structures. When they appear in a form which is integrated into the secondary process, their lifetime is increased: they have become further structuralized.

> . . . Anaximander's cosmogony . . . [is] a rationalization of an ancient Creation Myth. . . . He inherited from mythical thought a scheme of cosmogony in which the operating factors had originally been conceived as personal God. Expurgating the factors he could recognize as mythical, he substituted for the Gods the operation of powers, such as "the hot" and "the cold" which he took to be unquestionably natural. But he kept the fundamental framework of the myth [1950, pp. 121–122].
>
> What we claim to have established . . . is that the pattern of Ionian cosmogony, for all its appearance of complete rationalism, is not a free construction of the intellect, reasoning from direct observation of the existing world [1952, p. 201].

The Orphic myths and practices, just like the animistic conceptions and practices of primitives, were on the one hand dominated by primary-process mechanisms, and on the other hand were welded into a system by a synthetic function. The rationalized form the Milesian philosophers gave to the mythological world view, which made their assertions appear to be the results of observation, was but a new system, a new synthesis, a shift to a new level of the secondary process (see Freud, 1915a, pp. 124–125), which initiated a new integration of the primary processes by the secondary, an achievement which affected not only Greek civilization but ultimately all Western civilization.

Piaget showed that the dominance of primary-process forms of thought in children—which Freud inferred, by the genetic approach, from the reports of his adult patients—can be demonstrated by direct interviews. He showed (1924, 1927a, 1927b, 1931) that children's thinking develops from what he calls a naïve realism through animism to artificialism. These forms of thought characterize children's explanations of both familiar and unfamiliar phenomena, and are not limited to thought pertaining to instinctual-drive objects. Thus here too we encounter structured primary-process mechanisms, to use the terminology we suggested. The child's primary-processlike thinking orients his actions to his limited world and to his limited objectives more or less as adequately as the primitive's orients him to his.

In his studies of the first years of life Piaget (1936, 1937) demonstrated that "abstract" intelligence develops from sensorimotor intelligence. According to him, circular reflexes, i.e., reflexlike, but self-stimulating, behaviors (e.g., grasping which engenders further grasping) are the innate sensorimotor foundations of the development of intelligence. These behaviors are activated by appropriate objects (e.g., objects which are suckable, graspable, visible, etc.) to which they are "preadapted." When different—but not too different—objects activate these circular reflex behaviors, the behaviors (more precisely, the schemata underlying them) begin to accommodate to these objects and, in doing so, differentiate. When an object becomes the object of several of these circular reflexes (e.g., vision and prehension), the reflex behaviors begin to coordinate and a different kind of self-stimulating (circular) behavior (one which is capable of a primitive degree of anticipation), termed a "primary circular reaction," takes shape. The primary circular reactions lead progressively to secondary ones, which in turn initiate tertiary ones, which in turn yield to abstract, though primitive, thinking which can discover, anticipate, and intend without overt sensorimotor action. At each of these stages, behavior has its own form of integration, primitive though it may be, and is realistic and adaptive in its own way, that is to say, is not exclusively guided by somatic need or instinctual-drive satisfaction. Yet behavior at all of these stages is pervaded by phenomena similar to condensation, displacement, and substitution, which are characteristic of the primary process.

CONCLUSION

The most general propositions of psychoanalytic developmental psychology may be tentatively formulated as follows:

(1) Behavior is determined by both intrinsic maturational factors and experience.

(2) The central intrinsic maturational factors are instinctual drives and the structures restraining them.

(3) The process of development is not a continuous quantitative growth but a sequence of discontinuous, qualitatively distinct phases.

(4) The interaction of the instinctual drive with experience can be traced by the vicissitudes of its defining characteristics: the cathexes, modes, and objects.

(5) The development of thought is a progression from the dominance of primary-process forms to the dominance of secondary-process forms. Both of these forms involve intrinsic maturational factors, which can be modified by experience. The particular kind of integration of primary-process forms into the secondary process produces the thought form characteristic of a given culture or state of consciousness. The restraint of the primary process by the secondary process creates the balance between reality adaptation and instinctual-drive satisfaction in the individual.

While the interaction of the intrinsic motivational factors with experience has been demonstrated by psychoanalysis, and while many of the general effects of these interactions are known and understood, the specific mechanisms involved in these interactions—which may be termed learning—are yet to be explored.

REFERENCES

Armstrong, E. A. (1947). *Bird Display and Behaviour*. Oxford: Oxford University Press, 1948.

———— (1950). The Nature and Function of Displacement Activities. In *Physiological Mechanisms in Animal Behaviour*, Symposia of the Society for Experimental Biology. New York: Academic Press, pp. 361–382.

Beach, F. A., & Jaynes, J. (1954). Effects of Early Experience upon the Behavior of Animals. *Psychol. Bull.*, 51:239–263.

Benjamin, J. D. (1959). Prediction and Psychopathological Theory. In *Dynamic Psychopathology in Childhood*, ed. L. Jessner & E. Pavenstedt. New York: Grune & Stratton, pp. 6–77.

Bergman, P., & Escalona, S. (1949). Unusual Sensitivities in Very Young Children. *Psychoanal. Study Child*, 3/4:333–352. New York: International Universities Press.

Bernstein, L. (1952). A Note on Christie's: "Experimental Naïveté and Experiential Naïveté." *Psychol. Bull.*, 49:38–40.

Breuer, J., & Freud, S. (1893–95). Studies on Hysteria. *Standard Edition*, 2. London: Hogarth Press, 1955.

Christie, R. (1952). The Effect of Some Early Experiences in the Latent Learning of Adult Rats. *J. Exper. Psychol.*, 43:281–288.

Coleman, R. W., Kris, E., & Provence, S. (1953). The Study of Variations of Early Parental Attitudes. *Psychoanal. Study Child*, 8:20–47. New York: International Universities Press.

Cornford, F. M. (1950). *The Unwritten Philosophy and Other Essays*. Cambridge: Cambridge University Press.

———— (1952). *Principium Sapientiae; The Origins of Greek Philosophical Thought*. Cambridge: Cambridge University Press.

Craig, W. (1913). The Stimulation and the Inhibition of Ovulation in Birds and Mammals. *J. Animal Behav.*, 3:215–221.

———— (1914). Male Doves Reared in Isolation. *J. Animal Behav.*, 4:121–133.

———— (1918). Appetites and Aversions as Constituents of Instincts. *Biol. Bull.*, 34:91–107.

Erikson, E. H. (1937). Configurations in Play—Clinical Notes. *Psychoanal. Quart.*, 6:139–214.

———— (1939). Observations on Sioux Education. *J. Psychol.*, 7:101–156.

———— (1940). Problems of Infancy and Early Childhood. In *Cyclopedia of Medicine*. Philadelphia: Davis, pp. 714–730. Also in *Outline of Abnormal Psychology*, ed. G. Murphy & A. Bachrach. New York: Modern Library, 1954, pp. 3–36.

———— (1950a). Growth and Crises of the "Healthy Personality." In *Personality in Nature, Society, and Culture*, 2nd ed., ed. C. Kluckhohn & H. A. Murray. New York: Knopf, 1953, pp. 185–225. Also in Identity and the Life Cycle: Selected Papers. *Psychol. Issues*, No. 1, pp. 50–100, 1959.

———— (1950b). *Childhood and Society*. New York: Norton.

Escalona, S., et al. (1952). Early Phases of Personality Development: A Nonnormative Study of Infant Behavior. *Monogr. Soc. Res. Child Devel.*, 17(1), No. 54.

Ford, C. S., & Beach, F. A. (1951). *Patterns of Sexual Behavior.* New York: Harper.

Fredericson, E. (1951). Competition: The Effects of Infantile Experience upon Adult Behavior. *J. Abnorm. Soc. Psychol.,* 46:406–409.

Freud, A. (1936). *The Ego and the Mechanisms of Defence.* New York: International Universities Press, 1946.

———, & Burlingham, D. T. (1943). *War and Children.* New York: International Universities Press, 1944.

———, & Burlingham, D. T. (1944). *Infants without Families.* New York: International Universities Press.

———, & Dann, S. (1951). An Experiment in Group Upbringing. *Psychoanal. Study Child,* 6:127–168. New York: International Universities Press.

Freud, S. (1887–1902). *The Origins of Psychoanalysis: Letters to Wilhelm Fliess, Drafts and Notes: 1887–1902.* New York: Basic Books, 1954.

——— (1893–96). *Collected Papers,* 1:9–219. New York: Basic Books, 1959.

——— (1894). The Defence Neuro-Psychoses. *Collected Papers,* 1:59–75. New York: Basic Books, 1959.

——— (1900). The Interpretation of Dreams. *Standard Edition,* 4 & 5. London: Hogarth Press, 1953.

——— (1901). The Psychopathology of Everyday Life, tr. A. A. Brill. *The Basic Writings.* New York: Modern Library, 1938, pp. 33–178.

——— (1905). Three Essays on the Theory of Sexuality. *Standard Edition,* 7:123–245. London: Hogarth Press, 1953.

——— (1911). Formulations on the Two Principles of Mental Functioning. *Standard Edition,* 12:218–226. London: Hogarth Press, 1958.

——— (1913 [1912–13]). Totem and Taboo. *Standard Edition,* 13:1–161. London: Hogarth Press, 1955.

——— (1914). On Narcissism: An Introduction. *Standard Edition,* 14:73–102. London: Hogarth Press, 1957.

——— (1915a). Instincts and Their Vicissitudes. *Standard Edition,* 14:117–140. London: Hogarth Press, 1957.

——— (1915b). The Unconscious. *Standard Edition,* 14:166–215. London: Hogarth Press, 1957.

——— (1923). *The Ego and the Id,* tr. J. Riviere. London: Hogarth Press, 1947.

——— (1926 [1925]). *The Problem of Anxiety,* tr. H. A. Bunker. New York: Psychoanalytic Quarterly & Norton, 1936.

——— (1933). *New Introductory Lectures on Psycho-Analysis,* tr. W. J. H. Sprott. New York: Norton.

——— (1937). Analysis Terminable and Interminable. *Collected Papers,* 5:316–357. New York: Basic Books, 1959.

Hall, C. S., & Whiteman, P. H. (1951). The Effects of Infantile Stimulation upon Later Emotional Stability in the Mouse. *J. Comp. Physiol. Psychol.,* 44:61–66.

Harlow, H. F., & Zimmermann, R. R. (1959). Affectional Responses in the Infant Monkey. *Science,* 130:421–432.

Hartmann, H. (1939). *Ego Psychology and the Problem of Adaptation,* tr. D. Rapaport. New York: International Universities Press, 1958. See also (abridged) annotated version in Rapaport (1951), pp. 362–396.

—— (1948). Comments on the Psychoanalytic Theory of Instinctual Drives. *Psychoanal. Quart.*, 17:368–388.

—— (1950). Comments on the Psychoanalytic Theory of the Ego. *Psychoanal. Study Child*, 5:74–96. New York: International Universities Press.

—— (1952). The Mutual Influences in the Development of the Ego and Id. *Psychoanal. Study Child*, 7:9–30. New York: International Universities Press.

—— (1955). Notes on the Theory of Sublimation. *Psychoanal. Study Child*, 10:9–29. New York: International Universities Press.

—— (1956). Notes on the Reality Principle. *Psychoanal. Study Child*, 11:31–53. New York: International Universities Press.

——, & Kris, E. (1945). The Genetic Approach in Psychoanalysis. *Psychoanal. Study Child*, 1:11–30. New York: International Universities Press.

——, Kris, E., & Loewenstein, R. M. (1946). Comments on the Formation of Psychic Structure. *Psychoanal. Study Child*, 2:11–38. New York: International Universities Press.

Hebb, D. O. (1949). *The Organization of Behavior; A Neuropsychological Theory*. New York: Wiley.

Heinroth, O. (1910). Beiträge zur Biologie, namentlich Ethologie und Physiologie der Anatiden. *Verhandlungen des 5. Internationalen Ornithologischen Kongresses*, Berlin, pp. 589–702.

—— (1938). *Aus dem Leben der Vögel*. Leipzig.

Hess, E. H. (1959). Imprinting. *Science*, 130:133–141.

Hunt, J. McV. (1941). The Effects of Infant Feeding-Frustration upon Adult Hoarding in the Albino Rat. *J. Abnorm. Soc. Psychol.*, 36:338–360.

——, & Willoughby, R. R. (1939). The Effect of Frustration on Hoarding in Rats. *Psychosom. Med.*, 1:309–310.

Jaynes, J. (1956). Imprinting: the Interaction of Learned and Innate Behavior: I. Development and Generalization. *J. Comp. Physiol. Psychol.*, 49:201–206.

—— (1957). Imprinting: The Interaction of Learned and Innate Behavior: II. The Critical Peroid. *J. Comp. Physiol. Psychol.*, 50:6–10.

Kagan, J., & Beach, F. A. (1953). Effects of Early Experience on Mating Behavior in Male Rats. *J. Comp. Physiol. Psychol.*, 46:204–208.

Kahn, M. W. (1951). The Effect of Severe Defeat at Various Age Levels on the Aggressive Behavior of Mice. *J. Genet., Psychol.*, 79:117–130.

Kardiner, A. (1939). *The Individual and His Society: The Psychodynamics of Primitive Social Organization*. New York: Columbia University Press.

——, et al. (1945). *The Psychological Frontiers of Society*. New York: Columbia University Press.

Kinsey, A. C., et al. (1948). *Sexual Behavior in the Human Male*. Philadelphia: Saunders.

—— (1953). *Sexual Behavior in the Human Female*. Philadelphia: Saunders.

Kris, E. (1950). On Preconscious Mental Processes. In Rapaport (1951), pp. 474–493.

—— (1951). Some Comments and Observations on Early Autoerotic Activities. *Psychoanal. Study Child*, 6:95–116. New York: International Universities Press.

—— (1955). Neutralization and Sublimation: Observations on Young Children. *Psychoanal. Study Child,* 10:30–46. New York: International Universities Press.

Lashley, K. S. (1914). A Note on the Persistence of an Instinct. *J. Animal Behav.,* 4:293–294.

———— (1938). Experimental Analysis of Instinctive Behavior. *Psychol. Rev.,* 45:445–472.

Leitch, M. (1948). A Commentary on the Oral Phase of Psychosexual Development. *Bull. Menninger Clin.,* 12:117–125.

————, & Escalona, S. (1949). The Reaction of Infants to Stress. *Psychoanal. Study Child,* 3/4:121–140. New York: International Universities Press.

Levine, S. (1956). A Further Study of Infantile Handling and Adult Avoidance Learning. *J. Pers.,* 25:70–80.

Levy, D. M. (1934). Experiments on the Sucking Reflex and Social Behavior of Dogs. *Amer. J. Orthopsychiat.,* 4:203–224.

———— (1935). A Note on Pecking in Chickens. *Psychoanal. Quart.,* 4:612–613.

———— (1938). On Instinct-Satiation: An Experiment on the Pecking Behavior of Chickens. *J. Gen. Psychol.,* 18:327–348.

Lorenz, K. (1935). Companionship in Bird Life. In *Instinctive Behavior,* ed. & tr. C. Schiller. New York: International Universities Press, 1957, pp. 83–128.

———— (1937a). Über den Begriff der Instinkthandlung. *Folia Biotheor.,* 2:17–50.

———— (1937b). The Nature of Instinct. In *Instinctive Behavior,* ed. & tr. C. Schiller. New York: International Universities Press, 1957, pp. 129–175.

———— (1937c). The Companion in the Bird's World. *The Auk,* 54:245–273.

———— (1942–43). Die angeborenen Formen möglicher Erfahrung. *Z. Tierpsychol.,* 5:235–409.

———— (1950). The Comparative Method in Studying Innate Behaviour Patterns. In *Physiological Mechanisms in Animal Behaviour,* Symposia of the Society for Experimental Biology. New York: Academic Press, pp. 221–268.

———— (1957). The Role of Aggression in Group Formation. In *Group Processes,* Transactions of the Fourth Conference, October 13–16, 1957. New York: Josiah Macy, Jr., Foundation, 1959, pp. 181–252.

McKelvey, R. K., & Marx, M. H. (1951). Effects of Infantile Food and Water Deprivation on Adult Hoarding in the Rat. *J. Comp. Physiol. Psychol.,* 44:423–430.

Nissen, H. W., Chow, K. L., & Semmes, J. (1951). Effects of Restricted Opportunity for Tactual, Kinesthetic, and Manipulative Experience on the Behavior of a Chimpanzee. *Amer. J. Psychol.,* 64:485–507.

Orlansky, H. (1949). Infant Care and Personality. *Psychol. Bull.,* 46:1–48.

Paul, I. H. (1959). Studies in Remembering: The Reproduction of Connected and Extended Verbal Material. *Psychol. Issues,* No. 2.

Piaget, J. (1924). *Judgment and Reasoning in the Child.* New York: Harcourt, Brace, 1928.

———— (1927a). *The Child's Conception of the World.* New York: Harcourt, Brace, 1929.

—— (1927b). *The Child's Conception of Physical Causality*. London: Kegan, 1930.

—— (1931). Children's Philosophies. In *A Handbook of Child Psychology*, ed. C. Murchison. Worcester: Clark University Press, pp. 377–391.

—— (1936). *The Origins of Intelligence in Children*, 2nd ed. New York: International Universities Press, 1952.

—— (1937). *The Construction of Reality in the Child*. New York: Basic Books, 1954.

—— (1956). Essay on the General Problem of the Psychobiological Development of the Child. Unpublished ms.

Rapaport, D., ed. & tr. (1951). *Organization and Pathology of Thought*. New York: Columbia University Press.

—— (1952). Review of O. H. Mowrer, *Learning Theory and Personality Dynamics. This volume*, Chapter 37.

—— (1953a). Review of J. Dollard & N. E. Miller, *Personality and Psychotherapy: An Analysis in Terms of Learning, Thinking, and Culture. This volume*, Chapter 43.

—— (1953b). Some Metapsychological Considerations Concerning Activity and Passivity. *This volume*, Chapter 44.

—— (1957a). Cognitive Structures. *This volume*, Chapter 50.

—— (1957b). The Theory of Ego Autonomy: A Generalization. *This volume*, Chapter 57.

—— (1959). The Structure of Psychoanalytic Theory: A Systematizing Attempt. In *Psychology: A Study of a Science*, Vol. III, ed. S. Koch. New York: McGraw-Hill, pp. 55–183. Also in *Psychol. Issues*, No. 6, 1960.

Richter, C. P. (1941). Biology of Drives. *Psychosom. Med.*, 3:105–110.

Riesen, A. H. (1951). Post-partum Development of Behavior. *Chicago Med. School Quart.*, 13:17–23.

Schur, M. (1958). The Ego and the Id in Anxiety. *Psychoanal. Study Child*, 13:190–220. New York: International Universities Press.

—— (1960). Phylogenesis and Ontogenesis of Affect- and Structure-Formation and the Phenomenon of Repetition Compulsion. *Int. J. Psycho-Anal.*, 41:275–287.

Scott, J. H. (1955). Some Effects at Maturity of Gentling, Ignoring, or Shocking Rats during Infancy. *J. Abnorm. Soc. Psychol.*, 51:412–414.

Scott, J. P., Fredericson, E., & Fuller, J. L. (1951). Experimental Exploration of the Critical Period Hypothesis. *Personality*, 1:162–183.

——, & Marston, M.-V. (1950). Critical Periods Affecting the Development of Normal and Mal-adjustive Social Behavior of Puppies. *J. Genet. Psychol.*, 77:25–60.

Spitz, R. A. (1946a). Anaclitic Depression. *Psychoanal. Study Child*, 2:313–342. New York: International Universities Press.

—— (1946b). The Smiling Response: A Contribution to the Ontogenesis of Social Relations. *Genet. Psychol. Monogr.*, 34:57–125.

—— (1949). Autoerotism. *Psychoanal. Study Child*, 3/4:85–120. New York: International Universities Press.

Sullivan, H. S. (1953). *The Interpersonal Theory of Psychiatry*. New York: Norton.

Thompson, W. R., & Heron, W. (1954a). The Effects of Early Restriction on Activity in Dogs. *J. Comp. Physiol. Psychol.,* 47:77–82.

Thompson, W. R., & Heron, W. (1954b). The Effects of Restricting Early Experience on the Problem-Solving Capacity of Dogs. *Canad. J. Psychol.,* 8:17–31.

Thorpe, W. H. (1956). *Learning and Instinct in Animals.* Cambridge: Harvard University Press.

Tinbergen, N. (1951). *The Study of Instinct.* Oxford: Clarendon Press.

——— (1952). "Derived" Activities; Their Causation, Biological Significance, Origin and Emancipation during Evolution. *Quart. Rev. Biol.,* 27:1–32.

Weininger, O. (1956). The Effects of Early Experience on Behavior and Growth Characteristics. *J. Comp. Physiol. Psychol.,* 49:1–9.

Weiss, P. (1939). *Principles of Development.* New York: Holt.

Werner, H. (1948). *Comparative Psychology of Mental Development,* rev. ed. New York: International Universities Press, 1957.

——— (1957). The Concept of Development from a Comparative and Organismic Point of View. In *The Concept of Development,* ed. D. B. Harris. Minneapolis: University of Minnesota Press, pp. 125–148.

———, & Wapner, S. (1949). Sensory-Tonic Field Theory of Perception. *J. Pers.,* 18:88–107.

———, & Wapner, S. (1952). Toward a General Theory of Perception. *Psychol. Rev.,* 59:324–338.

Whitman, C. O. (1919). The Behaviour of Pigeons. *Posthumous Works of C. O. Whitman,* 3:1–161.

Wolff, P. H. (1959). Observations on Newborn Infants. *Psychosom. Med.,* 21:110–118.

——— (1960). The Developmental Psychologies of Jean Piaget and Psychoanalysis. *Psychol. Issues,* No. 5.

Young, P. T. (1949). Food-Seeking Drive, Affective Process, and Learning. *Psychol. Rev.,* 56:98–121.

65

ON THE PSYCHOANALYTIC THEORY
OF MOTIVATION

I. INTRODUCTION

1. THE COMPLEXITY OF THE PROBLEM

If I had announced this title twenty-five years ago, I would have been expected to speak exclusively about the psychoanalytic theory of instinctual drives, with the focus on the phases of libido development. I would probably have played down the general theory of instinctual drives (Freud, 1905a, 1915a), on which the first section of this presentation will center. Many of the other developments in psychoanalytic theory which I will dwell on would have been outside the picture: the complexities introduced by Freud's theory of the ego (1923, 1926; A. Freud, 1936) were not yet grasped, Hartmann's (1939), Kris's (1932–1952), and Erikson's (1937, 1939) contributions were not yet made. The confusion around and misunderstandings of the theory of instinctual drives introduced by Hull's (1936–38, 1939) and continued by Dollard and Miller's (1950) and

This study and the experiments of the author and his associates which are referred to were aided by the Ford Foundation's grant in support of research at the Austen Riggs Center. The study was completed during the author's sabbatical (1959–60) at the Research Center for Mental Health, New York University. Reprinted from Marshall Jones, ed., Nebraska Symposium on Motivation, 1960, *pp. 173–247, by permission of University of Nebraska Press. Copyright 1961 by the University of Nebraska Press.*

Mowrer's (1950) efforts to mate or equate the psychoanalytic theory of instinctual drives with their drive-learning-behavior theory were still in their first stages. Piaget's studies (1936, 1937) of development in infancy were not yet published. Those observations on activity, exploration, and curiosity which are the basis of R. W. White's reconsideration of the theory of motivation in his recent paper (1959) had not yet been made. The considerations concerning the causal texture of the environment, which Heider (1926–59) and Brunswik (1934, 1956) brought into focus, were not generally familiar; nor were the complications these considerations introduce into the discussion of any theory of motivation as yet envisaged. Finally, the question, How should motivation be defined? could, in those days, have been answered without all the sophistication necessitated by these symposia on motivation in general, by Littman's paper (1958) in particular, and by Peters' monograph (1958). But since all of this has now happened, it is impossible to do justice to the problem as a whole in the compass of a single paper.

All I will attempt, therefore, is the following: in the introduction I will sketch the outlines of the problems which must be faced by the psychoanalytic (and probably any other) theory of motivation. In the main part I will sketch the psychoanalytic theory of instinctual drives, and wherever possible relate it to the problems outlined in the introduction. In the final part, I will dwell on those aspects of the psychoanalytic theory—the theory of consciousness and attention cathexes—which may, in the long run, prove to be the bridge between the psychoanalytic theory as a whole and those relations to the environment on which Heider (1926–59, 1958) and White (1959) have centered. My aim in this paper is to put forth and to argue three propositions: (1) A theory of motivation must distinguish motivations from causes: all motivations are causes, but not all causes are motivations. (2) The psychoanalytic theory of motivation must distinguish between instinctual drive motivations, motivations derived from and dependent upon instinctual drive motivations, and motivations autonomous from instinctual drive motivations, whether they are derived from instinctual drives or are of a different origin. (3) The curiosity, exploratory, activity—or to use White's term, effectance—motivations are not motivations but causes of behavior, and may be accounted for by the psychoanalytic theory of consciousness, i.e., attention cathexes, which is a causal but not a motivational theory.

Since the psychoanalytic theory of instinctual drives has never been fully systematized, in culling it from its sources (mainly Freud's writings) I will have to use my own judgment of the evidence and of the requirements of theoretical consistency. The psychoanalytic theory of motivation is even less developed than the theory of instinctual drives. The present paper is an attempt to construct a psychoanalytic theory of motivation. It is inevitable that such an attempt be marred by lack of foresight, errors of judgment, and even errors of fact. I have no brief for it but that it makes a beginning at systematizing facts and problems, attempts to put the facts into a more or less cohesive framework, and gives a more or less cohesive set of answers to the problems. My hope is that it will serve as a point of departure for the criticism and further development of the theory.

2. THE MISUNDERSTANDINGS SURROUNDING THE THEORY OF INSTINCTUAL DRIVES

Of all the complexities I have enumerated, the most difficult is how to deal with the ingrained misunderstandings of the psychoanalytic theory of instinctual drive. As an illustration, I would like to quote from White's bold and sweeping paper. He writes:

> The chief theories against which the discontent is directed are those of Hull and of Freud. In their respective realms, drive-reduction theory and psychoanalytic instinct theory, which are basically very much alike, have acquired a considerable . . . orthodoxy. Both views have an appealing simplicity, and both have been argued long enough so that their main outlines are generally known [1959, p. 297].

This statement calls for three comments. (1) It can be demonstrated—and I will attempt to do so—that Hull's and Freud's theories are as different as any two theories can be, even if some Freudians, neo-Freudians, and others have failed to discover this. (2) The psychoanalytic theory—whether appealing or not—is by no means simple. (3) White's assertion that the main outlines of the psychoanalytic theory are generally known is an unwarranted assumption.

3. THE EXPLANATORY RANGE OF THE THEORY OF INSTINCTUAL DRIVES

There is no doubt that the theory of instinctual drives was always the center of Freud's psychoanalytic theory,[1] and in spite of all the changes and additions which have accrued with the development of the theory, it is still indispensable. Freud developed the theory of instinctual drives to make sense of his clinical observations. In his effort to do this he found that his theory must—and does—meet the following requirements:

(1) To explain certain pathological phenomena.

(2) To account for irrational ideas and behavior which are not necessarily pathological.

(3) To explain the origin of behaviors and thoughts that man experiences as being beyond his control in contrast to those which he experiences as subject to his "will."

(4) To account for the origin of behaviors and ideas which emerge "spontaneously," that is, which are not obvious responses to an external stimulation or a somatic condition.

No other theory has even attempted to solve this minimal inventory of

[1] See pp. 867–869 concerning his prepsychoanalytic theory.

problems the theory of instinctual drives was introduced to solve. Indeed, there is some doubt that any other theory has proposed a satisfactory solution for even a single one of these problems. The many theories of therapy, pathology, and motivation, neo-Freudian, psychiatric, and psychological, have been by and large oblivious to these phenomena which served as the point of departure for the psychoanalytic theory, which, according to Boring (1950, p. 713), gave present-day psychology the concept of motivation.

4. THE EXAGGERATED CLAIMS FOR THE THEORY OF INSTINCTUAL DRIVES

No doubt a theory as powerful as all this would deserve attention even if it should prove less simple and less easily understood than it is at times believed to be. What then are the dissatisfactions with this theory which grew up not only outside of psychoanalysis and among the neo-Freudians, but even among psychoanalysts?

The theory of instinctual drives, one of Freud's earliest and most radical inventions, preoccupied him for a long time at the expense of all his other empirical discoveries and conceptual inventions.[2] And when he turned his attention to his other discoveries and conceptual inventions, psychoanalysts and others found it hard to give up this old exclusive preoccupation which they had come to share with him. Thus a vague general impression remained abroad that the theory of instinctual drives was the only explanatory tool psychoanalysis had.

The dissatisfaction with the theory of instinctual drives was compounded of two elements: (1) a justified dissatisfaction with the overemphasis on its explanatory potency and with the corresponding underemphasis on the explanatory potency and study of the other determiners of behavior; (2) an unjustified assumption that psychoanalysis had no other explanatory tools besides the theory of instinctual drives. Those who did not share (1) but accepted (2) worked the theory of instinctual drives overtime. Those who shared the first and accepted the second considered it a sufficient ground for rejecting the whole theory of psychoanalysis. The main stream of psychoanalytic theory, with Freud in the lead, proceeded—slowly, to be sure—to develop the other explanatory tools of psychoanalysis into a systematic ego psychology.

What does it mean to work the theory of instinctual drives overtime? For

[2] Freud wrote: "I have ascribed to you a wish that I had begun the subject of the neuroses with a description of the neurotic's behaviour, and of the ways in which he suffers from his disorder, protects himself against it, and adapts himself to it. This is certainly a very interesting subject, well worth studying, and not difficult to treat: nevertheless there are reasons against beginning with this aspect. The danger is that the unconscious will be overlooked, the great importance of the libido ignored, and that everything will be judged as it appears to the patient's own ego" (1916–17, pp. 330–331).

instance, Freud wrote: ". . . *whatever interrupts the progress of analytic work is a resistance*" (1900, p. 517). But he added a footnote in 1925:

> The proposition laid down in these peremptory terms—'whatever interrupts the progress of analytic work is a resistance'—is easily open to misunderstanding. It is of course only to be taken as a technical rule, as a warning to analysts. It cannot be disputed that in the course of an analysis various events may occur the responsibility for which cannot be laid upon the patient's intentions. His father may die without his having murdered him; or a war may break out which brings the analysis to an end. But behind its obvious exaggeration the proposition is asserting something both true and new. Even if the interrupting event is a real one and independent of the patient, it often depends on him how great an interruption it causes; and resistance shows itself unmistakably in the readiness with which he accepts an occurrence of this kind or the exaggerated use which he makes of it [1900, p. 517].

Now, anyone disregarding Freud's warning in this footnote provides an example of working the theory overtime. What is implied is this: if the instinctual drives (even if the defenses, that is, resistances, are thrown in for good measure) are taken to be the *only* causes of behavior, the result is a disregard for the other intrapsychic determining factors (for instance, ego factors other than defenses) as well as for the external stimuli (and their configurations and contexts, for instance their social context) as determiners or codeterminers of behavior. Considering how alert the psychoanalyst must be in his everyday work to resistances and to the effects of instinctual drives, and how likely these are to be hidden behind reasonably assessed realities and rational intents, the psychoanalyst's practical predicament becomes obvious.

The exigencies of his therapeutic task alert him to the hidden, unconscious, determining instinctual drives and he may willy-nilly come to assume that they are the only significant determiners of behavior. Freud himself, however sharply he centered his theory upon instinctual drives, never made or intended such an assumption. The clearest evidence for this I will cite on pp. 872–873, but his "Formulations on the Two Principles of Mental Functioning" (1911) and his many other discussions of the rôle of the environment (e.g., 1916–17, pp. 303, 316) show this beyond a doubt.

5. THE LIMITATIONS ON THE EXPLANATORY RÔLE OF THE INSTINCTUAL DRIVES IMPOSED BY EGO PSYCHOLOGY

What then curbed the initial overemphasis on the explanatory rôle of the instinctual drives? The clinical observations which prompted Freud to change the emphasis are well represented in the two passages which follow here. In 1923 Freud wrote:

> . . . [the ego] in its relation to the id . . . is like a man on horse-back, who has to hold in check the superior strength of the horse . . . Often a rider, if he is not to be parted from his horse, is obliged to guide it where it wants to go; so in the same way the ego constantly carries into action the wishes of the id as if they were its own [1923, p. 30].

In 1926 he wrote:

> Just as the ego controls the path to action in regard to the external world, so it controls access to consciousness. In repression it exercises its power in both directions, acting in the one manner upon the instinctual impulse itself and in the other upon the representative of that impulse. At this point it is relevant to ask how I can reconcile this acknowledgement of the might of the ego with the description of its position which I gave in *The Ego and the Id*. In that book I drew a picture of its dependent relationship to the id and to the superego and revealed how powerless and apprehensive it was in regard to both and with what an effort it maintained its show of superiority over them. This view has been widely echoed in psycho-analytic literature. Many writers have laid much stress on the weakness of the ego in relation to the id and of our rational elements in the face of the daemonic forces within us; and they display a strong tendency to make what I have said into a corner-stone of a psycho-analytic *Weltanschauung*. Yet surely the psycho-analyst, with his knowledge of the way in which repression works, should, of all people, be restrained from adopting such an extreme and one-sided view [1926, p. 95].

I cannot summarize here the empirical findings and the theoretical considerations which required a revision of the theories of repression and anxiety and compelled Freud to the change of emphasis reflected in this passage. Nevertheless, I hope it will be plausible that this formulation implies the recognition of the ego as a determinant of behavior, along with (and often in opposition to) the instinctual drives. Freud's ego theory of 1926 was then generalized by Hartmann (1939) in his theory of ego autonomy, and later in his theory of neutralization (1950, 1952). Hartmann juxtaposed to the instinctual drives as determiners of behavior not only—as Freud did—the ego's defenses, but also a broad range of ego functions (synthesis, differentiation, and functions of apparatuses) and the whole hierarchy of instinctual drive derivatives of various degrees of neutralization. Moreover, both Hartmann's (1939) theory of adaptation and Erikson's (1950) psychosocial theory provided a place for the external environment as a specific determinant (see part III, below) of behavior, in the framework of the psychoanalytic theory.[3]

[3] There was never much doubt about the behavior-determining rôle of the superego,

So much for the intrapsychic determinants of behavior other than instinctual drives. But we must examine further the rôle of environmental stimulation as a determiner of behavior, because the academic psychological theories have, as a rule, given it a central position and because there is a general —not entirely unjustified—impression that psychoanalytic theory gave it none.

6. THE PROBLEM OF THE RÔLE OF EXTERNAL STIMULATION

In the discussion of the theory of instinctual drives below, it will become clear that the rôle of external stimulation has, for a long while, been grossly underestimated in the theory of psychoanalysis. But even if this underestimation were rectified, the theory would still have no answer to the question, What rôle do external stimulations play in behavior? Such a rectification would not settle, for instance, the claims of Hull, Dollard, Miller, and others that external stimuli can serve as "drives."

Nevertheless, Hartmann's (1939) adaptation theory and Erikson's (1950) psychosocial theory have gone a long way in accounting theoretically both for an independent rôle of external (social) stimulation in the determination of behavior and for the interaction of such stimulation with instinctual drives.

Moreover, although it has scarcely been noticed, in Chapter VII of *The Interpretation of Dreams* (1900) Freud laid the groundwork for a theory of the rôle of external stimulation in his conception of the secondary process and in his theory of consciousness. It is true that his conception of the secondary process (the concepts of delay, detour, identity of thought, and experimental action in thought with small amounts of cathexes to anticipate reality) still centers on the instinctual drive object and not on relations to the environment in general. But his theory of consciousness, even though not fully developed, extends beyond those external stimulations which are intimately tied to the discharge of instinctual drives and to the rediscovery of their objects in reality, and provides a means of accounting for the rôle of external stimulation without introducing a special motive for this purpose, as White did. Further below we will review this theory and examine whether or not it can account for what White attempted to explain in terms of competence and learning, when he wrote as follows:

> As used here, competence will refer to an organism's capacity to interact effectively with its environment . . . . fitness to interact with the environment is slowly attained through prolonged feats of learning. In view of the directedness and persistence of the behavior that leads to these feats of learning, I consider it necessary to treat competence as

---

but there was not much clarity about it either (see Rapaport, 1957c), nor much understanding of the detailed mechanisms of its determining effect. But this aspect of the psychoanalytic theory will not be discussed in this paper.

having a motivational aspect, and my central argument will be that the motivation needed to attain competence cannot be wholly derived from sources of energy currently conceptualized as drives or instincts [1959, p. 297].

To account for the phenomena subsumed by White under the concept of competence without resorting to the assumption of an "effectance motivation" is, in a sense, an acid test for Freud's theory of consciousness, because both this theory and White's concepts are, in essence, designed to account for the perception of and the orientation within reality relationships and thus to explain the relation between external stimuli and mental energies. White wrote:

> external stimuli play an important part, but in terms of "energy" this part is secondary, as one can see most clearly when environmental stimulation is actively sought (1959, p. 321).

So much for the behavior-determining rôle of external stimulation for the moment.

7. THE RELATION OF MOTIVATIONS TO PHYSIOLOGY

Littman (1958) and Peters (1958)[4] have both come to the conclusion that only psychological investigations can discover what the motives[5] of behavior are and how they exert their effects, and that physiological investigations of the relation of motivations to somatic processes can provide no answer to these questions.
Littman wrote:

> The recent work in motivational physiology is exciting because it is giving us *additional* information about motivation, not because it is telling us what motivation 'really' is. . . . Its significance arises from the fact that a correlation is being drawn. . . . attempts to define motives in terms of some central neurological process are misdirected . . . What is needed is some way of designating motivational phenomena so that the properties of physiological mechanisms can have some stable motivational properties with which to relate. So it will not do, *logically,* to define motivational phenomena in physiological terms [1958, pp. 133–134].

And Peters wrote:

---

[4] I will discuss Littman's and Peters' views in some detail here and further below. I will do so not because I agree with their general conceptions, but rather because they are the only two authors I have found who raise those questions about motivation to which a systematic consideration of the psychoanalytic theory, I believe, inevitably leads.
[5] The term is used at this point as in psychology in general, that is, without a generally agreed-upon definition.

Hebb (1949), for example, claims that "The term motivation then refers (1) to the existence of an organized phase sequence, (2) to its direction or content, and (3) to its persistence in a given direction, or stability of content." He then goes on to say that his "definition" means that motivation is not a distinctive process but is a reference in another context to the same process to which "insight" refers. This, surely, is a terrible logical muddle. He rejects, for good reasons, the assumption of drive-theorists that directed and persistent behaviour is always preceded by various extra-neural bodily irritants postulated as antecedent causal conditions. In their place he postulates a central "motive state," an organized phase sequence in the cells of the brain. He then proceeds to *define* motivation in terms not only of the directedness, organization and persistence of behaviour relative to a goal, but also in terms of this highly speculative condition of the brain. Now it might be the case that such a condition of the brain was *necessary* for the occurrence of motivated behaviour; but on his own showing it cannot be sufficient, since he claims that *all* voluntary behaviour, including "insight," is also preceded by such a condition. . . . The reference to phase sequences in the brain and to central motive states can only, surely, be a theory to *explain* motivation; it cannot be part of the *meaning* of motivation. And as a theory, it can at best, as I have suggested before, be only a statement of some of the necessary conditions of motivated behaviour. It cannot be a sufficient explanation of it. Physiological speculation is no substitute for empirical psychological research. Still less should it masquerade as part of the analysis of terms at a different logical level [1958, pp. 42–43].[6]

The psychoanalytic theory of instinctual drives implies—all appearances to the contrary notwithstanding—a stand analogous to that of Littman and Peters in regard to the relation of the instinctual drives to somatic processes. The clearest statement of this view is probably in "Instincts and Their Vicissitudes," where Freud wrote: "The study of the sources of instincts lies outside the scope of psychology. . . . An exact knowledge of the sources of an instinct is not invariably necessary for purposes of psychological investigation . . ." (1915a, p. 123).

[6] But in a later publication Hebb took a stand very much like the one Peters presents here: "Even a physiologically based or "neuropsychological" theory of behavior remains a *psychological* theory. Its main features must be determined by certain constructs; theoretical conceptions, whose *raison d'être* is behavioral instead of physiological. Such constructs may be presented in anatomical and physiological terms, which on the one hand help communication among biological scientists. On the other hand, however, this seems to mislead both psychologist and the nonpsychologist into regarding the theory as neurophysiological instead of psychological. The misunderstanding makes psychologists regard the theory as having narrower application than it really has, and leads the physiologist to expect something more concrete and directly verifiable than is in fact possible" (Hebb, 1958, pp. 459–460).

It is not questioned that motives, just like any other psychological processes, have a (neuro-) physiological substrate in the organism. What is denied is that motives can be equated with this substrate. Motives are concepts derived from observations of behavior, and any observed correlations between them and physiological conditions can indicate at best that one of the necessary conditions of their operation has been discovered.

The relation of behavior in general and motivation in particular to physiological processes is a problem which is interesting in its own right, and involves both the study of the origins of motives (including instinctual drives) and the study of the origins of determiners of behavior other than motives.

8. MOTIVES AND CAUSES

Madsen (1959), having studied much of what is pertinent to motivation in the psychological literature, defines it (leaning on P. T. Young's definition) as follows: "Motivation = all variables which arouse, sustain, and direct behavior" (p. 44). This definition does reflect correctly the consensus of the dominant psychological views. But it does not make a distinction between motives and causes toward which the recent writings of both Littman[7] and Peters[8] point, namely, that while all behaviors are causally determined, not all causes are motives, and not all behaviors are motivated (for a similar view, see Woodworth [1958, pp. 49–53; also 1918, pp. 61 ff.]).

To clarify these points, let us assume that motives in general, just like instinctual drives, are to account for "spontaneous" behavior or spontaneous characteristics of behavior (see part I. 3. above), that is to say, for all that in behavior cannot be explained directly by external physical conditions (e.g., in falling) or by patent somatic conditions (e.g., toxicity), or by social stimuli (e.g., attack or approach by another person). If we disregard for the moment the fact that the characteristics of a man's behavior as he is falling and of his toxic behavior and of his behavior in response to the action of another person may be codetermined by motivations, and that

---

[7] ". . . I am not saying that the kinds of things which we ordinarily regard as motivational do not have causal properties; nor am I saying that motives are not among the most important class of causal phenomena that we know. What I am saying is that, even in the conventional schema that is current today, it is not the case that only motives have causal properties, and it is also not the case that motivational causes are the only important ones. I am also implying that it is possible to have behavioral systems in which the kinds of things that we treat as motives do not appear at all as causes . . ." (1958, p. 154).

[8] ". . . to explain *everything* a man does in terms of 'motives' is logically inappropriate because it lumps together acting purposefully according to rules, acting with a goal but according to no established rules, and cases where something happens to a man and it is odd to say that he *acts* at all. Psychologists, therefore, who say that all behaviour is motivated are using the concept too widely if by this they mean that we have a motive for everything we do" (1958, p. 152).

indeed his motivations may have contributed to bringing about his fall, his toxicity, and the behavior of the other person, then we have constricted examples of what are *not* motivations, but nevertheless *causes* of behavior. Unless we "overuse" the theory of motives—in the same way that the theory of instinctual drives is overused at times, that is, by searching for and emphasizing in any behavior what can be regarded as a motivation, even if it plays only a codetermining rôle—we will find such examples of nonmotivational causation of behavior in abundance in everyday life.[9]

How then do those causes which are motivations differ from those which are not?

Madsen's (1959) three criteria of motivation do not help us very much. Our example shows that not only motives but causes too "arouse" (initiate) behavior and the behavior initiated by causes is "directed" too. What is more difficult to decide is whether the persistent character of motivated behavior, to which Madsen refers by the term "sustained," is also characteristic of behaviors determined by nonmotivational causes. The question is: How sustained is sustained? On the one hand, toxic behavior—caused but not necessarily motivated—can be quite sustained; on the other hand, motivated behaviors are sustained only until consummation has occurred. But perhaps what is meant here by "sustained" is something different, namely "appetitive," or "homing" behavior which persists even when, owing to changes of conditions, it has to change its direction to arrive at the object it was originally directed at.

Littman's attempt to define motives leads him to the significant realization that motives are the "actives" of psychology, and the perhaps even more significant one that "there is no foundation for treating anything as *absolutely* an active . . . to be an active is relative to the logical properties of the theoretical system in which it finds itself" (1958, p. 162; see also pp. 136 and 146–147). But now Littman, who saw clearly that not all behaviors are motivated, fails to define and indeed tends to do away with the distinction between causes and motives: ". . . if motivational concepts are the actives of psychology, anything can be a motive" (1958, p. 147).

Peters too realized that "activeness" plays a crucial rôle in distinguishing causes and motives (1958, pp. 12, 15), but he conceived "active" in an absolute and subjective sense: all that is "suffered" by the subject is caused, all that is actively intended is motivated. It is thus that Peters equates motive with "reason" and perhaps "will," while he relegates not only the physical, chemical, and social effects, but also the effects of instinctual drives, to the category of causes.

Other definitions of motivation list *energizing, selectiveness,* and *consummatory activity* as defining characteristics of motives. But there is no

[9] Clearly, the theories of physical, social, and somatic causation can be overused too; the result in each instance is a failure to recognize the rôle of motivations and of other causes.

agreement in regard to these either. White (1959, p. 34) characterizes what he terms effectance motivations as having no consummatory acts. Brown (1953) and Farber (1954), if I understand them rightly, admit only the "energizing" function and reject the "selecting" function as a defining characteristic of drive, which is apparently the only motivational concept of their theory.

To make the situation even more complicated, Dollard and Miller (1950) consider any stimulation of sufficient strength a drive, i.e., a motive. This concept of motive would surely make it almost impossible to distinguish between motive and cause.

This chaotic state of affairs is partly due to the confusion between physiological processes and motivations, and partly to the kind of stimulus concept of motivation of which Dollard and Miller's is an example. The two are not unrelated: intrasomatic stimuli are the bridge between the two factors (physiological processes and stimuli in general) with which motivations are confused to such a degree that without the resolution of this confusion no clear distinction between causes and motives seems feasible.

It is possible, however, to reach a resolution. Let us define motivations as *internal* forces,[10] thereby distinguishing them from external stimuli, and let us remind ourselves of the conclusion reached above (part I. 7.) that motivations cannot be equated with any specifiable physiological processes, thereby distinguishing them from any internal stimuli. Such a definition of motivations already distinguishes them from the causes we used as examples: gravitational force, chemical toxicity, social pressure.

This definition also clarifies, at least partly, the activity vs. passivity problem raised by Littman and Peters. Internal forces are defined here as motives, even if—Peters to the contrary notwithstanding—the subject experiences their working as a compulsion, as a peremptory necessity in relation to which he feels passive. The justification of this definition lies in the observation that the same motives (e.g., instinctual drives) are experienced subjectively at various times by the same person as actively willed (a state of affairs conceptualized by the term "ego-syntonic instinctual impulses"), and at times as passively suffered (a state of affairs conceptualized by the term "ego-dystonic instinctual impulses"). Peters is factually incorrect when he identifies the passively suffered as pathological. Actually both the active and passive experiencing of motives occurs in both normal and pathological conditions. For further discussions of these points, see part III. 2. below, also Hartmann (1939) and Rapaport (1953c, 1957d).

But this definition does not tell us whether or not all internal forces are to be considered motives. For instance, are those forces which manifest themselves as defenses against instinctual drives, motives (see part III. 3.

---

[10] Here I use *internal* in the same sense in which Hebb speaks of processes which intervene between stimuli and responses. For the sense in which the term *force* is used here, see pp. 873–874.

below)? Should we consider those forces which manifest themselves as "reasons," "rule-following," and "will" motives—as Peters does? Are the forces involved in curiosity and exploration motives, as White's concept of "effectance motivation" implies?

To make a decision on these questions possible, it is necessary to amend the definition proposed above: *motives are appetitive internal forces*. The defining characteristics of the concept of appetitiveness as I am using it here are the following: (a) peremptoriness, (b) cyclic character, (c) selectiveness, and (d) displaceability. I will take these up one by one, though only jointly do the four define appetitiveness.

(a) *Peremptoriness:* In contradistinction to voluntary behavior which we can "take or leave," motivated behaviors are those which we cannot help doing. It is this mandatory character of behavior that we designate by the term "peremptoriness." (For the relation of peremptoriness to the energies expended by the work of the motive force, see pp. 886 ff. below.) Nevertheless, peremptoriness does not provide a dichotomous classification of behavior: peremptory behaviors differ from each other in the degree to which we can *delay* performing them. Thus there are motives of various degrees of peremptoriness.[11] (For a further discussion of this point, see part II. 5. below.)

(b) *Cyclic character:* The peremptoriness of motives also has a cyclic rise and fall. The rise leads to consummatory activity, the consummation leads to a fall followed anew by a progressive rise in peremptoriness. This cyclic character is conceptualized in terms of the accumulation and discharge of the energies of the motive force. Just like peremptoriness, the cyclic character is subject to attenuation, and motivations differ in degree of cyclicity also, from those in which the rhythm of rise and fall is conspicuous to those in which its only vestige is the presence of a consummatory activity.

(c) *Selectiveness:* In contradistinction to some uses of this term, selectiveness here implies that the direction of the motive force is determined by its object and varies with the changes of the place of the object and with the changes in the conditions determining the path by which the object is obtainable. This formulation implies that there are objects which are the specific necessary conditions for the discharge of the energies of the motivations in question.

(d) *Displaceability:*[12] If the object of a motive is not available, the objects lying on the path toward it or related to it by other specifiable connections become its substitutes in triggering the consummatory action, that

---

[11] In quasi-need types of motivations, peremptoriness is reduced to the tendency toward consummation manifested in the resumption and recall of interrupted tasks.
[12] The displaceability discussed here is different from that which is observed in the secondary processes. For a discussion of these differences, see Gill [1966] and Holt [1962].

is, the discharge of the accumulated drive energy. Motivations differ in regard to their degree of displaceability also.

While it is the task of the body of this paper rather than of this introduction to answer the questions raised above, I will briefly sketch the core of the answers to prepare the reader for the arguments of the paper. By these defining characteristics of appetitiveness, the restraining force that defenses exert against instinctual drives is not a motive force, since it is not appetitive. It has no object in the sense that motives have, and has no independent cyclic character either; indeed, steadiness is one of its outstanding characteristics. "Reason" and "will" must be separated into those of their manifestations which are rationalizations of motives and thus are effectively motives with all the defining characteristics of motives, and those which are not rationalizations. Some of the latter are motives which are selective, but are of a low, yet discernible, degree of peremptoriness, cyclicity, and displaceability. Lewin's quasi needs are an example of these (see p. 899 below), but there are probably many other distinct groups of such motives about which we know little or nothing. But some "reasons," "willings," and "rule-followings" are not motives at all, even though they are selective, have consummations, and may even appear to be peremptory. They do not show displaceability or cyclicity, and their peremptoriness derives from the nonmotivational yet compelling causal texture of the environment that Heider and Brunswik speak of. Finally, curiosity and exploratory behaviors do not seem to be motivated, since they lack selectivity in the here defined sense and apply to any object or situation, and thus displaceability as a defining characteristic does not apply to them. A cyclic character is also absent from them. I will endeavor to show later on that they are nonmotivational causes rather than motives of behavior. (For a detailed discussion of them, see part III. 4. and 5.)

Defining motives as intrapsychic forces distinguishes them from internal and external stimuli which are nonmotivational causes of behavior. The criterion of appetitiveness distinguishes motives from intrapsychic forces which are nonmotivational causes of behavior. But this latter distinction is not as clear-cut as the former. Most of the distinguishing characteristics of motives vary on a continuum from a maximal to a minimal degree. Thus we may expect to find motivations which cannot be easily distinguished from nonmotivational causes.

The question will undoubtedly arise in the reader's mind whether the definition of motives given here is not simply the definition of instinctual drives, and if so, whether it implies that the instinctual drives are the only motives. Admittedly, this definition is modeled on the defining characteristics of instinctual drives, because this seems to be, for the moment, the only way to distinguish motives from causes. But as I indicate in part I. 1. above and in part II. 5. below, this does not imply that all motives are instinctual drives or even derivatives of them.

Definitions are matters of strategy. It seems to me that it is preferable to define all motives by one set of characteristics, and to define all the other determiners of behavior as causes, than to accept prematurely the possibility that motive is not a unitary concept but a collective term for a miscellany of concepts. If this distinction between nonmotive causes and motives is not contradicted by observations which will not fit the definition of motives or the definition of causes, or will fit both of them, the conceptual strategy I have followed here will have proved useful. If this distinction is contradicted by observations—well then, new and consistent distinctions will have to be sought.[13]

As a rule, behavior is determined by a multiplicity of causes and by a multiplicity of motives. The psychoanalytic concept expressing this state of affairs is *overdetermination*. We may conclude that behavior is overdetermined, and that nonmotivational causes as well as motivations usually play a rôle in causing behaviors. Whether there are purely nonmotivationally determined behaviors, what they are, and in which circumstances they occur are not theoretical but empirical questions. The observations conceptualized in the term "overdetermination" suggest that what the empirical findings are likely to show is not an absence of all motivations in behaviors which appear to be determined by nonmotivational causes, but rather the presence of highly neutralized derivative motivations (see part II. 5.) or motivations of little actual effect.

Since we are prepared for the idea that the instinctual drives are not the only motives nor are motives the only causes of behavior, and are aware of several of the various pitfalls awaiting us, we can now turn to a review of the psychoanalytic theory of instinctual drives.

II. THE THEORY OF INSTINCTUAL DRIVES

1. HISTORICAL INTRODUCTION

Freud observed that when certain ideas became conscious (accompanied by the corresponding affect), his patients' symptoms tended to disappear. He assumed that the ideas in question were memories of past experiences (traumatic experiences). Accordingly, his first theory (1887–1902; Breuer and Freud, 1893–95; see also Rapaport, 1958) was environmentalistic-

---

[13] Another question that is likely to arise is, What is the place in this conception of the so-called "reactive motives" like fear, anxiety, or affects in general? I cannot dwell on this question in this paper. In part II. 3. I discuss the place of affects in the psychoanalytic theory of motivation. In accord with that, affects are not, in general, motivations. Their rôle in learning would, in the present theory (part III. 5.), be explained by their being internal excitations which therefore attract attention cathexes.

empiricistic: experiences which clash with the moral standards of society are repressed, the corresponding affect is prevented from being discharged, is dammed up, and displaced or subjected to conversion so that it finds expression in a symptom.

Freud soon discovered, however, that these ideas which were purported to be memories of actual sexual experiences were usually fantasies expressing wishes (1887–1902), and he was faced with the problem of explaining the origin of these fantasies. This problem proved to be connected with others when Freud discovered that wishes also underlie the apparently meaningless and arbitrary manifest content of dreams (1900). It was to explain the origin of these fantasies and dream-wishes that Freud introduced the concept of *instinctual drives* (see pp. 855 and 880). It is clear that here we have the conceptualization of a determiner of behavior. This step was the beginning of the end of that phase of Freud's theory-making in which he considered the crucial factors determining behavior as predominantly environmental. It ushered in a new phase in which intrapsychic determiners—of the type I am defining as motivations—became the crucial causes of behavior postulated by the theory.

I must dwell further on history, in order to clarify why this concept of an intrapsychic cause remained so fuzzy not only to psychologists and psychiatrists, but even to many psychoanalysts.

First, we must note that in Freud's early environmentalistic theory (1894; Breuer and Freud, 1893–95) the only intrapsychic factor was affect (i.e., emotion), and that even after this theory was superseded by the theory of instinctual drives, many psychoanalysts, and even Freud at times, still spoke of affects or emotions as the intrapsychic factors which give rise to fantasies, wishes, and symptoms. The fact that it is common for the manifestations of instinctual drives to be accompanied by affects helped to perpetuate this conception of affect and emotion. This state of affairs is embalmed in the ubiquitous term "emotional disorder" and is also probably one of the factors contributing to the fact that to this day psychology has no generally accepted definition of emotions or affects (see Rapaport, 1942).

Second, we must remember that Freud did not develop the theory of instinctual drives immediately upon giving up the environmentalistic theory in 1897 (1887–1902). Not even in Chapter VII of *The Interpretation of Dreams* (1900) did he have a theory of instinctual drives. Instead, he simply explored the *modus operandi* of the intrapsychic factors which produce fantasies and dreams. He termed the totality of these methods of operation *the primary process,* which he contrasted with *the secondary process,* that is, the totality of those methods of operation which subserve ordered thinking and reality orientation, and are superimposed upon the primary process and restrain its operations. Chapter VII of *The Interpretation of Dreams* is such an intricately woven discussion that the actual beginnings of the theory of instinctual drives implied in it has seldom been noticed. Instead, the intrapsychic factor Freud spoke about was taken to be the "wish," which thus duly took its place alongside the "affects" in obscuring the theory of instinctual drives. Of the many concepts Freud introduced in Chapter VII, wish, repression, symbolization, and the mechanisms of displacement and condensation gained broad currency. The general concept of the primary process, which subsumed several of these, was for a long time almost ignored and not until recently recognized as the predecessor of the instinctual drive concept; similar, though even more extreme, was the fate of the secondary process as the predecessor both of the concept of instinctual-drive restraining factors (for instance, defenses) and of the concepts accounting for relationships to reality. The result was a hampered development of the theory of instinctual drives, a much delayed development of the theory of instinctual-drive restraints, and an extreme delay in the formulation of the theory of relations to reality.

The referents of the primary process are behavioral phenomena which are peremptory: will and conscious effort cannot curb them. The referents of the secondary process are behaviors which the individual can control more or less voluntarily, that is, he can take them or leave them, and these guarantee much of the effectiveness of dealings with reality. The distinction between "peremptory" and "take it or leave it" behaviors is so important that William James (1890) considered it one of the basic unsolved problems of psychology.

It was in 1905, in *Three Essays on the Theory of Sexuality* (1905a), that Freud finally introduced his theory of the instinctual drive. But what stood in the center of that volume and has attracted most attention was the development of the libido, that is, the epigenesis of the sexual drives and the relation of this development to pathology. The theory of instinctual drives was thus at its very introduction treated in a one-sided fashion and was understood in an even more one-sided way, and not until "Instincts and Their Vicissitudes" (1915a) did Freud make an attempt to present the theory of instinctual drives more systematically. But even this presentation yields a more or less complete form of the theory only in conjunction with the papers "Repression" (1915b) and "The Unconscious" (1915c). In the meanwhile, "On Narcissism: An Introduction" (1914) and later *Beyond the Pleasure Principle* (1920) and *The Ego and the Id* (1923) consistently distracted attention from the theory itself to the problem of what specific instinctual drives must be chosen to account for the observations.

No wonder, then, that the theory of instinctual drives has to be reconstructed and that this reconstruction may at first sight have some unfamiliar characteristics.

2. THE INSTINCTUAL DRIVES

Definition: ". . . an 'instinct' [14] appears to us as a concept on the frontier between the mental and the somatic, as the psychical representative of the stimuli originating from within the organism and reaching the mind, as a measure of the demand made upon the mind for work in consequence of its connection with the body" (1915a, pp. 121–122).

Now this formulation as a definition leaves much to be desired. It does not state the referents of the concept nor does it provide an operational anchorage or even an anchorage in other variables. Thus it might seem to be at best a poorly defined hypothetical construct with plenty of "surplus meaning." However, considering the grief which the much better defined concepts of drive of the various learning theories have come to, you may want to refrain from rejecting this concept out of hand. Maybe there is something to be gained from this poor definition and perhaps the further attributes of this concept, not so far included in the definition, may improve it.

However, let us first see what the implications of the formulation are. It states that the concept of instinctual drive is a psychological concept ("psychical representative"), that is to say, the phenomena which it conceptualizes are *not* somatic processes—neither deficit states, nor homeostatic imbalances, nor hormonal excesses, nor even neural centers or systems—but behaviors. But at the same time it postulates that the instinctual drives do not originate outside of the organism (in stimuli or interpersonal relations). A thoroughgoing psychological determinism—one of the implications of this definition—does not necessitate the assumption of a severance of the mental apparatus from the body, but leads to the following two working assumptions: (a) the laws of functioning of the mental apparatus (i.e., the laws of behavioral regulation) can and must be investigated by a study of behavior (or if you prefer, molar behavior) without reference to molecular, physiological, or neural processes; (b) the relationships of the explanatory constructs derived from behavior to somatic processes must be kept vague at least as long as our knowledge of both types of process is meager, lest psychological concepts (or even behaviors) be prematurely equated with or tied to specific physiological processes. (For a more stringent and probably more precise formulation, see I. 7.) If we consider Beach's (1942, 1956) "central excitatory state" or Morgan's (1957, 1959) "central motive state" as sufficiently vague and broad conceptions for all the neural, hormonal, or other excitations which have a determining

---

[14] While the *Standard Edition* translates *Trieb* as "instinct" and in common psychoanalytic parlance it is often termed "drive," I will, in agreement with Max Schur (1959), speak of *instinctual drive,* to distinguish Freud's concept both from the "instinct" of older and newer animal psychology and from the "drive" of learning theory.

effect on behavior, then we may have in them a conception of the factor whose "psychical representative" Freud termed the instinctual drive. (For a relevant discussion, see pp. 879–880).

I think that even if the "definition" we are discussing should yield no more than this much, it would deserve to be retained. For it indicates the sort of "neuropsychological" concepts which have a kinship to the concept of instinctual drive. It is to Beach's (1942, 1956) and Morgan's (1957, 1959) conceptions that the theory of instinctual drives may be considered complementary, rather than to Hull's (1943), Miller and Dollard's (1950), Mowrer's (1950), Spence's (1958), J. S. Brown's (1953), etc., with which it is usually considered kindred (Allport, 1947), and some of which were developed in a deliberate effort to attain a complementarity with the psychoanalytic concept. Indeed, in spite of Lindsley's (1957) inclination to identify the activation of behavior with the effects of the reticular activating system, and in spite of Hebb's inclination to equate drives with phase sequences of sufficient complexity, there is more of an essential complementarity between their theories and the psychoanalytic theory of motivation than between the latter and the theories which are derived from Hull's (see Rapaport, 1952, 1953a, 1957b, 1959). The S-R theories, in spite of all their concealing refinements, remain essentially "empty organism" theories (Rapaport, 1957b), and their concept of motivation remains a stimulus concept vulnerable to all of Morgan's (1957, 1959)[15] and others' arguments to which the psychoanalytic conception of instinctual drives is immune.

I want to sharpen up this point and the difference between the S-R concept of drive and the psychoanalytic concept of instinctual drive by quoting Freud on the distinction between excitations arising from external stimulation and excitations which originate in instinctual drives. Freud wrote:

> . . . all that is essential in a stimulus is covered if we assume that it operates with a single impact, so that it can be disposed of by a single expedient action. A typical instance of this is motor flight from the source of stimulation. These impacts may, of course, be repeated and summated, but that makes no difference to our notion of the process and to the conditions for the removal of the stimulus. An instinct, on

---

[15] ". . . peripherally aroused drives constitute the model that behavior theorists have used to regard all drives as stimuli. One might be inclined to say in this case that drives are indeed stimuli if it were not for the general state of tension or striving that they seem to build up within the organism. This striving or drive, though associated with noxious stimulation, is not mechanically switched on and off with momentary changes in the stimulus situation. Rather it tends to build up slowly and to persist, sometimes after the stimulus has changed, as one can see in experiments where shock is used as the incentive. Hence, even in the case of so-called sensory drives, motive states have some properties of their own. For that reason, they may still be regarded as central drives, though admittedly the central component depends primarily on sensory conditions" (1957, p. 17).

the other hand, never operates as a force giving a *momentary* impact but always as a *constant* one. Moreover, since it impinges not from without but from within the organism, no flight can avail against it. . . . What does away with . . . [it] is "satisfaction." This can be attained only by an appropriate ("adequate") alteration of the internal source of stimulation [1915a, pp. 118–119].

In discussions of motivation much has been said about the irrelevance of the distinction between internal and external stimulation (e.g., Nissen, 1954, pp. 282–285) and we should expect these arguments to be leveled against these formulations concerning the instinctual drive also. Yet in this case these arguments are bound to misfire. Instinctual drives are not anchored to any specific internal stimulation any more than to any external stimulation (see I. 7.). They are mental representations of certain—so far unspecified—internal excitations about which we know only what we have postulated about them, namely, that their representations (the instinctual drives) serve as forces which initiate and regulate behavior.[16]

The referents of the concept of instinctual drive are related to what Hebb spoke of when he insisted that the "nervous system" is not a stimulus-response mechanism but has a spontaneous activity, and that much goes on between stimulus input and response output. More generally, those psychologists who are not in the "empty organism" camp, but speak about "mediation" and make an attempt to furnish the "black box" somehow, are all trying to cope with the problem that Freud was trying to cope with when he introduced the concept of the instinctual drive. But there is one difference: while Freud, like Hebb in his "spontaneous activity of the nervous system," assumed an innate factor, many, if not most, psychologists are still trying to furnish the black box with "acquired" furniture.

The fact that Freud conceived of this basic causative factor of his theory as inborn made it appear to many psychologists and to the so-called neo-Freudians that he entirely disregarded the causative rôle of experiential-environmental factors. To clarify this misconception, I will quote from *Three Essays on the Theory of Sexuality* the passage in which Freud defined his concept of the complemental series:

It might be possible to include repressions and sublimations as a part of the constitutional disposition, by regarding them as manifestations of it in life; and anyone who does so is justified in asserting that the final shape taken by sexual life is principally the outcome of the innate constitution. No one with perception will, however, dispute that an

[16] Hunger, thirst, or other metabolic needs are poor paradigms for instinctual drives, partly because, unlike instinctual drives, they are usually treated as somatic conditions rather than as mental representations of somatic conditions, and partly because they cannot be delayed for any significant length of time nor are they flexible in their object choice and consummatory pattern.

interplay of factors such as this also leaves room for the modifying effects of accidental events experienced in childhood and later. It is not easy to estimate the relative efficacy of the constitutional and accidental factors. In theory one is always inclined to overestimate the former; therapeutic practice emphasizes the importance of the latter. It should, however, on no account be forgotten that the relation between the two is a co-operative and not a mutually exclusive one. The constitutional factor must await experiences before it can make itself felt; the accidental factor must have a constitutional basis in order to come into operation. To cover the majority of cases we can picture what has been described as a "complemental series," in which the diminishing intensity of one factor is balanced by the increasing intensity of the other; there is, however, no reason to deny the existence of extreme cases at the two ends of the series [1905a, pp. 239–240].

I will abandon further discussion of the "definition," and turn to the instinctual drive's defining characteristics, which are its pressure, aim, object, and source. We will take them one by one.

Pressure.   "By the pressure of an instinct we understand its motor factor, the amount of force or the measure of the demand for work which it represents. The characteristic of exercising pressure is common to all instincts; it is in fact their very essence" (1915a, p. 122).

This formulation speaks of pressure in terms of forces and energies (work). Since pressure is a characteristic of all instinctual drives, they are conceived of as forces which expend energy (cathexis) when they initiate and regulate behavior. Even though psychologists do occasionally use the term "energy" (e.g., Morgan explicitly, "The term drive refers here to the 'energy' or impetus of behavior. It implies movement, activity, striving, or effort" [1957, p. 2], or Hull implicitly in his "excitatory potential"), only Kurt Lewin both used it and took pains to explain his usage, which was like the one implied by the psychoanalytic concept of instinctual drive. Lewin wrote:

> When the concept of energy is used here and when later those of force, of tension, of systems, and others are employed, the question may be left quite open as to whether or not one should ultimately go back to physical forces and energies. In any event, these concepts are, in my opinion, general logical fundamental concepts of all dynamics (even though their treatment in logic is usually very much neglected). They are in no way a special possession of physics . . . . the treatment of causal dynamic problems compels psychology to employ the fundamental concepts of dynamics . . . . it is always necessary carefully to avoid certain very easy errors, for example, in the adequate comprehension of the psychical field forces; and it must always be kept in

mind that we have to do with forces in a *psychical* field and not in the psychical environment [1935, p. 46].

Lewin's injunction holds for us too. We must keep in mind that in dealing with instinctual drives and the energy they expend in their work, we are not speaking about the muscular or other physiological energy expended in the course of executing the behavior, but rather about the psychological energy expended in the initiation, regulation, and termination of behavior—the physiological, biochemical, biophysical, or neurophysiological substrate of which we know, so far, nothing, or at best have but the vaguest conjectures.

The formulation concerning pressure implies first that it is a concept of force, and second, that like all force concepts it involves a concept of energy. This second implication of the concept is rarely recognized by psychologists discussing motivation, and the question arises, does it need to be recognized?

In physics the concept of energy was introduced when it was recognized that forces can be transformed into other forces: mechanical force—via heat—into vapor tension, gravitational force—via mechanical force—into electromotor force. A quantity which is invariant throughout these transformations was sought and defined as energy: the quantity equal to the work done by the force, but unlike the force, which is a vector, i.e., directional, it is a scalar, directionless entity and therefore displaceable. Freud too found it necessary to introduce the concept of instinctual drive energy (cathexis) when he noted that an instinctual drive prevented from consummatory action may manifest itself in fantasies, symptoms, etc. He termed this phenomenon *displacement,* and explained it as a transformation of the instinctual drive force, which transformation necessitates—just as it does in physics—the assumption of the existence of a displaceable entity. As we have seen, in Freud's first theory this displaceable entity was termed "affect." In his theory of the instinctual drives it became the energy—the cathexis—of the instinctual drive.

The force and energy conception of the instinctual drive enabled him to explain: (a) behaviors occurring without any apparent external stimulus to elicit them; (b) apparently varied forms of behavior occurring when the same instinctual drive is at work; (c) apparently identical behaviors occurring when different instinctual drives are at work; (d) apparently varied forms of behavior occurring in apparently identical stimulus situations; and (e) apparently identical behaviors occurring in apparently different stimulus situations. These implications of the instinctual drive concept have been explicated in the psychological literature by Frenkel-Brunswik (1942) and by Gill (1959). Frenkel-Brunswik's argument—as it pertains to (d) and (e)—has been adopted by McClelland (1958), whom I would like to quote here:

> Frenkel-Brunswik has argued for the importance of 'alternative manifestations' as an index of the presence of motivation. She found that

while rated exuberance and rated irritability both correlated positively with rated need for aggression, these outward behavioral signs actually correlated negatively with each other. The explanation would appear to be that the same person was unlikely to be both exuberant and irritable, though each of these characteristics was taken to be a sign of *n* Aggression. As Wittenborn points out, eating large amounts of chicken or of steak might signify the presence of a strong hunger drive, and yet they might not be correlated responses across persons. That is, one individual might satisfy his drive one way, and another in another way. If one were dealing with ordinary habits, one would expect some generalization of response tendencies to edible stimuli (chicken and steak); if one finds a low correlation between two such responses and a similar pattern of correlations of each with other responses, one might be justified in deciding that a motive rather than a habit is involved . . . It is interesting to note that this relatively recent approach to inferring the presence of a motive is similar to one proposed by Murray some time ago to differentiate his motive concept from Allport's trait concept [1958, pp. 16–17].

Littman too is aware of this point: "The variation in behavior in the face of identical inputs and the constancy of behavior in the face of varying inputs leads us beneath the skin of the organism" (1958, p. 132).

Just the same, the psychoanalytic theory of instinctual drives was written off by most psychologists as the product of Freud's "mechanistic" bent, and the questions whether and how the nature of his data imposed this theory on him were never carefully considered.

Before abandoning the discussion of the instinctual drives' pressure, it will be worth noting that some of the ethologists have developed a concept of "energy" similar to that of psychoanalysis. Tinbergen's (1952) paper on derivative activities and parts of Thorpe's (1956) theoretical discussion are to the point. I have discussed some of the parallels between the psychoanalytic and ethological considerations in my paper on "Psychoanalysis as a Developmental Psychology" (1960).

Aim: "The aim of an instinct is in every instance satisfaction, which can only be obtained by removing the state of stimulation . . ." (1915a, p. 122). In other words, the discharge of the accumulated instinctual drive energy is the aim of the instinctual drive and the achievement of this aim is termed "satisfaction." The central implication of this formulation is the most frequently and most radically misunderstood psychoanalytic concept, "the pleasure principle."

Since I have repeatedly attempted to clear up the confusion which surrounds this concept in the minds of both psychologists and psychoanalysts (1951c, 1959), I will deal with it here very briefly. The tendency of instinctual drive energy toward discharge (*satisfaction* if the discharge takes place in action, *wish fulfillment* if it takes the cognitive form of fantasies, dreams, delusions, etc.) is termed the pleasure principle. This principle is the psychological counterpart of the physical principle of entropy (see Rapaport, 1959, pp. 21 and 50–52). Freud originally named it the pleasure-pain principle, since he observed that the accumulation of instinctual drive energy is accompanied by subjectively experienced pain and that discharge of instinctual drive energy is accompanied by subjectively experienced pleasure. However, once the concept of the pleasure principle was formulated, it soon became apparent that there is no such one-to-one coordination between accumulation and discomfort on the one hand, and discharge and pleasure on the other. Accumulation of cathexes may be pleasurable (as in sexual forepleasure) and discharge of cathexes may be painful (as in anxiety). His discussions, as early as 1900, of anxiety dreams makes this obvious. Indeed, the reformulation of the theory of anxiety in 1926 is intimately related to this lack of a one-to-one coordination. In "Instincts and Their Vicissitudes" too, Freud explicitly warned that the proposition,

> . . . the activity of even the most highly developed mental apparatus is subject to the pleasure principle, i.e. is automatically regulated by feelings belonging to the pleasure-unpleasure series . . . that these feelings reflect the manner in which the process of mastering stimuli takes place . . . [is an assumption which must be preserved] in its present highly indefinite form, until we succeed, if that is possible, in discovering what sort of relation exists between pleasure and unpleasure, on the one hand, and fluctuations in the amounts of stimulus affecting mental life, on the other. It is certain that many very various relations of this kind, and not very simple ones, are possible [1915a, pp. 120–121].

Taking into account this formulation, that of 1900, and those in *Beyond the Pleasure Principle* (1920), the only consistent view we can arrive at is that psychoanalysis certainly is concerned with the subjective experiences of pleasure and pain and does use these terms to designate subjective experiences, but when it does not specify that they are used in that sense, and particularly when they appear in the context of the pleasure principle, then these terms must be taken for concepts: the referent of the concept *pain* is the accumulation of cathexes (which may, but need not, be accompanied by a subjective experience of pain), that of *pleasure* the discharge of cathexes (which may, but need not, be accompanied by a subjective experience of pleasure). Once this is grasped, Freud's theory is freed of the misconceptions by virtue of which it is still so often considered a subjectivistic and hedonistic theory.

Freud himself is responsible for another misunderstanding of the theory. His introduction of the constancy principle, the nirvana principle, and the concept of the repetition compulsion gave two erroneous impressions: *first,* that he had given up the pleasure principle—which he never did; *second,* that the pleasure principle was actually a principle of total quietism, which did not allow the psychoanalytic theory to account for any phenomena of engendering and maintaining tension, but only for phenomena of discharge (tension reduction). Thus it was mistakenly assumed by some that the constancy principle was needed to supplement the pleasure principle to account for tension maintenance. The fact is, however, that the entropic tendency embodied in the pleasure principle always depends for its effectiveness and its limits upon the structural conditions of the system whose energy distribution is studied. Total entropy and total discharge would be possible only under extreme structural conditions never realized. The constancy principle, the nirvana principle, and the repetition compulsion are manifestations of the pleasure principle under various structural conditions, the characterization of which exceeds the scope of this paper.[17]

Thus the pleasure principle, which expresses the aim of the instinctual drive, is the psychological equivalent of the entropy principle that all energies are subject to.[18] It regulates the distribution and expenditure of the instinctual drive's energy.

And now we will turn to the directional aspect of the instinctual drive concept.

The object: "The object of an instinct is the thing in regard to which or through which the instinct is able to achieve its aim. It is what is most variable about an instinct and is not originally connected with it, but becomes assigned to it only in consequence of being peculiarly fitted to make satisfaction possible. The object is not necessarily something extraneous: it may equally well be a part of the subject's own body. It may be changed any number of times in the course of the vicissitudes which the instinct undergoes during its existence; and highly important parts are played by this displacement of instinct" (1915a, pp. 122–123).

Though *force* and *energy* are crucial defining characteristics of the instinctual drive, the defining characteristic *object* is the outstanding conceptual invention in Freud's theory of the instinctual drive. One of the basic problems of all psychology is how to resolve the paradox that as a science it is to give an explanation, in terms of causes, of behavior, which is a purposive, i.e., teleological, phenomenon in its very nature.[19] Freud's solution

[17] But I at least touch on these issues in the discussion of neutralization, in II. 5.

[18] It may be objected that such a reference to entropy conflicts with my insistence that the science of behavior is to be built on psychological assumptions and observations. I cannot dwell on this point here, and will therefore simply refer to the passage by Kurt Lewin which I quoted (pp. 873–874). It contains the resolution of this apparent contradiction.

[19] Tolman's formulation of this point reads: "Behavior as behavior, that is, as molar, *is* purposive and *is* cognitive. These purposes and cognitions are of its immediate descriptive warp and woof. It, no doubt, is strictly and completely dependent upon

of this paradox is to postulate the object as a defining characteristic. The instinctual drive energy tending toward discharge provides an explanation in terms of causes of the changes we refer to as behavior. However, unlike the direction of other (e.g., physical) causes, the direction of instinctual drive discharge is not unequivocally determined, but rather is contingent on the presence of the instinctual drive object. The latter can be reached in various ways which, to use Heider's (1958) term, are equifinal. Even though Freud stresses that no specific object is originally connected with the instinctual drive, his insistence that the object "becomes assigned to it only in consequence of being peculiarly fitted to make satisfaction possible" implies that the necessity for such objects and the range of objects "peculiarly fitted" are phylogenetically determined.[20] Hartmann (1939) expressed this when he postulated that man is born equipped to cope with an "average expectable environment."

I believe that these formulations show that instinctual drives are motives in the sense defined here and bring into sharp relief the difference between causes which *are not* and causes which *are* motivations. *Motives* are characterized by appetitiveness implying a coordination of the instinctual drive discharge with a definite (even if broad) range of objects, and an equifinality in regard to this range of objects. *Causes* have only a direction which does not change, that is, causes do not "home" appetitively on the object by changing the direction and path as the place or conditions of the object change.

It should be noted (see Rapaport, 1951c) that the rôle of the object in instinctual drive discharge also involves the "summation" of the excitation provided by the object as a stimulus and the excitation provided by instinctual drive energy. When the accumulation of instinctual drive energy has not as yet reached threshold intensity, this "summation" may raise it to that intensity and thus bring about discharge.

---

an underlying manifold of physics and chemistry, but initially and as a matter of first identification, behavior as behavior reeks of purpose and of cognition. And such purposes and such cognitions are just as evident, as we shall see later, if this behavior be that of a rat as if it be that of a human being" (1932, p. 12).

[20] Tolman's early formulations—if we disregard his stress on randomness—show a striking parallel to Freud's conceptual solution: "We may now . . . sum up the features of this . . . type of theory. (1) Whereas there are no innate connections of external response to original stimulating condition, there are innate connections of specific driving adjustments to original external or internal stimulating conditions. (2) These driving adjustments tend to release particular sets of random acts. (3) They also set a particular goal for the random acts in that these acts tend to continue until some one occurs which provides a stimulating condition which innately relaxes the driving adjustment itself. (4) These driving adjustments are definable in terms of the purely abstract types of success which they predicate. (5) As so defined they necessarily involve a teleological use of language. (6) The theory predicates no mysterious degree of preëstablished harmony between the nature of the environment and the nature of the organism. This theory, it seems to me, is in all essentials the one advocated by Woodworth" (1922, p. 17).

Freud's formulation of the changes in object in the course of life is predicated on the concept of displacement, discussed above in connection with the instinctual drive energies, and implies a wide scope for changes wrought by experience, that is, for learning. The question is, what sort of learning is this? It is doubtful whether it is the sort of learning which is predicated by the drive-reduction-reinforcement theories of learning. This should be clear, if from nothing else, from those observations which indicate that object relations (specific links between an instinctual drive and its object) do not "extinguish," but are given up with rather great difficulty, and the process by which this is accomplished (identifications; see Freud, 1923) has far-reaching consequences for the structure of the mental apparatus (ego and superego formation). If and when a learning theory is developed which can account for such consequences of those processes of learning and unlearning which are observed clinically, psychoanalysis as a theory will change in character. From a theory built to account for the general characteristics of *observed* processes, and based only on the requirement that its propositions be consistent with each other and with the empirical data it accounts for, it will change into a theory whose propositions will be translatable into terms of the "microanatomy" of processes of change wrought by experience (learning) and thus into a theory whose propositions will be amenable to *independent tests*. At present, psychoanalysis can make only statements of this sort: when, under such and such conditions, such and such experiences do or do not take place, the consequences will be such and such. But it cannot state *how* these consequences come about, it cannot state the details of the processes (changes wrought by experience) by *means* of which the antecedents bring about the consequences. Here we cannot go further into what little we do know about the learning theory required to complement the psychoanalytic theory and about how much it will have to differ from and in what little it may prove to be like S-R learning theories. Later on, however, I will return to the problem of learning (see II. 5.; also Rapaport, 1959, pp. 98–99, and 1952, 1953a).

Now we turn to the last of the defining characteristics of instinctual drives discussed by Freud.

Source: We will dwell on this defining characteristic very briefly: "By the source of an instinct is meant the somatic process which occurs in an organ or part of the body and whose stimulus is represented in mental life by an instinct. We do not know whether this process is invariably of a chemical nature or whether it may also correspond to the release of other, e.g. mechanical, forces. The study of the sources of instincts lies outside the scope of psychology. . . . An exact knowledge of the sources of an instinct is not invariably necessary for purposes of psychological investigation . . ." (1915a, p. 123). This discussion of the sources of instinctual drives is rarely noted, the earlier one in *Three Essays on the Theory of Sexuality* (1905a) being the usually quoted and generally familiar one.

Freud's (and particularly Abraham's) discussions of the oral, anal, and genital zones gave the impression that psychoanalysis implies a primitive peripheralist theory of instinctual drives. It seems to me that in these discussions we are faced with one of Freud's various inconsistencies. Neither his insistence on a thoroughgoing *psychological* determinism, touched on early in this paper, nor the just-quoted denial of the relevance of the sources of instinctual drives for psychology, are compatible with a peripheralist theory.[21] I have discussed this point in somewhat more detail in the paper (1957b) already referred to and will not dwell on it further here.

I would like to emphasize, however, that pointing out the irrelevance of zones as *sources* of instinctual drives does not do away with their *psychological* significance. Erikson's (1937, 1950) study of *zonal modes* in particular and *organ modes* in general demonstrates this. While Freud occasionally noted phenomena related to zonal modes of instinctual drives, he did not study them and therefore could not include them among the defining characteristics of instinctual drives. Likewise he did not include the ubiquitously implied but never explicitly considered discharge thresholds among the defining characteristics of instinctual drives either, though it goes without saying that discussions of energies refer—explicitly or implicitly—to a structure within which the energies in question operate and therefore always imply a threshold concept.

3. INSTINCTUAL-DRIVE REPRESENTATIONS

To round out the theory of instinctual drives, I will briefly discuss the instinctual-drive representations: idea and affect. I do so partly to counter-

---

[21] I would like to make it even more plausible that Freud's theory is not tied to the peripheralist conception which his discussion of the "sources" of instinctual drives suggests, and therefore I will quote a passage showing that the peripheralist expressions reflect simply the language and knowledge of his time and that Freud on occasion indicates that he does not subscribe to their implications. While in "Instincts and Their Vicissitudes" (1915a) he does discuss thirst and hunger in terms of the "mucous membrane of the pharynx" and the "irritation of the mucous membrane of the stomach," he comments on this in a footnote as follows: "Assuming, of course, that these internal processes are the organic basis of the respective needs of thirst and hunger" (p. 118). To my mind his intent is clear: it is as though he were saying, "if this should not prove to be the case, then I will substitute here whatever is found to be their organic basis." His intention is to keep his theory independent of the results of physiological inquiry.

But the inconsistency of the peripheralist conception with the rest of the theory becomes even clearer from a general consideration. The zones are conceived of as—so to speak—stopping stations in the course of libido development: this itself makes it clear that they are "points of application" of the libidinal instinct rather than sources of independent instinctual drives. The energy of the libidinal instinct remains unchanged during its developmental wandering. It is displaced from one zone to another, but the zones are not the sources of it except in the proximal sense. Fundamentally, the unitary conception of libido implies a "central" rather than a peripheralist theory.

act the still prevalent tendency to confound instinctual drives with affects (or emotions) as the motive force of behavior, and partly to point up the fact that these representations, being the manifestations of the peremptoriness and appetitiveness of the instinctual drive, are significant characteristics differentiating them from nonmotivational forces.

The direct manifestations of an instinctual drive are the observable consummatory actions. The other effects of the instinctual drives are termed instinctual-drive representations (or presentations). In regard to these, Freud said:

> In our discussion so far we have dealt with the repression of an instinctual representative, and by the latter we have understood an idea or group of ideas which is cathected with a definite quota of psychical energy (libido or interest) coming from an instinct. Clinical observation now obliges us to divide up what we have hitherto regarded as a single entity; for it shows us that besides the idea, some other element representing the instinct has to be taken into account, and that this other element undergoes vicissitudes of repression which may be quite different from those undergone by the idea. For this other element of the psychical representative the term *quota of affect* has been generally adopted. It corresponds to the instinct in so far as the latter has become detached from the idea and finds expression, proportionate to its quantity, in processes which are sensed as affects [1915b, p. 152];

and

> The whole difference arises from the fact that ideas are cathexes—basically of memory-traces—whilst affects and emotions correspond to processes of discharge, the final manifestations of which are perceived as feelings. In the present state of our knowledge of affects and emotions we cannot express this difference more clearly [1915c, p. 178].

Thus in this theory both ideas and affects are conceived of as indicators of and safety valves for accumulations of instinctual drive cathexes. The disposal of instinctual drive cathexes on memory traces and through affect discharge channels respectively is then one of the conditions for experiencing either ideas or affects.[22] The question whether these are both the necessary and sufficient conditions for such experiences must be bypassed here, though we will touch upon it further below. It must be pointed out, however, that psychoanalytic theory distinguishes between the *ideas* and the *affects* discussed here on the one hand, the *thoughts* and *tamed affects*[23] on the other. Ideas and affects are peremptory, in contrast to thoughts and

---

[22] Here I shall not take up the problem of unconscious ideas and affects.
[23] Tamed affects are the final products of the process of neutralization as it pertains to affects (see Fenichel, 1941; also Rapaport, 1953b). P. H. Wolff suggests (personal communication) the term "derivative affects" for them.

tamed affects, which are by and large under voluntary control. Psychoanalytic theory accounts for this distinction by assuming that ideas and affects involve instinctual drive cathexes, while thoughts and affect signals involve (neutralized) hypercathexes at the disposal of the ego (see II. 5.).[24] I must stress again that one of the phenomena the concept of instinctual drive was developed to account for is the compulsory, peremptory character of certain behaviors and ideas, which has scarcely ever been the subject matter of investigation in academic psychology. But the French school of psychiatry was keenly aware of these phenomena, which it termed automatisms, and which must be strictly distinguished from skills and kindred phenomena often described as automatized (see Hartmann, 1939).

One more point should be made concerning ideas as instinctual drive representations. I have described them as indicators and safety valves of instinctual drive energy accumulation, but did not specify whether such an accumulation is only a necessary or also a sufficient condition for the emergence of ideas into consciousness. This is a problem for the psychoanalytic theory of consciousness which will concern us further below. Moreover, I have not discussed how such ideas come about and what relations obtain among them, not to mention the rôle of energy accumulations or discharges in their acquisition (in learning them); nor has the psychoanalytic theory of instinctual drives, to my knowledge, anything specific[25] to say on these topics. One might say that the psychoanalytic theory of instinctual drives has been concerned with the rôle of instinctual drives in performance, but, unlike the reinforcement-drive-learning theories, not in learning. Later on, in discussing Freud's theory of consciousness and structure formation, we will see that instinctual drives do have some rôle in "learning," but this rôle is neither as central nor as direct as the rôle of drives in S-R theory.

4. INSTINCTUAL DRIVES AS MOTIVATIONS

The first point to be made is that *instinctual drives, according to the above considerations, are not the only causes of behavior.* Clearly, since instinctual drives are mental representatives of certain somatic conditions and their objects are only one class of external stimulations, somatic conditions other than those they represent and external stimulations other than their objects may be determiners, that is, causes of behavior. Even if the psychoanalytic concept of overdetermination allows for causes other than instinctual drives, the fact is that psychoanalytic theory, prior to the development of ego psychology, was far less concerned with these causes than with instinctual drives. Indeed, as I showed in my introduction, it gave the impression to many analysts and nonanalysts that it disclaimed the validity

[24] These distinctions, presented here as if they were categorical, actually represent two poles of a continuum.
[25] Nos. 4–7 on p. 898 indicate that it does have some *general* things to say about it.

of such causes, and used motivations, and particularly instinctual drives, as its only explanatory concept. This impression to the contrary notwithstanding, the theory even then had some conceptualization of the fact that besides the instinctual drives, motives other than instinctual drives (and about these we will have more to say soon) and causes other than motives may codetermine—and thus overdetermine—behavior. In fact, it seems likely that behaviors which are not overdetermined are rare: behaviors determined exclusively by stimuli or exclusively by an instinctual drive or, for that matter, by *any* single cause or motive, or *only* by causes or *only* by motives, are probably exceptional if they exist at all. It is often difficult, however, to determine what all the codetermining factors are and, once they are determined, it may be difficult to assess whether their presence has any appreciable effect on the behavior.[26] Here is the point where psychoanalysts tend to overestimate the causal rôle of instinctual drives and their derivatives, and psychologists (as well as laymen) tend to overestimate the rôle of other causes, particularly stimuli. Needless to say, these overestimations go with the corresponding underestimations. All this is only human. The real trouble begins when these errors are turned into theories, and this too has been done. Róheim is reputed to have said that chimneys first served as phallic symbols and only later as smoke stacks. At the other extreme, some S-R theorists with their "empty organism" have considered—and some still do—stimuli as the only significant causative agents. It is possible that Peters (1958) errs here in the same way as the S-R theorists. He insists that Freud's instinctual drives are only causes and not motives, and that they play even this rôle only in pathology and in the psychopathology of everyday life, where the person is passive in relation to them. To him, these situations represent a breakdown of motivated human behavior, which he conceives of as motivated by "reasons" involving social rules. He seems to disclaim the possibility that a behavior may be overdetermined and that both the "rule-following" model of "reasons" and the Freudian "causal" model can participate in bringing it about. The fact is, however, that this has been observed to be the case not only in instances of "rationalization" to which Peters does refer, but also whenever instinctual drives are ego syntonic, that is to say, coincide with ego interests. Peters errs in the service of a good cause: his goal is to establish that not all behaviors are caused by drives. Nevertheless, it is regrettable that he seems not only to overlook overdetermination and to deny that instinctual drives are motives, but also to fail to realize that rule- and reason-following behavior may be determined on the one hand by nonmotivational causes, such as "habits," or the causal texture of the environment mediated (Heider, 1926–59) by external excitation, and on the other hand by motives.

[26] A factor overdetermining a given behavior need not alter the manifest form of it. It might simply serve as a reserve guarantee that the behavior would come about even in the absence of some of the other factors.

The second point to be made is that *instinctual drives are causes of behavior*. Peters is right—within limits—when he points out that man is passive in relation to instinctual drives, in the same sense as he is in relation to nonmotivational causes. However, instinctual drives are not only causes but also belong to that special class of causes which we term motives, and for which Littman's (1958) insight that they are "actives" is valid. Thus we have a paradox: instinctual drives are both "actives" and "passives." I have discussed this paradox in a study (1953c) of activity and passivity; I cannot dwell on it here, though I will attempt to point toward the resolution of it later (III. 2.). For the moment I would just like to indicate the consequences of considering instinctual drives only as causes—as Peters does. Peters goes awry in two respects, I believe. First, he seems to believe that his proposition concerning passivity is an absolute one. Second, he seems to believe that nothing in relation to which man is passive can be purposive.

As to the first respect in which Peters seems to be mistaken: Littman—though he too seems to share Peters' second belief—has cogently argued that activity and passivity are relative to the system within which they appear. In my paper on activity and passivity (1953c) I offered some empirical evidence that this is indeed the case. It might be useful to quote Littman's summary of this point:

> It makes perfectly good sense to call some things passive and some things active. But it does not make good sense to think that there is anything which is, in some sense of the term, "absolutely" active or passive. Therefore, *anything*—as far as we are here concerned this means any event or condition that we might wish to call psychological—may be an active or a passive. In other words, to be an active or passive "agent" is relative to some framework, and as the framework changes so does the status. Therefore, what is motivational to some people may not be so to others. *Because, you see, I am arguing that "to be motivational" is to be anything which may be regarded as "active"* [1958, pp. 146–147].

It makes good sense to call some things causes and others motives—but it makes no sense to say, as Peters seems to imply, that a cause cannot be at one and the same time a motive too.

As to the second respect in which Peters seems to be mistaken: even though the behaviors determined by instinctual drives are as a rule experienced as peremptory and compulsory, the instinctual drives are nevertheless causes of a motivational, purposive character, by virtue of the fact that their definition includes the object as a defining characteristic, the presence of which is the condition for their effectiveness. A sharp light is cast upon this point by the ego-syntonic instinctual drives which unite active and passive characteristics. Peters' argument that the conception of motivation should be limited to "reasons," that is, to the "rule-following model," and that the causal-motivational conceptions are logically fallacious, overlooks the fact that the crucial defining characteristic of the "rule-following model" is, on his own showing, purposive directionality, and that this is an integral characteristic of some causes, e.g., instinctual drives, also. This naturally does not invalidate the point that such purposiveness is lacking in most causes—and that motivations of the "rule-following" type too must be accounted for in any theory of motivation. The problem of the "rule-following model" is to account for those of our purposive behaviors which are appropriate to the causal texture of our environment and to the rules of our society, and to do so realizing that their purposiveness, unlike that of instinctual drives, cannot be explained by a phylogenetically given coordination to the environment like that of the instinctual drives which is given through the objects. In other words, this problem is identical with that of relations to reality in general and that of the origin and motivation of the secondary process in particular.

5. MOTIVATIONS DERIVED FROM INSTINCTUAL DRIVES: NEUTRALIZATION

Instinctual drives are not the only motivations in the conceptual framework of psychoanalytic theory. In addition there are motivations which derive from instinctual drives. The explanation of the origin and nature of these derivative motivations is an essential part of the psychoanalytic theory of motivation; it is Hartmann's (1950, 1952) theory of neutralization which deals with the issue. Freud's concepts of sublimation and desexualization (1923) are the predecessors of the concept of neutralization. I cannot discuss in detail the history and framework of either Freud's or Hartmann's conception, and will give only a brief sketch of the origin and characteristics of derivative motivations.

When an instinctual drive reaches threshold intensity and the drive object is absent, and therefore no consummatory action can take place, a change in threshold is assumed to occur. This change is conceptualized as a heightening of threshold by means of a superimposed cathectic barrier termed "anticathexis." When such anticathexes structuralize, we speak of them as defenses. We will encounter these again in discussing their rôle as nonmotivational causes.

Anticathexis, like any other energy, manifests itself as a force. For instance, anticathexis (defense) against an aggressive instinctual drive may manifest itself as an altruistic motivation. But this is not the only effect of such defenses: in spite of them the instinctual drive motivation may break through in disguised form, a process termed *the return of the repressed*. Moreover, defenses also generalize to instinctual drives and motivations other than those to defend against which they developed; thus they may modify, attenuate, and control these other motivations, instead of defending against these also.

The establishment of defenses results in a differentiation of the original instinctual drive motivations into a variety of derivative motivations. If we now consider that the same defense development will occur in relation to one or more of these derivative motivations, we are envisaging the process by which the whole hierarchy of derivative motivations originates.

Now to the characteristics of these derivative motivations. A hierarchy of defense (and/or control) structures is erected over the basic and peremptory instinctual drive motivations, and it is with the genesis of these layers of defensive and/or controlling structures that the genesis of derivative motivations is synonymous. It is plausible that the originally peremptory discharge tendency of instinctual drive energy is increasingly hampered by the layers of structure superimposed on it. Thus, the higher in the hierarchy of mental structure a derivative motivation appears, the more scaled down its peremptoriness and appetitiveness: in other words, the more neutralized it is. This conception is similar to the control of a river by a system of locks.

If we add to this conception of hierarchy the conception of autonomy, with which we shall be occupied soon, it becomes clear that at least some of these more neutralized derivative motivations will be autonomous from— i.e., can be activated without being triggered by—the underlying less neutralized motivations. For instance, they may discharge when their autonomously accumulated energy reaches threshold intensity, or upon external excitation (see Rapaport, 1951b).

Some of Peters' "reasons" and "rule-followings" are probably highly neutralized derivatives of instinctual drives, though some others are of an entirely different origin and some are not motivations at all, but structures.

These derivative motivations discussed do not exhaust all the motivations other than instinctual drives. We will later touch on some of them of the order of Lewinian *quasi needs* (Lewin, 1926).

III. THE PSYCHOANALYTIC THEORY OF RELATIONS TO REALITY

I will now turn to the psychoanalytic theory of relations to reality in order to clarify whether the rôle of external stimuli in psychoanalytic theory is that of causes or motives.

1. INSTINCTUAL DRIVES AND REALITY

By and large, only one set of psychoanalytic formulations concerning the relations of instinctual drives to reality has become common knowledge. This is the one which was generally—and not without reason—construed as asserting that the reality principle and reality testing are imposed upon the instinctual drives by frustration (Freud, 1900, 1911). The formulations interpreted in this way were in general inconsistent with the rest of the theory, but it is not our task to argue this point here. But that these interpretations disregarded the relationship of the instinctual drive to its object will be plausible from what was said above about this relationship.

Disregarding this relationship was bad enough by itself; disregarding the fact that the concept of the secondary process (Freud, 1900) postulated a whole set of relationships to reality was worse. True, Freud only occasionally touched on the origins of the secondary process from roots other than frustration (e.g., in the discussions of the latency period [1905a], of wit [1905b], of the drive for research [1910], and of the synthetic or rationalizing function [1913]).[27] Moreover, it has been overlooked that Freud (1937) did come to recognize inborn ego functions and that Hartmann, Kris, and Loewenstein (1946) generalized his conception. They replaced the conception of the ego arising from the id by the conception of both arising out of the common, originally undifferentiated matrix of the earliest phase of ontogenesis. The relevance of these propositions for the psychoanalytic theory of motivation is considerable, because they imply that ego structures, energies, and motivations pertaining to them need not arise solely as the derivatives of instinctual drives. This means that ego-development does not consist solely of neutralization associated with frustration. And we have already seen that even neutralization involves, besides defense development, the generalization of defenses to other motivations, that is, *control* development (see Rapaport, 1951a, part VII). Thus even motivations which derive from instinctual drives need not originate from frustration, that is, conflict. Hartmann's (1939) concept of the "conflict-free sphere" refers, in part, to this state of affairs. Erikson's (1950, 1946–59) epigenetic conception carried these considerations further, postulating that the motivations involved in trust, autonomy (independence), initiative, industry, etc., have predecessors which are themselves ego motivations, and which arise in the course of psychosocial development, though he does not specify whether or not they arise from instinctual drives.

But here we are faced with the difficulty that the autonomous development of ego motivations is complex, and is so intertwined with the development of instinctual drives that it is hard to establish unequivocal evidence for the existence of autonomous ego motivations. Nevertheless, it is probable that besides reality relationships established by frustration and motivations deriving from instinctual drives in consequence of frustration, we must postulate autonomous and inborn apparatuses of contact with reality and perhaps even corresponding, and therefore reality-attuned, autonomous motivations.

2. THE RELATION OF THE EGO TO THE INSTINCTUAL DRIVES AND TO REALITY

The development of the ego has two effects on behavior. Each of these is frequently recognized but rarely are both simultaneously considered in their bearing on each other.[28] With the consolidation of the ego in the course of ontogenesis, behavior gains increasing independence from both instinctual

---

[27] I dwelt on these points in my paper, "Psychoanalysis as a Developmental Psychology" (1960), and will therefore not enlarge on them here. See also Hartmann (1939).
[28] I dealt with the problems which I sketch in this section in more detail in "The Theory of Ego Autonomy: A Generalization" (1957d).

drives and external stimulation. In pathological conditions the diminution of either or both these independences commonly occurs. Delusions and hallucinations are extreme manifestations of an increased dependence of behavior on instinctual drive motivation. "Command automatisms," echolalia, and echopraxia are extreme manifestations of an increased dependence of behavior on external stimulation. But the concepts of field dependence and field independence (Witkin, et al., 1954) and of concrete and abstract behavior and thinking (Werner, 1948, Goldstein and Scheerer, 1941) show that in normal conditions and in less extreme forms of pathology too we find individual (characterological) differences along these continua, though within the normal range we encounter them in that structuralized form which George Klein (1958; Gardner et al., 1959) terms cognitive controls.

In psychoanalytic ego psychology, Heinz Hartmann has conceptualized the increasing relative independence of behavior from instinctual drives as *ego autonomy* and the increasing relative independence from external stimulation as *internalization*. I have attempted to demonstrate (1957d) that these two ontogenetic processes of increasing relative independence of behavior are interdependent, in that the relative independence of behavior from instinctual drives is contingent upon its *dependence* on external stimulation, and that the relative independence of behavior from external stimulation is contingent upon its *dependence* on instinctual drives. I mustered evidence suggesting that it is the *ab initio* dependence of behavior on external stimulation which makes it possible for behavior to attain a degree of independence from instinctual drive excitation, and that when the possibility of the ego's relying on external stimulation is significantly interfered with (as in isolation experiments and other "extreme" situations; see Bettelheim, 1943) the already achieved relative independence of behavior from the instinctual drives becomes significantly diminished. Likewise I mustered evidence suggesting that it is the *ab initio* dependence of behavior on instinctual drives that makes it possible for behavior to attain a degree of independence from external stimulation, and that when the possibility of the ego's relying on such instinctual drive excitation and its gratification is interfered with (as when massive defenses or other "extreme" situations prevail), the relative independence of behavior from external stimulation is significantly diminished. I suggested that these relationships can be conceptualized as the relative autonomy of the ego from the id and the relative autonomy of the ego from the environment.[29]

But whence the interdependence of these autonomies and what is its bearing on the psychoanalytic theory of motivation?

[29] For a penetrating discussion and an important application of the theoretical issues dealt with in this section, see Gill and Brenman (1959).

3. THE STRUCTURES OF INSTINCTUAL DRIVE RESTRAINT

The specific clinical theory of psychoanalysis is a theory of conflict. In the earliest phase of the theory the conflict was conceived of as between the memory of the traumatic event and the *dominant mass of ideas* of the person, or as the conflict of the ideas and affects present in the traumatic situation with the moral standards of society. The result was conceived of as defense resulting in symptom formation (see Rapaport, 1958).

The first step in the development of the theory of instinctual drive (Freud, 1900) was formulating the conflict as one between the "wishful impulse" and the endopsychic censorship, or as between the primary and the secondary processes. The result was conceived of as a compromise between the repressed impulse and the repressing agent, expressed in symptoms and anxiety. It is to be noted that in this phase of the theory, repression was the cause of anxiety.

In the first fully developed form of the instinctual drive theory the conflict was conceived of as being between the libidinal instincts and the ego instincts (Freud, 1911, 1914). In relation to the just-preceding theory this meant: *first,* the concept of libidinal instincts, which was implied anyway in the "wishful impulses" and primary processes of the preliminary theory, was now explicitly stated; *second,* an attempt to solve the problem of the origins of the energies and forces of the censorship and the secondary process, a problem which was not actually raised in the preliminary theory, was made. Since this theory proposed that the energies of the censorship and secondary processes were those of the ego instincts, it amounted to an instinctual drive theory of ego energies. Why this theory proved unworkable we cannot discuss here. But it should be pointed out that Freud's attempt at this instinctual drive theory of the ego, of the factors restraining the instinctual drives, and of reality relations is in a way similar to White's invoking an effectance motivation to explain competence, i.e., "[the] capacity to interact effectively with . . . [the] environment" (1959, p. 297): both postulate a motivation to explain veridical, reality-attuned functions.

In the final form of the instinctual drive theory, the conflict is conceived of as a structural conflict between instinctual drives of the id and anticathexes of the ego, which are conceptualized as defensive structures. The resulting symptoms are conceived of as compromises between instinctual drives and defenses. However, in this theory the defenses are not considered as the causes of anxiety, but rather the anxiety signal is conceived of as an ego function by means of which the ego initiates and/or intensifies defensive operations (Freud, 1926; also Rapaport, 1953b).

The bearing of the conception of instinctual drive restraints on the theory of motivation is multiple. *First,* the defenses as structures may be conceived of, in analogy to physical structures, as exerting restraining forces. As structures they certainly play a causal rôle in determining behavior. As restraining forces which are directed against instinctual drive forces, they have a causal though not a motivational rôle in determining behavior. Here, then, we encounter for the first time a mental (psychological) factor which is a cause but not a motivation of behavior. This opens up the possibility that other mental structures (e.g. ideas, associative relations, etc.) too may likewise play a causal but nonmotivational rôle in determining behavior.

Second, defense structures are recognized clinically by the appearance of different motivations where the appearance of instinctual drive forces would be expected (overkindliness instead of aggression, overcleanliness instead of coprophilia). In this respect defenses function as motives, and as the mainspring of the hierarchy of derivative motivations.

Third, these defensive structures are conceived of as built of anticathexes which are part of the ego's hypercathexes, a concept with which we will be concerned again below in connection with relations to reality and attention cathexes. This conception of defenses makes the close link between instinctual drive restraint and secondary process (that is, contact with reality) plausible.

Fourth, the theory of instinctual drive restraints shows that the psychoanalytic theory is not a simple drive-reduction theory like that of Hull and his successors. Those psychologists (e.g., G. Allport, 1946) who argued against psychoanalysis and Hull by adducing evidence that human behavior is not only "tension reducing" but also "tension engendering" and "tension maintaining" have smitten Hull and his descendants only. The psychoanalytic theory has from its inception pointed to and accounted for the engendering and maintenance of tension just as much as for tension discharge. It did so in the theories of conflict, defenses, and anxiety.

Fifth, clinical evidence shows that the defense-motives are themselves subject to defense formation, and indeed whole hierarchies of such defense and derivative motivations layered one over the other must be postulated to explain even common clinical phenomena. Knight (1940a, 1940b) and Gill (1945) have demonstrated this for the relationships of aggression, homosexuality, and paranoia. This hierarchic layering of structures is conceived to be the means by which the neutralization of instinctual drive cathexes is brought about. These multiple structural obstacles transform the peremptory instinctual drives into delayable motivations by setting the structural conditions under which the pleasure principle must operate (see II. 5. above). Another consequence of this hierarchic development will be touched on below (see pp. 849–850).

Sixth, I have already indicated that the variability of behavior under identical stimulus conditions and the constancy of behavior under varying stimulus conditions were part of the empirical evidence necessitating a theory of instinctual drives. It goes without saying that the displaceability of instinctual drive energy is the main conceptual tool by which the psychoanalytic theory accounts for this variability. We must now add that the defenses contribute their share to this variability. This too is a clinical commonplace. However, Klein and his collaborators' (Klein, 1951, 1956; Gardner et al., 1959) experimental demonstration of the operation of structures, apparently belonging to a high level of the hierarchy of defenses,[30] in cognitive performances in general and in perception in particular, is not a commonplace. Klein (1958; Gardner et al., 1959) has termed these structures *cognitive controls*. He also succeeded in demonstrating—as reported in his paper, "Need and Regulation" (1954), presented at one of these symposia—that these structures as causes contribute significantly and predictably to variations in behavior over and above the contribution of motivations. Here again we encounter mental structures in a causal, but not motivational, rôle.

This discussion of the concept of instinctual-drive restraint has extended the psychoanalytic theory of motivation beyond the theory of instinctual drives. But except for reaffirming the rôle of neutralized derivative motivations in relations to reality, it still has not given a general answer to the question concerning the motivation of our rational actions, ordered thinking, and contact with reality. We are approaching that problem step by step.

4. MAINTENANCE OF STRUCTURES AND PIAGET'S CONCEPTION
OF SCHEMA

What maintains the defenses once they are established? It is generally assumed that the pressure of instinctual drives is mostly responsible for their maintenance. The most striking evidence for this assumption comes from those situations in which increased instinctual pressure results in an increase of the intensity of defenses (e.g., in puberty, in menopause, in prodromal phases of pathology, etc.). In making this assumption, however, we would overlook two complementary considerations.

One of these was advanced by Freud (1937): defenses may be maintained even when the conflict underlying them has long since become quiescent. The fact that under these conditions defenses usually undergo a change of function (Hartmann, 1939) and turn into mechanisms of adaptation does not do away with the problem: *first,* some defenses do not undergo such a change of function; *second,* what maintains the mechanisms of adaptation into which some defenses turn by means of a change of function? We are faced here with the issue of the autonomy of structures, and we do not have sufficient factual knowledge to decide between the possible explanations. One of these explanations might be that a sufficiently consolidated structure is self-sustaining—but evidence to show that there are

[30] G. S. Klein suggests (personal communication) that these structures may be "constitutional" givens, which are only *elaborated* in the course of experience and thus these structures may also be considered as belonging to a "lowest" level of hierarchic organization.

actual instances where this is the case is difficult to come by.[31] Another explanation—which I suggested (1957d) and for which I marshaled some evidence—is that structures do not stand in isolation but are integrated with other structures and can be nourished and maintained through their relation to these other structures.[32] A third explanation would set out from those defenses which have, by a change of function, become adaptive mechanisms and as such can be brought into action not only by motivations but also by external stimuli. I have suggested (1957d) that such activation by external stimuli also contributes to the maintenance of these structures. This leads us back to the maintenance of defenses in general, and to the other neglected consideration.

The second consideration which is neglected when the pressure of instinctual drives is accepted as a sufficient explanation for the maintenance of defenses pertains to the rôle of the environment. This neglect is the more surprising since the evidence for it consists of clinical commonplaces. *First,* there is the so-called *secondary gain,* the advantage the patient derives from his defensive and symptomatic behavior, which has such a powerful rôle in maintaining these structures that some psychiatrists, psychologists, and so-called neo-Freudian "psychoanalysts" have taken it to be *the* cause of illness. *Second,* there is the equally common observation that often all therapeutic efforts are of no avail if the patient is continuously exposed to situations with which he has no other way of coping but his characteristic defensive behavior.[33] In these situations the very defenses which the work of the patient and the therapist would have to weaken and penetrate are continuously maintained and strengthened by the environment. In fact, the vicious circle of neurosis crucially involves the fact that the patient persistently exposes himself to situations (stimulations) which tend to elicit his defensive behavior and to reinforce his defenses, and avoids other situations which would tend to elicit alternative behaviors and thus would facilitate giving up his defenses. *Third,* there is evidence that structures other than defenses are also dependent upon external stimulation for their maintenance. For instance, it has recently been demonstrated (Miller, 1957; Polansky, Miller, and White, 1955) that the passive regressive tendencies of psychiatric patients become exacerbated by hospitalization unless the hospital setting specifically combats these tendencies. The increased corruptibility of the superego of a person who is removed from his usual setting, the mores and standards of which have nourished and supported his superego, seems to be a further example.

---

[31] R. R. Holt points out (personal communication) that *fixations* and full recall of events or poems after many years of disuse are such examples. He suggests that their explanation may be found in their cohesive structure and their isolation which save them from what Hebb would refer to as "fractionation" due to "recruitment" of their parts by other "phase sequences."

[32] Retroactive facilitation might provide an experimental analogy to this process.

[33] This situation is particularly common in therapeutic work with children.

I have described (1957d) this rôle of the environment as one of providing "stimulus nutriment" for structures. If we consider that the defensive or controlling structures guarantee the autonomy of the ego from the id, and that these structures too are maintained by environmental "stimulus nutriment," we come to understand how it is that the ego's *ab initio* dependence on environmental stimulation guarantees that the ego can develop an autonomy from the id.

Piaget's studies (1936, 1937; see also Wolff, 1960), however, seem to have even more far-reaching implications. He concluded from them that the very development (establishment) of structures depends upon "alimentation" by stimuli (see also Hebb [1949] to the same effect). It may be worth recalling that Piaget's conception of development starts out with what he calls circular reflex behaviors and schemata pertaining to them. These schemata are not specifically adapted to any single stimulus, but only to a general range of stimuli. Thus upon the first stimulation the schema assimilates the stimulus and provides that a motor accommodation is made to it. But neither the assimilation nor the accommodation can be fully successful at first, and no adaptation results. The lack of adaptation (i.e., imbalance between assimilation and accommodation) corresponds to a disequilibrium in the schema, which Piaget terms "desirability" and considers to be the causal factor due to which the assimilation of the object and the accommodation to the object are repeated as long as equilibrium is not reached. "Desirability" is Piaget's causal concept for the explanation of the circular, self-perpetuating character of infantile behavior in particular and exploratory behavior in general.[34]

When the schema reaches an equilibrium, that is, when it has adapted to the object, it has become a new structure. But exposures to new objects to which the schema is not yet adapted disturb its equilibrium again, set up a new "desirability," and initiate the schema's differentiation into new schemata. The processes of such new structure-building are contingent upon continued availability of the initiating stimulation, which Piaget termed "aliment," and to which I have referred as "stimulus nutriment." It is worth noting that Piaget's structure concept, just like the psychoanalytic, assumes a hierarchic layering of progressively differentiating structures.

What is noteworthy about Piaget's concept of development is that "motivation," i.e., *desirability,* and external stimulation, i.e., *aliment,* play equally important rôles. But what sort of "motivation" is this desirability? As far as Piaget's material goes—if I understand it correctly—desirability differs from what we are considering here as motivation. It is not given from the beginning, but rather is brought about by external stimulation, and only the potentiality for the disequilibrium brought about by external stimulation —desirability—is innately given. During the early phases of development,

[34] The crucial rôle of this circularity in behavior development was quite clear to Baldwin (1895) and perhaps to Troland (1929), but was entirely disregarded by the mainstream of psychology.

before the conservation of objects is achieved, this disequilibrium gives rise to appetitiveness in only a limited sense, that is, only as long as the object is within "reach," abating as the object ceases to stimulate. True, the range of this appetitiveness does increase, particularly after object constancy is attained, but there are at least four reasons for considering desirability as stimulus determined, rather than appetitive in the sense that motivations are: (1) At the very age at which whatever appetitiveness desirability has is limited in its "reach" to the immediately stimulating object, other forms of appetitiveness, which do not have such limits, and their affective accompaniments, are already observable. (2) The range of the appetitiveness due to desirability seems to expand no faster than the mental representations (conservation of objects) develop and expand its immediate "reach." [35] (3) Desirability, unlike motivations in the sense in which I am trying to delineate them here, involves no rise and fall and no consummation, but rather a repetitive activity resulting in a progressive decline as assimilation and accommodation approach equilibrium and adaptation is slowly achieved. (4) Desirability, unlike motivations as I discuss them here, does not result in peremptory behavior, nor in the corresponding *displacements of energy*[36] which occur when instinctual drives reach threshold intensity and the drive object is absent. I will try to show later on that the sort of causation of behavior Piaget describes may be explainable without the postulation of a special kind of motivation.

There is yet further and independent evidence available indicating that it is the development and maintenance of structures rather than a special kind of motivation which prompts the organism to reach out for stimulation. Some of the results of isolation experiments seem to be amenable to an explanation based on the deprivation of stimulus nutriment (Rapaport, 1957d, Bexton, Heron, and Scott, 1954). The study of hypnosis (Brenman and Gill, 1947; Gill and Brenman, 1959) also provides such results. The implications of "sensory disarrangement" experiments are also relevant here (I. Kohler, 1952; Werner and Wapner, 1955). Particularly pertinent are Held's experiments (Held and Hein, 1958; Held and Schlank, 1959; Held and White, 1959): he found that (a) readaptation after disarrangement does not overshoot the normal mark, and (b) there is readaptation only in the presence of "reafferent stimulation" (Holst, 1954), and concluded that our usual spatial orientations, however stable they may seem to

---

[35] The observation on which White relies so strongly in considering competence and its acquisition motivated and appetitive, namely, that we do go to great lengths to encounter new objects, may also be at least partially explained by this kind of expansion of "reach," i.e., we go because we know that there is something to be seen. But it is possible that this very expansion of reach amounts to a transition from a causation of the "desirability" type to a real motivation in our sense.

[36] Piaget describes displacements observed in the course of sensorimotor development, but they do not seem to be displacements of "desirability energy." I cannot go into a detailed analysis of this issue here.

us, are in the normal course of life brought about and maintained by such reafferent stimulation. In our terms, structures of spatial orientation too depend upon a particular kind of stimulus nutriment for their maintenance.

Now all this may sound like Woodworth's (1918) and G. W. Allport's (1937a) point that motives are habits in the making, and, indeed, these authors may have intuitively grasped and expressed in this way just the kind of relationship which I am trying to demonstrate. The trouble is that the evidence I have referred to above seems to show that the maintenance of already fully formed structures may require stimulus nutriment[37] and that there is some question whether the need for stimulus nutriment can be justifiably considered a motivational rather than a nonmotivational cause.

At this point, the impression may arise that what I am after is a deficiency-state explanation of environmental relations and of the causal rôle of stimuli. That is not my intention, nor could I agree—if it were suggested —that I am talking about "growth needs" or "self-realization" as Maslow (1955) does. While I see nothing wrong in *describing* behavior in teleological terms, it seems to me to go without saying that anybody who does so should—as Maslow does not—exercise caution lest he or his audience come to regard a teleological description as an *explanation*.[38] I believe that we must find an *explanation* for phenomena of "stimulus hunger"—to use the term Fenichel (1934) introduced in a different, though not unrelated, context—including all those exploratory, curious, active, and other behaviors which White subsumed under the concept of competence and explained by an "effectance motivation." In labeling effectance a motive, we explain nothing unless we can demonstrate that it, like drives, is purposive, expends energy, aims at consummation, and is to some degree peremptory. On White's and Piaget's showing, these stimulus-directed activities subsumed under effectance do not involve consummatory acts, and there is no evidence that they are peremptory. White considers them energy-expending and purposive: "External stimuli play an important part, but in terms of 'energy' this part is secondary, as one can see most clearly when environmental stimulation is actively sought" (1959, p. 321). But the question is whether their purposiveness (this active seeking) is selective and their energy expenditure is cyclical, in the sense in which I defined selectiveness and cyclicity as characteristics of motives. White rejects the explanation of competence phenomena by neutralized instinctual drives, because that explanation "preserves an image of mobility of energies" and because to his

[37] This may not always be the case, however. I have pointed out elsewhere (1957d) that stimulus nutriment for structure maintenance may be replaced by nutriment provided by motivations as well as by other (e.g., superordinate) structures. But of equal interest is yet another possibility, discussed above p. 892, n. 31.

[38] Commenting on Maslow's paper presented in one of these symposia, Peters wrote: "Moral philosophers have never been able to make much of the concept of 'self-realization' when it has been used as an over-all end to *justify* actions; to use it as a concept to *explain* them seems scarcely an encouraging move" (1958, p. 134).

mind these phenomena do not involve consummatory acts. I cannot but agree that if his facts are right these phenomena fail to have two of the defining characteristics without which they certainly cannot be explained in terms of any instinctual drive, neutralized or otherwise. Indeed, by my definition they cannot be explained by any motivation whatsoever.

We have seen that Piaget's "desirability" motivation is initiated by the impact of stimulation and subsides (or remains dormant) when the stimulation is not available, though it does engender appetitive behavior toward immediately available stimulation. This "short-range appetitiveness" as compared with "long-range appetitiveness" seems to differentiate significantly between desirability and instinctual drives. P. H. Wolff (1960) has discussed this difference in some detail. Whether this distinction holds for all those phenomena White explained by an effectance motivation is an interesting problem which can be explored experimentally. But in the Piaget instance at least, White's proposition would have to be revised: in it the rôle of stimulation is greater than that of energy.

If we take Berlyne's (1951) experiment as our paradigm for White's motivations, another difference between an effectance motivation and what I have defined as motives also becomes clear. Berlyne has shown that while novelty has an initially great but progressively decreasing effect on behavior, this "motivating" effect reappears in full strength when a new object is encountered. This is a state of affairs quite unlike the one observed in relation to motives which rise and fall cyclically and much like the phenomena of declining desirability with increasing adaptation which Piaget has demonstrated. Both the Berlyne and the Piaget phenomena are akin rather to the Karsten-Lewin (Karsten, 1927) phenomena of recovery after satiation than to motivational effects. Again: whether or not this is also characteristic of the other phenomena White discussed, among them P. T. Young's "hedonic arousal," constitutes an interesting question to which experiments must provide the answer.

In all the phenomena just discussed, the relation between the mental energy and the external stimulation involved in the behavior is different from that which appears in behaviors motivated by instinctual drives. Instinctual drives and kindred motives may be brought to threshold intensity by objects, may be intensified by changing the object, and may even be rearoused by a new object, but it is a common observation which requires no proof that such intensification and rearousal soon begin to bring diminishing returns and terminate in total refractoriness. Motivations are basically regulated by their intrinsic appetitiveness, which implies cyclicity, and only secondarily and within limits by stimuli. The Berlyne and Piaget phenomena are regulated primarily by the impinging external stimulation. Yet it may be argued that the "effectance motivations," just like other motives, expend mental energy. But does the fact that mental energy is involved turn the causal rôle of external stimulation into a motivational rôle? Does psychoanalytic theory have anything to say about this rôle of energies? We shall now turn to the discussion of this question.

5. CONSCIOUSNESS AND ATTENTION CATHEXES

In *The Interpretation of Dreams* (1900), Freud proposed a theory of consciousness, to which he never returned. Some of the implications of this theory, however, appear in his later writings, particularly in his "Papers on Metapsychology" (1915–17), but also in "Negation" (1925a) and in "A Note upon the 'Mystic Writing-Pad' " (1925b). We also know (Jones, 1955) that he wrote a chapter on consciousness for the contemplated volume of which the "Papers on Metapsychology" were to be a part. This paper was never published, nor was the manuscript ever found. In a sense, what follows here may be regarded as an attempt to reconstruct Freud's missing manuscript, from his theory of consciousness of 1900 and from his "Papers on Metapsychology."

It is known to everyone who is familiar with psychoanalysis that Freud (1900) distinguished between *consciousness as a subjective experience* and the concept of the *system Conscious-Preconscious (Cs.-Pcs.)*. The latter was the predecessor of the *ego* concept of his later, so-called structural theory. It is less well known that he also postulated an *apparatus of consciousness*, which he distinguished from both the subjective experience of consciousness and the system *Cs.-Pcs.* (see Gill [1963]). The function of this apparatus was to account for the phenomenon of *subjective conscious experience*.

It is worth while, I believe, to stop here for a moment to remind ourselves that some psychologists have eschewed all reference to consciousness, i.e., to introspective reports, while others have made a more or less deliberate use of introspective reports in trying to discover the laws governing behavior. But it seems that Freud was the only one who proposed a psychological theory to explain the phenomenon of the subjective conscious experience. I would like to point out that whether the specific theory proposed by Freud is valid or not, the very program it implies, namely, the exploration of the processes underlying the phenomenon of subjective conscious experience by psychological methods, is one of his most significant and most overlooked contributions to psychological theory. It should be stressed that what he proposed in this theory was neither an explanation of the *contents* of consciousness, nor a physiological explanation of the phenomenon of consciousness, but a psychological explanation of the phenomenon of consciousness (see Rapaport, 1951a, 1956, 1957a).

It will justifiably be asked why I should dwell, in a paper on the theory of motivation, on Freud's theory of consciousness. The answers are: (1) The remaining task for this paper is to clarify what the behavior-determining rôle of external stimulation and relations to reality is. (2) The prerequisite of this task is a theory of consciousness which gives an account of the

processes by whose mediation external stimulations exert whatever behavior-determining rôle they have. (3) The hope is that a consideration of
this theory of consciousness will clarify whether the behavior-determining
rôle of external stimulation involves a *special kind of motivation,* as White
believes, or only nonmotivational causation.

The core of Freud's conception of the function of the hypothetical apparatus of consciousness may be condensed into the following propositions:

(1) The subjective conscious experience is determined by the distribution
of a limited quantity of mental energy termed attention cathexis.[39]

(2) The changes in the distribution of attention cathexes are conceptualized as the function of the apparatus of consciousness.

(3) Attention cathexis is part of the energy of the system *Cs.-Pcs.* (in
present-day terminology, the ego) which is termed hypercathexis.

(4) Excitations within the mental apparatus (internal) or on the receptor organs (external) attract attention cathexes proportionately to their
intensity.

(5) Attention cathexis, if so attracted and if exceeding a certain amount
(threshold), gives rise to the conscious experience of the excitation.

(6) Simultaneous or contiguous excitations compete for the limited quantity of attention cathexis.

(7) When an external excitation is congruent with or related to a representation[40] of the internal excitation which is simultaneous or contiguous
with it, then there is no competition, but rather both excitations attract
attention cathexis to the common representation.

(8) Internal excitations may be defended against in such a way (e.g., by
repression) that they cannot attract attention cathexes.

(9) Defenses and other processes utilizing great amounts of hypercathexes diminish the quantity of attention cathexis available.[41]

(10) When an excitation of short duration ceases, the attention cathexis
it attracted becomes available to other excitations.

(11) An excitation of long duration attracts cathexis proportionate to
its duration as well as intensity.

(12) Attention cathexis attracted by an excitation in a sufficient amount
and for a sufficient duration gives rise to a structure (e.g., memory trace).

(13) Structures so built retain only a small quantity of the attention
cathexes that were needed to give rise to them. The condition of these cathexes is termed *bound,* and the process itself *binding.*

[39] Dr. Robert R. Holt suggests (personal communication) that an "open-system" conception of attention cathexis—in which as much as is used up is replaced—would be
more plausible and more satisfying. He may well be right, and the assumption of a
"limited quantity" is certainly only a working hypothesis. But to carry out his suggestion, as it would affect the whole conception, seems to be far too complex a task
at present and not yet required by any specific findings.
[40] Concerning *representations,* pp. 380–382.
[41] For pertinent findings, see Rapaport, Gill, and Schafer (1945–46) and Rapaport
(1947).

(14) Once structure building is completed, the attention cathexes used in the process—except for those which have become bound in the structure—become available to other excitations.

These propositions hew closely to Freud's formulations in Chapter VII of *The Interpretation of Dreams* (1900) and in his theories of repression (1915b, 1915c) and anxiety (1926). The documentation of the roots of these assumptions in Freud's writings will be found in my various writings (1951a, 1951d, 1956, 1957a). Freud's theory of consciousness has also been discussed by Lewy and me (1944) and by Klein (1959). These propositions do not exhaust all that Freud seems to have implied. A more extensive reconstruction would hew less closely to Freud's writings and would be out of place here.

It would seem that these propositions have a bearing on the early studies of academic psychologists on attention, attention span, and memory span (Oberly, 1924; Gill and Dallenbach, 1926; Blankenship, 1938; Woodworth, 1938) and may put these in a different light. They also seem to bear on Lewin's concept of quasi needs.[42] Gill, Schafer, and I (1945–46; Rapaport, 1947) have used these propositions to explain the variability of digit-span performance encountered in clinical diagnostic work. I have also used them in the explanation of thought forms observed in various states of consciousness (1956, 1957a). The recent concern with the limited range of attention span, variously referred to as "the magic seven" (Miller, 1956) and channel capacity (Frick, 1959), the recent interest in vigilance and distraction (Deese, 1955; Broadbent, 1958), some of the newer investigations of immediate memory (Poulton, 1953; J. Brown, 1954, 1958; Peterson and Peterson, 1959) and incidental memory, and many of the studies of Russell and his associates on associative mediation, bidirectionality of associations, and "priming" (recency), provide testing grounds for the assumptions which can be derived from these propositions. Moreover, some of the findings in the areas of investigation just listed seem difficult to interpret in S-R terms, and there is some evidence—part of which I will discuss later on—to show that the kind of theory sketched in the above propositions may be able to solve some of these refractory problems.

The problem of the origin of attention cathexes is not touched on in these propositions. There are two equally tenable assumptions to account for their origin. The relatively simpler one posits that the autonomous ego apparatuses are themselves the sources of these energies. The more complicated one posits that attention cathexes are products of neutralization. This assumption implies that neutralization produces not only increasingly less peremptory derivative motivations, but also progressively neutralized ener-

---

[42] It is reasonable to assume—and such an assumption can be experimentally tested—that the "tension systems" underlying these quasi needs are temporarily segregated attention cathexes. As such, they would constitute a class of autonomous ego motivations which have a consummatory activity, do allow for displacement, have a degree of peremptoriness, however low, but do not have a cyclic rise and fall.

gies which are not motivationally organized but rather become energies at the disposal of the ego, i.e., hypercathexes. I cannot discuss this alternative in detail here. The observations of my associate, P. H. Wolff (1959), on infants seem to be compatible with the former assumption. He has demonstrated that infants from the first hours of their lives on can and do follow moving sounds and visual objects, provided that these are exposed to them at a time when they are no longer asleep and not yet in a state of hunger or other distress. The total of such times averages 30 minutes per 24 hours in the first days of life and progressively increases later on. But these observations are not incompatible with the assumption of a dual origin of attention cathexes. Be that as it may, the problem of the origin of attention cathexes may sooner or later become amenable to empirical study and decision.

But what does all this add up to for the theory of motivation?

6. MOTIVATION VS. ATTENTION CATHEXIS AS AN EXPLANATION OF COMPETENCE IN RELATIONS TO REALITY

White proposed the concept of an effectance motivation to account for competence in relations to reality, that is, for the "capacity to interact effectively with . . . [the] environment" (1959, p. 297) and for the slow attainment of this capacity through "learning." I have argued that the effectance motivation as White characterizes it is not a motivation in the sense in which psychoanalysis conceives of motivation. But White could well argue that psychoanalysis is not the arbiter of terms and that like Humpty-Dumpty we can make a word mean what we want it to mean. White would then have two choices. He could assert, with Littman (1958) and Peters (1958), that motivation is not a homogeneous concept, or else he could choose in whose sense he uses the term "motivation." But he does neither. He leaves motivation an undefined concept.[43] But even if this trouble with the concept of motivation were settled, there is still another difficulty with White's argument.

He argues cogently and effectively that the drive theories of learning cannot account for all the acquisition and exercise of this competence. Then, however, he proceeds to propose a new motivation, effectance, to account for the rest of it, without attempting to make plausible *how* this new motivation should be able to do what drive motivations have not been able to. My emphasis is on the *how,* because I have no doubt that White marshaled telling evidence that learning unexplainable by drive motivations *does* occur. What he did not show is that his new motivation accounts for such learning. White's crucial evidence that the drive theory is in trouble derives from studies of attention (curiosity, novelty) and learning. I believe

[43] Dr. White indicated (personal communication) that he considers the defining characteristics of motives to be persistence, direction, and selectiveness. Comparing these with the discussion I offered above, in I. 8., I am still left with the impression that motives are not sufficiently defined by these criteria.

that Freud's theory of consciousness and structure formation accounts for such learning without invoking a new motivational concept. (1) In contrast to the theory of motivations, the theory of attention cathexis implies energies under such structural conditions that they do not strive for discharge: these cathexes are conceived of as in an equilibrium which is disrupted by impinging excitations (Proposition 4) and is restored when either a temporary excitation ceases (Proposition 10) or a continuing excitation results in structure formation (Propositions 11 and 14). (2) The attention cathexes *per se,* unlike the motivational cathexes (including those of high neutralization), show no peremptoriness; they are commanded by excitations (Propositions 4 and 5). (3) White marshaled evidence which seems to suggest that some of the phenomena which he explains by the effectance motivation are appetitive. If this is so, attention cathexes which show no appetitiveness[44] could not explain the phenomena marshaled. But the question is whether the phenomena White refers to are or are not appetitive, and if they are, whether that appetitiveness could be explained by *representations* (memories, images) of the allegedly appetited objects impinging upon the apparatus of consciousness. (4) Attention cathexes, unlike motives, do not have goals or specific objects or selectiveness, and except for the factors determining their chances of winning out in competition with each other, that is, except for their intensity (Proposition 4), salience, and novelty (Propositions 15, 16, 17) (see p. 903 below), objects are equivalent in their ability to attract them if other conditions remain constant (Proposition 7).

Thus the psychoanalytic theory of consciousness, and the partial theory of relations to reality that it implies,[45] is not a motivational theory. To be sure, it is not unrelated to motivations: the internal excitations which do play a salient rôle in it *are* motivations, but they too operate by attracting attention cathexes. This theory assigns to both the attention cathexes and to the external stimulations a rôle that is not motivational, but causal.

In the final analysis, the psychoanalytic theory of relations to reality and White's conception of competence need not be contradictory. The psychoanalytic theory of the secondary process, as well as White's theory, maintains that the relationships to reality are governed by laws other than the primary process and instinctual drives. Both assert that the laws governing relations to reality are not in the main governed by tension reduction, but by tension maintenance, and indeed tension-engendering regulations. Even the divergence between the nonmotivational explanation of compe-

[44] Their being aroused by *any* excitation, their being attracted by competing excitations, their lacking intrinsic selectiveness, and their tendency to return to equilibrium correspond not to behavioral appetitiveness, but rather to a state of readiness for the impingement of new excitations. But the possibility that they could be shaped into quasi needs could serve as the basis for the phenomena White marshaled. However, such quasi-need types of motivations seem very different from White's conception of an effectance motivation.

[45] See Hartmann (1956) for the more general theory of reality relations.

tence by the psychoanalytic theory of consciousness and White's explanation by the effectance drive may be one of conceptual tactics which, since the necessary facts are not yet in, could well be considered a divergence between two different predictions as to what conceptual framework will have greatest heuristic advantage. It is possible that what little we know so far about attention cathexes is only a crude approximation and that a closer exploration will show that the function of attention cathexes too has motivational characteristics. For instance, it is possible that we will discover that attention cathexes have a permanent gradient toward the external excitations. Freud's (1911) formulation that attention meets the sense impressions halfway suggests something of this kind (see also Freud, 1915b, Section VI).[46] Be that as it may, the fact is that White set a task for us when he culled the evidence concerning competence, because that material is also evidence about the functioning of the secondary process. We must find an adequate explanation for the observations which he has systematized. If the psychoanalytic theory cannot find it, some other theory will. I believe that the psychoanalytic theory provides a promising point of departure, and I shall try to make this plausible in the section which follows.

7. SOME EXPERIMENTS BEARING ON FREUD'S THEORY OF CONSCIOUSNESS

I will now offer some evidence which tends to confirm Freud's theory of consciousness and suggests that this theory may be able to account for the acquisition of competence in relations to reality in White's sense.

Of the experiments and observations White refers to, I will choose the Berlyne experiments as an example on which to demonstrate that Freud's theory of consciousness applies to these observations and experiments. Berlyne (1951) has shown that (a) of several objects present, rats and men pay most attention to the one which is different from the others; (b) this preference declines in time; (c) if a new and different object is introduced at this point, it will attract the same amount of attention as the originally different object had to begin with. I choose this example assuming that it captures the central features of the Wisconsin (Harlow, 1953; Butler, 1954; Butler and Alexander, 1955) exploratory-drive experiments and Bindra's (1959) novelty experiments, and because I do not have the space here to deal with each of these individually.

If we add to the 14 propositions summarizing Freud's theory of consciousness three more, defining novelty and familiarity,[47] Berlyne's findings are readily explained:

[46] We may also discover that motivations of the quasi-need type play a greater rôle in the economics and dynamics of attention cathexis than has been suspected so far, and are responsible for many of the phenomena White explains by effectance.

[47] These propositions are not advanced *ad hoc* to explain Berlyne's findings; they are derived from our experiments, some of which will be reported below.

(15) An external excitation is novel when there exists no structure corresponding to it; if a structure exists, the excitation is termed "familiar."

(16) If there exists a structure corresponding to an external excitation, the excitation will attract attention cathexis to that structure, but, in keeping with Proposition 14, this structure will readily give off the attention cathexis.

(17) If the simultaneously impinging external excitations are all familiar, salience will determine their relative power to attract attention cathexis.

Berlyne's first finding can be explained by Propositions 4, 15, and 17. His second finding would follow from Propositions 14 and 16, and his third finding from Propositions 4 and 17. But this kind of *ex post facto* explanation is always suspect. It can only be justified either if it has demonstrable heuristic value or if the propositions used in the *ex post facto* explanation are supported by independent evidence. I believe that both these conditions are to some extent fulfilled in the case of the propositions we have before us.

As for their heuristic value: the Berlyne experiments involve unexplained temporal relationships, for instance the rate of loss of preferential attending. According to the propositions discussed here, this rate should correspond to the rate at which cathexes become available in the course of structure building. This rate can be experimentally explored by methods other than Berlyne's; see, for example, the Peterson and Peterson (1959) experiment. By measuring this rate, a whole range of problems will become amenable to experimental exploration guided by the theory.

As for the independent evidence supporting the theory: it must be remembered, first of all, that the theory is based on clinical evidence. But this sort of evidence says only that a variety of clinical observations can be explained without mutual contradiction if such theoretical assumptions are made. The desirable evidence is experimental. Though the gathering of such evidence is in its very beginnings, I will take the risk of giving a bird's-eye view of some of the results. I say "take the risk" because a complex theory is *not* proved by a few experiments and certainly not by a small sample of even those few.

My associates and I at the Austen Riggs Center have undertaken a series of preliminary experiments to test this theory. We have also found in the literature a number of experimental studies which seem pertinent to it. The first experiment attempt to test the following assumptions: (1) only a limited quantity of attention cathexis is available at any given time (Proposition 1); (2) the process of structure building requires a cathectic investment interfering with contiguous processes (Propositions 6 and 12); (3) once structure building is completed, most of the cathexes used in structure building become available again (Proposition 14).

Dr. Richard Rouse of Williams College, while on Sabbatical at the Riggs Center, proposed to test these assumptions first by an experiment using the retroactive inhibition paradigm. He assumed that if the degree of interpolated learning is slight, it will demand little attention cathexis and will result in little retroactive inhibition. With increasing degrees of interpolated learning the cathectic requirement and the degree of inhibition will reach a maximum. But beyond a certain point of overlearning (in Hartmann's [1939] terms, automatization), the cathexes will become available again and the degree of inhibition will decline. He did not carry out this experiment, because his study of the literature showed that this effect had already been demonstrated (McGeoch, 1932; Melton and Irwin, 1940; Thune and Underwood, 1943), and an *ad hoc* and after-the-fact explanation of it had been proposed by the experimenters who demonstrated it (Melton and Lackum, 1941; McGeoch and Underwood, 1943).

But Rouse reasoned that this effect was to be expected in proactive inhibition also. His search of the literature showed that the results of such experiments were by no means conclusive (Atwater, 1953; Underwood, 1945, 1949). He therefore tested this assumption in two experiments on the proactive inhibition of retention. The first, a group experiment which he also replicated, used work criteria to vary the degree of practice in both tasks (Rouse, 1959). The predicted function was obtained in those groups that had little practice on the second task. These results have been confirmed in a second experiment which was also replicated and used performance criteria to vary the degree of practice on the first task.

These experiments, however, did not refute other explanations of the findings, and therefore much work still has to be done. Our other experiments are also deficient in this respect. Critical experiments are hard to come by.

A further contribution toward the confirmation of the theory comes from the experiments of Bahrick, which we came upon in the study of the literature. I will sketch only three of his experiments, though all of them are pertinent. (The interpretation of these experiments which follows is mine and Bahrick has no responsibility for it.) In one of these experiments, Bahrick (1957) gave his subjects an intentional learning task and provided an opportunity for simultaneous incidental learning. He interrupted each of his groups of subjects at a different degree of intentional learning and tested at that point for the degree of incidental learning. He found that at low degrees of intentional learning the degree of incidental learning rises slowly, then stops completely for a while, and rises steeply when the intentional learning enters the overlearning phase. The plateau in incidental learning is around that degree of intentional learning at which, according to Rouse's experiments, we would expect the maximum inhibitory effect if the intentional learning were the proactively inhibiting task. We may put it thus: competition for attention cathexis between the intentional and incidental tasks took place (Proposition 6). The cathectic requirement of intentional learning (Proposition 12) brought incidental learning to a standstill (Proposition 6), but once a consolidation of the intentionally learned material had taken place, the cathexes became available again and incidental learning progressed apace (Proposition 14).

Another of Bahrick's (Bahrick, Noble, and Fitts, 1954) experiments demonstrated that if incidental learning accompanied motor performance, the more random and the less repetitive the intentional motor performance was, that is, the less it could be automatized, the less incidental learning occurred (Propositions 14 and 16). It is worth noting that Postman reported similar antagonistic relationships between incidental and intentional learning (Postman and Senders, 1946) and between the amount of learning in free recall as against recall in order of presentation (Postman, 1955).

A third of Bahrick's experiments (1954) tends to confirm another proposition of the theory. He demonstrated that with increased incentive on intentional learning, incidental learning declines. According to Proposition 7, the attention cathexis of the intentional task should be increased under these conditions, and therefore, according to Propositions 1 and 6, the amount of attention cathexis available for incidental learning should decrease.

In the experiments so far mentioned, the cathectic demands of two processes of structure formation (learning) were pitted against each other. But since what we wanted to prove was that other demands for cathexis interfere with structure formation (learning), and the other demand we used was also structure formation (learning), our independent and dependent variables were identical. Thus the experiments involved some circularity. To get away from this, Peter Schiller, a graduate student at Clark University collaborating with us, designed and carried out the following experiment. He used three pursuit rotor tasks, of different degrees of difficulty, as shown by mean time on target in performance. Around the edge of the rotating disk of each of these pursuit tasks he printed the same set of words, so that the subject saw them appear one by one during his pursuit performance. He gave his subjects only pursuit instructions without reference to the words appearing above the line to be pursued. After the pursuit task was completed, he tested for incidental recall (and recognition) of the words. These pursuit tasks did not involve learning, and provide (by the measure of time on target) independent demands for attention cathexes competing with the cathectic expenditure involved in the incidental learning of the words. The results showed statistically significant differences between the three groups, indicating that the harder the pursuit task, the less incidental learning occurs. He also found on each task taken separately a statistically significant negative correlation between time on target and amount of incidental learning. These findings are consistent with Propositions 1, 6, and 12.

This is not the place to review all our experiments and all the relevant experiments reported in the literature. The sketches of the experiments and their results that I have presented do not do justice either to the methods used or to all of the results obtained in them. These experiments were reported here solely to make the following points plausible:

(1) The explanation implicit in psychoanalytic theory for some of the phenomena White attempted to explain by an effectance motivation is not an *ad hoc* explanation but—right or wrong—one which has some experimental support.

(2) The much frowned-upon energy concept of psychoanalysis may lead to inferences which can be experimentally tested.

(3) The existing theories of learning seem to have disregarded the relation of learning to the phenomenon of span of immediate memory and thereby may have overlooked a quantity involved in learning other than those they have attempted to capture.

(4) The psychoanalytic theory so far has no theory of learning, but it does have, in its theory of consciousness, a possible point of departure for such a theory. This potential theory is deeply rooted in the psychoanalytic theory as a whole and is not a drive-reinforcement or law of effect type of theory; thus all the efforts to make the drive-reinforcement theory appear "psychoanalytic" seem to have been misguided.

(5) The relationship to reality, or as White calls it, "competence" in dealing with the environment, is acquired by learning (White, 1959, p. 297). But, as White correctly stressed, the potentiality for acquiring such competence must be assumed to be present from the very beginning. It is to be doubted, however, that an effectance motivation or any other motivation is the basis of this potentiality, and it is possible that its basis is an apparatus of consciousness of the sort which I have described. Learning is still an open question, even though it has been studied for a hundred years. An approach to the study of learning (structure formation) based on Freud's theory of consciousness is at least worth a try.

IV. RÉSUMÉ

In this paper I have attempted

(1) to clarify the difference between causes and motives;

(2) to make it plausible that causes of behavior may or may not be motives;

(3) to demonstrate that the instinctual drives and their derivatives are causes which are also motives, and that some motives may not be such derivatives;

(4) to show that motives must be considered in purely psychological terms, independent of their physiological and neurophysiological basis;

(5) to give a survey of the psychoanalytic theory of instinctual drives and derivative motivations, and to make it clear that the S-R drive theories are unrelated to it;

(6) to clarify the nature of instinctual-drive restraining factors and

structures (defenses, habits, other ego apparatuses, etc.) in general and to show that they may act either as nonmotivational psychological causes or as motivational causes;

(7) to argue that relations to reality in general and stimuli in particular play a causal but not a motivational rôle in determining behavior;

(8) to clarify the point that stimuli play this causal rôle as goals (objects) of motivations, and as "stimulus nutriment" required for the maintenance of structures in general and instinctual drive-restraining structures in particular;

(9) to suggest that contact with external reality and the stimulus nutriment for structure building and structure maintenance it involves seem to be the guarantee of the ego's autonomy from the id, and instinctual drive pressure seems to be the guarantee of the autonomy of the ego from the environment;

(10) to sketch the psychoanalytic theory of consciousness as an indispensable part of the theory of relations to reality;

(11) to make it plausible that both Piaget's theory of development and the psychoanalytic theory of consciousness imply a structure-formation theory of learning whose central ingredient is "stimulus nutriment";

(12) to argue that the referents of White's competence concept, which by his showing are not explainable by "drive" theories, are not explainable by any other motivational theory, including an effectance motivation;

(13) to substantiate the proposition that the explanation of the phenomena subsumed by White under the concept of competence requires a theory of relations to the environment and learning other than drive-reinforcement theory;

(14) to suggest that Freud's theory of consciousness may provide such an explanation;

(15) to bring forward some experimental evidence from the literature and from the work of my collaborators and me which begins to provide some confirmation, if not of the validity, then at least of the heuristic potential, of this theory of consciousness.

REFERENCES

Allport, G. W. (1935–47). *The Nature of Personality: Selected Papers.* Cambridge, Mass.: Addison-Wesley Press, 1950.

———— (1937a). *Personality.* New York: Holt.

———— (1937b). The Functional Autonomy of Motives. In Allport (1935–47), pp. 76–91.

———— (1946). Geneticism vs. Ego-Structure in Theories of Personality. In Allport (1935–47), pp. 158–169.

———— (1947). Scientific Models and Human Morals. In Allport (1935–47), pp. 187–197.

Atwater, S. K. (1953). Proactive Inhibition and Associative Facilitation as Affected by Degree of Prior Learning. *J. Exp. Psychol.,* 46:400–404.

Bahrick, H. P. (1954). Incidental Learning under Two Incentive Conditions. *J. Exp. Psychol.,* 47:170–172.

——— (1957). Incidental Learning at Five Stages of Intentional Learning. *J. Exp. Psychol.,* 54:259–261.

———, Noble, M., & Fitts, P. M. (1954). Extratask Performance as a Measure of Learning a Primary Task. *J. Exp. Psychol.,* 48:298–302.

Baldwin, J. M. (1895). *Mental Development in the Child and the Race. Methods and Processes,* 2nd ed. New York: Macmillan.

Beach, F. A. (1942). Analysis of Factors Involved in the Arousal, Maintenance and Manifestation of Sexual Excitement in Male Animals. *Psychosom. Med.,* 4:173–198.

——— (1956). Characteristics of Masculine "Sex Drive." In *Nebraska Symposium on Motivation, 1956,* ed. M. R. Jones. Lincoln: University of Nebraska Press, pp. 1–32.

Berlyne, D. E. (1951). Attention to Change. *Brit. J. Psychol.,* 42:269–278.

Bettelheim, B. (1943). Individual and Mass Behavior in Extreme Situations. *J. Abnorm. Soc. Psychol.,* 38:417–452.

Bexton, W. H., Heron, W., & Scott, T. H. (1954). Effects of Decreased Variation in the Sensory Environment. *Canad. J. Psychol.,* 8:70–76.

Bindra, D. (1959). Stimulus Change, Reactions to Novelty, and Response Decrement. *Psychol. Rev.,* 66:96–103.

Blankenship, A. B. (1938). Memory Span: A Review of the Literature. *Psychol. Bull.,* 35:1–25.

Boring, E. G. (1950). *A History of Experimental Psychology,* 2nd ed. New York: Appleton-Century-Crofts.

Brenman, M., & Gill, M. M. (1947). *Hypnotherapy; A Survey of the Literature.* New York: International Universities Press.

Breuer, J., & Freud, S. (1893–95). Studies on Hysteria. *Standard Edition,* 2. London: Hogarth Press, 1955.

Broadbent, D. E. (1958). *Perception and Communication.* New York: Pergamon Press.

Brown, J. (1954). The Nature of Set-to-Learn and of Intra-material Interference in Immediate Memory. *Quart. J. Exp. Psychol.,* 6:141–148.

——— (1958). Some Tests of the Decay Theory of Immediate Memory. *Quart. J. Exp. Psychol.,* 10:12–21.

Brown, J. S. (1953). Problems Presented by the Concept of Acquired Drives. In *Current Theory and Research in Motivation: A Symposium.* Lincoln: University of Nebraska Press, pp. 1–19.

Brunswik, E. (1934). *Wahrnehmung und Gegenstandswelt.* Leipzig: Deuticke.

——— (1956). *Perception and the Representative Design of Psychological Experiments,* 2nd ed. Berkeley: University of California Press.

Butler, R. A. (1954). Incentive Conditions Which Influence Visual Exploration. *J. Exp. Psychol.,* 48:19–23.

———, & Alexander, H. M. (1955). Daily Patterns of Visual Exploratory Behavior in the Monkey. *J. Comp. Physiol. Psychol.,* 48:247–249.

Deese, J. (1955). Some Problems in the Theory of Vigilance. *Psychol. Rev.,* 62:359–368.

Dollard, J., & Miller, N. E. (1950). *Personality and Psychotherapy: An Analysis in Terms of Learning, Thinking, and Culture.* New York: McGraw-Hill.

Erikson, E. H. (1937). Configurations in Play—Clinical Notes. *Psychoanal. Quart.*, 6:139–214.

———— (1939). Observations on Sioux Education. *J. Psychol.*, 7:101–156.

———— (1946–59). Identity and the Life Cycle: Selected Papers. *Psychol. Issues*, No. 1, 1959.

———— (1950). *Childhood and Society.* New York: Norton.

Farber, I. E. (1954). Anxiety as a Drive State. In *Nebraska Symposium on Motivation, 1954*, ed. M. R. Jones. Lincoln: University of Nebraska Press, pp. 1–46.

Fenichel, O. (1934). On the Psychology of Boredom. *Collected Papers*, 1:292–302. New York: Norton, 1953. Also in Rapaport (1951a), pp. 349–361.

———— (1941). The Ego and the Affects. *Collected Papers*, 2:215–227. New York: Norton, 1954.

Frenkel-Brunswik, E. (1942). Motivation and Behavior. *Genet. Psychol. Monogr.*, 26:121–265.

Freud, A. (1936). *The Ego and the Mechanisms of Defence.* New York: International Universities Press, 1946.

Freud, S. (1887–1902). *The Origins of Psychoanalysis: Letters to Wilhelm Fliess, Drafts and Notes, 1887–1902.* New York: Basic Books, 1954.

———— (1894). The Defence Neuro-Psychoses. *Collected Papers*, 1:59–75. New York: Basic Books, 1959.

———— (1900). The Interpretation of Dreams. *Standard Edition*, 4 & 5. London: Hogarth Press, 1953.

———— (1905a). Three Essays on the Theory of Sexuality. *Standard Edition*, 7:123–245. London: Hogarth Press, 1953.

———— (1905b). Wit and Its Relation to the Unconscious, tr. A. A. Brill. *The Basic Writings.* New York: Modern Library, 1938, pp. 631–803.

———— (1910). Leonardo da Vinci and a Memory of His Childhood. *Standard Edition*, 11:63–137. London: Hogarth Press, 1957.

———— (1911). Formulations on the Two Principles of Mental Functioning. *Standard Edition*, 12:218–226. London: Hogarth Press, 1958.

———— (1913 [1912–13]). Totem and Taboo. *Standard Edition*, 13:1–161. London: Hogarth Press, 1955.

———— (1914). On Narcissism: An Introduction. *Standard Edition*, 14:73–102. London: Hogarth Press, 1957.

———— (1915a). Instincts and Their Vicissitudes. *Standard Edition*, 14:117–140. London: Hogarth Press, 1957.

———— (1915b). Repression. *Standard Edition*, 14:146–158. London: Hogarth Press, 1957.

———— (1915c). The Unconscious. *Standard Edition*, 14:166–215. London: Hogarth Press, 1957.

———— (1915–17 [1915]). Papers on Metapsychology. *Standard Edition*, 14:105–258. London: Hogarth Press, 1957.

———— (1916–17 [1915–17]). *A General Introduction to Psychoanalysis*, tr. J. Riviere. New York: Garden City Publishing Co., 1938.

—— (1920). *Beyond the Pleasure Principle,* tr. C. J. M. Hubback. London: Hogarth Press, 1948.

—— (1923). *The Ego and the Id,* tr. J. Riviere. London: Hogarth Press, 1947.

—— (1925a). Negation. *Collected Papers,* 5:181–185. New York: Basic Books, 1959. Also in Rapaport (1951a), pp. 338–348.

—— (1925b [1924]). A Note upon the "Mystic Writing-Pad." *Collected Papers,* 5:175–180. New York: Basic Books, 1959. Also in Rapaport (1951a), pp. 329–337.

—— (1926). Inhibitions, Symptoms and Anxiety. *Standard Edition,* 20:87–172. London: Hogarth Press, 1959.

—— (1937). Analysis Terminable and Interminable. *Collected Papers,* 5:316–357. New York: Basic Books, 1959.

Frick, F. C. (1959). Information Theory. In *Psychology: A Study of a Science,* Vol. II, ed. S. Koch. New York: McGraw-Hill, pp. 611–636.

Gardner, R. W., et al. (1959). Cognitive Control. *Psychol. Issues,* No. 4.

Gill, M. M. (1945). Paranoia, Homosexuality, and Aggression. Unpublished ms.

—— (1959). The Present State of Psychoanalytic Theory. *J. Abnorm. Soc. Psychol.,* 58:1–8.

—— (1963). Topography and Systems in Psychoanalytic Theory. *Psychol. Issues,* No. 10.

—— (1966). The Primary Process. In Motives and Thought: Psychoanalytic Essays in Memory of David Rapaport, ed. R. R. Holt. *Psychol. Issues,* Nos. 18/19.

——, & Brenman, M. (1959). *Hypnosis and Related States: Psychoanalytic Studies in Regression.* New York: International Universities Press.

Gill, N. F., & Dallenbach, K. M. (1926). A Preliminary Study of the Range of Attention. *Amer. J. Psychol.,* 37:247–256.

Goldstein, K., & Scheerer, M. (1941). Abstract and Concrete Behavior; An Experimental Study with Special Tests. *Psychol. Monogr.,* 53, No. 2.

Harlow, H. F. (1953). Motivation as a Factor in the Acquisition of New Responses. In *Current Theory and Research in Motivation: A Symposium.* Lincoln: University of Nebraska Press, pp. 24–49.

Hartmann, H. (1939). *Ego Psychology and the Problem of Adaptation,* tr. D. Rapaport. New York: International Universities Press, 1958. Also (abridged) in Rapaport (1951a), pp. 362–396.

—— (1950). Comments on the Psychoanalytic Theory of the Ego. *Psychoanal. Study Child,* 5:74–96. New York: International Universities Press.

—— (1952). The Mutual Influences in the Development of the Ego and Id. *Psychoanal. Study Child,* 7:9–30. New York: International Universities Press.

—— (1956). Notes on the Reality Principle. *Psychoanal. Study Child,* 11:31–53. New York: International Universities Press.

——, Kris, E., & Loewenstein, R. M. (1946). Comments on the Formation of Psychic Structure. *Psychoanal. Study Child,* 2:11–38. New York: International Universities Press.

Hebb, D. O. (1949). *The Organization of Behavior: A Neuropsychological Theory.* New York: Wiley.

———— (1958). Alice in Wonderland, or, Psychology among the Biological Sciences. In *Biological and Biochemical Bases of Behavior*, ed. H. F. Harlow & C. N. Woolsey. Madison: University of Wisconsin Press, pp. 451–467.

Heider, F. (1926–59). On Perception and Event Structure, and the Psychological Environment; Selected Papers. *Psychol. Issues*, No. 3, 1959.

———— (1958). *The Psychology of Interpersonal Relations*. New York: Wiley.

Held, R., & Hein, A. V. (1958). Adaptation of Disarranged Hand-Eye Coordination Contingent upon Re-afferent Stimulation. *Percep. Motor Skills*, 8:87–90.

————, & Schlank, M. (1959). Adaptation to Disarranged Hand-Eye Coordination in the Distance-Dimension. *Amer. J. Psychol.*, 72:603–605.

————, & White, B. (1959). Sensory Deprivation and Visual Speed: An Analysis. *Science*, 130:860–861.

Holst, E. von (1954). Relations between the Central Nervous System and the Peripheral Organs. *Brit. J. Animal Behav.*, 2:89–94.

Holt, R. R. (1962). A Critical Examination of Freud's Concept of Bound vs. Free Cathexis. *J. Amer. Psychoanal. Assn.*, 10:475–525.

Hull, C. L. (1936–38). *Hull's Psychological Seminars 1936–1938*. Notices and Abstracts of Proceedings. Bound mimeographed material on file in the libraries of the University of Chicago, University of North Carolina, and Yale University, Institute of Human Relations.

———— (1939). Modern Behaviorism and Psychoanalysis. *Trans. N. Y. Acad. Sci.*, 1 (Series 2):78–82.

———— (1943). *Principles of Behavior: An Introduction to Behavior Theory*. New York: Appleton-Century.

James, W. (1890). *The Principles of Psychology*, 2 vols. New York: Dover, 1950.

Jones, E. (1955). *The Life and Work of Sigmund Freud*, Vol. II. New York: Basic Books.

Karsten, A. (1927). Psychische Sättigung. *Psychol. Forsch.*, 10:142–254.

Klein, G. S. (1951). The Personal World through Perception. In *Perception: An Approach to Personality*, ed. R. R. Blake and G. V. Ramsey. New York: Ronald Press, pp. 328–355.

———— (1954). Need and Regulation. In *Nebraska Symposium on Motivation, 1954*, ed. M. R. Jones. Lincoln: University of Nebraska Press, pp. 224–274.

———— (1956). Perception, Motives, and Personality: A Clinical Perspective. In *Psychology of Personality: Six Modern Approaches*, ed. J. L. McCary. New York: Logos Press, pp. 123–199.

———— (1958). Cognitive Control and Motivation. In *Assessment of Human Motives*, ed. G. Lindzey. New York: Rinehart, pp. 87–118.

———— (1959). Consciousness in Psychoanalytic Theory: Some Implications for Current Research in Perception. *J. Amer. Psychoanal. Assn.*, 7:5–34.

Knight, R. P. (1940a). Introjection, Projection and Identification. *Psychoanal. Quart.*, 9:334–341.

———— (1940b). The Relationship of Latent Homosexuality to the Mechanism of Paranoid Delusions. *Bull. Menninger Clin.*, 4:149–159.

Kohler, I. (1952). The Formation and Transformation of the Perceptual World. *Psychol. Issues*, No. 12, 1964, pp. 19–133.

Kris, E. (1932–52). *Psychoanalytic Explorations in Art.* New York: International Universities Press, 1952.

Lewin, K. (1926). Intention, Will and Need. In Rapaport (1951a), pp. 95–153.

———— (1935). *A Dynamic Theory of Personality.* New York: McGraw-Hill.

Lewy, E., & Rapaport, D. (1944). The Psychoanalytic Concept of Memory and Its Relation to Recent Memory Theories. *This volume,* Chapter 12.

Lindsley, D. B. (1957). Psychophysiology and Motivation. In *Nebraska Symposium on Motivation, 1957,* ed. M. R. Jones. Lincoln: University of Nebraska Press, pp. 44–104.

Littman, R. A. (1958). Motives, History and Causes. In *Nebraska Symposium on Motivation, 1958,* ed. M. R. Jones. Lincoln: University of Nebraska Press, pp. 114–168.

McClelland, D. C. (1958). Methods of Measuring Human Motivation. In *Motives in Fantasy, Action and Society,* ed. J. W. Atkinson. Princeton: Van Nostrand, pp. 7–42.

McGeoch, J. A. (1932). The Influence of Degree of Interpolated Learning upon Retroactive Inhibition. *Amer. J. Psychol.,* 44:695–708.

————, & Underwood, B. J. (1943). Tests of the Two-Factor Theory of Retroactive Inhibition. *J. Exp. Psychol.,* 32:1–16.

Madsen, K. B. (1959). *Theories of Motivation: A Comparative Study of Modern Theories of Motivation.* Copenhagen: Munksgaard.

Maslow, A. (1955). Deficiency Motivation and Growth Motivation. In *Nebraska Symposium on Motivation, 1955,* ed. M. R. Jones. Lincoln: University of Nebraska Press, pp. 1–30.

Melton, A. W., & Irwin, J. McQ. (1940). The Influence of Degree of Interpolated Learning on Retroactive Inhibition and the Overt Transfer of Specific Responses. *Amer. J. Psychol.,* 53:173–203.

————, & Lackum, W. J. von (1941). Retroactive and Proactive Inhibition in Retention: Evidence for a Two-Factor Theory of Retroactive Inhibition. *Amer. J. Psychol.,* 54:157–173.

Miller, G. A. (1956). The Magical Number Seven, Plus or Minus Two: Some Limits on Our Capacity for Processing Information. *Psychol. Rev.,* 63:81–97.

Miller, S. C. (1957). Determinants of the Role-Image of the Patient in a Psychiatric Hospital. In *The Patient and the Mental Hospital,* ed. M. Greenblatt, D. J. Levinson, & R. H. Williams. Glencoe, Ill.: Free Press, pp. 380–401.

Montgomery, K. C. (1953a). Exploratory Behavior as a Function of "Similarity" of Stimulus Situation. *J. Comp. Physiol. Psychol.,* 46:129–133.

———— (1953b). The Effect of the Hunger and Thirst Drives upon Exploratory Behavior. *J. Comp. Physiol. Psychol.,* 46:315–319.

———— (1953c). The Effect of Activity Deprivation upon Exploratory Behavior. *J. Comp. Physiol. Psychol.,* 46:438–441.

———— (1954). The Role of the Exploratory Drive in Learning. *J. Comp. Physiol. Psychol.,* 47:60–64.

————, & Zimbardo, P. G. (1957). Effect of Sensory and Behavioral Deprivation upon Exploratory Behavior in the Rat. *Percep. Motor Skills,* 7:223–229.

Morgan, C. T. (1957). Physiological Mechanisms of Motivation. In *Nebraska*

Symposium on Motivation, 1957, ed. M. R. Jones. Lincoln: University of Nebraska Press, pp. 1–35.

──── (1959). Physiological Theory of Drive. In *Psychology: A Study of a Science,* Vol. I, ed. S. Koch. New York: McGraw-Hill, pp. 644–671.

Mowrer, O. H. (1950). *Learning Theory and Personality Dynamics.* New York: Ronald Press.

Nissen, H. W. (1954). The Nature of the Drive as Innate Determinant of Behavioral Organization. In *Nebraska Symposium on Motivation, 1954,* ed. M. R. Jones. Lincoln: University of Nebraska Press, pp. 281–321.

Oberly, H. S. (1924). The Range for Visual Attention, Cognition and Apprehension. *Amer. J. Psychol.,* 35:332–352.

Peters, R. S. (1958). *The Concept of Motivation.* New York: Humanities Press.

Peterson, L. R., & Peterson, M. J. (1959). Short-Term Retention of Individual Verbal Items. *J. Exp. Psychol.,* 58:193–198.

Piaget, J. (1936). *The Origins of Intelligence in Children,* 2nd ed. New York: International Universities Press, 1952.

──── (1937). *The Construction of Reality in the Child.* New York: Basic Books, 1954.

Polansky, N. A., Miller, S. C., & White, R. B. (1955). Some Reservations Regarding Group Psychotherapy in Inpatient Psychiatric Treatment. *Group Psychother.,* 8:254–262.

Postman, L. (1955). The Analysis of Incidental Learning. In *Associative Processes in Verbal Behavior,* ed. J. J. Jenkins. University of Minnesota, Department of Psychology. Mimeographed, pp. 102–133.

────, & Senders, V. L. (1946). Incidental Learning and Generality of Set. *J. Exp. Psychol.,* 36:153–165.

Poulton, E. C. (1953). Memorization during Recall. *Brit. J. Psychol.,* 44:173–176.

Rapaport, D. (1942). *Emotions and Memory,* 2nd unaltered ed. New York: International Universities Press, 1950.

──── (1947). Psychological Testing: Its Practical and Its Heuristic Significance. *This volume,* Chapter 20.

────, ed. & tr. (1951a). *Organization and Pathology of Thought.* New York: Columbia University Press.

──── (1951b). The Autonomy of the Ego. *This volume,* Chapter 31.

──── (1951c). The Conceptual Model of Psychoanalysis. *This volume,* Chapter 34.

──── (1951d). States of Consciousness: A Psychopathological and Psychodynamic View. *This volume,* Chapter 33.

──── (1952). Review of O. H. Mowrer, *Learning Theory and Personality Dynamics. This volume,* Chapter 37.

──── (1953a). Review of J. Dollard & N. E. Miller, *Personality and Psychotherapy: An Analysis in Terms of Learning, Thinking, and Culture. This volume,* Chapter 43.

──── (1953b). On the Psychoanalytic Theory of Affects. *This volume,* Chapter 41.

──── (1953c). Some Metapsychological Considerations Concerning Activity and Passivity. *This volume,* Chapter 44.

—— (1956). The Psychoanalytic Theory of Consciousness and a Study of Dreams. Lecture to the Detroit Psychoanalytic Society, January 14.

—— (1957a). Cognitive Structures. *This volume,* Chapter 50.

—— (1957b). Discussion of C. E. Osgood, "A Behavioristic Analysis of Perception and Language as Cognitive Phenomena." *This volume,* Chapter 51.

—— (1957c). A Theoretical Analysis of the Superego Concept. *This volume,* Chapter 55.

—— (1957d). The Theory of Ego Autonomy: A Generalization. *This volume,* Chapter 57.

—— (1958). A Historical Survey of Psychoanalytic Ego Psychology. *This volume,* Chapter 58.

—— (1959). The Structure of Psychoanalytic Theory: A Systematizing Attempt. *Psychol. Issues,* No. 6, 1960.

—— (1960). Psychoanalysis as a Developmental Psychology. *This volume,* Chapter 64.

——, Gill, M. M., & Schafer, R. (1945–46). *Diagnostic Psychological Testing,* 2 vols. Chicago: Year Book Publishers.

Rouse, R. O. (1959). Proactive Inhibition as a Function of Degree of Practice of the Two Tasks. *Amer. Psychol.,* 14:385.

Russell, W. A. (1955). Bi-directional Effects in Word Association. In *Associative Processes in Verbal Behavior: A Report of the Minnesota Conference,* ed. J. J. Jenkins. University of Minnesota, Department of Psychology. Mimeographed, pp. 1–17.

Schur, M. (1959). Introductory Remarks at the Panel on Ethology. Meetings of the American Psychoanalytic Association, December 2–4.

Spence, K. W. (1958). Behavior Theory and Selective Learning. In *Nebraska Symposium on Motivation, 1958,* ed. M. R. Jones. Lincoln: University of Nebraska Press, pp. 73–107.

Thorpe, W. H. (1956). *Learning and Instinct in Animals.* Cambridge: Harvard University Press.

Thune, L. E., & Underwood, B. J. (1943). Retroactive Inhibition as a Function of Degree of Interpolated Learning. *J. Exp. Psychol.,* 32:185–200.

Tinbergen, N. (1952). "Derived" Activities; Their Causation, Biological Significance, Origin and Emancipation during Evolution. *Quart. Rev. Biol.,* 27:1–32.

Tolman, E. C. (1922). Can Instincts Be Given Up in Psychology? *Collected Papers in Psychology.* Berkeley: University of California Press, 1951, pp. 9–22.

—— (1932). *Purposive Behavior in Animals and Men.* Berkeley: University of California Press, 1949.

Troland, L. T. (1929). *The Principles of Psychophysiology.* New York: Van Nostrand.

Underwood, B. J. (1945). The Effect of Successive Interpolations on Retroactive and Proactive Inhibition. *Psychol. Monogr.,* 59, No. 3.

—— (1949). Proactive Inhibition as a Function of Time and Degree of Prior Learning. *J. Exp. Psychol.,* 39:24–34.

Werner, H. (1948). *Comparative Psychology of Mental Development,* rev. ed. New York: International Universities Press, 1957.

———, & Wapner, S. (1955). The Innsbruck Studies on Distorted Visual Fields in Relation to an Organismic Theory of Perception. *Psychol. Rev.,* 62:130–138.

White, R. W. (1959). Motivation Reconsidered: The Concept of Competence. *Psychol. Rev.,* 66:297–333.

Witkin, H. A., Lewis, H. B., Hertzman, M., Machover, K., Meissner, P. B., & Wapner, S. (1954). *Personality through Perception: An Experimental and Clinical Study.* New York: Harper.

Wolff, P. H. (1959). Observations on Newborn Infants. *Psychosom. Med.,* 21:110–118.

——— (1960). The Developmental Psychologies of Jean Piaget and Psychoanalysis. *Psychol. Issues,* No. 5.

Woodworth, R. S. (1918). *Dynamic Psychology.* New York: Columbia University Press, 1922.

——— (1938). *Experimental Psychology.* New York: Holt.

——— (1958). *Dynamics of Behavior.* New York: Holt.

Supplementary
Bibliography

(1938) *Az Asszociáció Fogalomtörténete* [The History of the Association Concept]. Budapest: Royal Hungarian Peter Pazmany University.

(1938) Lélektan [A Short Outline of the History of Psychology]. *Kis Enciklopedia.* Budapest: Pantheon, pp. 172–179.

(1940) Histamine in the Treatment of Psychosis. *Amer. J. Psychiat.,* 97:601–610 (with R. W. Robb & B. Kovitz).

(1941) Detecting the Feeble-Minded Registrant. *Bull. Menninger Clin.,* 5:146–149.

(1941) The Etiology of the Psychosis of Dementia Paralytica with a Preliminary Report of the Treatment of a Case of This Psychosis with Metrazol. *J. Nerv. Ment. Dis.,* 94:147–159 (with V. B. Kenyon).

(1941) Metrazol Convulsions in the Treatment of the Psychosis of Dementia Paralytica. *Arch. Neurol. Psychiat.,* 46:884–896 (with M. Lozoff & V. B. Kenyon).

(1941) The Role of the Psychologist in the Psychiatric Clinic. *Bull. Menninger Clin.,* 5:75–84 (with J. F. Brown).

(1941) The Szondi Test. *Bull. Menninger Clin.,* 5:33–39.

(1942) *Emotions and Memory.* Baltimore: William & Wilkins. 2nd unaltered ed.; New York: International Universities Press, 1950.

(1942) Freudian Mechanisms and Frustration Experiments. *Psychoanal. Quart.,* 11:503–511.

(1942) Recent Developments in Clinical Psychology. *Trans. Kans. Acad. Sci.,* 45:290–293.

(1943) The Clinical Application of the Thematic Apperception Test. *Bull. Menninger Clin.,* 7:106–113.

(1943) Comparison of Clinical Findings and Psychological Tests in Three Cases Bearing upon Military Personnel Selection. *Bull. Menninger Clin.,* 7:114–128 (with R. P. Knight, M. M. Gill, & M. Lozoff).

(1943) The Development of Concept Formation in Children. *Trans. Kans. Acad. Sci.,* 46:220–223 (with S. Reichard & M. Schneider).

(1943) The Role of Testing Concept Formation in Clinical Psychological Work. *Bull. Menninger Clin.,* 7:99–105 (with S. Reichard).

(1944) The Development of Concept Formation in Children. *Amer. J. Orthopsychiat.,* 14:156–161 (with S. Reichard & M. Schneider).

(1944–46) *Manual of Diagnostic Psychological Testing,* 2 vols. New York: Josiah Macy, Jr. Foundation Review Series (with R. Schafer & M. M. Gill).

(1944) The Psychological Testing of Children: Intelligence and Emotional Adjustment. *Bull. Menninger Clin.,* 8:205–210 (with S. K. Escalona).

(1944) The Scatter in Diagnostic Intelligence Testing. *Character & Pers.,* 12:275–284 (with R. Schafer).

(1945) Book Review: *Personality and the Behavior Disorders,* ed. J. McV. Hunt. *J. Consult. Psychol.,* 9:61–62.

(1945) Contribution to the Study of Amnesia and Allied Conditions. *Psychoanal. Quart.,* 14:199–220 (with E. Geleerd & F. Hacker).

(1945–46) *Diagnostic Psychological Testing,* 2 vols. Chicago: Year Book Publishers (with R. Schafer & M. M. Gill). Spanish translation: Argentina, Paidea Publishers, 1959.

(1945) The New Army Individual Test of General Mental Ability. *Bull. Menninger Clin.,* 9:107–110.

(1945) The Rorschach Test: A Clinical Evaluation. *Bull. Menninger Clin.,* 9:73–77 (with R. Schafer).

(1947) Diagnostic Testing in Convulsive Disorders. In *Epilepsy,* ed. P. H. Hoch & R. P. Knight. New York: Grune & Stratton, pp. 123–135 (with M. Mayman).

(1947) On Personality Testing. In *Redirecting the Delinquent.* New York: Yearbook of the National Probation and Parole Association, pp. 160–172.

(1951) Interpretation of the Wechsler-Bellevue Intelligence Scale in Personality Appraisal. In *An Introduction to Projective Techniques,* ed. H. H. Anderson & G. L. Anderson. New York: Prentice-Hall, 1951, pp. 541–580 (with M. Mayman & R. Schafer).

(1951) *Organization and Pathology of Thought,* tr. & ed. New York: Columbia University Press.

(1953–54) *The Collected Papers of Otto Fenichel,* 2 vols., ed. New York: Norton (with H. Fenichel).

(1953) *Medical Psychology,* by P. Schilder, ed. & tr. New York: International Universities Press, 1953.

(1957) Book Review: *Zur Psychologie und Psychopathologie der Erinnerungen,* by H. H. Wieck. *Int. J. Group Psychother.,* 7:220.

(1958) *Ego Psychology and the Problem of Adaptation,* by H. Hartmann, ed. & tr. New York: International Universities Press.

(1959) The Structure of Psychoanalytic Theory: A Systematizing Attempt. In

Psychology: A Study of a Science, Vol. III, ed. S. Koch. New York: McGraw-Hill, pp. 55–183. Also in *Psychol. Issues,* No. 6, 1960. German translation: *Zur Struktur der Psychoanalytischen Theorie.* Stuttgart: Klett, 1962.

Name Index

Eschenburg, B., 54
Euclid, 174, 175, 276

Farber, I. E., 864
Fauser, 57
Fechner, G. T., 409
Federn, P., 89, 486, 492, 503, 546
Fellows, R. M., 55, 63
Fenichel, H., 319, 499, 515, 770
Fenichel, O., 5, 14, 239, 318, 348, 477–
479, 489, 491, 494–496, 498–502,
507, 553, 554, 670, 698, 699, 733,
754, 759, 760, 767–771, 802, 804,
806, 807, 881, 895
Ferenczi, S., 57, 59, 60, 64, 67, 68, 69,
71, 603, 691
Fichte, J. G., 108
Finkelstein, M., 724
Fischer, L. K., 347, 388, 389
Fisher, C., 635, 645, 791, 795
Fitts, P. M., 786, 790, 905
Flugel, J. C., 470, 502
Ford, C. S., 829
Förster, H. von, 406
Fosdick, R. B., 238, 241
Frank, L. K., 77, 346, 406, 463
Frankhauser, 54
Frazer, J., 839
Fredericson, E., 827, 828
French, T. M., 361, 419, 547
Frenkel-Brunswik, E., 874
Freud, A., 11, 206, 208, 266, 267, 319,
358, 364, 458, 465, 477, 478, 500,
501, 527, 597, 640, 691, 702, 727,
746, 750, 754, 758, 799, 824, 825,
853
Freud, S., 6, 10, 11, 13, 19–25, 28, 38, 44,
45, 58, 76, 101, 102, 104, 106, 108,
117, 121–123, 125, 134, 136–151,
153, 156, 157, 167, 168, 172, 174,
189, 190, 193, 203, 208, 213, 253,
256, 270, 271, 277, 279, 291, 307,
311, 314–323, 330, 340, 345, 358,
359, 361, 363, 369–371, 373, 375–
379, 381, 387, 395, 399–402, 409,
411–419, 422, 423, 426, 433, 434,
447, 452–459, 462, 463, 471, 477,
480–494, 496–499, 501, 502, 504,
506, 508, 517, 525–528, 532, 533,
534, 539–541, 543–552, 554, 556,
558–560, 562, 569, 570, 573, 589,
592, 594–596, 599, 603, 606, 609,
611, 617, 628, 632, 637, 639, 640,
642, 645–647, 648, 652, 653, 657,
670–672, 680, 682, 683, 686–694,
698, 699, 700, 701, 703–705, 724,
729, 732, 735, 737, 740, 746–752,
754, 759–769, 779, 785, 786, 795–

799, 801–807, 813–815, 818, 821–
831, 833, 835–843, 845, 853–861,
867–869, 871, 872, 874, 874–883, 885–
887, 889, 891, 897–899, 901, 902,
906, 907
Frick, F. C., 899
Froeschels, E., 642
Fromm, E., 102, 103, 173, 310, 371, 375,
381, 448, 527, 592
Fuller, J. L., 827
Furrer, A., 54

Gardner, R. W., 12, 679, 791, 888, 891
Gelb, A., 262
Geleerd, E., 101, 388, 634
Gerstmann, W., 61
Gibson, J. J., 398, 418, 629, 656
Gill, M. M., 3, 8, 19, 20, 113, 137, 225,
232, 314, 322, 342, 346, 351, 388,
399, 422, 462, 466, 467, 534, 580,
583, 616, 626, 633–635, 643, 649,
654, 655, 658, 681, 728, 733, 738,
740, 748, 786, 791, 795, 865, 874,
889, 890, 894, 897, 898, 899
Gill, N. F., 899
Gillespie, R. D., 62, 121, 233, 320
Ginsburg, S., 572
Ginzberg, E., 572, 724
Glover, E., 321, 344, 500, 502, 503, 508,
795
Goldberger, L., 728, 736
Golden, L., 347
Goldstein, K., 76, 249, 262, 340, 342,
654, 681, 729, 888
Gollwitzer, H., 737–738
Gomperz, H., 109
Gonseth, F., 643
Goodman, C. C., 348, 637
Goodnow, J. J., 674
Gorgias, 108
Greenacre, P., 310
Greenson, R. R., 502
Gregg, A., 164, 240
Grinker, R. R., 89
Gross, A. A., 521
Grotjahn, M., 62, 63, 554
Grüninger, U., 491
Grünthal, E., 398, 400, 731
Gubler, A., 57
Guthrie, E. R., 252

Hacker, F. J., 344, 388, 634, 658
Hall, C. S., 828
Hall, S., 471
Hanawalt, N. G., 641
Hanfmann, E., 94, 350, 465, 681
Harlow, H. F., 792, 828, 902
Hart, H. H., 533

Subject Index

Abstractions, 563–564, 789
Achievement, differential, 268–269
Acting out, 818
Action, 75–77, 277–279, 286, 301, 315, 318, 340, 376, 421, 483, 595, 707, 783, 818–819
    experimental, 277, 315, 316, 321, 325, 326, 331, 375, 402, 423, 433, 506, 561, 859
    group, 584–585
    and thought, 106–107
Activity
    and ego control, 554–555
    model of, 539–541, 549
Activity and passivity, 23–24, 516, 530–566, 686, 695, 705–706, 749, 750, 752, 832, 864, 884
    in art, 572
    and defense, 537–538
    and ego autonomy, 739–741
    hierarchic layering of, 564
    illustrative case of, 535–539
    as instinctual aims, 543–545
    and internal and external stimuli, 539
    subjective experience of, 555, 556
    in thinking, 561–566
    usage of terms, 532–535, 543–551
Adaptation, 19, 20, 46, 169, 371, 381, 425, 508, 587–589, 592, 597, 600–605, 610–611, 618, 620, 659, 679, 699, 726, 739, 749–753, 770, 779, 786, 796–798, 806–807, 809, 825, 846, 858, 859, 891
    and drives, 835
    failure of, 269

guarantees of, 379
and primary-process mechanisms, 844
primitive, 843
and psychological tests, 344
see also Reality
Adaptedness, 19–20, 508, 599–603, 618, 725, 726, 751, 806–807, 809
Adaptive point of view, 20, 314, 507–508, 580, 582, 616, 806–809
    see also Metapsychological points of view
Adjustment, 604, 798, 807
Affect charge, 21, 413, 414, 483–485, 487, 489, 493, 501, 505–508, 803
Affects, 12, 38, 39, 41, 78, 126, 129, 133, 135, 154, 155, 254, 256, 258–259, 362, 426–427, 457, 749, 750, 799, 824–825, 830, 869, 880–882, 889
    adaptive aspects of, 507–508
    chronicity of, 426, 479, 502, 504, 508, 803
    classification of, 478–479, 502–504
    communication of, 203–204
    conflict theory of, 485–487, 503, 802
    and defenses, 477–478, 491–493, 500, 501, 507, 746
    discharge of, 151, 315, 321, 363, 482–485, 487–489, 493, 498, 501, 505, 506, 508, 548, 799–800, 803, 805, 881
    and drives, 478, 481, 487, 488
    drive theory of, 492
    experiments on, 286
    hierarchic layering of, 492, 500, 501, 504, 804

927

Superego (cont'd)
and ego, 749, 766, 768, 690–695, 698, 705–707
energies of, 707
formation of, 879
functions of, 694, 695, 697, 698, 707
and id, 692, 695, 705, 707
and identifications, 692, 704
and moral restrictions, 690
and narcissism, 687–689
nature of, 589–590
and neurosis, 455–457
origin of, 687–689, 692–693, 695
oversevere, 538, 542–543
predecessors of, 691
and reality, 458, 694, 695, 705
and repression, 690
Supplies, 769–770
Symbolism, 44–45, 125, 156, 219, 374
and scanning, 333
Syntax, 26
Synthetic function, 21–22, 26, 372–374, 564, 590, 593, 597, 750, 782–783, 803, 838, 841–845, 887
Synthetic statements, 293, 294
Systems, open and closed, 406, 407

Taboo, origin of, 838–840
Tasks, interrupted, 122, 154, 286, 781, 865
Teaching, 129, 279
Technology, 714
and the psychology of man, 276–284
Teleology, 80–90
Telepathy, 218–219
Tension maintenance, 877, 890, 901
Tension systems, 122, 126, 153–155, 405, 899
Tests
Babcock Mental Deterioration, 67–71
and behavior, 340–341, 345
B.R.L. Sorting, 94
concept-formation, 77, 94, 95, 224, 226, 228, 232, 233, 249, 262, 342, 347, 465–466, 626
determinants of responses to, 347
diagnostic, 12, 17–19, 334–353
digit-span, 784, 785, 790
Draw-a-Person, 340, 342, 346, 353
in general paresis, 67–71
intelligence, 18, 77, 95, 161, 162, 222, 224, 226, 228, 232, 233, 247, 249, 254–259, 261–262, 264, 267–271, 273, 274, 341–342, 347, 433, 461, 652, 780
and introspection, 343
and levels of personality, 227–228, 343

need for new, 350–352
nonprojective, 221–229, 463
objectivity of, 334–337
projective, 18, 222–223, 228, 247, 263, 346–349, 424, 639
and psychiatry, 245–250, 263, 334–339, 350–351
psychological, 4, 5, 18, 65, 67–71, 161–162, 164, 232–235, 245–250, 259–274, 301, 334–341, 343, 345, 348, 350–352, 514
psychometric, 52
scoring of, 336
sorting, 340, 342
statistical treatment of, 226–227
Strong Vocational Interest, 227–228
structured and unstructured subject matter of, 341–342, 345, 347, 349, 350
subject's knowledge of object of, 341
Szondi, 67, 69, 71, 77, 94–96, 342, 346, 462
theory of, 301, 461–462
word-association, 232, 246, 247, 249, 253–254, 467, 626, 632–633, 780, 787
see also Projective techniques; Thematic Apperception Test; Rorschach; Wechsler-Bellevue
Thematic Apperception Test, 77, 93, 95, 96, 232, 248, 249, 259, 262, 263, 336, 338, 340, 341, 343, 346, 350, 462, 464, 467, 639
Theory
and experiments, 16
and observation, 178, 202, 205, 209
Thing and medium, 656
Thought, 4, 5, 17–18, 20–21, 40, 43, 58, 69, 74–76, 102, 104, 108, 180, 269, 271, 272, 277, 280, 282, 294, 301, 316, 331, 332, 338–339, 345–346, 393, 424, 474, 499, 506, 595, 644, 671, 881–882
and action, 22, 106–107, 277–279, 402
activity and passivity in, 516, 561–566
adaptedness of, 371, 377, 379, 381
automatized, 561–562
autonomy of, 280, 364–365
biological utility of, 326
categories of, 110–112
and consciousness, 436–438
contagion of, 565
content of, 17–18, 370, 432–433
and development, 77–78, 371–372, 375, 402, 836–846
disorders of, 16–18, 58, 332, 371–374, 378
in dreams, 147–148, 152